ANCIENT ITALY AND SICILY
RAETIA
NORICUM
HELVETII
SEDUNI
VENONETES
ALPES
CARNI
PANNONIA
TRIDENTUM
FORUM IULIUM
AUGUSTA PRAETORIA
COMUM
GALLIA TRANSPADANA
CENOMANI
VENETIA
AQUILEIA
TERGESTE
HISTRIA
LIBURNIA
MEDIOLANUM
NOVARIA
VERONA
PATAVIUM
AUGUSTA TAURINORUM
TICINUM
CREMONA
MANTUA
ATRIA
IRIA
PLACENTIA
POLLENTIA
FIDENTIA
PARMA
POLA
LIGURIA
MUTINA
BONONIA
LINGONES
SPINA
RAVENNA
SAVO
GENUA
LIMA
PORTUS VENERIS
FORUM CLODII
ARIMINUM
PISAURUM
MONOECUS
NICAEA
ANTIPOLIS
PISTORIA
LUCA
FAESULAE
PISAE
Arnus F.
FLORENTIA
SENONES
SENA GALLICA
ANCONA
UMBRIA
APENNINUS
MARE ADRIATICUM s. SUPERUM
DALMATIA
SALONAE
SINUS LIGUSTICUS
VOLATERRAE
ARRETIUM
SAENA
CORTONA
L.Trasumenus
PERUSIA
FIRMUM
ISSA
CORCYRA NIGRA
ILVA
VETULONIA
CLUSIUM
PICENUM
CASTRUM NOVUM
PORTUS TRAIANUS
RUSELLAE
VOLSINII
SPOLETIUM
NARNIA
HADRIA
EPIDAURUM
MARIANA
ETRURIA
HORTA
REATE
MONS
FALERII
SABINI
ALERIA
TARQUINII
CORSICA
CAERE
Tiberis F.
TIBUR
AEQUI
MARE SARDOUM
ALISTA
PALLA
PORTUS AUGUSTI
OSTIA
ROMA
LAVINIUM
LATINI
PRAENESTE
SAMNIUM
TEANUM
APULIA
ARPI
SIPONTUM
Fretum Gallicum
VOLSCI
FREGELLAE
LUCERIA
SALAPIA
CANUSIUM
CANNAE
TURENUM
BARIUM
MARE TUSCUM s. TYRRHENUM s. INFERUM
BENEVENTUM
AUSCULUM
Aufidus F.
VOLTURNUM
CAPUA
NOLA
VENUSIA
GNATHIA
CUMAE
NEAPOLIS
ABELLINUM
BRUNDISIUM
Vesuvius M.
FERONIA
SARDINIA
PUTEOLI
SALERNUM
PAESTUM
(Posidonia)
POTENTIA
CALABRIA
LUCANIA
TARENTUM
GRUMENTUM
METAPONTUM
HERACLEA
VELIA
(Elia)
BUXENTUM
SINUS TARENTINUS
LAUS
NEAPOLIS
CARALES
NORA
THURII
CONSENTIA
TEMPSA
TERINA
BRUTTII
CROTON
Lacinium Pr.
Iapygum Pr.
LIPARAEAE Ins.
STRONGYLE
EUONYMOS
PHOENICUSSA
ERICUSSA
LIPARA
HIERA
(Thermessa)
(Volcani I.)
VIBO VALENTIA
SCYLACIUM
MEDMA
CAULONIA
Pelorum Pr.
LOCRI EPIZEPHYRII
PANORMUS
SOLUNTUM
MESSANA
SCYLLAEUM
RHEGIUM
Zephyrium Pr.
Heracleum Pr.
MARE SICULUM ET IONIUM
ERYX
SEGESTA
TAUROMENIUM
Fretum Siculum
MOTYE
LILYBAEUM
SICILIA
Aetna M.
SELINUS
HENNA
CATANA
HERACLEA MINOA
AGRIGENTUM
LEONTINI
MEGARA HYBLAEA
GELA
SYRACUSAE
MARE AFRICUM
HIPPO ZARYTUS
UTICA
CARTHAGO
HIPPO REGIUS
NUMIDIA
NEAPOLIS
NARAGGARA
SICCA VENERIA
THAGURA
AFRICA
MELITA

BY WILL DURANT

The Story of Philosophy

Transition

The Pleasures of Philosophy

Adventures in Genius

BY WILL AND ARIEL DURANT

THE STORY OF CIVILIZATION:

I. *Our Oriental Heritage*

II. *The Life of Greece*

III. *Caesar and Christ*

IV. *The Age of Faith*

V. *The Renaissance*

VI. *The Reformation*

VII. *The Age of Reason Begins*

VIII. *The Age of Louis XIV*

IX. *The Age of Voltaire*

X. *Rousseau and Revolution*

XI. *The Age of Napoleon*

The Lessons of History

Interpretations of Life

THE STORY OF CIVILIZATION: PART II

THE LIFE OF GREECE

Being a history of Greek civilization from the beginnings, and of civilization in the Near East from the death of Alexander, to the Roman conquest; with an introduction on the prehistoric culture of Crete.

By Will Durant

SIMON AND SCHUSTER
NEW YORK

Published by Simon and Schuster
A Division of Gulf & Western Corporation
Simon & Schuster Building, Rockefeller Center
1230 Avenue of the Americas, New York, New York 10020

MANUFACTURED IN THE UNITED STATES OF AMERICA
ISBN 0-671-41800-9

27 28 29 30

TO MY FRIEND

MAX SCHOTT

Preface

MY purpose is to record and contemplate the origin, growth, maturity, and decline of Greek civilization from the oldest remains of Crete and Troy to the conquest of Greece by Rome. I wish to see and feel this complex culture not only in the subtle and impersonal rhythm of its rise and fall, but in the rich variety of its vital elements: its ways of drawing a living from the land, and of organizing industry and trade; its experiments with monarchy, aristocracy, democracy, dictatorship, and revolution; its manners and morals, its religious practices and beliefs; its education of children, and its regulation of the sexes and the family; its homes and temples, markets and theaters and athletic fields; its poetry and drama, its painting, sculpture, architecture, and music; its sciences and inventions, its superstitions and philosophies. I wish to see and feel these elements not in their theoretical and scholastic isolation, but in their living interplay as the simultaneous movements of one great cultural organism, with a hundred organs and a hundred million cells, but with one body and one soul.

Excepting machinery, there is hardly anything secular in our culture that does not come from Greece. Schools, gymnasiums, arithmetic, geometry, history, rhetoric, physics, biology, anatomy, hygiene, therapy, cosmetics, poetry, music, tragedy, comedy, philosophy, theology, agnosticism, skepticism, stoicism, epicureanism, ethics, politics, idealism, philanthropy, cynicism, tyranny, plutocracy, democracy: these are all Greek words for cultural forms seldom originated, but in many cases first matured for good or evil by the abounding energy of the Greeks. All the problems that disturb us today—the cutting down of forests and the erosion of the soil; the emancipation of woman and the limitation of the family; the conservatism of the established, and the experimentalism of the unplaced, in morals, music, and government; the corruptions of politics and the perversions of conduct; the conflict of religion and science, and the weakening of the supernatural supports of morality; the war of the classes, the nations, and the continents; the revolutions of the poor against the economically powerful rich, and of the rich against the politically powerful poor; the struggle between democracy and dictatorship, between individualism and communism, between the East and the West—all these agitated, as if for our instruction, the brilliant and turbulent life of ancient Hellas. There is nothing in Greek civilization that does not illuminate our own.

We shall try to see the life of Greece both in the mutual interplay of its cultural elements, and in the immense five-act drama of its rise and fall. We shall begin with Crete and its lately resurrected civilization, because apparently from Crete, as well as from Asia, came that prehistoric culture of Mycenae and Tiryns which slowly transformed the immigrating Achaeans and the invading Dorians into civilized Greeks; and we shall study for a moment the virile world of warriors and lovers, pirates and troubadours, that has come down to us on the rushing river of Homer's verse. We shall watch the rise of Sparta and Athens under Lycurgus and Solon, and shall trace the colonizing spread of the fertile Greeks through all the isles of the Aegean, the coasts of Western Asia and the Black Sea, of Africa and Italy, Sicily, France, and Spain. We shall see democracy fighting for its life at Marathon, stimulated by its victory, organizing itself under Pericles, and flowering into the richest culture in history; we shall linger with pleasure over the spectacle of the human mind liberating itself from superstition, creating new sciences, rationalizing medicine, secularizing history, and reaching unprecedented peaks in poetry and drama, philosophy, oratory, history, and art; and we shall record with melancholy the suicidal end of the Golden Age in the Peloponnesian War. We shall contemplate the gallant effort of disordered Athens to recover from the blow of her defeat; even her decline will be illustrious with the genius of Plato and Aristotle, Apelles and Praxiteles, Philip and Demosthenes, Diogenes and Alexander. Then, in the wake of Alexander's generals, we shall see Greek civilization, too powerful for its little peninsula, bursting its narrow bounds, and overflowing again into Asia, Africa, and Italy; teaching the cult of the body and the intellect to the mystical Orient, reviving the glories of Egypt in Ptolemaic Alexandria, and enriching Rhodes with trade and art; developing geometry with Euclid at Alexandria and Archimedes at Syracuse; formulating in Zeno and Epicurus the most lasting philosophies in history; carving the *Aphrodite of Melos*, the *Laocoön*, the *Victory of Samothrace*, and the Altar of Pergamum; striving and failing to organize its politics into honesty, unity, and peace; sinking ever deeper into the chaos of civil and class war; exhausted in soil and loins and spirit; surrendering to the autocracy, quietism, and mysticism of the Orient; and at last almost welcoming those conquering Romans through whom dying Greece would bequeath to Europe her sciences, her philosophies, her letters, and her arts as the living cultural basis of our modern world.

Acknowledgments

I am grateful to Mr. Wallace Brockway for his scholarly help at every stage of this work; to Miss Mary Kaufman, Miss Ethel Durant, and Mr. Louis Durant for aid in classifying the material; to Miss Regina Sands for her expert preparation of the manuscript; and to my wife for her patient encouragement and quiet inspiration.

I am deeply indebted to Sir Gilbert Murray and to his publishers, the Oxford University Press, for permission to quote from his translations of Greek drama. These translations have enriched English literature.

I am also indebted to the Oxford University Press for permission to quote from its excellent *Oxford Book of Greek Verse in Translation.*

W. D.

Notes

ON THE USE OF THIS BOOK

1. This book, while forming the second part of the author's *Story of Civilization*, has been written as an independent unit, complete in itself. The next volume will probably appear in 1943 under the title of *Caesar and Christ*—a history of Roman civilization and of early Christianity.

2. To bring the book into smaller compass, reduced type (like this) has been used for technical or recondite material. Indented passages in reduced type are quotations.

3. The raised numbers in the text refer to the Notes at the end of the volume. Hiatuses in the numbering of the notes are due to last minute curtailments.

4. The chronological table given at the beginning of each period is designed to free the text as far as possible from minor dates and royal trivialities. All dates are B.C. unless otherwise stated or evident.

5. The maps at the beginning and the end of the book show nearly all the places referred to in the text. The glossary defines all unfamiliar foreign words used, except when these are explained where they occur. The starred titles in the bibliography may serve as a guide to further reading. The index pronounces ancient names, and gives dates of birth and death where known.

6. Greek words have been transliterated into our alphabet according to the rules formulated by the *Journal of Hellenic Studies*; certain inconsistencies in these rules must be forgiven as concessions to custom; e.g., *Hieron*, but *Plato(n)*; *Hippodameia*, but *Alexandr(e)ia*.

7. In pronouncing Greek words not established in English usage, *a* should be sounded as in *father*, *e* as in *neigh*, *i* as in *machine*, *o* as in *bone*, *u* as in *June*, *y* like French *u* or German *ü*, *ai* and *ei* like *ai* in *aisle*, *ou* as in *route*, *c* as in *car*, *ch* as in *chorus*, *g* as in *go*, *z* like *dz* in *adze*.

Table of Contents

BOOK I: AEGEAN PRELUDE: 3500-1000 B.C.

BOOK II: THE RISE OF GREECE: 1000-480 B.C.

BOOK III: THE GOLDEN AGE: 480-399 B.C.

BOOK IV

THE DECLINE AND FALL OF GREEK FREEDOM

399-322 B.C.

BOOK V: THE HELLENISTIC DISPERSION: 322-146 B.C.

List of Illustrations

(Illustration Section follows page 334)

Maps of the Hellenistic World, Ancient Greece and the Aegean, and Ancient Italy and Sicily will be found on the inside covers.

BOOK I

AEGEAN PRELUDE

3500-1000 B.C.

CHRONOLOGICAL TABLE FOR BOOK I

NOTES: All dates are approximate. Individuals are placed at their time of flourishing, which is assumed to be about forty years after their birth; their dates of birth and death, where possible, are given in the index. Dates of rulers are for their reigns. A question mark before an entry indicates a date given only by Greek tradition.

B.C. 9000: Neolithic Age in Crete
3400-3000: Early Minoan, Helladic, Cycladic, I
3400-2100: Neolithic Age in Thessaly
3400-1200: Bronze Age in Crete
3000-2600: Early Minoan, Helladic, Cycladic, II
3000: Copper mined in Cyprus
2870: First known settlement at Troy
2600-2350: Early Minoan, Helladic, Cycladic, III
2350-2100: Middle Minoan, Helladic, Cycladic, I
2200-1200: Bronze Age in Cyprus
2100-1950: Middle Minoan, Helladic, Cycladic, II; first series of Cretan palaces
2100-1600: Chalcolithic Age in Thessaly
1950-1600: Middle Minoan, Helladic, Cycladic, III
1900: Destruction of first series of Cretan palaces
1600-1500: Late Minoan, Helladic (Mycenaean), Cycladic, I; second series of Cretan palaces
1600-1200: Bronze Age in Thessaly
1582: ? Foundation of Athens by Cecrops
1500-1400: Late Minoan, Helladic (Mycenaean), Cycladic, II
1450-1400: Destruction of second series of Cretan palaces
1433: ? Deucalion and the Flood
1400-1200: Late Minoan, Helladic (Mycenaean), Cycladic, III; palaces of Tiryns and Mycenae
1313: ? Foundation of Thebes by Cadmus
1300-1100: Age of Achaean domination in Greece
1283: ? Coming of Pelops into Elis
1261-1209: ? Heracles
1250: Theseus at Athens; Oedipus at Thebes; Minos and Daedalus at Cnossus
1250-1183: "Sixth city" of Troy; age of the Homeric heroes
1225: ? Voyage of the Argonauts
1213: ? War of the Seven against Thebes
1200: ? Accession of Agamemnon
1192-1183: ? Siege of Troy
1176: ? Accession of Orestes
1104: ? Dorian invasion of Greece

CHAPTER I

Crete

I. THE MEDITERRANEAN

AS we enter the fairest of all waters, leaving behind us the Atlantic and Gibraltar, we pass at once into the arena of Greek history. "Like frogs around a pond," said Plato, "we have settled down upon the shores of this sea."[1] Even on these distant coasts the Greeks founded precarious, barbarian-bound colonies many centuries before Christ: at Hemeroscopium and Ampurias in Spain, at Marseilles and Nice in France, and almost everywhere in southern Italy and Sicily. Greek colonists established prosperous towns at Cyrene in northern Africa, and at Naucratis in the delta of the Nile; their restless enterprise stirred the islands of the Aegean and the coasts of Asia Minor then as in our century; all along the Dardanelles and the Sea of Marmora and the Black Sea they built towns and cities for their far-venturing trade. Mainland Greece was but a small part of the ancient Greek world.

Why was it that the second group of historic civilizations took form on the Mediterranean, as the first had grown up along the rivers of Egypt, Mesopotamia, and India, as the third would flourish on the Atlantic, and as the fourth may appear on the shores of the Pacific? Was it the better climate of the lands washed by the Mediterranean? There, then as now,[2] winter rains nourished the earth, and moderate frosts stimulated men; there, almost all the year round, one might live an open-air life under a warm but not enervating sun. And yet the surface of the Mediterranean coasts and islands is nowhere so rich as the alluvial valleys of the Ganges, the Indus, the Tigris, the Euphrates, or the Nile; the summer's drought may begin too soon or last too long; and everywhere a rocky basis lurks under the thin crust of the dusty earth. The temperate north and the tropic south are both more fertile than these historic lands where patient peasants, weary of coaxing the soil, more and more abandoned tillage to grow olives and the vine. And at any moment, along one or another of a hundred faults, earthquakes might split the ground beneath men's feet, and frighten them into a fitful piety. Climate did not draw civilization to Greece; probably it has never made a civilization anywhere.

What drew men into the Aegean was its islands. The islands were beautiful; even a worried mariner must have been moved by the changing colors of those shadowed hills that rose like temples out of the reflecting sea. Today there are few sights lovelier on the globe; and sailing the Aegean, one begins to understand why the men who peopled those coasts and isles came to love them almost more than life, and, like Socrates, thought exile bitterer than death. But further, the mariner was pleased to find that these island jewels were strewn in all directions, and at such short intervals that his ship, whether going between east and west or between north and south, would never be more than forty miles from land. And since the islands, like the mainland ranges, were the mountaintops of a once continuous territory that had been gradually submerged by a pertinacious sea,[3] some welcome peak always greeted the outlook's eye, and served as a beacon to ships that had as yet no compass to guide them. Again, the movements of wind and water conspired to help the sailor reach his goal. A strong central current flowed from the Black Sea into the Aegean, and countercurrents flowed northward along the coasts; while the northeasterly etesian winds blew regularly in the summer to help back to their southern ports the ships that had gone to fetch grain, fish, and furs from the Euxine Sea.* Fog was rare in the Mediterranean, and the unfailing sunshine so varied the coastal winds that at almost any harbor, from spring to autumn, one might be carried out by a morning, and brought back by an evening, breeze.

In these propitious waters the acquisitive Phoenicians and the amphibious Greeks developed the art and science of navigation. Here they built ships for the most part larger or faster, and yet more easily handled, than any that had yet sailed the Mediterranean. Slowly, despite pirates and harassing uncertainties, the water routes from Europe and Africa into Asia—through Cyprus, Sidon, and Tyre, or through the Aegean and the Black Sea—became cheaper than the long land routes, arduous and perilous, that had carried so much of the commerce of Egypt and the Near East. Trade took new lines, multiplied new populations, and created new wealth. Egypt, then Mesopotamia, then Persia withered; Phoenicia deposited an empire of cities along the African coast, in Sicily, and in Spain; and Greece blossomed like a watered rose.

---

* The Greeks called the Mediterranean *Ho Pontos*, the Passage or Road, and euphemistically termed the Black Sea *Ho Pontos Euxeinos*—the Sea Kindly to Guests—perhaps because it welcomed ships from the south with adverse currents and winds. The broad rivers that fed it, and the frequent mists that reduced its rate of evaporation, kept the Black Sea at a higher level than the Mediterranean, and caused a powerful current to rush through the narrow Bosporus (Ox-ford) and the Hellespont into the Aegean. The Sea of Marmora was the *Propontis*, Before the Sea.

II. THE REDISCOVERY OF CRETE

"There is a land called Crete, in the midst of the wine-dark sea, a fair, rich land, begirt with water; and therein are many men past counting, and ninety cities."[4] When Homer sang these lines, perhaps in the ninth century before our era,* Greece had almost forgotten, though the poet had not, that the island whose wealth seemed to him even then so great had once been wealthier still; that it had held sway with a powerful fleet over most of the Aegean and part of mainland Greece; and that it had developed, a thousand years before the siege of Troy, one of the most artistic civilizations in history. Probably it was this Aegean culture—as ancient to him as he is to us—that Homer recalled when he spoke of a Golden Age in which men had been more civilized, and life more refined, than in his own disordered time.

The rediscovery of that lost civilization is one of the major achievements of modern archeology. Here was an island twenty times larger than the largest of the Cyclades, pleasant in climate, varied in the products of its fields and once richly wooded hills, and strategically placed, for trade or war, midway between Phoenicia and Italy, between Egypt and Greece. Aristotle had pointed out how excellent this situation was, and how "it had enabled Minos to acquire the empire of the Aegean."[5] But the story of Minos, accepted as fact by all classical writers, was rejected as legend by modern scholars; and until sixty years ago it was the custom to suppose, with Grote, that the history of civilization in the Aegean had begun with the Dorian invasion, or the Olympic games. Then in A.D. 1878 a Cretan merchant, appropriately named Minos Kalokairinos, unearthed some strange antiquities on a hillside south of Candia.† The great Schliemann, who had but lately resurrected Mycenae and Troy, visited the site in 1886, announced his conviction that it covered the remains of the ancient Cnossus, and opened negotiations with the owner of the land so that excavations might begin at once. But the owner haggled and tried to cheat; and Schliemann, who had been a merchant before becoming an archeologist, withdrew in anger, losing a golden chance to add another civilization to history. A few years later he died.[6]

In 1893 a British archeologist, Dr. Arthur Evans, bought in Athens a number of milkstones from Greek women who had worn them as amulets. He was curious about the hieroglyphics engraved upon them, which no scholar could read. Tracing the stones to Crete, he secured passage thither,

* All dates in this volume are B.C. unless otherwise stated or obviously A.D.

† The modern capital, now officially renamed Heracleum.

and wandered about the island picking up examples of what he believed to be ancient Cretan writing. In 1895 he purchased a part, and in 1900 the remainder, of the site that Schliemann and the French School at Athens had identified with Cnossus; and in nine weeks of that spring, digging feverishly with one hundred and fifty men, he exhumed the richest treasure of modern historical research—the palace of Minos. Nothing yet known from antiquity could equal the vastness of this complicated structure, to all appearances identical with the almost endless Labyrinth so famous in old Greek tales of Minos, Daedalus, Theseus, Ariadne, and the Minotaur. In these and other ruins, as if to confirm Evans' intuition, thousands of seals and clay tablets were found, bearing characters like those that had set him upon the trail. The fires that had destroyed the palaces of Cnossus had preserved these tablets, whose undeciphered pictographs and scripts still conceal the early story of the Aegean.*

Students from many countries now hurried to Crete. While Evans was working at Cnossus, a group of resolute Italians—Halbherr, Pernier, Savignoni, Paribeni—unearthed at Hagia Triada (Holy Trinity) a sarcophagus painted with illuminating scenes from Cretan life, and uncovered at Phaestus a palace only less extensive than that of the Cnossus kings. Meanwhile two Americans, Seager and Mrs. Hawes, made discoveries at Vasiliki, Mochlos, and Gournia; the British—Hogarth, Bosanquet, Dawkins, Myres—explored Palaikastro, Psychro, and Zakro; the Cretans themselves became interested, and Xanthoudidis and Hatzidakis dug up ancient residences, grottoes, and tombs at Arkalochori, Tylissus, Koumasa, and Chamaizi. Half the nations of Europe united under the flag of science in the very generation in which their statesmen were preparing for war.

How was all this material to be classified—these palaces, paintings, statues, seals, vases, metals, tablets, and reliefs?—to what period of the past were they to be assigned? Precariously, but with increasing corroboration as research went on and knowledge grew, Evans dated the relics according to the depth of their strata, the gradation of styles in the pottery, and the agreement of Cretan finds, in form or motive, with like objects exhumed in lands or deposits whose chronology was approximately known. Digging down patiently beneath Cnossus, he found himself stopped, some forty-three feet below the surface, by the virgin rock. The lower half of the excavated area was occupied by remains characteristic of the Neolithic Age—primitive forms of handmade pottery with simple linear ornament, spindle whorls for spinning and weaving, fat-buttocked

---

* Evans labored brilliantly at Cnossus for many years, was knighted for his discoveries, and completed, in 1936, his monumental four-volume report, *The Palace of Minos.*

goddesses of painted steatite or clay, tools and weapons of polished stone, but nothing in copper or bronze.* Classifying the pottery, and correlating the remains with those of ancient Mesopotamia and Egypt, Evans divided the post-neolithic and prehistoric culture of Crete into three ages—Early, Middle, and Late Minoan—and each of these into three periods.†

The first or lowest appearance of copper in the strata represents for us, through a kind of archeological shorthand, the slow rise of a new civilization out of the neolithic stage. By the end of the Early Minoan Age the Cretans learn to mix copper with tin, and the Bronze Age begins. In Middle Minoan I the earliest palaces occur: the princes of Cnossus, Phaestus, and Mallia build for themselves luxurious dwellings with countless rooms, spacious storehouses, specialized workshops, altars and temples, and great drainage conduits that startle the arrogant Occidental eye. Pottery takes on a many-colored brilliance, walls are enlivened with charming frescoes, and a form of linear script evolves out of the hieroglyphics of the preceding age. Then, at the close of Middle Minoan II, some strange catastrophe writes its cynical record into the strata; the palace of Cnossus is laid low as if by a convulsion of the earth, or perhaps by an attack from Phaestus, whose palace for a time is spared. But a little later a like destruction falls upon Phaestus, Mochlos, Gournia, Palaikastro, and many other cities in the island; the pottery is covered with ashes, the great jars in the storerooms are filled with debris. Middle Minoan III is a period of comparative stagnation, in which, perhaps, the southeastern Mediterranean world is long disordered by the Hyksos conquest of Egypt.[8]

In the late Minoan Age everything begins again. Humanity, patient under every cataclysm, renews its hope, takes courage, and builds once more. New and finer palaces rise at Cnossus, Phaestus, Tylissus, Hagia Triada, and Gournia. The lordly spread, the five-storied height, the luxurious decoration of these princely residences suggest such wealth as Greece would not know till Pericles. Theaters are erected in the palace courts, and gladiatorial spectacles of men and women in deadly combat with animals amuse gentlemen and ladies whose aristocratic faces, quietly alert, still live

* Since the earliest layer of copper implements at Cnossus may be dated, by correlation with the remains of neighboring cultures, about 3400 B.C., i.e., about 5300 years ago, and since the neolithic strata at Cnossus occupy some fifty-five per cent of the total depth from surface to rock, Evans calculated that the Neolithic Age in Crete had lasted at least 4500 years before the coming of metals—approximately from 8000 to 3400. Such calculations of time from depth of strata are, of course, highly problematical; the rate of deposition may change from age to age. Allowance has been made for a slower rate after the abandonment of Cnossus as an urban site in the fourteenth century B.C.[7] No paleolithic remains have been found in Crete.

† For the approximate duration of these epochs cf. the Chronological Table on p. 2.

for us on the bright frescoes of the resurrected walls. Wants are multiplied, tastes are refined, literature flourishes; a thousand industries graciously permit the poor to prosper by supplying comforts and delicacies to the rich. The halls of the king are noisy with scribes taking inventories of goods distributed or received; with artists making statuary, paintings, pottery, or reliefs; with high officials conducting conferences, hearing judicial appeals, or dispatching papers stamped with their finely wrought seals, while wasp-waisted princes and jeweled duchesses, alluringly décolleté, crowd to a royal feast served on tables shining with bronze and gold. The sixteenth and fifteenth centuries before our era are the zenith of Aegean civilization, the classic and golden age of Crete.

III. THE RECONSTRUCTION OF A CIVILIZATION

If now we try to restore this buried culture from the relics that remain—playing Cuvier to the scattered bones of Crete—let us remember that we are engaging upon a hazardous kind of historical television, in which imagination must supply the living continuity in the gaps of static and fragmentary material artificially moving but long since dead. Crete will remain inwardly unknown until its secretive tablets find their Champollion.

1. Men and Women

As we see them self-pictured in their art, the Cretans curiously resemble the double ax so prominent in their religious symbolism. Male and female alike have torsos narrowing pathologically to an ultramodern waist. Nearly all are short in stature, slight and supple of build, graceful in movement, athletically trim. Their skin is white at birth. The ladies, who court the shade, have fair complexions conventionally pale; but the men, pursuing wealth under the sun, are so tanned and ruddy that the Greeks will call them (as well as the Phoenicians) *Phoinikes*—the Purple Ones, Redskins. The head is rather long than broad, the features are sharp and refined, the hair and eyes are brilliantly dark, as in the Italians of today; these Cretans are apparently a branch of the "Mediterranean race."* The men as well as the women wear their hair partly in coils on the head or the neck, partly in ring-

* Current anthropology divides post-neolithic Europeans into three types, respectively preponderating in north, central, and southern Europe: (1) "Nordic" man—long-headed, tall, and fair of skin and eyes and hair; (2) "Alpine" man—broad-headed, of medium height, with eyes tending to gray and hair to brown; and (3) "Mediterranean" man—long-headed, short, and dark. No people is exclusively any of these "races."

lets on the brow, partly in tresses falling upon the shoulders or the breast. The women add ribbons for their curls, while the men, to keep their faces clean, provide themselves with a variety of razors, even in the grave.[10]

The dress is as strange as the figures. On their heads—most often bare—the men have turbans or tam-o'-shanters, the women magnificent hats of our early twentieth-century style. The feet are usually free of covering; but the upper classes may bind them in white leather shoes, which among women may be daintily embroidered at the edges, with colored beads on the straps. Ordinarily the male has no clothing above the waist; there he wears a short skirt or waistcloth, occasionally with a codpiece for modesty. The skirt may be slit at the side in workingmen; in dignitaries and ceremonies it reaches in both sexes to the ground. Occasionally the men wear drawers, and in winter a long outer garment of wool or skins. The clothing is tightly laced about the middle, for men as well as women are resolved to be —or seem—triangularly slim.[11] To rival the men at this point, the women of the later periods resort to stiff corsets, which gather their skirts snugly around their hips, and lift their bare breasts to the sun. It is a pretty custom among the Cretans that the female bosom should be uncovered, or revealed by a diaphanous chemise;[12] no one seems to take offense. The bodice is laced below the bust, opens in a careless circle, and then, in a gesture of charming reserve, may close in a Medici collar at the neck. The sleeves are short, sometimes puffed. The skirt, adorned with flounces and gay tints, widens out spaciously from the hips, stiffened presumably with metal ribs or horizontal hoops. There are in the arrangement and design of Cretan feminine dress a warm harmony of colors, a grace of line, a delicacy of taste, that suggest a rich and luxurious civilization, already old in arts and wiles. In these matters the Cretans had no influence upon the Greeks; only in modern capitals have their styles triumphed. Even staid archeologists have given the name *La Parisienne* to the portrait of a Cretan lady with profulgent bosom, shapely neck, sensual mouth, impudent nose, and a persuasive, provocative charm; she sits saucily before us today as part of a frieze in which high personages gaze upon some spectacle that we shall never see.[13]

The men of Crete are evidently grateful for the grace and adventure that women give to life, for they provide them with costly means of enhancing their loveliness. The remains are rich in jewelry of many kinds: hairpins of copper and gold, stickpins adorned with golden animals or flowers, or heads of crystal or quartz; rings or spirals of filigree gold mingling with the hair, fillets or diadems of precious metal binding it; rings and pendants hanging from the ear, plaques and beads and chains on the breast, bands and bracelets on the arm, finger rings of silver, steatite, agate, carnelian, amethyst, or gold. The men keep some of the jewelry for themselves: if they are poor they carry necklaces and bracelets of common stones; if they can afford it they flaunt great rings engraved with scenes of battle or the chase. The famous Cupbearer wears on the biceps of his left arm a broad band of precious metal, and on the wrist a bangle inlaid with agate. Everywhere in Cretan life man expresses his vainest and noblest passion—the zeal to beautify.

This use of *man* to signify all humanity reveals the prejudice of a patriarchal age, and hardly suits the almost matriarchal life of ancient Crete. For the Minoan woman does not put up with any Oriental seclusion, any purdah or harem; there is no sign of her being limited to certain quarters of the house, or to the home. She works there, doubtless, as some women do even today; she weaves clothing and baskets, grinds grain, and bakes bread. But also she labors with men in the fields and the potteries, she mingles freely with them in the crowds, she takes the front seat at the theater and the games, she sweeps through Cretan society with the air of a great lady bored with adoration; and when her nation creates its gods it is more often in her likeness than in man's. Sober students, secretly and forgivably enamored of the mother image in their hearts, bow down before her relics, and marvel at her domination.[14]

2. *Society*

Hypothetically we picture Crete as at first an island divided by its mountains among petty jealous clans which live in independent villages under their own chiefs, and fight, after the manner of men, innumerable territorial wars. Then a resolute leader appears who unites several clans into a kingdom, and builds his fortress palace at Cnossus, Phaestus, Tylissus, or some other town. The wars become less frequent, more widespread, and more efficient in killing; at last the cities fight for the entire island, and Cnossus wins. The victor organizes a navy, dominates the Aegean, suppresses piracy, exacts tribute, builds palaces, and patronizes the arts, like an early Pericles.[19] It is as difficult to begin a civilization without robbery as it is to maintain it without slaves.*

The power of the king, as echoed in the ruins, is based upon force, re-

* The usually cautious and accurate Thucydides writes: "The first person known to us by tradition as having established a navy is Minos. He made himself master of what is now called the Hellenic Sea, and ruled over the Cyclades. . . . He did his best to put down piracy in those waters, a necessary step to secure the revenues for his own use."[20]

ligion, and law. To make obedience easier he suborns the gods to his use: his priests explain to the people that he is descended from Velchanos, and has received from this deity the laws that he decrees; and every nine years, if he is competent or generous, they reanoint him with the divine authority. To symbolize his power the monarch, anticipating Rome and France, adopts the (double) ax and the fleur-de-lis. To administer the state he employs (as the litter of tablets suggests) a staff of ministers, bureaucrats, and scribes. He taxes in kind, and stores in giant jars his revenues of grain, oil, and wine; and out of this treasury, in kind, he pays his men. From his throne in the palace, or his judgment seat in the royal villa, he settles in person such litigation as has run the gauntlet of his appointed courts; and so great is his reputation as a magistrate that when he dies he becomes in Hades, Homer assures us, the inescapable judge of the dead.[21] We call him Minos, but we do not know his name; probably the word is a title, like *Pharaoh* or *Caesar*, and covers a multitude of kings.

At its height this civilization is surprisingly urban. The *Iliad* speaks of Crete's "ninety cities," and the Greeks who conquer them are astonished at their teeming populations; even today the student stands in awe before the ruined mazes of paved and guttered streets, intersecting lanes, and countless shops or houses crowding about some center of trade or government in all the huddled gregariousness of timid and talkative men. It is not only Cnossus that is great, with palaces so vast that imagination perhaps exaggerates the town that must have been the chief source and beneficiary of their wealth. Across the island, on the southern shore, is Phaestus, from whose harbor, Homer tells us, "the dark-prowed ships are borne to Egypt by the force of the wind and the wave."[22] The southbound trade of Minoan Crete pours out here, swelled by goods from northern merchants who ship their cargoes overland to avoid a long detour by perilous seas. Phaestus becomes a Cretan Piraeus, in love with commerce rather than with art. And yet the palace of its prince is a majestic edifice, reached by a flight of steps forty-five feet wide; its halls and courts compare with those at Cnossus; its central court is a paved quadrangle of ten thousand square feet; its megaron, or reception room, is three thousand square feet in area, larger even than the great Hall of the Double Ax in the northern capital.

Two miles northwest is Hagia Triada, in whose "royal villa" (as archeological imagination calls it) the Prince of Phaestus seeks refuge from the summer heat. The eastern end of the island, in Minoan days, is rich in small towns: ports like Zakro or Mochlos, villages like Praesus or Pseira, residential quarters like Palaikastro, manufacturing centers like Gournia. The main street in Palaikastro is well paved, well drained, and lined with spacious homes; one of these has twenty-three rooms on the surviving floor. Gournia boasts of avenues paved with gypsum, of homes built with mortarless stone, of a blacksmith's shop with extant forge, of a carpenter shop with a kit of tools, of small factories noisy with metalworking, shoemaking, vasemaking, oil refining, or textile industry; the modern workmen who excavate it, and gather up its tripods, jars, pottery, ovens, lamps, knives, mortars, polishers, hooks, pins, daggers, and swords, marvel at its varied products and equipment, and call it *he mechanike polis*—"the town of machinery."[23] By our standards the minor streets are narrow, mere alleys in the style of a semitropical Orient that fears the sun; and the rectangular houses, of wood or brick or stone, are for the most part confined to a single floor. Yet some Middle Minoan plaques exhumed at Cnossus show us homes of two, three, even five stories, with a cubicle attic or turret here and there; on the upper floors, in these pictured houses, are windows with red panes of unknown material. Double doors, swinging on posts apparently of cypress wood, open from the ground-floor rooms upon a shaded court. Stairways lead to the upper floors and the roof, where the Cretan sleeps when the nights are very warm. If he spends the evening indoors he lights his room by burning oil, according to his income, in lamps of clay, steatite, gypsum, marble, or bronze.[24]

We know a trifle or two about the games he plays. At home he likes a form of chess, for he has bequeathed to us, in the ruins of the Cnossus palace, a magnificent gaming board with frame of ivory, squares of silver and gold, and a border of seventy-two daisies in precious metal and stone. In the fields he takes with zest and audacity to the chase, guided by half-wild cats and slender thoroughbred hounds. In the towns he patronizes pugilists, and on his vases and reliefs he represents for us a variety of contests, in which lightweights spar with bare hands and kicking feet, middleweights with plumed helmets batter each other manfully, and heavyweights, coddled with helmets, cheekpieces, and long padded gloves, fight till one falls exhausted to the ground and the other stands above him in the conscious grandeur of victory.[25]

But the Cretan's greatest thrill comes when he wins his way into the crowd that fills the amphitheater on a holiday to see men and women face death against huge charging bulls. Time and again he pictures the stages of this lusty sport: the daring hunter capturing the bull by jumping astride its neck as it laps up water from a pool; the professional tamer twisting the animal's head until it learns some measure of tolerance for the acrobat's annoying tricks; the skilled performer, slim and agile, meeting the bull in the arena, grasping its horns, leaping into the air, somersaulting over its back, and landing feet first on the ground in the arms of a female companion who lends her grace to the scene.[26] Even in Minoan Crete this is already an ancient art; a clay cylinder from Cappadocia, ascribed to 2400 B.C., shows a bull-grappling sport as vigorous and dangerous as in these frescoes.[27] For a moment our oversimplifying intellects catch a glimpse of the contradictory complexity of man as we perceive that this game of blood-lust and courage, still popular today, is as old as civilization.

3. Religion

The Cretan may be brutal, but he is certainly religious, with a thoroughly human mixture of fetishism and superstition, idealism and reverence. He worships mountains, caves, stones, the number 3, trees and pillars, sun and moon, goats and snakes, doves and bulls; hardly anything escapes his theology. He conceives the air as filled with spirits genial or devilish, and hands down to Greece a sylvan-ethereal population of dryads, sileni, and nymphs. He does not directly adore the phallic emblem, but he venerates with awe the generative vitality of the bull and the snake.[28] Since his death rate is high he pays devout homage to fertility, and when he rises to the notion of a human divinity he pictures a mother goddess with generous mammae and sublime flanks, with reptiles creeping up around her arms and breasts, coiled in her hair, or rearing themselves proudly from her head. He sees in her the basic fact of nature—that man's greatest enemy, death, is overcome by woman's mysterious power, reproduction; and he identifies this power with deity. The mother goddess represents for him the source of all life, in plants and animals as well as in men; if he surrounds her image with fauna and flora it is because these exist through her creative fertility, and therefore serve as her symbols and her emanations. Occasionally she appears holding in her arms her divine child Velchanos, whom she has borne in a mountain cave.[29] Contemplating this ancient image, we see through it Isis and Horus, Ishtar and Tammuz, Cybele and Attis, Aphrodite and Adonis, and feel the unity of prehistoric culture, and the continuity of religious ideas and symbols, in the Mediterranean world.

The Cretan Zeus, as the Greeks call Velchanos, is subordinate to his mother in the affections of the Cretans. But he grows in importance. He becomes the personification of the fertilizing rain, of the moisture that in this religion, as in the philosophy of Thales, underlies all things. He dies, and his sepulcher is shown from generation to generation on Mt. Iouktas, where the majestic profile of his face can still be seen by the imaginative traveler; he rises from the grave as a symbol of reviving vegetation, and the Kouretes priests celebrate with dances and clashing shields his glorious resurrection.[30] Sometimes, as a god of fertility, he is conceived as incarnate in the sacred bull; it is as a bull that he mates in Cretan myth with Minos' wife Pasiphaë, and begets by her the monstrous Minos-bull, or Minotaur.

To appease these deities the Cretan uses a lavish rite of prayer and sacrifice, symbol and ceremony, administered usually by women priests, sometimes by officials of the state. To ward off demons he burns incense; to arouse a negligent divinity he sounds the conch, plays the flute or the lyre, and sings, in chorus, hymns of adoration. To promote the growth of orchards and the fields, he waters trees and plants in solemn ritual; or his priestesses in nude frenzy shake down the ripe burden of the trees; or his women in festal procession carry fruits and flowers as hints and tribute to the goddess, who is borne in state in a palanquin. He has apparently no temple, but raises altars in the palace court, in sacred groves or grottoes, and on mountaintops. He adorns these sanctuaries with tables of libation and sacrifice, a medley of idols, and "horns of consecration" perhaps representative of the sacred bull. He is profuse with holy symbols, which he seems to worship along with the gods whom they signify: first the shield, presumably as the emblem of his goddess in her warrior form; then the cross—in both its Greek and its Roman shapes, and as the swastika—cut upon the forehead of a bull or the thigh of a goddess, or carved upon seals, or raised in marble in the palace of the king; above all, the double ax, as an instrument of sacrifice magically enriched with the virtue of the blood that it sheds, or as a holy weapon unerringly guided by the god, or even as a sign of Zeus the Thunderer cleaving the sky with his bolts.[a]

Finally he offers a modest care and worship to his dead. He buries them in clay coffins or massive jars, for if they are unburied they may return. To keep them content below the ground he deposits with them modest portions of food, articles for their toilette, and clay figurines of women to tend or console them through all eternity. Sometimes, with the sly economy of an incipient skeptic, he substitutes clay animals in the grave in place of actual food. If he buries a king or a noble or a rich trader he surrenders to the corpse a part of the precious plate or jewelry that it once possessed; with touching sympathy he buries a set of chess with a good player, a clay orchestra with a musician, a boat with one who loved the sea. Periodically he returns to the grave to offer a sustaining sacrifice of food to the dead. He hopes that in some secret Elysium, or Islands of the Blest, the just god Rhadamanthus, son of Zeus Velchanos, will receive the purified soul, and give it the happiness and the peace that slip so elusively through the fingers in this earthly quest.

4. Culture

The most troublesome aspect of the Cretan is his language. When, after the Dorian invasion, he uses the Greek alphabet, it is for a speech completely alien to what we know as Greek, and more akin in sound to the Egyptian, Cypriote, Hittite, and Anatolian dialects of the Near East. In the earliest age he confines himself to hieroglyphics; about 1800 B.C. he begins to shorten these into a linear script of some ninety syllabic signs; two centuries later he contrives another script, whose characters often resemble those of the Phoenician alphabet; perhaps it is from him, as well as from the Egyptians and the Semites, that the Phoenicians gather together those letters they will scatter throughout the Mediterranean to become the unassuming, omnipresent instrument of Western civilization. Even the common Cretan composes, and like some privy councilor, leaves on the walls of Hagia Triada the passing inspirations of his muse. At Phaestus we find a kind of prehistoric printing: the hieroglyphs of a great disk unearthed there from Middle Minoan III strata are impressed upon the clay by stamps, one for each pictograph; but here, to add to our befuddlement, the characters are apparently not Cretan but foreign; perhaps the disk is an importation from the East.[82]

The clay tablets upon which the Cretan writes may some day reveal to us his accomplishments in science. He has some astronomy, for he is famed as a navigator, and tradition hands down to Dorian Crete the ancient Minoan calendar. The Egyptians acknowledge their indebtedness to him for certain medical prescriptions, and the Greeks borrow from him, as the words suggest, such aromatic and medicinal herbs as mint (*mintha*), wormwood (*apsinthon*), and an ideal drug (*daukos*) reputed to cure obesity without disturbing gluttony.[83] But we must not mistake our guessing for history.

Though the Cretan's literature is a sealed book to us, we may at least contemplate the ruins of his theaters. At Phaestus, about 2000, he builds ten tiers of stone seats, running some eighty feet along a wall overlooking a flagged court; at Cnossus he raises, again in stone, eighteen tiers thirty-three feet long, and, at right angles to them, six tiers from eighteen to fifty feet in length. These court theaters, seating four or five hundred persons, are the most ancient playhouses known to us—older by fifteen hundred years than the Theater of Dionysus. We do not know what took place on those stages; frescoes picture audiences viewing a spectacle, but we cannot tell what it is that they see. Very likely it is some combination of music and dance. A painting from Cnossus preserves a group of aristocratic ladies, surrounded by their gallants, watching a dance by gaily petticoated girls in an olive grove; another represents a *Dancing Woman* with flying tresses and extended arms; others show us rustic folk dances, or the wild dance of priests, priestesses, and worshipers before an idol or a sacred tree. Homer describes the "dancing-floor which once, in broad Cnossus, Daedalus made for Ariadne of the lovely hair; there youths and seductive maidens join hands in the dance . . . and a divine bard sets the time to the sound of the lyre."[84] The seven-stringed lyre, ascribed by the Greeks to the inventiveness of Terpander, is represented on a sarcophagus at Hagia Triada a thousand years before Terpander's birth. There, too, is the double flute, with two pipes, eight holes, and fourteen notes, precisely as in classical Greece. Carved on a gem, a woman blows a trumpet made from an enormous conch, and on a vase we see the sistrum beating time for the dancers' feet.

The same youthful freshness and lighthearted grace that animate his dances and his games enliven the Cretan's work in the arts. He has not left us, aside from his architecture, any accomplishments of massive grandeur or exalted style; like the Japanese of samurai days he delights rather in the refinement of the lesser and more intimate arts, the adornment of objects daily used, the patient perfecting of little things. As in every aristocratic civilization, he accepts conventions in the form and subject of his work, avoids extravagant novelties, and learns to be free even within the limitations of reserve and taste. He excels in pottery, gem cutting, bezel carving, and reliefs, for here his microscopic skill finds every stimulus and opportunity. He is at home in the working of silver and gold, sets all the precious stones, and makes a rich diversity of jewels. Upon the seals that he cuts to serve as official signatures, commercial labels, or business forms, he engraves in delicate detail so much of the life and scenery of Crete that from them alone we might picture his civilization. He hammers bronze into basins, ewers, daggers, and swords ornamented with floral and animal designs, and inlaid with gold and silver, ivory and rare stones. At Gournia he has left us, despite the thieves of thirty centuries, a silver cup of finished artistry; and here and there he has molded for us rhytons, or drinking horns, rising out of human or animal heads that to this day seem to hold the breath of life.

As a potter he tries every form, and reaches distinction in nearly all of them. He makes vases, dishes, cups, chalices, lamps, jars, animals, and gods. At first, in Early Minoan, he is content to shape the vessel with his hands along lines bequeathed to him from the Neolithic Age, to paint it with a glaze of brown or black, and to trust the fire to mottle the color into haphazard tints. In Middle Minoan he has learned the use of the wheel, and rises to the height of his skill. He makes a glaze rivaling the consistency and delicacy of porcelain; he scatters recklessly black and brown, white and red, orange and yellow, crimson and vermilion, and mingles them happily into novel shades; he fines down the clay with such confident thoroughness that in his most perfect product—the graceful and brightly colored "eggshell" wares found in the cave of Kamares on Mt. Ida's slopes—he has dared to thin the walls of the vessel to a millimeter's thickness, and to pour out upon it all the motifs of his rich imagination. From 2100 to 1950 is the apogee of the Cretan potter; he signs his name to his work, and his trade-mark is sought throughout the Mediterranean. In the Late Minoan Age he brings to full development the technique of faïence, and forms the brilliant paste into decorative plaques, vases of turquoise blue, polychrome goddesses, and marine reliefs so realistic that Evans mistook an enamel crab for a fossil.[35] Now the artist falls in love with nature, and delights to represent on his vessels the liveliest animals, the gaudiest fish, the most delicate flowers, and the most graceful plants. It is in Late Minoan I that he creates his surviving masterpieces, the Boxers' Vase and the Harvesters' Vase: in the one he presents us crudely with every aspect and attitude of the pugilistic game, adding a zone of scenes from the bull-leaper's life; in the other he follows with fond fidelity a procession probably of peasants marching and singing in some harvest festival. Then the great tradition of Cretan pottery grows weak with age, and the art declines; reserve and taste are forgotten, decoration overruns the vase in bizarre irregularity and excess, the courage for slow conception and patient execution breaks down, and a lazy carelessness called freedom replaces the finesse and finish of the Kamares age. It is a forgivable decay, the unavoidable death of an old and exhausted art, which will lie in refreshing sleep for a thousand years, and be reborn in the perfection of the Attic vase.

Sculpture is a minor art in Crete, and except in bas-relief and the story of Daedalus, seldom graduates from the statuette. Many of these little figures are stereotyped crudities seemingly produced by rote; one is a delightful snapshot in ivory of an athlete plunging through the air; another is a handsome head that has lost its body on the way down the centuries. The best of them excels in anatomical precision and in vividness of action anything that we know from Greece before Myron's time. The strangest is the *Snake Goddess* of the Boston Museum—a sturdy figure of ivory and gold, half mammae and half snakes; here at last the Cretan artist treats the human form with some amplitude and success. But when he essays a larger scale he falls back for the most part upon animals, and confines himself to painted reliefs, as in the bull's head in the Heracleum Museum; in this startling relic the fixed wild eyes, the snorting nostrils, the gasping mouth, and the trembling tongue achieve a power that Greece itself will never surpass.

Nothing else in ancient Crete is quite so attractive as its painting. The sculpture is negligible, the pottery is fragmentary, the architecture is in ruins; but this frailest of all the arts, easy victim of indifferent time, has left us legible and admirable masterpieces from an age so old that it slipped quite out of the memory of that classic Greece of whose painting, by contrast so recent, not one original remains. In Crete the earthquakes or the wars that overturned the palaces preserved here and there a frescoed wall; and wandering by them we molt forty centuries and meet the men who decorated the rooms of the Minoan kings. As far back as 2500 they make wall coatings of pure lime, and conceive the idea of painting in fresco upon the wet surface, wielding the brush so rapidly that the colors sink into the stucco before the surface dries. Into the dark halls of the palaces they bring the bright beauty of the open fields; they make plaster sprout lilies, tulips, narcissi, and sweet marjoram; no one viewing these scenes could ever again suppose that nature was discovered by Rousseau. In the museum at Heracleum the Saffron Picker is as eager to pluck the crocus as when his creator painted him in Middle Minoan days; his waist is absurdly thin, his body seems much too long for his legs; and yet his head is perfect, the colors are soft and warm, the flowers still fresh after four thousand years. At Hagia Triada the painter brightens a sarcophagus with spiral scrolls and queer, almost Nubian figures engrossed in some religious ritual; better yet, he adorns a wall with waving foliage, and then places in the midst of it, darkly but vividly, a stout, tense cat preparing to spring unseen upon a proud bird preening its plumage in the sun. In Late Minoan the Cretan painter is at the top of his stride; every wall tempts him, every plutocrat calls him; he decorates not merely the royal residences but the homes of nobles and burghers with all the lavishness of Pompeii. Soon, however, success and a surfeit of commissions spoil him; he is too anxious to be finished to quite touch perfection; he scatters quantity about him, repeats his flowers monotonously, paints his men impossibly, contents himself with sketching outlines, and falls into the lassitude of an art that knows that it has passed its zenith and must die. But never before, except perhaps in Egypt, has painting looked so freshly at the face of nature.

All the arts come together to build the Cretan palaces. Political power, commercial mastery, wealth and luxury, accumulated refinement and taste commandeer the architect, the builder, the artisan, the sculptor, the potter, the metalworker, the woodworker, and the painter to fuse their skills in producing an assemblage of royal chambers, administrative offices, court theaters, and arenas, to serve as the center and summit of Cretan life. They build in the twenty-first century, and the twentieth sees their work destroyed; they build again in the seventeenth, not only the palace of Minos but many other splendid edifices at Cnossus, and in half a hundred other cities in the thriving island. It is one of the great ages in architectural history.

The creators of the Cnossus palace are limited in both materials and men. Crete is poor in metal and quite devoid of marble; therefore they build with limestone and gypsum, and use wood for entablatures, roofs, and all columns above the basement floor. They cut the stone blocks so sharply that they can put them together without mortar. Around a central court of twenty thousand square feet they raise to three or four stories, with spacious stairways of stone, a rambling maze of rooms—guardhouses, workshops, wine press, storerooms, administrative offices, servants' quarters, anterooms, reception rooms, bedrooms, bathrooms, chapel, dungeon, throne room, and a

"Hall of the Double Ax"; adding near by the conveniences of a theater, a royal villa, and a cemetery. On the lowest floor they plant massive square pillars of stone; on the upper floors they use circular columns of cypress, tapering strangely downward, to support the ceilings upon smooth round capitals, or to form shady porticoes at the side. Safe in the interior against a gracefully decorated wall they set a stone seat, simply but skillfully carved, which eager diggers will call the throne of Minos, and on which every tourist will modestly seat himself and be for a moment some inches a king. This sprawling palace in all likelihood is the famous Labyrinth, or sanctuary of the Double Ax (labrys), attributed by the ancients to Daedalus, and destined to give its name in aftertime to any maze—of rooms, or words, or ears.*[36]

As if to please the modern spirit, more interested in plumbing than in poetry, the builders of Cnossus install in the palace a system of drainage superior to anything else of its kind in antiquity. They collect in stone conduits the water that flows down from the hills or falls from the sky, direct it through shafts to the bathrooms† and latrines, and lead off the waste in terra-cotta pipes of the latest style—each section six inches in diameter and thirty inches long, equipped with a trap to catch the sediment, tapering at one end to fit into the next section, and bound to this firmly with a necking of cement.[38] Possibly they include an apparatus for supplying running hot water to the household of the king.‡[39]

To the complex interiors the artists of Cnossus add the most delicate decorations. Some of the rooms they adorn with vases and statuettes, some with paintings or reliefs, some with huge stone amphorae or massive urns, some with objects in ivory, faïence or bronze. Around one wall they run a limestone frieze with pretty triglyphs and half rosettes; around another a panel of spirals and frets on a surface painted to simulate marble; around another they carve in high relief and living detail the contests of man and bull. Through the halls and chambers the Minoan painter spreads all the glories of his cheerful art: here, caught chattering in a drawing room, are Ladies in Blue, with classic features, shapely arms, and cozy breasts; here

* The ascription of rooms is, of course, highly conjectural. It should be added that nearly all the exhumed decorations of the palace have been removed to the museum at Heracleum or elsewhere, while much of what remains in site has been tastelessly restored.

† It is no longer agreed that the square depressions found in the floors of some rooms were baths; they have no outlets, and are made of gypsum, which water would gradually dissolve.[37]

‡ Mosso found similar drainage pipes in the villa at Hagia Triada. "One day, after a heavy downpour of rain, I was interested to find that all the drains acted perfectly, and I saw the water flow from the sewers, through which a man could walk upright. I doubt if there is any other instance of a drainage system acting after four thousand years."[40]

are fields of lotus, or lilies, or olive spray; here are Ladies at the Opera, and dolphins swimming motionlessly in the sea. Here, above all, is the lordly Cupbearer, erect and strong, carrying some precious ointment in a slim blue vase; his face is chiseled by breeding as well as by art; his hair descends in a thick braid upon his brown shoulders; his ears, his neck, his arm, and his waist sparkle with jewelry, and his costly robe is embroidered with a graceful quatrefoil design; obviously he is no slave, but some aristocratic youth proudly privileged to serve the king. Only a civilization long familiar with order and wealth, leisure and taste, could demand or create such luxury and such ornament.

IV. THE FALL OF CNOSSUS

When in retrospect we seek the origin of this brilliant culture, we find ourselves vacillating between Asia and Egypt. On the one hand, the Cretans seem kin in language, race, and religion to the Indo-European peoples of Asia Minor; there, too, clay tablets were used for writing, and the shekel was the standard of measurement; there, in Caria, was the cult of Zeus Labrandeus, i.e., Zeus of the Double Ax (labrys); there men worshiped the pillar, the bull, and the dove; there, in Phrygia, was the great Cybele, so much like the mother goddess of Crete that the Greeks called the latter Rhea Cybele, and considered the two divinities one.[40a] And yet the signs of Egyptian influence in Crete abound in every age. The two cultures are at first so much alike that some scholars presume a wave of Egyptian emigration to Crete in the troubled days of Menes.[41] The stone vases of Mochlos and the copper weapons of Early Minoan I are strikingly like those found in Proto-Dynastic tombs; the double ax appears as an amulet in Egypt, and even a "Priest of the Double Ax"; the weights and measures, though Asiatic in value, are Egyptian in form; the methods used in the glyptic arts, in faïence, and in painting are so similar in the two lands that Spengler reduced Cretan civilization to a mere branch of the Egyptian.[42]

We shall not follow him, for it will not do, in our search for the continuity of civilization, to surrender the individuality of the parts. The Cretan quality is distinct; no other people in antiquity has quite this flavor of minute refinement, this concentrated elegance in life and art. Let us believe that in its racial origins the Cretan culture was Asiatic, in many of its arts Egyptian; in essence and total it remained unique. Perhaps it belonged to a complex of civilization common to all the Eastern Mediterranean, in which each nation inherited kindred arts, beliefs, and ways from a widespread neolithic culture parent to them all. From that common civilization

Crete borrowed in her youth, to it she contributed in her maturity. Her rule forged an order in the isles, and her merchants found entry at every port. Then her wares and her arts pervaded the Cyclades, overran Cyprus, reached to Caria and Palestine,[43] moved north through Asia Minor and its islands to Troy, reached west through Italy and Sicily to Spain,[44] penetrated the mainland of Greece even to Thessaly, and passed through Mycenae and Tiryns into the heritage of Greece. In the history of civilization Crete was the first link in the European chain.

We do not know which of the many roads to decay Crete chose; perhaps she took them all. Her once famous forests of cypress and cedar vanished; today two thirds of the island are a stony waste, incapable of holding the winter rains.[45] Perhaps there too, as in most declining cultures, population control went too far, and reproduction was left to the failures. Perhaps, as wealth and luxury increased, the pursuit of physical pleasure sapped the vitality of the race, and weakened its will to live or to defend itself; a nation is born stoic and dies epicurean. Possibly the collapse of Egypt after the death of Ikhnaton disrupted Creto-Egyptian trade, and diminished the riches of the Minoan kings. Crete had no great internal resources; her prosperity required commerce, and markets for her industries; like modern England she had become dangerously dependent upon control of the seas. Perhaps internal wars decimated the island's manhood, and left it disunited against foreign attack. Perhaps an earthquake shook the palaces into ruins, or some angry revolution avenged in a year of terror the accumulated oppressions of centuries.

About 1450 the palace of Phaestus was again destroyed, that of Hagia Triada was burned down, the homes of the rich burghers of Tylissus disappeared. During the next fifty years Cnossus seems to have enjoyed the zenith of her fortune, and a supremacy unquestioned throughout the Aegean. Then, about 1400, the palace of Cnossus itself went up in flames. Everywhere in the ruins Evans found signs of uncontrollable fire—charred beams and pillars, blackened walls, and clay tablets hardened against time's tooth by the conflagration's heat. So thorough was the destruction, and so complete the removal of metal even from rooms covered and protected by debris, that many students suspect invasion and conquest rather than earthquake.*[46] In any case, the catastrophe was sudden; the workshops of artists

* If archeological chronology would permit the deferment of this conflagration to the neighborhood of 1250 it would be convenient to interpret the tragedy as an incident in the Achaean conquest of the Aegean preliminary to the siege of Troy.

and artisans give every indication of having been in full activity when death arrived. About the same time Gournia, Pseira, Zakro, and Palaikastro were leveled to the ground.

We must not suppose that Cretan civilization vanished overnight. Palaces were built again, but more modestly, and for a generation or two the products of Crete continued to dominate Aegean art. About the middle of the thirteenth century we come at last upon a specific Cretan personality—that King Minos of whom Greek tradition told so many frightening tales. His brides were annoyed at the abundance of serpents and scorpions in his seed; but by some secret device his wife Pasiphaë eluded these,[47] and safely bore him many children, among them Phaedra (wife of Theseus and lover of Hippolytus) and the fair-haired Ariadne. Minos having offended Poseidon, the god afflicted Pasiphaë with a mad passion for a divine bull. Daedalus pitied her, and through his contrivance she conceived the terrible Minotaur. Minos imprisoned the animal in the Labyrinth which Daedalus had built at his command, but appeased it periodically with human sacrifice.[48]

Pleasanter even in its tragedy is the legend of Daedalus, for it opens one of the proudest epics of human history. Greek story represented him as an Athenian Leonardo who, envious of his nephew's skill, slew him in a moment of temperament, and was banished forever from Greece. He found refuge at Minos' court, astonished him with mechanical inventions and novelties, and became chief artist and engineer to the king. He was a great sculptor, and fable used his name to personify the graduation of statuary from stiff, dead figures to vivid portraits of possible men; the creatures made by him, we are informed, were so lifelike that they stood up and walked away unless they were chained to their pedestals.[49] But Minos was peeved when he learned of Daedalus' connivance with Pasiphaë's amours, and confined him and his son Icarus in the maze of the Labyrinth. Daedalus fashioned wings for himself and Icarus, and by their aid they leaped across the walls and soared over the Mediterranean. Disdaining his father's counsel, proud Icarus flew too closely to the sun; the hot rays melted the wax on his wings, and he was lost in the sea, pointing a moral and adorning a tale. Daedalus, empty-hearted, flew on to Sicily, and stirred that island to civilization by bringing to it the industrial and artistic culture of Crete.*[50]

* Pausanias, father of all Baedekers, credits Daedalus with several statues, mostly of wood, and a marble relief of Ariadne dancing, as all extant in the second century A.D.[51] The Greeks never doubted the reality of Daedalus, and the experience of Schliemann warns us to be skeptical even of our skepticism. Old traditions have a way of being easily rejected by one generation of scholars, and laboriously confirmed by the next.

More tragic still is the story of Theseus and Ariadne. Minos, victorious in a war against youthful Athens, exacted from that city, every ninth year, a tribute of seven girls and seven young men, to be devoured by the Minotaur. On the coming of the third occasion for this national humiliation the handsome Theseus—his father King Aegeus reluctantly consenting—had himself chosen as one of the seven youths, for he was resolved to slay the Minotaur and end the recurrent sacrifice. Ariadne pitied the princely Athenian, loved him, gave him a magic sword, and taught him the simple trick of unraveling thread from his arm as he penetrated the Labyrinth. Theseus killed the Minotaur, followed the thread back to Ariadne, and took her with him on his flight from Crete. On the isle of Naxos he married her as he had promised, but while she slept he and his companions sailed treacherously away.*[52]

With Ariadne and Minos, Crete disappears from history till the coming of Lycurgus to the island, presumably in the seventh century. There are indications that the Achaeans reached it in their long raid of Greece in the fourteenth and thirteenth centuries, and Dorian conquerors settled there towards the end of the second millennium before Christ. Here, said many Cretans and some Greeks,[53] Lycurgus, and in less degree Solon, had found the model for their laws. In Crete as in Sparta, after the island had come under Dorian sway, the ruling class led a life of at least outward simplicity and restraint; the boys were brought up in the army, and the adult males ate together in public mess halls; the state was ruled by a senate of elders, and was administered by ten *kosmoi* or orderers, corresponding to the ephors of Sparta and the archons of Athens.[54] It is difficult to say whether Crete taught Sparta, or Sparta Crete; perhaps both states were the parallel results of similar conditions—the precarious life of an alien military aristocracy amid a native and hostile population of serfs. The comparatively enlightened law code of Gortyna, discovered on the walls of that Cretan town in A.D. 1884, belongs apparently to the early fifth century; in an earlier form it may have influenced the legislators of Greece. In the sixth century Thaletas of Crete taught choral music at Sparta, and the Cretan sculptors Dipoenus and Scyllis instructed the artists of Argos and Sicyon. By a hundred channels the old civilization emptied itself out into the new.

* The Athenians counted all this as history. They treasured for centuries, by continually repairing it, the ship in which Theseus had sailed to Crete, and used it as a sacred vessel in sending envoys annually to the feast of Apollo at Delos.

CHAPTER II

Before Agamemnon

I. SCHLIEMANN

IN the year 1822 a lad was born in Germany who was to turn the spadework of archeology into one of the romances of the century. His father had a passion for ancient history, and brought him up on Homer's stories of the siege of Troy and Odysseus' wanderings. "With great grief I heard from him that Troy had been so completely destroyed that it had disappeared without leaving any trace of its existence."[1] At the age of eight, having given the matter mature consideration, Heinrich Schliemann announced his intention to devote his life to the rediscovery of the lost city. At the age of ten he presented to his father a Latin essay on the Trojan War. In 1836 he left school with an education too advanced for his means, and became a grocer's apprentice. In 1841 he shipped from Hamburg as cabin boy on a steamer bound for South America. Twelve days out the vessel foundered; the crew was tossed about in a small boat for nine hours, and was thrown by the tide upon the shores of Holland. Heinrich became a clerk, and earned a hundred and fifty dollars a year; he spent half of this on books, and lived on the other half and his dreams.[2] His intelligence and application had their natural results; at twenty-five he was an independent merchant with interests on three continents; at thirty-six he felt that he had enough money, retired from commerce, and gave all his time to archeology. "In the midst of the bustle of business I had never forgotten Troy, or the agreement I had made with my father to excavate it."[3]

In his travels as a merchant he had made it a practice to learn the language of each country he traded with, and to write in that language the current pages of his diary.[4] By this method he learned English, French, Dutch, Spanish, Portuguese, Italian, Russian, Swedish, Polish, and Arabic. Now he went to Greece, studied the language as a living speech, and was soon able to read both ancient and modern Greek as fluently as German.* Henceforth, he declared, "I should find it impossible to live anywhere but on classical soil."[6] Since his Russian wife refused to leave Russia, he advertised for a Greek wife, laid down precise specifications for the position, and at the age of forty-seven chose a bride of nineteen from among the photographs he received. He married her almost at sight, and unwittingly in the ancient style of purchase; her parents charged him for her a price commensurate with their conception of his fortune. When his new wife bore him children he reluctantly consented to baptize them, but solemnized the ceremony by laying a copy of the *Iliad* upon their heads and reading a hundred hexameters aloud. He named them Andromache and Agamemnon, called his servants Telamon and Pelops, and christened his Athenian home Bellerophon.[7] He was an old man mad about Homer.

In 1870 he went to the Troad—the northwest corner of Asia Minor—and made up his mind, against all current scholarly opinion, that Priam's Troy lay buried under the hill called Hissarlik. After a year of negotiations he secured permission from the Turkish Government to explore the site; he engaged eighty laborers, and set to work. His wife, who loved him for his eccentricities, shared his toil in the earth from sunrise to sunset. All winter long an icy gale from the north drove a blinding dust into their eyes, and swept with such violence through the cracks of their frail cottage that no lamp could be kept lit in the evening. Despite the fire in the hearth the water froze nearly every night. "We had nothing to keep us warm except our enthusiasm for the great work of discovering Troy."[8]

A year passed before they were rewarded. Then, blow by blow, a workman's pick exposed a large copper vessel, and this, opened, revealed an astonishing treasure of some nine thousand objects in silver and gold. The canny Schliemann hid the find in his wife's shawl, dismissed his workmen to an unexpected siesta, hurried to his hut, locked the door, spread out the precious things on the table, linked each one fondly with some passage in

---

* "In order to acquire quickly the Greek vocabulary," Schliemann writes, "I procured a modern Greek translation of *Paul et Virginie*, and read it through, comparing every word with its equivalent in the French original. When I had finished this task I knew at least one half the Greek words the book contained; and after repeating the operation I knew them all, or nearly so, without having lost a single minute by being obliged to use a dictionary. . . . Of the Greek grammar I learned only the declensions and the verbs, and never lost my precious time in studying its rules; for as I saw that boys, after being troubled and tormented for eight years and more in school with the tedious rules of grammar, can nevertheless none of them write a letter in ancient Greek without making hundreds of atrocious blunders, I thought the method pursued by the schoolmasters must be altogether wrong. . . . I learned ancient Greek as I would have learned a living language."[5]

Homer, adorned his wife with an ancient diadem, and sent messages to his friends in Europe that he had unearthed "the Treasury of Priam."[9] No one would believe him; some critics charged him with having placed the objects where he found them; and at the same time the Sublime Porte sued him for taking gold from Turkish soil. But scholars like Virchow, Dörpfeld, and Burnouf came to the site, verified Schliemann's reports, and carried on the work with him until one buried Troy after another was uncovered, and the problem was no longer whether Troy had existed, but which of the nine Troys exhumed had been the Ilios of the *Iliad*.

In 1876 Schliemann resolved to confirm the epic from another direction—to show that Agamemnon too was real. Guided by Pausanias' classic description of Greece,* he sank thirty-four shafts at Mycenae in the eastern Peloponnesus. Turkish officials interrupted the work by claiming half of the material that he had found at Troy. Unwilling to let the precious "Treasury of Priam" lie unseen in Turkey, Schliemann clandestinely dispatched the objects to the State Museum at Berlin, paid the Porte five times more damages than were required of him, and resumed his digging at Mycenae. Again he was rewarded; and when he saw his workers carrying up to him skeletons, pottery, jewelry, and golden masks, he telegraphed joyfully to the King of Greece that he had discovered the tombs of Atreus and Agamemnon.[10] In 1884 he moved on to Tiryns and, guided again by Pausanias, unearthed the great palace and cyclopean walls that Homer had described.[11]

Seldom had any man done so much for archeology. He had the faults of his virtues, for his enthusiasm drove him into a reckless haste that destroyed or confused many exhumed objects in order to reach at once the goal that he sought; and the epics that had inspired his labors misled him into thinking that he had discovered Priam's hoard at Troy, and the tomb of Agamemnon at Mycenae. The world of scholarship doubted his reports, and the museums of England, Russia, and France long refused to accept as genuine the relics that he had found. He consoled himself with vigorous self-appreciation, and went on digging courageously until disease struck him down. In his last days he hesitated whether to pray to the God of Christianity or to the Zeus of classic Greece. "To Agamemnon Schliemann, best beloved of sons, greeting!" he writes. "I am very glad that you are going to study Plutarch, and have finished Xenophon . . . I pray Zeus the Father and Pallas Athene that they will grant you a hundred returns of the

---

* Pausanias traveled through Greece about A.D. 160, and described it in his *Periegesis*, or Tour.

day in health and happiness."[12] He died in 1890, worn out by climatic hardships, scholastic hostility, and the incessant fever of his dream.

Like Columbus he had discovered a world stranger than the one he sought. These jewels were older by many centuries than Priam and Hecuba; these graves were not the tombs of the Atridae, but the ruins of an Aegean civilization, on the Greek mainland, as ancient as the Minoan Age in Crete. Unknowingly Schliemann had proved Horace's famous line—*vixerunt fortes ante Agamemnona*—"there lived many brave men before Agamemnon."* Year by year, as Dörpfeld and Muller, Tsountas and Stamatakis, Waldstein and Wace dug more widely into the Peloponnesus, and still others explored Attica and the islands, Euboea and Boeotia, Phocis and Thessaly, the soil of Greece gave up the ghostly relics of a culture before history. Here too men had been lifted from barbarism to civilization by the passage from nomadic hunting to settled agriculture, by the replacement of stone tools with copper and bronze, by the conveniences of writing and the stimulus of trade. Civilization is always older than we think; and under whatever sod we tread are the bones of men and women who also worked and loved, wrote songs and made beautiful things, but whose names and very being have been lost in the careless flow of time.

II. IN THE PALACES OF THE KINGS

On a long low hill five miles east of Argos and a mile north of the sea, stood, in the fourteenth century before our era, the fortress-palace of Tiryns. Today one reaches its ruins by a pleasant ride from Argos or Nauplia, and finds them half lost amid quiet fields of corn and wheat. Then, after a little climb up prehistoric stone steps, the traveler stands before the cyclopean walls built, said Greek tradition, for the Argive prince Proetus, two centuries before the Trojan War.† Even then the town itself was old,

* Towards the end of his life Dörpfeld and Virchow almost convinced him that he had found the remains not of Agamemnon but of a far earlier generation. After many heartaches Schliemann took the matter good-naturedly. "What?" he exclaimed, "so this is not Agamemnon's body, these are not his ornaments? All right, let's call him Schulze"; and thereafter they always spoke of "Schulze."[13]

† The Greeks gave the name Cyclopean to such structures as in their mythical fancy could have been built only by giants like the one-eyed Titans called Cyclopes (Round-Eyes), who labored at the forges of Hephaestus in the volcanoes of the Mediterranean. Architecturally the term implied large unmortared stones, unhewn or roughly cut, and filled in at the joints with pebbles laid in clay. Tradition added that Proetus had imported celebrated masons, called Cyclopes, from Lycia.

having been founded, said ancient memory, by the hero Tiryns, son of Argus of the hundred eyes, in the infancy of the world.[14] Proteus, the story went on, gave the palace to Perseus, who ruled Tiryns with the dusky Andromeda as his queen.

The walls that protected the citadel rose from twenty-five to fifty feet in height, and were so thick that at several places they contained spacious galleries, vaulted and arched with immense overlapping horizontal slabs. Many of the stones still in place measure six feet in length by three in breadth and depth; the smallest of them, said Pausanias, "could hardly be moved by a pair of mules."[15] Within the walls, behind a propylon or gateway that set a style for many an acropolis, lay a broad paved court bounded with colonnades; and around this, as at Cnossus, was a medley of rooms gathered about the megaron—a hall of state thirteen hundred square feet in area, with a pavement of painted cement, and a ceiling supported by four columns enclosing a hearth. Here, in contrast to merry Crete, was established a lasting principle of Greek architecture—the separation of the women's quarters, or gynaeceum, from the chambers of the men. The king's room and the queen's room were built side by side, but, so far as the remains reveal, they were eremitically sealed against intercommunication. Of this palace-castle Schliemann found only the ground plan, the column bases, and portions of the wall. At the foot of the hill were the remnants of stone or brick houses and bridges, and some fragments of archaic pottery; there, in prehistoric days, the town of Tiryns huddled for protection below the palace walls. We must picture the life of Bronze Age Greece as moving insecurely around and within such feudal fortresses.

Ten miles farther north, perhaps in the fourteenth century before Christ, Perseus (if we wish to believe Pausanias[16]) built Mycenae—the greatest capital of prehistoric Greece. Here too, around a forbidding citadel, a town of several villages grew, housing a busy population of peasants, merchants, artisans, and slaves, who had the happiness of eluding history. Six hundred years later Homer called Mycenae "a well-built city, broad-avenued and abounding in gold."[17] Despite a hundred despoiling generations some parts of these also cyclopean walls survive, to attest the immemorial cheapness of labor and uneasiness of kings. In a corner of the wall is the famous Lion Gate, where, carved upon a stone triangle over a massive lintel, two royal beasts, now worn and headless, dumbly stand guard over a grandeur that is gone. On the acropolis beyond are the ruins of the palace. Again, as at Tiryns and Cnossus, we can trace the divisions of throne room, altar room, storerooms, bathroom, and reception rooms. Here once were painted floors, columned porticoes, frescoed walls, and majestic flights of stairs.

Near the Lion Gate, in a narrow area enclosed by a ring of erect stone slabs, Schliemann's workers dug up nineteen skeletons, and relics so rich that one could forgive the great amateur for seeing in these shafts the burial chambers of the children of Atreus. Had not Pausanias described the royal graves as "in the ruins of Mycenae"?[18] Here were male skulls with crowns of gold, and golden masks on the bones of the face; here were osseous ladies with golden diadems on what had been their heads; here were painted vases, bronze caldrons, a silver rhyton, beads of amber and amethyst, objects of alabaster, ivory, or faïence, heavily ornamented daggers and swords, a gaming board like that at Cnossus, and almost anything in gold—seals and rings, pins and studs, cups and beads, bracelets and breastplates, vessels of toilette, even clothing embroidered with thin plates of gold.[19] These were assuredly royal jewels, royal bones.

In the hillside opposite the acropolis Schliemann and others discovered nine tombs altogether different from these "shaft graves." Leaving the road that comes down from the citadel, one enters at the right a corridor lined with walls of large, well-cut stones. At the end is a plain portal, once adorned with slim cylindrical columns of green marble, now in the British Museum; above it is a simple lintel of two stones, one extending thirty feet and weighing 113 tons. Within, the traveler finds himself under a dome, or tholos, fifty feet high and as many wide; the walls are built of sawn blocks reinforced with decorative bronze rosettes; each stratum of stones overlaps the one beneath, until the uppermost layer closes the top. This strange structure, Schliemann thought, was the tomb of Agamemnon, and a smaller tholos near by, discovered by his wife, was at once described as the tomb of Clytaemnestra. All the "beehive" tombs at Mycenae were found empty; thieves had anticipated the archeologists by several centuries.

These gloomy ruins are the reminders of a civilization as ancient to Pericles as Charlemagne to ourselves. Current opinion dates the shaft graves near to 1600 B.C. (some four hundred years before the traditional age of Agamemnon), and the beehive tombs about 1450; but prehistoric chronology is not a precision tool. We do not know how this civilization began, nor what people it was that built towns not only at Mycenae and Tiryns but at Sparta, Amyclae, Aegina, Eleusis, Chaeronea, Orchomenos, and Delphi. Probably, like most nations, it was already composite in stock and heritage; Greece was as diverse in blood before the Dorian invasion (1100 B.C.) as England before the Norman Conquest. So far as we can guess, the

Mycenaeans were akin to the Phrygians and Carians of Asia Minor, and to the Minoans of Crete.[20] The lions of Mycenae have a Mesopotamian countenance; this ancient motif probably came through Assyria and Phrygia to Greece.[20a] Greek tradition called the Mycenaeans "Pelasgi" (possibly meaning People of the *Sea—pelagos*), and pictured them as coming down from Thrace and Thessaly into Attica and the Peloponnesus in a past so distant that the Greeks termed them *autochthonoi*—aborigines. Herodotus accepted this account, and ascribed the Olympian gods to a Pelasgic origin, but he "could not say with any certainty what the language of the Pelasgi was."[21] No more can we.

Doubtless these *autochthonoi* were themselves late-comers into a land that had suffered cultivation since neolithic days; there are no aborigines. In their turn they too were overrun; for in the later years of Mycenaean history, towards 1600, we find many indications of a cultural-commercial, if not a military-political, conquest of the Peloponnesus by the products or emigrants of Crete.[22] The palaces at Tiryns and Mycenae, except for the gynaeceum, were designed and decorated in the Minoan manner; Cretan vases and styles reached into Aegina, Chalcis, and Thebes; Mycenaean ladies and goddesses adopted the charming fashions of Crete, and the art revealed in the later shaft graves is unmistakably Minoan.[23] Apparently it was this stimulating contact with a higher culture that lifted Mycenae to the peak of its civilization.

III. MYCENAEAN CIVILIZATION

The remains of this culture are too fragmentary to give us a picture as distinct as those that take form in the ruins of Crete or the poetry of Homer. Life on the mainland was a little nearer to the hunting stage than in Crete. The bones of deer, wild boars, goats, sheep, hares, oxen, and pigs among the Mycenaean leavings—not to speak of fishbones and marine shells—indicate an appetite already Homeric, and unfriendly to the Cretan waist. Here and there the relics reveal the strange contemporaneity of "ancient" and "modern" modes—obsidian arrowheads lying beside a hollow bronze drill apparently used in boring dowel holes into stones.[24]

Industry was less advanced than in Crete; there are no signs on the mainland of such industrial centers as Gournia. Trade grew slowly, for the seas were troubled with pirates, including the Mycenaeans; the kings of Mycenae and Tiryns had Cretan artists engrave for them, on their vases and rings, a proud record of their achievements in piracy.[25] To protect themselves against other pirates they built their cities inland, far enough from the sea to guard against sudden attack, close enough to take readily to their ships. Lying on the road from the Argolic Gulf to the Isthmus of Corinth, Tiryns and Mycenae were well situated both to plunder traders with feudal tolls, and to set out occasionally on buccaneering raids. Seeing Crete grow rich on orderly trade, Mycenae learned that piracy—like its civilized offspring, tariff dues—can strangle commerce and internationalize poverty; it reformed, and allowed piracy to subside into trade. By 1400 its mercantile fleet was strong enough to defy the sea power of Crete; it refused to ship its Africa-bound goods across the island, but sent them directly to Egypt; possibly this was the cause, or result, of a war that ended in the destruction of the Cretan citadels.

The wealth that grew from this trade was not accompanied by any commensurate culture visible in the remains. Greek tradition credited the Pelasgians with having learned the alphabet from Phoenician traders. At Tiryns and Thebes some jars have been found bearing unintelligible characters, but no clay tablets, or inscriptions, or documents have been discovered; probably when Mycenae decided to be literate it used perishable writing materials, as the Cretans did in their final period; and nothing has been preserved. In art the Mycenaeans followed Cretan models, and so faithfully that archeology suspects them of importing their major artists from Crete. But after Cretan art declined, painting flourished vigorously on the mainland. The decorative designs of borders and cornices are of the first order, and persist into classic Greece, while the surviving frescoes indicate a keen feeling for moving life. The Ladies in the Box are splendid dowagers, who might adorn any opera promenade today and be in full fashion of coiffure and gowns; they are more alive than the stiffly conscious Ladies in the Chariot, who are out for an afternoon drive in the park. Better still is the *Boar Hunt*, a fresco from Tiryns: the boar and the flowers are unconvincingly conventional, the incredibly pink hounds are disfigured with stylized spots of scarlet, black, or blue, and the hind quarters of the plunging boar taper away into the likeness of some high-heeled maiden falling from her palace bower; nevertheless the chase is real, the boar is desperate, the dogs are in fast flight through the air, and man, the most sentimental and terrible of all beasts of prey, stands ready with his murderous spear.[20] One may suspect from such samples the active and physical life of the Mycenaeans, the proud beauty of their women, the vivid adornment of their palaces.

The highest art of Mycenae was in metals. Here the mainland equaled Crete, and dared to use its own forms and decoration. If Schliemann did not quite find the bones of Agamemnon, he found their weight in silver and gold: jewelry of many kinds, in spendthrift quantities; stud buttons worthy of any king; intaglios alive with scenes of hunting, war, or piracy; and a cow's head in shining silver, with horns and frontal rosette of gold—at any moment one expects from it the plaintive mooing to which Schliemann, never at a loss for explanations, traced the name Mycenae (Mükenai).[27] The finest of these metal relics from Tiryns and Mycenae are two bronze daggers inlaid with electron and burnished gold, and elegantly engraved with wildcats chasing ducks, and lions pursuing leopards or fighting men.[29] Most peculiar of all the remains are the golden masks, apparently laid over the faces of dead royalty. One mask[30] looks for all the world like the face of a cat; however, the gallant Schliemann ascribed it not to Clytaemnestra but to Agamemnon.

The unquestioned masterpieces of Mycenaean art were found neither at Tiryns nor at Mycenae but in a tomb at Vaphio, near Sparta, where a minor prince once emulated the magnificence of the northern kings. Here, amid another treasure of jewelry, were two thin cups of beaten gold, simply formed and yet worked with the loving patience of all great art. The craftsmanship is so like the best Minoan that most students are inclined to attribute these cups to some Cretan Cellini; but it would be a pity to deprive the Mycenaean culture of its most perfect memorials. The subject—the snaring and taming of a bull—seems characteristically Cretan; and yet the frequency with which such scenes are engraved upon Mycenaean rings and seals or painted upon the palace walls shows that the bull sport was as popular on the mainland as on the island. On one of the cups the bull is caught in a net of heavy rope; his mouth and nostrils gape with breathless anger and fatigue as he struggles to get free and imprisons himself the more; while on the other side a second bull gallops off in terror, and a third charges at a cowboy who catches it bravely by the horns. On the companion cup the captured bull is being led away; as we turn the vessel around we see him already reconciled to the restraints of civilization, and engaged, as Evans puts it, in "amorous conversation" with a cow.[31] Many centuries were to pass before such skillful work would appear again in Greece.

The Mycenaean himself, as well as most of his art, is found in the tombs; for he folded and buried his dead in uncomfortable jars, and seldom cremated them as the Heroic Age would do. Apparently he believed in a future life, for many objects of use and value were placed in the graves. For the rest Mycenaean religion, so far as it reveals itself to us, gives every evidence of Cretan origin or kinship. Here as in Crete are the double ax, the sacred pillar, the holy dove, and the cult of a mother goddess associated with a young male deity, presumably her son; and here again are attendant divinities in the form of snakes. Through all the transformations of religion known to us in Greece the mother goddess has remained. After the Cretan Rhea came Demeter, the *Mater Dolorosa* of the Greeks; after Demeter the Virgin Mother of God. Today, standing on the ruins of Mycenae, one sees, in the little village below, a modest Christian church. Grandeur is gone; simplicity and consolation remain. Civilizations come and go; they conquer the earth and crumble into dust; but faith survives every desolation.

After the fall of Cnossus Mycenae prospered as never before; the rising wealth of the "Shaft Grave Dynasty" raised great palaces upon the hills of Mycenae and Tiryns. Mycenaean art took on a character of its own, and captured the markets of the Aegean. Now the commerce of the mainland princes reached eastward into Cyprus and Syria, southward through the Cyclades to Egypt, westward through Italy to Spain, northward through Boeotia and Thessaly to the Danube; and found itself balked only at Troy. Like Rome absorbing and disseminating the civilization of Hellas, so Mycenae, won by the culture of dying Crete, spread the Mycenaean phase of that culture throughout the Mediterranean world.

IV. TROY

Between the Greek mainland and Crete 220 islands dot the Aegean, forming a circle around Delos, and therefore called the Cyclades. Most of them are rugged and barren, precarious mountain survivals of a land half drowned in the sea; but some were rich enough in marble or metal to be already busy and civilized, as the world goes, long before Greek history comes into our view. In 1896 the British School of Athens dug into the soil of Melos at Phylakopi and found tools, weapons, and pottery remarkably akin, age by age, to the Minoan; and a like research in other islands has built up a prehistoric picture of the Cyclades conforming in time and character, though never comparable in artistic excellence, with the bioscope of Crete. The Cyclades were cramped for land, totaling less than a thousand square miles among them, and proved, like classic Greece, incapable of uniting under one political power. By the seventeenth century B.C. the little isles had passed in government and art, even, here and there, in language and writing, under Cretan domination. Then, in the final period (1400-1200), the imports from Crete fell away, and the islands increasingly took their pottery and their styles from Mycenae.

Moving eastward into the Sporades (Scattered) Islands, we find in Rhodes another prehistoric culture of the simpler Aegean type. In Cyprus the rich deposits of copper that gave the island its name brought it a measure of wealth throughout the Bronze Age (3400-1200), but its wares* remained crude and undistinguished before the coming of Cretan influence. Its population, predominantly Asiatic, used a syllabic script akin to the Minoan, and worshiped a

* Sedulously collected by General di Cesnola, and now in the Metropolitan Museum of Art in New York.

goddess apparently descended from the Semitic Ishtar, and destined to become the Aphrodite of the Greeks.[32] After 1600 the metal industry of the island developed rapidly; the mines, owned by the royal government, exported copper to Egypt, Crete, and Greece: the foundry at Enkomi made famous daggers, and the potters sold their globular bowls from Egypt to Troy. The forests were cut into timber, and *cypress* from Cyprus began to compete with the cedars of Lebanon. In the thirteenth century Mycenaean colonists founded the colonies that were to become the Greek cities of Paphos, sacred to Aphrodite, and Citium, birthplace of the Stoic Zeno, and Cyprian Salamis, where Solon paused in his wanderings to replace chaos with law.

From Cyprus Mycenaean trade and influence crossed to Syria and Caria, and thence, as well as by other "rowing-stones," they moved up the coasts and islands of Asia until they reached Troy. There, on a hill separated by three miles from the sea, Schliemann and Dörpfeld found nine cities, superimposed each upon its predecessor, as if Troy had had nine lives.

(1) In the lowest strata were the remains of a neolithic village coming down to 3000 B.C. Here were walls of rough stones, mortared with mud; clay whorls, bits of worked ivory, tools of obsidian, and pieces of hand-polished black pottery. (2) Above this lay the ruins of the Second City, which Schliemann believed to have been Homer's Troy. Its enclosing walls, like those of Tiryns and Mycenae, were of cyclopean stones; at intervals there were fortresses, and at the corners great double gates, of which two are well preserved. Some houses survive to a height of four feet, their walls built of brick and wood upon a stone foundation. The red-painted pottery, wheel-turned but crude, indicates a life span for this city from approximately 2400 to 1900. Bronze has replaced stone for tools and weapons, and jewelry abounds; but the statuettes are unprepossessingly primitive. The Second City was apparently destroyed by fire; signs of conflagration are numerous, and persuaded Schliemann that this was the work of Agamemnon's Greeks.

(3-5) Above the "Burnt City" are the relics of three successive hamlets, small and poor, and negligible in archeological content. (6) About 1600 another city rose on the historic hill. Through the passionate haste of his work, Schliemann mixed the objects of this stratum with those of the second, and dismissed the Sixth City as an unimportant "Lydian settlement."[33] But Dörpfeld, continuing the excavations after Schliemann's death, and for a time with Schliemann's money,[34] revealed a town considerably larger than the Second, ornate with substantial buildings in dressed stone, and enclosed by a thirty-foot wall of whose four gates three remain.

In the ruins were monochrome vases of finer workmanship than before, vessels like the "Minyan" ware of Orchomenos, and potsherds so like those found at Mycenae that Dörpfeld considered them to be importations from that city, and therefore contemporary with the Shaft Grave Dynasty (1400-1200). On these and other shifting grounds current opinion identifies the Sixth City with Homer's Troy,*[35] and assigns to it the "Treasury of Priam" that Schliemann thought he had found in the Second City—six bracelets, two goblets, two diadems, a fillet, sixty earrings, and 8700 other pieces, all in gold.[36] The Sixth City too, we are assured, perished by fire, shortly after 1200. Greek historians traditionally assigned the siege of Troy to 1194-1184 B.C.†

Who were the Trojans? An Egyptian papyrus mentions certain "Dardenui" as among the allies of the Hittites at the battle of Kadesh (1287); it is likely that these were the ancestors of the "Dardenoi" who in Homer's terminology are one with the Trojans.[37] Probably these Dardani were of Balkan origin, crossed the Hellespont in the sixteenth century with the kindred Phrygians, and settled in the lower valley of the Scamander.[38] Herodotus, however, identified the Trojans with the Teucrians, and the Teucrians, according to Strabo, were Cretans who settled in the Troad,‡ perhaps after the fall of Cnossus.[40] Both Crete and the Troad had a sacred Mt. Ida, the "many-fountained Ida" of Homer and Tennyson. Presumably the region was subject at various times to political and ethnic influences from the Hittite hinterland. All in all, the excavations indicate a civilization partly Minoan, partly Mycenaean, partly Asiatic, partly Danubian. Homer represents the Trojans as speaking the same language and worshiping the same gods as the Greeks; but later Hellenic imagination preferred to think of Troy as an Asiatic city, and of the famous siege as the first known episode in an endless contest between Semite and Aryan, East and West.[41]

More significant than the racial complexion of its people was the strategic

* Dr. Carl Blegen, field director of the University of Cincinnati excavations at Troy (1931f), believes that these have shown that Troy VI was destroyed about 1300, probably by earthquake, and that upon its ruins rose the Seventh City, which he calls Priam's Troy. Dörpfeld prefers to call this Troy VI*b*. Cf. *Journal of Hellenic Studies, LVI*, 156.

† (7) Troy VII was a small unfortified settlement, which occupied the site till (8) Alexander the Great, in 334, built upon it Troy VIII in homage to Homer. (9) About the beginning of the Christian era the Romans built *Novum Ilium*, or New Troy, which survived till the fifth century A.D.

‡ The name *Troy* was traced by Greek tradition to the eponymous hero Tros, father of Ilus, father of Laomedon, father of Priam.[39] Hence the variant names of the city—*Troas, Ilios, Ilion, Ilium.* An eponymous hero, or eponym, is a probably legendary person to whom a social or political group attributes its origin and name. The Dardani, for example, believed or pretended that they were descended from Dardanus, son of Zeus; so the Dorians traced themselves to Dorus, the Ionians to Ion, etc.

position of Troy near the entrance to the Hellespont and the rich lands about the Black Sea. Throughout history that narrow passage has been the battleground of empires; the siege of Troy was the Gallipoli adventure of 1194 B.C. The plain was moderately fertile, and precious metals lay in the soil to the east; but this alone would hardly account for the wealth of Troy, and the tenacious attack of the Greeks. The city was admirably placed to levy tolls upon vessels wishing to pass through the Hellespont, while it was too far inland to be conveniently assailed from the sea:[42] perhaps it was this, and not Helen's face, that launched a thousand ships upon Ilium. On a likelier theory the southward current and winds in the strait persuaded merchants to unload their cargoes at Troy and ship them overland into the interior; from the charges exacted for this service Troy may have derived its wealth and power.[43] In any case the city's trade grew rapidly, as may be judged from the varied provenance of its remains. From the lower Aegean came copper, olive oil, wine, and pottery; from the Danube and Thrace came pottery, amber, horses, and swords; from distant China came so great a rarity as jade.[44] In return Troy brought from the interior, and exported, timber, silver, gold, and wild asses. Seated proudly behind their walls, the "horse-taming Trojans" dominated the Troad, and taxed its trade on land and sea.

The picture that we derive from the *Iliad* of Priam and his household is one of Biblical grandeur and patriarchal benevolence. The King is polygamous, not as a diversion but as a royal responsibility to continue his high breed abundantly; his sons are monogamous, and as well behaved as the fictitious Victorians—excepting, of course, the gay Paris, who is as innocent of morals as Alcibiades. Hector, Helenus, and Troilus are more likable than the vacillating Agamemnon, the treacherous Odysseus, and the petulant Achilles; Andromache and Polyxena are as charming as Helen and Iphigenia; and Hecuba is a shade better than Clytaemnestra. All in all, the Trojans, as pictured by their enemies, seem to us less deceitful, more devoted, better gentlemen, than the Greeks who conquered them. The conquerors themselves felt this in later days; Homer had many a kind word to say for the Trojans, and Sappho and Euripides left no doubt as to where their sympathies and admiration lay. It was a pity that these noble Dardans stood in the way of an expanding Greece which, despite its multitude of faults, would in the end bring to this and every other region of the Mediterranean a higher civilization than they had ever known.

CHAPTER III

The Heroic Age

I. THE ACHAEANS

MODEST Hittite tablets from Boghaz Keui, of approximately 1325 B.C., speak of the "Ahhijava" as a people equal in power to the Hittites themselves. An Egyptian record towards 1221 B.C. mentions the "Akaiwasha" as joining other "Peoples of the Sea" in a Libyan invasion of Egypt, and describes them as a roving band "fighting to fill their bellies."[1] In Homer the Achaeans are, specifically, a Greek-speaking people of southern Thessaly;[2] often, however, because they had become the most powerful of the Greek tribes, Homer uses their name for all the Greeks at Troy. Greek historians and poets of the classic age called the Achaeans, like the Pelasgians, autochthonous—native to Greece as far back as memory could recall; and they assumed without hesitation that the Achaean culture described in Homer was one with that which has here been termed Mycenaean. Schliemann accepted this identification, and for a brief while the world of scholarship agreed with him.

In 1901 an unusually iconoclastic Englishman, Sir William Ridgeway,[3] upset this happy confidence by pointing out that though Achaean civilization agreed with the Mycenaean in many ways, it differed in vital particulars. (1) Iron is practically unknown to the Mycenaeans; the Achaeans are familiar with it. (2) The dead in Homer are cremated; in Tiryns and Mycenae they are buried, implying a different conception of the afterlife. (3) The Achaean gods are the Olympians, of whom no trace has been found in the culture of Mycenae. (4) The Achaeans use long swords, round shields, and safety-pin brooches; no objects of such form appear in the varied Mycenaean remains. (5) There are considerable dissimilarities in coiffure and dress. Ridgeway concluded that the Mycenaeans were Pelasgians, and spoke Greek; that the Achaeans were blond "Celts," or Central Europeans, who came down through Epirus and Thessaly from 2000 onward, brought with them the worship of Zeus, invaded the Peloponnesus about 1400, adopted Greek speech and many Greek ways, and established themselves as feudal chieftains ruling from their fortress-palaces a subjugated Pelasgian population.

The theory is illuminating, even if it must be substantially modified. Greek literature says nothing of an Achaean invasion; and it would not be wise to hang a rejection of so unanimous a tradition upon a gradual increase in the use of iron, a change in modes of burial or coiffure, a lengthening of swords or rounding of shields, or even a safety pin. It is more likely that the Achaeans, as all classic writers supposed, were a Greek tribe that, in its natural multiplication, expanded from Thessaly into the Peloponnesus during the fourteenth and thirteenth centuries, mingled their blood with the Pelasgo-Mycenaeans there, and, towards 1250 B.C., became the ruling class.[4] Probably it was they who gave Greek to the Pelasgians, instead of receiving it from them. In such place names as Corinth and Tiryns, Parnassus and Olympia,* we may have echoes of a Creto-Pelasgo-Mycenaean tongue.[5] In the same manner, presumably, the Achaeans superimposed their mountain and sky gods upon the "chthonic" or subterranean deities of the earlier population. For the rest there is no sharp line of separation between the Mycenaean culture and that later phase of it, the Achaean, which we find in Homer; the two ways of life seem to have mingled and melted into one. Slowly, as the amalgamation proceeded, Aegean civilization passed away, dying in the defeat of Troy, and Greek civilization began.

II. THE HEROIC LEGENDS

The legends of the Heroic Age suggest both the origins and the destinies of the Achaeans. We must not ignore these stories; for though a sanguinary fancy enlivens them, they may contain more history than we suppose; and they are so bound up with Greek poetry, drama, and art that we should be at a loss to understand these without them.†

---

* And in such Greek words as *sesamon* (sesame), *kyparissos* (cypress), *hyssopos* (hyssop), *oinos* (wine), *sandalon* (sandal), *chalkos* (copper), *thalassa* (sea), *molybdos* (lead), *zephyros* (zephyr), *kybernao* (steer), *sphongos* (sponge), *laos* (people), *labyrinthis, dithyrambos, kitharis* (zither), *syrinx* (flute), and *paian* (paean).

† "Perseus . . . Heracles . . . Minos, Theseus, Jason . . . it has been common in modern times to regard these and the other heroes of this age . . . as purely mythical creations. The later Greeks, in criticizing the records of their past, had no doubt that they were historical persons who actually ruled in Argos and other kingdoms; and after a period of extreme skepticism many modern critics have begun to revert to the Greek view as that which explains the evidence most satisfactorily. . . . The heroes of the tales, like the geographical scenes in which they moved, are real."—*Cambridge Ancient History*, II, 478. We shall assume that the major legends are true in essence, imaginative in detail.

Hittite inscriptions mention an Atarissyas as King of the Ahhijavas in the thirteenth century B.C.; he is probably Atreus, King of the Achaeans.[6] In Greek story Zeus begat Tantalus, King of Phrygia,* who begat Pelops, who begat Atreus, who begat Agamemnon. Pelops, being exiled, came to Elis in the western Peloponnesus about 1283, and determined to marry Hippodameia, daughter of Oenomaus, Elis' king. The east pediment of the great temple of Zeus at Olympia still tells us the story of their courtship. The King made a practice to test his daughter's suitors by competing with them in a chariot race: if the suitor won he would receive Hippodameia; if he lost he was put to death. Several suitors had tried, and had lost both race and life. To reduce the risks Pelops bribed the King's charioteer, Myrtilus, to remove the linchpins from the royal chariot, and promised to share the kingdom with him if their plan succeeded. In the contest that ensued the King's chariot broke down, and he was killed. Pelops married Hippodameia and ruled Elis, but instead of sharing the kingdom with Myrtilus he threw Myrtilus into the sea. As Myrtilus sank he laid an ominous curse upon Pelops and all his descendants.

Pelops' daughter married Sthenelus, son of Perseus and King of Argos; the throne passed down to their son Eurystheus, and, after the latter's death, to his uncle Atreus. Atreus' sons Agamemnon and Menelaus married Clytaemnestra and Helen, daughters of King Tyndareus of Lacedaemon; and when Atreus and Tyndareus died, Agamemnon and Menelaus between them ruled all the eastern Peloponnesus from their respective capitals at Mycenae and Sparta. The Peloponnesus, or Island of Pelops, came to be called after their grandfather, whose descendants had quite forgotten the curse of Myrtilus.

Meanwhile the remainder of Greece was also busy with heroes, usually founding cities. In the fifteenth century before our era, said Greek tradition, the iniquity of the human race provoked Zeus to overwhelm it with a flood, from which one man, Deucalion, and his wife Pyrrha, alone were saved, in an ark or chest that came to rest on Mt. Parnassus. From Deucalion's son Hellen had come all the Greek tribes, and their united name, Hellenes. Hellen was grandfather of Achaeus and Ion, who begot the

* Tantalus angered the gods by divulging their secrets, stealing their nectar and ambrosia, and offering them his son Pelops, boiled and sliced. Zeus put Pelops together again, and punished Tantalus, in Hades, with a raging thirst; Tantalus was placed in the midst of a lake whose waters receded whenever he tried to drink of them; over his head branches rich in fruit were hung, which withdrew when he sought to reach them; a great rock was suspended above him, which at every moment threatened to fall and crush him.[7]

Achaean and Ionian tribes, which, after many wanderings, peopled respectively the Peloponnesus and Attica. One of Ion's descendants, Cecrops, with the help of the goddess Athena, founded (on a site whose acropolis had already been settled by Pelasgians) the city that was named after her, Athens.[8] It was he, said the story, that gave civilization to Attica, instituted marriage, abolished bloody sacrifices, and taught his subjects to worship the Olympian gods—Zeus and Athena above the rest.

The descendants of Cecrops ruled Athens as kings. The fourth in line was Erechtheus, to whom the city, honoring him as a god, would later dedicate one of its loveliest temples. His grandson, Theseus, about 1250, merged the twelve demes or villages of Attica into one political unity, whose citizens, wherever they lived, were to be called Athenians; perhaps it was because of this historic *synoikismos*, or municipal cohabitation, that Athens, like Thebes and Mycenae, had a plural name. It was Theseus who brought order and power to Athens, ended the sacrifice of her children to Minos, and gave her people security on the roads by slaying the highwayman Procrustes, who had liked to stretch or cut the legs of his captives to make them fit his bed. After Theseus' death Athens worshiped him, too, as a god. As late as 476, in the skeptical age of Pericles, the city brought the bones of Theseus from Scyros and deposited them as sacred relics in the temple of Theseus.

To the north, in Boeotia, a rival capital had equally stirring traditions, destined to become the very substance of Greek drama in the classic age. Late in the fourteenth century B.C. the Phoenician or Cretan or Egyptian prince Cadmus founded the city of Thebes at the meeting of the roads that cross Greece from east to west and from north to south, taught its people letters, and slew the dragon (perhaps an ancient phrase for an infecting or infesting organism) that hindered the settlers from using the waters of the Areian spring. From the dragon's teeth, which Cadmus sowed in the earth, sprang armed men who, like the Greeks of history, attacked one another until only five survived; these five, said Thebes, were the founders of her royal families. The government established itself on a hill citadel called the Cadmeia, where in our own time a "palace of Cadmus" has been unearthed.* There, after Cadmus, reigned his son Polydorus, his grandson Labdacus, and his great-grandson Laius, whose son Oedipus, as all the world knows, slew his father and married his mother. When Oedipus died

* Assigned to 1400-1200 B.C. It contained fragments of writing in undeciphered characters, probably of Cretan lineage.

his sons quarreled over the scepter, as is the habit of princes. Eteocles drove out Polynices, who persuaded Adrastus, King of Argos, to attempt his restoration. Adrastus tried (ca. 1213), in the famous war of the Seven (Allies) against Thebes, and again sixteen years later in the war of the Epigoni, or sons of the Seven. This time both Eteocles and Polynices were killed, and Thebes was burned to the ground.

Among the Theban aristocrats was one Amphitryon, who had a charming wife, Alcmene. Her Zeus visited while Amphitryon was gone to the wars; and Heracles (Hercules) was their son.* Hera, who did not relish these jovial condescensions, sent two serpents to destroy the babe in the cradle; but the boy grasped one in each hand and strangled them both; therefore he was called Heracles, as having won glory through Hera. Linus, oldest name in the history of music, tried to teach the youth how to play and sing; but Heracles did not care for music, and slew Linus with the lyre. When he grew up—a clumsy, bibulous, gluttonous, kindly giant—he undertook to kill a lion that was ravaging the flocks of Amphitryon and Thespius. The latter, King of Thespiae, offered his home and his fifty daughters to Heracles, who rose to the occasion manfully.[10] He slew the lion, and wore its skin as his garb. He married Megara, daughter of Creon of Thebes, and tried to settle down; but Hera sent a madness upon him, and unwittingly he killed his own children. He consulted the oracle at Delphi, and was instructed to go and live at Tiryns and serve Eurystheus, the Argive king, for twelve years; after which he would become an immortal god. He obeyed, and carried out for Eurystheus his famous twelve labors.† Released by the king, Heracles returned to Thebes. He performed many

* "Zeus," says Diodorus, "made that night three times its normal length; and by the magnitude of the time expended on the procreation he presaged the exceptional might of the child."[9]

† He strangled the lion that troubled the flocks at Nemea; he destroyed the many-headed hydra that ravaged Lerna; he captured a fleet stag and carried it to Eurystheus; he caught a wild boar from Mt. Eurymanthus and carried it to Eurystheus; in one day he cleansed all the stables of Augeas' three thousand oxen by diverting the rivers Alpheus and Peneus into the stalls—and paused long enough in Elis to establish the Olympic games; he destroyed the murderous Stymphalian birds of Arcadia; he captured the mad bull that was devastating Crete, and carried it on his shoulders to Eurystheus; he caught and tamed the man-eating horses of Diomedes; he slew nearly all the Amazons; he set up two confronting promontories as the "Pillars of Hercules" at the mouth of the Mediterranean, captured the oxen of Geryon and brought them through Gaul, across the Alps, through Italy, and across the sea to Eurystheus; he found the apples of the Hesperides, and for a while held up the earth for Atlas; he descended into Hades, and delivered Theseus and Ascalaphus from torment.—The Hesperides, daughters of Atlas, had been entrusted by Hera with the golden apples given her by Gaea (Earth) at her wedding with Zeus. The apples were guarded by a dragon, and conferred semidivine qualities upon those who ate them.

other exploits; he joined the Argonauts, sacked Troy, helped the gods to win their battle against the giants, freed Prometheus, brought Alcestis back to life, and, now and then, killed his own friends by accident. After his death he was worshiped as hero and god; and since he had had countless loves, many tribes claimed him as their progenitor.*

His sons made their home at Trachis in Thessaly; but Eurystheus, fearing lest they depose him in revenge for the unnecessary labors that he had laid upon their father, ordered the Trachinian king to exile them from Greece. The Heracleidae (i.e., children of Heracles) found refuge in Athens; Eurystheus sent an army to attack them, but they defeated and killed him. When Atreus came against them with another force, Hyllus, one of the sons, offered to fight any of Atreus' men in single combat, on condition that if he won, the Heracleidae should receive the kingdom of Mycenae; if he lost, the Heracleidae would depart and not return for fifty years, after which time their children were to receive Mycenae.[12] He lost, and led his partisans into exile. Fifty years later a new generation of Heracleidae returned; it was they, not the Dorians, said Greek tradition, who, being resisted in their claims, conquered the Peloponnesus, and put an end to the Heroic Age.

If the tale of Pelops and his descendants suggests the Asia Minor origin of the Achaeans, the theme of their destiny is struck in the story of the Argonauts. Like so many of the legends that served as both the historical tradition and the popular fiction of the Greeks, it is an excellent narrative, with all the elements of adventure, exploration, war, love, mystery, and death woven into a fabric so rich that after the dramatists of Athens had almost worn it bare it was rewoven into a very passable epic, in Hellenistic days, by Apollonius of Rhodes. It begins in Boeotian Orchomenos on the harsh note of human sacrifice, like Agamemnon's tragedy. Finding his land stricken with famine, King Athamas proposed to offer his son Phrixus to the gods. Phrixus learned of the plan and escaped from Orchomenos with his sister Helle, riding with her through the air on a ram with a golden fleece. But the ram was unsteady, and Helle fell off and was drowned in the strait which after her was called the Hellespont. Phrixus reached land

* This amazing "culture hero," Diodorus thought, was a primitive engineer, a prehistoric Empedocles; the legends told about him meant that he had cleansed the springs, cleaved mountains, changed the courses of rivers, reclaimed waste areas, rid the woods of dangerous beasts, and made Greece a habitable land.[11] In another aspect Heracles is the beloved son of god who suffers for mankind, raises the dead to life, descends into Hades, and then ascends into heaven.

and found his way to Colchis, at the farther end of the Black Sea; there he sacrificed the ram and hung up its fleece as an offering to Ares, god of war. Aietes, King of Colchis, set a sleepless dragon to watch the fleece, for an oracle had said that he should die if a stranger carried it off; and to better assure himself he decreed that all strangers coming to Colchis should be put to death. His daughter Medea, who loved strange men and ways, pitied the wayfarers who entered Colchis, and helped them to escape. Her father ordered her to be confined; but she fled to a sacred precinct near the sea, and lived there in bitter brooding till Jason found her wandering on the shore.

Some twenty years before (Greek chronologists said about 1245), Pelias, son of Poseidon, had usurped the throne of Aeson, King of Iolcus in Thessaly. Aeson's infant son Jason had been hidden by friends, and had grown up in the woods to great strength and courage. One day he appeared in the market place, dressed in a leopard skin and armed with two spears, and demanded his kingdom. But he was simple as well as strong, and Pelias persuaded him to undertake a heavy task as the price of the throne—to recover the Golden Fleece. So Jason built the great ship *Argo* (the Swift), and called to the adventure the bravest spirits in Greece. Heracles came, with his beloved companion Hylas; and Peleus, father of Achilles; Theseus, Meleager, Orpheus, and the fleet-footed maiden Atalanta. As the vessel entered the Hellespont it was halted, seemingly by some force from Troy, for Heracles left the expedition to sack the city and kill its King Laomedon, and all his sons but Priam.

When, after many tribulations, the Argonauts reached their goal, they were warned by Medea of the death that awaited all strangers in Colchis. But Jason persisted; and Medea agreed to help him gain the Fleece if he would take her to Thessaly and keep her as his wife until he died. He pledged himself to her, captured the Fleece with her aid, and fled back to his ship with her and his men. Many of them were wounded, but Medea quickly healed them with roots and herbs. When Jason reached Iolcus he again asked for the kingdom, and Pelias again delayed. Then Medea, by the arts of a sorceress, deceived the daughters of Pelias into boiling him to death. Frightened by her magic powers, the people drove her and Jason from Iolcus, and debarred him forever from the throne.[13] The rest belongs to Euripides.

A myth is often a bit of popular wisdom personified in poetic figures, as the story of Eden suggests the disillusionment of knowledge and the liabilities of love; legend is often a fragment of history swelling with new fictions as it rolls down the years. It is probable that in the generation before the historic siege of Troy the Greeks had tried to force their way through the Hellespont and open the Black Sea to colonization and trade; the story of the Argonauts may be the dramatized memory of that commercial exploration; and the "golden fleece" may refer to the woolen skins or cloths anciently used in northern Asia Minor to catch particles of gold carried down by the streams.[14] A Greek settlement was actually made, about this time, on the island of Lemnós, not far from the Hellespont. The Black Sea proved inhospitable despite its propitiating name, and the fortress of Troy rose again after Heracles' visitation to discourage adventures in the strait. But the Greeks did not forget; they would come again, a thousand ships instead of one; and on the plain of Ilion the Achaeans would destroy themselves to free the Hellespont.

III. HOMERIC CIVILIZATION

How shall we reconstruct the life of Achaean Greece (1300-1100 B.C.) out of the poetry of its legends? Our chief reliance must be upon Homer, who may never have existed, and whose epics are younger by at least three centuries than the Achaean Age. It is true that archeology has surprised the archeologists by making realities of Troy, Mycenae, Tiryns, Cnossus, and other cities described in the *Iliad*, and by exhuming a Mycenaean civilization strangely akin to that which spontaneously takes form between the lines of Homer; so that our inclination today is to accept as real the central characters of his fascinating tales. None the less, it is impossible to say how far the poems reflect the age in which the poet lived, rather than the age of which he writes. We shall merely ask, then, what did Greek tradition, as gathered together in Homer, conceive the Homeric Age to be? In any case we shall have a picture of Hellas in buoyant transit from the Aegean culture to the civilization of historic Greece.

1. Labor

The Achaeans (i.e., the Greeks of the Heroic Age) impress us as less civilized than the Mycenaeans who preceded them, and more civilized than the Dorians who followed them. They are above all physical—the men tall and powerful, the women ravishingly lovely in an unusually literal sense. Like the Romans a thousand years after them, the Achaeans look down upon literary culture as effeminate degeneration; they use writing under protest, and the only literature they know is the martial lay and unwritten song of the troubadour. If we believe Homer we must suppose that Zeus had realized in Achaean society the aspiration of the American poet who wrote that if he were God he would make all men strong, and all women beautiful, and would then himself become a man. Homeric Greece is *kalligynaika*[15]—it is a dream of fair women. The men too are handsome, with their long hair and their brave beards; the greatest gift that a man can give is to cut off his hair and lay it as an offering upon the funeral pyre of his friend.[16] Nakedness is not yet cultivated; both sexes cover the body with a quadrangular garment folded over the shoulders, tied with a clasp pin, and reaching nearly to the knees; the women may add a veil or a girdle, and the men a loincloth—which, as dignity increases, will evolve into drawers and trousers. The well to do go in for costly robes, such as that which Priam brings humbly to Achilles in ransom for his son.[17] The men are barelegged, the women bare-armed; both wear shoes or sandals outdoors, but are usually barefoot within. Both sexes wear jewelry, and the women and Paris anoint the body with "rose-scented oil."[18]

How do these men and women live? Homer shows them to us tilling the soil, sniffing with pleasure the freshly turned dark earth, running their eyes with pride along the furrows they have ploughed so straight, winnowing the wheat, irrigating the fields, and banking up the streams against the winter floods;[19] he makes us feel the despair of the peasant whose months of toil are washed out by "the torrent at the full that in swift course shatters the dykes, neither can the long line of mounds hold it in, nor the walls of the fruitful orchards stay its sudden coming."[20] The land is hard to farm, for much of it is mountain, or swamp, or deeply wooded hill; the villages are visited by wild beasts, and hunting is a necessity before it becomes a sport. The rich are great stockbreeders, raising cattle, sheep, pigs, goats, and horses; one Erichthonius keeps three thousand brood mares with their foals.[21] The poor eat fish and grain, occasionally vegetables; warriors and the rich rely upon great portions of roast meat; they breakfast on meat and wine. Odysseus and his swineherd eat, between them, a small roast pig for luncheon, and a third of a five-year-old hog for dinner.[22] They have honey instead of sugar, meat fat instead of butter; instead of bread they eat cakes of grain, baked large and thin on a plate of iron or a hot stone. The diners do not recline, as the Athenians will do, but sit on chairs; not at a central table but along the walls, with little tables between the seats. There are no forks, spoons, or napkins, and only such knives as the guests may carry; eating is managed with the fingers.[23] The staple drink, even among the poor and among children, is diluted wine.

The land is owned by the family or the clan, not by the individual; the father administers and controls it, but he cannot sell it.[24] In the *Iliad* great tracts are called the King's Commons or Demesne (*temenos*); in effect it belongs to the community, and in its fields any man may pasture his flocks. In the *Odyssey* these common lands are being divided, and sold to—or appropriated by—rich or strong individuals; the commons disappears in ancient Greece precisely as in modern England.[25]

The soil might yield metal as well as food; but the Achaeans neglect to mine the earth, and are content to import copper and tin, silver and gold, and a strange new luxury, iron. A shapeless mass of iron is offered as a precious prize at the games held in honor of Patroclus,[26] it will make, says Achilles, many an agricultural implement. He says nothing of weapons, which are still of bronze.[27] The *Odyssey* describes the tempering of iron,* but that epic probably belongs to a later age than the *Iliad*.

The smith at his forge and the potter at his wheel work in their shops; other Homeric craftsmen—saddlers, masons, carpenters, cabinetmakers—go to work at the home that has ordered their product. They do not produce for a market, for sale or profit; they work long hours, but leisurely, without the sting and stimulus of visible competition.[29] The family itself provides most of its needs; everyone in it labors with his hands; even the master of the house, even the local king, like Odysseus, makes bed and chairs for his home, boots and saddles for himself; and unlike the later Greeks he prides himself on his manual skill. Penelope, Helen, and Andromache, as well as their servant women, are busy with spinning, weaving, embroidery, and household cares; Helen seems lovelier when she displays her needlework to Telemachus[30] than when she walks in beauty on the battlements of Troy.

The craftsmen are freemen, never slaves as in classic Greece. Peasants may in emergency be conscripted to labor for the king, but we do not hear of serfs bound to the soil. Slaves are not numerous, nor is their position degraded; they are mostly female domestics, and occupy a position in effect as high as that of household servants today, except that they are bought and sold for long terms instead of for precariously brief engagements. On occasion they are brutally treated; normally they are accepted as members of the family, are cared for in illness or depression or old age, and may develop a humane relation of affection with master or mistress. Nausicaa helps her bondwomen to wash the family linen in the stream, plays ball with them, and altogether treats them as companions.[31] If a slave woman bears a son to her master, the child is usually free.[32] Any man, however, may become a slave, through capture in battle or in piratical raids. This is the bitterest aspect of Achaean life.

Homeric society is rural and local; even the "cities" are mere villages nestling against hilltop citadels. Communication is by messenger or herald, or, over

* "When a smith tempers in cold water a great ax or an adze, it gives off a hissing; this is what gives iron its strength."[28]

long distances, by signal fires flashing from peak to peak.[33] Overland traffic is made difficult and dangerous by roadless mountains and swamps and bridgeless streams. The carpenter makes carts with four wheels boasting of spokes and wooden tires; even so most goods are carried by mules or men. Trade by sea is easier, despite pirates and storms; natural harbors are numerous, and only on the perilous four-day trip from Crete to Egypt does the ship lose sight of land. Usually the boat is beached at night, and crew and passengers sleep on trusty land. In this age the Phoenicians are still better merchants and mariners than the Greeks. The Greeks revenge themselves by despising trade, and preferring piracy.

The Homeric Greeks have no money, but use, as media for exchange, ingots of iron, bronze, or gold; the ox or cow is taken as a standard of value. A gold ingot of fifty-seven pounds is called a talent (*talanton*, weight).[34] Much barter remains. Wealth is computed realistically in goods, especially cattle, rather than in pieces of metal or paper that may lose or alter their value at any moment through a change in the economic theology of men. There are rich and poor in Homer as in life; society is a rumbling cart that travels an uneven road; and no matter how carefully the cart is constituted, some of the varied objects in it will sink to the bottom, and others will rise to the top; the potter has not made all the vessels of the same earth, or strength, or fragility. Already in the second book of the *Iliad* we hear the sound of the class war; and as Thersites flies oratorically at Agamemnon we recognize an early variation on a persistent theme.[35]

2. *Morals*

As we read Homer the impression forms that we are in the presence of a society more lawless and primitive than that of Cnossus or Mycenae. The Achaean culture is a step backward, a transition between the brilliant Aegean civilization and the Dark Age that will follow the Dorian conquest. Homeric life is poor in art, rich in action; it is unmeditative, buoyant, swift; it is too young and strong to bother much about manners or philosophy. Probably we misjudge it by seeing it in the violent crisis or disorderly aftermath of war.

There are, it is true, many tender qualities and scenes. Even the warriors are generous and affectionate; between parent and child there is a love as profound as it is silent. Odysseus kisses the heads and shoulders of the members of his family when, after their long separation, they recognize him; and in like manner they kiss him.[36] Helen and Menelaus weep when they learn that this noble lad, Telemachus, is the son of the lost Odysseus who fought so valiantly for them.[37] Agamemnon himself is capable of tears so abundant that they remind Homer of a stream pouring over rocks.[38] Friendships are firm among the heroes, though possibly a degree of sexual inversion enters into the almost neurotic attachment of Achilles to Patroclus, especially to Patroclus dead. Hospitality is lavish, for "from Zeus are all strangers and beggars."[39] Maids bathe the foot or the body of the guest, anoint him with unguents, and may give him fresh garments; he receives food and lodging if he needs them, and perhaps a gift.[40] "Lo," says "fair-cheeked Helen," as she places a costly robe in Telemachus' hands, "I too give thee this gift, dear child, a remembrance of the hands of Helen, against the day of thy longed-for marriage, for thy bride to wear."[41] It is a picture that reveals to us the human tenderness and fine feeling that in the *Iliad* must hide themselves under the panoply of war.

Even war does not thwart the Greek passion for games. Children and adults engage in skillful and difficult contests, apparently with fairness and good humor; Penelope's suitors play draughts, and throw the disk or javelin; the Phaeacian hosts of Odysseus play at quoits, and a strange medley of ball and dance.* When the dead Patroclus has been cremated, according to Achaean custom, games are played that set a precedent for Olympia—foot races, disk-throwing, javelin-throwing, archery, wrestling, chariot races, and single combat fully armed; all in excellent spirit, except that only the ruling class may enter, and only the gods may cheat.[43]

The other side of the picture is less pleasing. As a prize for the chariot race Achilles offers "a woman skilled in fair handiwork"; and on the funeral pyre horses, dogs, oxen, sheep, and human beings are sacrificed to keep the dead Patroclus well tended and fed.[44] Achilles treats Priam with fine courtesy, but only after dragging Hector's body in mangled ignominy around the pyre. To the Achaean male, human life is cheap; to take it is no serious matter; a moment's pleasure can replace it. When a town is captured the men are killed or sold into slavery; the women are taken as concubines if they are attractive, as slaves if they are not. Piracy is still a respected occupation; even kings organize marauding expeditions, plunder towns and villages, and enslave their population; "Indeed," says Thucydides, "this came to be the main source of livelihood among the early Hel-

* "Then Alcinous ordered Halias and Laodamas to dance, by themselves, for never did any one dare join himself with them. They took in their hands the fine ball, purple-dyed . . . and played. The first, bending his body right back, would hurl the ball towards the shadowy crowds, while the other in his turn would spring high into the air and catch it gracefully before his feet touched the ground. Then, after they had made full trial of tossing the ball high, they began passing it back and forth between them, all the while they danced upon the fruitful earth."[42]

lenes, no disgrace being yet attached to such an occupation,"[45] but some glory; very much as, in our times, great nations may conquer and subjugate defenseless peoples without loss of dignity or righteousness. Odysseus is insulted when he is asked is he a merchant, "mindful of the gains of his greed";[46] but he tells with pride how, on his return from Troy, his provisions having run low, he sacked the city of Ismarus and stored his ships with food; or how he ascended the river Aegyptus "to pillage the splendid fields, to carry off the women and little children, and to kill the men."[47] No city is safe from sudden and unprovoked attack.

To this lighthearted relish for robbery and slaughter the Achaeans add an unabashed mendacity. Odysseus can hardly speak without lying, or act without treachery. Having captured the Trojan scout Dolon, he and Diomed promise him life if he will give them the information they require; he does, and they kill him.[48] It is true that the other Achaeans do not quite equal Odysseus in dishonesty, but not because they would not; they envy and admire him, and look up to him as a model character; the poet who pictures him considers him a hero in every respect; even the goddess Athena praises him for his lying, and counts this among the special charms for which she loves him. "Cunning must he be and knavish," she tells him, smiling, and stroking him with her hand, "who would go beyond thee in all manner of guile, aye, though it were a god that met thee. Bold man, crafty in counsel, insatiate in deceit, not even in thine own land, it seems, wast thou to cease from guile and deceitful tales, which thou lovest from the bottom of thine heart."[49]

In truth we ourselves are drawn to this heroic Munchausen of the ancient world. We discover some likable traits in him, and in the hardy and subtle people to which he belongs. He is a gentle father, and in his own kingdom a just ruler, who "wrought no wrong in deed or word to any man in the land." "Never again," says his swineherd, "shall I find a master so kind, how far soever I go, not though I come again to the house of my father and mother!"[50] We envy Odysseus his "form like unto the immortals," his frame so athletic that though nearing fifty he throws the disk farther than any of the Phaeacian youths; we admire his "steadfast heart," his "wisdom like to Jove's";[51] and our sympathy goes out to him when, in his despair of ever seeing again "the smoke leaping up from his own land," he yearns to die, or when, in the midst of his perils and sufferings, he steels himself with words that old Socrates loved to quote: "Be patient now, my soul; thou hast endured still worse than this."[52] He is a man of iron in body and mind, yet every inch human, and therefore forgivable.

The secret of the matter is that the Achaean's standard of judgment is as different from ours as the virtues of war differ from those of peace. He lives in a disordered, harassed, hungry world, where every man must be his own policeman, ready with arrow and spear, and a capacity for looking calmly at flowing blood. "A ravening belly," as Odysseus explains, "no man can hide. . . . Because of it are the benched ships made ready that bear evil to foeman over the unresting sea."[53] Since the Achaean knows little security at home, he respects none abroad; every weakling is fair play; the supreme virtue, in his view, is a brave and ruthless intelligence. Virtue is literally *virtus*, manliness, *arete*, the quality of Ares or Mars. The good man is not one that is gentle and forbearing, faithful and sober, industrious and honest; he is simply one who fights bravely and well. A bad man is not one that drinks too much, lies, murders, and betrays; he is one that is cowardly, stupid, or weak. There were Nietzscheans long before Nietzsche, long before Thrasymachus, in the lusty immaturity of the European world.

3. *Sexes*

Achaean society is a patriarchal despotism tempered with the beauty and anger of woman, and the fierce tenderness of parental love.* Theoretically the father is supreme: he may take as many concubines as he likes,† he may offer them to his guests, he may expose his children on the mountaintops to die, or slaughter them on the altars of the thirsty gods. Such paternal omnipotence does not necessarily imply a brutal society, but only one in which the organization of the state has not yet gone far enough to preserve social order; and in which the family, to create such order, needs the powers that will later be appropriated by the state in a nationalization of the right to kill. As social organization advances, paternal authority and family unity decrease, freedom and individualism grow. In practice the Achaean male is usually reasonable, listens patiently to domestic eloquence, and is devoted to his children.

Within the patriarchal framework the position of woman is far higher in Homeric than it will be in Periclean Greece. In the legends and the

* There are vestiges of an earlier and "matriarchal" condition: before Cecrops, said Athenian tradition, "children did not know their own father"—i.e., presumably, descent was reckoned through the mother; and even in Homeric days many of the gods especially worshiped by Greek cities were goddesses—Hera at Argos, Athena at Athens, Demeter and Persephone at Eleusis—with no visible subordination to any male deity.[54]

† Theseus had so many wives that an historian drew up a learned catalogue of them.[55]

epics she plays a leading role, from Pelops' courtship of Hippodameia to Iphigenia's gentleness and Electra's hate. The gynaeceum does not confine her, nor does the home; she moves freely among men and women alike, and occasionally shares in the serious discourse of the men, as Helen does with Menelaus and Telemachus. When the Achaean leaders wish to fire the imagination of their people against Troy they appeal not to political or racial or religious ideas, but to the sentiment for woman's beauty; the loveliness of Helen must put a pretty face upon a war for land and trade. Without woman the Homeric hero would be a clumsy boor, with nothing to live for or die for; she teaches him something of courtesy, idealism, and softer ways.

Marriage is by purchase, usually in oxen or their equivalent, paid by the suitor to the father of the girl; the poet speaks of "cattle-bringing maidens."[56] The purchase is reciprocal, for the father usually gives the bride a substantial dowry. The ceremony is familial and religious, with much eating, dancing, and loose-tongued merriment. "Beneath a blaze of torches they led the brides from their chambers through the city, and loud rose the bridal song. The young men whirled in the dance, and high among them did sound the flute and the lyre";[57] so changeless are the essentials of our life. Once married, the woman becomes mistress in her home, and is honored in proportion to her children. Love in the truest sense, as a profound mutual tenderness and solicitude, comes to the Greeks, as to the French, after marriage rather than before; it is not the spark thrown off by the contact or nearness of two bodies, but the fruit of long association in the cares and industries of the home. The Homeric wife is as faithful as her husband is not. There are three adulteresses in Homer—Clytaemnestra, Helen, and Aphrodite; but they do injustice to the mortal average, if not to the divine.

Formed out of this background, the Homeric family (barring the enormities of legends that play no part in Homer) is a wholesome and pleasing institution, rich in fine women and loyal children. The women function not only as mothers but as workers; they grind the grain, card the wool, spin, weave, and embroider; they do little sewing, since garments are mostly without seams; and cooking is normally left to men. Amid these labors they bear and rear children, heal their hurts, pacify their quarrels, and teach them the manners, morals, and traditions of the tribe. There is no formal education, apparently no teaching of letters, no spelling, no grammar, no books; it is a boy's utopia. The girl is taught the arts of the home, the boy those of the chase and war; he learns to fish and swim, to till the fields, set snares, handle animals, aim the arrow and the lance, and take care of himself in all the emergencies of a half-lawless life. When the oldest boy grows up to manhood he becomes, in the absence of his father, the responsible head of the family. When he marries he brings his bride to his father's home, and the rhythm of the generations is renewed. The individual members of the family change with time, but the family is the lasting unit, surviving perhaps for centuries, and forging in the turbulent crucible of the home the order and character without which all government is in vain.

4. *The Arts*

The Achaeans leave to merchants and lowly scribes the art of writing, which has presumably been handed down to them from Mycenaean Greece; they prefer blood to ink and flesh to clay. In all of Homer there is but one reference to writing,[58] and there in a characteristic context; a folded tablet is given to a messenger, directing the recipient to kill the messenger. If the Achaeans have time for literature it is only when war and marauding allow a peaceful interlude; the king or prince gathers his retainers about him for a feast, and some wandering minstrel, stringing the lyre, recounts in simple verse the exploits of ancestral heroes; this is, for the Achaeans, both poetry and history. Homer, perhaps wishing like Pheidias to engrave his own portrait upon his work, tells how Alcinous, King of the Phaeacians, calls for such song in entertaining Odysseus. "Summon hither the divine minstrel, Demodocus; for to him above all others has the god granted skill in song. . . . Then the herald drew near, leading the good minstrel, whom the Muse loved above all other men, and gave him both good and evil; of his sight she deprived him, but gave him the gift of sweet song."[59]

The only art except his own that interests Homer is toreutics—the hammering of metals into plastic forms. He says nothing of painting or sculpture, but calls up all his inspiration to describe the scenes inlaid or damascened upon Achilles' shield, or raised in relief upon Odysseus' brooch. He speaks briefly but illuminatingly about architecture. The common dwelling in Homer is apparently of sun-dried brick with a footing of stone; the floor is ordinarily of beaten earth, and is cleaned by scraping; the roof is of reeds overlaid with clay, and slopes only enough to carry off the rain. The doors are single or double, and may have bolts or keys.[60] In the better dwellings the interior walls are of painted stucco, with ornamental border or frieze, and are hung with weapons, shields, and tapestries. There is no kitchen, no chimney, no windows; an opening in the roof of the central hall lets out some of the smoke that may rise from the hearth; the rest finds its way through the door, or settles in soot on the walls. Rich establishments have a bathroom; others content themselves with a tub.

The furniture is of heavy wood, often artistically carved and finished; Icmalius fashions for Penelope an armchair set with ivory and precious metals; and Odysseus makes for himself and his wife a massive bedstead designed to last for a century.

It is characteristic of the age that its architecture ignores temples and spends itself upon palaces, just as Periclean architecture will neglect palaces and lavish itself upon temples. We hear of the "sumptuous home of Paris, which that prince had built with the aid of the most cunning architects in Troy";[61] of King Alcinous' great mansion, with walls of bronze, frieze of blue-glass paste, doors of silver and gold, and other features that may belong rather to poetry than to architecture; we hear something of Agamemnon's royal residence at Mycenae, and a great deal about Odysseus' palace at Ithaca. This has a front court, paved in part with stone, surrounded by a palisade or plastered wall, and adorned with trees, stalls for horses, and a heap of steaming dung on which Odysseus' dog Argos makes his bed in the sun.* A large pillared porch leads to the house; here the slaves sleep and often the visitors. Within, an anteroom opens upon a central hall supported by pillars, and sometimes lighted not only by the opening in the roof, but by a narrow clerestory or open space between the architrave and the eaves. At night braziers burning on tall stands give an unsteady illumination. In the center of the hall is the hearth, around whose sacred fire the family gathers in the evening for warmth and good cheer, and debates the ways of neighbors, the willfulness of children, and the vicissitudes of states.

5. *The State*

How are these passionate and vigorous Achaeans ruled? In peace by the family, in crisis by the clan. The clan is a group (*genos*, literally a genus) of persons acknowledging a common ancestor and a common chieftain. The citadel of the chieftain is the origin and center of the city; there, as his force subsides into usage and law, clan after clan gathers, and makes a political as well as a kinship community. When the chieftain desires some united action from his clan or city, he summons its free males to a public assembly, and submits to them a proposal which they may accept or reject, but which only the most important members of the group may propose to change. In this village assembly—the one democratic element in an essentially feudal and aristocratic society—skilled speakers who can sway the people are valuable to the state; already, in old Nestor, whose voice "flows sweeter than honey from his tongue,"[62] and in wily Odysseus, whose words fall "like snowflakes upon the people,"[63] we have the beginnings of

* Argos dies of joy on recognizing his master after twenty years' separation.

that stream of eloquence which will reach greater heights in Greece than in any other civilization, and will finally submerge it in ruin.

When all the clans must act at once the chieftains follow the lead of the strongest of their number as king, and report to him with their armies of freemen and attendant slaves. Those chieftains who are nearest to the king in residence and respect are called the King's Companions; they will be called that again in Philip's Macedonia and in Alexander's camp. In their *boule*, or council, the nobles exercise full freedom of speech, and address the king as merely and temporarily first among equals. Out of these institutions—public assembly, council of nobles, and king—will come, in a hundred varieties and under a thousand shibboleths and phrases, the constitutions of the modern Western world.

The powers of the king are narrowly limited and very wide. They are limited in space, for his kingdom is small. They are limited in time, for he may be deposed by the Council, or by a right which the Achaeans readily recognize—the right of the stronger. Otherwise his rule is hereditary, and has only the vaguest boundaries. He is above all a military commander, solicitous for his army, without which he might be found in the wrong. He sees to it that it is well equipped, well fed, well trained; that it has poisoned arrows,[64] lances, helmets, greaves, spears, breastplates, shields, and chariots. So long as the army defends him he is the government—legislature, executive, judiciary. He is the high priest of the state religion, and sacrifices for the people. His decrees are the laws, and his decisions are final; there is as yet no word for law.[65] Below him the Council may sit occasionally to judge grave disputes; then, as if to set a precedent for all courts, it asks for precedents, and decides accordingly. Precedent dominates law because precedent is custom, and custom is the jealous older brother of law. Trials of any kind, however, are rare in Homeric society; there are hardly any public agencies of justice; each family must defend and revenge itself. Violence abounds.

To support his establishment the king does not levy taxes; he receives, now and then, "gifts" from his subjects. But he would be a poor king if he depended upon such presents. His chief income is derived, presumably, from tolls on the plunder that his soldiers and his ships gather on land or sea. Perhaps that is why, late in the thirteenth century, the Achaeans are found in Egypt and Crete; in Egypt as unsuccessful buccaneers, in Crete as passing conquerors. Then, suddenly, we hear of them inflaming their people with a tale of humiliating rape, collecting all the forces of all the tribes, equipping a hundred thousand men, and sailing in a vast and unparalleled armada of a thousand ships to try their fortunes against the spearhead of Asia on the plains and hill of Troy.

IV. THE SIEGE OF TROY

Was there such a siege? We only know that every Greek historian, and every Greek poet, and almost every temple record or legend in Greece, took it for granted; that archeology has placed the ruined city, generously multiplied, before our eyes; and that today, as until the last century, the story and its heroes are accepted as in essence real.[66] An Egyptian inscription of Rameses III reports that "the isles were restless" toward 1196 B.C.;[67] and Pliny alludes to a Rameses "in whose time Troy fell."[68] The great Alexandrian scholar Eratosthenes, on the basis of traditional genealogies collated late in the sixth century before Christ by the geographer-historian Hecataeus, calculated the date of the siege as 1194 B.C.

The ancient Persians and Phoenicians agreed with the Greeks in tracing the great war to four abductions of beautiful women. The Egyptians, they said, stole Io from Argos, the Greeks stole Europa from Phoenicia, and Medea from Colchis; did not a just balancing of the scales require that Paris should abduct Helen?*[69] Stesichorus in his penitent years, and after him Herodotus and Euripides, refused to admit that Helen had gone to Troy; she had only gone to Egypt, under constraint, and had merely waited there a dozen years for Menelaus to come and find her; besides, asked Herodotus, who could believe that the Trojans would fight ten years for one woman? Euripides attributed the expedition to excess population in Greece, and the consequent urge to expansion;[70] so old are the youngest excuses of the will to power.

Nevertheless it is possible that some such story was used to make the adventure digestible for the common Greek; men must have phrases if they are to give their lives. Whatever may have been the face and shibboleth of the war, its cause and essence lay, almost beyond doubt, in the struggle of two groups of powers for possession of the Hellespont and the rich lands lying about the Black Sea. All Greece and all western Asia saw it as a decisive conflict; the little nations of Greece came to the aid of Agamemnon, and the peoples of Asia Minor sent repeated reinforcements to Troy. It was the beginning of a struggle that would be renewed at Marathon and

* Helen, it need hardly be said, was the daughter of Zeus, who, in the form of a swan, seduced Leda, wife of Sparta's King Tyndareus.

Salamis, at Issus and Arbela, at Tours and Granada, at Lepanto and Vienna. . . .

Of the events and aftermath of the war we can relate only what the poets and dramatists of Greece have told us; we accept this as rather literature than history, but all the more for that reason a part of the story of civilization; we know that war is ugly, and that the *Iliad* is beautiful. Art (to vary Aristotle) may make even terror beautiful—and so purify it—by giving it significance and form. Not that the form of the *Iliad* is perfect; the structure is loose, the narrative is sometimes contradictory or obscure, the conclusion does not conclude; nevertheless the perfection of the parts atones for the disorder of the whole, and with all its minor faults the story becomes one of the great dramas of literature, perhaps of history.

(I)* At the opening of the poem the Greeks have already besieged Troy for nine years in vain; they are despondent, homesick, and decimated with disease. They had been delayed at Aulis by sickness and a windless sea; and Agamemnon had embittered Clytaemnestra, and prepared his own fate, by sacrificing their daughter Iphigenia for a breeze. On the way up the coast the Greeks had stopped here and there to replenish their supplies of food and concubines; Agamemnon had taken the fair Chryseis, Achilles the fair Briseis. A soothsayer now declares that Apollo is withholding success from the Greeks because Agamemnon has violated the daughter of Apollo's priest, Chryses. The King restores Chryseis to her father, but, to console himself and point a tale, he compels Briseis to leave Achilles and take Chryseis' place in the royal tent. Achilles convokes a general assembly, and denounces Agamemnon with a wrath that provides the first word and the recurring theme of the *Iliad*. He vows that neither he nor his soldiers will any longer stir a hand to help the Greeks.

(II) We pass in review the ships and tribes of the assembled force, and (III) see bluff Menelaus engaging Paris in single combat to decide the war. The two armies sit down in civilized truce; Priam joins Agamemnon in solemn sacrifice to the gods. Menelaus overcomes Paris, but Aphrodite snatches the lad safely away in a cloud and deposits him, miraculously powdered and perfumed, upon his marriage bed. Helen bids him return to the fight, but he counterproposes that they "give the hour to dalliance." The lady, flattered by desire, yields. (IV) Agamemnon declares Menelaus victor, and the war is apparently ended; but the gods, in imitative council on Olympus, demand more blood. Zeus votes for peace, but withdraws his vote in terrified retreat when Hera, his spouse, directs her speech upon him. She suggests that if Zeus will agree to the destruction of Troy she will allow him to raze Mycenae, Argos, and Sparta to the

* Parenthetical numbers indicate books of the *Iliad*.

ground. The war is renewed; many a man falls pierced by arrow, lance, or sword, and "darkness enfolds his eyes."

(v) The gods join in the merry slicing game; Ares, the awful god of war, is hurt by Diomed's spear, "utters a cry as of nine thousand men," and runs off to complain to Zeus. (vi) In a pretty interlude the Trojan leader Hector, before rejoining the battle, bids good-by to his wife Andromache. "Love," she whispers to him, "thy stout heart will be thy death; nor hast thou pity of thy child or me, who shall soon be a widow. My father and my mother and my brothers all are slain; but, Hector, thou art father to me and mother, and thou art the husband of my youth. Have pity, then, and stay here in the tower." "Full well I know," he answers, "that Troy will fall, and I foresee the sorrow of my brethren and the King; for them I grieve not; but to think of thee a slave in Argos unmans me almost. Yet, even so, I will not shirk the fight."[m] His infant son Astyanax, destined shortly to be flung over the walls to death by the victorious Greeks, screams in fright at Hector's waving plumes, and the hero removes his helmet that he may laugh, weep, and pray over the wondering child. Then he strides down the causeway to the battle, and (vii) engages Ajax, King of Salamis, in single combat. They fight bravely, and separate at nightfall with exchange of praise and gifts—a flower of courtesy floating on a sea of blood. (viii) After a day of Trojan victories Hector bids his warriors rest.

> Thus made harangue to them Hector; and roaring the Trojans applauded.
> Then from the yoke loosed their war-steeds sweating, and each by his chariot
> Tethered his horses with thongs. And then they brought from the city,
> Hastily, oxen and goodly sheep; and wine honey-hearted
> Gave them, . . . and corn from the houses.
> Firewood they gathered withal; and then from the plain to the heavens
> Rose on the winds the sweet savor. And these by the highways of battle
> Hopeful sat through the night, and many their watchfires burning.
>
> Even as when in the sky the stars shine out round the night-orb,
> Wondrous to see, and the winds are laid, and the peaks and the headlands
> Tower to the view, and the glades come out, and the glorious heaven
> Stretches itself to its widest, and sparkle the stars multitudinous,
> Gladdening the heart of the toil-wearied shepherd—even as countless

'Twixt the black ships and the river of Xanthus glittered the watch-fires
Built by the horse-taming Trojans by Ilium.
Meanwhile the war-wearied horses, champing spelt and white barley,
Close by their chariots, waited the coming of fair-thronèd Dawn.[72]

(IX) Nestor, King of Elian Pylus, advises Agamemnon to restore Briseis to Achilles; he agrees, and promises Achilles half of Greece if he will rejoin the siege; but Achilles continues to pout. (X) Odysseus and Diomed make a two-man sally upon the Trojan camp at night, and slay a dozen chieftains. (XI) Agamemnon leads his army valiantly, is wounded, and retires. Odysseus, surrounded, fights like a lion; Ajax and Menelaus cleave a path to him, and save him for a bitter life. (XII-XIII) When the Trojans advance to the walls that the Greeks have built about their camp (XIV) Hera is so disturbed that she resolves to rescue the Greeks. Oiled, perfumed, ravishingly gowned, and bound with Aphrodite's aphrodisiac girdle, she seduces Zeus to a divine slumber while Poseidon helps the Greeks to drive the Trojans back. (XV) Advantage fluctuates; the Trojans reach the Greek ships, and the poet rises to a height of fervid narrative as the Greeks fight desperately in a retreat that must mean death.

(XVI) Patroclus, beloved of Achilles, wins his permission to lead Achilles' troops against Troy; Hector slays him, and (XVII) fights Ajax fiercely over the body of the youth. (XVIII) Hearing of Patroclus' death, Achilles at last resolves to fight. His goddess-mother Thetis persuades the divine smithy, Hephaestus, to forge for him new arms and a mighty shield. (XIX) Achilles is reconciled with Agamemnon, (XX) engages Aeneas, and is about to kill him when Poseidon rescues him for Virgil's purposes. (XXI) Achilles slaughters a host of Trojans, and sends them to Hades with long genealogical speeches. The gods take up the fight: Athena lays Ares low with a stone, and when Aphrodite, going for a soldier, tries to save him, Athena knocks her down with a blow upon her fair breast. Hera cuffs the ears of Artemis; Poseidon and Apollo content themselves with words. (XXII) All Trojans but Hector fly from Achilles; Priam and Hecuba counsel Hector to stay behind the walls, but he refuses. Then suddenly, as Achilles advances upon him, Hector takes to his heels. Achilles pursues him three times around the walls of Troy; Hector makes a stand, and is killed.

(XXIII) In the subsiding finale of the drama Patroclus is cremated with ornate ritual. Achilles sacrifices to him many cattle, twelve captured Trojans, and his own long hair. The Greeks honor Patroclus with games, and (XXIV) Achilles drags the corpse of Hector behind his chariot three times around the pyre. Priam comes in state and sorrow to beg for the remains of his son. Achilles relents, grants a truce of twelve days, and allows the aged king to take the cleansed and anointed body back to Troy.

V. THE HOME-COMING

Here the great poem suddenly ends, as if the poet had used up his share of a common story, and must leave the rest to another minstrel's lay. We are told by the later literature how Paris, standing beside the battle, slew Achilles with an arrow that pierced his vulnerable heel, and how Troy fell at last through the stratagem of the wooden horse.

The victors themselves were vanquished by their victory, and returned in weary sadness to their longed-for homes. Many of them were shipwrecked, and some of these, stranded on alien shores, founded Greek colonies in Asia, the Aegean, and Italy.[73] Menelaus, who had vowed that he would kill Helen, fell in love with her anew when the "goddess among women" came to him in the calm majesty of her loveliness; gladly he took her back to be his queen again in Sparta. When Agamemnon reached Mycenae he "clasped his land and kissed it, and many were the hot tears that streamed from his eyes."[74] But during his long absence Clytaemnestra had taken his cousin Aegisthus for husband and king; and when Agamemnon entered the palace they slew him.

Sadder still was the home-coming of Odysseus; and here probably another Homer has told the tale in a poem less powerful and heroic, gentler and pleasanter, than the *Iliad.** Odysseus, says the *Odyssey*, is shipwrecked on the island of Ogygia, a fairyland Tahiti, whose goddess-queen Calypso holds him as her lover for eight years while secretly he pines for his wife Penelope and his son Telemachus, who pine for him at Ithaca.

(I) Athena persuades Zeus to bid Calypso let Odysseus depart. The goddess flies to Telemachus, and hears with sympathy the youth's simple tale: how the princes of Ithaca and its vassal isles are paying court to Penelope, seeking through her the throne, and how meanwhile they live gaily in Odysseus' palace, and consume his substance. (II) Telemachus bids the suitors disperse, but they laugh at his youth. Secretly he embarks upon the sea in search of his father, while Penelope, mourning now for both husband and son, holds off the suitors

* Very probably the narrative in this instance has less basis in history than the *Iliad.* The legend of the long-wandering mariner or warrior, whose wife cannot recognize him on his return, is apparently older than the story of Troy, and appears in almost every literature.[75] Odysseus is the Sinuhe, the Sinbad, the Robinson Crusoe, the Enoch Arden of the Greeks. The geography of the poem is a mystery that still exercises leisurely minds.

by promising to wed one of them when she has completed her web—of which she unweaves at night as much as she has woven by day. (III) Telemachus visits Nestor at Pylus and (IV) Menelaus at Sparta, but neither can tell him where to find his father. The poet paints an attractive picture of Helen settled and subdued, but still divinely beautiful; she has long since been forgiven her sins, and remarks that when Troy fell she had grown tired of the city anyway.*

(V) Now for the first time Odysseus enters the tale. "Sitting on the shore" of Calypso's isle, "his eyes were dry of tears, and his sweet life ebbed away, as he longed mournfully for his return. By night indeed he would sleep by Calypso's side perforce in the hollow caves, unwilling beside the willing nymph, but by day he would sit on the rocks and the sands, rocking his soul with tears and groans, and looking over the unresting sea."[78] Calypso, having detained him one night more, bids him make a raft and set out alone.

(VI) After many struggles with the ocean, Odysseus lands in the mythical country of Phaeacia (possibly Corcyra-Corfu), and is found by the maiden Nausicaa, who leads him to the palace of her father, King Alcinous. The lass falls in love with the strong-limbed, strong-hearted hero, and confides to her companions: "Listen, my white-armed maidens. . . . Erewhile this man seemed to me uncomely, but now he is like the gods that keep wide heaven. Would that such a one might be called my husband, dwelling here, and that it might please him here to abide."[79] (VII-VIII) Odysseus makes so good an impression that Alcinous offers him Nausicaa's hand. Odysseus excuses himself, but is glad to tell the story of his return from Troy.

(IX) His ships (he tells the King) were borne off their course to the land of the Lotus-Eaters, who gave his men such honey-sweet lotus fruit that many forgot their homes and their longing, and Odysseus had to force them back to their ships. There they sailed to the land of the Cyclopes, one-eyed giants who lived without law or labor on an island abounding in wild grain and fruit. Caught in a cave by the Cyclop Polyphemus, who ate several of his men, Odysseus saved the remnant by lulling the monster to sleep with wine, and then burning out his single eye. (X) The wanderers took again to the sea, and came to the land of the Laestrygonians; but these, too, were cannibals, and only Odysseus' ship escaped them. He and his mates reached next the isle of Aenea, where the lovely and treacherous goddess Circe lured most of them into her cave with song, drugged them, and turned them into swine. Odysseus was about to slay her when he changed his mind and accepted her love. He and his comrades, now restored to human form, remained with Circe a full year.

* After her death, said Greek tradition, she was worshiped as a goddess. It was a common belief in Greece that those who spoke ill of her were punished by the gods; even Homer's blindness, it was hinted, came upon him because he had lent his song to the calumnious notion that Helen had eloped to Troy, instead of being snatched off to Egypt against her will.[77]

(XI) Setting sail again, they came to a land perpetually dark, which proved to be the entrance to Hades; there Odysseus talked with the shades of Agamemnon, Achilles, and his mother. (XII) Resuming their voyage, they passed the island of the Sirens, against whose seductive strains Odysseus protected his men by putting wax into their ears. In the straits (Messina?) of Scylla and Charybdis his ship was wrecked, and he alone survived, to live for eight long years on Calypso's isle.

(XIII) Alcinous is so moved with sympathy by Odysseus' tale that he bids his men row Odysseus to Ithaca, but to blindfold him lest he learn and reveal the location of their happy land. On Ithaca the goddess Athena guides the wanderer to the hut of his old swineherd Eumaeus, who (XIV), though not recognizing him, receives him with Gargantuan hospitality. (XV) When Telemachus is led by the goddess to the same hut Odysseus (XVI) makes himself known to his son, and both "wail aloud vehemently." He unfolds to Telemachus a plan for slaying all the suitors. (XVII-XVIII) In the guise of a beggar he enters his palace, sees the wooers feasting at his expense, and rages inwardly when he hears that they lie with his maidservants at night even while courting Penelope by day. (XIX-XX) He is insulted and injured by the suitors, but he defends himself with vigor and patience. (XXI) By this time the wooers have discovered the trick of Penelope's web, and have forced her to finish it. She agrees to marry whichever of them can string Odysseus' great bow—which hangs on the wall—and shoot an arrow through the openings of twelve axes ranged in line. They all try, and all fail. Odysseus asks for a chance, and succeeds. (XXII) Then with a wrath that frightens everyone, he casts off his disguise, turns his arrows upon the suitors, and, with the help of Telemachus, Eumaeus, and Athena, slays them all. (XXIII) He finds it hard to convince Penelope that he is Odysseus; it is difficult to surrender twenty suitors for one husband. (XXIV) He meets the attack of the suitors' sons, pacifies them, and re-establishes his kingdom.

Meanwhile in Argos the greatest tragedy in Greek legend was pursuing its course. Orestes, son of Agamemnon, grown to manhood and aroused by his bitter sister Electra, avenged their father by murdering their mother and her paramour. After many years of madness and wandering Orestes ascended the throne of Argos-Mycenae (ca. 1176 B.C.) and later added Sparta to his kingdom.* But from his accession the house of Pelops began to decline. Perhaps the decline had begun with Agamemnon, and that

* Sir Arthur Evans has found, in a Mycenaean tomb in Boeotia, engravings representing a young man attacking a sphinx, and a youth killing an older man and a woman. He believes that these refer to Oedipus and Orestes; and as he ascribes these engravings to ca. 1450 B.C., he argues for a date for Oedipus and Orestes some two centuries earlier than the epoch tentatively assigned to these characters in the text.[80]

vacillating chieftain had used war as a means of uniting a realm that was already falling to pieces. But his victory completed his ruin. For few of his chieftains ever returned, and the kingdoms of many others had lost all loyalty to them. By the end of the age that had opened with the siege of Troy the Achaean power was spent, the blood of Pelops was exhausted. The people waited patiently for a saner dynasty.

VI. THE DORIAN CONQUEST

About the year 1104 B.C. a new wave of immigration or invasion came down upon Greece from the restlessly expanding north. Through Illyria and Thessaly, across the Corinthian Gulf at Naupactus, and over the Isthmus at Corinth, a warlike people, tall, roundheaded, letterless, slipped or marched or poured into the Peloponnesus, mastered it, and almost completely destroyed Mycenaean civilization. We guess at their origin and their route, but we know their character and their effect. They were still in the herding and hunting stage; now and then they stopped to till the soil, but their main reliance was upon their cattle, whose need for new pasturage kept the tribes ever on the move. One thing they had in unheard-of quantity—iron. They were the emissaries of the Hallstatt* culture to Greece; and the hard metal of their swords and souls gave them a merciless supremacy over Achaeans and Cretans who still used bronze to kill. Probably from both west and east, from Elis and Megara, they came down upon the separate little kingdoms of the Peloponnesus, put the ruling classes to the sword, and turned the Mycenaean remnant into helot-serfs. Mycenae and Tiryns went up in flames, and for some centuries Argos became the capital of Pelops' isle. On the Isthmus the invaders seized a commanding peak—the Acrocorinthus—and built around it the Dorian city of Corinth.[80a] The surviving Achaeans fled, some of them into the mountains of the northern Peloponnesus, some into Attica, some overseas to the islands and coasts of Asia. The conquerors followed them into Attica, but were repulsed; they followed them to Crete,[81] and made final the destruction of Cnossus; they captured and colonized Melos, Thera, Cos, Cnidus, and Rhodes. Throughout the Peloponnesus and Crete, where the Mycenaean culture had most flourished, the devastation was most complete.

This terminal catastrophe in the prehistory of Aegean civilization is what modern historians know as the Dorian conquest, and what Greek tradi-

* A town in Austria whose iron remains have given its name to the first period of the Iron Age in Europe.

tion called the Return of the Heracleidae. For the victors were not content to record their triumph as a conquest of a civilized people by barbarians; they protested that what had really happened was that the descendants of Heracles, resisted in their just re-entry into the Peloponnesus, had taken it by heroic force. We do not know how much of this is history, and how much is diplomatic mythology designed to transform a bloody conquest into a divine right. It is difficult to believe that the Dorians were such excellent liars in the very youth of the world. Perhaps, as disputants will never allow, both stories were true: the Dorians were conquerors from the north, led by the scions of Heracles.

Whatever the form of the conquest, its result was a long and bitter interruption in the development of Greece. Political order was disturbed for centuries; every man, feeling unsafe, carried arms; increasing violence disrupted agriculture and trade on land, and commerce on the seas. War flourished, poverty deepened and spread. Life became unsettled as families wandered from country to country seeking security and peace.[82] Hesiod called this the Age of Iron, and mourned its debasement from the finer ages that had preceded it; many Greeks believed that "the discovery of iron had been to the hurt of man."[83] The arts languished, painting was neglected, statuary contented itself with figurines; and pottery, forgetting the lively naturalism of Mycenae and Crete, degenerated into a lifeless "Geometrical Style" that dominated Greek ceramics for centuries.

But not all was lost. Despite the resolution of the invading Dorians to keep their blood free from admixture with that of the subject population—despite the racial antipathies between Dorian and Ionian that were to incarnadine all Greece—there went on, rapidly outside of Laconia, slowly within, a mingling of the new stocks with the old; and perhaps the addition of the vigorous seed of Achaeans and Dorians with that of the more ancient and volatile peoples of southern Greece served as a powerful biological stimulant. The final result, after centuries of mingling, was a new and diverse people, in whose blood "Mediterranean," "Alpine," "Nordic," and Asiatic elements were disturbingly fused.

Nor was Mycenaean culture entirely destroyed. Certain elements of the Aegean heritage—instrumentalities of social order and government, elements of craftsmanship and technology, modes and routes of trade, forms and objects of worship,[84] ceramic and toreutic skills, the art of fresco painting, decorative motives and architectural forms—maintained a half-stifled existence through centuries of violence and chaos. Cretan institutions, the Greeks believed, passed down into Sparta;[85] and the Achaean assembly remained the essential structure of even democratic Greece. The Mycenaean megaron probably provided the ground plan of the Doric temple,[86] to which the Dorian spirit would add freedom, symmetry, and strength. The artistic tradition, slowly reviving, lifted Corinth, Sicyon, and Argos to an early Renaissance, and made even dour Sparta, for a while, smile with art and song; it nourished lyric poetry through all this historyless Dark Age; it followed Pelasgian, Achaean, Ionian, Minyan exiles in their flight migration to the Aegean and Asia, and helped the colonial cities to leap ahead of their mother states in literature and art. And when the exiles came to the islands and Ionia they found the remains of Aegean civilization ready to their hands. There, in old towns a little less disordered than on the Continent, the Age of Bronze had kept something of its ancient craft and brilliance; and there on Asiatic soil would come the first reawakening of Greece.

In the end the contact of five cultures—Cretan, Mycenaean, Achaean, Dorian, Oriental—brought new youth to a civilization that had begun to die, that had grown coarse on the mainland through war and plunder, and effeminate in Crete through the luxury of its genius. The mixture of races and ways took centuries to win even a moderate stability, but it contributed to produce the unparalleled variety, flexibility, and subtlety of Greek thought and life. Instead of thinking of Greek culture as a flame that shone suddenly and miraculously amid a dark sea of barbarism, we must conceive of it as the slow and turbid creation of a people almost too richly endowed in blood and memories, and surrounded, challenged, and instructed by warlike hordes, powerful empires, and ancient civilizations.

BOOK II

THE RISE OF GREECE

1000-480 B.C.

CHRONOLOGICAL TABLE FOR BOOK II

NOTES: All dates before 480, except 776, are uncertain. A place name without other description indicates the traditional date of its first Greek settlement.

B.C.

1100-850: Aeolian and Ionian migrations
1000: Temple of Hera at Olympia
840: Probable period of Homer
776: First (?) Olympic Games
770: Sinope and Cumae
757-6: Cyzicus and Trapezus
752: First decennial archons
750-650: Greeks settle Thracian peninsula
750-594: Age of the aristocracies
750: Probable period of Hesiod
735: Naxos (Sicily)
734: Corcyra and Syracuse
730-29: Rhegium, Leontini, Catana
725-05: First Messenian War
725: Coinage in Lydia and Ionia
721: Sybaris; 710, Crotona
705: Taras; 700, Poseidonia; beginnings of Greek architecture in stone
683: First annual archons at Athens
680: Pheidon dictator at Argos; earliest state coinage in Greece
676: Orthagoras dictator at Sicyon
670: Terpander of Lesbos, poet and musician; Archilochus of Paros, poet; Homeric hymns to Apollo and Demeter
660: Laws of Zaleucus at Locri
658: Byzantium; 654, Lampsacus
655-25: Cypselus dictator at Corinth
651: Selinus; 650, Abdera and Olbia
648: Himera; Myron dictator at Sicyon
640-31: Second Messenian War; Tyrtaeus, poet, at Sparta
630: Laws of Lycurgus at Sparta (?)
630: Cyrene; 615, Abydos
625-585: Periander dictator at Corinth
620: Laws of Draco at Athens
615: Thrasybulus dictator at Miletus
610: Laws of Charondas at Catana
600: Naucratis; Massalia (Marseilles); Cleisthenes dictator at Sicyon, Pittacus at Mytilene; Sappho and Alcaeus, poets of Lesbos; Thales of Miletus, philosopher; Alcman, poet, at Sparta; rise of sculpture
595: First Sacred War
594: Laws of Solon at Athens
590: Age of the Seven Wise Men; rise of the Amphictyonic League and Orphism; second Temple of Artemis at Ephesus
582: First Pythian and Isthmian games; the Acropolis statues and the "Apollos"

B.C.

580: Acragas; Aesop of Samos, fabulist
576: First Nemean games
570: Phalaris dictator at Acragas; Stesichorus of Himera, poet; Anaximander of Miletus, philosopher
566: First Panathenaic games
561-60: First dictatorship of Peisistratus
560-46: Croesus of Lydia subjugates Ionia
558: Carthage conquers Sicily and Corsica
550: Emporium (Spain); 535, Elea (Italy)
546-27: Second dictatorship of Peisistratus
545: Persia subjugates Ionia
544: Anaximenes of Miletus, philosopher
540: Hipponax of Ephesus, poet
535-15: Polycrates dictator of Samos; Theodorus of Samos, artist; Anacreon of Teos, poet
534: Thespis establishes drama at Athens
530: Theognis of Megara, poet
529-00: Pythagoras, philosopher, at Crotona
527-10: Hippias dictator at Athens
520: Olympieum begun at Athens
517: Simonides of Ceos, poet
514: Conspiracy of Harmodius and Aristogeiton
511: Phrynichus of Athens, dramatist
510: Destruction of Sybaris by Crotona
507: Cleisthenes extends democracy at Athens
500: Hecataeus of Miletus, geographer
499: Ionia revolts; Aeschylus' first play
497: Ionian Greeks burn Sardis
494: Persians defeat Ionians at Lade
493: Themistocles archon at Athens
490: Marathon; temple of Aphaea at Aegina
489: Aristides archon; trial of Miltiades
488-72: Theron dictator at Acragas
487: First selection of archons by lot
485-78: Gelon dictator at Syracuse
485: Epicharmus establishes comedy at Syracuse
482: Ostracism of Aristides
480: Battles of Artemisium, Thermopylae, Salamis, and Himera; Ageladas of Argos, sculptor
479: Battles of Plataea and Mycale

CHAPTER IV

Sparta

I. THE ENVIRONMENT OF GREECE

LET us take an atlas of the classic world* and find our way among the neighbors of ancient Greece. By *Greece*, or *Hellas*, we shall mean all lands occupied, in antiquity, by peoples speaking Greek.

We begin where many invaders entered—over the hills and through the valleys of Epirus. Here the ancestors of the Greeks must have tarried many a year, for they set up at Dodona a shrine to their thundering sky-god Zeus; as late as the fifth century the Greeks consulted the oracle there, and read the divine will in the clangor of caldrons or the rustling leaves of the sacred oak.[1] Through southern Epirus flowed the river Acheron, amid ravines so dark and deep that Greek poets spoke of it as the portal or very scene of Hell. In Homer's day the Epirots were largely Greek in speech and ways; but then new waves of barbarism came down upon them from the north, and dissuaded them from civilization.

Farther up the Adriatic lay Illyria, sparsely settled with untamed herdsmen who sold cattle and slaves for salt.[2] On this coast, at Epidamnus (the Roman Dyrrachium, now Durazzo), Caesar disembarked his troops in pursuit of Pompey. Across the Adriatic the expanding Greeks snatched the lower coasts from the native tribes, and gave civilization to Italy. (In the end those native tribes would sweep back upon them, and one tribe, almost barbarous till Alexander's time, would swallow them up, along with their motherland, in an unprecedented empire.) Beyond the Alps ranged the Gauls, who were to prove very friendly to the Greek city of Massalia (Marseilles); and at the western end of the Mediterranean lay Spain, already half civilized and fully exploited by the Phoenicians and Carthaginians when, about 550, the Greeks established their timid colony at Emporium (Ampurias). On the coast of Africa, menacingly opposite Sicily, was imperial Carthage, founded by Dido and the Phoenicians, tradition said, in 813; no mere village, but a city of 700,000 population, monopolizing the commerce of the western Mediterranean, dominating Utica, Hippo, and three hundred other towns in Africa, and controlling prosperous lands, mines, and colonies in Sicily, Sardinia, and Spain. This fabulously wealthy metropolis was fated to lead the Oriental thrust against Greece in the west, as Persia would lead it in the east.

* Or the maps inside the covers of this book.

Farther east on the African coast lay the prosperous Greek city of Cyrene, against a dark Libyan hinterland. Then Egypt. It was the belief of most Greeks that many elements of their civilization had come to them from Egypt; their legends ascribed the foundation of several Greek cities to men who, like Cadmus and Danaus, had come from Egypt, or had brought Egyptian culture to Greece by way of Phoenicia or Crete.[3] Under the Saïte kings (663-525) Egyptian commerce and art revived, and the ports of the Nile were for the first time opened to Greek trade. From the seventh century onward many famous Greeks —Thales, Pythagoras, Solon, Plato, and Democritus may serve as examples— visited Egypt, and were much impressed by the fullness and antiquity of its culture. Here were no barbarians, but men who had had a mature civilization, and highly developed arts, two thousand years before the fall of Troy. "You Greeks," said an Egyptian priest to Solon, "are mere children, talkative and vain, and knowing nothing of the past."[4] When Hecataeus of Miletus boasted to the Egyptian priests that he could trace his ancestry through fifteen generations to a god, they quietly showed him, in their sanctuaries, the statues of 345 high priests, each the son of the preceding, making 345 generations since the gods had reigned on earth.[5] From the Egyptian cults of Isis and Osiris, in the belief of Greek scholars like Herodotus and Plutarch, came the Orphic doctrine of a judgment after death, and the resurrection ritual of Demeter and Persephone at Eleusis.[6] Probably in Egypt, Thales of Miletus learned geometry, and Rhoecus and Theodorus of Samos picked up the art of hollow casting in bronze; in Egypt the Greeks acquired new skills in pottery, textiles, metalworking, and ivory;[7] there, as well as from the Assyrians, Phoenicians, and Hittites, Greek sculptors took the style of their early statues—flat-faced, slant-eyed, closefisted, straight-limbed, stiff;* in the colonnades of Sakkara and Beni-Hasan, as well as in the remains of Mycenaean Greece, Greek architects found part of their inspiration for the fluted column and the Doric style.[8] And as Greece in its youth learned humbly from Egypt, so, when it was exhausted, it died, one might say, in the arms of Egypt; at Alexandria it merged its philosophies, its rites, and its gods with those of Egypt and Judea, in order that they might find a resurrected life in Rome and Christianity.

Second only to Egypt's was the influence of Phoenicia. The enterprising merchants of Tyre and Sidon acted like a circulating medium in the transmission of culture, and stimulated every Mediterranean region with the sciences, techniques, arts, and cults of Egypt and the Near East. They excelled and perhaps instructed the Greeks in the building of ships; they taught them better methods in metalworking, textiles, and dyes;[9] they played a part, with Crete and Asia Minor, in passing on to Greece the Semitic form of the alphabet that had been developed in Egypt, Crete, and Syria. Farther east, Babylonia gave

* Cf. the seated *Chares* from Miletus in the British Museum, or the *Head of Cleobis* by Polymedes in the museum at Delphi.

to the Greeks its system of weights and measures,[10] its water clock and sundial,[11] its monetary units of obol, mina, and talent,[12] its astronomical principles, instruments, records, and calculations, its sexagesimal system of dividing the year, the circle, and the four right angles that are subtended by a circle at its center, into 360 parts, each of the 360 degrees into 60 minutes, and each of the minutes into 60 seconds; it was presumably his acquaintance with Egyptian and Babylonian astronomy that enabled Thales to predict an eclipse of the sun.[13] Probably from Babylonia came Hesiod's notion of Chaos as the origin of all things; and the story of Ishtar and Tammuz is suspiciously like those of Aphrodite and Adonis, Demeter and Persephone.

Near the eastern end of the commercial complex that united the classic world lay the final enemy of Greece. In some ways—though few—the civilization of Persia was superior to that of contemporary Hellas; it produced a type of gentleman finer than the Greek in every respect except that of intellectual keenness and education, and a system of imperial administration that easily excelled the clumsy hegemonies of Athens and Sparta, and lacked only the Greek passion for liberty.—From Assyria the Ionian Greeks took a measure of skill in animal statuary, a certain thickness of figure and flatness of drapery in their early sculpture, many decorative motives in friezes and moldings, and occasionally a style of relief, as in the lovely stela of Aristion.[14]—Lydia maintained intimate relations with Ionia, and its brilliant capital, Sardis, was a clearinghouse for the traffic in goods and ideas between Mesopotamia and the Greek cities on the coast. The necessities of an extensive trade stimulated banking, and caused the Lydian government, about 680, to issue a state-guaranteed coinage. This boon to trade was soon imitated and improved by the Greeks, and had effects as momentous and interminable as those that came from the introduction of the alphabet.—The influence of Phrygia was older and subtler. Its mother goddess, Cybele, entered directly and deviously into Greek religion, and its orgiastic flute music became that "Phrygian mode" so popular among the populace, and so disturbing to the moralists, of Greece. From Phrygia this wild music crossed the Hellespont into Thrace, and served the rites of Dionysus. The god of wine was the chief gift of Thrace to Greece; but one Thracian city, Hellenized Abdera, sought to even the balance by giving Greece three philosophers—Leucippus, Democritus and Protagoras. It was from Thrace that the cult of the Muses passed down into Hellas; and the half-legendary founders of Greek music—Orpheus, Musaeus, and Thamyris—were Thracian singers and bards.

From Thrace we move southward into Macedonia, and our cultural circumvallation of Greece is complete. It is a picturesque land, with a soil once rich in minerals, plains fertile in grain and fruit, and mountains disciplining a hardy stock that was destined to conquer Greece. The mountaineers and peasants were of mixed race, predominantly Illyrian and Thracian; perhaps they were akin to the Dorians who conquered the Peloponnesus. The ruling aristocracy claimed Hellenic lineage (from Heracles himself), and spoke a dialect of Greek. The earlier capital, Edessa, stood on a vast plateau between the plains that stretched to Epirus and the ranges that reached to the Aegean. Farther east lay Pella, capital-to-be of Philip and Alexander; and near the sea was Pydna, where the Romans would conquer the conquering Macedonians, and win the right to transmit Greek civilization to the Western world.

This, then, was the environment of Greece: civilizations like Egypt, Crete, and Mesopotamia that gave it those elements of technology, science, and art which it would transform into the brightest picture in history; empires like Persia and Carthage that would feel the challenge of Greek commerce, and would unite in a war to crush Greece between them into a harmless vassalage; and, in the north, warlike hordes recklessly breeding, restlessly marching, who would sooner or later pour down over the mountain barriers and do what the Dorians had done—break through what Cicero was to call the Greek border woven on the barbarian robe,[15] and destroy a civilization that they could not understand. Hardly any of these surrounding nations cared for what to the Greeks was the very essence of life—liberty to be, to think, to speak, and to do. Every one of these peoples except the Phoenicians lived under despots, surrendered their souls to superstition, and had small experience of the stimulus of freedom or the life of reason. That was why the Greeks called them all, too indiscriminately, *barbaroi*, barbarians; a barbarian was a man content to believe without reason and to live without liberty. In the end the two conceptions of life—the mysticism of the East and the rationalism of the West—would fight for the body and soul of Greece. Rationalism would win under Pericles, as under Caesar, Leo X, and Frederick; but mysticism would always return. The alternate victories of these complementary philosophies in the vast pendulum of history constitute the essential biography of Western civilization.

II. ARGOS

Within this circle of nations little Greece expanded until its progeny peopled nearly every Mediterranean shore. For the gaunt hand that stretched its skeletal fingers southward into the sea was but a small part of the Greece whose history concerns us. In the course of their development the irrepressible Hellenes spread into every isle of the Aegean, into Crete, Rhodes, and Cyprus, into Egypt, Palestine, Syria, Mesopotamia, and Asia Minor, into the Sea of Marmora and the Black Sea, into the shores and peninsulas of the north Aegean, into Italy, Gaul, Spain, Sicily, and northern Africa. In all these regions they built city-states, independent and diverse, and yet Greek; they spoke the Greek tongue, worshiped Greek gods, read and wrote Greek literature, contributed to Greek science and philosophy, and practiced democracy in the Greek aristocratic way. They did not leave Greece behind them when they migrated from their motherland, they carried it with them, even the very soil of it, wherever they went. For nearly a thousand years they made the Mediterranean a Greek lake, and the center of the world.

The most discouraging task faced by the historian of classic civilization is that of weaving into one pattern and story these scattered members of the body of Greece.* We shall attempt it by the pleasant method of a tour: with a map at our elbow and no expenditure but of the imagination, we shall pass from city to city of the Greek world, and observe in each center the life of the people before the Persian war—the modes of economy and government, the activities of scientists and philosophers, the achievements of poetry, and the creations of art.† The plan has many faults: the geographical sequence will not quite agree with the historical; we shall be leaping from century to century as well as from isle to isle; and we shall find ourselves talking with Thales and Anaximander before listening to Homer and Hesiod. But it will do us no harm to see the irreverent *Iliad* against its actual background of Ionian skepticism, or to hear Hesiod's dour plaints after visiting the Aeolian colonies from which his harassed father came. When at last we reach Athens we shall know in some measure the rich variety of the civilization that it inherited, and which it preserved so bravely at Marathon.

If we begin at Argos, where the victorious Dorians established their government, we find ourselves in a scene characteristically Greek: a not too fertile plain, a small and huddled city of little brick-and-plaster houses, a temple on the acropolis, an open-air theater on the slope of the hill, a modest palace here and there, narrow alleys and unpaved streets, and in the distance the inviting and merciless sea. For Hellas is composed of mountains and ocean; majestic scenery is so usual there that the Greeks, though moved and inspired by it, seldom mention it in their books. The winter is wet and cold, the summer hot and dry; sowing is in our autumn, reaping is in our spring; rain is a heavenly

---

* "To write the history of Greece at almost any period without dissipating the interest is a task of immense difficulty . . . because there is no constant unity or fixed center to which the actions and aims of the numerous states can be subordinated or related."—Bury, *Ancient Greek Historians*, p. 22.

† To avoid returning too often to the same scene, the architectural history of minor cities will be carried in these chapters (Book II) down to the death of Alexander (323).

blessing, and Zeus the Rain Maker is god of gods. The rivers are short and shallow, torrents for a winter spell, dry smooth pebbles in the summer heat. There were a hundred cities like Argos in the gamut of Greece, a thousand like it but smaller; each of them jealously sovereign, separated from the rest by Greek pugnacity, or dangerous waters, or roadless hills.

The Argives ascribed the foundation of their city to Pelasgic Argus, the hero with a hundred eyes; and its first flourishing to an Egyptian, Danaus, who came at the head of a band of "Danaae" and taught the natives to irrigate their fields with wells. Such eponyms are not to be scorned; the Greeks preferred to end with myth that infinite regress which we must end with mystery. Under Temenus, one of the returning Heracleidae, Argos grew into the most powerful city of Greece, bringing Tiryns, Mycenae, and all Argolis under its sway. Towards 680 the government was seized by one of those *tyrannoi*, or dictators, who for the next two centuries became the fashion in the larger cities of Greece. Presumably Pheidon, like his fellow dictators, led the rising merchant class—allied in a passing marriage of convenience with the commoners—against a landowning aristocracy. When Aegina was threatened by Epidaurus and Athens Pheidon went to its rescue and took it for himself. He adopted—probably from the Phoenicians—the Babylonian system of weights and measures, and the Lydian plan of a currency guaranteed by the state; he established his mint on Aegina, and the Aeginetan "tortoises" (coins marked with the island's symbol) became the first official coinage in continental Greece.[16]

Pheidon's enlightened despotism opened a period of prosperity that brought many arts to Argolis. In the sixth century the musicians of Argos were the most famous in Hellas;[17] Lasus of Hermione won high place among the lyric poets of his time, and taught his skill to Pindar; the foundations were laid of that Argive school of sculpture which was to give Polycleitus and its canon to Greece; drama found a home here, in a theater with twenty thousand seats; and architects raised a majestic temple to Hera, beloved and especially worshiped by Argos as the goddess-bride who renewed her virginity every year.[18] But the degeneration of Pheidon's descendants—the nemesis of monarchy—and a long series of wars with Sparta weakened Argos, and forced it at last to yield to the Lacedaemonians the leadership of the Peloponnesus. Today it is a quiet town, lost amid its surrounding fields; remembering vaguely the glories of its past, and proud that in all its long history it has never been abandoned.

III. LACONIA

South of Argos, and away from the sea, rise the peaks of the Parnon range. They are beautiful, but still more pleasing to the eye is the Eurotas River that runs between them and the taller, darker, snow-tipped range of Taygetus on the west. In that seismic valley lay Homer's "hollow

Lacedaemon," a plain so guarded by mountains that Sparta, its capital, needed no walls. At its zenith Sparta ("The Scattered") was a union of five villages, totaling some seventy thousand population. Today it is a hamlet of four thousand souls; and hardly anything remains, even in the modest museum, of the city that once ruled and ruined Greece.

1. The Expansion of Sparta

From that natural citadel the Dorians dominated and enslaved the southern Peloponnesus. To these long-haired northerners, hardened by mountains and habituated to war, there seemed no alternative in life but conquest or slavery; war was their business, by which they made what seemed to them an honest living; the non-Dorian natives, weakened by agriculture and peace, were in obvious need of masters. So the kings of Sparta, who claimed a continuous lineage from the Heracleidae of 1104, first subjected the indigenous population of Laconia, and then attacked Messenia. That land, in the southwestern corner of the Peloponnesus, was relatively level and fertile, and was tilled by pacific tribes. We may read in Pausanias how the Messenian king, Aristodemus, consulted the oracle at Delphi for ways to defeat the Spartans; how Apollo bade him offer in sacrifice to the gods a virgin of his own royal race; how he put to death his own daughter, and lost the war.[19] (Perhaps he had been mistaken about his daughter.) Two generations later the brave Aristomenes led the Messenians in heroic revolt. For nine years their cities bore up under attack and siege; but in the end the Spartans had their way. The Messenians were subjected to an annual tax of half their crops, and thousands of them were led away to join the Helot serfs.

The picture that we are to form of Laconian society before Lycurgus has, like some ancient paintings, three levels. Above is a master class of Dorians, living for the most part in Sparta on the produce of fields owned by them in the country and tilled for them by Helots. Socially between, geographically surrounding, the masters and the Helots were the Perioeci ("Dwellers Around"): freemen living in a hundred villages in the mountains or on the outskirts of Laconia, or engaged in trade or industry in the towns; subject to taxation and military service, but having no share in the government, and no right of intermarriage with the ruling class. Lowest and most numerous of all were the Helots, so named, according to Strabo, from the town of Helus, whose people had been among the first to be enslaved by the Spartans.[20] By simple conquest of the non-Dorian population or by importing prisoners of war, Sparta had made Laconia a land of some 224,000 Helots, 120,000 Perioeci, and 32,000 men, women, and children of the citizen class.*[21]

The Helot had all the liberties of a medieval serf. He could marry as he pleased, breed without forethought, work the land in his own way, and live in a village with his neighbors, undisturbed by the absentee owner of his lot, so long as he remitted regularly to this owner the rental fixed by the government. He was bound to the soil, but neither he nor the land could be sold. In some cases he was a domestic servant in the town. He was expected to attend his master in war, and, when called upon, to fight for the state; if he fought well he might receive his freedom. His economic condition was not normally worse than that of the village peasantry in the rest of Greece outside of Attica, or the unskilled laborer in a modern city. He had the consolations of his own dwelling, varied work, and the quiet friendliness of trees and fields. But he was continually subject to martial law, and to secret supervision by a secret police, by whom he might at any moment be killed without cause or trial.[22]

In Laconia, as elsewhere, the simple paid tribute to the clever; this is a custom with a venerable past and a promising future. In most civilizations this distribution of the goods of life is brought about by the normally peaceful operation of the price system: the clever persuade us to pay more for the less readily duplicable luxuries and services that they offer us than the simple can manage to secure for the more easily replaceable necessaries that they produce. But in Laconia the concentration of wealth was effected by irritatingly visible means, and left among the Helots a volcanic discontent that in almost every year of Spartan history threatened to upset the state with revolution.

2. *Sparta's Golden Age*

In that dim past before Lycurgus came, Sparta was a Greek city like the rest, and blossomed out in song and art as it would never do after him. Music above all was popular there, and rivaled man's antiquity; for as far back as we can delve we find the Greeks singing. In Sparta, so frequently at war, music took a martial turn—the strong and simple "Doric mode"; and not only were other styles discouraged, but any deviation from this Doric style was punishable by law. Even Terpander, though he had quelled a sedition by his songs, was fined by the ephors, and his lyre nailed mute to the wall, because to suit his voice, he had dared to add another string

* These figures, of course, are conjectural, being based upon a few hints and many assumptions.

to the instrument; and in a later generation Timotheus, who had expanded Terpander's seven strings to eleven, was not allowed to compete at Sparta until the ephors had removed from his lyre the scandalously extra strings.[23]

Sparta, like England, had great composers when she imported them. Towards 670, supposedly at the behest of the Delphic oracle, Terpander was brought in from Lesbos to prepare a contest in choral singing at the festival of the Carneia. Likewise Thaletas was summoned from Crete about 620; and soon after came Tyrtaeus, Alcman, and Polymnestus. Their labors went mostly to composing patriotic music and training choruses to sing it. Music was seldom taught to individual Spartans;[24] as in revolutionary Russia, the communal spirit was so strong that music took a corporate form, and group competed with group in magnificent festivals of song and dance. Such choral singing gave the Spartans another opportunity for discipline and mass formations, for every voice was subject to the leader. At the feast of the Hyacinthia King Agesilaus sang obediently in the place and time assigned to him by the choral master; and at the festival of the Gymnopedia the whole body of Spartans, of every age and sex, joined in massive exercises of harmonious dance and antistrophal song. Such occasions must have provided a powerful stimulus and outlet to the patriotic sentiment.

Terpander (i.e., "Delighter of Men") was one of those brilliant poet-musicians who inaugurated the great age of Lesbos in the generation before Sappho. Tradition ascribed to him the invention of *scolia* or drinking songs, and the expansion of the lyre from four to seven strings; but the heptachord, as we have seen, was as old as Minos, and presumably men had sung the glories of wine in the forgotten adolescence of the world. Certainly he made a name for himself at Lesbos as a *kitharoedos*—i.e., a composer and singer of musical lyrics. Having killed a man in a brawl, he was exiled, and found it convenient to accept an invitation from Sparta. There, it seems, he lived the remainder of his days, teaching music and training choruses. We are told that he ended his life at a drinking party: while he was singing—perhaps that extra note which he had added at the top of the scale—one of his auditors threw a fig at him; which, entering his mouth and his windpipe, choked him to death in the very ecstasy of song.[25]

Tyrtaeus continued Terpander's work at Sparta during the Second Messenian War. He came from Aphidna—possibly in Lacedaemon, probably in Attica; certainly the Athenians had an old joke about the Spartans, that when the latter were losing the Second War they were saved by a lame Attic schoolmaster, whose songs of battle woke up the dull Spartans, and stirred them to victory.[26] Apparently he sang his own songs to the flute in public assembly, seeking to transform martial death into enviable glory. "It is a fine thing," says one of his surviving fragments, "for a brave man to die in the front rank of those who fight for their country. . . . Let each one, standing squarely on his feet, rooted to the ground and biting his lips, keep firm. . . . Foot to foot, shield to shield, waving plumes mingling and helmets clashing, let the warriors press breast to breast, each sword and spear-point meeting in the shock of battle."[27] Tyrtaeus, said the Spartan King Leonidas, "was an adept in tickling the souls of youth."[28]

Alcman sang in the same generation, as friend and rival of Tyrtaeus, but in a more varied and earthly strain. He came from far-off Lydia, and some said that he was a slave; nevertheless the Lacedaemonians welcomed him, not having yet learned the *xenelasia*, or hatred of foreigners, which was to become part of the Lycurgean code. The later Spartans would have been scandalized at his eulogies of love and food, and his roster of Laconia's noble wines. Tradition ranked him as the grossest eater of antiquity, and as an insatiable pursuer of women. One of his songs told how fortunate he was that he had not remained in Sardis, where he might have become an emasculate priest of Cybele, but had come to Sparta, where he could love in freedom his golden-haired mistress Megalostrata.[29] He begins for us that dynasty of amorous poets which culminates in Anacreon, and he heads the list of the "Nine Lyric Poets" chosen by Alexandrian critics as the best of ancient Greece.* He could write hymns and paeans as well as songs of wine and love, and the Spartans liked especially the *parthenia*, or maiden songs, which he composed for choruses of girls. A fragment now and then reveals that power of imaginative feeling which is the heart of poetry:

> Asleep lie mountain-top and mountain-gully, shoulder also and ravine; the creeping things that come from the dark earth, the beasts that lie upon the hillside, the generation of the bees, the monsters in the depths of the purple sea; all lie asleep, and with them the tribes of the winging birds.†[30]

---

* Alcman, Alcaeus, Sappho, Stesichorus, Ibycus, Anacreon, Simonides, Pindar, Bacchylides.

† How strangely similar this is—as if one feeling united two poets across twenty-five centuries—to Goethe's "Wanderer's Night-Song":

Über allen Gipfeln	O'er all the hill-tops
Ist Ruh,	Is quiet now,
In allen Wipfeln	In all the tree-tops
Spürest du	Hearest thou
Kaum einen Hauch;	Hardly a breath;
Die vögelein schweigen im Walde.	The birds are asleep in the trees.
Warte nur, balde	Wait; soon like these
Ruhest du auch.[31]	Thou, too, shalt rest.[32]

We may judge from these poets that the Spartans were not always Spartans, and that in the century before Lycurgus they relished poetry and the arts as keenly as any of the Greeks. The choral ode became so closely associated with them that when the Athenian dramatists wrote choral lyrics for their plays they used the Doric dialect, though they wrote the dialogue in the Attic speech. It is hard to say what other arts flourished in Lacedaemon in those halcyon days, for even the Spartans neglected to preserve or record them. Laconian pottery and bronze were famous in the seventh century, and the minor arts produced many refinements for the life of the fortunate few. But this little Renaissance was ended by the Messenian Wars. The conquered land was divided among the Spartans, and the number of serfs was almost doubled. How could thirty thousand citizens keep in lasting subjection four times their number of Perioeci, and seven times their number of Helots? It could be done only by abandoning the pursuit and patronage of the arts, and turning every Spartan into a soldier ready at any moment to suppress rebellion or wage war. The constitution of Lycurgus achieved this end, but at the cost of withdrawing Sparta, in every sense but the political, from the history of civilization.

3. *Lycurgus*

Greek historians from Herodotus onward took it for granted that Lycurgus was the author of the Spartan code, just as they accepted as historical the siege of Troy and the murder of Agamemnon. And as modern scholarship for a century denied the existence of Troy and Agamemnon, so today it hesitates to admit the reality of Lycurgus. The dates assigned to him vary from 900 to 600 B.C.; and how could one man take out of his head the most unpleasant and astonishing body of legislation in all history, and impose it in a few years not only upon a subject population but even upon a self-willed and warlike ruling class?[33] Nevertheless it would be presumptuous to reject on such theoretical grounds a tradition accepted by all Greek historians. The seventh century was peculiarly an age of personal legislators—Zaleucus at Locris (ca. 660), Draco at Athens (620), and Charondas at Sicilian Catana (ca. 610)—not to speak of Josiah's discovery of the Mosaic code in the Temple at Jerusalem (ca. 621). Probably we have in these instances not so much a body of personal legislation as a set of customs harmonized and clarified into specific laws, and named, for convenience's sake, from the man who codified them and in most cases gave them a written form.* We shall record the tradition, while remembering that it has in all likelihood personified and foreshortened a process of change, from custom to law, that required many authors and many years.

According to Herodotus,[34] Lycurgus, uncle and guardian of the Spartan King Charilaus, received from the oracle at Delphi certain *rhetra*, or edicts, which were described by some as the laws of Lycurgus themselves, or by others as a divine sanction for the laws that he proposed. Apparently the legislators felt that to alter certain customs, or to establish new ones, the safest procedure would be to present their proposals as commands of the god; it was not the first time that a state had laid its foundations in the sky. Tradition further relates that Lycurgus traveled in Crete, admired its institutions, and resolved to introduce some of them into Laconia.[35] The kings and most of the nobles grudgingly accepted his reforms as indispensable to their own security; but a young aristocrat, Alcander, resisted violently, and struck out one of the legislator's eyes. Plutarch tells the story with his usual simplicity and charm:

> Lycurgus, so far from being daunted or discouraged by this accident, stopped short, and showed his disfigured face, and eye beaten out, to his countrymen. They, dismayed and ashamed at the sight, delivered Alcander into his hands to be punished. . . . Lycurgus, having thanked them, dismissed them all, excepting only Alcander; and taking him with him into his house, neither did nor said anything severely to him, but . . . bade Alcander to wait upon him at table. The young man, who was of an ingenuous temper, without murmuring did as he was commanded; and being thus admitted to live with Lycurgus, he had an opportunity to observe in him, besides his gentleness and calmness of temper, an extraordinary sobriety and an indefatigable industry; and so, from being an enemy, became one of his most zealous admirers, and told his friends and relations that he was not that morose and ill-natured man they had taken him for, but the one mild and gentle character of the world.[36]

Having completed his legislation, Lycurgus (says a probably legendary coda to his story) pledged the citizens not to change the laws till his return. Then he went to Delphi, retired into seclusion, and starved himself to death, "thinking it a statesman's duty to make his very death, if possible, an act of service to the state."[37]

* Lycurgus, however, was believed to have forbidden the writing of his laws.

4. *The Lacedaemonian Constitution*

When we attempt to specify the reforms of Lycurgus the tradition becomes contradictory and confused. It is difficult to say which elements of the Spartan code preceded Lycurgus, which were created by him or his generation, and which were added after him. Plutarch and Polybius[38] assure us that Lycurgus redistributed the land of Laconia into thirty thousand equal shares among the citizens; Thucydides[39] implies that there was no such distribution. Perhaps old properties were left untouched, while the newly conquered land was equally divided. Like Cleisthenes of Sicyon and Cleisthenes of Athens, Lycurgus (*viz.*, the authors of the Lycurgean constitution) abolished the kinship organization of Laconian society, and replaced it with geographical divisions; in this way the power of the old families was broken, and a wider aristocracy was formed. To prevent the displacement of this landowning oligarchy by such mercantile classes as were gaining leadership in Argos, Sicyon, Corinth, Megara, and Athens, Lycurgus forbade the citizens to engage in industry or trade, prohibited the use or importation of silver or gold, and decreed that only iron should be used as currency. He was resolved that the Spartans (i.e., the landowning citizens) should be left free for government and war.

It was a boast of ancient conservatives[40] that the Lycurgean constitution endured so long because the three forms of government—monarchy, aristocracy, and democracy—were united in it, and in such proportions that each element neutralized the others against excess. Sparta's monarchy was really a duarchy, since it had concurrently two kings, descending from the invading Heraclids. Possibly this strange institution was a compromise between two related and therefore rival houses, or a device to secure without absolutism the psychological uses of royalty in maintaining social order and national prestige. Their powers were limited: they performed the sacrifices of the state religion, headed the judiciary, and commanded the army in war. In all matters they were subordinate to the Senate; and after Plataea they lost more and more of their authority to the ephors.

The aristocratic and predominant element of the constitution resided in the Senate, or *gerousia,* literally and actually a group of old men; normally citizens under sixty were considered too immature for its deliberations. Plutarch gives their number as twenty-eight, and tells an incredible story of their election. When a vacancy occurred candidates were required to pass silently and in turn before the Assembly; and he who was greeted with the loudest and longest shouts was pronounced elected.[41] Perhaps this was thought to be a realistic and economical abbreviation of the fuller democratic process. We do not know which of the citizens were eligible to such election; presumably they were the *homoioi*, or equals, who owned the soil of Laconia, had served in the army, and brought their quota of food to the public mess.[42] The Senate originated legislation, acted as a supreme court in capital crimes, and formulated public policy.

The Assembly, or *apella*, was Sparta's concession to democracy. Apparently all male citizens were admitted to it upon reaching the age of thirty; some eight thousand males were eligible in a population of 376,000. It met on each day of the full moon. All matters of great public moment were submitted to it, nor could any law be passed without its consent. Few laws, however, were ever added to the Lycurgean constitution; and these the Assembly might accept or reject, but not discuss or amend. It was essentially the old Homeric public meeting, listening in awe to the council of chiefs and elders, or to the army-commanding kings. Theoretically sovereignty resided in the *apella;* but an amendment made to the constitution after Lycurgus empowered the Senate, if it judged that the Assembly had decided "crookedly," to reverse the decision.[43] When an advanced thinker asked Lycurgus to establish a democracy Lycurgus replied, "Begin, my friend, by setting it up in your own family."[44]

Cicero compared the five ephors (i.e., overseers) to the Roman tribunes, since they were chosen annually by the Assembly; but they corresponded more to the Roman consuls, as wielding an administrative power checked only by the protests of the Senate. The ephorate existed before Lycurgus, and yet is not mentioned in such reports of his legislation as have reached us. By the middle of the sixth century the ephors had become equal in authority to the kings; after the Persian War they were practically supreme. They received embassies, decided disputes at law, commanded the armies, and directed, absolved, or punished the kings.

The enforcement of the government's decrees was entrusted to the army and the police. It was the custom of the ephors to arm certain of the younger Spartans as a special and secret police (the *krypteia*), with the right to spy upon the people, and, in the case of Helots, to kill at their discretion.[45] This institution was used at unexpected times, even to do away with Helots who, though they had served the state bravely in war, were feared by the masters as able and therefore dangerous men. After eight years of the Peloponnesian War, says the impartial Thucydides,

> the Helots were invited by a proclamation to pick out those of their number who claimed to have most distinguished themselves against

> the enemy, in order that they might receive their freedom; the object being to test them, as it was thought that the first to claim their freedom would be the most high-spirited and the most apt to rebel. As many as two thousand were selected accordingly, who crowned themselves and went round the temples, rejoicing in their new freedom. The Spartans, however, soon afterwards did away with them, and no one ever knew how each of them perished.[46]

The power and pride of Sparta was above all in its army, for in the courage, discipline, and skill of these troops it found its security and its ideal. Every citizen was trained for war, and was liable to military service from his twentieth to his sixtieth year. Out of this severe training came the hoplites of Sparta—those close-set companies of heavy-armed, spear-hurling citizen infantry that were the terror even of the Athenians, and remained practically undefeated until Epaminondas overcame them at Leuctra. Around this army Sparta formed its moral code: to be good was to be strong and brave; to die in battle was the highest honor and happiness; to survive defeat was a disgrace that even the soldier's mother could hardly forgive. "Return with your shield or on it," was the Spartan mother's farewell to her soldier son. Flight with the heavy shield was impossible.

5. *The Spartan Code*

To train men to an ideal so unwelcome to the flesh it was necessary to take them at birth and form them by the most rigorous discipline. The first step was a ruthless eugenics: not only must every child face the father's right to infanticide, but it must also be brought before a state council of inspectors; and any child that appeared defective was thrown from a cliff of Mt. Taygetus, to die on the jagged rocks below.[47] A further elimination probably resulted from the Spartan habit of inuring their infants to discomfort and exposure.[48] Men and women were warned to consider the health and character of those whom they thought of marrying; even a king, Archidamus, was fined for marrying a diminutive wife.[49] Husbands were encouraged to lend their wives to exceptional men, so that fine children might be multiplied; husbands disabled by age or illness were expected to invite young men to help them breed a vigorous family. Lycurgus, says Plutarch, ridiculed jealousy and sexual monopoly, and called it "absurd that people should be so solicitous for their dogs and horses as to exert interest and pay money to procure fine breeding, and yet keep their wives shut up, to be made mothers only by themselves, who might be foolish, infirm, or diseased." In the general opinion of antiquity the Spartan males were stronger and handsomer, their women healthier and lovelier, than the other Greeks.[50]

Probably more of this result was due to training than to eugenic birth. Thucydides makes King Archidamus say: "There is little difference" (at birth, presumably) "between man and man, but the superiority lies with him who is reared in the severest school."[51] At the age of seven the Spartan boy was taken from his family and brought up by the state; he was enrolled in what was at once a military regiment and a scholastic class, under a *paidonomos,* or manager of boys. In each class the ablest and bravest boy was made captain; the rest were instructed to obey him, to submit to the punishments he might impose upon them, and to strive to match or better him in achievement and discipline. The aim was not, as at Athens, athletic form and skill, but martial courage and worth. Games were played in the nude, under the eyes of elders and lovers of either sex. The older men made it their concern to provoke quarrels among the boys, individually and in groups, so that vigor and fortitude might be tested and trained; and any moment of cowardice brought many days of disgrace. To bear pain, hardship, and misfortune silently was required of all. Every year, at the altar of Artemis Orthia, some chosen youths were scourged till their blood stained the stones.[52] At twelve the boy was deprived of underclothing, and was allowed but one garment throughout the year. He did not bathe frequently, like the lads of Athens, for water and unguents made the body soft, while cold air and clean soil made it hard and resistant. Winter and summer he slept in the open, on a bed of rushes broken from the Eurotas' banks. Until he was thirty he lived with his company in barracks, and knew none of the comforts of home.

He was taught reading and writing, but barely enough to make him literate; books found few buyers in Sparta,[53] and it was easy to keep up with the publishers. Lycurgus, said Plutarch, wished children to learn his laws not by writing but by oral transmission and youthful practice under careful guidance and example; it was safer, he thought, to make men good by unconscious habituation than to rely upon theoretical persuasion; a proper education would be the best government. But such education would have to be moral rather than mental; character was more important than intellect. The young Spartan was trained to sobriety, and some Helots were compelled to drink to excess in order that the youth might see how foolish drunkenness can be.[54] He was taught, in preparation for war, to forage in the fields and find his own food, or starve; to steal in such cases was permissible, but to be detected was a crime punishable by flogging.[55] If he behaved well he was allowed to attend the public mess of the citizens, and was expected to listen carefully there so that he might become acquainted with the problems of the state, and learn the art of genial conversation. At the age of thirty, if he had survived with honor the hardships of youth, he was admitted to the full rights and responsibilities of a citizen, and sat down to dine with his elders.

The girl, though left to be brought up at home, was also subject to regulation by the state. She was to engage in vigorous games—running, wrestling, throwing the quoit, casting the dart—in order that she might become strong and healthy for easy and perfect motherhood. She should go naked in public dances and processions, even in the presence of young men, so that she might be stimulated to proper care of her body, and her defects might be discovered and removed. "Nor was there anything shameful in the nakedness of the young women," says the highly moral Plutarch; "modesty attended them, and all wantonness was excluded." While they danced they sang songs of praise for those that had been brave in war, and heaped contumely upon those that had given way. Mental education was not wasted upon the Spartan girl.

As to love, the young man was permitted to indulge in it without prejudice of gender. Nearly every lad had a lover among the older men; from this lover he expected further education, and in return he offered affection and obedience. Often this exchange grew into a passionate friendship that stimulated both youth and man to bravery in war.[56] Young men were allowed considerable freedom before marriage, so that prostitution was rare, and hetairai here found no encouragement.[57] In all of Lacedaemon we hear of only one temple to Aphrodite, and there the goddess was represented as veiled, armed with a sword, and bearing fetters on her feet, as if to symbolize the foolishness of marrying for love, the subordination of love to war, and the strict control of marriage by the state.

The state specified the best age of marriage as thirty for men and twenty for women. Celibacy in Sparta was a crime; bachelors were excluded from the franchise, and from the sight of public processions in which young men and women danced in the nude. According to Plutarch the bachelors themselves were compelled to march in public, naked even in winter, singing a song to the effect that they were justly suffering this punishment for having disobeyed the laws. Persistent avoiders of marriage might be set upon at any time in the streets by groups of women, and be severely handled.

Those who married and had no children were only less completely disgraced; and it was understood that men who were not fathers were not entitled to the respect that the youth of Sparta religiously paid to their elders.[58]

Marriages were usually arranged by the parents, without purchase; but after this agreement the bridegroom was expected to carry off the bride by force, and she was expected to resist; the word for marriage was *harpadzein*, to seize.[59] If such arrangements left some adults still unmarried, several men might be pushed into a dark room with an equal number of girls, and be left to pick their life mates in the darkness;[60] the Spartans thought that such choosing would not be blinder than love. It was usual for the bride to stay with her parents for a while; the bridegroom remained in his barracks, and visited his wife only clandestinely; "in this relation," says Plutarch, "they lived a long time, insomuch that they sometimes had children by their wives before even they saw their faces by daylight." When they were ready for parentage custom allowed them to set up a home. Love came after marriage rather than before, and marital affection appears to have been as strong in Sparta as in any other civilization.[61] The Spartans boasted that there was no adultery among them, and they may have been right, for there was much freedom before marriage, and many husbands could be persuaded to share their wives, especially with brothers.[62] Divorce was rare. The Spartan general Lysander was punished because he left his wife and wished to marry a prettier one.[63]

All in all, the position of woman was better in Sparta than in any other Greek community. There more than elsewhere she preserved her high Homeric status, and the privileges that survived from an early matrilinear society. Spartan women, says Plutarch,[64] "were bold and masculine, overbearing to their husbands . . . and speaking openly even on the most important subjects." They could inherit and bequeath property; and in the course of time—so great was their influence over men—nearly half the real wealth of Sparta was in their hands.[65] They lived a life of luxury and liberty at home while the men bore the brunt of frequent war, or dined on simple fare in the public mess.

For every Spartan male, by a characteristic ordinance of the constitution, was required from his thirtieth to his sixtieth year to eat his main meal daily in a public dining hall, where the food was simple in quality and slightly but deliberately inadequate in amount. In this way, says Plutarch, the legislator thought to harden them to the privations of war, and to keep them from the degeneration of peace; they "should not spend their lives at home, laid on costly couches at splendid tables, delivering themselves up to the hands of their tradesmen and cooks, to fatten them in corners like greedy brutes, and to ruin not their minds only but their very bodies, which, enfeebled by indulgence and excess, would stand in need of long sleep, warm bathing, freedom from work, and, in a word, of as much care and attendance as if they were continually sick."[66] To supply the food for this public meal each citizen was required to contribute to his dining club, periodically, stated quantities of corn and other provisions; if he failed in this his citizenship was forfeited.

Normally, in the earlier centuries of the code, the simplicity and asceticism to which Spartan youth was trained persisted into later years. Fat men were a rarity in Lacedaemon; there was no law regulating the size of the stomach, but if a man's belly swelled indecently he might be publicly reproved by the government, or banished from Laconia.[67] There was little of the drinking and the revelry that flourished in Athens. Differences of wealth were real, but hidden; rich and poor wore the same simple dress—a woolen peplos, or shirt, that hung straight from the shoulders without pretense to beauty or form. The accumulation of movable riches was difficult; to lay up a hundred dollars' worth of iron currency required a large closet, and to remove it, nothing less than a yoke of oxen.[68] Human greed remained, however, and found an outlet in official corruption. Senators, ephors, envoys, generals, and kings were alike purchasable, at prices befitting their dignity.[69] When an ambassador from Samos displayed his gold plate at Sparta, King Cleomenes I had him recalled lest the citizens be spoiled by alien example.[70]

The Spartan system, fearful of such contamination, was inhospitable beyond precedent. Foreigners were rarely welcomed. Usually they were made to understand that their visits must be brief; if they stayed too long they were escorted to the frontier by the police. The Spartans themselves were forbidden to go abroad without permission of the government, and to dull their curiosity they were trained to a haughty exclusiveness that would not dream that other nations could teach them anything.[71] The system had to be ungracious in order to protect itself; a breath from that excluded world of freedom, luxury, letters, and arts might topple over this strange and artificial society, in which two thirds of the people were serfs, and all the masters were slaves.

6. *An Estimate of Sparta*

What type of man, and what kind of civilization, did this code produce? First of all, a man of strong body, at home with hardship and privation. A luxury-loving Sybarite remarked of the Spartans that "it was no commendable thing in them to be so ready to die in the wars, since by that they were freed from much hard labor and miserable living."[72] Health was one of the cardinal virtues in Sparta, and sickness was a crime; Plato's heart must have been gladdened to find a land so free from medicine and democracy. And here was courage; only the Roman would equal the Spartan's record for fearlessness and victory. When the Spartans surrendered at Sphacteria, Greece could hardly believe it; it was unheard of that Spartans should not fight to the last man; even their common soldiers, on many occasions, killed themselves rather than survive defeat.[73] When the news of the Spartan disaster at Leuctra—so overwhelming that in effect it put an end to Sparta's history—was brought to the ephors as they presided over the Gymnopedia games, the magistrates said nothing, but merely added, to the roster of the holy dead whom the games honored, the names of the newly slain. Self-control, moderation, equanimity in fortune and adversity—qualities that the Athenians wrote about but seldom showed—were taken for granted in every Spartan citizen.

If it be a virtue to obey the laws, the Spartan was virtuous beyond most men. "Though the Lacedaemonians are free," the ex-king Demaratus told Xerxes, "yet they are not free in all things; for over them is set law as a master, whom they fear much more than thy people fear thee."[74] Seldom—probably never again except in Rome and medieval Jewry—has a people been so strengthened by reverence for its laws. Under the Lycurgean constitution Sparta, for at least two centuries, became always stronger. Though it failed to conquer Argos or Arcadia, it persuaded all the Peloponnesus except Argos and Achaea to accept its leadership in a Peloponnesian League that for almost two hundred years (560-380) kept the peace in Pelops' isle. All Greece admired Sparta's army and government, and looked to it for aid in deposing burdensome tyrannies. Xenophon tells of "the astonishment with which I first noted the unique position of Sparta among the states of Hellas, the relatively sparse population, and at the same time the extraordinary power and prestige of the community. I was puzzled to account for the fact. It was only when I came to consider the peculiar institutions of the Spartans that my wonderment ceased."[75] Like Plato and Plutarch, Xenophon was never tired of praising Spartan ways.

Here it was, of course, that Plato found the outlines of his utopia, a little blurred by a strange indifference to Ideas. Weary and fearful of the vulgarity and chaos of democracy, many Greek thinkers took refuge in an idolatry of Spartan order and law.

They could afford to praise Sparta, since they did not have to live in it. They did not feel at close range the selfishness, coldness, and cruelty of the Spartan character; they could not see from the select gentlemen whom they met, or the heroes whom they commemorated from afar, that the Spartan code produced good soldiers and nothing more; that it made vigor of body a graceless brutality because it killed nearly all capacity for the things of the mind. With the triumph of the code the arts that had flourished before its establishment died a sudden death; we hear of no more poets, sculptors, or builders in Sparta after 550.* Only choral dance and music remained, for there Spartan discipline could shine, and the individual could be lost in the mass. Excluded from commerce with the world, barred from travel, ignorant of the science, the literature, and the philosophy of exuberantly growing Greece, the Spartans became a nation of excellent hoplites, with the mentality of a lifelong infantryman. Greek travelers marveled at a life so simple and unadorned, a franchise so jealously confined, a conservatism so tenacious of every custom and superstition, a courage and discipline so exalted and limited, so noble in character, so base in purpose, and so barren in result; while, hardly a day's ride away, the Athenians were building, out of a thousand injustices and errors, a civilization broad in scope and yet intense in action, open to every new idea and eager for intercourse with the world, tolerant, varied, complex, luxurious, innovating, skeptical, imaginative, poetical, turbulent, free. It was a contrast that would color and almost delineate Greek history.

In the end Sparta's narrowness of spirit betrayed even her strength of soul. She descended to the sanctioning of any means to gain a Spartan aim; at last she stooped so far to conquer as to sell to Persia the liberties that Athens had won for Greece at Marathon. Militarism absorbed her, and made her, once so honored, the hated terror of her neighbors. When she fell, all the nations marveled, but none mourned. Today, among the scanty ruins of that ancient capital, hardly a torso or a fallen pillar survives to declare that here there once lived Greeks.

* Gitiadas adorned a temple of Athena with excellently wrought bronze plates; Bathycles of Magnesia built the stately throne of Apollo at Amyclae; and Theodorus of Samos built for Sparta a famous town hall. After that Spartan art, even by imported artists, is hardly heard of any more.

IV. FORGOTTEN STATES

Northward from Sparta the valley of the Eurotas reaches across the frontier of Laconia into the massed mountains of Arcadia. They would be more beautiful if they were not so dangerous. They have not welcomed the narrow roads cut out of their rock slopes, and seem to threaten gloomily all disturbers of these Arcadian retreats. No wonder the conquering Dorians and Spartans were both baffled here, and left Arcadia, like Elis and Achaea, to the Achaean and Pelasgian stocks. Now and then the traveler comes upon a plain or a plateau, and finds flourishing new towns like Tripolis, or the remains of ancient cities like Orchomenos, Megalopolis, Tegea, and Mantinea, where Epaminondas won both victory and death. But for the most part it is a land of scattered peasants and shepherds, living precariously with their flocks in these grudging hills; and though after Marathon the cities awoke to civilization and art, they hardly enter the story before the Persian War. Here in these perpendicular forests once roamed the great god Pan.

In southern Arcadia the Eurotas almost meets a yet more famous river. Swiftly the Alpheus wears its way through the Parrhasian range, meanders leisurely into the plains of Elis, and leads the traveler to Olympia. The Elians, Pausanias tells us,[76] were of Aeolic or Pelasgic origin, and came from Aetolia across the bay. Their first king, Aethlius, was father of that Endymion whose beauty so allured the moon that she closed his eyes in a perpetual sleep, sinned at leisure, and had by him half a hundred daughters. Here, where the Alpheus joins the Cladeus flowing from the north, was the holy city of the Greek world, so sacred that war seldom disturbed it, and the Elians had the boon of a history in which battles were replaced by games. In the angle of the merging streams was the Altis, or hallowed precinct, of Olympian Zeus. Wave after wave of invaders stopped here to worship him; periodically, in later days, their delegates returned to beseech his help and enrich his fane; from generation to generation the temples of Zeus and Hera grew in wealth and renown, until the greatest architects and sculptors of Greece were brought together, after the triumph over Persia, to restore and adorn them in lavish gratitude. The shrine of Hera went back to 1000 B.C.; its ruins are the oldest temple remains in Greece. Fragments of thirty-six columns and twenty Doric capitals survive to show how often and how variously the pillars were replaced. Originally, no doubt, they were of wood; and one shaft of oak still stood when Pausanias came there, notebook in hand, in the days of the Antonines.

From Olympia one passes by the site of the ancient capital, Elis, into Achaea. Hither some of the Achaeans fled when the Dorians took Argos and Mycenae. Like Arcadia it is a land of mountains, along whose slopes patient shepherds drive their flocks up or down as the seasons change. On the western coast is the still-thriving port of Patras, of whose women Pausanias said that they were "twice as numerous as the men, and devoted to Aphrodite if any women are."[77] Other cities huddled against the hills along the Corinthian Gulf–Aegium, Helice, Aegira, Pellene–now almost forgotten, but once alive with men, women, and children, every one of whom was the center of the world.

V. CORINTH

A few more mountains, and the traveler re-enters, in Sicyon, the area of Dorian settlement. Here, in 676, one Orthagoras taught the world a trick of politics that aftercenturies would use. He explained to the peasants that they were of Pelasgic or Achaean stock, while the landowning aristocracy that exploited them was descended from Dorian invaders; he appealed to the racial pride of the dispossessed, led them in a successful revolution, made himself dictator, and established the manufacturing and trading classes in power.* Under his able successors, Myron and Cleisthenes, these classes made Sicyon a semi-industrial city, famous for its shoes and its pottery, though still named from the cucumbers that it grew.

Farther east is the city that should have been, by all geographic and economic omens, the richest and most cultured center in Greece. For Corinth, on the isthmus, had an enviable position. It could lock the land door to or upon the Peloponnesus; it could serve and mulct the overland trade between northern and southern Greece; and it had harbors and shipping on both the Saronic and the Corinthian Gulf. Between these seas it built a lucrative *Diolcos* ("a slipping through")–a wooden tramway along which ships were drawn on rollers over four miles of land.† Its fortress was the impregnable Acrocorinthus, a mountain peak two thousand feet high, watered by its own inexhaustible spring. Strabo has described for us the stirring sight from the citadel, with the city spread out on two bright

* So in 1789 Camille Desmoulins, from his café rostra, urged the Gauls to overthrow their German (Frankish) aristocracy.

† The *Diolcos* was a grateful alternative to merchants who distrusted the rough waters off Cape Malea on the sea route to the western Mediterranean. The tramway was sturdy enough to carry the usual trading vessel of Greek times; indeed, Augustus transported his fleet over the *Diolcos* in pursuit of Antony and Cleopatra after the battle of Actium, and a Greek squadron was similarly carried over as late as A.D. 883.[78] Periander planned in his day to cut the canal that now joins the two gulfs, but his engineers found it too great a task.[79]

terraces below, the open-air theater, the great public baths, the colonnaded market place, the gleaming temples, and the protective walls that reached to the port of Lechaeum on the northern gulf. At the very summit of the mount, as if to symbolize a major industry of the city, was a temple to Aphrodite.[80]

Corinth had a history stretching back to Mycenaean times; even in Homer's day it was famous for its wealth.[81] After the Dorian conquest kings ruled it, then an aristocracy dominated by the family of the Bacchiadae. But here, too, as in Argos, Sicyon, Megara, Athens, Lesbos, Miletus, Samos, Sicily, and wherever Greek trade flourished, the business class, by revolution or intrigue, captured political power; this is the real meaning of the outbreak of "tyrannies" or dictatorships in seventh-century Greece. About 655 Cypselus seized the government. Having promised Zeus the entire wealth of Corinth if he succeeded, he laid a ten per cent tax on all property each year, and gave the proceeds to the temple, until, after a decade, he has fulfilled his vow, while leaving the city as rich as before.[82] His popular and intelligent rule, through thirty years, laid the basis of Corinthian prosperity.[83]

His ruthless son, Periander, in one of the longest dictatorships in Greek history (625-585), established order and discipline, checked exploitation, encouraged business, patronized literature and art, and made Corinth for a time the foremost city in Greece. He stimulated trade by establishing a state coinage,[84] and promoted industry by lowering taxes. He solved a crisis of unemployment by undertaking great public works, and establishing colonies abroad. He protected small businessmen from the competition of large firms by limiting the number of slaves that might be employed by one man, and forbidding their further importation.[85] He relieved the wealthy of their surplus gold by compelling them to contribute to a colossal golden statue as an ornament for the city; he invited the rich women of Corinth to a festival, stripped them of their costly robes and jewels, and sent them home with half their beauty nationalized. His enemies were numerous and powerful; he dared not go out without a heavy guard, and his fear and seclusion made him morose and cruel. To protect himself against revolt he acted on the cryptic advice of his fellow dictator Thrasybulus of Miletus, that he should periodically cut down the tallest ears of corn in the field.*[86] His concubines preyed upon him with accusations of his wife, until in a temper he threw her downstairs; she was pregnant, and died of the shock. He burnt the concubines alive, and banished to Corcyra

* Cf. the periodical "purges" in Communist Russia, 1935-38.

his son Lycophron, who so grieved for his mother that he would not speak to his father. When the Corcyreans put Lycophron to death Periander seized three hundred youths of their noblest families and sent them to King Alyattes of Lydia, that they might be made eunuchs; but the ships that bore them touched at Samos, and the Samians, braving Periander's anger, freed them. The dictator lived to a ripe old age, and after his death was numbered by some among the Seven Wise Men of ancient Greece.[87]

A generation after him the Spartans overthrew the dictatorship at Corinth and set up an aristocracy—not because Sparta loved liberty, but because she favored landowners against the business classes. Nevertheless it was upon trade that the wealth of Corinth was based, helped now and then by the devotees of Aphrodite, and the Panhellenic Isthmian games. Courtesans were so numerous in the city that the Greeks often used *corinthiazomai* as signifying harlotry.[88] It was a common matter in Corinth to dedicate to Aphrodite's temple women who served her as prostitutes, and brought their fees to the priests. One Xenophon (not the leader of the Ten Thousand) promises the goddess fifty hetairai, or courtesans, if she will help him to victory in the Olympic games; and the pious Pindar, celebrating this triumph, refers to the vow without flinching.[89] "The Temple of Aphrodite," says Strabo,[90] "was so rich that it owned more than a thousand temple slaves, courtesans whom both men and women had dedicated to the goddess. And therefore it was also on account of these women that the city was crowded with people and grew rich; for instance, the ship captains freely squandered their money here." The city was grateful, and looked upon these "hospitable ladies" as public benefactors. "It is an ancient custom at Corinth," says an early author quoted by Athenaeus,[91] "whenever the city addresses any supplication to Aphrodite . . . to employ as many courtesans as possible to join in the supplication." The courtesans had a religious festival of their own, the Aphrodisia, which they celebrated with piety and pomp.[92] St. Paul, in his First Epistle to the Corinthians,[93] denounced these women, who still in his time plied there their ancient trade.

In 480 Corinth had a population of fifty thousand citizens and sixty thousand slaves—an unusually high proportion of freemen to slaves.[94] The quest for pleasure and gold absorbed all classes, and left little energy for literature and art. We hear of a poet Eumelus in the eighth century, but Corinthian names seldom grace Greek letters. Periander welcomed poets at his court, and brought Arion from Lesbos to organize music in Corinth. In the eighth century the pottery and bronzes of Corinth were famous;

in the sixth her vase painters were at the top of their profession in Greece. Pausanias tells of a great cedar chest, in which Cypselus hid from the Bacchiadae, and upon which artists carved elegant reliefs, with inlays of ivory and gold.[95] Probably it was in the age of Periander that Corinth raised to Apollo a Doric temple famous for its seven monolithic columns, five of which still stand to suggest that Corinth may have loved beauty in more forms than one. Perhaps time and chance were ungrateful to the city, and her annals fell to be written by men of other loyalties. The past would be startled if it could see itself in the pages of historians.

VI. MEGARA

Megara loved gold as much as Corinth did, and like her thrived on commerce; it had, however, a great poet, in whose verses the ancient city lives as if its revolutions were one with our own. Standing at the very entrance to the Peloponnesus, with a port on either gulf, it was in a position to bargain with armies and levy tolls upon trade; to which it added a busy textile industry manned with men and women who, in the honest phraseology of the day, were called slaves. The city flourished best in the seventh and sixth centuries, when it disputed the commerce of the isthmus with Corinth; it was then that it sent out, as trading posts, colonies as far-flung as Byzantium on the Bosporus and Megara Hyblaea in Sicily. Wealth mounted, but the clever gathered it so narrowly into their hands that the mass of the people, destitute serfs amid plenty,[96] listened readily to men who promised them a better life. About 630 Theagenes, having decided to become dictator, praised the poor and denounced the rich, led a starving mob into the pastures of the wealthy breeders, had himself voted a bodyguard, increased it, and with it overthrew the government.[97] For a generation Theagenes ruled Megara, freed the serfs, humbled the mighty, and patronized the arts. Towards 600 the rich deposed him in turn; but a third revolution restored the democracy, which confiscated the property of leading aristocrats, commandeered rich homes, abolished debts, and passed a decree requiring the wealthy to refund the interest that had been paid them by their debtors.[98]

Theognis lived through these revolutions, and described them in bitter poems that might be the voice of our class war today. He was, he tells us (for he is our sole authority on this subject), a member of an ancient and noble family. He must have grown up in comfortable circumstances, for he was guide, philosopher, and lover to a youth named Cyrnus, who became one of the leaders of the aristocratic party. He gives Cyrnus much advice, and asks merely love in return. Like all lovers he complains of short measure, and his finest extant poem reminds Cyrnus that he will achieve immortality only through Theognis' poetry:

> Lo, I have given thee wings wherewith to fly
> Over the boundless ocean and the earth;
> Yea, on the lips of many shalt thou lie,
> The comrade of their banquet and their mirth.
> Youths in their loveliness shall bid thee sound
> Upon the silver flute's melodious breath;
> And when thou goest darkling underground
> Down to the lamentable house of death,
> Oh, yet not then from honor shalt thou cease,
> But wander, an imperishable name,
> Cyrnus, about the seas and shores of Greece,
> Crossing from isle to isle the barren main.
> Horses thou shalt not need, but lightly ride,
> Sped by the Muses of the violet crown,
> And men to come, while earth and sun abide,
> Who cherish song shall cherish thy renown.
> Yea, I have given thee wings, and in return
> Thou givest me the scorn with which I burn.[99]

He warns Cyrnus that the injustices of the aristocracy may provoke a revolution:

> Our state is pregnant, shortly to produce
> A rude avenger of prolonged abuse.
> The commons hitherto seem sober-minded,
> But their superiors are corrupt and blinded.
> The rule of noble spirits, brave and high,
> Never endangered peace and harmony.
> The supercilious, arrogant pretense
> Of feeble minds, weakness and insolence;
> Justice and truth and law wrested aside
> By crafty shifts of avarice and pride;
> These are our ruin, Cyrnus!—never dream
> (Tranquil and undisturbed as it may seem)
> Of future peace or safety to the state;
> Bloodshed and strife will follow soon or late.*[100]

* The ascription of this poem, and of those quoted below, to certain periods in Theognis' life is hypothetical.

The revolution came; Theognis was among the men exiled by the triumphant democracy, and his property was confiscated. He left his wife and children with friends, and wandered from state to state—Euboea, Thebes, Sparta, Sicily; at first welcomed and fed for his poetry, then lapsing into a bitter and unaccustomed poverty. Out of his resentment he addresses to Zeus the questions which Job would ask of Yahweh:

> Blessed, almighty Jove! with deep amaze
> I view the world, and marvel at thy ways. . . .
> How can you reconcile it to your sense
> Of right and wrong, thus loosely to dispense
> Your bounties on the wicked and the good?
> How can your laws be known or understood?[101]

He becomes bitter against the leaders of the democracy, and prays to this inscrutable Zeus for the boon of drinking their blood.[102] In the first known use of this metaphor he likens the state of Megara to a ship whose pilot has been replaced by disorderly and unskilled mariners.[103] He argues that some men are by nature abler than others, and that therefore aristocracy in some form is inevitable; already men had discovered that majorities never rule. He uses *hoi agathoi,* the good, as synonymous with the aristocrats, and *hoi kakoi,* the bad, base, worthless, as signifying the common people.[104] These native differences, he thinks, are ineradicable; "no amount of teaching will make a bad man good,"[105]—though he may merely mean here that no training can turn a commoner into an aristocrat. Like all good conservatives he is strong for eugenics: the evils of the world are due not to the greed of the "good" but to their misalliances and their infertility.[106]

He plots with Cyrnus another counterrevolution; he argues that even if one has taken a vow of loyalty to the new government it is permissible to assassinate a tyrant; and he pledges himself to work with his friends until they have taken full vengeance upon their foes. Nevertheless, after many years of exile and loneliness, he bribes an official to let him return to Megara.[107] He is revolted at his own duplicity, and writes lines of despair that hundreds of Greeks would quote:

> Not to be born, never to see the sun—
> No worldly blessing is a greater one!
> And the next best is speedily to die,
> And lapt beneath a load of earth to lie.[108]

In the end we find him back in Megara, old and broken, and promising, for safety's sake, never again to write of politics. He consoles himself with wine and a loyal wife,[109] and does his best to learn at last the lesson that everything natural is forgivable.

> Learn, Cyrnus, learn to bear an easy mind;
> Accommodate your humor to mankind
> And human nature; take it as you find.
> A mixture of ingredients good and bad—
> Such are we all, the best that can be had.
> The best are found defective, and the rest,
> For common use, are equal to the best.
> Suppose it had been otherwise decreed,
> How could the business of the world proceed?[110]

VII. AEGINA AND EPIDAURUS

Across the bay from Megara and Corinth earthquake had raised, or left, one of their earliest rivals in industry and trade—the island of Aegina. There, in Mycenaean times, a prosperous city developed, whose graves gave up much gold.[111] The conquering Dorians found the land too barren for tillage, but admirably placed for commerce. When the Persians came the island knew only an aristocracy of tradesmen, eager to sell the excellent vases and bronzes produced in their shops for the slaves whom they imported in great number to work in their factories, or for sale to the cities of Greece. Aristotle, about 350, calculated that Aegina had a population of half a million, of whom 470,000 were slaves.[112] Here the first Greek coins were made, and the Aeginetan weights and measures remained standard in Greece till its conquest by Rome.

That such a commercial community could graduate from wealth to art was revealed when, in 1811, a traveler discovered in a heap of rubbish the vigorous and finely carved figures that once adorned the pediment of the temple of Aphaea. Of the temple itself twenty-two Doric columns stand, still bearing their architrave. Probably the Aeginetans built it shortly before the Persian War; for though its architecture is classic, its statuary shows many traces of the archaic, semi-Oriental style. Possibly, however, it was raised after Salamis; for the statuary, which represents Aeginetans overcoming Trojans, may symbolize the perennial conflict between Greece and the Orient, and the recent victory won by the Greek fleet under the very brows of Aegina at Salamis. To that fleet the little island contributed thirty ships; and one of these, after the victory, was awarded by the Greeks the first prize for bravery.

A pleasant boat ride takes the traveler from Aegina to Epidaurus, now a village of five hundred souls, but once among the most famous cities of

Greece. For here—or rather ten miles out in a narrow gorge among the loftiest mountains of the Argolic peninsula—was the chief home of Asclepius, the hero-god of healing. "O Asclepius!" Apollo himself had said through his oracle at Delphi, "thou who art born a great joy to all mortals, whom lovely Coronis bare to me, the child of love, at rocky Epidaurus."[113] Asclepius cured so many people—even raising a man from the dead—that Pluto, god of Hades, complained to Zeus that hardly anyone was dying any more; and Zeus, who would hardly know what to do with the human race if it were not for death, destroyed Asclepius with a thunderbolt.[114] But the people, first in Thessaly, then in Greece, worshiped him as a savior god. At Epidaurus they raised to him the greatest of his temples, and there the physician-priests who from him were called Asclepiads established a sanitarium known throughout Hellas for its success in treating disease. Epidaurus became a Greek Lourdes; pilgrims flocked to it from every part of the Mediterranean world, seeking what to the Greeks seemed the greatest boon of all—health. They slept in the temple, submitted hopefully to the regimen prescribed, and recorded their cures, which they believed to be miraculous, on stone tablets that still lie here and there among the ruins of the sacred grove. It was out of the fees and gifts of these patients that Epidaurus built its theater, and the stadium whose seats and goals still lie in the lap of the neighboring hills, and the lovely tholos—a circular, colonnaded building whose surviving fragments, preserved in the little museum, are among the most exquisitely carved marbles in Greece. Today such patients go to Tenos in the Cyclades, where the priests of the Greek Church heal them[115] as those of Asclepius healed their forerunners two thousand five hundred years ago. And the gloomy peak where once the people of Epidaurus sacrificed to Zeus and Hera is now the sacred mount of St. Elias. The gods are mortal, but piety is everlasting.

What the student looks for most eagerly at Epidaurus is not the leveled ruins of the Asclepium. The land is well wooded here, and he does not see the perfect theater that he is seeking until a turn in the road spreads it out against the mountainside in a gigantic fan of stone. Polycleitus the Younger built it in the fourth century before our era, but even to this day it is almost completely preserved. As the traveler stands in the center of the *orchestra*, or dancing place—a spacious circle paved with stone—and sees before him fourteen thousand seats in rising tiers, so admirably designed that every seat directly faces him; as his glance follows the radiating aisles that rise in swift straight lines from the stage to the trees of the mountain slope above; as he speaks quietly to his friends on the farthest, highest seats, two hundred feet away, and perceives that his every word is understood: then he visions Epidaurus in the days of its prosperity, sees in his mind's eye the crowds coming out in gay freedom from shrine and city to hear Euripides, and feels, more than he can ever express, the vibrant, *plein-air* life of ancient Greece.

CHAPTER V

Athens

I. HESIOD'S BOEOTIA

EAST of Megara the road divides—south to Athens, north to Thebes. Northward the route is mountainous, and draws the traveler up to the heights of Mt. Cithaeron. Far to the west Parnassus is visible. Ahead, across lesser heights and far below, is the fertile Boeotian plain. At the foot of the hill lies Plataea, where 100,000 Greeks annihilated 300,000 Persians. A little to the west is Leuctra, where Epaminondas won his first great victory over the Spartans. Again a little west rises Mt. Helicon, home of the Muses and Keats's "blushful Hippocrene"—that famous fountain, the Horse's Spring, which, we are assured, gushed forth when the hoof of the winged steed Pegasus struck the earth as he leaped toward heaven.[1] Directly north is Thespiae, always at odds with Thebes; and close by is the fountain in whose waters Narcissus contemplated his shadow—or, another story said, that of the dead sister whom he loved.[2]

In the little town of Ascra, near Thespiae, lived and toiled the poet Hesiod, second only to Homer in the affection of the classic Greeks. Tradition gave 846 and 777 as the dates of his birth and death; some modern scholars bring him down to 650;[3] probably he lived a century earlier than that.[4] He was born at Aeolian Cyme in Asia Minor; but his father, tired of poverty there, migrated to Ascra, which Hesiod describes as "miserable in winter, insufferable in summer, and never good"[5]—like most of the places in which men live. As Hesiod, farm hand and shepherd boy, followed his flocks up and down the slopes of Helicon he dreamed that the Muses breathed into his body the soul of poetry. So he wrote and sang, and won prizes in musical contests,[6] even, some said, from Homer himself.[7]

Loving like any young Greek the marvels of mythology, he composed* a *Theogony*, or Genealogy of the Gods, of which we have a thousand halting lines, giving those dynasties and families of deities which are as vital to religion as the pedigrees of kings are to history. First he sang of the

* So all classical antiquity believed except some Boeotian literati of the second century A.D., who questioned Hesiod's authorship.[8]

Muses themselves, because they were, so to speak, his neighbors on Helicon, and in his youthful imagination he could almost see them "dancing with delicate feet" on the mountainside, and "bathing their soft skins" in the Hippocrene.[9] Then he described not so much the creation as the procreation of the world—how god begot god until Olympus overflowed. In the beginning was Chaos; "and next broad-bosomed Earth, ever secure seat of all the immortals"; in Greek religion the gods live on the earth or within it, and are always close to men. Next came Tartarus, god of the nether world; and after him Eros, or Love, "fairest of the gods."[10] Chaos begot Darkness and Night, which begot Ether and Day; Earth begot Mountains and Heaven, and Heaven and Earth, mating, begot Oceanus, the Sea. We capitalize these names, but in Hesiod's Greek there were no capitals, and for all we know he meant merely that in the beginning was chaos, and then the earth, and the inners of the earth, and night and day and the sea, and desire begetting all things; perhaps Hesiod was a philosopher touched by the Muses and personifying abstractions into poetry; Empedocles would use the same tricks a century or two later in Sicily.[11] From such a theology it would be but a step to the natural philosophy of the Ionians.

Hesiod's mythology revels in monsters and blood, and is not averse to theological pornography. Out of the mating of Heaven (Uranus) and Earth (Ge or Gaea) came a race of Titans, some with fifty heads and a hundred hands. Uranus liked them not, and condemned them to gloomy Tartarus. But Earth resenting this, proposed to them that they should kill their father. One of the Titans, Cronus, undertook the task. Then "huge Ge rejoiced, and hid him in ambush; in his hand she placed a sickle with jagged teeth, and suggested to him all the stratagem. Then came vast Heaven, bringing Night [Erebus] with him, and, eager for love, brooded around Earth, and lay stretched on all sides." Thereupon Cronus mutilated his father, and threw the flesh into the sea. From the drops of blood that fell upon the earth came the Furies; from the foam that formed around the flesh as it floated on the waters rose Aphrodite.*[12] The Titans captured Olympus, deposed Heaven-Uranus, and raised Cronus to the throne. Cronus married his sister Rhea, but Earth and Heaven, his parents, having predicted that he would be deposed by one of his sons, Cronus swallowed them all except Zeus, whom Rhea bore secretly in Crete. When Zeus grew up he deposed Cronus in turn, forced him to disgorge his children, and plunged the Titans back into the bowels of the earth.[13]

Such, according to Hesiod, were the births and ways of the gods. Here,

* From *aphros*, foam. The final syllable is of uncertain derivation.

too, is the tale of Prometheus, Far-Seer and Fire-Bringer; here, in tedious abundance, are some of the divine adulteries that enabled so many Greeks, like Mayflower Americans, to trace their pedigrees to the gods—one would never have guessed that adultery could be so dull. We do not know how far these myths were the popular outgrowth of a primitive and almost savage culture, and how far they are due to Hesiod; few of them are mentioned in the healthy pages of Homer. It is possible that some measure of the disrepute into which these tales brought the Olympians in days of philosophical criticism and moral development is to be ascribed to the gloomy fancy of Ascra's bard.

In the only poem universally conceded to Hesiod he descends from Olympus to the plains, and writes a vigorous georgic of the farmer's life. The *Works and Days* takes the form of a long reproof and counsel to the poet's brother Perseus, who is so strangely pictured that he may be only a literary device. "Now will I speak to thee with good intent, thou exceeding foolish Perseus."[14] This Perseus, we are told, has cheated Hesiod of Hesiod's inheritance; and now the poet, in the first of known sermons on the dignity of labor, tells him how much wiser honesty and toil are than vice and luxurious ease. "Behold, thou mayest choose vice easily, even in heaps; for the path is plain, and she dwells very near. But before excellence the immortal gods have placed the sweat of toil; long and steep is the road that leads to her, and rough it is at first; but when you reach the height then truly is it easy, though so hard before."[15] So the poet lays down rules for diligent husbandry, and the proper days for plowing, planting, and reaping, in rough saws that Virgil would polish into perfect verse. He warns Perseus against drinking heavily in summer, or dressing lightly in winter. He draws a chilly picture of winter in Boeotia—the "keenly piercing air that flays the steers," the seas and rivers tossed about by the northern wind, the moaning forests and crashing pines, the beasts "shunning the white snow" and huddling fearfully in their folds and stalls.[16] How cozy then is a well-built cottage, the lasting reward of courageous and prudent toil! There the domestic tasks go on despite the storm; then a wife is a helpmate indeed, and repays a man for the many tribulations she has caused him.

Hesiod cannot quite make up his mind about helpmates. He must have been a bachelor or a widower, for no man with a living wife would have spoken so acridly of woman. It is true that at the end of our fragment of the *Theogony* the poet begins a chivalrous Catalogue of Women, recounting the legends of those days when heroines were as numerous as men, and most of the gods were goddesses. But in both of his major works he tells with bitter relish how all human ills were brought to man by the beautiful Pandora. Angered by Prometheus' theft of fire from Heaven, Zeus bids the gods mold woman as a Greek gift for man. He

> bade Hephaestus with all speed mix earth with water, and endue it with man's voice and strength, and to liken in countenance to immortal goddesses the fair, lovely beauty of a maiden. Then he bade Athena teach her how to weave the highly wrought web, and golden Aphrodite to shed around her head grace, and painful desire, and cares that waste the limbs; but to endue her with a dog-like mind and tricky manners he charged the messenger Hermes. . . . They obeyed Zeus . . . and the herald of the gods placed within her a winning voice; and this woman he called Pandora, because all who dwelt in Olympian mansions bestowed on her a gift, a mischief to inventive men.[17]

Zeus presents Pandora to Epimetheus, who, though he has been warned by his brother Prometheus not to accept gifts from the gods, feels that he may yield to beauty this once. Now Prometheus has left with Epimetheus a mysterious box, with instructions that it should under no circumstances be opened. Pandora, overcome with curiosity, opens the box, whereupon ten thousand evils fly out of it and begin to plague the life of man, while Hope alone remains. From Pandora, says Hesiod, "is the race of tender women; from her is a pernicious race; and tribes of women, a great hurt, dwell with men, helpmates not of consuming poverty but of surfeit. . . . So to mortal men Zeus gave women as an evil."[18]

But alas, says our vacillating poet, celibacy is as bad as marriage; a lonely old age is a miserable thing, and the property of a childless man reverts at his death to the clan. So, after all, a man had better marry—though not before thirty; and he had better have children—though not more than one, lest the property be divided.

> When full matureness crowns thy manhood's pride,
> Lead to thy mansion the consenting bride;
> Thrice ten thy sum of years the nuptial prime,
> Nor fall far short, nor far exceed the time . . .
> A virgin choose, that morals chaste impress
> By this wise love may stamp her yielding breast.
> Some known and neighboring damsel be thy prize;
> And wary bend around thy cautious eyes,
> Lest by a choice imprudent thou be found

The merry mock of all the dwellers round.
No better lot has Providence assigned
Than a fair woman with a virtuous mind;
Nor can a worse befall than when thy fate
Allots a worthless, feast-continuing mate.
She with no touch of mere material flame
Shall burn to tinder thy care-wasted frame;
Shall send a fire thy vigorous bones within
And age unripe in bloom of years begin.[19]

Before this Fall of Man, says Hesiod, the human race lived through many happy centuries on the earth. First the gods, in the days of Cronus (Virgil's *Saturnia regna*), had made a Golden Race of men, who were themselves as gods, living without toil or care; of its own accord the earth bore ample food for them, and nourished their rich flocks; they spent many a day in joyous festival, and never aged; and when at last death came to them, it was like a painless and dreamless sleep. But then the gods, with divine whimsicality, made a Silver Race, far inferior to the first; these individuals took a century to grow up, lived through a brief maturity of suffering, and died. Zeus made then a Brazen Race, men with limbs and weapons and houses of brass, who fought so many wars with one another that "black Death seized them and they quitted the bright sunlight." Zeus tried again and made the Heroic Race, which fought at Thebes and Troy; when these men died "they dwelt with carefree spirit in the Isles of the Blest." Last and worst came the Iron Race, mean and corrupt, poor and disorderly, toiling by day and wretched by night; sons dishonoring parents, impious and stingy to the gods, lazy and factious, warring among themselves, taking and giving bribes, distrusting and maligning one another, and grinding the faces of the poor; "Would," cries Hesiod, "that I had not been born in this age, but either before or after it!" Soon, he hopes, Zeus will bury this Iron Race under the earth.[20]

Such is the theology of history with which Hesiod explains the poverty and injustice of his time. These ills he knew by sight and touch; but the past, which the poets had filled with heroes and gods, must have been nobler and lovelier than this; surely men had not always been as poor and harassed and petty as the peasants whom he knew in Boeotia. He does not realize how deeply the faults of his class enter into his own outlook, how narrow and earthly, almost commercial, are his views of life and labor, women and men. What a fall this is from the picture of human affairs in Homer, as a scene of crime and terror, but also of grandeur and nobility! Homer was a poet, and knew that one touch of beauty redeems a multitude of sins; Hesiod was a peasant who grudged the cost of a wife, and grumbled at the impudence of women who dared to sit at the same table with their husbands.[21] Hesiod, with rough candor, shows us the ugly basement of early Greek society—the hard poverty of serfs and small farmers upon whose toil rested all the splendor and war sport of the aristocracy and the kings. Homer sang of heroes and princes for lords and ladies; Hesiod knew no princes, but sang his lays of common men, and pitched his tune accordingly. In his verses we hear the rumblings of those peasant revolts that would produce in Attica the reforms of Solon and the dictatorship of Peisistratus.*

In Boeotia, as in the Peloponnese, the land was owned by absentee nobles who dwelt in or near the towns. The most prosperous of the cities were built around Lake Copais, now dry but once supplying a complex system of irrigation tunnels and canals. Late in the Homeric Age this tempting region was invaded by peoples who took their name from that Mt. Boeon, in Epirus, near which they had had their home. They captured Chaeronea (near which Philip was to put an end to Greek liberty), Thebes, their future capital, and finally the old Minyan capital, Orchomenos. These and other towns, in classic days, joined under the leadership of Thebes in a Boeotian Confederacy, whose common affairs were managed by annually chosen boeotarchs, and whose peoples celebrated together at Coronea the festival of Panboeotia.

It was the custom of the Athenians to laugh at the Boeotians as dull-witted, and to attribute this obtuseness to heavy eating and a moist and foggy climate—very much as the French used to diagnose the English. There may have been some truth in this, for the Boeotians play an unprepossessing part in Greek history. Thebes, for example, aided the Persian invaders, and was a thorn in the side of Athens for centuries. But in the other side of the scales we place the brave and loyal Plataeans, plodding Hesiod and soaring Pindar, the noble Epaminondas and the completely lovable Plutarch. We must beware of seeing Athens' rivals only through Athens' eyes.

* History knows nothing of Hesiod's death. Legend tells how, at the age of eighty, he seduced the maiden Clymene; how her brother killed him and threw his body into the sea; and how Clymene bore as his son the lyric poet Stesichorus—who, however, was born in Sicily.[22]

II. DELPHI

From Plutarch's city, Chaeronea, one passes at the continuous risk of his life over a dozen mountains into Phocis, to reach, on the very slope of Parnassus, the sacred city of Delphi. A thousand feet below is the Crisaean plain, bright with the silver leaves of ten thousand olive trees; five hundred feet farther down is an inlet of the Corinthian Gulf; ships move with the stately, silent slowness of distance over waters deceptively motionless. Beyond are other ranges, clothed for a moment in royal purple by the setting sun. At a turn in the road is the Castalian Spring, framed in a gorge of perpendicular cliffs; from the heights, legend said (adding another fable to his own), the citizens of Delphi hurled the wandering Aesop; over them, says history, Philomelus the Phocian drove the defeated Locrians in the Second Sacred War.*[23] Above are the twin peaks of Parnassus, where the Muses dwelt when they tired of Helicon. Greeks who climbed a hundred tortuous miles to stand on this mountainside—poised on a ledge between mist-shrouded heights and a sunlit sea, and surrounded on every side with beauty or terror—could hardly doubt that beneath these rocks lived some awful god. Time and again earthquake had rumbled here, frightening away the plundering Persians, and a century later the plundering Phocians, and a century later the plundering Gauls; it was the god protecting his shrine. As far back as Greek tradition could reach, worshipers had gathered here to find in the winds among the gorges, or the gases escaping from the earth, the voice and will of deity. The great stone that nearly closed the cleft from which the gases came was, to the Greeks, the center of Greece, and therefore the *omphalos*, as they called it, the umbilicus or very navel of the world.

Over that navel they built their altars, in older days to Ge, Mother Earth, later to her bright conqueror Apollo. Once a terrible serpent had guarded the gorge, holding it against men; Phoebus had slain him with an arrow, and, as the Pythian Apollo, had become the idol of the shrine. There, when an earlier temple was destroyed by fire (548), the rich Alcmaeonids, aristocrats exiled from Athens, rebuilt it with funds subscribed by all Greece and augmented by their own; they gave it a façade of marble, sur-

* Twice the Greeks waged Sacred Wars over the perquisites of Apollo's temple: once in 595-85, when the southern Greeks put an end to the exacting of greedy tolls by the people of neighboring Cirrha from pilgrims passing to Delphi through their port; and again in 356-46, when an allied Greek army under Philip of Macedon ousted the Phocians who had captured Delphi and appropriated the temple funds. The first war led to the neutralization of Delphi and the establishment of the Pythian games; the second led to the Macedonian conquest of Greece.

rounded it with a Doric peristyle, and supported it with Ionic colonnades within; seldom had Greece seen so magnificent a shrine. A Sacred Way wound up the slope to the sanctuary, adorned at every step with statues, porticoes, and "treasuries"—miniature temples built in the sacred precincts (at Olympia, Delphi, or Delos) by Greek cities as repositories for their funds, or as their individual tributes to the god. A hundred years before the battle of Marathon, Corinth and Sicyon raised such treasuries at Delphi; later, Athens, Thebes, and Cyrene rivaled them, Cnidus and Siphnos surpassed them. Amid them all, as a reminder that Greek drama was a part of Greek religion, a theater was built into the face of Parnassus. Far above all the rest was a stadium, where Greece practiced its favorite worship of health, courage, beauty, and youth.

Imagination pictures the scene in the days of Apollo's festival—fervent pilgrims crowding the road to the sacred city, filling noisily the inns and tents thrown up to shelter them, passing curiously and skeptically among the booths where subtle traders displayed their wares, mounting in religious procession or hopeful pilgrimage to Apollo's temple, laying before it their offering or sacrifice, chanting their hymns or saying their prayers, sitting awed in the theater, and plodding up half a thousand trying steps to witness the Pythian games or gaze in wonder at mountains and sea. Life once passed this way in all its eagerness.

III. THE LESSER STATES

In the western mainlands of Greece life was content to be rural and subdued throughout Greek history—and is so today. In Locris, Aetolia, Acarnania, and Aeniania men were too close to primitive realities, too far from the quickening currents of communication and trade, to have time or skill for literature, philosophy, or art; even the gymnasium and the theater, so dear to Attica, found no home here; and the temples were artless village shrines stirring no national sentiment. At long intervals modest towns arose, like Amphissa in Locris, or Aetolian Naupactus, or little Calydon, where once Meleager had hunted the boar with Atalanta.* On the west coast near Calydon is the modern Mesolongion, or Missolonghi, where Marco Bozzaris fought and Byron died.

* A wild boar having devastated the fields of Calydon, Meleager, son of Calydon's King Oeneus, organized a hunt for it, with such aides as Theseus, Castor and Pollux, Nestor, Jason, and the fair-faced, fleet-footed Atalanta. Several heroes were slain by the boar, but Atalanta shot it and Meleager killed it. Atalanta, sought by many wooers in her Arcadian home, agreed to marry any one of them that could outrun her, but those who lost were to be put to death. Hippomenes won by dropping as he ran the three golden apples of the Hesperides given him by Aphrodite; Atalanta stooped to pick them, and lost the race. Of Meleager's secret love for Atalanta, and his tragic death, the reader may learn in Swinburne's *Atalanta in Calydon*.

Between Acarnania and Aetolia runs the greatest river of Hellas—the Achelous, which the imaginative Greeks worshiped as a god, and appeased with prayer and sacrifice. Near its sources in Epirus rises the Spercheus, along whose banks in the little state of Aeniania once lived the pre-Homeric Achaeans, and a small tribe called Hellenes, whose name, by the whims of usage, was adopted by all the Greeks. Towards the east lay Thermopylae, called "Hot Gates" because of its warm sulphur springs and its narrow strategic pass, from north to south, between mountains and the Malic Gulf. Then over Mt. Othrys and through Achaea Phthiotis one descends into the great plains of Thessaly.

Here at Pharsalus Caesar's weary troops wiped out the forces of Pompey. Nowhere else in Greece were the crops so rich as in Thessaly, or the horses so spirited, or the arts so poor. Rivers ran from all directions into the Peneus, making a fertile alluvial soil from the southern boundary of the state to the foot of the northern ranges. Through these mountains the Peneus slashes its way across Thessaly to the Thracian Sea. Between the peaks of Ossa and Olympus it carves the Vale of Tempe (i.e., a cutting), where for four miles the angry river is hemmed in by precipitous cliffs rising a thousand feet above the stream. Along the great rivers were many cities—Pherae, Crannon, Tricca, Larisa, Gyrton, Elatea—ruled by feudal barons living on the toil of serfs. Here, in the extreme north, is Mt. Olympus, tallest of Greek peaks, and home of the Olympian gods. On its northern and eastern slopes lay Pieria, where the Muses had dwelt before they moved to Helicon.* Southward, and along the gulf, ran Magnesia, piling up mountains from Ossa to Pelion.

Beginning a few miles across the strait from Magnesia, the great island of Euboea stretches its length along the shores of the mainland between inner gulfs and outer Aegean, and pivots itself on a peninsula at Chalcis that almost binds it to Boeotia. The island's backbone is a range that continues Olympus, Ossa, Pelion, and Othrys, and ends in the Cyclades. Its coastal plains were rich enough to lure Ionians from Attica in the days of the Dorian invasion, and to lead to its conquest by Athens in 506 on the plea that Athens, if blockaded at the Piraeus, would starve without Euboean grain. Neighboring deposits of copper and iron and banks of murex shells gave Chalcis its wealth and its name; for a time it was the chief center of the metallurgical industry in Greece, making unrivaled swords and excellent vases of bronze. The trade of the island, helped by one of the first Greek coinages, passed out from Chalcis, enriched its citizens, and led them to found commercial colonies in Thrace, Italy, and Sicily. The Euboean system of weights and measures became almost universal in Greece; and the alphabet of Chalcis, given to Rome by the Euboean colony

* Hence the wise counsel of Alexander Pope's philosophical doggerel:

A little learning is a dangerous thing;
Drink deep or taste not the Pierian spring.[34]

of Italian Cumae, became through Latin the alphabet of modern Europe. A few miles to the south of Chalcis was its ancient rival, Eretria. There Menedemus, a pupil of Plato, established a school of philosophy, but for the rest neither Eretria nor Chalcis wrote its name very distinctly into the record of Greek thought or art.

From Chalcis a bridge, lineal descendant of the wooden span built in 411 B.C., leads the traveler across the Euripus strait back into Boeotia. A few miles south on the Boeotian coast lay the little town of Aulis, where Agamemnon sacrificed his daughter to the gods. In this region once lived an insignificant tribe, the Graii, who joined the Euboeans in sending a colony to Cumae, near Naples; from them the Romans gave to all the Hellenes whom they encountered the name *Graici*, Greeks; and from that circumstance all the world came to know Hellas by a term which its own inhabitants never applied to themselves.[25] Farther south is Tanagra, whose poetess Corinna won the prize from Pindar about 500 B.C., and whose potters, in the fifth and fourth centuries, would make the most famous statuettes in history. Five miles south again and we are in Attica. From the peaks of the Parnes range we can make out the hills of Athens.

IV. ATTICA

1. The Background of Athens

The very atmosphere seems different—clean, sharp, and bright; each year here has three hundred sunny days. We are at once reminded of Cicero's comment on "Athens' clear air, which is said to have contributed to the keenness of the Attic mind."[26] Rain falls in Attica in autumn and winter, but seldom in summer. Fog and mist are rare. Snow falls about once a year in Athens, four or five times a year on the surrounding mountaintops.[27] The summers are hot, though dry and tolerable; and in the lowlands, in ancient days, malarial swamps detracted from the healthiness of the air.[28] The soil of Attica is poor; nearly everywhere the basic rock lies close to the surface, and makes agriculture a heartbreaking struggle for the simplest goods of life.* Only adventurous trade, and the patient culture of the olive and the grape, made civilization possible in Attica.

It is all the more surprising that on this arid peninsula so many towns should have appeared. They are everywhere: at every harbor along the coast, in every valley among the hills. An active and enterprising people

* "Attica," says Thucydides (i, 1), "because of the poverty of its soil, enjoyed from a very remote period freedom from faction [?] and invasion."

had settled Attica in or before neolithic days, and had hospitably received and intermarried with Ionians—a mixture of Pelasgo-Mycenaeans and Achaeans[28a]—fleeing from Boeotia and the Peloponnesus in the face of the northern migrations and invasions. Here was no conquering alien race exploiting a native population, but a complex Mediterranean stock, of medium stature and dark features, directly inheriting the blood and culture of the old Helladic civilization, proudly conscious of its indigenous quality,[29] and excluding from its national sanctuary, the Acropolis, those half-barbarian upstarts, the Dorians.[30]

Relationships of blood gave them their social organization. Each family belonged to a tribe, whose members claimed the same divine heroic ancestor, worshiped the same deity, joined in the same religious ceremony, had a common archon (governor) and treasurer, owned together certain communal lands, enjoyed among themselves the rights of intermarriage and bequest, accepted obligations of mutual aid, vengeance, and defense, and slept at last in the tribal burial place. Each of the four tribes of Attica was composed of three phratries or brotherhoods, each phratry of thirty clans or *gentes* (*gene*), and each clan, as nearly as possible, of thirty heads of families.[31] This kinship classification of Attic society lent itself not only to military organization and mobilization, but to so clannish an aristocracy of old families that Cleisthenes had to redistribute the tribes before he could establish democracy.

Each town or village was probably in origin the home of a clan, and sometimes took its name from the clan, or from the god or hero whom it worshiped, as in the case of Athens. The traveler entering Attica from eastern Boeotia would come first to Oropus, and receive no very favorable impression; for Oropus was a frontier town, as terrifying to the tourist as any such today. "Oropus," says Dicaearchus (?) about 300 B.C., "is a nest of hucksters. The greed of the customhouse officials here is unsurpassed, their roguery inveterate and bred in the bone. Most of the people are coarse and truculent in their manners, for they have knocked the decent members of the community on the head."[32] From Oropus southward one moved through a close succession of towns: Rhamnus, Aphidna, Deceleia (a strategic point in the Peloponnesian War), Acharnae (home of Aristophanes' pugnacious pacifist Dicaeopolis), Marathon, and Brauron—in whose great temple stood that statue of Artemis which Orestes and Iphigenia had brought from the Tauric Chersonese, and where, every four years, as much of Attica as could come joined in the piety and debauchery of the Brauronia, or feast of Artemis.[33] Then Prasiae and Thoricus; then the silver-mining region of Laurium, so vital in the economic and military history of Athens:

then, at the very point of the peninsula, Sunium, on whose cliffs a lovely temple rose as a guide to mariners and their hopeful offering to the incalculable Poseidon. Then up the western coast (for Attica is half coast, and its very name is from *aktike*, coastland) past Anaphlystus to the isle of Salamis,* home of Ajax and Euripides; then to Eleusis, sacred to Demeter and her mysteries; and then back to the Piraeus. Into this sheltered port, neglected before Themistocles revealed its possibilities, ships were to bring the goods of all the Mediterranean world for the use and pleasure of Athens. The barrenness of the soil, the nearness of the coast, the abundance of harbors lured the people of Attica into trade; their courage and inventiveness won for them the markets of the Aegean; and out of that commercial empire came the wealth, the power, and the culture of Athens in the Periclean age.

2. *Athens under the Oligarchs*

These towns of Attica were not only the background but the members of Athens. We have seen how, according to Greek belief, Theseus with a benevolent "synoecism" had brought the people of Attica into one political organization, with one capital.† Five miles from the Piraeus, and in a nest of hills—Hymettus, Pentelicus, and Parnes—Athens grew around the old Mycenaean acropolis; and all the landowners of Attica were its citizens. The oldest families, and those with the largest holdings, wielded the balance of power; they had tolerated the kingship when disorder threatened, but when quiet and stability returned they reasserted their feudal domination of the central government. After King Codrus had died in heroic self-sacrifice against the invading Dorians,‡ they announced (so the story went) that no one was good enough to succeed him, and replaced the king with an archon chosen for life. In 752 they limited the tenure of the archonship to ten years, and in 683 to one. On the latter occasion they divided the powers of the office among nine archons: an archon *eponymos*, who gave his name to the year as a means of dating events; an archon *basileus*, who bore the name of king but was merely head of the state religion; a *polemarchos*, or military commander; and six *thesmothetai*, or lawmakers. As in Sparta and Rome, so in Athens the overthrow of the monarchy represented not a victory for the commons, or any intentional advance towards

* Probably named by the Phoenicians from *shalam*, peace; cf. Salem.[34]

† Tradition placed this event in the thirteenth century B.C.; but the union of Attica under Athens could hardly have been completed before 700, since the "Homeric" *Hymn to Demeter*, composed about that date, speaks of Eleusis as still having its own king.[35]

‡ A possibly legendary event attributed by tradition to 1068 B.C.

democracy, but a recapture of mastery by a feudal aristocracy—one more swing of the pendulum in the historical alternation between localized and centralized authority. By this piecemeal revolution the royal office was shorn of all its powers, and its holder was confined to the functions of a priest. The word *king* remained in the Athenian constitution to the end of its ancient history, but the reality was never restored. Institutions may with impunity be altered or destroyed from above if their names are left unchanged.

The Eupatrid oligarchs—i.e., the well-born ruling few—continued to govern Attica for almost five centuries. Under their rule the population was divided into three political ranks: the *hippes*, or knights, who owned horses* and could serve as cavalry; the *zeugitai*, who owned a yoke of oxen and could equip themselves to fight as hoplites or heavy-armed troops; and the *thetes*, hired laborers who fought as light-armed infantry. Only the first two were accounted citizens; and only the knights could serve as archons, judges, or priests. After completing their term of office the archons, if no scandal had tarnished them, became automatically and for life members of the *boule* or Council that met in the cool of the evening on the Areopagus, or Ares' hill, chose the archons, and ruled the state. Even under the monarchy this Senate of the Areopagus had limited the authority of the king; now, under the oligarchy, it was as supreme as its counterpart in Rome.[36]

Economically the population fell again into three groups. At the top were the Eupatrids, who lived in relative luxury in the towns while slaves and hired men tilled their holdings in the country, or merchants made profits for them on their loans. Next in wealth were the *demiurgoi*, or public workmen—i.e., professional men, craftsmen, traders, and free laborers. As colonization opened up new markets, and coinage liberated trade, the rising power of this class became the explosive force that under Solon and Peisistratus won for it a share in the government, and under Cleisthenes and Pericles raised it to the zenith of its influence. Most of the laborers were freemen; slaves were as yet in the minority, even in the lower classes.[37]—Poorest of all were the *georgoi*, literally land workers, small peasants struggling against the stinginess of the soil and the greed of money-lenders and baronial lords, and consoled only with the pride of owning a bit of the earth.

Some of these peasants had once held extensive tracts; but their wives had been more fertile than their land, and in the course of generations their

* The mark of a gentleman then, as in the days of Roman *equites*, French *chevaliers*, and English *cavaliers*.

holdings had been divided and redivided among their sons. The collective ownership of property by clan or patriarchal family was rapidly passing away, and fences, ditches, and hedges marked the rise of jealously individual property. As plots became smaller and rural life more precarious, many peasants sold their lands—despite the fine and disfranchisement that punished such sales—and went to Athens or lesser towns to become traders or craftsmen or laborers. Others, unable to meet the obligations of ownership, became tenant tillers of Eupatrid estates, *hectemoroi,* or "share-croppers" who kept a part of the produce as their pay.[38] Still others struggled on, borrowed money by mortgaging their land at high rates of interest, were unable to pay, and found themselves attached to the soil by their creditors, and working for them as serfs. The holder of the mortgage was considered to be the hypothetical owner of the property until the mortgage was satisfied, and placed upon the mortgaged land a stone slab announcing this ownership.[39] Small holdings became smaller, free peasants fewer, great holdings greater. "A few proprietors," says Aristotle, "owned all the soil, and the cultivators with their wives and children were liable to be sold as slaves," even into foreign parts, "on failure to pay their rent" or their debts.[40] Foreign trade, and the replacement of barter with coinage, hurt the peasant further; for the competition of imported food kept the prices of his products low, while the prices of the manufactured articles that he had to buy were determined by forces beyond his control, and rose inexplicably with every decade. A bad year ruined many farmers, and starved some of them to death. Rural poverty in Attica became so great that war was welcomed as a blessing: more land might be won, and fewer mouths would have to be fed.[41]

Meanwhile, in the towns, the middle classes, unhindered by law, were reducing the free laborers to destitution, and gradually replacing them with slaves.[42] Muscle became so cheap that no one who could afford to buy it deigned any longer to work with his hands; manual labor became a sign of bondage, an occupation unworthy of freemen. The landowners, jealous of the growing wealth of the merchant class, sold abroad the corn that their tenants needed for food, and at last, under the law of debt, sold the Athenians themselves.[43]

For a time men hoped that the legislation of Draco would remedy these evils. About 620 this *thesmothete*, or lawmaker, was commissioned to codify, and for the first time to put into writing, a system of laws that would restore order in Attica. So far as we know, the essential advances of his code were a moderate extension, among the newly rich, of eligibility to the archonship, and the replacement of feud vengeance with law: hereafter the Senate of the Areopagus was to try all cases of homicide. The last was a basic and progressive change; but to enforce it, indeed to persuade vengeful men to accept it as more certain and severe than their own revenge, he attached to his laws penalties so drastic that after most of his legislation had been superseded by Solon's he was remembered for his punishments rather than for his laws. Draco's code congealed the cruel customs of an unregulated feudalism; it did nothing to relieve debtors of slavery, or to mitigate the exploitation of the weak by the strong; and though it slightly extended the franchise it left to the Eupatrid class full control of the courts, and the power to interpret in their own way all laws and issues affecting their interests.[44] The owners of property were protected more zealously than ever before; petty theft, even idleness, was punished in the case of citizens with disfranchisement, in the case of others with death.*[45]

As the seventh century drew to a close the bitterness of the helpless poor against the legally entrenched rich had brought Athens to the edge of revolution. Equality is unnatural; and where ability and subtlety are free, inequality must grow until it destroys itself in the indiscriminate poverty of social war; liberty and equality are not associates but enemies. The concentration of wealth begins by being inevitable, and ends by being fatal. "The disparity of fortune between the rich and the poor," says Plutarch, "had reached its height, so that the city seemed to be in a truly dangerous condition, and no other means for freeing it from disturbances . . . seemed possible but a despotic power."[46] The poor, finding their situation worse with each year—the government and the army in the hands of their masters, and the corrupt courts deciding every issue against them[47]—began to talk of a violent revolt, and a thoroughgoing redistribution of wealth.[48] The rich, unable any longer to collect the debts legally due them, and angry at the challenge to their savings and their property, invoked ancient laws,[49] and prepared to defend themselves by force against a mob that seemed to threaten not only property but all established order, all religion, and all civilization.

3. *The Solonian Revolution*

It seems incredible that at this juncture in Athenian affairs, so often repeated in the history of nations, a man should have been found who, without any act of violence or any bitterness of speech, was able to persuade the rich and the poor to a compromise that not only averted social chaos

* "Those that stole a cabbage or an apple were to suffer even as villains that committed sacrilege or murder."—Plutarch, *Solon.*

but established a new and more generous political and economic order for the entire remainder of Athens' independent career. Solon's peaceful revolution is one of the encouraging miracles of history.

His father was a Eupatrid of purest blood, related to the descendants of King Codrus and, indeed, tracing his origin to Poseidon himself. His mother was cousin to the mother of Peisistratus, the dictator who would first violate and then consolidate the Solonian constitution. In his youth Solon participated lustily in the life of his time: he wrote poetry, sang the joys of "Greek friendship,"[50] and, like another Tyrtaeus, stirred the people with his verses to conquer Salamis.[51] In middle age his morals improved in inverse ratio to his poetry; his stanzas became dull, and his counsel excellent. "Many undeserving men are rich," he tells us, "while their betters are poor. But we will not exchange what we are for what they have, since the one gift abides while the other passes from man to man." The riches of the rich "are no greater than his whose only possessions are stomach, lungs and feet that bring him joy, not pain; the blooming charms of lad or maid; and an existence ever in harmony with the changing seasons of life."[52] Once, when a sedition occurred in Athens, he remained neutral, luckily before his own reputed legislation making such caution a crime.[53] But he did not hesitate to denounce the methods by which the wealthy had reduced the masses to a desperate penury.[54]

If we may believe Plutarch, Solon's father "ruined his estate in doing benefits and kindnesses to other men." Solon took to trade, and became a successful merchant with far-flung interests that gave him wide experience and travel. His practice was as good as his preaching, for he acquired among all classes an exceptional reputation for integrity. He was still relatively young—forty-four or forty-five—when, in 594, representatives of the middle classes asked him to accept election nominally as archon *eponymos*, but with dictatorial powers to soothe the social war, establish a new constitution, and restore stability to the state. The upper classes, trusting to the conservatism of a moneyed man, reluctantly consented.

His first measures were simple but drastic economic reforms. He disappointed the extreme radicals by making no move to redivide the land; such an attempt would have meant civil war, chaos for a generation, and the rapid return of inequality. But by his famous *Seisachtheia*, or Removal of Burdens, Solon canceled, says Aristotle, "all existing debts, whether owing to private persons or to the state";*[55] and at one blow cleared Attic lands of all mortgages. All persons enslaved or attached for debt were

* Probably this did not apply to commercial debts in which personal servitude was not involved.[56]

released; those sold into servitude abroad were reclaimed and freed; and such enslavement was forbidden for the future. It was characteristic of humanity that certain of Solon's friends, getting wind of his intention to cancel debts, bought on mortgage large tracts of land, and later retained these without paying the mortgages; this, Aristotle tells us with a rare twinkle in his style, was the origin of many fortunes, that were later "supposed to be of immemorial antiquity."[57] Solon was under suspicion of having connived at this and of having profited by it, until it was discovered that as a heavy creditor he himself had lost by his law.[58] The rich protested unanswerably that such legislation was confiscation; but within a decade opinion became almost unanimous that the act had saved Attica from revolution.[59]

Of another Solonian reform it is difficult to speak with clearness or certainty. Solon, says Aristotle, "superseded the Pheidonian measures"—that is, the Aeginetan coinage theretofore used in Attica—"by the Euboic system on a larger scale, and made the mina,* which had contained seventy drachmas, now contain a hundred."[60] According to Plutarch's fuller account, Solon "made the mina, which before passed for seventy-three drachmas, go for a hundred, so that, though the number of pieces in a payment was equal, the value was less; which proved a considerable benefit to those that were to discharge great debts, and no loss to the creditors."[61] Only the genial and generous Plutarch could devise a form of inflation that would relieve debtors without hurting creditors—except that doubtless in some cases half a loaf is better than none.†

More lasting than these economic reforms were those historic decrees that created the Solonian constitution. Solon prefaced them with an act of amnesty freeing or restoring all persons who had been jailed or banished for political offenses short of trying to usurp the government. He went on to repeal, directly or by implication, most of Draco's legislation; the law concerning murder remained.[64] It was in itself a revolution that the laws of Solon were applied without distinction to all freemen; rich and

* For the value of Athenian coins, see below, Chap. XII, sect. III.

† Grote and many others interpreted Plutarch's statement to mean that Solon had depreciated the currency by twenty-seven per cent and had thereby given relief to landlords who, themselves debtors to others, were deprived of the mortgage returns upon which they had depended for meeting their obligations.[62] Such inflation, however, would have fallen as a second blow upon those landlords who had lent sums to merchants; if it helped any class, it helped these merchants rather than the landlords or the peasants—whose mortgages had already been forgiven. Possibly Solon had no thought of debasing the currency, but wished merely to substitute, for a monetary standard that had been found convenient in trading with the Peloponnesus, another that would facilitate trade with the rich and growing markets of Ionia, where the Euboic standard was in common use.[63]

poor were now subject to the same restraints and the same penalties. Recognizing that his reforms had been made possible by the support of the mercantile and industrial classes and signified their accession to a substantial share in the government, Solon divided the free population of Attica into four groups according to their wealth: first, the *pentacosiomedimni*, or five-hundred-bushel men, whose annual income reached five hundred measures of produce, or the equivalent thereof;* second, the *hippes*, whose income was between three and five hundred measures; third, the *zeugitai*, with incomes between two and three hundred measures; and fourth, the *thetes*, all other freemen. Honors and taxes were determined by the same rating, and the one could not be enjoyed without paying the other; furthermore, the first class was taxed on twelve times, the second class on ten times, the third class on only five times, the amount of its annual income; the property tax was in effect a graduated income tax.[65] The fourth class was exempt from direct taxation. Only the first class was eligible to the archonship or to military commands; the second class was eligible to lower offices and to the cavalry; the third was privileged to join the heavy-armed infantry; the fourth was expected to provide the common soldiers of the state. This peculiar classification weakened the kinship organization upon which the oligarchy had rested its power, and established the new principle of "timocracy"—government by honor or prestige as frankly determined by taxable wealth. A similar "plutocracy" prevailed, throughout the sixth and part of the fifth century, in most of the Greek colonies.

At the head of the new government Solon's code left the old Senate of the Areopagus, a little shorn of its exclusiveness and powers, open now to all members of the first class, but still with supreme authority over the conduct of the people and the officers of the state.[66] Next below it he created a new *boule*, a Council of Four Hundred, to which each of the four tribes elected a hundred members; this Council selected, censored, and prepared all business that could be brought before the Assembly. Beneath this oligarchic superstructure, ingratiating to the strong, Solon, perhaps with good will aforethought, placed fundamentally democratic institutions. The old *ekklesia* of Homer's day was brought back to life, and all citizens were invited to join in its deliberations. This Assembly annually elected, from among the five-hundred-bushel men, the archons who heretofore had been appointed by the Areopagus; it could at any time question these officers, impeach them, punish them; and when their terms expired it scruti-

* A *medimnus*—about one and a half bushels—was considered equivalent to one drachma in money.

nized their official conduct during the year, and could debar them, if it chose, from their usual graduation into the Senate. More important still, though it did not seem so, was the admission of the lowest class of the citizens to full parity with the higher classes in being eligible to selection *by lot* to the *heliaea*—a body of six thousand jurors that formed the various courts before which all matters except murder and treason were tried, and to which appeal could be made from any action of the magistrates. "Some believe," says Aristotle, "that Solon intentionally introduced obscurity into his laws, to enable the commons to use their judicial power for their own political aggrandizement"; for since, as Plutarch adds, "their differences could not be adjusted by the letter, they would have to bring all their causes to the judges, who were in a manner masters of the laws."[67] This power of appeal to popular courts was to prove the wedge and citadel of Athenian democracy.

To this basic legislation, the most important in Athenian history, Solon added a miscellany of laws aimed at the less fundamental problems of the time. First he legalized that individualization of property which custom had already decreed. If a man had sons he was to divide his property among them at his death; if he died childless he might bequeath to anyone the property that in such cases had heretofore reverted automatically to the clan.[68] With Solon begins, in Athens, the right and law of wills. Himself a businessman, Solon sought to stimulate commerce and industry by opening citizenship to all aliens who had a skilled trade and came with their families to reside permanently at Athens. He forbade the export of any produce of the soil except olive oil, hoping to turn men from growing surplus crops to practicing an industry. He enacted a law that no son should be obliged to support a father who had not taught him some specific trade.[69] To Solon—not to the later Athenians—the crafts had their own rich honor and dignity.

Even into the dangerous realm of morals and manners Solon offered laws. Persistent idleness was made a crime, and no man who lived a life of debauchery was permitted to address the Assembly.[70] He legalized and taxed prostitution, established public brothels licensed and supervised by the state, and erected a temple to Aphrodite Pandemos from the revenues. "Hail to you, Solon!" sang a contemporary Lecky. "You bought public women for the benefit of the city, for the benefit of the morality of a city that is full of vigorous young men who, in the absence of your wise institution, would give themselves over to the disturbing annoyance of the better women."[71] He enacted the un-Draconian penalty of a hundred drachmas for the violation of a free woman, but anyone who caught an adulterer in the act was allowed to kill him there and then. He limited the size of dowries, wishing that marriages should be contracted by the affection of mates and for the rearing of children; and with childlike trustfulness he forbade women to extend their wardrobes beyond three suits. He was asked to legislate against bachelors, but refused, saying that, after all, "a wife is a heavy load to carry."[72] He made it a crime to speak evil of the dead, or to speak evil of the living in temples, courts, or public offices, or at the games; but even he could not tie the busy tongue of Athens, in which, as with us, gossip and slander seemed essential to democracy. He laid it down that those who remained neutral in seditions should lose their citizenship, for he felt that the indifference of the public is the ruin of the state. He condemned pompous ceremonies, expensive sacrifices, or lengthy lamentations at funerals, and limited the goods that might be buried with the dead. He established the wholesome law—a source of Athenian bravery for generations—that the sons of those who died in war should be brought up and educated at the expense of the government.

To all of his laws Solon attached penalties, milder than Draco's but still severe; and he empowered any citizen to bring action against any person whom he might consider guilty of crime. That his laws might be the better known and obeyed he wrote them down in the court of the archon *basileus* upon wooden rollers or prisms that could be turned and read. Unlike Lycurgus, Minos, Hammurabi, and Numa, he made no claim that a god had given him these laws; this circumstance, too, revealed the temper of the age, the city, and the man. Invited to make himself a permanent dictator he refused, saying that dictatorship was "a very fair spot, but there was no way down from it."[73] Radicals criticized him for failing to establish equality of possessions and power; conservatives denounced him for admitting the commons to the franchise and the courts; even his friend Anacharsis, the whimsical Scythian sage, laughed at the new constitution, saying that now the wise would plead and the fools would decide. Besides, added Anacharsis, no lasting justice can be established for men, since the strong or clever will twist to their advantage any laws that are made; the law is a spider's web that catches the little flies and lets the big bugs escape. Solon accepted all this criticism genially, acknowledging the imperfections of his code; asked had he given the Athenians the best laws, he answered, "No, but the best that they could receive"[74]—the best that the conflicting groups and interests of Athens could at that time be persuaded conjointly to accept. He followed the mean and preserved the state; he was a good pupil of Aristotle before the Stagirite was born. Tradition attributed to him the motto that was inscribed upon the temple of Apollo at Delphi—*meden agan*, nothing in excess;[75] and all Greeks agreed in placing him among the Seven Wise Men.

The best proof of his wisdom was the lasting effect of his legislation. Despite a thousand changes and developments, despite intervening dictatorships and superficial revolutions, Cicero could say, five centuries later, that the laws of Solon were still in force at Athens.[76] Legally his work marks the end of government by incalculable and changeable decrees, and the beginning of government by written and permanent law. Asked what made an orderly and well-constituted state, he replied, "When the people obey the rulers, and the rulers obey the laws."[77] To his legislation Attica owed the liberation of its farmers from serfdom, and the establishment of a peasant proprietor class whose ownership of the soil made the little armies of Athens suffice to preserve her liberties for many generations. When, at the close of the Peloponnesian War, it was proposed to limit the franchise to freeholders, only five thousand adult freemen in all Attica failed to satisfy this requirement.[78] At the same time trade and industry were freed from political disabilities and financial inconveniences, and began that vigorous development which was to make Athens the commercial leader of the Mediterranean. The new aristocracy of wealth put a premium upon intelligence rather than birth, stimulated science and education, and prepared, materially and mentally, for the cultural achievements of the Golden Age.

In 572, at the age of sixty-six, and after serving as archon for twenty-two years, Solon retired from office into private life; and having bound Athens, through the oath of its officials, to obey his laws unchanged for ten years,[79] he set out to observe the civilizations of Egypt and the East. It was now, apparently, that he made his famous remark—"I grow old while always learning."[80] At Heliopolis, says Plutarch, he studied Egyptian history and thought under the tutelage of the priests; from them, it is said, he heard of the sunken continent Atlantis, whose tale he told in an unfinished epic which two centuries later would fascinate the imaginative Plato. From Egypt he sailed to Cyprus and made laws for the city that in his honor changed its name to Soli.* Herodotus[81] and Plutarch describe with miraculous memory his chat at Sardis with Croesus, the Lydian king: how this

---

* Diogenes Laertius tells this story rather of Soli in Cilicia—the town whose preservation of old Greek speech into Alexander's day led to the word *solecism*.

paragon of wealth, having arrayed himself in all his paraphernalia, asked Solon did he not account him, Croesus, a happy man; and how Solon, with Greek audacity, replied:

> The gods, O King, have given the Greeks all other gifts in moderate degree; and so our wisdom, too, is a cheerful and a homely, not a noble and kingly, wisdom; and this, observing the numerous misfortunes that attend all conditions, forbids us to grow insolent upon our present enjoyment, or to admire any man's happiness that may yet, in course of time, suffer change. For the uncertain future has yet to come, with every possible variety of fortune; and him only to whom the divinity has continued happiness unto the end do we call happy; to salute as happy one that is still in the midst of life and hazard we think as little safe and conclusive as to crown and proclaim as victorious the wrestler that is yet in the ring.[82]

This admirable exposition of what the Greek dramatists mean by *hybris* —insolent prosperity—has the ring of Plutarch's eclectic wisdom; we can only say that it is better phrased than Herodotus' report, and that both accounts belong, presumably, to the realm of imaginary conversations. Certainly both Solon and Croesus, in the manner of their deaths, justified the skepticism of this homily. Croesus was dethroned by Cyrus in 546, and (if we may rephrase Herodotus with Dante) knew the bitterness of remembering, in his misery, the happy time of his splendor, and the stern warning of the Greek. And Solon, returning to Athens to die, saw in his last years the overthrow of his constitution, the establishment of a dictatorship, and the apparent frustration of all his work.

4. *The Dictatorship of Peisistratus*

The conflicting groups which he had dominated for a generation had resumed, upon his departure from Athens, the natural play of politics and intrigue. As in the passionate days of the French Revolution, three parties struggled for power: the "Shore," led by the merchants of the ports, who favored Solon; the "Plain," led by the rich landowners, who hated Solon; and the "Mountain," a combination of peasants and town laborers who still fought for a redistribution of the land. Like Pericles a century later, Peisistratus, though an aristocrat by birth and fortune, manners and tastes, accepted the leadership of the commons. At a meeting of the Assembly he displayed a wound, claiming that it had been inflicted upon him by the enemies of the people, and asked for a bodyguard. Solon protested; knowing the subtlety of his cousin, he suspected that the wound had been self-inflicted, and that the bodyguard would open the way to a dictatorship. "Ye men of Athens," he warned them, "I am wiser than some of you, and braver than others: wiser than those of you who do not perceive the treachery of Peisistratus, and braver than those who are aware of it, but out of fear hold their peace."[83] Nevertheless the Assembly voted that Peisistratus should be allowed a force of fifty men. Peisistratus collected four hundred men instead of fifty, seized the Acropolis, and declared a dictatorship. Solon, having published to the Athenians his opinion that "each man of you, individually, walketh with the tread of a fox, but collectively ye are geese,"[84] placed his arms and shield outside his door as a symbol of resigning his interest in politics, and devoted his last days to poetry.

The wealthy forces of the Shore and the Plain united for a moment and expelled the dictator (556). But Peisistratus secretly made his peace with the Shore, and, probably with their connivance, re-entered Athens under circumstances that seemed to corroborate Solon's judgment of the collective intelligence. A tall and beautiful woman, arrayed in the armor and costume of the city's goddess Athena, and seated proudly in a chariot, led the forces of Peisistratus into the city, while heralds announced that the patron deity of Athens was herself restoring him to power (550). "The people of the city, fully persuaded," says Herodotus, "that the woman was the veritable goddess, prostrated themselves before her, and received Peisistratus back."[85] The leaders of the Shore turned against him again and drove him into a second exile (549); but in 546 Peisistratus once more returned, defeated the troops sent out against him, and this time maintained his dictatorship for nineteen years, during which the wisdom of his policies almost redeemed the picturesque unscrupulousness of his means.

The character of Peisistratus was a rare union of culture and intellect, administrative vigor and personal charm. He could fight ruthlessly, and readily forgive; he could move in the foremost currents of the thought of his time, and govern without the intellectual's vacillation of purpose and timidity of execution. He was mild of manner, humane in his decisions, and generous to all. "His administration," says Aristotle, "was temperate, and showed the statesman rather than the tyrant."[86] He made few reprisals upon regenerate enemies, but he banished irreconcilable opponents, and distributed their estates among the poor. He improved the army and built up the fleet as security against external attack; but he kept Athens out of war, and maintained at home, in a city so recently disturbed by class hostility, such order and content that it was common to say that he had brought back the Golden Age of Cronus' reign.

He surprised everyone by making little change of detail in the Solonian constitution. Like Augustus he knew how to adorn and support dictatorship with democratic concessions and forms. Archons were elected as usual, and the Assembly and the popular courts, the Council of Four Hundred and the Senate of the Areopagus met and functioned as before, except that the suggestions of Peisistratus found a very favorable hearing. When a citizen accused him of murder he appeared before the Senate and offered to submit to trial, but the complainant decided not to press the charge. Year by year the people, in inverse proportion to their wealth, became reconciled to his rule; soon they were proud of him, at last fond of him. Probably Athens had needed, after Solon, just such a man as Peisistratus: one with sufficient iron in his blood to beat the disorder of Athenian life into a strong and steady form, and to establish by initial compulsion those habits of order and law which are to a society what the bony structure is to an animal—its shape and strength, though not its creative life. When, after a generation, the dictatorship was removed, these habits of order and the framework of Solon's constitution remained as a heritage for democracy. Peisistratus, perhaps not knowing it, had come not to destroy the law but to fulfill it.

His economic policies carried on that emancipation of the people which Solon had begun. He settled the agrarian question by dividing among the poor the lands that belonged to the state, as well as those of banished aristocrats; thousands of dangerously idle Athenians were settled upon the soil; and for centuries afterward we hear of no serious agrarian discontent in Attica.[87] He gave employment to the needy by undertaking extensive public works, building a system of aqueducts and roads, and raising great temples to the gods. He encouraged the mining of silver at Laurium, and issued a new and independent coinage. To finance these undertakings he laid a ten per cent tax upon all agricultural products; later he seems to have reduced this to 5 per cent.[88] He planted strategic colonies on the Dardanelles, and made commercial treaties with many states. Under his rule trade flourished, and wealth grew not among a few only, but in the community as a whole. The poor were made less poor, the rich not less rich. That concentration of wealth which had nearly torn the city into civil war was brought under control, and the spread of comfort and opportunity laid the economic bases of Athenian democracy.

Under Peisistratus and his sons Athens was physically and mentally transformed. Till their time it had been a second-rate city in the Greek world, lagging behind Miletus, Ephesus, Mytilene, and Syracuse in wealth and culture, in vitality of life and mind. Now new buildings of stone and marble reflected the radiance of the day; the old temple of Athena on the Acropolis was beautified with a Doric peristyle; and work was begun on that temple of Olympian Zeus whose stately Corinthian columns, even in their ruins, brighten the road from Athens to her port. By establishing the Panathenaic games and giving them a Panhellenic character, Peisistratus brought to his city not honor only, but the stimulus of foreign faces, competition, and ways; under his rule the Panathenaea became the great national festival, whose impressive ceremonial still moves on the frieze of the Parthenon. To his court, by public works and private beneficence, Peisistratus attracted sculptors, architects, and poets; in his palace was collected one of the earliest libraries of Greece. A committee appointed by him gave to the *Iliad* and the *Odyssey* the form in which we know them. Under his administration and encouragement Thespis and others lifted drama from a mummers' mimicry to a form of art ready to be filled out by the great triumvirate of the Athenian stage.

The "tyranny" of Peisistratus was part of a general movement in the commercially active cities of sixth-century Greece, to replace the feudal rule of a landowning aristocracy with the political dominance of the middle class in temporary alliance with the poor.* Such dictatorships were brought on by the pathological concentration of wealth, and the inability of the wealthy to agree on a compromise. Forced to choose, the poor, like the rich, love money more than political liberty; and the only political freedom capable of enduring is one that is so pruned as to keep the rich from denuding the poor by ability or subtlety and the poor from robbing the rich by violence or votes. Hence the road to power in Greek commercial cities was simple: to attack the aristocracy, defend the poor, and come to an understanding with the middle classes.[89] Arrived at power, the dictator abolished debts, or confiscated large estates, taxed the rich to finance public works, or otherwise redistributed the overconcentrated wealth; and while attaching the masses to himself through such measures, he secured the support of the business community by promoting trade with state coinage and commercial treaties, and by raising the social prestige of the *bourgeoisie*. Forced to depend upon popularity instead of hereditary

* The word *tyrant* had come from Lydia, perhaps from the town of Tyrrha, meaning a fortress; probably it is a distant cousin to our word *tower* (Gk. *tyrris*). Apparently it was applied first to Gyges, the Lydian king.

power, the dictatorships for the most part kept out of war, supported religion, maintained order, promoted morality, favored the higher status of women, encouraged the arts, and lavished revenues upon the beautification of their cities. And they did all these things, in many cases, while preserving the forms and procedures of popular government, so that even under despotism the people learned the ways of liberty. When the dictatorship had served to destroy the aristocracy the people destroyed the dictatorship; and only a few changes were needed to make the democracy of freemen a reality as well as a form.

5. *The Establishment of Democracy*

When Peisistratus died, in 527, he left his power to his sons; his wisdom had survived every test except that of parental love. Hippias gave promise of being a wise ruler, and for thirteen years continued the policies of his father. Hipparchus, his younger brother, was harmlessly, though expensively, devoted to love and poetry; it was at his invitation that Anacreon and Simonides came to Athens. The Athenians were not quite pleased to see the leadership of the state pass down without their consent to the young Peisistratids, and began to realize that the dictatorship had given them everything but the stimulus of freedom. Nevertheless Athens was prosperous, and the quiet reign of Hippias might have gone on to a peaceful close had it not been for the unsmooth course of true Greek love.

Aristogeiton, a man of middle age, had won the love of the young Harmodius, then, says Thucydides,[90] "in the flower of youthful beauty." But Hipparchus, equally careless of gender, also solicited the lad's love. When Aristogeiton heard of this he resolved to kill Hipparchus and at the same time, in self-protection, to overthrow the tyranny. Harmodius and others joined him in the conspiracy (514). They murdered Hipparchus as he was arranging the Panathenaic procession, but Hippias eluded them and had them slain. To complicate the tale a courtesan Leaena, mistress of Harmodius, died bravely under torture, having refused to betray the surviving conspirators; if we may believe Greek tradition, she bit off her tongue and spat it in the face of her torturers to make sure that she would not answer their questions.[91]

Though the people lent no visible support to this revolt, Hippias was frightened by it into replacing his hitherto mild rule with a regime of suppression, espionage, and terror. The Athenians, strengthened by a generation of prosperity, could afford now to demand the luxury of liberty;

gradually, as the dictatorship grew harsher, the cry for freedom grew louder; and Harmodius and Aristogeiton, who had conspired for love and passion rather than for democracy,* were transformed by popular imagination into the martyrs of liberty. Off in Delphi the Alcmaeonids, who had been re-exiled by Peisistratus, saw their opportunity, raised an army, and marched upon Athens with the announced intention of deposing Hippias. At the same time they bribed the Pythian oracle to tell all Spartans who consulted her that Sparta must overthrow the tyranny at Athens. Hippias successfully resisted the forces of the Alcmaeonids; but when a Lacedaemonian army joined them he withdrew to the Areopagus. Seeking the security of his children in the event of his own death, he sent them secretly out of Athens; but they were captured by the invaders, and Hippias, as the price of their safety, consented to abdication and exile (510). The Alcmaeonids, led by the courageous Cleisthenes,† entered Athens in triumph; and on their heels came the banished aristocrats, prepared to celebrate the return of their property and their power.

In the election that ensued, Isagoras, representing the aristocracy, was chosen to be chief archon. Cleisthenes, one of the defeated candidates, aroused the people to revolt, overthrew Isagoras, and set up a popular dictatorship. The Spartans again invaded Athens, seeking to restore Isagoras; but the Athenians resisted so tenaciously that the Spartans retired, and Cleisthenes, the Alcmaeonid aristocrat, proceeded to establish democracy (507).

His first reform struck at the very framework of Attic aristocracy—those four tribes and 360 clans whose leadership, by centuries of tradition, was in the hands of the oldest and richest families. Cleisthenes abolished this kinship classification, and replaced it with a territorial division into ten tribes, each composed of a (varying) number of demes. To prevent the formation of geographical or occupational blocs, such as the old parties of Mountain, Shore, and Plain, each tribe was to be composed of an equal number of demes, or districts, from the city, from the coast, and from the interior. To offset the sanctity that religion had given to the old division, religious ceremonies were instituted for each new tribe or deme, and a famous ancient hero of the locality was made its deity or patron saint. Freemen of foreign origin, who had rarely been admitted to the franchise under the aristocratic determination of citizenship by descent, now auto-

* One would not be surprised to learn that they represented a resentful aristocracy, like Brutus and Cassius in Rome. Brutus, too, became the hero of a revolution, after eighteen centuries had obscured his history.

† Grandson of Cleisthenes, dictator of Sicyon.

matically became citizens of the demes in which they lived. At one stroke the roll of voters was almost doubled, and democracy secured a new support and a broader base.

Each of the new tribes was entitled to name one of the ten *strategoi*, or generals, who now joined the polemarch in command of the army; and each tribe elected fifty members of the new Council of 501 which now replaced Solon's Council of Four Hundred and assumed the most vital powers of the Areopagus. These councilors were chosen for a year's term, not by election but by lot, from the list of all citizens who had reached the age of thirty and had not already served two terms. In this strange inauguration of representative government both the aristocratic principle of birth and the plutocratic principle of wealth were overridden by the new device of the lot, which gave every citizen an equal chance not only to vote, but to hold office in the most influential branch of the government. For the Council so elected determined all matters and proposals to be submitted for approval or rejection to the Assembly, reserved to itself various judicial powers, exercised wide administrative functions, and supervised all officials of the state.

The Assembly was enlarged by the access of new citizens, so that a full meeting of its membership would have meant an attendance of approximately thirty thousand men. All these were eligible for service in the *heliaea*, or courts; but the fourth class, or *thetes*, were still, as under Solon, ineligible to individual office. The powers of the Assembly were enlarged by the institution of ostracism, which Cleisthenes seems to have added as a protection for the young democracy. At any time, by a majority of votes written secretly upon potsherds (*ostraka*), the Assembly, in a quorum of six thousand members, might send into exile for ten years any man who in its judgment had become a danger to the state. In this way ambitious leaders would be stimulated to conduct themselves with circumspection and moderation, and men suspected of conspiracy could be disposed of without the law's delay. The procedure required that the Assembly should be asked, "Is there any man among you whom you think vitally dangerous to the state? If so, whom?" The Assembly might then vote to ostracize any one citizen—not excepting the mover of the motion.* Such exile involved no confiscation of property, and no disgrace; it was merely democracy's way of cutting off the "tallest ears of corn."[92] Nor did the Assembly abuse its power. In the ninety years between the introduction of ostracism and its disuse at Athens, only ten persons were banished by it from Attica.

* A similar institution was used at Argos, Megara, and Syracuse.

One of these, we are told, was Cleisthenes himself. But in truth we do not know his later history; it was absorbed and lost in the brilliance of his work. Beginning with a thoroughly unconstitutional revolt, he had established, in the face of the most powerful families in Attica, a democratic constitution that continued in operation, with only minor changes, to the end of Athenian liberty. The democracy was not complete; it applied only to freemen, and still placed a modest property limitation upon eligibility to individual office.* But it gave all legislative, executive, and judicial power to an Assembly and a Court composed of the citizens, to magistrates appointed by and responsible to the Assembly, and to a Council for whose members all citizens might vote, and in whose supreme authority, by the operation of the lot, at least one third of them actually shared for at least a year of their lives. Never before had the world seen so liberal a franchise, or so wide a spread of political power.

The Athenians themselves were exhilarated by this adventure into sovereignty. They realized that they had undertaken a difficult enterprise, but they advanced to it with courage and pride, and, for a time, with unwonted self-restraint. From that moment they knew the zest of freedom in action, speech, and thought; and from that moment they began to lead all Greece in literature and art, even in statesmanship and war. They learned to respect anew a law that was their own considered will, and to love with unprecedented passion a state that was their unity, their power, and their fulfillment. When the greatest empire of the age decided to destroy these scattered cities called Greece, or to lay them under tribute to the Great King, it forgot that in Attica it would be opposed by men who owned the soil that they tilled, and who ruled the state that governed them. It was fortunate for Greece, and for Europe, that Cleisthenes completed his work, and Solon's, twelve years before Marathon.

* A property qualification was placed upon the franchise in the earlier stages of American and French democracy.

CHAPTER VI

The Great Migration

I. CAUSES AND WAYS

IN carrying the story of Sparta and Athens down to the eve of Marathon we have sacrificed the unity of time to the unity of place. It is true that the cities of the mainland were older than the Greek settlements in the Aegean and Ionia, and that these cities, in many cases, sent out the colonies whose life we must now describe. But, by a confusing inversion of normal sequences, several of those colonies became greater than their mother cities, and preceded them in the development of wealth and art. The real creators of Greek culture were not the Greeks of what we now call Greece, but those who fled before the conquering Dorians, fought desperately for a foothold on foreign shores, and there, out of their Mycenaean memories and their amazing energy, made the art and science, the philosophy and poetry that, long before Marathon, placed them in the forefront of the Western world. Greek civilization was inherited by the parent cities from their children.

There is nothing more vital in the history of the Greeks than their rapid spread throughout the Mediterranean.* They had been nomadic before Homer, and all the Balkan peninsula had seemed fluid with this movement, but the successive Greek waves that broke upon the Aegean isles and the western coasts of Asia were stirred up above all by the Dorian invasion. From every part of Hellas men went out in search of homes and liberty beyond the grasp of the enslaving conquerors. Political faction and family feud in the older states contributed to the migration; the defeated sometimes chose exile, and the victors gave every encouragement to their exodus. Some of the Greek survivors of the Trojan War stayed in Asia; others, through shipwreck or adventure, settled in the islands of the Aegean; some, reaching home after a perilous journey, found their thrones or their wives occupied, and returned to their ships to build new homes and fortunes abroad.[2] In mainland Greece, as in modern Europe, colonization proved a blessing in varied ways: it provided outlets for surplus population and

* Cf. Pater: "Perhaps the most brilliant and animating episode in the entire history of Greece—its early colonization."[1]

adventurous spirits, and safety valves against agrarian discontent; it established foreign markets for domestic products, and strategic depots for the import of food and minerals. In the end it created a commercial empire whose thriving interchange of goods, arts, ways, and thoughts made possible the complex culture of Greece.

The migration followed five main lines—Aeolian, Ionian, Dorian, Euxine, Italian. The earliest began in the northern states of the mainland, which were the first to feel the brunt of the invasions from the north and the west. From Thessaly, Phthiotis, Boeotia, and Aetolia, throughout the twelfth and eleventh centuries, a stream of immigrants moved slowly across the Aegean to the region about Troy, and founded there the twelve cities of the Aeolian League. The second line took its start in the Peloponnesus, whence thousands of Mycenaeans and Achaeans fled on the "Return of the Heraclids." Some of them settled in Attica, some in Euboea; many of them moved out into the Cyclades, ventured across the Aegean, and established in western Asia Minor the twelve cities of the Ionian Dodecapolis. The third line was followed by Dorians who overflowed the Peloponnesus into the Cyclades, conquered Crete and Cyrene, and set up a Dorian Hexapolis around the island of Rhodes. The fourth line, starting anywhere in Greece, settled the coast of Thrace, and built a hundred cities on the shores of the Hellespont, the Propontis, and the Euxine Sea. The fifth line moved westward to what the Greeks called the Ionian Isles, thence across to Italy and Sicily, and finally to Gaul and Spain.

Only a sympathetic imagination or a keen recollection of our own colonial history can visualize the difficulties that were surmounted in this century-long migration. It was an adventure of high moment to leave the land consecrated by the graves of one's ancestors and guarded by one's hereditary deities, and go forth into strange regions unprotected, presumably, by the gods of Greece. Therefore the colonists took with them a handful of earth from their native state to strew upon the alien soil, and solemnly carried fire from the public altar of their mother city to light the civic fire at the hearth of their new settlement. The chosen site was on or near a shore, where ships—the second home of half the Greeks—might serve as a refuge from attack by land; better still if it were a coastal plain protected by mountains that provided a barrier in the rear, an acropolis for defense in the town, and a promontory-sheltered harbor in the sea; best of all if such a haven could be found on some commercial route, or by a river mouth that received the products of the interior for export or exchange; then prosperity was only a matter of time. Good sites were nearly always occupied, and had to be conquered by stratagem or force; the Greeks, in such matters, recognized no morals loftier than our own. In some cases the conquerors reduced the prior inhabitants to slavery, with all the irony of pilgrims seeking freedom; more often they made friends of the natives by bringing them Greek gifts, charming them with a superior culture, courting their women, and adopting their gods; the colonial Greeks did not bother about purity of race,[3] and could always find in their teeming pantheon some deity sufficiently like the local divinity to facilitate a religious entente. Above all, the colonists offered the products of the Greek handicrafts to the natives, secured grain, cattle, or minerals in return, and exported these throughout the Mediterranean—preferably to the *metropolis*, or mother city, from which the settlers had come, and to which they retained for centuries a certain filial piety.

One by one these colonies took form, until Greece was no longer the narrow peninsula of Homeric days, but a strangely loose association of independent cities scattered from Africa to Thrace and from Gibraltar to the eastern end of the Black Sea. It was an epochal performance for the women of Greece; we shall not always find them so ready to have children. Through these busy centers of vitality and intelligence the Greeks spread into all of southern Europe the seeds of that subtle and precarious luxury called civilization, without which life would have no beauty, and history no meaning.

II. THE IONIAN CYCLADES

Sailing south from the Piraeus along the Attic coast, and bearing east around Sunium's templed promontory, the traveler reaches the little isle of Ceos, where, if we may believe the incredible on the authority of Strabo and Plutarch, "there was once a law that appears to have commanded those who were sixty years of age to drink hemlock, in order that the food might be sufficient for the rest," and "there was no memory of a case of adultery or seduction over a period of seven hundred years."[4]

Perhaps that is why her greatest poet exiled himself from Ceos after reaching middle age; he might have found it difficult to attain, at home, the eighty-seven years that Greek tradition gives him. All the Hellenic world knew Simonides at thirty, and when he died, in 469, he was by common consent the most brilliant writer of his time. His fame as poet and singer won him an invitation from Hipparchus, codictator of Athens, at whose court he found it possible to live in amity with another poet, Anacreon. He survived the war with Persia, and was chosen again and again to write epitaphs for memorials of the honored dead. In his old age he lived at the court of Hieron I, dictator of Syracuse; and his repute was then so high that in 475 he made peace in the field between Hieron and Theron, dictator of Acragas, as hostilities were about to begin.[5] Plutarch, in his perennially pertinent essay on "Should Old Men Govern?" tells us that Simonides continued to win the prize for lyric poetry and choral song into very old age. When finally he consented to die he was buried at Acragas with the honors of a king.

He was a personality as well as a poet, and the Greeks denounced and loved him for his vices and eccentricities. He had a passion for money, and his muse was dumb in the absence of gold. He was the first to write poetry for pay, on the ground that poets had as much right to eat as anyone else; but the practice was new to Greece, and Aristophanes echoed the resentment of the public when he said that Simonides "would go to sea on a hurdle to earn a groat."[6] He prided himself on having invented a system of mnemonics, which Cicero adopted gratefully;[7] its essential principle lay in arranging the things to be remembered into some logical classification and sequence, so that each item would naturally lead to the next. He was a wit, and his sharp repartees passed like a mental currency among the cities of Greece; but in his old age he remarked that he had often repented of speaking, but never of holding his tongue.[8]

We are surprised to find, in the extant fragments of a poet so widely acclaimed and so liberally rewarded, that indispersible gloom which broods over so much of Greek literature after Homer—in whose days men were too active to be pessimists, and too violent to be bored.

> Few and evil are the days of our life; but everlasting will be our sleep beneath the earth. . . . Small is the strength of man, and invincible are his errors; grief treads upon the heels of grief through his short life; and death, whom no man escapes, hangs over him at last; to this come good and bad alike. . . . Nothing human is everlasting. Well said the bard of Chios that the life of man is even as that of a green leaf; yet few who hear this bear it in mind, for hope is strong in the breast of the young. When youth is in flower, and the heart of man is light, he nurses idle thought, hoping he will never grow old or die; nor does he think of sickness in good health. Fools are they who dream thus, nor know how short are the days of our youth and our life.[9]

No hope of Blessed Isles comforts Simonides, and the divinities of Olympus, like those of Christianity in some modern verse, have become instruments of poetry rather than consolations of the soul. When Hieron challenged him to define the nature and attributes of God he asked for a day's time to prepare his answer, and the next day begged for two days more, and on each occasion doubled the period that he required for thought. When at last Hieron demanded an explanation, Simonides replied that the longer he pondered the matter the more obscure it became.[10]

Out of Ceos came not only Simonides, but his nephew and lyric successor Bacchylides, and, in Alexandrian days, the great anatomist Erasistratus. We cannot say so much for Seriphos, or Andros, or Tenos, or Myconos, or Sicinos, or Ios. On Syros lived Pherecydes (ca. 550), who was reputed to have taught Pythagoras, and to have been the first philosopher to write in prose. On Delos, said Greek story, Apollo himself had been born. So sacred was the island as his sanctuary that both death and birth were forbidden within its borders; those about to give birth or to die were hurriedly conveyed from its shores; and all known graves were emptied that the island might be purified.[11] There, after the repulse of the Persians, Athens and her Ionian allies would keep the treasure of the Delian Confederacy; there, every fourth year, the Ionians met in pious but convivial assemblage to celebrate the festival of the handsome god. A seventh-century hymn describes the "women with fine girdles,"[12] the eager merchants busy at their booths, the crowds lining the road to watch the sacred procession; the tense ritual and solemn sacrifice in the temple; the joyous dances and choral hymns of Delian and Athenian maidens chosen for their comeliness as well as their song; the athletic and musical contests, and the plays in the theater under the open sky. Annually the Athenians sent an embassy to Delos to celebrate Apollo's birthday; and no criminal might be executed in Athens until this embassy's return. Hence the long interval, so fortunate for literature and philosophy, between the conviction of Socrates and his execution.

Naxos is the largest, as Delos is almost the smallest, of the Cyclades. It was famous for its wine and its marble, and became rich enough, in the sixth century, to have its own navy and its own school of sculpture. Southeast of Naxos lies Amorgos, home of the unamiable Semonides, whose ungallant satire on women has been carefully preserved by man-written history.* To the west lies Paros, almost composed of marble; its citizens

* Semonides compares women now to foxes, asses, pigs, and the changeful sea, and swears that no husband has ever passed through a day without some word of censure from his wife.[13]

made their homes of it, and Praxiteles found there the translucent stone which he would carve and polish into the warmth and texture of human flesh. On this island, about the end of the eighth century, Archilochus was born, son of a slave woman, but one of the greatest lyric singers of Greece. A soldier's fortune led him north to Thasos where, in a battle with the natives, he found his heels more valuable than his shield; he took to the one and abandoned the other, and lived to turn many a merry quip about his flight. Back in Paros he fell in love with Neobule, daughter of the rich Lycambes. He describes her as a modest lass with tresses falling over her shoulders, and sighs, as so many centuries have sighed, "only to touch her hand."[14] But Lycambes, admiring the poet's verses more than his income, put an end to the affair; whereupon Archilochus aimed at him and Neobule and her sister such barbs of satiric verse that all three of them, legend assures us, hanged themselves. Archilochus turned his back sourly upon the "figs and fishes" of Paros, and became again a soldier of fortune. Finally, his heels having failed him, he was killed in battle against the Naxians.

We learn from his poems that he was a man of rough speech to both friends and foes, with a disappointed lover's penchant for adultery.[15] We picture him as an inspired pirate, a melodious buccaneer coarse in prose and polished in verse; taking the iambic meter already popular in folk songs and fashioning it into short and stinging lines of six feet; this was the "iambic trimeter" that would become the classic medium of Greek tragedy. He experimented gaily with dactylic hexameters, trochaic tetrameters, and a dozen other meters,* and gave to Greek poetry the metrical forms that it would keep to the end. Only a few broken lines survive, and we must accept the word of the ancients that he was the most popular of all Greek poets after Homer. Horace loved to imitate his technical diversities; and the great Hellenistic critic, Aristophanes of Byzantium, when asked which of Archilochus' poems he liked best, voiced in two words the feeling of Greece when he answered, "The longest."[16]

A morning's sail west of Paros is Siphnos, famous for its mines of silver and gold. These were owned by the people through their government. The yield was so rich that the island could set up at Delphi the Siphnian Treasury with its placid caryatides, erect many another monument, and yet distribute a substantial balance among the citizens at the end of every

---

* Longfellow's *Evangeline*, his *Hiawatha*, and the final line of each stanza in *Childe Harold's Pilgrimage*, by Byron, may serve as examples respectively of dactylic hexameter, trochaic tetrameter, and iambic trimeter.

year.[17] In 524 a band of freebooters from Samos landed on the island and exacted a tribute of a hundred talents—the equivalent of $600,000 today. The rest of Greece accepted this heroic robbery with the equanimity and fortitude with which men are accustomed to bear the misfortunes of their friends.

III. THE DORIAN OVERFLOW

The Dorians, too, colonized the Cyclades, and tamed their warlike spirits to terrace the mountain slopes patiently, that the parsimonious rain might be held and coaxed to nourish their crops and vines. In Melos they took over from their Bronze Age predecessors the quarrying of obsidian, and made the island so prosperous that the Athenians, as we shall see, spared no pains to Melos to win its support in the struggle with Sparta. Here, in 1820, was found that *Aphrodite of Melos** which is now the most famous statue in the Western world.

Moving east and then south, the Dorians conquered Thera and Crete, and from Thera sent a further colony to Cyrene. A few of them settled in Cyprus, where, from the eleventh century, a small colony of Arcadian Greeks had struggled for mastery against the old Phoenician dynasties. It was one of these Phoenician kinglets, Pygmalion, of whom legend told how he so admired an ivory Aphrodite carved by his hands that he fell in love with it, begged the goddess to give it life, and married his creation when the goddess complied.[18] The coming of iron probably lessened the demand for Cyprian copper, and left the island off the main line of Greek economic advance. The cutting of the timber by the natives to burn the copper ore, by the Phoenicians for ships and by the Greeks for agricultural clearings, slowly transformed Cyprus into the hot and half-barren derelict that it is today. The art of the island, like its population, was in the Greek period a medley of Egyptian, Phoenician, and Hellenic influences, and never attained a homogeneous character of its own.†

The Dorians were but a minority of the Greek population in Cyprus; but in Rhodes and the southern Sporades and on the adjoining mainland they became the ruling class. Rhodes prospered in the centuries between Homer and Marathon, though its zenith would not come till the Hellenistic age. On a promontory jutting out from Asia, Dorian settlers developed the city of Cnidus,

---

* Or, as we know it, from the Roman name of the goddess and the Italian name of the island, the *Venus de Milo*.

† Cf. Case XIII of the Cesnola Collection of Cyprian Antiquities in the Metropolitan Museum of Art, New York. A bilingual tablet unearthed by British scholars in 1868 enabled them to decipher Cypriote writing as a dialect of Greek expressed by syllabic signs; but the results have not added anything of interest to universal history.

well situated to be a port of the coastal trade. Here the astronomer Eudoxus would be born, and the historian (or fabulist) Ctesias, and that Sostratus who was to build the Pharos at Alexandria. Here, among the ruins of ancient temples, would be found the sad and matronly *Demeter* of the British Museum.

Opposite Cnidus lay the island of Cos, home of Hippocrates and rival of Cnidus as a center of Greek medical science. Apelles the painter would be born here, and Theocritus the poet. A little to the north, on the coast, was Halicarnassus, birthplace of Herodotus and royal seat, in Hellenistic days, of the Carian King Mausolus and his fond Artemisia. This city, with Cos and Cnidus and the chief towns of Rhodes (Lindus, Camirus, and Ialysus) formed the Dorian Hexapolis, or Six Cities, of Asia Minor—weak rivals, for a time, of the Twelve Cities of Ionia.

IV. THE IONIAN DODECAPOLIS

1. *Miletus and the Birth of Greek Philosophy*

Running northwest of Caria for some ninety miles was the strip of mountainous coastland, twenty to thirty miles wide, anciently known as Ionia. Here, said Herodotus, "the air and climate are the most beautiful in the whole world."[19] Its cities lay for the most part at the mouths of rivers, or at the ends of roads, that carried the goods of the hinterland down to the Mediterranean for shipment everywhere.

Miletus, southernmost of the Ionian Twelve, was in the sixth century the richest city of the Greek world. The site had been inhabited by Carians from Minoan days; and when, about 1000 B.C., the Ionians came there from Attica, they found the old Aegean culture, though in a decadent form, waiting to serve as the advanced starting point of their civilization. They brought no women with them to Miletus, but merely killed the native males and married the widows;[20] the fusion of cultures began with a fusion of blood. Like most of the Ionian cities, Miletus submitted at first to kings who led them in war, then to aristocrats who owned the land, then to "tyrants" representing the middle class. Under the dictator Thrasybulus, at the beginning of the sixth century, industry and trade reached their peak, and the growing wealth of Miletus flowered forth in literature, philosophy, and art. Wool was brought down from the rich pasture lands of the interior, and turned into clothing in the textile mills of the city. Taking a lesson from the Phoenicians and gradually bettering their instruction, Ionian merchants established colonies as trading posts in Egypt, Italy, the

Propontis, and the Euxine. Miletus alone had eighty such colonies, sixty of them in the north. From Abydos, Cyzicus, Sinope, Olbia, Trapezus, and Dioscurias, Miletus drew flax, timber, fruit, and metals, and paid for these with the products of her handicrafts. The wealth and luxury of the city became a proverb and a scandal throughout Greece. Milesian merchants, overflowing with profits, lent money to enterprises far and wide, and to the municipality itself. They were the Medici of the Ionian Renaissance.

It was in this stimulating environment that Greece first developed two of its most characteristic gifts to the world—science and philosophy. The crossroads of trade are the meeting place of ideas, the attrition ground of rival customs and beliefs; diversities beget conflict, comparison, thought; superstitions cancel one another, and reason begins. Here in Miletus, as later in Athens, were men from a hundred scattered states; mentally active through competitive commerce, and freed from the bondage of tradition by long absences from their native altars and homes. Milesians themselves traveled to distant cities, and had their eyes opened by the civilizations of Lydia, Babylonia, Phoenicia, and Egypt; in this way, among others, Egyptian geometry and Babylonian astronomy entered the Greek mind. Trade and mathematics, foreign commerce and geography, navigation and astronomy, developed hand in hand. Meanwhile wealth had created leisure; an aristocracy of culture was growing up in which freedom of thought was tolerated because only a small minority could read. No powerful priesthood, no ancient and inspired text limited men's thinking; even the Homeric poems, which were to become in some sense the Bible of the Greeks, had hardly taken yet a definite form; and in that final form their mythology was to bear the imprint of Ionian skepticism and scandalous merriment. Here for the first time thought became secular, and sought rational and consistent answers to the problems of the world and man.*

Nevertheless the new plant, mutation though it was, had its roots and ancestry. The hoary wisdom of Egyptian priests and Persian Magi, perhaps even of Hindu seers, the sacerdotal science of the Chaldeans, the poetically personified cosmogony of Hesiod, were mingled with the natural realism of Phoenician and Greek merchants to produce Ionian philosophy. Greek religion itself had paved the way by talking of Moira, or Fate, as ruler of both gods and men: here was that idea of law, as superior to incalculable personal decree, which would mark the essential difference between science and mythology, as well as between despotism and democ-

* Similar movements, however, appeared in India and China in this sixth century B.C.

racy. Man became free when he recognized that he was subject to law. That the Greeks, so far as our knowledge goes, were the first to achieve this recognition and this freedom in both philosophy and government is the secret of their accomplishment, and of their importance in history.

Since life proceeds by heredity as well as by variation, by stabilizing custom as well as by experimental innovation, it was to be expected that the religious roots of philosophy would form as well as feed it, and there should remain in it, to the very end, a vigorous element of theology. Two currents run side by side in the history of Greek philosophy: one naturalistic, the other mystical. The latter stemmed from Pythagoras, and ran through Parmenides, Heracleitus, Plato, and Cleanthes to Plotinus and St. Paul; the other had its first world figure in Thales, and passed down through Anaximander, Xenophanes, Protagoras, Hippocrates, and Democritus to Epicurus and Lucretius. Now and then some great spirit—Socrates, Aristotle, Marcus Aurelius—merged the two currents in an attempt to do justice to the unformulable complexity of life. But even in these men the dominant strain, characteristic of Greek thought, was the love and pursuit of reason.

Thales was born about 640, probably at Miletus, reputedly of Phoenician parentage,[21] and derived much of his education from Egypt and the Near East; here, as if personified, we see the transit of culture from East to West. He appears to have engaged in business only so far as to provide himself with the ordinary goods of life; everyone knows the story of his successful speculation in oil presses.* For the rest he gave himself to study, with the absorbed devotion suggested by the tale of his falling into a ditch while watching the stars. Despite his solitude, he interested himself in the affairs of his city, knew the dictator Thrasybulus intimately, and advocated the federation of the Ionian states for united defense against Lydia and Persia.[23]

To him tradition unanimously ascribed the introduction of mathematical and astronomical science into Greece. Antiquity told how, in Egypt, he calculated the heights of the pyramids by measuring their shadows when a man's shadow equaled his height. Returning to Ionia, Thales pursued the fascinatingly logical study of geometry as a deductive science, and demon-

* Let Aristotle tell the story: "They say that Thales, perceiving by his skill in astrology (astronomy) that there would be great plenty of olives that year, while it was yet winter hired at a low price all the oil presses in Miletus and Chios, there being no one to bid against him. But when the season came for making oil, many persons wanting them, he all at once let them upon what terms he pleased; and raising a large sum of money by that means, convinced them that it was easy for philosophers to be rich if they chose it."[22]

strated several of the theorems later collected by Euclid.* As these theorems founded Greek geometry, so his studies of astronomy established that science for Western civilization, and disentangled it from its Oriental associations with astrology. He made several minor observations, and startled all Ionia by successfully predicting an eclipse of the sun for May 28, 585 B.C.,[25] probably on the basis of Egyptian records and Babylonian calculations. For the rest his theory of the universe was not appreciably superior to the current cosmology of the Egyptians and the Jews. The world, he thought, was a hemisphere resting on an endless expanse of water, and the earth was a flat disk floating on the flat side of the interior of this hemisphere. We are reminded of Goethe's remark that a man's vices (or errors) are common to him with his epoch, but his virtues (or insights) are his own.

As some Greek myths made Oceanus the father of all creation,[26] so Thales made water the first principle of all things, their original form and their final destiny. Perhaps, says Aristotle, he had come to this opinion from observing "that the nutriment of everything is moist, and that . . . the seeds of everything have a moist nature; . . . and that from which everything is generated is always its first principle."[27] Or perhaps he believed that water was the most primitive or fundamental of the three forms—gas, liquid, solid—into which, theoretically, all substances may be changed. The significance of his thought lay not in reducing all things to water, but in reducing all things to one; here was the first monism in recorded history. Aristotle describes Thales' view as materialistic; but Thales adds that every particle of the world is alive, that matter and life are inseparable and one, that there is an immortal "soul" in plants and metals as well as in animals and men; the vital power changes form, but never dies.[28] Thales was wont to say that there is no essential difference between living and dead. When someone sought to nettle him by asking why, then, he chose life instead of death, he answered, "Because there is no difference."[29]

In his old age he received by common consent the title of *sophos*, or sage; and when Greece came to name its Seven Wise Men it placed Thales first. Being asked what was very difficult, he answered, in a famous apophthegm, "To know thyself." Asked what was very easy, he answered, "To give advice." To the question, what is God? he replied, "That which has neither beginning nor end." Asked how men might live most virtuously

* That a circle is bisected by its diameter; that the angles at the base of any isosceles triangle are "similar" (i.e., equal); that the angle in a semicircle is a right angle; that the opposite angles formed by two intersecting straight lines are equal; that two triangles having two angles and one side respectively equal are themselves equal.[24]

and justly, he answered, "If we never do ourselves what we blame in others."[30] He died, says Diogenes Laertius,[31] "while present as a spectator at a gymnastic contest, being worn out with heat and thirst and weakness, for he was very old."

Thales, says Strabo,[32] was the first of those who wrote on *physiologia*—i.e., on the science of nature (*physis*), or on the principle of being and development in things. His work was vigorously advanced by his pupil Anaximander, who, though he lived from 611 to 549 B.C., expounded a philosophy surprisingly like that which Herbert Spencer, trembling before his own originality, published in A.D. 1860. The first principle, says Anaximander, was a vast Indefinite-Infinite (*apeiron*), a boundless mass possessing no specific qualities, but developing, by its inherent forces, into all the varied realities of the universe.* This animate and eternal but impersonal and unmoral Infinite is the only God in Anaximander's system; it is the unvarying and everlasting One, as distinguished from the mutable evanescent Many of the world of things. (Here stems the metaphysics of the Eleatic School—that only the eternal One is real.) From this characterless Infinite are born new worlds in endless succession, and to it in endless succession they return as they evolve and die. In the primordial Infinite all opposites are contained—hot and cold, moist and dry, liquid and solid and gas . . . ; in development these potential qualities become actual, and make diverse and definite things; in dissolution these opposed qualities are again resolved into the Infinite. (A source for Heracleitus as well as for Spencer.) In this rise and fall of worlds the various elements struggle with one another, and encroach upon each other as hostile opposites. For this opposition they pay with dissolution; "Things perish into those from which they have been born."

Anaximander, though he too can be guilty of astronomic *bizarreries* forgivable in an age without instruments, advanced on Thales by conceiving the earth as a cylinder freely suspended in the center of the universe, and sustained only by being equidistant from all things.[34] The sun, moon, and stars, he thought, moved in circles around the earth. To illustrate all this Anaximander, probably on Babylonian models, constructed at Sparta a *gnomon*, or sundial, on which he showed the movement of the planets, the

* Cf. Spencer's definition of evolution as substantially a change from "indefinite, incoherent homogeneity to a definite, coherent heterogeneity."[33]

obliquity of the ecliptic,* and the succession of solstices, equinoxes, and seasons.[35] With the collaboration of his fellow Milesian, Hecataeus, he established geography as a science by drawing—apparently upon a tablet of brass—the first known map of the inhabited world.†

In its earliest form, said Anaximander, the earth was in a fluid state; external heat dried some of it into land, and evaporated some of it into clouds; while the variations of heat in the atmosphere so formed caused the motions of the winds. Living organisms arose by gradual stages from the original moisture; land animals were at first fishes, and only with the drying of the earth did they acquire their present shape. Man too was once a fish; he could not at his earliest appearance have been born as now, for he would have been too helpless to secure his food, and would have been destroyed.[36]

A slighter figure is Anaximander's pupil Anaximenes, whose first principle was air. All other elements are produced from air by rarefaction, which gives fire, or by condensation, which forms progressively wind, cloud, water, earth, and stone. As the soul, which is air, holds us together, so the air, or *pneuma*, of the world is its pervasive spirit, breath, or God.[37] Here was an idea that would ride out all the storms of Greek philosophy, and find a haven in Stoicism and Christianity.

This heyday of Miletus produced not only the earliest philosophy, but the earliest prose, and the first historiography, in Greece.‡ Poetry seems natural to a nation's adolescence, when imagination is greater than knowledge, and a strong faith gives personality to the forces of nature in field, wood, sea, and sky; it is hard for poetry to avoid animism, or for animism to avoid poetry. Prose is the voice of knowledge freeing itself from imagination and faith; it is the language of secular, mundane, "prosaic" affairs; it is the emblem of a nation's maturity, and the epitaph of its youth. Up to this time (600) nearly all Greek literature had taken a poetic form; education had transmitted in verse the lore and morals of the race; even early philosophers, like Xenophanes, Parmenides, and Empedocles, gave their

* The ecliptic (so called because eclipses of the sun and moon take place in it) is the great circle made by the apparent annual path of the sun through the heavens. Since the plane of this circle or ecliptic is also the plane of the earth's orbit, the obliquity of the ecliptic is the oblique angle (about 23°) between the plane of the earth's equator and the plane of its orbit around the sun.

† The Egyptians had drawn maps, but of limited districts.

‡ The wise reader will always supply the word *known* after such words as *earliest* and *first*.

systems a poetic dress. Just as science was at first a form of philosophy, struggling to free itself from the general, the speculative, the unverifiable, so philosophy was at first a form of poetry, striving to free itself from mythology, animism, and metaphor.

It was therefore an event when Pherecydes and Anaximander expounded their doctrines in prose. Other men of the age, whom the Greeks called *logographoi*—reason writers, prose writers—began to chronicle in the new medium the annals of their states; so Cadmus (550) wrote a chronicle of Miletus, Eugaeon wrote of Samos, Xanthus wrote of Lydia. Towards the end of the century Hecataeus of Miletus advanced both history and geography in epochal works—the *Historiai*, or Inquiries, and the *Ges periodos*, or Circuit of the Earth. The latter divided the known planet into two continents, Europe and Asia, and included Egypt in Asia; if (as many doubt) the existing fragments are genuine, it was especially informative about Egypt, and provided a rich field for unacknowledged poaching by Herodotus. The *Histories* began with a skeptical blast: "I write what I consider to be the truth; for the traditions of the Greeks seem to me many and ridiculous." Hecataeus accepted Homer as history, and swallowed some tales with his eyes shut; nevertheless he made an honest effort to distinguish fact from myth, to trace real genealogies, and to arrive at a credible history of the Greeks. Greek historiography was old when the "Father of History" was born.

To Hecataeus and the other *logographoi* who appeared in this age in most of the cities and colonies of Hellas, *historia** meant any inquiry into the facts of any matter, and was applied to science and philosophy as well as to historiography in the modern sense. The term had a skeptical connotation in Ionia; it signified that the miracle stories of gods and demigod heroes were to be replaced with secular records of events, and rational interpretations of causes and effects. In Hecataeus the process begins; in Herodotus it advances; in Thucydides it is complete.

The poverty of Greek prose before Herodotus is bound up with the conquest and impoverishment of Miletus in the very generation in which prose literature began. Internal decay followed the custom of history in smoothing the path of the conqueror. The growth of wealth and luxury made epicureanism fashionable, while stoicism and patriotism seemed antiquated and absurd; it became a byword among the Greeks that "once upon a time the Milesians were brave."[88] Competition for the goods of the earth

* From *histor* or *istor*, knowing; a euphonism for *id-tor*, from the root *id* in *eidenai*, to know; cf. our *wit* and *wisdom*. *Story* is a shortened form of *history*.

became keener as the old faith lost its power to mitigate class strife by giving scruples to the strong and consolations to the weak. The rich, supporting an oligarchic dictatorship, became a united party against the poor, who wanted a democracy. The poor secured control of the government, expelled the rich, collected the remaining children of the rich on threshing floors, set oxen upon them, and had them trampled to death. The rich returned, recaptured power, coated the leaders of the democracy with pitch, and then burnt them alive.[39] *De nobis fabula narrabitur.* When, about 560, Croesus began to subject to Lydian rule the Greek coast of Asia from Cnidus to the Hellespont, Miletus saved its independence by refusing to help her sister states. But in 546 Cyrus conquered Lydia, and without much difficulty absorbed the faction-torn cities of Ionia into the Persian Empire. The great age of Miletus was over. Science and philosophy, in the history of states, reach their height after decadence has set in; wisdom is a harbinger of death.

2. *Polycrates of Samos*

Across the bay from Miletus, near the outlets of the Maeander, stood the modest town of Myus, and the more famous city of Priene. There, in the sixth century, lived Bias, one of the Seven Wise Men. As Hermippus said, the Seven Wise Men were seventeen; for different Greeks made different lists of them, most frequently agreeing upon Thales, Solon, Bias, Pittacus of Mytilene, Periander of Corinth, Chilon of Sparta, and Cleobolus of Lindus in Rhodes. Greece respected wisdom as India respected holiness, as Renaissance Italy respected artistic genius, as young America naturally respects economic enterprise. The heroes of Greece were not saints, or artists, or millionaires, but sages; and her most honored sages were not theorists but men who had made their wisdom function actively in the world. The sayings of these men became proverbial among the Greeks, and were in some cases inscribed in the temple of Apollo at Delphi. People liked to quote, for example, the remarks of Bias—that the most unfortunate of men is he who has not learned how to bear misfortune; that men ought to order their lives as if they were fated to live both a long and a short time; and that "wisdom should be cherished as a means of traveling from youth to old age, for it is more lasting than any other possession."[40]

West of Priene lay Samos, second largest of Ionia's isles. The capital stood on the southeastern shore; and as one entered the well-protected harbor, passing the famous red ships of the Samian fleet, the city rose as if in tiers on the hill: first the wharves and shops, then the homes, then the fortress-acropolis and the great temple of Hera; and behind these a succession of ranges and peaks rising to a height of five thousand feet. It was a sight to stir the patriotism of every Samian soul.

The zenith of Samos came in the third quarter of the sixth century, under Polycrates. The revenues from the busy port enabled the dictator to end a dangerous period of unemployment by a program of public works that called forth the admiration of Herodotus. The greatest of these undertakings was a tunnel that carried the city's water supply 4500 feet through a mountain; we catch some idea of Greek ability in mathematics and engineering when we learn that the two bores, begun at opposite ends, met in the center with an error of eighteen feet in direction and nine in height.*[41]

Samos had been a cultured center long before Polycrates. Here, about 590, the fabulous Aesop had been the Phrygian slave of the Greek Iadmon. An unconfirmed tradition tells how Iadmon freed him, how Aesop traveled widely, met Solon, lived at the court of Croesus, embezzled the money that Croesus had commissioned him to distribute at Delphi, and met a violent death at the hands of the outraged Delphians.[42] His fables, largely taken from Eastern sources, were well known at Athens in the classic age; Socrates, says Plutarch, put them into verse.[43] Though their form was Oriental, their philosophy was characteristically Greek. "Sweet are the beauties of Nature, the earth and sea, the stars, and the orbs of sun and moon. But all the rest is fear and pain,"[44] especially if one embezzles. We can still meet him in the Vatican, where a cup from the Periclean age represents him with half-bald head and Vandyke beard, listening profitably to a merry fox.[45]

The great Pythagoras was born in Samos, but left it in 529 to live at Crotona in Italy. Anacreon came from Teos to sing Polycrates' charms and to tutor his son. The greatest figure at the court was the artist Theodorus, the Leonardo of Samos, Jack-of-all-trades and master of most. The Greeks ascribed to him, perhaps as a cloture on research, the invention of the level, the square, and the lathe;[46] he was a skilled engraver of gems, a metalworker, stoneworker, woodworker, sculptor, and architect. He took part in designing the second temple of Artemis at Ephesus, built a vast *skias*, or pavilion, for Sparta's public assemblies, helped to introduce clay modeling

* Similar enterprises today make both ends meet with an error of only a few inches, or none.

into Greece, and shared with Rhoecus the honor of bringing from Egypt or Assyria to Samos the hollow casting of bronze.[47] Before Theodorus the Greeks had made crude bronze statues by riveting plates of the metal to a "bridge" of wood;[48] now they were prepared to produce such masterpieces in bronze as the *Charioteer of Delphi* and the *Discus Thrower* of Myron. Samos was famous also for its pottery; Pliny recommends it to us by telling us that the priests of Cybele would use nothing but Samian potsherds in depriving themselves of their manhood.[49]

3. *Heracleitus of Ephesus*

Across the Caystrian Gulf from Samos stood Ionia's most famous city—Ephesus. Founded about 1000 by colonists from Athens, it prospered by tapping the trade of both the Cayster and the Maeander. Its population, its religion, and its art contained a strong Eastern element; the Artemis worshiped there began and ended as an Oriental goddess of motherhood and fertility. Her renowned temple had many deaths, and almost as many resurrections. On the site of an ancient altar twice built and twice destroyed, the first temple was erected about 600, and was probably the earliest important edifice in the Ionic style. The second temple was raised about 540, partly through the generosity of Croesus; Paeonius of Ephesus, Theodorus of Samos, and Demetrius, a priest of the shrine, shared in designing it. It was the largest Greek temple that had yet been built, and was ranked without dispute among the Seven Wonders of the World.*

The city was known not only for its temple but for its poets, its philosophers, and its expensively gowned women.[51] Here, as early as 690 B.C., lived Callinus, the earliest known elegiac poet of Greece. Far greater and uglier was Hipponax, who, towards 550, composed poems so coarse in subject, obscure in language, pointed in wit, and refined in metrical style, that all Greece began to talk about him, and all Ephesus to hate him. He was short and thin, lame and deformed, and completely disagreeable. Woman, he tells us, in one of his surviving fragments, brings two days of happiness to a man—"one when he marries her, the other when he buries her."[52] He was a ruthless satirist, and lampooned every notable in Ephesus from the

* The other six were the Hanging Gardens of Babylon, the Pharos at Alexandria, the Colossus of Rhodes, the Pheidian Zeus at Olympia, the tomb of Mausolus at Halicarnassus, and the Pyramids. Pliny describes the second temple as 425 feet long by 225 feet wide, with 127 columns sixty feet in height—several of them adorned or disfigured with reliefs.[50] Completed in 420 B.C. after more than a century of labor, it was destroyed by fire in 356.

lowest criminal to the highest priest of the temple. When two sculptors, Bupalus and Athenis, exhibited an elegant caricature of him he attacked them with such corrosive verse that some of it has proved more durable than their stone, and sharper than the teeth of time. "Hold my coat," says a typically polished morsel; "I shall hit Bupalus in the eye. I am ambidextrous, and I never miss my aim."[53] Tradition said that Hipponax died by suicide; but perhaps this was only a universal wish.

The most illustrious son of Ephesus was Heracleitus the Obscure. Born about 530, he belonged to a noble family, and thought that democracy was a mistake. "There are many bad but few good," he said (111*), and "one man to me is as ten thousand if he be the best" (113). But even aristocrats did not please him, nor women, nor scholars. "Abundant learning," he wrote with genial particularity, "does not form the mind; if it did it would have instructed Hesiod, Pythagoras, Xenophanes and Hecataeus" (16). "For the only real wisdom is to know that idea which by itself will govern everything on every occasion" (19). So he went off, like a Chinese sage, to live in the mountains and brood over the one idea that would explain all things. Disdaining to expound his conclusions in words intelligible to common men, and seeking in obscurity of life and speech some safety from individuality-destroying parties and mobs, he expressed his views in pithy and enigmatical apophthegms *On Nature*, which he deposited in the temple of Artemis for the mystification of posterity.

Heracleitus has been represented in modern literature as building his philosophy around the notion of change; but the extant fragments hardly support this interpretation. Like most philosophers he longed to find the One behind the Many, some mind-steadying unity and order amid the chaotic flux and multiplicity of the world. "All things are one," he said, as passionately as Parmenides (1); the problem of philosophy was, what is this one? Heracleitus answered, Fire. Perhaps he was influenced by the Persian worship of fire; probably, as we may judge from his identification of Fire with Soul and God, he used the term symbolically as well as literally, to mean energy as well as fire; the fragments permit no certainty. "This world . . . was made neither by a god nor by man, but it ever was, and is, and shall be, ever-living Fire, in measures being kindled and in measures going out" (20). Everything is a form of Fire, either in Fire's "downward path" through progressive condensation into moisture, water,

* The parenthetical numbers refer to the fragments of Heracleitus as numbered by Bywater.

and earth; or in its "upward path" from earth to water to moisture to Fire.*[54]

Though he finds a consoling constancy in the Eternal Fire, Heracleitus is troubled by its endless transformations; and the second nucleus of his thought is the eternity and ubiquity of change. He finds nothing static in the universe, the mind, or the soul. Nothing is, everything becomes; no condition persists unaltered, even for the smallest moment; everything is ceasing to be what it was, and is becoming what it will be. Here is a new emphasis in philosophy: Heracleitus does not merely ask, like Thales, what things are, but, like Anaximander, Lucretius, and Spencer, how they became what they are; and he suggests, like Aristotle, that a study of the second question is the best approach to the first. The extant apophthegms do not contain the famous formula, *panta rei, ouden menei*—"all things flow, nothing abides"; but antiquity is unanimous in attributing it to Heracleitus.[56] "You cannot step twice into the same river, for other waters are ever flowing on to you" (41); "we are and we are not" (81); here, as in Hegel, the universe is a vast Becoming. Multiplicity, variety, change are as real as unity, identity, being; the Many are as real as the One.[57] The Many *are* the One; every change is a passage of things towards or from the condition of Fire. The One *is* the Many; in the very heart of Fire flickers restless change.

Hence Heracleitus passes to the third element in his philosophy—the unity of opposites, the interdependence of contraries, the harmony of strife. "God is day and night, winter and summer, war and peace, surfeit and hunger" (36). "Good and bad are the same; goodness and badness are one" (57-8); "life and death are the same; so are waking and sleeping, youth and age" (78). All these contraries are stages in a fluctuating movement, moments of the ever-changing Fire; each member in an opposing pair is necessary to the meaning and existence of the other; reality is the tension and interplay, the alternation and exchange, the unity and har-

* Possibly Heracleitus had in mind a nebular hypothesis: the world begins as fire (or heat or energy), it becomes gas or moisture, which is precipitated as water, whose chemical residue, after evaporation, forms the solids of the earth.[55] Water and earth (liquid and solid) are two stages of one process, two forms of one reality (25). "All things are exchanged for Fire, and Fire for all things" (22). All change is a "pathway down or up," a passage from one to another form—now more, now less, condensed—of energy or Fire. "The path upwards and downwards is one and the same" (69); rarefaction and condensation are movements in an eternal oscillation of change; all things are formed on the downward and condensing or on the upward and rarefying pathway of reality from Fire and back to Fire; all forms are modes of one underlying energy. In Spinoza's language: Fire or energy is the eternal and omnipresent substance, or basic principle; condensation and rarefaction (the downward and upward paths) are its attributes; its modes or specific forms are the visible things of the world.

mony, of opposites. "They understand not how that which is at variance with itself agrees with itself. There sits attunement of opposite tensions, like that of the bow and the harp" (45). As the tension of the string, loosened or drawn taut, creates the harmony of vibrations called music or a note, so the alternation and strife of opposites creates the essence and meaning and harmony of life and change. In the struggle of organism with organism, of man with man, of man with woman, of generation with generation, of class with class, of nation with nation, of idea with idea, of creed with creed, the warring opposites are the warp and woof on the loom of life, working at cross-purposes to produce the unseen unity and hidden concord of the whole. "From things that differ comes the fairest attunement" (46); any lover will understand.

All three of these principles—fire, change, and the tension unity of contraries—enter into Heracleitus' conception of soul and God. He smiles at men who "seek in vain to purify themselves from blood-guiltiness by defiling themselves with blood" (130), or who "offer prayers to these statues here—as if one should try to converse with houses; such men know nothing of the real nature of gods" (126). Nor will he admit personal immortality; man too, like everything else, is a changeful and fitful flame, "kindled and put out like a light in the night" (77). Even so, man is Fire; the soul or vital principle is part of the eternal energy in all things; and as such it never dies. Death and birth are arbitrary points taken in the current of things by the human analyzing mind; but from the impartial standpoint of the universe they are merely phases in the endless change of forms. At every instant some part of us dies while the whole lives; at every second one of us dies while Life lives. Death is a beginning as well as an ending; birth is an ending as well as a beginning. Our words, our thoughts, even our morals, are prejudices, and represent our interests as parts or groups; philosophy must see things in the light of the whole. "To God all things are beautiful and good and right; men deem some things wrong and some right" (61).

As the soul is a passing tongue of the endlessly changing flame of life, so God is the everlasting Fire, the indestructible energy of the world. He is the unity binding all opposites, the harmony of all tensions, the sum and meaning of all strife. This Divine Fire, like life (for the two are everywhere and one), is always altering its form, always passing upward or downward on the ladder of change, always consuming and remaking things; indeed, some distant day, "Fire will judge and convict all things" (26), destroy them, and make way for new forms, in a Last Judgment or cosmic catastrophe. Nevertheless, the operations of the Undying Fire are not without sense and order; if we could understand the world as a whole we should see in it a vast impersonal wisdom, a Logos or Reason or Word (65); and we should try to mold our lives into accord with this way of Nature, this law of the universe, this wisdom or orderly energy which is God (91). "It is wise to hearken not to me, but to the Word" (1), to seek and follow the infinite reason of the whole.

When Heracleitus applies to ethics these four basic concepts of his thought—energy, change, the unity of opposites, and the reason of the whole—he illuminates all life and conduct. Energy harnessed to reason, wedded to order, is the greatest good. Change is not an evil but a boon; "in change one finds rest; it is weariness to be always toiling at the same things and always beginning afresh" (72-3). The mutual necessity of contraries makes intelligible and therefore forgivable the strife and suffering of life. "For men to get all they wish is not the better thing; it is disease that makes health pleasant; evil, good; hunger, surfeit; toil, rest" (104). He rebukes those who desire an end of strife in the world (43); without this tension of opposites there would be no "attunement," no weaving of the living web, no development. Harmony is not an ending of conflict, it is a tension in which neither element definitely wins, but both function indispensably (like the radicalism of youth and the conservatism of old age). The struggle for existence is necessary in order that the better may be separated from the worse, and may generate the highest. "Strife is the father of all and the king of all; some he has marked out to be gods, and some to be men; some he has made slaves, and some free" (44). In the end, "strife is justice" (62); the competition of individuals, groups, species, institutions, and empires constitutes nature's supreme court, from whose verdict there is no appeal.

All in all, the philosophy of Heracleitus, concentrated for us now in 130 fragments, is among the major products of the Greek mind. The theory of the Divine Fire passed down into Stoicism; the notion of a final conflagration was transmitted through Stoicism to Christianity; the Logos, or reason in nature, became in Philo and Christian theology the Divine Word, the personified wisdom with which or through whom God creates and governs all things; in some measure it prepared for the early modern view of natural law. Virtue as obedience to nature became a catchword of Stoicism; the unity of opposites revived vigorously in Hegel; the idea of change came back into its own with Bergson. The conception of strife and struggle as determining all things reappears in Darwin, Spencer, and

Nietzsche—who carries on, after twenty-four centuries, the war of Heracleitus against democracy.

We know almost nothing of Heracleitus' life; and of his death we have only an unsupported story in Diogenes Laertius, which may illustrate the prosaic ends to which our poetry may return:

> And at last becoming a complete misanthrope, he used to spend his time walking about the mountains, feeding on grasses and plants; and in consequence of these habits he was attacked by the dropsy, and so he returned to the city, and asked the physicians, in a riddle, whether they were able to produce a drought after wet weather. And as they did not understand him, he shut himself up in a stable for oxen, and covered himself with cow dung, hoping to cause the wet to evaporate from him by the warmth that this produced. And as he did himself no good in this way, he died, having lived seventy years.[58]

4. *Anacreon of Teos*

Colophon, a few miles north of Ephesus, derived its name, presumably, from the hill on whose slope it rose.* Xenophanes the anticlerical, born among them about 576, described the Colophonians as "richly clothed in purple garments, proud of their luxuriously dressed hair wet with costly and sweet-smelling oils"; vanity has a long history.[60] Here, and perhaps at Smyrna, the poet Mimnermus (610) sang, for a people already infected with the languid pessimism of the East, his melancholy odes of fleeting youth and love. He lost his heart to Nanno, the girl who accompanied his songs with the plaintive obbligato of the flute; and when she rejected his love (perhaps on the ground that a poet married is a poet dead), he immortalized her with a sheaf of delicate elegiac verse.

> We blossom like the leaves that come in Spring,
> What time the sun begins to flame and glow,
> And in the brief span of youth's gladdening
> Nor good nor evil from the gods we know;
> But always at the goal dark spirits stand
> Holding, one grievous Age, one Death, within her hand.[61]

---

* Gk. *kolophon,* hill; cf. Latin *collis,* Eng. *hill.* Because the cavalry of the city was famous for giving the "finishing touch" to a defeated force, the word *kolophon* became in Greek a synonym for the final stroke, and passed into our language as a publisher's symbol, originally placed at the end of a book.[59]

A more famous poet lived a century later in the near-by town of Teos. Anacreon wandered much, but in Teos he was born (563) and died (478). Many a court sought him, for among his contemporaries only Simonides rivaled him in fame. We find him joining a band of emigrants to Thracian Abdera, serving as soldier for a campaign or two, abandoning his shield in the poetic fashion of the time, and thereafter content to brandish a pen; spending some years at the court of Polycrates in Samos; brought thence in official state, on a fifty-oared galley, to grace the palace of Hipparchus in Athens; and at last, after the Persian War, returning to Teos to ease his declining years with song and drink. He paid for his excesses by living to a great age, and died at eighty-five, we are told, of a grape pit sticking in his throat.[62]

Alexandria knew five books of Anacreon, but only disordered couplets remain. His subjects were wine, women, and boys; his manner was one of polished banter in tripping iambics. No topic seemed impure in his impeccable diction, or gross in his delicate verse. Instead of the vulgar virulence of Hipponax, or the trembling intensity of Sappho, Anacreon offered the urbane chatter of a court poet who would play Horace to any Augustus that pleased his fancy and paid for his wine. Athenaeus thinks that his tipsy songs and changeful loves were a pose;[63] perhaps Anacreon hid his fidelities that he might be interesting to women, and concealed his sobriety to augment his fame. A choice legend tells how, in his cups, he stumbled against a child and abused it with harsh words, and how, in his age, he fell in love with this lad and did penance with doting praise.[64] His Eros was ambidextrous, and reached impartially for either sex; but in his later years he gallantly gave the preference to women. "Lo, now," says a pretty fragment, "golden-haired Love strikes me with his purple ball, and calls me forth to play with a motley-slippered maid. But she hails from lofty Lesbos, and so finds fault with my white hair, and goes a-searching for other prey."[65] A wit of a later age wrote for Anacreon's grave a revealing epitaph:

> All-enchanting nurse of the wine, O Vine, grow lush and long above the tomb of Anacreon. So shall the tippling friend of neat liquor, who thrummed in night-long revel the lute of a lover of lads, yet sport above his buried head the glorious cluster of some teeming bough, and be wet evermore with the dew whose delicious scent was the breath of his mild old mouth.[66]

5. *Chios, Smyrna, Phocaea*

From Teos the mainland staggers westward in vacillating bays and promontories until, across ten miles of sea, the traveler reaches Chios. Here, amid groves of figs and olives, and Anacreontic vines, Homer may have spent his youth. Wine making was a major industry in Chios, and used many slaves; in 431 the island had 30,000 freemen, 100,000 slaves.[67] Chios became a clearing-house for slaves; slave dealers bought the families of insolvent debtors from their creditors, and purchased boys to make eunuchs of them for the palaces of Lydia and Persia.[68] In the sixth century Drimachus led his fellow slaves in revolt, defeated all armies sent against him, established himself in a mountain fastness, levied toll upon the richer citizens by discriminating robbery, offered them "protection" for a consideration after our own fashion, terrified them into dealing more justly with their slaves, gave his voluntarily severed head to his friends so that they might claim the reward that had been promised for it, and was worshiped for centuries afterward as the patron deity of slaves:[69] here is an excellent epic for some Spartacus of the pen. Art and literature flourished amid the wealth and bondage of Chios; here the Homeridae, a guild and succession of bards, had their seat; here Ion the dramatist and Theopompus the historian would be born; here Glaucus (tradition said) discovered, about 560, the technique of welding iron; here Archermus and his sons, Bupalus and Athenis, made the finest statuary in sixth-century Greece.

Returning to the mainland, the traveler passes by the sites of Erythrae and Clazomenae—birthplace of Pericles' teacher and friend, Anaxagoras. Farther east, on a well-sheltered inlet, is Smyrna. Settled by Aeolians as far back as 1015[70] it was changed by immigration and conquest into an Ionian city. Already famous in the days of Achilles, sacked by Alyattes of Lydia about 600 B.C., destroyed again and again, and recently by the Greeks in A.D. 1924, Smyrna, rivaling Damascus in age, has known all the vicissitudes of history.* The remains of the ancient town suggest its rich and varied life; a gymnasium, an acropolis, a stadium, and a theater have been dug out of the earth. The avenues were broad and well paved; temples and palaces adorned them; the main street, called Golden, was famous throughout Greece.

The northernmost of Ionia's cities was Phocaea, still functioning as Fokia. The river Hermus connected it almost with Sardis itself, and gave it a lucrative advantage in the commerce of the Greeks with Lydia. Phocaean merchants undertook distant voyages in the search for markets; it was they who brought Greek culture to Corsica, and founded Marseilles.

---

* Today, under the name of Ismir (this and *Smyrna* are probably connected with the ancient trade in myrrh), it is the second city of Turkey in population, and the largest in Asia Minor.

Such were the Twelve Cities of Ionia, seen superficially as if in an hour's flight through space and time. Though they were too competitive and jealous to form a union for mutual defense, their citizens acknowledged some solidarity of background and interest, and met periodically on the promontory of Mycale near Priene, in the great festival of the Panionium. Thales begged them to form a sympolity in which every adult male would be a citizen both of his city and of a Panionian union; but commercial rivalries were too strong, and led rather to internecine wars than to political unity. Hence, when the Persian attack came (546-5), the alliance improvised for defense proved rootlessly weak, and the Ionian cities came under the power of the Great King. Nevertheless this spirit of independence and rivalry gave to the Ionian communities the stimulus of competition and the zest of liberty. It was under these conditions that Ionia developed science, philosophy, history, and the Ionic capital, while at the same time it produced so many poets that the sixth century in Hellas seems almost as fertile as the fifth. When Ionia fell her cities bequeathed their culture to the Athens that had fought to save them, and transmitted to it the intellectual leadership of Greece.

V. SAPPHO OF LESBOS

Above the Ionian Dodecapolis lay the twelve cities of mainland Aeolis, settled by Aeolians and Achaeans from northern Greece soon after the fall of Troy had opened Asia Minor to Greek immigration. Most of these cities were small, and played a modest role in history; but the Aeolian isle of Lesbos rivaled the Ionian centers in wealth, refinement, and literary genius. Its volcanic soil made the island a very garden of orchards and vines. Of its five cities Mytilene was the greatest, almost as rich, through its commerce, as Miletus, Samos, and Ephesus. Towards the end of the seventh century a coalition of the mercantile classes with the poorer citizens overthrew the landed aristocracy, and made the brave, rough Pittacus dictator for ten years, with powers like those of his friend and fellow Wise Man, Solon. The aristocracy conspired to recapture power, but Pittacus foiled them and exiled their leaders, including Alcaeus and Sappho, first from Mytilene and then from Lesbos itself.

Alcaeus was a roistering firebrand who mingled politics with poetry and made every other lyric raise the tocsin of revolt. Of aristocratic birth, he attacked Pittacus with a lusty scurrility that merited the crown of banishment. He molded his own poetic forms, to which posterity gave the name "alcaics"; and every stanza, we are told, had melody and charm. For a while he sang of war, and described his home as hung with martial trophies and accouterments;[71] however, when his own chance for heroism came he threw away his shield, fled like Archilochus, and complimented himself lyrically on the valor of his discretion. Occasionally he sang of love, but dearest to his pen was the wine for which Lesbos was as famous as for its poetry. *Nun chre methusthen,* he advises us: *nunc bibamus*, let us drink deeply; in summer to cool our thirst, in autumn to put a bright color upon death, in winter to warm our blood, in spring to celebrate nature's resurrection.

> The rain of Zeus descends, and from high heaven
>   A storm is driven,
> And on the running water-brooks the cold
>   Lays icy hold.
> Then up! beat down the winter, make the fire
>   Blaze higher and higher;
> Mix wine as sweet as honey of the bee
>   Abundantly;
> Then drink, with comfortable wool around
>   Your temples bound.
> We must not yield our hearts to woe, or wear
>   With wasting care;
> For grief will profit us no whit, my friend,
>   Nor nothing mend;
> But this is our best medicine, with wine fraught
>   To cast out thought.[72]

It was his misfortune—though he bore it with lighthearted unconsciousness—to have among his contemporaries the most famous of Greek women. Even in her lifetime all Greece honored Sappho. "One evening over the wine," says Stobaeus, "Execestides, the nephew of Solon, sang a song of Sappho's which his uncle liked so much that he bade the boy teach it to him; and when one of the company asked, 'What for?' he answered, 'I want to learn it and die!' "[73] Socrates, perhaps hoping for similar lenience, called her "The Beautiful," and Plato wrote about her an ecstatic epigram:

> Some say there are Nine Muses. How careless they are!
> Behold, Sappho of Lesbos is the Tenth![74]

"Sappho was a marvelous woman," said Strabo; "for in all the time of which we have record I do not know of any woman who could rival her even in a slight degree in the matter of poetry."[75] As the ancients meant Homer when they said "the Poet," so all the Greek world knew whom men signified when they spoke of "the Poetess."

Psappha, as she called herself in her soft Aeolic dialect, was born at Eresus, on Lesbos, about 612; but her family moved to Mytilene when she was still a child. In 593 she was among the conspiring aristocrats whom Pittacus banished to the town of Pyrrha; already at nineteen she was playing a part in public life through politics or poetry. She was not known for beauty: her figure was small and frail, her hair and eyes and skin were darker than the Greeks desired;[76] but she had the charm of daintiness, delicacy, refinement, and a brilliant mind that was not too sophisticated to conceal her tenderness. "My heart," she says, "is like that of a child."[77] We know from her verses that she was of a passionate nature, one whose words, says Plutarch, "were mingled with flames";[78] a certain sensuous quality gave body to the enthusiasms of her mind. Atthis, her favorite pupil, spoke of her as dressed in saffron and purple, and garlanded with flowers. She must have been attractive in her minuscule way, for Alcaeus, exiled with her to Pyrrha, soon sent her an invitation to romance. "Violet-crowned, pure, sweet-smiling Sappho, I want to say something to you, but shame prevents me." Her answer was less ambiguous than his proposal: "If thy wishes were fair and noble, and thy tongue designed not to utter what is base, shame would not cloud thine eyes, but thou wouldst speak thy just desires."[79] The poet sang her praises in odes and serenades, but we hear of no further intimacy between them.

Perhaps they were separated by Sappho's second exile. Pittacus, fearing her maturing pen, banished her now to Sicily, probably in the year 591, when one would have thought her still a harmless girl. About this time she married a rich merchant of Andros; some years later she writes: "I have a little daughter, like a golden flower, my darling Cleis, for whom I would not take all Lydia, nor lovely Lesbos."[80] She could afford to reject the wealth of Lydia, having inherited that of her husband on his early death. After five years of exile she returned to Lesbos, and became a leader of the island's society and intellect. We catch the glamour of luxury in one of her surviving fragments: "But I, be it known, love soft living, and for me brightness and beauty belong to the desire of the sun."[81] She became deeply attached to her young brother Charaxus, and was vexed to her finger tips when, on one of his mercantile journeys to Egypt, he fell in love with the courtesan Doricha, and, ignoring his sister's entreaties, married her.[82]

Meanwhile Sappho too had felt the fire. Eager for an active life, she had opened a school for young women, to whom she taught poetry, music, and dancing; it was the first "finishing school" in history. She called her students not pupils but hetairai—companions; the word had not yet acquired a promiscuous connotation. Husbandless, Sappho fell in love with one after another of these girls. "Love," says one fragment, "has shaken my mind as a down-rushing wind that falls upon the oak-trees."[83] "I loved you, Atthis, long ago," says another fragment, "when my own girlhood was still all flowers, and you seemed to me an awkward little child." But then Atthis accepted the attentions of a youth from Mytilene, and Sappho expressed her jealousy with unmeasured passion in a poem preserved by Longinus and translated haltingly into "sapphic" meter by John Addington Symonds:

> Peer of gods he seemeth to me, the blissful
> Man who sits and gazes at thee before him,
> Close beside thee sits, and in silence hears thee
> Silverly speaking,
> Laughing love's low laughter. Oh, this, this only
> Stirs the troubled heart in my breast to tremble!
> For should I but see thee a little moment,
> Straight is my voice hushed;
> Yea, my tongue is broken, and through and through me,
> 'Neath the flesh, impalpable fire runs tingling.
> Nothing see mine eyes, and a voice of roaring
> Waves in my ear sounds;
> Sweat runs down in rivers, a tremor seizes
> All my limbs, and paler than grass in autumn,
> Caught by pains of menacing death, I falter,
> Lost in the love-trance.*[84]

Atthis' parents removed her from the school; and a letter ascribed to Sappho gives what may be her account of the parting.

> She (Atthis?) wept full sore to leave me behind, and said: "Alas, how sad our lot! Sappho, I swear 'tis against my will I leave you." And I answered her: "Go your way rejoicing, but remember me, for you know how I doted upon you. And if you remember not, oh, then I will remind you of what you forget, how dear and beautiful was the life we led together. For with many a garland of violets

* Swinburne has given us a better example of the meter, and described Sappho's love, in a profoundly beautiful poem called "Sapphics" ("All the night came not upon my eyelids"), in *Poems and Ballads*.

and sweet roses mingled you have decked your flowing locks by my side, and with many a woven necklet, made of a hundred blossoms, your dainty throat; and with unguent in plenty, both precious and royal, have you anointed your fair young skin in my bosom. And no hill was there, nor holy place, nor water-brook, whither we did not go; nor ever did the teeming noises of the early spring fill any wood with the medley-song of the nightingales but you wandered thither with me."[85]

After which, in the same manuscript, comes the bitter cry, "I shall never see Atthis again, and indeed I might as well be dead." This surely is the authentic voice of love, rising to a height of sincerity and beauty beyond good and evil.

The later scholars of antiquity debated whether these poems were expressions of "Lesbian love," or merely exercises of poetic fancy and impersonation. It is enough for us that they are poetry of the first order, tense with feeling, vivid with imagery, and perfect in speech and form. A fragment speaks of "the footfall of the flowering spring"; another of "Love the limb-loosener, the bitter-sweet torment"; another compares the unattainable love to "the sweet apple that reddens on the end of the bough, the very end of the bough, which the gatherers missed, nay missed not, but could not reach so far."[86] Sappho wrote of other topics than love, and used, even for our extant remains, half a hundred meters; and she herself set her poems to music for the harp. Her verse was collected into nine books, of some twelve thousand lines; six hundred lines survive, seldom continuous. In the year 1073 of our era the poetry of Sappho and Alcaeus was publicly burned by ecclesiastical authorities in Constantinople and Rome.[87] Then, in 1897, Grenfell and Hunt discovered, at Oxyrhynchus in the Fayum, coffins of papier-mâché, in whose making certain scraps of old books had been used; and on these scraps were some poems of Sappho.[88]

Male posterity avenged itself upon her by handing down or inventing the tale of how she died of unrequited love for a man. A passage in Suidas[89] tells how "the courtesan Sappho"—usually identified with the poetess—leaped to death from a cliff on the island of Leucas because Phaon the sailor would not return her love. Menander, Strabo, and others refer to the story, and Ovid recounts it in loving detail;[90] but it has many earmarks of legend, and must be left hovering nebulously between fiction and fact. In her later years, tradition said, Sappho had relearned the love of men. Among the Egyptian morsels is her touching reply to a proposal of marriage: "If my breasts were still capable of giving suck, and my womb were able to bear children, then to another marriage-bed not with trembling feet would I come. But now on my skin age has brought many lines, and Love hastens not to me with his gift of pain"—and she advises her suitor to seek a younger wife.[91] In truth we do not know when she died, or how; we know only that she left behind her a vivid memory of passion, poetry, and grace; and that she shone even above Alcaeus as the most melodious singer of her time. Gently, in a final fragment, she reproves those who would not admit that her song was finished:

> You dishonor the good gifts of the Muses, my children, when you say, "We will crown you, dear Sappho, best player of the clear, sweet lyre." Know you not that my skin is all wrinkled with age, and my hair is turned from black to white? . . . Surely as starry Night follows rose-armed Dawn and brings darkness to the ends of the earth, so Death tracketh everything living, and catcheth it in the end.[92]

VI. THE NORTHERN EMPIRE

North of Lesbos is little Tenedos, whose women were accounted by some ancient travelers to be the most beautiful in Greece.[93] Then one follows the adventurous Hellenes into the northern Sporades: to Imbros, and Lemnos, and Samothrace. The Milesians, seeking to control the Hellespont, founded, about 560, the still-living town of Abydos on its south shore;* here Leander and Byron swam the straits, and Xerxes' army crossed to Europe on a bridge of boats. Farther eastward the Phocaeans settled Lampsacus, birthplace of Epicurus. Within the Propontis lay two groups of islands: the Proconnesus, rich in the marble that gave the Propontis its current name, the Sea of Marmora; and the Arctonnesus, on whose southernmost tip the Milesians established in 757 the great port of Cyzicus. Along the coast rose one Greek city after another: Panormus, Dascylium, Apameia, Cius, Astacus, Chalcedon. Up through the Bosporus the Greeks advanced, hungry for metals, grain, and trade, founding Chrysopolis (now Scutari) and Nicopolis—"city of victory." Then they made their way along the southern shore of the Black Sea, depositing towns at Heracleia, Pontica, Tieum, and Sinope—a city splendidly adorned, says Strabo,[94] with gymnasium, agora, and shady colonnades; Diogenes the Cynic was not above being born here. Then Amisus, Oenoe, Tripolis, and Trapezus (Trebizond, Trabzon)—where Xenophon's Ten Thousand shouted with joy at the sight of the longed-for sea. The opening up of this region to Greek

* Nearly all the cities mentioned in this chapter are still in existence, though under altered names.

colonization, perhaps by Jason, later by the Ionians, gave the mother cities the same outlet for surplus population and trade, the same resources in food, silver, and gold, that the discovery of America gave to Europe at the beginning of modern times.[95]

Following the eastern shores of the Euxine northward into Medea's Colchis, the Greeks founded Phasis and Dioscurias, and Theodosia and Panticapaeum in the Crimea. Near the mouths of the Bug and the Dnieper they established the city of Olbia (Nikolaev); at the mouth of the Dniester, the town of Tyras; and on the Danube, Troesmis. Then, moving southward along the west shore of the Black Sea, they built the cities of Istrus (Constanta, Kustenje), Tomi (where Ovid died), Odessus (Varna), and Apollonia (Burgas). The historically sensitive traveler stands appalled at the antiquity of these living towns; but today's residents, engrossed in the tasks of their own generation, are undisturbed by the depth of the centuries that lie silent beneath them.

Then again at the Bosporus the Megarians, about 660, built Byzantium*—yesterday Constantinople, now Istanbul. Even before Pericles this strategic port was becoming what Napoleon would call it at the Peace of Tilsit—the key to Europe; in the third century B.C. Polybius described its maritime position as "more favorable to security and prosperity than that of any other city in the world known to us."[97] Byzantium grew rich by exacting tolls from passing vessels, and exporting to the Greek world the grain of southern Russia ("Scythia") and the Balkans, and the fish that were netted with shameful ease as they crowded through the narrow straits. It was its curving form, and the wealth derived from this fishing industry, that gave the city its later name, the "Golden Horn." Under Pericles Athens dominated Byzantine polities, levied tolls there to fill her treasury in time of emergency, and regulated the export of grain from the Black Sea as a contraband of war.[98]

Along the northern or Thracian shore of the Propontis the Greeks built towns at Selymbria, Perinthus (Eregli), Bisanthe, Callipolis (Gallipoli), and Sestus. Later settlements were established on the southwestern coast of Thrace at Aphrodisias, Aenus, and Abdera—where Leucippus and Democritus would propound the philosophy of atomistic materialism. Off the coast of Thrace lay the island of Thasos, "bare and ugly as a donkey's back in the sea," Archilochus described it,[99] but so rich in gold mines that their proceeds paid all the expenses of the government. On or near the eastern coast of Macedonia Greek goldseekers, chiefly Athenians, founded Neapolis and Amphipolis—whose capture by Philip would lead to the war in which Athens was to lose her liberty. Other Greeks, mostly from Chalcis and Eretria, conquered and named the three-fingered peninsula of Chalcidice, and by 700 had established thirty towns there,

* The name was probably taken from Byzas, a native king.[96]

several of them destined to play a role in Greek history: Stageirus (birthplace of Aristotle), Scione, Mende, Potidaea, Acanthus, Cleonae, Torone, and Olynthus—captured by Philip in 348 and known to us now through the oratory of Demosthenes. Recent excavations at Olynthus have unearthed a town of considerable extent, with many houses of two stories and some of twenty-five rooms. In the time of Philip Olynthus appears to have had 60,000 inhabitants; we may judge from this figure for a minor city the abounding fertility and energetic expansion of the pre-Periclean Greeks.

Finally, between Chalcidice and Euboea, Ionian migrants peopled the Euboean Isles—Gerontia, Polyaegos, Icos, Peparethos, Scandile, Scyros. The orbit of empire in east and north had come full turn, the circuit was complete; Greek enterprise had transformed the islands of the Aegean and the coasts of Asia Minor, the Hellespont, the Black Sea, Macedonia, and Thrace into a busy network of Hellenized cities, throbbing with agriculture, industry, trade, politics, literature, religion, philosophy, science, art, eloquence, chicanery, and venery. It only remained to conquer another Greece in the West, and build a bridge between ancient Hellas and the modern world.

CHAPTER VII

The Greeks in the West

I. THE SYBARITES

SKIRTING Sunium again, our ship of fancy, sailing westward, finds Cythera, island haunt of Aphrodite, and therefore the goal of Watteau's *Embarkation.** There, about A.D. 160, Pausanias saw "the most holy and ancient of all the temples that the Greeks have built to Aphrodite";[1] and there, in 1887, Schliemann dug its ruins out of the earth.[2] Cythera was the southernmost of the Ionian Islands that bordered the west coast of Greece, and so named because Ionian immigrants settled them; Zacynthos, Cephallenia, Ithaca, Leucas, Paxos, and Corcyra made the rest. Schliemann thought that Ithaca was the island of Odysseus, and vainly sought under its soil some confirmation of Homer's tale;[3] but Dörpfeld believed that Odysseus' home was on rocky Leucas. From the cliffs of Leucas, as an annual sacrifice to Apollo, the ancient Leucadians, says Strabo, were in the habit of hurling a human victim; but being men as well as theologians, they mercifully attached to him powerful birds whose wings might break his fall:[4] probably the story of Sappho's leap is bound up with memories of this rite. Corinthian colonists occupied Corcyra (Corfu) about 734 B.C., and soon became so strong that they defeated Corinth's navy and established their independence. From Corcyra some Greek adventurers sailed up the Adriatic as far as Venice; some made small settlements on the Dalmatian coast and in the valley of the Po;[5] others crossed at last through fifty miles of stormy water to the heel of Italy.

They found a magnificent shore line, curved into natural harbors and backed by a fertile hinterland that had been almost neglected by the aborigines.[6] The Greek invaders took possession of this coastal region by the ruthless law of colonial expansion—that natural resources unexploited by the native population will draw in, by a kind of chemical attraction, some other people to exploit them and pour them into the commerce and usage of the world. From Brentesium (Brindisi) the newcomers, chiefly Dorian, traversed the heel of the peninsula to establish a major city

* Watteau's painting, *Embarkation for Cythera*, symbolized the spirit of the upper classes in eighteenth-century France, which had shed just enough theology to be epicurean.

at Taras—the Roman Tarentum (Taranto).* There they grew olives, raised horses, manufactured pottery, built ships, netted fish, and gathered mussels to make a purple dye more highly valued than the Phoenician.[8] As in most of the Greek colonies, the government began as an oligarchy of landowners, passed under dictators financed by the middle class, and enjoyed vigorous and turbulent intervals of democracy. Here the romantic Pyrrhus would land, in 281 B.C., and undertake to play Alexander to the West.

Across the Tarentine Gulf a new wave of immigrants, mostly Achaeans, founded the cities of Sybaris and Crotona. The murderous jealousy of these kindred states illustrates the creative energy and destructive passions of the Greeks. Trade between eastern Greece and western Italy had a choice of two routes, one by water, the other in part by land. Ships following the water route touched at Crotona, and exchanged many goods there; thence they passed to Rhegium, paid tolls, and moved cautiously through pirate-ridden seas and the swirling currents of the Messina Straits to Elea and Cumae—the northernmost Greek settlement in Italy. To avoid these tolls and perils, and a hundred extra miles of rowing and sailing, merchants who chose the other route unloaded their cargoes at Sybaris, carried them overland some thirty miles to the western coast at Laus, and reshipped them to Poseidonia, whence they were marketed into the interior of Italy.

Strategically situated on this line of trade, Sybaris prospered until it had (if we may believe Diodorus Siculus[9]) 300,000 population and such wealth as few Greek cities could match. *Sybarite* became a synonym for *epicurean.* All physical labor was performed by slaves or serfs while the citizens, dressed in costly robes, took their ease in luxurious homes and consumed exotic delicacies.† Men whose work was noisy, such as carpenters and smiths, were forbidden to practice their crafts within the confines of the city. Some of the roads in the richer districts were covered with awnings as a protection against heat and rain.[11] Alcisthenes of Sybaris, says Aristotle, had a robe of such precious stuffs that Dionysius I of Syracuse later sold it for 120 talents ($720,000).[12] Smyndyrides of Sybaris, visiting Sicyon to sue for the hand of Cleisthenes' daughter, brought with him a thousand servants.[13]

* The traditional dates for the founding of the Greek cities in the West are given in the Chronological Table. These dates were taken by Thucydides from the old logographer Antiochus of Syracuse; they are highly uncertain, and Mahaffy believed that the Sicilian foundations came later than those in Italy. Thucydides' chronology, however, has still many supporters.[7]

† Cooks or confectioners who invented new dishes or sweets—Athenaeus reports—were allowed to patent them for a year.[10] Perhaps Athenaeus mistook caricature for history.

All went well with Sybaris until it slipped into war with its neighbor Crotona (510). We are unreliably informed that the Sybarites marched out to battle with an army of 300,000 men.[15] The Crotoniates, we are further assured, threw this force into confusion by playing the tunes to which the Sybarites had taught their horses to dance.[16] The horses danced, the Sybarites were slaughtered, and their city was so conscientiously sacked and burned that it disappeared from history in a day. When, sixty-five years later, Herodotus and other Athenians established near the site the new colony of Thurii, they found hardly a trace of what had been the proudest community in Greece.

II. PYTHAGORAS OF CROTONA

Crotona lasted longer; founded about 710 B.C., it is, as Crotone, still noisy with industry and trade. It had the only natural harbor between Taras and Sicily, and could not forgive those ships that discharged their cargoes at Sybaris. Enough trade remained to give the citizens a comfortable prosperity, while a wholesome defeat in war, a long economic depression, a brisk climate, and a certain Dorico-Puritan mood in the population conspired to keep them vigorous despite their wealth. Here grew famous athletes like Milo, and the greatest school of medicine in Magna Grecia.*

Perhaps it was its reputation as a health resort that drew Pythagoras to Crotona. The name means "mouthpiece of the Pythian" oracle at Delphi; many of his followers considered him to be Apollo himself, and some laid claim to having caught a flash of his golden thigh.[17] Tradition assigned his birth to Samos about 580, spoke of his studious youth, and gave him thirty years of travel. "Of all men," says Heracleitus, who praised parsimoniously, "Pythagoras was the most assiduous inquirer."[18] He visited, we are told, Arabia, Syria, Phoenicia, Chaldea, India, and Gaul, and came back with an admirable motto for tourists: "When you are traveling abroad look not back at your own borders";[19] prejudices should be checked at every port of entry. More surely he visited Egypt, where he studied with the priests and learned much astronomy and geometry, and perhaps a little nonsense.[20] Returning to Samos and finding that the dictatorship of Polycrates interfered with his own, he migrated to Crotona, being now over fifty years of age.[21]

There he set up as a teacher; and his imposing presence, his varied learning, and his willingness to receive women as well as men into his school,

*The name given by the Romans to the Greek cities in southern Italy.

soon brought him several hundred students. Two centuries before Plato he laid down the principle of equal opportunity for both sexes, and did not merely preach it but practiced it. Nevertheless he recognized natural differences of function; he gave his women pupils considerable training in philosophy and literature, but he had them instructed as well in maternal and domestic arts, so that the "Pythagorean women" were honored by antiquity as the highest feminine type that Greece ever produced.[22]

For the students in general Pythagoras established rules that almost turned the school into a monastery. The members bound themselves by a vow of loyalty, both to the Master and to one another. Ancient tradition is unanimous that they practiced a communistic sharing of goods while they lived in the Pythagorean community.[23] They were not to eat flesh, or eggs, or beans. Wine was not forbidden, but water was recommended—a dangerous prescription in lower Italy today. Possibly the prohibition of flesh food was a religious taboo bound up with the belief in the transmigration of souls: men must beware of eating their ancestors. Probably there were dispensations, now and then, from the letter of these rules; English historians in particular find it incredible that the wrestler Milo, who was a Pythagorean, had become the strongest man in Greece without the help of beef[24]—though the calf that became a bull in his arms* managed well enough on grass. The members were forbidden to kill any animal that does not injure man, or to destroy a cultivated tree. They were to dress simply and behave modestly, "never yielding to laughter, and yet not looking stern." They were not to swear by the gods, for "every man ought so to live as to be worthy of belief without an oath." They were not to offer victims in sacrifice, but they might worship at altars that were unstained with blood. At the close of each day they were to ask themselves what wrongs they had committed, what duties they had neglected, what good they had done.[25]

Pythagoras himself, unless he was an excellent actor, followed these rules more rigorously than any student. Certainly his mode of life won for him such respect and authority among his pupils that no one grumbled at his pedagogical dictatorship, and *autos epha—ipse dixit*—"he himself has said it"—became their formula for a final decision in almost any field of conduct or theory. We are told, with touching reverence, that the Master never drank wine by day, and lived for the most part on bread and honey, with vegetables as dessert; that his robe was always white and spotless;

* Cf. Chap. IX, sect. IV, below.

that he was never known to eat too much, or to make love; that he never indulged in laughter, or jests, or stories; that he never chastised any one, not even a slave.[26] Timon of Athens thought him "a juggler of solemn speech, engaged in fishing for men";[27] but among his most devoted followers were his wife Theano and his daughter Damo, who had facilities for comparing his philosophy with his life. To Damo, says Diogenes Laertius, "he entrusted his *Commentaries*, and charged her to divulge them to no person out of the house. And she, though she might have sold his discourses for much money, would not abandon them, for she thought obedience to her father's injunctions more valuable than gold; and that, too, though she was a woman."[28]

Initiation into the Pythagorean society required, in addition to purification of the body by abstinence and self-control, a purification of the mind by scientific study. The new pupil was expected to preserve for five years the "Pythagorean silence"—i.e., presumably, to accept instruction without questions or argument—before being accounted a full member, or being permitted to "see" (study under?) Pythagoras.[29] The scholars were accordingly divided into *exoterici*, or outer students, and *esoterici*, or inner members, who were entitled to the secret wisdom of the Master himself. Four subjects composed the curriculum: geometry, arithmetic, astronomy, and music. Mathematics came first;* not as the practical science that the Egyptians had made it, but as an abstract theory of quantities, and an ideal logical training in which thinking would be compelled to order and clarity by the test of rigorous deduction and visible proof. Geometry now definitely received the form of axiom, theorem, and demonstration; each step in the sequence of propositions raised the student to a new platform, as the Pythagoreans put it, from which he might view more widely the secret structure of the world.[31] Pythagoras himself, according to Greek tradition, discovered many theorems: above all, that the sum of the angles within any triangle equals two right angles, and that the square of the hypotenuse of a right-angled triangle equals the sum of the squares of the other two sides. Apollodorus tells us that when the Master discovered this theorem he sacrificed a hecatomb—a hundred animals—in thanksgiving;[32] but this would have been scandalously un-Pythagorean.

From geometry, inverting the modern order, Pythagoras passed to arith-

---

* The Pythagoreans appear to have been the first to use the word *mathematike* with the meaning of *mathematics*; before them it had been applied to the learning (*mathema*) of anything.[30]

metic—not as a practical art of reckoning, but as the abstract theory of numbers. The school seems to have made the first classification of numbers into odd or even, prime or factorable;[33] it formulated the theory of proportion, and through this and the "application of areas" created a geometrical algebra.[34] Perhaps it was the study of proportion that led Pythagoras to reduce music to number. One day, as he passed a blacksmith's shop, his ear was attracted by the apparently regular musical intervals of the sounds that came from the anvil. Finding that the hammers were of different weights, he concluded that tones depend upon numerical ratios. In one of the few experiments which we hear of in classical science, he took two strings of equal thickness and equal tension, and discovered that if one was twice as long as the other they sounded an octave when he plucked them; if one was half again the length of the other they gave a fifth (*do, sol*); if one was a third longer than the other they gave a fourth (*do, fa*);[35] in this way every musical interval could be mathematically calculated and expressed. Since all bodies moving in space produce sounds, whose pitch depends upon the size and speed of the body, then each planet in its orbit about the earth (argued Pythagoras) makes a sound proportioned to its rapidity of translation, which in turn rises with its distance from the earth; and these diverse notes constitute a harmony or "music of the spheres," which we never hear because we hear it all the time.[36]

The universe, said Pythagoras, is a living sphere, whose center is the earth. The earth too is a sphere, revolving, like the planets, from west to east. The earth, indeed the whole universe, is divided into five zones—arctic, antarctic, summer, winter, and equatorial. More or less of the moon is visible to us according to the degree in which that half of it which is facing the sun is also turned toward the earth. Eclipses of the moon are caused by the interposition of the earth, or some other body, between the moon and the sun.[37] Pythagoras, says Diogenes Laertius, "was the first person to call the earth round, and to give the name of *kosmos* to the world."[38]

Having with these contributions to mathematics and astronomy done more than any other man to establish science in Europe, Pythagoras proceeded to philosophy. The very word is apparently one of his creations. He rejected the term *sophia*, or wisdom, as pretentious, and described his own pursuit of understanding as *philosophia*—the love of wisdom.[39] In the sixth century *philosopher* and *Pythagorean* were synonyms.[40] Whereas Thales and the other Milesians had sought the first principle of all things in matter, Pythagoras sought it in form. Having discovered numerically regular relations and sequences in music, and having postulated them in the planets, he made the philosopher's leap at unity by announcing that such numerically regular relations and sequences existed everywhere, and that the essential factor in everything was number. Just as Spinoza would argue* that there were two worlds—one the people's world of things perceived by sense, the other the philosopher's world of laws and constancies perceived by reason—and that only the second world was permanently real; so Pythagoras felt that the only basic and lasting aspects of anything were the numerical relationships of its parts.† Perhaps health was a proper mathematical relationship, or proportion, in the parts or elements of the body. Perhaps even the soul was number.

At this point the mysticism in Pythagoras, nurtured in Egypt and the Near East, disported itself freely. The soul, he believed, is divided into three parts: feeling, intuition, and reason. Feeling is centered in the heart, intuition and reason in the brain. Feeling and intuition belong to animals as well as men;‡ reason belongs to man alone, and is immortal.[42] After death the soul undergoes a period of purgation in Hades; then it returns to earth and enters a new body in a chain of transmigration that can be ended only by a completely virtuous life. Pythagoras amused, or perhaps edified, his followers by telling them that he had been in one incarnation a courtesan, in another the hero Euphorbus; he could remember quite distinctly his adventures at the siege of Troy, and recognized, in a temple at Argos, the armor that he had worn in that ancient life.[43] Hearing the yelp of a beaten dog, he went at once to the rescue of the animal, saying that he distinguished in its cries the voice of a dead friend.[44] We catch again a glimpse of the trade in ideas that bound sixth-century Greece, Africa, and Asia when we reflect that this idea of metempsychosis was at one and the same time capturing the imagination of India, of the Orphic cult in Greece, and of a philosophical school in Italy.

We feel the hot breath of Hindu pessimism mingling, in the ethics of

---

* In the fragment "On the Improvement of the Intellect."

† Science tries to reduce all phenomena to quantitative, mathematical, verifiable statements; chemistry describes all things in terms of symbols and figures, arranges the elements mathematically in a periodic law, and reduces them to an intra-atomic arithmetic of electrons; astronomy becomes celestial mathematics, and physicists seek a mathematical formula to cover the phenomena of electricity, magnetism, and gravitation; some thinkers of our time have tried to express philosophy itself in mathematical form.

‡ We should note, in passing, that Pythagoras, slightly anticipating Pasteur, denied spontaneous generation, and taught that all animals are born from other animals through "seeds."[41]

Pythagoras, with the clear, bright air of Plato. The purpose of life in the Pythagorean system is to gain release from reincarnation; the method is through virtue; and virtue is a harmony of the soul within itself and with God. Sometimes this harmony can be artificially induced, and the Pythagoreans, like Greek priests and doctors, used music to heal nervous disorders. More often harmony comes to the soul through wisdom, a quiet understanding of underlying truths, for such wisdom teaches a man modesty, measure, and the golden mean. The opposite way—the way of discord, excess, and sin—leads by inevitable fate to tragedy and punishment; justice is a "square number," and sooner or later every wrong will be "squared" with an equivalent penalty.[45] Here in germ are the moral philosophies of Plato and Aristotle.

Pythagorean politics is Plato's philosophy realized before its conception. According to the common tradition of antiquity the school of Pythagoras was a communistic aristocracy: men and women pooling their goods, educated together, trained to virtue and high thinking by mathematics, music, and philosophy, and offering themselves as the guardian rulers of the state. Indeed it was Pythagoras' effort to make his society the actual government of his city that brought ruin upon himself and his followers. The initiates entered so actively into politics, and took so decidedly the aristocratic side, that the democratic or popular party of Crotona, in an ecstasy of rage, burned down the house in which the Pythagoreans were gathered, killed several of them, and drove the rest out of the city. Pythagoras himself, in one account, was captured and slain when, in his flight, he refused to tread upon a field of beans; another story lets him escape to Metapontum, where he abstained from food for forty days and—perhaps feeling that eighty years were enough—starved himself to death.[46]

His influence was lasting; even today he is a potent name. His society survived for three centuries in scattered groups throughout Greece, producing scientists like Philolaus of Thebes and statesmen like Archytas, dictator of Taras and friend of Plato. Wordsworth, in his most famous ode, was an unconscious Pythagorean. Plato himself was enthralled by the vague figure of Pythagoras. At every turn he takes from him—in his scorn of democracy, his yearning for a communistic aristocracy of philosopher-rulers, his conception of virtue as harmony, his theories of the nature and destiny of the soul, his love of geometry, and his addiction to the mysticism of number. All in all, Pythagoras was the founder, so far as we know them, of both science and philosophy in Europe—an achievement sufficient for any man.

III. XENOPHANES OF ELEA

West of Crotona lies the site of ancient Locri. The colony was founded, says Aristotle, by runaway slaves, adulterers, and thieves from Locris in mainland Greece; but perhaps Aristotle had an Old World disdain for the New. Suffering disorder from the defects of their qualities, the colonists applied to the oracle at Delphi for advice, and were told to get themselves laws. Possibly Zaleucus had instructed the oracle, for about 664 he gave to Locri ordinances which, as he said, Athena had dictated to him in a dream. This was the first written code of laws in the history of Greece, though not the first to be handed down by the gods. The Locrians liked it so well that they required any man who wished to propose a new law to speak with a rope around his neck, so that, if his motion failed, he might be hanged with a minimum of public inconvenience.*[47]

Rounding the toe of Italy northward, the traveler reaches flourishing Reggio, founded by the Messenians about 730 under the name of Rhegion, and known to the Romans as Rhegium. Slipping through the Straits of Messina—probably the "Scylla and Charybdis" of the *Odyssey*—one comes to where Laus stood; and then to ancient Hyele, the Roman Velia, known to history as Elea because Plato wrote it so, and because only its philosophers are remembered. There Xenophanes of Colophon came about 510, and founded the Eleatic School.

He was a personality as unique as his favorite foe, Pythagoras. A man of dauntless energy and reckless initiative, he wandered for sixty-seven years, he tells us,[48] "up and down the land of Hellas," making observations and enemies everywhere. He wrote and recited philosophical poems, denounced Homer for his impious ribaldry, laughed at superstition, found a port in Elea, and obstinately completed a century before he died.[49] Homer and Hesiod, sang Xenophanes, "have ascribed to the gods all deeds that are a shame and a disgrace among men—thieving, adultery, and fraud."[50] But he himself was not a pillar of orthodoxy.

> There never was, nor ever will be, any man who knows with certainty the things about the gods. . . . Mortals fancy that gods are born, and wear clothes, and have voice and form like themselves. Yet if oxen and lions had hands, and could paint and fashion images as men do, they would make the pictures and images of their gods in their own likeness; horses would make them like horses, oxen like oxen. Ethiopians make their gods black and snub-nosed; Thracians give

---

* The Greeks were so fond of this fable that they told it also of the laws of Catana and Thurii. The plan was especially pleasing to Michel de Montaigne, and may not have outlived its utility.

> theirs blue eyes and red hair. . . . There is one god, supreme among gods and men; resembling mortals neither in form nor in mind. The whole of him sees, the whole of him thinks, the whole of him hears. Without toil he rules all things by the power of his mind.[51]

This god, says Diogenes Laertius,[52] was identified by Xenophanes with the universe. All things, even men, taught the philosopher, are derived from earth and water by natural laws.[53] Water once covered nearly all the earth, for marine fossils are found far inland and on mountaintops; and at some future time water will probably cover the whole earth again.[54] Nevertheless all change in history, and all separateness in things, are superficial phenomena; beneath the flux and variety of forms is an unchanging unity, which is the innermost reality of God.

From this starting point Xenophanes' disciple, Parmenides of Elea, proceeded to that idealistic philosophy which was in turn to mold the thought of Plato and Platonists throughout antiquity, and of Europe even to our day.

IV. FROM ITALY TO SPAIN

Twenty miles north of Elea lay the city of Poseidonia—the Roman Paestum—founded by colonists from Sybaris as the main Italian terminus of Milesian trade. Today one reaches it by a pleasant ride from Naples through Salerno. Suddenly, by the roadside, amid a deserted field, three temples appear, majestic even in their desolation. For the river, by blocking its own mouth here with centuries of silt, has long since turned this once healthy valley into a swamp, and even the reckless race that tills the slopes of Vesuvius has fled in despair from these malarial plains. Fragments of the ancient walls remain; but better preserved, as if by solitude, are the shrines that the Greeks raised, in modest limestone but almost perfect form, to the gods of the corn and the sea. The oldest of the buildings, lately called the "Basilica," was more likely a temple to Poseidon; men who owed their living to the fruit and commerce of the Mediterranean dedicated it to him towards the middle of this amazing sixth century B.C., which created great art, literature, and philosophy from Italy to Shantung. The inner as well as the outer colonnades remain, and attest the columnar passion of the Greeks. The following generation built a smaller temple, also Dorically simple and strong; we call it the "temple of Ceres," but we do not know what god sniffed the savor of its offerings. A yet later generation, just before or after the Persian War,[55] erected the greatest and best-proportioned of the three temples, probably also to Poseidon—fittingly enough, since from its porticoes one gazes into the inviting face of the treacherous sea. Again almost everything is columns: a powerful and complete Doric peristyle without, and, within, a two-storied colonnade that once upheld a roof. Here is one of the most impressive sights in Italy; it seems incredible that this temple, better preserved than anything built by the Romans, was the work of Greeks almost five centuries before Christ. We can imagine something of the beauty and vitality of a community that had both the resources and the taste to raise such centers for its religious life; and then we can conjure up less inadequately the splendor of richer and vaster cities like Miletus, Samos, Ephesus, Crotona, Sybaris, and Syracuse.

Slightly north of where Naples stands today adventurers from Chalcis, Eretria, Euboean Cyme, and Graia founded, about 750, the great port of Cumae, oldest of Greek towns in the West. Taking the products of eastern Greece and selling them in central Italy, Cumae rapidly acquired wealth, colonized and controlled Rhegium, obtained command of the Straits of Messina, and excluded from them, or subjected to heavy tolls, the vessels of cities not leagued with it in trade.[56] Spreading southward, the Cumaeans founded Dicaearchia—which became the Roman port of Puteoli (Pozzuoli)—and Neapolis, or New City, our Naples. From these colonies Greek ideas as well as goods passed into the crude young city of Rome, and northward into Etruria. At Cumae the Romans picked up several Greek gods—Apollo and Heracles especially—and bought for more than they were worth the scrolls in which the Cumaean Sibyl—the aged priestess of Apollo—had foretold the future of Rome.

Near the beginning of the sixth century the Phocaeans of Ionia landed on the southern shore of France, founded Massalia (Marseilles), and carried Greek products up the Rhone and its branches as far as Arles and Nîmes. They made friends and wives of the natives, introduced the olive and the vine as gifts to France, and so familiarized southern Gaul with Greek civilization that Rome found it easy to spread its kindred culture there in Caesar's time. Ranging along the coast to the east, the Phocaeans established Antipolis (Antibes), Nicaea (Nice), and Monoecus (Monaco). Westward they ventured into Spain and built the towns of Rhodae (Rosas), Emporium (Ampurias), Hemeroscopium, and Maenaca (near Malaga). The Greeks in Spain flourished for a while by exploiting the silver mines of Tartessus; but in 535 the Carthaginians and Etruscans combined their forces to destroy the Phocaean fleet, and from that time Greek power in the western Mediterranean waned.

V. SICILY

We have left not quite to the last the richest of all the regions colonized by the Greeks. To Sicily nature had given what she had withheld from continental Greece—an apparently inexhaustible soil fertilized by rain and lava, and producing so much wheat and corn that Sicily was thought to be if not the birthplace at least a favorite haunt of Demeter herself. Here were orchards, vineyards, olive groves, heavy with fruit; honey as succulent as Hymettus', and flowers blooming in their turn from the beginning to the end of the year. Grassy plains pastured sheep and cattle, endless timber grew in the hills, and the fish in the surrounding waters reproduced faster than Sicily could eat them.

A neolithic culture had flourished here in the third millennium before Christ, a bronze culture in the second; even in Minoan days trade had bound the island with Crete and Greece.[57] Towards the end of the second millennium three waves of immigration broke upon Sicilian shores: the Sicans came from Spain, the Elymi from Asia Minor, the Sicels from Italy.[58] About 800 the Phoenicians established themselves at Motya and Panormus (Palermo) in the west. From 735 on* the Greeks poured in, and in quick succession founded Naxos, Syracuse, Leontini, Messana (Messina), Catana, Gela, Himera, Selinus, and Acragas. In all these cases the natives were driven from the coast by force of arms. Most of them retired to till the mountainous interior, some became slaves to the invaders, so many others intermarried with the conquerors that Greek blood, character, and morals in Sicily took on a perceptible native tint of passion and sensuality.[59] The Hellenes never quite conquered the island; the Phoenicians and Carthaginians remained predominant on the west coast, and for five hundred years periodic war marked the struggle of Greek and Semite, Europe and Africa, for the possession of Sicily. After thirteen centuries of domination by Rome that contest would be resumed, in the Middle Ages, between Norman and Saracen.

Catana was distinguished for its laws, the Lipari Islands for their communism, Himera for its poet, Segesta, Selinus, and Acragas for their temples, Syracuse for its power and wealth. The laws that Charondas gave to Catana, a full generation before Solon, became a model for many cities in Sicily and Italy, and served to create public order and sexual morality in communities unprotected by ancient mores and sacred precedents. A man might divorce his wife, or a wife her husband, said Charondas, but then he or she must not marry anyone younger than the divorced mate.[60] Charondas, according to a typically Greek tale, forbade the citizens to enter the assembly while armed. One day, however, he himself came to the public meeting forgetfully wearing his sword. When a voter reproached him for breaking his own law he answered, "I will rather confirm it," and slew himself.[61]

---

* Or perhaps a generation later; cf. note to p. 160 above.

If we wish to visualize the difficulties of life in colonies carved out by violent conquest we need only contemplate the curious communism of the Lipari—i.e., the Glorious—Islands, which lie to the north of eastern Sicily. Here, about 580, some adventurers from Cnidus organized a pirate's paradise. Preying upon the commerce about the Straits, they brought the booty to their island lairs and shared it with exemplary equality. The land was owned by the community, a part of the population was assigned to till it, and the products were distributed in like shares to all the citizens. In time, however, individualism reasserted itself: the land was divided into plots individually owned, and life resumed the uneven tenor of its competitive way.

On the northern coast of Sicily lay Himera, destined to be the Plataea of the West. There Stesichorus, "Maker of Choruses," at a time when the Greeks were tiring of epics, recast into the form of choral lyrics the legends of the race, and gave even to Helen and Achilles the passing novelty of "modern dress." As if to bridge the gap between the dying epic and the future novel, Stesichorus composed love stories in verse; in one of these a pure and timid lass dies of unrequited love, in the style of Provençal madrigals or Victorian fiction. At the same time he opened a pathway for Theocritus by writing a pastoral poem on the death of the shepherd Daphnis, whose love for Chloe was to be the main business of the Greek novel in the Roman age. Stesichorus had his own romance, and with no less a lady than Helen herself. Having lost his sight, he attributed this calamity to his having handed down the tale of Helen's infidelity; to atone to her (for she was now a goddess) he composed a "palinode," or second song, assuring the world that Helen had been kidnaped by force, had never yielded to Paris, had never gone to Troy, but had waited intact in Egypt until Menelaus came to rescue her. In his old age the poet warned Himera against giving dictatorial power to Phalaris of Acragas.* Being unheeded, he moved to Catana, where his monumental tomb was one of the sights of Roman Sicily.

West of Himera lay Segesta, of which nothing remains but a peristyle of unfinished Doric columns weirdly rising amid surrounding weeds. To find Sicilian architecture at its best we must cross the island southward to the once great cities of Selinus and Acragas. During its tragic tenure of life from its establishment in 651 to its destruction by Carthaginians in 409, Selinus raised to the silent gods seven Doric temples, immense in size but of imperfect workmanship, covered with painted plaster and decorated with crude reliefs. The demon of earthquake destroyed these temples at a date unknown, and little survives of them but broken columns and capitals sprawling on the ground.

* He cast his warning into the form of a fable. A horse, annoyed by the invasion of a stag into its pasturage, asked a man to help it punish the poacher. The man promised to do this if the horse would allow him to bestride it javelin in hand. The horse agreed, the stag was frightened away, and the horse found that he was now a slave to the man.

Acragas, the Roman Agrigentum, was in the sixth century the largest and richest city in Sicily. We picture it rising from its busy wharves through a noisy market place to the homes on the slope of the hill, and the stately acropolis whose shrines almost lifted their worshipers to the sky. Here, as in most of the Greek colonies, the landowning aristocracy yielded power to a dictatorship representing chiefly the middle class. In 570 Phalaris seized the government, and secured immortality by roasting his enemies in a brazen bull; he was particularly pleased by a contrivance that made the agonized cries of his victims sound through a mechanism of pipes like the bellowing of the animal.[62] Nevertheless it was to him and a later dictator, Theron, that the city owed the political order and stability that permitted its economic development. The merchants of Acragas, like those of Selinus, Crotona, and Sybaris, became the American millionaires of their time, upon whom the lesser plutocrats of older Greece looked with secret envy and compensatory scorn; the new world, said the old, was interested in size and show, but had no taste or artistry. The temple of Zeus at Acragas unquestionably sought size, for Polybius describes it as "second to none in Greece in dimensions and design";[63] we cannot directly judge its beauty, for wars and earthquakes destroyed it. A generation later, in the age of Pericles, Acragas raised more modest structures. One of them, the temple of Concord, survives almost completely, and of the temple of Hera there remains an impressive colonnade; enough in either case to show that Greek taste was not confined to Athens, and that even the commercial west had learned that "size is not development."—In Acragas the great Empedocles would be born; and perhaps it was there, and not in Etna's crater, that he would die.

Syracuse began as it is today—a village huddled on the promontory of Ortygia. As far back as the eighth century Corinth had sent colonists, armed with righteousness and superior weapons, to seize the little peninsula, which was then perhaps an island. They built or widened the connection with the mainland of Sicily, and drove most of the Sicels into the interior. They multiplied with all the rapidity of a vigorous people on a resource-full soil; in time their city became the largest in Greece, with a circumference of fourteen miles and a population of half a million souls. An aristocracy of landholders was overthrown about 495 by a revolt of the unfranchised plebs in alliance with the enslaved Sicels. The new democracy, if we may believe Aristotle,[64] proved incapable of establishing an orderly society, and in 485 Gelon of Gela, by a program of enlightened treachery, set up a dictatorship. Like many of his kind he was as able as he was unscrupulous. Scorning all moral codes and political restraints, he transformed Ortygia into an impregnable fortress for his government, conquered Naxos, Leontini, and

Messana, and taxed all eastern Sicily to make Syracuse the most beautiful of Greek capitals. "In this way," says Herodotus, sadly, "Gelon became a great king."*[65]

He redeemed himself, and became the idolized Napoleon of Sicily when, as Xerxes' fleet moved upon Athens, the Carthaginians sent an armada only less numerous than the Persian to wrest the island paradise from the Greeks. The fate of Sicily was joined with that of Greece when in the same month—tradition said on the same day—Gelon faced Hamilcar at Himera, and Themistocles confronted Xerxes at Salamis.

VI. THE GREEKS IN AFRICA

The Carthaginians had reason to be disturbed, for even on the north coast of Africa the Greeks had established cities and were capturing trade. As early as 630 the Dorians of Thera had sent a numerous colony to Cyrene, midway between Carthage and Egypt. There, on the desert's edge, they found good soil, with rain so abundant that the natives spoke of the site as the place where there was a hole in the sky. The Greeks used part of the land for pasturage, and exported wool and hides; they grew from the silphium plant a spice that all Greece was eager to buy; they sold Greek products to Africa, and developed their own handicrafts to such a point that Cyrenaic vases ranked among the best. The city used its wealth intelligently, and adorned itself with great gardens, temples, statuary, and gymnasiums. Here the first famous epicurean philosopher, Aristippus, was born, and here, after much wandering, he returned to found the Cyrenaic School.

Within Egypt itself, normally hostile to any foreign settlement, the Greeks gained a foothold, at last an empire. About 650 the Milesians opened a "factory," or trading post, at Naucratis on the Canopic branch of the Nile. Pharaoh Psamtik I tolerated them because they made good mercenaries, while their commerce provided rich prey for his collectors of customs revenues.[67] Ahmose II gave them a large measure of self-government. Naucratis became almost an industrial city, with manufactures of pottery, terra cotta, and faïence; still more it became an emporium of trade, bringing in Greek oil and wine, and sending out Egyptian wheat, linen, and wool, African ivory, frankincense, and gold. Gradually, amid these exchanges, Egyptian lore and techniques in religion,

* "Gelon of Syracuse," says Lucian, "had disagreeable breath, but did not find it out himself for a long time, no one venturing to mention such a circumstance to a tyrant. At last a foreign woman who had a connection with him dared to tell him; whereupon he went to his wife and scolded her for never having, with all her opportunities of knowing, warned him of it; she put in the defense that as she had never been familiar or at close quarters with any other man, she had supposed all men were like that."[66] He was disarmed.

architecture, sculpture, and science flowed into Greece, while in return Greek words and ways entered Egypt, and paved the way for Greek domination in the Alexandrian age.

If in imagination we take a merchant vessel from Naucratis to Athens, our tour of the Greek world will be complete. It was necessary that we should make this long circuit in order that we might see and feel the extent and variety of Hellenic civilization. Aristotle described the constitutional history of 158 Greek city-states, but there were a thousand more. Each contributed in commerce, industry, and thought to what we mean by Greece. In the colonies, rather than on the mainland, were born Greek poetry and prose, mathematics and metaphysics, oratory and history. Without them, and the thousand absorbing tentacles which they stretched out into the old world, Greek civilization, the most precious product in history, might never have been. Through them the cultures of Egypt and the Orient passed into Greece, and Greek culture spread slowly into Asia, Africa, and Europe.

CHAPTER VIII

The Gods of Greece

I. THE SOURCES OF POLYTHEISM

WHEN we look for unifying elements in the civilization of these scattered cities we find essentially five: a common language, with local dialects; a common intellectual life, in which only major figures in literature, philosophy, and science are known far beyond their political frontiers; a common passion for athletics, finding outlet in municipal and interstate games; a love of beauty locally expressed in forms of art common to all the Greek communities; and a partly common religious ritual and belief.

Religion divided the cities as much as it united them. Under the polite and general worship of the remote Olympians lay the intenser cults of local deities and powers who served no vassalage to Zeus. Tribal and political separatism nourished polytheism, and made monotheism impossible. In the early days every family had its own god; to him the divine fire burned unextinguished at the hearth, and to him offerings of food and wine were made before every meal. This holy communion, or sharing of food with the god, was the basic and primary act of religion in the home. Birth, marriage, and death were sanctified into sacraments by ancient ritual before the sacred fire; and in this way religion suffused a mystic poetry and a stabilizing solemnity over the elemental events of human life. In like manner the gene, the phratry, the tribe, and the city had each its special god. Athens worshiped Athena, Eleusis Demeter, Samos Hera, Ephesus Artemis, Poseidonia Poseidon. The center and summit of the city was the shrine of the city god; participation in the worship of the god was the sign, the privilege, and the requisite of citizenship. When the city marched out to war it carried the form and emblem of its god in the forefront of the troops, and no important step was taken without consulting him through divination. In return he fought for the city, and sometimes seemed to appear at the head or above the spears of the soldiers; victory was the conquest not only of a city by a city but of a god by a god. The city, like the family or the tribe, kept always burning, at a public altar in the prytaneum or town hall, a sacred fire symbolizing the mystically potent and persistent life of the city's founders and heroes; and periodically the citizens partook of a common meal before this fire. Just as in the family the father was also the priest, so in the Greek city the chief magistrate or archon was the high priest of the state religion, and all his powers and actions were sanctified by the god. By this conscription of the supernatural, man was tamed from a hunter into a citizen.

Liberated by local independence, the religious imagination of Greece produced a luxuriant mythology and a populous pantheon. Every object or force of earth or sky, every blessing and every terror, every quality—even the vices—of mankind was personified as a deity, usually in human form; no other religion has ever been so anthropomorphic as the Greek. Every craft, profession, and art had its divinity, or, as we should say, its patron saint; and in addition there were demons, harpies, furies, fairies, gorgons, sirens, nymphs, almost as numerous as the mortals of the earth. The old question—is religion created by priests?—is here settled; it is incredible that any conspiracy of primitive theologians should have begotten such a plethora of gods. It must have been a boon to have so many deities, so many fascinating legends, sacred shrines, and solemn or joyous festivals. Polytheism is as natural as polygamy, and survives as long, suiting well all the contradictory currents of the world. Even today, in Mediterranean Christianity, it is not God who is worshiped, so much as the saints; it is polytheism that sheds over the simple life the inspiring poetry of consolatory myth, and gives to the humble soul the aid and comfort that it would not venture to expect from a Supreme Being unapproachably awful and remote.

Each of the gods had a mythos, or story, attached to him, which accounted for his place in the city's life, or for the ritual that honored him. These myths, rising spontaneously out of the lore of the place and the people, or out of the inventions and embellishments of rhapsodists, became at once the faith and the philosophy, the literature and the history of the early Greek; from them came the subjects that adorned Greek vases, and suggested to artists countless paintings, statues, and reliefs. Despite the achievements of philosophy and the attempts of a few to preach a monotheistic creed, the people continued to the end of Hellenic civilization to create myths, and even gods. Men like Heracleitus might allegorize the myths, or like Plato adapt them, or like Xenophanes denounce them; but when Pausanias toured Greece five centuries after Plato he found still alive among the people the legends that had warmed the heart of the Homeric age. The mythopoetic, theopoetic process is natural, and goes on today as always; there is a birth rate as well as a death rate of the gods; deity is like energy, and its quantity remains, through all vicissitudes of form, approximately unchanged from generation to generation.

II. AN INVENTORY OF THE GODS

1. *The Lesser Deities*

We shall force some order and clarity upon this swarm of gods if we artificially divide them into seven groups: sky-gods, earth-gods, fertility-gods, animal gods, subterranean gods, ancestor or hero gods, and Olympians. "The names of all of them," as Hesiod said, "it were troublesome for a mortal man to tell."[1]

(1) Originally, so far as we can make out, the great god of the invading Greeks, as of the Vedic Hindus, was the noble and various sky itself; it was probably this sky-god who with progressing anthropomorphism became Uranus, or Heaven, and then the "cloud-compelling," rain-making, thunder-herding Zeus.[2] In a land surfeited with sunshine and hungry for rain, the sun, Helios, was only a minor deity. Agamemnon prayed to him,[3] and the Spartans sacrified horses to him to draw his flaming chariot through the skies;* the Rhodians, in Hellenistic days, honored Helios as their chief divinity, flung annually into the sea four horses and a chariot for his use, and dedicated to him the famous Colossus;[4] and Anaxagoras almost lost his life, even in Periclean Athens, for saying that the sun was not a god, but only a ball of fire. Generally, however, there was little worship of the sun in classic Greece; still less of the moon (Selene); least of all, of the planets or the stars.

(2) The earth, not the heavens, was the home of most Greek gods. And first the earth itself was the goddess Ge or Gaea, patient and bountiful mother, pregnant through the embrace of raining Uranus, the sky. A thousand lesser deities dwelt on the earth, in its waters, or in its surrounding air: spirits of sacred trees, especially the oak; Nereids, Naiads, Oceanids, in rivers, lakes, or the sea; gods gushing forth as wells or springs, or flowing as stately streams like the Maeander or the Spercheus; gods of the wind, like Boreas, Zephyr, Notus, and Eurus, with their master Aeolus; or the great god Pan, the horned, cloven-footed, sensual, smiling Nourisher, god of shepherds and flocks, of woods and the wild life lurking in them, he whose magic flute could be heard in every brook and dell, whose startling cry brought *pan*ic to any careless herd, and whose attendants were

* Phaëthon (the Brilliant), son of Helios, begged for the thrill of driving the sun's chariot across the heavens. He drove it recklessly, nearly set the world on fire, was struck by lightning, and fell into the sea. Perhaps the Greeks meant this tale, like that of Icarus, to serve as a sermon to youth.

merry fauns and satyrs, and those old satyrs called *sileni*, half goat and half Socrates. Everywhere in nature there were gods; the air was so crowded with spirits of good or evil that, said an unknown poet, "There is not one empty chink into which you could push the spike of a blade of corn."[5]

(3) The most mysterious and potent force in nature being reproduction, it was natural that the Greeks, like other ancient peoples, should worship the principle and emblems of fertility in man and woman along with their worship of fertility in the soil. The phallus, as symbol of reproduction, appears in the rites of Demeter, Dionysus, Hermes, even of the chaste Artemis.[6] In classical sculpture and painting this emblem recurs with scandalous frequency. Even the Great Dionysia, the religious festival at which the Greek drama was played, was introduced by phallic processions, to which Athenian colonies piously sent phalli.[7] Doubtless such festivals lent themselves to much lusty humor, as one may judge from Aristophanes; but all in all the humor was healthy, and perhaps served the purpose of stimulating Eros and promoting the birth rate.[8]

The more vulgar side of this fertility cult was expressed in the Hellenistic and Roman periods by the worship of Priapus, born of an amour between Dionysus and Aphrodite, and popular with vase painters and the mural artists of Pompeii. A lovelier variation of the reproductive theme was the veneration of goddesses representing motherhood. Arcadia, Argos, Eleusis, Athens, Ephesus, and other localities gave their greatest devotion to feminine deities, often husbandless; such goddesses presumably reflect a primitive matrilinear age before the coming of marriage;[9] the enthronement of Zeus as Father God over all gods represents the victory of the patriarchal principle.* The probable priority of women in agriculture may have helped to give form to the greatest of these mother deities, Demeter, goddess of the corn or the tilled earth. One of the most beautiful of Greek myths, skillfully narrated in the *Hymn to Demeter* once attributed to Homer, tells how Demeter's daughter Persephone, while gathering flowers, was kidnaped by Pluto, god of the underworld, and snatched down to Hades. The sorrowing mother searched for her everywhere, found her, and persuaded Pluto to let Persephone live on the earth nine months in every year—a pretty symbol for the annual death and rebirth of the soil. Because the people of Eleusis befriended the disguised Demeter as she "sat by the way, grieved in her inmost heart," she taught them and Attica the secret of agriculture, and sent Triptolemus, son of Eleusis' king, to spread the art among mankind. Essentially it was the same myth as that of Isis and Osiris in Egypt, Tammuz and Ishtar in Babylonia, Astarte and Adonis in Syria, Cybele and Attis in Phrygia. The cult of motherhood survived through classical times to take new life in the worship of Mary the Mother of God.

---

* Note the absence of mother goddesses in such strongly patriarchal societies as Judea, Islam, and Protestant Christendom.

(4) Certain animals, in early Greece, were honored as semideities. Greek religion was too anthropomorphic, in its sculptural age, to admit the divine menageries that we find in Egypt and India; but a vestige of a less classical past appears in the frequent association of an animal with a god. The bull was sacred because of its strength and potency; it was often an associate, disguise, or symbol of Zeus and Dionysus, and perhaps preceded them as a god.[10] In like manner the "cow-eyed Hera" may once have been a sacred cow.[11] The pig too was holy because of its fertility; it was associated with the gentle Demeter; at one of her festivals, the Thesmophoria, the sacrifice was ostensibly *of* a pig, possibly *to* it.[12] At the feast of the Diasia the sacrifice was nominally to Zeus, really to a subterranean snake that was now dignified with his name.[13] Whether the snake was holy as supposedly deathless, or as a symbol of reproductive power, we find it passing down as a deity from the snake-goddess of Crete into fifth-century Athens; in the temple of Athena, on the Acropolis, a sacred serpent dwelt to whom, each month, a honey cake was offered in appeasing sacrifice. In Greek art a snake is often seen about the figures of Hermes, Apollo, and Asclepius;[15] under the shield of Pheidias' *Athene Parthenos* was wreathed a mighty serpent; the *Farnese Athena* is half covered with snakes.[16] The snake was often used as a symbol or form of the guardian deity of temple or home;[17] perhaps because it prowled about tombs it was believed to be the soul of the dead.[18] The Pythian games are thought to have been celebrated, at first, in honor of the dead python of Delphi.

(5) The most terrible of the gods were under the earth. In caves and clefts and like nether chambers dwelt those chthonian or earthly deities whom the Greeks worshiped not by day with loving adoration, but at night with apotropaic rites of riddance and fear. These vague nonhuman powers were the real *autochthonoi* of Greece, older than the Hellenes, older perhaps than the Mycenaeans, who probably transmitted them to Greece; if we could trace them to their origin we might find that they were the vengeful spirits of the animals that had been driven into the forests or under the soil by the advance and multiplication of men. The greatest of these subterranean deities was called Zeus Chthonios; but *Zeus* here meant merely *god*.[19] Or he was called Zeus Meilichios, the Benevolent God; but here again the words were deceptive and propitiatory, for this god was a fearful snake.—Brother to Zeus was Hades, lord of the underworld that took his name. To placate him the Greeks called him Pluto, the giver of abundance, for he had it in his power to bless or blight the roots of all things that grew in the soil.* Still more ghostly and terrible was Hecate, an evil spirit that came up from the lower world and brought misfortune, through her evil

* Plutus, god of wealth, was a form of Pluto. In early Greece wealth took chiefly the form of corn either growing in the earth or stored in the earth in jars, in either case under Pluto's protection.[20]

eye, to all whom she visited. The less learned Greeks sacrificed puppies to keep her away.[21]

(6) Before the classical age the dead were regarded as spirits capable of good and evil to men, and were appeased with offerings and prayer. They were not quite gods, but the primitive Greek family, like the Chinese, honored its dead beyond any deity.[22] In classical Greece these vague ghosts were more dreaded than loved, and were propitiated with aversion rituals, as in the festival of Anthesteria. The worship of heroes was an extension of the cult of the dead. Great, noble, or beautiful men or women could be raised by the gods to immortal life and become minor deities. So the people of Olympia offered annual sacrifice to Hippodameia; Cassandra was worshiped at Laconian Leuctra, Helen at Sparta, Oedipus at Colonus. Or a god might descend into the body of a mortal, and transform him with divinity; or the god might cohabit with a mortal and beget a hero-god, as Zeus with Alcmena begot Heracles. Many cities, groups, even professions, traced their origin to some god-born hero; so the physicians of Greece looked back to Asclepius. The god was once a dead man, ancestor, or hero; the temple was originally a tomb; the church is still in most lands a shelter for relics of the sacred dead. In general the Greeks made less distinction between men and gods than we do; many of their gods were as human, except in birth, as our saints, and as close to their worshipers; and though they were called Immortals, some of them, like Dionysus, could die.

2. *The Olympians*

All these were the less famous, though not necessarily the less honored, gods of Greece. How is it that we hear so little of them in Homer, and so much of the Olympians? Probably because the gods of Olympus entered with the Achaeans and Dorians, overlaid the Mycenaean and chthonian deities, and conquered them as their worshipers were conquered. We see the change in action at Dodona and Delphi, where the older god of the earth, Gaea, was displaced in the one case by Zeus, in the other by Apollo. The defeated gods were not wiped out; they remained, so to speak, as subject deities, hiding bitterly underground, but still revered by the common people, while the victorious Olympians received on their mountaintop the worship of the aristocracy; hence Homer, who composed for the elite, says almost nothing of the nether gods. Homer, Hesiod, and the sculptors helped the political ascendancy of the conquerors to spread the cult of the Olympians. Sometimes the minor gods were combined or absorbed into the greater figures, or became their attendants or satellites, very much as minor states were now and then attached or subjected to greater ones; so the satyrs and sileni were given to Dionysus, the sea nymphs to Poseidon, the mountain and forest sprites to Artemis. The more savage rites and myths faded out; the chaos of a demon-haunted earth yielded to a semiorderly divine government that reflected the growing political stability of the Greek world.

At the head of this new regime was the majestic and patriarchal Zeus. He was not first in time; Uranus and Cronus, as we have seen, preceded him; but they and the Titans, like Lucifer's hosts, were overthrown.* Zeus and his brothers cast lots to divide the world amongst them; Zeus won the sky, Poseidon the sea, Hades the bowels of the earth. There is no creation in this mythology: the world existed before the gods, and the gods do not make man out of the slime but beget him by union among themselves, or with their mortal offspring; God is literally the Father in the theology of the Greeks. Nor are the Olympians omnipotent or omniscient; each limits the other, or even opposes the other; any one of them, especially Zeus, can be deceived. Nevertheless they acknowledge his suzerainty, and crowd his court like the retainers of a feudal lord; and though he consults them on occasion, and now and then yields his preference to theirs,[23] he frequently puts them in their place.[24] He begins as a sky-and-mountain-god, provider of the indispensable rain.† Like Yahweh he is, among his earlier forms, a god of war; he debates with himself whether to end the siege of Troy or "make the war more bloody," and decides for the latter course.[26] Gradually he becomes the calm and mighty ruler of gods and men, bestriding Olympus in bearded dignity. He is the head and source of the moral order of the world; he punishes filial neglect, guards family property, sanctions oaths, pursues perjurers, and protects boundaries, hearths, suppliants, and guests. At last he is the serene dispenser of judgment whom Pheidias carves for Olympia.

His one failing is the youthful readiness with which he falls in love. Not having created women, he admires them as wonderful beings, bearing even to the gods the inestimable gifts of beauty and tenderness; and he finds it beyond him to resist them. Hesiod draws up a long list of the divine amours and their glorious offspring.[27] His first mate is Dione, but he leaves her in

* This struggle between Zeus and his aides against the Titans became for the Greeks a symbol of the conquest of barbarism and brute strength by civilization and reason, and offered a frequent subject for art.

† The name *Zeus* is probably akin to the Latin *dies*, our day, and may come from an Indo-European root *di*, meaning to shine. Jupiter is *Zeu-pater*, Zeus the father; hence the genitive *Dios*. Today the haunts and peaks once sacred to Zeus are named, or dedicated to, St. Elias, the rain-giving saint of the Greek Church.[25]

Epirus when he moves to Thessalian Olympus. There his first wife is Metis, goddess of measure, mind, wisdom. Gossip says that her children will dethrone him; therefore he swallows her, absorbs her qualities, and becomes himself the god of wisdom. Metis is delivered of Athena within him, and his head has to be cut open that Athena may be born. Lonely for loveliness, he takes Themis for his mate, and begets by her the twelve Hours; then he takes Eurynome, and begets the three Graces; then Mnemosyne, and engenders the nine Muses; then Leto, and fathers Apollo and Artemis; then his sister Demeter, and has Persephone; finally, having sown his wild oats, he weds his sister Hera, makes her Queen of Olympus, and receives from her Hebe, Ares, Hephaestus, and Eileithyia. But he does not get along well with Hera. She is as old a god as he, and more honored in many states; she is the patron deity of matrimony and motherhood, protectress of the marriage tie; she is prim and grave and virtuous, and frowns upon his escapades; moreover, she is an excellent shrew. He thinks of beating her,[28] but finds it easier to console himself with new amours. His first mortal mate is Niobe; his last is Alcmena, who is descended from Niobe in the sixteenth generation.* He loves also, with Greek impartiality, the handsome Ganymede, and snatches him up to be his cupbearer on Olympus.

It was natural that so fertile a father should have some distinguished children. When Athena was born in full development and armament from the head of Zeus she provided the literature of the world with one of its most hackneyed similes. She was an appropriate goddess for Athens, consoling its maids with her proud virginity, inspiring its men with martial ardor, and symbolizing for Pericles the wisdom that belonged to her as the daughter of Metis and Zeus. When Pallas the Titan tried to make love to her she slew him, and added his name to hers as a warning to other suitors. To her Athens dedicated its loveliest temple and its most splendid festival.

More widely worshiped than Athena was her comely brother Apollo, bright deity of the sun, patron of music, poetry, and art, founder of cities, maker of laws, god of healing and father of Asclepius, "far-darting" archer and god of war, successor to Gaea and Phoebe† at Delphi as the holiest oracle of Greece. As god of the growing crops he received tithe offerings at harvest time, and in return he radiated his golden warmth and light from Delos and Delphi to enrich the soil. Everywhere he was associated with order, measure, and beauty; and whereas in other cults there were strange

---

* It should be added, in justice to the dead, that these adventures were probably invented by the poets, or by tribes anxious to trace their lineage to the greatest of the gods.

† From Phoebe he took the name Phoebus, "inspired."

elements of fear and superstition, in the worship of Apollo, and in his great festivals at Delphi and Delos, the dominant note was the rejoicing of a brilliant people in a god of health and wisdom, reason and song.

Happy, too, was his sister Artemis (Diana), maiden goddess of the chase, so absorbed in the ways of animals and the pleasures of the woods that she had no time for the love of men. She was the goddess of wild nature, of meadows, forests, hills, and the sacred bough. As Apollo was the ideal of Greek youth, so Artemis was the model of Greek girlhood—strong, athletic, graceful, chaste; and yet again she was the patroness of women in childbirth, who prayed to her to ease their pains. At Ephesus she kept her Asiatic character as a goddess of motherhood and fertility. In this way the ideas of virgin and mother became confused in her worship; and the Christian Church found it wise, in the fifth century of our era, to attach the remnants of this cult to Mary, and to transform the mid-August harvest festival of Artemis into the feast of the Assumption.[29] In such ways the old is preserved in the new, and everything changes except the essence. History, like life, must be continuous or die; character and institutions may be altered, but slowly; a serious interruption of their development throws them into national amnesia and insanity.

A thoroughly human figure in this pantheon was the master craftsman of Olympus, that lame Hephaestus whom the Romans knew as Vulcan. At first he seems a pitiful and ridiculous figure, this insulted and injured Quasimodo of the skies; but in the end our sympathies are with him rather than with the clever and unscrupulous gods who maltreat him. Perhaps in early days, before he became so human, he had been the leaping spirit of the fire and the forge. In the Homeric theogony he is the son of Zeus and Hera; but other myths assure us that Hera, jealous of Zeus's unaided delivery of Athena, gave birth to Hephaestus without the aid of any male. Seeing him to be ugly and weak, she cast him down from Olympus. He found his way back, and built for the gods the many mansions in which they dwelt. Though his mother had dealt so cruelly with him, he showed her all kindness and respect, and defended her so zealously in one of her quarrels with Zeus that the great Olympian seized him by the leg and hurled him down to the earth. A whole day Hephaestus fell; at last he landed on the island of Lemnos, and hurt his ankle; certainly thereafter (before that, says Homer) he was painfully lame. Again he found his way back to Olympus. In his resounding workshops he built a mighty anvil with twenty huge bellows, made the shield and armor of Achilles, statues that moved of their own accord, and other very wonderful things. The Greeks worshiped him as the god of all metal trades, then of all handicrafts, and pictured the volcanoes as the chimneys of his subterranean forges. It was his misfortune that he married Aphrodite, for it is difficult for beauty to be virtuous. Learning of her affair with Ares, Hephaestus fashioned a trap that fell upon the lovers as they loved; and then the limping deity had his lame revenge by bringing his fellow gods to look in laughter upon the bound divinities of love and war. But to Hermes, Homer tells us, Apollo said:

> "Hermes, son of Zeus . . . wouldst thou in sooth be willing, even though ensnared with strong bonds, to lie on a couch by the side of golden Aphrodite?" Then the messenger answered him: "Would that this might befall, Lord Apollo, that thrice as many bonds inextricable might clasp me about, and that ye gods—aye, and all the goddesses, too—might be looking on, but that I might sleep by the side of golden Aphrodite."[30]

Ares (Mars) was never distinguished for intelligence or subtlety; his business was war, and even the charms of Aphrodite could not give him the thrill that came to him from lusty and natural killing. Homer calls him "the curse of men," and tells with pleasure how Athena laid him low with a stone; "he covered, as he lay, seven acres of the field."[31] Hermes (Mercury) is more interesting. In origin he is a stone, and from the cult of sacred stones his worship is derived; the stages of his evolution are still visible. Then he is the tall stone placed upon graves, or he is the daimon, or spirit, in this stone. Then he is the boundary stone or its god, marking and guarding a field; and because his function there is also to promote fertility, the phallus becomes one of his symbols. Then he is the herm or pillar—with carved head, uncarved body, and prominent male member—which was placed before all respectable houses in Athens;[32] we shall see how the mutilation of these hermae on the eve of the expedition against Syracuse provided the proximate cause for the ruin of Alcibiades and Athens. Again he is the god of wayfarers and the protector of heralds; their characteristic staff, or caduceus, is one of his favorite insignia. As god of travelers he becomes a god of luck, trade, cunning, and gain, therefore an inventor and guarantor of measures and scales, a patron saint of perjurers, embezzlers, and thieves.[33] He is himself a herald, bearing the billets and decrees of Olympus from god to god or man, and he moves on winged sandals with the speed of an angry wind. His running-about gives him a lithe and graceful form, and prepares him for Praxiteles. As a swift and vigorous youth he is the patron saint of athletes, and his shamelessly virile image has a place in every palaestra.[34] As herald he is the god of eloquence; as celestial interpreter he is the first of a long *herme*neutical line. One of the "Homeric" Hymns tells how, in his youth, he stretched strings across a tortoise shell, and so invented the lyre. Finally it comes his turn to appease Aphrodite; and their offspring, we are told,[35] is a delicate hermaphrodite, sharing their charms and named from their names.

It was characteristic of Greece that in addition to deities of chastity, virginity, and motherhood it should have a goddess of beauty and love. Doubtless in her Near-Eastern origins, and in Cyprus her half-Oriental home, Aphrodite was first of all a mother goddess; to the end of her tenure she remained associated with reproduction and fertility in the whole realm of plant, animal, and human life. But as civilization developed, and increasing security obviated the need for a high birth rate, the esthetic sense was left free to see other values in woman than those of multiplication, and to make Aphrodite not only the embodiment of the ideal of beauty, but the deity of all heterosexual pleasure. The Greeks worshiped her in many forms: as Aphrodite Urania, the Heavenly, the goddess of chaste or sacred love; as Aphrodite Pandemos, the Popular, the goddess of profane love in all its modes; and even as Aphrodite Kallipygos, the Venus of the Lovely Nates.[36] At Athens and Corinth the courtesans built temples to her as their patron saint. At the beginning of April various cities in Greece celebrated her great festival, the Aphrodisia; and on that occasion, for those who cared to take part, sexual freedom was the order of the day.[37] She was the love goddess of the sensual and passionate south, ancient rival of Artemis, the love goddess of the cold and hunting north. Mythology, almost as ironic as history, made her the wife of the crippled Hephaestus, but she consoled herself with Ares, Hermes, Poseidon, Dionysus, and many a mortal like Anchises and Adonis.* To her, in competition with Hera and Athena, Paris awarded the golden apple as the prize of beauty. But perhaps she was never really beautiful until Praxiteles reconceived her, and gave her the loveliness for which Greece could forgive all her sins.

* The myth of Adonis is one more variation on the vegetation theme—the annual death and resurrection of the soil. This handsome youth was desired by both Aphrodite and Persephone, the goddesses of love and of death. Ares, jealous of Adonis' success with Aphrodite, disguised himself as a wild boar and killed him. The anemone was born of Adonis' blood, and rivers of poetry from Aphrodite's grief. Zeus persuaded the goddesses to divide Adonis' time and attentions by leaving him for half a year with Persephone in Hades, and restoring him for half a year to earthly life and love. In Phoenicia, Cyprus, and Athens the death of the boy was commemorated in the festival of the Adonia; women carried images of the Lord (for such was the meaning of his name), loudly bewailed his death, and triumphantly celebrated his resurrection.[38]

To the legitimate or illegitimate children of Zeus we must add, as major Olympians, his sister Hestia, goddess of the hearth, and his unruly brother Poseidon. This Greek Neptune, secure in his watery realms, considered himself fully the equal of Zeus. Even landlocked nations worshiped him, for he commanded not only the sea but the rivers and the springs; it was he who guided the mysterious subterranean streams, and made earthquakes with tidal waves.[39] To him Greek mariners prayed, and raised appeasing temples on perilous promontories.

Subordinate deities were numerous even on Olympus, for there was no end to personifications. There was Hestia (the Roman Vesta), goddess of the hearth and its sacred fire. There was Iris, the rainbow, sometimes messenger for Zeus; Hebe, goddess of youth; Eileithyia, who helped women in childbirth; Dike or Justice; Tyche, Chance; and Eros, Love, whom Hesiod made the creator of the world, whom Sappho called "a limb-dissolving, bitter-sweet, impracticable wild beast."[40] There was Hymeneus, the Marriage Song; Hypnos, Sleep; Oneiros, Dream; Geras, Old Age; Lethe, Oblivion; Thanatos, Death, and others beyond naming. There were nine Muses to inspire artists and poets: Clio for history, Euterpe for lyric poetry accompanied by the flute, Thalia for comic drama and idyllic poetry, Melpomene for tragedy, Terpsichore for choral dance and song, Erato for love verse and mimicry; Polymnia for hymns, Urania for astronomy, Calliope for epic poetry. There were three Graces, and their twelve attendants, the Hours. There was Nemesis, who meted out good and evil to men, and visited with disaster all who were guilty of *hybris*—insolence in prosperity. There were the terrible Erinnyes, the Furies who left no wrong unrevenged; the Greeks with deprecating euphemism called them Well-Wishers, Eumenides. And finally there were the Moirai, the Fates or Allotters who regulated inevitably the affairs of life, and ruled, some said, both gods and men. In that conception Greek religion found its limit, and flowed over into science and law.

We have left for the last the most troublesome, the most popular, the most difficult to classify, of all the Greek gods. Only late in his career was Dionysus received into Olympus. In Thrace, which gave him as a Greek gift to Greece, he was the god of liquor brewed from barley, and was known as Sabazius; in Greece he became a god of wine, the nourisher and guardian of the vine; he began as a goddess of fertility, became a god of intoxication, and ended as a son of god dying to save mankind. Many figures and legends were mingled to make his myth. The Greeks thought of him as

Zagreus, "the horned child" borne to Zeus by his daughter Persephone. He was the best beloved of his father, and was seated beside him on the throne of heaven. When the jealous Hera incited the Titans to kill him, Zeus, to disguise him, changed him into a goat, then a bull; in this form, nevertheless, the Titans captured him, cut his body into pieces, and boiled them in a caldron. Athena, like another Trelawney, saved the heart, and carried it to Zeus; Zeus gave it to Semele, who, impregnated with it, gave to the god a second birth under the name of Dionysus.*

Mourning for Dionysus' death, and joyful celebration of his resurrection, formed the basis of a ritual extremely widespread among the Greeks. In springtime, when the vine was bursting into blossom, Greek women went up into the hills to meet the reborn god. For two days they drank without restraint, and like our less religious bacchanalians, considered him witless who would not lose his wits. They marched in wild procession, led by Maenads, or mad women, devoted to Dionysus; they listened tensely to the story they knew so well, of the suffering, death, and resurrection of their god; and as they drank and danced they fell into a frenzy in which all bonds were loosed. The height and center of their ceremony was to seize upon a goat, a bull, sometimes a man (seeing in them incarnations of the god); to tear the live victim to pieces in commemoration of Dionysus' dismemberment; then to drink the blood and eat the flesh in a sacred communion whereby, as they thought, the god would enter them and possess their souls. In that divine enthusiasm† they were convinced that they and the god became one in a mystic and triumphant union; they took his name, called themselves, after one of his titles, *Bacchoi,* and knew that now they would never die. Or they termed their state an *ecstasis,* a going out of their souls to meet and be one with Dionysus; thus they felt freed from the burden of the flesh, they acquired divine insight, they were able to prophesy, they were gods. Such was the passionate cult that came down from Thrace into Greece like a medieval epidemic of religion, dragging one region after another from the cold and clear Olympians of the state worship into a faith and ritual that satisfied the craving for excitement and release, the longing for enthusiasm and possession, mysticism and mystery. The priests of

* Diodorus Siculus, as early as 50 B.C., interpreted the tale as a vegetation myth. Zagreus, the vine, is a child of Demeter, the earth, fertilized by Zeus, the rain. The vine, like the god, is cut (pruned) to give it new life; and the juice of the grape is boiled to make wine. Each year, under nourishing rains, the vine is reborn.[41] Herodotus found so many resemblances between the myths of Dionysus and Osiris that he identified the two gods in one of the first essays in comparative religion.[42]

† From *entheos,* "a god within"; "enthusiasm" originally meant possession by a god.

Delphi and the rulers of Athens tried to keep the cult at a distance, but failed; all they could do was to adopt Dionysus into Olympus, Hellenize and humanize him, give him an official festival, and turn the revelry of his worshipers from the mad ecstasy of wine among the hills into the stately processions, the robust songs, and the noble drama of the Great Dionysia. For a while they won Dionysus over to Apollo, but in the end Apollo yielded to Dionysus' heir and conqueror, Christ.

III. MYSTERIES

There were essentially three elements and stages in Greek religion: chthonian, Olympian, and mystic. The first was probably of Pelasgo-Mycenaean origin, the second probably Achaeo-Dorian, the third Egypto-Asiatic. The first worshiped subterranean, the second celestial, the third resurrected, gods. The first was most popular among the poor, the second among the well to do, the third in the lower middle class. The first predominated before the Homeric age, the second in it, the third after it. By the time of the Periclean Enlightenment the most vigorous element in Greek religion was the mystery. In the Greek sense a mystery was a secret ceremony in which sacred symbols were revealed, symbolic rites were performed, and only initiates were the worshipers. Usually the rites represented or commemorated, in semidramatic form, the suffering, death, and resurrection of a god, pointed back to old vegetation themes and magic, and promised the initiate a personal immortality.

Many places in Greece celebrated such mystic rites, but no other place in this respect could rival Eleusis. The mysteries there were of pre-Achaean origin, and appear to have been originally an autumn festival of plowing and sowing.[43] A myth explained how Demeter, rewarding the people of Attica for their kindness to her in her wanderings, established at Eleusis her greatest temple, which was destroyed and rebuilt many times during the history of Greece. Under Solon, Peisistratus, and Pericles the festival of Demeter at Eleusis was adopted by Athens, and raised to higher elaboration and pomp. In the Lesser Mysteries, held near Athens in the spring, candidates for initiation underwent a preliminary purification by self-immersion in the waters of the Ilissus. In September the candidates and others walked in grave but happy pilgrimage for fourteen miles along the Sacred Way to Eleusis, bearing at their head the image of the chthonian deity Iacchus. The procession arrived at Eleusis under torchlight, and solemnly placed the image in the temple; after which the day was ended with sacred dances and songs.

The Greater Mysteries lasted four days more. Those who had been purified with bathing and fasting were now admitted to the lesser rites; those who had received such rites a year before were taken into the Hall of Initiation, where the secret ceremony was performed. The *mystai*, or initiates, broke their fast by participating in a holy communion in memory of Demeter, drinking a holy mixture of meal and water, and eating sacred cakes. What mystic ritual was then performed we do not know; the secret was well kept throughout antiquity, under penalty of death; even the pious Aeschylus narrowly escaped condemnation for certain lines that might have given the secret away. The ceremony was in any case a symbolic play, and had a part in generating the Dionysian drama. Very probably the theme was the rape of Persephone by Pluto, the sorrowful wandering of Demeter, the return of the Maiden to earth, and the revelation of agriculture to Attica. The summary of the ceremony was the mystic marriage of a priest representing Zeus with a priestess impersonating Demeter. These symbolic nuptials bore fruit with magic speed, for it was soon followed, we are told, by a solemn announcement that "Our Lady has borne a holy boy"; and a reaped ear of corn was exhibited as symbolizing the fruit of Demeter's labor—the bounty of the fields. The worshipers were then led by dim torchlight into dark subterranean caverns symbolizing Hades, and, again, to an upper chamber brilliant with light, representing, it appears, the abode of the blessed; and they were now shown, in solemn exaltation, the holy objects, relics, or icons that till that moment had been concealed. In this ecstasy of revelation, we are assured, they felt the unity of God, and the oneness of God and the soul; they were lifted up out of the delusion of individuality, and knew the peace of absorption into deity.[44]

In the age of Peisistratus the mysteries of Dionysus entered into the Eleusinian liturgy by a religious infection: the god Iacchus was identified with Dionysus as the son of Persephone, and the legend of Dionysus Zagreus was superimposed upon the myth of Demeter.[45] But through all forms the basic idea of the mysteries remained the same: as the seed is born again, so may the dead have renewed life; and not merely the dreary, shadowy existence of Hades, but a life of happiness and peace. When almost everything else in Greek religion had passed away, this consoling hope, reunited in Alexandria with that Egyptian belief in immortality from which the Greek had been derived, gave to Christianity the weapon with which to conquer the Western world.

In the seventh century there came into Hellas, from Egypt, Thrace, and Thessaly, another mystic cult, even more important in Greek history than the mysteries of Eleusis. At its source we find, in the age of the Argonauts, the obscure but fascinating figure of Orpheus, a Thracian who "in culture, music, and poetry," says Diodorus, "far surpassed all men of whom we have a record."[46] Very probably he existed, though all that we now know of him bears the marks of myth. He is pictured as a gentle spirit, tender, meditative, affectionate; sometimes a musician, sometimes a reforming ascetic priest of Dionysus. He played the lyre so well, and sang to it so melodiously, that those who heard him almost began to worship him as a god; wild animals became tame at his voice, and trees and rocks left their places to follow the sound of his harp. He married the fair Eurydice, and almost went mad when death took her. He plunged into Hades, charmed Persephone with his lyre, and was allowed to lead Eurydice up to life again on condition that he should not look back upon her until the surface of the earth was reached. At the last barrier anxiety overcame him lest she should no longer be following; he looked back, only to see her snatched down once more into the nether world. Thracian women, resenting his unwillingness to console himself with them, tore him to pieces in one of their Dionysian revels; Zeus atoned for them by placing the lyre of Orpheus as a constellation among the stars. The severed head, still singing, was buried at Lesbos in a cleft that became the site of a popular oracle; there, we are told, the nightingales sang with especial tenderness.[47]

In later days it was claimed that he had left behind him many sacred songs; and perhaps it was so. At the behest of Hipparchus, says Greek tradition, a scholar named Onomacritus, about 520, edited these as the Homeric lays had been edited a generation before. In the sixth century, or earlier, these hymns had acquired a sacred character as divinely inspired, and formed the basis of a mystical cult related to that of Dionysus but far superior to it in doctrine, ritual, and moral influence. The creed was essentially an affirmation of the passion (suffering), death, and resurrection of the divine son Dionysus Zagreus, and the resurrection of all men into a future of reward and punishment. Since the Titans, who had slain Dionysus, were believed to have been the ancestors of man, a taint of original sin rested upon all humanity; and in punishment for this the soul was enclosed in the body as in a prison or a tomb. But man might console himself by knowing that the Titans had eaten Dionysus, and that therefore every man harbored, in his soul, a particle of indestructible divinity. In a mystic sacrament of communion the Orphic worshipers ate the raw flesh of a bull as a symbol of Dionysus to commemorate the slaying and eating of the god, and to absorb the divine essence anew.[48]

After death, said Orphic theology, the soul goes down to Hades, and must face judgment by the gods of the underworld; the Orphic hymns and ritual, like the Egyptian *Book of the Dead*, instructed the faithful in the art of preparing for this comprehensive and final examination. If the verdict was guilty there would be severe punishment. One form of the doctrine conceived this punishment as eternal,[49] and transmitted to later theology the notion of hell. Another form adopted the idea of transmigration: the soul was reborn again and again into lives happier or bitterer than before according to the purity or impurity of its former existence; and this wheel of rebirth would turn until complete purity was achieved, and the soul was admitted to the Islands of the Blest.[50] Another variant offered hope that the punishment in Hades might be ended through penances performed in advance by the individual, or, after his death, by his friends. In this way a doctrine of purgatory and indulgences arose; and Plato describes with almost the anger of a Luther the peddling of such indulgences in the Athens of the fourth century B.C.:

> Mendicant prophets go to rich men's doors and persuade them that they have a power committed to them of making atonement for their sins or those of their fathers by sacrifices or charms. . . . And they produce a host of books written by Musaeus and Orpheus . . . according to which they perform their ritual, and persuade not only individuals but whole cities that expiations and atonements may be made by sacrifices and amusements [ceremonies?] which fill a vacant hour, and are equally at the service of the living and the dead. The latter [ceremonies] they call mysteries, and these redeem us from the Pains of Hell; but if we neglect them no one knows what awaits us.[51]

Nevertheless there were in Orphism idealistic trends that culminated in the morals and monasticism of Christianity. The reckless looseness of the Olympians was replaced by a strict code of conduct, and the mighty Zeus was slowly dethroned by the gentle figure of Orpheus, even as Yahweh was to be dethroned by Christ. A conception of sin and conscience, a dualistic view of the body as evil and of the soul as divine, entered into Greek thought; the subjugation of the flesh became a main purpose of religion, as a condition of the release for the soul. The brotherhood of Orphic initiates had no ecclesiastical organization and no separate life; but they were distinguished by the wearing of white garments, the avoidance of flesh food, and a degree of asceticism not usually associated with Hellenic ways. They represented, in several aspects, a Puritan Reformation in the history of Greece. Their rites encroached more and more upon the public worship of the Olympian gods.

The influence of the sect was extensive and enduring. Perhaps it was here that the Pythagoreans took their diet, their dress, and their theory of transmigration; it is worthy of note that the oldest Orphic documents now extant were found in southern Italy.[52] Plato, though he rejected much in Orphism, accepted its opposition of body and soul, its puritan tendency, its hope of immortality. Part of the pantheism and asceticism of Stoicism may be traced to an Orphic origin. The Neo-Platonists of Alexandria possessed a large collection of Orphic writings, and based upon them much of their theology and their mysticism. The doctrines of hell, purgatory, and heaven, of the body versus the soul, of the divine son slain and reborn, as well as the sacramental eating of the body and blood and divinity of the god, directly or deviously influenced Christianity, which was itself a mystery religion of atonement and hope, of mystic union and release. The basic ideas and ritual of the Orphic cult are alive and flourishing amongst us today.

IV. WORSHIP

Greek ritual was as varied as the kinds of deities that it honored. The chthonian gods received a gloomy ritual of appeasement and riddance, the Olympians a joyful ritual of welcome and praise. Neither form of ceremony required a clergyman: the father acted as priest for the family, the chief magistrate for the state. Life in Greece was not as secular as it has been described; religion played a major part in it everywhere, and each government protected the official cult as vital to social order and political stability. But whereas in Egypt and the Near East the priesthood dominated the state, in Greece the state dominated the priesthood, took the leadership of religion, and reduced the clergy to minor functionaries in the temples. The property of the temples, in real estate, money, and slaves, was audited and administered by officials of the state.[53] There were no seminaries for the training of priests; anyone could be quietly chosen or appointed priest if he knew the rites of the god; and in many places the office was let out to the highest bidder.[54] There was no hierarchy of priestly caste; the priests of one temple or state had usually no association with those of another.[55] There was no church, no orthodoxy, no rigid creed; religion consisted not in professing certain beliefs, but in joining in the official ritual;[56] any man might have his own creed provided that he did not openly deny or blaspheme the city's gods. In Greece church and state were one.

The place of worship could be the domestic hearth, the municipal hearth in the city hall, some cleft in the earth for a chthonian deity, some temple for an Olympian god. The precincts of the temple were sacred and inviolable; here the worshipers met, and here all pursued persons, even if tainted with serious crime, could find sanctuary. The temple was not for the congregation but for the god; there, in his home, his statue was erected, and a light burned before it which was not allowed to die. Often the people identified the god with the statue; they washed, dressed, and tended the image carefully, and sometimes scolded it for negligence; they told how, at various times, the statue had sweated, or wept, or closed its eyes.[57] In the temple records a history was kept of the festivals of the god, and of the major events in the life of the city or group that worshiped him; this was the source and first form of Greek historiography.

The ceremony consisted of procession, chants, sacrifice, prayer, and sometimes a sacred meal. Magic and masquerade, tableaux and dramatic representations might be part of the procession. In most cases the basic ritual was prescribed by custom, and every movement of it, every word of the hymns and prayers, was preserved in a book kept sacred by the family or the state; rarely was any syllable or action altered, or any rhythm; the god might not like or comprehend the novelty. The living speech changed, the ritual speech remained as before; in time the worshipers ceased to understand the words they used,[58] but the thrill of antiquity supplied the place of understanding. Often the ceremony outlasted even the memory of the cause that had prompted it; then new myths were invented to explain its establishment: the myth or creed might change, but not the ritual. Music was essential to the whole process, for without music religion would be difficult; music generates religion as much as religion generates music. Out of the temple and processional chants came poetry, and the meters that later adorned the robust profanity of Archilochus, the reckless passion of Sappho, and the scandalous delicacies of Anacreon.

Having reached the altar—usually in front of the temple—the worshipers sought with sacrifice and prayer to avert the wrath or win the aid of their god. As individuals they might offer almost anything of value—statues, reliefs, furniture, weapons, caldrons, tripods, garments, pottery; when the gods could make no use of such articles the priests could. Armies might offer part of their spoils, as Xenophon's Ten Thousand did in their retreat.[59] Groups would offer the fruits of the field, the vines or the trees; more often an animal appetizing to the god; sometimes, on occasions of great need, a human being. Agamemnon offered Iphigenia for a wind; Achilles slaughtered twelve Trojan youths on the pyre of Patroclus;[60] human victims were hurled from the cliffs of Cyprus and Leucas to satiate Apollo; others were presented to Dionysus in Chios and Tenedos; Themistocles is said to have sacrificed Persian captives to Dionysus at the battle of Salamis;[61] the Spartans celebrated the festival of Artemis Orthia by flogging youths, sometimes to death, at her altar;[62] in Arcadia Zeus received human sacrifice till the second century A.D.;[63] at Massalia, in time of pestilence, one of the poorer citizens was fed at public expense, clad in holy garments, decorated with sacred boughs, and cast over a cliff to death with prayers that he might bear punishment for all the sins of his people.[64] In Athens it was the custom, in famine, plague, or other crisis, to offer to the gods, in ritual mimicry or in actual fact, one or more scapegoats for the purification of the city; and a similar rite, mimic or literal, was annually performed at the festival of the Thargelia.*[65] In the course of time human sacrifice was mitigated by restricting its victims to condemned criminals, and dulling their senses with wine; finally it was replaced by the sacrifice of an animal. When, on the night before the battle of Leuctra (371 B.C.), the Boeotian leader Pelopidas had a dream that seemed to demand a human sacrifice at the altar as the price of victory, some of his councilors advised it, but others protested against it, saying "that such a barbarous and impious obligation could not be pleasing to any Supreme Beings; that typhons and giants did not preside over the world, but the general father of gods and mortals; that it was absurd to imagine any divinities and powers delighting in slaughter and sacrifice of men."[68]

Animal sacrifice, then, was a major step in the development of civilization. The beasts who bore the brunt of this advance in Greece were the bull, the sheep, and the pig. Before any battle the rival armies sent up sacrifices in proportion to their desired victory; before any assembly in Athens the meeting place was purified by the sacrifice of a pig. The piety of the people, however, broke down at the crucial point: only the bones and a little flesh, wrapped in fat, went to the god; the rest was kept for the priests and the worshipers. To excuse themselves the Greeks told how, in the days of the giants, Prometheus had wrapped the edible portions of the sacrificial animal in skin, and the bones in fat, and had asked Zeus to choose which he preferred. Zeus had "with both hands" chosen the fat. It was true that Zeus was enraged upon finding that he had been deceived; but he had made his choice, and must abide by it forever.[69] Only in sacrifice to the chthonian gods was everything surrendered to the deity, and the entire animal burnt to ashes in a *holocaust;* the divinities of the lower world were

* These victims in Athens were called *pharmakoi,* which meant originally magicians; *pharmakon* meant a magic spell or formula, then a healing drug.[66] The question whether the *pharmakoi* were really slain is in dispute; but there is little doubt that the sacrifice was originally literal.[67]

more feared than those of Olympus. No common meal followed a chthonic sacrifice, for that might tempt the god to come and join the feast. But after sacrifice to the Olympians the worshipers, not in awed atonement to the god but in joyous communion with him, consumed the consecrated victim; the magic formulas pronounced over it had, they hoped, imbued it with the life and power of the god, which would now pass mystically into his communicants. In like manner wine was poured upon the sacrifice, and then into the cups of the worshipers, who drank, so to speak, with the gods.[70] In the *thiasoi,* or fraternities, into which so many trade and social groups in Athens were organized, this idea of divine communion in a common religious meal formed the binding tie.[71]

Animal sacrifice continued throughout Greece until ended by Christianity,[72] which wisely substituted for it the spiritual and symbolical sacrifice of the Mass. In some measure prayer too became a substitute for sacrifice; it was a clever amendment that commuted offerings of blood into litanies of praise. In this gentler way man, subject to chance and tragedy at every step, consoled and strengthened himself by calling to his aid the mysterious powers of the world.

V. SUPERSTITIONS

Between these upper and nether poles of Greek religion, the Olympian and the subterranean, surged an ocean of magic, superstition, and sorcery; behind and below the geniuses whom we shall celebrate were masses of people poor and simple, to whom religion was a mesh of fears rather than a ladder of hope. It was not merely that the average Greek accepted miracle stories—of Theseus rising from the dead to fight at Marathon, or of Dionysus changing water into wine:[73] such stories appear among every people, and are part of the forgivable poetry with which imagination brightens the common life. One could even pass over the anxiety of Athens to secure the bones of Theseus, and of Sparta to bring back from Tegea the bones of Orestes;[74] the miraculous power officially attributed to these relics may well have been part of the technique of rule. What oppressed the pious Greek was the cloud of spirits that surrounded him, ready and able, he believed, to spy upon him, interfere with him, and do him evil. These demons were always seeking to enter into him; he had to be on his guard against them at all times, and to perform magical ceremonies to disperse them.

This superstition verged on science, and in some measure forecast our germ theory of disease. All sickness, to the Greek, meant possession by an alien spirit; to touch a sick person was to contract his uncleanliness or "possession"; our bacilli and bacteria are the currently fashionable forms of what the Greeks called *keres* or little demons.[75] So a dead person was "unclean"; the *keres* had gotten him once for all. When the Greek left a house where a corpse lay, he sprinkled himself with water, from a vessel placed for such purposes at the door, to drive away from himself the spirit that had conquered the dead man.[76] This conception was extended to many realms where even our bacteriophobia would hardly apply it. Sexual intercourse rendered a person unclean; so did birth, childbirth, and homicide (even if unintentional). Madness was possession by an alien spirit; the madman was "beside himself." In all these cases a ceremony of purification was considered necessary. Periodically homes, temples, camps, even whole cities were purified, and very much as we disinfect them—by water, smoke, or fire.[77] A bowl of clean water stood at the entrance to every temple, so that those who came to worship might cleanse themselves,[78] perhaps by a suggestive symbolism. The priest was an expert in purification; he could exorcise spirits by striking bronze vessels, by incantations, magic, and prayer; even the intentional homicide might, by adequate ritual, be purified.[79] Repentance was not indispensable in such cases; all that was needed was to get rid of the evil possessive demons; religion was not so much a matter of morals as a technique of manipulating spirits. Nevertheless the multiplication of taboos and purificatory rites produced in the religious Greek a state of mind surprisingly akin to the Puritan sense of sin. The notion that the Greeks were immune to the ideas of conscience and sin will hardly survive a reading of Pindar and Aeschylus.

Out of this belief in an enveloping atmosphere of spirits came a thousand superstitions, which Theophrastus, successor to Aristotle, summarized in one of his *Characters:*

> Superstitiousness would seem to be a sort of cowardice with respect to the divine. . . . Your Superstitious Man will not sally forth for the day till he have washed his hands and sprinkled himself at the Nine Springs, and put a bit of bay-leaf from a temple in his mouth. And if a cat cross his path he will not proceed on his way till some one else be gone by, or he have cast three stones across the street. Should he espy a snake in his house, if it be one of the red sort he will call upon Dionysus; if it be a sacred snake he will build a shrine then and there. When he passes one of the smooth stones set up at crossroads he anoints it with oil from his flask, and will not go his ways till he have knelt down and worshiped it. If a mouse gnaw a bag of his meal, he will off to the wizard and ask what he must do; and if the advice be, "Send the bag to the cobblers to be patched," he neglects the advice and frees himself of the ill by rites of aversion.

> . . . If he catches sight of a madman or an epileptic, he shudders and spits into his bosom.[80]

The simpler Greeks believed, or taught their children to believe, in a great variety of bogies. Whole cities were disturbed, at short intervals, by "portents" or strange occurrences, like deformed births of animals or men.[81] The belief in unlucky days was so widespread that on such days no marriage might take place, no assembly might be held, no courts might meet, no enterprise might begin. A sneeze, a stumble, might be reason for abandoning a trip or an undertaking; a minor eclipse could stop or turn back armies, and bring great wars to a disastrous end. Again, there were persons gifted with the power of effective cursing: an angered parent, a neglected beggar might lay upon one a curse that would ruin one's life. Some persons possessed magic arts; they could mix love philters or aphrodisiacs, and could by secret drugs reduce a man to impotence or a woman to sterility.[82] Plato did not consider his *Laws* complete without an enactment against those who injure or slay by magic arts.[83] Witches are not medieval inventions; note Euripides' Medea, and Theocritus' Simaetha. Superstition is one of the most stable of social phenomena; it remains almost unchanged through centuries and civilizations, not only in its bases but even in its formulas.

VI. ORACLES

In a world so crowded with supernatural powers, the events of life seemed to depend upon the will of demons and gods. To discover that will the curious Greeks consulted soothsayers and oracles, who divined the future by reading the stars, interpreting dreams, examining the entrails of animals, or observing the flight of birds. Professional soothsayers hired themselves out to families, armies, and states;[84] Nicias, before setting out upon the expedition to Sicily, engaged a troop of sacrificers, augurs, diviners;[85] and though not all generals were as pious as this great slaveowner, nearly all were as superstitious. Men and women appeared who claimed inspiration and clairvoyance; in Ionia particularly certain women called Sibyls (i.e., the Will of God) issued oracles believed by millions of Greeks.[86] From Erythrae the Sibyl Herophila was said to have wandered through Greece to Cumae in Italy, where she became the most famous of her kind, and lived, we are told, a thousand years. Athens, like Rome, had a collection of ancient oracles, and the government maintained in the prytaneum men skilled in their interpretation.[87]

Public oracles were set up at many temples in all parts of Greece; but the most famous and honored were in early days the oracle of Zeus at

Dodona, and in the historical period that of Apollo at Delphi. "Barbarians" as well as Greeks consulted this oracle; even Rome sent messengers to ask or suggest the will of the god. Since the power of divination was supposed to belong particularly to the intuitive sex, three priestesses, each at least half a century old, were trained to consult Apollo through the medium of a trance. From a hollow in the earth below the temple came a peculiar gas, ascribed to the eternal decomposition of the python that Apollo had slain there; the officiating priestess, called Pythia, took her seat on a high tripod over this cleft, inhaled the divine stench, chewed narcotic laurel leaves, fell into delirium and convulsions, and, thus inspired, uttered incoherent words which the priests translated to the people. Very often the final reply admitted of diverse, even contrary, interpretations, so that the infallibility of the oracle was maintained whatever the event.[88] Possibly the priests were no less puppets than the priestesses; sometimes they accepted bribes;[89] and in most cases the voice of the oracle harmonized melodiously with the dominant influence in Greece.[90] Nevertheless, where external powers did not constrain them, the priests taught valuable lessons of moderation and political wisdom to the Greeks. Though they condoned human sacrifice even after the moral sense of Greece had begun to revolt against it, and made no protest against the immoralities of Olympus, they aided the establishment of law, encouraged the manumission of slaves, and bought many slaves in order to give them liberty.[91] They were not in advance of Greek thought, but they did not hinder it by doctrinal intolerance. They gave a helpful supernatural sanction to necessary Greek policies, and provided some degree of international conscience and moral unity for the scattered cities of Greece.

Out of this unifying influence came the oldest known confederation of Greek states. The Amphictyonic League was originally the religious alliance of the peoples "dwelling around" the sanctuary of Demeter near Thermopylae. The chief constituent states were Thessaly, Magnesia, Phthiotis, Doris, Phocis, Boeotia, Euboea, and Achaea. They met semiannually, in spring at Delphi, in autumn at Thermopylae. They bound themselves never to destroy one another's cities, never to allow the water supply of any member city to be shut off, never to plunder—or permit to be plundered—the treasury of Apollo at Delphi, and to attack any nation that violated these pledges. Here was the outline of a League of Nations; an outline whose completion was prevented by the natural fluctuations of wealth and power among states, and the inherent rivalries of men and groups. Thessaly formed a bloc of vassal states, and permanently dominated the League.[92]

Other amphictyonies were established; Athens, for example, belonged to the Amphictyony of Calauria; and the rival leagues, while promoting peace within their membership, became against other groups vast instruments of intrigue and war.

VII. FESTIVALS

If it could not end war Greek religion succeeded in alleviating the routine of economic life with numerous festivals. "How many victims offered to the gods!" cried Aristophanes; "how many temples, statues . . . sacred processions! At every moment of the year we see religious feasts and garlanded victims" of sacrifice.[93] The rich paid the cost, the state provided the *theorika*, or divine funds, to pay to the populace the price of admission to the games or plays that distinguished the holyday.

The calendar at Athens was essentially a religious calendar, and many months were named from their religious festivals. In the first month, Hecatombaion (July-August), came the Cronia (corresponding to the Roman Saturnalia), when masters and slaves sat down together to a joyful feast; in the same month, every fourth year, occurred the Panathenaea, when, after four days of varied contests and games, the entire citizenship formed a solemn and colorful procession to carry to the priestess of Athena the sacred peplos, a gorgeously embroidered robe which was to be placed upon the image of the city's goddess; this, as all the world knows, was the theme that Pheidias chose for the frieze of the Parthenon. In the second month, Metageitnion, came the Metageitnia, a minor festival in honor of Apollo. In the third month, Boedromion, Athens sallied forth to Eleusis for the Greater Mysteries. The fourth month, Pyanepsion, celebrated the Pyanepsia, the Oscophoria, and the Thesmophoria; in this the women of Athens honored Demeter Thesmophoros (the Lawgiver) with a strange chthonian ritual, parading phallic emblems, exchanging obscenities, and symbolically going down to Hades and returning, apparently as magical ceremonies to promote fertility in the soil and man.[94] Only the month of Maimakterion had no festival.

In the month of Poseideon Athens held the Italoa, a feast of first fruits; in Gamelion the Lenaea, in honor of Dionysus. In Anthesterion came three important celebrations: the Lesser or preparatory Mysteries; the Diasia, or sacrifice to Zeus Meilichios; and, above all, the Anthesteria, or Feast of Flowers. In this three-day spring festival to Dionysus wine flowed freely, and everybody was more or less drunk;[95] there was a competition in wine drinking, and the streets were alive with revelry. The king-archon's wife rode on a car beside the image of Dionysus, and was married to it in the temple as a symbol of the union of the god with Athens. Beneath this jolly ritual ran a somber undertone of fear and propitiation of the dead; the living ate a solemn meal in commemoration of their ancestors, and left for them pots full of food and drink. At the end of the feast the people chased the spirits of the departed from the house with a formula of exorcism: "Out of the door with you, souls! Anthesteria is over"—words that became a proverbial phrase for dismissing importunate beggars.*

In the ninth month, Elaphebolion, came the Great Dionysia, established by Peisistratus in 534; in that year Thespis inaugurated the drama at Athens as part of the festival. It was the end of March, spring was in the air, the sea was navigable, merchants and visitors crowded the city and swelled the attendance at the ceremonies and the plays. All business was suspended, all courts were closed; prisoners were released to let them share in the festivities. Athenians of every age and class, brilliantly attired, took part in the procession that brought the statue of Dionysus from Eleutherae and placed it in his theater. The rich drove chariots, the poor marched on foot; a long train of animals followed as destined gifts for the gods. Choruses from the towns of Attica joined or competed in song and dance.—In the tenth month, Munychion, Athens celebrated the Munychia, and Attica, every fifth year, celebrated the Brauronia in honor of Artemis. In Thargelion occurred the Thargelia, or feast of the grain harvest. In the twelfth month, Skirophorion, came the festivals of Skirophoria, Arretophoria, Dipolia, and Bouphonia. Not all these feasts were annual; but even for a four-year period they represented a grateful relief from daily toil.

Other states had similar holidays; and in the countryside every sowing and every harvest was greeted with festal conviviality. Greater than all these were the Panhellenic festivals, the *panegyreis*, or universal gatherings. There were the Panionia on Mycale, the feast of Apollo at Delos, the Pythian festival at Delphi, the Isthmian at Corinth, the Nemean near Argos, the Olympic in Elis. These were the occasions of interstate games, but basically they were holydays. It was the good fortune of Greece to have a religion human enough —in later days humane enough—to associate itself joyfully and creatively with art, poetry, music, and games, even, at last, with morality.

VIII. RELIGION AND MORALS

At first sight Greek religion does not seem to have been a major influence for morality. It was in origin a system of magic rather than of ethics, and remained so, in large measure, to the end; correct ritual received more

* In many parts of Europe the people still believe that the ghosts of the dead return to earth yearly, and must be entertained in a "Feast of All Souls."[96]

emphasis than good conduct, and the gods themselves, on Olympus or on earth, had not been exemplars of honesty, chastity, or gentleness. Even the Eleusinian Mysteries, though they offered supernatural hopes, made salvation depend upon ritual purifications rather than upon nobility of life. "Pataikion the thief," said the sarcastic Diogenes, "will have a better fate after his death than Agesilaus or Epaminondas, for Pataikion has been initiated at Eleusis."[97]

Nevertheless, in the more vital moral relations Greek religion came subtly to the aid of the race and the state. The purification ritual, however external in form, served as a stimulating symbol of moral hygiene. The gods gave a general, if vague and inconstant, support to virtue; they frowned upon wickedness, revenged themselves upon pride, protected the stranger and the suppliant, and lent their terror to the sanctity of oaths. Dike, we are told, punished every wrong, and the awful Eumenides pursued the murderer, like Orestes, to madness or death. The central acts and institutions of human life—birth, marriage, the family, the clan, the state—received a sacramental dignity from religion, and were rescued from the chaos of hasty desire. Through the worship or honoring of the dead, the generations were bound together in a stabilizing continuity of obligations, so that the family was not merely a couple and their children, or even a patriarchal assemblage of parents, children, and grandchildren, but a holy union and sequence of blood and fire stretching far into the past and the future, and holding the dead, the living, and the unborn in a sacred unity stronger than any state. Religion not only made the procreation of children a solemn duty to the dead, but encouraged it through the fear of the childless man that no posterity would inter him or tend his grave. So long as this religion kept its influence, the Greek people reproduced themselves vigorously, and as plentifully among the best as among the worst; and in this way, with the help of a merciless natural selection, the strength and quality of the race were maintained. Religion and patriotism were bound together in a thousand impressive rites; the god or goddess most revered in public ceremony represented the apotheosis of the city; every law, every meeting of the assembly or the courts, every major enterprise of the army or the government, every school and university, every economic or political association, was surrounded with religious ceremony and invocation. In all these ways Greek religion was used as a defense by the community and the race against the natural egoism of the individual man.

Art, literature, and philosophy first strengthened this influence, and then weakened it. Pindar, Aeschylus, and Sophocles poured their own ethical fervor or insight into the Olympian creed, and Pheidias ennobled the gods with beauty and majesty; Pythagoras and Plato associated philosophy with religion, and supported the doctrine of immortality as a stimulus to morals. But Protagoras doubted, Socrates ignored, Democritus denied, Euripides ridiculed the gods; and in the end Greek philosophy, hardly willing it, destroyed the religion that had molded the moral life of Greece.

CHAPTER IX

The Common Culture of Early Greece

I. THE INDIVIDUALISM OF THE STATE

THE two rival zeniths of European culture—ancient Hellas and Renaissance Italy—rested upon no larger political organization than the city-state. Geographical conditions presumably contributed to this result in Greece. Everywhere mountains or water intervened; bridges were rare and roads were poor; and though the sea was an open highway, it bound the city with its commercial associates rather than with its geographical neighbors. But geography does not altogether explain the city-state. There was as much separatism between Thebes and Plataea, on the same Boeotian plain, as between Thebes and Sparta; more between Sybaris and Crotona on the same Italian shore than between Sybaris and Syracuse. Diversity of economic and political interest kept the cities apart; they fought one another for distant markets or grain, or formed rival alliances for control of the sea. Distinctions of origin helped to divide them; the Greeks considered themselves to be all of one race,[1] but their tribal divisions—Aeolian, Ionian, Achaean, Dorian—were keenly felt, and Athens and Sparta disliked each other with an ethnological virulence worthy of our own age. Differences of religion strengthened, as they were strengthened by, political divisions. Out of the unique cults of locality and clan came distinct festivals and calendars, distinct customs and laws, distinct tribunals, even distinct frontiers; for the boundary stones limited the realm of the god as well as of the community; *cujus regio, ejus religio.* These and many other factors united to produce the Greek city-state.

It was not a new administrative form: we have seen that there were city-states in Sumeria, Babylonia, Phoenicia, and Crete hundreds or thousands of years before Homer or Pericles. Historically the city-state was the village community in a higher stage of fusion or development—a common market, meeting ground, and judgment seat for men tilling the same hinterland, belonging to the same stock, and worshiping the same god. Politically it was to the Greek the best available compromise between those two hostile and fluctuating components of human society—order and liberty; a smaller community would have been insecure, a larger one tyrannical. Ideally—in the aspirations of philosophers—Greece was to consist of sovereign city-states co-operating in a Pythagorean harmony. Aristotle conceived the state as an association of freemen acknowledging one government and capable of meeting in one assembly; a state with more than ten thousand citizens, he thought, would be impracticable. In the Greek language one word—*polis*—sufficed for both *city* and *state.*

All the world knows that this political atomism brought to Hellas many a tragedy of fraternal strife. Because Ionia was unable to unite for defense it fell subject to Persia; because Greece, despite confederacies and leagues, was unable to stand together, the freedom which it idolized was in the end destroyed. And yet Greece would have been impossible without the city-state. Only through this sense of civic individuality, this exuberant assertion of independence, this diversity of institutions, customs, arts, and gods, was Greece stimulated, by competition and emulation, to live human life with a zest and fullness and creative originality that no other society had ever known. Even in our own times, with all our vitality and variety, our mechanisms and powers, is there any community of like population or extent that pours into the stream of civilization such a profusion of gifts as flowed from the chaotic liberty of the Greeks?

II. LETTERS

Nevertheless there were common factors in the life of these watchfully separatist states. As far back as the thirteenth century B.C. we find one language throughout the Greek peninsula. It belonged to the "Indo-European" group, like Persian and Sanskrit, Slavonic and Latin, German and English; thousands of words denoting the primary relations or objects of life have common roots in these tongues, and suggest not only the predispersion antiquity of the things denoted, but the kinship or association of the peoples who used them in the dawn of history.* It is true that the Greek language was diversified into dialects—Aeolic, Doric, Ionic, Attic; but these were mutually intelligible, and yielded, in the fifth and fourth centuries, to a *koine dialektos*, or common dialect, which emanated principally from Athens, and was spoken by nearly all the educated classes of the Hellenic world. Attic Greek was a noble tongue, vigorous, supple, melodious; as irregular as any vital speech, but lending itself readily to expressive combinations, delicate gradations and dis-

* Cf. in addition to numerals and family terms, such words as Sanskrit *dam(as)* (house), Greek *domos.* Latin *domus*, English *tim-ber*; *dvaras, thyra, fores, door*; *venas, (f)oinos, vinum, wine*; *naus, naus, navis, nave*; *akshas, axon, axis, axle*; *iugam, zygon, iugum, yoke*, etc.

tinctions of meaning, subtle philosophical conceptions, and every variety of literary excellence from the "many-billowed surge" of Homer's verse to the placid flow of Plato's prose.*

Greek tradition attributed the introduction of writing into Greece to Phoenicians in the fourteenth century B.C., and we know nothing to the contrary. The oldest Greek inscriptions, dating from the eighth and seventh centuries, show a close resemblance to the Semitic characters on the ninth-century Moabite stone.[3] These inscriptions were written, in Semitic fashion, from right to left; sixth-century inscriptions (e.g., at Gortyna) were made alternately from right to left and from left to right; later inscriptions are from left to right throughout, and certain letters are turned around accordingly, as ꓭ and Ǝ to B and E. The Semitic names for the letters were adopted with minor modifications;† but the Greeks made several basic changes. Above all, they added vowels, which the Semites had omitted; certain Semitic characters denoting consonants or breathings were used to represent *a, e, i, o,* and *ü.* Later the Ionians added the long vowels *eta* (long *e*) and *o-mega* (long or double *o*). Ten different Greek alphabets struggled for ascendancy as part of the war of the city-states; in Greece the Ionian form prevailed, and was transmitted to eastern Europe, where it survives today; in Rome the Chalcidian form was adopted from Cumae to become the Latin alphabet, and ours. The Chalcidic alphabet lacked the long *e* and *o,* but, unlike the Ionian, retained the Phoenician *vau* as a consonant (a *v* with approximately the sound of *w*); hence the Athenians called wine *oinos,* the Chalcidians called it *voinos,* the Romans called it *vinum,* we call it *wine.* Chalcis kept the Semitic *koppa* or *q,* and passed it on to Rome and ourselves; Ionia abandoned it, content with *k.* Ionia represented L as Λ, Chalcis as *L*; Rome straightened up the latter form and gave it to Europe. The Ionians used P for R, but in Greek Italy the P sprouted a tail, and became R.[4]

The earliest uses of writing in Greece were probably commercial or religious; apparently priestly charms and chants are the mother of poetry, and bills of lading are the father of prose. Writing split into two varieties: the formal for literary or epigraphic purposes, the cursive for ordinary use. There were no accents, no spaces between words, no punctuation points;[5] but a change of topic was marked off by a horizontal dividing stroke called the *paragraphos*—i.e., a sign "written on the side." The materials used to receive writing were various: at first, if we may believe Pliny, leaves or the bark of trees;[6] for inscrip-

---

* We do not know how ancient Greek was pronounced.[2] The accents that trouble us so much were seldom used by the classical Greeks, but were inserted into ancient texts by Aristophanes of Byzantium in the third century B.C. These accents should be ignored in reading Greek poetry.

† Cf. Greek *alpha,* Phoenician *aleph* (bull); *beta, beth* (tent); *gamma, gimel* (camel); *delta, daleth* (door); *e-psilon, he* (window); *zeta, zain* (lance); *heta, kheth* (paling); *iota, yod* (hand), etc.

tions, stone, bronze, or lead; for ordinary writing, clay tablets as in Mesopotamia;* then wooden tablets covered with wax, which were popular, in retrospect, with schoolboys;[7] for more permanent purposes papyrus, which the Phoenicians brought from Egypt, and (in the Hellenistic and Roman periods) parchment, made from the skins or membranes of goats or sheep. A metal stylus was used on wax tablets; on papyrus or parchment a reed dipped in ink. Wax writing was erased with the flat butt of the stylus, ink with a sponge; so the poet Martial sent a sponge with his poems to his friend, so that they might be wiped out with a stroke.[8] Many a critic will mourn the passing of this courtesy.

In no field have the old words so regularly come down to us as in that of writing. *Paper*, of course, is *papyrus*, and once again, in the cycle of fashion, the substance is a compressed plant. A line of writing was a *stichos* or row; the Latins called it a *versus* or verse—i.e., a turning back. The text was written in columns upon a strip of papyrus or parchment from twenty to thirty feet long, wound about a stick. Such a roll was called a *biblos*, from the Phoenician city, so named, whence papyrus came to Greece. A smaller roll was called *biblion;* our Bible was originally *ta biblia*, the rolls.† When a roll formed part of a larger work it was called a *tomos*, or cutting. The first sheet of a roll was called the *protokollon*—i.e., the first sheet glued to the stick. The edges‡ of the roll were smoothed with pumice and sometimes colored; if the author could afford the expense, or the roll contained important matter, it might be wrapped in a *diphthera* (membrane), or, as the Latins called it, a *vellum.* Since a large roll would be inconvenient for handling or reference, literary works were usually divided into several rolls, and the word *biblos*, or book, was applied not to each work as a whole, but to each roll or part. These divisions were seldom made by the author; later editors divided the *Histories* of Herodotus into nine books, the *Peloponnesian War* of Thucydides into eight, Plato's *Republic* into ten, the *Iliad* and the *Odyssey* into twenty-four. Since papyrus was costly, and each copy had to be written by hand, books were very limited in the classic world; it was easier than now to be educated, though as hard as now to be intelligent. Reading was not a universal accomplishment; most knowledge was handed down by oral tradition from one generation or craftsman to the next; most literature was read aloud by trained reciters to persons who learned through the ear.§ There was no reading public in Greece before the seventh century; there were no Greek libraries till those collected by Polycrates

---

**Graphein*, which we translate *to write*, originally meant *to engrave.*

† The Latins called a roll *volumen*—wound up.

‡ Latin *frontes*, whence our *frontispiece.*

§ Though we have been eye-minded since the development of printing, and writing is seldom read aloud, style and punctuation are still formed with a view to easy breathing in the reader, and a rhythmic sound in the words. Probably our descendants will be ear-minded again.

and Peisistratus in the sixth.[9] In the fifth century we hear of the private libraries of Euripides and the archon Eucleides; in the fourth, of Aristotle's. We know of no public library before Alexandria's, none in Athens till Hadrian.[10] Perhaps the Greeks of Pericles' day were so great because they did not have to read many books, or any long one.

III. LITERATURE

Literature, like religion, divided and united Greece. The poets sang in their local dialects, and often of their native scenes; but all Hellas listened to the more eloquent voices, and stirred them now and then to broader themes. Time and prejudice have destroyed too much of this early poetry to let us feel its wealth and scope, its reputed vigor of utterance and finish of form; but as we move through the isles or cities of sixth-century Greece our wonder rises at the abundance and excellence of Greek literature before the Periclean age. The lyric poetry reflected an aristocratic society in which feeling, thought, and morals were free so long as they observed the amenities of breeding; this style of urbane and polished verse tended to disappear under the democracy. It had a rich variety of structure and meter, but seldom shackled itself with rhyme; poetry meant to the Greeks, feeling imaginatively and rhythmically expressed.*

While the lyric singers tuned their lyres to love and war, the wandering bards, in great men's halls, recited in epic measures the heroic deeds of the race. Guilds of "rhapsodes"† built up through generations a cycle of lays centering around the sieges of Thebes and Troy and the homing of the warriors. Song was socialized among these minstrels; each stitched his story together from earlier fragments, and none pretended to have composed a whole sequence of these tales. In Chios a clan of such rhapsodes called themselves Homeridae, and claimed descent from a poet Homer who, they said, was the author of the epics that they recited throughout eastern Greece.[11] Perhaps this blind bard was but an eponym, the imaginary ancestor of a tribe or group, like Hellen, Dorus, or Ion.[12] The Greeks of the sixth century attributed to Homer not only the *Iliad* and the *Odyssey* but all the other epics then existing. The Homeric poems are the oldest epics known to us; but their very excellence, as well as their many references to earlier bards, suggest that the surviving epics stand at the end of a long line of development from simple lays to lengthy "stitched" songs. In

---

* Rhyme was mostly confined to oracles and religious prophecies.

† From *raptein,* to stitch together, and *oide*, a song.

sixth-century Athens—possibly under Solon,[13] probably under Peisistratus—a governmental commission selected or collated the *Iliad* and the *Odyssey* from the epic literature of the preceding centuries, assigned them to Homer, and edited—perhaps wove—them into substantially their present shape.[14]

It is one of the miracles of literature that poems so complex in origin achieved in the end so artistic a result. It is quite true that both in language and in structure the *Iliad* falls considerably this side of perfection: that Aeolian and Ionic forms are mingled as if by some polyglot Smyrnan, and that the meter requires now one dialect and now the other; that the plot is marred by inconsistencies, changes of plan and emphasis, and contradictions of character; that the same heroes are killed two or three times over in the course of the tale; that the original theme—the wrath of Achilles and its results—is interrupted and obscured by a hundred episodes apparently taken from other lays and sewn into the epic at every seam. Nevertheless, in its larger aspects the story is one, the language is powerful and vivid, the poem is all in all "the greatest that ever sounded on the lips of men."[15] Such an epic could have been begun only in the active and exuberant youth of the Greeks, and could have been completed only in their artistic maturity. Its characters are nearly all warriors or their women; even the philosophers, like Nestor, put up an enviably good fight. These individuals are intimately and sympathetically conceived; and perhaps the finest thing in all Greek literature is the unbiased manner in which we are made to feel now with Hector and now with Achilles. In his tent Achilles is a thoroughly unheroic and unlikable figure, complaining to his mother that his luck does not befit his semidivinity, and that Agamemnon has stolen his plum, the unhappy Briseis; letting the Greeks die by the thousands while he eats and pouts and sleeps in his ship or his tent; sending Patroclus unaided to death, and then rending the air with unmanly lamentations. When finally he goes into battle he is not stirred by patriotism but mad with grief over the loss of his friend. In his rage he loses all decency, and sinks to savage cruelty with both Lycaon and Hector. In truth he is an undeveloped mind, unsettled and uncontrolled, and overshadowed with prophecies of death. "Nay, friend," he says to the fallen Lycaon, who sues for mercy, "die like another! What wouldst thou vainly weeping? Patroclus died, who was far better than thou. Look upon me! Am I not beautiful and tall, and sprung of a good father, and a goddess the mother that bare me? Yet, lo, Death is over me, and the mighty hand of Doom. There cometh a dawn of day, a noon or an evening, and a hand that I know not shall lay me dead."[16] So he stabs the unresisting Lycaon through the neck, flings the body into the river, and makes one of those grandiose speeches that adorn the slaughter in the *Iliad*, and laid the foundation for oratory among the Greeks. Half of Hellas worshiped Achilles for centuries as a god;[17] we accept him, and forgive him, as a child. At the worst he is one of the supreme creations of the poetic mind.

What carries us along through the *Iliad* when we do not have to study or translate it is not merely these characterizations, so numerous and diverse, nor merely the flow and turmoil of the tale, but the rushing splendor of the verse. It must be admitted that Homer repeats as well as nods; it is part of his plan to recall as in refrain certain epithets and lines; so he sings with fond repetition, of *Emos d'erigeneia phane rhododactylos Eos*—"when appeared the morning's daughter, rosy-fingered Dawn."[18] But if these are flaws they are lost in the brilliance of the language, and the wealth of similes that now and then, amid the shock of war, calm us with the quiet beauty of peaceful fields. "As when flies in swarming myriads haunt the herdsman's stalls in spring time, when new milk has filled the pails—in such vast multitudes mustered the long-haired Greeks upon the plain."[19] Or

As when, among
The deep dells of an arid mountain-side,
A great fire burns its way, and the thick wood
Before it is consumed, and shifting winds
Hither and thither sweep the flames—so ranged
Achilles in his fury through the field
From side to side, and everywhere o'ertook
His victims, and the earth ran dark with blood.[20]

The *Odyssey* is so different from all this that from the outset one suspects its separate authorship. Even some of the Alexandrian scholars suggested this, and all the critical authority of Aristarchus was required to hush the dispute.[21] The *Odyssey* agrees with the *Iliad* in certain standard phrases—"owl-eyed Athena," "long-haired Greeks," "wine-dark sea," "rosy-fingered Dawn"—which may have been taken from the same hoard and poetical tradition into which the authors of the *Iliad* had dipped their pens. But the *Odyssey* contains an array of words apparently brought into use after the *Iliad* was composed.[22] In the second epic we hear frequently of iron, where the earlier one spoke of bronze; we hear of writing, of private property in land, of freedmen and emancipation—none of which are mentioned in the *Iliad;* the very gods and their functions are different.[23] The meter is the same dactylic hexameter, as in all the Greek epics; but the style and spirit and substance are so far from the *Iliad* that if one author wrote both poems he was a paragon of complexity and a master of all moods. The new poet is more literary and philosophical, less violent and warlike, than the old; more self-conscious and meditative, leisurely and civilized; so gentle, indeed, that Bentley thought the *Odyssey* had been composed for the special benefit of women.[24]

Whether here too we have poets rather than a poet is harder to say than in the case of the *Iliad*. There are signs of suture, but the stitching seems more skillful than in the older epic; the plot, though devious, turns out in the end to be remarkably consistent, worthy almost of contemporary fictioneers. From the beginning the conclusion is foreshadowed, every episode advances it, and its coming binds all the books into a whole. Probably the epic was built upon pre-existing lays, as in the case of the *Iliad;* but the work of unification is far more complete. We may conclude with a high degree of diffidence that the *Odyssey* is a century younger than the *Iliad*, and is predominantly the work of one man.

The characters are less vigorously and vividly conceived than in the *Iliad*. Penelope is shadowy, and never quite emerges from behind her loom except in the end, when a moment of doubt, perhaps of regret, flits through her mind at the return of her master. Helen is clearer, and unique; here the launcher of a thousand ships and the cause of ten thousand deaths is still "a goddess among women," maturely lovely in her middle age, gentler and quieter than before, but as proud as ever, and taking gracefully for granted all the attentions that hedge in a queen.[25] Nausicaa is a pretty essay in the male understanding of women; we hardly expected so delicate and romantic a picture from a Greek. Telemachus is uncertainly drawn, infected with hesitation as by some Hamlet touch; but Odysseus is the most complete and complex portrait in Greek poetry. All in all, the *Odyssey* is a fascinating novel in engaging verse, full of tender sentiment and adventurous surprise; more interesting, to an unwarlike and aging soul, than the majestic and bloody *Iliad*.

These poems—sole survivors of a long succession of epics—became the most precious element in the literary heritage of Greece. "Homer" was the staple of Greek education, the repository of Greek myth, the source of a thousand dramas, the foundation of moral training, and—strangest of all—the very Bible of orthodox theology. It was Homer and Hesiod, said Herodotus (probably with some hyperbole), who gave definite and human form to the Olympians, and order to the hierarchy of heaven.[26] There is much that is magnificent in Homer's gods, and we come to like them for their failings; but scholars have long since detected in the poets who pictured them a rollicking skepticism hardly befitting a national Bible. These deities quarrel like relatives, fornicate like fleas, and share with mankind what seemed to Alexander the stigmata of mortality—the need for love and sleep; they do everything human but hunger and die. Not one of them could bear comparison with Odysseus in intelligence, with Hector in heroism, with Andromache in tenderness, or with Nestor in dignity. Only a poet of the sixth century, versed in Ionian doubt, could have made such farcelings of the gods.[27] It is one of the humors of history that these epics, in which the Olympians have essentially the function of comic relief, were reverenced throughout Hellas as props of respectable morality and belief. Eventually the anomaly proved explosive; the humor destroyed the belief, and the moral development of men rebelled against the superseded morals of the gods.

IV. GAMES

Religion failed to unify Greece, but athletics—periodically—succeeded. Men went to Olympia, Delphi, Corinth, and Nemea not so much to honor the gods—for these could be honored anywhere—as to witness the heroic contests of chosen athletes, and the ecumenical assemblage of varied Greeks. Alexander, who could see Greece from without, considered Olympia the capital of the Greek world.

Here under the rubric of athletics we find the real religion of the Greeks—the worship of health, beauty, and strength. "To be in health," said Simonides, "is the best thing for man; the next best, to be of form and nature beautiful; the third, to enjoy wealth gotten without fraud; and the fourth, to be in youth's bloom among friends."[27a] "There is no greater glory for a man as long as he lives," said the *Odyssey*,[28] "than that which he wins by his own hands and feet." Perhaps it was necessary for an aristocratic people, living among slaves more numerous than themselves and frequently called upon to defend their soil against more populous nations, to keep in good condition. Ancient war depended upon physical vigor and skill, and these were the original aim of the contests that filled Hellas with the noise of their fame. We must not think of the average Greek as a student and lover of Aeschylus or Plato; rather, like the typical Briton or American, he was interested in sport, and his favored athletes were his earthly gods.

Greek games were private, local, municipal, and Panhellenic. Even the fragmentary remains of antiquity reveal an interesting range of sports.

A relief in the Athens Museum shows on one side a wrestling match, on another a hockey game.[29] Swimming, bareback riding, throwing or dodging missiles while mounted, were not so much sports as general accomplishments of all citizens. Hunting became a sport when it ceased to be a necessity. Ball games were as varied then as now, and as popular; at Sparta the terms *ballplayer* and *youth* were synonyms. Special rooms were built in the palaestra for games of ball; these rooms were called *sphairisteria*, and the teachers were *sphairistai*. On another relief we see men bouncing a ball against the floor or the wall, and striking it back with the flat of the hand;[30] we do not know whether the players did this in turn as in modern handball. One ball game resembled Canadian lacrosse, being a form of hockey played with racquets. Pollux, writing in the second century of our era, describes it in almost modern terms:

> Certain youths, divided into two equal groups, leave in a level place—which they have prepared and measured—a ball made of leather, about the size of an apple. They rush at it, as if it were a prize lying between them, from their fixed starting-points. Each of them has in his right hand a racquet (*rhabdon*) . . . ending in a sort of flat bend whose center is woven with gut strings . . . plaited like a net. Each side strives to be the first to drive the ball to the opposite end of the ground from that allotted to them.[31]

The same author pictures a game in which one team tries to throw a ball over or through an opposed group, "until one side drives the other back over their goal line." Antiphanes, in an imperfect fragment from the fourth century B.C., describes a "star": "When he got the ball he delighted to give it to one player while dodging another; he knocked it away from one and urged on another with noisy cries. Outside, a long pass, beyond him, overhead, a short pass. . . ."[32]

From these private sports came local and incidental games, as after the death of a hero like Patroclus, or the successful issue of some great enterprise, like the march of Xenophon's Ten Thousand to the sea. Then came municipal games, in which the contestants represented various localities and groups within one city-state. Almost but not quite international were the quadrennial Panathenaic games, established by Peisistratus in 566; here the entries were mostly from Attica, but outsiders were welcomed. Besides the usual athletic events there were chariot races, a torch race, a rowing race, musical competitions for voice, harp, lyre, and flute, dances, and recitations, chiefly from Homer. Each of the ten divisions of Attica was represented by twenty-four men chosen for their health, vigor, and good looks; and a prize was awarded to the most impressive twenty-four for "fine manhood."[33]

Since athletics were necessary for war, and yet would die without competitions, the cities of Greece, to provide the highest stimulus, arranged Panhellenic games. The oldest of these were organized as a regular quadrennial event at Olympia in 776 B.C.—the first definite date in Greek history. Originally confined to Eleans, within a century they were drawing entries from all Greece; by 476 the list of victors ranged from Sinope to Marseilles. The feast of Zeus became an international holyday; a truce was proclaimed to all wars in Greece for the month of the festival, and fines were levied by the Eleans upon any Greek state in whose territory a traveler to the games suffered molestation. Philip of Macedon humbly paid a fine because some of his soldiers had robbed an Athenian en route to Olympia.

We picture the pilgrims and athletes starting out from distant cities, a month ahead of time, to come together at the games. It was a fair as well as a festival; the plain was covered not only with the tents that sheltered the visitors from the July heat, but with the booths where a thousand concessionaires exposed for sale everything from wine and fruit to horses and statuary, while acrobats and conjurors performed their tricks for the crowd. Some juggled balls in the air, others performed marvels of agility and skill, others ate fire or swallowed swords: modes of amusement, like forms of superstition, enjoy a reverend antiquity. Famous orators like Gorgias, famous sophists like Hippias, perhaps famous writers like Herodotus, delivered addresses or recitations from the porticoes of the temple of Zeus. It was a special holiday for men, since married women were not allowed to attend the festival; these had their own games at the feast of Hera. Menander summed up such a scene in five words: "crowd, market, acrobats, amusements, thieves."[34]

Only freeborn Greeks were allowed to compete in the Olympic games. The athletes (from *athlos*, a contest) were selected by local and municipal elimination trials, after which they submitted for ten months to rigorous training under professional *paidotribai* (literally, youth rubbers) and *gymnastai*. Arrived at Olympia, they were examined by the officials, and took an oath to observe all the rules. Irregularities were rare; we hear of Eupolis bribing other boxers to lose to him,[35] but the penalty and dishonor attached to such offenses were discouragingly great. When everything was ready the athletes were led into the stadium; as they entered, a herald announced their names and the cities that had entered them. All the contestants, whatever their age or rank, were naked; occasionally a girdle might be worn at the loins.[36] Of the stadium itself nothing remains but the narrow stone slabs toed by the runners at the starting point. The 45,000 spectators kept their places in the stadium all day long, suffering from insects, heat, and thirst; hats were forbidden, the water was bad, and flies and mosquitoes infested the place as they do today. Sacrifices were offered at frequent intervals to Zeus Averter of Flies.[37]

The most important events were grouped together as the pentathlon, or five contests. To promote all-around development in the athlete each entry in any of these events was required to compete in all of them; to secure the victory it was necessary to win three contests out of the five. The first was a broad jump; the athlete held weights like dumbbells in his hands, and leaped from a standing start. Ancient writers assure us that some jumpers spanned fifty feet;[38] but it is not necessary to believe everything that we read. The second event was throwing the discus, a circular plate of metal or stone weighing about twelve pounds; the best throws are said to have covered a hundred feet.[39] The third contest was in hurling the javelin or spear, with the aid of a leather thong attached to the center of the shaft. The fourth and principal event of the group was the stadium sprint—i.e., for the length of the stadium, usually some two hundred yards. The fifth contest was wrestling. It was a highly popular form of competition in Greece, for the very name *palaistra* was taken from it, and many a story was told of its champions.

Boxing was an ancient game, almost visibly handed down from Minoan Crete and Mycenaean Greece. The boxers practiced with punching balls hung on a level with the head and filled with fig seeds, meal, or sand. In the classic age of Greece (i.e., the fifth and fourth centuries), they wore "soft gloves" of oxhide dressed with fat and reaching almost to the elbow. Blows were confined to the head, but there was no rule against hitting a man who was down. There were no rests or rounds; the boxers fought till one surrendered or succumbed. They were not classified by weight; any man of any weight might enter the lists. Hence weight was an asset, and boxing degenerated in Greece from a competition in skill into a contest in brawn.

In the course of time, as brutality increased, boxing and wrestling were combined into a new contest called the pankration, or game of all powers. In this everything but biting and eye-gouging was permitted, even to a kick in the stomach.[40] Three heroes whose names have come down to us won by breaking the fingers of their opponents;[41] another struck so ferociously with straight extended fingers and strong sharp nails that he pierced the flesh of his adversary and dragged out his bowels.[42] Milo of Crotona was a more amiable pugilist. He had developed his strength, we are told, by carrying a calf every day of its life until it was a full-grown bull. People loved him for his tricks: he would hold a pomegranate so fast in his fist that no one could get it from him, and yet the fruit was uninjured; he would stand on an oiled quoit and resist all efforts to dislodge him; he would tie a cord around his forehead and burst the cord by holding his breath and so forcing blood to his head. In the end he was destroyed by his virtues. "For he chanced," says Pausanias, "on a withered tree, into which some wedges had been driven to separate the wood, and he took it into his head to keep the wood apart with his hands. But the wedges slipped out, he was imprisoned in the tree, and became a prey to the wolves."[43]

In addition to the pentathlon sprint, there were other foot races at the games. One was for four hundred yards, another for twenty-four stadia, or 2⅔ miles; a third was an armed race, in which each runner carried a heavy shield. We have no knowledge of the records made in these races; the stadium differed in length in different cities, and the Greeks had no instruments for measuring small intervals of time. Stories tell of a Greek runner who could outdistance a hare; of another who raced a horse from Coronea to Thebes (some twenty miles) and beat it; and of how Pheidippides ran from Athens to Sparta—150 miles—in two days[44] and, at the cost of his life, brought to Athens the news of the victory at Marathon, twenty-four miles away. But there were no "marathon races" in Greece.

In the plain below the stadium Olympia built a special hippodrome for horse races. Women as well as men might enter their horses, and, as now, the prize went to the owner and not to the jockey, though the horse was sometimes rewarded with a statue.[45] The culminating events of the games were the chariot races, with two or four horses running abreast. Often ten four-horse chariots competed together; and as each had to negotiate twenty-three turns around the posts at the ends of the course, accidents were the chief thrill of the game; in one race with forty starters a single chariot finished. We may imagine the tense excitement of the spectators at these contests, their wordy arguments about their favorites, their emotional abandonment as the survivors rounded the last turn.

When the toils of five days were over the victors received their rewards. Each bound a woolen fillet about his head, and upon this the judges placed a crown of wild olive, while a herald announced the name and city of the winner. This laurel wreath was the only prize given at the Olympic games, and yet it was the most eagerly contested distinction in Greece. So important were the games that not even the Persian invasion stopped them; and while a handful of Greeks withstood Xerxes' army at Thermopylae the customary thousands watched Theagenes of Thasos, on the very day of the battle, win the pancratiast's crown. "Good heavens!" exclaimed a Persian to his general; "what manner of men are these against whom you have brought us to fight?—men who contend with one another not for money but for honor!"[46] He, or the Greek inventor of the tale, did the Greeks too much credit, and not merely because the Greeks should on that day have been at Thermopylae rather than at Olympia. Though the direct prize at the games was little, the indirect rewards were great. Many cities voted substantial sums to the victors on their return from their triumphs; some cities made them generals; and the crowd idolized them so openly that jealous philosophers complained.[47] Poets like Simonides and Pindar were engaged by the victor or his patrons to write odes in his honor, which were sung by choruses of boys in the procession that welcomed him home; sculptors were paid to perpetuate him in bronze or stone; and sometimes he was given free sustenance in the city hall. We may judge the cost of this item when we learn, on questionable authority, that Milo ate a four-year-old heifer, and Theagenes an ox, in a day.[48]

The sixth century saw the peak of the splendor and popularity of athletics in Greece. In 582 the Amphictyonic League established the Pythian games in honor of Apollo at Delphi; in the same year the Isthmian games were instituted at Corinth in honor of Poseidon; six years later the Nemean games were inaugurated to celebrate the Nemean Zeus; and all three occasions became Panhellenic festivals. Together with the Olympic games they formed a *periodos*, or cycle, and the great ambition of a Greek athlete was to win the crown at all of them. In the Pythian games contests in music and poetry were added to the physical competitions; and indeed such musical tilts had been celebrated at Delphi long before the establishment of the athletic games. The original event was a hymn in honor of Apollo's victory over the Delphic python; in 582 contests were added in singing, and in playing the lyre and the flute. Similar musical contests were held at Corinth, Nemea, Delos, and elsewhere; for the Greeks believed that by frequent public competitions they could stimulate not only the ability of the performer but the taste of the public as well. The principle was applied to almost every art—to pottery, poetry, sculpture, painting, choral singing, oratory, and drama.[49] In this way and others the games had a profound influence upon art and literature, and even upon the writing of history; for the chief method of reckoning time, in later Greek historiography, was by Olympiads, designated by the name of the victor in the one-stadium foot race. The physical perfection of the all-around athlete in the sixth century generated that ideal of statuary which reached its fullness in Myron and Polycleitus. The nude contests and games in the palaestra and at the festivals gave the sculptor unequaled opportunities to study the human body in every natural form and pose; the nation unwittingly became models to its artists, and Greek athletics united with Greek religion to generate Greek art.

V. ARTS

Now that we come at last to the most perfect products of Greek civilization we find ourselves tragically limited in the quantity of the remains. The devastation caused in Greek literature by time and bigotry and mental fashions is negligible compared with the destruction of Greek art. One classic bronze survives—the *Charioteer of Delphi;* one classic marble statue —the *Hermes* of Praxiteles; not one temple—not even the Theseum—has come down to us in the form and color that it had for ancient Greece. Greek work in textiles, in wood, in ivory, silver, or gold, is nearly all gone; the material was too perishable or too precious to escape vandalism and time. We must reconstruct the ship from a few planks of the wreckage.

The sources of Greek art were the impulses to representation and decoration, the anthropomorphic quality of Greek religion, and the athletic character and ideal. The early Greek, like other primitives, when he outgrew the custom of sacrificing living beings to accompany and serve the dead, buried carved or painted figures as substitutes. Later he placed images of his ancestors in his home; or he dedicated in the temple likenesses of himself, or of those whom he loved, as votive figurines that might magically win for their models the protection of the god. Minoan religion, Mycenaean religion, even the chthonic cults of Greece, were too vague and impersonal, sometimes too horrible and grotesque, to lend themselves to esthetic form; but the frank humanity of the Olympian gods, and their need of temple homes for their earthly stays, opened a wide road for sculpture, architecture, and a hundred ancillary arts. No other religion—possibly excepting Catholicism—has so stimulated and influenced literature and art: almost every book or play, statue or building or vase, that has come down to us from ancient Greece touches upon religion in subject, purpose, or inspiration.

But inspiration alone would not have made Greek art great. There was needed a technical excellence rising out of cultural contacts and the transmission and development of crafts; indeed art to the Greek was a form of handicraft, and the artist grew so naturally out of the artisan that Greece never quite distinguished them. There was needed a knowledge of the human body, as in its healthy development the norm of proportion, symmetry, and beauty; there was needed a sensuous, passionate love of beauty, that would hold no toil too great that might give to the living moment of loveliness a lasting form. The women of Sparta placed in their sleeping chambers figures of Apollo, Narcissus, Hyacinthus, or some other handsome deity, in order that they might bear beautiful children.[50] Cypselus established a beauty contest among women far back in the seventh century; and according to Athenaeus this periodical competition continued down to the Christian era.[51] In some places, says Theophrastus, "there are contests between the women in respect of modesty and good management . . . ; and also there are contests about beauty, as for instance . . . in Tenedos and Lesbos."[52]

1. Vases

There was a pretty legend in Greece that the first cup was molded upon Helen's breast.[53] If so, the mold was lost in the Dorian invasion, for what pottery has come down to us from early Greece does not remind us of Helen. The invasion must have profoundly disturbed the arts, impoverishing craftsmen, scattering schools, and ending for a time the transmission of technology; for Greek vases after the invasion begin again with primitive simplicity and crudity, as if Crete had never lifted pottery into an art.

Probably the rough mood of the Dorian conquerors, using what survived of Minoan-Mycenaean techniques, produced that Geometric style which dominates the oldest Greek pottery after the Homeric age. Flowers, scenery, and plants, so luxuriant in Cretan ornament, were swept away, and the stern spirit that made the glory of the Doric temple contrived the passing ruin of Greek pottery. The gigantic jars that characterize this period made small pretense to beauty; they were designed to store wine or oil or grain rather than to interest a ceramic connoisseur. The decoration was almost all by repeated triangles, circles, chains, checkers, lozenges, swastikas, or simple parallel horizontal lines; even the human figures that intervened were geometrical—torsos were triangles, thighs and legs were cones. This lazy style of ornament spread through Greece, and determined the form of the Dipylon vases* at Athens; but on these enormous containers (usually made to receive the human dead) black silhouettes of mourners, chariots, and animals were drawn, however awkwardly, between the pattern's lines. Towards the end of the eighth century more life entered into the painting of Greek pottery; two colors were used for the ground, curves replaced straight lines, palmettes and lotuses, prancing horses and hunted lions took form upon the clay, and the ornate Oriental succeeded the bare Geometric style.

An age of busy experimentation followed. Miletus flooded the market with its red vases, Samos with its alabasters, Lesbos with its black wares, Rhodes with its whites, Clazomenae with its grays, and Naucratis exported faïence and translucent glass. Erythrae was famous for the thinness of its vases, Chalcis for brilliance of finish, Sicyon and Corinth for their delicate "Proto-Corinthian" scent bottles and elaborately painted jugs like the Chigi vase in Rome. A kind of ceramic war engaged the potters of the rival cities; one or another of them found purchasers in every port of the Mediterranean, and in the interior of Russia, Italy, and Gaul. In the seventh century Corinth seemed to be winning; its wares were in every land and hand, its potters had found new techniques of incision and coloring, and had shown a fresh inventiveness in forms. But about 550 the masters of the Ceramicus—the potters' quarter on the outskirts of Athens—came to the front, threw off Oriental influence, and captured with their Black-Figure ware the markets of the Black Sea, Cyprus, Egypt, Etruria, and Spain. From that time onward the best ceramic craftsmen migrated to Athens or were born there; a great school and tradition formed as through many generations son succeeded father in the art; and the making of fine pottery became one of the great industries, finally one of the conceded monopolies, of Attica.

The vases themselves, now and then, bear pictures of the potter's shop, the master working with his apprentices, or watchfully supervising the various processes: mixing the pigments and the clay, molding the form, painting the ground, engraving the picture, firing the cup, and feeling the happiness of those who see beauty taking form under their hands. More than a hundred of these Attic potters are known to us; but time has broken up their masterpieces, and they are only names. Here on a drinking cup are the proud words, *Nikosthenes me poiesen*—"Nicosthenes made me."[53a] A greater than he was Execias, whose majestic amphora is in the Vatican; he was one of many artists encouraged by patronage and peace under the Peisistratids. From the hands of Clitias and Ergotimus came, about 560, the famous François vase, found in Etruria by a Frenchman of that name, and now treasured in the Archeological Museum at Florence—a great mixing bowl covered with row upon row of figures and scenes from Greek mythology.[54] These men were the outstanding masters of the Black-

* So called because they were found chiefly near the Double Gate of the city at the Ceramicus.

Figure style in sixth-century Attica. We need not exaggerate the excellence of their work; it cannot compare, either in conception or in execution, with the best work of the T'ang or Sung Chinese. But the Greek had a different aim from the Oriental: he sought not color but line, not ornament but form. The figures on the Greek vases are conventional, stylized, improbably magnificent in the shoulders and thin in the legs; and as this continued through the classic age, we must assume that the Greek potter never dreamed of realistic accuracy. He was writing poetry, not prose, speaking to the imagination rather than the eye. He limited himself in materials and pigments: he took the fine red clay of the Ceramicus, quieted its color with yellow, carefully engraved the figures, and filled out the silhouettes with brilliant black glaze. He transformed the earth into a profusion of vessels that wedded beauty and use: hydria, amphora, oenochoë, kylix, krater, lekythos—i.e., water jug, two-handled jar, wine bowl, drinking cup, mixing bowl, and unguent flask. He conceived the experiments, created the subjects, and developed the techniques that were taken up by bronzeworkers, sculptors, and painters; he made the first essays in foreshortening, perspective, chiaroscuro, and modeling;[55] he paved the way for statuary by molding terra-cotta figures in a thousand themes and forms. He freed his own art from Dorian geometry and Oriental excess, and made the human figure the source and center of its life.

Towards the last quarter of the sixth century the Athenian potter tired of black figures on a red ground, inverted the formula, and created that Red-Figure style which ruled the markets of the Mediterranean for two hundred years. The figures were still stiff and angular, the body in profile with the eyes in full view; but even within these limits there was a new freedom, a wider scope, of conception and execution. He sketched the figures upon the clay with a light point, drew them in greater detail with a pen, filled in the background with black, and added minor touches with colored glaze. Here, too, some of the masters made lasting names. One amphora is signed, "Painted by Euthymides, son of Pollias, as never Euphronius"[56]—which was to challenge Euphronius to equal it. Nevertheless this Euphronius is still rated as the greatest potter of his age; to him, some think, belongs the great krater on which Heracles wrestles with Antaeus. To his contemporary Sosias is attributed one of the most famous of Greek vases, whereon Achilles binds the wounded arm of Patroclus; every detail is lovingly carried out, and the silent pain of the young warrior has survived the centuries. To these men, and now nameless others, we owe such masterpieces as the cup in whose interior we see Dawn mourning over her dead son, and the hydria, in the Metropolitan Museum of Art at New York, that shows a Greek soldier, perhaps Achilles, plunging his lance into a fair and not breastless Amazon. It was before such a vase as one of these that John Keats stood enthralled one day, until its "wild ecstasy" and "mad pursuit" fired his brain with an ode greater than any Grecian urn.

2. *Sculpture*

The Greek settlement of western Asia, and the opening of Egypt to Greek trade towards 660 B.C., allowed Near Eastern and Egyptian forms and methods of statuary to enter Ionia and European Greece. About 580 two Cretan sculptors, Dipoenus and Scyllis, accepted commissions at Sicyon and Argos, and left behind them there not only statues but pupils; from this period dates a vigorous school of sculpture in the Peloponnese. The art had many purposes: it commemorated the dead first with simple pillars, then with herms whose head alone was carved, then with forms completely chiseled in the round, or with funeral-stelae reliefs; it made statues of victorious athletes, first as types, later as individuals; and it was encouraged by the lively imagination of Greek faith to make countless images of the gods.

Until the sixth century its material was most frequently wood. We hear a great deal of the chest of Cypselus, dictator of Corinth. According to Pausanias, it was made of cedar, inlaid with ivory and gold, and adorned with complicated carvings. As wealth increased, wooden statues might be covered, in whole or part, by precious materials; indeed it was thus that Pheidias made his chryselephantine (i.e., gold and ivory) statues of *Athene Parthenos* and the Olympian *Zeus*. Bronze rivaled stone as sculptural material to the end of classical art. Few ancient bronzes have survived the temptation to melt them down, but we may judge from the perhaps too ministerial *Charioteer* of the Delphi Museum (ca. 490) how near to perfection the art of hollow casting had been carried since Rhoecus and Theodorus of Samos had introduced it into Greece. The most famous group in Athenian statuary, the *Tyrannicides* (Harmodius and Aristogeiton), was cast in bronze by Antenor at Athens shortly after the expulsion of Hippias. Many forms of soft stone were used before the sculptors of Greece undertook to mold harder varieties with hammer and chisel; but once they had learned the art they almost denuded Naxos and Paros of marble. In the archaic period (1100-490) the figures were often painted; but towards the end of that age it was found that a better effect could be secured, in representing the delicate skin of women, by leaving the polished marble without artificial tint.

The Greeks of Ionia were the first to discover the uses of drapery as a sculptural element. Egypt and the Near East had left the clothing rigid—a vast stone apron nullifying the living form; but in sixth-century Greece the sculptors introduced folds into the drapery, and used the garment to reveal that ultimate source and norm of beauty, the healthy human body. Nevertheless the Egypto-Asiatic influence remained so strong that in most archaic Greek sculpture the figure is heavy, graceless, and stiff; the legs are strained even in repose; the arms hang helpless at the sides; the eyes have the almond form, and occasionally an Oriental slant; the face is stereotyped, immobile, passionless. Greek statuary, in this period, accepted the Egyptian rule of frontality—i.e., the figure was made to be seen only from the front, and so rigidly bisymmetrical that a vertical line would pass through the nose, mouth, navel, and genitals with never a right or left deviation, and no flexure of either motion or rest. Perhaps convention was responsible for this dull rigidity: the law of the Greek games forbade a victor to set up a portrait statue of himself unless he had won all contests in the pentathlon; only then, the Greeks argued, would he achieve the harmonious physical development that would merit individual modeling.[57] For this reason, and perhaps because, as in Egypt, religious convention before the fifth century governed the representation of the gods, the Greek sculptor confined himself to a few poses and types, and devoted himself to their mastery.

Two types above all won his study: the youth, or *kouros*, nearly nude, slightly advancing the left leg, with arms at the side or partly extended, fists closed, countenance quiet and stern; and the *kore*, or maiden, carefully coiffured, modestly posed and draped, one hand gathering up the robe, the other offering some gift to the gods. History till lately called the *kouroi* "Apollos," but they were more probably athletes or funerary monuments. The most famous of the type is the *Apollo* of Tenea; the largest, the *Apollo* of Sunium; the most pretentious, the *Throne of Apollo* at Amyclae, near Sparta. One of the finest is the small *Strangford Apollo* in the British Museum; finer still is the *Choiseul-Gouffier Apollo*, a Roman copy of an early fifth-century original.[58] To at least the male eye the *korai* are more pleasing: their bodies are gracefully slender, their faces are softened with a Mona Lisa smile, their drapery begins to escape the stiffness of convention; some of them, like those in the Athens Museum would be called masterpieces in any other land;[59] one of them, which we may call the *Kore* of Chios,* is a masterpiece even in Greece. In them the sensuous Ionian touch breaks through the Egyptian immobility and Dorian austerity of the "Apollos." Archermus of Chios created another type, or followed lost models, in the *Nike*, or *Victory*, of Delos; out of this would come the lovely *Nike* of Paeonius at Olympia, the *Winged Victory* of Samothrace, and, in Christian art, the winged figures of cherubim.[60] Near Miletus unknown sculptors carved a series of draped and seated females for the temple of the Branchidae, figures powerful but crude, dignified but ponderous, profound but dead.†

Sculpture in relief was so old that a pretty legend could undertake to describe its origin. A lass of Corinth drew upon a wall the outline of the shadow that the lamplight cast of her lover's head. Her father Butades, a potter, filled in the outline with clay, pressed the form to hardness, took it down, and baked

* No. 682 in the National Museum at Athens.

† Now in the British Museum; there are copies in the Metropolitan Museum in New York. The Branchidae were the hereditary priests of the temple.

it; so, Pliny assures us, bas-relief was born.[61] The art became even more important than sculpture in the adornment of temples and graves. Already in 520 Aristocles made a funeral relief of Aristion, which is one of the many treasures of the Athens Museum.

Since reliefs were nearly always painted, sculpture, relief, and painting were allied arts, usually handmaids to architecture; and most artists were skilled in all four forms. Temple moldings, friezes, metopes, and pediment backgrounds were usually painted, while the main structure was ordinarily left in the natural color of the stone. Of painting as a separate art we have only negligible remains from Greece; but we know through passages in the poets that panel painting, with colors mixed in melted wax, was already practiced in the days of Anacreon.[62] Painting was the last great art to develop in Greece, and the last to die.

All in all, the sixth century failed to rise, in any Greek art except architecture, to the boldness of conception or the perfection of form attained in the same age by Greek philosophy and poetry. Perhaps artistic patronage was slow to develop in an aristocracy still rural and poor, or in a business class too young to have graduated from wealth to taste. Nevertheless the age of the dictators was a period of stimulation and improvement in every Greek art—above all, under Peisistratus and Hippias in Athens. Towards the end of this period the old rigidity of sculpture began to thaw, the rule of frontality was broken down; legs began to move, arms to leave the side, hands to open up, faces to take on feeling and character, bodies to bend in a variety of poses revealing new studies in anatomy and action. This revolution in sculpture, this animation of stone with life, became a major event in Greek history; the escape from frontality was one of the signal accomplishments of Greece. Egyptian and Oriental influences were set aside, and Greek art became Greek.

3. *Architecture*

The science of building recovered slowly from the Dorian invasion, and redeemed beyond its deserts the Dorian name. Across the Dark Age from Agamemnon to Terpander, the Mycenaean megaron transmitted the essentials of its structure to Greece; the rectangular shape of the building, the use of columns within and without, the circular shaft and simple square capital, the triglyphs and metopes of the entablature, were all preserved in the greatest achievement of Greek art, the Doric style. But whereas Mycenaean architecture was apparently secular, devoted to palaces and homes, classical Greek architecture was almost entirely religious. The royal megaron was transformed into a civic temple as monarchy waned and religion and democracy united the affections of Greece in honoring the personified city in its god.

The earliest Greek temples were of wood or brick, as befitted the poverty of the Dark Age. When stone became the orthodox material of temple building the architectural features remained as set by timber construction; the rectangular naos or temple proper, the circular shafts, the "master-beam" architraves, the beam-end triglyphs, the gabled roof, confessed the wooden origin of their form; even the first Ionic spiral was apparently a floral figure painted upon a block of wood.[63] The use of stone increased as Greek wealth and travel grew; the transition was most rapid after the opening of Egypt to Greek trade about 660 B.C. Limestone was the favored material of the new styles before the sixth century; marble came in towards 580, at first for decorative portions, then for façades, finally for the entire temple from base to tiles.

Three "orders" of architecture were developed in Greece: the Doric, the Ionic, and, in the fourth century, the Corinthian. Since the interior of the temple was reserved for the god and his ministrants, and worship was held outside, all three orders devoted themselves to making the exterior impressively beautiful. They began at the ground, usually in some elevated place, with the stereobate—two or three layers of foundation stone in receding steps. From the uppermost layer, or stylobate, rose directly, without individual base, the Doric column—"fluted" with shallow, sharp-edged grooves, and widening perceptibly at the middle in what the Greeks called entasis, or stretching. Furthermore, the Doric column tapered slightly towards the top, thereby emulating the tree, and successfully contradicting the Minoan-Mycenaean style. (An undiminished shaft—worse yet, one that tapers downward—seems top-heavy and graceless to the eye, while the wider base heightens that sense of stability which all architecture should convey. Perhaps, however, the Doric column is too heavy, too thick in proportion to its height, too stolidly engrossed in sturdiness and strength.) Upon the Doric column sat its simple and powerful capital: a "necking" or circular band, a cushionlike echinus, and, topmost, a square abacus to spread the supporting thrust of the pillar beneath the architrave.

While the Dorians were developing this style from the megaron, modified probably by acquaintance with the Egyptian "proto-Doric" colonnades of Der-el-Bahri and Beni-Hasan, the Ionian Greeks were altering the same fundamental form under Asiatic influence. In the resultant Ionic order a slender column rose upon an individual base, and began at the bottom, as it ended at the top, with a narrow fillet or band; its height was usually greater, and its diameter smaller, than in the Doric shaft; the upward tapering was scarcely perceptible; the flutings were deep, semicircular grooves separated by flat edges. The Ionic capital was composed of a narrow echinus, a still narrower abacus, and between them—almost concealing them—emerged the twin spirals of a volute, like an infolded scroll—a graceful element adapted from Hittite, Assyrian, and other Oriental forms.[64] These characteristics, together with the elaborate adornment of the entablature, described not only a style but a people; they represented in stone the Ionian expressiveness, suppleness, sentiment, elegance, and love of delicate detail, even as the Doric order conveyed the proud reserve, the massive strength, the severe simplicity of the Dorian; the sculpture, literature, music, manners, and dress of the rival groups differed in harmony with their architectural styles. Dorian architecture is mathematics, Ionian architecture is poetry, both seeking the durability of stone; the one is "Nordic," the other Oriental; together they constitute the masculine and feminine themes in a basically harmonious form.

Greek architecture distinguished itself by developing the column into an element of beauty as well as a structural support. The essential function of the external colonnade was to uphold the eaves, and to relieve the walls of the naos, or inner temple, from the outward thrust of the gabled roof. Above the columns rose the entablature—i.e., the superstructure of the edifice. Here again, as in the supporting elements, Greek architecture sought a clear differentiation, and yet an articulated connection, of the members. The architrave—the great stone that connected the capitals—was in the Doric order plain, or carried a simple painted molding; in Ionic it was composed of three layers, each projecting below, and was topped with a marble cornice segmented with a confusing variety of ornamental details. Since the sloping beams that made the framework of the roof in the Doric style came down, and were secured, between two horizontal beams at the eaves, the united ends of the three beams formed—at first in wood, then imitatively in stone—a triglyph or triply divided surface. Between each triglyph and the next a space was left as an open window when the roof was of wood or of terra-cotta tiles; when translucent marble tiles were used these metopes, or "seeing-between" places, were filled in with marble slabs carved in low relief. In the Ionic style a band or frieze of reliefs might run around the upper outer walls of the naos or cella; in the fifth century both forms of relief—metopes and frieze—were often used in the same building, as in the Parthenon. In the pediments—the triangles formed by the gabled roof in front and rear—the sculptor found his greatest opportunity; the figures here might be drawn out in high relief and enlarged for view from below; and the cramped corners, or tympana, tested the subtlest skill. Finally, the roof itself might be a work of art, with brilliantly colored tiles and decorative rain-disposing acroteria, or pinnacle figures, rising from the angles of the pediments. All in all, there was probably a surplus of sculpture on the Greek temple, between the columns, along the walls, or within the edifice. The painter also was involved: the temple was colored in whole or in part, along with its statues, moldings, and reliefs. Perhaps we do the Greeks too much honor today, when time has worn the paint from their temples and divinities, and ferrous strains have lent to the marble natural and incalculable hues that set off the brilliance of the stone under the clear Greek sky. Some day even contemporary art may become beautiful.

The two rival styles achieved grandeur in the sixth century, and perfection in the fifth. Geographically they divided Greece unevenly: Ionic prevailed in Asia and the Aegean, Doric on the mainland and in the west. The salient achievements of sixth-century Ionic were the temples of Artemis at Ephesus, of Hera at Samos, and of the Branchidae near Miletus; but only ruins survive of Ionic architecture before Marathon. The finest extant buildings from the sixth century are the older temples of Paestum and Sicily, all in the Doric style. The ground plan remains of the great temple built at Delphi, between 548 and 512, from the designs of the Corinthian Spintharus; it was destroyed by earthquake in 373, was rebuilt on the same plan, and in that form still stood when Pausanias made his tour of Greece. Athenian architecture of the period was almost wholly Doric: in this style Peisistratus began, about 530, the gigantic temple of the Olympian Zeus, on the plain at the foot of the Acropolis. After the Persian conquest of Ionia in 546, hundreds of Ionian artists migrated to Attica, and introduced or developed the Ionic style in Athens. By the end of the century Athenian architects were using both orders, and had laid all the technical groundwork for the Periclean age.

4. Music and the Dance

The word *mousike* among the Greeks meant originally any devotion to any Muse. Plato's Academy was called a *Museion* or Museum—i.e., a place dedicated to the Muses and the many cultural pursuits which they patronized; the Museum at Alexandria was a university of literary and scientific activity, not a collection of museum pieces. In the narrower and modern sense music was at least as popular among the Greeks as it is among ourselves today. In Arcadia all freemen studied music to the age of thirty; everyone knew some instrument; and to be unable to sing was accounted a disgrace.[65] Lyric poetry was so named because, in Greece, it was composed to be sung to the accompaniment of the lyre, the harp, or the flute. The poet usually wrote the music as well as the words, and sang his own songs; to be a lyric poet in ancient Greece was far more difficult than to compose, as poets do today, verses for silent and solitary reading. Before the sixth century there was hardly any Greek literature divorced from music. Education and letters, as well as religion and war, were bound up with music: martial airs played an important part in military training, and nearly all instruction of the memory was through verse. By the eighth century Greek music was already old, with hundreds of varieties and forms.

The instruments were simple, and were based, like our vaster armory of sound, upon percussion, wind, or strings. The first class were not popular. The flute was favored at Athens until Alcibiades, laughing at his music master's inflated cheeks, refused to play so ridiculous an instrument, and set a fashion against it among Athenian youth. (Besides, said the Athenians, the Boeotians surpassed them with the flute, which branded the art as a vulgar one.[66]) The simple flute, or aulos, was a tube of cane or bored wood with a detachable mouthpiece and from two to seven finger holes into which movable stopples might be inserted to modify the pitch. Some players used the double flute—a "masculine" or bass flute in the right hand and a "feminine" or treble flute in the left, both held to the mouth by a strap around the cheeks, and played in simple harmony. By attaching the flute to a distensible bag the Greeks made a bagpipe; by uniting several graduated flutes they made a syrinx, or Pipe of Pan; by extending and opening the end, and closing the finger holes, they made a salpinx, or trumpet.[67] Flute music, says Pausanias,[68] was usually gloomy, and was always used in dirges or elegies; but the *auletridai*—the flute-playing geisha girls of Greece—do not seem to have purveyed gloom. String music was confined to plucking the strings with finger or plectrum; bowing was unknown.[69] The lyre, phorminx, or kithara were essentially alike—four or more strings of sheep gut stretched over a bridge across a resonant body of metal or tortoise shell. The kithara was a small harp, used for accompanying narrative poetry; the lyre was like a guitar, and was chosen to accompany lyric poetry and songs.

The Greeks told many strange tales of how the gods—Hermes, Apollo, Athena—had invented these instruments; how Apollo had pitted his lyre against the pipes and flutes of Marsyas (a priest of the Phrygian goddess Cybele), had won—unfairly, as Marsyas thought—by adding his voice to the instrument, and had topped the performance by having poor Marsyas flayed alive: so legend personified the conquest of the flute by the lyre. Prettier stories were told of ancient musicians who had established or developed the musical art: of Olympus, Marsyas' pupil, who, towards 730, invented the enharmonic scale;* of Linus, Heracles' teacher, who invented Greek musical notation and established some of the "modes";[70] of Orpheus, Thracian priest of Dionysus; and of his pupil Musaeus, who said that "song

* A scale employing quarter tones; e.g., E E′ F A B B′ C E—where the accent indicates a quarter tone above the preceding note.

is a sweet thing to mortals."[71] These tales reflect the probable fact that Greek music derived its forms from Lydia, Phrygia, and Thrace.*[72]

Song entered into almost every phase of Greek life. There were dithyrambs for Dionysus, paeans for Apollo, hymns for any god; there were *enkomia*, or songs of praise, for rich men, and *epinikia*, or songs of victory, for athletes; there were *symposiaka, skolia, erotika, hymenaioi, elegiai,* and *threnoi* for dining, drinking, loving, marrying, mourning, and burying; herdsmen had their *bukolika*, reapers their *lityerses*, vinedressers their *epilenia*, spinners their *iouloi*, weavers their *elinoi*.[77] And then as now, presumably, the man in the market or the club, the lady in the home and the woman of the streets, sang songs not quite as learned as Simonides'; vulgar music and polite music have come down distantly together through the centuries.

The highest form of music, in the belief and practice of the Greeks, was choral singing; to this they gave the philosophical depth, the structural complexity, the emotional range, which in modern music tend to find place in the concerto or the symphony. Any festival—a harvest, a victory, a marriage, a holyday—might be celebrated with a chorus; and now and then cities and groups would organize great contests in choral song. The performance was in most cases prepared far in advance: a composer was appointed to write the words and music, a rich man was persuaded to pay the expense, professional singers

---

* The music of Hellas was played in a variety of scales far more numerous and complex than ours. Our diatonic scale makes no smaller division than the half tone, and twelve half tones constitute our octave; the Greeks used quarter tones, and had forty-five scales of eighteen notes apiece.[73] These scales were in three groups: the diatonic scales, based upon the tetrachord E D C B; the chromatic, upon E C♯ C B; and the enharmonic, upon E C C♭ B. From the Greek scales, by simplification, came those of medieval church music, and, through these, our own.

Within the diatonic tetrachord seven modes (*harmoniai*) were produced by tuning the strings to alter the position of the semitones in the octave. The most important modes were the Dorian (E F G A B C D E), martial and grave though in a minor key; the Lydian (C D E F G A B C), tender and plaintive though in a major key; and the Phrygian (D E F G A B C D), minor in key, and orgiastically passionate and wild.[74] It is amusing to read of the violent controversies concerning the musical, ethical, and medical effects, restorative or disastrous, which the Greeks—chiefly the philosophers—ascribed to these half-tone variations. Dorian music, we are told, made men brave and dignified, the Lydian made them sentimental and weak, the Phrygian made them excited and headstrong. Plato saw effeminate luxury and gross immorality as the offspring of most music, and wished to banish all instrumental performances from his ideal state. Aristotle would have had all youths trained in the Dorian mode.[75] Theophrastus had a good word to say even for the Phrygian mode; serious diseases, he tells us, can be made painless by playing a Phrygian air near the affected part.[76]

Greek musical notation used not ovals and stems on a staff of lines, but the letters of the alphabet, varied by inversion or transversion, augmented by dots and dashes to make sixty-four signs, and placed above the words of the song. A few scraps of such notation have come down to console us for the loss of the rest; they indicate melodies akin rather to Oriental than to European strains, and would be more bearable to the Hindus, the Chinese, or the Japanese than to our dull Occidental ears, untrained to quarter tones.

were engaged, and the chorus was carefully trained. All the singers sang the same note, as in the music of the Greek Church today; there was no "part song" except that in later centuries the accompaniment was played a fifth above or below the voice, or ran counter to it; this is as near as the Greeks seem to have come to harmony and counterpoint.[78]

The dance in its highest development was woven into one art with choral singing, just as many forms and terms of modern music were once associated with the dance;* and dancing rivaled music in age and popularity among the Greeks. Lucian, unable to trace its earthly beginnings, sought the origins of the dance in the regular motions of the stars.[80] Homer tells us not only of the dancing floor made by Daedalus for Ariadne, but of an expert dancer among the Greek warriors at Troy, Meriones, who, dancing while he fought, could never be found by any lance.[81] Plato described *orchesis*, or dancing, as "the instinctive desire to explain words by gestures of the entire body"—which is rather a description of certain modern languages; Aristotle better defined the dance as "an imitation of actions, characters, and passions by means of postures and rhythmical movements."[82] Socrates himself danced, and praised the art as giving health to every part of the body;[83] he meant, of course, Greek dancing.

For the Greek dance was quite different from ours. Though in some of its forms it may have served as a sexual stimulant, it rarely brought men into physical contact with women. It was an artistic exercise rather than a walking embrace, and, like the Oriental dance, it used arms and hands as much as legs and feet.[84] Its forms were as varied as the types of poetry and song; ancient authorities listed two hundred.[85] There were religious dances, as among the Dionysiac devotees; there were athletic dances, like Sparta's Gymnopedia, or Festival of Naked Youth; there were martial dances, like the Pyrrhic, taught to children as part of military drill; there was the stately *hyporchema*, a choral hymn or play performed by two choirs of which one alternately sang or danced while the other danced or sang; there were folk dances for every major event of life and every season or festival of the year. And as for everything else, there were dance contests, usually involving choral song.

All these arts—lyric poetry, song, instrumental music, and the dance—were closely allied in early Greece, and formed in many ways one art. As time went on, and already in the seventh century, specialization and professionalism set in. The rhapsodes abandoned song for recitation, and separated narrative verse from music.[86] Archilochus sang his lyrics without accompaniment,[87] and began that long degeneration which at last reduced

* The word *foot*, as meaning part of a verse, owes its origin to the dance that accompanied the song;[79] *orchestra*, to the Greek, meant a dancing platform, usually in front of the stage.

poetry to a fallen angel silent and confined. The choral dance broke up into singing without dancing, and dancing without singing; for, as Lucian put it, "The violent exercise caused shortness of breath, and the song suffered for it."[88] In like manner there appeared musicians who played without singing, and won the applause of devotees by their precise and rapid execution of quarter tones.[89] Some famous musicians, then as now, engrossed the receipts; Amoebeus, harpist and singer, received a talent ($6000) each time that he performed.[90] The common player, doubtless, lived from hand to mouth, for the musician, like other artists, belongs to a profession that has had the honor of starving in every generation.

The highest repute went to those who, like Terpander, Arion, Alcman, or Stesichorus, were skilled in all forms, and wove choral song, instrumental music, and the dance into a complex and harmonious whole probably more profoundly beautiful and satisfying than the operas and orchestras of today. The most famous of these masters was Arion. About him the Greeks told the tale how, on a voyage from Taras to Corinth, the sailors stole his money, and then gave him a choice between being stabbed to death or drowned. Having sung a final song, he dived into the sea, and was carried on the back of a dolphin (perhaps his harp) to the shore. It was he who, chiefly at Corinth and towards the close of the seventh century, transformed the inebriated singers of impromptu Dionysiac dithyrambs into a sober and trained "cycle" chorus of fifty voices, singing in strophe and antistrophe, with arias and recitatives as in our oratorios. The theme was usually the suffering and death of Dionysus; and in honor of the god's traditional attendants the chorus was dressed in goatlike satyr guise. Out of this, in fact and name, came the tragic theater of the Greeks.

5. *The Beginnings of the Drama*

The sixth century, already distinguished in so many fields and lands, crowned its accomplishments by laying the foundations of the drama. It was one of the creative moments in history; never before, so far as we know, had men passed from pantomime or ritual to the spoken and secular play.

Comedy, says Aristotle,[91] developed "out of those who led the phallic procession." A company of people carrying sacred phalli, and singing dithyrambs to Dionysus, or hymns to some other vegetation god, constituted, in Greek terminology, a *komos*, or revel. Sex was essential, for the culmination of the ritual was a symbolic marriage aimed at the magic stimulation of the soil;[92] hence in early Greek comedy, as in most modern comedies and novels, marriage and presumptive procreation form the proper ending of the tale. The comic drama of Greece remained till Menander obscene because its origin was frankly phallic; it was in its beginnings a joyous celebration of reproductive powers, and sexual restraints were in some measure removed. It was a day's moratorium on morals; free speech (*parrhasia*) was then particularly free;[93] and many of the paraders, dressed in Dionysian satyr style, wore a goat's tail and a large artificial phallus of red leather as part of their costume. This garb became traditional on the comic stage; it was a matter of sacred custom, religiously observed in Aristophanes; indeed, the phallus continued to be the inseparable emblem of the clown until the fifth century of our era in the West, and the last century of the Byzantine Empire in the East.[94] Along with the phallus, in the Old Comedy, went the licentious *kordax* dance.[95]

Strange to say, it was in Sicily that the rustic vegetation revel was first transformed into the comic drama. About 560 one Susarion of Megara Hyblaea, near Syracuse, developed the processional mirth into brief plays of rough satire and comedy.[96] From Sicily the new art passed into the Peloponnesus and then into Attica; comedies were performed in the villages by traveling players or local amateurs. A century passed before the authorities—to quote Aristotle's phrase[97]—treated the comic drama seriously enough to give it (465 B.C.) a chorus for representation at an official festival.

Tragedy—*tragoidia*, or the goat song—arose in like manner from the mimic representations, in dancing and singing, of satyrlike Dionysian revelers dressed in the costume of goats.[98] These satyr plays remained till Euripides an essential part of the Dionysian drama; each composer of a tragic trilogy was expected to make a concession to ancient custom by offering, as the fourth part of his presentation, a satyr play in honor of Dionysus. "Being a development of the satyr play," says Aristotle,[99] "it was quite late before tragedy rose from short plots and comic diction to its full dignity." Doubtless other seeds matured in the birth of tragedy; perhaps it took something from the ritual worship and appeasement of the dead.[100] But essentially its source lay in mimetic religious ceremonies like the representation, in Crete, of the birth of Zeus, or, in Argos and Samos, his symbolic marriage with Hera, or, in Eleusis and elsewhere, the sacred mysteries of Demeter and Persephone, or, above all, in the Peloponnesus and Attica, the mourning and rejoicing over the death and resurrection of Dionysus. Such representations were called *dromena*—things performed; *drama* is a kindred word, and means, as it should, an action. At Sicyon tragic choruses, till the days of the dictator Cleisthenes, commemorated, we are told, the "sufferings of Adrastus," the ancient king. At Icaria, where Thespis grew up, a goat was sacrificed to Dionysus; perhaps the "goat song" from which tragedy derived its name was a chant sung over the dismembered symbol or embodiment of the drunken god.[101] The Greek drama, like ours, grew out of religious ritual.

Hence the Athenian drama, tragic and comic, was performed as part of the festival of Dionysus, under the presidency of his priests, in a theater named after him, by players called "the Dionysian artists." The statue of Dionysus was brought to the theater and so placed before the stage that he might enjoy the spectacle. The performance was preceded by the sacrifice of an animal to the god. The theater was endowed with the sanctity of a temple, and offenses committed there were punished severely as sacrileges rather than as merely crimes. Just as tragedy held the place of honor on the stage at the City Dionysia, so comedy held the foreground at the festival of the Lenaea; but this festival too was Dionysian. Perhaps originally the theme, as in the drama of the Mass, was the passion and death of the god; gradually the poets were allowed to substitute the sufferings and death of a hero in Greek myth. It may even be that in its early forms the drama was a magic ritual, designed to avert the tragedies it portrayed, and to purge the audience of evils, in a more than Aristotelian sense, by representing these as borne and finished with by proxy.[102] In part it was this religious basis that kept Greek tragedy on a higher plane than that of the Elizabethan stage.

The chorus as developed for mimetic action by Arion and others became the foundation of dramatic structure, and remained an essential part of Greek tragedy until the later plays of Euripides. The earlier dramatists were called dancers because they made their plays chiefly a matter of choral dancing, and were actually teachers of dancing.[103] Only one thing was needed to turn these choral representations into dramas, and that was the opposition of an actor, in dialogue and action, to the chorus. This inspiration came to one of these dancing instructors and chorus trainers, Thespis of Icaria—a town close to the Peloponnesian Megara, where the rites of Dionysus were popular, and not far from Eleusis, where the ritual drama of Demeter, Persephone, and Dionysus Zagreus was annually performed. Helped no doubt by the egoism that propels the world, Thespis separated himself from the chorus, gave himself individual recitative lines, developed the notion of opposition and conflict, and offered the drama in its stricter sense to history. He played various roles with such verisimilitude that when his troupe performed at Athens, Solon was shocked at what seemed to him a kind of public deceit, and denounced this newfangled art as immoral[104]—a charge that it has heard in every century. Peisistratus was more imaginative, and encouraged the competitive performance of dramas at the Dionysian festival. In 534 Thespis won the victory in such a contest. The new form developed so rapidly that Choerilus, only a generation later, produced 160 plays. When, fifty years after Thespis, Aeschylus and Athens returned victorious from the battle of Salamis, the stage was set for the great age in the history of the Greek drama.

VI. RETROSPECT

Looking back upon the multifarious civilization whose peaks have been sketched in the foregoing pages, we begin to understand what the Greeks were fighting for at Marathon. We picture the Aegean as a beehive of busy, quarrelsome, alert, inventive Greeks, establishing themselves obstinately in every port, developing their economy from tillage to industry and trade, and already creating great literature, philosophy, and art. It is amazing how quickly and widely this new culture matured, laying in the sixth century all the foundations for the achievements of the fifth. It was a civilization in certain respects finer than that of the Periclean period—superior in epic and lyric poetry, enlivened and adorned by the greater freedom and mental activity of women, and in some ways better governed than in the later and more democratic age. But even of democracy the bases had been prepared; by the end of the century the dictatorships had taught Greece enough order to make possible Greek liberty.

The realization of self-government was something new in the world; life without kings had not yet been dared by any great society. Out of this proud sense of independence, individual and collective, came a powerful stimulus to every enterprise of the Greeks; it was their liberty that inspired them to incredible accomplishments in arts and letters, in science and philosophy It is true that a large part of the people, then as always, harbored and loved superstitions, mysteries, and myths; men must be consoled. Despite this, Greek life had become unprecedentedly secular; politics, law, literature, and speculation had one by one been separated and liberated from ecclesiastical power. Philosophy had begun to build a naturalistic interpretation of the world and man, of body and soul. Science, almost unknown before, had made its first bold formulations; the elements of Euclid were established; clarity and order and honesty of thought had become the ideal of a saving minority of men. A heroic effort of flesh and spirit rescued these achievements, and the promise they held, from the dead hand of alien despotism and the darkness of the Mysteries, and won for European civilization the trying privilege of freedom.

CHAPTER X

The Struggle for Freedom

I. MARATHON

"IN the reigns of Darius, Xerxes, and Artaxerxes," says Herodotus, "Greece suffered more sorrows than in twenty generations before."[1] The Greek nation had to pay the penalty of its development; spreading everywhere, it was bound sooner or later to come into conflict with a major power. Using water as their highway, the Hellenes had opened up a trade route that extended from the eastern coast of Spain to the farthest ports of the Black Sea. This European water route—Greco-Italian-Sicilian—competed more and more with the Oriental land and water route—Indo-Perso-Phoenician; and thereby arose a lasting and bitter rivalry in which war, by all human precedents, was inevitable, and in which the battles of Lade, Marathon, Plataea, Himera, Mycale, the Eurymedon, the Granicus, Issus, Arbela, Cannae, and Zama were merely incidents. The European system won against the Oriental partly because transport by water is cheaper than transport by land, and partly because it is almost a law of history that the rugged, warlike north conquers the easygoing, art-creating south.

In the year 512 Darius I of Persia crossed the Bosporus, invaded Scythia, and, marching westward, conquered Thrace and Macedon. When he returned to his capitals he had enlarged his realm to embrace Persia, Afghanistan, northern India, Turkestan, Mesopotamia, northern Arabia, Egypt, Cyprus, Palestine, Syria, Asia Minor, the eastern Aegean, Thrace, and Macedonia; the greatest empire that the world has yet seen had overextended itself to include and awaken its future conqueror. Only one important nation remained outside this vast system of government and trade, and that was Greece. By 510 Darius had hardly heard of it outside Ionia. "The Athenians," he asked—"who are they?"[2] About 506 the dictator Hippias, deposed by revolution at Athens, fled to the Persian satrap at Sardis, begged for help in regaining his power, and offered, in that event, to hold Attica under the Persian dominion.

To this temptation there was added in 500 a timely provocation. The Greek cities of Asia Minor, under Persian rule for half a century, suddenly dismissed their satraps and declared their independence. Aristagoras of

Miletus went to Sparta to enlist its aid, without success; he passed on to Athens, mother city of many Ionian towns, and pleaded so well that the Athenians sent a fleet of twenty ships to support the revolt. Meanwhile the Ionians were acting with a chaotic vigor characteristic of the Greeks; each rebel city raised its own troops, but kept them under separate command; and the Milesian army, led with more bravery than wisdom, marched upon Sardis and burned the great city to the ground. The Ionian Confederacy organized a united fleet, but the Samian contingent secretly made terms with the Persian satrap, and when, in 494, the Persian navy met the Ionian at Lade, in one of the major sea battles of history, the half hundred ships of the Samians sailed away without fighting, and many other contingents followed their example.[3] The defeat of the Ionians was complete, and Ionian civilization never quite recovered from this physical and spiritual disaster. The Persians laid siege to Miletus, captured it, killed the males, enslaved the women and children, and so completely plundered the city that Miletus became from that day a minor town. Persian rule was re-established throughout Ionia, and Darius, resentful of Athenian interference, resolved to conquer Greece. Little Athens, as the result of her generous assistance to her daughter cities, found herself face to face with an empire literally a hundred times greater than Attica.

In the year 491 a Persian fleet of six hundred ships under Datis struck across the Aegean from Samos, stopped on the way to subdue the Cyclades, and reached the coast of Euboea with 200,000 men. Euboea submitted after a brief struggle, and the Persians crossed the bay to Attica. They pitched their camp near Marathon, because Hippias had advised them that in that plain they could use their cavalry, in which they were overwhelmingly superior to the Greeks.[4]

All Greece was in turmoil at the news. The Persian arms had never yet been defeated, the advance of the Empire had never yet been stopped; how could a nation so weak, so scattered, so unused to unity, hold back this wave of Oriental conquest? The northern Greek states were loath to resist so monstrous a power; Sparta hesitatingly prepared, but allowed superstition to delay its mobilization; little Plataea acted quickly, and sent a large proportion of its citizens by forced marches to Marathon. At Athens Miltiades freed and enlisted slaves as well as freemen, and led them over the mountains to the battlefield. When the rival armies met, the Greeks had some twenty thousand men, the Persians probably one hundred thousand.[5] The Persians were brave, but they were accustomed to individual fighting, and were not trained for the mass defense and attack of the Greeks. The Greeks united discipline with courage, and though they committed the folly of dividing the command among ten generals, each supreme for a day, they were saved by the example of Aristides, who yielded his leadership to Miltiades.[6] Under this blunt soldier's vigorous strategy the small Greek force routed the Persian horde in what was not only one of the decisive battles, but also one of the most incredible victories, of history. If we may accept Greek testimony on such a matter, 6,400 Persians, but only 192 Greeks, fell at Marathon. After the battle was over the Spartans arrived, mourned their tardiness, and praised the victors.

II. ARISTIDES AND THEMISTOCLES

The strange mixture of nobility and cruelty, idealism and cynicism, in Greek character and history was illustrated by the subsequent careers of Miltiades and Aristides. Inflated by the praise of all Greece, Miltiades asked the Athenians to equip a fleet of seventy ships, to be under his unchecked command. When the ships were ready Miltiades led them to Paros, and demanded of its citizens one hundred talents ($600,000) on pain of wholesale death. The Athenians recalled him and fined him fifty talents; but Miltiades died soon after, and the fine was paid by his son Cimon, the future rival of Pericles.[8]

The man who had yielded place to him at Marathon survived the pitfalls of success. Aristides was in life and manners a Spartan at Athens. His quiet, staid character, his modest simplicity and undiscourageable honesty won him the title of the Just; and when, in a drama of Aeschylus', the passage occurred—

> For not at seeming just, but being so,
> He aims; and from his depth of soil below
> Harvests of wise and prudent counsels grow—

all the audience turned to look at Aristides, as the living embodiment of the poet's lines.[9] When the Greeks captured the camp of the Persians at Marathon, and found great wealth in their tents, Aristides was left in charge of it, and "neither took anything for himself, nor suffered others to do it";[10] and when, after the war, the allies of Athens were induced to contribute annually to the treasury of Delos as a fund for common defense, Aristides was chosen by them to fix their payments, and none protested his decisions. Nevertheless, he was more admired than popular. Though a close friend of Cleisthenes, who had so extended democracy, he was of the opinion that democracy had gone far enough, and that any further empowerment of the Assembly would lead to administrative corruption and public disorder. He exposed malfeasance wherever he found it, and made many enemies. The democratic party, led by Themistocles, used Cleisthenes' recently established device of ostracism to get rid of him, and in 482 the only man in Athenian history that was at once famous and honest was exiled at the height of his career. All the world knows—though again it may be only a fable—how Aristides inscribed his own name on the *ostracon* for a letterless citizen who did not know him, but who, with the resentment of mediocrity for excellence, was tired of hearing him called the Just. When Aristides learned of the decision he expressed the hope that Athens would never have occasion to remember him.[11]

The historian is constrained to admit that the public men of Athens were properly equipped with the unscrupulousness that sometimes enters into statesmanship. As much as Alcibiades at a later age, Themistocles was a very flame of ability; "he has a claim on our admiration quite extraordinary and unparalleled," says the always moderate Thucydides.[12] Like Miltiades, he saved Athens, but could not save himself; he could defeat a great empire, but not his own lust for power. "He received reluctantly and carelessly," says Plutarch, "instructions given him to improve his manners and behavior, or to teach him any pleasing or graceful accomplishment; but whatever was said to improve him in sagacity, or in the management of affairs, he would give attention to beyond his years, confident in his natural capacity for such things."[13] It was Athens' misfortune that both Themistocles and Aristides fell in love with the same girl, Stesilaus of Ceos, and that their animosity outlived the beauty that had aroused it.[14] Nevertheless it was Themistocles whose foresight and energy prepared for, and carried through, the victory of Salamis—the most crucial battle in Greek history. As far back as 493 he had planned and begun a new harbor for Athens at the Piraeus; now, in 482, he persuaded the Athenians to forego a distribution of money due them from the proceeds of the silver mines at Laurium, and to devote the sum to the building of a hundred triremes. Without this fleet there could have been no resistance to Xerxes.

III. XERXES

Darius I died in 485, and was succeeded by Xerxes I. Both father and son were men of ability and culture, and it would be an error to think of the Greco-Persian War as a contest between civilization and barbarism. When Darius, before invading Greece, sent heralds to Athens and Sparta to demand earth and water as symbols of submission, both cities had put the heralds to death. Troubled by portents, Sparta now repented of this violation of international custom, and asked for two citizens to go to Persia and surrender themselves to any punishment that the Great King might exact in retribution. Sperthias and Bulis, both of old and wealthy families, volunteered, made their way to Xerxes, and offered to die in atonement for the killing of Darius' messengers. Xerxes, says Herodotus,[15] "answered with true greatness of soul that he would not act like the Lacedaemonians, who, by killing the heralds, had broken the laws which all men held in common. As he had blamed such conduct in them, he would never be guilty of it himself."

Xerxes prepared leisurely but thoroughly for the second Persian attack upon Greece. For four years he collected troops and materials from all the provinces of his realm; and when, in 481, he at last set forth, his army was probably the largest ever assembled in history before our own century. Herodotus reckoned it, without moderation, at 2,641,000 fighting men, and an equal number of engineers, slaves, merchants, provisioners, and prostitutes; he tells us, with perhaps a twinkle in his eye, that when Xerxes' army drank water whole rivers ran dry.[16] It was, naturally and fatally, a highly heterogeneous force. There were Persians, Medes, Babylonians, Afghans, Indians, Bactrians, Sogdians, Sacae, Assyrians, Armenians, Colchians, Scyths, Paeonians, Mysians, Paphlagonians, Phrygians, Thracians, Thessalians, Locrians, Boeotians, Aeolians, Ionians, Lydians, Carians, Cilicians, Cypriotes, Phoenicians, Syrians, Arabians, Egyptians, Ethiopians, Libyans, and many more. There were footmen, cavalrymen, chariots, elephants, and a fleet of transports and fighting triremes numbering, according to Herodotus, 1207 ships in all. When Greek spies were caught in the camp, and a general ordered their execution, Xerxes countermanded the order, spared the men, had them conducted through his forces, and then set them free, trusting that when they had reported to Athens and Sparta the extent of his preparations, the remainder of Greece would hasten to surrender.[17]

In the spring of 480 the great host reached the Hellespont, where Egyptian and Phoenician engineers had built a bridge that was among the most admired mechanical achievements of antiquity. If again we may follow Herodotus, 674 ships of trireme or penteconter size were distributed in two rows athwart the strait, each vessel facing the current, and moored with a heavy anchor. Then the builders stretched cables of flax or papyrus over each row of ships from bank to bank, bound the cables to every ship, and made them taut with capstans on the shore. Trees were cut and sawn into planks, and these, laid across the cables, were fastened to them and to one another. The planks were covered with brushwood, and this with earth, and the whole was trodden down to resemble a road. A bulwark was erected on each side of the causeway high enough to keep animals from taking fright at sight of the sea.[18] Nevertheless many of the beasts, and some of the soldiers, had to be driven by the lash to trust themselves to the bridge. It stood the burden well, and in seven days and nights the entire host had passed over it successfully. A native of the region, seeing the spectacle, concluded that Xerxes was Zeus, and asked why the master of gods and men had taken so much trouble to conquer little Greece when he might have destroyed the presumptuous nation with one thunderbolt.[19]

The army marched overland through Thrace and down into Macedonia and Thessaly, while the Persian fleet, hugging the coasts, avoided the storms of the Aegean by passing southward through a canal dug by forced labor across the isthmus at Mt. Athos to the length of a mile and a quarter. Wherever the army ate two meals, we are told, the city that fed it was utterly ruined; Thasos spent four hundred silver talents—approximately a million dollars—in playing host to Xerxes for a day.[20] The northern Greeks. even to the Attic frontier, surrendered to fear or bribery, and allowed their troops to be added to Xerxes' millions. Only Plataea and Thespiae, in the north, prepared to fight.

IV. SALAMIS

How can we imagine, today, the terror and desperation of the southern Greeks at the approach of this polyglot avalanche? Resistance seemed insane; the loyal states could not muster one tenth of Xerxes' force. For once Athens and Sparta worked together with single mind and heart. Delegates were sped to every city in the Peloponnesus to beg for troops or supplies; most of the states co-operated; Argos refused, and never lived down her disgrace. Athens fitted out a fleet that sailed north to meet the Persian armada, and Sparta dispatched a small force under King Leonidas to halt Xerxes for a while at Thermopylae. The two navies met at Artemisium, off the northern coast of Euboea. When the Greek admirals saw the overwhelming number of the enemy's vessels they were of a mind to withdraw. The Euboeans, fearing a descent of the Persians upon their shores, sent to Themistocles, commander of the Athenian contingent, a bribe of thirty talents ($180,000) on condition that he persuade the Greek leaders to fight; he succeeded by sharing the bribe.[21] With characteristic subtlety Themistocles had sailors inscribe upon the rocks messages to the Greeks in the Persian fleet begging them to desert, or in any case not to fight against their motherland; he hoped that if the Ionians saw these words they would be moved by them, and that if Xerxes saw and understood them, the King would not dare to use Hellenes in the battle. All day the rival fleets fought, until night put an end to the engagement before either side could win; the Greeks then retired to Artemisium, the Persians to Aphetae. Considering the inequality of numbers, the Greeks justifiably looked upon the battle as a victory. When news came of the disaster at Thermopylae the surviving Greek fleet sailed south to Salamis, to provide a refuge for Athens.

Meanwhile Leonidas, despite the most heroic resistance in history, had been overwhelmed at the "Hot Gates," not so much by the bravery of the Persians as by the treachery of Hellenes. Certain Greeks from Trachis not only betrayed to Xerxes the secret of the indirect route over the mountains, but led the Persian force by that approach to attack the Spartans in the rear. Leonidas and his three hundred elders (for he had chosen only fathers of sons to go with him, lest any Spartan family should be extinguished) died almost to the last man. Of the two Spartan survivors one fell at Plataea, the other hanged himself for shame.[22] The Greek historians assure us that the Persians lost 20,000, the Greeks 300.[23] Over the tomb of the latter heroes was placed the most famous of Greek epitaphs: "Go, stranger, and tell the Lacedaemonians that we lie here in obedience to their laws."[24]

When the Athenians learned that no barrier now remained between Athens and the Persians, proclamation was made that every Athenian should save his family as best he could. Some fled to Aegina, some to Salamis, some to Troezen; some of the men were enlisted to fill up the crews of the fleet that was returning from Artemisium. Plutarch paints[25] a touching picture of how the tame animals of the city followed their masters to the shore, and howled when the overladen vessels drew off without them; one dog, belonging to Pericles' father, Xanthippus, leaped into the sea and swam alongside his ship to Salamis, where it died of exhaustion.[26] We may judge of the excitement and passion of those days when we learn that an Athenian who, in the Assembly, advised surrender, was killed there and then, and that a crowd of women went to his house and stoned his wife and children to death.[27] When Xerxes arrived he found the city almost deserted, and gave it over to pillage and fire.

Soon afterward the Persian fleet, twelve hundred strong, entered the Bay of Salamis. Against it were ranged three hundred Greek triremes, still under divided command. The majority of the admirals were opposed to risking an engagement. Resolved to force action upon the Greeks, Themistocles resorted to a stratagem that would have cost him his life had the Persians won. He sent a trusted slave to Xerxes to tell him that the Greeks were intending to sail away during the night, and that the Persians could prevent this only by surrounding the Greek fleet. Xerxes accepted the advice, and on the next morning, with every escape blocked, the Greeks were compelled to give fight. Xerxes, seated in state at the foot of Mt. Aegaleus, on the Attic shore across from Salamis, watched the action, and noted the names of those of his men who fought with especial bravery. The superior tactics and seamanship of the Hellenes, and the confusion of tongues, minds, and superfluous ships among the Orientals, finally decided the issue in favor of Greece. According to Diodorus the invaders lost two hundred vessels, the defenders forty; but we do not have the Persian side of the story. Few of the Greeks, even from the lost ships, died; for being all excellent swimmers, they swam to land when their boats foundered.[28] The remnant of the Persian fleet fled to the Hellespont, and the subtle Themistocles sent his slave again to Xerxes to say that he had dissuaded the Greeks from pursuit. Xerxes left 300,000 men under command of Mardonius, and with the rest of his troops marched back in humiliation to Sardis, a large part of his force dying of pestilence and dysentery on the way.

In the same year as Salamis—possibly, as the Greeks would have it, on the same day (September 23, 480 B.C.)—the Greeks of Sicily fought the Carthaginians at Himera. We do not know that the Phoenicians of Africa were acting in concert with those who supported Xerxes and so largely manned his fleet; perhaps it was only a coincidence that Greece found itself assaulted in east and west at once.[29] In the traditional account Hamilcar, the Carthaginian admiral, arrived at Panormus with 3000 ships and 300,000 troops; he proceeded thence to lay siege to Himera, where he was met by Gelon of Syracuse with 55,000 men. After the fashion of Punic generals, Hamilcar stood aside from the battle, and burned sacrificial victims to his gods as the contest raged; when his defeat became evident he threw himself into the fire. A tomb was erected to him on the site; and there his grandson Himilcon, seventy years afterwards, slaughtered 3000 Greek captives in revenge.[30]

A year later (August, 479) the liberation of Greece was completed by almost simultaneous engagements on land and sea. Mardonius' army, living leisurely on the country, had pitched its camp near Plataea on the Boeotian plain. There, after two weeks of waiting for propitious omens, a Greek force of 110,000 men, led by the Spartan king Pausanias, joined issue with them in the greatest land battle of the war. The non-Persians in the invading force had no heart for the conflict, and took to flight as soon as the Persian contingent, which bore the point of the attack, began to waver. The Greeks won so overwhelming a victory that (according to their historians) they lost but 159 men, while of the Persian force 260,000 were slain.* On the same day, the Greeks aver, a Greek squadron met a Persian flotilla off the coast of Mycale, the central meeting place of all Ionia. The Persian fleet was destroyed, the Ionian cities were freed from Persian rule, and control of the Hellespont and the Bosporus was won by the Greeks as they had won it from Troy seven hundred years before.

The Greco-Persian War was the most momentous conflict in European history, for it made Europe possible. It won for Western civilization the opportunity to develop its own economic life—unburdened with alien tribute or taxation—and its own political institutions, free from the dictation of Oriental kings. It won for Greece a clear road for the first great experiment in liberty; it preserved the Greek mind for three centuries from the enervating mysticism of the East, and secured for Greek enterprise full freedom of the sea. The Athenian fleet that remained after Salamis now opened every port in the Mediterranean to Greek trade, and the commercial expansion that ensued provided the wealth that financed the leisure and culture of Periclean Athens. The victory of little Hellas against such odds stimulated the pride and lifted up the spirit of its people; out of very gratitude they felt called upon to do unprecedented things. After centuries of preparation and sacrifice Greece entered upon its Golden Age.

* These figures from Herodotus[31] are presumably an outburst of patriotic imagination. Plutarch, trying to be impartial, raises the Greek loss to 1360, and Diodorus Siculus, though always generous with numbers, lowers the Persian loss to 100,000;[32] but even Plutarch and Diodorus were Greeks.

BOOK III

THE GOLDEN AGE

480-399 B.C.

CHRONOLOGICAL TABLE FOR BOOK III

Note: Where no city is named for a person, "of Athens" is understood.

B.C.

478: Pindar of Thebes, poet
478-67: Hieron I dictator at Syracuse
478: Pythagoras of Rhegium, sculptor
477: Delian Confederacy founded
472: Polygnotus, painter; Aeschylus' *Persae*
469: Birth of Socrates
468: Cimon defeats Persians at the Eurymedon; first contest between Aeschylus and Sophocles
467: Bacchylides of Ceos, poet; Aeschylus' *Seven against Thebes*
464-54: Helot revolt; siege of Ithome
463-31: Public career of Pericles
462: Ephialtes limits the Areopagus; pay for jurors; Anaxagoras at Athens
461: Cimon ostracized; Ephialtes killed
460: Empedocles of Acragas, philosopher; Aeschylus' *Promotheus Bound*
459-54: Athenian expedition to Egypt fails
458: Aeschylus' *Oresteia;* the Long Walls
456: Temple of Zeus at Olympia; Paeonius of Mende, sculptor
454: Delian treasury removed to Athens
450: Zeno of Elea, philosopher; Hippocrates of Chios, mathematician; Callimachus develops the Corinthian order; Philolaus of Thebes, astronomer
448: Peace of Callias with Persia
447-31: The Parthenon
445: Leucippus of Abdera, philosopher
443: Herodotus of Halicarnassus, historian, joins colonists founding Thurii (Italy); Gorgias of Leontini, Sophist
442: Sophocles' *Antigone;* Myron of Eleutherae, sculptor
440: Protagoras of Abdera, Sophist
438: Pheidias' *Athene Parthenos;* Euripides' *Alcestis*
437: The Propylaea
435-34: War between Corinth and Corcyra
433: Alliance of Athens and Corcyra
432: Revolt of Potidaea; trials of Aspasia, Pheidias, and Anaxagoras
431-04: Peloponnesian War
431-24: Euripides' *Medea, Andromache,* and *Hecuba*; Sophocles' *Electra*
430: Plague at Athens; trial of Pericles
429: Death of Pericles; Cleon in power; Sophocles' *Oedipus the King*
428: Revolt of Mytilene; Euripides' *Hippolytus;* death of Anaxagoras

B.C.

427: Embassy of Gorgias at Athens; Prodicus and Hippias, Sophists
425: Siege of Sphacteria; Aristophanes' *Acharnians*
424: Brasidas takes Amphipolis; exile of Thucydides, historian; Aristophanes' *Knights*
423: Aristophanes' *Clouds*; Zeuxis of Heraclea and Parrhasius of Ephesus, painters
422: Aristophanes' *Wasps*; death of Cleon and Brasidas
421: Peace of Nicias; Aristophanes' *Peace*
420: Hippocrates of Cos, physician; Democritus of Abdera, philosopher; Polycleitus of Sicyon, sculptor
420-04: The Erechtheum
419: Lysias, orator
418: Spartan victory at Mantinea; Euripides' *Ion*
416: Massacre at Melos; Euripides' *Electra* (?)
415-13: Athenian expedition to Syracuse
415: Mutilation of the Hermae; disgrace of Alcibiades; Euripides' *Trojan Women*
414: Siege of Syracuse; Aristophanes' *Birds*
413: Athenian defeat at Syracuse; Euripides' *Iphigenia in Tauris*
412: Euripides' *Helen* and *Andromeda*
411: Revolt of the Four Hundred; Aristophanes' *Lysistrata* and *Thesmophoriazusae*
410: Restoration of the democrary; victory of Alcibiades at Cyzicus
408: Timotheus of Miletus, poet and musician; Euripides' *Orestes*
406: Athenian victory at Arginusae; deaths of Euripides and Sophocles; Euripides' *Bacchae* and *Iphigenia in Aulis*
405-367: Dionysius I dictator at Syracuse
405: Spartan victory at Aegospotami; Aristophanes' *Frogs*
404: End of the Peloponnesian War; rule of the Thirty at Athens
403: Restoration of the democracy
401: Defeat of Cyrus II at Cunaxa; retreat of Xenophon's Ten Thousand; Sophocles' *Oedipus at Colonus*
399: Trial and death of Socrates

CHAPTER XI

Pericles and the Democratic Experiment

I. THE RISE OF ATHENS

"THE period which intervened between the birth of Pericles and the death of Aristotle," wrote Shelley,[1] "is undoubtedly, whether considered in itself or with reference to the effect which it has produced upon the subsequent destinies of civilized man, the most memorable in the history of the world." Athens dominated this period because she had won the allegiance—and the contributions—of most Aegean cities by her leadership in saving Greece; and because, when the war was over, Ionia was impoverished and Sparta was disordered by demobilization, earthquake, and insurrection, while the fleet that Themistocles had created now rivaled with the conquests of commerce its victories at Artemisium and Salamis.

Not that the war was quite over: intermittently the struggle between Greece and Persia continued from the conquest of Ionia by Cyrus to the overthrow of Darius III by Alexander. The Persians were expelled from Ionia in 479, from the Black Sea in 478, from Thrace in 475; and in 468 a Greek fleet under Cimon of Athens decisively defeated the Persians on land and sea at the mouth of the Eurymedon.* The Greek cities of Asia and the Aegean, for their protection against Persia, now (477) organized under Athenian leadership the Delian Confederacy, and contributed to a common fund in the temple of Apollo on Delos. Since Athens donated ships instead of money, it soon exercised, through its sea power, an effective control over its allies; and rapidly the Confederacy of equals was transformed into an Athenian Empire.

In this policy of imperial aggrandizement all the major statesmen of Athens—even the virtuous Aristides and later the impeccable Pericles—joined with the unscrupulous Themistocles. No other man had deserved so well of Athens as Themistocles, and no one was more resolved than he to be repaid for it. When the Greek leaders met to give first and second

* A river in Pamphylia, in southern Asia Minor.

awards to those men who had most ably defended Greece in the war, each of them voted for himself first, and for Themistocles second. It was he who set the course of Greek history by persuading Athens that the road to supremacy lay not on land but on the sea, and not by war so much as by trade. He negotiated with Persia, and sought to end the strife between the old and the young empire in order that unimpeded commerce with Asia might bring prosperity to Athens. Under his prodding the men, even the women and children, of Athens raised a wall around the city, and another around the ports at the Piraeus and Munychia; under his lead, carried forward by Pericles, great quays, warehouses, and exchanges were erected at the Piraeus, providing every convenience for maritime trade. He knew that these policies would arouse the jealousy of Sparta, and might lead to war between the rival states; but he was stirred on by his vision of Athens' development, and his confidence in the Athenian fleet.

His aims were as magnificent as his means were venal. He used the navy to force tribute from the Cyclades, on the ground that they had yielded too quickly to the Persians, and had lent Xerxes their troops; and he appears to have accepted bribes to let some cities off.[2] For like considerations he arranged the recall of exiles, sometimes keeping the money, says Timocreon, though he had failed to obtain the recall.[3] When Aristides was placed in charge of the public revenue he found that his predecessors had embezzled public funds, and not least lavishly Themistocles.[4] Toward 471 the Athenians, fearing his unmoral intellect, passed a vote of ostracism upon him, and he sought a new home in Argos. Shortly thereafter the Spartans found documents apparently implicating Themistocles, in the secret correspondence of their regent Pausanias, whom they had starved to death for entering into traitorous negotiations with Persia. Happy to destroy her ablest enemy, Sparta revealed these papers to Athens, which at once sent out an order for Themistocles' arrest. He fled to Corcyra, was denied refuge there, found brief asylum in Epirus, and thence sailed secretly to Asia, where he claimed from Xerxes' successor some reward for restraining the Greek pursuit of the Persian fleet after Salamis. Lured by Themistocles' promise to help him subjugate Greece,[5] Artaxerxes I received him into his counsels, and assigned the revenues of several cities for his maintenance. Before Themistocles could carry out the schemes that never let him rest he died at Magnesia in 449 B.C., at the age of sixty-five, admired and disliked by all the Mediterranean world.

After the passing of Themistocles and Aristides the leadership of the democratic faction at Athens descended to Ephialtes, and that of the oligarchic or conservative faction to Cimon, son of Miltiades. Cimon had most of the virtues that Themistocles lacked, but none of the subtlety that ability must depend upon for political success. Unhappy amid the intrigues of the city, he secured command of the fleet, and consolidated the liberties of Greece by his victory at the Eurymedon. Returning to Athens in glory, he at once lost his popularity by advising a reconciliation with Sparta. He won the Assembly's reluctant consent to lead an Athenian force to the aid of the Spartans against their revolted Helots at Ithome; but the Spartans suspected the Athenians even when bringing gifts, and so clearly distrusted Cimon's soldiers that these returned to Athens in anger, and Cimon was disgraced. In 461 he was ostracized at the instigation of Pericles, and the oligarchic party was so demoralized by his fall that for two generations the government remained in the hands of the democrats. Four years later Pericles, repentant (or, rumor said, enamored of Cimon's sister Elpinice), secured his recall, and Cimon died with honors in a naval campaign in Cyprus.

The leader of the democratic party at this time was a man of whom we know strangely little, and yet his activity was a turning point in the history of Athens. Ephialtes was poor but incorruptible, and did not long survive the animosities of Athenian politics. The popular faction had been strengthened by the war, for in that crisis all class divisions among freemen had for a moment been forgotten, and the saving victory at Salamis had been won not by the army—which was dominated by the aristocrats—but by the navy, which was manned by the poorer citizens and controlled by the mercantile middle class. The oligarchic party sought to maintain its privileges by making the conservative Areopagus the supreme authority in the state. Ephialtes replied by a bitter attack upon this ancient senate.* He impeached several of its members for malfeasance, had some of them put to death,[7] and persuaded the Assembly to vote the almost complete abolition of the powers that the Areopagus still retained. The conservative Aristotle later approved this radical policy, on the ground that "the transfer to the commons of the judicial functions that had belonged to the Senate appears to have been an advantage, for corruption finds an easier

* Grote's statement, written about 1850, of the case against the Areopagus recalls certain criticisms of the Supreme Court of the United States in 1937. "The Areopagus, standing alone in the enjoyment of a life-tenure, appears to have exercised an undefined and extensive control which long continuance had gradually consecrated. It was invested with a kind of religious respect. . . . The Areopagus also exercised a supervision over the public assembly, taking care that none of the proceedings . . . should be such as to infringe the established laws of the country. These were powers immense, undefined, not derived from any formal grant of the people."[6]

material in a small number than in a large one."[8] But the conservatives of the time did not see the issue so calmly. Ephialtes, having been found unpurchasable, was assassinated in 461 by an agent of the oligarchy,[9] and the perilous task of leading the democratic party passed down to the aristocratic Pericles.

II. PERICLES

The man who acted as commander in chief of all the physical and spiritual forces of Athens during her greatest age was born some three years before Marathon. His father, Xanthippus, had fought at Salamis, had led the Athenian fleet in the battle of Mycale, and had recaptured the Hellespont for Greece. Pericles' mother, Agariste, was a granddaughter of the reformer Cleisthenes; on her side, therefore, he belonged to the ancient family of the Alcmaeonids. "His mother being near her time," says Plutarch, "fancied in a dream that she was brought to bed of a lion, and a few days after was delivered of Pericles—in other respects perfectly formed, only his head was somewhat longish and out of proportion";[10] his critics were to have much fun with this very dolicocephalic head. The most famous music teacher of his time, Damon, gave him instruction in music, and Pythocleides in music and literature; he heard the lectures of Zeno the Eleatic at Athens, and became the friend and pupil of the philosopher Anaxagoras. In his development he absorbed the rapidly growing culture of his epoch, and united in his mind and policy all the threads of Athenian civilization—economic, military, literary, artistic, and philosophical. He was, so far as we know, the most complete man that Greece produced.

Seeing that the oligarchic party was out of step with the time, he attached himself early in life to the party of the *demos*—i.e., the *free* population of Athens; then, as even in Jefferson's day in America, the word "people" carried certain proprietary reservations. He approached politics in general, and each situation in it, with careful preparation, neglecting no aspect of education, speaking seldom and briefly, and praying to the gods that he might never utter a word that was not to the point. Even the comic poets, who disliked him, spoke of him as "the Olympian," who wielded the thunder and lightning of such eloquence as Athens had never heard before; and yet by all accounts his speech was unimpassioned, and appealed to enlightened minds. His influence was due not only to his intelligence but to his probity; he was capable of using bribery to secure state ends, but was himself "manifestly free from every kind of corruption, and superior to all considerations of money";[11] and whereas Themistocles had entered public office poor and left it rich, Pericles, we are told, added nothing to his patrimony by his political career.[12] It showed the good sense of the Athenians in this generation that for almost thirty years, between 467 and 428, they elected and re-elected him, with brief intermissions, as one of their ten *strategoi* or commanders; and this relative permanence of office not only gave him supremacy on the military board, but enabled him to raise the position of *strategos autokrator* to the place of highest influence in the government. Under him Athens, while enjoying all the privileges of democracy, acquired also the advantages of aristocracy and dictatorship. The good government and cultural patronage that had adorned Athens in the age of Peisistratus were continued now with equal unity and decisiveness of direction and intelligence, but also with the full and annually renewed consent of a free citizenship. History through him illustrated again the principle that liberal reforms are most ably executed and most permanently secured by the cautious and moderate leadership of an aristocrat enjoying popular support. Greek civilization was at its best when democracy had grown sufficiently to give it variety and vigor, and aristocracy survived sufficiently to give it order and taste.

The reforms of Pericles substantially extended the authority of the people. Though the power of the *heliaea* had grown under Solon, Cleisthenes, and Ephialtes, the lack of payment for jury service had given the well to do a predominating influence in these courts. Pericles introduced (451) a fee of two obols (34 cents), later raised to three, for a day's duty as juror, an amount equivalent in each case to half a day's earnings of an average Athenian of the time.[13] The notion that these modest sums weakened the fiber and corrupted the morale of Athens is hardly to be taken seriously, for by the same token every sta .hat pays its judges or its jurymen would long since have been destroyed. Pericles seems also to have established a small remuneration for military service. He crowned this scandalous generosity by persuading the state to pay every citizen two obols annually as the price of admission to the plays and games of the official festivals; he excused himself on the ground that these performances should not be a luxury of the upper and middle classes, but should contribute to elevate the mind of the whole electorate. It must be confessed, however, that Plato, Aristotle, and Plutarch—conservatives all—were agreed that these pittances injured the Athenian character.[14]

Continuing the work of Ephialtes, Pericles transferred to the popular courts the various judicial powers that had been possessed by the archons and magistrates, so that from this time the archonship was more of a bureaucratic or administrative office than one that carried the power of forming policies, deciding cases, or issuing commands. In 457 eligibility to the archonship, which had been confined to the wealthier classes, was extended to the third class, or *zeugitai;* soon thereafter, without any legal form, the lowest citizen class, the *thetes,* made themselves eligible to the office by romancing about their income; and the importance of the *thetes* in the defense of Athens persuaded the other classes to wink at the fraud.[15] Moving for a moment in the opposite direction, Pericles (451) carried through the Assembly a restriction of the franchise to the legitimate offspring of an Athenian father and an Athenian mother. No legal marriage was to be permitted between a citizen and a noncitizen. It was a measure aimed to discourage intermarriage with foreigners, to reduce illegitimate births, and perhaps to reserve to the jealous burghers of Athens the material rewards of citizenship and empire. Pericles himself would soon have reason to regret this exclusive legislation.

Since any form of government seems good that brings prosperity, and even the best seems bad that hinders it, Pericles, having consolidated his political position, turned to economic statesmanship. He sought to reduce the pressure of population upon the narrow resources of Attica by establishing colonies of poor Athenian citizens upon foreign soil. To give work to the idle,[16] he made the state an employer on a scale unprecedented in Greece: ships were added to the fleet, arsenals were built, and a great corn exchange was erected at the Piraeus. To protect Athens effectively from siege by land, and at the same time to provide further work for the unemployed, Pericles persuaded the Assembly to supply funds for constructing eight miles of "Long Walls," as they were to be called, connecting Athens with the Piraeus and Phalerum; the effect was to make the city and its ports one fortified enclosure, open in wartime only to the sea—on which the Athenian fleet was supreme. In the hostility with which unwalled Sparta looked upon this program of fortification the oligarchic party saw a chance to recapture political power. Its secret agents invited the Spartans to invade Attica and, with the aid of an oligarchic insurrection, to put down the democracy; in this event the oligarchs pledged themselves to level the Long Walls. The Spartans agreed, and dispatched an army which defeated the Athenians at Tanagra (457); but the oligarchs failed to make their revolution. The Spartans returned to the Peloponnesus empty-handed, dourly awaiting a better opportunity to overcome the flourishing rival that was taking from them their traditional leadership of Greece.

Pericles rejected the temptation to retaliate upon Sparta, and instead, devoted his energies now to the beautification of Athens. Hoping to make his city the cultural center of Hellas, and to rebuild the ancient shrines—which the Persians had destroyed—on a scale and with a splendor that would lift up the soul of every citizen, he devised a plan for using all the genius of Athens' artists, and the labor of her remaining unemployed, in a bold program for the architectural adornment of the Acropolis. "It was his desire and design," says Plutarch, "that the undisciplined mechanic multitude . . . should not go without their share of public funds, and yet should not have these given them for sitting still and doing nothing; and to this end he brought in these vast projects of construction."[117] To finance the undertaking he proposed that the treasury accumulated by the Delian Confederacy should be removed from Delos, where it lay idle and insecure, and that such part of it as was not needed for common defense should be used to beautify what seemed to Pericles the legitimate capital of a beneficent empire.

The transference of the Delian treasury to Athens was quite acceptable to the Athenians, even to the oligarchs. But the voters were loath to spend any substantial part of the fund in adorning their city—whether through some qualm of conscience, or through a secret hope that the money might be appropriated more directly to their needs and enjoyment. The oligarchic leaders played upon this feeling so cleverly that when the matter neared a vote in the Assembly the defeat of Pericles' plan seemed certain. Plutarch tells a delightful story of how the subtle leader turned the tide. " 'Very well,' said Pericles; 'let the cost of these buildings go not to your account but to mine; and let the inscription upon them stand in my name.' When they heard him say this, whether it were out of a surprise to see the greatness of his spirit, or out of emulation of the glory of the works, they cried aloud, bidding him spend on . . . and spare no cost till all were finished."

While the work proceeded, and Pericles' especial protection and support were given to Pheidias, Ictinus, Mnesicles, and the other artists who labored to realize his dreams, he lent his patronage also to literature and philosophy; and whereas in the other Greek cities of this period the strife of parties consumed much of the energy of the citizens, and literature languished, in Athens the stimulus of growing wealth and democratic freedom was combined with wise and cultured leadership to produce the Golden Age. When Pericles, Aspasia, Pheidias, Anaxagoras, and Socrates attended a play by Euripides in the Theater of Dionysus, Athens could see visibly the zenith and unity of the life of Greece—statesmanship, art, science, philosophy, literature, religion, and morals living no separate career as in the pages of chroniclers, but woven into one many-colored fabric of a nation's history.

The affections of Pericles wavered between art and philosophy, and he might have found it hard to say whether he loved Pheidias or Anaxagoras the more; perhaps he turned to Aspasia as a compromise between beauty and wisdom. For Anaxagoras he entertained, we are told, "an extraordinary esteem and admiration."[18] It was the philosopher, says Plato,[19] who deepened Pericles into statesmanship; from long intercourse with Anaxagoras, Plutarch believes, Pericles derived "not merely elevation of purpose and dignity of language, raised far above the base and dishonest buffooneries of mob eloquence, but, besides this, a composure of countenance, and a serenity and calmness in all his movements, which no occurrence whilst he was speaking could disturb." When Anaxagoras was old, and Pericles was absorbed in public affairs, the statesman for a time let the philosopher drop out of his life; but later, hearing that Anaxagoras was starving, Pericles hastened to his relief, and accepted humbly his rebuke, that "those who have occasion for a lamp supply it with oil."[20]

It seems hardly credible, and yet on second thought most natural, that the stern "Olympian" should have been keenly susceptible to the charms of woman; his self-control fought against a delicate sensibility, and the toils of office must have heightened in him the normal male longing for feminine tenderness. He had been many years married when he met Aspasia. She belonged to—she was helping to create—the type of hetaira that was about to play so active a part in Athenian life: a woman rejecting the seclusion that marriage brought to the ladies of Athens, and preferring to live in unlicensed unions, even in relative promiscuity, if thereby she might enjoy the same freedom of movement and conduct as men, and participate with them in their cultural interests. We have no testimony to Aspasia's beauty, though ancient writers speak of her "small, high-arched foot," "her silvery voice," and her golden hair.[21] Aristophanes, an unscrupulous political enemy of Pericles, describes her as a Milesian courtesan who had established a luxurious brothel at Megara, and had now imported some of her girls into Athens; and the great comedian delicately suggests that the quarrel of Athens with Megara, which precipitated the Peloponnesian War, was brought about because Aspasia persuaded Pericles to revenge her upon Megarians who had kidnaped some of her personnel.[22] But Aristophanes was not an historian, and may be trusted only where he himself is not concerned.

Arriving in Athens about 450, Aspasia opened a school of rhetoric and philosophy, and boldly encouraged the public emergence and higher education of women. Many girls of good family came to her classes, and some husbands brought their wives to study with her.[23] Men also attended her lectures, among them Pericles and Socrates, and probably Anaxagoras, Euripides, Alcibiades, and Pheidias. Socrates said that he had learned from her the art of eloquence,[24] and some ancient gossips would have it that the statesman inherited her from the philosopher.[25] Pericles now found it admirable that his wife had formed an affection for another man. He offered her her freedom in return for his own, and she agreed; she took a third husband,[26] while Pericles brought Aspasia home. By his own law of 451 he could not make her his wife, since she was of Milesian birth; any child he might have by her would be illegitimate, and ineligible to Athenian citizenship. He seems to have loved her sincerely, even uxoriously, never leaving his home or returning to it without kissing her, and finally willing his fortune to the son that she bore him. From that time onward he forewent all social life outside his home, seldom going anywhere except to the agora or the council hall; the people of Athens began to complain of his aloofness. For her part Aspasia made his home a French Enlightenment *salon,* where the art and science, the literature, philosophy, and statesmanship of Athens were brought together in mutual stimulation. Socrates marveled at her eloquence, and credited her with composing the funeral oration that Pericles delivered after the first casualties of the Peloponnesian War.[27] Aspasia became the uncrowned queen of Athens, setting fashion's tone, and giving to the women of the city an exciting example of mental and moral freedom.

The conservatives were shocked at all this, and turned it to their purposes. They denounced Pericles for leading Greeks out to war against Greeks, as in Aegina and Samos; they accused him of squandering public funds; finally, through the mouths of irresponsible comic dramatists abusing the free speech that prevailed under his rule, they charged him with turning his home into a house of ill fame, and having relations with the wife of his son.[28] Not daring to bring any of these matters to open trial, they attacked him through his friends. They indicted Pheidias for embezzling, as they alleged, some of the gold assigned to him for his chryselephantine *Athena,* and apparently succeeded in convicting him; they indicted Anaxagoras on the ground of irreligion, and the philosopher, on Pericles' advice, fled into exile; they brought against Aspasia a like writ of impiety (*graphe asebeias*), complaining that she had shown disrespect for the gods of Greece.[29] The comic poets satirized her mercilessly as a Deianeira who had ruined Pericles,* and called her, in plain Greek, a concubine; one of them, Hermippus, doubtless in turn a dishonest penny, accused her of serving as Pericles' procuress, and of bringing freeborn women to him for his pleasure.[30] At her trial, which took place before a court of fifteen hundred jurors, Pericles spoke in her defense, using all his eloquence, even to tears; and the case was dismissed. From that moment (432) Pericles began to lose his hold upon the Athenian people; and when, three years later, death came to him, he was already a broken man.

III. ATHENIAN DEMOCRACY

1. Deliberation

These strange indictments suffice to show how real was the limited democracy that functioned under the supposed dictatorship of Pericles. We must study this democracy carefully, for it is one of the outstanding experiments in the history of government. It is limited, first, by the fact that only a small minority of the people can read. It is limited physically by the difficulty of reaching Athens from the remoter towns of Attica. The franchise is restricted to those sons, of two free Athenian parents, who have reached the age of twenty-one; and only they and their families enjoy civil rights, or directly bear the military and fiscal burdens of the state. Within this jealously circumscribed circle of 43,000 citizens out of an Attic population of 315,000, political power, in the days of Pericles, is formally equal; each citizen enjoys and insists upon *isonomia* and *isegoria*—equal rights at law and in the Assembly. To the Athenian a citizen is a man who not only votes, but takes his turn, by lot and rote, as magistrate or judge; he must be free, ready, and able to serve the state at any time. No one who is subject to another, or who has to labor in order to live, can have the time or the capacity for these services; and therefore the manual worker seems to most Athenians unfit for citizenship, though, with human inconsistency they admit the peasant proprietor. All of the 115,000

* Deianira, wife of Heracles, caused his death by presenting him with a poisoned robe. Cf. Sophocles' *Trachinian Women*.

slaves of Attica, all women, nearly all workingmen, all of the 28,500 "metics" or resident aliens,* and consequently a great part of the trading class, are excluded from the franchise.†

The voters are not gathered into parties, but are loosely divided into followers of the oligarchic or the democratic factions according as they oppose or favor the extension of the franchise, the dominance of the Assembly, and the governmental succor of the poor at the expense of the rich. The active members of each faction are organized into clubs called *hetaireiai*, companionships. There are clubs of all kinds in Periclean Athens—religious clubs, kinship clubs, military clubs, workers' clubs, actors' clubs, political clubs, and clubs honestly devoted to eating and drinking. The strongest of all are the oligarchic clubs, whose members are sworn to mutual aid in politics and law, and are bound by a common passionate hostility to those lower enfranchised ranks that press upon the toes of the landed aristocracy and the moneyed merchant class.[31] Against them stand the relatively democratic party of small businessmen, of citizens who have become wage workers, and of those who man the merchant ships and the Athenian fleet; these groups resent the luxuries and privileges of the rich, and raise up to leadership in Athens such men as Cleon the tanner, Lysicles the sheep dealer, Eucrates the tow seller, Cleophon the harp manufacturer, and Hyperbolus the lampmaker. Pericles holds them off for a generation by a subtle mixture of democracy and aristocracy; but when he dies they inherit the government and thoroughly enjoy its perquisites. From Solon to the Roman conquest this bitter conflict of oligarchs and democrats is waged with oratory, votes, ostracism, assassination, and civil war.

Every voter is of right a member of the basic governing body—the *ekklesia*, or Assembly; there is at this level no representative government. Since transportation is difficult over the hills of Attica, only a fraction of the eligible members ever attend any one meeting; there are rarely more than two or three thousand. Those citizens who live in Athens or at the Piraeus come by a kind of geographical determinism to dominate the Assembly; in this way the democrats gain ascendancy over the conservatives, who are for the most part scattered among the farms and estates of Attica. The Assembly meets four times a month, on important occasions in the agora, in the Theater of Dionysus, or at the Piraeus, ordinarily in a semicircular place called the Pnyx on the slope of a hill west of the Areopagus;

* The Greek word, *metoikoi*, means "sharing the home."

† The figures are from Gomme, A. W., *The Population of Athens in the Fifth and Fourth Centuries B.C.*, pp. 21, 26, 47. They are frankly conjectural. The total figure includes the wives and minor children of the citizens.

in all these cases the members sit on benches under the open sky, and the sitting begins at dawn. Each session opens with the sacrifice of a pig to Zeus. It is usual to adjourn at once in case of a storm, earthquake, or eclipse, for these are accounted signs of divine disapproval. New legislation may be proposed only at the first session of each month, and the member who offers it is held responsible for the result of its adoption; if these are seriously evil another member may within a year of the vote invoke upon him the *graphe paranomon*, or writ of illegality, and have him fined, disfranchised, or put to death; this is Athens' way of discouraging hasty legislation. By another form of the same writ a new proposal may be checked by a demand that before its enactment one of the courts shall pass upon its constitutionality—i.e., its agreement with existing law.[32] Again, before considering a bill, the Assembly is required to submit it to the Council of Five Hundred for preliminary examination, very much as a bill in the American Congress, before discussion of it on the floor, is referred to a committee presumed to have especial knowledge and competence in the matter involved. The Council may not reject a proposal outright; it may only report it, with or without a recommendation.

Ordinarily the presiding officer opens the Assembly by presenting a *probouleuma*, or reported bill. Those who wish to speak are heard in the order of their age; but anyone may be disqualified from addressing the Assembly if it can be shown that he is not a landowner, or is not legally married, or has neglected his duties to his parents, or has offended public morals, or has evaded a military obligation, or has thrown away his shield in battle, or owes taxes or other money to the state.[33] Only trained orators avail themselves of the right to speak, for the Assembly is a difficult audience. It laughs at mispronunciations, protests aloud at digressions, expresses its approval with shouts, whistling, and clapping of hands, and, if it strongly disapproves, makes such a din that the speaker is compelled to leave the *bema*, or rostrum.[34] Each speaker is allowed a given time, whose lapse is measured by a clepsydra or water clock.[35] Voting is by a show of hands unless some individual is directly and specially affected by the proposal, in which case a secret ballot is taken. The vote may confirm, amend, or override the Council's report on a bill, and the decision of the Assembly is final. Decrees for immediate action, as distinct from laws, may be enacted more expeditiously than new legislation; but such decrees may with equal expedition be canceled, and do not enter into the body of Athenian law.

Above the Assembly in dignity, inferior to it in power, is the *boule*, or

Council. Originally an upper house, it has by the time of Pericles been reduced in effect to a legislative committee of the *ekklesia.* Its members are chosen by lot and rote from the register of the citizens, fifty for each of the ten tribes; they serve for a year only, and receive, in the fourth century, five obols per day. Since each councilor is disqualified for re-election until all other eligible citizens have had a chance to serve, every citizen, in the normal course of events, sits on the *boule* for at least one term during his life. It meets in the *bouleuterion,* or council hall, south of the agora, and its ordinary sessions are public. Its functions are legislative, executive, and consultative: it examines and reformulates the bills proposed to the Assembly; it supervises the conduct and accounts of the religious and administrative officials of the city; it controls public finances, enterprises, and buildings; it issues executive decrees when action is called for and the Assembly is not in session; and, subject to later revision by the Assembly, it controls the foreign affairs of the state.

To perform these varied tasks the Council divides itself into ten prytanies, or committees, each of fifty members; and each prytany presides over the Council and the Assembly for a month of thirty-six days. Every morning the presiding prytany chooses one of its members to serve as chairman of itself and the Council for the day; this position, the highest in the state, is therefore open by lot and turn to any citizen; Athens has three hundred presidents every year. The lot determines at the last moment which prytany, and which member of it, shall preside over the Council during the month or the day; by this device the corrupt Athenians hope to reduce the corruption of justice to the lowest point attainable by human character. The acting prytany prepares the agenda, convokes the Council, and formulates the conclusions reached during the day. In this way, through Assembly, Council, and prytany, the democracy of Athens carries out its legislative functions. As for the Areopagus, its powers are in the fifth century restricted to trying cases of arson, willful violence, poisoning, or premeditated murder. Slowly the law of Greece has been changed "from status to contract," from the whim of one man, or the edict of a narrow class, into the deliberate agreement of free citizens.

2. *Law*

The earliest Greeks appear to have conceived of law as sacred custom, divinely sanctioned and revealed; *themis** meant to them both these customs and

* I.e., what is laid down, from *ti-themi,* I place; cf. our *doom* in its early sense of law, and the Russian *duma.*

a goddess who (like India's Rita or China's Tao or Tien) embodied the moral order and harmony of the world. Law was a part of theology, and the oldest Greek laws of property were mingled with liturgical regulations in the ancient temple codes.[36] Perhaps as old as such religious law were the rules established by the decrees of tribal chieftains or kings, which began as force and ended, in time, as sanctities.

The second phase of Greek legal history was the collection and co-ordination of these holy customs by lawgivers (*thesmothetai*) like Zaleucus, Charondas, Draco, Solon; when such men put their new codes into writing, the *thesmoi*, or sacred usages, became *nomoi*, or man-made laws.* In these codes law freed itself from religion, and became increasingly secular; the intention of the agent entered more fully into judgment of the act; family liability was replaced by individual responsibility, and private revenge gave way to statutory punishment by the state.[37]

The third step in Greek legal development was the accumulative growth of a body of law. When a Periclean Greek speaks of the law of Athens he means the codes of Draco and Solon, and the measures that have been passed—and not repealed—by the Assembly or the Council. If a new law contravenes an old one, the repeal of the latter is prerequisite; but scrutiny is seldom complete, and two statutes are often found in ludicrous contradiction. In periods of exceptional legal confusion a committee of *nomothetai*, or law determiners, is chosen by lot from the popular courts to decide which laws shall be retained; in such cases advocates are appointed to defend the old laws against those who propose to repeal them. Under the supervision of these *nomothetai* the laws of Athens, phrased in simple and intelligible language, are cut upon stone slabs in the King's Porch; and thereafter no magistrate is allowed to decide a case by an unwritten law.

Athenian law makes no distinction between a civil and a criminal code, except that it reserves murder cases for the Areopagus, and in civil suits leaves the complainant to enforce the court's decree himself, going to his aid only if he meets with resistance.[38] Murder is infrequent, for it is branded as a sacrilege as well as a crime, and the dread of feud revenge remains if the law fails to act. Under certain conditions direct retaliation is still tolerated in the fifth century; when a husband finds his mother, wife, concubine, sister, or daughter in illicit relations he is entitled to kill the male offender at once.[39] Whether a killing is intentional or not it has to be expiated as a pollution of the city's soil, and the rites of purification are painfully rigid and complex. If the victim has granted pardon before dying, no action can be brought against the killer.[40] Beneath the

* In Periclean Athens the name *thesmothetai* was given to the six minor archons who recorded, interpreted, and enforced the laws; in Aristotle's day they presided over the popular courts.

Areopagus are three tribunals for homicide cases, according to the class and origin of the victim, and according as the act was intentional, or excusable, or not. A fourth tribunal holds court at Phreattys on the coast, and tries those who, while exiled for unpremeditated homicide, are now charged with another and premeditated murder; being polluted by the first crime, they are not allowed to touch Attic soil, and their defense is conducted from a boat near the shore.

The law of property is uncompromisingly severe. Contracts are rigorously enforced; all jurors are required to swear that they "will not vote for an abolition of private debts, or for a distribution of the lands or houses belonging to Athenians"; and every year the head archon, on taking office, has proclamation made by a herald that "what each possesses he shall remain possessor and absolute master thereof."[41] The right of bequest is still narrowly limited. Where there are male children the old religious conception of property, as bound up with a given family line and the care of ancestral spirits, demands that the estate should automatically pass to the sons; the father owns the property only in trust for the family dead, living, and to be born. Whereas in Sparta (as in England) the patrimony is indivisible and goes to the eldest son, in Athens (very much as in France) it is apportioned among the male heirs, the oldest receiving a moderately larger share than the others.[42] As early as Hesiod we find the peasant limiting his family in Gallic fashion, lest his estate be ruinously divided among many sons.[43] The husband's property never descends to the widow; all that remains to her is her dowry. Wills are as complex in Pericles' day as in our own, and are couched in much the same terms as now.[44] In this as in other matters Greek legislation is the basis of that Roman law which in turn has provided the legal foundations of Western society.

3. *Justice*

Democracy reaches the judiciary last of all; and the greatest reform accomplished by Ephialtes and Pericles is the transfer of judicial powers from the Areopagus and the archons to the *heliaea*. The establishment of these popular courts gives to Athens what trial by jury will win for modern Europe. The *heliaea** is composed of six thousand dicasts, or jurors, annually drawn by lot from the register of the citizens; these six thousand are distributed into ten dicasteries, or panels, of approximately five hundred each, leaving a surplus for vacancies and emergencies. Minor and local cases are settled by thirty judges who periodically visit the demes or counties of Attica. Since no juror may serve more than a year at a time, and

* Strictly, *heliaea* is the name of the place where the courts met, and was so called (from *helios*, sun) because the sessions were held in the open air.

eligibility is determined by rotation, every citizen, in the average of chance, becomes a juror every third year. He does not have to serve, but the payment of two—later three—obols per day obtains an attendance of two or three hundred jurors for each panel. Important cases, like that of Socrates, may be tried before vast dicasteries of twelve hundred men. To reduce corruption to a minimum, the panel before which a case is to be tried is determined by lot at the last minute; and as most trials last but a day we do not hear much of bribery in the courts; even the Athenians find it difficult to bribe in a moment three hundred men.

Despite expedition, the courts of Athens, like courts the world over, are usually behind their calendar, for the Athenians itch to litigate. To cool this fever public arbitrators are chosen by lot from the roster of citizens who have reached their sixtieth year; the parties to a dispute submit their complaint and defense to one of these, again chosen by lot at the last minute; and each party pays him a small fee. If he fails to reconcile them he gives his judgment, solemnized by an oath. Either party may then appeal to the courts, but these usually refuse to hear minor cases that have not been submitted to arbitration. When a case is accepted for trial the plea is entered or sworn to, the witnesses make their depositions and swear to them, and all these statements are presented to the court in written form. They are sealed in a special box, and at a later date they are opened and examined, and judgment is given, by a panel chosen by lot. There is no public prosecutor; the government relies upon private citizens to accuse before the courts anyone guilty of serious offenses against morals, religion, or the state. Hence arises a class of "sycophants," who make such charges a regular practice, and develop their profession into an art of blackmail; in the fourth century they earn a good living by bringing—or, better, threatening to bring—actions against rich men, believing that a popular court will be loath to acquit those who can pay substantial fines.* The expenses of the courts are mostly covered by fines imposed upon convicted men. Plaintiffs who fail to substantiate their charges are also fined; and if they receive less than a fifth of the jurors' votes they are subject to a lashing, or to a penalty of a thousand drachmas ($1000). Each party in a trial usually acts as his own lawyer, and has to make in person the first presentation of his case. But as the complexity of procedure rises, and litigants detect in the jurors a certain sensitivity to eloquence, the practice grows of engaging a rhetor or orator, versed in the law, to support the complaint or defense, or to prepare, in his client's name and

* Crito, rich friend of Socrates, complained that it was difficult for one who wished to mind his own business to live at Athens. "For at this very time," he said, "there are people bringing actions against me, not because they have suffered any wrongs from me, but because they think that I would rather pay them a sum of money than have the trouble of law proceedings."[45]

character, a speech that the client may read to the court. From these special rhetor-pleaders comes the lawyer. His antiquity in Greece appears from a remark in Diogenes Laertius that Bias, Wise Man of Priene, was an eloquent pleader of causes, who always reserved his talents for the just side. Some of these lawyers are attached to the courts as *exegetai*, or interpreters; for many of the jurors have no more legal knowledge than the parties to the case.

Evidence is ordinarily presented in writing, but the witness must appear and swear to its accuracy when the *grammateus*, or clerk of the court, reads it to the jurors. There is no cross-examination. Perjury is so frequent that cases are sometimes decided in the face of explicit sworn evidence. The testimony of women and minors is accepted only in murder trials; that of slaves is admitted only when drawn from them by torture; it is taken for granted that without torture they will lie. It is a barbarous aspect of Greek law, destined to be outdone in Roman prisons and Inquisition chambers, and perhaps rivaled in the secret rooms of police courts in our time. Torture, in Pericles' day, is forbidden in the case of citizens. Many masters decline to let their slaves be used as witnesses, even when their case may depend upon such testimony; and any permanent injury done to a slave by torture must be made good by those who inflicted it.[46]

Penalties take the form of flogging, fines, disfranchisement, branding, confiscation, exile, and death; imprisonment is seldom used as a punishment. It is a principle of Greek law that a slave should be punished in his body, but a freeman in his property. A vase painting shows a slave hung up by his arms and legs, and mercilessly lashed.[47] Fines are the usual penalty for citizens, and are assessed on a scale that opens the democracy to the charge of fattening its purse through unjust condemnations. On the other hand a convicted person and his accuser are in many cases allowed to name the fine or punishment that they think just; and the court then chooses between the suggested penalties. Murder, sacrilege, treason, and some offenses that seem minor to us are punished with both confiscation and death; but a prospective death penalty may usually be avoided before trial by voluntary exile and the abandonment of property. If the accused disdains flight, and is a citizen, death is inflicted as painlessly as possible by administering hemlock, which gradually benumbs the body from the feet upward, killing when it reaches the heart. In the case of slaves the death penalty may be effected by a brutal cudgeling.[48] Sometimes the condemned, before or after death, may be hurled over a cliff into a pit called the *barathron*. When a sentence of death is laid upon a murderer it is carried out by the public executioner in the presence of the relatives of the victim, as a concession to the old custom and spirit of revenge.

The Athenian code is not as enlightened as we might expect, and advances only moderately upon Hammurabi's. Its basic defect is the limitation of legal rights to freemen constituting hardly a seventh of the population. Even free women and children are excluded from the proud *isonomia* of the citizens; metics, foreigners, and slaves can bring suit only through a patron citizen. Sycophantic blackmail, frequent torture of slaves, capital punishment for minor offenses, personal abuse in forensic debate, the diffusion and weakening of judicial responsibility, the susceptibility of jurors to oratorical displays, their inability to temper present passions with a knowledge of the past or a wise calculation of the future—these are black marks against a system of law envied throughout Greece for its comparative mildness and integrity, and sufficiently dependable and practical to give to Athenian life and property that orderly protection which is so necessary for economic activity and moral growth. One test of Athenian law is the reverence that nearly every citizen feels for it: the law is for him the very soul of his city, the essence of its beneficence and strength. The best judgment of the Athenian code is the readiness with which other Greek states adopt a large part of it. "Everyone would admit," says Isocrates, "that our laws have been the source of very many and very great benefits to the life of humanity."[49] Here for the first time in history is a government of laws and not of men.

Athenian law prevails throughout the Athenian Empire of two million souls while that Empire endures; but for the rest Greece never achieves a common system of jurisprudence. International law makes as sorry a picture in fifth-century Athens as in the world today. Nevertheless external trade requires some legal code, and commercial treaties (*symbola*) are described by Demosthenes as so numerous in his time that the laws governing commercial disputes "are everywhere identical."[50] These treatises establish consular representation, guarantee the execution of contracts, and make the judgments given in one signatory nation valid in the others.[51] This, however, does not put an end to piracy, which breaks out whenever the dominant fleet is weakened, or relaxes its watchfulness. Eternal vigilance is the price of order as well as of liberty; and lawlessness stalks like a wolf about every settled realm, seeking some point of weakness which may give it entry. The right of a city to lead foraging expeditions upon the persons and property of other cities is accepted by some Greek states so long as no treaty specifically forbids it.[52] Religion succeeds in making temples inviolable unless used as military bases; it protects heralds and pilgrims to Panhellenic festivals; it requires a formal declaration of war before hostilities, and the granting of a truce, when asked, for the return and burial of the dead in battle. Poisoned weapons are avoided by general custom, and prisoners are usually exchanged or ransomed at the recognized tariff of two minas—later one mina ($100)—each;[53] otherwise war is nearly as brutal among the Greeks as in modern Christendom. Treaties are numerous, and are solemnized with pious oaths; but they are almost always broken. Alliances are frequent, and sometimes generate lasting leagues, like the Delphic Amphictyony in the sixth century and the Achaean and Aetolian Leagues in the third. Occasionally two cities exchange the courtesy of *isopoliteia*, by which each gives to the other's freemen the rights of citizenship. International arbitration may be arranged, but the decisions arrived at in such cases are as often as not rejected or ignored. Towards foreigners the Greek feels no moral obligation, and no legal one except by treaty; they are *barbaroi**—not quite "barbarians," but outsiders—aliens speaking outlandish tongues. Only in the Stoic philosophers of the cosmopolitan Hellenistic era will Greece rise to the conception of a moral code embracing all mankind.

4. Administration

As early as 487, perhaps earlier, the method of election in the choice of archons is replaced by lot; some way must be found to keep the rich from buying, or the knaves from smiling, their way into office. To render the selection less than wholly accidental, all those upon whom the lot falls are subjected, before taking up their duties, to a rigorous *dokimasia*, or character examination, conducted by the Council or the courts. The candidate must show Athenian parentage on both sides, freedom from physical defect and scandal, the pious honoring of his ancestors, the performance of his military assignments, and the full payment of his taxes; his whole life is on this occasion exposed to challenge by any citizen, and the prospect of such a scrutiny presumably frightens the most worthless from the sortition. If he passes this test the archon swears an oath that he will properly perform the obligations of his office, and will dedicate to the gods a golden statue of life-size if he should accept presents or bribes.[54] The fact that chance is allowed to play so large a part in the naming of the nine archons suggests the diminution which the office has suffered since Solon's day; its functions are now in the nature of administrative routine. The archon basileus, whose name preserves the empty title of king, has become merely the chief religious official of the city. Nine times yearly the archon is required to obtain a vote of confidence from the Assembly; his actions and judgments may be appealed to the *boule* or the *heliaea;* and any citizen may indict him for malfeasance. At the end of his term all his official acts, accounts, and documents are reviewed by a board of *logistai* responsible to

* The word is cousin to the Sanskrit *barbara* and the Latin *balbus,* both of which mean stammering; cf. our *babble.* The Greeks implied by *barbaros* rather strangeness of speech than lack of civilization, and used *barbarismos* precisely as we, following them, use *barbarism* —to mean an alien or quasi-alien distortion of a nation's idiom.

the Council; and severe penalties, even death, may avenge serious misconduct. If the archon escapes these democratic dragons he becomes, at the end of his year of office, a member of the Areopagus; but this, in the fifth century, is a well-nigh empty honor, since that body has lost nearly all its powers.

The archons are but one of many committees which, under the direction and scrutiny of the Assembly, the Council, and the courts, administer the affairs of the city. Aristotle names twenty-five such groups, and estimates the number of municipal officials at seven hundred. Nearly all of these are chosen annually by lot; and since no man may be a member of the same committee twice, every citizen may expect to be a city dignitary for at least one year of his life. Athens does not believe in government by experts.

More importance is attached to military than to civil office. The ten *strategoi,* or commanders, though they too are appointed for a year only, and are at all times subject to examination and recall, are chosen not by lot but by open election in the Assembly. Here ability, not popularity, is the road to preferment; and the *ekklesia* of the fourth century shows its good sense by choosing Phocion general forty-five times, despite the fact that he is the most unpopular man in Athens and makes no secret of his scorn for the crowd. The functions of the *strategoi* expand with the growth of international relations, so that in the later fifth century they not only manage the army and the navy, but conduct negotiations with foreign states, and control the revenues and expenditures of the city. The commander in chief, or *strategos autokrator,* is therefore the most powerful man in the government; and since he may be re-elected year after year, he can give to the state a continuity of purpose which its constitution might otherwise render impossible. Through this office Pericles makes Athens for a generation a democratic monarchy, so that Thucydides can say of the Athenian polity that though it is a democracy in name it is really government by the greatest of the citizens.

The army is identical with the electorate; every citizen must serve, and is subject, until the age of sixty, to conscription in any war. But Athenian life is not militarized; after a period of youthful training there is little of martial drill, no strutting of uniforms, no interference of soldiery with the civilian population. In active service the army consists of light-armed infantry, chiefly the poorer citizens, carrying slings or spears; the heavy-armed infantry, or hoplites, those prosperous citizens who can afford armor, shield, and javelin; and the cavalry of rich men, clad in armor and helmet, and equipped with lance and sword. The Greeks excel the Asiatics in military discipline, and perhaps owe their achievements to a striking combination of loyal obedience on the battlefield with vigorous independence in civil affairs. Nevertheless there is no science of war among them, no definite principles of tactics on strategy, before Epaminondas and Philip. Cities are usually walled, and defense is—among the Greeks as among ourselves—more effective than offense; otherwise man might have no civilization to record. Siege armies bring up great beams suspended by chains, and, drawing the beams back, drive them forward against the wall; this is as far as siege machinery develops before Archimedes. As for the navy, it is kept up by choosing, each year, four hundred trierarchs, rich men whose privilege it is to recruit a crew, equip a trireme with materials supplied by the state, pay for its building and launching, and keep it in repair; in this way Athens supports in peacetime a fleet of some sixty ships.[55]

The maintenance of the army and the navy constitutes the chief expenditure of the state. Revenues come from traffic tolls, harbor dues, a two per cent tariff on imports and exports, a twelve-drachma annual poll tax on metics, a half-drachma tax on freedmen and slaves, a tax on prostitutes, a sales tax, licenses, fines, confiscations, and the imperial tribute. The tax on farm produce, which financed Athens under Peisistratus, is abandoned by the democracy as derogatory to the dignity of agriculture. Most taxes are farmed out to publicans, who collect them for the state and pocket a share as their profit. Considerable income is derived from state ownership of mineral resources. In emergencies the city resorts to a capital levy, the rate rising with the amount of property owned; by this method, for example, the Athenians in 428 raise two hundred talents ($1,200,000) for the siege of Mytilene. Rich men are also invited to undertake certain *leiturgiai*, i.e., public services, such as equipping embassies, fitting out ships for the fleet, or paying for plays, musical contests, and games. These "liturgies" are voluntarily undertaken by some of the wealthy, and are forced by public opinion upon others. To add to the discomfort of the well to do, any citizen assigned to a liturgy may compel any other to take it from him, or exchange fortunes with him, if he can prove the other to be richer than himself. As the democratic faction grows in power it finds ever more numerous occasions and reasons for using this device; and in return the financiers, merchants, manufacturers, and landed proprietors of Attica study the arts of concealment and obstruction, and meditate revolution.

Excluding such gifts and levies, the total internal revenue of Athens in the time of Pericles amounts to some four hundred talents ($2,400,000) a year; to which is added six hundred talents of contributions from subjects and allies. This income is spent without any budget, or advance estimate and allocation of funds. Under Pericles' thrifty management, and despite his unprecedented expenditures, the treasury shows a growing surplus, which in 440 stands at 9700 talents ($58,200,000); a pretty sum for any city in any age, and quite extraordinary in Greece, where few states—in the Peloponnesus none—have any surplus at all.[56] In cities that have such a reserve it is deposited, usually, in the temple of the city's god—at Athens, after 434, in the Parthenon. The state claims the right to use not only this surplus, but, as well, the gold in the statues which it raises to its god; in the case of Pheidias' *Athene Parthenos* this amounts to forty talents ($240,000), and is so affixed as to be removable.[57] In the temple the city keeps also its "theoric fund," from which it makes the payments annually due the citizens for attendance at the sacred plays and games.

Such is Athenian democracy—the narrowest and fullest in history: narrowest in the number of those who share its privileges, fullest in the directness and equality with which all the citizens control legislation, and administer public affairs. The faults of the system will appear vividly as its history unfolds; indeed, they are already noised about in Aristophanes. The irresponsibility of an Assembly that may without check of precedent or revision vote its momentary passion on one day, and on the next day its passionate regret, punishing then not itself but those who have misled it; the limitation of legislative authority to those who can attend the *ekklesia;* the encouragement of demagogues and the wasteful ostracism of able men; the filling of offices by lot and rotation, changing the personnel yearly and creating a chaos of government; the disorderliness of faction perpetually disturbing the guidance and administration of the state—these are vital defects, for which Athens will pay the full penalty to Sparta, Philip, Alexander, and Rome.

But every government is imperfect, irksome, and mortal; we have no reason to believe that monarchy or aristocracy would govern Athens better, or longer preserve it; and perhaps only this chaotic democracy can release the energy that will lift Athens to one of the peaks of history. Never before or since has political life, within the circle of citizenship, been so intense or so creative. This corrupt and incompetent democracy is at least a school: the voter in the Assembly listens to the cleverest men in Athens, the juror in the courts has his wits sharpened by the taking and sifting of evidence, the holder of office is molded by executive responsibility and experience into a deeper maturity of understanding and judgment; "the city," says Simonides, "is the teacher of the man."[68] For these reasons, it may be, the Athenians can appreciate, and thereby call into existence, Aeschylus and Euripides, Socrates and Plato; the audience at the theater has been formed in the Assembly and the courts, and is ready to receive the best. This aristocratic democracy is no laissez-faire state, no mere watchman of property and order; it finances the Greek drama, and builds the Parthenon; it makes itself responsible for the welfare and development of its people, and opens up to them the opportunity *ou monon tou zen, alla tou eu zen*—"not only to live, but to live well." History can afford to forgive it all its sins.

CHAPTER XII

Work and Wealth in Athens

I. LAND AND FOOD

AT the base of this democracy and this culture lies the production and distribution of wealth. Some men can govern states, seek truth, make music, carve statues, paint pictures, write books, teach children, or serve the gods because others toil to grow food, weave clothing, build dwellings, mine the earth, make useful things, transport goods, exchange them, or finance their production or their movement. Everywhere this is the foundation.

Supporting all society is the peasant, the poorest and most necessary of men. In Attica he has at least the franchise; only citizens are permitted to own land, and nearly all peasants own the soil that they till. Clan control of the land has disappeared, and private ownership is solidly established. As in modern France and America, this great class of small proprietors is a steadying conservative force in a democracy where the propertyless city dwellers are always driving toward reform. The ancient war between the country and the city—between those who want high returns for agriculture and low prices for manufactured goods, and those who want low prices for food and high wages or profits in industry—is especially conscious and lively in Attica. Whereas industry and trade are accounted plebeian and degrading by the Athenian citizen, the pursuits of husbandry are honored as the groundwork of national economy, personal character, and military power; and the freemen of the countryside tend to look down upon the denizens of the city as either weakling parasites or degraded slaves.[1]

The soil is poor: of 630,000 acres in Attica a third is unsuitable for cultivation, and the rest is impoverished by deforestation, meager rainfall, and rapid erosion by winter floods. The peasants of Attica shirk no toil—for themselves or their handful of slaves—to remedy this dry humor of the gods; they gather the surplus flow of headwaters into reservoirs, dike the channels of the streams to control the floods, reclaim the precious humus of the swamps, build thousands of irrigation canals to bring to their thirsty fields the trickle of the rivulets, patiently transplant vegetables to improve their size and quality, and let the land lie fallow in alternate years to regain its strength. They alkalinize the soil with salts like carbonate of lime, and fertilize it with potassium nitrate, ashes, and human waste;[2] the gardens and groves about Athens are enriched with the sewage of the city, brought by a main sewer to a reservoir outside the Dipylon, and led thence by brick-lined canals into the valley of the Cephisus River.[3] Different soils are mixed to their mutual benefit, and green crops like beans in flower are plowed in to nourish the earth. Plowing, harrowing, sowing, and planting are crowded into the brief days of the fall; the grain harvest comes at the end of May, and the rainless summer is the season of preparation and rest. With all this care Attica produces only 675,000 bushels of grain yearly—hardly enough to supply a quarter of its population. Without imported food Periclean Athens would starve; hence the urge to imperialism, and the necessity for a powerful fleet.

The countryside tries to atone for its parsimonious grain by generous harvests of olives and grapes. Hillsides are terraced and watered, and asses are encouraged to make the vine more fruitful by gnawing off the twigs.[4] Olive trees cover many a landscape in Periclean Greece, but it is Peisistratus and Solon who deserve the credit for introducing them. The olive tree takes sixteen years to come to fruit, forty years to reach perfection; without the subsidies of Peisistratus it might never have grown on Attic soil; and the devastation of the olive orchards in the Peloponnesian War will play a part in the decline of Athens. To the Greek the olive has many uses: one pressing gives oil for eating, a second, oil for anointing, a third, oil for illumination; and the remainder is used as fuel.[5] It becomes Attica's richest crop, so valuable that the state assumes a monopoly of its export, and pays with it and wine for the grain that it must import.

It forbids altogether the export of figs, for these are a main source of health and energy in Greece. The fig tree grows well even in arid soil; its spreading roots gather whatever moisture the earth will yield, and its stinted foliage offers scant surface for evaporation. Furthermore, the husbandman learns from the East the secret of caprification: he hangs branches of the wild male goat fig (*caprificus*) among the boughs of the female cultivated tree, and relies upon gall wasps to carry the fertilizing pollen of the male into the fruit of the female, which then bears richer and sweeter figs.

These products of the soil—cereals, olive oil, figs, grapes, and wine—are the staples of diet in Attica. Cattle rearing is negligible as a source of food; horses are bred for racing, sheep for wool, goats for milk, asses, mules, cows, and oxen for transport, but chiefly pigs for food; and bees are kept as providers of honey for a sugarless world. Meat is a luxury; the poor have it only on feast days; the heroic banquets of Homeric days have disappeared. Fish is both a commonplace and a delicacy; the poor man buys it salted and dried; the rich man celebrates with fresh shark meat and eels.[6] Cereals take the form of porridge, flat loaves, or cakes, often mixed with honey. Bread and cake are seldom baked at home, but are bought from women peddlers or in market stalls. Eggs are added, and vegetables—particularly beans, peas, cabbage, lentils, lettuce, onions, and garlic. Fruits are few; oranges and lemons are unknown. Nuts are common, and condiments abound. Salt is collected in salt pans from the sea, and is traded in the interior for slaves; a cheap slave is called a "salting," and a good one is "worth his salt." Nearly everything is cooked and dressed with olive oil, which makes an excellent substitute for petroleum. Butter is hard to keep in Mediterranean lands, and olive oil takes its place. Honey, sweetmeats, and cheese provide dessert; cheesecakes are so fancied that many classic treatises are devoted to their esoteric art.[7] Water is the usual drink, but everyone has wine, for no civilization has found life tolerable without narcotics or stimulants. Snow and ice are kept in the ground to cool wine in the hot months.[8] Beer is known but scorned in Periclean days. All in all, the Greek is a moderate eater, and contents himself with two meals daily. "Yet there are many," says Hippocrates, "who, if accustomed to it, can easily bear three full meals a day."[9]

II. INDUSTRY

Out of the earth come minerals and fuels as well as food. Lighting is provided by graceful lamps or torches—burning refined olive oil, or resin—or by candles. Heat is derived from dry wood or charcoal, burning in portable braziers. The cutting of trees for fuel and building denudes the woods and hills near the towns; already in the fifth century timber for houses, furniture, and ships is imported. There is no coal.

Greek mining is not for fuels but for minerals. The soil of Attica is rich in marble, iron, zinc, silver, and lead. The mines at Laurium, near the southern tip of the peninsula, are in the phrase of Aeschylus "a fountain running silver"[10] for Athens; they are a main support of the government, which retains all subsoil rights, and leases the mines to private operators for a talent ($6000) fee and one twenty-fourth of the product yearly.[11] In 483 a prospector discovers the first really profitable veins at Laurium, and a silver rush takes place to the region of the mines. Only citizens are allowed to lease the properties, and only slaves perform the work. The pious Nicias, whose superstition will help to ruin Athens, makes $170 a day by leasing a thousand slaves to the mine operators at a rental of one obol (17 cents) each per day; many an Athenian fortune is made in this way, or by lending money to the enterprise. The slaves in the mine number some twenty thousand, and include the superintendents and engineers. They work in ten-hour shifts, and the operations continue without interruption, night and day. If the slave rests he feels the foreman's lash; if he tries to escape he is attached to his work by iron shackles; if he runs away and is captured his forehead is branded with a hot iron.[12] The galleries are but three feet high and two feet wide; the slaves, with pick or chisel and hammer, work on their knees, their stomachs, or their backs.[13] The broken ore is carried out in baskets or bags handed from man to man, for the galleries are too narrow to let two men pass each other conveniently. The profits are enormous: in 483 the share received by the government is a hundred talents ($600,000)—a windfall that builds a fleet for Athens and saves Greece at Salamis. Even for others than the slaves there is evil in this as well as good; the Athenian treasury becomes dependent upon the mines, and when, in the Peloponnesian War, the Spartans capture Laurium the whole economy of Athens is upset. The exhaustion of the veins in the fourth century co-operates with many other factors in Athenian decay. For Attica has no other precious metal in her soil.

Metallurgy advances with mining. The ore at Laurium is crushed in huge mortars with a heavy iron pestle worked by slave power; then it goes to mills where it is ground between revolving stones of hard trachyte; then it is sized by screening; the material that passes through the screen is sent to an ore washer, where jets of water are discharged from cisterns upon inclined rectangular tables of stone covered with a smooth thin coat of hard cement; the current is turned at sharp angles, where pockets snare the metal particles. The collected metal is thrown into small smelting furnaces equipped with blowers to raise the heat; at the bottom of each furnace are openings through which the molten metal is drawn. Lead is separated from the silver by heating the molten metal on cupels of porous material and exposing it to the air; by this simple process the lead is converted into litharge, and the silver is freed. The processes of smelting and refining are competently performed, for the silver coins of Athens are ninety-eight per cent pure. Laurium pays the price of the wealth it produces, as mining always pays the price for metal industry; plants and men wither and die from the furnace fumes, and the vicinity of the works becomes a scene of dusty desolation.[14]

Other industries are not so toilsome. Attica has many of them now, small in scale but remarkably specialized. It quarries marble and other stones, it makes a thousand shapes of pottery, it dresses hides in great tanneries like those owned by Cleon, rival of Pericles, and Anytus, accuser of Socrates; it has wagon-makers, shipbuilders, saddlers, harness makers, shoe manufacturers; there are saddlers who make only bridles, and shoemakers who make only men's or women's shoes.[15] In the building trades are carpenters, molders, stonecutters, metalworkers, painters, veneerers. There are blacksmiths, swordmakers, shieldmakers, lampmakers, lyre tuners, millers, bakers, sausage men, fishmongers—everything necessary to an economic life busy and varied, but not mechanized or monotonous. Common textiles are still for the most part produced in the home; there the women weave and mend the ordinary clothing and bedding of the family, some carding the wool, some at the spinning wheel, some at the loom, some bent over an embroidery frame. Special fabrics come from workshops, or from abroad—fine linens from Egypt, Amorgos, and Tarentum, dyed woolens from Syracuse, blankets from Corinth, carpets from the Near East and Carthage, colorful coverlets from Cyprus; and the women of Cos, late in the fourth century, learn the art of unwinding the cocoons of the silkworm and weaving the filaments into silk.[16] In some homes the women become so highly skilled in textile arts that they produce more than their families can use; they sell the surplus at first to consumers, then to middlemen; they employ helpers, freedmen or slaves; and in this way a domestic industry develops as a step to a factory system.

Such a system begins to take form in the age of Pericles. Pericles himself, like Alcibiades, owns a factory.[17] No machinery is available, but slaves can be had in abundance; it is because muscle power is cheap that there is no incentive to develop machinery. The *ergasteria* of Athens are rather workshops than factories; the largest of them, Cephalus' shield factory, has 120 workmen, Timarchus' shoe factory has ten, Demosthenes' cabinet factory twenty, his armor factory thirty.[18] At first these shops produce only to order; later they manufacture for the market, and finally for export; and the spread and abundance of coinage, replacing barter, facilitates their operations. There are no corporations; each factory is an independent unit, owned by one or two men; and the owner often works beside his slaves. There are no patents; crafts are handed down from father to son, or are learned by apprentices; the Athenians are exempted by law from caring for the old age of parents who have failed to teach them a trade.[19] Hours are long but work is leisurely; master and man labor from dawn to twilight, with a siesta at summer noons. There are no vacations, but there are some sixty workless holydays every year.

III. TRADE AND FINANCE

When an individual, a family, or a city creates a surplus, and wishes to exchange it, trade begins. The first difficulty here is that transport is costly, for roads are poor, and the sea is a snare. The finest road is the Sacred Way from Athens to Eleusis; but this is mere dirt, and is often too narrow to let vehicles pass. The bridges are precarious causeways formed by earthen dikes, which as likely as not have been washed away by floods. The usual draft animal is the ox, who is too philosophical to enrich the trader that depends upon him for transport; wagons are fragile, and always break down, or get bogged in the mud; it is better to pack the goods on the back of a mule, for he goes a trifle faster, and does not take up so much of the road. There is no postal service in Greece, even for the governments; they are content with runners, and private correspondence must wait the chance of using these. Important news can be flashed by fire beacons from hill to hill, or sent by carrier pigeons.[20] There are inns here and there on the road, but they are favored by robbers and vermin; even the god Dionysus, in Aristophanes, inquires of Heracles for "the eating-houses and hostels where there are the fewest bugs."[21]

Sea transport is cheaper, especially if voyages are limited, as most of them are, to the calm summer months. Passenger tariffs are low: for two drachmas ($2) a family can secure passage from the Piraeus to Egypt or the Black Sea,[22] but ships do not cater to passengers, being made to carry goods or wage war or do either at need. The main motive power is wind upon a sail, but slaves ply the oars when the wind is contrary or dead. The smallest seagoing merchant vessels are triaconters with thirty oars, all on one level; the penteconter has fifty. Back about 700 the Corinthians launched the first trireme, with a crew of two hundred men plying three banks or tiers of oars; by the fifth century such ships, beautiful with their long and lofty prows, have grown to 256 tons, carry seven thousand bushels of grain, and become the talk of the Mediterranean by making eight miles an hour.[23]

The second problem of trade is to find a reliable medium of exchange. Every city has its own system of weights and measures, and its own individual coinage; at every one of a hundred frontiers one must transvalue all values skeptically, for every Greek government except the Athenian cheats by debasing its coins.[24] "In most cities," says an anonymous Greek, "merchants are compelled to ship goods for the return journey, for they cannot get money that is of any use to them elsewhere."[25] Some cities mint coins of electrum—a compound of silver and gold—and rival one another in getting as little gold as possible into the mixture. The Athenian government, from Solon onward, helps Athenian trade powerfully by establishing a reliable coinage, stamped with the owl of Athena; "taking owls to Athens" is the Greek equivalent of "carrying coals to Newcastle."[26] Because Athens, through all her vicissitudes, refuses to depreciate her silver drachmas, these "owls" are accepted gladly throughout the Mediterranean world, and tend to displace local currencies in the Aegean. Gold at this stage is still an article of merchandise, sold by weight, rather than a vehicle of trade; Athens mints it only in rare emergencies, usually in a ration to silver of 14 to 1.[27] The smallest Athenian coins are of copper; eight of these make an obol—a coin of iron or bronze, named from its resemblance to nails or spits (*obeliskoi*). Six obols make a drachma, i.e., a handful; two drachmas make a gold stater; one hundred drachmas make a mina; sixty minas make a talent. A drachma in the first half of the fifth century buys a bushel of grain, as a dollar does in twentieth-century America.*[28] There is no paper money in Athens, no government bonds, no joint-stock corporations, no stock exchange.

But there are banks. They have a hard struggle to get a footing, for those who have no need for loans denounce interest as a crime, and the philosophers agree with them. The average fifth-century Athenian is a hoarder; if he has savings he prefers to hide them rather than entrust them to the banks. Some men lend money on mortgages, at 16 to 18 per cent; some lend it, without interest, to their friends; some deposit their money in temple treasuries. The temples serve as banks, and lend to individuals and states at a moderate interest; the temple of Apollo at Delphi is in some measure an international bank for all Greece. There are no private loans to governments, but occasionally one state lends to another. Meanwhile the money-changer at his table (*trapeza*) begins in the fifth century to receive money on deposit, and to lend it to merchants at interest rates that vary from 12 to 30 per cent according to the risk; in this way he becomes a banker, though to the end of ancient Greece he keeps his early name of *trapezite*, the man at the table. He takes his methods from the Near East, improves them, and passes them on to Rome, which hands them down to modern Europe. Soon after the Persian War Themistocles deposits seventy talents ($420,000) with the Corinthian banker Philostephanus, very much as political adventurers feather foreign nests for themselves today; this is the earliest known allusion to secular—nontemple—banking. Towards the end of the century Antisthenes and Archestratus establish what will become, under Pasion, the most famous of all private Greek banks. Through such *trapezitai* money circulates more freely and rapidly, and so does more work, than before; and the facilities that they offer stimulate creatively the expansion of Athenian trade.

---

* In this volume an obol is reckoned as equivalent in buying power to 17 cents in United States currency in 1938, a drachma as $1, a talent as $6000. These equivalents are only approximate, for prices rose throughout Greek history; cf. section V of this chapter.

Trade, not industry or finance, is the soul of Athenian economy. Though many producers still sell directly to the consumer, a growing number of them require the intermediary of the market, whose function it is to buy and store goods until the consumer is ready to purchase them. In this way a class of retailers arises, who peddle their wares through the streets, or in the wake of armies, or at festivals or fairs, or offer them for sale in shops or stalls in the agora or elsewhere in the town. To the shops come freemen or metics or slaves to haggle with tradesmen and buy for the home. One of the severest disabilities suffered by the "free" women of Athens is that custom does not allow them to shop.[29]

Foreign commerce advances even faster than domestic trade, for the Greek states have learned the advantages of an international division of labor, and each specializes in some product; the shieldmaker, for example, no longer goes from city to city at the call of those who need him, but makes his shields in his shop and sends them out to the markets of the classic world. In one century Athens moves from household economy—wherein each household makes nearly all that it needs—to urban economy—wherein each town makes nearly all that it needs—to international economy—where each state is dependent upon imports, and must make exports to pay for them. The Athenian fleet for two generations keeps the Aegean clear of pirates, and from 480 to 430 commerce thrives as it never will again until Pompey suppresses piracy in 67 B.C. The docks, warehouses, markets, and banks of the Piraeus offer every facility for trade; soon the busy port becomes the chief center of distribution and reshipment for the commerce between the East and the West. "The articles which it is difficult to get, one here, one there, from the rest of the world," says Isocrates, "all these it is easy to buy in Athens."[30] "The magnitude of our city," says Thucydides, "draws the produce of the world into our harbor, so that to the Athenian the fruits of other countries are as familiar a luxury as those of his own."[31] From the Piraeus merchants carry the wine, oil, wool, minerals, marble, pottery, arms, luxuries, books, and works of art produced by the fields and shops of Attica; to the Piraeus they bring grain from the Byzantium, Syria, Egypt, Italy, and Sicily, fruit and cheese from Sicily and Phoenicia, meat from Phoenicia and Italy, fish from the Black Sea, nuts from Paphlagonia, copper from Cyprus, tin from England, iron from the Pontic coast, gold from Thasos and Thrace, timber from Thrace and Cyprus, embroideries from the Near East, wools, flax, and dyes from Phoenicia, spices from Cyrene, swords from Chalcis, glass from Egypt, tiles from Corinth, beds from Chios and Miletus, boots and bronzes from

Etruria, ivory from Ethiopia, perfumes and ointments from Arabia, slaves from Lydia, Syria, and Scythia. The colonies serve not only as markets, but as shipping agents to send Athenian goods into the interior; and though the cities of Ionia decay in the fifth century because the trade that once passed there is diverted to the Propontis and Caria during and after the Persian War, Italy and Sicily replace them as outlets for the surplus products and population of mainland Greece. We may estimate the amount of Aegean commerce from the return of 1200 talents from a 5 per cent tax laid in 413 upon the imports and exports of the cities in the Athenian Empire, indicating a trade of $144,000,000 a year.

The danger lurking in this prosperity is the growing dependence of Athens upon imported grain; hence her insistence upon controlling the Hellespont and the Black Sea, her persistent colonizing of the coasts and isles on the way to the straits, and her disastrous expeditions to Egypt in 459 and to Sicily in 415. It is this dependence that persuades Athens to transform the Confederacy of Delos into an empire; and when, in 405, the Spartans destroy the Athenian fleet in the Hellespont, the starvation and surrender of Athens are inevitable results. Nevertheless it is this trade that makes Athens rich, and provides, with the imperial tribute, the sinews of her cultural development. The merchants who accompany their goods to all quarters of the Mediterranean come back with changed perspective, and alert and open minds; they bring new ideas and ways, break down ancient taboos and sloth, and replace the familial conservatism of a rural aristocracy with the individualistic and progressive spirit of a mercantile civilization. Here in Athens East and West meet, and jar each other from their ruts. Old myths lose their grasp on the souls of men, leisure rises, inquiry is supported, science and philosophy grow. Athens becomes the most intensely alive city of her time.

IV. FREEMEN AND SLAVES

Who does all this work? In the countryside it is done by citizens, their families, and free hired men; in Athens it is done partly by citizens, partly by freedmen, more by metics, mostly by slaves. The shopkeepers, artisans, merchants, and bankers come almost entirely from the voteless classes. The burgher looks down upon manual labor, and does as little of it as he may. To work for a livelihood is considered ignoble; even the professional practice or teaching of music, sculpture, or painting is accounted by many

Greeks "a mean occupation."* Hear blunt Xenophon, who speaks, however, as a proud member of the knightly class:

> The base mechanic arts, so called . . . are held in ill repute by civilized communities, and not unreasonably; seeing they are the ruin of the bodies of all concerned in them, workers and overseers alike, who are forced to remain in sitting postures or to hug the gloom, or else to crouch whole days confronting a furnace. Hand in hand with physical enervation follows apace an enfeebling of soul, while the demand which these base mechanic arts make on the time of those employed in them leaves them no leisure to devote to the claims of friendship and the state.[32]

Trade is similarly scorned; to the aristocratic or philosophical Greek it is merely money-making at the expense of others; it aims not to create goods but to buy them cheap and sell them dear; no respectable citizen will engage in it, though he may quietly invest in it and profit from it so long as he lets others do the work. A freeman, says the Greek, must be free from economic tasks; he must get slaves or others to attend to his material concerns, even, if he can, to take care of his property and his fortune; only by such liberation can he find time for government, war, literature, and philosophy. Without a leisure class there can be, in the Greek view, no standards of taste, no encouragement of the arts, no civilization. No man who is in a hurry is quite civilized.

Most of the functions associated in history with the middle class are in Athens performed by metics—freemen of foreign birth who, though ineligible to citizenship, have fixed their domicile in Athens. For the most part they are professional men, merchants, contractors, manufacturers, managers, tradesmen, craftsmen, artists, who, in the course of their wandering, have found in Athens the economic liberty, opportunity, and stimulus which to them is far more vital than the vote. The most important industrial undertakings, outside of mining, are owned by metics; the ceramic industry is theirs completely; and wherever middlemen can squeeze themselves in between producer and consumer they are to be found. The law harasses them and protects them. It taxes them like citizens, lays "liturgies" upon them, exacts military service from them, and adds a poll tax for good measure; it forbids them to own land or to marry into the family of a citizen; it excludes them from its religious organization, and

---

* Plutarch, *Pericles*. Zimmern, *The Greek Commonwealth*, 272, and Ferguson, *Greek Imperialism*, 61, feel that the Athenian disdain for manual labor has been exaggerated; but cf. Glotz, *Ancient Greece at Work*, 160.

from direct appeal to its courts. But it welcomes them into its economic life, appreciates their industry and skill, enforces their contracts, gives them religious freedom, and guards their wealth against violent revolution. Some of them flaunt their riches vulgarly, but some of them, too, work quietly in science, literature, and the arts, practice law or medicine, and create schools of rhetoric and philosophy. In the fourth century they will provide the authors and subject of the comic drama, and in the third they will set the cosmopolitan tone of Hellenistic society. They itch for citizenship, but they love Athens proudly, and contribute painfully to finance her defense against her enemies. Through them, chiefly, the fleet is maintained, the empire is supported, and the commercial supremacy of Athens is preserved.

Mingled with the metics in political disabilities and economic opportunities are the freedmen—those who once were slaves. For though it is inconvenient to liberate a slave, since usually he must be replaced by another, yet the promise of freedom is an economical stimulus to a young slave; and many Greeks, as death approaches, reward their most loyal slaves with manumission. The slave may be freed through ransoming by relatives or friends, as in the case of Plato; or the state, indemnifying his owner, may free him for service in war; or he himself may save his obols until he can buy his liberty. Like the metic, the freedman engages in industry, trade, or finance; at the lowest he may do for pay the work of a slave, at the top he may become a magnate of industry. Mylias manages Demosthenes' armor factory; Pasion and Phormio become the richest bankers in Athens. The freedman is especially valued as an executive, for no one is more severe with slaves than the man who has come up from slavery,[33] and has known only oppression all the days of his life.

Beneath these three classes—citizens, metics, and freedmen—are the 115,000 slaves of Attica.* They are recruited from unransomed prisoners of war, victims of slave raids, infants rescued from exposure, wastrels, and criminals. Few of them in Greece are Greeks. The Hellene looks upon foreigners as natural slaves, since they so readily give absolute obedience to a king, and he does not account the servitude of such men to Greeks as

* The figure is Gomme's, l.c. Possibly the number was much greater: Suidas, on the authority of a speech uncertainly attributed to Hypereides in 338, gives the number of adult male slaves alone as 150,000;[34] and according to the unreliable Athenaeus the census of Attica by Demetrius Phalereus about 317 gave 21,000 citizens, 10,000 metics and freedmen, and 400,000 slaves. Timaeus about 300 reckoned the slaves of Corinth at 460,000, and Aristotle, about 340, those of Aegina at 470,000.[35] Perhaps these high figures are due to including slaves transiently offered for sale in the slave marts of Corinth, Aegina, and Athens.

unreasonable. But he balks at the enslavement of a Greek, and seldom stoops to it. Greek traders buy slaves as they would merchandise, and offer them for sale at Chios, Delos, Corinth, Aegina, Athens, and wherever else they can find purchasers. The slave dealers at Athens are among the richest of the metics. In Delos it is not unusual for a thousand slaves to be sold in a day; Cimon, after the battle of the Eurymedon, puts 20,000 prisoners on the slave market.[36] At Athens there is a mart where slaves stand ready for naked inspection and bargaining purchase at any time. They cost from half a mina to ten minas ($50 to $1000). They may be bought for direct use, or for investment; men and women in Athens find it profitable to buy slaves and rent them to homes, factories, or mines; the return is as high as 33 per cent.[37] Even the poorest citizen has a slave or two; Aeschines, to prove his poverty, complains that his family has only seven; rich homes may have fifty.[38] The Athenian government employs a number of slaves as clerks, attendants, minor officials, or policemen; many of these receive their clothing and a daily "allowance" of half a drachma, and are permitted to live where they please.

In the countryside the slaves are few, and are chiefly women servants in the home; in northern Greece and most of the Peloponnesus serfdom makes slavery superfluous. In Corinth, Megara, and Athens slaves do most of the manual labor, and women slaves most of the domestic toil; but slaves do also a great part of the clerical, and some of the executive work, in industry, commerce, and finance. Most skilled labor is performed by freemen, freedmen or metics; and there are no learned slaves as there will be in the Hellenistic period and in Rome. The slave is seldom allowed to bring up children of his own, for it is cheaper to buy a slave than to rear one. If the slave misbehaves he is whipped; if he testifies he is tortured; when he is struck by a freeman he must not defend himself. But if he is subjected to great cruelty he may flee to a temple, and then his master must sell him. In no case may his master kill him. So long as he labors he has more security than many who in other civilizations are not called slaves; when he is ill, or old, or there is no work for him to do, his master does not throw him upon public relief, but continues to take care of him. If he is loyal he is treated like a faithful servant, almost like a member of the family. He is often allowed to go into business, provided he will pay his owner a part of his earnings. He is free from taxation and from military service. Nothing in his costume distinguishes him, in fifth-century Athens, from the freeman; indeed the "Old Oligarch" who about 425 writes a pamphlet on *The Polity of the Athenians* complains that the slave does not make way for citizens on the street, that he talks freely, and acts in every detail as if he were the equal of the citizen.[39] Athens is known for mildness to her slaves; it is a common judgment that slaves are better off in democratic Athens than poor freemen in oligarchic states.[40] Slave revolts, though feared, are rare in Attica.[41]

Nevertheless the Athenian conscience is disturbed by the existence of slavery, and the philosophers who defend it reveal almost as clearly as those who denounce it that the moral development of the nation has outrun its institutions. Plato condemns the enslavement of Greeks by Greeks, but for the rest accepts slavery on the ground that some people have underprivileged minds.[42] Aristotle looks upon the slave as an animate tool, and thinks that slavery will continue in some form until all menial work can be done by self-operating machines.[43] The average Greek, though kind to his slaves, has no notion of how a cultured society can get along without slavery; to abolish slavery, he feels, it would be necessary to abolish Athens. Others are more radical. The Cynic philosophers condemn slavery outright; their successors, the Stoics, will condemn it more politely; Euripides again and again stirs his audiences by sympathetic pictures of war-captured slaves; and the sophist Alcidamas goes about Greece preaching, unmolested, the doctrine of Rousseau almost in the words of Rousseau: "God has sent all men into the world free, and nature has made no man a slave."[44] But slavery goes on.

V. THE WAR OF THE CLASSES

The exploitation of man by man is less severe in Athens and Thebes than in Sparta or Rome, but it is adequate to the purpose. There are no castes among the freemen in Athens, and a man may by resolute ability rise to anything but citizenship; hence, in part, the fever and turbulence of Athenian life. There is no tense class distinction between employer and employee except in the mines; usually the master works beside his men, and personal acquaintance dulls the edge of exploitation. The wage of nearly all artisans, of whatever class, is a drachma for each actual day of work;[45] but unskilled workers may get as low as three obols (50 cents) a day.[46] Piecework tends to replace timework as the factory system develops; and wages begin to vary more widely. A contractor may hire slaves from their owner for a rental of one to four obols a day.[47] We may estimate the buying power of these wages by comparing Greek prices with our own. In 414 a house and estate in Attica cost twelve hundred drachmas; a *medimnus*, or 1½ bushels, of barley costs a drachma in the sixth century, two at the close of the fifth, three in the fourth, five in the time of Alexander; a sheep costs a drachma in Solon's day, ten to twenty at the end of the fifth century;[48] in Athens as elsewhere currency tends to increase faster than goods, and prices rise. At the close of the fourth century prices are five times as high as at the opening of the sixth; they double from 480 to 404, and again from 404 to 330.[49]

A single man lives comfortably on 120 drachmas ($120) a month;[50] we may judge from this the condition of the worker who earns thirty drachmas per month, and has a family. It is true that the state comes to his relief in times of great stress, and then distributes corn at a nominal price. But he observes that the goddess of liberty is no friend to the goddess of equality, and that under the free laws of Athens the strong grow stronger, the rich richer, while the poor remain poor.*[51] Individualism stimulates the able, and degrades the simple; it creates wealth magnificently, and concentrates it dangerously. In Athens, as in other states, cleverness gets all that it can, and mediocrity gets the rest. The landowner profits from the rising value of his land; the merchant does his best, despite a hundred laws, to secure corners and monopolies; the speculator reaps, through the high rate of interest on loans, the lion's share of the proceeds of industry and trade. Demagogues arise who point out to the poor the inequality of human possessions, and conceal from them the inequality of human economic ability; the poor man, face to face with wealth, becomes conscious of his poverty, broods over his unrewarded merits, and dreams of perfect states. Bitterer than the war of Greece with Persia, or of Athens with Sparta, is, in all the Greek states, the war of class with class.

In Attica it begins with the conflict between the new rich and the landed aristocracy. The ancient families still love the soil, and live for the greater part on their estates. Division of the patrimony through many generations has made the average holding small[53] (the rich Alcibiades has only seventy acres), and the squire in most cases labors personally on the soil, or in the management of his property. But though the aristocrat is not rich, he is proud; he adds his father's name to his own as a title of nobility, and he remains aloof as long as he can from the mercantile *bourgeoisie* which is capturing the wealth of Athens' growing trade. His wife, however, cries for a city home and the varied life and opportunities of the metropolis; his

* The great fortunes of Greek antiquity were of course modest in amount by modern standards. Callias, the wealthiest of the Athenians, is said to have had two hundred talents ($1,200,000); Nicias, one hundred.[52]

daughters wish to live in Athens and snare rich husbands; his sons hope to find hetairai there and to give gay parties in the style of the *nouveaux riches*. As the aristocrat cannot compete in luxury with the merchants and manufacturers, he accepts them, or their children, as sons-in-law or daughters-in-law; they are anxious to climb, and willing to pay. The upshot is a union of the rich in land with the rich in money, and the formation of an upper class of oligarchs, envied and hated by the poor, angry at the excesses and extravagance of democracy, and fearful of revolution.

It is the insolence of the new wealth that brings on the second phase of the class war—the struggle of the poorer citizens against the rich. Many of the *bourgeoisie* flaunt their wealth like Alcibiades, but few others can so charm the "mechanic multitude" by dramatic audacity and elegance of person or speech. Young men conscious of ability and frustrated with poverty translate their personal need for opportunity and place into a general gospel of revolt; and intellectuals eager for new ideas and the applause of the oppressed formulate for them the aims of their rebellion.[54] They call not for the socialization of industry and trade but for the abolition of debts and the redistribution of the land—among the citizens; for the radical movement in fifth-century Athens is confined to the poorer voters, and never dreams, at this stage, of liberating the slaves, or letting the metics in on the reallotment of the soil. The leaders talk of a golden past in which all men were equal in possessions, but they do not wish to be taken too literally when they speak of restoring that paradise. It is an aristocratic communism that they have in mind—not a nationalization of the land by the state, but an equal sharing of it by the citizens. They point out how unreal is the equality of the franchise in the face of mounting economic inequality; but they are resolved to use the political power of the poorer citizenry to persuade the Assembly to sluice into the pockets of the needy—by fines liturgies, confiscations, and public works[55]—some of the concentrated wealth of the rich.[56] And to give a lead to future rebels they adopt red as the symbolic color of their revolt.[57]

In the face of this threat the rich band themselves in secret organizations pledged to take common action against what Plato, despite his communism, will call the "monstrous beast" of the aroused and hungry mob.[58] The free workers also organize—have at least since Solon organized—themselves into clubs (*eranoi, thiasoi*) of stonemasons, marble cutters, woodworkers, ivory-workers, potters, fishermen, actors, etc.; Socrates is a member of a sculptor's *thiasos*.*[59] But these groups are not so much trade-unions as mutual benefit

* The sculptors and architects of Greece formed a guild of builders, with their own religious mysteries, and became the forerunners of the Freemasons of later Europe.[60]

societies: they come together in meeting places called synods or synagogues, have banquets and games, and worship a patron deity; they make payments to sick members, and contract collectively for specific enterprises; but they do not enter visibly into the Athenian class war. The battle is fought on the fields of literature and politics. Pamphleteers like the "Old Oligarch" issue denunciations or defenses of democracy. The comic poets, since their plays require rich men to finance their production, are on the side of the drachmas, and pour ridicule upon the radical leaders and their utopias. In the *Ecclesiazusae* (392) Aristophanes introduces us to the lady communist Praxagora, who makes an oration as follows:

> I want all to have a share of everything, and all property to be in common; there will no longer be either rich or poor; no longer shall we see one man harvesting vast tracts of land, while another has not ground enough to be buried in. . . . I intend that there shall only be one and the same condition of life for all. . . . I shall begin by making land, money, everything that is private property, common to all. . . . Women shall belong to all men in common.[61]

"But who," asks Blepyrus, "will do the work?" "The slaves," is her reply. In another comedy, the *Plutus* (408), Aristophanes allows Poverty, who is threatened with extinction, to defend herself as the necessary goad to human toil and enterprise:

> I am the sole cause of all your blessings, and your safety depends upon me alone. . . . Who would wish to hammer iron, build ships, sew, turn, cut up leather, bake bricks, bleach linen, tan hides, or break up the soil with the plow and garner the gifts of Demeter if he could live in idleness and free from all this work? . . . If your system [communism] is applied . . . you will not be able to sleep in a bed, for no more will ever be manufactured; nor on carpets, for who would weave them if he had gold?[62]

The reforms of Ephialtes and Pericles are the first achievement of the democratic revolt. Pericles is a man of judgment and moderation; he does not wish to destroy the rich but to preserve them and their enterprise by easing the condition of the poor; but after his death (429) the democracy becomes so radical that the oligarchic party conspires again with Sparta, and makes in 411, and once more in 404, a rich man's revolution. Nevertheless, because wealth is great in Athens and trickles down to many, and because fear of a slave uprising gives the citizenry pause, the class war in Athens is milder, and sooner reaches a working compromise, than in Greek states where the middle class is not strong enough to mediate between rich and poor. At Samos, in 412, the radicals seize the government, execute two hundred aristocrats, banish four hundred more, divide up the lands and houses among themselves,[63] and develop another society like that which they have overthrown. At Leontini, in 422, the commoners expel the oligarchs, but soon afterward take to flight. At Corcyra, in 427, the oligarchs assassinate sixty leaders of the popular party; the democrats seize the government, imprison four hundred aristocrats, try fifty of them before a kind of Committee of Public Safety, and execute all fifty at once; seeing which a considerable number of the surviving prisoners slay one another, others kill themselves, and the rest are walled up in the temple in which they have sought sanctuary, and are starved to death. Thucydides describes the class war in Greece in a timeless passage:

> During seven days the Corcyraeans were engaged in butchering those of their fellow-citizens whom they regarded as their enemies; and although the crime imputed was that of attempting to put down the democracy, some were slain also for private hatred, others by their debtors because of the monies owed to them. Death thus raged in every shape, and as usually happens at such times, there was no length to which violence did not go; sons were killed by their fathers, and suppliants were dragged from the altar or slain upon it. . . . Revolution thus ran its course from city to city, and the places where it arrived last, from having heard what had been done before, carried to a still greater excess the refinement of their inventions . . . and the atrocity of their reprisals. . . . Corcyra gave the first example of these crimes . . . of the revenge exacted by the governed —who had never experienced equitable treatment, or, indeed, aught but violence from their rulers—when their hour came; of the iniquitous resolves of those who desired to get rid of their accustomed poverty, and ardently coveted their neighbors' goods; and the savage and pitiless excesses into which men who had begun the struggle not in a class but in a party spirit, were hurried by their passions. . . . In the confusion into which life was now thrown in the cities, human nature, always rebelling against the law and now its master, gladly showed itself ungoverned in passion, above respect for justice, and the enemy of all superiority. . . . Reckless audacity came now to be considered the courage of a loyal ally; prudent hesitation, specious cowardice; moderation was held to be a cloak for unmanliness; ability to see all sides of a question was accounted inability to act on any. . . .
>
> The cause of all these evils was the lust for power arising from greed and ambition. . . . The leaders in the cities, each provided

> with the fairest professions, on the one side with the cry of the political equality of the people, on the other of a moderate aristocracy, sought prizes for themselves in those public interests which they pretended to cherish; and, recoiling from no means in their struggle for ascendancy, engaged in the direst excesses. . . . Religion was in honor with neither party, but the use of fair phrases to arrive at guilty ends was in high reputation. . . . The ancient simplicity into which honor so largely entered was laughed down, and disappeared; and society became divided into camps in which no man trusted his fellow. . . . Meanwhile the moderate part of the citizens perished between the two, either for not joining in the quarrel, or because envy would not suffer them to escape. . . . The whole Hellenic world was convulsed.[64]

Athens survives this turbulence because every Athenian is at heart an individualist, and loves private property; and because the Athenian government finds a practicable medium between socialism and individualism in a moderate regulation of business and wealth. The state is not afraid to regulate: it sets a limit upon the size of dowries, the cost of funerals, and the dress of women;[65] it taxes and supervises trade, enforces fair weights and measures and honest quality so far as the ingenuity of human rascality permits;[66] it limits the export of food, and enacts sharp laws to govern and chasten the practices of merchants and tradesmen. It watches the grain trade carefully, and legislates severely against corners—even to the death penalty—by forbidding the purchase of more than seventy-five bushels of wheat at a time; it interdicts loans on outgoing cargoes unless the return shipment is to bring grain to the Piraeus; it requires that all corn loaded by vessels owned in Athens shall be brought to the Piraeus; and it prohibits the export of more than a third of any corn cargo that reaches that port.[67] By keeping a reserve of grain in state-owned storehouses, and pouring this upon the market when prices rise too rapidly, Athens sees to it that the price of bread shall never be exorbitant, that millionaires shall not be created out of the hunger of the people, and that no Athenian shall starve.[68] The state regulates wealth through taxation and liturgies, and persuades or compels rich men to supply funds for the fleet, the drama, and the theoric payments that enable the poor to attend the plays and the games. For the rest Athens protects freedom of trade, private property, and the opportunity to profit, deeming them the necessary implements of human liberty, and the most powerful stimuli to industry, commerce, and prosperity.

Under this system of economic individualism tempered with socialistic regulation, wealth accumulates in Athens, and spreads sufficiently to prevent a radical revolution; to the end of ancient Athens private property remains secure. The number of citizens with a comfortable income doubles between 480 and 431;[69] the public revenue grows, public expenditures rise, and yet the treasury is full beyond any precedent in Greek history. The economic basis of Athenian freedom, enterprise, art, and thought is firmly laid, and will bear without strain every extravagance of the Golden Age except the war by which all Greece will be ruined.

CHAPTER XIII

The Morals and Manners of the Athenians

I. CHILDHOOD

EVERY Athenian citizen is expected to have children, and all the forces of religion, property, and the state unite to discountenance childlessness. Where no offspring comes, adoption is the rule, and high prices are paid for prepossessing orphans. At the same time law and public opinion accept infanticide as a legitimate safeguard against excess population and a pauperizing fragmentation of the land; any father may expose a newborn child to death either as doubtfully his, or as weak or deformed. The children of slaves are seldom allowed to live. Girls are more subject to exposure than boys, for every daughter has to be provided with a dowry, and at marriage she passes from the home and service of those who have reared her into the service of those who have not. Exposure is effected by leaving the infant in a large earthenware vessel within the precincts of a temple or in some other place where it can soon be rescued if any wish to adopt it. The parental right to expose permits a rough eugenics, and co-operates with a rigorous natural selection by hardship and competition to make the Greeks a strong and healthy people. The philosophers almost unanimously approve of family limitation: Plato will call for the exposure of all feeble children, and of those born of base or elderly parents;[1] and Aristotle will defend abortion as preferable to infanticide.[2] The Hippocratic code of medical ethics will not allow the physician to effect abortion, but the Greek midwife is an experienced hand in this field, and no law impedes her.*[3]

On or before the tenth day after birth the child is formally accepted into the family with a religious ritual around the hearth, and receives presents and a name. Usually a Greek has but one name, like Socrates or Archimedes; but since it is customary to call the eldest son after the paternal grandfather, repetition is frequent, and Greek history is confounded with a multiplicity of Xenophons, Aeschineses, Thucydideses, Diogeneses, and Zenos. To avoid ambiguity the father's name or the place of birth may be added, as with *Kimon Miltiadou*

* We have no evidence of contraceptive devices among the Greeks.[4]

—Cimon son of Miltiades—or *Diodorus Siculus*—Diodorus of Sicily; or the problem may be solved by some jolly nickname, like *Callimedon*—The Crab.[5]

Once the child is so accepted into the family it cannot lawfully be exposed, and is reared with all the affection that parents lavish upon their children in every age. Themistocles describes his son as the real ruler of Athens; for he, Themistocles, the most influential man in the city, is ruled by his wife, who is ruled by their child.[6] Many an epigram in *The Greek Anthology* reveals a tender parental love:

> I wept at the death of my Theonoe, but the hopes centered in our child lightened my sorrows. And now envious Fate has bereaved me of the boy as well. Alas! I am cheated of thee, my child, all that was left to me. Persephone, hear this cry of a father's grief, and lay the child upon his dead mother's breast.[7]

The tragedies of adolescence are eased with many games, some of which will survive the memory of Greece. On a white perfume vase made for a child's grave a little boy is seen taking his toy cart with him down to Hades.[8] Babies have terra-cotta rattles containing pebbles; girls keep house with their dolls, boys fight great campaigns with clay soldiers and generals, nurses push children on swings or balance them on seesaws, boys and girls roll hoops, fly kites, spin tops, play hide-and-seek or blindman's buff or tug of war, and wage a hundred merry contests with pebbles, nuts, coins, and balls. The marbles of the Golden Age are dried beans shot from the fingers, or smooth stones shot or tossed into a circle to dislodge enemy stones and come to rest as near as possible to the center. As children approach the "age of reason"—seven or eight—they take up the game of dice by throwing square knucklebones (*astragali*), the highest throw, six, being counted the best.[9] The games of the young are as old as the sins of their fathers.

II. EDUCATION

Athens provides public gymnasiums and palaestras, and exercises some loose supervision over teachers; but the city has no public schools or state universities, and education remains in private hands. Plato advocates state schools,[10] but Athens seems to believe that even in education competition will produce the best results. Professional schoolmasters set up their own schools, to which freeborn boys are sent at the age of six. The name *paidagogos* is given not to the teacher but to the slave who conducts the boy daily to and from school; we hear of no boarding schools. Attendance at school continues till fourteen or sixteen, or till a later age among the well to do.[11] The schools have no desks but only benches; the pupil holds on his knee the roll from which he reads or the material upon which he writes. Some schools, anticipating much later fashions, are adorned with statues of Greek heroes and gods; a few are elegantly furnished. The teacher teaches all subjects, and attends to character as well as intellect, using a sandal.*[12]

The curriculum has three divisions—writing, music, and gymnastics; eager modernists will add, in Aristotle's day, drawing and painting.[14] Writing includes reading and arithmetic, which uses letters for numbers. Everyone learns to play the lyre, and much of the material of instruction is put into poetical and musical form.[15] No time is spent in acquiring any foreign language, much less a dead one, but great care is taken in learning the correct usage of the mother tongue. Gymnastics are taught chiefly in the gymnasium and the palaestra, and no one is considered educated who has not learned to wrestle, swim, and use the bow and the sling.

The education of girls is carried on at home, and is largely confined to "domestic science." Outside of Sparta girls take no part in public gymnastics. They are taught by their mothers or nurses to read and write and reckon, to spin and weave and embroider, to dance and sing and play some instrument. A few Greek women are well educated, but these are mostly hetairai; for respectable ladies there is no secondary education, until Aspasia lures a few of them into rhetoric and philosophy. Higher education for men is provided by professional rhetors and sophists, who offer instruction in oratory, science, philosophy, and history. These independent teachers engage lecture halls near the gymnasium or palaestra, and constitute together a scattered university for pre-Platonic Athens. Only the prosperous can study under them, for they charge high fees; but ambitious youths work by night in mill or field in order to be able to attend by day the classes of these nomadic professors.

When boys reach the age of sixteen they are expected to pay special attention to physical exercises, as fitting them in some measure for the tasks of war. Even their sports give them indirectly a military preparation: they run, leap, wrestle, hunt, drive chariots, and hurl the javelin. At eighteen they enter upon the second of the four stages of Athenian life (*pais*, *ephebos*, *aner*, *geron*—child, youth, man, elder), and are enrolled into the ranks of Athens' soldier youth, the epheboi.† Under moderators chosen by the leaders of their tribes they are trained for two years in the duties of citizenship and war. They live and eat together, wear an impressive uniform, and submit to moral supervision night and day. They organize themselves democratically on the model of the city, meet in assembly, pass resolutions, and erect laws for their own governance;

* In one of the pictures at Pompeii, probably copied from the Greek, we see a pupil supported upon the shoulders of another, and held at his heels by a third, while the teacher flogs him.[13]

† This institution, however, cannot yet be traced back beyond 336 B.C.

they have archons, *strategoi*, and judges.[16] For the first year they are schooled with strenuous drill, and hear lectures on literature, music, geometry, and rhetoric.[17] At nineteen they are assigned to garrison the frontier, and are entrusted for two years with the protection of the city against attack from without and disorder within. Solemnly, in the presence of the Council of Five Hundred, with hands stretched over the altar in the temple of Agraulos, they take the oath of the young men of Athens:

> I will not disgrace the sacred arms, nor will I abandon the man next to me, whoever he may be. I will bring aid to the ritual of the state, and to the holy duties, both alone and in company with many. I will transmit my native commonwealth not lessened, but larger and better than I have received it. I will obey those who from time to time are judges; I will obey the established statutes, and whatever other regulations the people shall enact. If anyone shall attempt to destroy the statutes I will not permit it, but will repel him both alone and with all. I will honor the ancestral faith.[18]

The epheboi are assigned a special place at the theater, and play a prominent role in the religious processions of the city; perhaps it is such young men that we see riding so handsomely on the Parthenon frieze. Periodically they exhibit their accomplishments in public contests, above all in the relay torch race from the Piraeus to Athens. All the city comes out for this picturesque event, and lines the four-and-a-half-mile road; the race is run at night, and the way is not illuminated; all that can be seen of the runners is the leaping light of the torches that they carry forward and pass on. When, at the age of twenty-one, the training of the epheboi is completed, they are freed from parental authority, and formally admitted into the full citizenship of the city.

Such is the education—eked out by lessons learned in the home and in the street—that produces the Athenian citizen. It is an excellent combination of physical and mental, moral and esthetic, training, of supervision in youth with freedom in maturity; and in its heyday it turns out young men as fine as any in history. After Pericles theory grows and beclouds practice; philosophers debate the goals and methods of education—whether the teacher should aim chiefly at intellectual development or at moral character, chiefly at practical ability or the promotion of abstract science. But all agree in attaching the highest importance to education. When Aristippus is asked in what way the educated are superior to the untutored he answers, "as broken horses are to the unbroken"; and Aristotle to the same question replies, "as the living are to the dead." At least, adds Aristippus, "If the pupil derives no other good, he will not, when he attends the theater, be one stone upon another."[19]

III. EXTERNALS

The citizens of Athens, in the fifth century, are men of medium height, vigorous, bearded, and not all as handsome as Pheidias' horsemen. The ladies of the vases are graceful, and those of the stelae have a dignified loveliness, and those molded by the sculptors are supremely beautiful; but the actual ladies of Athens, limited in their mental development by an almost Oriental seclusion, are at best as pretty as their Near Eastern sisters, but no more. The Greeks admire beauty even beyond other nations, but they do not always embody it. Greek women, like others, find their figures a little short of perfection. They lengthen them with high cork soles on their shoes, pad out deficiencies with wadding, compress abundances with lacing, and support the breasts with a cloth brassiere.*[20]

The hair of the Greeks is usually dark; blondes are exceptional, and much admired; many women, and some men, dye their hair to make it blonde, or to conceal the grayness of age.[22] Both sexes use oils to help the growth of the hair and to protect it against the sun; the women, and again some men, add perfumes to the oil.[23] Both sexes, in the sixth century, wear the hair long, usually bound in braids around or behind the head. In the fifth century the women vary their coiffure by knotting the hair low on the nape of the neck, or letting it fall over the shoulders, or around the neck and upon the breast. The ladies like to bind their hair with gay ribbons, and to adorn these with a jewel on the forehead.[24] After Marathon the men begin to cut their hair; after Alexander they will shave their mustaches and beards with sickle-shaped razors of iron. No Greek ever wears a mustache without a beard. The beard is neatly trimmed, usually to a point. The barber not only cuts the hair and shaves or trims the beard, but he manicures his customer and otherwise polishes him up for presentation; when he has finished he offers him a mirror in the most modern style.[25] The barber has his shop, which is a center for the "wineless symposia" (as Theophrastus calls them) of the local gossips and gadflies; but he often works outside it under the sky. He is garrulous by profession; and when one of his kind asks King Archelaus of Macedon how he would like to have his hair cut the king answers, "In silence."[26] The women also shave here and there, using razors or depilatories of arsenic and lime.

Perfumes—made from flowers, with a base of oil—are numbered in the

* Plutarch tells a pretty story of how an epidemic of suicide among the women of Miletus was suddenly and completely ended by an ordinance decreeing that self-slain women should be carried naked through the marketplace to their burial.[21]

hundreds; Socrates complains that men make so much use of them.[27] Every lady of class has an armory of mirrors, pins, hairpins, safety pins, tweezers, combs, scent bottles, and pots for rouge and creams. Cheeks and lips are painted with sticks of minium or alkanet root; eyebrows are penciled with lampblack or pulverized antimony; eyelids are shaded with antimony or kohl; eyelashes are darkened, and then set with a mixture of egg white and gum ammoniac. Creams and washes are used for removing wrinkles, freckles, and spots; disagreeable applications are kept on the face for hours in the patient lust to seem, if one cannot be, beautiful. Oil of mastic is employed to prevent perspiration, and specific perfumed unguents are applied to various parts of the body; a proper lady uses palm oil on the face and breast, marjoram on the eyebrows and hair, essence of thyme on the throat and knees, mint on the arms, myrrh on the legs and feet.[28] Against this seductive armament men protest to as much effect as in other ages. A character in Athenian comedy reproves a lady in cosmetic detail: "If you go out in summer, two streaks of black run from your eyes; perspiration makes a red furrow from your cheeks to your neck; and when your hair touches your face it is blanched by the white lead."[29] Women remain the same, because men do.

Water is limited, and cleanliness seeks substitutes. The well to do bathe once or twice daily, using a soap made of olive oil mixed with an alkali into a paste; then they are anointed with fragrant essences. Comfortable homes have a paved bathroom in which stands a large marble basin, usually filled by hand; sometimes water is brought by pipes and channels into the house and through the wall of the bathroom, where it spouts from a metal nozzle in the shape of an animal's head, and falls upon the floor of a small shower-bath enclosure, whence it runs out into the garden.[30] Most people, unable to spare water for a bath, rub themselves with oil, and then scrape it off with a crescent-shaped strigil, as in Lysippus' *Apoxyomenos*. The Greek is not fastidiously clean; his hygiene is not so much a matter of indoor toilette as of abstemious diet and an active outdoor life. He seldom sits in closed homes, theaters, churches, or halls, rarely works in closed factories or shops; his drama, his worship, even his government, proceed under the sun; and his simple clothing, which lets the air reach every part of his body, can be thrown aside with one swing of the arm for a bout of wrestling or a bath of sunshine.

Greek dress consists essentially of two squares of cloth, loosely draped about the body, and seldom tailored to fit the individual; it varies in minor detail from city to city, but remains constant for generations. The chief garment at Athens is for men the chiton, or tunic, for women the peplos, or robe, both made of wool. If the weather requires it these may be covered with a mantle (himation) or cloak (chlamys), suspended like them from the shoulders, and falling freely in those natural folds that so please us in Greek statuary. In the fifth century clothing is usually white; women, rich men, and gay youths, however, go in for color, even for purple and dark red, and colored stripes and embroidered hems; and the women may bind a colored girdle about the waist. Hats are unpopular on the ground that they keep moisture from the hair and so make it prematurely gray;[31] the head is covered only in traveling, in battle, and at work under the hot sun; women may wear colored kerchiefs or bandeaux; workers sometimes wear a cap and nothing else.[32] Shoes are sandals, high shoes, or boots; usually of leather, black for men, colored for women. The ladies of Thebes, says Dicaearchus, "wear low purple shoes laced so as to show the bare feet."[33] Most children and workingmen dispense with shoes altogether; and no one bothers with stockings.[34]

Both sexes announce or disguise their incomes with jewelry. Men wear at least one ring; Aristotle wears several.[35] The walking sticks of the men may have knobs of silver or gold. Women wear bracelets, necklaces, diadems, earrings, brooches and chains, jeweled clasps and buckles, and sometimes jeweled bands about the ankles or the upper arms. Here, as in most mercantile cultures, luxury runs into excess among those to whom wealth is a novelty. Sparta regulates the headdress of its ladies, and Athens forbids women to take more than three dresses on a journey.[36] Women smile at these restrictions, and, without lawyers, get around them; they know that to most men and to some women dress makes the woman; and their behavior in this matter reveals a wisdom gathered through a thousand centuries.

IV. MORALS

The Athenians of the fifth century are not exemplars of morality; the progress of the intellect has loosened many of them from their ethical traditions, and has turned them into almost unmoral individuals. They have a high reputation for legal justice, but they are seldom altruistic to any but their children; conscience rarely troubles them, and they never dream of loving their neighbors as themselves. Manners vary from class to class; in the dialogues of Plato life is graced with a charming courtesy, but in the comedies of Aristophanes there are no manners at all, and in public oratory personal abuse is relied upon as the very soul of eloquence; in such matters the Greeks have much to learn from the time-polished "barbarians" of Egypt or Persia or Babylon. Salutation is cordial but simple; there is no bowing, for that seems to the proud citizens a vestige of monarchy; hand-shaking is reserved for oaths or solemn farewells; usually the greeting is merely *Chaire*—"Rejoice"—followed, as elsewhere, by some brilliant remark about the weather.[37]

Hospitality has lessened since Homeric days, for travel is a little more secure than then, and inns provide food and shelter for transients; even so it remains an outstanding virtue of the Athenians. Strangers are welcomed though without introduction; if they come with letters from a common friend, they receive bed and board, and sometimes parting gifts. An invited guest is always privileged to bring an uninvited guest with him. This freedom of entry gives rise in time to a class of parasites—*parasitoi*—a word originally applied to the clergy who ate the "corn left over" from the temple supplies. The well to do are generous givers in both public and private philanthropy; the practice as well as the word is Greek. Charity—*charitas,* or love—is also present; there are many institutions for the care of strangers, the sick, the poor, and the old.[38] The government provides pensions for wounded soldiers, and brings up war orphans at the expense of the state; in the fourth century it will make payments to disabled workmen.[39] In periods of drought, war, or other crisis, the state pays two obols (34 cents) a day to the needy, in addition to the regular fees for attendance at the Assembly, the courts, and the plays. There are the normal scandals; a speech of Lysias concerns a man who, though on public relief, has rich men for his friends, earns money by his handicraft, and rides horses for recreation.[40]

The Greek might admit that honesty is the best policy, but he tries everything else first. The chorus in Sophocles' *Philoctetes* expresses the tenderest sympathy for the wounded and deserted soldier, and then takes advantage of his slumber to counsel Neoptolemus to betray him, steal his weapons, and leave him to his fate. Everyone complains that the Athenian retailers adulterate their goods, give short weight and short change despite the government inspectors, shift the fulcrum of their scales towards the measuring weights,[40a] and lie at every opportunity; the sausages, for example, are accused of being dogs.[41] A comic dramatist calls the fishmongers "assassins"; a gentler poet calls them "burglars."[42] The politicians are not much better; there is hardly a man in Athenian public life that is not charged with crookedness;[43] an honest man like Aristides is considered exciting news, almost a monstrosity; even Diogenes' daytime lantern does not find another. Thucydides reports that men are more anxious to be called clever than honest, and suspect honesty of simplicity.[44] It is an easy matter to find Greeks who will betray their country: "At no time," says Pausanias, "was Greece wanting in people afflicted with this itch for treason."[45] Bribery is a popular way to political advancement, criminal impunity, diplomatic accomplishments; Pericles has large sums voted to him for secret uses, presumably for lubricating international negotiations. Morality is strictly tribal; Xenophon, in a treatise on education, frankly advises lying and robbery in dealing with the enemies of one's country.[46] The Athenian envoys at Sparta in 432 defend their empire in plain terms: "It has always been the law that the weaker should be subject to the stronger . . . no one has ever allowed the cry for justice to hinder his ambition when he had a chance of gaining anything by might"[47]—though this passage, and the supposed speech of the Athenian leaders at Melos,[48] may be exercises of Thucydides' philosophical imagination, inflamed by the cynical discourses of certain Sophists; it would be as fair to judge the Greeks from the unconventional ethics of Gorgias, Callicles, Thrasymachus, and Thucydides as it would be to describe the modern European by the brilliant *bizarreries* of Machiavelli, La Rochefoucauld, Nietzsche, and Stirner—not saying how fair that would be. That something of this superiority to morals is an active ingredient in the Greek character appears in the readiness with which the Spartans agree with the Athenians on these mooted points of morals. When the Lacedaemonian Phoebidas, despite a treaty of peace, treacherously seizes upon the citadel of Thebes, and the Spartan King Agesilaus is questioned about the justice of this action, he replies: "Inquire only if it is useful; for whenever an action is useful to our country it is right." Time and again truces are violated, solemn promises are broken, envoys are slain.[49] Perhaps, however, the Greeks differ from ourselves not in conduct but in candor; our greater delicacy makes it offensive to us to preach what we practice.

Custom and religion among the Greeks exercise a very modest restraint upon the victor in war. It is a regular matter, even in civil wars, to sack the conquered city, to finish off the wounded, to slaughter or enslave all unransomed prisoners and all captured noncombatants, to burn down the houses, the fruit trees, and the crops, to exterminate the live stock, and to destroy the seed for future sowings.[50] At the opening of the Peloponnesian War the Spartans butcher as enemies all Greeks whom they find on the sea, whether allies of Athens or neutrals;[51] at the battle of Aegospotami, which closes the war, the Spartans put to death three thousand Athenian prisoners[52]—almost the selected best of Athens' depleted citizenry. War of some kind—of city against city or of class against class—is a normal condition in Hellas. In this way the Greece that defeated the King of Kings turns upon itself, Greek meets Greek in a thousand battles, and in the course of a century after Marathon the most brilliant civilization in history consumes itself in a prolonged national suicide.

V. CHARACTER

If we are still attracted to these reckless disputants it is because they cover the nakedness of their sins with an exhilarating vigor of enterprise and intellect. The nearness of the sea, the opportunities of trade, the freedom of economic and political life form the Athenian to an unprecedented excitability and resilience of temper and thought, a very fever of mind and sense. What a change from the Orient to Europe, from the drowsy southern regions to these intermediate states where winter is cold enough to invigorate without dulling, and summer warm enough to liberate without enfeebling body and soul! Here is faith in life and man, a zest of living never rivaled again until the Renaissance.

Out of this stimulating milieu comes courage, and an impulsiveness all the world away from the *sophrosyne*—self-control—which the philosophers vainly preach, or the Olympian serenity which young Winckelmann and old Goethe will foist upon the passionate and restless Greeks. A nation's ideals are usually a disguise, and are not to be taken as history. Courage and temperance—*andreia*, or manliness, and the *meden agan*, or "nothing in excess" of the Delphic inscription—are the rival mottoes of the Greek; he realizes the one frequently enough, but the other only in his peasants, philosophers, and saints. The average Athenian is a sensualist, but with a good conscience; he sees no sin in the pleasures of sense, and finds in them the readiest answer to the pessimism that darkens his meditative intervals. He loves wine, and is not ashamed to get drunk now and then; he loves women, in an almost innocently physical way, easily forgives himself for promiscuity, and does not look upon a lapse from virtue as an irremediable disaster. Nevertheless he dilutes two parts of wine with three of water, and considers repeated drunkenness an offense against good taste. Though he seldom practices moderation he sincerely worships it, and formulates more clearly than any other people in history the ideal of self-mastery.

The Athenians are too brilliant to be good, and scorn stupidity more than they abominate vice. They are not all sages, and we must not picture their woman as all lovely Nausicaas or stately Helens, or their men as combining the courage of Ajax with Nestor's wisdom; history has remembered the geniuses of Greece and has ignored her fools (except Nicias); even our age may seem great when most of us are forgotten, and only our mountain peaks have escaped the obscurity of time. Discounting the pathos of distance, the average Athenian remains as subtle as an Oriental, as enamored of novelty as an American; endlessly curious and perpetually mobile; always preaching a Parmenidean calm and always tossed upon a Heracleitean sea. No people ever had a livelier fancy, or a readier tongue. Clear thought and clear expression seem divine things to the Athenian; he has no patience with learned obfuscation, and looks upon informed and intelligent conversation as the highest sport of civilization. The secret of the exuberance of Greek life and thought lies in this, that to the Greek, man is the measure of all things. The educated Athenian is in love with reason, and seldom doubts its ability to chart the universe. The desire to know and understand is his noblest passion, and as immoderate as the rest. Later he will discover the limits of reason and human effort, and by a natural reaction will fall into a pessimism strangely discordant with the characteristic buoyancy of his spirit. Even in the century of his exuberance the thought of his profoundest men—who are not his philosophers but his dramatists—will be clouded over with the elusive brevity of delight and the patient pertinacity of death.

As inquisitiveness generates the science of Greece, so acquisitiveness establishes and dominates its economy. "Love of wealth wholly absorbs men," says Plato, with the exaggeration usual in moralists, "and never for a moment allows them to think of anything but their own private possessions; on this the soul of every citizen hangs suspended."[53] The Athenians are competitive animals, and stimulate one another with nearly ruthless rivalry. They are shrewd, and give the Semites a close run in cunning and stratagem; they are every bit as stiff-necked as the Biblical Hebrews, as pugnacious, obstinate, and proud. They bargain virulently in buying and selling, argue every point in conversation, and, when they cannot make war upon other countries, quarrel among themselves. They are not given to sentiment, and disapprove of Euripides' tears. They are kind to animals and cruel to men: they regularly use torture upon unaccused slaves, and sleep heartily, to all appearances, after slaughtering a cityful of noncombatants. Nevertheless they are generous to the poor or the disabled; and when the Assembly learns that the granddaughter of Aristogeiton the tyrannicide is living in destitution on Lemnos, it provides funds to bring her to Athens and to give her a dowry and a husband. The oppressed and hunted of other cities find a sympathetic refuge in Athens.

In truth the Greek does not think of character in our terms. He aspires neither to the conscience of the good bourgeois, nor to the sense of honor of the aristocrat. To the Greek the best life is the fullest one, rich in health, strength, beauty, passion, means, adventure, and thought. Virtue is *arete*, manly—literally and originally, martial—excellence (Ares, Mars); precisely what the Romans called *vir-tus*, man-liness. The Athenian ideal man is the *kalokagathos*, who combines beauty and justice in a gracious art of living that frankly values ability, fame, wealth, and friends as well as virtue and humanity; as with Goethe, self-development is everything. Along with this conception goes a degree of vanity whose candor is hardly to our taste: the Greeks never tire of admiring themselves, and announce at every turn their superiority to other warriors, writers, artists, peoples. If we wish to understand the Greeks as against the Romans we must think of the French vs. the English; if we wish to feel the Spartan spirit as opposed to the Athenian we must think of the Germans vs. the French.

All the qualities of the Athenians come together to make their city-state. Here is the creation and summation of their vigor and courage, their brilliance and loquacity, their unruliness and acquisitiveness, their vanity and patriotism, their worship of beauty and freedom. They are rich in passions but poor in prejudices. Now and then they tolerate religious intolerance, not as a check upon thought but as a weapon in partisan politics, and as a bound to moral experimentation; otherwise they insist upon a degree of liberty that seems fantastically chaotic to their Oriental visitors. But because they are free, because, ultimately, every office is open to every citizen, and each is ruled and ruler in turn, they give half their lives to their state. Home is where they sleep; they *live* in the market place, in the Assembly, in the Council, in the courts, in the great festivals, athletic contests, and dramatic spectacles that glorify their city and its gods. They recognize the right of the state to conscript their persons and their wealth for its needs. They forgive its exactions because it gives more opportunity for human development than man has ever known before; they fight for it fiercely because it is the mother and guardian of their liberties. "Thus," says Herodotus, "did the Athenians increase in strength. And it is plain enough, not from this instance only but from many examples, that freedom is an excellent thing; since even the Athenians, who, while they continued under the rule of dictators, were not a whit more valiant than any of their neighbors, no sooner shook off the yoke than they became decidedly the first of all."[54]

VI. PREMARITAL RELATIONS

In morality, as in alphabet, measures, weights, coinage, costume, music, astronomy, and mystic cults, classic Athens seems more Oriental than European. The physical basis of love is accepted frankly by both sexes; the love philters that anxious ladies brew for negligent men have no merely Platonic aim. Premarital chastity is required of respectable women, but among unmarried men after the ephebic period there are few moral restraints upon desire. The great festivals, though religious in origin, are used as safety valves for the natural promiscuity of humanity; sexual license on such occasions is condoned in the belief that monogamy may be more easily achieved during the balance of the year. No stigma is attached in Athens to the occasional intercourse of young men with courtesans; even married men may patronize them without any greater moral penalty than a scolding at home and a slightly tarnished reputation in the city.[58] Athens officially recognizes prostitution, and levies a tax upon its practitioners.[59]

With a career so open to talent, harlotry becomes in Athens, as in most other cities of Greece, a well-plied profession with many specialties. The lowest order of them, the *pornai*, live chiefly at the Piraeus, in common brothels marked for the convenience of the public with the phallic symbol of Priapus. An obol secures admission to these houses, where the girls, so lightly clad that they are called *gymnai* (naked), allow their prospective purchasers to examine them like dogs in a kennel. A man may strike a bargain for any period of time, and may arrange with the madam of the house to take a girl to live with him for a week, a month, or a year; sometimes a girl is hired out in this way to two or more men, distributing her time among them according to their means.[61] Higher than these girls in the affection of the Athenians are the auletrides, or flute-players, who, like the geisha of Japan, assist at "stag" entertainments, provide music and gaiety, perform dances artistic or lascivious, and then, if properly induced, mingle with the guests and spend the night with them.[62] A few old courtesans may stave off destitution by developing training schools for such flute girls, and teaching them the science of cosmetic adornment, personal transfiguration, musical entertainment, and amorous dalliance. Tradition hands down carefully from one generation of courtesans to another, like a precious heritage, the arts of inspiring love by judicious display, holding it by coy refusal, and making it pay.[63] Nevertheless some of the auletrides, if we may take Lucian's word for it from a later age, have tender hearts, know real affection, and ruin themselves, Camille-like, for their lovers' sakes. The honest courtesan is an ancient theme hoary with the dignity of age.

The highest class of Greek courtesans is composed of the hetairai—literally, companions. Unlike the *pornai*, who are mostly of Oriental birth, the hetairai are usually women of the citizen class, who have fallen from the respectability or fled from the seclusion required of Athenian maids and matrons. They live independently, and entertain at their own homes the lovers whom they lure. Though they are mostly brunettes by nature, they dye their hair yellow in the belief that Athenians prefer blondes; and they distinguish themselves, apparently under legal compulsion, by wearing flowery robes.[64] By occasional reading, or attending lectures, some of them acquire a modest education, and amuse their cultured patrons with learned conversation. Thais, Diotima, Thargelia, and Leontium, as well as Aspasia, are celebrated as philosophical disputants, and sometimes for their polished literary style.[65] Many of them are renowned for their wit, and Athenian literature has an anthology of hetairai epigrams.[66] Though all courtesans are denied civil rights, and are forbidden to enter any temple but that of their own goddess, Aphrodite Pandemos, a select minority of the hetairai enjoy a high standing in male society at Athens; no man is ashamed to be seen with these; philosophers contend for their favors; and an historian chronicles their history as piously as Plutarch.[67]

In such ways a number of them achieve a certain scholastic immortality. There is Clepsydra, so named because she accepts and dismisses her lovers by the hourglass; Thargelia, who, as the Mata Hari of her time, serves the Persians as a spy by sleeping with as many as possible of the statesmen of Athens;[68] Theoris, who consoles the old age of Sophocles, and Archippe, who succeeds her about the ninth decade of the dramatist's life;[69] Archeanassa, who amuses Plato,[70] and Danae and Leontium, who teach Epicurus the philosophy of pleasure; Themistonoe, who practices her art until she has lost her last tooth and her last lock of hair; and the businesslike Gnathaena, who, having spent much time in the training of her daughter, demands a thousand drachmas ($1000) as the price of the young lady's company for a night.[71] The beauty of Phryne is the talk of fourth-century Athens, since she never appears in public except completely veiled, but, at the Eleusinian festival, and again on the feast of the Poseidonia, disrobes in the sight of all, lets down her hair, and goes to bathe in the sea.[72] For a time she loves and inspires Praxiteles, and poses for his *Aphrodites;* from her, too, Apelles takes his *Aphrodite Anadyomene.*[73] So rich is Phryne from her loves that she offers to rebuild the walls of Thebes if the Thebans will inscribe her name on the structure, which they stubbornly refuse to do. Perhaps she asks too large an honorarium from Euthias; he revenges himself by indicting her on a charge of impiety. But a member of the court is one of her clients, and Hypereides, the orator, is her devoted lover;

Hypereides defends her not only with eloquence but by opening her tunic and revealing her bosom to the court. The judges look upon her beauty, and vindicate her piety.[74]

Lais of Corinth, says Athenaeus, "appears to have been superior in beauty to any woman that had ever been seen."[75] As many cities as claimed Homer dispute the honor of having witnessed her birth. Sculptors and painters beg her to pose for them, but she is coy. The great Myron, in his old age, persuades her; when she disrobes he forgets his white hair and beard, and offers her all his possessions for one night; whereupon she smiles, shrugs her rounded shoulders, and leaves him statueless. The next morning, burning with readolescence, he has his hair trimmed, and his beard cut off; he puts on a scarlet robe and a golden girdle, a chain of gold around his neck and rings on all his fingers. He colors his cheeks with rouge, and perfumes his garments and his flesh. He seeks out Lais, and announces that he loves her. "My poor friend," she replied, seeing through his metamorphosis, "you are asking me what I refused to your father yesterday."[76] She lays up a great fortune, but does not refuse herself to poor but comely lovers; she restores the ugly Demosthenes to virtue by asking ten thousand drachmas for an evening,[77] and from the well-to-do Aristippus she earns such sums as scandalize his servant;[78] but to the penniless Diogenes she gives herself for a pittance, being pleased to have philosophers at her feet. She spends her wealth generously upon temples, public buildings, and friends, and finally returns, after the custom of her kind, to the poverty of her youth. She plies her trade patiently to the end; and when she dies she is honored with a splendid tomb as the greatest conqueror that the Greeks have ever known.[79]

VII. GREEK FRIENDSHIP

Stranger than this strange entente between prostitution and philosophy is the placid acceptance of sexual inversion. The chief rivals of the hetairai are the boys of Athens; and the courtesans, scandalized to the very depths of their pockets, never tire of denouncing the immorality of homosexual love. Merchants import handsome lads to be sold to the highest bidder, who will use them first as concubines and later as slaves;[80] and only a negligible minority of males think it amiss that the effeminate young aristocrats of the city should arouse and assuage the ardor of aging men. In this matter of genders Sparta is as careless as Athens; when Alcman wishes to compliment some girls he calls them his "female boy-friends."[81] Athenian law disfranchises those who receive homosexual attentions,[82] but public opinion tolerates the practice humorously; in Sparta and Crete no stigma of any kind is attached to it;[83] in Thebes it is accepted as a valuable source of military organization and bravery. The greatest heroes in the fond remembrance of Athens are Harmodius and Aristogeiton, tyrannicides and lovers; the most popular in Athens in his day is Alcibiades, who boasts of the men who love him; as late as Aristotle "Greek lovers" plight their troth at the tomb of Iolaus, comrade of Heracles;[84] and Aristippus describes Xenophon, leader of armies and hardheaded man of the world, as infatuated with young Cleinias.[85] The attachment of a man to a boy, or of a boy to a boy, shows in Greece all the symptoms of romantic love—passion, piety, ecstasy, jealousy, serenading, brooding, moaning, and sleeplessness.[86] When Plato, in the *Phaedrus*, talks of human love, he means homosexual love; and the disputants in his *Symposium* agree on one point—that love between man and man is nobler and more spiritual than love between man and woman.[87] A similar inversion appears among the women, occasionally among the finest, as in Sappho, frequently among the courtesans; the auletrides love one another more passionately than they love their patrons, and the *pornaia* are hothouses of Lesbian romance.[88]

How shall we explain the popularity of this perversion in Greece? Aristotle attributes it to fear of overpopulation,[89] and this may account for part of the phenomenon; but there is obviously a connection between the prevalence of both homosexuality and prostitution in Athens, and the seclusion of women. After the age of six the boys of Periclean Athens are taken from the gynaeceum in which respectable women spend their lives, and are brought up chiefly in companionship with other boys, or men; little opportunity is given them, in their formative and almost neutral period, to know the attractiveness of the tender sex. The life of the common mess hall in Sparta, of the agora, gymnasium, and palaestra in Athens, and the career of the ephebos, show the youth only the male form; even art does not announce the physical beauty of woman until Praxiteles. In married life the men seldom find mental companionship at home; the rarity of education among women creates a gulf between the sexes, and men seek elsewhere the charms that they have not permitted their wives to acquire. To the Athenian citizen his home is not a castle but a dormitory; from morning to evening, in a great number of cases, he lives in the city, and rarely has social contacts with respectable women other than his wife and daughters. Greek society is unisexual, and misses the disturbance, grace, and stimulation that the spirit and charm of women will give to Renaissance Italy and Enlightenment France.

VIII. LOVE AND MARRIAGE

Romantic love appears among the Greeks, but seldom as the cause of marriage. We find little of it in Homer, where Agamemnon and Achilles frankly think of Chryseis and Briseis, even of the discouraging Cassandra, in terms of physical desire. Nausicaa, however, is a warning against too broad a generalization, and legends as old as Homer tell of Heracles and Iola, of Orpheus and Eurydice. The lyric poets, again, talk abundantly of love, commonly in the sense of amorous appetite; stories like that which Stesichorus tells of a maiden dying for love[90] are exceptional; but when Theano, wife of Pythagoras, speaks of love as "the sickness of a longing soul,"[91] we feel the authentic note of romantic rut. As refinement grows, and superimposes poetry upon heat, the tender sentiment becomes more frequent; and the increasing delay that civilization places between desire and fulfillment gives imagination leisure to embellish the object of hope. Aeschylus is still Homeric in his treatment of sex; but in Sophocles we hear of "Love" who "rules at will the gods,"*[92] and in Euripides many a passage proclaims Eros' power. The later dramatists often describe a youth desperately enamored of a girl.[93] Aristotle suggests the real quality of romantic adoration when he remarks that "lovers look at the eyes of the beloved, in which modesty dwells."[94]

Such affairs in classic Greece lead rather to premarital relations than to matrimony. The Greeks consider romantic love to be a form of "possession" or madness, and would smile at anyone who should propose it as a fit guide in the choice of a marriage mate.[95] Normally marriage is arranged by the parents as in always classic France, or by professional matchmakers,[96] with an eye not to love but to dowries. The father is expected to provide for his daughter a marriage portion of money, clothing, jewelry, and perhaps slaves.[97] This remains to its end the property of the wife, and reverts to her in case of a separation from her husband—a consideration that discourages divorce by the male. Without a dowry a girl has little chance of marriage; therefore where the father cannot give it to her the relatives combine to provide it. Marriage by purchase, so frequent in Homeric days, has by this means been inverted in Periclean Greece: in effect, as Euripides' Medea complains,[98] the woman has to buy her master. The Greek, then, marries not for love, nor because he enjoys matrimony (for he prates endlessly about its tribulations), but to continue himself and the state through a wife suitably dowered, and children who will ward off the evil fate of an untended soul. Even with these inducements he avoids wedlock as long

---

* Cf. *Antigone*, 781f.:

When Love disputes
He carries his battles!
Love, he loots
The rich of their chattels!
By delicate cheeks
On maiden's pillow
Watches he all the night-time long;
His prey he seeks
Over the billow,
Pastoral haunts he preys among.
Gods are deathless, and they
Cannot elude his whim;
And oh, amid us whose life's a day,
Mad is the heart that broodeth him![92a]

as he can. The letter of the law forbids him to remain single, but the law is not always enforced in Periclean days; and after him the number of bachelors mounts until it becomes one of the basic problems of Athens.[99] There are so many ways of being amused in Greece! Those men who yield marry late, usually near thirty, and then insist upon brides not much older than fifteen.[100] "To mate a youth with a young wife is ill," says a character in Euripides; "for a man's strength endures, while the bloom of beauty quickly leaves the woman's form."[101]

A choice having been made, and the dowry agreed upon, a solemn betrothal takes place in the home of the girl's father; there must be witnesses, but her own presence is not necessary. Without such a formal betrothal no union is valid in Athenian law; it is considered to be the first act in the complex rite of marriage. The second act, which follows in a few days, is a feast in the house of the girl. Before coming to it the bride and bridegroom, in their separate homes, bathe in ceremonial purification. At the feast the men of both families sit on one side of the room, the women on the other; a wedding cake is eaten, and much wine is drunk. Then the bridegroom escorts his veiled and white-robed bride—whose face he may not yet have seen—into a carriage, and takes her to his father's dwelling amid a procession of friends and flute-playing girls, who light the way with torches and raise the hymeneal chant. Arrived, he carries the girl over the threshold, as if in semblance of capture. The parents of the youth greet the girl, and receive her with religious ceremony into the circle of the family and the worship of its gods; no priest, however, takes any part in the ritual. The guests then escort the couple to their room with an epithalamion, or marriage-chamber song, and linger boisterously at the door until the bridegroom announces to them that the marriage has been consummated.

Besides his wife a man may take a concubine. "We have courtesans for the sake of pleasure," says Demosthenes, "concubines for the daily health of our bodies, and wives to bear us lawful offspring and be the faithful guardians of our homes":[102] here in one startling sentence is the Greek view of woman in the classic age. Draco's laws permit concubinage; and after the Sicilian expedition of 415, when the roll of citizens has been depleted by war and many girls cannot find husbands, the law explicitly allows double marriages; Socrates and Euripides are among those who assume this patriotic obligation.[103] The wife usually accepts concubinage with Oriental patience, knowing that the "second wife," when her charms wear off, will become in effect a household slave, and that only the offspring of the first wife are accounted legitimate. Adultery leads to divorce only when committed by the wife; the husband in such case is spoken of as "carrying horns" (*keroesses*), and custom requires him to send his wife away.[104] The law makes adultery by woman, or by a man with a married woman, punishable with death, but the Greeks are too lenient to concupiscence to enforce this statute. The injured husband is usually left to deal with the adulterer as he will and can—sometimes killing him in *flagrante delicto*, sometimes sending a slave to beat him, sometimes contenting himself with a money indemnity.[105]

For the man divorce is simple; he may dismiss his wife at any time, without stating the cause. Barrenness is accepted as sufficient reason for divorcing a wife, since the purpose of marriage is to have children. If the man is sterile, law permits, and public opinion recommends, the reinforcement of the husband by a relative; the child born of such a union is considered to be the son of the husband, and must tend his departed soul. The wife may not at will leave her husband, but she may ask the archons for a divorce on the ground of the cruelty or excesses of her mate.[106] Divorce is also allowed by mutual consent, usually expressed in a formal declaration to the archon. In case of separation, even where the husband has been guilty of adultery, the children remain with the man.[107] All in all, in the matter of sex relations, Athenian custom and law are thoroughly man-made, and represent an Oriental retrogression from the society of Egypt, Crete, and the Homeric Age.

IX. WOMAN

As surprising as anything else in this civilization is the fact that it is brilliant without the aid or stimulus of women. With their help the Heroic Age achieved splendor, the age of the dictators a lyric radiance; then, almost overnight, married women vanish from the history of the Greeks, as if to confute the supposed correlation between the level of civilization and the status of woman. In Herodotus woman is everywhere; in Thucydides she is nowhere to be seen. From Semonides of Amorgos to Lucian, Greek literature is offensively repetitious about the faults of women; and towards the close of it even the kindly Plutarch repeats Thucydides:[108] "The name of a decent woman, like her person, should be shut up in the house."[109]

This seclusion of woman does not exist among the Dorians; presumably it comes from the Near East to Ionia, and from Ionia to Attica; it is part of the tradition of Asia. Perhaps the disappearance of inheritance through the mother, the rise of the middle classes, and the enthronement of the commercial view of life enter into the change: men come to judge women in terms of utility, and find them especially useful in the home. The Oriental nature of Greek marriage goes with this Attic purdah; the bride is cut off from her kin, goes to live almost as a menial in another home, and worships other gods. She cannot make contracts, or incur debts beyond a trifling sum; she cannot bring actions at law; and Solon legislates that anything done under the influence of woman shall have no validity at law.[110] When her husband dies she does not inherit his property. Even physiological error enters into her legal subjection; for just as primitive ignorance of the male role in reproduction tended to exalt woman, so the male is exalted by the theory popular in classic Greece that the generative power belongs only to man, the woman being merely the carrier and nurse of the child.[111] The older age of the man contributes to the subordination of the wife; he is twice her years when he marries her, and can in some degree mold her mind to his own philosophy. Doubtless the male knows too well the license allowed to his sex in Athens to risk his wife or daughter at large; he chooses to be free at the cost of her seclusion. She may, if properly veiled and attended, visit her relatives or intimates, and may take part in the religious celebrations, including attendance at the plays; but for the rest she is expected to stay at home, and not allow herself to be seen at a window. Most of her life is spent in the women's quarters at the rear of the house; no male visitor is ever admitted there, nor does she appear when men visit her husband.

In the home she is honored and obeyed in everything that does not contravene the patriarchal authority of her mate. She keeps the house, or superintends its management; she cooks the meals, cards and spins the wool, makes the clothing and bedding for the family. Her education is almost confined to household arts, for the Athenian believes with Euripides that a woman is handicapped by intellect.[112] The result is that the respectable women of Athens are more modest, more "charming" to men, than their like in Sparta, but less interesting and mature, incapable of being comrades to husbands whose minds have been filled and sharpened by a free and varied life. The women of sixth-century Greece contributed significantly to Greek literature; the women of Periclean Athens contribute nothing.

Toward the end of the period a movement arises for the emancipation of woman. Euripides defends the sex with brave speeches and timid innuendoes; Aristophanes makes fun of them with boisterous indecency. The women go to the heart of the matter and begin to compete with the hetairai in making themselves as attractive as the progress of chemistry will permit. "What sensible thing are we women capable of doing?" asks Cleonica in Aristophanes' *Lysistrata*. "We do nothing but sit around with our paint and lipstick and transparent gowns, and all the rest of it."[113] From 411 onward female roles become more prominent in Athenian drama, and reveal the growing escape of women from the solitude to which they have been confined.

Through it all the real influence of woman over man continues, making her subjection largely unreal. The greater eagerness of the male gives woman an advantage in Greece as elsewhere. "Sir," says Samuel Johnson, "nature has given woman so much power that the law cannot afford to give her more."[114] Sometimes this natural sovereignty is enhanced by a substantial dowry, or an industrious tongue, or uxorious affection; more often it is the result of beauty, or the bearing and rearing of fine children, or the slow fusion of souls in the crucible of a common experience and task. An age that can portray such gentle characters as Antigone, Alcestis, Iphigenia, and Andromache, and such heroines as Hecuba, Cassandra, and Medea, could not be unaware of the highest and the deepest in woman. The average Athenian loves his wife, and will not always try to conceal it; the funeral stelae reveal surprisingly the tenderness of mate for mate, and of parents for children, in the intimacy of the home. *The Greek Anthology* is vivid with erotic verse, but it contains also many a touching epigram to a beloved comrade. "In this stone," says one epitaph, "Marathonis laid Nicopolis, and bedewed the marble chest with tears. But it was of no avail. What profit hath a man whose wife is gone, and who is left solitary on earth?"[115]

X. THE HOME

The Greek family, like the Indo-European household in general, is composed of the father, the mother, sometimes a "second wife," their unmarried daughters, their sons, their slaves, and their sons' wives and children and slaves. It remains to the end the strongest institution in Greek civilization, for both in agriculture and in industry it is the unit and instrument of economic production. The power of the father in Attica is extensive, but much narrower than in Rome. He can expose the newborn child, sell the labor of his minor sons and unwedded daughters, give his daughters in marriage, and, under certain conditions, appoint another husband for his widow.[116] But he cannot, in Athenian law, sell the persons of his children; and each son, on marrying, escapes from parental authority, sets up his own home, and becomes an independent member of the gene.

The Greek house is unpretentious. The exterior is seldom more than a stout blank wall with a narrow doorway, dumb witnesses to the insecurity of Greek life. The material is sometimes stucco, usually sun-baked brick. In the city the houses are crowded together in narrow streets; often they rise to two stories, occasionally they are tenements housing several families; but nearly every *citizen* owns an individual home. Dwellings in Athens are small till Alcibiades sets a fashion of magnificence; there is a democratic taboo, reinforced by aristocratic precaution, against display; and the Athenian, living for the most part in the open air, does not endow the home with the significance and affection that it receives in colder zones. A rich house may have a colonnaded porch facing the street, but this is highly exceptional. Windows are a luxury, and are confined to the upper story; they have no panes, but may be closed with shutters, or screened with lattices against the sun. The entrance door is ordinarily made of double leaves, turning upon vertical pivots running into the threshold and the lintel. On the door of many well-to-do houses is a metal knocker, often in the form of a ring in a lion's mouth.[117] The entrance hallway, except in the poorer dwellings, leads into an *aule*, or uncovered court, commonly paved with stones. Around the court may run a columned portico; in the center may be an altar, or a cistern, or both, perhaps also adorned with columns, and paved with a mosaic floor. Light and air come to the house chiefly through this court, for upon it open nearly all the rooms; to pass from one room to another it is usually necessary to enter the portico or the court. In the shade and privacy of the court and the portico much of the family's life is lived, and much of its work is done.

Gardens are rare in the city, and are confined to small areas in the court or behind the house. Country gardens are more spacious and numerous; but the scarcity of rain in summer, and the cost of irrigation, make gardens a luxury in Attica. The average Greek has no Rousseauan sensitivity to nature; his mountains are still too troublesome to be beautiful, though his poets, despite its dangers, intone many paeans to the sea. He is not sentimental about nature, so much as animistically imaginative; he peoples the woods and streams of his country with gods and sprites, and thinks of nature as not a landscape but a Valhalla; he names his mountains and rivers from the divinities that inhabit them; and instead of painting nature directly he draws or carves symbolic images of the deities that in his poetic theology give it life. Not till Alexander's armies bring back Persian ways and gold will the Greek build himself a pleasure garden or "paradise." Nevertheless, flowers are loved in Greece as much as anywhere, and gardens and florists supply them all the year round. Flower girls peddle roses, violets, hyacinths, narcissi, irises, myrtles, lilacs, crocuses, and anemones from house to house. Women wear flowers in their hair, dandies wear them behind the ear; and on festal occasions both sexes may come forth with flower garlands, lei-like, around the neck.[118]

The interior of the house is simple. Among the poor the floors are of hardened earth; as income rises this basis may be covered with plaster, or paved with flat stones or with small round stones set in cement, as in the Near East immemorially; and all this may be covered with reed mats or rugs. The brick walls are plastered and whitewashed. Heating, which is needed for only three months of the year, is furnished by a brazier whose smoke has to find a way out through the door to the court. Decoration is minimal; but at the end of the fifth century the homes of the rich may have pillared halls, walls paneled with marble or painted imitations of it, mural paintings and tapestries, and ceiling arabesques. Furniture is scanty in the average home—some chairs, some chests, a few tables, a bed. Cushions take the place of upholstery on chairs, but the seats of the rich may be carefully carved, and inlaid with silver, tortoise, or ivory. Chests serve as both closets and chairs. Tables are small, and usually three-legged, whence their name *trapezai;* they are brought in and removed with the food, and are hardly used for other purposes; writing is done upon the knee. Couches and beds are favorite objects for adornment, being often inlaid or elaborately carved. Leather thongs stretched across the bedstead serve as a spring; there are mattresses and pillows, and embroidered covers, and commonly a raised headrest. Lamps may be hung from the ceiling, or placed upon stands, or take the form of torches elegantly wrought.

The kitchen is equipped with a great variety of iron, bronze, and earthenware vessels; glass is a rare luxury, not made in Greece. Cooking is done over an open fire; stoves are a Hellenistic innovation. Athenian meals are simple, like the Spartan and unlike the Boeotian, Corinthian, or Sicilian; but when honored guests are expected it is customary to engage a professional cook, who is always male. Cooking is a highly developed art, with many texts and heroes; some Greek cooks are as widely known as the latest victor in the Olympic games. To eat alone is considered barbarous, and table manners are looked upon as an index of a civilization's development. Women and boys sit at meals before small tables; men recline on couches, two on each. The family eats together when alone; if male guests come, the women of the family retire to the gynaeceum. Attendants remove the sandals or wash the feet of the guests before the latter recline, and offer them water to cleanse their hands; sometimes they anoint the heads of the guests with fragrant oils. There are no knives or forks, but there are spoons; solid food is eaten with the fingers. During the meal the fingers are cleaned with scraps or crumbs of bread; after it with water. Before dessert the attendants fill the cup of each guest from a krater, or mixing bowl, in which wine has been diluted with water. Plates are of earthenware; silver plate appears as the fifth century ends. Epicures grow in number in the fourth century; one Pithyllus has coverings made for his tongue and fingers so that he may eat food as hot as he likes.[119] There are a few vegetarians, whose guests make the usual jokes and complaints; one diner flees from a vegetarian feast for fear that he will be offered hay for dessert.[120]

Drinking is as important as eating. After the *deipnon*, or dinner, comes the *symposion*, or drinking together. At Sparta as well as at Athens there are drinking clubs whose members become so attached to one another that such organizations become potent political instruments. The procedure at banquets is complicated, and philosophers like Xenocrates and Aristotle think it desirable to set down laws for them.[121] The floor, upon which uneaten material has been thrown, is swept clean after the meal; perfumes are passed around, and much wine. The guests may then dance, not in pairs or with the other sex (for usually only males are invited), but in groups; or they may play games like kottabos;* or they may match poems, witticisms, or riddles, or watch professional performers like the female acrobat in Xenophon's *Symposium*, who tosses twelve hoops at once and then dances somersaults through a hoop "set all around with upright swords."[122] Flute girls may appear, play, sing, dance, and love as arranged for. Educated Athenians prefer, now and then, a symposium of conversation, conducted in an orderly manner by a symposiarch chosen by a throw of the dice to act as chairman. The guests take care not to break up the talk into small groups, which usually means small talk; they keep the conversation general, and listen, as courteously as their vivacity will permit, to each man in turn. So elegant a discourse as that which Plato offers us is doubtless the product of his brilliant imagination; but probably Athens has known dialogues as lively as his, perhaps profounder; and in any case it is Athenian society that suggests and provides the background. In that exciting atmosphere of free wits the Athenian mind is formed.

XI. OLD AGE

Old age is feared and mourned beyond wont by the life-loving Greeks. Even here, however, it has its consolations; for as the used-up body is returned like worn currency to the mint, it has the solace of seeing, before it is consumed, the fresh new life through which it cheats mortality. It is true that Greek history reveals cases of selfish carelessness or coarse insolence towards the old. Athenian society, commercial, individualistic, and innovating, tends to be unkind to old age; respect for years goes with a religious and conservative society

* This consisted in throwing liquid from a cup so that it would strike some small object placed at a distance.

like Sparta's, while democracy, loosening all bonds with freedom, puts the accent on youth, and favors the new against the old. Athenian history offers several instances of children taking over their parents' property without proof of imbecility in the elders;[123] but Sophocles rescues himself from such an action simply by reading to the court some passages from his latest play. Athenian law commands that sons shall support their infirm or aged parents;[124] and public opinion, which is always more fearful than the law, enjoins modesty and respect in the behavior of the young towards the old. Plato takes it for granted that a well-bred youth will be silent in the presence of his seniors unless he is asked to speak.[125] There are in the literature many pictures of modest adolescence, as in the earlier dialogues of Plato or the *Symposium* of Xenophon; and there are touching stories of filial devotion, like that of Orestes to Agamemnon, and of Antigone to Oedipus.

When death comes, every precaution is taken that the soul of the departed shall be spared all avoidable suffering. The body must be buried or burned; else the soul will wander restlessly about the world, and will revenge itself upon its negligent posterity; it may, for example, reappear as a ghost, and bring disease or disaster to plants and men. Cremation is more popular in the Heroic Age, burial in the classic. Burial was Mycenaean, and will survive into Christianity; cremation apparently entered Greece with the Achaeans and the Dorians, whose nomad habits made impossible the proper care of graves. One or the other is so obligatory among Athenians that the victorious generals at Arginusae are put to death for allowing a severe storm to deter them from recovering and burying their dead.

Greek burial customs carry on old ways into the future. The corpse is bathed, anointed with perfumes, crowned with flowers, and dressed in the finest garments that the family can afford. An obol is placed between the teeth to pay Charon, the mythical boatman who ferries the dead across the Styx to Hades.* The body is placed in a coffin of pottery or wood; to "have one foot in the coffin" is already a proverb in Greece.[126] Mourning is elaborate: black garments are worn, and the hair, or part of it, is shorn as a gift for the dead. On the third day the corpse is carried on a bier in procession through the streets, while the women weep and beat their breasts; professional wailers or dirge singers may be hired for the occasion. Upon the sod of the covered grave wine is poured to slake the dead soul's thirst, and animals may be sacrificed for its food. The mourners lay wreaths of flowers or cypress upon the tomb,[127] and then return home to the funeral feast. Since the departed soul is believed to be present at this feast, sacred custom requires that "of the dead nothing but good" shall be spoken;[128] this is the source of an ancient saw, and perhaps of the unfailing lauds of our epitaphs. Periodically the children visit the graves

* It was the custom among the Greeks to carry small change in the mouth.

of their ancestors, and offer them food and drink. After the battle of Plataea, where the Greeks of many cities have fallen, the Plataeans pledge themselves to provide for all the dead an annual repast; and six centuries later, in the days of Plutarch, this promise will still be performed.

After death the soul, separated from the body, dwells as an insubstantial shade in Hades. In Homer only spirits guilty of exceptional or sacrilegious offense suffer punishment there; all the rest, saints and sinners alike, share an equal fate of endless prowling about dark Pluto's realm. In the course of Greek history a belief arises, among the poorer classes, in Hades as a place of expiation for sins; Aeschylus pictures Zeus as judging the dead there and punishing the guilty, though no word is said about rewarding the good.[129] Only rarely do we find mention of the Blessed Isles, or the Elysian Fields, as heavens of eternal happiness for a few heroic souls. The thought of the gloomy fate awaiting nearly all the dead darkens Greek literature, and makes Greek life less bright and cheerful than is fitting under such a sun.

CHAPTER XIV

The Art of Periclean Greece

I. THE ORNAMENTATION OF LIFE

"IT is beautiful," says a character in Xenophon's *Economics*,

> to see the footgear ranged in a row according to its kind; beautiful to see garments sorted according to their use, and coverlets; beautiful to see glass vases and tableware so sorted; and beautiful, too, despite the jeers of the witless and flippant, to see cooking-pots arranged with sense and symmetry. Yes, all things without exception, because of symmetry, will appear more beautiful when placed in order. All these utensils will then seem to form a choir; the center which they unite to form will create a beauty that will be enhanced by the distance of the other objects in the group.[1]

This passage from a general reveals the scope, simplicity, and strength of the esthetic sense in Greece. The feeling for form and rhythm, for precision and clarity, for proportion and order, is the central fact in Greek culture; it enters into the shape and ornament of every bowl and vase, of every statue and painting, of every temple and tomb, of every poem and drama, of all Greek work in science and philosophy. Greek art is reason made manifest: Greek painting is the logic of line, Greek sculpture is a worship of symmetry, Greek architecture is a marble geometry. There is no extravagance of emotion in Periclean art, no *bizarrerie* of form, no striving for novelty through the abnormal or unusual;* the purpose is not to represent the indiscriminate irrelevancy of the real, but to catch the illuminating essence of things, and to portray the ideal possibilities of men. The pursuit of wealth, beauty, and knowledge so absorbed the Athenians that they had no time for goodness. "I swear by all the gods," says one of Xenophon's banqueters, "that I would not choose the power of the Persian king in preference to beauty."[3]

The Greek, whatever the romanticists of less virile ages may have fancied of him, was no effeminate esthete, no flower of ecstasy murmuring mys-

* *Philokaloumen met' euteleias,* says Thucydides' Pericles: "We love beauty without extravagance."[2]

teries of art for art's sake; he thought of art as subordinate to life, and of living as the greatest art of all; he had a healthy utilitarian bias against any beauty that could not be used; the useful, the beautiful, and the good were almost as closely bound together in his thought as in the Socratic philosophy.* In his view art was first of all an adornment of the ways and means of life: he wanted his pots and pans, his lamps and chests and tables and beds and chairs to be at once serviceable and beautiful, and never too elegant to be strong. Having a vivid "sense of the state," he identified himself with the power and glory of his city, and employed a thousand artists to embellish its public places, ennoble its festivals, and commemorate its history. Above all, he wished to honor or propitiate the gods, to express his gratitude to them for life or victory; he offered votive images, lavished his resources upon his temples, and engaged statuaries to give to his gods or his dead an enduring similitude in stone. Hence Greek art belonged not to a museum, where men might go to contemplate it in a rare moment of esthetic conscience, but to the actual interests and enterprises of the people; its "Apollos" were not dead marbles in a gallery, but the likenesses of beloved deities; its temples no mere curiosities for tourists, but the homes of living gods. The artist, in this society, was not an insolvent recluse in a studio, working in a language alien to the common citizen; he was an artisan toiling with laborers of all degrees in a public and intelligible task. Athens brought together, from all the Greek world, a greater concourse of artists, as well as of philosophers and poets, than any other city except Renaissance Rome; and these men, competing in fervent rivalry and cooperating under enlightened statesmanship, realized in fair measure the vision of Pericles.

Art begins at home, and with the person; men paint themselves before they paint pictures, and adorn their bodies before building homes. Jewelry, like cosmetics, is as old as history. The Greek was an expert cutter and engraver of gems. He used simple tools of bronze—plain and tubular drills, a wheel, and a polishing mixture of emery powder and oil;[5] yet his work was so delicate and minute that a microscope was probably required in executing the details, and is certainly needed in following them.[6] Coins were not especially pretty at Athens, where the grim owl ruled the mint. Elis led all the mainland in this field, and towards the close of the fifth century Syracuse issued a dekadrachma that has never been surpassed in numismatic art. In metalwork the masters of Chalcis maintained their leadership; every Mediterranean city sought their iron, copper, and silver wares. Greek mirrors were more pleasing than mirrors by

* "Among the ancients," said Stendhal, "the beautiful is only the high relief of the useful."[4]

their nature can frequently be; for though one might not see the clearest of reflections in the polished bronze, the mirrors themselves were of varied and attractive shapes, often elaborately engraved, and upheld by figures of heroes, fair women, or gods.

The potters carried on the forms and methods of the sixth century, with their traditional banter and rivalry. Sometimes they burnt into the vase a word of love for a boy; even Pheidias followed this custom when he carved upon the finger of his *Zeus* the words, "Pantarkes is fair."[7] In the first half of the fifth century the red-figure style reached its apex in the *Achilles and Penthesilea* vase, the *Aesop and the Fox* cup in the Vatican, and the Berlin Museum *Orpheus among the Thracians.* More beautiful still were the white lekythoi of the mid-century; these slender flasks were dedicated to the dead, and were usually buried with them, or thrown upon the pyre to let their fragrant oils mingle with the flames. The vase painters ventured into individuality, and sometimes fired the clay with subjects that would have startled the staid masters of the Archaic age; one vase allows Athenian youths to embrace courtesans shamelessly; another shows men vomiting as they come from a banquet; other vases do what they can for sex education.[8] The heroes of Periclean vase painting—Brygus, Sotades, and Meidias—abandoned the old myths, and chose scenes from the life of their times, delighting above all in the graceful movement of woman and the natural play of the child. They drew more faithfully than their predecessors: they showed the body in three-quarters view as well as in profile; they produced light and shade by using thin or thick solutions of the glaze; they modeled the figures to show contours and depth, and the folds of feminine drapery. Corinth and Sicilian Gela were also centers of fine vase painting in this age, but no one questioned the superiority of the Athenians. It was not the competition of other potters that overcame the artists of the Ceramicus; it was the rise of a rival art of decoration. The vase painters tried to meet the attack by imitating the themes and styles of the muralists; but the taste of the age went against them, and slowly, as the fourth century advanced, pottery resigned itself to being more and more an industry, less and less an art.

II. THE RISE OF PAINTING

Four stages vaguely divide the history of Greek painting. In the sixth century it is chiefly ceramic, devoted to the adornment of vases; in the fifth it is chiefly architectural, giving color to public buildings and statues; in the fourth it hovers between the domestic and the individual, decorating dwellings and making portraits; in the Hellenistic Age it is chiefly individual, producing easel pictures for private purchasers. Greek painting begins as an offshoot of drawing, and remains to the end a matter essentially of drawing and design. In its development it uses three methods: fresco, or painting upon wet plaster; tempera, or painting upon wet cloth or boards with colors mixed with the white of eggs; and encaustic, which mixed the colors with melted wax; this is as near as antiquity comes to painting in oils. Pliny, whose will to believe sometimes rivals that of Herodotus, assures us that the art of painting was already so advanced in the eighth century that Candaules, King of Lydia, paid its weight in gold for a picture by Bularchus;[9] but all beginnings are mysteries. We may judge the high repute of painting in Greece from the fact that Pliny gives it more space than to sculpture; and apparently the great paintings of the classic and Hellenistic periods were as much discussed by the critics, and as highly regarded by the people, as the most distinguished specimens of architecture or statuary.[10]

Polygnotus of Thasos was as famous in fifth-century Greece as Ictinus or Pheidias. We find him in Athens about 472; perhaps it was the rich Cimon who procured him commissions to adorn several public buildings with murals.* Upon the Stoa, which thereafter was called *Poecile*, or the Painted Portico, and which, three centuries later, would give its name to the philosophy of Zeno, Polygnotus depicted the *Sack of Troy*—not the bloody massacre of the night of victory, but the somber silence of the morning after, with the victors quieted by the ruin around them, and the defeated lying calm in death. On the walls of the temple of the Dioscuri he painted the *Rape of the Leucippidae*, and set a precedent for his art by portraying the women in transparent drapery. The Amphictyonic Council was not shocked; it invited Polygnotus to Delphi, where, in the Lesche, or Lounge, he painted *Odysseus in Hades*, and another *Sack of Troy*. All these were vast frescoes, almost empty of landscape or background; but so crowded with individualized figures that many assistants were needed to fill in with color the master's carefully drawn designs. The Lesche mural of Troy showed Menelaus' crew about to spread sail for the return to Greece; in the center sat Helen; and though many other women were in the picture, all appeared to be gazing at her beauty. In a corner stood Andromache, with Astyanax at her breast; in another a little boy clung to an altar in fear; and in the distance a horse rolled around on the sandy beach.[12] Here, half a century before Euripides, was all the drama of *The Trojan Women*. Polygnotus refused to take pay for these pictures, but gave them to Athens and Delphi out of the generosity of confident strength. All Hellas acclaimed him: Athens conferred citizenship upon him, and the Amphictyonic Council arranged that wherever he went in Greece he should be (as Socrates wished to be) maintained at the public expense.[13] All that remains of him is a little pigment on a wall at Delphi to remind us that artistic immortality is a moment in geological time.

---

* He repaid Cimon by making love to his sister Elpinice, and painting her portrait as Laodicea among the women of Troy.[11]

About 470 Delphi and Corinth established quadrennial contests in painting as part of the Pythian and Isthmian games. The art was now sufficiently advanced to enable Panaenus, brother (or nephew) of Pheidias, to make recognizable portraits of the Athenian and Persian generals in his *Battle of Marathon*. But it still placed all figures in one plane, and made them of one stature; it indicated distance not by a progressive diminution of size and a modeling with light and shade, but by covering more of the lower half of the farther figures with the curves that represented the ground. Towards 440 a vital step forward was taken. Agatharchus, employed by Aeschylus and Sophocles to paint scenery for their plays, perceived the connection between light and shade and distance, and wrote a treatise on perspective as a means of creating theatrical illusion. Anaxagoras and Democritus took up the idea from the scientific angle, and at the end of the century Apollodorus of Athens won the name of *skiagraphos*, or shadow painter, because he made pictures in chiaroscuro—i.e., in light and shade; hence Pliny spoke of him as "the first to paint objects as they really appeared."[14]

Greek painters never made full use of these discoveries; just as Solon frowned upon the theatrical art as a deception, so the artists seem to have thought it against their honor, or beneath their dignity, to give to a plane surface the appearance of three dimensions. Nevertheless it was through perspective and chiaroscuro that Zeuxis, pupil of Apollodorus, made himself the supreme figure in fifth-century painting. He came from Heracleia (Pontica?) to Athens about 424; and even amid the noise of war his coming was considered an event. He was a "character," bold and conceited, and he painted with a swashbuckling brush. At the Olympic games he strutted about in a checkered tunic on which his name was embroidered in gold; he could afford it, since he had already acquired "a vast amount of wealth" from his paintings.[15] But he worked with the honest care of a great artist, and when Agatharchus boasted of his own speed of execution, Zeuxis said quietly, "I take a long time."[16] He gave away many of his masterpieces, on the ground that no price could do them justice; and cities and kings were happy to receive them.

He had only one rival in his generation—Parrhasius of Ephesus, almost as great and quite as vain. Parrhasius wore a golden crown on his head, called himself "the prince of painters," and said that in him the art had reached perfection.[17] He did it all in lusty good humor, singing as he painted.[18] Gossip said that he had bought a slave and tortured him to study facial expression in pain for a picture of Prometheus;[19] but people tell many stories about artists. Like Zeuxis he was a realist; his *Runner* was portrayed with such verisimilitude that those who beheld it expected the perspiration to fall from the picture, and the athlete to drop from exhaustion. He drew an immense mural of *The People of Athens*, representing them as implacable and merciful, proud and humble, fierce and timid, fickle and generous—and so faithfully that the Athenian public, we are informed, realized for the first time its own complex and contradictory character.[20]

A great rivalry brought him into public competition with Zeuxis. The latter painted some grapes so naturally that birds tried to eat them. The judges were enthusiastic about the picture, and Zeuxis, confident of victory, bade Parrhasius draw aside the curtain that concealed the Ephesian's painting. But the curtain proved to be a part of the picture, and Zeuxis, having himself been deceived, handsomely acknowledged his defeat. Zeuxis suffered no loss of reputation. At Crotona he agreed to paint a *Helen* for the temple of Lacinian Hera, on condition that the five loveliest women of the city should pose in the nude for him, so that he might select from each her fairest feature, and combine them all in a second goddess of beauty.[21] Penelope, too, found new life under his brush; but he admired more his portrait of an athlete, and wrote under it that men would find it easier to criticize him than to equal him. All Greece enjoyed his conceit, and talked about him as much as of any dramatist, statesmen, or general. Only the prize fighters outdid his fame.

III. THE MASTERS OF SCULPTURE

1. Methods

None the less painting remained slightly alien to the Greek genius, which loved form more than color, and made even the painting of the classic age (if we may judge it from hearsay) a statuesque study in line and design rather than a sensuous seizure of the colors of life. The Hellene delighted rather in sculpture: he filled his home, his temples, and his graves with terracotta statuettes, worshiped his gods with images of stone, and marked the tombs of his departed with stelae reliefs that are among the commonest and most moving products of Greek art. The artisans of the stelae were simple workers who carved by rote, and repeated a thousand times the familiar theme of the quiet parting, with clasped hands, of the living from the dead. But the theme itself is noble enough to bear repetition, for it shows classic restraint at its best, and teaches even a romantic soul that feeling speaks with most power when it lowers its voice. These slabs show us the dead most often in some characteristic occupation of life—a child playing with a hoop, a girl carrying a jar, a warrior proud in his armor, a young woman admiring her jewels, a boy reading a book while his dog lies content but watchful under his chair. Death in these stelae is made natural, and therefore forgivable.

More complex, and supreme in their kind, are the sculptural reliefs of this age. In one of them Orpheus bids a lingering farewell to Eurydice, whom Hermes has reclaimed for the nether world;[22] in another Demeter gives to Triptolemus the golden grain by which he is to establish agriculture in Greece; here some of the coloring still adheres to the stone, and suggests the warmth and brilliance of Greek relief in the Golden Age.[23] Still more beautiful is *The Birth of Aphrodite,* carved on one side of the "Ludovisi Throne"* by an unknown sculptor of presumably Ionian training. Two goddesses are raising Aphrodite from the sea; her thin wet garment clings to her form and reveals it in all the splendor of maturity; the head is semi-Asiatic, but the drapery of the attendant deities, and the soft grace of their pose, bear the stamp of the sensitive Greek eye and hand. On another side of the "throne" a nude girl plays the double flute. On a third side a veiled woman prepares her lamp for the evening; perhaps the face and garments here are even nearer to perfection than on the central piece.

The advance of the fifth-century sculptor upon his forebears is impressive. Frontality is abandoned, foreshortening deepens perspective, stillness gives place to movement, rigidity to life. Indeed, when Greek statuary breaks through the old conventions and shows man in action, it is an artistic revolution; rarely before, in Egypt or the Near East, or in pre-Marathon Greece, has any sculpture in the round been caught in action. These developments owe much to the freshened vitality and buoyancy of Greek life after Salamis, and more to the patient study of motile anatomy by master and apprentice through many generations. "Is it not by modeling your works on living beings," asks Socrates, sculptor and philosopher, "that you make your statues appear alive? . . . And as our different attitudes cause the play of certain muscles of our body, upwards or downwards, so that some are contracted and some stretched, some wrung and some relaxed, is it not by expressing these efforts that you give greater truth and verisimilitude to your works?"[24] The Periclean sculptor is interested in every feature of the

* A block of marble discovered in Rome in 1887 when the Villa Ludovisi was torn down. The original is in the Museo delle Terme in Rome; there is a good copy in the Metropolitan Museum of Art in New York.

body—in the abdomen as much as the face, in the marvelous play of the elastic flesh over the moving framework of the bones, in the swelling of muscles, tendons, and veins, in the endless wonders of the structure and action of hands and ears and feet; and he is fascinated by the difficulty of molding the extremities. He does not often use models to pose for him in a studio; for the most part he is content to watch the men stripped and active in the palaestra or on the athletic field, and the women solemnly marching in the religious processions, or naturally absorbed in their domestic tasks. It is for this reason, and not through modesty, that he centers his studies of anatomy upon the male, and in his portraits of women substitutes the refinements of drapery for anatomical detail—though he makes the drapery as transparent as he dares. Tired of the stiff skirts of Egypt and archaic Greece he loves to show feminine robes agitated by a breeze, for here again he catches the quality of motion and life.

He uses almost any workable material that comes to his hand—wood, ivory, bone, terra cotta, limestone, marble, silver, gold; sometimes, as in the chryselephantine statues of Pheidias, he uses gold on the raiment and ivory for the flesh. In the Peloponnesus bronze is the sculptor's favorite material, for he admires its dark tints as well adapted to represent the bodies of men tanned by nudity under the sun; and—not knowing the rapacity of man—he dreams that it is more durable than stone. In Ionia and Attica he prefers marble; its difficulty stimulates him, its firmness lets him chisel it safely, its translucent smoothness seems designed to convey the rosy color and delicate texture of a woman's skin. Near Athens the sculptor discovers the marble of Mt. Pentelicus, and observes how its iron content mellows with time and weather into a vein of gold glowing through the stone; and with the obstinate patience that is half of genius he slowly carves the quarries into living statuary. When he works in bronze the fifth-century sculptor uses the method of hollow casting by the process of *cire perdu*, or lost wax: i.e., he makes a model in plaster or clay, overlaps it with a thin coat of wax, covers it all with a mold of plaster or clay perforated at many points, and places the figure in a furnace whose heat melts the wax, which runs out through the holes; then he pours molten bronze into the mold at the top till the metal fills all the space before occupied by the wax; he cools the figure, removes the outer mold, and files and polishes, lacquers or paints or gilds, the bronze into the final form. If he prefers marble he begins with the unshaped block, unaided by any system of pointing;* he works freehand, and

* A method of indicating the depth to which, at various points, a block of sculptural material is to be cut by a carver before the artist takes it in hand. This process came into use in Hellenistic Greece.[25]

for the most part guides himself by the eye instead of by instruments;[26] blow by blow he removes the superfluous until the perfection that he has conceived takes shape in the stone, and, in Aristotle's phrase, matter becomes form.

His subjects range from gods to animals, but they must all be physically admirable; he has no use for weaklings, for intellectuals, for abnormal types, or for old women or men. He does well with the horse, but indifferently with other animals. He does better with women, and some of his anonymous masterpieces, like the meditative young lady holding her robe on her breast in the Athens Museum, achieve a quiet loveliness that does not lend itself to words. He is at his best with athletes, for these he admires without stint, and can observe without hindrance; now and then he exaggerates their prowess, and crosses their abdomens with incredible muscles; but despite this fault he can cast bronzes like that found in the sea near Anticythera, and alternatively named an *Ephebos*, or a *Perseus* whose hand once held Medusa's snake-haired head. Sometimes he catches a youth or a girl absorbed in some simple and spontaneous action, like the boy drawing a thorn from his foot.* But his country's mythology is still the leading inspiration of his art. That terrible conflict between philosophy and religion which runs through the thought of the fifth century does not show yet on the monuments; here the gods are still supreme; and if they are dying they are nobly transmuted into the poetry of art. Does the sculptor who shapes in bronze the powerful *Zeus* of Artemisium† really believe that he is modeling the Law of the World? Does the artist who carves the gentle and sorrowful *Dionysus* of the Delphi Museum know, in the depths of his inarticulate understanding, that Dionysus has been shot down by the arrows of philosophy, and that the traditional features of Dionysus' successor, Christ, are already previsioned in this head?

2. *Schools*

If Greek sculpture achieved so much in the fifth century, it was in part because each sculptor belonged to a school, and had his place in a long lineage of masters and pupils carrying on the skills of their art, checking the extravagances of independent individualities, encouraging their specific abilities, disciplining them with a sturdy grounding in the technology and achievements of the past, and forming them, through this interplay of talent

* In the Capitoline Museum, Rome; probably a copy of a fifth-century Greek original.
† In the Athens Museum; reproduced in the Metropolitan Museum of Art.

and law, into a greater art than often comes to genius isolated and unruled. Great artists are more frequently the culmination of a tradition than its overthrow; and though rebels are the necessary variants in the natural history of art, it is only when their new line has been steadied with heredity and chastened with time that it generates supreme personalities.

Five schools performed this function in Periclean Greece: those of Rhegium, Sicyon, Argos, Aegina, and Attica. About 496 another Pythagoras of Samos settled at Rhegium, cast a *Philoctetes* that won him Mediterranean fame, and put into the faces of his statues such signs of passion, pain, and age as shocked all Greek sculptors till those of the Hellenistic period decided to imitate him. At Sicyon Canachus and his brother Aristocles carried on the work begun a century earlier by Dipoenus and Scyllis of Crete. Callon and Onatas brought distinction to Aegina by their skill with bronze; perhaps it was they who made the Aegina pediments. At Argos Ageladas organized the transmission of sculptural technique in a school that reached its apex in Polycleitus.

Coming from Sicyon, Polycleitus made himself popular in Argos by designing for its temple of Hera, about 422, a gold and ivory statue of the matron goddess, which the age ranked second only to the chryselephantine immensities of Pheidias.* At Ephesus he joined in a competition with Pheidias, Cresilas, and Phradmon to make an *Amazon* for the temple of Artemis; the four artists were made judges of the result; each, the story goes, named his own work best, Polycleitus' second best; and the prize was given to the Sicyonian.†[27] But Polycleitus loved athletes more than women or gods. In the famous *Diadumenos* (of which the best surviving copy is in the Athens Museum) he chose for representation that moment in which the victor binds about his head the fillet over which the judges are to place the laurel wreath. The chest and abdomen are too muscular for belief, but the body is vividly posed upon one foot, and the features are a definition of classic regularity. Regularity was the fetish of Polycleitus; it was his life aim to find and establish a canon or rule for the correct proportion of every part in a statue; he was the Pythagoras of sculpture, seeking a divine mathematics of symmetry and form. The dimensions of any part of a perfect body, he thought, should bear a given ratio to the dimensions of any one part, say the index finger. The Polycleitan canon called for a round head, broad shoulders, stocky torso, wide hips, and short legs, making all in all a

---

* We have perhaps an echo of its majesty in the noble head of Juno in the British Museum, reputed to be a copy from Polycleitus.

† Perhaps an *Amazon* in the Vatican is a Roman copy of this work.

figure rather of strength than of grace. The sculptor was so fond of his canon that he wrote a treatise to expound it, and molded a statue to illustrate it. Probably this was the *Doryphoros*, or *Spear Bearer*, of which the Naples Museum has a Roman copy; here again is the brachycephalic head, the powerful shoulders, the short trunk, the corrugated musculature overflowing the groin. Lovelier is the *Westmacott Ephebos* of the British Museum, where the lad has feelings as well as muscles, and seems lost in a gentle meditation on something else than his own strength. Through these figures the canon of Polycleitus became for a time a law to the sculptors of the Peloponnesus; it influenced even Pheidias, and ruled till Praxiteles overthrew it with that rival canon of tall, slim elegance which survived through Rome into the statuary of Christian Europe.

Myron mediated between the Peloponnesian and the Attic schools. Born at Eleutherae, living at Athens, and (says Pliny[28]) studying for a while with Ageladas, he learned to unite Peloponnesian masculinity with Ionian grace. What he added to all the schools was motion: he saw the athlete not, like Polycleitus, before or after the contest, but in it; and realized his vision so well in bronze that no other sculptor in history has rivaled him in portraying the male body in action. About 470 he cast the most famous of athletic statues—the *Discobolos* or *Discus Thrower*.* The wonder of the male frame is here complete: the body carefully studied in all those movements of muscle, tendon, and bone that are involved in the action; the legs and arms and trunk bent to give the fullest force to the throw; the face not distorted with effort, but calm in the confidence of ability; the head not heavy or brutal, but that of a man of blood and refinement, who could write books if he would condescend. This chef-d'oeuvre was only one of Myron's achievements; his contemporaries valued it, but ranked even more highly his *Athena and Marsyas*† and his *Ladas*. Athena here is too lovely for the purpose; no one could guess that this demure virgin is watching with calm content the flaying of the defeated flutist. Myron's Marsyas is George Bernard Shaw caught in an unseemly but eloquent pose; he has played for the last time, and is about to die; but he will not die without a speech. Ladas was an athlete who succumbed to the exhaustion of victory; Myron portrayed him so realistically that an old Greek, seeing the statue, cried out: "Like as thou wert in life, O Ladas, breathing forth thy panting soul, such

---

* The Museo delle Terme has the torso of a fine marble copy by a Roman artist. The Munich Antiquarium has a late copy in bronze; the Metropolitan Museum of Art has a copy uniting the Vatican torso with the head from the Palazzo Lancelotti.

† There is a good copy of the Lateran copy in the Metropolitan Museum of Art.

hath Myron wrought thee in bronze, stamping on all thy body thine eagerness for the victor's crown." And of Myron's *Heifer* the Greeks said that it could do everything but moo.[29]

The Attic or Athenian school added to the Peloponnesians and to Myron what woman gives to man—beauty, tenderness, delicacy, and grace; and because in doing this it still retained a masculine element of strength, it reached a height that sculpture may never attain again. Calamis was still a little archaic, and Nesiotes and Critius, in casting a second group of *Tyrannicides*, did not free themselves from the rigid simplicity of the sixth century; Lucian warns orators not to behave like such lifeless figures. But when, about 423, Paeonius of Thracian Mende, after studying sculpture at Athens, made for the Messenians a *Nike*, or *Victory*, he touched heights of grace and loveliness that no Greek would reach again until Praxiteles; and not even Praxiteles would surpass the flow of this drapery, or the ecstasy of this motion.*

3. Pheidias

From 447 to 438 Pheidias and his aides were absorbed in carving the statues and reliefs of the Parthenon. As Plato was first a dramatist and then became a dramatic philosopher, so Pheidias was first a painter and then became a pictorial sculptor. He was the son of a painter, and studied for a while under Polygnotus; from him, presumably, he learned design and composition, and the grouping of figures for a total effect; from him, it may be, he acquired that "grand style" which made him the greatest sculptor in Greece. But painting did not satisfy him; he needed more dimensions. He took up sculpture, and perhaps studied the bronze technique of Ageladas. Patiently he made himself master of every branch of his art.

He was already an old man when, about 438, he formed his *Athene Parthenos*, for he depicted himself on its shield as aged and bald, and not unacquainted with grief. No one expected him to carve with his own hands the hundreds of figures that filled the metopes, frieze, and pediments of the Parthenon; it was enough that he superintended all Periclean building, and designed the sculptural ornament; he left it to his pupils, above all to Alcamenes, to execute the plans. He himself, however, made three statues

* The *Nike* was pieced together from fragments unearthed by the Germans at Olympia in 1890, and is now in the Olympia Museum.—Almost as beautiful are the *Nereids*, or *Sea Maidens*, which were found headless among the ruins of a monument in Lycian Xanthus, and are now in the British Museum. The Greek spirit had penetrated even into non-Greek Asia.

of the city's goddess for the Acropolis. One was commissioned by Athenian colonists in Lemnos; it was of bronze, a little larger than life, and so delicately molded that Greek critics considered this *Lemnian Athena* the most beautiful of Pheidias' works.*[30] Another was the *Athene Promachos*, a colossal bronze representation of the goddess as the warlike defender of her city; it stood between the Propylaea and the Erechtheum, rose with its pedestal to a height of seventy feet, and served as a beacon to mariners and a warning to enemies.† The most famous of the three, the *Athene Parthenos*, stood thirty-eight feet high in the interior of the Parthenon, as the virgin goddess of wisdom and chastity. For this culminating figure Pheidias wished to use marble, but the people would having nothing less than ivory and gold. The artist used ivory for the visible body, and forty-four talents (2545 lbs.) of gold for the robe;[32] furthermore, he adorned it with precious metals, and elaborate reliefs on the helmet, the sandals, and the shield. It was so placed that on Athena's feast day the sun would shine through the great doors of the temple directly upon the brilliant drapery and pallid face of the Virgin.‡

The completion of the work brought no happiness to Pheidias, for some of the gold and ivory assigned to him for the statue disappeared from his studio and could not be accounted for. The foes of Pericles did not overlook this opportunity. They charged Pheidias with theft, and convicted him.§ But the people of Olympia interceded for him, and paid his bail of forty (?) talents, on condition that he come to Olympia and make a chryselephantine statue for the temple of Zeus;[34] they were glad to trust him with more ivory and gold. A special workshop was built for him and his assistants near the temple precincts, and his brother Panaenus was commissioned to decorate the throne of the statue and the walls of the temple with paintings.[35] Pheidias was enamored of size, and made his seated *Zeus* sixty feet high, so that when it was placed within the temple critics complained that the god would break through the roof if he should take it into his head to stand up. On the "dark brows" and "ambrosial locks"[36] of the Thunderer, Pheidias placed a crown of gold in the form of olive branches and leaves; in

---

* No authentic copy remains.

† It was carried off to Constantinople about A.D. 330, and appears to have been destroyed in a riot there in 1203.[31]

‡ If we may judge from the "Lenormant" and "Varvaka" models of this statue that are preserved in the Athens Museum, we should not have cared much for the *Athene Parthenos*. The first has a stout frame and a swollen face, and the breast of the second is crawling with sacred snakes.

§ Ca. 438. There is much uncertainty about the date, and about the sequence of events in the later years of Pheidias' life.[33]

the right hand he set a small statue of Victory, also in ivory and gold; in the left hand a scepter inlaid with precious stones; on the body a golden robe engraved with flowers; and on the feet sandals of solid gold. The throne was of gold, ebony, and ivory; at its base were smaller statues of Victory, Apollo, Artemis, Niobe, and Theban lads kidnaped by the Sphinx.[37] The final result was so impressive that legend grew around it: when Pheidias had finished, we are told, he begged for a sign from heaven in approval; whereupon a bolt of lightning struck the pavement near the statue's base—a sign which, like most celestial messages, admitted of diverse interpretations.* The work was listed among the Seven Wonders of the World, and all who could afford it made a pilgrimage to see the incarnate god. Aemilius Paullus, the Roman who conquered Greece, was struck with awe on seeing the colossus; his expectations, he confessed, had been exceeded by the reality.[38] Dio Chrysostom called it the most beautiful image on earth, and added, as Beethoven was to say of Beethoven's music: "If one who is heavy-laden in mind, who has drained the cup of misfortune and sorrow in life, and whom sweet sleep visits no more, were to stand before this image, he would forget all the griefs and troubles that befall the life of man."[39] "The beauty of the statue," said Quintilian, "even made some addition to the received religion; the majesty of the work was equal to the god."[40]

Of Pheidias' last years there is no unchallenged account. One story pictures him as returning to Athens and dying in jail;[41] another lets him stay in Elis, only to have Elis put him to death in 432;[42] there is not much to choose between these denouements. His pupils carried on his work, and attested his success as a teacher by almost equaling him. Agoracritus, his favorite, carved a famous *Nemesis;* Alcamenes made an *Aphrodite of the Gardens* which Lucian ranked with the highest masterpieces of statuary.†[43] The school of Pheidias came to an end with the fifth century, but it left Greek sculpture considerably further advanced than it had found it. Through Pheidias and his followers the art had neared perfection at the very moment when the Peloponnesian War began the ruin of Athens. Technique had been mastered, anatomy was understood, life and movement and grace had been poured into bronze and stone. But the characteristic achievement of Pheidias was the attainment and definitive expression of the *classic* style, the "grand style" of Winckelmann: strength reconciled with beauty, feeling with restraint, motion with repose, flesh and bone with mind and soul. Here, after five centuries of effort, the famed "serenity" so imaginatively

* Nothing remains of this *Zeus* but fragments of the pedestal.

† A *Draped Venus* in the Louvre may be a copy of this statue.

ascribed to the Greeks was at least conceived; and the passionate and turbulent Athenians, contemplating the figures of Pheidias, might see how nearly, if only in creative sculptury, men for a moment had been like gods.

IV. THE BUILDERS

1. The Progress of Architecture

During the fifth century the Doric order consolidated its conquest of Greece. Among all the Greek temples built in this prosperous age only a few Ionic shrines survive, chiefly the Erechtheum and the temple of Nike Apteros on the Acropolis. Attica remained faithful to Doric, yielding to the Ionic order only so far as to use it for the inner columns of the Propylaea, and to place a frieze around the Theseum and the Parthenon; perhaps a tendency to make the Doric column longer and slenderer reveals a further influence of the Ionic style. In Asia Minor the Greeks imbibed the Oriental love of delicate ornament, and expressed it in the complex elaboration of the Ionic entablature, and the creation of a new and more ornate order, the Corinthian. About 430 (as Vitruvius tells the tale) an Ionian sculptor, Callimachus, was struck by the sight of a basket of votive offerings, covered with a tile, which a nurse had left upon the tomb of her mistress; a wild acanthus had grown around the basket and the tile; and the sculptor, pleased with the natural form so suggested, modified the Ionic capitals of a temple that he was building at Corinth, by mingling acanthus leaves with the volutes.[44] Probably the story is a myth, and the nurse's basket had less influence than the palm and papyrus capitals of Egypt in generating the Corinthian style. The new order made little headway in classic Greece; Ictinus used it for one isolated column in the court of an Ionic temple at Phigalea, and towards the end of the fourth century it was used for the choragic monument of Lysicrates. Only under the elegant Romans of the Empire did this delicate style reach its full development.

All the Greek world was building temples in this period. Cities almost bankrupted themselves in rivalry to have the fairest statuary and the largest shrines. To her massive sixth-century edifices at Samos and Ephesus Ionia added new Ionic temples at Magnesia, Teos, and Priene. At Assus in the Troad Greek colonists raised an almost archaic Doric fane to Athena. At the other end of Hellas Crotona built, about 480, a vast Doric home for Hera; it survived till 1600, when a bishop thought he could make better use of its stones.[45] To the fifth century belong the greatest of the temples at Poseidonia (Paestum), Segesta, Selinus, and Acragas, and the temple of Asclepius at Epidaurus. At Syracuse the columns still stand of a temple raised to Athena by Gelon I, and partly preserved by its transformation into a Christian church. At Bassae, near

Phigalea in the Peloponnesus, Ictinus designed a temple of Apollo strangely different from his other masterpiece, the Parthenon; here the Doric periptery enclosed a space occupied by a small naos and a large open court surrounded by an Ionic colonnade; and around the interior of this court, along the inner face of the Ionic columns, ran a frieze almost as graceful as the Parthenon's, and having the added virtue of being visible.*

At Olympia the Elian architect Libon, a generation before the Parthenon, raised a rival to it in a Doric shrine to Zeus. Six columns stood at each end, thirteen on either side; perhaps too stout for beauty, and unfortunate in their material—a coarse limestone coated with stucco; the roof, however, was of Pentelic tiles. Paeonius and Alcamenes, Pausanias tells us,[46] carved for the pediments powerful figures† portraying on the eastern gable the chariot race between Pelops and Oenomaus, and on the western gable the struggle of Lapiths and centaurs. The Lapiths, in Greek legend, were a mountain tribe of Thessaly. When Pirithous, their king, married Hippodameia, daughter of King Oenomaus of Pisa in Elis, he invited the centaurs to the wedding feast. The centaurs dwelt in the mountains about Pelion; Greek art represented them as half man and half horse, possibly to suggest their untamed woodland nature, or because the centaurs were such excellent horsemen that each man and his mount seemed to be one animal. At the feast these horsemen got drunk, and tried to carry off the Lapith women. The Lapiths fought bravely for their ladies, and won. (Greek art never tired of this story, and perhaps used it to symbolize the clearing of the wilderness from wild beasts, and the struggle between the human and the bestial in man.) The figures on the east pediment are archaically stiff and still; those on the west seem hardly of the same period, for though some of them are crude, and the hair is stylized in ancient fashion, they are alive with action, and show a mature grasp of sculptural grouping. Startlingly beautiful is the bride, a woman of no fragile slenderness, but of a full-bodied loveliness that quite explains the war. A bearded centaur has one arm around her waist, one hand upon her breast; she is about to be snatched from her nuptials, and yet the artist portrays her features in such calm repose that one suspects him of having read Lessing or Winckelmann; or perhaps, like any woman, she is not insensitive to the compliment of desire. Less ambitious and massive, but more delicately finished, are the extant metopes of the temple, recounting certain labors of Heracles; one, wherein Heracles holds up the world for Atlas, stands out as a work of complete mastery. Heracles here is no abnormal giant, rock-ribbed with musculature, but simply a man of full and harmonious development. Before him is Atlas, whose head would adorn the shoulders of Plato. At the left is one of Atlas' daughters, perfect in the natural beauty of healthy

* Thirty-eight of the columns remain, the walls of the naos, and parts of the inner colonnade. Fragments of the frieze are in the British Museum.

† Now in the Olympia Museum.

womanhood; perhaps the artist had some symbolism in mind when he showed her gently helping the strong man to bear the weight of the world. The specialist finds some faults of execution and detail in these half-ruined metopes; but to an amateur observer the bride, and Heracles, and the daughter of Atlas, are as near to perfection as anything in the history of sculptural relief.

2. *The Reconstruction of Athens*

Attica leads all Greece in the abundance and excellence of its fifth-century building. Here the Doric style, which tends elsewhere to a bulging corpulence, takes on Ionian grace and elegance; color is added to line, ornament to symmetry. On a dangerous headland at Sunium those who risked the sea raised to Poseidon a shrine of which eleven columns stand. At Eleusis Ictinus designed a spacious temple to Demeter, and under Pericles' persuasion Athens contributed funds to make this edifice worthy of the Eleusinian festival. At Athens the proximity of good marble on Mt. Pentelicus and in Paros encouraged the artist with the finest of building materials. Seldom, until our periods of economic breakdown, has a democracy been able or willing to spend so lavishly on public construction. The Parthenon cost seven hundred talents ($4,200,000); the *Athene Parthenos* (which, however, was a gold reserve as well as a statue) cost $6,000,000; the unfinished Propylaea, $2,400,000; minor Periclean structures at Athens and the Piraeus, $18,000,000; sculpture and other decoration, $16,200,000; altogether, in the sixteen years from 447 to 431, the city of Athens voted $57,600,000 for public buildings, statuary, and painting.[47] The spread of this sum among artisans and artists, executives and slaves, had much to do with the prosperity of Athens under Pericles.

Imagination can picture vaguely the background of this courageous adventure in art. The Athenians, on their return from Salamis, found their city almost wholly devastated by the Persian occupation; every edifice of any value had been burned to the ground. Such a calamity when it does not destroy the citizens as well as the city, makes them stronger; the "act of God" clears away many eyesores and unfit habitations; chance accomplishes what human obstinacy would never allow; and if food can be found through the crisis, the labor and genius of men create a finer city than before. The Athenians, even after the war with Persia, were rich in both labor and genius, and the spirit of victory doubled their will for great enterprise. In a generation Athens was rebuilt; a new council chamber rose, a new prytaneum, new homes, new porticoes, new walls of defense, new wharves and warehouses at a new port. About 446 Hippodamus of Miletus, chief town-planner of antiquity, laid out a new Piraeus, and set a new style, by replacing the old chaos of haphazard and winding alleys with broad, straight streets crossing at right angles. On an elevation a mile northwest of the Acropolis unknown artists raised that smaller Parthenon known as the Theseum, or temple of Theseus.* Sculptors filled the pediments with statuary and the metopes with reliefs, and ran a frieze above the inner columns at both ends. Painters colored the moldings, the triglyphs, metopes, and frieze, and made bright murals for an interior dimly lit by light shining through marble tiles.†

The finest work of Pericles' builders was reserved for the Acropolis, the ancient seat of the city's government and faith. Themistocles began its reconstruction, and planned a temple one hundred feet long, known therefore as the Hecatompedon. After his fall the work was abandoned; the oligarchic party opposed it on the ground that any dwelling for Athena, if it was not to bring bad luck to Athens, must be built upon the site of the old temple of Athene Polias (i.e., Athena of the City), which the Persians had destroyed. Pericles, caring nothing about superstitions, adopted the site of the Hecatompedon for the Parthenon, and, though the priests protested to the end, went on with his plans. On the southwestern slope of the Acropolis his artists erected an Odeum, or Music Hall, unique in Athens for its cone-shaped dome. It offered a handle to conservative satirists, who thenceforth referred to Pericles' conical head as his *odeion*, or hall of song. The Odeum was built for the most part of wood, and soon succumbed to time. In this auditorium musical performances were presented, and the Dionysian dramas were rehearsed; and there, annually, were held the contests instituted by Pericles in vocal and instrumental music. The versatile statesman himself often acted as a judge in these competitions.

The road to the summit, in classical days, was devious and gradual, and was flanked with statues and votive offerings. Near the top was a majestically broad flight of marble steps, buttressed with bastions on either side.

* The name is a mistake, since this temple, erected in 425, could not have been the Theseum to which, in 469, Cimon brought the supposed bones of Theseus; but time sanctifies error as well as theft, and the traditional name is commonly retained for lack of a certain designation.

† The Theseum is the best preserved of all ancient Greek buildings; even so it lacks its marble tiles, its murals, its interior statuary, its pedimental sculptures, and nearly all of its external coloring. The metopes are so badly damaged that their reliefs are almost undistinguishable.

On the south bastion Callicrates raised a miniature Ionic temple to Athena as Nike Apteros, or the Wingless Victory.* Elegant reliefs (partly preserved in the Athens Museum) adorned the external balustrade with figures of winged Victories bringing to Athens their far-gathered spoils. These *Nikai* are in the noblest style of Pheidias, less vigorous than the massive goddesses of the Parthenon, but even more graceful in motion, and more delicate and natural in their protrayal of drapery. The *Victory* tying her sandals deserves her name, for she is one of the triumphs of Greek art.

At the top of the Acropolis steps Mnesicles built, in elaboration of Mycenaean pylons, an entrance with five openings, before each of which stood a Doric portico; these colonnades in time gave to the whole edifice their name of Propylaea, or Before the Gates. Each portico carried a frieze of triglyphs and metopes, and was crowned with a pediment. Within the passageway was an Ionic colonnade, boldly inserted within a Doric form. The interior of the northern wing was decorated with paintings by Polygnotus and others, and contained votive tablets (*pinakes*) of terra cotta or marble; hence its name of Pinakotheka, or Hall of Tablets. A small south wing remained unfinished; war, or the reaction against Pericles, put a stop to the work, and left an ungainly mass of beautiful parts as a gateway to the Parthenon.

Within these gates, on the left, was the strangely Oriental Erechtheum. This, too, was overtaken by war: not more than half of it was finished when the disaster of Aegospotami reduced Athens to chaos and poverty. It was begun after Pericles' death, under the prodding of conservatives who feared that the ancient heroes Erechtheus and Cecrops, as well as the Athena of the older shrine, and the sacred snakes that haunted the spot, would punish Athens for building the Parthenon on another site. The varied purposes of the structure determined its design, and destroyed its unity. One wing was dedicated to Athene Polias, and housed her ancient image; another was devoted to Erechtheus and Poseidon. The naos or cella, instead of being enclosed by a unifying peristyle, was here buttressed with three separate porticoes. The northern and eastern porches were upheld by slender Ionic

* Statues of Nike, or Victory, were often made without wings, so that she might not be able to abandon the city. The temple was pulled down by the Turks in A.D. 1687 to make a fortress. Lord Elgin rescued some slabs of the frieze and sent them to the British Museum. In 1835 the stones of the temple were put together again; the restored building was replaced on the original site, and terra-cotta casts were substituted for the missing parts of the badly damaged frieze.

columns as beautiful as any of their kind.* In the northern porch was a perfect portal, adorned with a molding of marble flowers. In the cella was the primitive wooden statue of Athena, which the pious believed had fallen from heaven; there, too, was the great lamp whose fire was never extinguished, and which Callimachus, the Cellini of his time, had fashioned of gold and embellished with acanthus leaves, like his Corinthian capitals. The south portico was the famous Porch of the Maidens, or Caryatids.† These patient women were descended, presumably, from the basket bearers of the Orient; and an early caryatid at Tralles, in Asia Minor, betrays the Eastern—probably the Assyrian—origin of the form. The drapery is superb, and the natural flexure of the knee gives an impression of ease; but even these substantial ladies seem hardly strong enough to convey that sense of sturdy and reliable support which the finest architecture gives. It was an aberration of taste that Pheidias would probably have forbidden.

3. The Parthenon

In 447 Ictinus, aided by Callicrates, and under the general supervision of Pheidias and Pericles, began to build a new temple for Athene Parthenos. In the western end of the structure he placed a room for her maiden priestesses, and called it the room "of the virgins"—*ton parthenon;* and in the course of careless time this name of a part, by a kind of architectural metaphor, was applied to the whole. Ictinus chose as his material the white marble of Mt. Pentelicus, veined with iron grains. No mortar was used; the blocks were so accurately squared and so finely finished that each stone grasped the next as if the two were one. The column drums were bored to let a small cylinder of olivewood connect them, and permit each drum to be turned around and around upon the one below it until the meeting surfaces were ground so smooth that the division between drums was almost invisible.[49]

* These columns, rather than those of the Parthenon, set the style for later architecture. The foot of each was modulated into the stylobate by an "Attic base" of three members, articulated by fillets or bands. The top of the column was graduated into the voluted capital by a band of flowers. The entablature had a richly decorated molding, a frieze of black stone, and, under the cornice, a series of reliefs. The egg-and-dart and honeysuckle ornament of the molding was as carefully carved as the sculpture; the artists were paid as much for a foot of such molding as for a figure in the frieze.[48]

† This term was applied to the figures by the Roman architect Vitruvius, from the name given to the priestesses of Artemis at Caryae in Laconia. The Athenians called them simply *korai,* or Maidens.

The style was pure Doric, and of classic simplicity. The design was rectangular, for the Greeks did not care for circular or conical forms; hence there were no arches in Greek architecture, though Greek architects must have been familiar with them. The dimensions were modest: 228 x 101 x 65 feet. Probably a system of proportion, like the Polycleitan canon, prevailed in every part of the building, all measurements bearing a given relation to the diameter of the column.[60] At Poseidonia the height of the column was four times its diameter; here it was five; and the new form mediated successfully between Spartan sturdiness and Attic elegance. Each column swelled slightly (three quarters of an inch in diameter) from base to middle, tapered toward the top, and leaned toward the center of its colonnade; each corner column was a trifle thicker than the rest. Every horizontal line of stylobate and entablature was curved upward towards its center, so that the eye placed at one end of any supposedly level line could not see the farther half of the line. The metopes were not quite square, but were designed to appear square from below. All these curvatures were subtle corrections for optical illusions that would otherwise have made stylobate lines seem to sink in the center, columns to diminish upward from the base, and corner columns to be thinner and outwardly inclined. Such adjustments required considerable knowledge of mathematics and optics, and constituted but one of those mechanical features that made the temple a perfect union of science and art. In the Parthenon, as in current physics, every straight line was a curve, and, as in a painting, every part was drawn toward the center in subtle composition. The result was a certain flexibility and grace that seemed to give life and freedom to the stones.

Above the plain architrave ran an alternating series of triglyphs and metopes. In the ninety-two metopes were high reliefs recounting once more the struggle of "civilization" against "savagery" in the wars of Greeks and Trojans, Greeks and Amazons, Lapiths and centaurs, giants and gods. These slabs are clearly the work of many hands and unequal skills; they do not match in excellence the reliefs of the cella frieze, though some of the centaur heads are Rembrandts in stone. In the gable pediments were statuary groups carved in the round and in heroic size. In the east pediment, over the entrance, the spectator was allowed to see the birth of Athena from the head of Zeus. Here was a powerful recumbent "Theseus,"* a giant capable of philosophical meditation and civilized repose; and a fine figure of Iris, the female Hermes, with drapery clinging and yet blown by the wind—for

* The naming of the Parthenon figures is mostly conjectural.

Pheidias considers it an ill wind that does not disturb some robe. Here also was a majestic "Hebe," the goddess of youth, who filled the cups of the Olympians with nectar; and here were three imposing "Fates." In the left corner four horses' heads—eyes flashing, nostrils snorting, mouths foaming with speed—announced the rising of the sun, while in the right corner the moon drove her chariot to her setting; these eight are the finest horses in sculptural history. In the west pediment Athena contested with Poseidon the lordship of Attica. Here again were horses, as if to redeem the forked absurdity of man; and reclining figures that represented, with unrealistic magnificence, Athens' modest streams. Perhaps the male figures are too muscular, and the female too spacious; but seldom has statuary been grouped so naturally, or so skillfully adjusted to the narrowing spaces of a pediment. "All other statues," said Canova, with some hyperbole, "are of stone; these are of flesh and blood."

More attractive, however, are the men and women of the frieze. For 525 feet along the top of the outer wall of the cella, within the portico, ran this most famous of all reliefs. Here, presumably, the youths and maids of Attica are bearing homage and gifts to Athena on the festival day of the Panathenaic games. One part of the procession moves along the west and north sides, another along the south side, to meet on the east front before the goddess, who proudly offers to Zeus and other Olympians the hospitality of her city and a share of her spoils. Handsome knights move in graceful dignity on still handsomer steeds; chariots support dignitaries, while simple folk are happy to join in on foot; pretty girls and quiet old men carry olive branches and trays of cakes; attendants bear on their shoulders jugs of sacred wine; stately women convey to the goddess the peplos that they have woven and embroidered for her in long anticipation of this holy day; sacrificial victims move with bovine patience or angry prescience to their fate; maidens of high degree bring utensils of ritual and sacrifice; and musicians play on their flutes deathless ditties of no tone. Seldom have animals or men been honored with such painstaking art. With but two and a quarter inches of relief the sculptors were able, by shading and modeling, to achieve such an illusion of depth that one horse or horseman seems to be beyond another, though the nearest is raised no farther from the background than the rest.[51] Perhaps it was a mistake to place this extraordinary relief so high that men could not comfortably contemplate it, or exhaust its excellence. Pheidias excused himself, doubtless with a twinkle in his eye, on the ground that the gods could see it; but the gods were dying while he carved.

Beneath the seated deities of the frieze was the entrance to the inner

FIG. 1—*Hygiaea, Goddess of Health*
Athens Museum
(See page 499)

FIG. 2—*The Cup-Bearer*
From the Palace of Minos.
Heracleum Museum
(See page 20)

FIG. 3—*The "Snake Goddess"*
Boston Museum
(See page 17)

FIG. 4—*Wall Fresco and "Throne of Minos"*
Heracleum Museum
(See page 18)

FIG. 5–*A Cup from Vaphio*
Athens Museum
(See page 32)

FIG. 6–*Mask of "Agamemnon"*
Athens Museum
(See page 32)

FIG. 7—*Warrior, from temple of Aphaea at Aegina*
Munich Glyptothek
(See page 95)

FIG. 8—*Theater of Epidaurus*

(See page 96)

FIG. 9—*Temple of Poseidon*
Paestum
(See page 109)

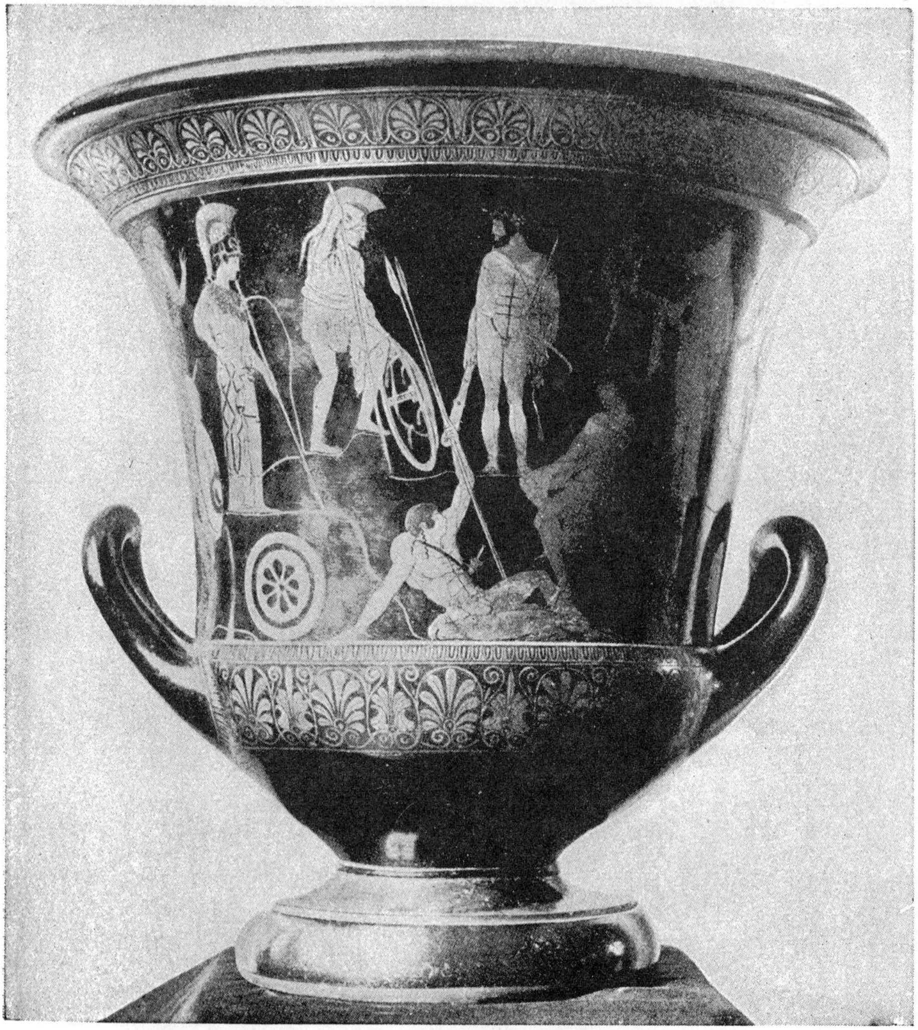

Fig. 10—*A Krater Vase, With Athena and Heracles*
Louvre, Paris
(See page 220)

FIG. 11—*The Portland Vase*
British Museum
(See page 616)

FIG. 12—*The François Vase*
Archeological Museum, Florence
(See page 219)

FIG. 13–*A Kore, or Maiden*
Acropolis Museum, Athens
(See page 222)

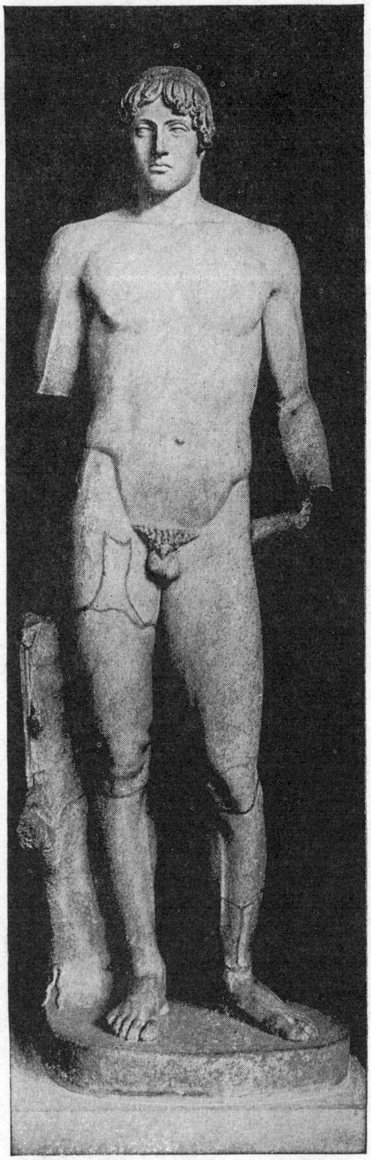

FIG. 14–*The "Choiseul-Gouffier Apollo"*
Acropolis Museum, Athens
(See page 222)

FIG. 15—*Pericles*
British Museum
(See page 248)

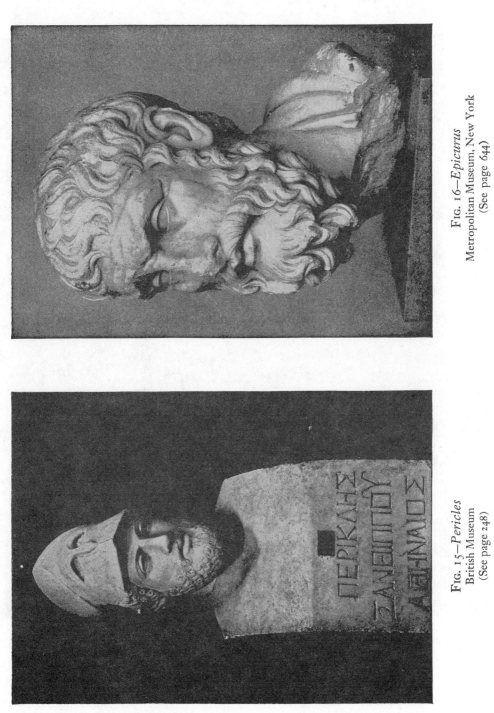

FIG. 16—*Epicurus*
Metropolitan Museum, New York
(See page 644)

FIG. 17—*Orpheus, Eurydice, and Hermes*
Naples Museum
(See page 319)

FIG. 18—"*Birth of Aphrodite*"
From the "Ludovisi Throne." Museo delle Terme, Rome
(See page 319)

FIG. 19—"*Ludovisi Throne,*" *Right Base*
Museo delle Terme, Rome
(See page 319)

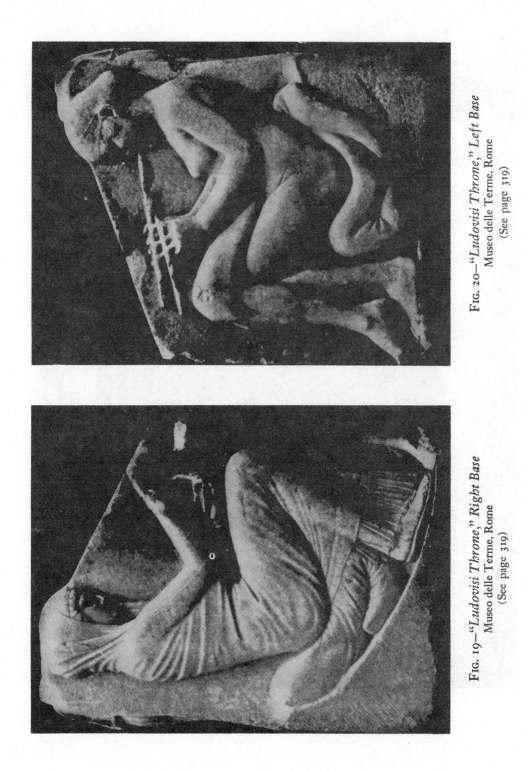

FIG. 20—"*Ludovisi Throne,*" *Left Base*
Museo delle Terme, Rome
(See page 319)

FIG. 21—*The Diadumenos.*
Roman copy, after Polycleitus (?)
Athens Museum
(See page 322)

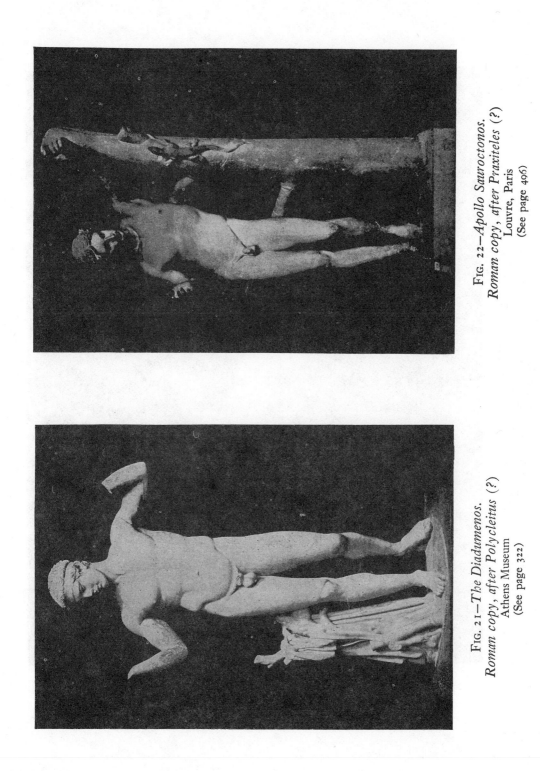

FIG. 22—*Apollo Sauroctonos.*
Roman copy, after Praxiteles (?)
Louvre, Paris
(See page 496)

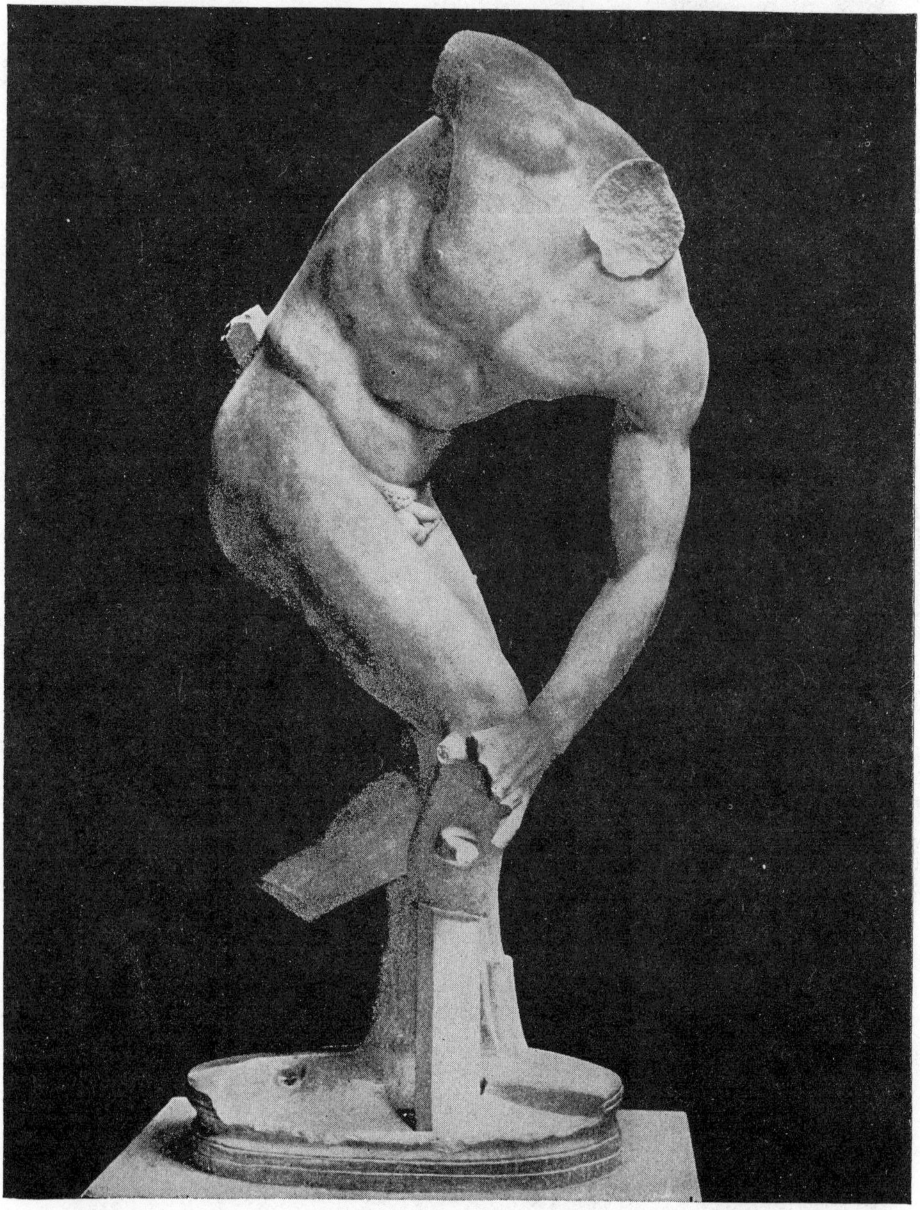

FIG. 23—*The Discus Thrower. Roman copy, after Myron (?)*
Museo delle Terme, Rome
(See page 323)

FIG. 24—*The "Dreaming Athena"*
An anonymous relief, probably of the fifth century.
Acropolis Museum, Athens
(See page 319)

Fig. 25—*The Rape of the Lapith Bride*
From the west pediment of the temple of Zeus. Olympia Museum
(See page 328)

FIG. 26—*Stela of Damasistrate*
Athens Museum
(See page 318)

FIG. 27—*Heracles and Atlas*
Metope from the temple of Zeus. Olympia Museum
(See page 328)

Fig. 28—*Nike Fixing Her Sandal*
From the temple of Nike Apteros. Acropolis Museum, Athens
(See page 331)

Fig. 29—*Propylaea and temple of Nike Apteros*

(See page 331)

Fig. 30—*The Charioteer of Delphi*
Delphi Museum
(See page 221)

Fig. 31—*A Caryatid from the Erechtheum*
British Museum
(See page 332)

FIG. 32—*The Parthenon*

(See page 332)

FIG. 33—*Goddesses and "Iris"*
East pediment of the Parthenon. British Museum
(See page 333)

FIG. 34—"*Cecrops and Daughter*"
West pediment of the Parthenon. British Museum
(See page 334)

Fig. 35—*Horsemen, from the West Frieze of the Parthenon*
British Museum
(See page 334)

FIG. 36—*Sophocles*
Lateran Museum, Rome
(See page 391)

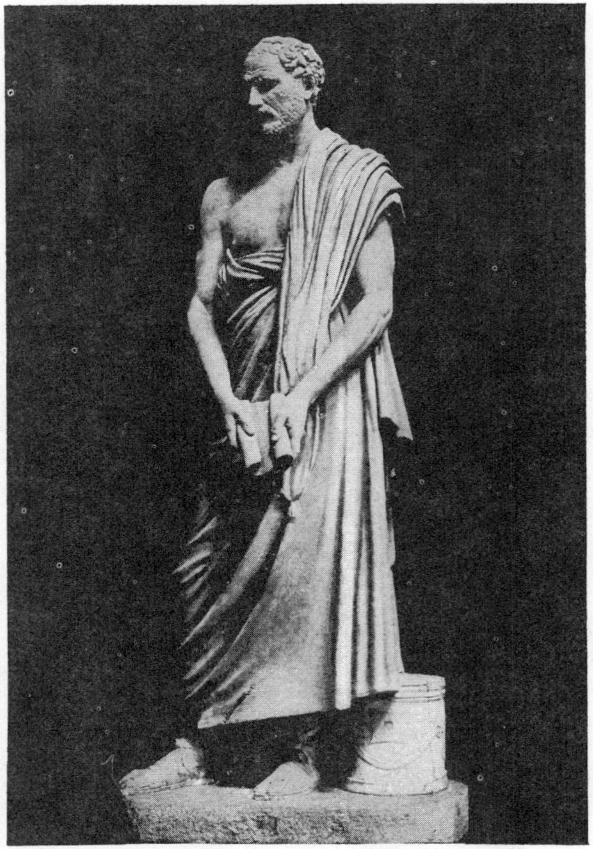

FIG. 37—*Demosthenes*
Vatican, Rome
(See page 478)

FIG. 38—*A Tanagra Statuette*
Metropolitan Museum, New York
(See page 492)

FIG. 39—*The Mausoleum of Halicarnassus*

A reconstruction. After Adler

(See page 494)

FIG. 40—*Relief from the Mausoleum of Halicarnassus*
British Museum
(See page 494)

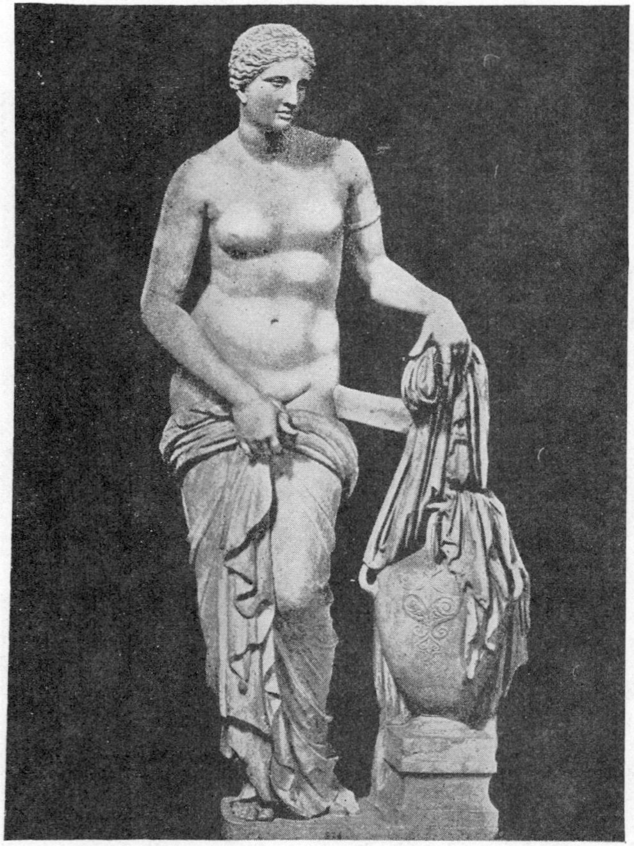

Fig. 41—*The "Aphrodite of Cnidus"*
Vatican, Rome
(See page 495)

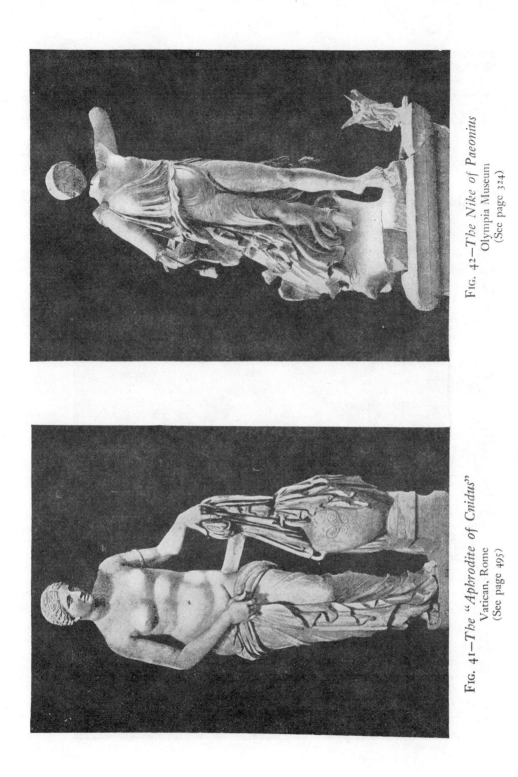

Fig. 42—*The Nike of Paeonius*
Olympia Museum
(See page 324)

FIG. 43—*The Hermes of Praxiteles*
Olympia Museum
(See page 496)

Fig. 44—*Head of Praxiteles' Hermes*
Olympia Museum
(See page 496)

Fig. 45—*The Doryphoros of Polycleitus. As reproduced by Apollonius*
Naples Museum
(See page 323)

Fig. 46—*Head of Meleager. Roman copy, after Scopas (?)*
Villa Medici, Rome
(See page 497)

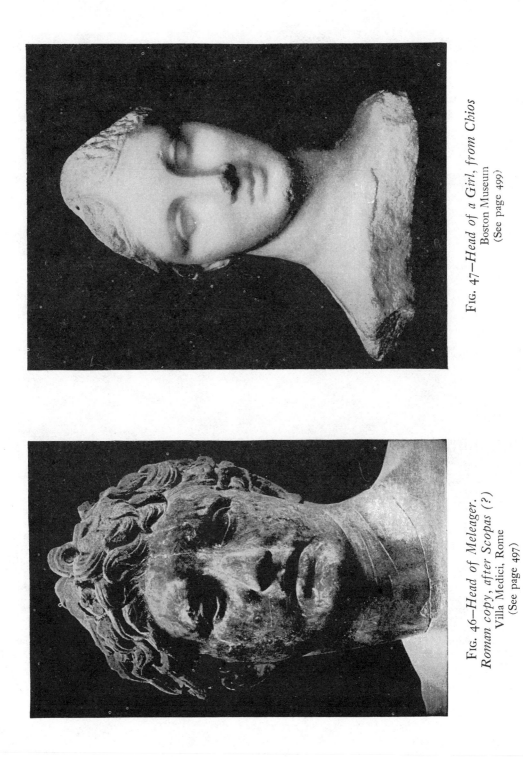

Fig. 47—*Head of a Girl, from Chios*
Boston Museum
(See page 499)

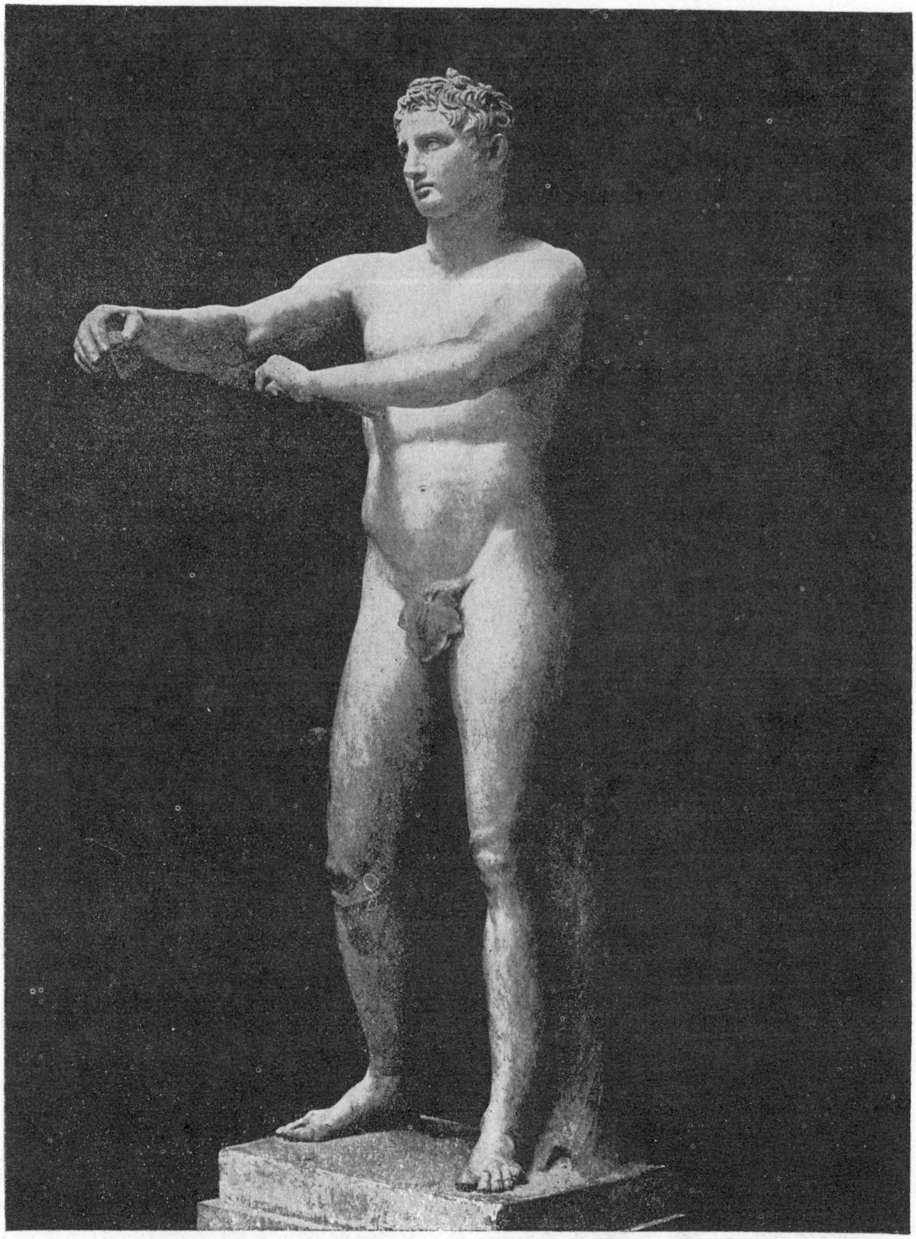

FIG. 48—*The Apoxyomenos. A Roman copy, after Lysippus (?)*
Vatican, Rome
(See page 498)

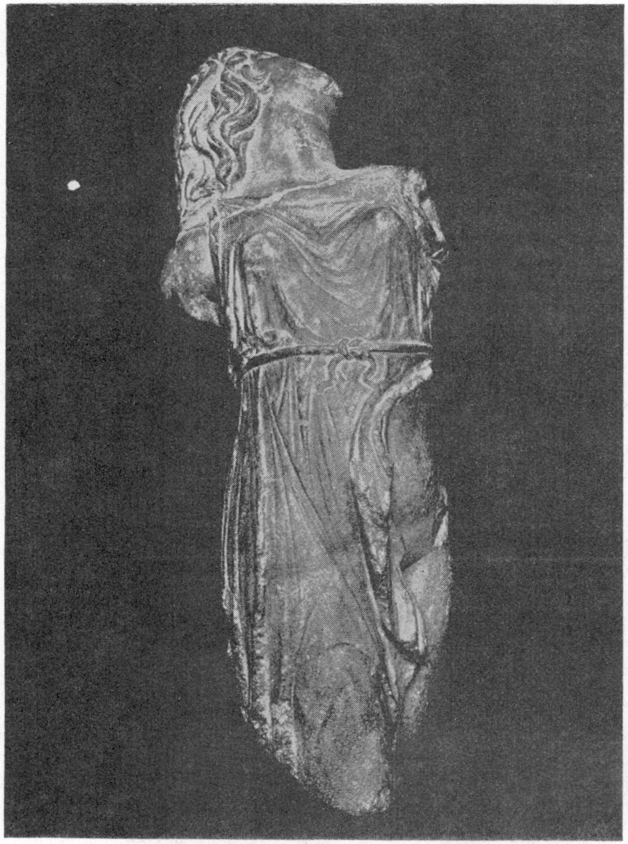

Fig. 49—*The Raging (or Dancing) Maenad*
Roman copy, after Scopas (?)
Dresden Albertinum
(See page 498)

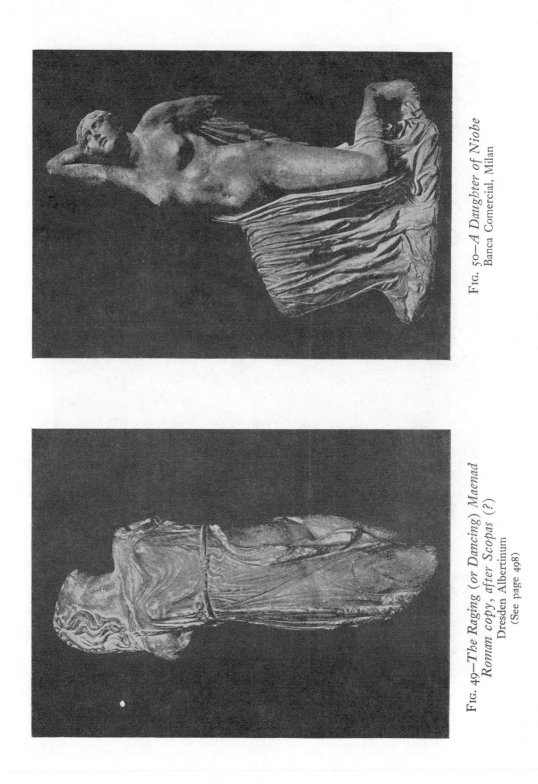

Fig. 50—*A Daughter of Niobe*
Banca Comercial, Milan

FIG. 51—*The Aphrodite of Cyrene*
Museo delle Terme. Rome

FIG. 52—*The Demeter of Cnidus*
British Museum
(See page 499)

FIG. 53—*Altar of Zeus at Pergamum*
A reconstruction. State Museum, Berlin
(See page 618)

Fig. 54—*Frieze from the Altar of Zeus at Pergamum*
State Museum, Berlin
(See page 623)

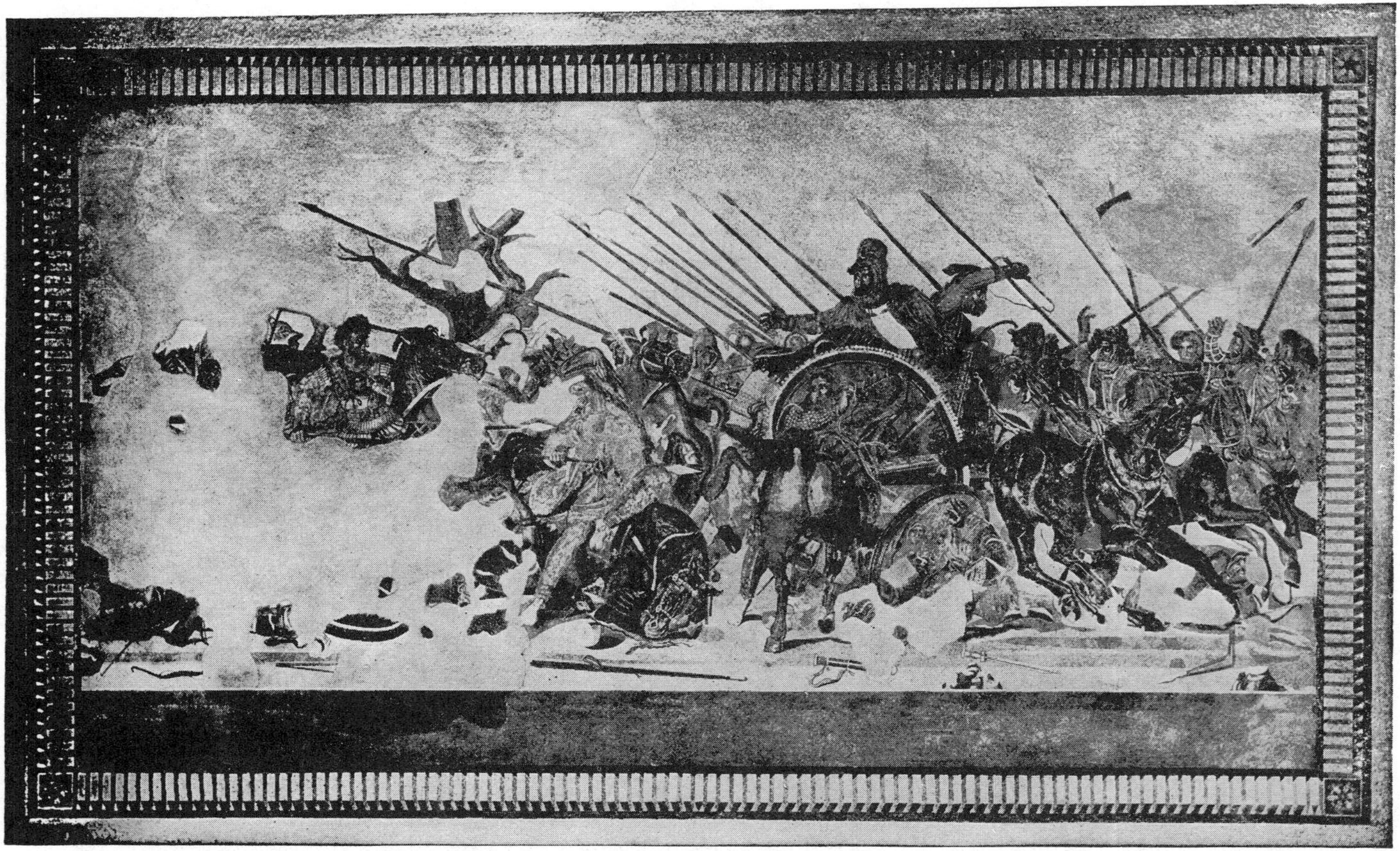

FIG. 55—*The Battle of Issus. Mosaic found at Pompeii*
Naples Museum
(See page 620)

FIG. 56—*The Laocoön*
Vatican, Rome
(See page 622)

FIG. 57—*The Farnese Bull*
Naples Museum
(See page 623)

FIG. 58—*The "Alexander" Sarcophagus*
Constantinople Museum
(See page 623)

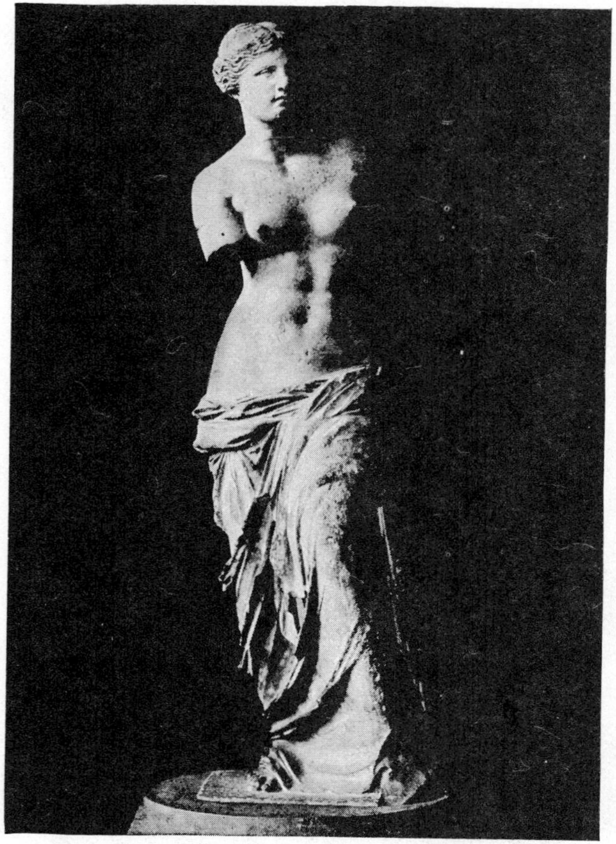

Fig. 59—*The Aphrodite of Melos*
Louvre, Paris
(See page 624)

Fig. 60—*The Venus de' Medici*
Uffizi Gallery, Florence
(See page 624)

Fig. 61—*The "Victory of Samothrace"*
Louvre, Paris
(See page 624)

FIG. 62—*Hellenistic Portrait Head*
Naples Museum

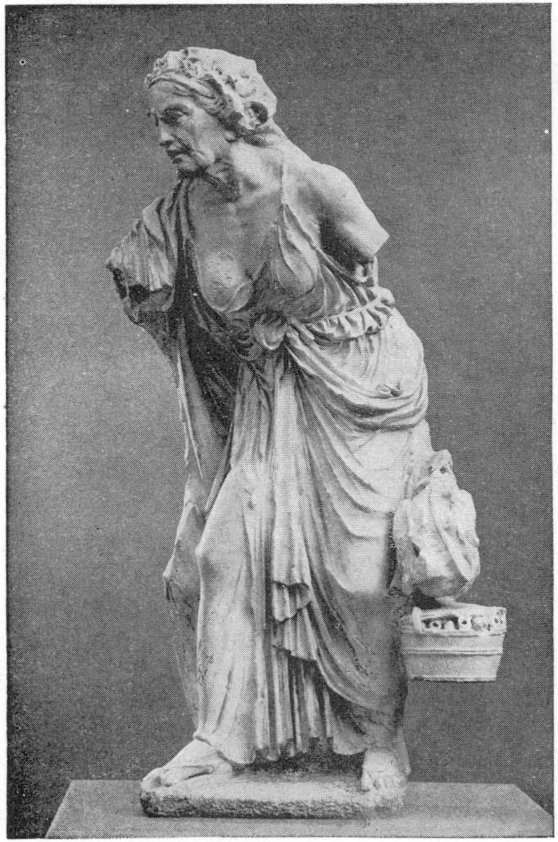

FIG. 63—*The "Old Market Woman"*
Metropolitan Museum, New York
(See page 626)

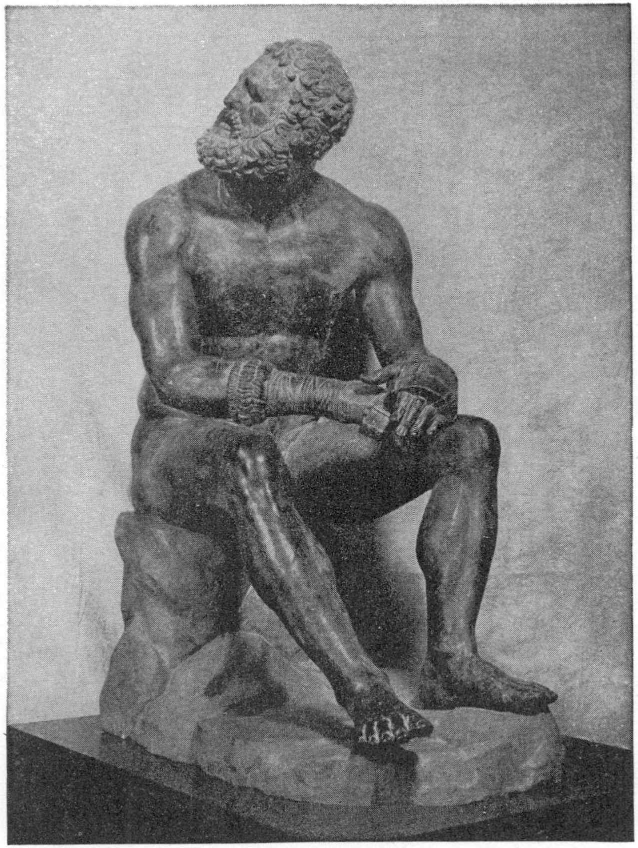

FIG. 64—*The Prize Fighter*
Museo delle Terme, Rome

temple. The interior was relatively small; much of the space was taken up by two double-storied Doric colonnades that supported the roof, and divided the naos into a nave and two aisles; while in the western end Athene Parthenos blinded her worshipers with the gold of her raiment, or frightened them with her spear and shield and snakes. Behind her was the Room of the Virgins, adorned with four columns in the Ionic style. The marble tiles of the roof were sufficiently translucent to let some light into the nave, and yet opaque enough to keep out the heat; moreover, piety, like love, deprecates the sun. The cornices were decorated with careful detail, surmounted with terra-cotta acroteria, and armed with gargoyles to carry off the rain. Many parts of the temple were painted, not in subdued colors but in bright tints of yellow, blue, and red. The marble was washed with a stain of saffron and milk; the triglyphs and parts of the molding were blue; the frieze had a blue background, the metopes a red, and every figure in them was colored.[52] A people accustomed to a Mediterranean sky can bear and relish brighter hues than those that suit the clouded atmosphere of northern Europe. Today, shorn of its colors, the Parthenon is most beautiful at night, when through every columned space come changing vistas of sky, or the ever worshipful moon, or the lights of the sleeping city mingling with the stars.*

Greek art was the greatest of Greek products; for though its masterpieces have yielded one by one to the voracity of time, their form and spirit still survive sufficiently to be a guide and stimulus to many arts, many generations, and many lands. There were faults here, as in all that men do. The

* The Parthenon, like the Erechtheum and the Theseum, was preserved through its use as a Christian church; it needed no great change of name, being in each case dedicated to the Virgin. After the Turkish occupation in 1456 it was transformed into a mosque, and acquired a minaret. In 1687, when the Venetians besieged Athens, the Turks used the temple to store each day's supply of powder for their artillery. The Venetian commander, so informed, ordered his gunners to fire upon the Parthenon. A shell pierced the roof, exploded the powder, and laid half the building in ruins. After capturing the city Morosini tried also to take the pediment statuary, but his workmen dropped and smashed the figures in lowering them. In 1800 Lord Elgin, British ambassador to Turkey, secured permission to remove a part of the sculptures to the British Museum, on the ground that they would be safer there than at Athens against weather and war. His spoils included twelve statues, fifteen metopes, and fifty-six slabs of the frieze. The Museum's expert on sculpture advised against buying this material; it was only after ten years of negotiations that the Museum agreed to pay $175,000 for them, which was less than half what Lord Elgin had spent in securing and transporting them.[53] A few years later, during the Greek War of Independence (1821-1830), the Acropolis was twice bombarded, and much of the Erechtheum was destroyed.[54] Some metopes of the Parthenon are still in place; a few slabs of the frieze are in the Athens Museum, and a few others in the Louvre. The citizens of Nashville, Tennessee, have built a replica of the Parthenon, in the same dimensions as the original, with like materials, and, so far as our knowledge goes, with the same decorations and coloring; and the Metropolitan Museum of Art contains a small hypothetical reproduction of the interior.

sculpture was too physical, and rarely reached the soul; it moves us more often to admire its perfection than to feel its life. The architecture was narrowly limited in form and style, and clung across a thousand years to the simple rectangle of the Mycenaean megaron. It achieved almost nothing in secular fields; it attempted only the easier problems of construction, and avoided difficult tasks like the arch and the vault, which might have given it greater scope. It held up its roofs with the clumsy expedient of internal and superimposed colonnades. It crowded the interior of its temples with statues whose size was out of proportion to the edifice, and whose ornamentation lacked the simplicity and restraint that we expect of the classic style.*

But no faults can outweigh the fact that Greek art created the classic style. The essence of that style—if the theme of this chapter may be restated in closing—is order and form: moderation in design, expression, and decoration; proportion in the parts and unity in the whole; the supremacy of reason without the extinction of feeling; a quiet perfection that is content with simplicity, and a sublimity that owes nothing to size. No other style but the Gothic has had so much influence; indeed, Greek statuary is still the ideal, and until yesterday the Greek column dominated architecture to the discouragement of more congenial forms. It is good that we are freeing ourselves from the Greeks; even perfection becomes oppressive when it will not change. But long after our liberation is complete we shall find instruction and stimulus in that art which was the life of reason in form, and in that classic style which was the most characteristic gift of Greece to mankind.

---

* One might also note the lack of order in the arrangement of the buildings on the Acropolis, or in the sacred enclosure at Olympia; but it is difficult to say whether this disorder was a defect of taste or an accident of history.

CHAPTER XV

The Advancement of Learning

THE cultural activity of Periclean Greece takes chiefly three forms—art, drama, and philosophy. In the first, religion is the inspiration; in the second it is the battleground; in the third it is the victim. Since the organization of a religious group presumes a common and stable creed, every religion sooner or later comes into opposition with that fluent and changeful current of secular thought that we confidently call the progress of knowledge. In Athens the conflict was not always visible on the surface, and did not directly affect the masses of the people; the scientists and the philosophers carried on their work without explicitly attacking the popular faith, and often mitigated the strife by using the old religious terms as symbols or allegories for their new beliefs; only now and then, as in the indictments of Anaxagoras, Aspasia, Diagoras of Melos, Euripides, and Socrates, did the struggle come out into the open, and become a matter of life and death. But it was there. It ran through the Periclean age like a major theme, played in many keys and elaborated in many variations and forms; it was heard most distinctly in the skeptical discourses of the Sophists and in the materialism of Democritus; it sounded obscurely in the piety of Aeschylus, in the heresies of Euripides, even in the irreverent banter of the conservative Aristophanes; and it was violently recapitulated in the trial and death of Socrates. Around this theme the Athens of Pericles lived its mental life.

I. THE MATHEMATICIANS

Pure science, in fifth-century Greece, was still the handmaiden of philosophy, and was studied and developed by men who were philosophers rather than scientists. To the Greeks higher mathematics was an instrument not of practice but of logic, directed less to the conquest of the physical environment than to the intellectual construction of an abstract world.

Popular arithmetic, before the Periclean period, was almost primitively clumsy.* One upright stroke indicated 1, two strokes 2, three 3, and four 4; 5, 10, 100, 1000, and 10,000 were expressed by the initial letter of the Greek word

* On later (possibly Periclean) arithmetical notation cf. Chap. XXVIII, sect. 1, below.

for the number—*pente, deka, hekaton, chilioi, myrioi.* Greek mathematics never achieved a symbol for zero. Like our own it betrayed its Oriental origin by taking from the Egyptians the decimal system of counting by tens, and from the Babylonians, in astronomy and geography, the duodecimal or sexagesimal system of counting by twelves or sixties, as still on our clocks, globes, and charts. Probably an abacus helped the people with the simpler calculations. Fractions were painful for them: to work with a complex fraction they reduced it to an accumulation of fractions having 1 as their common numerator; so $\frac{23}{32}$ was broken down into $\frac{1}{2} + \frac{1}{8} + \frac{1}{16} + \frac{1}{32}$.[1]

Of Greek algebra we have no record before the Christian era. Geometry, however, was a favorite study of the philosophers, again less for its practical value than for its theoretical interest, the fascination of its deductive logic, its union of subtlety and clarity, its imposing architecture of thought. Three problems particularly attracted these mathematical metaphysicians: the squaring of the circle, the trisection of the angle, and the doubling of the cube. How popular the first puzzle became appears in Aristophanes' *Birds*, in which a character representing the astronomer Meton enters upon the stage armed with ruler and compasses, and undertakes to show "how your circle may be made a square"—i.e., how to find a square whose area will equal that of a given circle. Perhaps it was such problems as these that led the later Pythagoreans to formulate a doctrine of irrational numbers and incommensurable quantities.* It was the Pythagoreans, too, whose studies of the parabola, the hyperbola, and the ellipse prepared for the epochal work of Apollonius of Perga on conic sections.[2] About 440 Hippocrates of Chios (not the physician) published the first known book on geometry, and solved the problem of squaring the lune.† About 420 Hippias of Elia accomplished the trisection of an angle through the quadratrix curve.[3] About 410 Democritus of Abdera announced that "in constructing lines according to given conditions no one has ever surpassed me, not even the Egyptians;"[4] he almost made the boast forgivable by writing four books on geometry, and finding formulas for the areas of cones and pyramids.[5] All in all, the Greeks were as excellent in geometry as they were poor in arithmetic. Even into their art geometry entered actively, making many forms of ceramic and architectural ornament, and determining the proportions and curvatures of the Parthenon.

---

* Irrational numbers are those that cannot be expressed by either a whole number or a fraction, like the square root of 2. Incommensurable quantities are those for which no third quantity can be found which bears to each of them a relation expressible by a rational number, like the side and diagonal of a square, or the radius and circumference of a circle.

† A moonlike figure made by the arcs of two intersecting circles.

II. ANAXAGORAS

It was part of the struggle between religion and science that the study of astronomy was forbidden by Athenian law at the height of the Periclean age.[6] At Acragas Empedocles suggested that light takes time to pass from one point to another.[7] At Elea Parmenides announced the sphericity of the earth, divided the planet into five zones, and observed that the moon always has its bright portion turned toward the sun.[8] At Thebes Philolaus the Pythagorean deposed the earth from the center of the universe, and reduced it to the status of one among many planets revolving about a "central fire."[9] Leucippus, pupil of Philolaus, attributed the origin of the stars to the incandescent combustion and concentration of material "drawn onward in the universal movement of the circular vortex."[10] At Abdera Democritus, pupil of Leucippus and student of Babylonian lore, described the Milky Way as a multitude of small stars, and summarized astronomic history as the periodical collision and destruction of an infinite number of worlds.[11] At Chios Oenopides discovered the obliquity of the ecliptic.[11a] Nearly everywhere among the Greek colonies the fifth century saw scientific developments remarkable in a period almost devoid of scientific instruments.

But when Anaxagoras tried to do similar work at Athens he found the mood of the people and the Assembly as hostile to free inquiry as the friendship of Pericles was encouraging. He had come from Clazomenae about 480 B.C., at twenty years of age. Anaximenes so interested him in the stars that when someone asked him the object of life he answered, "The investigation of sun, moon, and heaven."[12] He neglected his patrimony to chart the earth and the sky, and fell into poverty while his book *On Nature* was acclaimed by the intelligentsia of Athens as the greatest scientific work of the century.

It carried on the traditions and speculations of the Ionian school. The universe, said Anaxagoras, was originally a chaos of diverse seeds (*spermata*), pervaded by a *nous*, or Mind, tenuously physical, and akin to the source of life and motion in ourselves. And as mind gives order to the chaos of our actions, so the World Mind gave order to the primeval seeds, setting them into a rotatory vortex,* and guiding them toward the development of organic forms.[13] This rotation sorted the seeds into the four elements—fire, air, water, and earth—and separated the world into two revolving layers, an outer one of "ether," and an inner one of air. "In consequence of this violent

* This is the Vortex that Aristophanes, in *The Clouds*, so effectively satirized as Socrates' substitute for Zeus.

whirling motion, the surrounding fiery ether tore away stones from the earth, and kindled them into stars."[14] The sun and the stars are glowing masses of rock: "The sun is a red-hot mass many times larger than the Peloponnesus."[15] When their revolving motion wanes, the stones of the outer layer fall upon the earth as meteors.[16] The moon is an incandescent solid, having on its surface plains, mountains, and ravines;[17] it receives its light from the sun, and is of all heavenly bodies the nearest to the earth.[18] "The moon is eclipsed through the interposition of the earth . . . the sun through the interposition of the moon."[19] Probably other celestial bodies are inhabited like the earth; upon them "men are formed, and other animals that have life; the men dwell in cities, and cultivate fields as we do."[20] Out of the inner or gaseous layer of our planet successive condensations produced clouds, water, earth, and stones. Winds are due to rarefactions of the atmosphere produced by the heat of the sun; "thunder is caused by the collision of clouds, and lightning by their friction."[21] The quantity of matter never changes, but all forms begin and pass away; in time the mountains will become the sea.[22] The various forms and objects of the world are brought into being by increasingly definite aggregations of homogeneous parts (*homoiomeria*).[23] All organisms were originally generated out of earth, moisture, and heat, and thereafter from one another.[24] Man has developed beyond other animals because his erect posture freed his hands for grasping things.[25]

These achievements—the foundation of meteorology, the correct explanation of eclipses, a rational hypothesis of planetary formation, the discovery of the borrowed light of the moon, and an evolutionary conception of animal and human life—made Anaxagoras at once the Copernicus and Darwin of his age. The Athenians might have forgiven him these *aperçus* had he not neglected his *nous* in explaining the events of nature and history; perhaps they suspected that this *nous*, like Euripides' *deus ex machina*, was a device for saving the author's skin. Aristotle notes that Anaxagoras sought natural explanations everywhere.[26] When a ram with a single horn in the center of its forehead was brought to Pericles, and a soothsayer interpreted it as a supernatural omen, Anaxagoras had the animal's skull cleft, and showed that the brain, instead of filling both sides of the cranium, had grown upward towards the center, and so had produced the solitary horn.[27] He aroused the simple by giving a natural explanation of meteors, and reduced many mythical figures to personified abstractions.[28]

The Athenians took him good-humoredly for a time, merely nicknaming him *nous*.[29] But when no other way could be found of weakening Pericles,

Cleon, his demagogic rival, brought a formal indictment of impiety against Anaxagoras on the charge that he had described the sun (still to the people a god) as a mass of stone on fire; and pursued the case so relentlessly that the philosopher, despite Pericles' brave defense of him, was convicted.* Having no taste for hemlock, Anaxagoras fled to Lampsacus on the Hellespont, where he kept himself alive by teaching philosophy.† When news was brought to him that the Athenians had condemned him to death, he said, "Nature has long since condemned both them and me."[33] He died a few years later, aged seventy-three.

The backwardness of the Athenians in astronomy was reflected in their calendar. There was no general Greek calendar: every state had its own; and each of the four possible points for beginning a new year was adopted somewhere in Greece; even the months changed their names across frontiers. The Attic calendar reckoned months by the moon, and years by the sun.[34] As twelve lunar months made only 360 days, a thirteenth month was added every second year to bring the calendar into harmony with the sun and the seasons.[35] Since this made the year ten days too long, Solon introduced the custom of having alternate months of twenty-nine and thirty days, arranged into three weeks (*dekades*) of ten (occasionally nine) days each;[36] and as an excess of four days still remained, the Greeks omitted one month every eighth year. In this incredibly devious way they at last arrived at a year of 365¼ days.‡

Meanwhile a modest degree of progress was made in terrestrial science. Anaxagoras correctly explained the annual overflow of the Nile as due to the spring thaws and rains of Ethiopia.[38] Greek geologists attributed the Straits of Gibraltar to a cleaving earthquake, and the Aegean isles to a subsiding sea.[39] Xanthus of Lydia, about 496, surmised that the Mediterranean and the Red Sea were formerly connected at Suez; and Aeschylus noted the belief of his time that Sicily had been torn asunder from Italy by a convulsion of the earth.[40] Scylax of Caria (521-485) explored the whole coast of the Mediterranean and the Black Sea. No Greek seems to have dared so adventurous a voyage of discovery as that which the Carthaginian Hanno, with a fleet of sixty ships, led through Gibraltar some 2600 miles down the west coast of Africa (ca. 490). Maps of the Mediterranean world were common in Athens at the end of the fifth century. Physics, so far as we know, remained undeveloped, though the curvatures of the Parthenon show considerable knowledge of optics. The

---

* Ca. 434.[30] Another account places the trial in 450.[31]

† According to a rival story he was imprisoned at Athens, and was awaiting the fatal cup when Pericles arranged his escape.[32]

‡ Herodotus remarks on the superior calendar of the Egyptians.[37] From Egypt the Greeks took the gnomon, or sundial, and from Asia the clepsydra, or water clock, as their instruments for measuring time.

Pythagoreans, towards 450, announced the most lasting of Greek scientific hypotheses—the atomic constitution of matter. Empedocles and others expounded a theory of the evolution of man from lower forms of life, and described the slow advance of man from savagery to civilization.[41]

III. HIPPOCRATES

The epochal event in the history of Greek science during the Periclean age was the rise of rational medicine. Even in the fifth century Greek medicine was in large measure bound up with religion, and the treatment of disease was still practiced by the temple priests of Asclepius. This temple therapy used a combination of empirical medicine with impressive ritual and charms that touched and released the imagination of the patient; possibly hypnosis and some form of anesthesia were also employed.[42] Secular medicine competed with this ecclesiastical medicine. Though both groups ascribed their origin to Asclepius, the profane Asclepiads rejected religious aids, made no claim to miraculous cures, and gradually placed medicine upon a rational basis.

Secular medicine, in fifth-century Greece, took form in four great schools: at Cos and Cnidus in Asia Minor, at Crotona in Italy, and in Sicily. At Acragas Empedocles, half philosopher and half miracle man, shared medical honors with the rational practitioner Acron.[43] As far back as 520 we read of the physician Democedes, who, born at Crotona, practiced medicine in Aegina, Athens, Samos, and Susa, cured Darius and Queen Atossa, and returned to spend his last days in the city of his birth.[44] At Crotona, too, the Pythagorean school produced the most famous of Greek physicians before Hippocrates. Alcmaeon has been called the real father of Greek medicine,[45] but he is clearly a late name in a long line of secular medicos whose origin is lost beyond the horizons of history. Early in the fifth century he published a work *On Nature* (*peri physeos*)—the usual title, in Greece, for a general discussion of natural science. He, first of the Greeks, so far as we know, located the optic nerve and the Eustachian tubes, dissected animals, explained the physiology of sleep, recognized the brain as the central organ of thought, and defined health Pythagoreanly as a harmony of the parts of the body.[46] At Cnidus the dominating figure was Euryphron, who composed a medical summary known as the *Cnidian Sentences*, explained pleurisy as a disease of the lungs, ascribed many illnesses to constipation, and became famous for his success as an obstetrician.[47] An unmerry war raged between the schools of Cos and Cnidus; for the

Cnidians, disliking Hippocrates' penchant for basing "prognosis" upon general pathology, insisted upon a careful classification of each ailment, and a treatment of it on specific lines. In the end, by a kind of philosophical justice, many of the Cnidian writings found their way into the Hippocratic Collection.

As we see Hippocrates in Suidas' thumbnail biography, he appears as the outstanding physician of his time. He was born in Cos in the same year as Democritus; despite their far-separated homes the two became great friends, and perhaps the "laughing philosopher" had some share in the secularization of medicine. Hippocrates was the son of a physician, and grew up and practiced among the thousands of invalids and tourists who came to "take the waters" in the hot springs of Cos. His teacher, Herodicus of Selymbria, formed his art by accustoming him to rely upon diet and exercise rather than upon drugs. Hippocrates won such repute that rulers like Perdiccas of Macedon and Artaxerxes I of Persia were among his patients; and in 430 Athens sent for him to try his hand at staying the great plague. His friend Democritus shamed him by completing a century, while the great physician died at the age of eighty-three.

Nothing in medical literature could be more heterogeneous than the collection of treatises anciently ascribed to Hippocrates. Here are textbooks for physicians, counsels for laymen, lectures for students, reports of researches and observations, clinical records of interesting cases, and essays by Sophists interested in the scientific or philosophical aspects of medicine. The forty-two clinical records are the only examples of their kind for the next seventeen hundred years; and they set a high standard of honesty by confessing that in sixty per cent of the cases the disease, or the treatment, proved fatal.[48] Of all these compositions only four are by general consent from the pen of Hippocrates—the "Aphorisms," the "Prognostic," the "Regimen in Acute Diseases," and the monograph "On Wounds in the Head"; the remainder of the *Corpus Hippocraticum* is by a variety of authors ranging from the fifth to the second century B.C.[49] There is a fair amount of nonsense in the assortment, but probably not more than the future will find in the treatises and histories of the present day. Much of the material is fragmentary, and takes a loose aphoristic form verging now and then upon Heracleitean obscurity. Among the "Aphorisms" is the famous remark that "Art is long, but time is fleeting."[50]

The historical role of Hippocrates and his successors was the liberation of medicine from both religion and philosophy. Occasionally, as in the treatise on "Regimen," prayer is advised as an aid; but the page-by-page tone of the Collection is a resolute reliance upon rational therapy. The essay on "The Sacred Disease" directly attacks the theory that ailments are caused by the gods; all diseases, says the author, have natural causes. Epilepsy, which the people explained as possession by a demon, is not excepted: "Men continue to believe in its divine origin because they are at a loss to understand it. . . . Charlatans and quacks, having no treatment that would help, concealed and sheltered themselves behind superstition, and called this illness sacred in order that their complete ignorance might not be revealed."[51] The mind of Hippocrates was typical of the Periclean time spirit—imaginative but realistic, averse to mystery and weary of myth, recognizing the value of religion, but struggling to understand the world in rational terms. The influence of the Sophists can be felt in this move for the emancipation of medicine; and indeed, philosophy so powerfully affected Greek therapy that the science had to fight against philosophical as well as theological impediments. Hippocrates insists that philosophical theories have no place in medicine, and that treatment must proceed by careful observation and accurate recording of specific cases and facts. He does not quite realize the value of experiment; but he is resolved to be guided by experience.[52]

The natal infection of Hippocratic medicine with philosophy appears in the once famous doctrine of "humors." The body, says Hippocrates, is compounded of blood, phlegm, yellow bile, and black bile; that man enjoys the most perfect health in whom these elements are duly proportioned and mingled; pain is the defect or excess of one "humor," or its isolation from the rest.[53] This theory outlived all the other medical hypotheses of antiquity; it was abandoned only in the last century, and perhaps survives by transmigration in the doctrine of hormones or glandular secretions today. Since the behavior of the "humors" was considered subject to climate and diet, and the most prevalent ailments in Greece were colds, pneumonia, and malaria, Hippocrates (?) wrote a brief treatise on "Airs, Waters, Places" in relation to health. "One may expose oneself confidently to cold," we are told, "except after eating or exercise. . . . It is not good for the body not to be exposed to the cold of winter."[54] The scientific physician, wherever he settles, will study the effects, upon the local population, of the winds and the seasons, the water supply and the nature of the soil.

The weakest point in Hippocratic medicine was diagnosis. There was, apparently, no taking of the pulse; fever was judged by simple touch, and auscultation was direct. Infection was understood in the case of scabies, ophthalmia, and phthisis.[55] The *Corpus* contains excellent clinical pictures of epilepsy, epidemic parotitis, puerperal septicemia, and quotidian, tertian, and quartan fevers. There is no mention in the Collection of smallpox, measles, diphtheria, scarlet fever, or syphilis; and no clear mention of typhoid fever.[56] The treatises on "Regimen" move towards preventive medicine by advocating "prodiagnosis"—an attempt to catch the first symptoms of a disease, and nip it in the bud.[57] Hippocrates was particularly fond of "prognosis": the good physician, he believed, will learn by experience to foresee the effects of various bodily conditions, and be able to predict from the first stages of a disease the course that it will follow. Most diseases reach a crisis in which either the illness or the patient comes to an end; the almost Pythagorean calculation of the day on which the crisis should appear was a characteristic element of Hippocratic theory. If in these crises the natural heat of the body can overcome the morbid matter and discharge it, the patient is cured. In any cure nature—i.e., the powers and constitution of the body—is the principal healer; all that the physician can do is to remove or reduce the impediments to this natural defense and recuperation. Hence Hippocratic treatment makes little use of drugs, but depends chiefly upon fresh air, emetics, suppositories, enemas, cupping, bloodletting, fomentations, ointments, massage, and hydrotherapy. The Greek pharmacopoeia was reassuringly small, and consisted largely of purgatives. Skin troubles were treated with sulphur baths, and by administering the oil of dolphin livers.[58] "Live a healthy life," Hippocrates advises, "and you are not likely to fall ill, except through epidemic or accident. If you do fall ill, proper regimen will give you the best chance of recovery."[59] Fasting was often prescribed, if the strength of the patient allowed; for "the more we nourish unhealthy bodies the more we injure them."[60] In general "a man should have only one meal a day, unless he have a very dry belly."[61]

Anatomy and physiology made slow progress in Greece, and owed much of this to the examination of animal entrails in the practice of augury. A little brochure "On the Heart," in the Hippocratic Collection, describes the ventricles, the great vessels, and their valves. Syennesis of Cyprus and Diogenes of Crete wrote descriptions of the vascular system, and Diogenes knew the significance of the pulse.[62] Empedocles recognized that the heart is the center of the vascular system, and described it as the organ by which the *pneuma*, or vital breath (oxygen?), is carried through the blood vessels to every part of the body.[63] The *Corpus*, following Alcmaeon, makes the brain the seat of consciousness and thought; "Through it we think, see, hear, and distinguish the ugly from the beautiful, the bad from the good."[64]

Surgery was still for the most part an unspecialized activity of advanced general practitioners, though the armies had surgeons on their staffs.[65] The Hippocratic literature describes trephining operations, and its treatment for dislocations of shoulder or jaw are "modern" in everything except anesthesia.[66] A votive tablet from the temple of Asclepius at Athens shows a folding case containing scalpels of various forms.[67] The little museum at Epidaurus has preserved for us ancient forceps, probes, scalpels, catheters, and specula essentially like those that are used today; and certain statues there are apparently models illustrating methods for reducing dislocations of the hip.[68] The Hippocratic treatise "On the Physician" gives detailed directions for the preparation of the operating room, the arrangement of natural and artificial light, the cleanliness of the hands, the care and use of instruments, the position of the patient, the bandaging of wounds, etc.[69]

It is clear from these and other passages that Greek medicine in Hippocrates' days had made great advances, technically and socially. Heretofore Greek physicians had migrated from city to city as need called them, like the Sophists of their time or the preachers of our own. Now they settled down, opened *iatreia*—"healing places," or offices—and treated patients there or at the patients' homes.[70] Women physicians were numerous, and were usually employed for diseases of their sex; some of them wrote authoritative treatises on the care of the skin and the hair.[71] The state exacted no public examination of prospective practitioners, but required satisfactory evidence of an apprenticeship or tutelage to a recognized physician.[72] City governments reconciled socialized with private medicine by engaging doctors to attend to public health, and to give medical treatment to the poor; the best of such state physicians, like Democedes, received two talents ($12,000) a year.[73] There were, of course, many quacks and, as always, an inexhaustible supply of omniscient amateurs. The profession, as in all generations, suffered from its dishonest or incompetent minority;[74] and like other peoples the Greeks revenged themselves upon the uncertainties of medicine by jokes almost as endless as those that wreak their vengeance upon marriage.

Hippocrates raised the profession to a higher standing by his emphasis on medical ethics. He was a teacher as well as a practitioner, and the famous oath ascribed to him may have been designed to ensure the loyalty of the student to his instructor.*

* The oath is regarded as deriving from the Hippocratic school rather than from the master himself; but Erotian, writing in the first century A.D., attributes it to Hippocrates.[75]

The Hippocratic Oath

> I swear by Apollo Physician, by Asclepius, by Hygiaea, by Panacea, and by all the gods and goddesses, making them my witnesses, that I will carry out, according to my ability and judgment, this oath and this indenture. To hold my teacher in this art equal to my own parents; to make him partner in my livelihood; when he is in need of money to share mine with him; to consider his family as my own brothers, and to teach them this art, if they want to learn it, without fee or indenture; to impart precept, oral instruction, and all other instruction to my own sons, to the sons of my teacher, and to indentured pupils who have taken the physician's oath, but to nobody else. I will use treatment to help the sick according to my ability and judgment, but never with a view to injury and wrongdoing. Neither will I administer a poison to anybody when asked to do so, nor will I suggest such a course. Similarly I will not give to a woman a pessary to cause abortion. But I will keep pure and holy both my life and my art. I will not use the knife, not even, verily, on sufferers from stone, but I will give place to such as are craftsmen therein. Into whatsoever houses I enter I will enter to help the sick, and I will abstain from all intentional wrongdoing and harm, especially from abusing the bodies of man or woman, bond or free. And whatsoever I shall see or hear in the course of my profession, as well as outside my profession in my intercourse with men, if it be what should not be published abroad, I will never divulge, holding such things to be holy secrets. Now if I carry out this oath, and break it not, may I gain forever reputation among all men for my life and for my art; but if I transgress it and forswear myself, may the opposite befall me.[76]

The physician, Hippocrates adds, should maintain a becoming exterior, keeping his person clean and his clothing neat. He must always remain calm, and must make his behavior inspire the patient with confidence.[77] He must

> keep a careful watch over himself, and . . . say only what is absolutely necessary. . . . When you enter a sick man's room, bear in mind your manner of sitting, reserve, arrangement of dress, decisive utterance, brevity of speech, composure, bedside manners . . . self-control, rebuke of disturbance, readiness to do what has to be done. . . . I urge you not to be too unkind, but to consider carefully your patient's superabundance or means. Sometimes give your services

> for nothing; and if there be an opportunity of serving a stranger who is in financial straits, give him full assistance. For where there is love of man, there is also love of the art.[78]

If, in addition to all this, the physician studies and practices philosophy, he becomes the ideal of his profession; for "a physician who is a lover of wisdom is the equal of a god."[79]

Greek medicine shows no essential advance upon the medical and surgical knowledge of Egypt a thousand years before the various Fathers of Medicine; in the matter of specialization the Greek development seems to have fallen short of the Egyptian. From another point of view we must hold the Greeks in high esteem, for not until the nineteenth century of our era was any substantial improvement made upon their medical practice or theory. In general, Greek science went as far as could be expected without instruments of observation and precision, and without experimental methods. It would have done better had it not been harassed by religion and discouraged by philosophy. At a time when many young men in Athens were taking up with enthusiasm the study of astronomy and comparative anatomy, the progress of science was halted by obscurantist legislation, and the persecutions of Anaxagoras, Aspasia, and Socrates; while the famous "turning around" of Socrates and the Sophists from the external to the internal world, from physics to ethics, drew Greek thought from the problems of nature and evolution to those of metaphysics and morals. Science stood still for a century while Greece succumbed to the charms of philosophy.

CHAPTER XVI

The Conflict of Philosophy and Religion

I. THE IDEALISTS

THE age of Pericles resembled our own in the variety and disorder of its thought, and in the challenge that it offered to every traditional standard and belief. But no age has ever rivaled that of Pericles in the number and grandeur of its philosophical ideas, or in the vigor and exuberance with which they were debated. Every issue that agitates the world today was bruited about in ancient Athens, and with such freedom and eagerness that all Greece except its youth was alarmed. Many cities—above all, Sparta—forbade the public consideration of philosophical problems, "on account of the jealousy and strife and profitless discussions" (says Athenaeus) "to which they give rise."[1] But in Periclean Athens the "dear delight" of philosophy captured the imagination of the educated classes; rich men opened their homes and salons in the manner of the French Enlightenment; philosophers were lionized, and clever arguments were applauded like sturdy blows at the Olympic games.[2] When, in 432, a war of swords was added to the war of words, the excitement of the Athenian mind became a fever in which all soberness of thought and judgment was consumed. The fever subsided for a time after the martyrdom of Socrates, or was dissipated from Athens to other centers of Greek life; even Plato, who had known the very height and crisis of it, became exhausted after sixty years of the new game, and envied Egypt the inviolable orthodoxy and quiet stability of its thought. No age until the Renaissance would know such enthusiasm again.

Plato was the culmination of a development that began with Parmenides; he played Hegel to Parmenides' Kant; and though he scattered condemnation lavishly, he never ceased to reverence his metaphysical father. In the little town of Elea, on the western coast of Italy, 450 years before Christ, there began for Europe that philosophy of idealism which was to wage through every subsequent century an obstinate war against materialism.* The mysterious problem of knowledge, the distinction between noumenon and phenomenon, between the unseen real and the unreal seen, was flung into the caldron of European thought, and was to boil or simmer there through Greek and medieval days until, in Kant, it would explode again in a philosophical revolution.

As Kant was "awakened" by Hume, so Parmenides was aroused to philosophy by Xenophanes; perhaps his was one of many minds stirred by Xenophanes' declaration that the gods were myths, and that there was only one reality, which was both world and God. Parmenides studied with the Pythagoreans also, and absorbed something of their passion for astronomy. But he did not lose himself in the stars. Like most Greek philosophers he was interested in living affairs and the state; Elea commissioned him to draw up for it a code of laws, which it liked so well that its magistrates were thenceforth required to decide all cases by that code.[3] Possibly as a recreational aside in a busy life he composed a philosophical poem *On Nature*, of which some 160 verses survive, enough to make us regret that Parmenides did not write prose. The poet announces, with a twinkle in his eye, that a goddess has delivered to him a revelation: that all things are one; that motion, change, and development are unreal—phantasms of superficial, contradictory, untrustworthy sense; that beneath these mere appearances lies an unchanging, homogeneous, indivisible, indissoluble, motionless unity, which is the only Being, the only Truth, and the only God. Heracleitus said, *Panta rei*, all things change; Parmenides says, *Hen ta panta*, all things are one, and never change. At times, like Xenophanes, he speaks of this One as the universe, and calls it spheroidal and finite; at times, in an idealistic vision, he identifies Being with Thought, and sings, "One thing are Thinking and Being,"[4] as if to say that for us things exist only in so far as we are conscious of them. Beginning and end, birth and death, formation and destruction, are of forms only; the One Real never begins and never ends; there is no Becoming, there is only Being. Motion, too, is unreal, it assumes the passage of something from where it is to where there is nothing, or empty space; but empty space, Not Being, cannot be; there is no void; the One fills every nook and cranny of the world, and is forever at rest.†

* The Hindus had seen the problem long before, and were to remain Parmenideans to the end; perhaps the antisensationism of the *Upanishads* had penetrated through Ionia or Pythagoras to Parmenides.

† This strains the imagination; but almost in Parmenidean fashion we speak of a table as at rest though it is composed (we are told) of the most excitably mobile "electrons." Parmenides saw the world as we see the table; the electron would see the table as we see the world.

It was not to be expected that men would listen patiently to all this; and apparently the Parmenidean Rest became the target of a thousand metaphysical assaults. The significance of Parmenides' subtle follower, Zeno of Elea, lay in an attempt to show that the ideas of plurality and motion were, at least theoretically, as impossible as Parmenides' motionless One. As an exercise in perversity, and to amuse his youth, Zeno published a book of paradoxes, of which nine have come down to us, and of which three will suffice. *First,* said Zeno, any body, in order to move to point A, must reach B, the middle of its course toward A; to arrive at B it must reach C, the middle of its course toward B; and so on to infinity. Since an infinity of time would be required for this infinite series of motions, the motion of any body to any point is impossible in a finite time. *Second,* as a variant of the first, swift-footed Achilles can never overtake the leisurely tortoise; for as often as Achilles reaches the point which the tortoise occupied, in that same moment the tortoise has moved beyond that point. *Third,* a flying arrow is really at rest; for at any moment of its flight it is at only one point in space, that is, is motionless; its motion, however actual to the senses, is logically, metaphysically unreal.*[5]

Zeno came to Athens about 450, perhaps with Parmenides, and set the impressionable city astir by his skill in reducing any kind of philosophical theory to absurd consequences. Timon of Phlius described

> The two-edged tongue of mighty Zeno, who,
> Say what one would, would argue it untrue.[8]

This pre-Socratic gadfly was (in the relative sense which our ignorance of the past compels us to give to such phrases) the father of logic, as Parmenides was for Europe the father of metaphysics. Socrates, who denounced Zeno's dialectical method,[9] imitated it so zealously that men had to kill him in order to have peace of mind. Zeno's influence upon the skeptical Sophists was decisive, and in the end it was his skepticism that triumphed in Pyrrho and Carneades. In his old age, having become a man "of great wisdom and learning,"[10] he complained that the philosophers had taken too seriously the intellectual pranks of his youth. His final escapade was more fatal to him: he joined in an attempt to depose the tyrant Nearches at Elea, was foiled and arrested, tortured and killed.[11] He bore his sufferings bravely, as if to associate his name so soon with the Stoic philosophy.

---

* The discussion of these paradoxes has gone on from Plato[6] to Bertrand Russell,[7] and may continue as long as words are mistaken for things. The assumptions that invalidate the puzzles are that "infinite" is a thing instead of merely a word indicating the inability of the mind to conceive an absolute end; and that time, space, and motion are discontinuous, i.e., are composed of separate points or parts.

II. THE MATERIALISTS

As Parmenides' denial of motion and change was a reaction against the fluid and unstable metaphysics of Hercleitus, so his monism was a counterblast to the atomism of the later Pythagoreans. For these had developed the number theory of their founder into the doctrine that all things are composed of numbers in the sense of indivisible units.[12] When Philolaus of Thebes added that "all things take place by necessity and by harmony,"[13] everything was ready for the Atomic school in Greek philosophy.

About 435 Leucippus of Miletus came to Elea, and studied under Zeno; there, perhaps, he heard of the number atomism of the Pythagoreans, for Zeno had aimed some of his subtlest paradoxes at this doctrine of plurality.[14] Leucippus finally settled in Abdera, a flourishing Ionian colony in Thrace. Of his direct teaching only one fragment remains: "Nothing happens without a reason, but all things occur for a reason, and of necessity."[15] Presumably it was in answer to Zeno and Parmenides that Leucippus developed the notion of the void, or empty space; in this way he hoped to make motion theoretically possible as well as sensibly actual. The universe, said Leucippus, contains atoms and space and nothing else. Atoms tumbling about in a vortex fall by necessity into the first forms of all things, like attaching itself to like; in this way arose the planets and the stars.[16] All things, even the human soul, are composed of atoms.

Democritus was the pupil or associate of Leucippus in developing the atomistic philosophy into a rounded system of materialism. His father was a man of wealth and position in Abdera;[17] from him, we are told, Democritus inherited a hundred talents ($600,000), most of which he spent in travel.[18] Unconfirmed stories send him as far as Egypt and Ethiopia, Babylonia, Persia, and India.[19] "Among my contemporaries," he says, "I have traveled over the largest portion of the earth in search of things the most remote, and have seen the most climates and countries, and heard the largest number of thinkers."*[20] At Boeotian Thebes he stopped long enough to imbibe the number atomism of Philolaus.[22] Having spent his money he became a philosopher, lived simply, devoted himself to study and contemplation, and said, "I would rather discover a single demonstration" (in geometry) "than win the throne of Persia."[23] There was some modesty in him, for he shunned dialectic and discussion, founded no school, and sojourned in Athens without making himself known to any of the philosophers there.[24]

* "To the wise and good man," he writes, "the whole earth is his fatherland."[21]

Diogenes Laertius gives a long list of his publications in mathematics, physics, astronomy, navigation, geography, anatomy, physiology, psychology, psychotherapy, medicine, philosophy, music, and art.[25] Thrasyllus called him *pentathlos* in philosophy, and some contemporaries gave him the very name of Wisdom (*sophia*).[26] His range was as wide as Aristotle's, his style as highly praised as Plato's.[27] Francis Bacon, in no perverse moment, called him the greatest of ancient philosophers.[28]

He begins, like Parmenides, with a critique of the senses. For practical purposes we may trust them; but the moment we begin to analyze their evidence we find ourselves taking away from the external world layer after layer of the color, temperature, flavor, savor, sweetness, bitterness, and sound that the senses lay upon it; these "secondary qualities" are in ourselves or in the total process of perception, not in the objective thing; in an earless world a falling forest would make no noise, and the ocean, however angry, would never roar. "By convention (*nomos*) sweet is sweet, bitter is bitter, hot is hot, cold is cold, color is color; but in truth there are only atoms and the void."[29] Hence the senses give us only obscure knowledge, or opinion; genuine knowledge comes only by investigation and thought. "Verily, we know nothing. Truth is buried deep. . . . We know nothing for certain, but only the changes produced in our body by the forces that impinge upon it."[30] All sensations are due to atoms discharged by the object and falling upon our sense organs.[31] All senses are forms of touch.[32]

The atoms that constitute the world differ in figure, size, and weight; all have a tendency downward; in the resultant rotatory motion like atoms combine with like and produce the planets and the stars. No *nous*, or intelligence, guides the atoms, no Empedoclean "love" or "hate" assorts them, but necessity—the natural operation of inherent causes—rules over all.[33] There is no chance; chance is a fiction invented to disguise our ignorance.[34] The quantity of matter remains always the same; none is ever created, none ever destroyed;[35] only the atom combinations change. Forms, however, are innumerable; even of worlds there is probably an "infinite" number, coming into being and passing away in an interminable pageantry.[36] Organic beings arose originally from the moist earth.[37] Everything in man is made of atoms; the soul is composed of tiny, smooth, round atoms, like those of fire. Mind, soul, vital heat, vital principle, are all one and the same thing; they are not confined to men or animals, but are diffused throughout the world; and in man and other animals the mental atoms whereby we think are distributed throughout the body.*[38]

Nevertheless these fine atoms that constitute the soul are the noblest and most wonderful part of the body. The wise man will cultivate thought, will free himself from passion, superstition, and fear, and will seek in contemplation and understanding the modest happiness available to human life. Happiness does not come from external goods; a man "must become accustomed to finding within himself the sources of his enjoyment."[42] "Culture is better than riches. . . . No power and no treasure can outweigh the extension of our knowledge."[43] Happiness is fitful, and "sensual pleasure affords only a brief satisfaction"; one comes to a more lasting content by acquiring peace and serenity of soul (*ataraxia*), good cheer (*euthumia*), moderation (*metriotes*), and a certain order and symmetry of life (*biou symmetria*).[44] We may learn much from the animals—"spinning from the spider, building from the swallow, singing from the nightingale and the swan";[45] but "strength of body is nobility only in beasts of burden, strength of character is nobility in man."[46] So, like the heretics of Victorian England, Democritus raises upon his scandalous metaphysics a most presentable ethic. "Good actions should be done not out of compulsion but from conviction; not from hope of reward, but for their own sake. . . . A man should feel more shame in doing evil before himself than before all the world."[47]

He illustrated his own precepts, and perhaps justified his counsels, by living to the age of a hundred and nine, or, as some say, to merely ninety, years.[48] Diogenes Laertius relates that when Democritus read in public his most important work, the *megas diakosmos*, or *Great World*, the city of Abdera presented him with a hundred talents ($600,000); but perhaps Abdera had depreciated its currency. When someone asked the secret of his longevity, he answered that he ate honey daily, and bathed his body with oil.[49] Finally, having lived long enough, he reduced his food each day, determined to starve himself by easy degrees.[50] "He was exceedingly old," says Diogenes,[51]

> and appeared to be at the point of death. His sister lamented that he would die during the festival of the Thesmophoria, which would prevent her from discharging her duties to the goddess. So he bade her be of good cheer, and to bring him hot loaves (or a little honey[52]) every day. And by applying these to his nostrils he kept himself

* Lucretius attributes a kind of psychophysical parallelism to "the great Democritus," who laid it down that the atoms of body and the atoms of mind are placed one beside one alternately in pairs, and so link the frame together."[39]

alive over the festival. But when the three days of the feast were passed he expired without any pain, as Hipparchus assures us, having lived one hundred and nine years.

His city gave him a public funeral, and Timon of Athens praised him.[53] He founded no school; but he formulated for science its most famous hypothesis, and gave to philosophy a system which, denounced by every other, has survived them all, and reappears in every generation.

III. EMPEDOCLES

Idealism offends the senses, materialism offends the soul; the one explains everything but the world, the other everything but life. To merge these half-truths it was necessary to find some dynamic principle that could mediate between structure and growth, between things and thought. Anaxagoras sought such a principle in a cosmic Mind; Empedocles sought it in the inherent forces that made for evolution.

This Leonardo of Acragas was born in the year of Marathon, of a wealthy family whose passion for horse racing gave no promise of philosophy. He studied for a while with the Pythagoreans, but in his exuberance he divulged some of their esoteric doctrine, and was expelled.[54] He took very much to heart the notion of transmigration, and announced with poetic sympathy that he had been "in bygone times a youth, a maiden, and a flowering shrub; a bird, yes, and a fish that swims in silence through the deep sea."[55] He condemned the eating of animal food as a form of cannibalism; for were not these animals the reincarnation of human beings?[56] All men, he believed, had once been gods, but had forfeited their heavenly place by some impurity or violence; and he was certain that he felt in his own soul intimations of a prenatal divinity. "From what glory, from what immeasurable bliss, have I now sunk to roam with mortals on this earth!"[57] Convinced of his divine origin, he put golden sandals upon his feet, clothed his body with purple robes, and crowned his head with laurel; he was, as he modestly explained to his countrymen, a favorite of Apollo; only to his friends did he confess that he was a god. He claimed supernatural powers, performed magic rites, and sought by incantations to wrest from the other world the secrets of human destiny. He offered to cure diseases by the enchantment of his words, and cured so many that the populace half believed his claims. Actually he was a learned physician fertile in suggestions to medical science, and skilled in the psychology of the medical art. He was a brilliant orator; he "invented," says Aristotle,[58] the principles of rhetoric, and taught them to Gorgias, who peddled them in Athens. He was an engineer who freed Selinus from pestilence by draining marshes and changing the courses of streams.[59] He was a courageous statesman who, though himself an aristocrat, led a popular revolution against a narrow aristocracy, refused the dictatorship, and established a moderate democracy.[60] He was a poet, and wrote *On Nature* and *On Purifications* in such excellent verse that Aristotle and Cicero ranked him high among the poets, and Lucretius complimented him with imitation. "When he went to the Olympic games," says Diogenes Laertius, "he was the object of general attention, so that there was no mention made of anybody else in comparison with him."[61] Perhaps, after all, he was a god.

The 470 lines that survive give us only hazardous intimations of his philosophy. He was an eclectic, and saw some wisdom in every system. He deprecated Parmenides' wholesale rejection of the senses, and welcomed each sense as an "avenue to understanding."[63] Sensation is due to effluxes of particles proceeding from the object and falling upon the "pores" (*poroi*) of the senses; therefore light needs time to come from the sun to us.[64] Night is caused by the earth intercepting the rays of the sun.[65] All things are composed of four elements—air, fire, water, and earth. Operating upon these are two basic forces, attraction and repulsion, Love and Hate. The endless combinations and separations of the elements by these forces produce the world of things and history. When Love or the tendency to combine is dominant, matter develops into plants, and organisms take higher and higher forms. Just as transmigration weaves all souls into one biography, so in nature there is no sharp distinction between one species or genus and another; e.g., "Hair and leaves and the thick feathers of birds, and the scales that form on tough limbs, are the same thing."[68] Nature produces every kind of organ and form; Love unites them, sometimes into monstrosities that perish through maladaptation, sometimes into organisms capable of propagating themselves and meeting the conditions of survival.[69] All higher forms develop from lower forms.[70] At first both sexes are in the same body; then they become separated, and each longs to be reunited with the other.*[71] To this process of evolution corresponds a process of dissolution, in which Hate, or the force of division, tears down the complex structure that Love has built. Slowly organisms and planets revert to more and more primitive forms, until all things are merged again in a

* Perhaps Plato poached here for Aristophanes' speech in the *Symposium*.

primeval and amorphous mass.[72] These alternating processes of development and decay go on endlessly, in each part and in the whole; the two forces of combination and separation, Love and Hate, Good and Evil, fight and balance each other in a vast universal rhythm of Life and Death. So old is the philosophy of Herbert Spencer.[73]

The place of God in this process is not clear, for in Empedocles it is difficult to separate fact from metaphor, philosophy from poetry. Sometimes he identifies deity with the cosmic sphere itself, sometimes with the life of all life, or the mind of all mind; but he knows that we shall never be able to form a just idea of the basic and original creative power. "We cannot bring God near so as to reach him with our eyes and lay hold of him with our hands. . . . For he has no human head attached to bodily members, nor do two branching arms dangle from his shoulders; he has neither feet nor knees nor any hairy parts. No; he is only mind, sacred and ineffable mind, flashing through the whole universe with swift thoughts."[74] And Empedocles concludes with the wise and weary counsel of old age:

> Weak and narrow are the powers implanted in the limbs of men; many the woes that fall on them and blunt the edge of thought; short is the measure of the life in death through which they toil. Then are they borne away; like smoke they vanish into air; and what they dream they know is but the little that each hath stumbled upon in wandering about the world. Yet boast they all that they have learned the whole. Vain fools! For what that is, no eye hath seen, no ear hath heard, nor can it be conceived by the mind of man.[75]

In his last years he became more distinctly a preacher and prophet, absorbed in the theory of reincarnation, and imploring his fellow men to purge away the guilt that had exiled them from heaven. With the assorted wisdom of Buddha, Pythagoras, and Schopenhauer he warned the human race to abstain from marriage, procreation,[76] and beans.[77] When, in 415, the Athenians besieged Syracuse, Empedocles did what he could to help its resistance, and thereby offended Acragas, which hated Syracuse with all the animosity of kinship. Banished from his native city, he went to the mainland of Greece and died, some say, in Megara.[78] But Hippobotus, says Diogenes Laertius,[79] tells how Empedocles, after bringing back to full life a woman who had been given up for dead, rose from the feast that celebrated her recovery, disappeared, and was never seen again. Legend said that he had leaped into Etna's fiery mouth so that he might die without leaving a trace behind him, and thereby confirm his divinity. But the elemental fire betrayed him; it flung up his brazen slippers and left them, like heavy symbols of mortality, upon the crater's edge.[80]

IV. THE SOPHISTS

It is a reproof to those who think of Greece as synonymous with Athens, that none of the great Hellenic thinkers before Socrates belonged to that city, and only Plato after him. The fate of Anaxagoras and Socrates indicates that religious conservatism was stronger in Athens than in the colonies, where geographical separation had broken some of the bonds of tradition. Perhaps Athens would have remained obscurantist and intolerant to the point of stupidity had it not been for the growth of a cosmopolitan trading class, and the coming of the Sophists to Athens.

The debates in the Assembly, the trials before the *heliaea,* and the rising need for the ability to think with the appearance of logic and to speak with clarity and persuasion, conspired with the wealth and curiosity of an imperial society to create a demand for something unknown in Athens before Pericles—formal higher education in letters, oratory, science, philosophy, and statesmanship. The demand was met at first not by the organization of universities but by wandering scholars who engaged lecture halls, gave there their courses of instruction, and then passed on to other cities to repeat them. Some of these men, like Protagoras, called themselves *sophistai*—i.e., teachers of wisdom.[81] The word was accepted as equivalent to our "university professor," and bore no derogatory connotation until the conflict between religion and philosophy led to conservative attacks upon the Sophists, and the commercialism of certain of them provoked Plato to darken their name with the imputations of venal sophistry that now cling to it. Perhaps the general public entertained a vague dislike for these teachers from their first appearance, since their costly instruction in logic and rhetoric could be bought only by the well to do, and gave these an advantage in trying their cases before the courts.[82] It is true that the more famous Sophists, like most skilled practitioners in any field, charged all that their patrons could be persuaded to pay; this is the final law of prices everywhere. Protagoras and Gorgias, we are told, demanded ten thousand drachmas ($10,000) for the education of a single pupil. But lesser Sophists were content with reasonably moderate fees; Prodicus, famous throughout Greece, asked from one to fifty drachmas for admission to his courses.[83]

Protagoras, the most renowned of the Sophists, was born in Abdera a generation before Democritus. In his lifetime he was the better known of the two, and the more influential; we surmise his repute from the furore created by his visits to Athens.*[84] Even Plato, who was not often intentionally fair to the Sophists, respected him, and described him as a man of high character. In the Platonic dialogue that is named after him Protagoras makes a much better showing than the argumentative young Socrates; here it is Socrates who talks like a Sophist, and Protagoras who behaves like a gentleman and a philosopher, never losing his temper, never jealous of another's brilliance, never taking the argument too seriously, and never anxious to speak. He admits that he undertakes to teach his pupils prudence in private and public matters, the orderly management of home and family, the art of rhetoric or persuasive speaking, and the ability to understand and direct affairs of state.[86] He defends his high fees by saying that it is his custom, when a pupil objects to the sum asked, to agree to receive as adequate whatever amount the pupil may name as just in a solemn statement before some sacred shrine[87]—a rash procedure for a teacher who doubted the existence of the gods. Diogenes Laertius accuses him of being the first to "arm disputants with the weapon of sophism," a charge that would have pleased Socrates; but Diogenes adds that Protagoras "was also the first to invent that sort of argument which is called Socratic"[88]—which might not have pleased Socrates.

It was but one of his many distinctions that he founded European grammar and philology. He treated of the right use of words, says Plato,[89] and was the first to distinguish the three genders of nouns, and certain tenses and moods of verbs.[90] But his chief significance lay in this, that with him, rather than with Socrates, began the subjective standpoint in philosophy. Unlike the Ionians he was less interested in things than in thought—i.e., in the whole process of sensation, perception, understanding, and expression. Whereas Parmenides rejected sensation as a guide to truth, Protagoras, like Locke, accepted it as the only means of knowledge, and refused to admit any transcendental—suprasensual—reality. No absolute truth can be found, said Protagoras, but only such truths as hold for given men under given conditions; contradictory assertions can be equally true for different persons or at different times.[91] All truth, goodness, and beauty are relative and subjective; "man is the measure of all things—of those that are, that they are, and of those that are not, that they are not."[92] To the historical eye a whole world begins to tremble when Protagoras announces this simple principle of humanism and relativity; all established truths and sacred

* These probably occurred in 451-45, 432, 422, and 415.[85]

principles crack; individualism has found a voice and a philosophy; and the supernatural bases of social order threaten to melt away.

The far-reaching skepticism implicit in this famous pronouncement might have remained theoretical and safe had not Protagoras applied it for a moment to theology. Among a group of distinguished men in the home of the unpopular freethinker, Euripides, Protagoras read a treatise whose first sentence made a stir in Athens. "With regard to the gods I know not whether they exist or not, or what they are like. Many things prevent our knowing: the subject is obscure, and brief is the span of our mortal life."[93] The Athenian Assembly, frightened by that ominous prelude, banished Protagoras, ordered all Athenians to surrender any copies they might have of his writings, and burned the books in the market place. Protagoras fled to Sicily, and, story tells us, was drowned on the way.[94]

Gorgias of Leontini carried on this skeptical revolution, but had the good sense to spend most of his life outside of Athens. His career was typical of the union between philosophy and statesmanship in Greece. Born about 483, he studied philosophy and rhetoric with Empedocles, and became so famous in Sicily as an orator and a teacher of oratory that in 427 he was sent by Leontini as an ambassador to Athens. At the Olympic games of 408 he captivated a great crowd by an address in which he appealed to the warring Greeks to make peace among themselves in order to face with unity and confidence the resurrected power of Persia. Traveling from city to city, he expounded his views in a style of oratory so euphuistically ornate, so symmetrically antithetical in idea and phrase, so delicately poised between poetry and prose, that he had no difficulty in attracting students who offered him a hundred minas for a course of instruction. His book *On Nature* sought to prove three startling propositions: (1) Nothing exists; (2) if anything existed it would be unknowable; and (3) if anything were knowable the knowledge of it could not be communicated from one person to another.*[95] Nothing else remains of Gorgias' writings. After enjoying the hospitality and fees of many states he settled down in Thessaly, and had the wisdom to consume most of his great fortune before his death.[96] He lived, as all authorities assure us, to at least one hundred and five; and an ancient writer tells us that "though Gorgias attained to the age of one hundred and eight, his body was not weakened by old age, but to the end of his life he was in sound condition, and his senses were those of a youth."[97]

* These propositions, aiming to discredit the transcendentalism of Parmenides, meant: (1) Nothing exists beyond the senses; (2) if anything existed beyond the senses it would be unknowable, for all knowledge comes through the senses; (3) if anything suprasensual were knowable, the knowledge of it would be incommunicable, since all communication is through the senses.

If the Sophists together constituted a scattered university, Hippias of Elis was a university in himself, and typified the polymath in a world where knowledge was not yet so vast as to be clearly beyond the grasp of one mind. He taught astronomy and mathematics, and made original contributions to geometry; he was a poet, a musician, and an orator; he lectured on literature, morals, and politics; he was an historian, and laid the foundations of Greek chronology by compiling a list of victors at the Olympic games; he was employed by Elis as an envoy to other states; and he knew so many arts and trades that he made with his own hands all his clothing and ornaments.[98] His work in philosophy was slight but important: he protested against the degenerative artificiality of city life, contrasted nature with law, and called law a tyrant over mankind.[99] Prodicus of Ceos carried on the grammatical work of Protagoras, fixed the parts of speech, and pleased the elders with a fable in which he represented Heracles choosing laborious Virtue instead of easy Vice.[100] Other Sophists were not so pious: Antiphon of Athens followed Democritus into materialism and atheism, and defined justice in terms of expediency; Thrasymachus of Chalcedon (if we may take Plato's word for it) identified right with might, and remarked that the success of villains cast doubt upon the existence of the gods.[101]

All in all, the Sophists must be ranked among the most vital factors in the history of Greece. They invented grammar and logic for Europe; they developed dialectic, analyzed the forms of argument, and taught men how to detect and practice fallacies. Through their stimulus and example reasoning became a ruling passion with the Greeks. By applying logic to language they promoted clarity and precision of thought, and facilitated the accurate transmission of knowledge. Through them prose became a form of literature, and poetry became a vehicle of philosophy. They applied analysis to everything; they refused to respect traditions that could not be supported by the evidence of the senses or the logic of reason; and they shared decisively in a rationalist movement that finally broke down, among the intellectual classes, the ancient faith of Hellas. "The common opinion" of his time, says Plato, derived "the world and all animals and plants . . . and inanimate substances from . . . some spontaneous and unintelligent cause."[102] Lysias tells of an atheistic society that called itself the *kakodaimoniotai*, or Devils' Club, and deliberately met and dined on holydays set apart for fasting.[103] Pindar, at the opening of the fifth century, accepted the oracle of Delphi piously; Aeschylus defended it politically; Herodotus, about 450, criticized it timidly; Thucydides, at the end of the century, openly rejected it. Euthyphro complained that when in the Assembly he spoke of oracles, the people laughed at him as an antiquated fool.[104]

The Sophists must not be blamed or credited for all of this; much of it was in the air, and was a natural result of growing wealth, leisure, travel, research, and speculation. Their role in the deterioration of morals was likewise contributory rather than basic; wealth of itself, without the aid of philosophy, puts an end to puritanism and stoicism. But within these modest limits the Sophists unwittingly quickened disintegration. Most of them, barring a thoroughly human love of money, were men of high character and decent life; but they did not transmit to their pupils the traditions or the wisdom that had made or kept them reasonably virtuous despite their discovery of the secular origin and geographical mutability of morals. Their colonial derivation may have led them to underestimate the value of custom as a peaceful substitute for force or law in maintaining morality and order. To define morality or human worth in terms of knowledge, as Protagoras did a generation before Socrates,[105] was a heady stimulus to thought, but an unsteadying blow to character; the emphasis on knowledge raised the educational level of the Greeks, but it did not develop intelligence as rapidly as it liberated intellect. The announcement of the relativity of knowledge did not make men modest, as it should, but disposed every man to consider himself the measure of all things; every clever youth could now feel himself fit to sit in judgment upon the moral code of his people, reject it if he could not understand and approve it, and then be free to rationalize his desires as the virtues of an emancipated soul. The distinction between "Nature" and convention, and the willingness of minor Sophists to argue that what "Nature" permitted was good regardless of custom or law, sapped the ancient supports of Greek morality, and encouraged many experiments in living. Old men mourned the passing of domestic simplicity and fidelity, and the pursuit of pleasure or wealth unchecked by religious restraints.[106] Plato and Thucydides speak of thinkers and public men who rejected morals as superstitions, and acknowledged no right but strength. This unscrupulous individualism turned the logic and rhetoric of the Sophists into an instrument of legal chicanery and political demagogy, and degraded their broad cosmopolitanism into a cautious reluctance to defend their country, or an unprejudiced readiness to sell it to the highest bidder. The religious peasantry and the conservative aristocrats began to agree with the common citizen of the urban democracy that philosophy had become a danger to the state.

Some of the philosophers themselves joined in the attack upon the Sophists. Socrates condemned them (as Aristophanes was to condemn Socrates) for making error specious with logic and persuasive with rhetoric, and scorned them for taking fees.[107] He excused his ignorance of grammar on the ground that he could not afford the fifty-drachma course of Prodicus, but only the one-drachma course, which gave merely the rudiments.[108] In an ungenial moment he used a merciless and revealing comparison:

> It is believed among us, Antiphon, that it is possible to dispose of beauty or of wisdom alike honorably or dishonorably; for if a person sells his beauty for money to anyone that wishes to purchase it, men call him a male prostitute; but if anyone makes a friend of a person whom he knows to be an honorable and worthy admirer, we regard him as prudent. In like manner those who sell their wisdom for money to any that will buy, men call sophists, or, as it were, prostitutes of wisdom; but whoever makes a friend of a person whom he knows to be deserving, and teaches him all the good that he knows, we consider him to act the part which becomes a good and honorable citizen.[109]

Plato could afford to agree with this view, being a rich man. Isocrates began his career with a speech *Against the Sophists*, became a successful professor of rhetoric, and charged a thousand drachmas ($1000) for a course.[110] Aristotle continued the attack; he defined a Sophist as one who "is only eager to get rich off his apparent wisdom,"[111] and accused Protagoras of "promising to make the worse appear the better reason."[112]

The tragedy was deepened by the fact that both sides were right. The complaint about fees was unjust: short of a state subsidy no other way was then open to finance higher education. If the Sophists criticized traditions and morals it was, of course, with no evil intent; they thought that they were liberating slaves. They were the intellectual representatives of their time, sharing its passion for the free intellect; like the Encyclopedists of Enlightenment France they swept away the dying past with magnificent *élan,* and did not live long enough, or think far enough, to establish new institutions in place of those that loosened reason would destroy. In every civilization the time comes when old ways must be re-examined if the society is to readjust itself to irresistible economic change; the Sophists were the instrument of this re-examination, but failed to provide the statesmanship for the readjustment. It remains to their credit that they powerfully stimulated the pursuit of knowledge, and made it fashionable to think. From every corner of the Greek world they brought new ideas and challenges to Athens, and aroused her to philosophical consciousness and maturity. Without them Socrates, Plato, and Aristotle would have been impossible.

V. SOCRATES

1. *The Mask of Silenus*

It is pleasant to stand at last face to face with a personality apparently so real as Socrates. But when we consider the two sources upon which we must rely for our knowledge of Socrates we find that one of them, Plato, writes imaginative dramas, that the other, Xenophon, writes historical novels, and that neither product can be taken as history. "They say," writes Diogenes Laertius, "that Socrates having heard Plato read the *Lysis*, cried out, 'O Heracles! what a number of lies the young man has told about me!' For Plato had set down a great many things as sayings of Socrates which he had never said."[113] Plato does not pretend to limit himself to fact; probably it never occurred to him that the future might have scant means of distinguishing, in his work, imagination from biography. But he draws so consistent a picture of his master throughout the Dialogues, from Socrates' youthful timidity in the *Parmenides* and his insolent loquacity in the *Protagoras* to the subdued piety and resignation of the *Phaedo*, that if this was not Socrates, then Plato is one of the greatest character creators in all literature. Aristotle accepts as authentically Socratic the views attributed to Socrates in the *Protagoras*.[114] Recently discovered fragments of an *Alcibiades* written by Aeschines of Sphettos, an immediate disciple of Socrates, tend to confirm the portrait given in the earlier dialogues of Plato, and the story of the philosopher's attachment to Alcibiades.[115] On the other hand, Aristotle classes Xenophon's *Memorabilia* and *Banquet* as forms of fiction, imaginary conversations in which Socrates becomes, more often than not, a mouthpiece for Xenophon's ideas.*[116] If Xenophon honestly played Eckermann to Socrates' Goethe we can only say that he has carefully collected the master's safest platitudes; it is incredible that so virtuous a man should have upset a civilization. Other ancient writers did not make the old sage into such a saint; Aristoxenus of Tarentum, about 318, reported, on the testimony of his father—who claimed to have known Socrates—that the philosopher was a person without education, "ignorant and debauched";[117] and Eupolis, the comic poet, rivaled his rival Aristophanes

* So in Book III of the *Memorabilia* Socrates is made to expound the principles of military strategy.

in abusing the great gadfly.[118] Making due discount for polemic vitriol it is at least clear that Socrates was a man, hated and loved beyond any other figure of his time.

His father was a sculptor, and he himself was said to have carved a *Hermes*, and three *Graces* that stood near the entrance to the Acropolis.[119] His mother was a midwife: it was a standing joke with him that he merely continued her trade, but in the realm of ideas, helping others to deliver themselves of their conceptions. One tradition describes him as the son of a slave;[120] it is improbable, for he served as a hoplite (a career open only to citizens), inherited a house from his father, and had seventy minas ($7000) invested for him by his friend Crito;[121] for the rest he is represented as poor.[122] He paid much attention to the training of the body, and was usually in good physical condition. He made a reputation for himself as a soldier during the Peloponnesian War: in 432 he fought at Potidaea, in 424 at Delium, in 422 at Amphipolis. At Potidaea he saved both the life and the arms of the young Alcibiades, and gave up in the youth's favor his claim to the prize for valor; at Delium he was the last Athenian to give ground to the Spartans, and seems to have saved himself by glaring at the enemy; even the Spartans were frightened. In these campaigns, we are told, he excelled all in endurance and courage, bearing without complaint hunger, fatigue, and cold.[124] At home, when he condescended to stay there, he worked as a stonecutter and statuary. He had no interest in travel, and seldom went outside the city and its port. He married Xanthippe, who berated him for neglecting his family; he recognized the justice of her complaint,[125] and defended her gallantly to his son and his friends. Marriage disturbed him so little that he seems to have taken an additional wife when the mortality of males in the war led to the temporary legalization of polygamy.[128]

All the world knows the face of Socrates. Judging precariously from the bust in the Museo delle Terme at Rome, it was not typically Greek;[129] its spacious spread, its flat, broad nose, its thick lips, and heavy beard suggest rather Solon's friend of the steppes, Anacharsis, or that modern Scythian, Tolstoi. "I say," Alcibiades insists, even while protesting his love, "that Socrates is exactly like the masks of Silenus, which may be seen sitting in the statuaries' shops, having pipes and flutes in their mouths; and they are made to open in the middle, and there are images of gods inside them. I say also that he is like Marsyas the satyr. You will not deny, Socrates, that your face is that of a satyr."[130] Socrates raises no objection; to make matters worse he confesses to an unduly large paunch, and hopes to reduce it by dancing.[131]

Plato and Xenophon agree in describing his habits and his character. He was content with one simple and shabby robe throughout the year, and liked bare feet better than sandals or shoes.[132] He was incredibly free from the acquisitive fever that agitates mankind. Viewing the multitude of articles exposed for sale in the market place, he remarked, "How many things there are that I do not want!"[133]—and felt himself rich in his poverty. He was a model of moderation and self-control, but all the world away from a saint. He could drink like a gentleman, and needed no timid asceticism to keep him straight.* He was no recluse; he liked good company, and let the rich entertain him now and then; but he made no obeisance to them, could get along very well without them, and rejected the gifts and invitations of magnates and kings.[135] All in all he was fortunate: he lived without working, read without writing, taught without routine, drank without dizziness, and died before senility, almost without pain.

His morals were excellent for his time, but would hardly satisfy all the good people who praise him. He "took fire" at the sight of Charmides, but controlled himself by asking if this handsome lad had also a "noble soul."[136] Plato speaks of Socrates and Alcibiades as lovers, and describes the philosopher "in chase of the fair youth."[137] Though the old man seems to have kept these amours for the most part Platonic, he was not above giving advice to homosexuals and hetairai on how to attract lovers.[138] He gallantly promised his help to the courtesan Theodota, who rewarded him with the invitation: "Come often to see me."[139] His good humor and kindliness were so unfailing that those who could stomach his politics found it simple to put up with his morals. When he had passed away Xenophon spoke of him as "so just that he wronged no man in the most trifling affair . . . so temperate that he never preferred pleasure to virtue; so wise that he never erred in distinguishing better from worse . . . so capable of discerning the character of others, and of exhorting them to virtue and honor, that he seemed to be such as the best and happiest of men would be."[140] Or, as Plato put it, with moving simplicity, he "was truly the wisest, and justest, and best of all the men whom I have ever known."[141]

* "So far as drinking is concerned," Xenophon makes Socrates say, "wine does of a truth 'moisten the soul' and lull our griefs to sleep. . . . But I suspect that men's bodies fare like those of plants. . . . When God gives the plants water in floods to drink they cannot stand up straight or let the breezes blow through them; but when they drink only as much as they enjoy they grow up straight and tall, and come to full and abundant fruitage."[134]

2. *Portrait of a Gadfly*

Being curious and disputatious he became a student of philosophy, and was for a time fascinated by the Sophists who invaded Athens in his youth. There is no evidence that Plato invented the fact as well as the content of Socrates' meetings with Parmenides, Protagoras, Gorgias, Prodicus, Hippias, and Thrasymachus; it is likely that he saw Zeno when the latter came to Athens about 450, and that he was so infected with Zeno's dialectic that it never left him.[142] Probably he knew Anaxagoras, if not in person then in doctrine; for Archelaus of Miletus, pupil of Anaxagoras, was for a time the teacher of Socrates. Archelaus began as a physicist and ended as a student of morals; he explained the origin and basis of morals on rationalistic lines, and perhaps turned Socrates from science to ethics.[143] By all these avenues Socrates came to philosophy, and thenceforth found his "greatest good in daily converse about virtue, examining myself and others; for a life unscrutinized is unworthy of a man."* So he went prowling among men's beliefs, prodding them with questions, demanding precise answers and consistent views, and making himself a terror to all who could not think clearly. Even in Hades he proposed to be a gadfly, and "find out who is wise, and who pretends to be wise and is not."[144] He protected himself from a similar cross-examination by announcing that he knew nothing; he knew all the questions, but none of the answers; he modestly called himself an "amateur in philosophy."[145] What he meant, presumably, was that he was certain of nothing except man's fallibility, and had no hard and fast system of dogmas and principles. When the oracle at Delphi, to Chaerephon's alleged inquiry, "Is any man wiser than Socrates?" gave the alleged reply, "No one,"[146] Socrates ascribed the response to his profession of ignorance.

From that moment he set himself to the pragmatic task of getting clear ideas. "For himself," he said, "he would hold discourse, from time to time, on what concerned mankind, considering what was pious, what impious; what was just, what unjust; what was sanity, what insanity; what was courage, what cowardice; what was the nature of government over men, and the qualities of one skilled in governing them; and touching on other subjects . . . of which he thought that those who were ignorant might justly be deemed no better than slaves."[147] To every vague notion, easy generalization, or secret prejudice he pointed the challenge, "What is it?" and asked for precise definitions. It became his habit to rise early and go to the market place, the gymnasiums, the palaestras, or the workshops of artisans, and

* *De anexetastos bios ou biotos anthropo.*—Plato, *Apology*, 37.

engage in discussion any person who gave promise of a stimulating intelligence or an amusing stupidity. "Is not the road to Athens made for conversation?" he asked.[148] His method was simple: he called for the definition of a large idea; he examined the definition, usually to reveal its incompleteness, its contradictoriness, or its absurdity; he led on, by question after question, to a fuller and juster definition, which, however, he never gave. Sometimes he proceeded to a general conception, or exposed another, by investigating a long series of particular instances, thereby introducing a measure of induction into Greek logic; sometimes, with the famous Socratic irony, he unveiled the ridiculous consequences of the definition or opinion he wished to destroy. He had a passion for orderly thinking, and liked to classify individual things according to their genus, species, and specific difference, thereby preparing for Aristotle's method of definition as well as for Plato's theory of Ideas. He liked to describe dialectic as the art of careful distinctions. And he salted the weary wastes of logic with a humor that died an early death in the history of philosophy.

His opponents objected that he tore down but never built, that he rejected every answer but gave none of his own, and that the results demoralized morals and paralyzed thought. In many cases he left the idea that he had set out to clarify more obscure than before. When a resolute fellow like Critias tried to question him he turned his reply into another question, and at once recaptured the advantage. In the *Protagoras* he offers to answer instead of asking, but his good resolution lasts but a moment; whereupon Protagoras, being an old hand at the game of logic, quietly withdraws from the argument.[149] Hippias rages at Socrates' elusiveness: "By Zeus!" he cries, "you shall not hear [my answer] until you yourself declare what you think justice to be; for it is not enough that you laugh at others, questioning and confuting everybody, while you yourself are unwilling to give a reason to anybody, or to declare your opinion on any subject."[150] To such taunts Socrates replied that he was only a midwife like his mother. "The reproach which is often made against me, that I ask questions of others and have not the wit to answer them myself, is very just. The reason is that the god compels me to be a midwife, but forbids me to bring forth"[151] —a *deus ex machina* worthy of his friend Euripides.

In many ways he resembled the Sophists, and the Athenians applied the name to him without hesitation, and usually without reproach.[152] Indeed, he was often a Sophist in the modern sense: he was rich in crafty dodges and argumentative tricks, slyly changed the scope or meaning of terms, drowned the problem in loose analogies, quibbled like a schoolboy, and beat the wind bravely with words.[153] The Athenians might be excused for giving him hemlock, since there is no pest like a conscious logician. In four points he differed from the Sophists: he despised rhetoric, he wished to strengthen morality, he did not profess to teach anything more than the art of examining ideas, and he refused to take pay for his instruction—though he appears to have accepted occasional help from his rich friends.[154] With all his irritating faults his students loved him deeply. "Perhaps," he says to one of them, "I may be able to assist you in the pursuit of honor and virtue, from being mutually disposed to love; for whenever I conceive a liking for persons I devote myself with ardor, and with my whole mind, to love them, and be loved by them in return, regretting their absence and having mine regretted by them, and longing for their society while they long for mine."[155]

Aristophanes' *Clouds* represents the pupils of Socrates as forming a school with a regular meeting place; and a passage in Xenophon lends some color to this conception.[156] Usually he is pictured as teaching wherever he found a pupil or a listener. But no common doctrine united his followers; they differed so widely among themselves that they became the leaders of the most diverse philosophical schools and theories in Greece—Platonism, Cynicism, Stoicism, Epicureanism, Skepticism. There was the proud and humble Antisthenes, who took from his master the doctrine of simplicity in life and needs, and founded the Cynic school; perhaps he was present when Socrates said to Antiphon: "You seem to think that happiness consists in luxury and extravagance; but I think that to want nothing is to resemble the gods, and that to want as little as possible is to make the nearest approach to the gods."[157] There was Aristippus, who derived from Socrates' placid acceptance of pleasure as a good the doctrine which he later developed at Cyrene, and which Epicurus would preach at Athens. There was Eucleides of Megara, who sharpened the Socratic dialectic into a skepticism that denied the possibility of any real knowledge. There was the young Phaedo, who had been reduced to slavery, and had been ransomed by Crito at the behest of Socrates; Socrates loved the lad, and "made him a philosopher."[158] There was the restless Xenophon who, though he gave up philosophy for soldiering, testified that "nothing was of greater benefit than to associate with Socrates, and to converse with him, on any occasion, on any subject whatever."[159] There was Plato, upon whose vivid imagination the sage made so lasting an impression that the two minds are mingled forever in philosophical history. There was the rich Crito, who "looked upon Socrates with the greatest affection, and took care that he should never be in want of anything."[160] There was the dashing young Alcibiades, whose infidelities were to discredit and endanger his teacher, but who now loved Socrates with characteristic abandon, and said:

> When we hear any other speaker, even a very good one, his words produce absolutely no effect upon us in comparison, whereas the very fragments of your words, Socrates, even at second hand, and however imperfectly reported, amaze and possess the souls of every man, woman and child who comes within hearing of them. . . . I am conscious that if I did not shut my ears against him and fly from the voice of the siren, he would detain me until I grew old sitting at his feet. . . . I have known in my soul, or in my heart . . . that greatest of pangs, more violent in ingenuous youth than any serpent's tooth, the pang of philosophy. . . . And you, Phaedrus, you, Agathon, you, Eryximachus, you, Pausanias, you, Aristodemus, you, Aristophanes, all of you, and I need not say Socrates himself, have all had experience of the same madness and passion for philosophy.[161]

There was the oligarchic leader Critias, who enjoyed Socrates' quips against democracy, and helped to incriminate him by writing a play in which he described the gods as the invention of clever statesmen who used them as night watchmen to frighten men into decency.[162] And there was the son of the democratic leader Anytus, a lad who preferred to hear Socrates discourse rather than to attend to his business, which was dealing in leather. Anytus complained that Socrates had unsettled the boy with skepticism, that the boy no longer respected his parents or the gods; moreover, Anytus resented Socrates' criticisms of democracy.*[163] "Socrates," says Anytus, "I think you are too ready to speak evil of men; and if you will take my advice, I would recommend you to be careful. Perhaps there is no city in which it is not easier to do men harm than to do them good; and this is certainly the case at Athens."[165] Anytus bided his time.

3. *The Philosophy of Socrates*

Behind the method was a philosophy, elusive, tentative, unsystematic, but so real that in effect the man died for it. At first sight there is no Socratic philosophy; but this is largely because Socrates, accepting the relativism of Protagoras, refused to dogmatize, and was certain only of his ignorance.

---

* Possibly, as Plutarch and Athenaeus assure us, Anytus loved Alcibiades, who rejected him for Socrates.[164]

Though condemned for irreligion, Socrates gave at least lip service to the gods of his city, participated in its religious ceremonies, and was never known to utter an impious word.[166] He professed to follow, in all important negative decisions, an inner *daimonion* which he described as a sign from heaven. Perhaps this spirit was another play of the Socratic irony; if so, it was remarkably well sustained; and it is but one class of many appeals, in Socrates, to oracles and dreams as messages from the gods.[167] He argued that there were too many instances of amazing adaptation and apparent design to allow us to ascribe the world to chance or any unintelligent cause. On immortality he was not so definite; he pleads for it tenaciously in the *Phaedo*, but in the *Apology* he says, "Were I to make any claim to be wiser than others, it would be because I do not think that I have any sufficient knowledge of the other world, when in fact I have none."[168] In the *Cratylus* he applies the same agnosticism to the gods: "Of the gods we know nothing."[169] He advised his followers not to dispute of such matters; like Confucius, he asked them did they know human affairs so well that they were ready to meddle with those of heaven?[170] The best thing to do, he felt, was to acknowledge our ignorance, and meanwhile to obey the oracle at Delphi, which, when asked how one should worship the gods, answered, "According to the law of your country."[171]

He applied this skepticism even more rigorously to the physical sciences. One should study them only so far as to guide his life; beyond that they are an inscrutable maze; each mystery, when solved, reveals a deeper mystery.[173] In his youth he had studied science with Archelaus; in his maturity he turned from it as a more or less plausible myth, and interested himself no longer in facts and origins but in values and ends. "He discoursed," says Xenophon, "always of human affairs."[174] The Sophists had also "turned around" from natural science to man, and had begun the study of sensation, perception, and knowledge; Socrates went further inward to study human character and purpose. "Tell me, Euthydemus, have you ever gone to Delphi?" "Yes, twice." "And did you observe what is written on the temple wall—Know thyself?" "I did." "And did you take no thought of that inscription, or did you attend to it, and try to examine yourself, and ascertain what sort of character you are?"[175]

Philosophy, therefore, was for Socrates neither theology nor metaphysics nor physics, but ethics and politics, with logic as an introduction and a means. Coming at the close of the Sophistic period, he perceived that the Sophists had created one of the most critical situations in the history of any culture—the weakening of the supernatural basis of morals. Instead of a

frightened return to orthodoxy, he moved forward to the profoundest question that ethics can ask: is a natural ethic possible? Can morality survive without supernatural belief? Can philosophy, by molding an effective secular moral code, save the civilization which its freedom of thought has threatened to destroy? When, in the *Euthyphro,* Socrates argues that the good is not good because the gods approve of it, but that the gods approve of it because it is good, he is proposing a philosophical revolution. His conception of good, so far from being theological, is earthly to the point of being utilitarian. Goodness, he thinks, is not general and abstract, but specific and practical, "good for something." Goodness and beauty are forms of usefulness and human advantage; even a dung basket is beautiful if it is well formed for its purpose.[176] Since (Socrates thought) there is nothing else so useful as knowledge, knowledge is the highest virtue, and all vice is ignorance[178]—though "virtue" (*arete*) here means excellence rather than sinlessness. Without proper knowledge right action is impossible; with proper knowledge right action is inevitable. Men never do that which they know to be wrong—i.e., unwise, injurious to themselves. The highest good is happiness, the highest means to it is knowledge or intelligence.

If knowledge is the highest excellence, Socrates argues, aristocracy is the best form of government, and democracy is nonsense. "It is absurd," says Xenophon's Socrates, "to choose magistrates by lot where no one would dream of drawing lots for a pilot, a mason, a flute-player, or any craftsman at all, though the shortcomings of such men are far less harmful than those that disorder our government."[179] He condemns the litigiousness of the Athenians, their noisy envy of one another, the bitterness of their political factions and disputes: "On these accounts," he says, "I am constantly in the greatest fear lest some evil should happen to the state too great for it to bear."[180] Nothing could save Athens, he thought, except government by knowledge and ability; and this was no more to be determined by voting than the qualifications of a pilot, a musician, a physician, or a carpenter. Nor should power or wealth choose the officials of the state; tyranny and plutocracy are as bad as democracy; the reasonable compromise is an aristocracy in which office would be restricted to those mentally fit and trained for it.[181] Despite these criticisms of Athenian democracy Socrates recognized its advantages, and appreciated the liberties and opportunities that it gave him. He smiled at the tendency of some followers to preach a "return to Nature," and adopted towards Antisthenes and the Cynics the same attitude that Voltaire would take towards Rousseau—that with all its

faults civilization is a precious thing, not to be abandoned for any primeval simplicity.[182]

Nevertheless the majority of the Athenians looked upon him with irritated suspicion. The orthodox in religion considered him to be the most dangerous of the Sophists; for while he observed the amenities of the ancient faith he rejected tradition, wished to subject every rule to the scrutiny of reason, founded morality in the individual conscience rather than in social good or the unchanging decrees of heaven, and ended with a skepticism that left reason itself in a mental confusion unsettling to every custom and belief. To him, as well as to Protagoras and Euripides, praisers of the past like Aristophanes attributed the irreligion of the age, the disrespect of the young for the old, the loosened morals of the educated classes, and the disorderly individualism that was consuming Athenian life. Though Socrates refused to support the oligarchic faction, many of its leaders were his pupils or his friends. When one of them, Critias, led the oligarchs in a rich man's revolution and a ruthless terror, democrats like Anytus and Meletus branded Socrates as the intellectual source of the oligarchic reaction, and determined to remove him from Athenian life.

They succeeded, but they could not destroy his immense influence. The dialectic he had received from Zeno was passed down through Plato to Aristotle, who turned it into a system of logic so complete that it remained unaltered for nineteen hundred years. Upon science his influence was injurious: students were turned away from physical research, and the doctrine of external design offered no encouragement to scientific analysis. The individualist and intellectualist ethic of Socrates had a modest share, perhaps, in undermining Athenian morals; but its emphasis on conscience as above the law became one of the cardinal tenets of Christianity. Through his pupils the many suggestions of his thought became the substance of all the major philosophies of the next two centuries. The most powerful element in his influence was the example of his life and character. He became for Greek history a martyr and a saint; and every generation that sought an exemplar of simple living and brave thinking turned back to nourish its ideals with his memory. "In contemplating the man's wisdom and nobility of character," said Xenophon, "I find it beyond my power to forget him, or, in remembering him, to refrain from praising him. And if, among those who make virtue their aim, any one has ever been brought into contact with a person more helpful than Socrates, I count that man worthy to be called most blessed."[183]

CHAPTER XVII

The Literature of the Golden Age

I. PINDAR

NORMALLY the philosophy of one age is the literature of the next: the ideas and issues that in one generation are fought out on the field of research and speculation provide in the succeeding generation the background of drama, fiction, and poetry. But in Greece the literature did not lag behind the philosophy; the poets were themselves philosophers, did their own thinking, and were in the intellectual vanguard of their time. That same conflict between conservatism and radicalism which agitated Greek religion, science, and philosophy found expression also in poetry and drama, even in the writing of history. Since excellence of artistic form was added, in Greek letters, to depth of speculative thought, the literature of the Golden Age reached heights never touched again until the days of Shakespeare and Montaigne.

Because of this burden of thought, and the decay of royal or aristocratic patronage, the fifth century was less rich than the sixth in lyric poetry as an independent art. Pindar is the transition between the two periods: he inherits the lyric form, but fills it with dramatic magnificence; after him poetry breaks through its traditional limits, and, in the Dionysian drama, combines with religion, music, and the dance to make a greater vehicle for the splendor and passion of the Golden Age.

Pindar came of a Theban family that traced its lineage back to primitive times, and claimed to include many of the ancient heroes commemorated in his verse. His uncle, an accomplished flutist, passed down to Pindar much of his love for music, and something of his skill. For advanced musical instruction the parents sent the boy to Athens, where Lasus and Agathocles taught him choral composition. Before he was twenty—i.e., by 502—he returned to Thebes, and studied with the poetess Corinna. Five times he competed against Corinna in public song, and five times was beaten; but Corinna was very pleasing to behold, and the judges were men.[1] Pindar called her a sow, Simonides a crow, himself an eagle.[2] Despite this myopia his reputation rose so high that his fellow Thebans soon concocted a story that told how once, as the young poet slept in the fields, some bees had settled upon his lips, and had left their honey there.[3] Soon he was handsomely commissioned to write odes in honor of princes and rich men; he was the guest of noble families in Rhodes, Tenedos,

Corinth, and Athens, and for a time lived as royal bard at the courts of Alexander I of Macedon, Theron of Acragas, and Hieron I of Syracuse. Usually his songs were paid for in advance, very much as if a city should in our days engage a composer to celebrate it with an original composition for chorus and dance, and to conduct the performance himself. When Pindar returned to Thebes, towards his forty-fourth year, he was acclaimed as Boeotia's greatest gift to Greece.

He worked painstakingly, composing the music for each poem, and often training a chorus to sing it. He wrote hymns and paeans for deities, dithyrambs for the festivals of Dionysus, *parthenaia* for maidens, *enkomia* for celebrities, *skolia* for banquets, *threnoi*, or dirges, for funerals, and *epinikia*, or songs of victory, for winners at the Panhellenic competitions. Of all these only forty-five odes remain, named after the games whose heroes they honored. Of these odes, again, only the words survive, none of the music; in judging them, we are in the position of some future historian who, having the librettos of Wagner's operas but nothing of the scores, should list him as a poet rather than a composer, and should rank him by the words that once attended upon his harmonies. Or if we picture some Chinese scholar, unfamiliar with Christian story, reading in one evening, in lame translation, ten Bach chorals divorced from their music and ritual, we shall measure our justice to Pindar. When read today, ode after ode, in the silence of the study, he is beyond comparison the dreariest outpost in the classical landscape.

Only the analogy of music can explain the structure of these poems. To Pindar, as to Simonides and Bacchylides, the form to be followed in an epinician ode was as compulsory as sonata form in the sonatas and symphonies of modern Europe. First came the statement of the theme—the name and story of the athlete who had gained the prize, or of the nobleman whose horses had drawn their chariot to victory. In general Pindar celebrates "the wisdom of man, and his beauty, and the splendor of his fame."[4] In truth he was not much interested in his formal subject; he sang in praise of runners, courtesans, and kings, and was willing to accept any promptly paying tyrant as a patron saint[5] if the occasion gave scope to his rich imagination and his proudly intricate verse. His topic might be anything from a mule race to the glory of Greek civilization in all its variety and spread. He was loyal to Thebes, and not more inspired than the Delphic oracle when he defended Theban neutrality in the Persian War; but later he was ashamed of his error, and went out of his way to praise the leader of the Greek defense as "renowned Athens, rich, violet-crowned, worthy of song, bulwark of Hellas, god-protected city."[6] The Athenians are said to have given him ten thousand drachmas ($10,000) for the dithyrambs, or processional song, in which these lines occurred;[7] Thebes, we are less reliably informed, fined him for his implied reproof, and Athens paid the fine.[8]

The second part of a Pindaric ode was a selection from Greek mythology. Here Pindar was discouragingly lavish; as Corinna complained, he "sowed with the whole sack rather than with the hand."[9] He had a high conception of the gods, and honored them as among his best clients. He was the favorite poet of the Delphic priesthood; during his life he received many privileges from them, and after his death his spirit was, with Caledonian generosity, invited to share in the first fruits offered at Apollo's shrine.[10] He was the last defender of the orthodox faith; even the pious Aeschylus seems wildly heretical beside him; Pindar would have been horrified by the blasphemies of *Prometheus Bound*. Sometimes he rises to an almost monotheistic conception of Zeus as "the All, governing all things and seeing all things."[11] He is a friend of the Mysteries, and shares the Orphic hope of paradise. He preaches the divine origin and destiny of the individual soul,[12] and offers one of the earliest descriptions of a Last Judgment, a Heaven, and a Hell. "Immediately after death the lawless spirits suffer punishment, and the sins committed in this realm of Zeus are judged by One who passeth sentence stern and inevitable."

> But in sunshine ever fair
>   Abide the good, and all their nights and days
> An equal splendor wear.
> And never as of old with thankless toil
> For their poor empty needs they vex the soil,
>   And plough the watery seas;
> But dwelling with the glorious gods in ease
>   A tearless life they pass,
>   Whose joy on earth it was
> To keep their plighted word. But, far from these,
>   Torments the rest sustain too dark for human gaze.[13]

The third and concluding section of a Pindaric ode was usually a word of moral counsel. We must not expect any subtle philosophy here; Pindar was no Athenian, and had probably never met or read a Sophist; his intellect was consumed in his art, and no force remained for original thought. He was satisfied to urge his victorious athletes or princes to be modest in their success, and to show respect for the gods, their fellow men, and their own best selves. Now and then he mingled reproof with praise, and dared to warn Hieron against greed;[14] but neither was he afraid to say a kind word for that most maligned and loved of all goods—money. He abhorred the revolutionists of Sicily, and warned them almost in the words of Confucius: "Even for the feeble it is an easy thing to shake a city to its foundation, but it is a sore struggle to set it in its place again."[15] He liked the moderate democracy of Athens after Salamis, but sincerely believed aristocracy to be the least harmful of all forms of government. Ability, he thought, lies in the blood rather than in schooling, and tends to appear in families that have shown it before. Only good blood can prepare a man for those rare deeds that ennoble and justify human life. "Things of a day! What are we and what not? A dream about a shadow is man; yet when some god-given splendor falls, a glory of light comes over him, and his life is sweet."[16]

Pindar was not popular in his lifetime, and for some centuries yet he will continue to enjoy the lifeless immortality of those writers whom all men praise and no one reads. While the world was moving forward he asked it to stand still, and it left him so far behind that though younger than Aeschylus he seems older than Alcman. He wrote a poetry as compact, involved, and devious as Tacitus' prose, in an artificial and deliberately archaic dialect of his own, in meters so elaborate that few poets have ever cared to follow them,* and so varied that only two of the forty-five odes have the same metrical form. He is so obscure, despite the naïveté of his thought, that grammarians spend a lifetime unraveling his Teutonic constructions, only to find, beneath them, a mine of sonorous platitudes. If despite these faults, and his frigid formality, and turgid metaphors, and tiresome mythology, some curious scholars are still persuaded to read him, it is because his narratives are swift and vivid, his simple morality is sincere, and the splendor of his language lifts to a passing grandeur even the humblest themes.

He lived to the age of eighty, secure in Thebes from the turmoil of Athenian thought. "Dear to a man," he sang, "is his own home city, his comrades and his kinsmen, so that he is well content. But to foolish men belongeth a love for things afar."[17] Ten days before his end (442), we are told, he sent to ask the oracle of Ammon, "What is best for man?"—to which the Egyptian oracle answered, like a Greek, "Death."[18] Athens put up a statue to him at the public cost, and the Rhodians inscribed his seventh Olympian ode—a panegyric of their island—in letters of gold upon a temple wall. When, in 335, Alexander ordered rebellious Thebes to be burned to the ground he commanded his soldiers to leave unharmed the house in which Pindar had lived and died.

II. THE DIONYSIAN THEATER

The story is told in the *Lexicon* of Suidas[19] that during the performance of a play by Pratinas, about 500 B.C., the wooden benches upon which the auditors sat gave way, injuring some, and causing such alarm that the Athenians built, on the southern slope of the Acropolis, a theater of stone,

* A notable exception is Dryden's *Alexander's Feast.*

which they dedicated to the god Dionysus.* In the next two centuries similar theaters rose at Eretria, Epidaurus, Argos, Mantinea, Delphi, Tauromenium (Taormina), Syracuse, and elsewhere in the scattered Greek world. But it was on the Dionysian stage that the major tragedies and comedies were first played, and fought out the bitterest phase of that war, between the old theology and the new philosophy, which binds into one vast process of thought and change the mental history of the Periclean age.

The great theater is, of course, open to the sky. The fifteen thousand seats, rising in a fanlike semicircle of tiers toward the Parthenon, face Mt. Hymettus and the sea; when the persons of the drama invoke the earth and the sky, the sun and the stars and the ocean, they are addressing realities which most of the audience, as it listens to the speech or chant, can directly see and feel. The seats, originally of wood, later of stone, have no backs; many people bring cushions; but they sit through five plays in a day with no other known support for their spines than the unaccommodating knees of the auditors behind them. In the front rows are a few marble seats with backs for the local high priests of Dionysus and the officials of the city.† At the foot of the auditorium is an *orchestra*, or dancing space, for the chorus. At the rear of this is a small wooden building known as the *skene*, or scene, which serves to represent now a palace, now a temple, now a private dwelling, and probably also to house the players while off stage.‡ There are such simple "properties"—altars, furniture, etc.—as the story may require; in the case of Aristophanes' *Birds* there are important adjuncts of scenery and costume;[20] and Agatharchus of Samos paints backgrounds in such a way as to produce the illusion of distance. Several mechanical devices help to vary the action or the place.§ To show an action that has transpired within the *skene*, a wooden platform (*ekkyklema*) may be wheeled out, and have human figures arranged on it in a tableau suggestive

* This was not the Theater of Dionysus that tourists see today; the surviving structure was built under the direction of the Finance Minister Lycurgus about 338. Some parts of it are conjecturally traced back to 421; some others appear to have been added in the first and third centuries after Christ.

† This and the remarks about the stage presume that the theater built by Lycurgus followed the general plan of the structure that it replaced.

‡ Whether the action took place on the roof of the *skene*, or upon the *proskenion*, or proscenium, before it, is uncertain; perhaps the action moved from one level to the other as the location of the story changed.

§ A drop curtain was used in the Roman period, being lowered into a crevice at the beginning of a scene, and raised at the end; but our extant plays from the fifth century give no evidence of this, and apparently rely on choral interludes to serve the purpose of a curtain between the "acts."

of what has occurred; so a corpse may be on it, with the murderers holding bloody weapons in their hands; it is against the traditions of the Greek drama to represent violence directly on the stage. At either side of the proscenium is a large, triangular, upright prism that turns on a pivot; each face of the prism has a different scene painted on it; and by revolving these *periaktoi* the background can be altered in a moment. A still stranger apparatus is the *mechane*, or machine, a crane with pulley and weights; it is placed upon the *skene* at the left, and is used to lower gods or heroes from heaven down to the stage, or to raise them back to heaven, or even to exhibit them suspended in the air. Euripides in particular is fond of using this mechanism to let down a god—a *deus ex machina*, as the Romans put it—who piously unties the knot of his agnostic plays.

The tragic drama at Athens is not a secular or perennial affair, but part of the annual celebration of the feast of Dionysus.* From among many plays offered to the archon a few are selected for performance. Each of the ten tribes or demes of Attica chooses one of its rich citizens to serve as choragus, i.e., director of the chorus; it is his privilege to pay the cost of training the singers, dancers, and actors, and to meet the other expenses of presenting one of the compositions. Sometimes a choragus spends a fortune upon scenery, costumes, and "talent"—in this way every play financed by Nicias obtains a prize;[21] some other choragi economize by hiring second-hand robes from dealers in theatrical costumes.[22] The actual training of the chorus is usually undertaken by the dramatist himself.

The chorus is in many ways the most important as well as the most costly part of the spectacle. Often it gives its name to the drama; and through it, for the most part, the poet expresses his views on religion and philosophy. The history of the Greek theater is a losing struggle of the chorus to dominate the play: at first the chorus is everything; in Thespis and Aeschylus its role diminishes as the number of actors increase; in the drama of the third century it disappears. Usually the chorus is composed not of professional singers but of amateurs chosen from the civic roster of the tribe. They are all men, and number, after Aeschylus, fifteen. They dance as well as sing, and move in dignified procession across the long and narrow stage, interpreting through the poetry of motion the words and moods of the play.

Music holds in the Greek drama a place second only to the action and the poetry. Usually the dramatist composes the music as well as the

---

* Plays were also presented during the lesser Dionysia, or Lenaea, usually at the Piraeus; and at various times in the local theaters of the Attic towns.

words.[23] Most of the dialogue is spoken or declaimed; some of it is chanted in recitative; but the leading roles contain lyrical passages that must be sung as solos, duets, trios, or in unison or alternation with the chorus.[24] The singing is simple, without "parts" or harmony. The accompaniment is usually given by a single flute, and accords with the voices note for note; in this way the words can be followed by the audience, and the poem is not drowned out in the song. These plays cannot be judged by reading them silently; to the Greeks the words are but a part of a complex art form that weaves poetry, music, acting, and the dance into a profound and moving unity.*

Nevertheless the play is the thing, and the prize is awarded less for the music than for the drama, and less for the drama than for the acting; a good actor can make a success of a middling play.[26] The actor—who is always a male—is not disdained as in Rome, but is much honored; he is exempt from military service, and is allowed safe passage through the lines in time of war. He is called *hypokrites*, but this word means answerer—i.e., to the chorus; only later will the actor's role as an impersonator lead to the use of the word as meaning hypocrite. Actors are organized in a strong union or guild called the Dionysian Artists, which has members throughout Greece. Troupes of players wander from city to city, composing their own plays and music, making their own costumes, and setting up their own stages. As in all times, the incomes of leading actors are very high, that of secondary actors precariously low;[27] and the morals of both are what might be expected of men moving from place to place, fluctuating between luxury and poverty, and too high-strung to be capable of a stable and normal life.

In both tragedy and comedy the actor wears a mask, fitted with a resonant mouthpiece of brass. The acoustics of the Greek theater, and the visibility of the stage from every seat, are remarkable; but even so it is found advisable to reinforce the voice of the actor, and help the eye of the distant spectator to distinguish readily the various characters portrayed. All subtle play of vocal or facial expression is sacrificed to these needs. When real individuals are represented on the stage, like the Euripides of the *Eccle-*

---

* Music continued to play a central role in the culture of the classic period (480-323). The great name among the fifth-century composers was Timotheus of Miletus; he wrote nomes in which the music dominated the poetry, and represented a story and an action. His extension of the Greek lyre to eleven strings, and his experiments in complex and elaborate styles, provoked the conservatives of Athens to such denunciation that Timotheus, we are told, was about to take his own life when Euripides comforted him, collaborated with him, and correctly prophesied that all Greece would soon be at his feet.[25]

siazusae and the Socrates of the *Clouds*, the masks imitate, and largely caricature, their actual features. The masks have come down into the drama from religious performances, in which they were often instruments of terror or humor; in comedy they continue this tradition, and are as grotesque and extravagant as Greek fancy can make them. Just as the actor's voice is strengthened and his countenance enlarged by the mask, so his dimensions are extended with padding, and his height is enhanced by an *onkos*, or projection on his head, and by *kothornoi*, or thick-soled shoes, on his feet. All in all, as Lucian puts it, the ancient actor makes a "hideous and appalling spectacle."[28]

The audience is as interesting as the play. Men and women of all ranks are admitted,[29] and after 420 all citizens who need it receive from the state the two obols required for entrance. Women sit apart from men, and courtesans have a place to themselves; custom keeps all but the looser ladies away from comedy.[30] It is a lively audience, not less or more mannerly than such assemblages in other lands. It eats nuts and fruit and drinks wine as it listens; Aristotle proposes to measure the failure of a play by the amount of food eaten during the presentation. It quarrels about seats, claps and shouts for its favorites, hisses and groans when it is displeased; when moved to more vigorous protest it kicks the benches beneath it; if it becomes angry it may frighten an actor off the stage with olives, figs, or stones.[31] Aeschines is almost stoned to death for an offensive play; Aeschylus is nearly killed because the audience believes that he has revealed some secrets of the Eleusinian Mysteries. A musician who has borrowed a supply of stones to build a house promises to repay it with those that he expects to collect from his next performance.[32] Actors sometimes hire a claque to drown out with applause the hisses they fear, and comic actors may throw nuts to the crowd as a bribe to peace.[33] If it wishes, the audience can by deliberate noise prevent a drama from continuing, and compel the performance of the next play;[34] in this way a long program may be shortened within bearing.

There are three days of drama at the city Dionysia; on each day five plays are presented—three tragedies and a satyr play by one poet, and a comedy by another.[35] The performance begins early in the morning and continues till dusk. Only in exceptional cases is a play performed twice in the Theater of Dionysus; those who have missed it there may see it in the theaters of other Greek cities, or with less splendor on some rural stage in Attica. Between 480 and 380 some two thousand new dramas are performed at Athens.[36] In early times the prize for the best tragic trilogy was a goat, for

the best comedy a basket of figs and a jug of wine; but in the Golden Age the three prizes for tragedy and the single prize for comedy take the form of grants of money by the state. The ten judges are chosen by lot in the theater itself on the first morning of the competition, out of a large list of candidates nominated by the Council. At the end of the last play each of the judges writes his selections for first, second, and third prizes upon a tablet; the tablets are placed in an urn, and an archon draws out five tablets at random. These five judgments, summed up, constitute the final award, and the other five are destroyed unread; no one, therefore, can know in advance who the judges are to be, or which of them will really judge. Despite these precautions there is some corruption or intimidation of judges.[37] Plato complains that the judges, through fear of the crowd, almost always decide according to the applause, and argues that this "theatrocracy" is debasing both the dramatists and the audience.[38] When the contest is over the victorious poet and his choragus are crowned with ivy, and sometimes the victors set up a monument, like the choragic monument of Lysicrates, to commemorate their triumph. Even kings compete for this crown.

The size of the theater and the traditions of the festival determine in large measure the nature of the Greek drama. Since nuances cannot be conveyed by facial expression or vocal inflection, subtle character portraits are rare in the Dionysian theater. The Greek drama is a study of fate, or of man in conflict with the gods; the Elizabethan drama is a study of action, or of man in conflict with man; the modern drama is a study of character, or of man in conflict with himself. The Athenian audience knows in advance the destiny of each person represented, and the issue of each action; for religious custom is still strong enough in the fifth century to limit the theme of the Dionysian drama to some story from the accepted myths and legends of the early Greeks.* There is no suspense and no surprise, but, instead, the pleasures of anticipation and recognition. Dramatist after dramatist tells the same tale to the same audience; what differs is the poetry, the music, the interpretation, and the philosophy. Even the philosophy, before Euripides, is determined in large measure by tradition: throughout

* There were a few dramas about later history; of these the only extant example is Aeschylus' *Persian Women.* About 493 Phrynichus presented *The Fall of Miletus;* but the Athenians were so moved to grief by contemplating the capture of their daughter city by the Persians that they fined Phrynichus a thousand drachmas for his innovation, and forbade any repetition of the play.[39] There are some indications that Themistocles had secretly arranged for the performance as a means of stirring up the Athenians to active war against Persia.[40]

Aeschylus and Sophocles the prevailing theme is the nemesis of punishment, by jealous gods or impersonal fate, for insolent presumption and irreverent pride (*hybris*); and the recurring moral is the wisdom of conscience, honor, and a modest moderation (*aidos*). It is this combination of philosophy with poetry, action, music, song, and dance that makes the Greek drama not only a new form in the history of literature, but one that almost at the outset achieves a grandeur never equaled again.

III. AESCHYLUS

Not quite at the outset; for as many talents, in heredity and history, prepare the way for a genius, so some lesser playwrights, who may here be forgotten with honor, intervened between Thespis and Aeschylus. Perhaps it was the successful resistance to Persia that gave Athens the pride and stimulus necessary to an age of great drama, while the wealth that came with trade and empire after the war provided for the costly Dionysian contests in dithyrambic singing and the choral play. Aeschylus felt both the stimulus and the pride in person. Like so many Greek writers of the fifth century, he lived as well as wrote, and knew how to do as well as to speak. In 499, at the age of twenty-six, he produced his first play; in 490 he and his two brothers fought at Marathon, and so bravely that Athens ordered a painting to commemorate their deeds; in 484 he won his first prize at the Dionysian festival; in 480 he fought at Artemisium and Salamis, and in 479 at Plataea; in 476 and 470 he visited Syracuse, and was honored at the court of Hieron I; in 468, after dominating Athenian literature for a generation, he lost the first prize for drama to the youthful Sophocles; in 467 he recaptured supremacy with his *Seven against Thebes;* in 458 he won his last and greatest victory with the *Oresteia* trilogy; in 456 he was again in Sicily; and there, in that year, he died.

It took a man of such energy to mold the Greek drama into its classic form. It was Aeschylus who added a second actor to the one drawn out from the chorus by Thespis, and thereby completed the transformation of the Dionysian chant from an oratorio into a play.* He wrote seventy (some say ninety) dramas, of which seven remain. Of these, the earliest

* Though in Aeschylus the actors were only two, the roles they played in a drama were limited only in the sense that no more than two characters could be on the stage at once. The leader of the chorus was sometimes individualized into a third actor. Minor characters—attendants, soldiers, etc.—were not counted as actors.

three are minor works;* the most famous is the *Prometheus Bound;* the greatest make up the *Oresteia* trilogy.

The *Prometheus Bound,* too, may have been part of a trilogy, though no ancient authority vouches for this. We hear of a satyr play by Aeschylus called *Prometheus the Fire Bringer;* but it was produced apart from the *Prometheus Bound,* in a quite different combination.[41] Fragments survive of a *Prometheus Unbound* by Aeschylus; these are well-nigh meaningless, but anxious scholars assure us that if we had the full text we should find Aeschylus answering satisfactorily all the heresies which the extant play puts into the hero's lines. Even so it is noteworthy that an Athenian audience, at a religious festival, should have put up with the Titan's blasphemies. As the play opens we find Prometheus being chained to a rock in the Caucasus by Hephaestus at the command of a Zeus irate because Prometheus has taught men the art of fire. Hephaestus speaks:

High-thoughted son of Themis, who is sage!
Thee loath I loath must rivet fast in chains
Against this rocky height unclomb by man,
Where never human voice nor face shall find
Out thee who lov'st them; and thy beauty's flower,
Scorched in the sun's clear heat shall fade away.
Night shall come up with garniture of stars
To comfort thee with shadow, and the sun
Disperse with retrickt beams the morning frosts;
But through all dangers sense of present woe
Shall vex thee sore, because with none of them
There comes a hand to free. Such fruit is plucked
From love of man! . . . For Zeus is stern,
And new-made kings are cruel.[42]

Hanging helpless on the crag, Prometheus hurls defiance to Olympus, and recounts proudly the steps by which he brought civilization to primitive men, who till then

lived like silly ants beneath the ground
In hollow caves unsunned. There came to them
No steadfast sign of winter, nor of spring
Flower-perfumed, nor of summer full of fruit;

---

* *The Suppliant Women* is of the primitive type, in which the chorus predominates; *The Persians* is also mostly choral, and vividly describes the battle of Salamis; the *Seven against Thebes* was the third play in a trilogy that told the story of King Laius and his queen Jocasta, the patricide and incest of their son Oedipus, and the conflict between the sons of Oedipus for the Theban throne.

> But blindly and lawlessly they did all things,
> Until I taught them how the stars do rise
> And set in mystery, and devised for them
> Number, the inducer of philosophies,
> The synthesis of letters, and besides,
> The artificer of all things, memory
> That sweet muse-mother. I was first to yoke
> The servile beasts. . . .
> And none but I originated ships. . . .
> And I,
> Who did devise for mortals all these arts,
> Have no device left now to save myself.[43]

The whole earth mourns with him. "There is a cry in the waves of the sea as they fall together, and a groaning in the deep; a wail comes up from the cavern realms of death." All the nations send their condolences to this political prisoner, and bid him remember that suffering visits all: "Grief walks the earth, and sits down at the feet of each by turns." But they do nothing to free him. Oceanus advises him to yield, "seeing that who reigns, reigns by cruelty instead of right"; and the chorus of Oceanids, daughters of the sea, wonder whether humanity deserves to be suffered for with such a crucifixion. "Nay, thine was a helpless sacrifice, O beloved. . . . Didst thou not see the race of men, how little in effort and energy, dreamers bound in chains?"[44] Nevertheless they so admire him that when Zeus threatens to hurl him down into Tartarus they stay by him, and face with him the thunderbolt that blasts them and Prometheus into the abyss. But Prometheus, being a god, is denied the easement of death. In the lost conclusion of the trilogy he is raised up from Tartarus to be again chained to a mountain rock, and a vulture is commissioned by Zeus to gnaw out the Titan's heart. The heart grows by night as fast as the vulture consumes it by day; in this way Prometheus suffers through thirteen generations of men. Then the kindly giant Heracles kills the vulture, and persuades Zeus to free Prometheus. The Titan repents, makes his peace with Omnipotence, and places upon his finger the iron ring of necessity.

In this simple and powerful trilogy Aeschylus set the theme of Greek drama—the struggle of human will against inescapable destiny—and the theme of the life of Greece in the fifth century—the conflict between rebellious thought and traditional belief. His conclusion is conservative, but he knows the case for the rebel, and gives it all his sympathy; not even in Euripides shall we find so critical a view of Olympus. This is another

Paradise Lost in which the Fallen Angel, despite the poet's piety, is the hero of the tale. Probably Milton often recalled Aeschylus' Titan when he composed such eloquent speeches for Satan. Goethe was fond of this play, and used Prometheus as a mouthpiece in irreverent youth; Byron made him the model of nearly all his selves; and Shelley, always at odds with fate, brought the story back to life in *Prometheus Unbound*, where the rebel never yields. The legend hides a dozen allegories: suffering is the fruit of the tree of knowledge; to know the future is to gnaw one's heart away; the liberator is always crucified; and in the end one must accept limits, *man muss entsagen*, must accomplish his purpose within the nature of things. This is a noble theme, and helps the majestic language of Aeschylus to make the *Prometheus* a tragedy in the "grand style." Never has the war between knowledge and superstition, enlightenment and obscurantism, genius and dogma, been more powerfully pictured, or lifted to a higher reach of symbol and utterance. "The other productions of the Greek tragedians," said Schlegel, "are so many tragedies; but this is Tragedy herself."[45]

Nevertheless the *Oresteia* is greater still—by common consent the finest achievement in Greek drama, perhaps in all drama.[46] It was produced in 458, probably two years after *Prometheus Bound*, and two years before the author's death. The theme is the fateful breeding of violence by violence, and the inescapable punishment, through generation after generation, of insolent pride and excess. We call it a legend but the Greeks, perhaps rightly, called it history. The story, as told by each of the greater dramatists of Greece, might be called *The Children of Tantalus*, for it was he, the Phrygian king so recklessly proud in his wealth, who began the long chain of crime, and called down the vengeance of the Furies, by stealing the nectar and ambrosia of the gods, and giving the divine food to Pelops, his son; in every age some men acquire more wealth than befits a man, and use it to spoil their children. We have seen how Pelops, by foul means, won the throne of Elis, slew his accomplice, and married the daughter of the king whom he had deceived and killed. By Hippodameia he had three children: Thyestes, Aerope, and Atreus. Thyestes seduced Aerope; Atreus, to avenge his sister, served up his brother's children to him at a banquet; whereupon Aegisthus, son of Thyestes by Thyestes' daughter, vowed vengeance upon Atreus and his line. Atreus had two sons, Agamemnon and Menelaus. Agamemnon married Clytaemnestra, and had by her two daughters, Iphigenia and Electra, and one son, Orestes. At Aulis,

and lays upon it a lock of his hair. Hearing the approach of the Libation Bearers, the young men withdraw, and listen in fascination as Electra, Orestes' brooding sister, comes with the women, stands over the grave, and calls upon Agamemnon's spirit to arouse Orestes to avenge him. Orestes reveals himself; and from her bitter heart she pours into his simple mind the thought that he must kill their mother. The youths, disguised as merchants, proceed to the royal palace; Clytaemnestra softens them with hospitality; but when Orestes tests her by saying that the boy she sent to Phocis is dead, he is shocked to see a secret joy hiding in her grief. She calls Aegisthus to share with him the news that the avenger whom they feared is no more. Orestes slays him, drives his mother into the palace, and comes out a moment later already half insane with the consciousness that he is a matricide.

> While I am still not mad I here declare
> To all who love me, and confess, that I
> Have slain my mother.[50]

In the third play Orestes is pursued, in the poet's externalization of the boy's wild fancy, by the Erinnyes, or Furies, whose task it is to punish crime; and from their euphemistic, deprecatory title, the Eumenides, or Well-Wishers, the play derives its name. Orestes is an outcast, shunned by all men; wherever he goes the Furies hang over him as black ghosts crying out for his blood. He flings himself upon the altar of Apollo at Delphi, and Apollo comforts him; but the shade of Clytaemnestra rises from the earth to urge the Furies not to desist from torturing her son. Orestes goes to Athens, kneels before Athena's shrine, and cries out to her for deliverance. Athena hears him, and calls him "perfect by suffering." When the Erinnyes protest she summons them to try Orestes' case before the Council of the Areopagus; the concluding scene shows this strange trial, symbolical of the replacement of blood revenge with law. Athena, goddess of the city, presides; the Furies state the case for vengeance against Orestes, and Apollo defends him. The court divides evenly; Athena casts the deciding ballot in favor of Orestes, and declares him free. She solemnly establishes the Council of the Areopagus as henceforth the supreme court of Attica, whose swift condemnation of the murderer shall free the land from feuds, and whose wisdom will guide the state through the dangers that beset every people. The goddess by her fair speech appeases the disappointed Furies, and so wins them that their leader says, "This day a new Order is born."

After the *Iliad* and the *Odyssey*, the *Oresteia* is the highest achievement in Greek literature. Here is a breadth of conception, a unity of thought and execution, a power of dramatic development, an understanding of character, and a splendor of style which in their sum we shall not find again before Shakespeare. The trilogy is as closely knit as the three acts of a well-designed drama; each part foreshadows and requires the next with logical inevitability. As play succeeds play the terror of the theme grows until we begin dimly to realize how deeply this story must have moved the Greeks. It is true that there is too much talk, even for four murders; that the lyrics are often obscure, their metaphors exaggerated, their language sometimes heavy and rough and strained. Nevertheless these chorals are supreme in their kind, full of grandeur and tenderness, eloquent with their plea for a new religion of forgiveness, and for the virtues of a political order that was passing away.

For the *Oresteia* is as conservative as the *Prometheus* is radical, though only two years seem to have separated them in time. In 462 Ephialtes deprived the Areopagus of its powers; in 461 he was assassinated; in 458 Aeschylus offered in the *Oresteia* a defense of the Council of the Areopagus as the wisest body in the Athenian government. The poet was now full of years, and could understand the old more easily than the young; like Aristophanes he longed for the virtues of the men of Marathon. Athenaeus would have us believe that Aeschylus was a great drinker;[51] but in the *Oresteia* he is a Puritan preaching a sermon in buskins on sin and its punishment, and the wisdom born of suffering. The law of *hybris* and *nemesis* is another doctrine of karma, or of original sin; every evil deed will be found out, and be avenged in one life or another. In this way Greek thought made its trial at reconciling evil with God: all suffering is due to sin, even if it is the sin of a generation that is dead. The author of *Prometheus* was no naïve pietist; his plays, even in the *Oresteia*, are studded with heresies; he was attacked for revealing ritual secrets, and was saved only by the intercession of his brother Ameinias, who bared before the Assembly the wounds he had received at Salamis.[52] But Aeschylus was convinced that morality, to hold its own against unsocial impulse, required supernatural sanctions; he hoped that

One there is who heareth on high—
  Some Pan or Zeus, some seer Apollo—
And sendeth down, for the law transgressed,
  The Wrath of the Feet that follow.[53]

—i.e., the Furies of conscience and retribution. Therefore he speaks with a solemn reverence for religion, and makes an effort to reach beyond polytheism to the conception of one God.

Zeus, Zeus, whate'er He be,
If this name He love to hear,
This He shall be called of me.
Searching earth and sea and air
Refuge nowhere can I find
Save Him only, if my mind
Will cast off, before it die,
The burden of this vanity.[54]

He identifies Zeus with the personified Nature of Things, the Law or Reason of the World; "The Law that is Fate and the Father and All-comprehending are here met together as one."[55]

Perhaps these concluding lines of his masterpiece were his last words as a poet. Two years after the *Oresteia* we find him again in Sicily. Some believe that the audience, being more radical than the judges, did not like the trilogy; but this hardly accords with the fact that the Athenians, a few years later, and directly contrary to custom, decreed that his plays might be repeated in the Theater of Dionysus, and that a chorus should be granted to anyone who offered to produce them. Many did, and Aeschylus continued to win prizes after his death. Meanwhile in Sicily, says an old story, an eagle had killed him by dropping a tortoise upon his bald head, mistaking it for a stone.[56] There he was buried over his own epitaph, so strangely silent about his plays, so humanly proud of his scars:

Beneath this stone lies Aeschylus;
Of his noble prowess the grove of Marathon can speak,
Or the long-haired Persian, who knows it well.

IV. SOPHOCLES

The first prize for tragedy was won from Aeschylus in 468 by a newcomer, aged twenty-seven, and bearing a name that meant the Wise and Honored One. Sophocles was the most fortunate of men, and almost the darkest of pessimists. He came from Colonus, a suburb of Athens, and was the son of a sword manufacturer, so that the Persian and Peloponnesian Wars, which impoverished nearly all Athenians, left the dramatist a comfortable income.[57] In addition to wealth he had genius, beauty, and good health. He won the double prize for wrestling and music—a combination that would have pleased Plato; his skill as a ballplayer and a harpist enabled him to give public performances in both fields; and after the battle of Salamis it was he who was chosen by the city to lead the nude youths of Athens in a dance and song of victory.[58] Even in later years he was handsome; the Lateran Museum statue shows him old and bearded and rounded, but still vigorous and tall. He grew up in the happiest age of Athens; he was the friend of Pericles, and held high offices under him; in 443 he was Imperial Treasurer; in 440 he was one of the generals who commanded the Athenian forces in Pericles' expedition against Samos—though it should be added that Pericles preferred his poetry to his strategy. After the Athenian debacle in Syracuse he was appointed to the Committee of Public Safety;[59] and in this capacity he voted for the oligarchical constitution of 411. His character pleased the people more than his politics; he was genial, witty, unassuming, pleasure-loving, and endowed with a charm that atoned for all his errors. He had a fancy for money[60] and boys,[61] but in his old age he turned his favor to courtesans.[62] He was very pious, and occasionally filled the office of priest.[63]

He wrote 113 plays; we have only seven, and do not know the order in which they were produced. Eighteen times he won the first award at the Dionysian, twice at the Lenaean, festivals; he received his first prize at twenty-five, his last at eighty-five; for thirty years he ruled the Athenian stage more completely than Pericles contemporaneously ruled Athens. He increased the number of actors to three, and played a role himself until he lost his voice. He (and after him Euripides) abandoned the Aeschylean form of trilogy, preferring to compete with three independent plays. Aeschylus was interested in cosmic themes that overshadowed the persons of his drama; Sophocles was interested in character, and was almost modern in his flair for psychology. *The Trachinian Women* is on its surface a sensational melodrama: Deianeira, jealous of her husband and Heracles' love for Iola, sends him unwittingly a poisoned robe, and, when it consumes him, kills herself; what draws Sophocles here is not the punishment of Heracles, which would have seemed central to Aeschylus—nor even the passion of love, which would have attracted Euripides—but the psychology of jealousy. So in the *Ajax* no attention is paid to the mighty deeds of the hero; what lures the author is the study of a man going mad. In the *Philoctetes* there is almost no action, but a frank analysis of injured simplicity and diplomatic dishonesty. In the *Electra* the story is as slight as it is old; Aeschylus was fascinated by the moral issues involved; Sophocles almost ignores them in his eagerness to study with psychoanalytic ruthlessness the young woman's hatred of her mother. The play has given its name to a neurosis once widely discussed, as *Oedipus the King* has provided a name for another.

Oedipus Tyrannus is the most famous of Greek dramas. Its opening scene is impressive: a motley throng of men, women, boys, girls, and infants sit before the royal palace in Thebes, carrying boughs of laurel and olive as symbols of supplication. A plague has fallen upon the city, and the people have gathered to beg King Oedipus to offer some appeasing sacrifice to the gods. An oracle announces that the plague will leave Thebes with the unknown assassin of Laius, the former king. Oedipus lays a bitter curse upon the murderer, whoever he may be, whose crime has brought such misery to Thebes. This is a perfect instance of that method which Horace advised, of plunging *in medias res*, and letting explanations enter afterward. But the audience, of course, knew the story, for the tale of Laius, Oedipus, and the Sphinx was part of the folklore of the Greeks. Tradition said that a curse had been laid upon Laius and his children because he had introduced an unnatural vice into Hellas;[64] the consequences of this sin, ruining generation after generation, formed a typical theme for Greek tragedy. Laius and his queen Jocasta, said an oracle, would have a son who would slay his father and marry his mother. For once in the world's history two parents wanted a girl for their first child. But a son came; and to avoid fulfillment of the oracle he was exposed on the hills. A shepherd found him, called him Oedipus from his swollen feet, and gave him to the king and queen of Corinth, who reared him as their son. Grown to manhood, Oedipus learned, again from the oracle, that he was destined to kill his father and marry his mother. Believing the king and queen of Corinth to be his parents, he fled from that city and took the road to Thebes. On the way he met an old man, quarreled with him, and slew him, not knowing that the old man was his father. Nearing Thebes he encountered the Sphinx, a creature with the face of a woman, the tail of a lion, and the wings of a bird. To Oedipus the Sphinx presented its renowned riddle: "What is that which is four-footed, three-footed, and two-footed?" All who failed to answer correctly were destroyed by the Sphinx; and the terrified Thebans, longing to clear the highway of this monster, had vowed to have as their next king whoever should solve the riddle, for the Sphinx had agreed to commit suicide if anyone answered it. Oedipus replied: "Man; for as a child he crawls on four feet, as an adult he walks on two, and as an old man he adds a cane." It was a lame answer, but the Sphinx accepted it, and loyally plunged to its death. The Thebans hailed Oedipus as their savior, and when Laius failed to return they made the newcomer king. Obeying the custom of the land, Oedipus married the queen, and had by her four children: Antigone, Polynices, Eteocles, and Ismene. In the second scene in Sophocles' play—the most powerful scene in Greek drama—an old high priest, commanded by Oedipus to reveal, if he can, the identity of Laius' murderer, names Oedipus himself. Nothing could be more tragic than the King's reluctant and terrified realization that he is the slayer of his father and the mate of his mother. Jocasta refuses to believe it, and explains it away as a Freudian dream: "It has been the lot of many men in dreams," she reassures Oedipus, "to think themselves partners of their mother's bed; but he passes through life most easily to whom these things become trifles."[65] When the identification is complete she hangs herself; and Oedipus, mad with remorse, gouges out his own eyes, and leaves Thebes as an exile, with only Antigone to help him.

In *Oedipus at Colonus*, the second play of an unintentional trilogy,* the former king is a white-haired outcast leaning upon his daughter's arm and begging his bread from town to town. He comes in his wandering to shady Colonus, and Sophocles takes the opportunity to sing to his native village, and its faithful olive groves, an untranslatable song which ranks high in Greek poetry:

Stranger, where thy feet now rest
In this land of horse and rider,
Here is earth all earth excelling,
White Colonus here doth shine.
Oftenest here, and homing best
Where the close green coverts hide her,
Warbling her sweet mournful tale,
Sings the melodious nightingale . . .
Fresh with heavenly dews, and crowned
With earliest white in shining cluster,
Each new morn the young narcissus
Blooms. . . .

And a marvelous herb of the soil grows here,
  Whose match I never had heard it sung
In the Dorian Isle of Pelops near
  Or in Asia far hath sprung.

* *Oedipus the King*, *Oedipus at Colonus*, and *Antigone* were produced separately.

'Tis a plant that flourishes unsubdued,
Self-engendering, self-renewed,
  To her armed foes' dismay:
That never so fair but in this land bloomed,—
With the grey-blue silvery leaf soft-plumed,
  Her nurturing Olive-Spray.
No force, no ravaging hand shall raze it,
  In youth so rash or in age so wise,
For the orb of Zeus in heaven surveys it,
  And blue-grey light of Athena's eyes.[66]

An oracle has foretold that Oedipus will die in the precincts of the Eumenides; and when he learns that he is now in their sacred grove at Colonus the old man, having found no loveliness in life, thinks that here it would be sweet to die. To Theseus, King of Athens, he speaks lines that sum up with clairvoyant insight the forces that were weakening Greece—the decay of the soil, of faith, of morals, and of men:

Only to gods in heaven
Comes no old age, nor death of anything;
All else is turmoiled by our master Time.
The earth's strength fades, and manhood's glory fades,
Faith dies, and unfaith blossoms like a flower.
And who shall find in the open streets of men,
Or secret places of his own heart's love,
One wind blow true forever?[67]

Then, seeming to hear the call of a god, Oedipus bids a tender farewell to Antigone and Ismene, and walks into the dark grove, Theseus alone accompanying him.

Going on
A little space we turned. And lo, we saw
The man no more; but he, the King,* was there,
Holding a hand to shade his eyes, as one
To whom there comes a vision drear and dread
He may not bear to look upon. . . .
What form of death
He died, knows no man but our Theseus only. . . .
But either some one whom the gods had sent
To guide his steps, or else the abyss of earth
In friendly mood had opened wide its jaws

* Theseus.

Without one pang. And so the man was led
With naught to mourn for—did not leave the world
As worn with pain and sickness; but his end,
If any ever was, was wonderful.[68]

The last play in the sequence, but apparently the first of the three to be composed, carries the faithful Antigone to her grave. Hearing that her brothers Polynices and Eteocles are warring for the kingdom, she hurries back to Thebes in the hope of bringing peace. But she is ignored, and the brothers fight to their death. Creon, ally of Eteocles, seizes the throne, and, as punishment for Polynices' rebellion, forbids his burial. Antigone, sharing the Greek belief that the spirit of the dead is tortured so long as the corpse is not interred, violates the edict and buries Polynices. Meanwhile the chorus sings one of the most renowned of Sophocles' odes:

Many wonders there be, but naught more wondrous than man.
Over the surging sea, with a whitening south wind wan,
Through the foam of the firth man makes his perilous way;
And the eldest of deities, Earth that knows not toil or decay,
Ever he furrows and scores, as his team, year in year out,
With breed of the yoked horse the ploughshare turneth about.

The light-witted birds of the air, the beasts of the weald and the
wood,
He traps with his woven snare, and the brood of the briny flood.
Master of cunning he: the savage bull, and the hart
Who roams the mountain free, are tamed by his infinite art;
And the shaggy rough-maned steed is broken to bear the bit.

Speech, and the wind-swift speed of counsel and civic wit,
He hath learned for himself all these; and the arrowy rain to fly,
And the nipping airs that freeze, 'neath the open winter sky.
He hath provision for all; fell plague he hath learned to endure;
Safe whate'er may befall: yet for death he hath found no cure.[69]

Antigone is condemned by Creon to be buried alive. Creon's son Haemon protests against the awful sentence, and, being repulsed swears to his father "thou shalt never more set eyes upon my face." Here for a moment love plays a part in a Sophoclean tragedy and the poet intones to Eros a hymn long remembered in antiquity:

Love resistless in fight, all yield at a glance of thine eye;
Love who pillowed all night on a maiden's cheek doth lie;

Over the upland folds thou roamest, and the trackless sea.
Love the gods captive holds; shall mortals not yield to thee?[70]

Haemon disappears; and in search for him Creon orders his soldiers to open the cave in which Antigone has been entombed. There they find Antigone dead and beside her Haemon, resolved to die.

We looked, and in the cavern's vaulted gloom
I saw the maiden lying strangled there,
A noose of linen twined about her neck;
And hard beside her, clasping her cold form,
Her lover lay bewailing his dead bride . . .
When the King saw him, with a terrible groan
He moved towards him, crying, "O my son,
What hast thou done? What ailed thee? What mischance
Has reft thee of thy reason? Oh, come forth,
Come forth, my son; thy father supplicates."
But the son glared at him with tiger eyes,
Spat in his face, and then, without a word,
Drew his two-hilted sword and smote, but
Missed his father flying backwards. Then the boy,
Wroth with himself, poor wretch, incontinent,
Fell on his sword and drove it through his side
Home; but, yet breathing, clasped in his lax arms
The maid, her pallid cheek incarnadined
With his expiring gasps. So there they lay
Two corpses, one in death.[71]

The dominant qualities of these plays, surviving time and translation, are beauty of style and mastery of technique. Here is the typically "classic" form of utterance: polished, placid, and serene; vigorous but restrained, dignified but graceful, with the strength of Pheidias and the smooth delicacy of Praxiteles. Classic too is the structure; every line is relevant, and moves towards that moment in which the action finds its climax and its significance. Each of these plays is built like a temple, wherein every part is carefully finished in detail, but has its proper and subordinate place in the whole; except that the *Philoctetes* lazily accepts the *deus ex machina* (which is a jest in Euripides) as a serious solution of a knotty plot. Here, as in Aeschylus, the drama moves upward towards the *hybris* of some crowning insolence (as in Oedipus' bitter curse upon the unknown murderer); turns around some *anagnorisis* or sudden recognition, some *peripeteia* or reversal of fortune; and moves downward toward the *nemesis* of inevitable punishment. Aristotle, when he wished to illustrate perfection of dramatic structure, always referred to *Oedipus the King*, and the two plays that deal with Oedipus illustrate well the Aristotelian definition of tragedy as a purging of pity and terror through their objective presentation. The characters are more clearly drawn than in Aeschylus, though not as realistically as in Euripides. "I draw men as they ought to be drawn," said Sophocles, "Euripides draws them as they are"[72]—as if to say that drama should admit some idealization, and that art should not be photography. But the influence of Euripides appears in the argumentativeness of the dialogue and the occasional exploitation of sentiment; so Oedipus wrangles unroyally with Teiresias, and, blinded, gropes about touchingly to feel the faces of his daughters. Aeschylus, contemplating the same situation, would have forgotten the daughters and thought of some eternal law.

Sophocles, too, is a philosopher and a preacher, but his counsels rely less than those of Aeschylus upon the sanctions of the gods. The spirit of the Sophists has touched him, and though he maintains a prosperous orthodoxy, he reveals himself as one who might have been Euripides had he not been so fortunate. But he has too much of the poet's sensitivity to excuse the suffering that comes so often undeserved to men. Says Lyllus, over Heracles' writhing body:

We are blameless, but confess
That the gods are pitiless.
Children they beget, and claim
Worship in a father's name,
Yet with apathetic eye
Look upon such agony.[73]

He makes Jocasta laugh at oracles, though his plays turn upon them creakingly; Creon denounces the prophets as "all a money-getting tribe"; and Philoctetes asks the old question, "How justify the ways of Heaven, finding Heaven unjust?"[74] Sophocles answers hopefully that though the moral order of the world may be too subtle for us to understand it, it is there, and right will triumph in the end.[75] Following Aeschylus, he identifies Zeus with this moral order, and comes even more closely to monotheism. Like a good Victorian he is uncertain of his theology, but strong in his moral faith; the highest wisdom is to find that law which is Zeus, the moral compass of the world, and follow it.

Oh, may my constant feet not fail,
Walking in paths of righteousness.

Sinless in word and deed,
True to those eternal laws
That scale forever the high steep
Of heaven's pure ether, whence they sprang:
For only in Olympus is their home,
Nor mortal wisdom gave them birth;
And howsoe'er men may forget,
They will not sleep.[76]

It is the pen of Sophocles, but the voice of Aeschylus, faith making the last stand against unbelief. In this piety and resignation we see the figure of Job repentant and reconciled; but between the lines we catch premonitions of Euripides.

Like Solon, Sophocles counts that man most blessed who has never been born, and him next happiest who dies in infancy. A modern pessimist has taken pleasure in translating the somber lines of the chorus on the death of Oedipus, lines that reflect a world-weariness brought on by old age, and the bitter fratricide of the Peloponnesian War:

What man is he that yearneth
  For length unmeasured of days?
Folly mine eye discerneth
  Encompassing all his ways.
For years over-running the measure
  Shall change thee in evil wise:
Grief draweth nigh thee; and pleasure,
  Behold it is hid from thine eyes.
This to their wage have they
Which overlive their day. . . .

Thy portion esteem I highest
  Who wast not ever begot;
Thine next, being born, who diest
  And straightway again art not.
With follies light as the feather
  Doth Youth to man befall;
Then evils gather together,
  There wants not one of them all—
    Wrath, envy, discord, strife,
    The sword that seeketh life.
And sealing the sum of trouble
  Doth tottering Age draw nigh,
  Whom friends and kinsfolk fly;

Age, upon whom redouble
  All sorrows under the sky. . . .

And he that looseth from labor
  Doth one with other befriend,
  Whom bride nor bridesmen attend,
Song, nor sound of the tabor,
  Death that maketh an end.[77]

Every scholastic gossip knows that Sophocles consoled his old age with the hetaira Theoris, and had offspring by her.[78] His legitimate son Iophon, fearing, perhaps, that the poet would bequeath his wealth to Theoris' child, brought his father to court on a charge of financial incompetence. Sophocles read to the jury, as evidence of his mental clarity, certain choruses from the play which he was writing, probably the *Oedipus at Colonus;* whereupon the judges not only acquitted him, but escorted him to his home.[79] Born many years before Euripides, he lived to put on mourning for him; and then, in that same year 406, he too died. Legend tells how, as the Spartans besieged Athens, Dionysus, god of the drama, appeared to Lysander and obtained a safe-conduct for the friends of Sophocles, who wished to bury him in the sepulcher of his fathers at Deceleia. The Greeks rendered him divine honors, and the poet Simmias composed for him a quiet epitaph:

Creep gently, ivy, ever gently creep,
  Where Sophocles sleeps on in calm repose;
Thy pale green tresses o'er the marble sweep,
  While all around shall bloom the purple rose.
There let the vine with rich full clusters hang,
  Its fair young tendrils flung around the stone;
Due meed for that sweet wisdom which he sang,
  By Muses and by Graces called their own.

V. EURIPIDES

1. The Plays

As Giotto rough-hewed the early path of Italian painting, and Raphael subdued the art with a quiet spirit into technical perfection, and Michelangelo completed the development in works of tortured genius; as Bach with incredible energy forced open a broad road to modern music, and

Mozart perfected its form in melodious simplicity, and Beethoven completed the development in works of unbalanced grandeur; so Aeschylus cleared the way and set the forms for Greek drama with his harsh verse and stern philosophy, Sophocles fashioned the art with measured music and placid wisdom, and Euripides completed the development in works of passionate feeling and turbulent doubt. Aeschylus was a preacher of almost Hebraic intensity; Sophocles was a "classic" artist clinging to a broken faith; Euripides was a romantic poet who could never write a perfect play because he was distracted by philosophy. They were the Isaiah, Job, and Ecclesiastes of Greece.

Euripides was born in the year—some say on the day—of Salamis, probably on the island itself, to which, we are told, his parents had fled for refuge from the invading Medes.[80] His father was a man of some property and prominence in the Attic town of Phyla; his mother was of noble family,[81] though the hostile Aristophanes insists that she kept a grocer's shop and hawked fruit and flowers on the street. In later life he lived on Salamis, loving the solitude of its hills, and its varied prospects of blue sea. Plato wished to be a dramatist and became a philosopher; Euripides wished to be a philosopher and became a dramatist. He "took the entire course of Anaxagoras," says Strabo;[82] he studied for a while with Prodicus, and was so intimate with Socrates that some suspected the philosopher of having a hand in the poet's plays.[83] The whole Sophistic movement entered into his education, and through him captured the Dionysian stage. He became the Voltaire of the Greek Enlightenment, worshiping reason with destructive innuendo in the midst of dramas staged to celebrate a god.

The records of the Dionysian Theater credit him with seventy-five plays, from *The Daughters of Pelias* in 455 to *The Bacchae* in 406; eighteen survive, and a medley of fragments from the rest.* Their subject matter tells again the legends of the early Greeks, but with a note of skeptical protest sounding timidly and then boldly between the lines. The *Ion* presents the reputed founder of the Ionian tribes in a delicate dilemma: the oracle of Apollo declares Xuthus to be his father, but Ion discovers that he is the son of Apollo, who seduced his mother and then palmed her off on Xuthus; can it be, Ion asks, that the noble god is a liar? In *Heracles* and *Alcestis* the mighty son of Zeus and Alcmena is described as a good-natured drunkard, with the appetite of Gargantua and the brains of Louis XVI. The

* The major plays appeared in approximately the following order: *Alcestis*, 438; *Medea*, 431; *Hippolytus*, 428; *Andromache*, 427; *Hecuba*, ca. 425; *Electra*, ca. 416; *The Trojan Women*, 415; *Iphigenia in Tauris*, ca. 413; *Orestes*, 408; *Iphigenia in Aulis*, 406; *The Bacchae*, 406.

Alcestis recounts the unprepossessing story of how the gods, as a condition of allowing further life to Admetus (king of Thessalian Pherae), required that some other should consent to die in his stead. His wife offers herself as a sacrifice, and bids him a hundred-line farewell, which he hears with magnanimous patience. Alcestis is carried out for dead; but Heracles, between solitary drinking bouts and banquets, goes forth, argues and browbeats Death into relinquishing Alcestis, and brings her back alive. The play can be understood only as a subtle attempt to make the legend ridiculous.*

The *Hippolytus* applies with more finesse and grace the same method of reduction to the absurd. The handsome hero is a youthful huntsman who vows to Artemis, virgin goddess of the chase, that he will always be faithful to her; will ever shun women, and will find his greatest pleasure in the woods. Aphrodite, incensed by this insulting celibacy, pours into the heart of Phaedra, Theseus' wife, a mad passion for Hippolytus, Theseus' son by the Amazon Antiope. Here is the first love tragedy in extant literature, and here at the outset are all the symptoms of love at the crisis of its fever: Phaedra, rejected by Hippolytus, languishes and fades to the point of death. Her nurse, suddenly become a philosopher, muses with Hamlet-like skepticism about a life beyond the grave:

> Yet all man's life is but ailing and dim,
> And rest upon the earth comes never.
> But if any far-off state there be,
> Dearer than life to mortality,
> The hand of the Dark hath hold thereof,
> And mist is under and mist above.
> And some are sick for life, and cling
> On earth to this nameless and shining thing;
> For other life is a fountain sealed,
> And the deeps below us are unrevealed,
> And we drift on legends forever.[84]

The nurse bears a message to Hippolytus that Phaedra's bed will welcome him; he, knowing that she is his father's wife, is horrified, and bursts into one of those passages that earned Euripides a reputation for misogyny:

> Oh God, why hast thou made this gleaming snare,
> Woman, to dog us on the happy earth?

* It was presented in 438 as the fourth play in a group by Euripides; perhaps it was intended as a half-serious satyr play rather than as a half-comic tragedy. In *Balaustion's Adventure* Browning, with generous simplicity, has taken the play at its face value.

Was it thy will to make man, why his birth
Through love and woman?[85]

Phaedra dies; and in her hand her husband finds a note saying that Hippolytus seduced her. Theseus wildly calls upon Poseidon to slay Hippolytus. The youth protests his innocence, but is not believed. He is driven out of the land by Theseus; and as his chariot passes along the shore a sea lion emerges from the waves and pursues him; his horses run away, upset the chariot, and drag the entangled Hippolytus (i.e., "torn by horses") over the rocks to a mangled death. And the chorus cries out, in lines that must have startled Athens,

Ye gods that did snare him,
Lo, I cast in your faces
  My hate and my scorn!

In the *Medea* Euripides forgets for a while his war against the gods, and transforms the story of the Argonauts into his most powerful play. When Jason reaches Colchis, the royal princess Medea falls in love with him, helps him to get the Golden Fleece, and, to shield him, deceives her father and kills her brother. Jason vows eternal love to her, and takes her back with him to Iolcus. There the almost savage Medea poisons King Pelias to secure the throne that Pelias promised to Jason. Since the law of Thessaly forbids him to marry a foreigner, Jason lives with Medea in unwedded love, and has two children by her. But in time he tires of her barbarian intensity, looks about him for a legal wife and heir, and proposes to marry the daughter of Creon, King of Corinth. Creon accepts him, and exiles Medea. Medea, brooding upon her wrongs, speaks one of the famous passages of Euripides in defense of woman:

Of all things upon earth that bleed and grow,
A herb most bruised is woman. We must pay
Our store of gold, hoarded for that one day,
To buy us some man's love; and lo, they bring
A master of our flesh! There comes the sting
Of the whole shame. And then the jeopardy,
For good or ill, what shall that master be. . . .
Home never taught her that—how best to guide
Toward peace the thing that sleepeth at her side.
And she who, laboring long, shall find some way
Whereby her lord may bear with her, nor fray
His yoke too fiercely, blessed is the breath
That woman draws! Else let her pray for death.

Her lord, if he be wearied of her face
Within doors, gets him forth; some merrier place
Will ease his heart; but she waits on, her whole
Vision enchained on a single soul.
And then they say 'tis they that face the call
Of war, while we sit sheltered, hid from all
Peril! False mocking! Sooner would I stand
Three times to face their battles, shield in hand,
Than bear one child.[86]

Then follows the terrible story of her revenge. She sends to her rival, in pretended reconciliation, a set of costly robes; the Corinthian princess puts one on, and is consumed in fire; Creon, trying to rescue her, is burned to death. Medea kills her own children and drives off with their dead bodies before Jason's eyes. The chorus chants a philosophic end:

Great treasure halls hath Zeus in heaven,
From whence to man strange dooms be given,
  Past hope or fear.
And the end men looked for cometh not,
And a path is there where no man thought:
  So hath it fallen here.

The remaining plays turn for the most part upon the tale of Troy. In *Helen* we get the revised version of Stesichorus and Herodotus:[87] the Spartan queen does not elope with Paris to Troy; she is carried against her will to Egypt, and chastely awaits her master there; all Greece, Euripides suggests, has been hoodwinked by the legend of Helen in Troy. In *Iphigenia in Aulis* he pours into the old story of Agamemnon's sacrifice a profusion of sentiment new to the Greek drama, and a Lucretian horror of the crimes to which the ancient faith persuaded men. Aeschylus and Sophocles had also written on this theme, but their plays were soon forgotten in the brilliance of this new performance. The arrival of Clytaemnestra and her daughter is visioned with Euripidean tenderness; Orestes, "yet a wordless babe," is present to witness the superstitious murder that will dictate his destiny. The girl is all shyness and happiness as she runs to greet the King:

Iphig. Fain am I, father, on thy breast to fall,
After so long! Though others I outrun—
For oh, I yearn for thy face!—be not wroth . . .
So glad to see me—yet what troubled look!
Agam. On kings and captains weigheth many a care.

Iphig. This hour be mine—this one! Yield not to care!
Agam. Yea, I am all thine now; my thoughts stray not . . .
Iphig. And yet—and yet—thine eyes are welling tears!
Agam. Yea, for the absence yet to come is long.
Iphig. I know not, know not, dear my sire, thy meaning.
Agam. Thy wise discernment stirs my grief the more.
Iphig. So I may please thee, folly will I talk.[88]

When Achilles comes she finds that he knows nothing of their supposed marriage; instead she learns that the army is impatient for her sacrifice. She throws herself at Agamemnon's feet, and begs for her life.

I was thy first-born—first I called thee Sire,
And sat, thy child, upon thy knees the first;
And we exchanged sweet charities of life.
And this was thy discourse with me—"My child,
Shall I behold thee happy in the home
Of thy liege lord and husband, as befits?"
And nestling in the beard which now I clasp
A suppliant, I made answer unto thee:
"I too will welcome thee, when grey with years,
In the sweet shelter of my home, my Sire,
And with fond fostering recompense thy love."
Such were our words, which I remember well;
But thou forgettest, and wouldst take my life.[89]

Clytaemnestra denounces Agamemnon's surrender to a savage ritual, and utters a threat that contains many tragedies—"Constrain me not to turn traitress to thee." She encourages Achilles' attempt to rescue the girl, but Iphigenia, changing her mood, refuses to escape.

Hear the thing that flashed upon me, mother, as I thought hereon:
Lo, I am resolved to die; and fain am I that this be done
Gloriously—that I thrust ignoble thoughts away. . . .
Unto me all mighty Hellas looks; I only can bestow
Boons upon her—sailing of her galleys, Phrygia's overthrow,
Safety for her daughters from barbarians in the days to come,
That the ravisher no more may snatch them from a happy home,
When the penalty is paid for Paris' outrage, Helen's shame.
All this great deliverance I in death shall compass, and my name,
As of one who gave to Hellas freedom, shall be blessing-crowned.[90]

When the soldiers come for her she forbids them to touch her, and moves of her own accord to the sacrificial pyre.

In the *Hecuba* the war is over; Troy has been taken, and the victors are apportioning the spoils. Hecuba, widow of King Priam, sends her youngest son Polydorus with a treasure of gold to Priam's friend Polymnestor, King of Thrace. But Polymnestor, thirsting for the gold, slays the boy and throws his corpse into the sea; it is cast up on the shores of Ilion, and is brought to Hecuba. Meanwhile the shade of dead Achilles holds the winds from blowing the Greek fleet homeward till he has received in human sacrifice the fairest of Priam's daughters, Polyxena. The Greek herald, Talthybius, comes to take the girl from Hecuba. Finding her prostrate, disheveled, and distraught who had so recently been a queen, he utters some lines of Euripidean doubt:

What shall I say, Zeus?—that thou look'st on men?
Or that this fancy false we vainly hold
For naught, who deem there is a race of gods,
While chance controlleth all things among men?[91]

The next act of the composite drama takes the form of *The Trojan Women.* It was produced in 415, shortly after the Athenian destruction of Melos (416), and almost on the eve of the expedition that aimed to conquer Sicily for the Athenian Empire. It was at this moment that Euripides, shocked by the massacre in Melos and by the brutal imperialism of the proposed attack upon Syracuse, dared to present a powerful plea for peace, a brave portrayal of victory from the standpoint of the defeated, "the greatest denunciation of war in ancient literature."[92] He begins where Homer ends—after the capture of Troy. The Trojans lie dead after a general slaughter, and their women, bereaved to madness, pass down from their ruined city to be the concubines of the victors. Hecuba enters with her daughters Andromache and Cassandra. Polyxena has already been sacrificed, and now Talthybius comes to lead Cassandra to Agamemnon's tent. Hecuba falls to the ground in grief. Andromache tries to console her, but she too breaks down, as clasping the little prince Astyanax to her breast, she thinks of his dead father.

Andromache. And I . . . long since I drew my bow
Straight at the heart of good fame; and I know
My shaft hit; and for that am I the more
Fallen from peace. All that men praise us for,
I loved for Hector's sake, and sought to win.
I knew that always, be there hurt therein
Or utter innocence, to roam abroad

Hath ill report for women; so I trod
Down the desire thereof, and walked my way
In mine own garden. And light words and gay
Parley of women never passed my door.
The thoughts of mine own heart—I craved no more—
Spake with me, and I was happy. Constantly
I brought fair silence and a tranquil eye
For Hector's greeting, and watched well the way
Of living, where to guide and where obey . . .

One night—aye, men have said it—maketh tame
A woman in a man's arms. O shame, shame!
What woman's lips can so forswear her dead,
And give strange kisses in another's bed?
Why, not a dumb beast, not a colt will run
In the yoke untroubled, when her mate is gone . . .
O my Hector! best beloved
That, being mine, wast all in all to me,
My prince, my wise one, O my majesty
Of valiance! No man's touch had ever come
Near me, when thou from out my father's home
Didst lead me and make me thine . . . And thou art dead,
And I war-flung to slavery and the bread
Of shame in Hellas, over bitter seas!

Hecuba, dreaming of some distant revenge, bids Andromache accept her new master graciously, that he may allow her to rear Astyanax, and that Astyanax may some day restore the house of Priam and the splendor of Troy. But the Greeks have thought of this too; and Talthybius comes to announce that Astyanax must die: " 'Tis their will thy son from this crested wall of Troy be dashed to death." He tears the child from its mother's arms, and Andromache, holding it for a last moment, bids it an hysterical farewell.

Go, die, my best beloved, my cherished one,
In fierce men's hands, leaving me here alone.
Thy father was too valiant; that is why
They slay thee. . . .
And none to pity thee! . . . Thou little thing
That curlest in my arms, what sweet scents cling
All round thy neck! Beloved, can it be
All nothing, that this bosom cradled thee
And fostered, all the weary nights wherethrough

I watched upon thy sickness, till I grew
Wasted with watching? Kiss me. This one time;
Not ever again. Put up thine arms, and climb
About my neck; now kiss me, lips to lips . . .
Oh, ye have found an anguish that outstrips
All tortures of the East, ye gentle Greeks! . . .
Quick, take him; drag him; cast him from the wall,
If cast ye will! Tear him, ye beasts, be swift!
God hath undone me, and I cannot lift
One hand, one hand, to save my child from death.

She becomes delirious, and swoons; soldiers carry her away. Menelaus appears, and bids his soldiers bring Helen to him. He has sworn that he will kill her, and Hecuba is comforted at the thought that punishment is at last to find Helen.

I bless thee, Menelaus, I bless thee,
If thou wilt slay her! Only fear to see
Her visage, lest she snare thee and thou fall!

Helen enters, untouched and unafraid, proud in the consciousness of her beauty.

Hecuba. And comest thou now
Forth, and hast decked thy bosom and thy brow,
And breathest with thy lord the same blue air,
Thou evil heart? Low, low, with ravaged hair,
Rent raiment, and flesh shuddering, and within,
Oh, shame at last, not glory for thy sin. . . .
Be true, O King; let Hellas bear the crown
Of justice. Slay this woman. . . .
Menelaus. Peace, aged woman, peace. . . . (*To the soldiers*)
Have some chambered galley set for her,
Where she may sail the seas. . . .
Hecuba. A lover once, will always love again.

As Helen and Menelaus leave, Talthybius returns, bearing the dead body of Astyanax.

Talth. Andromache . . . hath charmed these tears into mine eyes,
Weeping her fatherland, as o'er the wave.
She gazed, speaking words to Hector's grave.
Howbeit, she prayed us that due rites be done
For burial of this babe. . . . And in thine hands
She bade me lay him, to be swathed in bands

Of death and garments... (*Hecuba takes the body.*)
Hecuba. Ah, what a death hath found thee, little one! . . .
Ye tender arms, the same dear mold have ye
As his. . . . And dear proud lips, so full of hope,
And closed forever! What false words ye said
At daybreak, when ye crept into my bed,
Called me kind names, and promised, "Grandmother,
When thou art dead, I will cut close my hair
And lead out all the captains to ride by
Thy tomb." Why didst thou cheat me so? 'Tis I,
Old, homeless, childless, that for thee must shed
Cold tears, so young, so miserably dead.
Dear God! the pattering welcomes of thy feet,
The nursing in my lap; and oh, the sweet
Falling asleep together! All is gone.
How should a poet carve the funeral stone
To tell thy story true? "There lieth here
A babe whom the Greeks feared, and in their fear
Slew him." Aye, Greece will bless the tale it tells! . . .
Oh, vain is man,
Who glorieth in his joy and hath no fears,
While to and fro the chances of the years
Dance like an idiot in the wind! . . . (*She wraps the child in the burial garments.*)
Glory of Phrygian raiment, which my thought
Kept for thy bridal day with some far-sought
Queen of the East, folds thee for evermore . . .[98]

In the *Electra* the ancient theme is far advanced. Agamemnon is dead, Orestes is in Phocis, and Electra has been married off by her mother to a peasant whose simple fidelity, and awe of her royal descent, survive her brooding negligence of him. To her, wondering will Orestes never find her, Orestes comes, bidden by Apollo himself (Euripides drives this point home) to avenge Agamemnon's death. Electra stirs him on; if he will not kill the murderers she will. The lad finds Aegisthus and slays him, and then turns upon his mother. Clytaemnestra is here a subdued and aging woman, gray-haired and frail, haunted by the memory of her crimes, at once fearing and loving the children who hate her; asking, but not begging, for mercy; and half reconciled to the penalty of her sins. When the killing is over Orestes is overcome with horror.

Sister, touch her again,
Oh, veil the body of her,

Shed on her raiment fair,
And close that death-red stain.—
Mother! And didst thou bear,
Bear in thy bitter pain,
To life, thy murderer?[94]

The final act of the drama, in Euripides, is called *Iphigenia in Tauris*—i.e., Iphigenia among the Tauri. Artemis, it now appears, substituted a deer for Agamemnon's daughter on the pyre at Aulis, snatched the girl from the flames, and made her a priestess at the shrine of Artemis among the half-savage Tauri of the Crimea. The Tauri make it a rule to sacrifice to the goddess any stranger who sets foot unasked upon their shores; and Iphigenia is the unhappy, brooding ministrant who consecrates the victims. Eighteen years of separation from Greece and those she loved have dulled her mind with grief. Meanwhile the oracle of Apollo has promised Orestes peace if he will capture from the Tauri the sacred image of Artemis, and bring it to Attica. Orestes and Pylades set sail, and at last reach the land of the Tauri, who gladly accept them as gifts of the sea for Artemis, and hurry them off to be slain at her altar. Orestes, exhausted, falls in an epileptic fit at Iphigenia's feet; and though she does not recognize him, she is overwhelmed with pity as she sees the two comrades, in the fairest years of youth, faced with death.

Iphig. To none is given
To know the coming nor the end of woe;
So dark is God, and to great darkness go
His paths, by blind chance mazed from our ken.
Whence are ye come, O most unhappy men? . . .
What mother then was yours, O strangers, say,
And father? And your sister, if you have
A sister: both at once, so young and brave
To leave her brotherless. . . .
Orestes. Would that my sister's hand could close mine eyes!
Iphig. Alas, she dwelleth under distant skies,
Unhappy one, and vain is all thy prayer.
Yet, oh, thou art from Argos; all of care
That can be I will give, and fail thee not.
Rich raiment to thy burial shall be brought,
And oil to cool thy pyre in golden floods,
And sweet that from a thousand mountain buds
The murmuring bee hath garnered, I will throw
To die with thee in fragrance.

She promises to save them if they will carry back to Argos the message which she bids them store in their memories.

> *Iphig.* Say, "To Orestes, Agamemnon's son,
> She that was slain in Aulis, dead to Greece
> Yet quick, Iphigenia, sendeth peace."
> *Orestes.* Iphigenia! Where? Back from the dead?
> *Iphig.* 'Tis I. But speak not, lest thou break my thread.
> "Take me to Argos, brother, ere I die."

Orestes wishes to clasp her in his arms, but the attendants forbid it; no man may touch the priestess of Artemis. He declares himself Orestes, but she cannot believe him. He convinces her by recalling the tales Electra told them.

> *Iphig.* Is this the babe I knew,
> The little babe, light-lifted like a bird? . . .
> O Argos land, O hearth and holy flame
> That old Cyclopes lit,
> I bless ye that he lives, that he is grown,
> A light and strength, my brother and mine own;
> I bless your name for it.[95]

They offer to rescue her, and in turn she helps them to capture the image of Artemis. By her subtle ruse they reach their ship safely, and carry the statue to Brauron; there Iphigenia becomes a priestess, and there, after her death, she is worshiped as a deity. Orestes is released from the Furies, and knows some years of peace. The thirst of the gods is sated, and the drama of *The Children of Tantalus* is complete.

2. *The Dramatist*

We must agree with Aristotle that these plays, from the viewpoint of dramatic technique, fall short of the standards set by Aeschylus and Sophocles.[96] The *Medea*, the *Hippolytus*, and *The Bacchae* are well planned, but even they cannot compare with the structural integrity of the *Oresteia*, or the complex unity of *Oedipus the King*. Instead of plunging at once into the action, and explaining its antecedents gradually and naturally in the course of the story, Euripides employs the artificial expedient of a pedagogical prologue, and, worse still, puts it sometimes into the mouth of a god. Instead of showing us the action directly, which is the function of drama, he too often introduces a messenger to describe the action, even when no violence is involved. Instead of making the chorus a part of the action he transforms it into a philosophical aside, or uses it to interrupt the development with lyrics always beautiful, but often irrelevant. Instead of presenting ideas through action, he sometimes displaces action with ideas, and turns the stage into a school for speculation, rhetoric, and argument. Too often his plots depend upon coincidences and "recognition"—though these are well arranged and dramatically presented. Most of the plays (like a few by his predecessors) end with intervention by the *deus ex machina,* the god from the crane—a device that can be forgiven only on the assumption that for Euripides the real play ended before this theophany, and the god was let down to provide the orthodox with a virtuous conclusion to what would otherwise have been a scandalous performance.[97] With such prologues and epilogues the great humanist won the privilege of presenting his heresies on the stage.

The material, like the form, is a medley of genius and artifice. Euripides is above all sensitive, as every poet must be; he feels the problems of mankind intensely, and expresses them with passion; he is the most tragic and the most human of all dramatists. But his feeling is too frequently sentimentality; his "droppings of warm tears"[98] are too easily released; he loses no chance to show a mother parting from her children, and wrings all possible pathos out of every situation. These scenes are always moving, and sometimes are described with a power unequaled in tragedy before or since; but they descend occasionally to melodrama, and a surfeit of violence and horror, as at the close of the *Medea.* Euripides is the Byron and Shelley and Hugo of Greece, a Romantic Movement in himself.

He easily surpasses his rivals in the delineation of character. Psychological analysis replaces with him, even more than with Sophocles, the operation of destiny; he is never weary of investigating the morals and motives of human conduct. He studies a great variety of men, from Electra's peasant husband to the kings of Greece and Troy; no other dramatist has drawn so many types of women, or drawn them with such sympathy; every shade of vice and virtue interests him, and is realistically portrayed. Aeschylus and Sophocles were too absorbed in the universal and eternal to see the temporal and the particular clearly; they created profound types, but Euripides creates living individuals; neither of the older men, for example, realized Electra so vividly. In these plays the drama of the conflict with fate yields more and more to the drama of situation and character, and the way is prepared by which, in the following centuries, the Greek stage will be captured by the comedy of manners under Philemon and Menander.

3. *The Philosopher*

But it would be foolish to judge Euripides chiefly as a playwright; his ruling interest is not dramatic technique but philosophical inquiry and political reform. He is the son of the Sophists, the poet of the Enlightenment, the representative of the radical younger generation that laughed at the old myths, flirted with socialism, and called for a new social order in which there should be less exploitation of man by man, of women by men, and of all by the state. It is for these rebel souls that Euripides writes; for them he adds his skeptical innuendoes, and inserts a thousand heresies between the lines of supposedly religious plays. He covers his tracks with pious passages and patriotic odes; he presents a sacred myth so literally that its absurdity is manifest and yet his orthodoxy cannot be impeached; he gives the body of his plays over to doubt, but surrenders the first and last words to the gods. His subtlety and brilliance, like those of the French Encyclopedists, is due in some part to the compulsion laid upon him to speak his mind while saving his skin.

His theme is that of Lucretius—

Tantum religio potuit suadere malorum

—so great are the evils to which religion has led men: oracles that breed violence upon violence, myths that exalt immorality with divine example, and shed supernatural sanctions upon dishonesty, adultery, theft, human sacrifice, and war. He describes a soothsayer as "a man who speaks few truths but many lies";[99] he calls it "sheer folly" to chart the future from the entrails of birds;[100] he denounces the whole apparatus of oracles and divination.[101] Above all he resents the immoral implications of the legends:

> Men shall know there is no God, no light
> In heaven, if wrong to the end shall conquer right. . . .
> Say not there be adulterers in heaven,
> Nor prisoner gods and gaolers: long ago
> My heart hath named it vile, and shall not alter. . . .
> These tales be false, false as those feastings wild
> Of Tantalus, and gods that tare a child.
> This land of murderers to its gods hath given
> Its own lust. Evil dwelleth not in heaven. . . .
> All these
> Are dead unhappy tales of minstrelsy.[102]

Sometimes such passages are softened with hymns to Dionysus, or psalms of pantheistic piety; but occasionally a character extends the Euripidean doubt to all the gods:

> Doth some one say that there be gods above?
> There are not, no, there are not. Let no fool,
> Led by the old false fable, thus deceive you.
> Look at the facts themselves, yielding my words
> No undue credence; for I say that kings
> Kill, rob, break oaths, lay cities waste by fraud,
> And doing thus are happier than those
> Who live calm pious lives day after day.[103]

He begins his lost *Melanippe* with a startling couplet—

> O Zeus, if there be a Zeus,
> For I know of him only by report—

whereupon the audience, we are told, rose to its feet in protest. And he concludes:

> The gods, too, whom mortals deem so wise,
> Are nothing clearer than some winged dream;
> And all their ways, like man's ways, but a stream
> Of turmoil. He who cares to suffer least,
> Not blind as fools are blinded by a priest,
> Goes straight . . . to what death, those who know him know.[104]

The fortunes of men, he thinks, are the result of natural causes, or of aimless chance; they are not the work of intelligent supernatural beings.[105] He suggests rational explanations of supposed miracles; Alcestis, for example, did not really die, but was sent off to burial while still alive; Heracles caught up with her before she had time to die.[106] He does not clearly tell us what his belief is, perhaps because he feels that the evidence does not lend itself to clear belief; but his most characteristic expressions are those of the vague pantheism that was now replacing polytheism among the educated Greeks.

> Thou deep Base of the World, and thou high Throne
> Above the World, whoe'er thou art, unknown
> And hard of surmise, Chain of Things that be,
> Or Reason of our Reason; God to thee
> I lift my praise, seeing the silent road
> That bringeth justice ere the end be trod
> To all that breathes and dies.[107]

Social justice is the minor theme of his songs; like all sympathetic spirits he longs for a time when the strong will be more chivalrous to the weak, and there will be an end to misery and strife.[108] Even in the midst of war, with all its compulsion to a patriotic belligerency, he presents the woes and horrors of war with unsparing realism.

> How are ye blind,
> Ye treaders down of cities, ye that cast
> Temples to desolation, and lay waste
> Tombs, the untrodden sanctuaries where lie
> The ancient dead; yourselves so soon to die.[109]

He gnaws his heart out at the sight of Athenians fighting Spartans for half a century, each enslaving the other, and both killing off their best; and he indites in a late play a touching apostrophe to peace:

> O Peace, thou givest plenty as from a deep spring; there is no beauty like unto thine; no, not even among the blessed gods. My heart yearneth within me, for thou tarriest; I grow old and thou returnest not. Shall weariness overcome mine eyes before they see thy bloom and thy comeliness? When the lovely songs of the dancers are heard again, and the thronging feet of them that wear garlands, shall grey hairs and sorrow have destroyed me utterly? Return, thou holy one, to our city; abide not far from us, thou that quencheth wrath. Strife and bitterness shall depart if thou art with us; madness and the edge of the sword shall flee from our doors.[109a]

Almost alone among the great writers of his time he dares to attack slavery; during the Peloponnesian War it became obvious that most slaves were such not by nature but by the accidents of life. He does not recognize any natural aristocracy; environment rather than heredity makes the man. The slaves in his dramas play important parts, and often speak his finest lines. With the imaginative sympathy of a poet he considers women. He knows the faults of the sex, and exposes them so realistically that Aristophanes was able to make him out a misogynist; but he did more than any other playwright of antiquity to present the case for women, and to support the dawning movement for their emancipation Some of his plays are almost modern, post-Ibsen studies in the problems of sex, even of sexual perversion.[110] He describes men with realism, but women with gallantry; the terrible Medea gets more compassion from him than he accords to the heroic but unfaithful Jason. He is the first dramatist to make a play turn upon love; his famous ode to Eros in the lost *Andromeda* was mouthed by thousands of young Greeks:

O Love, our Lord, of gods and men the king,
Either teach not how beauteous beauty is,
Or help poor lovers, whom like clay thou moldest,
Through toil and labor to a happy end.[111]

Euripides is naturally a pessimist, for every romantic becomes a pessimist when reality impinges upon romance. "Life," said Horace Walpole, "is a comedy to those who think, a tragedy to those who feel."[112] "Long ago," says our poet,

I looked upon man's days, and found a grey
Shadow. And this thing more I surely say
That those of all men who are counted wise,
Strong wits, devisers of great policies,
Do pay the bitterest toll. Since life began
Hath there in God's eye stood one happy man?[113]

He wonders at the greed and cruelty of men, the resourcefulness of evil, and the obscene indiscriminateness of death. At the beginning of the *Alcestis* Death says, "Is it not my function to take the doomed?"—to which Apollo answers, "No; only to dispatch those who have ripened into full old age." When death comes after life has been fully lived it is natural, and does not offend us. "We should not lament our fate if, like the harvests that follow each other in the passage of the years, one generation of men after another flowers, fades, and is carried off. So it is ordered in the course of Nature; and we must not be dismayed by anything that is rendered inevitable by her laws."[114] His conclusion is stoicism: "Do thou endure as men must, chafing not."[115] Now and then, following Anaximenes and anticipating the Stoics, he consoles himself with the thought that the spirit of man is part of the divine Air or *pneuma*, and will, after death, be preserved in the Soul of the World.[116]

Who knows if that be life which we call death,
And life be dying?—save alone that men
Living bear grief, but when they yield their breath
They have no sorrow then, and grieve no more.[117]

4. *The Exile*

The man whom we picture from these plays resembles sufficiently the sitting statue in the Louvre, and the busts at Naples, to let us believe that these are faithful copies of authentic Greek originals. The bearded face is handsome, but overwrought with meditation, and softened with a tender melancholy. His friends agreed with his enemies that he was gloomy, almost morose, not given to conviviality or laughter, and spending his later years in the seclusion of his island home. He had three sons, and derived some happiness from their childhood.[118] He found solace in books, and was the first private citizen in Greece, so far as we know, to collect a substantial library.*[119] He had excellent friends, including Protagoras and Socrates; the latter, who ignored other dramas, said that to see a play by Euripides he would walk to the Piraeus—a serious matter for a stout philosopher. The younger generation of emancipated souls looked up to him as their leader. But he had more enemies than any other writer in Greek history. The judges, who felt themselves bound, presumably, to protect religion and morals from his skeptical arrows, crowned only five of his efforts with victory; even so it was liberal of the archon basileus to admit so many Euripidean plays to a religious stage. Conservatives in all fields looked upon the dramatist as responsible with Socrates for the growth of unbelief among Athenian youth. Aristophanes declared war upon him at the outset in *The Acharnians*, satirized him with hilarious caricature in *The Thesmophoriazusae*, and, in the year after the poet's death, continued the attack in *The Frogs;* nevertheless, we are told, the tragic and the comic dramatist were on friendly terms to the end.[120] As for the audience, it denounced his heresies and crowded to his plays. When, at line 612 of the *Hippolytus*, the young hunter said, "My tongue hath sworn, but my mind remains unbound," the crowd protested so loudly against what seemed to be an outrageously immoral proposition that Euripides had to rise in his seat and comfort them with the assurance that Hippolytus would suffer edifyingly before the story closed—a safe promise for almost any character in Greek tragedy.

* There had already been royal or state libraries in Greece, as we have seen; and such collections in Egypt can be traced back to the Fourth Dynasty. A Greek library consisted of scrolls arranged in pigeonholes in a chest. Publication meant that an author had allowed his manuscript to be copied, and the copies to be circulated; thereafter further copies could be made without permission or "copyright." Copies of popular works were numerous, and not costly; Plato tells us in the *Apology* that Anaxagoras' treatise *On Nature* could be bought for a drachma ($1). Athens, in the age of Euripides, became the chief center of the book trade in Greece.

About 410 he was indicted on a charge of impiety; and soon afterward Hygiaonon brought against him another suit, involving much of the poet's fortune, and adduced Hippolytus' line as proof of Euripides' dishonesty. Both accusations failed; but the wave of public resentment that met *The Trojan Women* led Euripides to feel that he had hardly a friend left in Athens. Even his wife, it is said, turned against him because he could not join in the martial enthusiasm of the city. In 408, at the age of seventy-two, he accepted the invitation of King Archelaus to be his guest in the Macedonian capital. At Pella, under the protection of this Frederick—who had no fears for the orthodoxy of his people—Euripides found peace and comfort; there he wrote the almost idyllic *Iphigenia in Aulis*, and the profound religious play, *The Bacchae*. Eighteen months after his arrival he died, attacked and dismembered, said pious Greeks, by the royal hounds.[121]

A year later his son produced the two dramas at the city Dionysia, and the judges gave them the first prize. Even modern scholars have thought that *The Bacchae* was Euripides' apology to Greek religion;[122] and yet the play may have been intended as a bitter allegory of Euripides' treatment by the public of Athens. It is the story of how Pentheus, King of Thebes, was torn to pieces by a mob of female Dionysian orgiasts, led by his own mother Agave because he had denounced their wild superstition and intruded upon their revelry. It was no invention; the tale belonged to the religious tradition; the dismemberment and sacrifice of an animal, or of any man who dared to attend the ceremonies, was part of the Dionysian rite; and this powerful drama, by returning for its plot to the legend of Dionysus, bound Greek tragedy at its culmination with Greek tragedy at its birth. The play was composed among the Macedonian mountains which it describes in lyrics of unfailing power; and perhaps it was intended for performance in Pella, where the Bacchic cult was especially strong. Euripides enters with surprising insight into the mood of religious ecstasy, and puts into the mouths of the Bacchantes psalms of passionate devotion; it may indeed be that the old poet had gone to the limits of rationalism and beyond it, and recognized now the frailty of reason, and the persistency of the emotional needs of women and men. But the story does dubious honor to the Dionysian religion; its theme is once more the evils that may come of superstitious creeds.

The god Dionysus visits Thebes in disguise as a Bacchus, or incarnation of himself, and preaches the worship of Dionysus. The daughters of Cadmus reject the message; he hypnotizes them into pious ecstasy, and they go up into the hills to worship him with wild dances. They clothe themselves with the skins of animals, girdle themselves with snakes, crown themselves with ivy, and suckle the young of wolves and deer. The Theban king Pentheus opposes the cult as hostile to reason, morals, and order, and imprisons its preacher, who bears his punishment with Christian gentleness. But the god in the preacher asserts himself, opens the prison walls, and uses his miraculous power to hypnotize the young ruler. Under this influence Pentheus dresses himself as a woman, climbs the hills, and joins the revelers. The women discover that he is a man, and tear him limb from limb; his own mother, drunk with "possession," carries Pentheus' severed head in her hands, thinking it the head of a lion, and sings a song of triumph over it. When she comes to her senses and sees that it is the head of her son, she is revolted with the cult that intoxicated her; and when Dionysus says, "Ye mocked me, being God; this is your wage," she answers, "Should God be like a proud man in his rage?" The last lesson is the same as the first; even in his dying play the poet remained Euripides.

After his death he achieved popularity even in Athens. The ideas for which he had fought became the dominant conceptions of the following centuries, and the Hellenistic age looked back to him and to Socrates as the greatest intellectual stimuli that Greece had ever known. He had dealt with living problems rather than "dead tales of minstrelsy," and it took the ancient world a long time to forget him. The plays of his predecessors slipped into oblivion while his own were repeated in every year, and wherever the Greek world had a stage. When, in the collapse of that expedition to Syracuse (415) whose failure had been forecast in *The Trojan Women*, the captive Athenians faced a living death as chained slaves in the quarries of Sicily, those were given their freedom (Plutarch tells us) who could recite passages from the plays of Euripides.[123] The New Comedy molded itself upon his dramas, and grew out of them; one of its leaders, Philemon, said, "If I were sure that the dead have consciousness, I would hang myself to see Euripides."[124] The revival of skepticism, liberalism, and humanitarianism in the eighteenth and nineteenth centuries made Euripides almost a contemporary figure, more modern than Shakespeare. All in all, only Shakespeare has equaled him; and Goethe did not think so. "Have all the nations of the world since Euripides," asked Goethe of Eckermann, "produced one dramatist worthy to hand him his slippers?"[125] Not more than one.

VI. ARISTOPHANES

1. Aristophanes and the War

Greek tragedy is more somber than the Elizabethan, because it seldom employs that principle of comic relief by which, through a humorous interruption of the tragical, the auditor's tolerance for tragedy is increased. The Greek playwright preferred to keep his tragic drama on a persistently high plane, and relegated comedy to a "satyr" play which carried no serious import, but allowed the excited emotions of the audience to subside into humor and ease. In the course of time the comic drama declared its independence of tragedy, and a day was allotted to it, at the Dionysian festivals, when the entire program consisted of three or four comedies, written by different authors, played in succession, and competing for a separate prize.

Comedy, like oratory, had its first Greek bloom in Sicily. About 484 there came to Syracuse from Cos a philosopher, physician, poet, and dramatist, Epicharmus, who expounded Pythagoras, Heracleitus, and rationalism in thirty-five comedies, of which only occasional quotations remain. Twelve years after Epicharmus' arrival in Sicily the Athenian archon allowed its first chorus to comedy. The new art developed rapidly under the stimulus of democracy and freedom, and became the principal medium, in Athens, of moral and political satire. The wide license of speech permitted to comedy was a tradition of the Dionysian phallic procession. The abuse of this freedom led in 440 to a law against personal attacks in comedy; but this prohibition was repealed three years later, and full freedom of criticism and abuse continued even during the Peloponnesian War. The Greek comedy took the place, as political critic, of a free press in modern democracies.

We hear of many comic dramatists before Aristophanes, and the great Rabelais of antiquity even condescended to praise some of them when the smoke of his battles with them had cleared away. Cratinus was the mouthpiece of Cimon, and made rabid war against Pericles, whom he called "the squill-headed God Almighty";[126] merciful time has spared us the necessity of reading him. Another forerunner was Pherecrates, who, about 420, satirized, in *The Wild Men*, those Athenians who professed to dislike civilization and to long for a "return to nature": so old are the brave innovations of our youth. The ablest competitor of Aristophanes was Eupolis; they at first co-operated, then quarreled and parted, after which they satirized each other vigorously, but still agreed in attacking the democratic party. If comedy throughout the fifth century was hostile to democracy, it was partly because poets like money and the aristocracy was rich, but chiefly because the function of Greek comedy was to amuse with criticism, and the democratic party was in power. Since the leader of the democracy, Pericles, was sympathetic to new ideas like the emancipation of woman and the development of a rationalist philosophy, the comic dramatists ranged themselves, with suspicious unanimity, against all forms of radicalism, and called for a return to the ways and reputed morals of the "Men of Marathon." Aristophanes became the voice of this reaction, as Socrates and Euripides were the protagonists of the new ideas. The conflict between religion and philosophy captured the comic stage.

Aristophanes had some excuse for liking aristocracy, since he came of a cultured and prosperous family, and appears to have owned land in Aegina. His very name was a patent of nobility, meaning "the best made manifest." Born about 450, he was in the springtime of life when Athens and Sparta began that war which was to be a bitter theme of his plays. The Spartan invasion of Attica compelled him to abandon his country estate and come to live in Athens. He disliked city life, and resented the sudden demand upon him to hate Megarians, Corinthians, and Spartans; he denounced this conflict of Greek killing Greek, and called, in play after play, for peace.

After the death of Pericles in 429 supreme power in Athens passed into the hands of the rich tanner, Cleon, who represented those commercial interests that wanted a "knock-out blow"—i.e., the utter destruction of Sparta as a competitor for the mastery of Greece. In a lost play, *The Babylonians* (426), Aristophanes subjected Cleon and his policies to such stinging ridicule that the burly *strategos* prosecuted him for treason, and had him fined. Two years later Aristophanes revenged himself by presenting *The Knights*. Its leading character was Demos (i.e., the People), whose major-domo was called the Tanner; everyone understood the transparent allegory, including Cleon, who saw the play. The satire was so sharp that no actor would play the part of the Tanner for fear of political misfortune, whereupon Aristophanes took the role himself. Nicias (the name of the superstitious leader of the oligarchic faction) announces that an oracle has told him that the next ruler of Demos' house will be a sausage-seller. Such a huckster comes along, and the slaves hail him as "Chief that shall be of our glorious Athens!" "Prithee," says the Sausage-Seller, "let me go wash my tripes . . . you make a fool of me." But one Demosthenes assures him that he has just the qualifications for ruling the people—is he not a rascal, and free from all education? The Tanner, fearing that he is to be deposed, protests his services and his loyalty to Demos; no one except the harlots, he urges, has done so much for Demos as he. There is the usual Aristophanic burlesque: the Sausage-Seller belabors the Tanner with tripe, and primes himself for an oratorical contest in the Assembly by eating garlic. A contest in adulation ensues, to see which of the candidates can praise Demos the more lavishly, and "deserve better of Demos and his belly." The rivals bring a feast of good things and lay them before Demos like a platter of pre-election promises. The Sausage-Seller proposes that as a test of their honesty each candidate's locker shall be searched. In the Tanner's locker a heap of succulent dainties is found, in particular a massive cake, from which he has cut only a tiny slice for Demos (a reference to a current charge that Cleon had embezzled state funds). The Tanner is dismissed, and the Sausage-Seller becomes the ruler of Demos' house.

The Wasps (422) continues the satire on democracy in a milder and weaker vein; the chorus is composed of idle citizens—dressed as wasps—who seek to make an obol or two every day by serving as jurymen, in order that they may, by listening to "sycophants" and levying confiscatory fines, vote the money of the rich into the coffers of the state and the pockets of the poor. But Aristophanes' ruling interest in these early plays is to ridicule war and promote peace. The hero of *The Acharnians* (425) is Diceopolis ("Honest Citizen"), a farmer who complains that his land has been devastated by armies, so that he can no longer live by squeezing wine from his vineyards. He sees no reason for war, and is clear that he himself has no quarrel with the Spartans. Tired of waiting for the generals or the politicians to make peace, he signs a personal treaty with the Lacedaemonians; and when a chorus of war-patriotic neighbors denounces him he replies:

> Well, the very Spartans even, I've my doubts and scruples whether
> They've been totally to blame, in every instance, altogether.
> *Chorus.* Not to blame in every instance? Villain, vagabond, how
> dare ye,
> Talking treason to our faces, to suppose that we will spare ye?

He agrees to let them kill him if he cannot prove that Athens is as much to blame for the war as Sparta. His head is laid upon a chopping block, and he begins his argument. Presently an Athenian general enters, defeated, blustering, and profane; the Chorus is disgusted with him, and releases Diceopolis, who pleases all by selling a wine called Peace. It was a play of considerable audacity, possible only among a people trained to hear the other side. Taking advantage of the parabasis or digression in which the custom of comedy allowed the author to address the audience through the chorus or one of the characters, Aristophanes explained his function as a comic gadfly among the Athenians:

> Never since our poet presented comedies has he praised himself upon the stage. . . . But he maintains that he has done you much that is good. If you no longer allow yourselves to be too much hoodwinked by strangers or seduced by flattery, if in politics you are no longer the ninnies you once were, it is thanks to him. Formerly, when delegates from other cities wanted to deceive you, they had but to style you "the people crowned with violets"; at the word "violets" you at once sat erect on the tips of your bums. Or if, to tickle your vanity, some one spoke of "rich and sleek Athens," he would get all, because he spoke of you as he would have of anchovies in oil. In cautioning you against such wiles, the poet has done you great service.[127]

In *The Peace* (421) the poet was triumphant: Cleon was dead, and Nicias was about to sign for Athens a treaty pledging peace and friendship with Sparta for fifty years. But a few years later hostilities were resumed; and in 411 Aristophanes, abandoning hope in his fellow citizens, invited the women of Greece to end the bloodshed. As the *Lysistrata* opens, the ladies of Athens, while their men are still asleep, gather at dawn in council near the Acropolis. They agree to withhold the comforts of love from their spouses until these come to terms with the enemy; and they send an embassy to the women of Sparta to invite their co-operation in this novel campaign for peace. The men, awake at last, call to the women to come home; when these refuse, the men besiege them, but the attackers are repulsed with pails of hot water and torrents of speech. Lysistrata ("Dissolver of Armies") reads the men a lesson:

> During the wars of old we bore with you. . . . But we observed you carefully; and oftentimes, when we were at home, we used to hear that you had decided some matter badly. When we inquired about it, the men would answer, "What's that to you? Be silent." And we asked, "How is it, husband, that you men manage these affairs so foolishly?"

The leader of the men answers that women must keep out of public matters because they cannot manage the treasury. (As they debate, some of the women steal away to their husbands, muttering Aristophanic excuses.)

Lysistrata replies, "Why not? The wives have long had the management of their husbands' purses, to the great advantage of both." She argues so well that the men are finally persuaded to call a conference of the warring states. When the delegates are gathered, Lysistrata arranges that they shall have all the wine they can drink. Soon they are in a happy mood, and the long-delayed treaty is signed. The chorus ends the play with a paean to peace.

2. *Aristophanes and the Radicals*

Behind the disintegration of Athenian public life, in the view of Aristophanes, lay two basic evils: democracy and irreligion. He agreed with Socrates that the sovereignty of the people had become a sovereignty of politicians; but he was convinced that the skepticism of Socrates, Anaxagoras, and the Sophists had helped to loosen those moral bonds which had once made for social order and personal integrity. In *The Clouds* he made uproarious fun of the new philosophy. An old-fashioned gentleman by the name of Strepsiades, who is looking for an argument that may justify him in repudiating his debts, is delighted to hear that Socrates operates a Thinking Shop where one may learn to prove anything, even if it is false. He finds his way to the "School of Very Hard Thinkers." In the middle of the classroom he sees Socrates suspended from the ceiling in a basket, engrossed in thought, while some of the students are bent down with noses to the ground.

> *Strep.* What are those people doing, stooping so oddly?
>
> *Student.* They are probing the secrets that lie deep as Tartarus.
>
> *Strep.* But why—excuse me, but—their hind quarters—why are they stuck up so strangely in the air?
>
> *Stud.* Their other ends are studying astronomy.
>
> (*Strepsiades asks Socrates for lessons.*)
>
> *Socr.* By what gods do you swear? For the gods are not a current coin with us. (*Points to the chorus of clouds.*) These are the real gods.
>
> *Strep.* But come, is there no Zeus?
>
> *Socr.* There is no Zeus.
>
> *Strep.* But who makes it rain, then?
>
> *Socr.* These clouds. For have you ever seen rain without clouds? But if it were Zeus he ought to rain in fine weather as well as when clouds appear. . . .

Strep. But tell me, who is it that thunders? This makes me tremble.

Socr. These clouds, as they roll, thunder.

Strep. How?

Socr. When they are full of water, and are driven along, they fall heavily upon each other, and burst with a clap.

Strep. But who drives them? Is it not Zeus?

Socr. Not at all; the ethereal Vortex drives them on.

Strep. So the greatest of gods is Vortex. But what makes the clap of thunder?

Socr. I will teach you from your own case. Were you ever, after being stuffed with broth at a festival, later disturbed in your stomach, and did a tumult suddenly rumble through you?

In another scene Pheidippides, son of Strepsiades, meets in personification Just Argument and Unjust Argument. The first tells him that he must imitate the stoic virtues of the men of Marathon, but the other preaches to him the new morality. What good, asks Unjust Argument, have men ever gained by justice, or virtue, or moderation? For one honest successful and respected man there can always be found ten dishonest successful and respected men. Consider the gods themselves: they lied, stole, murdered, and committed adultery; and they are worshiped by all the Greeks. When Just Argument doubts that most successful men have been dishonest, Unjust Argument asks him:

Come now, from what class do our lawyers spring?

J. A. Well—from the blackguards.

U. A. Surely. Tell me, again, what are our tragic poets?

J. A. Blackguards.

U. A. And our public orators?

J. A. Blackguards all.

U. A. Now look about you. (*Turning and pointing to the audience.*) Which class among our friends here seems the most numerous? (*J. A. gravely examines the audience.*)

J. A. The blackguards have it by a large majority.

Pheidippides is so apt a pupil of Unjust Argument that he beats his father, on the ground that he is strong enough to do it and enjoys it; and besides, he asks, "Did you not beat me when I was a boy?" Strepsiades begs for mercy in the name of Zeus, but Pheidippides informs him that Zeus no longer exists, having been replaced by Vortex. The enraged father runs out into the streets, and calls upon all good citizens to destroy this new philosophy. They attack and burn down the Thinking Shop, and Socrates barely escapes with his life.

We do not know what part this comedy played in the tragedy of Socrates. It was brought out in 423, twenty-four years before the famous trial. Its good-humored satire does not seem to have offended the philosopher; we are told that he stood throughout the performance,[128] to give his enemies a better shot. Plato pictures Socrates and Aristophanes as friends after the performance; Plato himself recommended the play to Dionysius I of Syracuse as a jolly extravaganza, and maintained his own friendship with Aristophanes even after his master's death.[129] Of the three accusers of Socrates in 399 one, Meletus, was a child when the comedy was presented, and another Anytus, was on friendly terms with Socrates after the play.[130] Probably the later circulation of the play as literature did the sage more harm than its original performance; Socrates himself, in Plato's report of his defense, referred to the play as one of the major sources of that bad reputation which was prejudicing his case with the jurors.

There was another target in Athens at which Aristophanes aimed his satire; and in this case the mood was one of implacable hostility. He distrusted the skepticisms of the Sophists, the moral, economic, and political individualism that was undermining the state, the sentimental feminism that was agitating the women, and the socialism that was arousing the slaves. All these evils he saw at their clearest in Euripides; and he resolved to destroy with laughter the influence of the great dramatist upon the mind of Greece.

He began in 411 with a play which he called *The Thesmophoriazusae*, from the women who celebrated in sexual exclusiveness the feast of Demeter and Persephone. The assembled devotees discuss the latest quips of Euripides against their sex, and plan revenge. Euripides gets wind of the proceedings, and persuades his father-in-law Mnesilochus to dress as a woman and enter the meeting to defend him. The first complainant alleges that the tragic dramatist has deprived her of a living: formerly she made wreaths for the temples, but since Euripides has shown that there are no gods, the temple business has been ruined. Mnesilochus defends Euripides on the ground that his worst sayings about women are visibly and audibly true, and are mild compared with what women themselves know to be their faults. The ladies suspect that this traducer of the sex cannot be a woman; they tear off Mnesilochus' disguise, and he saves himself from dismemberment only by snatching a babe from a woman's arms and

threatening to kill it if they touch him. As they nevertheless attack him, he unwraps the child, and finds that it is a wineskin disguised to escape the collector of internal revenue. He proposes to cut its throat just the same, much to the distress of its owner. "Spare my darling!" she cries; "or at least bring a bowl, and if it must die, let us catch its blood." Mnesilochus solves the problem by drinking the wine, and meanwhile sending an appeal to Euripides for rescue. Euripides appears in various parts from his plays—now as Menelaus, now as Perseus, now as Echo—and finally arranges Mnesilochus' escape.

The Frogs (405) returns to the assault despite Euripides' death. Dionysus, god of the drama, is dissatisfied with the surviving playwrights of Athens, and descends to Hades to bring back Euripides. As he is ferried over to the lower world a choir of frogs greets him with a croaking chorus that must have provided a month's catchword for young Athenians. Aristophanes pokes much fun at Dionysus in passing, and boldly parodies the Mysteries of Eleusis. When the god arrives in Hades he finds Euripides attempting to unseat Aeschylus as king of all dramatists. Aeschylus accuses Euripides of spreading skepticism and a dangerous casuistry, and of corrupting the morals of Athenian women and youth; ladies of refinement, he says, have been known to kill themselves through shame at having heard Euripides' obscenities. A pair of scales is brought in, and each poet throws into it lines from his plays; one mighty phrase of Aeschylus (here the satire strikes the older poet too) tips the scale against a dozen of Euripides. At last Aeschylus proposes that the younger dramatist shall leap into one scale with wife, children, and baggage, while he will guarantee to find a couplet that will outweigh them all. In the end the great skeptic loses the contest, and Aeschylus is brought back to Athens as victor.* This oldest known essay in literary criticism received the first prize from the judges, and so pleased the audience that another performance of it was given a few days afterward.

In a middling play called *The Ecclesiazusae* (393)—i.e., The Assemblywomen—Aristophanes turned his laughter upon the radical movement in general. The ladies of Athens disguise themselves as men, pack the Assembly, outvote their husbands, brothers, and sons, and elect themselves rulers of the state. Their leader is a fiery suffragette, Praxagora, who berates her sex as fools for letting themselves be ruled by such dolts as men, and proposes that all wealth shall be divided equally among the *citizens*, leaving the slaves uncontaminated with gold. The attack upon Utopia takes a

* Possibly a reference to the repetition of Aeschylus' plays.

more graceful form in Aristophanes' masterpiece, *The Birds* (414). Two citizens who despair of Athens climb up to the abode of the birds, hoping to find there an ideal life. With the help of the birds they build, between earth and heaven, a Utopian city, Nephelococcygia, or Cloud-Cuckoo-Land. The birds, in a chorus as lyrically perfect as anything in the tragic poets, apostrophize mankind:

Ye children of man, whose life is a span,
Protracted with sorrow from day to day,
Naked and featherless, feeble and querulous,
Sickly calamitous creatures of clay,
Attend to the words of the sovereign birds,
Immortal, illustrious lords of the air,
Who survey from on high, with a merciful eye,
Your struggles of misery, labor, and care.

The birds plan to intercept all communication between the gods and men; no sacrifices shall be allowed to mount to heaven; soon, say the reformers, the old gods will starve, and the birds will be supreme. New gods are invented in the image of birds, and those conceived in the image of men are deposed. Finally an embassy comes from Olympus, seeking a truce; the leader of the birds agrees to take as his wife the handmaiden of Zeus, and the play ends in a happy marriage.

3. *The Artist and the Thinker*

Aristophanes is an unclassifiable mixture of beauty, wisdom, and filth. When the mood is upon him he can write lyrics of purest Greek serene, which no translator has ever yet conveyed. His dialogue is life itself, or perhaps it is swifter, racier, more vigorous than life dares be. He belongs with Rabelais, Shakespeare, and Dickens in the lusty vitality of his style; and like theirs his characters give us more keenly the shape and aroma of the time than all the works of the historians; no one who has not read Aristophanes can know the Athenians. His plots are ridiculous, and are put together with an almost extempore carelessness; sometimes the main theme is exhausted before the play is half through, and the remainder limps forward on the crutches of burlesque. The humor is generally of a low order; it cracks and groans with facile puns, drags itself out to tragic lengths, and too often depends upon digestion, reproduction, and excretion. In *The Acharnians* we hear of a character who eases himself con-

tinuously for eight months;[131] in *The Clouds* the major forms of human waste are mingled with sublime philosophy;[132] every second page offers us rumps, wind, bosoms, gonads, coitus, pederasty, onanism; everything is here.[133] He charges his old rival, Cratinus, with nocturnal incontinence.[134] He is the most contemporary of ancient poets, for nothing is so timeless as obscenity. Coming to him after any other Greek author—worst of all, after Euripides—he seems depressingly vulgar, and we find it difficult to imagine the same audience enjoying them both.

If we are good conservatives we can stomach all this on the ground that Aristophanes attacks every form of radicalism, and upholds devotedly every ancient virtue and vice. He is the most immoral of all Greek writers known to us, but he hopes to make up for it by attacking immorality. He is always found on the side of the rich, but he denounces cowardice; he lies pitilessly about Euripides, living and dead, but he assails dishonesty; he describes the women of Athens as unbelievably coarse, but he exposes Euripides for defaming them; he burlesques the gods so boldly* that in comparison with the pious Socrates we must picture him as an hilarious atheist—but he is all for religion, and accuses the philosophers of undermining the gods. Yet it took real courage to caricature the powerful Cleon, and to paint the faults of Demos to Demos' face; it took insight to see, in the trend of religion and morals from sophistic skepticism to epicurean individualism, a basic danger to the life of Athens. Perhaps Athens would have fared better if it had taken some of his advice, moderated her imperialism, made an early peace with Sparta, and mitigated with aristocratic leadership the chaos and corruption of post-Periclean democracy.

Aristophanes failed because he did not take his own counsels seriously enough to observe them himself. His excesses of pornography and abuse were partly responsible for the law forbidding personal satire; and though the law was soon repealed, the Old Comedy of political criticism died before the death of Aristophanes (385), and was replaced, even in his later plays, by the Middle Comedy of manners and romance. But the vitality of the Greek comic theater disappeared along with its extravagance and brutality. Philemon and Menander rose and passed and were forgotten, while Aristophanes survived all changes of moral and literary fashions to come down to our own time with eleven of his forty-two plays intact. Even today, despite all difficulties of understanding and translation, Aristophanes is alive; and, if we hold our noses, we can read him with profane delight.

---

* Some of the gods, he tells us, keep brothels in heaven.[135]

VII. THE HISTORIANS

Prose was not completely forgotten in this heyday of dramatic poetry. Oratory, stimulated by democracy and litigation, became one of the passions of Greece. As early as 466 Corax of Syracuse wrote a treatise, *Techne Logon* (The Art of Words), to guide the citizen who wished to address an assembly or a jury; here already are the traditional divisions of an oration into introduction, narrative, argument, subsidiary remarks, and peroration. Gorgias brought the art to Athens, and Antiphon used the ornate style of Gorgias in speeches and pamphlets devoted to oligarchical propaganda. In Lysias Greek oratory became more natural and vivid; but it was only in the greatest statesmen, like Themistocles and Pericles, that the public address rose above all visible artifice, and proved the effectiveness of simple speech. The new weapon was sharpened by the Sophists, and so thoroughly exploited by their pupils that when the oligarchic party seized power in 404 it forbade the further teaching of rhetoric.[136]

The great achievement of Periclean prose was history. In a sense it was the fifth century that discovered the past, and consciously sought for a perspective of man in time. In Herodotus historiography has all the charm and vigor of youth; in Thucydides fifty years later, it has already reached a degree of maturity which no later age has ever surpassed. What separates and distinguishes these two historians is the Sophist philosophy. Herodotus was the simpler, perhaps the kindlier, certainly the more cheerful spirit. He was born in Halicarnassus about 484, of a family exalted enough to participate in political intrigue; because of his uncle's adventures he was exiled at the age of thirty-two, and began those far-reaching travels that supplied the background for his *Histories*. He passed down through Phoenicia to Egypt, as far south as Elephantine; he moved west to Cyrene, east to Susa, and north to the Greek cities on the Black Sea. Wherever he went he observed and inquired with the eye of a scientist and the curiosity of a child; and when, about 447, he settled down in Athens, he was armed with a rich assortment of notes concerning the geography, history, and manners of the Mediterranean states. With these notes, and a little plagiarizing of Hecataeus and other predecessors, he composed the most famous of all historical works, recording the life and history of Egypt, the Near East, and Greece from their legendary origins to the close of the Persian War. An ancient story tells how he read parts of his book publicly at Athens and Olympia, and so pleased the Athenians with his account of the war,

and their exploits in it, that they voted him twelve talents ($60,000)—which any historian will consider too pleasant to be true.[137]

The introduction announces the purpose of the book in grand style:

> This is a presentation of the Inquiries (*Historiai*) of Herodotus of Halicarnassus, to the end that time may not obliterate the great and marvelous deeds of the Hellenes and the Barbarians; and especially that the causes for which they waged war with one another may not be forgotten.

Since all the nations of the eastern Mediterranean are brought into the narrative, the book is, in a limited sense, a "universal history," much broader in its scope than the narrow subject of Thucydides. The story is unconsciously unified by the contrast of barbarian despotism with Greek democracy, and moves, though by halting steps and confusing digressions, to a foreshadowed and epic end at Salamis. The purpose is to record "wondrous deeds and wars,"[138] and in truth the tale sometimes recalls Gibbon's regrettable misunderstanding of history as "little more than the register of the crimes, follies, and misfortunes of mankind."[139] Nevertheless Herodotus, though he speaks in only the most incidental way of literature, science, philosophy, and art, finds room for a thousand interesting illustrations of the dress, manners, morals, and beliefs of the societies he describes. He tells us how Egyptian cats jump into the fire, how the Danubians get drunk on smells, how the walls of Babylon were built, how the Massagetae eat their parents, and how the priestess of Athena at Pedasus grew a mighty beard. He presents not only kings and queens, but men of all degrees; and women, who are excluded from Thucydides, enliven these pages with their scandals, their beauty, their cruelties, and their charm.

There is, as Strabo says, "much nonsense in Herodotus";[140] but our historian, like Aristotle, covers a vast field, and has many opportunities to err. His ignorance is as wide as his learning, his credulity is as great as his wisdom. He thinks that the semen of Ethiopians is black,[141] accepts the legend that the Lacedaemonians won battles because they had brought the bones of Orestes to Sparta,[142] and reports incredible figures for the size of Xerxes' army, the casualties of the Persians, and the almost woundless victories of the Greeks. His account is patriotic, but not unjust; he gives both sides of most political disputes,* signalizes the heroism of the invaders, and testifies to the honor and chivalry of the Persians. When he depends upon

* Cf. the imaginative but excellent discussion of monarchy, aristocracy, and democracy, in iii, 80-2.

foreign informants he makes his greatest mistakes; so he thinks that Nebuchadrezzar was a woman, that the Alps are a river, and that Cheops came after Rameses III. But when he deals with matters that he has had a chance to observe in person he is more reliable, and his statements are increasingly confirmed as our knowledge grows.

He swallows many superstitions, records many miracles, quotes oracles piously, and darkens his pages with omens and auguries; he gives the dates of Semele, Dionysus, and Heracles; and presents all history, like a Greek Bossuet, as the drama of a Divine Providence rewarding the virtues and punishing the sins, crimes, and insolent prosperity of men. But he has his rationalistic moments, perhaps having heard the Sophists in his later years: he suggests that Homer and Hesiod gave name and form to the Olympian deities, that custom determines men's faiths, and that one man knows as much as another about the gods;[143] having accepted Providence as the final arbiter of history, he puts it aside, and looks for natural causes; he compares and identifies the myths of Dionysus and Osiris in the manner of a scientist; he smiles tolerantly at some tales of divine intervention, and offers a possible natural explanation;[144] and he reveals his general method with a twinkle in his eye when he says: "I am under obligation to tell what is reported, but I am not obliged to believe it; and let this hold for every narrative in this history."[145] He is the first Greek historian whose works have come down to us; and in that sense Cicero may be forgiven for calling him the Father of History. Lucian, like most of the ancients, ranked him above Thucydides.[146]

Nevertheless the difference between the mind of Herodotus and that of Thucydides is almost the difference between adolescence and maturity. Thucydides is one of the phenomena of the Greek Enlightenment, a descendant of the Sophists as Gibbon was a spiritual nephew of Bayle and Voltaire. His father was a rich Athenian who owned gold mines in Thrace; his mother was a Thracian of distinguished family. He received all the education available in Athens, and grew up in the odor of skepticism. When the Peloponnesian War broke out he kept a record of it from day to day. In 430 he suffered from the plague. In 424, aged thirty-six (or forty), he was chosen one of two generals to command a naval expedition to Thrace. Because he failed to lead his forces to Amphipolis in time to relieve it from siege, he was exiled by the Athenians. He spent the next twenty years of his life in travel, especially in the Peloponnesus; to this direct acquaintance with the enemy we owe something of the impressive impartiality that distinguishes his book. The oligarchic revolution of 404 ended his exile, and he returned to Athens. He died—some say by murder—in or before 396, leaving unfinished his *History of the Peloponnesian War.*

He begins it simply:

> Thucydides, an Athenian, wrote the history of the war between the Peloponnesians and the Athenians from the moment that it broke out, believing that it would be an important war, and more worthy of relation than any that had preceded it.

He opens his introductory narrative where Herodotus left off, at the close of the Persian War. It is a pity that the genius of the greatest Greek historians saw nothing worthier of relation in Greek life than its wars. Herodotus wrote partly with an eye to entertain the educated reader; Thucydides writes to furnish information for future historians, and the guidance of precedent for future statesmanship. Herodotus wrote in a loose and easygoing style, inspired perhaps by the rambling epics of Homer; Thucydides, like one who has heard the philosophers, the orators, and the dramatists, writes in a style often involved and obscure because it attempts to be at once brief, precise, and profound, a style occasionally spoiled by Gorgian rhetoric and embellishment, but sometimes as terse and vivid as Tacitus, and rising, in the more crucial moments, to a dramatic power as intense as anything in Euripides; nothing in the dramatists can surpass the pages that describe the expedition to Syracuse, the vacillations of Nicias, and the horrors that followed his defeat. Herodotus ranged from place to place and from age to age; Thucydides forces his story into a rigid chronological frame of seasons and years, sacrificing the continuity of his narrative. Herodotus wrote in terms of personalities rather than processes, feeling that processes operate through personalities; Thucydides, though he recognizes the role of exceptional individuals in history, and occasionally lightens his theme with a portrait of Pericles or Alcibiades or Nicias, leans rather to impersonal recording and the consideration of causes, developments, and results. Herodotus wrote of far-off events reported to him in most cases at second or third hand; Thucydides speaks often as an eyewitness, or as one who has spoken with eyewitnesses, or has seen the original documents; in several instances he gives the documents concerned. He has a keen conscience for accuracy; even his geography has been verified in detail. He seldom passes moralistic judgments upon men or events; he lets his patrician scorn of Athenian democracy get the better of him in picturing Cleon, but for the greater part he keeps himself aloof from his story, gives the facts with fairness to both sides, and recounts the story of Thucydides' brief military career as if he had never known, much less been, the man. He is the father of scientific method in history, and is proud of the care and industry with which he has worked. "On the whole," he says, with a glance at Herodotus,

> the conclusions I have drawn from the proofs quoted may, I believe, be safely relied on. Assuredly they will not be disturbed either by the lays of a poet displaying the exaggeration of his craft, or by the compositions of the chroniclers that are attractive at truth's expense—the subjects they treat being out of the reach of evidence, and time having robbed most of them of historical value by enthroning them in the region of legend. Turning from these, we can rest satisfied with having proceeded upon the clearest data, and having arrived at conclusions as exact as can be expected in matters of such antiquity. . . . The absence of romance in my history will, I fear, detract somewhat from its interest; but if it be judged useful by those inquirers who desire an exact knowledge of the past as an aid to the interpretation of the future—which, in the course of human affairs, must resemble, if it does not reflect, the past—I shall be content. In fine, I have written my work not as an essay which is to win the applause of the moment, but as a possession for all time.[147]

Nevertheless, he yields accuracy to interest in one particular: he has a passion for putting elegant speeches into the mouths of his characters. He frankly admits that these orations are mostly imaginary, but they help him to explain and vivify personalities, ideas, and events. He claims that each speech represents the substance of an address actually given at the time; if this is true, all Greek statesmen and generals must have studied rhetoric with Gorgias, philosophy with the Sophists, and ethics with Thrasymachus. The speeches have all the same style, the same subtlety, the same realism of view; they make the laconic Laconian as windy as any Sophist-bred Athenian. They put the most undiplomatic arguments into the mouths of diplomats,* and the most compromising honesty into the words of generals. The "Funeral Oration" of Pericles is an excellent essay on the virtues of Athens, and comes with fine grace from the pen of an exile; but Pericles was famous for simplicity of speech rather than for rhetoric; and Plutarch spoils the romance by saying that Pericles left nothing written, and that of his sayings hardly anything was preserved.[148]

* E.g., the speech of Alcibiades at Sparta, vi, 20.89.

Thucydides has defects corresponding to his virtues. He is as severe as a Thracian, and lacks the vivacity and wit of the Athenian spirit; there is no humor in his book. He is so absorbed in "this war, of which Thucydides is the historian" (a proudly recurring phrase) that he has an eye only for political and military events. He fills his pages with martial details, but makes no mention of any artist, or any work of art. He seeks causes sedulously, but seldom sinks beneath political to economic factors in the determination of events. Though writing for future generations, he tells us nothing of the constitutions of the Greek states, nothing of the life of the cities, nothing of the institutions of society. He is as exclusive towards women as towards the gods; he will not have them in his story; and he makes the gallant Pericles, who risked his career for a courtesan advocate of feminine freedom, say that "a woman's best fame is to be as seldom as possible mentioned by men, either for censure or for praise."[149] Face to face with the greatest age in the history of culture, he loses himself in the logic-chopping fluctuations of military victory and defeat, and leaves unsung the vibrant life of the Athenian mind. He remains a general even after he has become an historian.

We are grateful for him, nevertheless, and must not complain too much that he did not write what he did not undertake to write. Here at least is an historical method, a reverence for truth, an acuteness of observation, an impartiality of judgment, a passing splendor of language and fascination of style, a mind both sharp and profound, whose ruthless realism is a tonic to our naturally romantic souls. Here are no legends, no myths, and no miracles. He accepts the heroic tales, but tries to explain them in naturalistic terms. As for the gods, he is devastatingly silent; they have no place in his history. He is sarcastic about oracles and their safe ambiguity,[150] and scornfully exposes the stupidity of Nicias in relying upon oracles rather than knowledge. He recognizes no guiding Providence, no divine plan, not even "progress"; he sees life and history as a tragedy at once sordid and noble, redeemed now and then by great men, but always relapsing into superstition and war. In him the conflict between religion and philosophy is decided; and philosophy wins.

Plutarch and Athenaeus refer to hundreds of Greek historians. Nearly all of them but Herodotus and Thucydides, in the Golden Age, have been covered up by the silt of time; and of the later historians only paragraphs remain. The case is no different with the other forms of Greek literature. Of the hundreds of tragic dramatists who won prizes at the Dionysia, we have a few plays by three; of the many comic writers we have one; of the great philosophers we have two. All in all, not more than one-twentieth survives from the critically acclaimed literature of fifth-century Greece; and from the earlier and later centuries even less.[151] Most of what we have comes from Athens; the other cities, as we can tell from the philosophers that they sent to Athens, were fertile in genius too, but their culture was sooner engulfed by barbarism from without and from below, and their manuscripts were lost in the disorder of revolution and war. We must judge the whole from the fragments of a part.

Even so it is a rich heritage, if not in quantity (but who has absorbed it all?), surely in form. Form and order are the essence of the classic style in literature as well as in art: the typical Greek writer, like the Greek artist, is never satisfied with mere expression, but longs to give form and beauty to his material. He cuts his matter down to brevity, rearranges it into clarity, transforms it into a complex simplicity; he is always direct, and seldom obscure; he shuns exaggeration and bias, and even when he is romantic in feeling he struggles to be logical in thought. This persistent effort to subordinate fancy to reason is the dominant quality of the Greek mind, even of Greek poetry. Therefore Greek literature is "modern," or rather contemporary; we find it hard to understand Dante or Milton, but Euripides and Thucydides are kin to us mentally, and belong to our age. And that is because, though myths may differ, reason remains the same, and the life of reason makes brothers of its lovers in all times, and everywhere.

CHAPTER XVIII

The Suicide of Greece

I. THE GREEK WORLD IN THE AGE OF PERICLES

LET us, before facing the melancholy spectacle of the Peloponnesian War, glance at the Greek world outside of Attica. Our knowledge of these other states in this period is so fragmentary that we are left to assume—what we cannot prove—that they shared to a minor degree in the cultural blossoming of the Golden Age.

In 459 Pericles, anxious to control Egyptian grain, sent a great fleet to expel the Persians from Egypt. The expedition failed, and thereafter Pericles adopted the policy of Themistocles—to win the world by commerce rather than by war. Throughout the fifth century Egypt and Cyprus continued under Persian rule. Rhodes remained free, and the merger of its three cities into one in 408 prepared it to become in the Hellenistic period one of the richest commercial centers in the Mediterranean. The Greek cities of Asia preserved their independence, won at Mycale in 479, until the destruction of the Athenian Empire left them helpless again before the tribute collectors of the Great King. The Greek colonies in Thrace and on the Hellespont, the Propontis, and the Euxine prospered under Athenian domination, but were impoverished by the Peloponnesian War. Under Archelaus Macedonia passed out of barbarism and became one of the powers of the Greek world: good roads were laid down, a disciplined army was formed out of the hardy mountaineers, a handsome new capital was built at Pella, and many Greek geniuses, like Timotheus, Zeuxis, and Euripides, found welcome at the court. Boeotia in this period produced Pindar, and gave to Greece, in the Boeotian Confederacy, an unappreciated example of how independent states might live in peace and co-operation.

In Italy the Greek cities suffered from frequent wars, and from Athenian ascendancy in maritime trade. In 443 Pericles sent out a group of Hellenes, gathered from different states, to establish near the site of Sybaris the new colony of Thurii, as an experiment in Panhellenic unity. Protagoras drew up a code of laws for the city, and Hippodamus the architect laid out the streets on a rectangular plan that was to be widely imitated in the following centuries. Within a few years the colonists divided into factions according to their origin, and most of the Athenians, probably including Herodotus, went back to Athens.

Sicily, always turbulent but always fertile, continued to grow in wealth and culture. Selinus and Acragas built massive temples; and under Theron Acragas became so rich that Empedocles remarked: "The men of Acragas devote themselves wholly to luxury as if they were to die tomorrow, but they furnish their houses as if they were to live forever."[1] Gelon I, when he died in 478, left Syracuse a system of administration almost as effective as that which Napoleon bequeathed to modern France. Under his brother and successor, Hieron I, the city became a center not only of trade and wealth, but of literature, science, and art. There, too, luxury reached dizzy heights: Syracusan banquets became a byword for extravagance, and "Corinthian girls" were so numerous in the city that any man who slept at home was considered a saint.[2] The citizens were quick of mind and sharp of tongue; they enjoyed good oratory to their ruin, and crowded to hear, in their magnificent open-air theater, the comedies of Epicharmus and the tragedies of Aeschylus.* Hieron was a tyrant of bad temper and good will, cruel to his enemies and generous to his friends. He opened his court and purse to Simonides, Bacchylides, Pindar, and Aeschylus, and with their help made Syracuse for a moment the intellectual capital of Greece.

But man cannot live on art alone. The Syracusans thirsted for the wine of freedom, and after the death of Hieron they deposed his brother and set up a limited democracy. The other Greek cities in the island took courage and likewise expelled their dictators; the trading classes overthrew the landowning aristocracies, and established a commercial democracy superimposed upon a system of ruthless slavery. After some sixty years, war ended this interlude of liberty as it had ended another through Gelon I. In 409 the Carthaginians, who had kept alive through three generations the memory of Hamilcar's defeat at Himera, invaded Sicily with an armada of fifteen hundred ships and twenty thousand men under Hamilcar's grandson, Hannibal. He laid siege to Selinus, which had become pacific under prosperity, and had neglected to keep its defenses in repair. The surprised city appealed for help to Acragas and Syracuse, whose comfortable citizens responded with Spartan leisureliness. Selinus was taken, all the survivors were massacred and mutilated, and the city became a part of the Carthaginian Empire. Hannibal proceeded to Himera, captured it with ease, and put three thousand prisoners to torture and death to appease the shade of his grandfather. A plague decimated his troops and took off Hannibal himself as they besieged Acragas, but his successor mollified the gods of Carthage by burning alive his own son as an offering. The Carthaginians took the city, took Gela and Camarina, and marched on toward Syracuse. The terrified Syracusans, interrupted in their banquets, gave absolute power to their ablest

* The theater was probably built under Hieron I (478-67), and rebuilt under Hieron II (270-16). Much of it survives; and many ancient Greek dramas have been staged in it in our century.

general, Dionysius. But Dionysius made peace with the Carthaginians, ceded to them all southern Sicily, and used his troops to establish a second dictatorship (405). It was not all treachery. Dionysius knew that resistance was useless; he surrendered everything but his army and his city, and resolved to strengthen both until he too, like Gelon, could expel the invaders from Sicily.

II. HOW THE GREAT WAR BEGAN

Just as the simple soul must picture deity in the form of a man, so the simple citizen must conceive the causes of war to be personal—usually one person. Even Aristophanes, like some gossips of his time, would have it that Pericles brought on the Peloponnesian War by attacking Megara, because Megara had offended Aspasia.[3]

It is probable that Pericles, who had not hesitated to conquer Aegina, had dreamed of completing Athens' control of Greek trade by dominating not only Megara but Corinth, which was to Greece what Istanbul is to the eastern Mediterranean today—a door and a key to half a continent's trade. But the basic cause of the war was the growth of the Athenian Empire, and the development of Athenian control over the commercial and political life of the Aegean. Athens allowed free trade there in time of peace, but only by imperial sufferance; no vessel might sail that sea without her consent. Athenian agents decided the destination of every vessel that left the grain ports of the north; Methone, starving with drought, had to ask Athens' leave to import a little corn.[4] Athens defended this domination as a vital necessity; she was dependent upon imported food, and was determined to guard the routes by which that food came. In policing the avenues of international trade Athens performed a real service to peace and prosperity in the Aegean, but the process became more and more irksome as the pride and wealth of the subject cities grew. The funds that these had contributed for defense against Persia were being used for the adornment of Athens, even for the financing of Athenian wars upon other Greeks.[5] Periodically the assessment had been increased until it was now, in 432, some 460 talents ($2,300,000) per year. Athens reserved to Athenian courts the right to try all cases, arising within the Confederacy, that involved Athenian citizens or major crimes. If any city resisted, it was reduced by force; so Pericles with efficient dispatch suppressed rebellions in Aegina (457), Euboea (446), and Samos (440). If we may believe Thucydides, the democratic leaders at Athens, while making liberty the idol of their policy among Athenians, frankly recognized that the Con-

federacy of free cities had become an empire of force. "You should remember," says Thucydides' Cleon to the Assembly (427), "that your empire is a despotism exercised over unwilling subjects who are always conspiring against you; they do not obey in return for any kindness which you do them to your own injury, but only in so far as you are their master; they have no love for you, but they are held down by force."[6] The inherent contradiction between the worship of liberty and the despotism of empire co-operated with the individualism of the Greek states to end the Golden Age.

The resistance to Athenian policy came from nearly every state in Greece.[7] Boeotia fought off at Coronea (447) the attempt of Athens to include it in the Empire. Some subject cities, and others that feared to become subject, appealed to Sparta to check the Athenian power. The Spartans were not eager for war, knowing the strength and valor of the Athenian fleet; but the old racial antipathy between Dorian and Ionian inflamed them, and the Athenian custom of establishing in every city democracies dependent upon the Empire seemed to the landowning oligarchy of Sparta a threat to aristocratic government everywhere. For a time the Spartans contented themselves with supporting the upper classes in every city, and slowly forging a united front against Athens.

Surrounded by enemies abroad and at home, Pericles worked for peace and prepared for war. The army, he calculated, could protect Attica, or all of Attica's population gathered within Athens' walls; and the navy could keep open the routes by which Euxine or Egyptian grain might enter Athens' walled port. It was his judgment that no real concessions could be made without endangering that supply of food; it seemed to him, as now to England, a choice between empire and starvation. Nevertheless he sent envoys to all the Greek states, inviting them to an Hellenic Conference which would seek a peaceful solution of the problems that were leading to war. Sparta refused to attend, feeling that her acceptance would be construed as an acknowledgment of Athenian hegemony, and at her secret suggestion[8] so many other states rejected the invitation that the project fell through. Meanwhile, says Thucydides, in a sentence that explains much history, "The Peloponnesus and Athens were both full of young men whose inexperience made them eager to take up arms."[9]

These basic factors being present, the coming of war awaited some provocative incident. In 435 Corcyra, a Corinthian colony, declared itself independent of Corinth; and presently she joined the Athenian Confederacy for protection. Corinth sent a fleet to reduce the island; Athens, ap-

pealed to by the victorious democrats of Corcyra, sent a fleet to help them. An indecisive battle took place, in which the navies of Corcyra and Athens fought against those of Megara and Corinth. In 432 Potidaea, a city in Chalcidice tributary to Athens but Corinthian in blood, attempted to expel the Athenian power. Pericles sent an army to besiege it, but its resistance continued for two years, and weakened the military resources and prestige of Athens. When Megara gave further help to Corinth Pericles ordered all Megarian products excluded from the markets of Attica and the Empire. Megara and Corinth appealed to Sparta; Sparta proposed to Athens a repeal of this Megarian decree; Pericles agreed on condition that Sparta permit foreign states to trade with Laconia. Sparta refused; instead, she laid down as a prerequisite to peace, that Athens should acknowledge the full independence of all Greek cities—i.e., that Athens should surrender her Empire. Pericles persuaded the Athenians to reject this demand; and Sparta declared war.[10]

III. FROM THE PLAGUE TO THE PEACE

Nearly all Greece ranged itself on one or the other side. Every state in the Peloponnesus except Argos supported Sparta; so did Corinth, Megara, Boeotia, Locris, and Phocis. Athens, at the outset, had the half-hearted help of the Ionian and Euxine cities and the Aegean isles. Like the World War of our own time, the first phase of the struggle was a contest between sea power and land power. The Athenian fleet laid waste the coastal towns of the Peloponnesus, while the Spartan army invaded Attica, seized the crops, and ruined the soil. Pericles called the population of Attica within the walls of Athens, refused to let his troops go out to battle, and advised the excited Athenians to bide their time and wait for their navy to win the war.

His calculations were strategically sound, but they ignored a factor that almost decided the conflict. The crowding of Athens led (430) to a plague —probably malaria[11]—which raged for nearly three years, killing a fourth of the soldiers and a great number of the civilian population.* The people, desperate with the combined sufferings of epidemic and war, accused Pericles of responsibility for both. Cleon and others indicted him on the charge of misusing public funds; since he had apparently employed state money to bribe the Spartan kings to peace, he was unable to give a satisfactory accounting; he was convicted, deposed from office, and fined the

* Cf. Lucretius' powerful description of this plague in *De Rerum Natura*, vi, 1138-1286.

enormous sum of fifty talents ($300,000). About the same time (429) his sister and his two legitimate sons died of the plague. The Athenians, finding no leader to replace him, recalled him to power (429); and, to show their esteem for him, and their sympathy in his bereavement, they overrode a law that he himself had passed, and bestowed citizenship upon the son that Aspasia had borne to him. But the aging statesman had himself been infected by the plague; he grew weaker day by day, and died within a few months after his restoration to office. Under him Athens had reached her zenith; but because that height had been attained in part through the wealth of an unwilling Confederacy, and through a power that invited almost universal hostility, the Golden Age was unsound in its foundations, and was doomed to disaster when Athenian statesmanship failed in the strategy of peace.

Perhaps, as Thucydides suggests, Athens might have come through to victory nevertheless, if it had pursued to the end the Fabian policy laid down by Pericles. But his successors were too impatient to carry out a program that required a proud self-control. The new masters of the democratic party were merchants like Cleon the dealer in leather, Eucrates the rope seller, Hyperbolus the lampmaker; and these men demanded an active war on land as well as sea. Cleon was the ablest of them, the most eloquent, unscrupulous, and corrupt. Plutarch describes him as "the first orator among the Athenians that pulled off his cloak and smote his thigh when addressing the people";[12] Cleon made it a point, says Aristotle, to appear on the rostrum in the garb of a workingman.[13] He was the first in a long line of demagogues that ruled Athens from the death of Pericles to the loss of Athenian independence at Chaeronea (338).

Cleon's ability was proved in 425 when the Athenian fleet besieged a Spartan army on the island of Sphacteria, near Messenian Pylus. No admiral seemed capable of taking the stronghold; but when the Assembly gave Cleon charge of the siege (half hoping that he would be killed in action), he surprised all by carrying through the attack with a skill and courage that forced the Lacedaemonians to an unprecedented surrender. Sparta, humbled, offered peace and alliance in return for the captured men, but Cleon's oratory persuaded the Assembly to reject the offer and continue the war. His hold on the populace was strengthened by a proposal, easily carried, that the Athenians should henceforth pay no taxes to the support of the war, but should finance it by raising the tribute exacted of the subject cities in the Empire (424). In these cities, as in Athens, the policy of Cleon was to get as much money out of the rich as he could find.

When the upper classes of Mytilene rebelled, overthrew the democracy, and declared Lesbos free of allegiance to Athens (429), Cleon moved that all adult males in the disaffected city be put to death. The Assembly—perhaps a mere quorum—agreed, and sent a ship with orders to that effect to Paches, the Athenian general who had put down the revolt. When word of the ruthless edict got about Athens the steadier heads called for another meeting of the Assembly, secured the repeal of the decree, and dispatched a second ship which reached Paches just in time to prevent a massacre. Paches sent to Athens a thousand ringleaders, who, at Cleon's suggestion, and in accordance with the custom of the age, were all put to death.[14]

Cleon redeemed himself by dying in battle against the Spartan hero Brasidas, who was capturing one after another of the cities subject or allied to Athens in the mainland north. It was in this campaign that Thucydides lost his naval commission and his Athenian residence by coming up too tardily to the relief of Amphipolis, which commanded the gold mines of Thrace. Brasidas having died in the same campaign, Sparta, left leaderless in the face of a threatened Helot revolt, offered peace again; and Athens, for once taking the advice of the oligarchic leader, signed the Peace of Nicias (421). The rival cities not only declared the war ended, but signed an alliance for fifty years; and Athens committed herself to go to the help of Sparta should the Helots rise.[15]

IV. ALCIBIADES

Three factors turned this pledge of a half century of friendship into a brief truce of six years: the diplomatic corruption of the peace into "war by other means"; the rise of Alcibiades as the leader of a faction that favored renewed hostilities; and the attempt of Athens to conquer the Dorian colonies in Sicily. Sparta's allies refused to sign the agreement; they fell away from Sparta as now a weakened state, and transferred their alliance to Athens. Alcibiades, while keeping Athens formally at peace, maneuvered them into a war with Sparta, and united them in battle against her at Mantinea (418). Sparta won, and Greece relapsed into an angry truce.

Meanwhile Athens sent a fleet to the Dorian isle of Melos to demand its entrance as a subject state into the Athenian Empire (416). According to Thucydides, who here probably sinks the historian into the sophistical philosopher or the revengeful exile, the Athenian envoys gave no other reason for their action than that might is right. "Of the gods we believe, and of men we know, that by a necessary law of their nature they rule wherever they can. And it is not as if we were the first to make this law, or to act upon it; we found it existing before, and shall leave it to exist forever after us; all we do is to make use of it, knowing that you and everybody else, having the same power as we have, would do the same as we do."[16] The Melians refused to yield, and announced that they would put their trust in the gods. Later, as irresistible reinforcements came to the Athenian fleet, they surrendered at the discretion of the conquerors. The Athenians put to death all adult males who fell into their hands, sold the women and children as slaves, and gave the island to five hundred Athenian colonists. Athens rejoiced in the conquest, and prepared to illustrate in a living tragedy the theme of her dramatists, that a vengeful nemesis pursues all insolent success.

Alcibiades was one of those who, in the Assembly, defended the resolution condemning the male population of Melos to death.[17] His support for any motion usually sufficed to carry it, for he was now the most famous man in Athens, admired for his eloquence, his good looks, his versatile genius, even his faults and crimes. His father, the rich Cleinias, had been killed at the battle of Coronea; his mother, an Alcmaeonid and near relative of Pericles, had persuaded the statesman to bring up Alcibiades in his home. The boy was troublesome, but intelligent and brave; at twenty he fought beside Socrates at Potidaea, and at twenty-six at Delium (424). The philosopher seems to have felt a warm attachment for the youth, and called him to virtue, says Plutarch, with words that "so overcame Alcibiades as to draw tears from his eyes, and disturb his very soul. Yet sometimes he would abandon himself to flatterers, when they proposed to him varieties of pleasure, and would desert Socrates, who would then pursue him as if he had been a fugitive slave."[18]

The wit and pranks of the young man became the shocked and fascinated gossip of Athens. When Pericles reproved his immodest dogmatism by saying that he too had talked cleverly in his youth, Alcibiades answered, "Pity I couldn't have known you when your brain was at its best."[19] Purely to meet the challenge of his fellow roisterers, he publicly struck in the face one of Athens' richest and most powerful men, Hipponicus. The next morning he entered the house of the frightened magnate, bared his body, and begged Hipponicus to scourge him in punishment. The old man was so overwhelmed that he gave the youth his daughter Hipparete in marriage, with a dowry of ten talents; Alcibiades persuaded him to double it, and spent most of it on himself. He lived on a scale of luxury never known in Athens before. He filled his home with costly furniture, and engaged artists to paint pictures on the walls. He kept a stud of racing horses, and often won the chariot race at Olympia; once his entries took the first, second, and fourth prizes in one contest, whereupon he feasted the whole Assembly.[20] He fitted out triremes, and paid the expenses of choruses; and when the state called for war contributors his donations topped all the rest. Free from any inhibition of conscience, convention, or fear, he frolicked through youth and early manhood with such animal spirits that all Athens seemed to enjoy his happiness. He lisped a little, but with a charm that made all fashionable young men lisp; he wore a new cut of shoe, and soon all the gilded youth of the city were wearing "Alcibiades shoes." He violated a hundred laws and injured a hundred men, but no one dared bring him before a court. His popularity with the hetairai was so general that he wore on his golden shield an Eros with a thunderbolt, as if to announce his victories in love.[21] His wife, after bearing his infidelities with patience, returned to her father's house, and prepared to sue for divorce; but when she appeared before the archon Alcibiades caught her up in his arms and carried her home through the market place, no one venturing to oppose him. Thereafter she gave him full freedom, and contented herself with the crumbs of his love; but her early death suggests a heart broken by his inconstancy.

Entering politics after the death of Pericles, he found only one rival—the rich and pious Nicias. But Nicias favored the aristocracy, and peace; therefore Alcibiades set himself to favor the commercial classes, and preached an imperialism that touched Athenian pride; the Peace of Nicias was sufficiently discredited in his eyes by bearing his rival's name. In 420 he was elected one of the ten generals, and began those ambitious schemes that led Athens back into war. When the Assembly acclaimed him Timon the misanthrope rejoiced, predicting great calamities.[22]

V. THE SICILIAN ADVENTURE

It was the imagination of Alcibiades that ruined the work of Pericles. Athens had recovered from the plague and the war, and trade was again bringing her the wealth of the Aegean. But the law of every being is self-development; no ambition, no empire, is ever content. Alcibiades dreamed of carving out a new realm for Athens in the rich cities of Italy and Sicily; there Athens would find grain, materials, and men; there she would control the foreign food supply of the Peloponnesus; there she might double the tribute that was making her the greatest city in Greece. Only Syracuse could rival her; and that was a thought hard for Athens to bear. If she could take Syracuse all the western Mediterranean would fall into her lap, and a splendor would come to Athens such as even Pericles had not conceived.

In 427 Sicily, imitating the mainland, had divided into warring camps, one led by Dorian Syracuse, the other by Ionian Leontini. Leontini sent Gorgias to Athens to seek help, but Athens was then too weak to respond. Now, in 416, Segesta dispatched envoys to Athens to say that Syracuse was planning to subjugate all Sicily, make the island Dorian in government, and supply food and money to Sparta should the great war be renewed. Alcibiades leaped to his opportunity. He argued that the Sicilian Greeks were hopelessly divided, even within each city; that it would be a simple matter—given a little courage—to annex the whole island to the Empire; that the Empire must continue to grow, or begin to decay; and that a little war now and then was a necessary training for an imperial race.[23] Nicias pled with the Assembly not to listen to any man whose personal extravagance tempted him to wild schemes of aggrandizement; but the eloquence of Alcibiades and the imagination of a people now dangerously free from moral scruples won the day. The Assembly declared war against Syracuse, voted funds for a vast armada, and, as if to ensure defeat, divided the command between Alcibiades and Nicias.

Preparations went on with the characteristic fever of war, and the occasion of the fleet's departure was awaited as a patriotic festival. But shortly before this appointed day a strange occurrence shocked a city that had lost much of its piety but none of its superstitions. Some unknown persons, under cover of night, had knocked off the noses, ears, and phalli from the figures of the god Hermes that stood before public buildings and many private dwellings as an emblem of fertility and a guardian of the home. An excited investigator brought forward the unreliable evidence of aliens and slaves that the prank had been perpetrated by a drunken party of Alcibiades' friends, led by Alcibiades himself. The young general protested his innocence, and demanded to be tried at once, that he might be convicted or cleared before the departure of the fleet; but his enemies, foreseeing his acquittal, succeeded in postponing the trial. And so in 415 the great flotilla set sail, led by a timid pacifist who hated war, and by an audacious militarist whose genius of leadership was frustrated by the divided command, and the dread, among the crews, that he had incurred the enmity of the gods.

The fleet had been gone some days when new evidence, as unreliable as before, was brought out to the effect that Alcibiades and his friends had participated in an impious mimicry of the Eleusinian Mysteries. Urged on by an enraged populace, the Assembly sent the swift galley *Salaminia* to overtake Alcibiades and bring him back for trial. Alcibiades accepted the summons and went aboard the *Salaminia;* but when the vessel stopped at Thurii he secretly made his way to shore, and escaped. The Athenian Assembly, baffled, pronounced judgment of exile upon him, with confiscation of all his property, and a decree of death in case the Athenians should ever capture him. Bitter at the thought that his plans for empire and glory had been frustrated by a condemnation which he continued to call unjust, Alcibiades took refuge in the Peloponnesus, and, appearing before the Spartan Assembly, proposed to help Sparta defeat Athens and establish there an aristocratic government. "As for democracy," Thucydides makes him say, "the men of sense among us knew what it was, and I perhaps as well as any, as I have the more cause to complain of it; but there is nothing new to be said of a patent absurdity."[24] He advised them to send a fleet to help Syracuse and an army to capture Deceleia—an Attic town whose possession should give Sparta military command of everything in Attica but Athens. The silver mines at Laurium would cease to finance Athenian resistance, and the subject cities, foreseeing the defeat of Athens, would stop their payment of tribute. Sparta took his advice.

The intensity of his own resolution appeared in the completeness with which he, so accustomed to luxury, took up the Spartan way of life. He became frugal and reserved, eating coarse food, wearing a rough tunic and no shoes, bathing in the Eurotas winter and summer, and observing all Lacedaemonian laws and customs faithfully. Even so his good looks and personal fascination ruined his plans. The Queen fell in love with him, bore him a son, and proudly whispered to her friends that he was the father. He excused himself to his intimates on the ground that he could not resist the chance to establish his race as kings over Laconia. King Agis, who had been away with the army, started home, and Alcibiades conveniently secured a commission in a Spartan squadron that was sailing to Asia. The King disowned the child and sent out secret orders for the assassination of Alcibiades; but the latter's friends warned him, and he escaped and joined the Persian admiral Tissaphernes at Sardis.

At the other end of the war front Nicias was encountering a resistance which only Alcibiades' genius for strategy and intrigue could have overcome. Nearly all of Sicily came to the aid of Syracuse. In 414 a Spartan fleet under Gylippus helped the Sicilian navy to bottle up the Athenian ships in the harbor of Syracuse, cutting them off from any supply of food. A final chance to escape was lost because of an eclipse of the moon, which frightened Nicias and many of his soldiers into awaiting an opportunity more satisfactory to the gods. On the next day, however, they found themselves surrounded, and were forced to give battle. They were defeated, first on sea and then on land. Nicias, though ill and weak, fought bravely, and at last surrendered to the mercy of the Syracusans. He was at once put to death; and the surviving Athenians, almost all of the citizen class, were sent to die at hard labor in the quarries of Sicily, where they tasted the fate of the men who for generations had worked the mines of Laurium.

VI. THE TRIUMPH OF SPARTA

The disaster broke the spirit of Athens. Nearly half the citizen body was now enslaved or dead; half the women of the citizen class were in effect widows, and the children were orphans. The funds that Pericles had accumulated in the treasury were almost exhausted; in another year the last penny would be gone. Thinking the fall of Athens imminent, the subject cities refused further tribute; most of her allies abandoned her, and many flocked to the side of Sparta. In 413 Sparta, claiming that the "fifty years" peace had been repeatedly violated by Athens, renewed the war. The Lacedaemonians now took and fortified Deceleia; the supply of food from Euboea and of silver from Laurium stopped; the slaves in the mines at Laurium revolted, and went over to the Spartans in a body of twenty thousand men. Syracuse sent an army to join in the attack; and the Persian King, seeing an opportunity to avenge Marathon and Salamis, provided funds for the growing Spartan fleet, on the shameful understanding that Sparta would assist Persia in regaining mastery over the Greek cities of Ionia.[25]

It was a proof of Athenian courage, ana of the vitality of Athenian democracy, that Athens stood off her enemies for ten years more. The government was put upon an economical footing, taxes and capital levies were collected to build a new fleet, and within a year of the defeat at Syracuse Athens was ready to contest Sparta's new mastery of the sea.

Just as recovery seemed assured, the oligarchic faction, which had never favored the war, and, indeed, looked to a Spartan victory to revive aristocracy in Athens, organized a revolt, seized the organs of government, and set up a supreme Council of Four Hundred (411). The Assembly, cowed by the assassination of many democratic leaders, voted its own abdication. The rich supported the rebellion as the only way of controlling the class war that had crossed the lines of the war between Athens and Sparta—much as the struggle of the middle classes against aristocracy united the liberal factions in England and America in the American Revolution. Once in power, the oligarchs sent envoys to make peace with Sparta, and secretly prepared to admit the Spartan army into Athens. Meanwhile Theramenes, leader of a center party of moderate aristocrats, led a counterrevolution, and replaced the Four Hundred—which had ruled some four months—with a Council of Five Thousand (411). For a brief while Athens enjoyed that combination of democracy and aristocracy which seemed to Thucydides and Aristotle[26] (aristocrats both) to have been the best and fairest government that Athens had known since Solon. But the second revolt, like the first, had forgotten that Athens depended for its food and life upon its navy, whose personnel, barring a few leaders, had been disfranchised by both revolutions. Incensed at the news, the sailors announced that unless the democracy were restored they would besiege Athens. The oligarchs waited hopefully for a Spartan army; the Spartans as usual were tardy; the new government took to its heels, and the victorious democrats restored the old constitution (411).

Alcibiades had secretly supported the oligarchic revolt, hoping that it might smooth a way for his return to Athens. Now the re-empowered democracy, perhaps ignorant of these intrigues, but knowing how badly Athens had fared since his exile, called him home with a promise of amnesty. Deferring his triumph at Athens, he took charge of the fleet at Samos, and moved into action with a celerity and success that brought Athens a brief moment of happiness. Speeding through the Hellespont, he met and completely destroyed a Spartan fleet at Cyzicus (410). After a year's siege he captured Chalcedon and Byzantium, and thereby restored Athens' control of the food supply from the Bosporus. Sailing back south he encountered another Spartan squadron near the isle of Andros, and defeated it with ease. Returning now (407) to Athens, he was welcomed with universal acclaim: his sins were forgotten, only his genius was remembered, and Athens' desperate need of an able general.[27] But Athens, while celebrating his victories, neglected to send him money for the pay of his crews.

Once again Alcibiades' lack of moral scruple ruined him. Leaving the greater number of his vessels at Notium (near Ephesus) in command of one Antiochus, with strict instructions to stay in port and under no circumstances to give battle, he himself went with a small force to Caria to raise funds for his men by something less than due process of law. Antiochus, itching for fame, left his haven and challenged a Spartan flotilla under Lysander. Lysander accepted the taunt, killed Antiochus in a hand-to-hand fight, and sank or captured most of the Athenian ships (407). When news of this catastrophe came to Athens the Assembly acted with characteristic haste; it censured Alcibiades for leaving his fleet, and removed him from command. Alcibiades, fearing now both Athens and Sparta, fled to a refuge in Bithynia.

Desperate, the Athenians ordered that the gold and silver in the statues and offerings on the Acropolis should be melted down for the building of a new flotilla of 150 triremes, and offered freedom to those slaves, and citizenship to those aliens, who would fight for the city. The new armada defeated a Spartan fleet off the Arginusae Islands (south of Lesbos) in 406, and Athens again thrilled with the news of victory. But the Assembly was furious when it learned that its generals* had allowed the crews of twenty-five ships, sunk by the enemy, to drown in a storm. Hotheads protested that these souls, for lack of proper burial, would wander restlessly about the universe; and accusing the survivors of negligence in not attempting a rescue, they proposed that the eight victorious generals (including the son of Pericles by Aspasia) should be put to death. Socrates, who happened to be a member of the presiding prytany for the day, refused to put the motion to a vote. It was presented and passed over his protests, and the sentence was carried out with the same precipitation with which it had been decreed. A few days later the Assembly repented, and condemned to death those who had persuaded it to execute the generals. Meanwhile the Spartans, weakened by the defeat, offered peace again; but the Assembly, moved by the oratory of the drunken Cleophon, refused.[28]

Led now by second-rate men, the Athenian fleet sailed north to meet the Spartans under Lysander in the Sea of Marmora. From his hiding place in the hills Alcibiades saw that the Athenian ships had taken up a strategically perilous position at Aegospotami, near Lampsacus. He risked his life to ride down to the shore and advise the Athenian admirals to seek a more sheltered place; but they distrusted his counsel, and reminded him that he was no longer in command. On the next day the decisive battle was fought;

* The term *strategos* was applied to naval as well as military commanders.

all but eight of the 208 Athenian ships were scuttled or taken, and Lysander ordered the execution of three thousand Athenian captives.[29] Learning that Lysander had issued orders for his assassination, Alcibiades sought refuge in Phrygia with the Persian general Pharnabazus, who assigned him a castle and a courtesan. But the Persian King, persuaded by Lysander, ordered Pharnabazus to kill his guest. Two assassins besieged Alcibiades in his castle, and set fire to it; he came out naked and desperate, seeking the privilege of fighting for his life; but before his sword could touch his assailants he was pierced by their arrows and javelins. He died at the age of forty-six, the greatest genius and most tragic failure in the military history of Greece.

Lysander, now absolute master of the Aegean, sailed down from city to city, overthrowing the democracies and setting up oligarchic governments subject to Sparta. Entering the Piraeus unresisted, he proceeded to blockade Athens. The Athenians resisted with their accustomed bravery, but within three months their stock of food was exhausted, and the streets were full of dead or dying men. Lysander gave Athens bitter and yet lenient terms: he would not, he said, destroy a city that had in time past performed such honorable services for Greece, nor would he enslave its population; but he demanded the leveling of the Long Walls, the recall of the oligarchic exiles, the surrender of all but eight of the surviving Athenian ships, and a pledge to support Sparta actively in any further war. Athens protested, and yielded.

Supported by Lysander, and led by Critias and Theramenes, the returning oligarchs seized the government, and established a Council of Thirty to rule Athens (404). These Greek Bourbons had learned nothing; they confiscated the property and alienated the support of many rich merchants; they plundered the temples, sold for three talents the wharves of the Piraeus which had cost a thousand,[30] exiled five thousand democrats, and put fifteen hundred others to death; they assassinated all Athenians who were distasteful to them politically or personally; they put an end to freedom of teaching, assemblage, and speech, and Critias himself, once his pupil, forbade Socrates to continue his public discourses. Seeking to compromise the philosopher to their cause, the Thirty ordered him and four others to arrest the democrat Leon. The others obeyed, but Socrates refused.

All the sins of the democracy were forgotten as the crimes of the oligarchs increased and multiplied. The number of men, even of substantial means, who began to seek an end to this bloody tyranny grew from day to day. When a thousand armed democrats under Thrasybulus approached the Piraeus, the Thirty found that hardly any but their immediate partisans could be persuaded to fight for them. Critias organized a small army, went out to battle, and was defeated and killed. Thrasybulus entered Athens, and restored the democracy (403). Under his guidance the Assembly behaved with unwonted moderation: it decreed death for only the highest surviving leaders of the revolution, and allowed them to escape this sentence by exile; it declared a general amnesty to all others who had supported the oligarchs; it even repaid to Sparta the hundred talents that the ephors had lent to the Thirty.[31] These acts of humanity and statesmanship gave to Athens at last the peace that she had not known for a generation.

VII. THE DEATH OF SOCRATES

Strange to say, the only cruelty of the restored democracy was committed upon an old philosopher whose seventy years should have put him beyond the possibility of being a danger to the state. But among the leaders of the victorious faction was the same Anytus who years before had threatened to revenge himself upon Socrates for dialectical slights and the "corruption" of his son. Anytus was a good man: he had fought bravely under Thrasybulus, had saved the lives of oligarchs who had been taken captive by his soldiers, had been instrumental in arranging the amnesty, and had left in undisturbed enjoyment of his property those to whom it had been sold after confiscation by the Thirty. But his generosity failed when it came to Socrates. He could not forget that when he had gone into exile his son had stayed in Athens with Socrates, and had become a drunkard.[32] It did not appease Anytus to observe that Socrates had refused to obey the Thirty, and (if we may take Xenophon's word for it) had denounced Critias as a bad ruler.[33] To Anytus it seemed that Socrates, more than any Sophist, was an evil influence both on morals and on politics; he was undermining the religious faith that had supported morality, and his persistent criticism was weakening the belief of educated Athenians in the institutions of democracy. The murderous tyrant Critias had been one of Socrates' pupils; the immoral and treasonable Alcibiades had been his lover; Charmides, his early favorite, had been a general under Critias, and had just died in battle against the democracy.* It seemed fitting to Anytus that Socrates should leave Athens, or die.

The indictment was brought forward by Anytus, Meletus, and Lycon

* Critias and Alcibiades had left the tutelage of Socrates early in his career as a teacher, not liking the restraints which he preached to them.[34]

in 399, and read as follows: "Socrates is a public offender in that he does not recognize the gods that the state recognizes, but introduces new demoniacal beings" (the Socratic *daimonion*); "he has also offended by corrupting the youth."*[35] The trial was held before a popular court, or *dikasterion*, of some five hundred citizens, mostly of the less educated class. We have no means of knowing how accurately Plato and Xenophon have reported Socrates' defense; we do know that Plato was present at the trial,[37] and that his account of Socrates' "apology" agrees in many points with Xenophon's. Socrates, says Plato, insisted that he believed in the state gods, even in the divinity of the sun and moon. "You say first that I do not believe in gods, and then again that I believe in demigods. . . . You might as well affirm the existence of mules, and deny that of horses and asses."[38] And then he referred sadly to the effects of Aristophanes' satire:

> I have had many accusers, who accused me of old, and their false charges have continued during many years; and I am more afraid of them than of Anytus and his associates. . . . For they began when you were children, and took possession of your minds with their falsehoods, telling of one Socrates, a wise man, who speculated about the heavens above, and searched into the earth beneath, and made the worse appear the better cause. These are the accusers I dread; for they are the circulators of this rumor, and their hearers are too apt to fancy that speculators of this sort do not believe in the gods. And they are many, and their charges against me are of ancient date, and they made them in days when you were impressionable—in childhood, or perhaps in youth—and the cause when heard went by default, for there was none to answer. And hardest of all, their names I do not know and cannot tell, unless in the chance case of a comic poet. . . . That is the nature of the accusation, and that is what you have seen yourselves in the comedy of Aristophanes.[39]

He lays claim to a divine mission to teach the good and simple life, and no threat will deter him.

> Strange, indeed, would be my conduct, O men of Athens, if I who, when I was ordered by the generals whom you chose to command me at Potidaea and Amphipolis and Delium, remained where

* Croiset believed that the real cause of the indictment was the hostility of the Attic peasantry to anyone who cast doubt upon the state gods. One of the chief markets for cattle was provided by the pious who bought the animals to offer in sacrifice; any decrease in faith would lessen this market. Aristophanes, in this interpretation, was the mouthpiece of these peasants, before whom his plays, if successful, would be repeated.[36]

> they placed me, like any other man, facing death—if, I say, now when, as I conceive and imagine, God orders me to fulfil the philosopher's mission of searching into myself and other men, I were to desert my post through fear of death. . . . If you say to me, Socrates, this time we will let you off, but upon one condition, that you are not to inquire and speculate in this way any more . . . I should reply: Men of Athens, I honor and love you; but I shall obey God rather than you, and while I have life and strength I shall never cease from the practice and teaching of philosophy, exhorting anyone whom I meet, after my manner, and convincing him, saying: O my friend, why do you, who are a citizen of the great and mighty and wise city of Athens, care so much about laying up the greatest amount of money and honor and reputation, and so little about wisdom and truth? Wherefore, O men of Athens, I say to you, do as Anytus bids, and either acquit me or not; but whatever you do, know that I shall never alter my ways, not even if I have to die many times.[40]

The judges appear to have interrupted him at this point, and to have bidden him desist from what seemed to them insolence; but he continued in even haughtier vein.

> I would have you know that if you kill such a one as I am, you will injure yourselves more than you will injure me. . . . For if you kill me you will not easily find another like me, who, if I may use such a ludicrous figure of speech, am a sort of gadfly, given to the state by the God; and the state is like a great and noble steed who is tardy in his motions owing to his very size, and requires to be stirred into life. . . . And as you will not easily find another like me, I would advise you to spare me.[41]

The sentence of guilty was pronounced upon him by the small majority of sixty; had his defense been more conciliatory it is likely that he would have been acquitted. He had the privilege of proposing an alternative penalty in place of death. At first he refused to make even this concession; but on the appeal of Plato and other friends, who underwrote his pledge, he offered to pay a fine of thirty minas ($3000). The second polling of the jury condemned him by eighty more votes than the first.[42]

It still remained open to him to escape from the prison; Crito and other friends (if we may follow Plato) prepared the way with bribery,[43] and probably Anytus had hoped for such a compromise. But Socrates remained himself to the last. He felt that he had but a few more years to live, and that "he relinquished only the most burdensome part of life, in which all feel their powers of intellect diminished."[46] Instead of accepting Crito's proposal he examined it from an ethical point of view, discussed it dialectically, and played the game of logic to the end.[47] His disciples visited him daily in his cell during the month between his trial and his execution, and he seems to have discoursed with them calmly until the final hour. Plato pictures him as fondling the hair and head of the young Phaedo, and saying, "Tomorrow, Phaedo, I suppose that these fair locks will be cut"—in mourning.[48] Xanthippe came in tears, with their youngest child in her arms; he comforted her, and asked Crito to have her escorted home. "You die undeservedly," said an ardent disciple; "Would you, then," Socrates answered, "have me deserve death?"[49]

After he was gone, says Diodorus,[50] the Athenians regretted their treatment of him, and put his accusers to death. Suidas makes Meletus die by public stoning.[51] Plutarch varies the tale: the accusers became so unpopular that no citizen would light their fires, or answer their questions, or bathe in the same water with them; so that they were at last driven in despair to hang themselves.[52] Diogenes Laertius reports that Meletus was executed, Anytus exiled, and a bronze statue put up by Athens in memory of the philosopher.[53] We do not know if these stories are true.*

The Golden Age ended with the death of Socrates. Athens was exhausted in body and soul; only the degradation of character by prolonged war and desperate suffering could explain the ruthless treatment of Melos, the bitter sentence upon Mytilene, the execution of the Arginusae generals, and the sacrifice of Socrates on the altar of a dying faith. All the foundations of Athenian life were disordered: the soil of Attica had been devastated by the Spartan raids, and the slow-growing olive trees had been burned to the ground; the Athenian navy had been destroyed, and control of trade and the food supply had been lost; the state treasury was empty, and private fortunes had been taxed almost to extinction; two thirds of the citizen body had been killed. The damage done to Greece by the Persian invasions could not compare with the destruction of Greek life and property by the Peloponnesian War. After Salamis and Plataea Greece was left poor, but exalted with courage and pride; now Greece was poor again, and Athens had suffered a wound to her spirit which seemed too deep to be healed.

---

* Grote[54] doubts them, and they are rendered dubious by the efforts of Plato and Xenophon to defend Socrates' reputation. But these accounts were generally accepted in antiquity (e.g., by Tertullian and Augustine[55]), and accord admirably with the habits of the Athenians.

Two things sustained her: the restoration of democracy under men of judgment and moderation, and the consciousness that during the last sixty years, even during the War, she had produced such art and literature as surpassed the like product of any other age in the memory of man. Anaxagoras had been exiled and Socrates had been put to death; but the stimulus that they had given to philosophy sufficed to make Athens henceforth, and despite herself, the center and summit of Greek thought. What before had been formless tentatives of speculation were now to mature into great systems that would agitate Europe for centuries to come; while the haphazard provision of higher education by wandering Sophists was to be replaced by the first universities in history—universities that would make Athens, as Thucydides had prematurely called her, "the school of Hellas." Through the bloodshed and turmoil of conflict the traditions of art had not quite decayed; for many centuries yet the sculptors and architects of Greece were to carve and build for all the Mediterranean world. Out of the despair of her defeat Athens lifted herself with startling virility to new wealth, culture, and power; and the autumn of her life was bountiful.

BOOK IV

THE DECLINE AND FALL OF GREEK FREEDOM

399-322 B.C.

CHRONOLOGICAL TABLE FOR BOOK IV

B.C.

399-60: Agesilaus king at Sparta
397: War between Syracuse and Carthage
396: Aristippus of Cyrene and Antisthenes of Athens, philosophers
395: Athens rebuilds the Long Walls
394: Battles of Coronea and Cnidus
?393: Plato's *Apology;* Xenophon's *Memorabilia;* Aristophanes' *Ecclesiazusae*
391-87: Dionysius subjugates south Italy
391: Isocrates opens his school
390: Evagoras Hellenizes Cyprus
387: Peace of Antalcidas, or King's Peace; Plato visits Archytas of Taras, mathematician, and Dionysius I
386: Plato founds the Academy
383: Spartans occupy Cadmeia at Thebes
380: Isocrates' *Panegyricus*
379: Pelopidas and Melon liberate Thebes
378-54: Second Athenian Empire
375: Theaetetus, mathematician
372: Diogenes of Sinope, philosopher
371: Epaminondas victorious at Leuctra
370: Diocles of Euboea, embryologist; Eudoxus of Cnidus, astronomer
367-57: Dionysius II dictator at Syracuse; Dion plans reforms
367: Plato visits Dionysius II
362: Epaminondas wins and dies at Mantinea
361: Plato's third visit to Syracuse
360: Praxiteles of Athens and Scopas of Paros, sculptors; Ephorus of Cyme and Theopompus of Chios, historians
359: Philip II regent in Macedonia
357-46: War between Athens and Macedonia
357-46: Exile of Dionysius II
356-46: Second Sacred War
356: Birth of Alexander the Great; burning of second temple at Ephesus; Isocrates' *On the Peace*
355: Isocrates' *Areopagiticus*

B.C.

354: Assassination of Dion
353-49: The Mausoleum at Halicarnassus
351: Demosthenes' *Philippic I*
349: Philip attacks Olynthus; Demosthenes' *Olynthiacs I and II*
348: Heracleides of Pontus, astronomer; Speusippus succeeds Plato as head of the Academy
346: Demosthenes' *On the Peace;* Isocrates' *Letter to Philip*
344: Timoleon rescues Syracuse; Demosthenes' *Philippic II*
343: Trial and acquittal of Aeschines
342-38: Aristotle tutor of Alexander
340: Timoleon defeats the Carthaginians
338: Philip defeats Athenians at Chaeronea; death of Isocrates
336: Assassination of Philip; accession of Alexander and Darius III
335: Alexander burns down Thebes, and begins his Persian campaigns
334: Aristotle opens the Lyceum; battle of the Granicus; choragic monument of Lysicrates
333: Battle of Issus
332: Siege and capture of Tyre; surrender of Jerusalem; foundation of Alexandria
331: Battle of Gaugamela (Arbela); Alexander at Babylon and Susa
330: Apelles of Sicyon, painter; Lysippus of Argos, sculptor; Aeschines' *Against Ctesiphon;* Demosthenes' *On the Crown*
329-8: Alexander invades central Asia
327: Deaths of Cleitus and Callisthenes
327-5: Alexander in India
325: Voyage of Nearchus
324: Exile of Demosthenes
323: Death of Alexander; Lamian War
322: Deaths of Aristotle, Demosthenes, and Diogenes

CHAPTER XIX

Philip

I. THE SPARTAN EMPIRE

SPARTA now assumed for a spell the naval mastery of Greece, and offered to history another tragedy of success brought low by pride. Instead of the freedom which she had promised to the cities once subject to Athens, she levied upon them an annual tribute of a thousand talents ($6,000,000), and established in each of them an aristocratic rule controlled by a Lacedaemonian harmost, or governor, and supported by a Spartan garrison. These governments, responsible only to the distant ephors, practiced such corruption and tyranny that soon the new empire was hated more intensely than the old.

In Sparta itself the influx of money and gifts from oppressed cities and obsequious oligarchs strengthened the internal forces that had long been leading to decay. By the fourth century the ruling caste had learned how to add private luxury to public simplicity, and even the ephors had ceased, except in outward show, to observe the Lycurgean discipline. Much of the land, by dowries and bequests, had fallen into the hands of women; and the wealth so accumulated gave to the Spartan ladies—free from the care of male children—an ease of life and morals hardly befitting their name.[1] The repeated division of some estates had impoverished many families to a point where they could no longer contribute their quota to the public mess, and therefore lost the rights of citizenship; while the formation of large properties through intermarriage and legacies had created in the few remaining "Equals" a provocative concentration of wealth.* "Some Spartans," Aristotle writes, "own domains of vast extent, the others have nearly nothing; all the land is in the hands of a few."[3] The disfranchised gentry, the excluded Perioeci, and the resentful Helots made a population too restless and hostile to permit the government to engage, on any large scale of space or time, in those external military operations which imperial rule required.

Meanwhile civil war among the Persians was affecting the fortunes of

* The *homoioi*, or Equals, numbered eight thousand in 480, two thousand in 371, seven hundred in 341.[2]

Greece. In 401 the younger Cyrus rebelled against his brother Artaxerxes II, enlisted Sparta's aid, and recruited an army from the thousands of Greek and other mercenaries left idle in Asia by the sudden termination of the Peloponnesian War. The two brothers met at Cunaxa, between the converging Tigris and Euphrates; Cyrus was defeated and slain, and all of his army was captured or destroyed except a contingent of twelve thousand Greeks whose quickness of mind and foot enabled them to escape into the interior of Babylonia. Hunted by the King's forces, the Greeks chose, in their rough democratic way, three generals to lead them to safety. Among these was Xenophon, once a pupil of Socrates, now a young soldier of fortune, destined to be remembered above all by the *Anabasis*, or *Ascent*, in which he later described with engaging simplicity the long "Retreat of the Ten Thousand" up along the Tigris and over the hills of Kurdistan and Armenia to the Black Sea. It was one of the great adventures in human history. We are amazed at the inexhaustible courage of these Greeks, fighting their way on foot, day by day for five months, through two thousand miles of enemy country, across hot and foodless plains, and over perilous mountain passes covered with eight feet of snow, while armies and guerrilla bands attacked them in the rear and in front and on either flank, and hostile natives used every device to kill them, or mislead them, or bar their way. As we read this fascinating story, made so dull for us in youth by the compulsion to translate it, we perceive that the most important weapon for an army is food, and that the skill of a commander lies as much in finding supplies as in organizing victory. More of these Greeks died from exposure and starvation than from battle, though the battles were as numerous as the days. When at last the 8600 survivors sighted the Euxine at Trapezus (Trebizond), their hearts overflowed.

> As soon as the vanguard got to the top of the mountains, a great cry went up. And when Xenophon and the rear guard heard it they imagined that other enemies were attacking in front—for enemies were following behind them. . . . They pushed ahead to lend aid, and in a moment they heard the soldiers shouting, "The sea! the sea!" and passing the word along. Then all the troops of the rear guard likewise broke into a run, and the pack animals began racing ahead. . . . And when all had reached the summit, then indeed they fell to embracing one another, and generals and captains as well, with tears in their eyes.[4]

For this was a Greek sea, and Trapezus a Greek city; they were safe now, and could rest without fear of death surprising them in the night. The news of their exploit resounded proudly through old Hellas, and encouraged Philip, two generations later, to believe that a well-trained Greek force could be relied upon to defeat a Persian army many times its size. Unwittingly Xenophon opened the way for Alexander.

Perhaps this influence was already felt by Agesilaus, who in 399 had succeeded to the throne of Sparta. Persia might have been persuaded to overlook Sparta's aid to Cyrus. But to the ablest of the Spartan kings a war with Persia seemed only an interesting adventure, and he set out with a small force to free all Greek Asia from Persian rule.* When Artaxerxes II learned that Agesilaus was easily defeating all Persian troops sent against him, he dispatched messengers with abundant gold to Athens and Thebes to bribe these cities into declaring war upon Sparta.[6] The effort readily succeeded, and after nine years of peace the conflict between Athens and Sparta was renewed. Agesilaus was recalled from Asia to meet, and barely defeat, the combined forces of Athens and Thebes at Coronea; but in the same month the united fleets of Athens and Persia under Conon destroyed the Spartan navy near Cnidus, and put an end to Sparta's brief domination of the seas. Athens rejoiced, and set to work energetically, with funds supplied by Persia, to rebuild her Long Walls. Sparta defended herself by sending an envoy, Antalcidas, to the Great King, offering to surrender the Greek cities of Asia to Persian rule if Persia would enforce among the mainland Greeks a peace that would protect Sparta. The Great King agreed, withdrew his financial support from Athens and Thebes, and compelled all parties to sign at Sardis (387) the "Peace of Antalcidas," or the "King's Peace." Lemnos, Imbros, and Scyros were conceded to Athens, and the major Greek states were guaranteed autonomy; but all the Greek cities of Asia, along with Cyprus, were declared the property of the King. Athens signed under protest, knowing that this was the most disgraceful event in Greek history. For a generation all the fruits of Marathon were lost; the Greek states of the mainland remained free in name, but in effect the power of Persia had engulfed them. All Greece looked upon Sparta as a traitor, and waited eagerly for some nation to destroy her.

II. EPAMINONDAS

As if to strengthen this feeling, Sparta assumed the authority to interpret and enforce the King's Peace among the Greek states. To weaken Thebes

* "In what respect," he asked, "is the 'Great King' greater than I, unless he is more upright and self-restrained?"[5]

she insisted that the Boeotian Confederacy violated the autonomy clause of the treaty, and must be dissolved. With this excuse the Spartan army set up in many Boeotian cities oligarchic governments favorable to Sparta and in several cases upheld by Spartan garrisons. When Thebes protested, a Lacedaemonian force captured her citadel, the Cadmeia, and established an oligarchy subject to Spartan domination. The crisis aroused Thebes to unwonted heroism. Pelopidas and six companions assassinated the four "Laconizing" dictators of Thebes, and reasserted Theban liberty. The Confederacy was reorganized, and named Pelopidas its leader, or boeotarch. Pelopidas called to his aid his friend and lover Epaminondas, who trained and led the army that reduced Sparta to her ancient isolation.

Epaminondas came of a distinguished but impoverished family which proudly traced its origin to the dragon's teeth sown by Cadmus a thousand years before. He was a quiet man, of whom it was said that no one talked less or knew more.[7] His modesty and integrity, his almost ascetic life, his devotion to his friends, his prudence in counsel, his courage and yet self-restraint in action, endeared him to all the Thebans despite the military discipline to which he subjected them. He did not love war, but he was convinced that no nation could lose all martial spirit and habits and yet maintain its freedom. Elected and many times re-elected boeotarch, he warned those who proposed to vote for him: "Bethink yourselves once more; for if I am made general you will be compelled to serve in my army."[8] Under his command the lax Thebans were drilled into good soldiers; even the "Greek lovers" who were so numerous in the city were formed by Pelopidas into a "Sacred Band" of three hundred hoplites, each of whom was pledged to stand by his friend, in battle, to the death.

When a Spartan army of ten thousand troops under King Cleombrotus invaded Boeotia, Epaminondas met it at Leuctra, near Plataea, with six thousand men, and won a victory that influenced the political history of Greece and the military methods of Europe. He was the first Hellene to make a careful study of tactics; he counted on facing odds in every battle, and concentrated his best fighters upon one wing for offense, while the remainder were ordered to follow a policy of defense; in this way the enemy, advancing in the center, could be disordered by a flank attack on its left. After Leuctra Epaminondas and Pelopidas marched into the Peloponnesus, freed Messenia from its century-long vassalage to Sparta, and founded the city of Megalopolis as a stronghold for all Arcadians. Even into Laconia the Theban army descended—an event without precedent for hundreds of years past. Sparta never recovered from her losses in this campaign: "She could not stand up against a single defeat," says Aristotle, "but was ruined through the small number of her citizens."[9]

Winter coming, the Thebans withdrew to Boeotia. Epaminondas, overreaching himself in typical Greek style, began to dream now of establishing a Theban Empire to replace the unity that Athenian or Spartan leadership had once given to Greece. His plans involved him in a war with the Athenians; and Sparta, thinking to rehabilitate herself, made an alliance with Athens. The hostile armies met at Mantinea in 362. Epaminondas won, but was killed in action by Gryllus, son of Xenophon. The brief hegemony of Thebes left no permanent boon to Hellas; it liberated Greece from the despotism of Sparta, but failed, like its predecessors, to create beyond Boeotia a coherent unity; and the conflicts that it engendered left the Greek states disordered and weakened when Philip came down upon them from the north.

III. THE SECOND ATHENIAN EMPIRE

Athens made a final attempt to forge such a unity. Through her rebuilt walls and fleet, the dependability of her coinage, her long-established facilities for finance and trade, she slowly won back commercial supremacy in the Aegean. Her former subjects and allies had learned from the wars of the last half century the need for a larger security than individual sovereignty could bring; and in 378 the majority of them combined again under Athens' leadership. By 370 Athens was once more the greatest power in the eastern Mediterranean.

Industry and trade were now the substance of her economic life. The soil of Attica had never been propitious to common tillage; patient labor had made it fruitful through tending the olive tree and the vine; but the Spartans had destroyed these, and few of the peasants were willing to wait half a generation for new olive orchards to yield. Most of the farmers of prewar days were dead; many of the survivors were too discouraged to go back to their ruined holdings, and sold them at low prices to absentee owners who could afford long-term investments. In this way, and through the eviction of peasant debtors, the ownership of Attica passed into a few families, who worked many of the large estates with slaves.[10] The mines at Laurium were reopened, fresh victims were sent into the pits, and new riches were transmuted out of silver ore and human blood. Xenophon[11] proposed a genial plan whereby Athens might replenish her treasury through the purchase of ten thousand slaves and their lease to the contractors at Laurium. Silver was mined in such abundance that the supply of the metal outran the production of goods, prices rose faster than wages, and the poor bore the burden of the change.

Industry flourished. The quarries at Pentelicus and the potteries in the Ceramicus had orders from all the Aegean world. Fortunes were made by buying cheap the products of domestic handicraft or small factories, and selling them dear in the home market or abroad. The growth of commerce and the accumulation of wealth in money instead of in land rapidly multiplied the number of bankers in Athens. They received cash or valuables for safekeeping, but apparently paid no interest on deposits. Soon discovering that under normal conditions not all deposits were reclaimed at once, the bankers began to lend funds at substantial rates of interest, providing, at first, money instead of credit. They acted as bail for clients, and made collections for them; they lent money on the security of land or precious articles, and helped to finance the shipment of goods. Through their aid, and even more through speculative loans by private individuals, the merchant might hire a ship, transport his goods to a foreign market, and buy there a return cargo—which, on reaching the Piraeus, remained the property of the lenders until the loan was repaid.[12] As the fourth century progressed, a real credit system developed: the bankers, instead of advancing cash, issued letters of credit, money orders, or checks; wealth could now pass from one client to another merely by entries in the banker's books.[13] Businessmen or bankers issued bonds for mercantile loans, and every large inheritance included a number of such bonds. Some bankers, like the ex-slave Pasion, developed so many connections, and acquired by a discriminating honesty so widespread a reputation for reliability, that their bond was honored throughout the Greek world. Pasion's bank had many departments and employees, mostly slaves; it kept a complex set of books, in which every transaction was so carefully recorded that these accounts were usually accepted in court as indisputable evidence. Bank failures were not uncommon, and we hear of "panics" in which bank after bank closed its doors.[14] Serious charges of malfeasance were brought against even the most prominent banks, and the people looked upon the bankers with that same mixture of envy, admiration, and dislike with which the poor favor the rich in all ages.[15]

The change from landed to movable wealth produced a feverish struggle for money, and the Greek language had to invent a word, *pleonexia*, to denote this appetite for "more and more," and another word, *chrematistike*, for the busy pursuit of riches. Goods, services, and persons were increasingly judged in terms of money and property. Fortunes were made and unmade with a new rapidity, and were spent in lavish displays that would have shocked the Athens of Pericles. The *nouveaux riches* (the Greeks had a name for them—*neoplutoi*) built gaudy houses, bedecked their women with costly robes and jewels, spoiled them with a dozen servants, and made it a principle to feed their guests with none but expensive drinks and foods.[16]

In the midst of this wealth poverty increased, for the same variety and freedom of exchange that enabled the clever to make money allowed the simple to lose it faster than before. Under the new mercantile economy the poor were *relatively* poorer than in the days of their serfdom on the land. In the countryside the peasants laboriously turned their sweat into a little oil or wine; in the towns the wages of free labor were kept down by the competition of slaves. Hundreds of citizens depended for their maintenance upon the fees paid for attendance at the Assembly or the courts; thousands of the population had to be fed by the temples or the state. The number of voters (not to speak of the general population) who had no property was in 431 some forty-five per cent of the electorate; in 355 it had mounted to fifty-seven per cent.[17] The middle classes, which had provided by their aggregate number and power a balance between the aristocracy and the commons, had lost much of their wealth, and could no longer mediate between the rich and the poor, between an unyielding conservatism and a utopian radicalism; Athenian society divided itself into Plato's "two cities"—"one the city of the poor, the other of the rich, the one at war with the other."[18] The poor schemed to despoil the rich by legislation or revolution, the rich organized themselves for protection against the poor. The members of some oligarchic clubs, says Aristotle, took a solemn oath: "I will be an adversary of the people" (i.e., the commons), "and in the Council I will do it all the evil that I can."[19] "The rich have become so unsocial," writes Isocrates, about 366, "that those who own property had rather throw their possessions into the sea than lend aid to the needy, while those who are in poorer circumstances would less gladly find a treasure than seize the possessions of the rich."[20]

In this conflict more and more of the intellectual classes took the side of the poor.[21] They disdained the merchants and bankers whose wealth seemed to be in inverse proportion to their culture and taste; even rich men among them, like Plato, began to flirt with communistic ideas. Pericles had used colonization as a safety valve to reduce the intensity of the class struggle;[22] but Dionysius controlled the west, Macedonia was expanding in the north, and Athens found it ever more difficult to conquer and settle new lands. Finally the poorer citizens captured the Assembly, and began to vote the property of the rich into the coffers of the state, for redistribution among the needy and the voters through state enterprises and fees.[23] The politicians strained their ingenuity to discover new sources of public revenue. They doubled the indirect taxes, the customs dues on imports and exports, and the hundredth on real-estate transfers; they continued the extraordinary taxes of war time into peace; they appealed for "voluntary" contributions, and laid upon the rich ever new opportunities ("liturgies") to finance public enterprises from their private funds; they resorted every now and then to confiscations and expropriations; and they broadened the field of the property-income tax to include lower levels of wealth.[24] Any man burdened with a liturgy could by law compel another to take it over if he could prove that the other was wealthier than he, and had borne no liturgy within two years. To facilitate the collection of revenue the taxpayers were divided into a hundred "symmories" (cosharers); the richest members of each group were required to pay, at the opening of each tax year, the whole tax due from the group for the year, and were left to collect during the year, as best they could, the shares due from the other members of the group. The result of these imposts was a wholesale hiding of wealth and income. Evasion became universal, and as ingenious as taxation. In 355 Androtion was appointed to head a squad of police empowered to search for hidden income, collect arrears, and imprison tax evaders. Houses were entered, goods were seized, men were thrown into jail. But the wealth still hid itself, or melted away. Isocrates, old and rich, and furious at being saddled with a liturgy, complained in 353: "When I was a boy, wealth was regarded as a thing so secure as well as admirable that almost everyone affected to own more property than he actually possessed. . . . Now a man has to be ready to defend himself against being rich as if it were the worst of crimes."[25] In other cities the process of decentralizing wealth was not so legal: the debtors of Mytilene massacred their creditors en masse, and excused themselves on the ground that they were hungry; the democrats of Argos (370) suddenly fell upon the rich, killed twelve hundred of them, and confiscated their property. The moneyed families of otherwise hostile states leagued themselves secretly for mutual aid against popular revolts. The middle classes, as well as the rich, began to distrust democracy as empowered envy, and the poor began to distrust it as a sham equality of votes stultified by a gaping inequality of wealth. The increasing bitterness of the class war left Greece internally as well as internationally divided when Philip pounced down upon it; and many rich men in the Greek cities welcomed his coming as the alternative to revolution.[26]

Moral disorder accompanied the growth of luxury and the enlightenment of the mind. The masses cherished their superstitions and clung to their myths; the gods of Olympus were dying, but new ones were being born; exotic divinities like Isis and Ammon, Atys and Bendis, Cybele and Adonis were imported from Egypt or Asia, and the spread of Orphism brought fresh devotees to Dionysus every day. The rising and half-alien *bourgeoisie* of Athens, trained to practical calculation rather than to mystic feeling, had little use for the traditional faith; the patron gods of the city won from them only a formal reverence, and no longer inspired them with moral scruples or devotion to the state.* Philosophy struggled to find in civic loyalty and a natural ethic some substitute for divine commandments and a surveillant deity; but few citizens cared to live with the simplicity of Socrates, or the magnanimity of Aristotle's "great-minded man."

As the state religion lost its hold upon the educated classes, the individual freed himself more and more from the old moral restraints—the son from parental authority, the male from marriage, the woman from motherhood, the citizen from political responsibility. Doubtless Aristophanes exaggerated these developments; and though Plato, Xenophon, and Isocrates agreed with him, they were all conservatives who might be relied upon to tremble at any doings of the growing generation. The morals of war improved in the fourth century, and a wave of Enlightenment humanitarianism followed the teachings of Euripides and Socrates, and the example of Agesilaus.[27] But sexual and political morality continued to decline. Bachelors and courtesans increased in fashionable co-operation, and free unions gained ground on legal marriage.[28] "Is not a concubine more desirable than a wife?" asks a character in a fourth-century comedy. "The one has on her side the law that compels you to retain her, no matter how displeasing she may be; the other knows that she must hold a man by behaving well, or else look for another."[29] So Praxiteles and then Hypereides lived with Phryne, Aristippus with Lais, Stilpo with Nicarete, Lysias with Metaneira, the austere Isocrates with Lagiscium.[30] "The young men," says Theopompus, with a moralist's exaggeration, "spent all their time among flute-girls and courtesans; those who were a little older devoted themselves to gam-

* "Now that a certain portion of mankind," says Plato (*Laws*, 948), "do not believe at all in the existence of the gods . . . a rational legislation ought to do away with the oaths of the parties on either side."

bling and profligacy; and the whole people spent more on public banquets and entertainments than on the provision necessary for the well-being of the state."[31]

The voluntary limitation of the family was the order of the day, whether by contraception, by abortion, or by infanticide. Aristotle notes that some women prevent conception "by anointing that part of the womb upon which the seed falls with oil of cedar, or ointment of lead, or frankincense commingled with olive oil."*[32] The old families were dying out; they existed, said Isocrates, only in their tombs; the lower classes were multiplying, but the citizen class in Attica had fallen from 43,000 in 431 to 22,000 in 400 and 21,000 in 313.[33] The supply of citizens for military service suffered a corresponding decrease, partly from the dysgenic carnage of war, partly from the reduced number of those who had a property stake in the state, partly from unwillingness to serve; the life of comfort and domesticity, of business and scholarship, had replaced the Periclean life of exercise, martial discipline, and public office.[34] Athletics were professionalized; the citizens who in the sixth century had crowded the palaestra and the gymnasium were now content to exert themselves vicariously by witnessing professional exhibitions. Young men received some grounding, as epheboi, in the art of war; but adults found a hundred ways of escaping military service. War itself had become professionalized by technical complications, and required the full time of specially trained men; citizen soldiers had to be replaced with mercenaries—an omen that the leadership of Greece must soon pass from statesmen to warriors. While Plato talked of philosopher kings, soldier kings were growing up under his nose. Greek mercenaries sold themselves impartially to Greek or "barbarian" generals, and fought as often against Greece as for her; the Persian armies that Alexander faced were full of Greeks. Soldiers shed their blood now not for a fatherland, but for the best paymaster that they could find.

Making honorable exceptions for the archonship of Eucleides (403) and the financial administration of Lycurgus (338-26), the political corruption and turbulence that had followed the death of Pericles continued during the fourth century. According to the law, bribery was punished with death; according to Isocrates,[35] it was rewarded with military and political preferment. Persia had no difficulty in bribing the Greek politicians to make war upon other Greek states or upon Macedon; at last even Demos-

---

* On a similar use of olive oil in our own time, cf. Himes, *Medical History of Contraception*, 80.

thenes illustrated the morals of his time. He was one of the noblest of one of the lowest groups in Athens—the rhetors or hired orators who in this century became professional lawyers and politicians. Some of these men, like Lycurgus, were reasonably honest; some of them, like Hypereides, were gallant; most of them were no better than they had to be. If we may take Aristotle's word for it, many of them specialized in invalidating wills.[36] Several of them laid up great fortunes through political opportunism and reckless demagogy. The rhetors divided into parties, and tore the air with their campaigns. Each party organized committees, invented catchwords, appointed agents, and raised funds; those who paid the expenses of all this frankly confessed that they expected to "reimburse themselves doubly."[37] As politics grew more intense, patriotism waned; the bitterness of faction absorbed public energy and devotion, and left little for the city. The constitution of Cleisthenes and the individualism of commerce and philosophy had weakened the family and liberated the individual; now the free individual, as if to avenge the family, turned around and destroyed the state.

In or near 400 the triumphant democrats, to insure the presence of the poorer citizens at the *ekklesia* and thereby to prevent its domination by the propertied classes, extended state payment to attendance at the Assembly. At first each citizen received an obol (17 cents); as the cost of living rose this was increased to two obols, then to three, until in Aristotle's time it stood at a drachma ($1) per day.[38] It was a reasonable arrangement, for the ordinary *citizen* towards the end of the fourth century, earned a drachma and a half for a day's work; he could not be expected to leave his employment without some recompense. The plan soon gave the poor a majority in the Assembly; more and more the well to do, despairing of victory, stayed home. It was of no use that a revision of the constitution in 403 confined the power of legislation to a body of five *nomothetai*, or lawmakers, selected from the citizens chosen by lot for jury service; this new group also inclined to the side of the commons, and its interposition lowered the prestige and authority of the more conservative Council. Perhaps in consequence of the payment for attendance, the level of intelligence in the Assembly seems to have fallen in the fourth century—though our authorities for this are prejudiced reactionaries like Aristophanes and Plato.[39] Isocrates thought that the Assembly should be paid by Athens' enemies to meet frequently, since it made so many mistakes.[40]

These mistakes cost Athens both her empire and her freedom. The same lust for wealth and power that had undermined the first Confederacy now wrecked the second. After the fall of Sparta at Leuctra Athens felt that it might again expand. In organizing the new empire she had pledged herself not to permit the appropriation of land outside of Attica by Athenian subjects.[41] Now she conquered Samos, the Thracian Chersonese, and the cities of Pydna, Potidaea, and Methone on the coasts of Macedonia and Thrace, and colonized them with Athenian citizens. The allied states protested, and many of them withdrew from the Confederation. Methods of coercion and punishment that had been used and had failed in the fifth century were used, and failed, again. In 357 Chios, Cos, Rhodes, and Byzantium declared a "Social War" of rebellion. When two of Athens' ablest generals, Timotheus and Iphicrates, judged it unwise to give battle in a storm to the rebel fleet in the Hellespont, the Assembly indicted them for cowardice. Timotheus was fined the impossible sum of one hundred talents ($600,000), and fled; Iphicrates was acquitted, but never served Athens again. The rebels fought off all attempts to subdue them, and in 355 Athens signed a peace acknowledging their independence. The great city was left without allies, without leaders, without funds, and without friends.

Possibly subtler factors entered into the weakening of Athens. The life of thought endangers every civilization that it adorns. In the earlier stages of a nation's history there is little thought; action flourishes; men are direct, uninhibited, frankly pugnacious and sexual. As civilization develops, as customs, institutions, laws, and morals more and more restrict the operation of natural impulses, action gives way to thought, achievement to imagination, directness to subtlety, expression to concealment, cruelty to sympathy, belief to doubt; the unity of character common to animals and primitive men passes away; behavior becomes fragmentary and hesitant, conscious and calculating; the willingness to fight subsides into a disposition to infinite argument. Few nations have been able to reach intellectual refinement and esthetic sensitivity without sacrificing so much in virility and unity that their wealth presents an irresistible temptation to impecunious barbarians. Around every Rome hover the Gauls; around every Athens some Macedon.

IV. THE RISE OF SYRACUSE

Despite a full measure of political turbulence, Syracuse, throughout the fourth century, was one of the richest and most powerful cities in Greece. Dionysius I, unscrupulous, treacherous, and vain, was the most capable administrator of his time. By turning the island of Ortygia into a fortress-residence for himself, and walling in the causeway that bound it with the mainland, he had rendered his position almost immune to attack; and by doubling the pay of his soldiers, and leading them to easy victories, he secured from them a personal loyalty that kept him on the throne for thirty-eight years. Having established his government, he changed his early policy of severity to one of conciliatory mildness, and a kind of egalitarian despotism.* He gave choice tracts of land to his officers and his friends, and (as a military measure) assigned nearly all the residences on Ortygia and the causeway to his soldiers; all the remaining soil of Syracuse and its environs he distributed equally among the population, free and slave. Under his guidance Syracuse flourished, though he taxed the people almost as severely as the Assembly taxed the Athenians. When the women became too ornate Dionysius announced that Demeter had appeared to him in a dream and bidden him order all feminine jewelry to be deposited in her temple. He obeyed the goddess, and the women for the most part obeyed him. Soon afterward he "borrowed" the jewelry from Demeter to finance his campaigns.[43]

For at the bottom of all his plans lay the resolve to expel the Carthaginians from Sicily. Envious of Hannibal's resort to battering machines in the siege of Selinus, Dionysius gathered into his service the best mechanics and engineers of western Greece, and set them to improve the tools of war. These men invented, among many new engines of offense and defense, the *katapeltes*, or catapult, for throwing heavy stones and similar projectiles; this and other military innovations passed from Sicily to Greece, and were taken up by Philip of Macedon. A call was sent out for mercenaries, and the armorers of Syracuse manufactured in unheard-of quantities weapons and shields to fit the habits and skills of each group of soldiers engaged. Land battles among the Greeks had heretofore been fought by infantry. Dionysius organized a large body of cavalry, and here, too, gave hints to Philip and Alexander. At the same time he poured funds into the building of two hundred ships, mostly quadriremes or quinqueremes; in speed and power this was such an armada as Greece had never seen.†

---

* When he condemned the Pythagorean Phintias (less correctly Pythias) to death for conspiracy, Phintias asked leave to go home for a day to settle his affairs. His friend Damon (not the music master of Pericles and Socrates) offered himself as hostage, and volunteered to suffer death in case Phintias should not return. Phintias returned; and Dionysius, as surprised as Napoleon at any sincere friendship, pardoned Phintias, and begged to be admitted into so steadfast a comradeship.[42]

† A bireme was a galley with two banks or decks of oars; a trireme, quadrireme, or quinquereme probably had not three, four, or five banks of oars, but so many men on each bench. handling so many oars through one oarlock or port.

By 397 all was ready, and Dionysius sent an embassy to Carthage to demand the liberation of all Greek cities in Sicily from Carthaginian rule. Anticipating a refusal, he invited these cities to expel their foreign governments. They did; and still enraged by the memory of Hannibal's massacres, they put to death, with tortures seldom used by Greeks, all Carthaginians who fell into their hands. Dionysius did his best to stop the carnage, hoping to sell the captives as slaves. Carthage ferried over a vast army under Himilcon, and war went on at intervals in 397, 392, 383, and 368. In the end Carthage recovered all that Dionysius had won from her, and after the bloodshed matters stood as before.

Whether through lust for power, or feeling that only a united Sicily could end Carthaginian rule, Dionysius had meanwhile turned his arms against the Greek cities in the island. Having subjugated them, he crossed over into Italy, conquered Rhegium, and mastered all southwest Italy. He attacked Etruria and took a thousand talents from its temple at Agylla; he planned to plunder the shrine of Apollo at Delphi, but time did not permit. Greece mourned that in the same year (387) liberty had fallen in the west, and in the east had been sold to Persia by the King's Peace. Three years before, Brennus and the Gauls had stood in triumph at the gates of Rome. Everywhere the barbarians on the fringe of the Greek world were growing stronger; and the ravages of Dionysius in southern Italy paved the way for the conquest of its Greek settlements first by the surrounding natives, and then by the half-barbarous Romans. At the next Olympic games the orator Lysias called upon Greece to denounce the new tyrant. The multitude attacked the tents of Dionysius' embassy, and refused to hear his poetry.

The same despot who, after capturing Rhegium, offered freedom to its inhabitants if they would bring him nearly all their hoarded wealth as ransom, and then, when the wealth had been surrendered, sold them as slaves, was a man of wide culture, not prouder of his sword than of his pen. When the poet Philoxenus, asked by the dictator for his opinion of the royal verses, pronounced them worthless, Dionysius sentenced him to the quarries. The next day the King repented, had Philoxenus released, and gave a banquet in his honor. But when Dionysius read more of his poetry, and asked Philoxenus to judge it, Philoxenus bade the attendants take him back to the quarries.[44] Despite such discouragements Dionysius patronized literature and the arts, and was pleased for a moment to entertain Plato, who was then (387) traveling in Sicily. According to a widespread tradition reported by Diogenes Laertius, the philosopher condemned dictatorship. "Your words," said Dionysius, "are those of an old dotard." "Your language," said Plato, "is that of a tyrant." Dionysius, we are told, sold him into slavery, but the philosopher was soon ransomed by Anniceris of Cyrene.[45]

The dictator's life was ended not by any of the assassins whom he feared, but by his own poetry. In 367 his tragedy, *The Ransom of Hector*, received first prize at the Athenian Lenaea. Dionysius was so pleased that he feasted with his friends, drank much wine, fell into a fever, and died.

The harassed city, which had borne with him as an alternative to subjection by Carthage, accepted hopefully the succession of his son to the throne. Dionysius II was now a youth of twenty-five, weak in body and mind, and therefore, thought the crafty Syracusans, likely to give them a mild and negligent rule. He had able advisers in Dion his uncle, and Philistius the historian. Dion was a man of wealth, but also a lover of letters and philosophy, and a devoted disciple of Plato. He became a member of the Academy, and lived, at home and abroad, a life of philosophical simplicity. It occurred to him that the malleable youth of the new dictator offered an opportunity of establishing, if not quite the Utopia that Plato had described to him,[46] at least a constitutional regime capable of uniting all Sicily for the expulsion of the Carthaginian power. At Dion's suggestion Dionysius II invited Plato to his court, and submitted himself to Plato's tutoring.

Doubtless the young autocrat put his best foot forward, and concealed from his teacher that addiction to drink and lechery[47] which had drawn from his father the prediction that the dynasty would die with his son. Deceived by the youth's apparent willingness, Plato led him towards philosophy by its most difficult approaches—mathematics and virtue. The ruler was told, as Confucius had told the Duke of Lu, that the first principle of government is good example, that to improve his people he must make himself a model of intelligence and good will. All the court began to study geometry, and to stand in diplomatic awe over figures traced in the sand. But Philistius, eclipsed by Plato's ascendancy, whispered to the dictator that all this was merely a plot by which the Athenians, who had failed to conquer Syracuse with an army and a fleet, would capture it through a single man; and that Plato, having taken the impregnable citadel with diagrams and dialogues, would depose Dionysius and put Dion on the throne. Dionysius saw in these whispers an excellent escape from geometry. He banished Dion, confiscated his property, and gave Dion's wife to a courtier whom she feared. Despite the dictator's protestations of affection, Plato left Syracuse and joined Dion in Athens. Six years later he returned at the King's invitation, and pled for Dion's recall. Dionysius refused, and Plato resigned himself to the Academy.[48]

In 357 Dion, poor in funds but rich in friends, recruited in mainland Greece a force of eight hundred men, and sailed for Syracuse. Landing secretly, he found the people eager to aid him. With one battle—in which, though he was now fifty, his own heroic fighting turned the tide—he so completely defeated the army of Dionysius that the frightened youth fled to Italy. At this juncture, with Greek impulsiveness, the Syracusan Assembly that he had convened removed Dion from command, lest he should make himself dictator. Dion withdrew peaceably to Leontini; but the forces of Dionysius, liking this turn of events, made a sudden attack upon the popular army, and defeated it. The leaders who had deposed him sent appeals to Dion to hurry back and take charge. He came, won another victory, forgave the men who had opposed him, and then announced a temporary dictatorship as necessary to order. Despite the advice of his friends he refused a personal guard, being "quite ready to die," he said, "rather than live perpetually on the watch against friends and foes alike."[49] Instead he maintained, amid surroundings of wealth and power, his accustomed modesty of life. For though, says Plutarch,

> all things had now succeeded to his wish, yet he desired not to enjoy any present advantage of his good fortune. . . . He was content with a very frugal and moderate competency, and was indeed the wonder of all men, that when not only Sicily and Carthage but all Greece looked to him as in the height of prosperity, and no man living greater than he, no general more renowned for valor and success, yet in his guard, his attendance, his table, he seemed as if he rather communed with Plato in the Academy than lived among hired captains and paid soldiers, whose solace of their toils and dangers it is to eat and drink their fill, and enjoy themselves plentifully every day.[50]

If we may credit Plato, it was Dion's aim to establish a constitutional monarchy, to reform Syracusan life and manners on the Spartan model, to rebuild and unify the enslaved or desolate Greek cities of Sicily, and then to expel the Carthaginians from the island. But the Syracusans had set their hearts on democracy, and were no more hungry for virtue than either Dionysius. A friend of Dion murdered him, and chaos broke loose. Dionysius hurried home, recaptured Ortygia and the government, and ruled with the bitter cruelty of a despot deposed and restored.

Undeserved fates come sometimes to individuals, but rarely to nations.

The Syracusans appealed for aid to their mother city, Corinth. The call came at a time when a Corinthian of almost legendary nobleness was waiting for a summons to heroism. Timoleon was an aristocrat who so loved liberty that when his brother Timophanes tried to make himself tyrant of Corinth, Timoleon killed him. Cursed by his mother and brooding over his deed, the tyrannicide withdrew to a woodland retreat, shunning all men. Hearing nevertheless of Syracuse's need, he came out of his retirement, organized a small force of volunteers, sailed to Sicily, and deployed his little band with such strategy that the royal army yielded after a brief taste of his generalship, and without killing any one of his men. Timoleon gave the humbled tyrant money enough to take himself to Corinth, where Dionysius spent the remainder of his life teaching school and sometimes begging his bread.[51] Timoleon re-established democracy, tore down the fortifications that had made Ortygia a buttress of tyranny, repulsed a Carthaginian invasion, restored freedom and democracy in the Greek cities, and made Sicily for a generation so peaceful and prosperous that new settlers were drawn to it from every part of the Hellenic world. Then, refusing public office, he retired to private life; but the island democracies, appreciating his wisdom and integrity, submitted all major matters to his judgment, and freely followed his advice. Two "sycophants" having indicted him on a charge of malfeasance, he insisted, over the protests of a grateful people, on being tried without favor according to the laws, and thanked the gods that freedom of speech and equality before the law had been restored in Sicily. When he died (337) all Greece looked upon him as one of the greatest of her sons.

V. THE ADVANCE OF MACEDONIA

While Timoleon was restoring democracy for its last respite in ancient Sicily, Philip was destroying it on the mainland. Macedonia, despite the cultural hospitality of Archelaus, was still for the most part a barbarous country of hardy but letterless mountaineers when Philip came to the throne (359); indeed, to the end of its career, though it used Greek as its official language, it contributed no author, or artist, or scientist, or philosopher, to the life of Greece.

Having lived for three years with the relatives of Epaminondas in Thebes, Philip had imbibed there a modicum of culture and a wealth of military ideas. He had all the virtues except those of civilization. He was strong in body and will, athletic and handsome, a magnificent animal trying, now and then, to be an Athenian gentleman. Like his famous son he was a man of violent temper and abounding generosity, loving battle as much, and strong drink more. Unlike Alexander he was a jovial laugher, and raised to high office a slave who amused him. He liked boys, but liked women better, and married as many of them as he could. For a time he tried monogamy with Olympias, the wild and beautiful Molossian princess who gave him Alexander; but later his fancy traveled, and Olympias brooded over her revenge. Most of all he liked stalwart men, who could risk their lives all day and gamble and carouse with him half the night. He was literally (before Alexander) the bravest of the brave, and left a part of himself on every battlefield. "What a man!" exclaimed his greatest enemy, Demosthenes. "For the sake of power and dominion he had an eye struck out, a shoulder broken, an arm and a leg paralyzed."[52] He had a subtle intelligence, capable of patiently awaiting his chance, and of moving resolutely through difficult means to distant ends. In diplomacy he was affable and treacherous; he broke a promise with a light heart, and was always ready to make another; he recognized no morals for governments, and looked upon lies and bribes as humane substitutes for slaughter. But he was lenient in victory, and usually gave the defeated Greeks better terms than they gave one another. All who met him—except the obstinate Demosthenes—liked him, and ranked him as the strongest and most interesting character of his time.

His government was an aristocratic monarchy in which the king's powers were limited by the duration of his superior strength of arm or mind, and by the willingness of the nobles to support him. Eight hundred feudal barons made up the "King's Companions"; they were great landowners who despised the life of cities, crowds, and books; but when, with their consent, the King announced a war, they came out of their estates physically fit and drunkenly brave. In the army they served as cavalry, riding the sturdy horses of Macedonia and Thrace, and trained by Philip to fight in a close formation that could change its tactics at once and as one at the commander's word. Beside these was an infantry of rugged hunters and peasants, arrayed in "phalanxes": sixteen rows of men pointing their lances over the heads—or resting them on the shoulders—of the rows ahead of them, making each phalanx an iron wall. The lance, twenty-one feet long, was weighted at the rear, so that when held aloft it projected fifteen feet forward. As each row of soldiers marched three feet before the next, the lances of the first five rows projected beyond the phalanx, and the lances of the first three rows had a greater reach than the six-foot javelin of the nearest Greek hoplite. The Macedonian soldier, after hurling his lance, fought with a short sword, and protected himself with a brass helmet, a coat of mail, greaves, and a lightweight shield. Behind the phalanx came a regiment of old-fashioned archers, who shot their arrows over the heads of the lancers; then came a siege train with catapults and battering rams. Resolutely and patiently—playing Frederick William I to Alexander's Frederick—Philip drilled this army of ten thousand men into the most powerful fighting instrument that Europe had yet known.

With this force he was determined to unify Greece under his leadership; then, with the help of all Hellas, he proposed to cross the Hellespont and drive the Persians out of Greek Asia. At every step toward this end he found himself running counter to the Hellenic love of freedom; and in trying to overcome this resistance he almost forgot the end in the means. His first move brought him into conflict with Athens, for he sought to win possession of the cities that Athens had acquired on the Macedonian and Thracian coasts; these cities not only blocked his way to Asia, they also controlled rich gold mines and a taxable trade. While Athens was absorbed in the "Social War" that ended her second empire, Philip seized Amphipolis (357), Pydna, and Potidaea (356), and answered the protests of Athens with fine compliments to Athenian literature and art. In 355 he took Methone, losing an eye in the siege; in 347, after a long campaign of chicanery and bravery, he captured Olynthus. He now controlled all the European coast of the north Aegean, had an income of a thousand talents a year from the mines of Thrace,[53] and could turn his thoughts to winning the support of Greece.

To finance his campaigns he had sold thousands of captives—many of them Athenians—into slavery, and had lost the good will of Hellenes. It was fortunate for him that during these years the Greek states were exhausting themselves in a second "Sacred War" (356-46) over the spoliation of the Delphic treasury by the Phocians. The Spartans and Athenians fought for the Phocians, the Amphictyonic League—Boeotia, Locris, Doris, Thessaly—fought against them. Losing, the Amphictyonic Council besought the help of Philip. He saw his opportunity, came swiftly down through the open passes, overwhelmed the Phocians (346), was received into the Delphic Amphictyony, was acclaimed as the protector of the shrine, and accepted an invitation to preside over all the Greeks at the Pythian games. He cast his eyes upon the divided states of the Peloponnesus, and felt that he could win all of them except weakened Sparta to accept him as leader in a Greek Confederacy that might free all Greeks in the east and the west. But Athens, listening at last to Demosthenes, saw in Philip not a liberator but an enslaver, and decided to fight for the jealous sovereignty of the city-state, and the preservation of that free democracy which had made her the light of the world.

VI. DEMOSTHENES

The Vatican statue of the great orator is one of the masterpieces of Hellenistic realism. It is a careworn face, as if every advance of Philip had cut another furrow into the brow. The body is thin and wearied; the aspect is that of a man who is about to make a final appeal for a cause that he considers lost; the eyes reveal a restless life, and foresee a bitter death.

His father was a manufacturer of swords and bedframes, who bequeathed to him a business worth some fourteen talents ($84,000). Three executors administered the property for the boy, and squandered it so generously on themselves that when Demosthenes reached the age of twenty (363) he had to sue his guardians to recover the remains of his inheritance. He spent most of this in fitting out a trireme for the Athenian navy, and then settled down to earn his bread by writing speeches for litigants. He could compose better than he could speak, for he was weak in body and defective in articulation. Sometimes, says Plutarch, he prepared pleas for both the opposed parties to a dispute. Meanwhile, to overcome his impediments, he addressed the sea with a mouth full of pebbles, or declaimed as he ran up a hill. He worked hard, and his only distractions were courtesans and boys. "What can one do with Demosthenes?" his secretary complained. "Everything that he has thought of for a whole year is thrown into confusion by one woman in one night."[54] After years of effort he became one of the richest lawyers at the Athenian bar, learned in technicalities, convincing in discourse, and flexible in morals. He defended the banker Phormio against precisely such charges as he had brought against his guardians, took substantial fees from private persons for introducing and pressing legislation, and never answered the accusation of his colleague Hypereides that he was receiving money from the Persian King to stir up war against Philip.[55] At his zenith his fortune was ten times as large as that which his father had left him.

Nevertheless he had the integrity to suffer and die for the views that he was paid to defend. He denounced the dependence of Athens upon mercenary troops, and insisted that the citizens who received money from the theoric fund should earn it by serving in the army; his courage rose to the point of demanding that this fund should be used not to pay citizens to attend religious ceremonies and plays, but to organize a better force for the defense of the state.* He told the Athenians that they were degenerate slackers who had lost the military virtues of their progenitors. He refused to admit that the city-state had stultified itself with faction and war, and that the times called for the unity of Greece; this unity, he warned, was a phrase to conceal the subjugation of Greece to one man. He detected the ambitions of Philip from their first symptoms, and begged the Athenians to fight to retain their allies and colonies in the north.

Against Demosthenes and Hypereides and the party of war stood Aeschines and Phocion and the party of peace. Very likely both sides were bribed, the one by Persia, the other by Philip,[57] and both were sincerely moved by their own agitation. Phocion was by common consent the most honest statesman of his time—a Stoic before Zeno, a philosophical product of Plato's Academy, an orator who so despised the Assembly that when it applauded him he asked a friend, "Have I not unconsciously said something bad?"[58] Forty-five times he was chosen *strategos*, far surpassing the record of Pericles; he served ably as a general in many wars, but spent most of his life in advocating peace. His associate Aeschines was no stoic, but a man who had risen from bitter poverty to a comfortable income. His youth as a teacher and an actor helped him to become a fluent speaker, the first Greek orator, we are told, to speak extempore with success;[59] his rivals wrote out their speeches in advance. Having served with Phocion in several engagements, he adopted Phocion's policy of compromising with Philip instead of making war; and when Philip paid him for his efforts his enthusiasm for peace became an edifying devotion.

Twice Demosthenes indicted Aeschines on the charge of receiving Macedonian gold, and twice failed to convict him. Finally, however, the martial eloquence of Demosthenes, and the southward advance of Philip, persuaded the Athenians to forego for a time the distribution of the theoric fund, and to employ it in war. In 338 an army was hastily organized, and marched north to face the phalanxes of Philip at Boeotian Chaeronea. Sparta

* The theoric (i.e., spectacle) fund had now been extended to so many festivals as almost to pauperize a large part of the citizenry. "The Athenian Republic," says Glotz, "had become a mutual benefit society, demanding from one class the wherewithal to support another."[56] The Assembly had made it a capital crime to propose any diversion of this fund to other purposes.

refused to help, but Thebes, feeling Philip's fingers at her throat, sent her Sacred Band to fight beside the Athenians. Every one of its three hundred members died on that battlefield. The Athenians fought almost as bravely, but they had waited too long, and were not equipped to meet so novel an army as the Macedonian. They broke and fled before the sea of lances that moved upon them, and Demosthenes fled with them. Alexander, Philip's eighteen-year-old son, led the Macedonian cavalry with reckless courage, and won the honors of a bitter day.

Philip was diplomatically generous in victory. He put to death some of the anti-Macedonian leaders in Thebes, and set up his partisans there in oligarchic power. But he freed the two thousand Athenian prisoners that he had taken, and sent the charming Alexander and the judicious Antipater to offer peace on condition that Athens recognize him as the general of all Greece against the common foe. Athens, which had expected harsher terms, not only consented, but passed resolutions showering compliments upon the new Agamemnon. Philip convened at Corinth a *synedrion*, or assembly, of the Greek states, formed them (except Sparta) into a federation modeled on the Boeotian, and outlined his plans for the liberation of Asia. He was unanimously chosen commander in this enterprise; each state pledged him men and arms, and promised that no Greek anywhere should fight against him. Such sacrifices were a small price to pay for his distance.

The results of Chaeronea were endless. The unity that Greece had failed to create for itself had been achieved, but only at the point of a half-alien sword. The Peloponnesian War had proved Athens incapable of organizing Hellas, the aftermath had shown Sparta incapable, the Theban hegemony in its turn had failed; the wars of the armies and the classes had worn out the city-states, and left them too weak for defense. Under the circumstances they were fortunate to find so reasonable a conqueror, who proposed to withdraw from the scene of his victory, and leave to the conquered a large measure of freedom. Indeed Philip, and Alexander after him, watchfully protected the autonomy of the federated states, lest any one of them, by absorbing others, should grow strong enough to displace Macedon. One great liberty, however, Philip took away—the right of revolution. He was a frank conservative who considered the stability of property an indispensable stimulus to enterprise, and a necessary prop to government. He persuaded the synod at Corinth to insert into the articles of federation a pledge against any change of constitution, any social transformation, any political reprisals. In each state he lent his influence to the side of property, and put an end to confiscatory taxation.

He had laid his plans well, except for Olympias; in the end his fate was determined not by his victories in the field but by his failure with his wife. She frightened him not only by her temper but by participating in the wildest Dionysian rites. One night he found a snake lying beside her in bed, and was not reassured by being told that it was a god. Worse, Olympias informed him that he was not the real father of Alexander; that on the night of their wedding a thunderbolt had fallen upon her and set her afire; it was the great god Zeus-Ammon who had begotten the dashing prince. Discouraged by such varied competition, Philip turned his amours to other women; and Olympias began her revenge by telling Alexander the secret of his divine paternity.[60] One of Philip's generals, Attalus, made matters worse by proposing a toast to Philip's expected child by a second wife, as promising a "legitimate" (i.e., completely Macedonian) heir to the throne. Alexander flung a goblet at his head, crying, "Am I, then, a bastard?" Philip drew his sword against his son, but was so drunk that he could not stand. Alexander laughed at him: "Here," he said, "is a man preparing to cross from Europe into Asia, who cannot step surely from one couch to another." A few months later one of Philip's officers, Pausanias, having asked redress from Philip for an insult from Attalus, and receiving no satisfaction, assassinated the King (336). Alexander, idolized by the army and supported by Olympias,* seized the throne, overcame all opposition, and prepared to conquer the world.

* Who was suspected of having urged on Pausanias.

CHAPTER XX

Letters and Arts in the Fourth Century

I. THE ORATORS

THROUGH all this turmoil literature reflected the declining virility of Greece. Lyrical poetry was no longer the passionate expression of creative individuals, but a polite exercise of *salon* intellectuals, a learned echo of schoolday tasks. Timotheus of Miletus wrote an epic, but it did not accord with an argumentative age, and remained as unpopular as his early music. Dramatic performances continued, but on a more modest scale and in a lower key. The impoverishment of the public treasury and the weakened patriotism of private wealth reduced the splendor and significance of the chorus; more and more the dramatists contented themselves with unrelated musical intermezzi in place of choruses organically united with the play. The name of the choragus disappeared from public notice, then the name of the poet; only the name of the actor remained. The drama became less and less a poem, more and more a histrionic exhibition; it was an era of great actors and small dramatists. Greek tragedy had been built upon religion and mythology, and required some faith and piety in its auditors; it naturally faded away in the twilight of the gods.

Comedy prospered as tragedy decayed, and took over something of the subtlety, refinement, and subject matter of the Euripidean stage. This Middle Comedy (400-323) lost its taste or courage for political satire precisely when politics most needed a "candid friend"; possibly such satire was forbidden or the audience was weary of politics now that Athens was ruled by second-rate men. The general retirement of the fourth-century Greek from public to private life inclined his interest from affairs of state to those of the home and the heart. The comedy of manners appeared; love began to dominate the scene, and not always by its virtue; the ladies of the demimonde mingled on the boards with fishwives, cooks, and bewildered philosophers—though the honor of the protagonists and the dramatist was saved by a marriage at the end. These plays were not coarsened by Aristophanes' vulgarity and burlesque, but neither were they vitalized by his exuberance and his imagination. We know the names, and have none of the works, of thirty-nine poets of the Middle Comedy; but we may judge from their fragments that they did not write for the ages. Alexis of Thurii wrote 245 plays, Antiphanes 260. They made hay while the sun shone, and died with its setting.

It was a century of orators. The rise of industry and trade turned men's minds to realism and practicality, and the schools that once had taught the poems of Homer now trained their pupils in rhetoric. Isaeus, Lycurgus, Hypereides, Demades, Deinarchus, Aeschines, Demosthenes were orator-politicians, leaders of political factions, masters of what the Germans have called the *Advokatenrepublik*. Similar men appeared in the democratic interludes of Syracuse; the oligarchic states did not suffer them. The Athenian orators were clear and vigorous in language, averse to ornate eloquence, capable, now and then, of noble patriotic flights, and given to such dishonesty of argument and abusiveness of speech as would not be tolerated even in a modern campaign. The heterogeneous quality of the Athenian Assembly and the popular courts had a debasing as well as a stimulating effect upon Greek oratory, and through it upon Greek literature. The Athenian citizen enjoyed bouts of oratorical invective almost as much as he enjoyed a prize fight; when a duel was expected between such word warriors as Aeschines and Demosthenes, men came from distant villages and foreign states to hear them. Often the appeal was to pride and prejudice; Plato, who hated oratory as the poison that was killing democracy, defined rhetoric as the art of governing men by addressing their feelings and passions.

Even Demosthenes, with all his vigor and nervous intensity, his frequent ascent to passages of patriotic fervor, his withering fire of personal attack, his clever and relieving alternation of narrative and argument, the carefully rhythmic quality of his language, and the overwhelming torrent of his speech—even Demosthenes strikes us as a little less than great. He laid the secret of oratory in acting (*hypocrisis*), and so believed this that he rehearsed his speeches patiently, and recited them before a mirror. He dug himself a cave and lived in it for months, practicing secretly; in these periods he kept one half of his face shaved to deter himself from leaving his retreat.[1] On the rostrum he contorted his figure, whirled round and round, laid his hand upon his forehead as in reflection, and often raised his voice to a scream.[2] All this, says Plutarch, "was wonderfully pleasing to the common people, but by well-educated persons, as, for example, by Demetrius of Phalerum, it was looked upon as mean, humiliating, and unmanly." We are amused by Demosthenes' histrionics, amazed by his self-esteem, confused by his digressions, and appalled by his ungracious scurrility. There is little wit in him, little philosophy. Only his patriotism redeems him, and the apparent sincerity of his despairing cry for freedom.

The historic climax of Greek oratory came in 330. Six years before, Ctesiphon had carried through the Council a preliminary proposal to award Demosthenes a crown or wreath in appreciation not only of his statesmanship but of his many financial gifts to the state. To keep this honor from his rival, Aeschines indicted Ctesiphon on the ground (technically correct) of having introduced an unconstitutional proposal. The case of Ctesiphon, repeatedly postponed, finally came to trial before a jury of five hundred citizens. It was, of course, a *cause célèbre;* all who could came, even from afar, to hear it; for in effect the greatest of Athenian orators was fighting for his good name and his political life. Aeschines spent little time attacking Ctesiphon, but turned his assault upon the character and career of Demosthenes, who replied in kind with his famous speech *On the Crown.* Every line of the two orations still vibrates with excitement, and is hot with the hatred of enemies brought face to face in war. Demosthenes, knowing that offense is better than defense, charged that Philip had chosen the most corruptible of the orators as his mouthpieces in Athens. Then he etched in acid a life portrait of Aeschines:

> I must let you know who this man really is who embarks upon vituperation so glibly . . . and what is his parentage. Virtue? You renegade!—what have you or your family to do with virtue? . . . Where did you get your right to talk about education? . . . Shall I relate how your father was a slave who kept an elementary school near the Temple of Theseus, and how he wore shackles on his legs and a timber collar round his neck, or how your mother practiced daylight nuptials in an outhouse? . . . You helped your father in the drudgery of a grammar school, grinding the ink, sponging the benches, sweeping the room, holding the position of a menial. . . . After getting yourself enrolled on the register of your parish—no one knows how you managed it, but let that pass—you chose a most gentlemanly occupation, that of clerk and errand-boy to minor officials. After committing all the offenses with which you reproach other people, you were relieved of that employment. . . . You entered the service of those famous players, Simylus and Socrates, better known as the Growlers. You played small parts to their lead, picking up figs and grapes and olives, and making a better living out of those missiles than by all the battles you fought for dear life.

> For there was no truce or armistice in the warfare between you and your audience. . . .
>
> Compare, then, Aeschines, your life and mine. You taught reading, I attended school. You danced, I was choragus. . . . You were a public scribe, I a public orator. You were a third-rate actor, I a spectator at the play. You failed in your part, and I hissed you.[3]

It was a powerful speech; not a model of order and courtesy, but so eloquent with passion that the jury acquitted Ctesiphon by a vote of five to one. In the following year the Assembly voted Demosthenes the disputed crown. Aeschines, unable to pay the fine that was automatically levied upon so unsuccessful a persecution, fled to Rhodes, where he made a precarious living by teaching rhetoric. An old tradition says that Demosthenes sent him money to alleviate his poverty.[4]

II. ISOCRATES

This duel of oratory has been loudly lauded and devoutly studied in every generation. But in truth it represents almost the nadir of Athenian politics; we cannot see nobility in this street-corner contest in vituperation, this mean quarrel for public praise between two secret recipients of foreign gold. Isocrates is a little more attractive, and carries down into the fourth century something of the grandeur of the fifth. Born in 436, he lived till 338, and died with Greek liberty. His father had made a fortune by manufacturing flutes; he gave his son every educational advantage, even sending him to study rhetoric with Gorgias in Thessaly. The Peloponnesian War, and the example of Alcibiades, ruined the flute business, and destroyed the family fortune; Isocrates had to go forth and earn his living by the sweat of his pen. He began by writing speeches for others, and thought of becoming an orator. But he suffered from shyness and a weak voice, and a strong distaste for the crudities of political strife. He abominated the demagogues who had captured the Assembly, and shrank for a time into a quiet pedagogic life.

In 391 he opened the most successful of Athenian schools of rhetoric. Students came to him from all the Greek world; perhaps their variety of origin and outlook helped to form his Panhellenic philosophy. He thought that all other teachers were on the wrong track. In a pamphlet *Against the Sophists* he denounced both those who professed to turn any numbskull into a pundit for three or four minas, and those who, like Plato, hoped to prepare men for government by training them in science and metaphysics. As for himself, he admitted that he could get results only when the student possessed some natural talent. He would not teach metaphysics or science, for these, he argued, were hopeless inquiries into insoluble mysteries. Nevertheless, he gave the name of philosophy to the instruction provided in his school. The curriculum centered upon the arts of writing and speaking, but these were taught in connection with literature and politics;[5] Isocrates offered, as we should say, a cultural course as opposed to the mathematical course given in Plato's Academy. The art of speech was the goal, as being then the chief medium of public advancement; the Athenian state was governed by argument. So Isocrates taught his pupils the use of words: how to arrange them in the clearest order, in rhythmic but not metrical sequence, in polished but not ornate diction, in smooth transitions of sound and thought,* in balanced clauses and cumulative periods; such prose, he believed, would please the refined ear as much as poetry. Out of this school came many leaders of the Demosthenic age: Timotheus the general, Ephorus and Theopompus the historians, Isaeus, Lycurgus, Hypereides, and Aeschines the orators, Speusippus the successor of Plato, and, some say, Aristotle himself.[6]

Isocrates was not content with forming great men; he wished to play some part in the affairs of his time. Unable to be either an orator or a statesman, he became a pamphleteer. He addressed long speeches to the Athenian public, to leaders like Philip, or to the assembled Greeks at the Panhellenic games; instead of delivering these he published them, and thereby unconsciously invented the essay as a literary form. Twenty-nine of his discourses remain, and rank among the most interesting survivals of Greek antiquity. His first great pronouncement, the *Panegyricus*,† struck the theme of all his thought—the theme of his old master Gorgias—a call to Greece to forget its little sovereignties, and become a state. Isocrates was a proud Athenian—"So far has our city distanced the rest of mankind in thought and speech that her pupils have become the teachers of all the world." But he was a prouder Greek; to him, as to the Hellenistic age, Hellenism meant not membership in a race, but participation in a culture; and that culture, he felt, was the finest that men had yet created anywhere.[7] But all around this culture were "barbarians"—in Italy, Sicily, Africa, Asia, and what we should now call the Balkans. It saddened him to see the barbarians becoming stronger, and Persia consolidating her control of Ionia, while the Greek states consumed themselves in civil war.

> For many as are the ills that are incident to the nature of man, we have ourselves invented more than those that nature lays upon us, by engendering wars and factions among ourselves. . . . Against these ills no one has ever protested; and people are not ashamed to weep over the calamities that have been fabricated by the poets,

* E.g., Isocrates—and most Greek writers after him—counted it a literary sin to end one word, and begin the next, with a vowel.

† So named because addressed to the *panegyris*, or General Assembly (*pan-agora*) of the Greeks, at the hundredth Olympiad.

> while they view complacently the real sufferings, the many terrible sufferings, that result from our state of war; and they are so far from feeling pity that they even rejoice more in each other's sorrows than in their own blessings.[8]

If the Greeks must fight, why not fight a real enemy? Why not drive the Persians back to their plateau? A small detachment of Greeks, he prophesied, would defeat a large army of Persians.[9] Such a holy war might at last give unity to Greece; and the choice was between Greek unity or triumphant barbarism.

Two years after publishing this appeal (378) Isocrates, turning theory into practice, toured the Aegean with his ex-pupil Timotheus, and helped to formulate the terms of the second Athenian Confederacy. The rise and fall of this new hope of unity formed one more disappointment in his long life. In a brave and vigorous pamphlet *On the Peace* he condemned Athens for again corrupting an alliance into an empire, and called upon her to sign a peace that would assure every Greek state against Athenian encroachments. "What we call empire is in reality misfortune, for by its very nature it depraves all who have to do with it."[10] Imperialism, he said, had ruined democracy by teaching Athenians to live on foreign tribute; losing that, they now wished to live on state contributions, and exalted to the highest offices those who promised them most.

> Whenever you deliberate on the business of the state you distrust and dislike men of superior intelligence, and cultivate instead the most depraved of the orators who come before you; you prefer . . . those who are drunk to those who are sober, those who are witless to those who are wise, and those who dole out the public money to those who perform public services at their own expense.[11]

In his next address, the *Areopagiticus,* he spoke more leniently of democracy. "We sit around in our shops denouncing the present order," says a timeless passage, "but we perceive that even badly constituted democracies are responsible for fewer disasters than are oligarchies."[12] Had not Sparta made a worse mistress for Greece than Athens had been?—and, "Have not we all of us, because of the madness of the Thirty, become greater enthusiasts for democracy than those who occupied Phyle?"*[13] But Athens had ruined itself by carrying to excess the principles of liberty and equality, by "training the citizens in such fashion that they looked upon insolence as democracy, lawlessness as liberty, impudence of speech as equality, and license to do what they pleased as happiness."[14] All men are not equal, and should not be equally free to hold office. The institution of the lot, Isocrates felt, had lowered disastrously the level of Athenian statesmanship. Better than this "mob rule" was the "timocracy" of Solon and Cleisthenes; for then amiable ignorance and eloquent venality had

* Thrasybulus, Anytus, and the other restorers of democracy in 404.

less chance of being raised to leadership; able men rose naturally to the top, and the Areopagus, receiving them after their term of office, became automatically the mature brain of the state.

In 346, when Athens came to terms with Philip, Isocrates, now ninety, addressed an open letter to the Macedonian King. He foresaw that Philip would make himself master of Greece, and begged him to use his power not as a tyrant, but as the unifier of autonomous Greek states in a war for the liberation of Greece from the King's Peace, and of Ionia from Persian rule. The war party denounced the letter as a surrender to despotism, and for seven years Isocrates held his pen. He spoke once more in 339, addressing his pamphlet to the Greeks who were gathering for the Panathenaic games. The *Panathenaicus* is a weak and prolix repetition of the *Panegyricus;* the style trembles in the old man's hand; but it is an astonishing performance for one who was only three years short of a century. Then in 338 came Chaeronea; Athens was defeated, but Isocrates' dream of a unified Greece was about to come true. A late Greek tradition says that when the news came he forgot about Philip and unity, and thought only of his native city humiliated, the days of her glory ended; and that, at the age of ninety-eight, having at last lived long enough, he starved himself to death.[15] We do not know if this is true; but Aristotle tells us that within five days after Chaeronea, Isocrates was dead.

III. XENOPHON

The influence of "the old man eloquent"[16] upon the statesmen of his time is open to doubt, but his influence upon letters was immediate and enduring.* It was felt first by the historians. Xenophon and others imitated his sketch of Evagoras,† and biography became a popular form of Greek literature, culminating in the gossipy masterpieces of Plutarch. To one of his pupils, Ephorus of Cyme, Isocrates committed the task of writing a general history of Greece—a record not of any one state, but of Greece as a whole. Ephorus carried out the assignment so well that his contemporaries ranked his *Universal History* with the books of Herodotus. To another pupil, Theopompus of Chios, Isocrates committed the field of recent events; Theopompus covered it in his *Hellenica* and *Philippica*, lively and rhetorical works highly praised by his contemporaries. About 340 Dicaearchus of Messana wrote a history of Greek civilization under the title of *Bios Hellados—The Life of Greece;* so ancient is our present enterprise, even, by chance, to its name.

* Cicero, Milton, Massillon, Jeremy Taylor, and Edmund Burke formed their prose style upon the balanced clauses and long periods of Isocrates.

† The enlightened dictator who had imported Greek culture into Cyprus, 410-387.

The only one of the fourth-century historians who has survived is Xenophon. Diogenes Laertius describes him in his youth:

> Xenophon was a man of great modesty, and as handsome as can be imagined. They say that Socrates met him in a narrow lane, and put his stick across it, and prevented him from passing by, asking where all kinds of necessary things were sold. And when Xenophon had answered him, he asked, again, where men were made good and virtuous. And as Xenophon did not know, Socrates said, "Follow me, then, and learn." And from that time forth Xenophon became a follower of Socrates.[17]

He was among the more practical of Socrates' students. He liked his master's fascinating sleight-o'-mind, and loved him as a philosophic saint. But he enjoyed action as well as thought, and became a soldier of fortune while some other scholars, as Aristophanes disdainfully put it, were "measuring the air."[18] About the age of thirty he took service under the younger Cyrus, fought at Cunaxa, and led the Ten Thousand to safety. At Byzantium he joined the Spartans in their war against Persia, captured a wealthy Mede, accepted a rich ransom for him, and lived on it for the rest of his life. He became a friend and admirer of the Spartan King Agesilaus, and made him the subject of a worshipful biography. Returning to Greece with Agesilaus after Athens had declared war upon Sparta, he chose to be loyal to him rather than to his city; whereupon Athens decreed him an exile, and confiscated his property. He fought on the side of the Lacedaemonians at Coronea, and received as a reward an estate at Scillus in Elis, then under Spartan domination. There he spent twenty years as a country gentleman, farming, hunting, writing, and bringing up his sons sternly on the Spartan plan.[19]

To his banishment we owe the varied works that lifted him to the front rank among the authors of his time. He wrote as his mood inclined him, about breaking in dogs, managing horses, training a wife, educating princes, fighting with Agesilaus, or raising revenues for Athens. In the *Anabasis*, with the fresh style of one who had seen or done the things he described, he told the thrilling (but quite uncorroborated) story of the Ten Thousand's long trek to the sea. In the *Hellenica* he took up the history of Greece where Thucydides had left off, and brought it down to the battle of Mantinea, in which his own son Gryllus died fighting bravely after slaying Epaminondas. The book is a dreary chronicle, in which history is conceived as an endless chain of battles, a vain logic-chopping alternation of victory and defeat. The style is lively, the character sketches are vivid; but the facts are judiciously chosen to prove the superiority of Spartan ways. Superstition, which disappeared from history in Thucydides, returns with Xenophon, and supernatural agency is invoked to explain the trajectory of events. With like simplicity or duplicity, the *Memorabilia* transforms Socrates into a monster of perfection, orthodox in religion, in ethics, in genderless love, in everything except that scorn for democracy which particularly endeared him to the banished and Laconizing Xenophon. Still more unreliable is the *Banquet*, which reports conversations alleged to have occurred when Xenophon was a child.

In the *Oeconomicus*, however, Xenophon speaks in his own right, and with such frank conservatism that we are charmed despite ourselves. Asked for instruction in agriculture, Socrates modestly confesses his ignorance, but recalls the advice and example of the rich landowner Ischomachus. The latter voices the knightly Xenophon's disdain for any occupation except husbandry and war. He expounds not only the secrets of successful tillage, but the art of managing one's property and one's wife. In pages that for a moment rival the grace of Plato, Ischomachus tells how he taught his bride—only half his age—the business of caring for the home, keeping all things in place, governing her servants with kindness but without familiarity, and building a good name for herself not through artificial beauty but through a faithful performance of her obligations as wife, mother, and friend. In the view of Ischomachus-Xenophon marriage is an economic as well as a physical association, and decays when the silent partner does all the work. Perhaps the readiness with which the young bride accepts all this is merely the devout wish of a general who won no victories on the domestic battlefield; but we should be willing to believe everything in the account except the tale of how Ischomachus, with but a moment's reasoning, persuaded his wife to abandon powder and rouge.[20]

Having expounded the art of marriage, Xenophon describes in the *Cyropaedia* (i.e., The Education of Cyrus) his ideals of schooling and government, as if in answer to Plato's *Republic*. Cleverly adapting fictitious biography to the uses of philosophy, he gives an imaginary account of the training, career, and administration of Cyrus the Great. He makes the story dramatically personal, enlivens it with dialogue, and decorates it with the oldest romantic love story in extant literature. He almost ignores cultural education, and concentrates upon making the boy a healthy, able, and honorable man; the youth learns the virile sports, the arts of war, the habit of silent obedience, and finally the capacity for effective and persuasive command over subordinates. The best government, Xenophon thinks, is an enlightened monarchy supported and checked by an aristocracy devoted to agricultural and military pursuits. He admires the laws of Persia for rewarding good as well as punishing evil,[21] and points out to the individualistic Greeks, from the example of Persia, the possibility of uniting many cities and states in an empire enjoying internal order and peace. Xenophon began, like Philip, with a vision of conquest; he ends, like Alexander, captivated by the people whom he thought to conquer.

He is a masterly storyteller, but a middling philosopher. He is an amateur in everything but war; he considers a hundred subjects, but always from the viewpoint of a general. He exaggerates the virtues of order and has not a word to say for liberty; we may judge from this how far disorder had gone in Athens. If antiquity ranked him with Herodotus and Thucydides it must have been because of his style—the fresh charm of its Attic purity, the harmonious flow of a prose that Cicero called "sweeter than honey,"[22] the human touches of personality, the transparent simplicity of language that allows the reader to see through the clear medium the thought or subject in hand. Xenophon and Plato stand to Thucydides and Socrates in the same relation as Apelles and Praxiteles to Polygnotus and Pheidias—the culmination of artistry and grace after an age of creative originality and power.

IV. APELLES

The highest excellence of the fourth century lay not in literature but in philosophy and art. In art, as in politics, the individual liberated himself from the temple, the state, the tradition, and the school. As patriotic devotion yielded to private loyalties, architecture took on a more modest scale, and became increasingly secular; the great choral forms of music and dance made way for private performances by professionals; painting and sculpture continued to adorn public buildings with the representation of gods or noble human types, but at the same time they entered upon that service and portrayal of living individuals which characterized the succeeding age. Where cities could still afford to patronize art on a national scale it was because—like Cnidus, Halicarnassus, or Ephesus—they had not been deeply touched by war, or, like Syracuse, had found in natural resources and governmental order the means of a rapid recovery.

On the mainland architecture marked time. In 338 Lycurgus rebuilt the Theater of Dionysus, the Stadium, and the Lyceum; and under his administration Philon raised an impressive arsenal at the Piraeus. As the tendency to a delicate refinement increased, the Doric order became less fashionable, its stern simplicity finding no counterpart in the soul; the Ionic style rose in popularity, and served as an architectural analogue to Praxiteles' elegance and Plato's charm; while the Corinthian order made modest conquests in the Tower of the Winds and the choragic monument of Lysicrates. At Arcadian Tegea Scopas raised a temple of Athena in all three styles—one colonnade Doric, another Ionic, another Corinthian[23]—and beautified it with statuary from his own masculine hand.

Vaster and more famous was the third temple of Artemis at Ephesus. The second temple had burned down on the day of Alexander's birth in 356, a coincidence which, says the usually kindly Plutarch, Hegesias of Magnesia "made the occasion of a conceit frigid enough to have stopped the conflagration."[24] The new building was begun soon afterward, and was completed by the end of the century. Alexander offered to bear the whole cost of the work if his name as donor were recorded on the edifice; but the proud Greeks of Ephesus refused for the disarming (or possibly satirical) reason that "it was not meet for one god to build a temple to another."[25] Nevertheless, Alexander's favorite architect, Dinocrates, designed the temple, on a scale that made it the largest in Hellas. Thirty-six of the columns were carved with bas-reliefs by various sculptors, including the ubiquitous Scopas; one sculptured column drum survives in the British Museum, as if to prove by its drapery alone that Greek sculpture was still near the height of its curve. The heads of the figures are not immobile and idealized types, but individualized faces alive with feeling and character—a premonition of Hellenistic realism.

At the opposite extreme of size the fourth century distinguished itself in terra-cotta statuettes. Boeotian Tanagra made its name synonymous with little figures in baked and unglazed clay, cast in generalized types but then molded and painted by hand into a thousand individual shapes quick with the color and variety of common life. As in earlier centuries, painting was called in to aid other arts; but now it acquired an independent status and dignity, and its masters received commissions from all the Greek world. Pamphilus of Amphipolis, who taught Apelles, refused to take any pupil for less than twelve years, and charged $6000 for the course. Mnason, dictator of Locrian Elatea, paid ten minas for each of the hundred figures in a battle scene by Aristides of Thebes, making $100,000 for one painting; and the same enthusiast gave Asclepiodorus $360,000 for a panel of the twelve major Olympians. Lucullus paid $12,000 for a *copy* of the portrait that Pausias of Sicyon had painted of Menander's mistress Glycera.[26] A picture by Apelles, says Pliny, sold for a sum equal to the treasuries of whole cities.[27]

"Apelles of Cos," says the same enthusiastic amateur, "surpassed all the other painters who either preceded or succeeded him. Singlehanded, he contributed more to painting than all the others together."[28] Apelles must have been supreme in his day and art, since he could afford the rare extravagance of praising other painters. Learning that his greatest rival, Protogenes, was living in poverty, Apelles sailed for Rhodes to visit him. Protogenes, unwarned, was not in his studio when Apelles came. An old woman attendant asked Apelles whom she should name as visitor when her master returned. Apelles replied only by taking a brush and tracing upon a panel, with one stroke, an outline of exceeding fineness. When Protogenes came back the old woman regretted that she could not tell him the name of his departed visitor; but Protogenes, seeing the outline and noting its delicacy, exclaimed: "Only Apelles could have drawn that line." Then he drew a still finer line within that of Apelles, and bade the woman show it if the stranger should return. Apelles came, marveled at the absent Protogenes' skill, but drew, between the two lines, a third of such slenderness and grace that when Protogenes saw it he confessed himself surpassed, and rushed to the harbor to detain and welcome Apelles. The panel was transmitted as a masterpiece from generation to generation, until it was bought by Julius Caesar and perished in the fire that destroyed his palace on the Palatine Hill. Anxious to awaken the Greek world to Protogenes' worth, Apelles asked him what he wanted for some of his paintings; Protogenes mentioned a modest sum, but Apelles offered him, instead, fifty talents ($300,000), and then circulated a report that he intended to sell these works as his own. The Rhodians, aroused to a better appreciation of their artist, paid Protogenes more than the sum Apelles had named, and kept the pictures among the public treasures of the city.[29]

Apelles meanwhile had captured the plaudits of the Greek world by his painting of *Aphrodite Anadyomene*—i.e., Aphrodite rising from the sea. Alexander sent for him, and sat for many portraits. The young conqueror was not satisfied with the representation of his horse Bucephalus in one of these pictures, and had the animal brought closer to the panel for comparison. Bucephalus, looking at the picture, whinnied; whereupon Apelles remarked, "Your Majesty's horse seems to know more about painting than you do."[30] On another occasion, when the King was holding forth about art in Apelles' studio, Apelles begged him to talk of anything else, lest the boys who were grinding the colors should laugh at him. Alexander took it good-naturedly; and when he engaged the artist to paint his favorite concubine, and Apelles fell in love with her, the King sent her to him as a gift.[31] —Over his finished pictures Apelles painted a thin coat of varnish, which preserved the colors, softened their glare, and yet made them livelier than before. He worked to the last, and death came upon him while he was once more delineating the eternal Aphrodite.

V. PRAXITELES

The sculptural masterpiece of the period was the great mausoleum dedicated to King Mausolus of Halicarnassus. Nominally a satrap of Persia, Mausolus had extended his personal sway over Caria and parts of Ionia and Lycia, and had used his rich revenues to build a fleet and beautify his capital. When he died (353), his devoted sister and wife, Artemisia, held a famous oratorical contest in his honor, and summoned the best artists of Greece to collaborate upon a tomb that should be a fitting memorial to his genius. She was a queen by nature as well as by marriage; when the Rhodians took advantage of the King's death to invade Caria, she defeated them by clever strategy, captured their fleet and their capital, and soon brought the rich merchants to terms.[32] But her grief over the death of Mausolus weakened her, and she died two years after him, before she could see the completed monument that was to give a word to every Western tongue. Slowly Scopas, Leochares, Bryaxis, and Timotheus raised a rectangular tomb of white marble slabs over a base of bricks, covered it with a pyramidal roof, and adorned it with thirty-six columns and a wealth of statuary and reliefs. A statue of Mausolus,* calm and strong, was found among the ruins of Halicarnassus by the English in 1857. Still more finished in workmanship is a frieze* showing again the struggle of Greeks and Amazons. These men, women, and horses are among the *chefs-d'oeuvres* of the world's bas-reliefs. The Amazons are not masculine females built for battle; they are women of a voluptuous beauty that should have tempted the Greeks to something gentler than war. The Mausoleum took its place, with the third temple at Ephesus, among the Seven Wonders of the World.

In many respects sculpture now reached its apogee. It lacked the stimulus of religion, and fell short of the majestic power of the Parthenon pediments; but it took a new inspiration from feminine grace, and achieved a loveliness never equaled before or since. The fifth century had modeled nude men and draped women; the fourth preferred to carve nude women and clothed men. The fifth century had idealized its types, and had cast or chiseled the harassed life of man into an emotionless repose; the fourth century tried to realize in stone something of human individuality and

* Now in the British Museum.

feeling. In male statuary the head and face took on more importance, the body less; the study of character replaced the idolatry of muscle; portraits in stone became the fashion for any subject who could pay. The body abandoned its stiff, straight pose, and leaned at ease upon a stick or tree; and the surface was modeled to let in the living play of light and shade. Anxious for realism, Lysistratus of Sicyon, apparently first among the Greeks, fitted a plaster mold upon the subject's face, and made a preliminary cast.[33]

The representation of sensuous beauty and grace came to perfection in Praxiteles. All the world knows that he courted Phryne, and gave a lasting form to her loveliness, but no one knows when he was born or when he died. He was both the son and father of sculptors named Cephisodotus, so that we picture him as the climax of a family tradition of patient artistry. He worked in bronze as well as marble, and won such repute that a dozen cities competed for his services. About 360 Cos commissioned him to carve an *Aphrodite;* with Phryne's help he did, but the Coans were scandalized to find the goddess quite nude. Praxiteles mollified them by making another *Aphrodite,* clothed, while Cnidus bought the first. King Nicomedes of Bithynia offered to pay the heavy public debt of the city in return for the statue, but Cnidus preferred immortality. Tourists came from every nook of the Mediterranean to see the work; critics pronounced it the finest statue yet made in Greece, and gossip said that men had been stirred to amorous frenzy by viewing it.*[34]

As Cnidus achieved fame through the *Aphrodite,* so the little town of Thespiae in Boeotia, birthplace of Phryne, attracted travelers because Phryne had dedicated there a marble *Eros* by Praxiteles. For she had asked of him, as a proof of his love, the most beautiful of the works in his studio. He wished to leave the choice to her; but Phryne, hoping to discover his own estimate, ran to him one day with news that his studio was on fire; whereupon he cried out, "I am lost if my *Satyr* and my *Eros* are burned."[35] Phryne chose the *Eros,* and gave it to her native town.† Eros, once the creator god of Hesiod, became in Praxiteles' conception a delicate and dreamy youth, symbolizing the power of love to capture the soul; he had not yet become the mischievous and sportive Cupid of Hellenistic and Roman art.

Presumably the *Satyr* of the Capitoline Museum in Rome, known to us

* A Roman copy in the Vatican corresponds to the representation of the statue on exhumed Cnidian coins.

† Nero had it brought to Rome, where it perished in the conflagration of A.D. 64. The Vatican *Cupid of Centocelle* may be a copy.

as Hawthorne's *Marble Faun*, is a copy of the work that Praxiteles preferred to his *Eros*. Some have thought that a torso in the Louvre is part of the original itself.[36] The satyr is represented as a well-formed and happy lad, whose only animal element is his long and pointed ears. He is resting lazily against a tree trunk, with one foot crossed behind the other. Seldom has marble conveyed so fully the sense of idle ease; all the charming carelessness of boyhood is in the relaxed limbs and trustful face. Perhaps the limbs are too rounded and soft; Praxiteles looked too long at Phryne to be able to model a man. The *Apollo Sauroctonus*—Apollo the Lizard-Killer—is so feminine that we are half inclined to class him with the hermaphrodites that abound in Hellenistic statuary.

Pausanias remarks with regrettable brevity that among the statues in the Heraeum at Olympia was "a stone *Hermes* carrying Dionysus as a babe, by Praxiteles."[37] German excavators digging on the site in 1877 crowned their labors by finding this figure, buried under centuries of rubbish and clay. Descriptions, photographs, and casts miss the quality of the work; one must stand before it in the little museum at Olympia, and clandestinely pass the fingers over its surface, to realize the smooth and living texture of this marble flesh. The messenger god has been entrusted with the task of rescuing the infant Dionysus from the jealousy of Hera, and taking him to the nymphs who are to rear him in secret. Hermes pauses on the way, leans against a tree, and holds up a cluster of grapes before the child. The infant is crudely done, as if the inspiration of the artist had been exhausted on the older god. The right arm of the *Hermes* is gone, and parts of the legs have been restored; the remainder is apparently as it came from the sculptor's hand. The firm limbs and broad chest show a healthy physical development; the head is in itself a masterpiece, with its aristocratic shapeliness, its chiseled refinement of features, and its curly hair; and the right foot is perfect where perfection in statuary is rare. Antiquity considered this a minor work; we may judge from this the artistic wealth of the age.

Another passage in Pausanias[38] describes a marble group set up by Praxiteles in Mantinea. Excavation has found the base alone, bearing the figures of three Muses, carved probably by the pupils rather than by the master. If we put together the references in extant Greek writings to statues by Praxiteles, we find some forty major works;[39] and these were doubtless but a part of his abundant production. We miss in the remains the sublimity and strength, the dignity and reverence of Pheidias; the gods have made way for Phryne, and the great issues of national life have been put aside for private love. But no sculptor has ever surpassed the sureness of Praxiteles' technique, the almost miraculous power to pour into hard stone ease and grace and the tenderest sentiment, sensuous delight and woodland joyousness. Pheidias was Doric, Praxiteles is Ionic; in him again we have a premonition of that cultural conquest of Europe which was to follow Alexander's victories.

VI. SCOPAS AND LYSIPPUS

Scopas played Byron to Pheidias' Milton and Praxiteles' Keats. We know nothing about his life except through his works, which are the real biography of any man; but even of his works we know none with certainty. The stocky and pugnacious heads of the statues that are attributed to him, or of the copies that are ascribed to his originals, stamp him as a man of passionate individuality and force. At Tegea, as we have seen, he served as both architect and sculptor, showing a versatility and power unsurpassed in all the centuries between Pheidias and Michelangelo. Excavations have found only a few fragments of a pediment, chiefly two badly damaged heads marked by a brachycephalic roundness, and a moody distant look, which are typical of Scopas' work; together with a battered and masculine figure of Atalanta. Strangely like these remains is the *Meleager* head in the Villa Medici at Rome; here again are the full cheeks, the sensual lips, the brooding eyes, the slightly projecting ridge of the forehead above the nose, and the half-disheveled curly hair; perhaps it is a Roman copy of a *Meleager* set up by Scopas as part of a group representing the Calydonian hunt. Another head, in the Metropolitan Museum at New York, is almost surely by Scopas, or copied from him; blunt and powerful, and yet handsome and intelligent, it is one of the most characterful remains of ancient statuary.

At Elis, says Pausanias,[40] Scopas cast "a brazen statue of the Pandemian Aphrodite sitting on a brazen he-goat." At Sicyon he made a marble *Heracles*, of which, perhaps, we have a Roman copy in the Lansdowne House at London: the body a relapse into Polycleitan stylized musculature, the head small and round as usual, the face almost as refined as in Praxiteles. He paused long enough at Megara, Argos, Thebes, and Athens to make statues that Pausanias saw there five centuries later; and perhaps he had a hand in rebuilding the sanctuary at Epidaurus. Crossing the Aegean, he made an *Athena* and a *Dionysus* for Cnidus, and played a major role in the sculptures of the Mausoleum. Going north, he carved one of the column drums of the third temple at Ephesus. At Pergamum he made a colossal seated *Ares;* at Chrysa in the Troad he set up an *Apollo Smintheus* to scare mice from the fields. He contributed to the fame of Samothrace with an *Aphrodite;* and in far-off Byzantium he carved a *Bacchante* of which the Dresden Albertinum may have a Roman copy in the *Raging Maenad.* This marble statuette, though only eighteen inches high, is worthy of a great artist—powerful in figure, magnificent in drapery, unique in pose, alive with anger, and beautiful from every side. Pliny refers to many other statues by Scopas, which in his day stood in the palaces of Rome: an *Apollo* probably copied in the *Apollo Citharoedus* of the Vatican; a group of *Poseidon, Thetis, Achilles, and Nereids,* "an admirable piece of workmanship," says Pliny, "even if it had taken a whole life to complete it"; and a "naked *Aphrodite,* sufficient to establish the renown of any city."[41]

All in all, these works, if a judgment may be based upon a few hypothetical survivals, suggest for Scopas a rank very near to Praxiteles. Here is originality without extravagance, strength without brutality, and a dramatic portrayal of impulse, emotion, and mood, without disfigurement by any strained intensity. Praxiteles loved beauty, Scopas was drawn to character; Praxiteles wished to reveal the grace and tenderness of womanhood, the buoyant health and gaiety of youth; Scopas chose to portray the pains and tragedies of life, and ennobled them with artistic representation. Perhaps, if we had more of his works, we should place him second only to Pheidias.

Lysippus of Sicyon began as a humble artisan in brass. He longed to be an artist, but could not afford a teacher; he took courage, however, when he heard Eupompus the painter announce that for his part he would imitate nature herself, not any artist.[42] Lysippus thereupon turned his face to the study of living beings, and formed a new canon of sculptural proportions to replace the stern rule of Polycleitus; he made the legs longer and the head shorter, extended the limbs into the third dimension, and gave the figure more vitality and ease. His *Apoxyomenos* is a vagrant son of the *Diadumenos;* Polycleitus' athlete bound a fillet above his brow, Lysippus' scrapes the oil and dust from his arm with a bronze strigil, and achieves a greater slenderness and grace. More attractive and alive, if we judge from the marble copy in the Delphi Museum, was his portrait of Agias, a young Thessalian nobleman. Once free, Lysippus struck out into new fields, abandoning the type for the individual, the conventional for the impressionistic,* and almost creating portrait sculpture among the Greeks. Philip interrupted his wars and amours to sit for Lysippus; Alexander was so pleased with the artist's busts of him that he made him the official royal sculptor, as he had given the exclusive right to Apelles to paint his likeness, and to Pyrgoteles to engrave it upon gems.

Some of the finest sculptural remains of the fourth century are anony-

* Other artists, said Lysippus, in a sentence that would have pleased Manet, made men as they were, while he made them "as they *appeared.*"[43]

mous: the bronze statue of a youth found in the sea near Marathon, an ancient copy of a fourth-century *Hermes of Andros*, and a modest, pensive, delicate *Hygiaea* found at Tegea*—all three in the Athens Museum; and in the Boston Museum, from Chios, a profoundly beautiful *Head of a Girl.* To this period, so far as we can make out, belong most of the Niobid figures that came to Rome from Asia Minor in the days of Augustus, and are now scattered among the museums of Europe. And perhaps to this age must be assigned the *originals* of three *Aphrodites* in the Praxitelean tradition: the hesitant *Venus of Capua* in the Naples Museum, the Vatican's *Crouching Venus*, and the modest *Venus of Arles* in the Louvre. Greater than these in mature beauty and quiet depth of feeling is the seated *Demeter* found at Cnidus in 1858, and now among the noblest figures in the British Museum. The subject is uncertain; perhaps it is merely the finest funerary piece that has come down to us from antiquity; perhaps it represents the corn goddess as a *mater dolorosa,* silently mourning the rape of Persephone. The emotion is conveyed with classic restraint; all the tenderness of motherhood, and its silent resignation, are in the face and eyes. This and the *Hermes,* and not those ingratiating *Aphrodites,* are the living sculptural masterpieces of fourth-century Greece.

* This lovely head, which has been used as symbol and first illustration for this volume, was stolen from the little museum at Tegea, and, after nine years' search, was found in a granary in a village of Arcadia by Alexandre Philadelpheus, the gracious curator of the National Museum at Athens. Both the subject and the period are uncertain; but the Praxitelean style seem to date it in the fourth century. M. Philadelpheus considers it "the pearl of the National Museum."

CHAPTER XXI

The Zenith of Philosophy

I. THE SCIENTISTS

COMPARED with the bold advance of the fifth century, and the revolutionary achievements of the third, science in the fourth marked time, and contented itself, in great part, with recording its accumulations. Xenocrates wrote a history of geometry, Theophrastus a history of natural philosophy, Menon a history of medicine, Eudemus histories of arithmetic, geometry, and astronomy.[1] The problems of religion, morals, and politics appearing to be more vital and pressing than the problems of nature, men turned with Socrates from the objective study of the material world to a consideration of the soul and the state.

Plato loved mathematics, dipped his philosophy into it deeply, dedicated the Academy to it, almost, in Syracuse, gave a kingdom for it. But arithmetic was for him a half-mystical theory of number; geometry was not a measuring of the earth, it was a discipline of pure reason, a portal to the mind of God. Plutarch tells of Plato's "indignation" at Eudoxus and Archytas for carrying on experiments in mechanics, "as the mere corruption and annihilation of the one good of geometry, which was thus shamefully turning its back upon the unembodied objects of pure intelligence to recur to sensation, and to ask help . . . from matter." In this way, Plutarch continues, "Mechanics came to be separated from geometry, and, repudiated or neglected by philosophers, took its place as a military art."[2] Nevertheless, in his own abstract way, Plato served mathematics well. He redefined the point as the beginning of a line,[3] formulated a rule for finding square numbers that are the sum of two squares,[4] and invented or developed mathematical analysis[5]—i.e., the proof or disproof of a proposition by considering the results that follow from assuming it; the *reductio ad absurdum* is one form of this method. The emphasis on mathematics, in the curriculum of the Academy, helped the science if only by training such creative pupils as Eudoxus of Cnidus and Heracleides of Pontus.

Plato's friend Archytas, besides being seven times chosen *strategos* of Taras, and writing several tracts of Pythagorean philosophy, developed the mathematics of music, doubled the cube, and wrote the first known treatise on mechanics. Antiquity credited him with three epochal inventions—the pulley, the screw, and the rattle; the first two laid the foundations of machine industry, the third, says the grave Aristotle, "gave children something to occupy them, and so prevented them from breaking things about the house."[6] In this same age Dinostratus "squared the circle" by using the quadratrix curve. His brother Menaechmus, a pupil of Plato, founded the geometry of conic sections,* doubled the cube, formulated the theoretical construction of the five regular solids,† advanced the theory of irrational numbers, and gave the world a famous phrase. "O King," he said to Alexander, "for traveling over the country there are both royal roads and roads for common citizens; but in geometry there is one road for all."‡[8]

The great name in fourth-century science is Eudoxus, who helped Praxiteles to give Cnidus a niche in history. Born there about 408, he set out at the age of twenty-three to study medicine with Philistion at Locri, geometry with Archytas at Taras, and philosophy with Plato at Athens. He was poor, and lived cheaply at the Piraeus, whence he walked to the Academy every scholastic day. After a stay in Cnidus he went to Egypt and spent sixteen months studying astronomy with the priests of Heliopolis. We find him next in Propontine Cyzicus, lecturing on mathematics. At the age of forty he moved with his pupils to Athens, opened there a school of science and philosophy, and for a time rivaled Plato. Finally he returned to Cnidus, set up an observatory, and was entrusted with the task of giving the city a new code of laws.[9]

His contributions to geometry were fundamental. He invented the theory of proportion,§ and most of the propositions, transmitted to us in the fifth book of Euclid; and he devised the method of exhaustion which made it possible to calculate the area of the circle and the volume of the sphere, the pyramid, and the cone; without this preliminary work Archimedes would have been impossible. But the absorbing interest of Eudoxus was in astronomy. We catch the spirit of the scientist in his remark that he would gladly be consumed like Phaethon if he might thereby discover the nature, size, and form of the sun.[10] The word *astrology* was then used to include what we call astronomy, but Eudoxus advised his pupils to ignore the Chaldean theory that a person's fortune could be told by noting the position of the stars at the time of his birth. He longed to reduce all celestial motions to fixed laws; and in his *Phainomena*—which antiquity considered its greatest book on astronomy—he laid the foundation for the scientific predicton of the weather.

* The Greeks defined conic sections as the figures—ellipse, parabola, and hyperbola—produced by cutting an acute-angled, a right-angled, and an obtuse-angled cone with a plane perpendicular to an element.[7] Modern mathematics adds the circle and intersecting lines.

† The tetrahedron (pyramid), hexahedron (cube), octahedron, dodecahedron, and icosahedron—convex solids enclosed by four, six, eight, twelve, or twenty regular polygons.

‡ The Royal Roads, or King's Highways, usually referred to the great roads of the Persian Empire. The story is told also of Euclid and Ptolemy I.[8a]

§ One of his favorite problems was to find the "golden section"—i.e., to divide a line at such a point that the whole line should have the same proportion to the larger part as the larger to the smaller.

His most famous theory was a brilliant failure. He suggested that the universe was composed of twenty-seven transparent and therefore invisible spheres, revolving in diverse directions and at various speeds about the center of the earth; and that the heavenly bodies were fixed upon the periphery or shell of these concentric spheres. The system now seems fantastic, but it was one of the first attempts to give a scientific explanation of celestial behavior. In accord with it Eudoxus calculated with considerable accuracy (if we may rashly take our present "knowledge" of these matters as a norm) the synodic and zodiacal periods of the planets.* The theory did more than any other in antiquity to stimulate astronomic research.

Ecphantus of Syracuse wrote, about 390: "The earth moves about its own center in an eastward direction."[12] Heracleides of Pontus, one of the great polymaths of antiquity—the author of famous works on grammar, music, poetry, rhetoric, history, geometry, logic, and ethics—took up the suggestion, or advanced it independently, arguing that instead of the whole universe revolving about the earth, the relevant phenomena can be explained by supposing that the earth itself rotates daily upon its axis.[13] Venus and Mercury, said Heracleides, revolve around the sun. For one brilliant moment, perhaps, Heracleides anticipated Aristarchus and Copernicus, for we read in the fragments of Geminus (ca. 70 B.C.): "Heracleides of Pontus said that, even on the assumption that the earth moves in a certain way, while the sun is in a certain way at rest, the apparent irregularity with reference to the sun can be saved."[14] We shall probably never know just what Heracleides meant.

Meanwhile a modest progress was being made in the sciences. In geography Dicaearchus of Messana, the biographer of Greece, measured the height of mountains, established the circumference of the earth at some thirty thousand miles, and noted the influence of the sun upon the tides. In 325 Nearchus, one of Alexander's generals, sailed from the mouth of the Indus along the southern coast of Asia to the Euphrates; his log, partly preserved in Arrian's *Indica*,[15] was one of the classics of ancient geography. Geodesy—the measurement of land surfaces, elevations, depressions, positions, and volumes—had already been christened (*geodaisia*) as distinct from geometry.[16] Philistion of Italian Locri, at the beginning of the century, practiced animal dissection, and called the heart the main regulator of life, the seat of the *pneuma*, or soul. Diocles of

* The synodic period of a heavenly body is the time between two successive conjunctions of it with the sun, as seen from the earth; the zodiacal period is the time between two successive appearances of a heavenly body in the same part of the sky as imaginatively divided into the twelve signs of the zodiac. Eudoxus' figure for the synodic period of Saturn was 390 days, ours is 378; for Jupiter, 390, ours 399; for Mars, 260, ours 780; for Mercury, 110 (one manuscript says 116), ours 116; for Venus, 570, ours 584. The zodiacal period given by Eudoxus for Saturn was 30 years, our figure, 29 years, 166 days; for Jupiter, 12 years, our figure, 11 years, 315 days; for Mars, 2 years, our figure, 1 year, 322 days; for Mercury and Venus, 1 year, our figure, 1 year.[11]

Euboean Carystus, about 370, dissected the womb of animals, described human embryos of twenty-seven to forty days, advanced anatomy, embryology, gynecology, and obstetrics, and scotched a favorite Greek error by announcing that both sexes contribute "seed" to form the embryo.[17] A second Aspasia became one of the famous physicians of fourth-century Athens, renowned for her work in women's diseases, surgery, and other branches of medicine.[18] And lest medical science should lower the death rate too fast for the means of subsistence, Aeneas Tacticus, the Arcadian, published about 360, in time for Philip and Alexander, the first Greek classic on the art of war.

II. THE SOCRATIC SCHOOLS

1. Aristippus

If it was a middling age in science the fourth century was the heyday of philosophy. The early thinkers had propounded vague cosmologies; the Sophists had doubted everything but rhetoric; Socrates had raised a thousand questions and answered none; now all the seeds that had been planted in two hundred years sprouted into great systems of metaphysical, ethical, and political speculation. Athens, too poor to maintain its state medical service, nevertheless opened private universities that made it, as Isocrates said, the "school of Hellas," the intellectual capital and arbiter of Greece. Having weakened the old religion, the philosophers struggled to find in nature and reason some substitute for it as a prop of morals and a guide to life.

They explored first the paths opened up by Socrates. While the Sophists relapsed for the most part into the teaching of rhetoric, and disappeared as a class, the pupils of Socrates became the storm centers of violently divergent philosophies. Eucleides of Megara, who had often traveled to Athens to hear Socrates, stirred up his native city with "a rage of disputes," as Timon of Athens phrased it,[19] and developed the dialectic of Zeno and Socrates into an eristic, or art of argument, that questioned every conclusion, and led in the next century to the skepticism of Pyrrho and Carneades. After Eucleides' death his brilliant disciple Stilpo led the Megarian school more and more towards the Cynic point of view: since every philosophy can be refuted, wisdom lies not in metaphysical speculation but in such simple living as will liberate the individual from dependence upon the external factors in well-being. When, after the sack of Megara, Demetrius Poliorcetes inquired how much Stilpo had lost, the sage replied that he had never possessed anything but knowledge, and no one had taken this away.[20] In his later years he numbered among his students the founder of the Stoic philosophy, so that the Megarian school may be said to have begun with one Zeno, and ended with another.

The elegant Aristippus, after Socrates' death, traveled to various cities, spent some time with Xenophon at Scillus but more with Lais in Corinth,[21] and then settled down to found a school of philosophy in his native Cyrene, on the coast of Africa. The wealth and luxury of the upper classes in the half-Oriental city had formed his habits, and he agreed most with that part of his master's doctrine which called happiness the greatest good. Handsome in figure, refined in manners, clever in speech, he made a way for himself everywhere. Shipwrecked and penniless in Rhodes, he went to a gymnasium, discoursed, and so fascinated the men there that they provided him and his companions with all comforts; whereupon he remarked that parents should arm their children with such wealth that even after a shipwreck it should be able to swim to land with its owner.[22]

His philosophy was simple and candid. Whatever we do, said Aristippus, is done through hope of pleasure or fear of pain—even when we impoverish ourselves for our friends, or give our lives for our generals. Therefore, by common consent, pleasure is the ultimate good, and everything else, including virtue and philosophy, must be judged according to its capacity to bring us pleasure. Our knowledge of things is uncertain; all that we know directly and surely is our feelings; wisdom, then, lies in the pursuit not of abstract truth but of pleasurable sensations. The keenest pleasures are not intellectual or moral, they are physical or sensual; therefore the wise man will seek physical delights above all. Nor will he sacrifice a present good to a conjectural future good; only the present exists, and the present is probably as good as the future, if not better; the art of life lies in plucking pleasures as they pass, and making the most of what the moment gives.[23] The use of philosophy is that it may guide us not away from pleasures, but to the most pleasant choice and use of them. It is not the ascetic who abstains that is pleasure's master, but rather the man who enjoys pleasures without being their slave, and can prudently distinguish between those that endanger him and those that do not; hence the wise man will show a discriminating respect for public opinion and the laws, but will seek as far as possible "to be neither the master nor the slave of any man."[24]

If it is a credit to a man that he practices what he preaches, Aristippus deserves some honor. He bore poverty and riches with equal grace, but made no pretense to impartiality between them. He insisted on being paid for his instructions, and did not hesitate to flatter tyrants to gain his end. He smiled patiently when Dionysius I spat upon him: "A fisherman," he said, "must put up with more moisture than this to catch even a smaller fish."[25] When a friend reproached him for kneeling before Dionysius he answered that it was not his fault if the King "had his ears in his feet"; and when Dionysius asked him why philosophers haunt the doors of the rich, but the rich do not frequent the presence of philosophers, he replied, "Because the first know what they want but the second do not."[26] Nevertheless he despised men who pursued wealth for its own sake. When the rich Phrygian Simus displayed to him an ornate house paved with marble, Aristippus spat in his face; and when Simus protested he excused himself on the ground that he could not find, amid all this marble, "a more suitable place to spit in."[27] Having made money, he spent it lavishly on good food, good clothing, good lodging, and (as they seemed to him) good women. Being reproved for living with a courtesan, he answered that he had no objection to living in a house, or sailing in a ship, that other men had used before him.[28] When his mistress said to him, "I am in a family way by you," he replied, "You can no more tell that it was I, than you could tell, after going through a thicket, which thorn had scratched you."[29]

People liked him despite his honest ways, for he was a person of pleasant manner, refined culture (*pace* Simus), and kindly heart. Doubtless his blunt hedonism was in part due to his delight in scandalizing the respectable sinners of the town. He gave himself away by reverencing Socrates, loving philosophy,* and confessing that the most impressive spectacle in life is the sight of a virtuous man steadily pursuing his course in the midst of vicious people.[31] Before his death (356) he remarked that the greatest legacy he was leaving to his daughter Arete was that he had taught her "to set a value on nothing that she can do without"[32]—a strange surrender to Diogenes. She succeeded him as head of the Cyrenaic school, wrote forty books, had many distinguished pupils, and earned from her city an honorable epitaph—"The Light of Hellas."[33]

2. *Diogenes*

Antisthenes agreed with the conclusion, but not the arguments, of this philosophy, and drew out of the same Socrates an ascetic theory of life.

* Those who omit philosophy from their education, said Aristippus, "are like the suitors of Penelope; they . . . find it easier to win over the maidservants than to marry the mistress."[30]

The founder of the Cynic school was the son of an Athenian citizen and a Thracian slave. He fought bravely at Tanagra in 426. He studied for a time with Gorgias and Prodicus, and then set up his own school; but having heard Socrates discourse, he went over—taking his pupils with him—to learn the wisdom of the older man. Like Eudoxus he lived at the Piraeus, and walked to Athens nearly every day—four or five miles each way. Perhaps he was present when Socrates (or Plato) discussed with a complaisant interlocutor the problem of pleasure.

> *Socr.* Do you think that the philosopher ought to care about the pleasures of . . . eating and drinking?
>
> *Simmias.* Certainly not.
>
> *Socr.* And what do you say of the pleasures of love—should he care about them?
>
> *Sim.* By no means.
>
> *Socr.* And will he think much of the other ways of indulging the body—for example, the acquisition of costly raiment, or sandals, or other adornments of the body? Instead of caring about these does he not rather despise anything beyond what nature needs?
>
> *Sim.* I should say that the true philosopher would despise them.[34]

This is the essence of the Cynic philosophy: to reduce the things of the flesh to bare necessities in order that the soul may be as free as possible. Antisthenes took the doctrine literally, and became a Greek Franciscan without theology. Aristippus' motto was, "I possess, but am not possessed"; Antisthenes' was, "I do not possess, in order not to be possessed." He had no property,[35] and dressed in so ragged a cloak that Socrates twitted him: "I can see your vanity, Antisthenes, through the holes of your cloak."[36] Aside from this his only weakness was the writing of books, of which he left ten; one of them was a history of philosophy. After Socrates died Antisthenes resumed his role as teacher. He chose as his lecture center the gymnasium Cynosarges (Dogfish) because it was maintained for people of low, or alien, or illegitimate birth; the name *Cynic* became attached to the school rather from the place than from the creed.[37] Antisthenes dressed like a workman, took no pay for his teaching, and preferred the poor for his pupils; anyone unwilling to practice poverty and hardship was driven away by Antisthenes' tongue or his club.

He refused at first to take Diogenes as a pupil; Diogenes insisted, bore insult patiently, was received, and made his teacher's doctrine famous throughout Hellas by living it completely. Antisthenes had been half slave in origin; Diogenes was a bankrupt banker from Sinope. Diogenes had begged from actual want, and was pleased to learn that this was a part of virtue and wisdom. He adopted the beggar's garb, wallet, and staff, and for a time made his home in a tub or cask in the court of the temple of Cybele at Athens.[38] He envied the simple life of animals, and tried to imitate it; he slept on the ground, ate what he could find wherever he found it, and (we are assured) performed the duties of nature and the rites of love in the sight of all.[39] Seeing a child drink from its hands, he threw away his cup.[40] Sometimes he carried a candle or a lantern, saying that he was looking for a man.[41] He injured no one, but refused to recognize laws, and announced himself, long before the Stoics, a *kosmopolites*, or Citizen of the World. He traveled leisurely, and we hear of him living for a time in Syracuse. On one of his journeys he was captured by pirates, who sold him as a slave to Xeniades of Corinth. When his owner asked him what he could do, he answered, "Govern men." Xeniades made him tutor of his sons and manager of his household, in which capacities Diogenes did so well that his master called him "a good genius," and took his advice in many things. Diogenes continued to live his simple life, so consistently that he became, next to Alexander, the most famous man in Greece.

He was something of a poseur, and evidently relished his renown. He had a gift for debate, and his namesake reports that he never lost an argument.[42] He called freedom of speech the greatest of social goods, and made much use of it, with coarse humor and unfailing wit. He rebuked a woman who knelt with head to the ground before a holy image: "Are you not afraid," he asked her, "to be in so indecent an attitude, when some god may be behind you, for every place is full of them?"[43] When he saw the son of a courtesan throw a stone at a crowd he warned him, "Take care lest you hit your father."[44] He disliked women, and despised men who behaved like them; when a richly dressed and perfumed young Corinthian asked him a question he said, "I will not answer you until you tell me whether you are a boy or a girl."[45] All the world knows the story of how Alexander, at Corinth, came upon Diogenes lying in the sun. "I am Alexander the Great King," said the ruler. "I am Diogenes the dog," said the philosopher. "Ask of me any favor you choose," said the King. "Stand out of the sun," answered Diogenes. "If I were not Alexander," said the young warrior, "I would be Diogenes";[46] but we do not hear that the philosopher returned the compliment. The two men died, we are asked to believe, on the same day in 323: Alexander at Babylon in his thirty-third year, Diogenes at Corinth in his nineties.[47] The Corinthians placed a marble dog over his grave; and Sinope, which had banished him, raised a monument to his memory.

Nothing could be clearer than the Cynic philosophy. It dallied with logic only long enough to dismiss as moonshine that theory of Ideas with which Plato was bewildering the intellectuals of Athens. Metaphysics, too, seemed to the Cynics a vain game; we should study nature not in order to explain the world, which is impossible, but that we may learn the wisdom of nature as a guide to life. The only real philosophy is ethics. The aim of life is happiness; but this is to be found not in the pursuit of pleasure but in a simple and natural life, independent as possible of all external aids. For though pleasure is legitimate if it results from one's own labor and effort, and is not followed by remorse,[48] yet it so often eludes us in the chase, or disappoints us when captured, that it may more wisely be called an evil than a good. A modest and virtuous life is the only road to abiding content; wealth destroys peace, and envious desire, like a rust, eats away the soul. Slavery is unjust but unimportant; the sage will find it as easy to be happy in bondage as in freedom; only internal freedom counts. The gods, said Diogenes, gave man an easy existence, but man has complicated it by itching for luxuries. Not that the Cynics put much faith in the gods. When a priest explained to Antisthenes how many good things the virtuous will enjoy after death, he asked, "Why, then, do you not die?"[49] Diogenes smiled at the Mysteries, and remarked of the offerings set up in Samothrace by those who had survived shipwreck, "The offerings would have been much more numerous if those who were lost had offered them instead of those who were saved."[50] Everything in religion but the practice of virtue seemed to the Cynics superstition. Virtue must be accepted as its own reward and should not depend upon the existence or justice of the gods. Virtue consists in eating, possessing, and desiring as little as possible, drinking only water, and injuring no one. Asked how to defend oneself against an adversary, Diogenes answered, "By proving honorable and upright."[51] Only sexual desire seemed reasonable to the Cynics. They avoided marriage as an external bond, but patronized prostitutes. Diogenes advocated free love and a community of wives,[52] and Antisthenes, seeking independence in everything, complained that he could not satisfy his hunger as solitarily as he could assuage his lust.[53] Having accepted sexual desire as normal and natural, like hunger, the Cynics professed themselves unable to understand why men should be ashamed to satisfy the one appetite, like the other, in public.[54] Even in death a man should be independent, choosing for it his own place and time; suicide is legitimate. Diogenes, some say, killed himself by holding his breath.[55]

The Cynic philosophy was part of a "back-to-nature" movement which arose in fifth-century Athens as a reaction of maladjustment to an irksomely complex civilization. Men are not civilized by nature, and bear the restraints of ordered life only because they fear punishment or solitude. Diogenes stood to Socrates in somewhat the same relation as Rousseau to Voltaire: he thought that civilization was a mistake, and that Prometheus had deserved his crucifixion for bringing it to mankind.[56] The Cynics, like the Stoics and Rousseau, idealized "nature peoples";[57] Diogenes tried to eat meat raw because cooking was unnatural.[58] The best society, he thought, would be one without artifices or laws.

The Greeks smiled upon the Cynics, and tolerated them as medieval society tolerated its saints. After Diogenes the Cynics became a religious order without religion; they made a rule of poverty, lived on alms, tempered their celibacy with promiscuity, and opened schools of philosophy. They had no homes, but taught and slept in the street or the temple porticoes. Through Diogenes' disciples, Stilpo and Crates, the Cynic doctrine passed down into the Hellenistic age, and formed the basis of Stoicism. The school disappeared as an entity about the end of the third century; but its influence remained strong in the Greek tradition, and perhaps reappeared in the Essenes of Judea and the monks of early Christian Egypt. How far all these movements were influenced by, or influenced, similar sects in India, scholarship cannot yet say. The "back-to-nature" devotees of our own day are the intellectual descendants of those men and women of Oriental or Greek antiquity who, tired of unnatural and cramping restraints, thought that they could turn and live with the animals. No full life is without a touch of this urban fantasy.

III. PLATO

1. The Teacher

Even Plato was moved by the Cynic ideal. In the second book of the *Republic*[59] he describes with relish and sympathy a communistic and naturalistic Utopia. He rejects it, and goes on to portray a "second-best" state; but when he comes to picture his philosopher-kings we find the Cynic dream—of men without property and without wives, dedicated to plain living and high philosophy—capturing the citadel of the finest imagination in Greek history. Plato's plan for a communistic aristocracy was the brilliant endeavor of a rich conservative to reconcile his scorn of democracy with the radical idealism of his time.

He came of a family so ancient that on his mother's side his pedigree went back to Solon, and on his father's side to the early kings of Athens, even to Poseidon, god of the sea.[60] His mother was the sister of Charmides and the niece of Critias, so that opposition to democracy was almost in his blood. Named Aristocles—"best and renowned"—the youth distinguished himself in almost every field: he excelled in the study of music, mathematics, rhetoric, and poetry; he charmed the women, and doubtless the men, with his good looks; he wrestled at the Isthmian games, and was nicknamed *Platon*, or broad, because of his robust frame; he fought in three battles, and won a prize for bravery.[61] He wrote epigrams, amorous verses, and a tragic tetralogy; he was hesitating between poetry and politics as a career when, at the age of twenty, he succumbed to the fascination of Socrates. He must have known him before, since the great gadfly had long been a friend of his uncle Charmides; but now he could understand Socrates' teaching, and enjoy the sight of the old man tossing ideas, like an acrobat, into the air, and impaling them on the prongs of his questioning. He burned his poems, forgot Euripides, athletics, and women, and followed the master as if under an hypnotic spell. Perhaps he took notes every day, feeling with an artist's sensitivity the dramatic possibilities of this grotesque and lovable Silenus.

Then, when Plato was twenty-three, came the tory revolution of 404, led by his own relatives; the tense days of the oligarchic terror, and the brave defiance of the Thirty by Socrates; the death of Critias and Charmides, the restoration of the democracy, the trial and death of Socrates: all the world seemed to collapse about the once carefree youth, and he fled from Athens as if it were a haunted city. He found some comfort at Megara in the home of Eucleides, and then at Cyrene, perhaps with Aristippus; thence he appears to have gone to Egypt and studied the mathematical and historical lore of the priests.[62] About 395 he was back in Athens, and a year later fought for the city at Corinth. About 387 he set forth again, studied the Pythagorean philosophy with Archytas at Taras and with Timaeus at Locri, passed over to Sicily to see Mt. Etna, formed a friendship with Dion of Syracuse, was introduced to Dionysius I, was sold into slavery, and was back safe in Athens in 386. With the three thousand drachmas raised to reimburse his ransomer, and which Anniceris refused, Plato's friends now bought for him a suburban recreation grove named from its local god Academus;[62a] and there Plato founded the university that was destined to be the intellectual center of Greece for nine hundred years.*

The Academy was technically a religious fraternity, or *thiasos*, dedicated to the worship of the Muses. The students paid no fees, but as they came for the most part from upper-class families their parents could be expected to make substantial donations to the institution; rich men, says Suidas, "from time to time bequeathed in their wills, to the members of the school, the means of living a life of philosophic leisure."[63] Dionysius II was reported to have given Plato eighty talents ($480,000)[64]—which might explain the philosopher's patience with the King. The comic poets of the time satirized the students as affected in their manners and overnice in their dress—with elegant caps and canes, and a short cloak or academic gown;[65] so old are the manners of Eton, and the black robes of scholarship. Women were admitted to the student body, for Plato remained to this extent a radical, that he was an ardent feminist. The chief studies were mathematics and philosophy. Over the portal was a warning inscription—*medeis ageometretos eisito*—"Let no one without geometry enter here"; perhaps a considerable measure of mathematics formed a requirement for admission. Most of the mathematical advances of the fourth century were made by men who had studied in the Academy. The mathematical course included arithmetic (theory of number), advanced geometry, "spheric" (astronomy), "music" (probably including literature and history), law, and philosophy.[66] Moral and political philosophy came last, if Plato followed the advice which —half justifying Anytus and Meletus—he puts into the mouth of Socrates:

> *Socr.* You know that there are certain principles about justice and good which were taught us in childhood; and under their parental authority we have been brought up, obeying and honoring them.
>
> *Glaucon.* That is true.
>
> *Socr.* And there are also opposite maxims and habits of pleasure which flatter and attract our soul, but they do not influence those who have any sense of right, and who continue to honor the maxims of their fathers and obey them.
>
> *Gl.* True.
>
> *Socr.* Now, when a man is in this state, and the questioning spirit asks what is fair and honorable, and he answers as the law directs, and

* It was not the first university: the Pythagorean school of Crotona, as far back as 520, had offered a variety of courses to a united scholastic community; and the school of Isocrates antedated the Academy by eight years.

then arguments come and refute the word of the legislator, and he is driven into believing that nothing is fair any more than foul, or just and good any more than the opposite, and the same of all his time-honored notions, do you think that he will still honor and obey them?

Gl. That is impossible.

Socr. And when he ceases to think them honorable and natural as heretofore, and he fails to discover the true, can he be expected to pursue any life other than that which flatters his desires?

Gl. He cannot.

Socr. And from being an observer of the law he is converted into a lawless person?

Gl. Unquestionably. . . .

Socr. Therefore every care must be taken in introducing our thirty-year-old citizens to dialectic. . . . They must not be allowed to taste the dear delight too early; that is one thing specially to be avoided; for young men, as you may have observed, when they first get the taste in their mouths, argue for amusement, and are always contradicting and refuting others in imitation of those who refute them; they are like puppy-dogs, who delight to tear and pull at all who come near them.

Gl. Yes, that is their great delight.

Socr. And when they have made many conquests and received defeats at the hands of many, they violently and speedily get into a way of not believing anything that they believed before, and hence . . . philosophy has a bad name with the rest of the world.

Gl. That is very true.

Socr. But when a man begins to get older, he will no longer be guilty of that sort of insanity; he will follow the example of the reasoner who is seeking for truth, and not of the eristic who is contradicting for the sake of amusement; and the greater consideration of his character will increase and not diminish the honor of the pursuit.[67]

Plato and his aides taught by lecturing, by dialogue, and by setting problems to the students. One problem was to find "the uniform and ordered movements by the assumption of which the apparent motions of the planets can be accounted for";[68] possibly Eudoxus and Heracleides derived some stimulus from these tasks. The lectures were technical, and sometimes disappointed those who had hoped for practical gain; but pupils like Aristotle, Demosthenes, Lycurgus, Hypereides, and Xenocrates were deeply influenced by them, and in many cases published the notes they had taken.

Antiphanes said humorously that just as, in a far northern city, words froze into ice as they were spoken, and were heard in the summer when they thawed, so the words spoken by Plato to his students in their youth were finally understood by them only in their old age.[69]

2. *The Artist*

Plato himself professed never to have written any technical treatises,[70] and Aristotle refers to the teaching in the Academy as Plato's "unwritten doctrine."[71] How far this differed from the teaching of the Dialogues we do not know.* Probably these were undertaken originally as a recreation, and in a half-humorous vein.[72] It is one of the playful ironies of history that the philosophical works most reverenced and studied in European and American universities today were composed in an attempt to make philosophy intelligible to the layman by binding it up with a human personality. It was not the first time that philosophical dialogues had been written; Zeno of Elea and several others had used this method,[73] and Simon of Athens, a leather cutter, had published, in dialogue, a report of the Socratic conversations held in his shop.[74] It was in Plato a literary, not an historical, form; he did not pretend to give accurate accounts of conversations held thirty or fifty years before, nor even to keep his references consistent. Gorgias, as well as Socrates, was astounded to hear the words that the young dramatist-philosopher had put into his mouth.[75] The Dialogues were written independently of one another, and perhaps at long intervals; we must not be shocked by slips of memory, much less by changes of view. There is no design unifying the whole, except as the continuing search of a visibly developing mind for a truth which it never finds.†

The Dialogues are cleverly and yet poorly constructed. They vivify the drama of ideas, and build up a coherent and affectionate portrait of Socrates; but they seldom achieve unity or continuity, they often wander from subject to subject, and they are frequently cast into a clumsily indirect mood by being presented as narrative reports, by one man, of other men's

* Certain passages in Aristotle suggest a different understanding of Plato—especially of the theory of Ideas—than that which we get from the Dialogues.

† The thirty-six Dialogues cannot be dated or authoritatively classified. We may arbitrarily divide them into (1) an early group—chiefly the *Apology, Crito, Lysis, Ion, Charmides, Cratylus, Euthyphro,* and *Euthydemus;* (2) a middle group—chiefly *Gorgias, Protagoras, Phaedo, Symposium, Phaedrus,* and *Republic;* and (3) a later group—chiefly *Parmenides, Theaetetus, Sophist, Statesman, Philebus, Timaeus,* and *Laws.* The first group was probably composed before the age of thirty-four, the second before forty, the third after sixty, the interval being devoted to the Academy.[76]

conversations. Socrates tells us that he has "a wretched memory,"[77] and then recites to a friend, verbatim, fifty-four pages of a discussion which he had carried on in his youth with Protagoras. Most of the Dialogues are weakened by the absence of vigorous interlocutors capable of saying to Socrates something other than "yes" or its equivalent. But these faults are lost in the clear brilliance of the language, the humor of situation, expression, and idea, the living world of varied characters humanly realized, and the frequent opening of windows into a profound and noble mind. We may judge the value that the ancients unconsciously put upon these Dialogues when we consider that they are the most complete product that has come down to us from any Greek author. Their form entitles them to as high a place in the annals of literature as their content has given them in the history of thought.

The earlier Dialogues are excellent examples of the youthful "eristic" condemned in the passage quoted a while back, but they are redeemed by the charming pictures they give of Athenian youth. The *Symposium* is the masterpiece of its genre, and the best introduction to Plato; its dramatic *mise en scène* ("Imagine," says Agathon to his servants, "that you are our hosts, and that I and the company are your guests"[78]), its living picture of Aristophanes, "hiccoughing because he had eaten too much," its lively episode of the drunken and scandalous Alcibiades, above all, its subtle combination of merciless realism in the portrayal of Socrates with the loftiest idealism in his conception of love—these qualities make the *Symposium* one of the peaks in the history of prose. The *Phaedo* is more subdued, and more beautiful; here the main argument, however weak, is honest, and gives its opponents a fair chance; the style flows more smoothly over a scene whose noble calm overcomes its tragedy, making the death of Socrates come as quietly as the turn of a river out of sight around a bend. Part of the dialogue of the *Phaedrus* takes place on the banks of the Ilissus, while Socrates and his pupil are cooling their feet in the stream. Greatest of all dialogues, of course, is the *Republic*, being the fullest exposition of Plato's philosophy, and in its earlier parts a dramatic conflict of personalities and ideas. The *Parmenides* is the worst specimen of empty logic-chopping in all literature, and the bravest example in the history of philosophy of a thinker irrefutably refuting his own most beloved doctrine—the theory of Ideas. Then, in the later Dialogues, the artistry of Plato wanes, Socrates fades from the picture, metaphysics loses its poetry, politics its youthful ideals; until, in the *Laws*, the weary inheritor of all the culture of many-sided Athens surrenders to the lure of Sparta, and gives up freedom, and poetry, and art, and philosophy itself.

3. *The Metaphysician*

There is no system in Plato, and if here, for order's sake, his ideas are summarized under the classic heads of logic, metaphysics, ethics, esthetics, and politics, it should be remembered that Plato himself was too intense a poet to shackle his thought in a frame. Because he is a poet he has most difficulty with logic; he wanders about seeking definitions, and loses his way in perilous analogies; "then we got into a labyrinth, and, when we thought we were at the end, came out again at the beginning, having still to see as much as ever."[79] He concludes: "I am not certain whether there is such a science of science" as logic "at all."[80] Nevertheless he makes a beginning. He examines the nature of language, and derives it from imitative sound.[81] He discusses analysis and synthesis, analogies and fallacies; he accepts induction, but prefers deduction;[82] he creates, even in these popular dialogues, technical terms—*essence*, *power*, *action*, *passion*, *generation*—which will be useful to later philosophy; he names five of the ten "categories" that will make up part of Aristotle's fame. He rejects the Sophist view that the senses are the best test of truth, that the individual "man is the measure of all things"; if that were so, he argues, any man's, any sleeper's, any madman's, any baboon's report of the world would be as good as any other.[83]

All that the "rabble of the senses" gives us is a Heracleitean flux of change; if we had only sensations, we should never have any knowledge or truth at all. Knowledge is possible through Ideas, through generalized images and forms that mold the chaos of sensation into the order of thought.[84] If we could be conscious only of individual things thought would be impossible. We learn to think by grouping things into classes according to their likenesses, and expressing the class as a whole by a common noun; *man* enables us to think of all men, *table* of all tables, *light* of every light that ever shone on land or sea. These Ideas (*ideai*, *eida*) are not objective to the senses but they are real to thought, for they remain, and are unchanged, even when all the sense objects to which they correspond are destroyed. Men are born and die, but man survives. Every individual triangle is only imperfectly a triangle, sooner or later passes away, and therefore is relatively unreal; but triangle—the form and law of all triangles

—is perfect and everlasting.[85] All mathematical forms are Ideas, eternal and complete;* everything that geometry says of triangles, circles, squares, cubes, spheres would remain true, and therefore "real," even if there had never been, and never would be, any such figures in the physical world. Abstractions also are real in this sense; individual acts of virtue have a brief existence, but virtue remains as a permanent reality for thought, and an instrument of thought; so with beauty, largeness, likeness, and so forth; these are as real to the mind as beautiful, large, or like things are real to the sense.[87] Individual acts or things are what they are by partaking of, and more or less realizing, these perfect forms or Ideas. The world of science and philosophy is composed not of individual things, but of Ideas;†[88] history, as distinct from biography, is the story of *man;* biology is the science not of specific organisms, but of *life;* mathematics is the study not of concrete things but of number, relation, and form independently of things and yet as valid for all things. Philosophy is the science of Ideas.

Everything in Plato's metaphysics turns upon the theory of Ideas. God, the Prime Mover Unmoved, or Soul of the World,[91] moves and orders all things according to the eternal laws and forms, the perfect and changeless Ideas which constitute, as the Neo-Platonists would say, the *Logos,* or Divine Wisdom or Mind of God. The highest of the Ideas is the Good. Sometimes Plato identifies this with God himself;[92] more often it is the guiding instrument of creation, the supreme form towards which all things are drawn. To perceive this Good, to vision the molding ideal of the creative process, is the loftiest goal of knowledge.[93] Motion and creation are not mechanical; they require in the world, as in ourselves, a soul or principle of life as their originative power.[94]

Only that which has power is real;[95] therefore matter is not basically real

* In his later years Plato tried to prove the Pythagorean converse, that all Ideas are mathematical forms.[86]

† Cf. Carrel: "For modern scientists, as for Plato, Ideas are the sole reality."[89] Cf. Spinoza: "I do not understand, by the series of causes and real entities, a series of individual mutable things, but rather the series of fixed and eternal things. For it would be impossible for human weakness to follow up the series of individual mutable things, not only because their number surpasses all counting, but because . . . the existence of particular things has no connection with their essence, and is not an eternal truth." (In order that the geometry of triangles may be true, it is not necessary that any particular triangle should exist.) "However, there is no need that we should understand the series of individual mutable things, for their essence . . . is only to be found in fixed and eternal things, and from the laws inscribed in those things as their true codes, according to which all individual things are made and arranged."[90] Note that in Plato's theory of Ideas Heracleitus and Parmenides are reconciled: Heracleitus is right, and flux is true, in the world of sense; Parmenides is right, and changeless unity is true, in the world of Ideas.

(*to me on*), but is merely a principle of inertia, a possibility waiting for God or soul to give it specific form and being according to some Idea. The soul is the self-moving force in man, and is part of the self-moving Soul of all things.[96] It is pure vitality, incorporeal and immortal. It existed before the body, and has brought with it from antecedent incarnations many memories which, when awakened by new life, are mistaken for new knowledge. All mathematical truths, for example, are innate in this way; teaching merely arouses the recollection of things known by the soul many lives ago.[97] After death the soul or principle of life passes into other organisms, higher or lower according to the deserts it has earned in its previous avatars. Perhaps the soul that has sinned goes to a purgatory or hell, and the virtuous soul goes to the Islands of the Blest.[98] When through various existences the soul has been purified of all wrongdoing, it is freed from reincarnation, and mounts to a paradise of everlasting happiness.*[99]

4. *The Moralist*

Plato knows that many of his readers will be skeptics, and for a while he struggles to find a natural ethic that shall stir men's souls to righteousness without relying on heaven, purgatory, and hell.[101] The Dialogues of his middle period turn more and more from metaphysics to morals and politics: "The greatest and fairest sort of wisdom by far is that which is concerned with the ordering of states and families."[102] The problem of ethics lies in the apparent conflict between individual pleasure and social good. Plato presents the problem fairly, and puts into the mouth of Callias as strong an argument for selfishness as any immoralist has ever given.[103] He recognizes that many pleasures are good; intelligence is needed to discriminate between good and harmful pleasures; and for fear that intelligence may come too late we must inculcate in the young a habit of temperance, a sense of the golden mean.[104]

The soul or principle of life has three levels or parts—desire, will, and thought; each part has its own virtue—moderation, courage, and wisdom; to which should be added piety and justice—the fulfillment of one's obligations to his parents and his gods. Justice may be defined as the co-operation of the parts in a whole, of the elements in a character, or of the people in a state, each part performing its fittest function properly.[105] The Good

* How much of this Hindu-Pythagorean-Orphic doctrine of immortality was protective coloration it is hard to say. Plato presents it half playfully, as if it were merely a useful myth, a poetic aid to decency.[100]

is neither reason alone nor pleasure alone, but that mingling of them, in proportion and measure, which produces the Life of Reason.[106] The supreme good lies in pure knowledge of the eternal forms and laws. Morally "the highest good . . . is the power or faculty, if there be such, which the soul has of loving the truth, and of doing all things for the sake of truth."[107] He who so loves truth will not care to return evil for evil;[108] he will think it better to suffer injustice than to do it; he will "go forth by sea and land to seek after men who are incorruptible, whose acquaintance is beyond price. . . . The true votaries of philosophy abstain from all fleshly lusts; and when philosophy offers them a purification and release from evil, they feel that they ought not to resist her influence; to her they incline, and whither she leads they follow her."[109]

Plato had burned his poems, and lost his religious faith. But he remained a poet and a worshiper; his conception of the Good was suffused with esthetic emotion and ascetic piety; philosophy and religion became one in him, ethic and esthetic were fused. As he grew older he became incapable of seeing any beauty apart from goodness and truth. He would censor, in his ideal state, all art and poetry that might seem to the government to have an immoral or unpatriotic tendency; all rhetoric and all nonreligious drama would be barred; even Homer–seductive painter of an immoral theology–would have to go. The Dorian and Phrygian modes of music might be allowed; but there must be no complicated instruments, no virtuosos making "a beastly noise" with their technical displays,[110] and no radical novelties.

> The introduction of a new kind of music must be shunned as imperiling the whole state, for styles of music are never disturbed without affecting the most important political institutions. . . . The new style, gradually gaining a lodgment, quietly insinuates itself into manners and customs, and from these it . . . goes on to attack laws and constitutions, displaying the utmost impudence, until it ends by overturning everything.[111]

Beauty, like virtue, lies in fitness, symmetry, and order. A work of art should be a living creature, with head, trunk, and limbs all vitalized and unified by one idea.[112] True beauty, thinks our passionate puritan, is intellectual rather than physical; the figures of geometry are "eternally and absolutely beautiful," and the laws whereby the heavens are made are fairer than the stars.[113] Love is the pursuit of beauty, and has three stages, according as it is love of the body, or of the soul, or of truth. Love of the body, between man and woman, is legitimate as a means to generation, which is a kind of immortality;[114] nevertheless this is a rudimentary form of love, unworthy of a philosopher. Physical love between man and man, or woman and woman, is unnatural, and must be suppressed as frustrating reproduction.[115] This can be done by sublimating it in the second or spiritual stage of love: here the older man loves the younger because his comeliness is a symbol and reminder of pure and eternal beauty, and the younger loves the older because his wisdom opens a way to understanding and honor. But the highest love is "the love of the everlasting possession of the Good," that love which seeks the absolute beauty of the perfect and eternal Ideas or forms.[116] This, and not fleshless affection between man and woman, is "Platonic love"—the point at which the poet and the philosopher in Plato merge in the passionate desire for understanding, an almost mystic longing for the Beatific Vision of the law and structure and life and goal of the world.

> For he, Adeimantus, whose mind is fixed upon true being, has no time to look down upon the affairs of men, or to be filled with jealousy and enmity in the struggle against them; his eye is ever directed towards fixed and immutable principles, which he sees neither injuring nor injured by one another, but all in order moving according to reason; these he imitates, and on these, so far as he can, he will mold his life.[117]

5. *The Utopian*

Nevertheless he is interested in the affairs of men. He sees a social vision too, and dreams of a society in which there shall be no corruption, no poverty, no tyranny, and no war. He is appalled at the bitterness of political faction in Athens, "strife and enmity and hatred and suspicion forever recurring."[118] Like a blue blood, he despises the plutocratic oligarchy, "the men of business . . . pretending never so much as to see those whom they have already ruined, inserting their sting—that is, their money—into anybody else who is not on his guard against them, and recovering the principal sum many times over: this is the way in which they make drones and paupers to abound in the state."[119] "And then democracy comes into being, after the poor have conquered their opponents, slaughtering some and banishing some, while to the remainder they give an equal share of freedom and power."[120] The democrats turn out to be as bad as the plutocrats: they use the power of their number to vote doles to the people and offices to themselves; they flatter and pamper the multitudes until liberty becomes anarchy, standards are debased by omnipresent vulgarity, and manners are coarsened by unhindered insolence and abuse. As the mad pursuit of wealth destroys the oligarchy, so the excesses of liberty destroy democracy.

> *Socr.* In such a state the anarchy grows and finds a way into private houses, and ends by getting among the animals and infecting them. . . . The father gets accustomed to descend to the level of his sons . . . and the son to be on a level with his father, having no fear of his parents, and no shame. . . . The master fears and flatters his scholars, and the scholars despise their masters and tutors. . . . Young and old are alike, and the young man is on a level with the old, and is ready to compete with him in word or deed; and old men . . . imitate the young. Nor must I forget to tell of the liberty and equality of the two sexes in relation to each other. . . . Truly, the horses and asses come to have a way of marching along with all the rights and dignities of freemen . . . all things are just ready to burst with liberty. . . .
>
> *Adeimantus.* But what is the next step? . . .
>
> *Socr.* The excessive increase of anything often causes a reaction in the opposite direction. . . . The excess of liberty, whether in states or individuals, seems only to pass into slavery . . . and the most aggravated form of tyranny arises out of the most extreme form of liberty.[121]

When liberty becomes license, dictatorship is near. The rich, afraid that democracy will bleed them, conspire to overthrow it;[122] or some enterprising individual seizes power, promises everything to the poor, surrounds himself with a personal army, kills first his enemies and then his friends "until he has made a purgation of the state," and establishes a dictatorship.[123] In such a conflict of extremes the philosopher who preaches moderation and mutual understanding is like "a man fallen among wild beasts"; if he is wise he will "retire under the shelter of a wall while the hurrying wind and the storm go by."[124]

Some students, in such crises, take refuge in the past, and write history; Plato takes refuge in the future, and models a utopia. First, he fancies, we must find a good king who will let us experiment with his people. Then we must send away all the adults except those necessary to maintain order and teach the young, for the ways of their elders would corrupt the young into an image of the past. To all the young, of whatever sex or class, twenty years of education will be given. It will include the teaching of myths—

not the immoral myths of the old faith, but new myths that may tame the soul into obedience to parents and the state.* At twenty all are to be given physical, mental, and moral tests. Those that fail will become the economic classes of our state—businessmen, workingmen, farmers; they will have private property, and different degrees of wealth (within limits) according to their ability; but there will be no slaves. The survivors of the first test will receive ten further years of education and training. At thirty they will be tested again. Those that fail will become soldiers; they shall have no private property, and shall not engage in business, but shall live in a military communism. Those that pass the second test will now (and none before) take up for five years the study of "divine philosophy"[125] in all its branches, from mathematics and logic to politics and law. At thirty-five the survivors, with all their theory on their heads, will be flung into the practical world to earn their living and make themselves a place. At fifty such of them as are still alive shall become, without election, members of the guardian or ruling class.

They shall have all powers, but no possessions. There will be no laws; all cases and issues will be decided by the philosopher-kings according to a wisdom untrammeled by precedent. Lest they abuse these powers, they shall have no property, no money, no families, no permanent individual wives; the people will hold the power of the purse, the soldiers the power of the sword. Communism is not democratic, it is aristocratic; the common soul is incapable of it; only soldiers and philosophers can bear it. As for marriage, it must in all classes be strictly regulated by the guardians as a eugenic sacrament: "The best of either sex should be united with the best as often as possible, and the inferior with the inferior; and they are to rear the offspring of one sort of union, but not of the other; for this is the only way of keeping the flock in prime condition."[126] All children are to be brought up by the state, and given equal educational opportunity; classes are not to be hereditary. Girls shall have an equal chance with boys, and no office in the state shall be closed to women because they are women. By this combination of individualism, communism, eugenics, feminism, and aristocracy Plato thinks that a society might be produced in which a philosopher would be glad to live. And he concludes: "Until philosophers are kings, or the kings and princes of this world have the spirit and power of philosophy . . . cities will never cease from ill, nor the human race."[127]

* I.e., Plato concludes that a natural ethic is inadequate.

6. *The Lawmaker*

He thought that he had found such a prince in Dionysius II. He felt, like Voltaire, that monarchy has this advantage over democracy, that in a monarchy the reformer has only to convince one man.[128] To make a better state "you would assume a dictator young, temperate, quick at learning, having a good memory, courageous, of a noble nature . . . and fortunate; his good fortune must be that he is the contemporary of a great legislator, and that some happy chance brings them together."[129] It was, as we have seen, an unhappy chance.

In his declining years, still longing to be a legislator, Plato offered a third-best state. The *Laws*, besides being the earliest extant classic of European jurisprudence, is an instructive study in the senile aftermath of youthful romanticism. The new city, says Plato, must be placed inland, lest foreign ideas undermine its faith, foreign trade its peace, and foreign luxuries its self-contained simplicity.[130] The number of free citizens shall be limited to the conveniently divisible number of 5040; in addition to these will be their families and their slaves. The citizens shall elect 360 guardians, divided into groups of thirty, each group administering the state for a month. The 360 shall choose a Nocturnal Council of twenty-six, which shall meet at night and legislate on all vital affairs.[131] These councilors shall allot the land in equal, indivisible, and inalienable parcels among the citizen families. The guardians "shall provide against the rains doing harm instead of good to the land . . . and shall keep them back by works and ditches, and make" irrigation "streams furnish even to the dry places plenty of water."[132] To control the growth of economic inequality, trade is to be held to a minimum; no gold or silver is to be kept by the people, and there shall be no lending of money at interest;[133] everyone is to be discouraged from living by investment, and is to be encouraged to live as an active farmer on the land. Any man who acquires more than four times the value of one share of land must surrender the surplus to the state; and severe limits are to be placed upon the power of bequest.[134] Women are to have equal educational and political opportunity with men.[135] Men must marry between thirty and thirty-five, or pay heavy annual fines;[136] and they are to beget children for only ten years. Drinking and other public amusements are to be regulated to preserve the morals of the people.[137]

To accomplish all this peaceably there must be complete state control of education, publication, and other means of forming public opinion and personal character. The highest official in the state is to be the minister of education. Authority will replace liberty in education, for the intelligence of children is too undeveloped to excuse us for leaving to them the guidance of their own lives. Literature, science, and the arts are to be under censorship; they will be forbidden to express ideas which the councilors consider hurtful to public morals and piety. Since obedience to parents and the laws can be secured only through supernatural sanctions and aids, the state shall determine what gods are to be worshiped, and how, and when. Any citizen who questions this state religion is to be imprisoned; if he persists he is to be killed.[138]

A long life is not always a blessing; it would have been better for Plato to have died before writing this indictment of Socrates, these prolegomena to all future Inquisitions. His defense would be that he loved justice more than truth; that his aim was to abolish poverty and war; that he could do this only by strict state control of the individual; and that this required either force or religion. The degenerative Ionian looseness of Athenian morals and politics, he thought, would be cured only by the Dorian discipline of the Spartan code. Through all of Plato's thought runs the fear of the abuses of freedom, and the conception of philosophy as the policeman of the people and the regulator of the arts. The *Laws* offers the surrender of a dying Athens that had completely lived to a Sparta that, ever since Lycurgus, had been dead. When Athens' most famous philosopher could find so little to say for freedom Greece was ripe for a king.

Looking back over this body of speculation we are surprised to see how fully Plato anticipated the philosophy, the theology, and the organization of medieval Christianity, and how much of the modern Fascist state. The theory of Ideas became the "realism" of the Scholastics—the objective reality of "universals." Plato is not only a *prä-existent Christlich*, as Nietzsche called him, but a pre-Christian Puritan. He distrusts human nature as evil, and thinks of it as an original sin tainting the soul. He breaks up into an evil body and a divine spirit[139] that unity of body and soul which had been the educated Greek ideal of the sixth and fifth centuries; like a Christian ascetic he calls the body the tomb of the soul. He takes from Pythagoras and Orphism an Oriental faith in transmigration, karma, sin, purification, and "release"; he adopts, in his last works, the other-worldly tone of a converted and repentant Augustine. One would almost say that Plato was not Greek if it were not for his perfect prose.

He remains the most likable of the Greek thinkers because he had the attractive faults of his people. He was so sensitive that like Dante he could see perfect and eternal beauty behind the imperfect and temporal form;

he was an ascetic because at every moment he had to rein in a rich and impetuous temperament.[140] He was a poet possessed by imagination, allured by every whimsy of thought, enthralled by the tragedy and comedy of ideas, flushed with the intellectual excitement of the free mental life of Athens. But it was his fate that he was a logician as well as a poet; that he was the most brilliant reasoner of antiquity, subtler than Zeno of Elea or Aristotle; that he loved philosophy more than he loved any woman or any man; and that in the end, like Dostoevski's Grand Inquisitor, he concluded to a suppression of all free reasoning, a conviction that philosophy must be destroyed in order that man may live. He himself would have been the first victim of his Utopias.

IV. ARISTOTLE

1. Wander-Years

When Plato died Aristotle built an altar to him, and gave him almost divine honors; for he had loved Plato even if he could not like him. He had come to Athens from his native Stageirus, a small Greek settlement in Thrace. His father had been court physician to Philip's father, Amyntas II, and (if Galen was not mistaken) had taught the boy some anatomy before sending him to Plato.[141] The two rival strains in the history of thought —the mystical and the medical—met and warred in the conjunction of the two philosophers. Perhaps Aristotle would have developed a thoroughly scientific mind had he not listened so long to Plato (some say for twenty years); the doctor's son struggled in him with the Puritan's pupil, and neither side won; Aristotle never quite made up his mind. He gathered about him scientific observations sufficient for an encyclopedia, and then tried to force them into the Platonic mold in which his scholastic mind had been formed. He refuted Plato at every turn because he borrowed from him on every page.

He was an earnest student, and soon caught the eye of his master. When Plato read at the Academy his treatise on the soul, Aristotle, says Diogenes Laertius, "was the only person who sat it out, while all the rest rose up and went away."[142] After Plato's death (347) Aristotle went to the court of Hermeias, who had studied with him at the Academy and had raised himself from slavery to be the dictator of Atarneus and Assus in upper Asia Minor. Aristotle married Hermeias' daughter Pythias (344), and was about to settle in Assus when Hermeias was assassinated by the Persians, who suspected him of planning to help Philip's proposed invasion of Asia.[143] Aristotle fled with Pythias to near-by Lesbos, and spent some time there in studying the natural history of the island.[144] Pythias died after giving him a daughter. Later Aristotle married, or lived with, the hetaira Herpyllis;[145] but he maintained to the end a tender devotion to the memory of Pythias, and at his death asked that his bones be laid beside hers; he was not quite the emotionless bookworm that one might picture from his works. In 343 Philip, who probably had known him as a youth at Amyntas' court, invited him to undertake the education of Alexander, then a wild lad of thirteen. Aristotle came to Pella and labored at the task for four years. In 340 Philip commissioned him to direct the restoration and repeopling of Stageirus, which had been laid waste in the war with Olynthus, and to draw up a code of laws for it; all of which he accomplished to the satisfaction of the city, which commemorated its re-establishment by him in an annual holiday.[146]

In 334 he returned to Athens, and—probably aided by funds from Alexander—opened a school of rhetoric and philosophy. He chose as its home the most elegant of Athens' gymnasiums, a group of buildings dedicated to Apollo Lyceus (God of Shepherds), surrounded with shady gardens and covered walks. In the morning he taught advanced subjects to regular students; in the afternoon he lectured to a more popular audience, probably on rhetoric, poetry, ethics, and politics. He collected here a large library, a zoological garden, and a museum of natural history. The school came to be called the Lyceum, and the group and its philosophy were named Peripatetic from the covered walks (*peripatoi*) along which Aristotle liked to move with his students as he discoursed.[147] A sharp rivalry developed between the Lyceum, whose students were mostly of the middle class, the Academy, which drew its membership largely from the aristocracy, and the school of Isocrates, which was frequented chiefly by colonial Greeks. The rivalry was eased in time by the emphasis of Isocrates on rhetoric, of the Academy on mathematics, metaphysics, and politics, and of the Lyceum on natural science. Aristotle set his pupils to gathering and co-ordinating knowledge in every field: the customs of barbarians, the constitutions of the Greek cities, the chronology of victors in the Pythian games and the Athenian Dionysia, the organs and habits of animals, the character and distribution of plants, and the history of science and philosophy. These researches became a treasury of data upon which he drew, sometimes too confidently, for his varied and innumerable treatises.

For the layman he wrote some twenty-seven popular dialogues, which Cicero and Quintilian considered equal to Plato's; it was chiefly by these that he was known in antiquity.[148] These dialogues were among the casualties of the barbarian conquest of Rome. What remains to us is a mass of technical, highly abstract, and inimitably dull works rarely referred to by ancient scholars, and apparently composed, in the last twelve years of his life, of notes made for his lectures by himself, or from his lectures by his pupils. These technical compendiums were not known outside the Lyceum until they were published by Andronicus of Rhodes in the first century B.C.[149] Forty of them survive, but Diogenes Laertius mentions 360 more—probably brief monographs. In these ashes of scholarship we must seek the once living thought that in later ages won for Aristotle the title of The Philosopher. We must approach him expecting no brilliance like Plato's and no wit like Diogenes', but only a rich argosy of knowledge, and such conservative wisdom as befits the friend and pensioner of kings.*

2. *The Scientist*

Aristotle has traditionally been considered as primarily a philosopher. Perhaps this is a mistake. Let us, if only for a fresh view, consider him chiefly as a scientist.

His curious mind is interested, to begin with, in the process and technique of reasoning; and so acutely does he analyze these that his "Organon," or Instrument—the name given after his death to his logical treatises—became the textbook of logic for two thousand years. He longs to think clearly, though he seldom, in his extant works, succeeds; he spends half his time defining his terms, and then feels that he has solved the problem. Definition itself he defines definitively as the specification of an object or idea by naming the genus or class to which it belongs ("man is an *animal*")

* The most important of the extant treatises may be arranged under six heads:

I. LOGIC: *Categories, Interpretation, Prior Analytics, Posterior Analytics, Topics, Sophist Reasonings.*

II. SCIENCE:

1. Natural Science: *Physics, Mechanics, On the Heavens, Meteorology.*
2. Biology: *History of Animals, Parts of Animals, Movements of Animals, Locomotion of Animals, Reproduction of Animals.*
3. Psychology: *On the Soul, Little Essays on Nature.*

III. *Metaphysics.*

IV. ESTHETICS: *Rhetoric, Poetics.*

V. ETHICS: *Nicomachean Ethics, Eudemian Ethics.*

VI. POLITICS: *Politics, The Constitution of Athens.*

and the specific difference that distinguishes it from all other members of that class ("man is a *rational* animal"). It is characteristic of his methodical way that he arranged in ten "categories" the basic aspects under which anything may be considered: substance, quantity, quality, relation, place, time, position, possession, activity, passivity—a classification that some writers have found an aid in the amplification of their flagging thought.

He accepts the senses as the only source of knowledge. Universals are generalized ideas, not innate but formed from many perceptions of like objects; they are conceptions, not things.[150] He lays down resolutely, as the axiom of all logic, the principle of contradiction: "It is impossible for the same attribute at once to belong and not to belong to the same thing in the same relation."[151] He exposes the fallacies into which sophists fall or lure us. He criticizes his predecessors for having drawn the universe, or their theories of it, out of their heads, instead of devoting themselves to patient observation and experiment.[152] His ideal of deductive reasoning is the syllogism—a trio of propositions of which the third follows necessarily from the others; but he recognizes that a syllogism, to avoid begging the question, must presuppose a wide induction to make its major premise probable. Though in his philosophical treatises he too often loses himself in deductive reasoning, he lauds induction, accumulates in his scientific works a mass of specific observations, and occasionally records his own or others' experiments.* With all his errors he is the father of scientific method, and the first man known to have organized co-operative scientific research.

He takes up science where Democritus left it, and dares to enter every field. He is weakest in mathematics and physics, and confines himself there to a study of first principles. He seeks in the *Physics* not new discoveries but clear definitions of the terms used—*matter, motion, space, time, continuity, infinite, change, end.* Motion and space are continuous, they are not made up, as Zeno assumed, of small indivisible moments or parts; the "infinite" exists potentially, but not actually.[153] He feels, though he does nothing to solve, the problems that were to arouse Newton—inertia, gravity, motion, velocity; he has some idea of the parallelogram of forces, and states the law of the lever: "The moving weight will more easily move" (the object) "the farther away it is from the fulcrum."[154]

He argues that the heavenly bodies—certainly the earth—are spherical, for only a spherical earth could explain the shape of the moon when it is

* E.g., in the *Reproduction of Animals* (iv. 6.1) he refers to the regrowth of the eyes when experimentally cut out in young birds; and he rejects the theory that the right testicle produces male, and the left testicle female, offspring, by showing that a man whose right testicle had been removed had continued to have children of either sex.

eclipsed by the intervention of the earth between it and the sun.[155] He has an admirable sense of geological time; periodically but imperceptibly, he tells us, the sea is replaced by land and land by the sea;[156] countless nations and civilizations have appeared and disappeared, whether through swift catastrophe or slow time: "Probably every art and philosophy has been repeatedly developed to the utmost and has perished again."[157] Heat is the chief agent of geological and meteorological changes. He hazards explanations of clouds, fog, dew, frost, rain, snow, hail, wind, thunder, lightning, the rainbow, and meteors. His theories are often bizarre; but the epochal importance of the little treatise on meteorology is that it invokes no supernatural agencies, but seeks to account for the apparent whims of the weather through natural causes operating in certain sequences and regularities. Natural science could go no further until invention gave it instruments of greater scope and precision in observation and measurement.

It is in biology that Aristotle is most at home, observes most widely and abundantly, and makes the most mistakes. The consolidation of previous discoveries in the final establishment of this vital science is his supreme achievement. With the help of his pupils, he gathered data on the fauna and flora of the Aegean countries, and brought together the first scientific collections of animals and plants. If we may follow Pliny,[158] Alexander gave orders to his hunters, gamekeepers, fishermen, and others to supply Aristotle with whatever species and information he might request. The philosopher apologizes for his interest in lowly things: "In all natural objects there lies some marvel, and if any one despises the contemplation of the lower animals, he must despise himself."[159]

He classifies the animal kingdom into *enaima* and *anaima*—blooded and bloodless—approximately corresponding to our "vertebrates" and "invertebrates." He subdivides the bloodless animals into testaceans, crustaceans, mollusks, and insects; the sanguineous into fishes, amphibians, birds, and mammals. He covers an impressively vast and varied field: organs of digestion, excretion, sensation, locomotion, reproduction, and defense; the types and ways of fishes, birds, reptiles, apes, and hundreds of other groups; their pairing seasons and their methods of bearing and rearing their young; the phenomena of puberty, menstruation, conception, pregnancy, abortion, heredity, twins; the habitats and migrations of animals, their parasites and diseases, their modes of sleep and hibernation. . . . He gives an excellent account of the life of the bee.[160] He is full of queer incidental observations: that the blood of oxen coagulates more rapidly than that of most other animals; that some male animals, especially the goat, have been known to give milk; that "in both sexes the horse is the most salacious of animals after man."*[161]

He is particularly interested in the reproductive structures and habits of animals, and marvels at the multiplicity of ways in which nature achieves the continuance of species, "preserving the type when she is unable to preserve the individual";[162] in this field his work remained unequaled until the last century. The life of animals moves about two foci—eating and procreation.[163] "The female has an organ which must be regarded as an ovary, for it contains that which at first is undifferentiated egg, and which becomes by differentiation many eggs."†[164] The female element contributes to the embryo material and food, the male element contributes energy and movement; the female is the passive element, the male is the activating agent.[165] Aristotle rejects the opinions of Empedocles and Democritus, that the sex of the embryo is determined by the temperature of the womb, or by the preponderance of one reproductive element over the other, and then reformulates the theories as his own: "Whenever the formative (male) principle fails to gain the upper hand, and from deficient warmth fails properly to cook the material and so fashion it into its own shape, then will this material pass over into . . . the female."[166] "Sometimes," he adds, "women bring forth three or even four children, especially in certain parts of the world. The largest number ever brought forth is five, and such an occurrence has been witnessed on several occasions. There was once upon a time a woman who had twenty children at four births; and most of them grew up."[167]

He anticipates many theories of nineteenth-century biology. He believes that the organs and characteristics of the embryo are formed by tiny particles (the "gemmules" of Darwin's "pangenesis") that pass from every part of the adult into the reproductive elements.[168] Like Von Baer he teaches that in the embryo the characters belonging to the genus appear first, those belonging to the species second, those belonging to the individual third.[169] He states a principle on which Herbert Spencer prided himself, that the fertility of organisms, by and large, varies inversely as the complexity of their development.[170] His description of the chick embryo shows him at his best:

---

* References in the *History of Animals* indicate that Aristotle prepared a volume of anatomical sketches, and that some of them were reproduced on the walls of the Lyceum; his text uses letters, in modern style, to refer to various organs or points in the drawings.

† Aristotle failed to distinguish between ovaries and uterus; but his description was not materially bettered before the work of Stensen in 1669.

If you wish, try this experiment. Take twenty or more eggs and let them be incubated by two or more hens. Then each day, from the second to that of hatching, remove an egg, break it, and examine it. . . . With the common hen the embryo becomes first visible after three days. . . . The heart appears like a speck of blood, beating and moving as though endowed with life; and from it two veins with blood in them pass in a convoluted course, and a membrane carrying bloody fibers from the vein-ducts now envelops the yolk. . . . When the egg is ten days old, the chick and all its parts are distinctly visible.[171]

The human embryo, Aristotle believes, develops like the chick: "In the same way the infant lies within its mother's womb . . . for the nature of the bird can be likened to that of man."[172] His theory of analogous organs enables him to see the animal world as one: "A nail is the analogue of a claw, a hand of a crab's nipper, a feather of a fish's scale."[173] At times he comes close to a doctrine of evolution:

Nature proceeds little by little from things lifeless to animal life in such a way that it is impossible to determine the exact line of demarcation. . . . Thus, next after lifeless things in the upward scale comes the genus of plants, relatively lifeless as compared with animals, but alive as compared with corporeal objects. There is in plants a continuous scale of ascent towards the animal. There are certain objects in the sea concerning which one would be at a loss to determine whether they be animal or vegetable. . . . The sponge is in every respect like a vegetable. . . . Some animals are rooted, and perish if detached. . . . In regard to sensibility, some animals give no sign of it, others indicate it obscurely. . . . And so throughout the animal scale there is a graduated differentiation.[174]

He considers the ape an intermediate form between man and other viviparous animals.[175] He rejects Empedocles' notion of the natural selection of accidental mutations; there is no fortuity in evolution; the lines of development are determined by the inherent urge of each form, species, and genus to develop itself to the fullest realization of its nature. There is design, but it is less a guidance from without than an inner drive or "entelechy"* by which each thing is drawn to its natural fulfillment.

Intermingled with these brilliant suggestions there are (as might be expected from the hindsight of twenty-three centuries) errors so numerous, and some so gross, that we are warranted in suspecting that the zoological works of Aristotle have suffered some admixture of his own notes with

*From *echo*, I have—*telos*, my goal or purpose—*en*, within.

those of his students.[176] The *History of Animals* is a mine of mistakes. We learn there that mice die if they drink in summer; that elephants suffer from only two diseases—catarrh and flatulence; that all animals but man develop rabies when bitten by a mad dog; that eels are generated spontaneously; that only men have palpitation of the heart; that the yolk of several eggs shaken together collects into the middle; that eggs float in strong brine.[177] Aristotle knows the internal organs of animals better than those of men, for neither he nor Hippocrates seems to have overridden religious taboos and practiced human dissection.[178] He thinks that man has only eight ribs, that women have fewer teeth than men,[179] that the heart lies higher than the lungs, that the heart and not the brain is the seat of sensation,*[180] that the function of the brain is (literally) to cool the blood.[181] Finally he (or some ponderous proxy) carries the theory of design to depths that make the judicious smile. "It is evident that plants are created for the sake of animals, and animals for the sake of men." "Nature has made the buttocks for repose, since quadrupeds can stand without fatigue, but man needs a seat."[182] And yet even this last passage reveals the scientist: the author takes it for granted that man is an animal, and seeks natural causes for the anatomical differences between beasts and men. All in all, the *History of Animals* is Aristotle's supreme work, and the greatest scientific product of fourth-century Greece. Biology waited twenty centuries for its equal.

3. *The Philosopher*

Whether through a sincere piety, or through a cautious respect for the opinions of mankind, Aristotle becomes less of a scientist and more of a metaphysician as he turns to the study of man. He defines the soul (*psyche*), or vital principle as "the primary entelechy of an organism"—i.e., the organism's inherent and destined form, its urge and directon of growth. The soul is not something added to, or residing in, the body, it is coextensive with the body; it is the body itself in its "powers of self-nourishment, self-growth, and self-decay"; it is the sum of the functions of the organism; it is to the body as vision is to the eye.[183] Nevertheless, this functional aspect is basic; it is the functions that make the structures, the desires that mold the organs, the soul that forms the body: "All natural bodies are organs of the soul."†[184]

The soul has three grades—nutritive, sensitive, and rational. Plants share

* He was misled by the insensitivity of cerebral tissue to direct stimulus.

† "The soul," Aristotle adds in a startling idealistic aside, "is in a certain way all existing things; for all things are either perceptions or thoughts."[185] Having bowed to Berkeley, Aristotle also bows to Hume: "Mind is one and continuous in the sense in which the process of thinking is so; and thinking is identical with the thoughts which are its parts."[186]

with animals and men the nutritive soul—the capacity for self-nourishment and internal growth; animals and men have in addition the sensitive soul—the capacity for sensation; the higher animals as well as men have the "passive rational" soul—the capacity for the simpler forms of intelligence; man alone has the "active rational" soul—the capacity to generalize and originate. This last is a part or emanation of that creative and rational power of the universe which is God; and as such it cannot die.[187] But this immortality is impersonal; what survives is the power, not the personality; the individual is a unique and mortal compound of nutritive, sensitive, and rational faculties; he achieves immortality only relatively, through reproduction, and only impersonally, through death.*

Just as the soul is the "form" of the body, so God is the "form" or "entelechy" of the world—its inherent nature, functions, and purposes.† All causes‡ at last go back to the First Cause Uncaused, all motions to the Prime Mover Unmoved; we must assume some origin or beginning for the motion and power in the world, and this source is God. As God is the sum and source of all motion, so he is the sum and goal of all purposes in nature; he is the Final, as well as the First, Cause. Everywhere we see things moving to specific ends; the front teeth grow sharp to cut food, the molars grow flat to grind it; the eyelid winks to protect the eye, the pupil expands in the dark to let in more light; the tree sends its roots into the earth, its shoots toward the sun.[189] As the tree is drawn by its inherent nature, power, and purposes toward the light, so the world is drawn by its inherent nature, power, and purposes, which are God. God is not the creator of the material world, but its energizing form; he moves it not from behind, but as an inner direction or goal, as something beloved moves the lover.[190] Finally, says Aristotle, God is pure thought, rational soul, contemplating itself in the eternal forms that constitute at once the essence of the world, and God.

The purpose of art, like that of metaphysics, is to capture the essential form of things. It is an imitation or representation of life,[191] but no mechanical copy; that which it imitates is the soul of the matter, not the body or matter itself; and through this intuition and mirroring of essence even the representation of an ugly object may be beautiful. Beauty is unity, the

---

* Other interpretations of Aristotle's contradictory pronouncements on this point are possible. The text follows the *Cambridge Ancient History*, VI, 345; Grote, *Aristotle*, II, 233; and Rohde, *Psyche*, 493.

† The essential aspect of anything, in Aristotle as in Plato, is the "form" (*eidos*), not the matter which is formed; the matter is not the "real being," but a negative and passive potentiality which acquires specific existence only when actuated and determined by form.

‡ Every effect, says Aristotle, is produced by four causes: material (the component stuff), efficient (the agent or his act), formal (the nature of the thing), and final (the goal). He gives a peculiar example: "What is the material cause of a man? The menses" (i.e., the provision of an ovum). "What is the efficient cause? The semen" (i.e., the act of insemination). "What is the formal cause? The nature" (of the agents involved). "What is the final cause? The purpose in view."[188]

co-operation and symmetry of the parts in a whole. In drama this unity is primarily a unity of action; the plot must concern itself with one action chiefly, and may admit other actions only to advance or illuminate this central tale. If the work is to be of high excellence the action must be noble or heroic. "Tragedy," says Aristotle's celebrated definition, "is a representation of an action that is heroic and complete and of a certain magnitude, by means of language enriched with all kinds of ornament . . . it represents men in action, and does not use narrative; and through pity and fear it brings relief to these and similar emotions."[192] By arousing our profoundest feelings, and then quieting them through a subsiding denouement, the tragic drama offers us a harmless and yet soul-deepening expression of emotions that might otherwise accumulate to neurosis or violence; it shows us pains and sorrows more awful than our own, and sends us home discharged and cleansed. In general there is a pleasure in contemplating any work of true art; and it is the mark of a civilization to provide the soul with works worthy of such contemplation. For "nature requires not only that we should be properly employed, but that we should be able to enjoy our leisure in an honorable way."[193]

What, then, is the good life? Aristotle answers, with frank simplicity, that it is the happy life; and he proposes to consider, in his *Ethics*,* not (like Plato) how to make men good, but how to make them happy. All other things than happiness, he thinks, are sought with some other end in view; happiness alone is sought for its own sake.[194] Certain things are necessary to lasting happiness: good birth, good health, good looks, good luck, good reputation, good friends, good money, and goodness.[195] "No man can be happy who is absolutely ugly."[196] "As for those who say that he who is being tortured on the wheel, or falls into great misfortunes, is happy provided only he be good, they talk nonsense."[197] Aristotle quotes, with a candor rare in philosophers, the answer of Simonides to Hieron's wife, who had asked whether it was better to be wise or to be rich: "Rich, for we see the wise spending their time at the doors of the rich."[198] But wealth is merely means; it does not of itself satisfy anyone but the miser; and since it is relative, it seldom satisfies a man long. The secret of happiness is action, the exercise of energy in a way suited to a man's nature and circumstances. Virtue is a practical wisdom, an intelligent appraisal of one's own good.[199] Usually it is a golden mean between two extremes; intelligence is needed

* The *Nicomachean Ethics* (so called because edited by Aristotle's son Nicomachus) and the *Politics* were originally one book. The plural title forms—*ta ethika* and *ta politika*—were used by the Greek editors to suggest the treatment of various moral and political problems; and these forms have been retained in the English adoption of the words.

to find the mean, and self-control (*enkrateia*, inner strength) to practice it. "He who is angry at what and with whom he ought," says a typically Aristotelian sentence, "and further, in right manner and time, and for a proper length of time, is praised."[200] Virtue is not an act but a *habit* of doing the right thing. At first it has to be enforced by discipline, since the young cannot judge wisely in these matters; in time that which was the result of compulsion becomes a habit, "a second nature," and almost as pleasant as desire.

Aristotle concludes, quite contrary to his initial placing of happiness in action, that the best life is the life of thought. For thought is the mark or special excellence of man, and "the proper work of man is a working of the soul in accordance with reason."[201] "The most fortunate of men is he who combines a measure of prosperity with scholarship, research, or contemplation; such a man comes closest to the life of the gods."[202] "Those who wish for an independent pleasure should seek it in philosophy, for all other pleasures need the assistance of men."[203]

4. The Statesman

As ethics is the science of individual happiness, so politics is the science of collective happiness. The function of the state is to organize a society for the greatest happiness of the greatest number. "A state is a collective body of citizens sufficient in themselves for all the purposes of life."[204] It is a natural product, for "man is by nature a political animal"[205]—i.e., his instincts lead him to association. "The state is by nature prior to the family and the individual": man as we know him is born into an already organized society, which molds him in its image.

Having collected and studied, with his students, 158 Greek constitutions,* Aristotle divided them into three types: monarchy, aristocracy, and timocracy—government respectively by power, by birth, and by excellence. Any one of these forms may be good according to time, place, and circumstance. "Though one form of government may be better than others," reads a sentence which every American should memorize, "yet there is no reason to prevent another from being preferable to it under particular conditions."[206] Each form of government is good when the ruling power seeks the good of all rather than its own profit; in the contrary case each is bad. Each type, therefore, has a degenerate analogue when it becomes government for the governors instead of for the governed; then monarchy

* Only one of these studies survives—the *Athenaion Politeia*, found in 1891. It is an admirable constitutional history of Athens.

lapses into despotism, aristocracy into oligarchy, timocracy into democracy in the sense of rule by the common man.[207] When the single ruler is good and able, monarchy is the best form of government; when he is a selfish autocrat we have tyranny, which is the worst form of government. An aristocratic government may be beneficial for a time, but aristocracies tend to deteriorate. "Noble character is now seldom found among those of noble birth, most of whom are good for nothing. . . . Highly gifted families often degenerate into maniacs, as, for example, the descendants of Alcibiades and the elder Dionysius; those that are stable often degenerate into fools and dullards, like the descendants of Cimon, Pericles, and Socrates."[208] When aristocracy decays it is usually replaced by a plutocratic oligarchy, which is government by wealth. This is better than the despotism of a king or a mob; but it gives power to men whose souls have been cramped by the petty calculations of trade, or the villainous taking of interest,[209] and issues, as like as not, in the conscienceless exploitation of the poor.[210]

Democracy—which here means government by the *demos*, by the common citizen—is just as dangerous as oligarchy, for it is based upon the passing victory of the poor over the rich in the struggle for power, and leads to a suicidal chaos. Democracy is at its best when it is dominated by peasant proprietors; it is at its worst when ruled by the urban rabble of mechanics and tradesmen.[211] It is true that the "multitude judge of many things better than any one person, and that from their numbers they are less liable to corruption, as water is from its quantity."[212] But government requires special ability and knowledge; and "it is impossible for one who lives the life of a mechanic or hired servant to acquire excellence"[213]—i.e., good character, training, and judgment. All men are created unequal; "equality is just, but only between equals";[214] and the upper classes will as readily make seditions if an unnatural equality is enforced, as the lower classes will rebel when inequality is unnaturally extreme.*[215] When a democracy is dominated by the lower classes the rich are taxed to provide funds for the poor. "The poor receive it and again want the same supply, while the giving it is like pouring water into a sieve."[217] And yet a wise conservative will not let people starve. "The true patriot in a democracy ought to take care that the majority are not too poor . . . he should endeavor that they may enjoy perpetual plenty; and as this is also advantageous to the rich, what can be saved out of the public money should be divided among the poor in such quantity as may enable each of them to buy a little field."[218]

* Even slavery is legitimate, Aristotle thinks: as it is right that the mind should rule the body, so it is just that those who excel in intelligence should rule those who excel only in strength.[216]

Having thus given back almost as much as he took away, Aristotle offers some modest recommendations, not for a utopia but for a moderately better society.

> We proceed to inquire what form of government and manner of life is best for communities in general, not adapting it to that superior virtue which is above the reach of the common people, or that education which only every advantage of nature and fortune can furnish, nor to those imaginary plans which may be formed at pleasure; but to that mode of life which the greater part of mankind can attain to, and that government which most cities may establish.[219] . . . Whoever would establish a government upon community of goods ought to consult the experience of many years, which would plainly enough inform him whether such a scheme is useful; for almost all things have already been found out.[220] . . . What is common to many is taken least care of; for all men have greater regard for what is their own than for what they possess in common with others.[221] . . . It is necessary to begin by assuming a principle of general application, viz., that the part of the state which desires the continuance of the new constitution ought to be stronger than that which does not.[222] . . . It is plain, then, that those states are best instituted wherein the middle classes are a larger and more formidable part than either the rich or the poor. . . . Whenever the number of those in the middle state has been too small, those who were the more numerous, whether the rich or the poor, always overpowered them, and assumed to themselves the administration of public affairs. . . . When either the rich get the better of the poor, or the poor of the rich, neither of them will establish a free state.[223]

To avoid these illiberal dictatorships from above or below, Aristotle proposes a "mixed constitution" or "timocracy"—a combination of aristocracy and democracy, in which the suffrage will be restricted to landowners, and a strong middle class will be the balance wheel and pivot of power. "The land ought to be divided into two parts, one of which should belong to the community in general, the other to the individuals separately."[224] All the citizens will own land; they "are to eat at public tables in certain companies"; and only they shall vote or bear arms. They will constitute a small minority—ten thousand at most—of the population. "None of them should be permitted to exercise any mechanic employment or live by trade, for these are ignoble, and destroy excellence."[225] But "neither should they be husbandmen; . . . the husbandmen should be a separate order of people"—presumably slaves. The citizens will elect the public officials, and hold each to account at the end of his term. "Laws, properly enacted, should define the issue of all cases as far as possible, and leave as little as possible to the discretion of the judges. . . ."[226] "It is better that law should rule than any individual. . . . He who entrusts any man with the supreme power gives it to a wild beast, for such his appetites sometimes make him; passion influences those who are in power, even the very best of men; but law is reason without desire."[227] The state so constructed shall regulate property, industry, marriage, the family, education, morals, music, literature, and art. "It is even more necessary to take care that the increase of the people should not exceed a certain number . . . to neglect this is to bring certain poverty upon the citizens."[228] "Nothing imperfect or maimed shall be brought up."[229] Out of these sound foundations will grow the flowers of civilization and tranquillity. "Since the highest virtue is intelligence, the pre-eminent duty of the state is not to train the citizens to military excellence, but to educate them for the right use of peace."[230]

It is unnecessary to sit in judgment upon Aristotle's work. Never before, so far as we know, had anyone reared so impressive an edifice of thought. When a man covers a vast field many errors may be forgiven him if the result adds to our comprehension of life. Aristotle's faults—or those of the volumes that we perhaps wrongly count as the considered product of his pen—are too obvious to need retailing. He is a logician, but is quite capable of bad reasoning; he lays down the laws of rhetoric and poetry, but his books are a jungle of disorder, and no breath of imagination stirs their dusty leaves. And yet, if we penetrate this verbiage we find a wealth of wisdom, and an intellectual industry that opened many paths in the country of the mind. He did not quite found biology, or constitutional history, or literary criticism—there are no beginnings—but he did more for them than any other ancient whom we know. To him science and philosophy owe a multitude of terms that in their Latin forms have facilitated learned communication and thought—*principle*, *maxim*, *faculty*, *mean*, *category*, *energy*, *motive*, *habit*, *end*. . . . He was, as Pater called him, "the first of the Schoolmen";[231] and his long ascendancy over philosophical method and speculation suggests the fertility of his ideas and the depth of his insight. His treatises on ethics and politics stand above every rival in fame and influence. When all deductions have been made he still remains "the master of those who know," an encouraging testimony to the elastic range of the human intellect, and a comforting inspiration to those who labor to bring man's scattered knowledge together into perspective and understanding.

CHAPTER XXII

Alexander

I. THE SOUL OF A CONQUEROR

THE intellectual career of Aristotle, after he left his royal pupil, paralleled the military career of Alexander; both lives were expressions of conquest and synthesis. Perhaps it was the philosopher who instilled into the mind of the youth that ardor for unity which gave some grandeur to Alexander's victories; more probably that resolve descended to him from his father's ambitions, and was fused into a passion by his maternal blood. If we would understand Alexander we must always remember that he bore in his veins the drunken vigor of Philip and the barbaric intensity of Olympias. Furthermore, Olympias claimed descent from Achilles. Therefore the *Iliad* had a special fascination for Alexander; when he crossed the Hellespont he was, in his interpretation, retracing the steps of Achilles; when he conquered Hither Asia he was completing the work that his ancestor had begun at Troy. Through all his campaigns he carried with him a copy of the *Iliad* annotated by Aristotle; often he placed it under his pillow at night beside his dagger, as if to symbolize the instrument and the goal.

Leonidas, an austere Molossian, trained the boy's body, Lysimachus taught him letters, Aristotle tried to form his mind. Philip was anxious that Alexander should study philosophy, "so that," he said, "you may not do a great many things of the sort that I am sorry to have done."[1] To some extent Aristotle made a Hellene of him; through all his life Alexander admired Greek literature, and envied Greek civilization. To two Greeks sitting with him at the wild banquet at which he slew Cleitus he said, "Do you not feel like demigods among savages when you are sitting in company with these Macedonians?"[2]

Physically, Alexander was an ideal youth. He was good in every sport: a swift runner, a dashing horseman, a brilliant fencer, a practiced bowman, a fearless hunter. His friends wished him to enter the foot races at Olympia; he answered that he would be willing, if his opponents were kings. When all others had failed to tame the giant horse Bucephalus, Alexander succeeded; seeing which, says Plutarch, Philip acclaimed him with prophetic words: "My son, Macedonia is too small for you; seek out a larger empire, worthier of you."[3] Even on the march his wild energy found vent in shooting arrows at passing objects, or in alighting from, and remounting, his chariot at full speed. When a campaign lagged he would go hunting and, unaided and on foot, face any animal in combat; once, after an encounter with a lion, he was pleased to hear it said that he had fought as though it had been a duel to decide which of the two should be king.[4] He liked hard work and dangerous enterprises, and could not bear to rest. He laughed at some of his generals, who had so many servants that they themselves could find nothing to do. "I wonder," he told them, "that you with your experience do not know that those who work sleep more soundly than those for whom other people work. Have you yet to learn that the greatest need after our victories is to avoid the vices and the weaknesses of those whom we have conquered?"[5] He grudged the time given to sleep, and said that "sleep and the act of generation chiefly made him sensible that he was mortal."[6] He was abstemious in eating, and, until his last years, in drinking, though he loved to linger with his friends over a goblet of wine. He despised rich foods, and refused the famous chefs who were offered him, saying that a night march gave him a good appetite for breakfast, and a light breakfast gave him an appetite for dinner.[7] Perhaps in consequence of these habits his complexion was remarkably clear, and his body and breath, says Plutarch, "were so fragrant as to perfume the clothes that he wore."[8] Discounting the flattery of those who painted or carved or engraved his likeness, we know from his contemporaries that he was handsome beyond all precedents for a king, with expressive features, soft blue eyes, and luxuriant auburn hair. He helped to introduce into Europe the custom of shaving the beard, on the ground that whiskers offered too ready a handle for an enemy to grasp.[8a] In this little item, perhaps, lay his greatest influence upon history.

Mentally he was an ardent student, who was too soon consumed with responsibilities to reach maturity of mind. Like so many men of action, he mourned that he could not be also a thinker. "He had," says Plutarch, "a violent thirst and passion for learning, which increased as time went on. . . . He was a lover of all kinds of reading and knowledge," and it was his delight, after a day of marching or fighting, to sit up half the night conversing with scholars and scientists. "For my part," he wrote to Aristotle, "I had rather surpass others in the knowledge of what is excellent, than in the extent of my power and dominion."[9] Possibly at Aristotle's suggestion he sent a commission to explore the sources of the Nile, and he gave funds generously for a variety of scientific inquiries. Whether a longer life would have brought him to Caesar's clear intelligence, or the subtle understanding of Napoleon, is to be doubted. Royalty found him at twenty, after which warfare and administration absorbed him; in consequence he remained uneducated to the end. He could talk brilliantly, but fell into a hundred errors when he wandered from politics and war. With all his campaigns he seems never to have gained such acquaintance with geography as the science of his time could have given him. He rose at times above the narrowness of dogma, but remained to the last a slave to superstition. He put great confidence in the soothsayers and astrologers that crowded his court; before the battle of Arbela he spent the night performing magic ceremonies with the magician Aristander, and offered sacrifices to the god Fear; he who faced all men and beasts with a very ecstasy of courage was "easily alarmed by portents and prodigies," even to changing important plans.[10] He could lead many thousands of men, could conquer and rule millions, but he could not control his own temper. He never learned to recognize his own faults or limitations, but allowed his judgment to be soaked and drowned in praise. He lived in a frenzy of excitement and glory, and so loved war that his mind never knew an hour of peace.

His moral character hovered between similar contradictions. He was at bottom sentimental and emotional, and had, we are told, "melting eyes"; he was moved sometimes beside himself by poetry and music; he played the harp with great feeling in his early youth. Teased about this by Philip, he abandoned the instrument, and thereafter, as if to overcome himself, refused to listen to any but martial airs.[11] Sexually he was almost virtuous, not so much on principle as by preoccupation. His incessant activity, his long marches and frequent battles, his complex plans and administrative burdens, used up his resources, and left him little appetite for love. He took many wives, but as a sacrifice to statesmanship; he was gallant to ladies, but preferred the company of his generals. When his aides brought a beautiful woman to his tent late at night he asked her, "Why at this time?" "I had to wait," she replied, "to get my husband to bed." Alexander dismissed her, and rebuked his servants, saying that because of them he had narrowly escaped becoming an adulterer.[12] He had many of the qualities of a homosexual, and loved Hephaestion to madness; but when Theodorus of Taras offered to sell him two boys of great beauty he sent the Tarentine packing, and begged his friends to tell him what baseness of soul he had shown that anyone should make such a proposal to him.[13] He gave to friendship the tenderness and solicitude that most men give to love. No statesman known to us, much less any general, ever surpassed him in simple trustfulness and warmheartedness, in open sincerity of affection and purpose, or in generosity even to acquaintances and enemies.[14] Plutarch remarks "upon what slight occasions he would write letters to serve friends." He endeared himself to his soldiers by his kindliness; he risked their lives, but not heedlessly; and he seemed to feel all their wounds. As Caesar forgave Brutus and Cicero, and Napoleon Fouché and Talleyrand, so Alexander forgave Harpalus, the treasurer who had absconded with his funds and had returned to beg forgiveness; the young conqueror reappointed him treasurer to all men's astonishment, and apparently with good results.[15] At Tarsus, in 333, Alexander being ill, his physician Philip offered him a purgative drink. At that moment a letter was brought to the King from Parmenio, warning him that Philip had been bribed by Darius to poison him. Alexander handed the letter to Philip, and as the latter read it, Alexander drank the draught—with no ill effect. His reputation for generosity helped him in his wars; many of the enemy allowed themselves to be taken prisoner, and cities, not fearing to be sacked, opened their gates at his coming.—Nevertheless, the Molossian tigress was in him, and it was his bitter fate to be ruined by his occasional paroxysms of cruelty. Having taken Gaza by siege and assault, and infuriated by its long resistance, Alexander caused the feet of Batis, its heroic commandant, to be bored, and brazen rings passed through them; then, intoxicated with memories of Achilles, he dragged the now dead Persian, tied by cords to the royal chariot, at full speed around the city.[16] His increasing resort to drink as a means of quieting his nerves led him more and more frequently, in his last years, to outbreaks of blind ferocity, followed by brooding fits of violent remorse.

One quality in him dominated all the rest—ambition. As a youth he had fretted over Philip's victories: "Father," he complained to his friends, "will get everything done before we are ready, and will leave me and you no chance of doing anything great and important."[17] In his passion for achievement he assumed every task, and faced every risk. At Chaeronea he was the first man to charge the Theban Sacred Band; at the Granicus he indulged to the full what he called his "eagerness for encountering danger."[18] This, too, became an uncontrollable passion; the sound and sight of battle intoxicated him; he forgot then his duties as a general, and plunged ahead into the thickest of the fight; time and again his soldiers, fearful of losing him, had to plead with him to go to the rear. He was not a great general; he was a brave soldier whose obstinate perseverance marched on, with boyish heedlessness of impossibilities, to unprecedented victories. He supplied the inspiration; probably his generals, who were able men, contributed organization, training, tactics, and strategy. He led his troops by the brilliance of his imagination, the fire of his unstudied oratory, the readiness and sincerity with which he shared their hardships and griefs. Without question he was a good administrator: he ruled with kindness and firmness the wide domain which his arms had won; he was loyal to the agreements which he signed with commanders and cities; and he tolerated no oppression of his subjects by his appointees. Amid all the excitement and chaos of his campaigns he kept clearly at the center of his thoughts the great purpose that even his death would not defeat: the unification of all the eastern Mediterranean world into one cultural whole, dominated and elevated by the expanding civilization of Greece.

II. THE PATHS OF GLORY

On his accession Alexander found himself at the head of a tottering empire. The northern tribes in Thrace and Illyria revolted; Aetolia, Acarnania, Phocis, Elis, Argolis renounced their allegiance; the Ambraciotes expelled the Macedonian garrison; Artaxerxes III boasted that he had instigated the killing of Philip, and that Persia now had nothing to fear from the immature stripling of twenty who had succeeded to the throne. When the glad tidings of Philip's death reached Athens, Demosthenes donned festal garb, placed a garland of flowers upon his head, and moved in the Assembly that a crown of honor should be voted to the assassin Pausanias.[19] Within Macedonia a dozen factions conspired against the young King's life.

Alexander rose to the situation with a decisive energy that ended all internal opposition, and set the tempo of his career. Having arrested and decapitated the chief plotters at home, he marched south into Greece (336), and within a few days reached Thebes. The Greek states hastened to renew their allegiance; Athens sent him a profuse apology, voted him two crowns, and conferred upon him divine honors. Alexander, appeased, declared all dictatorships abolished in Greece, and decreed that each city should live in freedom according to its own laws. The Amphictyonic Council confirmed him in all the rights and honors that it had given to Philip; and a congress of all Greek states except Sparta, meeting at Corinth, proclaimed him captain general of the Greeks, and promised to contribute men and supplies for the Asiatic campaign. Alexander returned to Pella, put the capital in order, and then marched north to suppress the rebellion of the barbarian tribes (335). With Napoleonic swiftness he led his troops as far as the modern Bucharest, and planted his standards upon the northern bank of the Danube. Then, hearing that the Illyrians were advancing upon Macedonia, he marched two hundred miles through Serbia, surprised the invaders in the rear, defeated them, and drove the remnant back to their mountains.

But in the meantime a rumor had stirred Athens that Alexander had been killed in fighting on the Danube. Demosthenes called for a war of independence, and felt justified in accepting large sums from Persia to further his plans. At his instigation Thebes revolted, killed the Macedonian officials left there by Alexander, and besieged the Macedonian garrison in the Cadmeia. Athens sent help to Thebes, and invited Greece and Persia to join in an alliance against Macedon. Alexander, furious over what seemed to him not a passion for freedom but the crudest ingratitude and treachery, marched his weary troops down again into Greece. Reaching Thebes after thirteen days, he defeated the army sent out against him. He left the fate of the defenseless city to her ancient enemies—Plataea, Orchomenos, Thespiae, and Phocis; they voted that Thebes should be burned to the ground, and her inhabitants sold as slaves. Hoping to give other rebels a lesson, Alexander signed the order, but stipulated that the victorious troops should spare the home of Pindar, and the lives of priests and priestesses, and of all Thebans who could prove that they had opposed the revolt. Later he looked back with shame upon this violent revenge, and "was sure to grant without the least difficulty whatsoever any Theban asked of him."[20] He atoned in part by his leniency with Athens; he forgave her violation of the pledges made to him a year before, and did not press his demand for the surrender of Demosthenes and the other anti-Macedonian leaders. To the end of his life he maintained an attitude of respect and affection for Athens: he dedicated on the Acropolis various spoils from his Asiatic victories, sent back to Athens the Tyrannicide statues that Xerxes had taken away, and remarked, after an arduous campaign, "O ye Athenians, will you believe what dangers I incur to merit your praise?"[21]

Having received again the allegiance of all the Greek states except Sparta, Alexander returned to Macedonia, and prepared for the invasion of Asia. He found his state treasury almost empty, with a deficit of five hundred talents ($3,000,000) as a legacy from Philip's reign.[22] He borrowed eight hundred talents, and set out to conquer not the world but his debts. He had hoped to fight Persia as the champion of all Hellas, but he knew that half of Greece was praying that he would soon be killed. It was reported that the Persians could muster a million men; Alexander's expeditionary force did not exceed thirty thousand infantry and five thousand cavalry.

Nevertheless the new Achilles, leaving twelve thousand soldiers under Antipater to guard Macedonia and watch Greece, set out in 334 upon the most daring and romantic enterprise in the history of kings. He would live eleven years more, but would never see home or Europe again. While his army crossed the Hellespont from Sestos to Abydos, he himself chose to land at Cape Sigeum, and retrace what he believed to have been Agamemnon's path to Troy. At every step he quoted to his comrades passages from the *Iliad*, which he knew almost by heart. He anointed the reputed tomb of Achilles, crowned it with garlands, and ran naked around it according to the custom of antiquity. "Happy Achilles!" he exclaimed, "to have had in life so faithful a friend, and, after his death, so famous a poet to celebrate him."[23] He vowed now to carry through to a successful end that long struggle, between Europe and Asia, which had begun at Troy.

It is not necessary to our purpose to tell again the story of his victories. He met the first Persian contingent at the river Granicus, and overwhelmed it. There Cleitus saved his life by severing the arm of the Persian who was about to strike Alexander from behind; a whimsical student might build upon such events an accidental interpretation of history. After giving his men a rest he marched down into Ionia, offering the Greek cities democratic self-government under his protectorate. Most of them opened their gates without resistance. At Issus he met the main force of the Persians, 600,000 men, under Darius III. Once more he won by using his cavalry for attack, his infantry for defense. Darius fled, leaving his purse and his family behind him, to be treated the one with gratitude, the other with chivalry. After peaceably taking Damascus and Sidon Alexander laid siege to Tyre, which was harboring a large Phoenician squadron in the pay of Persia. The ancient city resisted so long that when at last he captured it Alexander lost his head and allowed his men to massacre eight thousand Tyrians, and to sell thirty thousand as slaves. Jerusalem surrendered quietly, and was well treated; Gaza fought till every man in the city was dead and every woman raped.

The triumphant march of the Macedonians was resumed through the Sinai desert into Egypt, where, when he showed a tactful respect for the country's gods, Alexander was welcomed as a divinely sent liberator from Persian rule. Knowing that religion is stronger than politics, he crossed another desert to the oasis of Siwa, and paid his respects to the god Ammon—his very father if Olympias could be believed. The pliant priests crowned him Pharaoh with the ancient rites, and so eased the way for the Ptolemaic dynasty. Returning to the Delta, Alexander conceived or approved the idea of building a new capital at one of the Nile's many mouths; perhaps the Greek merchants at near-by Naucratis suggested it as providing a more convenient depot for the enlarged Greek trade that might now be expected between Egypt and Greece. He marked out the orbit of the walls of Alexandria, the outline of the principal streets, and the sites for temples to the Egyptian and Grecian gods; further details he left to his architect, Dinocrates.*

Marching back into Asia, he met the vast polyglot army of Darius at Gaugamela, near Arbela, and was dismayed by their multitude; he knew that one defeat would cancel all his victories. His soldiers comforted him: "Be of good cheer, Sire; do not fear the great number of the enemy, for they will not be able to stand the very smell of goat that clings to us."[25] He spent the night in reconnoitering the ground on which he was to give battle, and in offering sacrifices to the gods. His victory was decisive. The disorderly hosts of Darius could make no headway against the phalanxes, and knew not how to defend themselves against the swift and incalculable dashes of the Macedonian cavalry; they broke and fled, and Darius was not the last to go. While Darius' generals assassinated him as a coward, Alexander received the submission of Babylon, partook of its wealth, distributed some of it to his soldiers, but charmed the city by making obeisance to its gods, and decreeing the restoration of its sacred shrines. By the end of the year (331) he had reached Susa, whose population, still remembering the ancient glory of Elam, welcomed him as a deliverer. He protected the city from pillage, but comforted his troops by dividing among them some of the fifty thousand talents ($300,000,000) that he found in Darius' vaults. To the people of Plataea he sent a substantial sum because they had so bravely resisted the Persians in 480; and to the Greek cities of Asia he appears to have remitted the "donations" that he had elicited from them at the outset of his campaign.[26] And he announced proudly to the Greeks of the world that they were now completely free from Persian rule.

Hardly stopping to rest at Susa, he marched over mountains in the depth of winter to seize Persepolis; and so rapidly did he move that he was in Darius' palace before the Persians could conceal the royal treasury. Here again his good judgment left him, and he burned the magnificent city to the ground. His soldiers looted the houses, ravaged the women, and killed

* Dinocrates had pleased Alexander by proposing to carve Mt. Athos—six thousand feet high—into a figure of Alexander standing waist deep in the sea, holding a city in one hand and a harbor in the other.[24] The project was never carried out.

the men. Perhaps they had been infuriated by seeing, on their approach to the town, eight hundred Greeks who, for various reasons, had suffered mutilation at the hands of Persians by the cutting off of legs, arms, or ears, or the gouging out of the eyes. Alexander, moved to tears by the sight, gave them lands, and assigned dependents to work for them.

Still insatiate, he attempted now what Cyrus the Great had failed to accomplish—the subjugation of the tribes that hovered on the eastern borders of Persia. Perhaps in his simple geography he hoped to find, beyond that mystic East, the ocean that would serve as a natural frontier for his conquered realm. Entering Sogdiana, he came upon a village inhabited by the descendants of those Branchidae who, in 480, had surrendered to Xerxes the treasures of their temple near Miletus. Fevered with the thought that he was revenging the pillaged god, he ordered all the inhabitants slain, including the women and children—visiting the sins of the fathers upon the fifth generation. His campaign in Sogdiana, Ariana, and Bactriana was bloody and bootless; he achieved some victories, found some gold, and left enemies everywhere behind him. Near Bokhara his men captured Bessus, who had slain Darius. Alexander, suddenly making himself the avenger of the Great King, had Bessus whipped almost to death, had his nose and ears cut off, and then sent him to Ecbatana, where he was executed by having his arms tied to one, and his legs to the other, of two trees that had been drawn together by ropes, so that when the ropes were cut the trees pulled the body to pieces.[27] At every new remove from Greece Alexander was becoming less and less a Greek, more and more a barbarian king.

The year 327 found him passing over the Himalayas into India. Vanity conspired with curiosity to lead him into such distant territory; his generals advised against it, his army obeyed him unwillingly. Crossing the Indus, he defeated King Porus, and announced that he would continue to the Ganges. But his soldiers refused to go farther. He pled with them, and for three days, like a scion of Achilles, pouted in his tent; but they had had enough. Sadly he turned back, loath to face west again, and forced his way through hostile tribes with such personal bravery that his soldiers wept at their inability to realize all his dreams. He was the first to scale the walls of the Mallians; after he and two others had leaped into the city the ladders broke, and they found themselves alone amidst the enemy. Alexander fought till he sank exhausted by his wounds. Meanwhile his troops had made their way into the town, and soldier after soldier sacrificed his life to protect the fallen King. When the battle was over Alexander was carried to his tent, and his veterans kissed his garments as he passed. After three months of convalescence he renewed his march along the Indus, and at last reached the Indian Ocean. There he sent on part of his forces by water under Nearchus, who skillfully accomplished the long voyage in unfamiliar seas. Alexander himself led the rest of his army northwest along the coast of India and through the desert of Gedrosia (Baluchistan), where the sufferings of his men rivaled those of Napoleon's army on the return from Moscow. Heat killed thousands, thirst killed more. A little water was found, and was brought to Alexander, but he deliberately poured it out upon the ground.[28] When the remnants of his force reached Susa some ten thousand had died, and Alexander was half insane.

III. THE DEATH OF A GOD

He had now spent nine years in Asia, and he had changed the continent by his victories less than it had transformed him by its ways. He had been told by Aristotle to treat Greeks as freemen, "barbarians" as slaves. But he had been surprised to find among the Persian aristocrats a degree of refinement and good manners not often seen in the turbulent democracies of Greece; he admired the manner in which the Great Kings had organized their empire, and wondered how his rough Macedonians could replace such governors. He concluded that he could give some permanence to his conquests only by reconciling the Persian nobles to his leadership, and using them in administrative posts. More and more charmed by his new subjects, he abandoned the idea of ruling over them as a Macedonian, and conceived himself as a Greco-Persian emperor governing a realm in which Persians and Greeks would be on an equal footing, and would peaceably mingle their culture and their blood. The long quarrel of Europe and Asia would end in a wedding feast.

Already thousands of his soldiers had married native women, or were living with them; should he not do likewise, marry the daughter of Darius, and reconcile the nations by begetting a king who would unite both dynasties in his veins? He had already married Roxana, a Bactrian princess; but this was a negligible impediment. He broached the plan to his officers, and suggested that they, too, should take Persian wives. They smiled at his hopes of uniting the two nations, but they had been a long time away from home, and the Persian ladies were beautiful. So in one great nuptial at Susa (324) Alexander married Statira, daughter of Darius III, and Parysatis, daughter of Artaxerxes III, attaching himself in this way to both branches of Persian royalty, while eighty of his officers took Persian brides. Thousands of similar marriages were soon afterward celebrated among the soldiers. Alexander gave each officer a substantial dowry, and paid the debts of the marrying soldiers—which amounted (if we may believe Arrian) to twenty thousand talents ($120,000,000).[29] To further this union of peoples he opened lands in Mesopotamia and Persia to Greek colonists, thereby reducing the pressure of population in some of the Greek states, and mitigating the class war; now began those Hellenized Asiatic cities which were to be a vital part of the Seleucid Empire. At the same time he drafted thirty thousand Persian youths, had them educated on Greek lines, and taught them the Greek manual of war.

Possibly his wives had something to do with his rapid adoption of Oriental ways; possibly it was a failure of modesty, or a part of his plan. "In Persia," says Plutarch, "he first put on the barbaric" (i.e., foreign) "dress, perhaps with the view of making the work of civilizing the Persians easier, as nothing gains more upon men than a conformity to their customs. . . . However, he followed not the Median fashion . . . but taking a middle way between the Persian mode and the Macedonian, so contrived his habit that it was not so flaunting as the one, and yet more pompous and magnificent than the other."[30] His soldiers saw in this change the conquest of Alexander by the Orient; they felt that they had lost him, and they mournfully missed the signs of solicitude and affection which he had once showered upon them. The Persians made every obeisance to him, and flattered him to his heart's content; the Macedonians, themselves softened by Oriental luxury, grumbled at the tasks that he laid upon them, forgot his beneficence, murmured of desertion, and even plotted against his life. He began to prefer the society of the Persian grandees.

His culminating apostasy, or diplomacy, was his announcement of his own divinity. In 324 he sent word to all the Greek states except Macedonia (where the insult to Philip might have aroused resentment) that he wished hereafter to be publicly recognized as the son of Zeus-Ammon. Most of the states complied, feeling it to be merely a form; even the obstinate Spartans agreed, saying, "Let Alexander be a god if he wants to." It was not so much for a man to be a god in the Greek sense of the term; the chasm between humanity and deity was not as wide then as it was to become in modern theology; several Greeks had overleaped it, like Hippodameia, Oedipus, Achilles, Iphigenia, and Helen. The Egyptians had always thought of their Pharaohs as gods; if Alexander had neglected to rank himself similarly the Egyptians might have been disturbed by so bold a violation of precedent. The priests at Siwa, Didyma, and Babylon, who were believed to have special sources of information in this field, had all assured him of his divine origin. That (as Grote thought[31]) Alexander actually believed himself to be a god in a more than metaphorical sense is quite unlikely. It is true that after his self-deification he became increasingly irritable and arrogant; that he sat on a golden throne, wore sacred vestments, and sometimes adorned his head with the horns of Ammon.[32] But when he was not playing his divinity for world stakes he smiled at his own honors. Being injured by an arrow, he remarked to some friends, "This, you see, is blood, and not such ichor as flows from the wounds of the Immortals."[33] That he had not taken too seriously his mother's tale of the thunderbolt appears from his flaming anger at Attalus' imputations on his birth, and his remark about the need of sleep as distinguishing man from the gods. Even Olympias laughed when she heard that Alexander had made her legend official. "When," she asked, "will Alexander stop slandering me to Hera?"[34] Despite his godhead Alexander continued to offer sacrifice to the gods—an unheard-of thing for a divinity. Plutarch and Arrian, able to judge the matter as Greeks, took it for granted that Alexander deified himself as a means to easier rule over a superstitious and heterogeneous population.[35] Doubtless he felt that the task of unifying two hostile worlds would be facilitated by the reverence which the common people would give him if his claims to divinity were accepted by the upper classes. Perhaps, indeed, he thought to overcome the disruptive diversity of faiths in his empire by providing, in his own person, the beginning of a sacred myth and a common unifying faith.*

The Macedonian officers could not fathom Alexander's policy. The Greek spirit had touched them to the point of mental emancipation, but not to the point of philosophical toleration; they found it humiliating to prostrate themselves, as he now demanded, in approaching the King. One of his bravest officers, Philotas, son of his ablest and most favored general, Parmenio, entered into a conspiracy to kill the new god. Alexander got wind of it, had Philotas arrested, and wrung from him by torture a confession implicating his own father. Philotas was forced to repeat the confession before the soldiers, who, in accord with their custom in such cases, at once stoned him to death; Parmenio was executed by messenger as prob-

* Lucian gives the ancient view in one of his *Dialogues of the Dead:* "*Philip.* You cannot deny that you are my son, Alexander; if you had been Ammon's son you would not have died. *Alex.* I knew all the time that you were my father. I only accepted the statement of the oracle because I thought it was good policy. . . . When the barbarians thought they had a god to deal with, they gave up the struggle; which made their conquest an easy matter."[36]

ably guilty, and in any case a presumptive enemy. From that moment to the end, the relations between Alexander and his army became increasingly strained—the troops ever more discontent, the King ever more suspicious, severe, and lonely.

His solitary exaltation and the growing multitude of his cares inclined him to seek forgetfulness in heavy draughts of wine. At a banquet in Samarkand Cleitus, who had saved his life at the Granicus, drank himself into such candor as to tell Alexander that his victories had been won by his soldiers rather than by him, and that Philip's achievement had been much greater. Alexander, equally drunk, rose to strike him, but Ptolemy Lagus (soon to be ruler of Egypt) hurried Cleitus away. Cleitus, however, had more to say; he escaped from Ptolemy, and went back to finish his tirade. Alexander hurled a lance at him and killed him. Overcome with remorse, the King secluded himself for three days, refused to eat, fell into hysteria, and tried to end his own life. Soon afterward Hermolaus, a page whom Alexander had unjustly punished, formed another conspiracy against him. The boy was apprehended, and under torture made a confession incriminating Aristotle's nephew Callisthenes. The latter, who was accompanying the expedition as official historian, had already offended the King by refusing to prostrate himself before him, openly criticizing him for his Oriental ways, and boasting that Alexander would be known to posterity only through Callisthenes the historian. Alexander had him put in prison, where, seven months later, he died.* This incident put an end to the friendship between Alexander and Aristotle, who had for years been risking his life to defend Alexander's cause in Athens.

In the end the discontent in the army verged on open mutiny. When the King announced that he would send back to Macedon the oldest of the soldiers, each richly paid for his services,† he was shocked to hear many muttering that they wished he would dismiss them all, since, being a god, he had no need of men to realize his purposes. He ordered the leaders of the sedition executed, and then addressed to his troops an affecting (but probably apocryphal) speech[39] in which he reminded them of all that they had done for him, and he for them, and asked which of them could show more scars than he, whose body bore the marks of every weapon used in war. Finally he gave them all permission to go home: "Go back and report

---

* There are conflicting stories about his guilt and his death.[37] He left three main works: *Hellenica*, a history of Greece from 387 to 337; a *History of the Sacred War*, and a *History of Alexander*.

† Each of them, Arrian assures us, received a talent in addition to his pay—which continued till he reached his home.[38]

that you deserted your king and left him to the protection of conquered foreigners." Then he retired to his rooms, and refused to see anyone. His soldiers, stricken with remorse, came and lay down before the palace, saying that they would not leave till he had forgiven them and reaccepted them into his army. When at last he appeared they broke into tears and insisted on kissing him; and after being reconciled with him they went back to their camp shouting a song of thanksgiving.

Deceived by this show of affection, Alexander dreamed now of further campaigns and victories; he planned the subjugation of hidden Arabia, sent a mission to explore the Caspian regions, and thought of conquering Europe to the Pillars of Hercules. But his strong frame had been weakened by exposure and drink, and his spirit by the conspiracies of his officers and the mutinies of his men. While the army was in Ecbatana his dearest companion, Hephaestion, fell sick and died. Alexander had loved him so much that when Darius' queen, entering the conqueror's tent, bowed first to Hephaestion, thinking him Alexander, the young King said, graciously, "Hephaestion is also Alexander"[40]—as if to say that he and Hephaestion were one. The two often shared one tent, and drank from one cup; in battle they fought side by side. Now the King, feeling that half of him had been torn away, broke down in uncontrolled grief. He lay for hours upon the corpse, weeping; he cut off his hair in mourning, and for days refused to take food. He sentenced to death the physician who had left the sick youth's side to attend the public games. He ordered a gigantic funeral pile to be erected in Hephaestion's memory, at a cost, we are told, of ten thousand talents ($60,000,000), and sent to inquire of the oracle of Ammon whether it was permitted to worship Hephaestion as a god. In his next campaign a whole tribe was slain, at his orders, as a sacrifice to Hephaestion's ghost. The thought that Achilles had not long survived Patroclus haunted him like a sentence of death.

Back in Babylon, he abandoned himself more and more to drink. One night, reveling with his officers, he proposed a drinking match. Promachus quaffed twelve quarts of wine, and won the prize, a talent; three days later he died. Shortly afterward, at another banquet, Alexander drained a goblet containing six quarts of wine. On the next night he drank heavily again; and cold weather suddenly setting in, he caught a fever, and took to his bed. The fever raged for ten days, during which Alexander continued to give orders to his army and his fleet. On the eleventh day he died, being in the thirty-third year of his age (323). When his generals asked him to whom he left his empire he answered, "To the strongest."[41]

Like most great men he had been unable to find a successor worthy of him, and his work fell unfinished from his hands. Even so his achievement was not only immense, but far more permanent than has usually been supposed. Acting as the agent of historical necessity, he put an end to the era of city-states, and, by sacrificing a substantial measure of local freedom, created a larger system of stability and order than Europe had yet known. His conception of government as absolutism using religion to impose peace upon diverse nations dominated Europe until the rise of nationalism and democracy in modern times. He broke down the barriers between Greek and "barbarian," and prepared for the cosmopolitanism of the Hellenistic age; he opened Hither Asia to Greek colonization, and established Greek settlements as far east as Bactria; he united the eastern Mediterranean world into one great web of commerce, liberating and stimulating trade. He brought Greek literature, philosophy, and art to Asia, and died before he could realize that he had also made a pathway for the religious victory of the East over the West. His adoption of Oriental dress and ways was the beginning of Asia's revenge.

It was just as well that he died at his zenith; added years would almost surely have brought him disillusionment. Perhaps if he had lived he might have been deepened by defeat and suffering, and might have learned—as he was beginning—to love statesmanship more than war. But he had undertaken too much; the strain of holding his swollen realm together, and watching all its parts, was probably disordering his brilliant mind. Energy is only half of genius; the other half is harness; and Alexander was all energy. We miss in him—though we have no right to expect—the calm maturity of Caesar, or the subtle wisdom of Augustus. We admire him as we admire Napoleon, because he stood alone against half the world, and because he encourages us with the thought of the incredible power that lies potential in the individual soul. And we feel a natural sympathy for him, despite his superstitions and his cruelties, because we know that he was at least a generous and affectionate youth, as well as incomparably able and brave; that he fought against a maddening heritage of barbarism in his blood; and that through all battles and all bloodshed he kept before his eyes the dream of bringing the light of Athens to a larger world.

IV. THE END OF AN AGE

When the news of his death reached Greece, revolts against the Macedonian authority broke out everywhere. Theban exiles in Athens organized a force of patriots, and besieged the Macedonian garrison in the Cadmeia. In Athens itself, where many had prayed for an end to Alexander, the anti-Macedonian party, feeling that its prayers had been heard, crowned themselves with garlands and feasted over the death of him whom they had courted as a god—singing, says Plutarch, "triumphant songs of victory, as if by their own valor they had vanquished him."[42]

For a moment Demosthenes was in his glory. He had not fared well during Alexander's campaigns: he had been convicted of accepting a heavy bribe from Harpalus, and had been flung into jail; he had been allowed to escape, and had lived nine months of fretting exile in Troezen. Now he was recalled, and was sent as envoy to the Peloponnesus to raise allies for Athens in a war of liberation. A united force marched north, met Antipater at Crannon, and was destroyed. The old soldier, who lacked Alexander's sensitivity to Athenian culture, laid the most arduous terms upon the city, requiring it to pay the cost of the war, to receive a Macedonian garrison, to abandon its democratic constitution and courts, to disfranchise and deport to colonial settlements all citizens (12,000 out of 21,000) possessing less than two thousand drachmas' worth of property, and to surrender Demosthenes, Hypereides, and two other anti-Macedonian orators. Demosthenes fled to Calauria and took refuge in a temple sanctuary. Surrounded by Macedonian pursuers, he drank a phial of poison, and died before he could drag himself out of the sacred court.

The same tragic year saw the end of Aristotle. He had long been unpopular in Athens: the Academy and the school of Isocrates disliked him as a critic and a rival, while the patriots looked upon him as a leader of the pro-Macedonian party. Advantage was taken of Alexander's death to bring an accusation of impiety against Aristotle; heretical passages from his books were brought in as evidence; he was charged with having offered divine honors to the dictator Hermeias, who, being a slave, could not have been a god. Aristotle quietly left the city, saying that he would not give Athens a chance to sin a second time against philosophy.[43] He withdrew to the home of his mother's family in Chalcis, leaving the Lyceum in the care of Theophrastus. The Athenians passed sentence of death upon him, but had neither opportunity nor need to execute it. For either through a stomach illness aggravated by his flight, or, as some say,[44] by taking poison, Aristotle died a few months after leaving Athens, in the sixty-third year of his age. His will was a model of kindly consideration for his second wife, his family, and his slaves.

The death of Greek democracy was both a violent and a natural death, in which the fatal agents were the organic disorders of the system; the sword of Macedon merely added the final blow. The city-state had proved incapable of solving the problems of government: it had failed to preserve order within, and defense without; despite the appeals of Gorgias, Isocrates, and Plato for some Dorian discipline to tame Ionian freedom, it had discovered no way of reconciling local autonomy with national stability and power; and its love of liberty had seldom interfered with its passion for empire. The class war had become bitter beyond control, and had turned democracy into a contest in legislative looting. The Assembly, a noble body in its better days, had degenerated into a mob hating all superiority, rejecting all restraint, ruthless before weakness but cringing before power, voting itself every favor, and taxing property to the point of crushing initiative, industry, and thrift. Philip, Alexander, and Antipater did not destroy Greek freedom; it had destroyed itself; and the order that they forged preserved for centuries longer, and disseminated through Egypt and the East, a civilization that might otherwise have died of its own tyrannous anarchy.

And yet, had oligarchy or monarchy done any better? The Thirty had committed more atrocities against life and property in the few months of their power than the democracy in the preceding hundred years.[45] And while democracy was producing chaos in Athens, monarchy was producing chaos in Macedonia—a dozen wars of succession, a hundred assassinations, and a thousand interferences with freedom—with no redeeming glory of literature, science, philosophy, or art. The weakness and smallness of the state in Greece had been a boon to the individual, if not in body, certainly in soul; that freedom, costly though it was, had generated the achievements of the Greek mind. Individualism in the end destroys the group, but in the interim it stimulates personality, mental exploration, and artistic creation. Greek democracy was corrupt and incompetent, and had to die. But when it was dead men realized how beautiful its heyday had been; and all later generations of antiquity looked back to the centuries of Pericles and Plato as the zenith of Greece, and of all history.

BOOK V

THE HELLENISTIC DISPERSION

322–146 B.C.

CHRONOLOGICAL TABLE FOR BOOK V

B.C.

348-39: Speusippus head of the Academy
339-14: Xenocrates head of the Academy
323-285: Ptolemy I (Soter) founds Ptolemaic dynasty in Egypt
323: Judea made a satrapy of Syria
322-288: Theophrastus head of the Lyceum
321: Partition of Alexander's empire; Menander's first play
320: Ptolemy I captures Jerusalem; Pyrrho of Elis and Crates of Thebes, philosophers
319: Philemon and the New Comedy
318: Aristoxenus of Tarentum, theorist of music
317-07: Demetrius of Phalerum in power at Athens
316: Cassander King of Macedonia
315-01: Antigonus I (Cyclops) King of Macedonia
314: Antigonus I proclaims freedom of Greece; Zeno comes to Athens
314-270: Polemo head of the Academy
312-198: Judea under the Ptolemies
312-280: Seleucus I (Nicator) establishes Seleucid Empire
311: Hamilcar invades Sicily
310: Agathocles, dictator of Syracuse, invades Africa
307: Law against the philosophers
307-287: Demetrius Poliorcetes King of Macedonia
306: Epicurus opens his school at Athens
306-02: War between Cassander and Demetrius Poliorcetes for mastery of Greece

B.C.

305: Timaeus of Tauromenium, historian
301: Zeno opens his school at the Stoa; Seleucus I founds Antioch; Lysimachus defeats Antigonus I at Ipsus
300: Euclid of Alexandria, mathematician; Euhemerus, rationalist
295-72: Pyrrhus King of the Molossians
290: Rhodian school of sculpture
288-70: Strato head of the Lyceum
285-46: Ptolemy II (Philadelphus); Alexandrian Museum and Library
285: Zenodotus head of the Library; Herophilus of Chalcedon, anatomist
283-39: Antigonus II (Gonatas) King of Macedonia
280: Aristarchus of Samos, astronomer; rise of Achaean League; Pyrrhus helps Tarentum against Rome
280-62: Antiochus I (Soter) Seleucid emperor
280-79: Gauls invade Macedonia and Greece
279: Pyrrhus invades Sicily
278: The *Colossus* of Rhodes
277: Gauls invade Asia Minor
275: Aratus of Soli, poet
271: Timon of Phlius, satirist
270: Callimachus of Alexandria and Theocritus of Cos, poets; Berosus of Babylon, historian
270-69: Crates of Athens head of the Academy
270-16: Hieron II Dictator of Syracuse

CHRONOLOGICAL TABLE FOR BOOK V

B.C.

269-41: Arcesilaus head of the Middle Academy
266-61: Chremonidean War
261: Antigonus II takes Athens
261-47: Antiochus II (Theos) Seleucid emperor
261-32: Cleanthes head of the Stoa
260: Herodas of Cos, poet
258: Erasistratus of Ceos, physiologist
257-180: Aristophanes of Byzantium, philologist
251: Aratus of Sicyon frees his city
250: Arsaces founds kingdom of Parthia; the *Laocoön;* Manetho, Egyptian historian; Lycophron of Chalcis, poet
247: Archimedes of Syracuse, scientist
247-26: Seleucus II (Callinicus)
246-21: Ptolemy II (Euergetes I)
243: Aratus leads Achaean League against Macedonia
242: Agis IV attempts reforms in Sparta
240: Apollonius of Rhodes, poet
239-29: Demetrius II King of Macedonia
235-197: Attalus I establishes kingdom of Pergamum
235-195: Eratosthenes librarian at Alexandria
232-07: Chrysippus head of the Stoa
229: Aratus frees Athens
229-21: Antigonus III (Doson) King of Macedonia
226-24: Reforms of Cleomenes III in Sparta
226-23: Seleucus III (Soter)
225: Earthquake destroys Rhodes
223-187: Antiochus III (the Great) Seleucid emperor
221: Antigonus III defeats Cleomenes III at Sellasia
221-179: Philip V King of Macedonia
221-03: Ptolemy IV (Philopator)
220: Apollonius of Perga, mathematician
217: Ptolemy IV defeats Antiochus III at Raphia
215: Alliance of Philip V and Hannibal
214-05: First Macedonian War with Rome
212: Marcellus takes Syracuse; death of Archimedes
210: Sicily becomes a Roman province
208: Zeno of Tarsus, philosopher
207: Revolution of Nabis in Sparta
205: Egypt a Roman protectorate
203-181: Ptolemy V (Epiphanes)
200-197: Second Macedonian War
200: Diogenes of Seleucia, philosopher

B.C.

197: Battle of Cynoscephalae
197-160: Zenith of Pergamum under Eumenes II
196: Flamininus proclaims freedom of Greece; foundation of Pergamene Library
195-80: Aristophanes of Byzantium librarian at Alexandria
190: The *Farnese Bull*
189: Romans defeat Antiochus III at Magnesia
188: Philopoemen abolishes Lycurgean constitution in Sparta
187-75: Seleucus IV (Philopator)
181-45: Ptolemy VI (Philometor)
180: Great altar of Pergamum; Aristarchus of Samothrace librarian at Alexandria
179-68: Perseus King of Macedonia
175-63: Antiochus IV (Epiphanes) Seleucid emperor
175-38: Mithradates I King of Parthia
174: Antiochus IV rebuilds Olympieum
173: Carneades head of New Academy
171-68: Third Macedonian War
168: Aemilius Paullus defeats Perseus at Pydna; Antiochus IV despoils the Temple at Jerusalem
167: Deportation of the Achaeans, including Polybius, historian
166: First rising of the Maccabees; Book of Daniel
165: Judas Maccabee restores the Temple services
163-62: Antiochus V (Eupator) Seleucid emperor
162-50: Demetrius I (Soter) Seleucid emperor
161: Judas Maccabee makes treaty with Rome
160: Defeat and death of Judas Maccabee
160-39: Attalus II King of Pergamum
157: Judea becomes an independent priestly state
155: Carneades in Rome
150-45: Alexander Balas, Seleucid emperor
150: Hipparchus of Nicaea and Seleucus of Seleucia, astronomers; Moschus of Smyrna, poet
146: Mummius sacks Corinth; Greece and Macedonia become a province of Rome

CHAPTER XXIII

Greece and Macedon

I. THE STRUGGLE FOR POWER

HISTORIANS divide the past into epochs, years, and events, as thought divides the world into groups, individuals, and things; but history, like nature, knows only continuity amid change: *historia non facit saltum*—history makes no leaps. Hellenistic Greece did not feel Alexander's death as "the end of an age"; it looked upon him as the beginning of "modern" times, and as a symbol of vigorous youth rather than a factor in decay; it was convinced that it had now entered upon its richest maturity, and that its leaders were as magnificent as any in the past except the incomparable young King himself.[1] In many ways it was right. Greek civilization did not die with Greek freedom; on the contrary it conquered new areas and spread in three directions as the formation of vast empires broke down the political barriers to communication, colonization, and trade. Still enterprising and alert, the Greeks moved by hundreds of thousands into Asia and Egypt, Epirus and Macedon; and not only did Ionia flower again, but Hellenic blood, language, and culture made its way into the interior of Asia Minor, into Phoenicia and Palestine, through Syria and Babylonia, across the Euphrates and the Tigris, even to Bactria and India. Never had the Greek spirit shown more zest and courage; never had Greek letters and arts won so wide a victory.

Perhaps that is why historians are wont to end their histories of Greece with Alexander; after him the extent and complexity of the Greek world baffle any unified view or continuous narrative. There were not only three major monarchies—Macedonia, Seleucia, and Egypt; there were a hundred Greek city-states, of all degrees of independence; there was a maze of alliances and leagues; there were half-Greek states in Epirus, Judea, Pergamum, Byzantium, Bithynia, Cappadocia, Galatia, Bactria; and in the west were Greek Italy and Sicily, torn between aging Carthage and youthful Rome. Alexander's rootless empire was too loosely bound together by language, communication, customs, and faith to survive him. He had left not one but several strong men behind him, and none could be content with less than sovereignty. The size and diversity of the new realm dismissed all thought of democracy; self-government, as the Greeks understood it, presupposed a city-state whose citizens could come periodically to a common meeting place; and besides, had not the philosophers of democratic Athens denounced democracy as the enthronement of ignorance, envy, and chaos? Alexander's successors—who were therefore termed *Diadochi*—had been Macedonian chieftains, long accustomed to rule by the sword; democracy, except as the occasional consultation of their aides, never entered their heads. After some minor trials at arms which disposed of lesser contenders, they divided the empire into five parts (321)—Antipater taking Macedonia and Greece, Lysimachus Thrace, Antigonus Asia Minor, Seleucus Babylonia, and Ptolemy Egypt. They did not bother to call a confirming synod of the Greek states. From that moment, except for some fitful interludes in Greece, and the aristocratic republic of Rome, monarchy ruled Europe until the French Revolution.

The basic principle of democracy is freedom inviting chaos; the basic principle of monarchy is power inviting tyranny, revolution, and war. From Philip to Perseus, from Chaeronea to Pydna (338-168), the foreign and civil wars of the city-states were supplemented by the external and internal wars of the kingdoms, for the perquisites of government tempted a hundred generals to contests for thrones. Violence was as popular, *condottieri* as numerous and brilliant, in Hellenistic Greece as in Renaissance Italy. When Antipater died Athens revolted again, and put to death old Phocion, who had ruled it as justly as possible in Antipater's name. Cassander, Antipater's son, recaptured the city for Macedon (318), widened the franchise to holders of a thousand drachmas, and left as his regent the philosopher, scholar, and dilettante Demetrius of Phalerum, who gave the city ten years of prosperity and peace. Meanwhile Antigonus I ("Cyclops") dreamed of uniting all of Alexander's empire under his one eye; he was defeated at Ipsus (301) by a coalition, and lost Asia Minor to Seleucus I. His son Demetrius Poliorcetes ("Taker of Cities") liberated Greece from Macedonian rule, gave Athens twelve years more of democracy, was lodged as the grateful city's guest in the Parthenon, brought courtesans to live with him there,[2] drove some young men to desperation by his amorous attentions,* won a brilliant naval victory over Ptolemy I at Cyprus (308), besieged Rhodes for six years with new siege instruments but without success, made himself king of Macedon (294), ended Athenian liberty with a garrison, fell into ever new wars, was defeated and captured by Seleucus, and drank himself to death.

* Damocles, sought out everywhere by Demetrius and at last about to be captured, killed himself by plunging into a caldron of boiling water.[3] We must not misjudge the Athenians from one such instance of virtue.

Four years later (279), taking advantage of the disorder brought on by the struggle for power in the eastern Mediterranean, a horde of Celts, or "Gauls," under Brennus* marched down through Macedonia into Greece. Brennus, says Pausanias, "pointed out the weak state of Greece, the immense wealth of her cities, the votive offerings in the temples, the great quantities of silver and gold."[4] At the same time a revolution broke out in Macedonia under the leadership of Apollodorus; part of the army joined in, and helped the angry poor in their periodical revenge of despoiling the rich. The Gauls, doubtless guided by a Greek, found their way through secret passes around Thermopylae, killed and plundered indiscriminately, and advanced upon the rich temple at Delphi. Repulsed there by a Greek force and a storm that in Greek belief was Apollo's defense of his shrine, Brennus retreated and killed himself in shame. The surviving Gauls crossed over into Asia Minor. "They butchered all the males," writes Pausanias,

> and likewise old women, and babes at their mothers' breasts; they drank the blood, and feasted on the flesh of infants that were fat. High-spirited women, and maidens in their flower, committed suicide . . . those that survived were subjected to every kind of outrage. . . . Some of the women rushed upon the swords of the Gauls, and voluntarily courted death; to others death came from absence of food or sleep, as these merciless barbarians ravished them in turn, and wreaked their lusts upon them whether dying or dead.†[5]

After suffering years of such devastation, the Greeks of Asia bought off the invaders, and persuaded them to retire into northern Phrygia (where their settlements become known as Galatia), Thrace, and the Balkans. For two generations the Gauls levied fear tribute from Seleucus I and the Greek cities of the Asiatic coasts and the Black Sea; Byzantium alone paid them $240,000 a year.‡[6] As the emperors and generals of Rome were to be occupied, in the third century after Christ, in repelling barbarian inroads, so the kings and generals of Pergamum, Seleucia, and Macedonia gave much of their resources and energies, in the third century before Christ, to driving back the recurring waves of Celtic invasion. Throughout its history ancient civilization lived on the edge of a sea of barbarism that repeatedly threatened to inundate it. The stoic courage of citizens perpetually pre-

* Not the Brennus who had invaded Italy in 390 B.C.

† We have no Gallic version of these matters, nor any "barbarian" account of Greek invasions into Asia, Italy, or Sicily.

‡ In the following pages, to allow for the rise of prices in the Hellenistic age, the talent will be reckoned as equivalent to $3000 in the United States of 1939.

pared had once kept back the peril; but stoicism was dying in Greece precisely at the time that devised its classic formulation and its name.

Antigonus II, son of Demetrius Poliorcetes and called "Gonatas" for reasons now unknown, drove the Gauls out of Macedonia, put down the revolt of Apollodorus, and ruled Macedonia with ability and moderation for thirty-eight years (277-39). He gave generously to literature, science, and philosophy, brought poets like Aratus of Soli to his court, and formed a lifelong friendship with Zeno the Stoic; he was the first of that very discontinuous line of philosopher-kings which ended in Marcus Aurelius. Nevertheless it was during his reign that Athens made a last bid for freedom. In 267 the nationalist party came into power under the leadership of a young pupil of Zeno's, Chremonides. It secured the aid of Egypt, ousted the Macedonian troops, and announced the liberation of Athens. Antigonus came down at his leisure and recaptured the city (262), but dealt with it as became one who respected philosophy and old age. He established garrisons in the Piraeus, on Salamis, and at Sunium, and enjoined Athens from engaging in alliances or wars; for the rest he left the city completely free.

Other Greek states were solving in other ways the problem of reconciling liberty with order. About 279 little Aetolia, peopled like Macedon with half-barbarous and never-conquered mountaineers, began to organize the cities of northern Greece—chiefly those of the Delphic Amphictyony—into the Aetolian League; and about the same time the Achaean League of Patrae, Dyme, Pellene, and other towns attracted to its membership many cities of the Peloponnese. In either league the constituent municipalities kept control of all local government, but surrendered their armed forces and foreign relations to a federal council, and a *strategos,* elected by such of the citizens as could attend the annual assembly at Aegium in Achaea, or at Thermus in Aetolia. Each league maintained peace, and established common-measures, weights, and coinages throughout its area—an achievement in co-operation that makes the third century in some ways politically superior to the age of Pericles.

The Achaean League was transformed into a first-class power by Aratus of Sicyon. At the age of twenty this new Themistocles freed Sicyon from its dictator by a night attack with a handful of men. By eloquence and subtle negotiation he persuaded all the Peloponnesus except Sparta and Elis to join the League, which chose him as its *strategos* annually for ten years (245-35). With a few hundred men he secretly entered Corinth, scaled the almost inaccessible Acrocorinthus, routed the Macedonian troops, and restored the city to freedom. Passing on to the Piraeus, he bribed the Macedonian garrison to surrender, and announced the liberation of Athens. From that moment to the Roman conquest Athens enjoyed a unique self-government—militarily powerless, but left inviolate by the Hellenistic states because her universities had made her the intellectual capital of the Greek world. Athens turned to philosophy, and contentedly disappeared from political history.

Now at the height of their power, the two leagues began to weaken themselves by war with each other and class war within. In 220 the Aetolian League, with Sparta and Elis, fought the bitter "Social" War against the Achaean League and Macedon. Aratus, the defender of freedom, was also the protector of wealth; in each city the League supported the party of property. The poorer citizens complained that they could not afford to attend the distant assemblies of the League, and were thereby in effect disfranchised; they were skeptical of a liberty that meant the full privilege of the clever and the strong to exploit the simple and the weak; more and more they gave their applause to demagogues who called for a redistribution of the land. Like the rich of a century before, the poor began to favor Macedonia against their own governments.

Macedonia, however, was ruined by the honesty of Antigonus III. He had assumed power as regent for his stepson, Philip, and had promised to surrender the throne upon Philip's coming of age. The cynics of the time called him "Doson"—the Promiser—apparently because they took it for granted that he was lying. But he kept his word, and in 221 Philip V, aged seventeen, began a long reign of intrigue and war. He was a man of courage and capacity, but of unscrupulous subtlety. He seduced the wife of Aratus' son, poisoned Aratus, killed his own son on suspicion of conspiracy, and arranged banquets of poisoned wine for those who stood in the way of his plans.[7] He enlarged and enriched Macedonia, and left it more populous and prosperous than for one hundred and fifty years past. But in 215, fearful of the growing power of Rome, he made the historic mistake of allying himself with Hannibal and Carthage. A year later Rome declared war upon Macedonia, and began the conquest of Greece.

II. THE STRUGGLE FOR WEALTH

Athenaeus, who is as reliable as any gossip, tells us that Demetrius of Phalerum, about 310, took a census of Athens, and reported 21,000 citizens, 10,000 metics or aliens, and 400,000 slaves.[8] The last figure is incredible, but we know nothing that contradicts it. Very probably the number of rural slaves had grown; estates were becoming larger, and were being worked more and more by slaves under a slave overseer managing for an absentee landlord.[9] Under this system a more scientific agriculture developed; Varro knew fifty Greek manuals of the art. But the processes of erosion and deforestation had already gutted much of the land. Even in the fourth century Plato had expressed the belief that rain and flood, in the flow of time, had carried away much of the arable surface of Attica; the surviving hills, in his metaphor, were a skeleton from which the flesh had been washed away.[10] Many areas of Attica were in the third century so denuded of topsoil that their ancient farms were abandoned. The forests of Greece were vanishing, and timber, like food, had to be brought in from abroad.[11] The mines at Laurium were worn out and almost deserted; silver could be gotten more cheaply from Spain; and the gold mines of Thrace, which had once poured their wealth into Athens, now enriched the treasury and beautified the coinage of Macedon.

While the source of a virile and independent citizenry was drying up in the villages, industry and the class war were progressing in the towns. Small factories, and the slaves in them, were growing in number at Athens, as in all the larger cities of the Hellenistic world. Slave dealers accompanied the armies, bought unransomed captives, and sold them at three or four minas ($150 or $200) a head in the great slave markets of Delos and Rhodes. Some scruples, moral or economic, were felt about this ancient institution. A humanitarian sentiment arose as a by-product of philosophy; the cosmopolitan spirit of the age was negligent of racial distinctions; and casual hired labor, which could be thrown upon public relief whenever it ceased to be privately profitable, was in many circumstances cheaper than slave labor that had to be continuously maintained.[12] Towards the close of this period there was a substantial rise in manumissions.

Commerce languished in the older cities, but flourished in the new. The Greek ports of Asia and Egypt grew at the expense of the Piraeus; and even on the mainland it was Chalcis and Corinth that caught the swelling currents of Hellenistic trade. Through these strategically situated and well-equipped centers, as through Antioch, Seleucia, Rhodes, Alexandria, and Syracuse, a busy stream of merchants flowed, spreading a cosmopolitan and skeptical point of view. Bankers multiplied, and lent not only to traders and proprietors but to cities and governments.[13] Some cities, like Delos and Byzantium, had public or national banks holding government funds and managed by state officials.[14] In 324 Antimenes of Rhodes organized the first known system of insurance by guaranteeing owners, for a premium of eight per cent, against loss from the flight of their slaves.[15] The release of Persian accumulations and the quickened circulation of capital reduced the rate of interest to ten per cent in the third century and seven per cent in the second. Speculation was widespread, but not organized. Some manipulators sought to raise prices by limiting production; there were advocates of restricting crops to keep up the purchasing power of the farming community.[16] Prices in general were high, again because of the Achaemenid treasuries that Alexander had poured into the currency of the world; but at the same time, and partly by the same cause, trade was facilitated, production was stimulated, and prices gradually fell back to a normal range. The wealth of the wealthy grew beyond any precedent in Greek history. Homes became palaces, furniture and carriages more sumptuous, servants more numerous; dinners became orgies, and women became show windows of their husbands' prosperity.[17]

Wages lagged behind rising prices, and rapidly followed their fall. They could support a single man only, and made for celibacy, pauperism, and depopulation; they left a diminishing economic distance between free worker and slave. Employment was irregular, and thousands of men abandoned the mainland cities for mercenary soldiering abroad, or to hide their poverty in rural isolation.[18] The Athenian government relieved the destitute with grants of corn; the rich amused them with free tickets to celebrations and games. The wealthy stinted in wages but were generous in charity; often they lent money to their cities without interest, or rescued them from bankruptcy with large gifts, or built public works out of their private funds, or endowed temples or universities, or paid handsomely for the statues or the poems that published their features or their largess. The poor organized themselves into unions for mutual aid, but they could do little against the power and cleverness of the rich, the conservatism of the peasants, and the readiness of otherwise rival governments and leagues to exchange armed assistance in suppressing revolts.[19] The freedom of unequal ability to accumulate or starve brought on again, as in Solon's days, an extreme concentration of wealth. The poor lent readier ear to socialistic gospels; their spokesmen called for the cancellation of debts, the redivision of the land, and the confiscation of large fortunes; the boldest now and then proposed the liberation of the slaves.[20]

The decay of religious belief promoted the growth of compensatory utopias: Zeno the Stoic described an ideal communism in his *Republic* (ca. 300), and his follower Iambulus (ca. 250) inspired Greek rebels with a romance in which he described a Blessed Isle in the Indian Ocean (perhaps Ceylon); there, he reported, all men were equal, not only in rights but in ability and intelligence; all worked equally, and shared equally in the product; all took equal part, turn by turn, in administering the government; neither wealth nor poverty existed there, nor any war of the classes; nature produced fruit abundantly of her own accord, and men lived in harmony and universal love.[20a]

Some governments nationalized certain industries: Priene took over the saltworks, Miletus the textile factories, Rhodes and Cnidus the potteries; but the governments paid as low wages as the private employer, and squeezed all possible profit from the labor of their slaves. The gulf between rich and poor widened;[21] the class war became bitterer than before. Every city, young or old, echoed with the hatred of class for class, with uprisings, massacres, suppressions, banishments, and the destruction of property and life. When one faction won it exiled the other and confiscated its goods; when the exiles returned to power they revenged themselves in kind, and slaughtered their enemies; imagine the stability of an economic system subject to such decerebrations and disturbances. Some ancient Greek cities were so devastated by class strife that industry and men fled from them, grass grew in the streets, cattle came there to graze.[22] Polybius, writing about 150 B.C., describes certain timeless phases of the war from the viewpoint of a rich conservative:

> When they (the radical leaders) have made the populace ready and greedy to receive bribes, the virtue of democracy is destroyed, and it is transformed into a government of violence and the strong hand. For the mob, habituated to feed at the expense of others, and to have its hopes of a livelihood in the property of its neighbors, as soon as it has found a leader sufficiently ambitious and daring, . . . produces a reign of violence. Then come tumultuous assemblies, massacres, banishments, redivisions of land.[23]

It was war and class war that weakened mainland Greece to the point of being easily overcome by Rome. The bitter ruthlessness of the victors—the destruction of crops, vineyards, and orchards, the razing of farmhouses, the selling of captives into slavery—ruined one locality after another, and left an empty shell for the ultimate enemy. A land so wasted by strife, by erosion, deforestation, and the listless tillage of impoverished tenants or slaves, could not compete with the alluvial plains of the Orontes, the Euphrates, the Tigris, and the Nile. The northern cities were no longer on the great routes of trade; they had lost their navies, and could not control the sources and avenues of the grain supply that Athens and Sparta had mastered in their imperial days. The centers of power, even of literary and artistic creation, passed back again to Asia and Egypt, from which, a thousand years before, Greece had humbly learned her letters and her arts.

III. THE MORALS OF DECAY

The failure of the city-state accelerated the decay of the orthodox religion; the gods of the city had proved helpless to defend it, and had forfeited belief. The population was intermingled with foreign merchants who had no share in the city's civic or religious life, and whose amused skepticism spread among the citizens. The mythology of the ancient local gods survived among the peasantry and the simple townsfolk, and in the official rites; the educated used it for poetry and art, the half-liberated attacked it bitterly, the upper classes supported it as an aid to order, and discountenanced open atheism as bad taste. The growth of large states brought on a sympolity of the gods and made for a vague monotheism, while philosophers strove to formulate pantheism for the literate in a manner not too obviously incompatible with orthodox belief. About 300 Euhemerus of Messana in Sicily published his *Hiera Anagrapha* (literally *Holy Scriptures*, or *Records*), in which he argued that the gods were either personified powers of nature, or, more often, human heroes deified by popular imagination or gratitude for their benefits to mankind; that myths were allegories, and that religious ceremonies were originally exercises in commemoration of the dead. So Zeus was a conqueror who had died in Crete, Aphrodite was the founder and patroness of prostitution, and the story of Cronus eating his children was only a way of saying that cannibalism had once existed on the earth. The book had a sharply atheistic effect in third-century Greece.*[23a]

Skepticism, however, is uncomfortable; it leaves the common heart and imagination empty, and the vacuum soon draws in some new and encouraging creed. The victories of philosophy and Alexander cleared the way for novel cults. Athens in the third century was so disturbed by exotic faiths, nearly all of them promising heaven and threatening hell, that Epicurus, like Lucretius in first-century Rome, felt called upon to denounce religion as hostile to peace of mind and joy of life. The new temples, even

* Perhaps it reflected and aided the Hellenistic deification of kings.

in Athens, were now usually dedicated to Isis, Serapis, Bendis, Adonis, or some other alien deity. The Eleusinian mysteries flourished, and were imitated in Egypt, Italy, Sicily, and Crete; Dionysus Eleutherios—the Liberator—remained popular until he was absorbed into Christ; Orphism won fresh devotees as it renewed contact with the Eastern faiths from which it had sprung. The old religion had been aristocratic, and had excluded foreigners and slaves; the new Oriental cults accepted all men and women, alien or bond or free, and held out to all classes the promise of eternal life.

Superstition spread while science reached its apogee. Theophrastus' portrait of the Superstitious Man reveals how frail was the film of culture even in the capital of enlightenment and philosophy. The number seven was unspeakably holy; there were seven planets, seven days of the week, seven Wonders, seven Ages of Man, seven heavens, seven gates of hell. Astrology was rejuvenated by commerce with Babylonia; people took it for granted that the stars were gods who ruled in detail the destinies of individuals and states; character, even thought, was determined by the star or planet under which one had been born, and would therefore be jovial, or mercurial, or saturnine; even the Jews, the least superstitious of all peoples, expressed good wishes by saying *Mazzol-tov*—"May your planet be favorable."[24] Astronomy fought for its life against astrology, but finally succumbed in the second century A.D. And everywhere the Hellenistic world worshiped Tyche, the great god Chance.

Only an act of persistent imagination, or a gift for observation, can enable us to realize what it means to a nation to have its traditional religion die. Classic Greek civilization had been built upon a patriotic devotion to the city-state, and classic morality, though rooted in folkways rather than in faith, had been powerfully reinforced by supernatural belief. But now neither faith nor patriotism survived in the educated Greek; civic frontiers had been erased by empires; and the growth of knowledge had secularized morals, marriage, parentage, and law. For a time the Periclean Enlightenment helped morality, as in modern Europe; humanitarian feelings were developed, and aroused—ineffectually—a keener resentment against war; arbitration grew among cities and men. Manners were more polished, argument more urbane; courtesy trickled down, as in our Middle Ages, from the courts of the kings, where it was a matter of personal safety and royal prestige; when the Romans came Greece was amazed at their bad manners and blunt ways. Life was more refined; women moved about in it more freely, and stimulated the males to unwonted elegance. Men shaved now, especially in Byzantium and Rhodes, where the laws forbade it as effeminate.[25] But the pursuit of pleasure consumed the adult life of the upper classes. The old problem of ethics and morals—to reconcile the natural epicureanism of the individual with the necessary stoicism of the state—found no solution in religion, statesmanship, or philosophy.

Education spread, but spread thin; as in all intellectual ages it stressed knowledge more than character, and produced masses of half-educated people who, uprooted from labor and the land, moved about in unplaced discontent like loosened cargo in the ship of state. Some cities, like Miletus and Rhodes, established public—i.e., government-supported—schools; at Teos and Chios boys and girls were educated together, with an impartiality that only Sparta had shown.[26] The gymnasium developed into a high school or college, with classrooms, lecture hall, and library. The palaestra flourished, and proved popular in the East; but public games had degenerated into professional contests, chiefly boxing, in which strength counted for more than skill; the Greeks, who had once been a nation of athletes, became now a nation of spectators, content to witness rather than to do.

Sexual morality was relaxed even beyond the loose standards of the Periclean age. Homosexualism remained popular; the youth Delphis "is in love," says Theocritus' Simaetha, "but whether for a woman or for a man I cannot say."[27] The courtesan still reigned: Demetrius Poliorcetes levied a tax of two hundred and fifty talents ($750,000) upon the Athenians, and then gave it to his mistress Lamia on the ground that she needed it for soap; which led the angry Athenians to remark how unclean the lady must be.[28] Dances of naked women were accepted as part of the mores, and were performed before a Macedonian king.[29] Athenian life was portrayed in Menander's plays as a round of triviality, seduction, and adultery.

Greek women participated actively in the cultural pursuits of the time, and contributed to letters, science, philosophy, and art. Aristodama of Smyrna gave recitals of her poetry throughout Greece, and received many honors. Some philosophers, like Epicurus, did not hesitate to admit women into their schools. Literature began to stress the physical loveliness of woman rather than her worth and charm as a mother; the literary cult of feminine beauty arose in this period alongside the poetry and fiction of romantic love. The partial emancipation of woman was accompanied by a revolt against wholesale maternity, and the limitation of the family became the outstanding social phenomenon of the age. Abortion was punishable only if practiced by a woman against the wish of her husband, or at the instigation of her seducer. When a child came it was in many cases exposed. Only one family in a hundred, in the old Greek cities, reared more than one daughter: "Even a rich man," reports Poseidippus, "always exposes a daughter." Sisters were a rarity. Families with no child, or only one, were numerous. Inscriptions enable us to trace the fertility of seventy-nine families in Miletus about 200 B.C.: thirty-two had one child, thirty-one had two; altogether they had one hundred and eighteen sons and twenty-eight daughters.[30] At Eretria only one family in twelve had two sons; hardly any had two daughters. Philosophers condoned infanticide as reducing the pressure of population; but when the lower classes took up the practice on a large scale, the death rate overtook the birth rate. Religion, which had once frightened men into fertility lest their dead souls be untended, no longer had the power to outweigh considerations of comfort and cost. In the colonies immigration replaced the old families; in Attica and the Peloponnesus immigration trickled down to a negligible figure, and population declined. In Macedonia Philip V forbade the limitation of the family, and in thirty years raised the man power of the country fifty per cent;[31] we may judge from this how widespread the practice of limitation had become, even in half-primitive Macedon. "In our time," wrote Polybius about 150 B.C.,

> the whole of Greece has been subject to a low birth rate and a general decrease of the population, owing to which cities have become deserted and the land has ceased to yield fruit. . . . For as men had fallen into such a state of luxury, avarice, and indolence that they did not wish to marry, or, if they married, to rear the children born to them, or at most but one or two of them, so as to leave these in affluence and bring them up to waste their substance—the evil insensibly but rapidly grew. For in cases where, of one or two children, the one was carried off by war and the other by sickness, it was evident that the houses must have been left empty . . . and by small degrees cities became resourceless and feeble.[32]

IV. REVOLUTION IN SPARTA

Meanwhile that concentration of wealth, which everywhere in Greece was enflaming the eternal conflict of classes, produced in Sparta two attempts at revolutionary reform. Isolated by its mountain barriers, Sparta had maintained its independence, had fought back the Macedonians, and had bravely defeated the immense army of Pyrrhus (272). But the greed of the strong generated from within the ruin that enemy forces had failed to bring from without. The Lycurgean laws against alienating the land from the family by sale, or dividing it in bequests, had been abrogated,* and the fortunes made by Spartans in empire or war had gone to buying

* Perhaps because the latter had led to family limitation, as in modern France.

up the soil.[33] By 244 the 700,000 acres of Laconia were owned by one hundred families,[34] and only seven hundred men had preserved the rights of citizenship. Even these no longer ate in common; the poor could not make the necessary contribution, while the rich preferred to feast in private. A large majority of the families that had once enjoyed the franchise had sunk into poverty, and called for a cancellation of debts and a redivision of the land.

It is to the credit of monarchy that the attempt to reform this condition came from the Spartan kings. In 242 Agis IV and Leonidas succeeded to the dual throne. Convinced that Lycurgus had meant the land to be equally divided among all freemen, Agis proposed to redistribute it, to annul all debts, and to restore the semicommunism of Lycurgus. Those landowners whose property was mortgaged supported the move for cancellation; but when the measure had been passed they resisted violently the remaining elements of Agis' reforms. At the instigation of Leonidas, Agis was murdered, along with his mother and his grandmother, both of whom had volunteered to surrender their great estates for division among the people. In this royal drama the noblest characters were women. Chilonis, daughter of Leonidas, was the wife of Cleombrotus, who supported Agis. When Leonidas was exiled, and Cleombrotus seized his throne, Chilonis left her triumphant husband to share her father's banishment; when Leonidas recaptured power and exiled Cleombrotus, Chilonis chose exile with her husband.[35]

Leonidas, to get the rich property of Agis' widow into his family, compelled her to marry his son Cleomenes. But Cleomenes fell in love with his wife, and imbibed from her the ideas of the dead king. When he came to the throne as Cleomenes III he resolved to carry out Agis' reforms. Having won over the army by his courage in war, and the people by the simplicity of his life, he abolished the oligarchic ephorate on the ground that Lycurgus had never sanctioned it; he killed fourteen resisters, exiled eighty, canceled all debts, divided the land among the free population, and restored the Lycurgean discipline. Not content, he set out to conquer the Peloponnese for the revolution. The proletariat everywhere hailed him as a liberator, and many towns surrendered to him gladly; he took Argos, Pellene, Phlius, Epidaurus, Hermione, Troezen, at last even rich Corinth. The ferment of his program spread: in Boeotia the payment of debts was abandoned, and the state appropriated funds to appease the poor; in Megalopolis the philosopher Cercidas pled with the rich to aid the needy before revolution destroyed all wealth.[36] When Cleomenes invaded Achaea and defeated Aratus all upper-class Greece trembled for its property. Aratus appealed to Macedonia. Antigonus Doson came down, overwhelmed Cleomenes at Sellasia (221), and restored the oligarchic regime in Lacedaemon. Cleomenes fled to Egypt, tried and failed to win the help of Ptolemy III, tried and failed to rouse the Alexandrians to revolution, and killed himself.[37]

The class war continued. A generation after Cleomenes the people of Sparta overthrew the government, and set up a revolutionary dictatorship. Philopoemen, who had succeeded Aratus as head of the Achaean League, invaded Laconia, and restored the rule of property. As soon as Philopoemen had gone the people rose again, and set up Nabis as dictator (207). Nabis was a Syrian Semite who had been captured in war and sold into slavery at Megalopolis; smarting under suppressed ability, he had revenged himself by organizing a revolt among the Helots. Now he gave Spartan citizenship to all freemen, and freed all the Helots with one word. When the rich obstructed him he confiscated their wealth and cut off their heads. The news of his doings went abroad, and he found it a simple matter, with the help of the poorer classes, to conquer Argos, Messenia, Elis, and part of Arcadia. Everywhere he nationalized large estates, redistributed the land, and abolished debts.[38] The Achaean League, unable to overthrow him, appealed to Rome for aid. Flamininus came, but Nabis offered so resolute a resistance that the Roman accepted a truce by which Nabis was to release the imprisoned rich, but would retain his power. At this juncture Nabis was assassinated by an agent of the Aetolian League (192).[39] Four years later Philopoemen marched in again, propped up the oligarchs, abolished the Lycurgean regimen, and sold three thousand of Nabis' followers into slavery. The revolution was ended, but so was Sparta; it continued to exist, but it played no further part in the history of Greece.

V. THE ASCENDANCY OF RHODES

Frightened by the violence of faction and drawn by the movements of population, trade and capital passed from the mainland and sought new havens in the Aegean. Delos, once rich through Apollo, flourished in the second century as a free port under the protection of Rome and the management of Athens. The little isle was crowded with alien merchants, business offices, palaces and hovels, and the diverse temples of exotic faiths.

Rhodes reached her zenith in the third century, and was then by common consent the most civilized and beautiful city in Hellas. Strabo described the great port as "so far superior to all others in harbors, roads, walls, and improvements that I am unable to speak of any other city as equal to it, or even as almost equal to it."[40] Situated at one of the crossroads of the Mediterranean, in a position to take advantage of that expanding trade which Alexander's conquests had made possible between Europe, Egypt, and Asia, Rhodes' spacious harbors replaced Tyre and the Piraeus as a port of reshipment for goods, and as a clearinghouse for the organization and financing of commerce in the eastern sea. Her merchants established a profitable reputation for honesty, her banks and her government for stability, in a world of treachery and change; her powerful fleet, manned by her citizens, cleared the Aegean of pirates, maintained an equal security for the merchant vessels of all nations, and established a code of maritime law so ably devised and so widely accepted that it governed Mediterranean trade for centuries, and passed down into the marine law of Rome, Constantinople, and Venice.

Having freed herself from Macedonian domination by her heroic resistance to Demetrius Poliorcetes (305), Rhodes steered successfully through the troubled politics of the age by maintaining a wise neutrality, or by going to war only to check the growth of an aggressor state, or to preserve the freedom of the seas. She united many of the Aegean cities in an "Island League," and exercised her presidency so fairly that no one questioned her right to lead. Her government—an aristocracy resting on a democratic base as in republican Rome—ruled the synoecized cities of Lindus, Camirus, Ialysus, and Rhodes with skill and comparative justice, gave to alien residents such privileges as Athens had never yielded to her metics, protected a large population of slaves so well that when in danger it dared to arm them, and laid upon the rich men of the city the obligation to take care of the poor.[41] The state met its expenses by a two per cent tax upon imports and exports. It lent money generously, sometimes without interest, to cities in distress.

When Rhodes herself was physically ruined by an earthquake (225), all the Greek world came to her aid, for everyone recognized that her disappearance from the Aegean would lead to commercial and financial chaos. Hieron II sent one hundred gold talents ($300,000), and set up in the restored city a statuary group showing the people of Rhodes being crowned by the people of Syracuse. Ptolemy III sent three hundred talents* of silver; Antigonus III sent three thousand, together with great quantities of timber and pitch for building; his queen Chryseis gave three thousand talents of lead, and 150,000 bushels of corn. Seleucus III sent 300,000 bushels of corn and ten fully equipped quinqueremes. "As for the towns that contributed each according to its means," says Polybius, "it would be difficult to enumerate them."[42] It was a bright interlude in the dark annals of political history, one of the rare occasions when all the Greek world thought and acted as one.

* A Greek talent weighed fifty-eight pounds avoirdupois.

CHAPTER XXIV

Hellenism and the Orient

I. THE SELEUCID EMPIRE

AS we move from the mainland through the Aegean into the Greek settlements in Asia and Egypt we are surprised to find a fresh and flourishing life, and we perceive that the Hellenistic age saw not so much the decay as the dissemination of Greek civilization. From the end of the Peloponnesian War a stream of Greek soldiers and immigrants had entered Asia. Alexander's conquests widened this stream by offering new opportunities and avenues to Hellenic enterprise.

Seleucus, called "Nicator" (Victor), was distinguished among Alexander's generals as a man of courage, imagination, and unscrupulous generosity. It was characteristic of him that he gave his second wife, the beautiful Stratonice, to his son Demetrius when he learned that the boy was pining away for love of her. Antigonus I, challenging the allotment of Babylonia to Seleucus, set out to conquer for himself all the Near East; Seleucus and Ptolemy I defeated him at Gaza in 312. From that moment the house of Seleucus dated the Seleucid Empire, and a new era—a mode of reckoning that survived in western Asia till Mohammed. Seleucus united under his scepter the old kingdoms and cultures of Elam, Sumeria, Persia, Babylonia, Assyria, Syria, Phoenicia, and, at times, Asia Minor and Palestine. At Seleucia and Antioch he built capitals richer and more populous than any ever known in mainland Greece. For Seleucia he chose a site near the aged Babylon and the future Baghdad, almost at the junction of the Euphrates and the Tigris; it was conveniently located to attract commerce between Mesopotamia and the Persian Gulf and beyond; within half a century it had a population of 600,000 souls—a motley mass of Asiatics dominated by a minority of Greeks.* Antioch was similarly situated on the Orontes, not too far from its mouth to be reached by ocean shipping, yet sufficiently inland to be safe from naval attack, to tap the fertile fields of the river valley, and to draw the Mediterranean trade of northern Mesopotamia and Syria. Here the later Seleucid emperors established their residence, until under Antiochus IV it became the wealthiest city of Seleucid Asia, adorned with temples, porticoes, theaters, gym-

* On this site Professor Leroy Waterman in 1931 exhumed tablets indicating that one of the richest citizens of Seleucia had avoided the payment of taxes for twenty-five years.[1]

nasiums, palaestras, flower gardens, landscaped boulevards, and parks so beautiful that the Garden of Daphne was known throughout Greece for its laurels and cypresses, its fountains and streams.

Seleucus I was assassinated in 281, after thirty-five years of beneficent and popular rule. From his death his empire began to disintegrate, torn with geographical and racial divisions, violent struggles for the throne, and barbarian invasions on every side. Antiochus I Soter (Savior) fought gallantly against the Gauls. Antiochus II Theos (the God) lived in a perpetual intoxication, as if again to illustrate the gamble of hereditary monarchy; his wife Laodice began that chain of intrigue which disrupted and finally ruined the royal house. Antiochus III the Great was a man of capacity and culture; his bust in the Louvre shows a Greco-Macedonian with the courage of Macedon and the intelligence of Greece. He recaptured by untiring war most of the territory which the empire had lost since Seleucus I. He established a library at Antioch, and promoted the literary movement that culminated in Meleager of Gaza at the close of the second century. He preserved the Greek custom of municipal autonomy, writing to the cities that "if he should order anything contrary to the laws they should pay no attention, but assume that he had acted in ignorance."[2] He was ruined by ambition, imagination, and a flair for love. In 217 he was defeated by Ptolemy IV at Raphia, and lost Phoenicia, Syria, and Palestine; he consoled himself by a victorious expedition into Bactria and India (208), duplicating the exploits of Alexander. Lured by Hannibal into helping him against Rome, he landed an army in Euboea, fell in love at fifty with a pretty maid of Chalcis, courted her honorably, married her elaborately, forgot the war, and spent the winter enjoying his happiness.[3] The Romans defeated him at Thermopylae, drove him into Asia Minor, and overwhelmed him at Magnesia. Restless, he plunged into another eastern campaign, and died in its course (187), after a reign of thirty-six years.

His son Seleucus IV loved peace, administered the empire with economy and wisdom, and was assassinated in 175. At that time his younger brother was serving as archon at Athens, where he had gone to study philosophy. Hearing of Seleucus' death, he organized an army, marched to Antioch, deposed the assassin, and took the throne (175). Antiochus IV was both the most interesting and the most erratic of his line, a rare mixture of intellect, insanity, and charm. He governed his kingdom ably despite a thousand injustices and absurdities. He allowed his delegates to abuse their power, and gave his mistress authority over three cities. He was generous and cruel without judgment, often forgiving or condemning by whim, surprising simple folk with costly gifts, and tossing money with a child's ecstasy among the crowds in the street. He loved wine, women, and art; he drank to excess, and left his royal seat, at banquets, to dance naked with the entertainers, or to carouse with wastrels;[4] he was a Bohemian whose dream of power had come true. He despised the solemnity and trappings of the court, played practical jokes upon his dignitaries, and disguised himself to know the luxury of anonymity; it delighted him to mingle with the people and overhear their comments on the King. He liked to wander among the shops of the artisans, watching and studying the work of engravers and jewelers, and discussing with them the technical details of their craft. He felt a sincere enthusiasm for Greek art, literature, and thought. He made Antioch for a century the art center of the Greek world; he paid artists handsomely to set up statuary and temples in other cities of Hellas; he redecorated the shrine of Apollo at Delos, built a theater for Tegea, and financed the completion of the Olympieum at Athens. Having lived fourteen impressionable years in Rome, he had imbibed a taste for republican institutions; and as if to foreshadow Augustus, it pleased his humor and policy to clothe his monarchical power in the forms of republican freedom. The chief effect of his passion for things Roman was the introduction of gladiatorial games in Antioch, his capital. The people resented the brutal sport, but Antiochus won them over by lavish and spectacular displays; when they became accustomed to the butchery he considered their degeneration a personal victory. It was characteristic of him that he began as an ardent follower of the Stoics, and ended as an easy convert to the Epicureans. He enjoyed his own qualities so keenly that he labeled his coins Antiochus Theos Epiphanes—the God Made Manifest. Overreaching himself in the manner of his imaginative kind, he attempted in 169 to conquer Egypt. He was succeeding when Rome, herself a candidate for the Egyptian plum, ordered him to retire from African soil. Antiochus asked time to consider; but the Roman envoy, Popilius, drew a circle in the sand around Antiochus, and bade him decide before stepping over its line. Antiochus yielded in fury, plundered the Temple at Jerusalem to restore his treasury, sought glory like his father in a campaign against the eastern tribes, and died in Persia on the way, of epilepsy, madness, or disease.[8]

II. SELEUCID CIVILIZATION

The function of the Seleucid Empire in history was to give to the Near East that economic protection and order which Persia had provided before Alexander, and which Rome would restore after Caesar. Despite the wars, revolutions, spoliations, and corruption normal to human affairs, that function was performed. The Macedonian conquest broke down a thousand barriers of government and speech, and invited the East and the West to fuller economic exchange. The result was a brilliant resurrection of Greek Asia. While division and strife, the poverty of the soil, and the migrations of trade routes ruined the mainland, the comparative unity and peace preserved by the Seleucids encouraged agriculture, commerce, and industry. The Greek cities of Asia were no longer free to make revolutions or experiments; *homonoia*, Harmony, was enforced by the kings, and was literally worshiped by the people as a god.[6] Old cities like Miletus, Ephesus, and Smyrna had a second blooming.

The valleys of the Tigris, the Euphrates, the Jordan, the Orontes, the Maeander, the Halys, and the Oxus were fertile then beyond the conception of present imagination, obsessed with the vision of the deserts and rocky wastes that cover so much of the Near East after two thousand years of erosion, deforestation, and neglectful tenant tillage.[7] The soil was irrigated by a system of canals maintained under the supervision of the state. The land was owned by the king, or his nobles, or the cities, or the temples, or private individuals; in all cases the labor was performed by serfs transmitted with the soil in bequest or sale. The government considered as national property all the riches contained in the earth,[8] but did little to exploit them. Trades, and even cities, were now highly specialized. Miletus was a busy textile center; Antioch imported raw materials and turned them into finished goods. Some large factories, manned with slaves, achieved a modest degree of mass production for the general market.[9] But domestic consumption lagged behind production; the people were so poor that no adequate home market encouraged large-scale industry.

Commerce was the life of Hellenistic economy. It made the great fortunes, built the great cities, and employed a growing proportion of the expanding population. Money transactions now almost completely replaced the barter that had survived for four centuries the coinage of Croesus. Egypt, Rhodes, Seleucia, Pergamum, and other governments issued currencies sufficiently stable and similar to facilitate international trade. Bankers provided public and private credit. Ships were larger, made four to six knots per hour, and shortened voyages by crossing the open sea. On land the Seleucids developed and extended the great highways left as part of Persia's legacy to the East. Caravan routes converged from inner Asia upon Seleucia, and opened out thence to Damascus, Berytus (Beirut), and Antioch. Enriched by trade, and enriching it in turn, populous centers rose there and at Babylon, Tyre, Tarsus, Xanthus, Rhodes, Halicarnassus, Miletus, Ephesus, Smyrna, Pergamum, Byzantium, Cyzicus, Apamea, Heracleia, Amisus, Sinope, Panticapaeum, Olbia, Lysimacheia, Abydos, Thessalonica (Salonika), Chalcis, Delos, Corinth, Ambracia, Epidamnus (Durazzo), Taras, Neapolis (Naples), Rome, Massalia, Emporium, Panormus (Palermo), Syracuse, Utica, Carthage, Cyrene, and Alexandria. One busy web of trade bound together Spain under Carthage and Rome, Carthage under Hamilcar, Syracuse under Hieron II, Rome under the Scipios, Macedonia under the Antigonids, Greece under the Leagues, Egypt under the Ptolemies, the Near East under the Seleucids, India under the Mauryas, and China under the Hans. The routes from China passed through Turkestan, Bactria, and Persia, or over the Aral, Caspian, and Black Seas. The routes from India passed through Afghanistan and Persia to Seleucia, or through Arabia and Petra to Jerusalem and Damascus, or across the Indian Ocean to Adana (Aden), then through the Red Sea to Arsinoë (Suez), and thence to Alexandria. It was for control of the last two routes that the Seleucid and Ptolemaic dynasties fought those "Syrian Wars" that finally weakened them both to the point of falling vassal to Rome.

The Seleucid monarchy, inheriting the Asiatic tradition, was absolute; no assembly limited its power. The court was planned on the Oriental style, with chamberlains and lace, eunuchs and uniforms, incense and music; only the speech and the inner dress remained Greek. The nobles were not half-independent chieftains as in Macedonia or medieval Europe, but administrative or military appointees of the king. It was this structure of monarchy that passed down from Persia through the Seleucids and Sassanids to the Rome of Diocletian and the Byzantium of Constantine. Knowing that their power, in an alien scene, rested upon the loyalty of the Greek population, the Seleucid kings labored to restore the old Greek cities and to establish new ones. Seleucus I founded nine Seleucias, six Antiochs, five Laodiceas, three Apameas, one Stratonice; and his successors imitated him to the best of their lesser ability. Cities grew and multiplied as in nineteenth-century America.

Through them the Hellenization of western Asia proceeded, on the surface, at a rapid pace. The process, of course, was old; it had begun with the Great Migration, and the Hellenistic Dispersion was in part the Renaissance of Ionia, a return of Greek civilization to its early Asiatic homes. Even before Alexander Greeks had held high offices in the Persian Empire, and Greek merchants had dominated the trade routes of the nearer East. Now the opening of political, commercial, and artistic opportunities drew from old Greece, Magna Graecia, and Sicily an emigrant flow of adventurers, settlers, scribes, soldiers, traders, doctors, scholars, and courtesans. Greek sculptors and engravers made statues and coins for Phoenician, Lycian, Carian, Cilician, Bactrian kings. Greek dancing girls became the rage of Asiatic ports.[10] Sexual immorality took on a Greek grace, and Greek palaestras and gymnasiums aroused in some Orientals an unwonted devotion to athletics and baths. Cities secured new water supplies and drainage systems; avenues were paved and cleaned. Schools, libraries, and theaters stimulated reading and literature; collegians (*epheboi*) and university students roamed the streets and played their ancient pranks upon one another and the populace. No one was counted cultured unless he understood Greek and could enjoy the plays of Menander and Euripides. This imposition of Greek civilization upon the Near East is one of the startling phenomena of ancient history; no change so swift and far-reaching had ever been seen in Asia. We know too little of its details and its results. We are poorly informed about the literature, philosophy, and science of Seleucid Asia; if we find in it few figures of prime magnitude—Zeno the Stoic, Seleucus the astronomer, and, in the Roman period, Meleager the poet and Poseidippus the polymath—we cannot be sure that there were not many more. It was a flourishing culture, full of variety, refinement, and verve, and as fertile in art as any preceding age. Never before, so far as our knowledge goes, had a civilization achieved so wide a spread and such complex unity amid so many diverse environments. For a century western Asia belonged to Europe. The way was prepared for the Pax Romana, and the embracing synthesis of Christendom.

But the East was not conquered. It was too deeply and anciently itself to yield its soul. The masses of the people continued to speak their native tongues, to pursue their long-accustomed ways, and to worship their ancestral gods. Beyond the Mediterranean coasts the Greek veneer grew thin, and such Hellenic centers as Seleucia on the Tigris were Greek islands in an Oriental sea. There was no such fusion of races and cultures as Alexander had dreamed of; there were Greeks and Greek civilization on the top, and a medley of Asiatic peoples and cultures underneath. The qualities of the Greek intellect made no entry into the Oriental mind; the energy and love of novelty, the zest for worldliness and the passion for perfection, the expressiveness and individualism of the Greek effected no change in the Oriental character. On the contrary, as time moved on, Eastern ways of thought and feeling surged up from below into the ruling Greeks, and through them flowed westward to transform the "pagan" world. In Babylon the patient Semitic merchant and the temple banker regained ascendancy over the volatile Hellene, preserved the cuneiform writing, and forced back the Greek language into second place in the business world. Astrology and alchemy corrupted Greek astronomy and physics; Oriental monarchy proved more powerful than Greek democracy, and finally impressed its form upon the West; Greek kings and Roman emperors became gods in the manner of the East, and the Asiatic theory of the divine right of kings passed down through Rome and Constantinople into modern Europe. Through Zeno the East insinuated its quietism and fatalism into Greek philosophy; through a hundred channels it poured its mysticism and its piety into the vacuum left by the decay of the orthodox Greek faith. The Greek readily accepted the gods of the Orient as essentially identical with his own; but as the Greek did not really believe, and the Asiatic did, the Oriental god survived while the Greek god died. Artemis of the Ephesians became again an Eastern maternity goddess, with a dozen breasts. Babylonian, Phoenician, and Syrian cults captured great numbers of the invading Hellenes. The Greeks offered the East philosophy, the East offered Greece religion; religion won because philosophy was a luxury for the few, religion was a consolation for the many. In the rhythmic historic alternation of belief and unbelief, mysticism and naturalism, religion and science, religion returned to power because it recognized the secret helplessness and loneliness of man, and gave him inspiration and poetry; a disillusioned, exploited, war-wearied world was glad to believe and hope again. The least expected and most profound effect of Alexander's conquest was the Orientalization of the European soul.

III. PERGAMUM

The gradual absorption of the Greeks by Asia weakened the Seleucid power, and generated independent kingdoms on the edge of the Hellenistic world. As early as 280 Armenia, Cappadocia, Pontus, and Bithynia set up their own monarchies; and soon the Greek cities of the Black Sea fell subject to Asiatic rule. Bactria and Sogdiana broke away about 250. In 247 Arsaces, chief of the Parni—an Iranian nomad tribe—killed the Seleucid governor of Persia and set up the kingdom of Parthia, destined to plague Rome for centuries. In 282 Philataerus, entrusted by Lysimachus with the care of nine thousand talents and the fortified hill of Pergamum in Asia Minor, appropriated the money and declared his independence. His nephew Eumenes I absorbed Pitane and Atarneus, and made Pergamum a sovereign monarchy (262). Attalus I earned the gratitude of Greek Asia by driving back the Gauls who had penetrated to his city walls (230); his eldest son, Eumenes II, continued his competent rule, but shocked Greece by calling in the aid of Rome against Antiochus III. After their defeat of Antiochus at Magnesia the Romans gave Eumenes nearly all of Asia Minor. His brother and successor, Attalus II, distrusted the power of his sons to keep Pergamum free, and at his death (139) bequeathed his kingdom to Rome.

The little state did what it could to redeem the treachery of its birth and growth by making itself the rival of Alexandria as a center of art and learning. The wealth that came from the mines, vines, and cornfields, from the manufacture of woolens, parchments, and perfumes, from the making of bricks and tiles, and the mastery of north Aegean trade went not only to maintain a strong army and navy, but to encourage literature and art. The Pergamene kings believed that government and private business could fruitfully compete, supplying a mutual check on inefficiency and greed. The king cultivated large tracts of land with slaves, and operated, though not as monopolies, many factories, quarries, and mines. Under this unique system wealth increased and multiplied. Pergamum became an ornate capital, famous for its altar to Zeus, its luxurious palaces, its library and theater, its palaestras and baths; even its public lavatories upheld the municipal pride.[11] The library was second only to Alexandria's in the number of its volumes and the repute of its scholars; and the *pinakotheka* housed, for the public enjoyment, a great collection of paintings. For half a century Pergamum was the finest flower of Hellenic civilization.

Meanwhile the House of Seleucus had fallen into decay. The rise of independent kingdoms almost confined its power to Mesopotamia and Syria. Parthia, Pergamum, Egypt, and Rome patiently labored to weaken the dynasty by supporting pretenders at every succession, and fomenting faction and civil war. In 153, just as Demetrius I was restoring vigor to the Seleucid government, Rome collected mercenaries from every quarter to bolster up the false claims of a Smyrnean adventurer to the throne. Pergamum and Egypt joined in the attack; Demetrius fought and died heroically, and the Seleucid power fell into the hands of the worthless Alexander Balas, the puppet of his mistresses and of Rome.

IV. HELLENISM AND THE JEWS

The history of Judea in the Hellenistic age turns on two conflicts: the external struggle between Seleucid Asia and Ptolemaic Egypt for Palestine, and the internal struggle between the Hellenic and the Hebraic ways of life. The first conflict is dead history, and may be briefly dismissed; Matthew Arnold believed the second conflict to be one of the lasting cleavages of human feeling and thought. In the original division of Alexander's empire Judea (i.e., Palestine south of Samaria) had been awarded to Ptolemy. The Seleucids never accepted this decision; they saw themselves separated from the Mediterranean, and coveted the wealth that might come from the trade that passed through Damascus and Jerusalem. In the resultant wars Ptolemy I won, and Judea remained subject to the Ptolemies for more than a century (312-198). It paid an annual tribute of eight thousand talents, but despite this burden the land prospered. Judea was left a large measure of self-government under the hereditary high priest of Jerusalem and the Great Assembly. This *gerousia*, or Council of *Elders*, which Ezra and Nehemiah had formed two centuries back, became both a senate and a supreme court. Its seventy or more members were chosen from the heads of the leading families, and from the most learned scholars (*Soferim*) of the land. Its regulations—the *Dibre Soferim*—set the pattern of orthodox Judaism from the Hellenistic age to our own.

The basis of Judaism was religion: the idea of a surveillant and upholding deity entered into every phase and moment of Jewish life. Morals and manners were ordained by the *gerousia* in strictness and detail. Entertainments and games were few and restrained. Intermarriage with non-Jews was forbidden; so were celibacy and infanticide. Hence the Jews bred abundantly, and reared all their children; despite war and famine their numbers grew throughout antiquity, until in the time of Caesar there were some seven million Jews in the Roman Empire. The bulk of the population, before the Maccabean era, was agricultural. The Jews were not yet a nation of traders; even as late as the first century A.D. Josephus wrote: "We are not a commercial people";[13] the great trading peoples of the age were the Phoenicians, the Arabs, and the Greeks. Slavery existed in Judea as elsewhere, but the class war was relatively mild. Art was undeveloped; only music flourished. The flute, the drum, the cymbal, the "ram's horn" or trumpet, the lyre, and the harp were used to accompany the single voice, the folk song, or the solemn religious antiphons. Jewish religion scorned the concessions of Greek ritual to popular imagination; it would have nothing to do with images, oracles, or birds' entrails; it was less anthropomorphic and superstitious, less colorful and joyful, than the religion of the Greeks. Face to face with the naïve polytheism of Hellenic cults, the rabbis chanted the sonorous refrain still heard in every Jewish synagogue: *Shammai Israel, Adonai eleënu, Adonai echod*—"Hear, O Israel: the Lord is our God, the Lord is one."

Into this simple and puritan life the invading Greeks brought all the distractions and temptations of a refined and epicurean civilization. Around Judea was a ring of Greek settlements and cities: Samaria, Neapolis (Shechem), Gaza, Ascalon, Azotus (Ashdod), Joppa (Jaffa), Apollonia, Doris, Sycamina, Polis (Haifa), and Acco (Acre). Just across the Jordan was a leagued decapolis of Greek cities: Damascus, Gadara, Gerasa, Dium, Philadelphia, Pella, Raphia, Hippo, Scythopolis, and Canetha. Each of these had Greek institutions and establishments—temples to Greek gods and goddesses, schools and academies, gymnasiums and palaestras, and nude games. From such cities, and from Alexandria, Antioch, Delos, and Rhodes, Greeks and Jews came to Jerusalem, bringing the infection of

a Hellenism devoted to science and philosophy, art and literature, beauty and pleasure, song and dance, drinking and feasting, athletics and courtesans and handsome boys, along with a gay sophistication that questioned all morals, and an urbane skepticism that undermined all supernatural belief. How could Jewish youth resist these invitations to delight, this easy liberation from a thousand irksome restraints? Young wits among the Jews began to laugh at the priests as moneygrubbers, and at their pious followers as fools who allowed old age to come upon them without having ever known the pleasures, luxuries, and subtleties of life. Rich Jews were also won over, for they could afford to yield to temptation. Jews who sought appointment from Greek officials felt it the part of policy to speak the Greek language, to live in the Greek way, even to say a few kind words to the Greek gods.

Against this powerful assault upon both the intellect and the senses three forces defended the Jews: the persecution under Antiochus IV, the protection of Rome, and the power and prestige of a Law believed to be divinely revealed. Like antibodies gathering to attack an infection, the more religious among the Jews formed themselves into a sect called Chasidim—the Pious. They began (about 300 B.C.) with a simple pledge to avoid wine for a given period; later, by the inevitable psychology of war, they went to the extremes of Puritanism, and frowned upon all physical pleasure as a surrender to Satan and the Greeks. The Greeks marveled at them, and classified them with the strange "gymnosophists," or nude ascetic philosophers, whom Alexander's army had come upon in India. Even the common Jew deprecated the severe religiosity of the Chasidim, and sought for some middle way. Perhaps a compromise would have been reached had it not been for the attempt of Antiochus Epiphanes to force Hellenism upon Judea by persuasion of the sword.

In 198 Antiochus III defeated Ptolemy V, and made Judea a part of the Seleucid Empire. Tired of the Egyptian yoke, the Jews supported Antiochus, and welcomed his capture of Jerusalem as a liberation. But his successor, Antiochus IV, thought of Judea as a source of revenue; he was planning great campaigns, and needed funds. He ordered the Jews to pay in taxes one third of their grain crops and one half of the fruit of their trees.[14] Ignoring the usual inheritance of the office, he appointed as high priest the sycophantic Jason, who represented the Hellenizing party in Jerusalem and sought permission to establish Greek institutions in Judea. Antiochus heard him gladly, for he was disturbed by the diversity and persistence of Oriental cults in Greek Asia, and dreamed of unifying his

polyglot empire through one law and one faith. When Jason went about these matters with insufficient haste Antiochus replaced him with Menelaus, who gave him larger promises and a fatter bribe.[15] Under Menelaus Yahweh was identified with Zeus, Temple vessels were sold to raise funds, and in some Jewish communities sacrifices were offered to Hellenic deities. A gymnasium was opened in Jerusalem, and Jewish youths, even priests, took part, naked, in athletic games; some young Jews, in the ardor of their Hellenism, underwent operations to remedy the physiological shortcomings that might reveal their race.[16]

Shocked by these developments, and feeling their religion challenged in its very existence, the majority of the Jewish people went over to the side and view of the Chasidim. When Antiochus IV was expelled from Egypt by Popilius (168), the news reached Jerusalem in the form of a report that he had been killed. The rejoicing Jews deposed his appointees, massacred the leaders of the Hellenizing party, and cleansed the Temple of what they felt to be pagan abominations. Antiochus, not dead but humiliated, moneyless, and convinced that the Jews had obstructed his campaign against Egypt and were conspiring to return Judea to the Ptolemies,[17] marched up to Jerusalem, slaughtered Jews of either sex by the thousand, desecrated and looted the Temple, appropriated for the royal coffers its golden altar, its vessels, and its treasuries, restored Menelaus to supreme power, and gave orders for the compulsory Hellenization of all Jews (167). He commanded that the Temple be rededicated as a shrine to Zeus, that a Greek altar be built over the old one, and that the usual sacrifices be replaced with a sacrifice of swine. He forbade the keeping of the Sabbath or the Jewish festivals, and made circumcision a capital crime. Throughout Judea the old religion and its rites were interdicted, and the Greek ritual was made compulsory on pain of death. Every Jew who refused to eat pork, or who was found possessing the Book of the Law, was to be jailed or killed, and the Book wherever found was to be burned.[18] Jerusalem itself was put to the flames, its walls were destroyed, and its Jewish population was sold into slavery. Foreign peoples were brought in to resettle the site, a new fortress was built upon Mt. Zion, and a garrison of troops was left in it to rule the city in the name of the King.[19] At times, it seems, Antiochus thought of establishing and requiring the worship of himself as a god.[20]

The orgy of persecution became intensified as its proceeded. There is always, in any society, a minority whose instincts rejoice in the permission to persecute; it is a release from civilization. The agents of Antiochus, having put an end to all visible expression of Judaism in Jerusalem, passed like a searching fire into the towns and villages. Everywhere they gave

the people a choice between death and participation in Hellenic worship, which included the eating of sacrificial swine.[21] All synagogues and Jewish schools were closed. Those who refused to work on the Sabbath were outlawed as rebels. On the day of the Bacchanalia the Jews were compelled to deck themselves with ivy like the Greeks, to take part in the processions, and to sing wild songs in honor of Dionysus. Many Jews conformed to the demands, waiting for the storm to pass. Many others fled into caves or mountain retreats, lived on clandestine gleanings from the fields, and resolutely carried on the ordinances of Jewish life. The Chasidim circulated among them, preaching courage and resistance. A detachment of royal troops, coming upon some caves in which thousands of Jews—men, women, and children—were hiding, ordered them to come forth. The Jews refused; and because it was the Sabbath, they would not move the stones that might have blocked the entrance to the caves. The soldiers attacked with fire and sword, killing many of the refugees and asphyxiating the remainder with smoke.[22] Women who had circumcized their newborn sons were cast with their infants over the city walls to death.[23] The Greeks were surprised to find the strength of the old faith; not for centuries had they seen such loyalty to an idea. The stories of martyrdom went from mouth to mouth, filled books like the First and Second Maccabees, and gave to Christianity the prototypes of its martyrs and its martyrology. Judaism, which had been near assimilation, became intensified in religious and national consciousness, and withdrew into a protective isolation.

Among the Jews who in those days fled from Jerusalem were Mattathias —of the family of Hasmonai, of the tribe of Aaron—and his five sons— Johannan Caddis, Simon, Judas, Eleazar, and Jonathan. When Apelles, an agent of Antiochus, came to Modin, where these six had sought refuge, he summoned the inhabitants to repudiate the Law and sacrifice to Zeus. The aged Mattathias came forward with his sons and said: "Even should all the people in the kingdom obey the order to depart from the faith of their fathers, I and my sons will abide by the Covenant of our ancestors." As one of the Jews approached the altar to make the required sacrifice Mattathias slew him, and slew also the King's commissioner. Then he said to the people: "Whoever is zealous for the Law, and wishes to support the Covenant, let him follow me."[24] Many of the villagers retired with him and his sons to the mountains of Ephraim; and there they were joined by a small band of young rebels, and by such of the Chasidim as were still alive.

Soon afterward Mattathias died, having designated as captain of his band

his son Judas, called Maccabee.* Judas was a warrior whose courage equaled his piety; before every battle he prayed like a saint, but in the hour of battle "he was like a lion in his rage." The little army "lived in the mountains after the manner of beasts, feeding on herbs." Every now and then it descended upon a neighboring village, killed backsliders, pulled down pagan altars, and "what children soever they found uncircumcized, those they circumcized valiantly."[25] These things being reported to Antiochus, he sent an army of Syrian Greeks to destroy the Maccabean force. Judas met them in the pass of Emmaus; and though the Greeks were trained mercenaries fully armed, and Judas' band was poorly armed and clad, the Jews won a complete victory (166). Antiochus sent a larger force, whose general was so confident that he brought slave merchants with him to buy the Jews whom he expected to capture, and posted in the towns the prices that he would ask.[26] Judas defeated these troops at Mizpah, and so decisively that Jerusalem fell into his hands without resistance. He removed all pagan altars and ornaments from the Temple, cleansed and rededicated it, and restored the ancient service amid the acclaim of the returning orthodox Jews (164).†

As the regent Lysias advanced with a new army to recapture the capital, the news came—this time true—that Antiochus was dead (163). Desiring to be free for action elsewhere, Lysias offered the Jews full religious freedom on condition that they lay down their arms. The Chasidim consented, the Maccabeans refused; Judas announced that Judea, to be safe from further persecutions, must achieve political as well as religious liberty. Intoxicated with power, the Maccabeans now took their turn at persecution, pursuing the Hellenizing faction vengefully not only in Jerusalem but in the cities that bordered the frontier.[27] In 161 Judas defeated Nicanor at Adasa, and strengthened himself by making an alliance with Rome; but in the same year, fighting against great odds at Elasa, he was slain. His brother Jonathan carried on the war bravely, but was himself killed at Acco (143). The only surviving brother, Simon, supported by Rome, won from Demetrius II, in 142, an acknowledgment of Judean independence. By popular decree Simon was appointed both high priest and general; and as these offices were made hereditary in his family, he became the founder of the Hasmonean dynasty. The first year of his reign was counted as the beginning of a new era, and an issue of coinage proclaimed the heroic rebirth of the Jewish state.

* Usually but uncertainly interpreted as "The Hammer."

† The anniversary of this Rededication (Hanukkah) is still celebrated in nearly every Jewish home.

CHAPTER XXV

Egypt and the West

I. THE KINGS' REGISTER

THE smallest but richest morsel of Alexander's legacy was allotted to the ablest and wisest of his generals. With characteristic loyalty—perhaps as a visible sanction of his authority—Ptolemy, son of Lagus, brought the body of the dead king to Memphis, and had it entombed in a sarcophagus of gold.* He brought with him also Alexander's occasional mistress Thais, married her, and had by her two sons. He was a plain, blunt soldier, capable both of generous feeling and of realistic thinking. While other inheritors of Alexander's realm spent half their lives in war, and dreamed of undivided sovereignty, Ptolemy devoted himself to consolidating his position in an alien country, and to promoting Egyptian agriculture, commerce, and industry. He built a great fleet, and made Egypt as secure against naval attack as nature had made it almost unassailable by land. He helped Rhodes and the Leagues to preserve their independence of Macedon, and so won the title of *Soter*. Only when, after eighteen years of labor, he had firmly organized the political and economic life of his new realm did he call himself king (305). Through him and his successor Greek Egypt established its rule over Cyrene, Crete, the Cyclades, Cyprus, Syria, Palestine, Phoenicia, Samos, Lesbos, Samothrace, and the Hellespont. In his old age he found time to write astonishingly truthful commentaries on his campaigns, and to establish, about 290, the Museum and Library that were to make the fame of Alexandria. In 285, feeling his eighty-two years, he appointed his second son, Ptolemy Philadelphus, to the throne, yielded the government to him, and took his place as a subject in the young king's court. Two years later he died.

Already the fertile valley and delta had poured great wealth into the royal treasury. Ptolemy I, to give a dinner to his friends, had had to borrow their silver and rugs; Ptolemy II spent $2,500,000 on the feast that climaxed his coronation.[2] The new Pharaoh was a convert to the philoso-

* Ptolemy Philadelphus had the sarcophagus removed to Alexandria. Ptolemy Cocces melted down the gold for his use, and exposed the mortal remains of Alexander in a glass coffin.[1]

phy of Cyrene, and was resolved to enjoy each *monochronos hedone*—every pleasure that the moment gave. He ate himself into obesity, tried a variety of mistresses, repudiated his wife, and finally married his sister Arsinoë.[3] The new queen ruled the Empire and managed its wars while Ptolemy II reigned among the chefs and scholars of his court. Following and improving upon the example of his father, he invited to Alexandria as his guests famous poets, savants, critics, scientists, philosophers, and artists, and made his capital beautiful with architecture in the Greek style. During his long reign Alexandria became the literary and scientific capital of the Mediterranean, and Alexandrian literature flourished as it would never do again. Nevertheless Philadelphus was unhappy in his old age; his gout and his cares increased with the extent of his wealth and his power. Looking out from his palace window he saw and envied a beggar who lay at ease in the sun on the harbor dunes, and he mourned, "Alas, that I was not born one of these!"[4] Haunted by the fear of death, he sought in the lore of Egyptian priests the magic elixir of eternal life.[5]

He had so enlarged and lavishly financed the Museum and Library that later history named him as their founder. In 307 Demetrius of Phalerum, expelled from Athens, had taken refuge in Egypt. Ten years later we find him at the court of Ptolemy I. It was he, apparently, who suggested to Ptolemy Soter that the capital and the dynasty might be made illustrious by establishing a Museum—i.e., a House of the Muses—i.e., of the arts and sciences—which would rival the universities of Athens. Inspired, probably, by Aristotle's industry in collecting and classifying books, knowledge, animals, plants, and constitutions, Demetrius appears to have recommended the erection of a group of buildings capable not only of sheltering a great collection of books, but also of housing scholars who would devote their lives to research. The plan appealed to the first two Ptolemies; funds were provided, and the new university slowly took form near the royal palaces. There was a general mess hall, where the scholars seem to have had their meals; there was an exedra, or lecture hall, a court, a cloister, a garden, an astronomical observatory, and the great Library. The head of the entire institution was technically a priest, since it was formally dedicated to the Muses as actual goddesses. Living in the Museum were four groups of scholars: astronomers, writers, mathematicians, and physicians. All of these men were Greeks, and all received a salary from the royal treasury. Their function was not to teach, but to make researches, studies, and experiments. In later decades, as students multiplied about the Museum, its members undertook to give lectures, but the Museum remained to the end an

Institute for Advanced Studies rather than a university. It was, so far as we know, the first establishment ever set up by a state for the promotion of literature and science. It was the distinctive contribution of the Ptolemies and Alexandria to the history of civilization.

Ptolemy Philadelphus died in 246, after a long and largely beneficent reign. Ptolemy III Euergetes (Well-Doer) was another Thothmes III, intent on conquering the Near East; he took Sardis and Babylon, marched as far as India, and so effectually disorganized the Seleucid Empire that it crumbled at the touch of Rome. We shall not follow the record of his wars, for though there is drama in the details of strife, there is a dreary eternity in its causes and results; such history becomes a menial attendance upon the vicissitudes of power, in which victories and defeats cancel one another into a resounding zero. Euergetes' young wife Berenice gave thanks for his successes by dedicating a lock of her hair to the gods; the poets celebrated the story, and the astronomers lauded her to the skies by naming one of the constellations Coma Berenices—Berenice's Hair.

Ptolemy IV Philopator so loved his father that he imitated his wars and his triumphs. But his victory over Antiochus III at Raphia (217) had been won with native troops—their first use by any Ptolemy; and the Egyptians, now armed and conscious of their strength, began from this time onward to break down the authority of the Greeks on the Nile. Philopator gave himself to amusement, spent much time on his spacious pleasure boat, introduced the Bacchanalia into Egypt, and half persuaded himself that he was descended from Dionysus. In 205 his wife was killed by his mistress; and shortly afterward Philopator himself passed away. In the ensuing chaos Philip V of Macedon and Antiochus III of Seleucia were about to dismember and absorb Egypt when Rome—with which the second Ptolemy had made a treaty of friendship—entered upon the scene, defeated Philip, sent Antiochus packing, and made Egypt a Roman protectorate (205).

II. SOCIALISM UNDER THE PTOLEMIES

By far the most interesting aspect of Ptolemaic Egypt is its extensive experiment in state socialism. Royal ownership of the land had long been a sacred custom in Egypt; the Pharaoh, as king and god, had full right to the soil and all that it produced. The fellah was not a slave, but he could not leave his place without the permission of the government, and he was required to turn over the larger part of his crops to the state.[8] The Ptolemies accepted this system, and extended it by appropriating the great tracts which, under previous dynasties, had belonged to the Egyptian nobles or priests. A great bureaucracy of governmental overseers, supported by armed guards, managed all Egypt as a vast state farm.[7] Nearly every peasant in Egypt was told by these officials what soil to till and what crops to grow; his labor and his animals could at any time be requisitioned by the state for mining, building, hunting, and the making of canals or roads; his harvest was gauged by state measurers, registered by the scribes, threshed on the royal threshing floor, and conveyed by a living chain of fellahs into the granaries of the king.[8] There were exceptions to the system: the Ptolemies allowed the farmer to own his house and garden; they resigned the cities to private property; and they gave a right of leasehold to soldiers whose services were rewarded with land. But this leasehold was usually confined to areas which the owner agreed to devote to vineyards, orchards, or olive groves; it excluded the power of bequest, and might at any time be canceled by the king. As Greek energy and skill improved these cleruchic (shareholders') lands, a demand arose for the right to transmit the property from father to son. In the second century such bequest was permitted by custom, but not by law; in the last century before Christ it was recognized by law,[9] and the usual evolution from common property to private property was complete.

Doubtless this system of socialism had been evolved because the conditions of tillage in Egypt required more co-operation, more unison of action in time and space, than individual ownership could be expected to provide. The amount and character of the crops to be sown depended upon the extent of the annual inundation, and the efficiency of irrigation and drainage; these matters naturally made for central control. Greek engineers in the employ of the government improved the ancient processes, and applied a more scientific and intensive agriculture to the land. The ancient shaduf was replaced by the noria, a large wheel sometimes forty feet in diameter, equipped with buckets hanging freely on the interior rim; at the top of the revolution each bucket was tilted by an obstructing bar, and emptied its contents into an irrigation reservoir; better still, the "screw of Archimedes" and the pump of Ctesibius* raised water with a speed unknown before the Ptolemies.[10] The centralization of economic management in the hands of the government, and the institution of forced labor, made possible great public works of flood control, road construction, irrigation, and building, and prepared the way for the engineering feats of

* See Chap. XXVII below.

Rome. Ptolemy II drained Lake Moeris, and turned its bed into a great tract of fertile land for distribution among the soldiers. In 285 he began to restore the canal from the Nile near Heliopolis to the Red Sea near Suez;[11] Pharaoh Necho and Darius I had built and rebuilt this, but twice the shifting sands had choked it up, as in a century they would do again.

Industry operated under similar conditions. The government not only owned the mines, but either worked them itself, or appropriated the ore.[12] The Ptolemies opened up valuable gold deposits in Nubia, and had a stable gold coinage. They controlled the copper mines of Cyprus and Sinai. They had a monopoly of oil—derived not from the soil but from plants like linseed, croton, and sesame. The government fixed, each year, the amount of land to be sown to such plants; it took the whole produce at its own price; it extracted the oil in state factories through great beam presses worked by serfs; it sold the oil to retailers at its own price, and excluded foreign competition by a heavy tariff; its profit ranged from seventy to three hundred per cent.[13] Apparently there were similar governmental subsidies in salt, natron (carbonate of soda used as soap), incense, papyrus, and textiles; there were some private textile factories, but they had to sell all their product to the state.[14] Minor industries were left in private hands; the state merely licensed and supervised them, bought a large share of their output at fixed prices, and taxed a good part of the profits into the royal treasury. Handicrafts were carried on by ancient guilds, whose members were by tradition bound to their trade, their village, even to their domicile.[15] Industry was well developed; chariots, furniture, terra cotta, carpets, cosmetics were produced in abundance; glass blowing and the weaving of linen were Alexandrian specialties. Invention was more advanced in Ptolemaic Egypt than in any economy before imperial Rome's; the screw chain, the wheel chain, the cam chain, the ratchet chain, the pulley chain, and the screw press were all in use;[16] and the chemistry of dyes had progressed to the point of treating cloths with diverse reagents which brought forth, from immersion in one dye, a variety of fast colors.[17] In general the factories of Alexandria were worked by slaves, whose low cost of maintenance enabled the Ptolemies to undersell in foreign trade the products of Greek handicraft.[18]

All commerce was controlled and regulated by the government; retail traders were usually state agents distributing state goods.[19] All caravan routes and waterways were owned by the state. Ptolemy II introduced the camel into Egypt, and organized a camel post to the south; this carried only governmental communications, but these included nearly all the commercial correspondence of the country. The Nile was busy with passenger and freight traffic, apparently under private management subject to state regulation.[20] For the Mediterranean trade the Ptolemies built the largest commercial fleet of the time, with vessels of three hundred tons burden.[21] The warehouses of Alexandria invited world trade; its double harbor was the envy of other cities; its lighthouse was one of the Seven Wonders.* The fields, factories, and workshops of Egypt supplied a great surplus, which found markets as far east as China, as far south as central Africa, as far north as Russia and the British Isles. Egyptian explorers sailed down to Zanzibar and Somaliland, and told the world about the Troglodytes who lived along the east African coast on sea food, ostriches, carrots, and roots.[24] To break the Arab hold on Indian trade with the Near East, Egyptian ships sailed directly from the Nile to India. Under the wise encouragement of the Ptolemies Alexandria became the leading port of reshipment for Eastern merchandise destined for the markets of the Mediterranean.

This flowering of commerce and industry was quickened by excellent banking conveniences. Payment in kind survived to some degree, as a legacy from ancient Egypt; and the grain of the royal treasuries was used as part of the bank reserve; but deposits, withdrawals, and transfers of grain might be made on paper instead of being physically performed.[25] Beside this modified barter rose a complex money economy. Banking was a government monopoly, but its operations might be delegated to private firms.[26] Bills were paid by drafts on bank balances; banks lent money at interest, and paid the accounts of the royal treasury. The central bank, at Alexandria, had branches in all the important towns. Never in known history had agriculture, industry, commerce, and finance reached so rich, so unified, and so brutal a development.

The masters and beneficiaries of this system were the free Greeks of the capital. At the head of all was the Pharaoh-god-king. From the viewpoint of the Greek population the Ptolemy was truly a *Soter* or Savior, a *Euergetes* or Benefactor; he gave them a hundred thousand places in the bureaucracy, endless eco-

---

* Sostratus of Cnidus designed it for Ptolemy II, at a cost of eight hundred talents (about $2,400,000).[22] It rose in several setbacks to a height of four hundred feet; it was covered with white marble and adorned with sculptures in marble and bronze; above the pillared cupola that contained the light rose a twenty-one-foot statue of Poseidon. The flame came from the burning of resinous wood, and was made visible, probably by convex metal mirrors, to a distance of thirty-eight miles.[23] The structure was completed in 279 B.C., and was destroyed in the thirteenth century A.D. The island of Pharos, on which it stood, is now the Ras-et-Tin quarter of Alexandria; the site of the lighthouse has been covered by the sea.

nomic opportunities, unprecedented facilities for the life of the mind, and a wealthy court as the source and center of a luxurious social life. Nor was the king an incalculable despot. Egyptian tradition combined with Greek law to build up a system of legislation which borrowed from, and improved upon, the Athenian code in every respect except freedom. The edicts of the king had full legal force; but the cities enjoyed considerable self-government, and the Egyptian, Greek, and Jewish population lived each under its own system of law, chose its own magistrates, and pled before its own courts.[27] A Turin papyrus gives us the record of an Alexandrian lawsuit; the issues are precisely defined, the evidence is carefully presented, precedents are summarized, and the final judgment is given with judicial impartiality. Other papyri preserve Alexandrian wills, and reveal the antiquity of legal forms: "This is the will of Peisias the Lycian, son of X, of sound mind and deliberate intention."[28]

The Ptolemaic was the most efficiently organized government in the Hellenistic world. It took its national form from Egypt and Persia, its municipal form from Greece, and passed them on to Imperial Rome. The country was divided into nomes or provinces, each administered by appointees of the king. Nearly all these officials were Greek. The idea of Alexander, that Greek and Oriental or Egyptian should live and mingle on equal terms, was forgotten as unlucrative; the valley of the Nile became frankly a conquered land. The Greek overseers brought an advanced technology and management to the economic life of Egypt, and enormously expanded the wealth of the nation; but they took the increase. The state charged high prices for the products which it controlled, and barred competition with a tariff wall; hence olive oil that cost twenty-one drachmas in Delos cost fifty-two in Alexandria. Everywhere the government took rentals, taxes, customs, and tolls, sometimes labor and life itself. The peasant paid a fee to the state for the right to keep cattle, for the fodder that he fed them, and for the privilege of grazing them on the common pasture land. The private owner of gardens, vineyards, or orchards paid a sixth—under Ptolemy II a half—of his produce to the state.[29] All persons except soldiers, priests, and government officials paid a poll tax. There were taxes on salt, legal documents, and bequests; a five per cent tax on rentals, a ten per cent tax on sales, a twenty-five per cent levy on all fish caught in Egyptian waters, a toll on goods passing from village to town, or along the Nile; there were high export as well as import duties at all Egyptian ports; there were special taxes to maintain the fleet and the lighthouse, to keep the municipal physicians and police in good humor, and to buy a gold crown for every new king;[30] nothing was overlooked that could fatten the state. To keep track of all taxable products, income, and transactions the government maintained a swarm of scribes, and a vast system of personal and property registration; to collect the taxes it farmed them out to specialists, supervised their operations, and held their possessions as security till the returns were in. The total revenue of the Ptolemies, in money and kind, was probably the greatest gathered by any government between the fall of Persia and the ascendancy of Rome.

III. ALEXANDRIA

Most of this wealth came to Alexandria. The nome capitals and a few other towns were also prosperous, with paved and lighted streets, police protection, and a good water supply; but nothing quite so "modern" as Alexandria had ever been seen before. Strabo describes it in the first century A.D. as over three miles long and a mile wide; Pliny reckons the city wall as fifteen miles in length.[31] Dinocrates of Rhodes and Sostratus of Cnidus laid out the city on the rectangular plan, with a central avenue one hundred feet wide running from east to west, crossed by an equally wide avenue from north to south. Each of these thoroughfares, and probably some others, was well lighted at night, and was kept cool during the day by mile after mile of shaded colonnades. Of the four quarters into which the main arteries divided the city the westernmost, Rhacotis, was occupied chiefly by Egyptians; the northeast portion formed the Jewish quarter; the southeast corner, or Brucheum, contained the royal palace, the Museum, the Library, the tombs of the Ptolemies, the sarcophagus of Alexander (the Hôtel des Invalides of the age), the arsenal, the chief Greek temples, and many spacious parks. One park had a portico six hundred feet in length; another contained the royal zoological collection. In the center of the city were the administrative buildings, the government storehouses, the courthouse, the main gymnasium, and a thousand shops and bazaars. Outside the gates were a stadium, a hippodrome or race track, an amphitheater, and a vast cemetery known as the Necropolis, or City of the Dead.[32] Along the beach ran a succession of bathing establishments and resorts. A dike or mole, called Heptastadium because it was seven stadia long, connected the city with the island of Pharos, and made two harbors out of one. Behind the city lay Lake Mareotis, which provided ports and outlets for the traffic on the Nile; here the Ptolemies kept their pleasure boats and took their royal ease.*

The population of Alexandria about 200 B.C. was as varied as in a modern metropolis: from four to five hundred thousand Macedonians, Greeks,

---

* Hardly anything but a few catacombs and pillars have been preserved from ancient Alexandria. Its remains lie directly under the present capital, making excavation expensive; probably they have sunk beneath the water level; and parts of the old city have been covered by the Mediterranean.

Egyptians, Jews, Persians, Anatolians, Syrians, Arabs, and negroes.*[33] The growth of commerce had swelled the lower middle class, and filled the cosmopolitan capital with a busy, talkative, litigious crowd of shopkeepers and traders, always on the alert for a bargain, and with no prejudice in favor of honesty. At the top were the Macedonians and the Greeks, living in such luxury as astonished the Roman ambassadors who were appointed to the court in 273. Athenaeus recounts the delicacies that burdened the tables and digestions of the master class,[34] and Herodas writes: "Alexandria is the house of Aphrodite, and everything is to be found there—wealth, playgrounds, a large army, a serene sky, public displays, philosophers, precious metals, fine young men, a good royal house, an academy of science, exquisite wines, and beautiful women."[35] Alexandria's poets were discovering the literary value of virginity, and its novelists would soon make it the theme and final casualty of many a tale; but the city was notorious for the generosity of its women and the number of its stepdaughters of joy; Polybius complained that the finest private homes in Alexandria belonged to courtesans.[36] Women of all classes moved freely through the streets, shopped in the stores, and mingled with the men. Some of them made a name for themselves in literature and scholarship.[37] The Macedonian queens and ladies of the court, from Ptolemy II's Arsinoë to Antony's Cleopatra, took an active part in politics, and served policy rather than love with their crimes; but they retained sufficient charm to arouse the men to unprecedented gallantry, at least in poetry and prose, and brought into Alexandrian society an element of feminine influence and grace unknown in classic Greece.

Probably a fifth of Alexandria's population was Jewish. As far back as the seventh century there had been Hebrew settlements in Egypt; many Jewish traders had entered in the wake of the Persian conquest. Alexander had urged Jews to emigrate to Alexandria, and had, according to Josephus, offered them equal political and economic rights with the Greeks.[38] Ptolemy I, after taking Jerusalem, carried with him into Egypt thousands of Jewish captives, who were freed by his successor;[39] at the same time he invited well-to-do Hebrews to establish their homes and businesses in Alexandria.[40] By the beginning of the Christian era there were a million Jews in Egypt.[41] A large number of these lived in the Jewish quarter of the capital. It was no ghetto, for the Jews were free to live in any quarter but the Brucheum, which was restricted to official families and their servi-

* The population of Alexandria in 1927 was 570,000.

tors. They chose their own *gerousia* or senate, and followed their own worship. In 169 the high priest Onias III built a great temple at Leontopolis, a suburb of Alexandria, and Ptolemy VI, his personal friend, assigned the revenues of Heliopolis for its maintenance. Such temples served as schools and meeting places as well as for religious services; hence they were called by the Greek-speaking Jews *synagogai*, i.e., places of assembly. Since few Egyptian Jews after the second or third generation in Egypt knew Hebrew, the reading of the Law was followed by an interpretation in Greek. Out of these explanations and applications rose the custom of preaching a sermon on a text; and out of the ritual came the first forms of the Catholic Mass.[42]

This religious and racial separation combined with economic rivalries to arouse, towards the end of this period, an anti-Semitic movement in Alexandria. The Greeks and Egyptians alike were habituated to the union of church and state, and frowned upon the cultural independence of the Jews; furthermore, they felt the competition of the Jewish artisan or businessman, and resented his energy, tenacity, and skill. When Rome began to import Egyptian grain it was the Jewish merchants of Alexandria who carried the cargoes in their fleets.[42a] The Greeks, perceiving their failure to Hellenize the Jews, feared for their own future in a state where the majority remained persistently Oriental, and bred so vigorously. Forgetting the legislation of Pericles, they complained that the Jewish law forbade mixed marriages, and that the Jews for the most part kept to themselves. Anti-Semitic literature multiplied. Manetho, the Egyptian historian, gave currency to the story that the Jews had been expelled from Egypt, centuries back, because they had been afflicted with scrofula or leprosy.[43] Feeling mounted on both sides until, in the first century of the Christian era, it broke out into destructive violence.

The Jews did what they could to allay the resentment against their *amixia*—their social separation—and their success. Though they clung to their religion they spoke Greek, studied and wrote about Greek literature, and translated their sacred books and their histories into Greek. To acquaint the Greeks with the Jewish religious tradition, and to enable the Jew who knew no Hebrew to read his own scriptures, a group of Alexandrian Jewish scholars began, probably under Ptolemy II, a Greek translation of the Hebrew Bible. The kings favored the undertaking in the hope that it would make the Jews of Egypt more independent of Jerusalem, and would lessen the flow of Jewish-Egyptian funds to Palestine. Legend told how Ptolemy Philadelphus, at the suggestion of Demetrius of Phalerum, had invited some seventy Jewish scholars to come from Judea about 250 to translate the scriptures of their people; how the King had lodged each of them in a separate room on Pharos, and had kept them without intercommunication until each had made his own rendering of the Pentateuch; how all the seventy versions, when finished, agreed word for word, proving the divine inspiration of the text and of the translators; how the King rewarded the scholars with costly presents of gold; and how from these circumstances the Greek version of the Hebrew Bible came to be known as the *hermeneia kata tous hebdomekonta*—the *Interpretation according to the Seventy*—in Latin, *Interpretatio Septuaginta* (*sc. Seniorum*)—in a word, the "Septuagint."*[44] Whatever the process of translation, the Pentateuch seems to have appeared in Greek before the close of the third century, and the Prophetic books in the second.[46] This was the Bible used by Philo and St. Paul.

The process of Hellenization in Egypt failed as completely with the natives as with the Jews. Outside of Alexandria the Egyptians sullenly maintained their own religion, their own dress or nudity, their own immemorial ways. The Greeks thought of themselves as conquerors, not as fellow men; they did not bother to build Greek cities south of the Delta, or to learn the language of the people; and their laws did not recognize the marriage of an Egyptian with a Greek. Ptolemy I tried to unite the Greek and native faiths by identifying Serapis and Zeus; later Ptolemies encouraged the cult of themselves as gods to offer a common and convenient object of worship to their heterogeneous population; but those Egyptians who were not courting office paid little attention to these artificial cults. The Egyptian priests, shorn of their wealth and power, and dependent for their sustenance upon grants of money from the state, waited patiently for the Greek wave to recede. In the end it was not Hellenism that won in Alexandria, but mysticism; now were laid the foundations of Neo-Platonism and the medley of promissory cults that competed for the Alexandrian soul in the centuries that surrounded the birth of Christ. Osiris as Serapis became the favorite god of the later Egyptians, and of many Egyptian Greeks; Isis regained popularity as the goddess of women and motherhood. When Christianity came neither the clergy nor the people found it impossible to change Isis into Mary, and Serapis into Christ.

---

* The story was based upon a letter purporting to have been written by one Aristeas in the first century A.D. The letter was proved spurious by Hody of Oxford in 1684.[45]

IV. REVOLT

The lesson of Ptolemaic socialism is that even a government may exploit. Under the first two Ptolemies the system worked reasonably well: great engineering enterprises were completed, agriculture was improved, marketing was brought into order, the overseers behaved with a modest measure of injustice and partiality, and though the exploitation of materials and men was thorough, its profits went in large degree to develop and adorn the country, and to finance its cultural life. Three factors ruined the experiment. The Ptolemies went to war, and spent more and more of the people's earnings upon armies, navies, and campaigns. After Philadelphus there was a rapid deterioration in the quality of the kings; they ate and drank and mated, and allowed the administration of the system to fall into the hands of rascals who ground every possible penny out of the poor. The fact that the exploiters were foreigners was never forgotten by the Egyptians, nor by the priests who dreamed of the fleshpots of Egypt that their class had enjoyed before the Persian and Greek domination.

The Ptolemaic conception of socialism was essentially one of intensified production rather than of wide distribution. The fellah received enough of his product to keep him alive, but not enough to encourage him in his work or in the business of rearing a family. Generation after generation the government's exactions grew. The system of detailed national control became intolerable, like the relentlessly watchful eye of a despotic parent. The state lent seed-corn to the peasant to plant his crop, and then bound him to the farm until the harvest was in. No peasant might use any of his own product until all his debts had been paid to the state. The fellah was patient, but even he began to grumble. By the second century a substantial part of the soil had been abandoned for lack of peasants to work it; the cleruchs or lessees of royal land could get no tenants to till it for them; they tried to do it themselves, but were not up to the task; gradually the desert crept back upon civilization. In the gold mines of Nubia the slaves worked naked in dark and narrow galleries, in cramping positions, loaded with chains, and encouraged by the whip of the overseer; their food was poor, not even enough to keep them alive; thousands of them succumbed from malnutrition and fatigue; and the only welcome event in their lives was death.[47] The common laborer in the factories received one obol (nine cents) a day, the skilled worker two or three. Every tenth day was a day of rest.

Complaints multiplied, and strikes grew more frequent: strikes among the miners, the quarrymen, the boatmen, the peasants, the artisans, the tradesmen, even the overseers and the police; strikes seldom for better pay, since the toilers had ceased to hope for this, but of simple exhaustion and despair. "We are worn out," says a papyrus record of one strike; "we will run away"—i.e., seek sanctuary in a temple.[48] Nearly all the exploiters were Greeks, nearly all the exploited were Egyptians or Jews. The priests clandestinely appealed to the religious feelings of the natives, while the Greeks resented any concession made to Jews or Egyptians by the government. In the capital the populace was bribed by state bounties and spectacles, but it was excluded from the royal quarter, was watched by a large military force, and was allowed no voice in national affairs; in the end it became an irresponsible and violent mob.[49] In 216 the Egyptians revolted, but were put down; in 189 they revolted again, and the mutiny continued for five years. The Ptolemies won for a time by the force of their army, and by raising their contributions to the priests; but the situation had become impossible. The country had been milked to depletion, and even the exploiters felt that nothing remained.

Disintegration set in on every side. The Ptolemies passed from natural to unnatural vice, from intelligence to stupidity; they married with a freedom and haste that forfeited the esteem of their people; luxury unfitted them for war or government, at last even for thought. Lawlessness and dishonesty, incompetence and hopelessness, the absence of competition and of the stimulus that comes from ownership, lowered year by year the productivity of the land. Literature waned, creative art died; after the third century Alexandria added little to either. The Egyptians lost respect for the Greeks; the Greeks, if such a thing can be believed, lost respect for themselves. Year by year they forgot their own language, and spoke a corrupt mixture of Greek and Egyptian; more and more of them married their sisters, after native custom, or married into Egyptian families and were absorbed; thousands of them worshiped Egyptian gods. By the second century the Greeks had ceased to be the dominant race even politically; the Ptolemies, to preserve their authority, had adopted the Egyptian faith and ritual, and had increased the power of the priests. As the kings sank into epicurean ease the clergy reasserted its leadership, and won back year by year the lands and privileges which the earlier Ptolemies had taken away.[50] The Rosetta Stone, dated 196 B.C., describes the coronation ceremonies of Ptolemy V as following almost completely the Egyptian forms. Under Ptolemy V (203-181) and Ptolemy VI (181-145) dynastic feuds absorbed the energies of the royal house, while Egyptian agriculture and industry decayed. Order and peace were not restored until Caesar, as a mere incident in his career, took Egypt with hardly a blow, and Augustus made it a province of Rome (30 B.C.).

V. SUNSET IN SICILY

The Hellenistic age faced east and south, and almost ignored the west. Cyrene prospered as usual, having learned that it is better to trade than to war; out of it, in this period, came Callimachus the poet, Eratosthenes the philosopher, and Carneades the philosopher. Greek Italy was worried and weakened by the double challenge of multiplying natives and rising Rome, while Sicily lived in daily fear of the Carthaginian power. Twenty-three years after the coming of Timoleon a rich man's revolution suppressed the Syracusan democracy, and put the government into the hands of six hundred oligarchic families (320). These divided into factions, and were in turn overthrown by a radical revolution in which four thousand persons were killed and six thousand of the well to do were sent into banishment. Agathocles won dictatorship by promising a cancellation of debts and a redistribution of the land.[51] So, periodically, the concentration of wealth becomes extreme, and gets righted by taxation or by revolution.

After forty-seven years of chaos, during which the Carthaginians repeatedly invaded the island, and Pyrrhus came, won, lost, and went, Syracuse by unmerited good fortune fell into the power of Hieron II, the most beneficent of the many dictators thrown up by the passions and turbulence of the Sicilian Greeks. Hieron ruled for fifty-four years, says the astonished Polybius, "without killing, exiling, or injuring a single citizen, which indeed is the most remarkable of all things."[52] Surrounded by all the means of luxury, he led a modest and temperate life, and lived to the age of ninety. On several occasions he wished to resign his authority, but the people begged him to retain it.[53] He had the good judgment to make an alliance with Rome, and thereby kept the Carthaginians at bay for half a century. He gave the city order and peace, and considerable freedom; he executed great public works, and without oppressive taxation left a full treasury at his death. Under his protection or patronage Archimedes brought ancient science to its culmination, and Theocritus sang, in the last perfect Greek, the loveliness of Sicily and the expected bounty of its king. Syracuse became now the most populous and prosperous city in Hellas.[54]

Hieron amused his leisure by watching his artisans, under the supervision of Archimedes, construct for him a pleasure boat that embodied all the shipbuilding art and science of antiquity. It was half a stadium (407 feet) in length; it had a sport deck with a gymnasium and a large marble bath, and a shaded garden deck with a great variety of plants; it was manned by six hundred seamen in twenty groups of oars, and could carry in addition three hundred passengers or marines; it had sixty cabins, some with mosaic floors, and doors of ivory and precious woods; it was elegantly furnished in every part, and was adorned with paintings and statuary. It was protected against attack by armor and turrets; from each of the eight turrets great beams extended, with a hole at the end through which large stones could be dropped upon enemy vessels; throughout its length Archimedes constructed a great catapult capable of hurling stones of three talents' weight (174 pounds), or arrows twelve cubits (eighteen feet) long. It could carry 3900 tons of cargo, and itself weighed a thousand tons. Hieron had hoped to use it in regular service between Syracuse and Alexandria; but finding it too large for his own docks, and extravagantly expensive to maintain, he filled it with corn and fish from Sicily's abounding fields and seas, and sent it, vessels and contents, as a gift to Egypt, which was suffering an unusual dearth of corn.[55]

Hieron died in 216. He had wished to establish a democratic constitution before his death, but his daughters prevailed upon his dotage to bequeath his power to his grandson.[56] Hieronymus turned out to be a weakling and a scoundrel; he abandoned the Roman alliance, received envoys from Carthage, and permitted them to become in effect the rulers of Syracuse. Rome, not abounding in corn, prepared to fight Carthage for the wealth of an island that had never learned to govern itself. All the Mediterranean world, like a decaying fruit, prepared to fall into the hands of a greater and more ruthless conqueror than Greek history had ever known.

CHAPTER XXVI

Books

I. LIBRARIES AND SCHOLARS

IN every field of Hellenistic life except the drama we find the same phenomenon—Greek civilization not destroyed but dispersed. Athens was dying, and the Greek settlements of the west, barring Syracuse, were in decay; but the Greek cities of Egypt and the East were at their material and cultural zenith. Polybius, a man of wide experience, historical knowledge, and careful judgment, spoke, about 148 B.C., of "the present day, when the progress of the arts and sciences has been so rapid";[1] the words have a familiar ring. Through the dissemination of Greek as a common tongue a cultural unity was now established which would last in the eastern Mediterranean for nearly a thousand years. All men of education in the new empires learned Greek as the medium of diplomacy, literature, and science; a book written in Greek could be understood by almost any educated non-Greek in Egypt or the Near East. Men spoke of the *oikoumene*, or inhabited world, as one civilization, and developed a cosmopolitan outlook less stimulating but perhaps more sensible than the proud and narrow nationalism of the city-state.

For this enlarged audience thousands of writers wrote hundreds of thousands of books. We know the names of eleven hundred Hellenistic authors; the unknown are an incalculable multitude. A cursive script had developed to facilitate writing; indeed, as early as the fourth century B.C. we hear of systems of shorthand whereby "certain vowels and consonants can be expressed by strokes placed in various positions."[2] Books were written on Egyptian papyrus until Ptolemy VI, hoping to check the growth of the library at Pergamum, forbade the export of the material from Egypt. Eumenes II countered by encouraging the mass production of the treated skins of sheep and calves, which had long been used for writing purposes in the East; and soon "parchment," from the city and the name of Pergamum, rivaled paper as a vehicle of communication and literature.

Books having grown to such numbers, libraries became a necessity. These had existed before as the luxury of Egyptian or Mesopotamian potentates; but apparently Aristotle's library was the first extensive private collection. We may conjecture its size and worth from the fact that he paid $18,000 for that part of it which he bought from Plato's successor Speusippus. Aristotle bequeathed his books to Theophrastus, who bequeathed them (287) to Neleus, who took them to Scepsis in Asia Minor, where they were buried, says tradition, to escape the literary cupidity of the Pergamene kings. After almost a century of this damaging interment the volumes were sold about 100 B.C. to Apellicon of Teos, an Athenian philosopher. Apellicon found that many passages had been eaten away by the damp; he made new copies, filling in the gaps as intelligently as he could;[3] this may explain why Aristotle is not the most fascinating philosopher in history. When Sylla captured Athens (86) he appropriated Apellicon's library and transported it to Rome. There the Rhodian scholar Andronicus reordered and published the texts of Aristotle's works[4]—an event almost as stimulating in the history of Roman thought as the rediscovery of Aristotle was to prove in the awakening of medieval philosophy.

The adventures of this collection suggest the debt that literature owes to the Ptolemies for establishing and maintaining, as part of the Museum, the famous Alexandrian Library. Ptolemy I began it, Ptolemy II completed it, and added a smaller library in the suburban sanctuary of Serapis. By the end of Philadelphus' reign the number of rolls had reached 532,000 —making probably 100,000 books in our sense of this word.[5] For a time the enlargement of this collection rivaled the strategy of power in the affections of the Egyptian kings. Ptolemy III ordered that every book brought to Alexandria should be deposited with the Library; that copies should be made, the owner to receive the copy, the Library to retain the original. The same autocrat asked Athens to lend him the manuscripts of Aeschylus, Sophocles, and Euripides, and deposited $90,000 as security for their return; he kept the originals, sent back copies, and told the Athenians to keep his money as a forfeit.[6] The ambition to possess old books became so widespread that men arose who specialized in dyeing and spoiling new manuscripts to sell them as antiquities to collectors of first editions.[7]

The Library soon eclipsed the rest of the Museum in importance and interest. The office of librarian was one of the highest in the king's gift, and included the obligation of tutoring the crown prince. The names of these librarians have been preserved, with variations, in different manuscripts; the latest list[8] gives, as the first six, Zenodotus of Ephesus, Apollonius of Rhodes, Eratosthenes of Cyrene, Apollonius of Alexandria, Aristophanes of Byzantium, and Aristarchus of Samothrace; their diversity of origin suggests again the unity of Hellenistic culture. Quite as important as these was the poet and scholar Callimachus, who classified the collection in a catalogue running to one hundred and twenty rolls. We picture a corps of copyists, presumably slaves, making duplicates of precious originals, and a hive of scholars separating the materials into groups. Some of these men wrote histories of various departments of literature or science, others edited definitive editions of the masterpieces, others composed commentaries on these texts for the enlightenment of laity and posterity. Aristophanes of Byzantium effected a literary revolution by separating the clauses and sentences of the ancient writings with capitals and marks of punctuation; and it was he who invented the accents that so disturb us in reading Greek. Zenodotus began, Aristophanes advanced, Aristarchus completed, the recension of the *Iliad* and the *Odyssey*, establishing the present text, and illuminating its obscurities in learned scholia. By the end of the third century the Museum, the Library, and their scholars had made Alexandria, in everything but philosophy, the intellectual capital of the Greek world.

Doubtless other Hellenistic cities had libraries. Austrian archeologists have exhumed the remains of an ornate municipal library at Ephesus, and we hear of a great library being consumed in the destruction of Carthage by Scipio. But the only one that evoked comparison with Alexandria's was that of Pergamum. The kings of this transient state looked with enlightened envy upon the cultural enterprises of the Ptolemies. In 196 Eumenes II established the Pergamene Library, and brought to its halls some of the finest scholars of Greece. The collection grew rapidly; when Antony presented it to Cleopatra to replace that part of the Alexandrian Library which was burned in the uprising against Caesar in 48 B.C., it numbered some 200,000 rolls. Through this library, and the Attic taste of the Attalid kings, Pergamum became, towards the end of the Hellenistic period, the center of a purist school of Greek prose, which considered no word clean that had not come down from classic days. To the enthusiasm of these classicists we owe the preservation of the chef-d'oeuvres of Attic prose.

It was above all an age of intellectuals and scholars. Writing became a profession instead of a devotion, and generated cliques and coteries whose appreciation of talent varied inversely as the square of its distance from themselves. Poets began to write for poets, and became artificial; scholars began to write for scholars, and became dull. Thoughtful men felt that the creative inspiration of Greece was nearing exhaustion, and that the most lasting service they could render was to collect, shelter, edit, and expound the literary achievements of a bolder time. They established the methods of textual and literary criticism in almost all its forms. They tried to sift out the best from the mass of existing manuscripts, and to guide the reading of the people; they made lists of "best books," the "four heroic poets," the "nine historians," the "ten lyric poets," the "ten orators," etc.[9] They wrote biographies of great writers and scientists; they gathered and saved the fragmentary data which are now all that we know concerning these men. They composed outlines of history, literature, drama, science, and philosophy;[10] some of these "short cuts to knowledge" helped to preserve, some replaced and unwittingly obliterated the original works that they summarized. Saddened by the degeneration of Attic Greek into the Orientalized "pidgin" Greek of their time, Hellenistic scholars compiled dictionaries and grammars, and the Library of Alexandria, in the manner of the French Academy, issued edicts on the correct usage of the ancient tongue. Without their learned and patient "ant industry" the wars, revolutions, and catastrophes of two thousand years would have destroyed even those "precious minims" which have been transmitted to us as the shipwrecked legacy of Greece.

II. THE BOOKS OF THE JEWS

Through all the turmoil of the time the Jews maintained their traditional love of scholarship, and produced more than their share of the lasting literature of the age. To this period belong some of the finest portions of the Bible. Near the close of the third century a Jewish poet (or poetess?) composed the lovely Song of Songs: here is all the artistry of Greek verse from Sappho to Theocritus, but with something undiscoverable in any Greek author of the time—an intensity of imagination, a depth of feeling, and an idealist devotion strong enough to welcome the body, as well as the soul, of love, and to turn the flesh itself into spirit. Partly in Jerusalem, mostly in Alexandria, partly in other cities of the eastern Mediterranean, Hellenistic Jews wrote—in Hebrew, Aramaic, or Greek—such masterpieces as Ecclesiastes, Daniel, part of Proverbs and Psalms, and most of the greater Apocrypha. They composed histories like Chronicles, novelettes like Esther and Judith, and idyls of family life like the Book of Tobit. The *Soferim* changed the Hebrew script from the old Assyrian to the square Syrian style, which has remained to this day.[11] Since most of the Jews in the Near East now spoke Aramaic rather than Hebrew, the scholars explained the Scriptures in brief Aramaic Targums, or interpretations. Schools were opened for the study of the Torah, or Law, and the explanation of its moral code to growing youth; such explanations, commentaries, and illustrations, handed down from teacher to pupil across the generations, supplied in a later age most of the material of the Talmud.

By the close of the third century the scholars of the Great Assembly had completed the editing of the older literature, and had closed the canon of the Old Testament;[12] it was their judgment that the age of the prophets was ended, and that literal inspiration had ceased. The result was that many works of this epoch, full of wisdom and beauty, lost the chance of divine collaboration, and fell into the unfortunate category of Apocrypha.* The two books of Esdras may owe something of their literary excellence to King James' translators; but these can hardly be credited with the touching account of how Esdras asked the angel Uriel to explain why the wicked prosper, the good suffer, and Israel is in bondage; to which the angel answers, in powerful similes and yet simple speech, that it is not given to the part to understand or judge the whole.

The prologue of Ecclesiasticus describes it as a Greek translation, completed in 132, of discourses written in Hebrew two generations before by the translator's grandfather, Jesus the son of Sirach. This Joshua ben Sirach was both a scholar and a man of affairs; after seeing something of the world through travel he had settled down to make his home a school for students; and to them he delivered these essays on the wisdom of life.[13] He denounces the rich Jews who have abandoned their faith to cut a better figure in the Gentile world; he warns youth against the courtesans who wait for it everywhere; and he offers the Law as still the best guide amid the evils and pitfalls of the world. But he is no puritan. Unlike the Chasidim he has a good word to say for harmless pleasure; and he protests against the mystics who reject medicine on the ground that all maladies, having come from God, can be cured by God alone. The book is rich in epigrams, of which the most renowned brings together the rod and the child. "The number of whippings laid to his account," said Renan, "must be incalculable."[14] It is a noble book, wiser and kinder than Ecclesiastes.

---

* The Old Testament Apocrypha (lit. hidden) are those books that were excluded from the Jewish canon of the Old Testament as uninspired, but were included in the Roman Catholic Vulgate—i.e., the Latin translation, by St. Jerome, of the Hebrew and Greek texts of the Bible. The chief O. T. Apocrypha are Ecclesiasticus, I and II Esdras, and I and II Maccabees. The apocalyptic (i.e., revealing) books are those that purport to contain prophetic divine revelations; such writings began to appear about 250 B.C., and continued into the Christian era. Some apocalypses, like the Book of Enoch, are considered apocryphal and uncanonical; others, like the Book of Revelation, are considered canonical.

In the twenty-fourth chapter of Ecclesiasticus we are told that "Wisdom is the first product of God, created from the beginning of the world." Here and in the first chapter of Proverbs are the earliest Hebrew forms of the doctrine of the Logos—Wisdom as a "demiurge," or intermediate creator, delegated by God to design the world. This hypostatizing of Wisdom as personified intelligence becomes a dominating idea of Jewish theology in the last centuries before Christ. Alongside of it runs increasingly the conception of personal immortality. In the Book of Enoch, written apparently by several authors in Palestine between 170 and 66 B.C., the hope of heaven has become a vital need; the success of wicked power and the misfortunes of a pious and loyal people could no longer be borne unless that hope might be entertained; without it life and history seemed to be the work of Satan rather than of God. A Messiah will come who will establish the Kingdom of Heaven on earth, and will reward the virtuous with everlasting happiness after death.

In the Book of Daniel the whole terror of the age of Antiochus IV finds a voice. About 166, when the faithful had been persecuted to the death for their beliefs, and ever larger enemies were advancing upon the Maccabean band, one of the Chasidim, probably, undertook to rekindle the courage of the people by describing the sufferings and prophecies of Daniel in the days of Nebuchadrezzar in Babylon. Copies of the book passed secretly among the Jews; it was given out as the work of a prophet who had lived three hundred and seventy years before, had borne greater trials than any Jew under Antiochus, had emerged victorious, and had predicted a like triumph for his race. And even if the virtuous and faithful found indifferent fortune here, their reward would come at the Last Judgment, when the Lord would welcome them into a heaven of unending happiness, and plunge their persecutors into everlasting hell.

All in all, the extant Jewish writings of this period may be described as a mystic or imaginative literature of instruction, edification, and consolation. To the Jews of earlier ages life itself had been enough, and religion was not a flight from the world but a dramatization of morals by the poetry of faith; a powerful God, ruling and seeing all things, would reward virtue and punish vice in this existence on earth. The Captivity had shaken this belief, the restoration of the Temple had renewed it; it broke down under the bludgeoning of Antiochus. Pessimism now had a clear field; and in the writings of the Greeks the Jews found the most eloquent exposures of the injustices and tragedies of life. Meanwhile Jewish contact with Persian ideas of heaven and hell, of a struggle between good and evil, and the final triumph of good, offered an escape from the philosophy of despair, and perhaps the ideas of immortality that had come down from Egypt to Alexandria, and those that had animated the mysteries of Greece, co-operated to inspire in the Jews of the Greek and Roman periods that consoling hope which bore them up through all the vicissitudes of their Temple and their state. From these Jews, and from the Egyptians, Persians, and Greeks, the idea of eternal reward and punishment would flow down into a new and stronger faith, and help it to win a disintegrating world.

III. MENANDER

Like the other arts, the drama enjoyed in this age its greatest quantitative prosperity. Every city, almost every third-rate town, had its theater. The actors, better organized than ever, were in great demand, enjoyed high fees, and lived with characteristic superiority to the morals of their time. Dramatists continued to turn out tragedies, but, whether by accident or good taste, tradition has covered them with oblivion's balm. The mood of Hellenistic Athens, like ours today, preferred the lighthearted, lightheaded, sentimental, happy-ending stories of the New Comedy. Of this, too, only fragments remain; but we have some discouraging samples of it in the pilferings of Plautus and Terence, who composed their plays by translating and adapting Hellenistic comedies. The high concerns of state and soul that aroused Aristophanes are in the New Comedy put aside as too perilous for the literary neck; usually the theme is domestic or private, and traces the devious roads by which women are led to generosity, and men nevertheless to matrimony. Love enters upon its triumphant career as master of the boards; a thousand damsels in distress cross the stage, but achieve honor and wedlock in the end. The old phallic dress is abandoned, and the old phallic bawdiness; but the story circles narrowly about the virginity of the leading lady, and virtue plays as small a role in it as in our daily press. Since the actors wore masks, and the number of masks was limited, the comic dramatist wove his plots of intrigue and mistaken identity around a few stock characters whom the audience was always delighted to recognize—the cruel father, the benevolent old man, the prodigal son, the heiress mistaken for a poor girl, the bragging soldier, the clever slave, the flatterer, the parasite, the physician, the priest, the philosopher, the cook, the courtesan, the procuress, and the pimp.

The masters of this comedy of manners in third-century Athens were Philemon and Menander. Of Philemon hardly anything survives except the echo of his renown. The Athenians liked him better than Menander, and gave him more prizes; but Philemon had raised to high excellence the art of organizing a claque. Posterity, being ignored in the subsidy, reversed the judgment, and gave the crown to Menander's bones. This Congreve of Athens was a nephew of the fertile dramatist Alexis of Thurii, the pupil of Theophrastus, and the friend of Epicurus; from them he learned the secrets of drama, philosophy, and tranquillity. He almost realized Aristotle's ideal: he was handsome and rich, contemplated life with serenity and understanding, and took his pleasures like a gentleman. He was an inconstant lover, content to repay Glycera's devotion by touching her name with immortality. When Ptolemy I invited him to Alexandria he sent Philemon in his stead, saying, "Philemon has no Glycera"; Glycera, who had suffered much, rejoiced at having triumphed over a king.[15] Thereafter, we are assured, he lived faithfully with her until, at the age of fifty-two, he died of a cramp while swimming at the Piraeus (292).[16]

His first play, as if announcing a new epoch, appeared in the year that followed Alexander's death. Thereafter he wrote one hundred and four comedies, eight of which won the first prize. Some four thousand lines remain, all in brief fragments except for a papyrus discovered in Egypt in 1905; this contains half of the *Epitrepontes*, or *The Arbitrants*, and has lowered Menander's reputation. We shall waste our reproaches if we complain that the themes of these plays are as monotonous as those of Greek sculpture, architecture, and pottery; we must remind ourselves that the Greeks judged a work not by the story it told—which is a child's criterion—but by the manner of its telling. What the Greek mind relished in Menander was the neat polish of his style, the philosophy concentrated in his wit, and so realistic a portrayal of common scenes that Aristophanes of Byzantium asked, "O Menander, O Life, which of you imitated the other?"[17] In a world that had fallen forfeit to soldiers nothing remained, in Menander's view, but to contemplate human affairs as a spectator indulgent but uninvolved. He notes the vanities and vacillations of woman, but concedes that the average wife is a blessing. The action of *The Arbitrants* turns in part upon a rejection of the double standard;[18] and of course one play is about the virtuous prostitute who, like Dumas' Lady of the Camellias, refuses the man whom she loves in order to get him respectably married to a profitable wife.[19] Lines that are now proverbs appear in the fragments, like "Evil communications corrupt good manners" (quoted by St. Paul[20]), and "Conscience makes cowards of the bravest men";[21] some credit Menander with the original of Terence's famous line—*Homo sum, humani nil a me alienum puto*—"I am a man, and consider nothing human to be alien to me." Occasionally we come upon jewels of insight, as in "Everything that dies dies by its own corruption; all that injures is within";[22] or in these typical verses, prophetic of Menander's early death:

> Whom the gods love, die young; that man is blest
> Who, having viewed at ease this solemn show
> Of sun, stars, ocean, fire, doth quickly go
> Back to his home with calm uninjured breast.

Be life or short or long, 'tis manifest
Thou ne'er wilt see things goodlier, Parmeno,
Than these; then take thy sojourn here as though
Thou wert some playgoer or wedding guest,
The sooner sped, the safelier to thy rest.
Well-furnished, foe to none, with strength at need,
Shalt thou return; while he who tarries late
Faints on the road out-worn, with age oppressed,
Harassed by foes whom life's dull tumults breed;
Thus ill dies he for whom death long doth wait.[23]

IV. THEOCRITUS

When Philemon died (262) Greek comedy, and in large measure Athenian literature, died with him. The theater flourished, but it produced no masterpieces that time or scholarship thought fit to preserve; and the repetition of old comedies—chiefly those of Menander and Philemon—more and more crowded out original productions. As the third century ended, the spirit of the gay society that had generated the New Comedy died away, and was replaced in Athens by the serious mood of the philosophical schools. Other cities, Alexandria in particular, tried to transplant the dramatic art, but failed.

The great Library and the scholars whom it had attracted set the tone of Alexandrian literature. Books had to meet the tastes of a learned and critical audience, sophisticated by science and history. Even poetry became erudite, and tried to cover up the poverty of its fancy with recondite allusions and subtle turns of phrase. Callimachus wrote dead hymns to dead gods, pretty epigrams that sparkled for a day, judicious eulogies like *The Lock of Berenice*, and a didactic poem on *Causes (Aitia)* which contained much learned lore from geography, mythology, and history, and one of the earliest love stories in literature. Acontius, hero of this tale, is incredibly handsome, and Cydippe is painfully beautiful; they fall in love at first sight, are opposed by their money-minded parents, threaten suicide, half die of broken hearts, and finally end the romance with marriage; this is the story that a million poets and novelists have told since then, and which a million more will tell. It must be added, however, that in one of his epigrams Callimachus returned to more orthodox Greek tastes:

Drink now, and love, Democrates; for we
Shall not have wine and boys eternally.[24]

His only rival in his century was his pupil Apollonius of Rhodes. When the student poached upon the master's verses and competed for the favor of the Ptolemies, the two men quarreled in life and print, and Apollonius returned to

Rhodes. He proved his courage by writing, in an age that preferred brevity, a very passable epic, the *Argonautica.* Callimachus dismissed it with an epigram—"A big book is a big evil"—of whose truth the reader may find an instance at close hand. In the end Apollonius was rewarded; he received the coveted appointment of librarian, and even persuaded some of his contemporaries to read his epic. It still survives, and contains an excellent psychological study of Medea's love; but it is not indispensable to a modern education.*

The rise of pastoral poetry betrays almost statistically the growth of an urban civilization. The Greeks of earlier centuries had said little about the beauty of the countryside because most of them had once lived on farms or near them, and knew the lonely hardships, as well as the quiet beauty, of rural life. Doubtless the Alexandria of the Ptolemies was as hot and dusty as Alexandria is today, and the Greeks who lived in it looked back with idealizing memory upon the hills and fields of their motherland; the great city was just the place to breed bucolic poetry. Thither came, about 276, a confident young man with the pleasant name of Theocritus. He had begun life in Sicily, and had continued it in Cos; he had returned to Syracuse to seek the patronage of Hieron II, and had failed; but he could never forget the beauty of Sicily, its mountains and flowers, its coasts and bays. He moved to Alexandria, composed a panegyric on Ptolemy II, and won the passing favor of the court. For some years he seems to have lived amid royalty and scholarship, while his melodious pictures of country life made him popular among the sophisticates of the capital. His Praxinoa describes the terror of Alexandria's crowded streets:

> O Heavens, what a mob! I can't imagine
> How we're to squeeze through, or how long it'll take;
> An ant-heap is nothing to this hurly-burly . . .
> O Gorgon, darling, look!—what shall we do?
> The royal cavalry! Don't ride us down!
> Eunoa, get out of the way![26]

How could a man with the soul of a poet and memories of Sicily be happy in such an environment? He praised the King for bread, but fed his spirit on fancies of his native island, and perhaps of Cos; he envied the simple life of the shepherd pacing with his placid animals grassy slopes overlooking sunny seas. In this mood he perfected the idyl—the *eidyllion* or little picture—and gave it the connotation that it keeps today, of a rustic cameo or a poetic tale. Only ten of the thirty-two pieces that have come

* Virgil copied it in form, sometimes in substance, sometimes line for line, in the *Aeneid.*[25]

down to us from Theocritus are pastoral poetry; but these have set a half-rural stamp upon the name that covers them all. Here at last nature entered Greek literature, not as a goddess merely, but as the living and lovable features of the earth. Never before had Greek literature conveyed so feelingly the secret sense of kinship that stirs the soul with gratitude and affection for rocks and streams, water and soil and sky.

But another theme reaches even more deeply into the heart of Theocritus —romantic love. He is still a Greek, indites two lyrics (*xii* and *xxix*) to homosexual friendship, and tells with vivid sentiment the story of Heracles and Hylas (*xiii*)—how the giant, "who withstood the ferocity of the lion, loved a youth and taught him like a father everything by which he might become a good and illustrious man; nor would he leave the lad at dawn, or noon, or evening, but sought continually to fashion him after his own heart, and to make him a right yoke-fellow with him in mighty deeds." A more famous idyl (*i*) rehearses Stesichorus' tale of Daphnis the Sicilian shepherd, who piped and sang so well that legend made him the inventor of bucolic (i.e., cow-tending) poetry. For a while Daphnis watched his herd, and envied their amorous play. When the first hair had sprouted on his lip a divine nymph fell in love with him, and had him for her mate. But as the price of her favors, she made him swear that he would never love another woman. He tried hard to keep his vow, and succeeded till a king's daughter became enamored of his youth and gave herself to him in the fields. Aphrodite saw it, and revenged her fellow goddess by making Daphnis waste away with unrequited love. As he died he bequeathed his pipe to Pan in a song to which the narrator adds a haunting refrain:

"Master, approach; take to thee this fair pipe
Bedded in wax that breathes of honey still,
Bound at the lips with twine. For Love has come
To hale me off unto the house of Death."
    Muses, forego, forego the pastoral song.

"Now let the briar and the thistle flower
With violets, and the fair narcissus bloom
On junipers; let all things go awry,
And pines grow pears, since Daphnis is for death.
Let stags pursue the hounds, and from the hills
The screeching owls outsing the nightingales."
    Muses, forego, forego the pastoral song.

So said he then—no more. And Aphrodite
Was fain to raise him; but the Destinies
Had spun his thread right out. So Daphnis went
Down-stream; the whirlpool closed above his head,
The head of him whom all the Muses loved,
Of him from whom the Nymphs were not estranged.
    Muses, forego, forego the pastoral song.[27]

The second idyl continues the theme of love, but in a fiercer mood. Simaetha, maid of Syracuse, seduced and deserted by Delphis, seeks to command his love by filters and charms; if she fails she is resolved to poison him. Standing under the stars she tells Selene, goddess of the moon, with what hot jealousy she saw Delphis walking with his comrade.

Scarce had we reached the midpoint of the road by the dwelling of
  Lycon,
Delphis when I beheld with Eudanippus advancing:
Blonder of cheek and chin were the youths than yellowing ivy,
Yea, and their breasts far brighter of sheen than thou, O Selene,
Showing they just had come from the noble toil of the wrestlers.
    Think on my love, and think whence it came, thou Lady Selene.

I, when I saw, how I raged, how the flame took hold of my bosom,
Burned my love-lost heart! My beauty waned, and no longer
Watched I the pomp as it passed; nor how I returned to my home-
  stead
Knew I, for some fell bane, some parching disease had undone me.
Ten days, stretched on my bed, and ten nights dwelt I in anguish.
    Think on my love, and think whence it came, thou Lady Selene.

Often the bloom of my flesh grew dry and yellow as dye-wood,
Yea, and the hairs of my head fell off, and of all that I once was
Naught but skin was left, and bones; and to whom did I not turn,
Whose road left I unsought where an old crone chanted a love-
  charm?
Still no solace I found, and time sped ever a-flying.
    Think on my love, and think whence it came, thou Lady Selene.

The third idyl introduces us to the nymph Amaryllis, and her unattainable charms; the fourth to the shepherd Corydon, the seventh to the poetic goatherd Lycidas—names destined to be invoked by a thousand poets again from Virgil to Tennyson. These rustics are idealized, and speak the most exquisite Greek; any one of them can sing hexameters lovelier than Homer's; but we learn to accept their incredible gifts as a tolerable convention when we surrender to the plaintive lilt of their songs. Theocritus redeems their reality with the smell of their jackets and the occasional obscenity of their thoughts; a lusty vein of humor salts their sentiment, and makes them men. All in all, this is the most perfect Greek poetry written after Euripides, the only extant Hellenistic verse that has the breath of life.

V. POLYBIUS

If the Hellenistic age inspired but one great poet, it produced an unprecedented quantity and variety of prose. It invented the imaginary conversation, the essay, and the encyclopedia; it continued the tradition of writing brief and vivid biographies; and in the Roman sequel Greek literature would add the sermon and the novel. Oratory was a dying mode, for it had depended upon the game of politics, litigation before popular courts, and the democratic right to talk. The letter became a favorite vehicle, for both communication and literature; now were established the epistolary forms and phrases that we find in Cicero, and even the famous exordium dear to our grandfathers: "Hoping that this finds you as well as it leaves me."[28]

Historiography flourished. Ptolemy I, Aratus of Achaea, and Pyrrhus of Epirus wrote memoirs of their campaigns, establishing a tradition that culminated in Caesar. The Egyptian high priest Manetho wrote in Greek an *Aigyptiaka*, or *Annals of Egypt*, which bundled the Pharaohs somewhat arbitrarily into those dynasties that classify them to this day. Berosus, high priest of the Chaldeans, dedicated to Antiochus I a history of Babylon based upon the cuneiform records. Megasthenes, ambassador of Seleucus I to Chandragupta Maurya, startled the Greek world, about 300, with a book on India. "There is among the Brahmans," said a suggestive passage, "a sect of philosophers who . . . hold that God is the Word, by which they mean not articulate speech but the discourse of reason";[29] here again was that doctrine of Logos which was destined to make such an impress upon Christian theology. Timaeus af Tauromenium (Taormina), having been exiled from Sicily by Agathocles (317), traveled widely in Spain and Gaul, and then settled down in Athens to write a history of Sicily and the West. He was an industrious student, so anxious to include everything that some of his rivals called him "an old ragpicker."[30] He labored to arrive at an accurate chronology, and hit upon the scheme of dating events by Olympiads. He criticized his predecessors severely, and was lucky enough to die before seeing the brutal attack made upon his work by Polybius.[31]

The greatest of the Hellenistic historians, and the only Greek fit to make a triad with Herodotus and Thucydides, was born at Megalopolis, in Arcadia (208). His father, Lycortas, was one of the leading men of the Achaean League, being ambassador to Rome in 189 and *strategos* in 184. The boy was brought up in the odor of politics, was trained as a soldier under Philopoemen, fought in the Roman campaign against the Gauls in Asia Minor, was associated with his father on an embassy to Egypt (181), and was made the League's *hipparchos*, or commander of the cavalry, in 169.[32] He paid for his prominence: when the Romans punished the League for supporting Perseus against them they took a thousand leading Achaeans to Rome as hostages, and Polybius was among them (167). For sixteen years he suffered exile, and at times, he tells us, "utter loss of spirit and paralysis of mind."[33] But the younger Scipio befriended him, introduced him to the Scipionic circle of educated Romans, and persuaded the Senate, when it was scattering the other exiles throughout Italy, to let Polybius live with him in Rome. He accompanied Scipio on many campaigns, gave him valuable military advice, explored for him the coasts of Spain and Africa, and stood beside him at the burning of Carthage (146). He had received his freedom in 151, and in 149 he was employed as the representative of Rome in arranging a *modus vivendi* between the cities of Greece and their distant master, the Roman Senate. He must have performed this ungrateful task well, for several cities honored him with monuments—though one can never tell in what tense man's gratitude is felt. Having lived through sixty full years of action, he retired to write a *Treatise on Tactics*, a *Life of Philopoemen*, and his immense *Histories*. He died like a gentleman by falling from his horse as he was returning from a hunt, at the age of eighty-two.

No man ever wrote history from a wider background of education, travel, and experience. His work was conceived on a grand scale, and proposed to tell the story, not only of Greece but of "the whole world" (i.e., the Mediterranean nations) from 221 to 146 B.C. "Such is the plan I propose; but all depends upon Fortune's granting me a life long enough to execute it."[34] He rightly felt that the center of political history, in the period which he covered, lay in Rome; he gave his book unity by making Rome the focus of its events, and studying with a diplomat's curiosity the methods by which Rome, with British casualness, had mastered the Mediterranean world.[35] He admired the Romans intensely, for he had seen them in their greatest epoch, and had known chiefly the best of them in Scipio's group; they had, he felt, just those qualities that were fatally lacking in Greek character and government. Himself an aristocrat, and befriended by aristocrats, he had no sympathy with what seemed to him mere mob rule in the later stages of Greek democracy. Political history appeared to him to be a repetitious cycle of monarchy (or dictatorship), aristocracy, oligarchy, democracy, and monarchy. The best escape from this cycle, he thought, was through a "mixed constitution" like that of Lycurgus or Rome—an enfranchised but limited citizenry choosing its own magistrates, but checked by the power of a continuous and aristocratic senate.[36] It was from this viewpoint that he wrote down the record of his times.

Polybius is "the historians' historian" because he is as interested in his method as in his subject. He likes to talk about his plan of procedure, and philosophizes at every opportunity. Humanly he pictures his own qualifications as ideal. He insists that history should be written by those who have seen—or have directly consulted others who have seen—the events to be described. He denounces Timaeus for having relied on his ears rather than his eyes, and tells with pride of his own travels in search of data, documents, and geographical veracity; he reminds us how, in returning from Spain to Italy, he crossed the Alps by the same pass that Hannibal had used, and how he went down into the very toe of Italy to decipher an inscription left by Hannibal in Brutium.[37] He proposes to make his history as accurate as "the magnitude of the work and its comprehensive treatment" will allow;[38] and he succeeds, so far as we can say, better than any other Greek except Thucydides. He argues that the historian should have been a man of affairs, versed in the actual processes of statesmanship, politics, and war; otherwise he will never understand the behavior of states or the course of history.[39] He is a realist and a rationalist; he pierces the moral phrases of diplomats to the actual motives of policy. It amuses him to observe how easily men can be deceived, singly or en masse, and even repeatedly by the same tricks.[40] "What is good," says a scandalous presage of Machiavelli, "very seldom coincides with what is advantageous, and few are those who can combine the two and adapt them to each other."[41] He accepts the Stoic theology of a Divine Providence, but he merely pities the popular cults of his day, and smiles at stories of supernatural intervention.[42] He recognizes the role of chance in history, and the occasional efficacy of great men,[43] but he is resolved to lay bare the factual and often impersonal chain of causes and effects, so that history may be a lantern of understanding held up to the present and the future.[44] "There is no more ready corrective of conduct than knowledge of the past"; and "the soundest education and training for a life of active politics is the study of history";[45] "it is history, and history alone, which, without involving us in actual danger, will mature our judgment and prepare us to take right views, whatever may be the crisis or the posture of affairs."[46] The best method of history, he thinks, will be that which sees the life of a nation as an organic unity, and weaves the story of each part into the life history of the whole. "He who believes that by studying isolated histories he can acquire a just view of history as a whole is, as it seems to me, much in the case of one who, after having looked at the dissevered limbs of an animal once alive and beautiful, fancies he has been as good as an eyewitness of the creature itself in all its action and grace."[47]

Of the forty books into which Polybius divided his *Histories*, time has preserved five, and the epitomists have rescued substantial fragments of the rest. It is a great pity that the execution of this vast conception is marred by degenerate Greek, peevish critiques of other historians, an almost exclusive preoccupation with politics and war, and an absurd segmentation of the narrative into Olympiads, giving the history of all the Mediterranean nations in each four-year period, and leading to exasperating digressions and a baffling discontinuity. Sometimes, as in the story of Hannibal's invasion, Polybius mounts to drama and eloquence, but he reacts so strongly against the florid rhetoric popular among his immediate predecessors that he makes it a point of honor to be dull.[48] "No one," said an ancient critic, "ever read him through."[49] The world has almost forgotten him; but historians will long continue to study him because he was one of the greatest theorists and practitioners of historiography; because he dared to take a wide view and write a "universal history"; and because, above all, he understood that mere facts are worthless except through their interpretation, and that the past has no value except as our roots and our illumination.

CHAPTER XXVII

The Art of the Dispersion

I. A MISCELLANY

THE decline of Greek civilization was longest deferred in the sphere of art. Here the Hellenistic age bears comparison, not only in fertility but even in originality, with any period in history. Certainly the minor arts suffered no deterioration. Skilled workers in wood, ivory, silver, and gold were scattered throughout the expanded Greek world. The engraving of gems and coins now reached its highest excellence; as far east as Bactria Hellenized kings lavished art upon their currency, and in the west the dekadrachma of Hieron II might be defended as the finest coin in numismatic record. Alexandria became famous for its goldsmiths and silversmiths, whose artistry rivaled the faultless style of its poets; for its delightful cameos—precious stones or shells carved in colored relief; for its blue or green faïence, its skillfully glazed pottery, its delicately designed and many-colored glass. The Portland Vase, very likely a product of Alexandria, shows this art at its best: elegant figures cut into a layer of milk-white glass superimposed upon a body of blue glass; this is, so to speak, the Josiah Wedgwood masterpiece of antiquity.*

Music remained popular in all classes of the population. Scales and modes changed in the direction of refinement and novelty;[1] transient discords were admitted into harmony; instruments and compositions increased in complexity.[2] Towards 240, at Alexandria, the old "pipes of Pan" were enlarged into an organ of bronze pipes; and about 175 Ctesibius improved this into an organ operated by a combination of water and air and enabling the player to control vast waves of sound. We know nothing more of its construction; but we shall see how rapidly it developed, in Roman days, into the organ of Christian and modern times.[3] Instruments were combined into orchestras, and semisymphonic performances of purely instrumental music, sometimes in five movements, were given in the theaters of Alexandria, Athens, and Syracuse.[4] Professional virtuosos rose to great prominence, and to a social standing commensurate with their high fees. About

* It derives its name from the Duke of Portland, who bought it in Rome. It is now in the British Museum.

318 Aristoxenus of Taras, a pupil of Aristotle, wrote a small treatise, *Harmonics*, which became the classic ancient text in musical theory. Aristoxenus was a very serious man, and like most philosophers he did not enjoy the music of his time. Athenaeus represents him as saying, in words that many generations have heard: "We also, since the theaters have become completely barbarized, and since music has become utterly ruined and vulgar—we, being but a few, will recall to our minds, sitting by ourselves, what music used to be."[5]

The architecture of the Hellenistic age cannot impress us, for time has leveled it away with indiscriminate hostility. And yet we know, from literature and the remains, that the Greek building art spread its sway in this period from Bactria to Spain. The mutual influence of Greece and the Orient brought in a mixture of styles: the colonnade and the architrave invaded inner Asia, while the arch, the vault, and the cupola entered the West; even so ancient an Hellenic center as Delos raised Egyptian and Persian capitals. The Doric order seemed too stern and stiff for an age that loved refinement and ornament; it gave ground city by city, while the ornate Corinthian style advanced to its highest excellence. The secularization of art kept pace with the secularization of government, law, morals, letters, and philosophy; stoas, porticoes, market places, courts, assembly rooms, libraries, theaters, gymnasiums, and baths began to crowd out the temples, and regal or private palaces gave a new outlet to Greek design and decoration. Domestic interiors were adorned with paintings, statues, and wall reliefs. Private gardens surrounded the more palatial homes. Royal parks, gardens, lakes, and pavilions were built in the capitals, and were usually opened to public use. Town planning developed as a sister art to architecture; streets were laid out on Hippodamus' rectangular scheme, with main avenues as wide as thirty feet—an ample width for horse-and-chariot days. Smyrna boasted of paved thoroughfares,[6] but presumably most Hellenistic streets were trampled dirt, and knew all the vicissitudes of mud.

Fine buildings developed beyond any precedent. At Athens, in the second century, the lofty Corinthian columns of the Olympieum were set up, and the general design of the extended edifice, the most magnificent in Athens, was laid down by the Roman architect Cossutius—a strange inversion of Rome's usual dependence upon the artists of Greece. Livy described this temple of the Olympian Zeus as the only structure he had seen that could be a fit dwelling for the god of gods.[7] Sixteen columns of it stand—the most beautiful existing specimens of the Corinthian style. At Eleusis the dying piety of Athens and the genius of Philon completed the majestic temple of the Mysteries which Pericles had begun on a site already sacred in Mycenaean times; only fragments are left, but some of them show Greek design and carving still at their best. At Delos the French have excavated the ground plan of Apollo's sanctuary, and have revealed a city once crowded with edifices devoted to commerce or the protection of a hundred Greek or foreign gods. At Syracuse Hieron II raised many impressive buildings, and restored and enlarged the extant municipal theater; to this day we may read his name on its stones. In Egypt the Ptolemies adorned Alexandria with edifices that gave the city a reputation for beauty, but no sign of them survives. Ptolemy III erected at Edfu a temple which is the noblest architectural relic of the Grecian occupation, and his successors built or rebuilt the temple of Isis at Philae. In Ionia new homes were given to the gods at Miletus, Priene, Magnesia, and elsewhere; the third temple of Artemis at Ephesus was finished about 300 B.C. A still vaster fane was raised by the architects Paeonius and Daphnis at Didyma, near Miletus, in honor of Apollo (332 B.C.–A.D. 41); some drums of the superb Ionic columns still remain. At Pergamum Eumenes II made his capital the talk of Greece by building, among many noble structures, that famous Altar to Zeus which the Germans exhumed in 1878, and have skillfully reconstructed in the Pergamum Museum in Berlin. A majestic flight of steps mounted between two porticoes to a spacious colonnaded court; and around one hundred and thirty feet of the base ran a frieze as supreme in its period as that of the Mausoleum in the fourth century, or the Parthenon in the fifth. Never had Greece been so handsomely adorned; and never had the enthusiasm of its citizens and the skill of its artists transformed with such splendor so many habitations of men.

II. PAINTING

Painting is usually the last great art to mature in a civilization; in the early stages of a culture it is subordinated to religious architecture and statuary, and it acquires independence only when private life and private wealth invite the decoration of the home or the commemoration of a name. The death of democracy having weakened the sense of the state, the individual returned to domestic consolations. Rich men built themselves palatial residences, and gave high fees to artists who could adorn a fountain or brighten a wall. Alexandria used painting on glass as one form of mural ornament; all Hellenistic cities employed for this purpose movable panels of wood; princes and magnates preferred to have immense pictures painted on detachable marble slabs. Pausanias describes a prodigious number of paintings seen by him in his tour of Greece, but nothing of this flourishing art has cheated time except some faded tints on pottery or stone. We are left to guess at its quality from the pale and middling copies found at Pompeii, Herculaneum, and Rome.

Greece continued to rank its painters as high as its sculptors and architects, perhaps higher. It paid them American commissions, and told a thousand fond stories about their lives. Ctesicles of Ephesus, failing to receive a desired boon from Queen Stratonice, painted her romping with a fisherman, exhibited the picture, and then took ship to safety; Stratonice, because "the likenesses of the two figures were so admirably expressed," forgave him and let him return.[8] When Aratus took Sicyon he ordered all portraits of its past dictators destroyed; one dictator, Archestratus, had been shown by Melanthus (a fourth-century painter) beside his chariot, and so vividly that the artist Neacles entreated Aratus to spare the picture; Aratus consented, on condition that the figure of Archestratus be replaced by some less offensive form.[9] Protogenes, says Strabo, painted a satyr with a partridge so realistically that live partridges called to it; the painter finally blotted out the bird so that people might appreciate the excellence of his satyr.[10] The same artist, Pliny tells us, applied four coats of paint to his most famous picture, *Ialysus* (supposed founder of the town of that name in Rhodes), so that when time wore out the uppermost layer the colors might still be fresh and clear. Vexed by his inability to represent with sufficient verisimilitude the foam that dripped from the mouth of Ialysus' dog, Protogenes lost his temper and hurled a sponge at the picture, willing to destroy it; the sponge, of course, struck just at the right place, and, when it fell, left a blotch of color marvelously like the foam of a panting hound. When Demetrius Poliorcetes besieged Rhodes he refrained from setting fire to the town lest this painting be destroyed. During the siege Protogenes continued at work in his village studio, in the direct line of the Macedonian advance. Demetrius sent for him and asked why he had not, like the other villagers, taken refuge within the city walls. "Because I know," answered Protogenes, "that you are waging war with the Rhodians, and not with the arts." The King assigned a guard to protect him, and neglected the siege to watch the artist work.[11]

Hellenistic painters knew the tricks of perspective, foreshortening, lighting, and grouping. Though they used landscapes only as background and decoration, and rendered them (if we may judge from the Pompeian copies) in a lifeless and conventional way, they at least realized the existence of nature, and brought it into art at the same time that Theocritus was importing it into poetry. But they were so interested in man and all his works that they had little time for trees and flowers. Their predecessors had painted only the gods and the rich; the Hellenistic artists were fascinated by anything human, and discovered that an ugly subject might make a beautiful painting, or at least a handsome fee. They turned to common life with a Dutch zest, and delighted in picturing barbers, cobblers, prostitutes, seamstresses, donkeys, deformed men, or peculiar animals. To these genre pictures they added representations of still life—cakes and eggs, fruit and vegetables, fish and game, wine and all the paraphernalia of its ancient ritual. Sosus of Pergamum amused his contemporaries by imitating, in a deceptively realistic floor mosaic, an unswept floor still littered with the leavings of a feast.[12] The sedate were scandalized, and denounced these glorifiers of common things as *pornographoi* and *rhyparographoi*—portrayers of obscenity and filth. In Thebes the representation of ugly objects was forbidden by law.[13]

Certain larger masterpieces of the age were rescued not from anonymity but from oblivion by the lava of Vesuvius. A fresco found at Ostia is apparently a weak copy of a Hellenistic original; we know it as *The Aldobrandini Wedding* from the Italian family to which it belonged before it found a place in the Vatican. Aphrodite, Rubensianly robust, warms up the courage of the timid bride while the bridegroom, needing no prodding, waits impatiently beside the couch; finer than these central personages is a graceful woman playing some hymeneal strain on a faded lute. A Pompeian mural, traced uncertainly to a third-century Greek original, shows Achilles, with Patroclus beside him, angrily surrendering Briseis to Agamemnon's lust. The figures in these paintings seem to our wont and taste more ample than beautiful; we are accustomed to less body and longer legs; but it must be conceded that ancient artists knew Greek men and women better than we shall ever know them. Time has taken the bloom from these works; only an act of historical imagination can restore the brilliance and freshness that doubtless were once the admiration of multitudes and kings.

More impressive are certain Roman mosaics that have apparently been derived from Hellenistic paintings. Mosaic was an old art in Egypt and Mesopotamia; the Greeks took it over, and lifted it to the peak of its history. A painting was divided by lines into little squares, and tiny cubes of marble were so colored that when put together they reproduced the picture in a form surprisingly durable; several mosaics, though trodden by innumerable feet through many centuries, still retain their color and tell their ancient tale. *The Battle of Issus*, found in the House of the Faun at Pompeii, and dubiously connected with a fourth-century Greek painting by Philoxenus,* is composed of approximately 1,500,000 stones, each some two or three millimeters square, the whole mosaic measuring eight by sixteen feet. It was badly injured by the earthquake and eruption that overwhelmed Pompeii in A.D. 79, but enough remains to attest the skill and vigor of the work. Alexander, black and disheveled with the heat and

* This mosaic, and the *Achilles and Briseis*, are in the Naples Museum.

filth of war, is leading the attack, and has ridden his Bucephalus to within a few feet of the chariot that carries Darius. A Persian grandee has flung himself between the kings, and has received Alexander's lance in his body. Darius, ignoring his own danger—for the conqueror's next lance is aimed at him—leans from his chariot towards his fallen friend, his face full of anxiety and grief. Persian cavalrymen rush up to rescue their ruler, and Alexander's weapon stays poised in the air. The representation of complex emotions in Darius' face is the outstanding accomplishment of the work; but the most attractive head in the composition is that of Alexander's horse. There is no greater mosaic than this.

III. SCULPTURE

Never has statuary been more abundant than in the Hellenistic age. Temples and palaces, homes and streets, gardens and parks were crowded with it; every phase of human life, and many aspects of the plant and animal world, were represented in it; portrait busts immortalized for a moment dead heroes and living celebrities; at last even abstractions like Fortune, Peace, Calumny, or the Nick of Time, became concrete in stone. Eutychides of Sicyon, a pupil of Lysippus, molded for Antioch a famous *Tyche*, or *Fortune*, to serve as the incarnation of the city's soul and hope. The sons of Praxiteles—Timachus and Cephisodotus—carried on the refined tradition of Athenian sculpture; and in the Peloponnesus Damophon of Messene scaled the heights of fame with a colossal group of *Demeter, Persephone, and Artemis*. But most of the new sculptors followed the line of least starvation to the palaces and courts of Greco-Oriental magnates and kings.

Rhodes, in the third century, developed a school of sculpture characteristically its own. There were a hundred colossal statues in the island, any one of which, says Pliny,[14] would have made a city famous. The greatest of them was the bronze colossus of the sun-god Helios, set up in successive blocks by Chares of Lindus about 280. Chares, says a naïve tradition, committed suicide when the cost seriously exceeded his estimate; and Laches, also of Lindus, completed the work. It did not bestride the harbor, but rose near it to a height of one hundred and five feet. Its dimensions might suggest that Rhodian taste ran to display and size; but perhaps the Rhodians proposed to use it as a lighthouse and a symbol. If we may believe a poem in *The Greek Anthology*,[15] the statue held a light aloft, and symbolized the freedom that Rhodes enjoyed—a curious anticipation of a famous statue in a modern port.* It was, of course, included among the Seven Wonders of the World. "This statue," Pliny reports,

* The Statue of Liberty is one hundred and fifty-one feet high from base to torch.

> was thrown down by an earthquake fifty-six years after it was erected. Few men can clasp the thumb in their arms, and its fingers are larger than most statues. When the limbs are broken asunder vast caverns are seen yawning in the interior. Within it, too, are to be seen large masses of rock by whose weight the artist steadied it while in process of erection. It is said that it was twelve years in the making, and that three hundred talents were spent upon it—a sum raised from the engines of war abandoned by Demetrius after his futile siege.*[16]

Almost as famous in history was another product of the Rhodian school, the *Laocoön.* Pliny saw it in the palace of the Emperor Titus; it was found in the ruins of the Baths of Titus in A.D. 1506, and is almost certainly the original work of Agesander, Polydorus, and Athenodorus, who carved it out of two blocks of marble in the second or first century B.C.[18] Its discovery stirred Renaissance Italy and profoundly impressed Michelangelo, who tried, without success, to restore the lost right arm of the central figure.† Laocoön was a Trojan priest who, when the Greeks sent the wooden horse to Troy, advised against receiving it, saying (says Virgil), *Timeo Danaos et dona ferentes*—"I fear the Greeks even when they bring gifts."[19] To punish his wisdom Athena, who favored the Greeks, commissioned two serpents to kill him. They seized first upon his two sons, seeing which Laocoön rushed to their aid, only to be caught in the coils; in the end all three were crushed, and died from the venom of the fangs. The sculptors took the liberty assumed by Virgil (and, in the *Philoctetes*, by Sophocles) to describe pain vigorously, but the result does not accord with the natural repose of stone. In literature, and usually in life, pain passes; in the *Laocoön* the cry of agony has been given an unnatural permanence, and the spectator is not so moved as by Demeter's silent grief.‡ What nevertheless evokes our admiration is the mastery of design and technique; the musculature is exaggerated, but the old priest's limbs, and the bodies of his sons, are molded with dignity and restraint. Perhaps if we had known the story before seeing the group we should have been as impressed as Pliny, who thought this the greatest achievement of ancient plastic art.[20]

---

* It remained where it fell till A.D. 653, when the Saracens sold the materials. Nine hundred camels were required to remove them.[17]

† The restored arm in the Vatican is the work of Bernini, well done in detail, but ruinous to the centripetal unity of the composition. Winckelmann nevertheless liked the group so well that Lessing was aroused, by reading him, to write a book of esthetic criticism around it, and occasionally about it.

‡ In the *Demeter* of the British Museum.

Many other Greek centers had flourishing schools of sculpture in this underestimated age. Alexandria turned over its soil and its buildings too often in the long course of its history to preserve the works that Greek artists made for the Ptolemies. The sole important survivor is the serene *Nile* of the Vatican, humorously supported by sixteen water babies symbolizing the sixteen cubits of the river's annual rise. At Sidon Greek sculpture cut for unknown dignitaries a series of sarcophagi of which the best, misnamed the Sarcophagus of Alexander, is the pride of the Constantinople Museum. Its carving is equal, on a smaller scale, to that of the Parthenon frieze; the figures are handsome and well proportioned; the action is vigorous but clear, and the soft tints that still cling to the stone exemplify the aid that Greek painting gave to Greek sculpture. At Tralles, in Caria, about 150 B.C., Apollonius and Tauriscus cast for Rhodes a colossal bronze group now known as the *Farnese Bull:* two handsome youths are lashing the lovely Dirce to the horns of a wild bull, because she has ill-treated their mother Antiope—who looks on in repulsively calm satisfaction.* At Pergamum Greek sculptors cast in bronze several battle groups, which Attalus first dedicated in his capital to celebrate his repulse of the Gauls. To express the debt which all Greek culture felt to Athens, and perhaps to spread his fame, Attalus presented marble replicas of these figures to be set up on the Athenian Acropolis. Fragmentary marble copies have survived in *The Dying Gaul* of the Capitoline Museum, in the miscalled *Paetus and Arria*†—a Gaul who, preferring death to capture, kills first his wife and then himself—and in several smaller pieces now scattered through Egypt and Europe. Perhaps to the same group belongs a *Dead Amazon*,‡ impeccably molded in every detail except the incredibly perfect breasts. These figures show a classic restraint in the expression of emotion: the conquered men suffer the extremes of pain and grief, but die without opera; and the conquerors have allowed the artists to portray the virtues, as well as the defeat, of their enemies. There is no sign here of any falling off in power of conception, accuracy of anatomical observation, or skill and patience of technique. Almost as perfect is the great relief that ran along the base of the Altar of Zeus on the Acropolis of Pergamum, and told again the story of the war between the gods and the giants—presumably a modest allegory for Pergamenes and Gauls. The work is overcrowded, and sometimes theatrically violent; but some figures stand out as in the best tradition of Greek art. The headless *Zeus* is carved with the strength of Scopas, and the goddess Hecate is a lyric of grace and beauty amid the terror and carnage of war.

* The original is lost. A Roman marble copy of the third century A.D. was found in the sixteenth century in the Baths of Caracalla, was repaired by Michelangelo, was housed for a time in the Palazzo Farnese, and is now in the Naples Museum.

† In the Museo delle Terme at Rome.

‡ In the Naples Museum.

The age was rich in now anonymous masterpieces that almost call the roll of the major gods. The majestic *Head of Zeus* found at Otricoli, and the *Ludovisi Hera* now in the Museo delle Terme so pleased the young Goethe that he took casts of them with him to Germany as, so to speak, the authentic autographs of Jove and Juno. The once acclaimed *Apollo Belvedere** is academically cold and lifeless; and yet, two centuries ago, it set Winckelmann aflame.[21] A world away from this smooth weakling is the *Farnese Heracles*, copied by Glycon of Athens from an original attributed to Lysippus—all muscle in the overdone body, all weariness, kindliness, and wonder in the face—as if power was asking itself its never answered question: what should be its goal? Of Aphrodite the age had representatives only less numerous than her devotees; several of these statues have survived, mostly through Roman copies. The *Aphrodite of Melos*—the *Venus de Milo* of the Louvre—is apparently an original Greek work of the second century B.C. It was found on the island of Melos in 1820, near a pedestal fragment bearing the letters—*sandros;* perhaps Agesander of Antioch carved this modest nudity. The face is not as delicately fair as that which forms the symbol of this volume, but the figure itself is a poem of that health whose natural flower is beauty; the wasp waist finds no encouragement in this full body and these sturdy hips. Not so near perfection, but still pleasant to the eye, are the *Capitoline Venus* and the *Venus de Medici.*† Candidly and disarmingly sensual is the *Venus Callipyge*, or Venus of the Lovely Buttocks,‡ who drapes her charms to reveal them, and turns to admire her nates in the pool. More impressive than any of these is the superb *Nike*, or *Victory of Samothrace*, found there in 1863, and now the sculptural masterpiece of the Louvre.§ The goddess of victory is shown as if alighting in full flight upon the prow of a swiftly moving ship and leading the vessel on to attack; her great wings seem to pull the craft along in the face of the breeze that confuses her robes. Again the Greek conception of woman as no mere delicacy, but as a strong mother, dominates the work; this is not the frail and passing beauty of youth, but the lifelong call of the woman to the man to lift himself up to achievement, as if the artist had wished to illustrate the last lines of Goethe's *Faust*. The civilization that could conceive and carve this figure was yet far from dead.

The gods were not the chief interest of the sculptors who brightened the evening of Greek art. These men looked upon Olympus as a quarry of subjects, and no more. When that quarry had been worn down by repetition they turned

---

* So called from the pavilion in the Vatican where the statue was formerly placed.

† In the Capitoline Museum at Rome, and the Uffizi at Florence.

‡ In the Naples Museum.

§ It was formerly described as a dedication set up by Demetrius Poliorcetes in 305 to commemorate his defeat of Ptolemy I off Cyprian Salamis in 306; but recent discussion tends to connect it with the battle of Cos (ca. 258), in which the fleets of Macedonia, Seleucia, and Rhodes defeated Ptolemy II.[22]

to the earth and took delight in representing the wisdom and loveliness, the strangeness and absurdities of human life. They carved or cast impressive heads of Homer, Euripides, and Socrates. They made a number of smooth and delicate *Hermaphrodites*, whose equivocal beauty arrests the eye in the Archeological Museum at Constantinople, or the Borghese Gallery in Rome, or the Louvre. Children offered refreshingly natural poses, like the boy who removes a thorn from his foot, and another who struggles with a goose,* and—finest of this class—the trustful *Praying Youth* attributed to Lysippus' pupil Boëthus.† Or the sculptors went to the woods and depicted sylvan sprites like the *Barberini Faun* of Munich, or hilarious satyrs like the *Drunken Silenus* of the Naples Museum. And here and there, with jolly frequency, they inserted among their figures the rosy cheeks and impish pranks of the god of love.

IV. COMMENTARY

This sudden irruption of humor into the once formal sanctuaries of Greek sculpture is a distinctive mark of Hellenistic art. Every museum has preserved from the ruins of the age some laughing faun, some singing Pan, some rioting Bacchus, some urchin serving as a fountain with alarming indecency. Perhaps the return of Greek art to Asia restored to it the variety, feeling, and warmth which it had almost lost in its classic subordination to religion and the state. Nature, which had been adored, began now to be enjoyed. Not that classic moderation disappeared: the *Youth of Subiaco* in the Museo delle Terme, the *Sleeping Ariadne* of the Vatican, the *Sitting Maiden* of the Palace of the Conservatori continue the delicate tradition of Praxiteles; and in Athens, throughout this period, many sculptors fought the "modernistic" tendencies of their time by deliberately going back to fourth- and fifth-century styles, even, now and then, to the archaic dignity of the sixth. But the spirit of the age was for experiment, individualism, naturalism, and realism, with a strong countercurrent toward imagination, idealism, sentiment, and dramatic effect. Artists carefully followed the progress of anatomy, and worked more from models in studios; sculptors carved their figures to be seen not only from in front, but from all sides. They used novel materials—crystal, chalcedony, topaz, glass, dark basalt, black marble, porphyry—to imitate the pigment of Negroes or the ruddy faces of satyrs illumined with wine.

Their fertility of invention equaled their mastery of technique. They

* Both in the Vatican.

† In the State Museum, Berlin.

were tired of repeating types; they anticipated Ruskin's criticism,* and were resolved to show the reality and individuality of the persons and objects they portrayed. They no longer confined themselves to the perfect and the beautiful, to athletes, heroes, and gods; they made genre pictures or terra cottas of workingmen, fishermen, musicians, market men, jockeys, eunuchs; they sought unhackneyed subjects in children and peasants, in characterful features like those of Socrates, in bitter old men like Demosthenes, in powerful, almost brutal faces like that of Euthydemus the Greco-Bactrian king, in desolate derelicts like the *Old Market Woman* of the Metropolitan Museum in New York; they recognized and relished the variety and complexity of life. They did not hesitate to be sensual; they were not parents anxious about the chastity of their daughters, nor philosophers disturbed by the social consequences of an epicurean individualism; they saw the charms of the flesh, and carved them into a beauty that might for a while laugh at wrinkles and time. Freed from the conventions of the classic age, they indulged themselves in tender sentiment, and pictured, possibly with sincere feeling, shepherds dying of undisillusioned love, pretty heads lost in romantic reverie, mothers fondly contemplating their children: these, too, seemed to them a part of the reality they would record. And finally they faced the facts of pain and grief, of tragic catastrophes and untimely death; and they resolved to find a place for them in their representation of human life.

No student with a mind of his own will join in any sweeping judgment about Hellenistic decay; a general conclusion to this effect serves too easily as an excuse for ending the story of Greece before the task is done. We feel in this period a slackening of creative impulse, but we are compensated by the lavish abundance of an art now completely master of its tools. Youth cannot last forever, nor are its charms supreme; the life of Greece, like every life, had to have a natural subsidence, and accept a ripe old age. Decadence had set in, it had bitten into religion, morals, and letters, and had left its stigmata upon individual works here and there; but the impetus of the Greek genius kept Greek art, like Greek science and philosophy, near their zenith to the end. And never in its isolated youth had the Greek passion for beauty, or the Greek power and patience to embody it, spread so triumphantly, or with such rich stimulation and result, into the sleeping cities of the East. There Rome would find it, and pass it on.

---

* "There is no personal character in Greek art—abstract ideas of youth and age, strength and swiftness, virtue and vice—yes; but there is no individuality."[23] Ruskin thought only of fifth- and fourth-century Greek art, just as Winckelmann and Lessing knew chiefly the art of the Hellenistic age.

CHAPTER XXVIII

The Climax of Greek Science

I. EUCLID AND APOLLONIUS

THE fifth century saw the zenith of Greek literature, the fourth the flowering of philosophy, the third the culmination of science. The kings proved more tolerant and helpful to research than the democracies. Alexander sent to the Greek cities of the Asiatic coast camel loads of Babylonian astronomical tablets, most of which were soon translated into Greek; the Ptolemies built the Museum for advanced studies, and gathered the science as well as the literature of the Mediterranean cultures into the great Library; Apollonius dedicated his *Conics* to Attalus I, and under the protection of Hieron II Archimedes drew his circles and reckoned the sand. The fading of frontiers and the establishment of a common language, the fluid interchange of books and ideas, the exhaustion of metaphysics and the weakening of the old theology, the rise of a secularly minded commercial class in Alexandria, Rhodes, Antioch, Pergamum, and Syracuse, the multiplication of schools, universities, observatories, and libraries, combined with wealth, industry, and royal patronage to free science from philosophy, and to encourage it in its work of enlightening, enriching, and endangering the world.

About the opening of the third century—perhaps long before it—the tools of the Greek mathematician were sharpened by the development of a simpler notation. The first nine letters of the alphabet were used for the digits, the next letter for 10, the next nine for 20, 30, etc., the next for 100, the next for 200, 300, and so forth. Fractions and ordinals were expressed by an acute accent after the letter; so, according to the context, ι′ stood for *one tenth* or *tenth;* and a small ι under a letter indicated the corresponding thousand. This arithmetical shorthand provided a convenient system of computation; some extant Greek papyri crowd complicated calculations, ranging from fractions to millions, into less space than similar reckonings would require in our own numerical notation.*

Nevertheless the greatest victories of Hellenistic science were in geometry. To this period belongs Euclid, whose name would for two thousand years pro-

* These papyri are not older than Alexandria; but since they use the primitive digamma to represent 6, it is probable that the alphabetical notation antedated the Hellenistic age.

vide geometry with a synonym. All that we know of his life is that he opened a school at Alexandria, and that his students excelled all others in their field; that he cared nothing about money, and when a pupil asked, "What shall I profit from learning geometry?" bade a slave give him an obol, "since he must make a gain out of what he learns";[1] that he was a man of great modesty and kindliness; and that when, about 300, he wrote his famous *Elements*, it never occurred to him to credit the various propositions to their discoverers, because he made no pretense at doing more than to bring together in logical order the geometrical knowledge of the Greeks.* He began, without preface or apology, with simple definitions, then postulates or necessary assumptions, then "common notions" or axioms. Following Plato's injunctions, he confined himself to such figures and proofs as needed no other instruments than ruler and compasses. He adopted and perfected a method of progressive exposition and demonstration already familiar to his predecessors: proposition, diagrammatic illustration, proof, and conclusion. Despite minor flaws the total result was a mathematical architecture that rivaled the Parthenon as a symbol of the Greek mind. Actually it outlived the Parthenon as an integral form; for until our own century the *Elements* of Euclid constituted the accepted textbook of geometry in nearly every European university. One must go to the Bible to find a rival for it in enduring influence.

A lost work of Euclid, the *Conics*, summarized the studies of Menaechmus, Aristaeus, and others on the geometry of the cone. Apollonius of Perga, after years of study in Euclid's school, took this treatise as the starting point of his own *Conics*, and explored in eight "books" and 387 propositions the properties of the curves generated by the intersection of a cone by a plane. To three of these curves (the fourth being the circle) he gave their lasting names—parabola, ellipse, and hyperbola. His discoveries made possible the theory of projectiles, and substantially advanced mechanics, navigation, and astronomy. His exposition was laborious and verbose, but his method was completely scientific; his work was as definitive as Euclid's, and its seven extant books are to this day the most original classic in the literature of geometry.

II. ARCHIMEDES

The greatest of ancient scientists was born at Syracuse about 287 B.C., son of the astronomer Pheidias, and apparently cousin to Hieron II, the most enlightened ruler of his time. Like many other Hellenistic Greeks who were interested in science and could afford the expense, Archimedes went to Alexandria; there he studied under the successors of Euclid, and derived

* Books I and II summarize the geometrical work of Pythagoras; Book III, Hippocrates of Chios; Book V, Eudoxus; Books IV, VI, XI, and XII, the later Pythagorean and Athenian geometricians. Books VII-X deal with higher mathematics.

an inspiration for mathematics that gave him two boons—an absorbed life and a sudden death. Returning to Syracuse, he devoted himself monastically to every branch of mathematical science. Often, like Newton, he neglected food and drink, or the care of his body, in order to pursue the consequences of a new theorem, or to draw figures in the oil on his body, the ashes on the hearth, or the sand with which Greek geometers were wont to strew their floors.[2] He was not without humor: in what he considered his best book, *The Sphere and the Cylinder*, he deliberately inserted false propositions (so we are assured), partly to play a joke upon the friends to whom he sent the manuscript, partly to ensnare poachers who liked to appropriate other men's thoughts.[3] Sometimes he amused himself with puzzles that brought him to the verge of inventing algebra, like the famous Cattle Problem that so beguiled Lessing;[4] sometimes he made strange mechanisms to study the principles on which they operated. But his perennial interest and delight lay in pure science conceived as a key to the understanding of the universe rather than as a tool of practical construction or expanding wealth. He wrote not for pupils but for professional scholars, communicating to them in pithy monographs the abstruse conclusions of his research. All later antiquity was fascinated by the originality, depth, and clarity of these treatises. "It is not possible," said Plutarch, three centuries later, "to find in all geometry more difficult and intricate questions, or more simple and lucid explanations. Some ascribe this to his natural genius; others think that these easy and unlabored pages were the result of incredible effort and toil."[5]

Ten of Archimedes' works survive, after many adventures in Europe and Arabia. (1) *The Method* explains to Eratosthenes, with whom he had formed a friendship in Alexandria, how mechanical experiments can extend geometrical knowledge. This essay ended the ruler-and-compass reign of Plato and opened the door to experimental methods; even so it reveals the different mood of ancient and modern science: the one tolerated practice for the sake of theoretical understanding, the other tolerates theory for the sake of possible practical results. (2) A *Collection of Lemmas* discusses fifteen "choices," or alternative hypotheses, in plane geometry. (3) *The Measurement of a Circle* arrives at a value between $3\frac{1}{7}$ and $3\frac{10}{71}$ for π—the ratio of the circumference to the diameter of a circle—and "squares the circle" by showing, through the method of exhaustion, that the area of a circle equals that of a right-angled triangle whose perpendicular equals the radius, and whose base equals the circumference, of the circle. (4) *The Quadrature of the Parabola* studies, by a form of integral calculus, the area cut off from a parabola by a chord, and the problem of finding the area of an ellipse. (5) *On Spirals* defines a spiral as the figure made by a point moving from a fixed point at a uniform rate along a straight line which is revolving in a plane at a uniform rate about the same fixed point; and finds the area enclosed by a spiral curve and two radii vectores by methods approximating differential calculus. (6) *The Sphere and the Cylinder* seeks formulas for the volume and surface area of a pyramid, a cone, a cylinder, and a sphere. (7) *On Conoids and Spheroids* studies the solids generated by the revolution of conic sections about their axes. (8) *The Sand-Reckoner* passes from geometry to arithmetic, almost to logarithms, by suggesting that large numbers may be represented by multiples, or "orders," of 10,000; by this method Archimedes expresses the number of grains of sand which would be needed to fill the universe—assuming, he genially adds, that the universe has a reasonable size. His conclusion, which anyone may verify for himself, is that the world contains not more than sixty-three "ten-million units of the eighth order of numbers"—or, as we should put it, 10^{63}. References to lost works of Archimedes indicate that he had also discovered a way of finding the square root of nonsquare numbers. (9) *On Plane Equilibriums* applies geometry to mechanics, studies the center of gravity of various bodily configurations, and achieves the oldest extant formulation of scientific statics. (10) *On Floating Bodies* founds hydrostatics by arriving at mathematical formulas for the position of equilibrium of a floating body. The work begins with the then startling thesis that the surface of any liquid body at rest and in equilibrium is spherical, and that the sphere has the same center as the earth.

Perhaps Archimedes was led to the study of hydrostatics by an incident almost as famous as Newton's apple. King Hieron had given to a Syracusan Cellini some gold to be formed into a crown. When the crown was delivered it weighed as much as the gold; but some doubt arose whether the artist had made up part of the weight by using silver, keeping the saved gold for himself. Hieron turned over to Archimedes his suspicion and the crown, presumably stipulating that the one should be resolved without injuring the other. For weeks Archimedes puzzled over the problem. One day, as he stepped into a tub at the public baths, he noticed that the water overflowed according to the depth of his immersion, and that his body appeared to weigh—or press downward—less, the more it was submerged. His curious mind, exploring and utilizing every experience, suddenly formulated the "principle of Archimedes"—that a floating body loses in weight an amount equal to the weight of the water which it displaces. Surmising that a *submerged* body would displace water according to its volume, and perceiving that this principle offered a test for the crown, Archimedes (if we may believe the staid Vitruvius) dashed out naked into the street and rushed to his dwelling, crying out "*Eureka! eureka!*"—I have found it! I have found it! Home, he soon discovered that a given weight of silver, since it had more volume per weight than gold, displaced more water, when immersed, than an equal weight of gold. He observed also that the submerged crown displaced more water than a quantity of gold equaling the crown in weight. He concluded that the crown had been alloyed with some metal less dense than gold. By replacing gold with silver in the gold weight which he was using for comparison, until the compound displaced as much water as the crown, Archimedes was able to say just how much silver had been used in the crown, and how much gold had been stolen.

That he had satisfied the curiosity of the King did not mean so much to him as that he had discovered the law of floating bodies, and a method for measuring specific gravity. He made a planetarium representing the sun, the earth, the moon, and the five planets then known (Saturn, Jupiter, Mars, Venus, and Mercury), and so arranging them that by turning a crank one could set all these bodies in motions differing in direction and speed;[6] but he probably agreed with Plato that the laws that govern the movements of the heavens are more beautiful than the stars.* In a lost treatise partly preserved in summaries, Archimedes so accurately formulated the laws of the lever and the balance that no advance was made upon his work until A.D. 1586. "Commensurable magnitudes," said Proposition VI, "will balance at distances inversely proportional to their gravities"[8]—a useful truth whose brilliant simplification of complex relationships moves the soul of a scientist as the *Hermes* of Praxiteles moves the artist. Almost intoxicated with the vision of power which he saw in the lever and the pulley, Archimedes announced that if he had a fixed fulcrum to work with he could move anything: "*Pa bo, kai tan gan kino,*" he is reported to have said, in the Doric dialect of Syracuse: "Give me a place to stand on, and I will move the earth."[9] Hieron challenged him to do as well as say, and pointed to the difficulty which his men were experiencing in beaching a large ship in the royal fleet. Archimedes arranged a series of cogs and pulleys in such wise that he alone, sitting at one end of the mechanism, was able to draw the fully loaded vessel out of the water onto the land.[10]

Delighted with this demonstration, the King asked Archimedes to design some engines of war. It was characteristic of the two men that Archimedes,

* Cicero saw the apparatus two centuries later, and marveled at its complex synchronism. "When Gallus moved the globe," he writes, "it was actually true that the moon was always as many revolutions behind the sun on the bronze contrivance as would agree with the number of days it was behind it in the sky. Thus the same eclipse of the sun happened on the globe as would happen in actuality."[7]

having designed them, forgot them, and that Hieron, loving peace, never used them. Archimedes, says Plutarch,

> possessed so high a spirit, so profound a soul, and such treasures of scientific knowledge, that though these inventions had now obtained for him the renown of more than human sagacity, he yet would not deign to leave behind him any writing on such subjects; but, repudiating as sordid and ignoble . . . every sort of art that lends itself to mere use and profit, he placed his whole affection and ambition in those purer speculations where there can be no reference to the vulgar needs of life—studies whose superiority to all others is unquestioned, and in which the only doubt can be whether the beauty and grandeur of the subjects examined, or the precision and cogency of the methods and means of proof, most deserve our admiration.[11]

But when Hieron was dead Syracuse became embroiled with Rome, and the doughty Marcellus assailed it by land and sea. Though Archimedes was now (212) a man of seventy-five, he superintended the defense on both fronts. Behind the walls that protected the harbor he set up catapults able to hurl heavy stones to a considerable distance; their rain of projectiles was so devastating that Marcellus retreated until he could advance by night. But when the ships were seen near the shore the sailors were harassed by bowmen who shot at them through the holes that Archimedes' aides had pierced in the wall. Moreover, the inventor had arranged within the walls great cranes which, when the Roman vessels came within reach, were turned by cranks and pulleys so as to drop upon the ships heavy weights of stone or lead that sank many of them. Other cranes, armed with gigantic hooks, grasped vessels, lifted them into the air, dashed them against the rocks, or plunged them end-foremost into the sea.*[12] Marcellus withdrew his fleet, and put his hopes in an attack by land. But Archimedes bombarded the troops with large stones thrown by catapults to such effect that the Romans fled, saying that they were being opposed by gods; and they refused to advance again.[14] "Such a great and marvelous thing," comments Polybius, "does the genius of one man show itself to be when properly applied. The Romans, strong both by sea and by land, had every hope of capturing the town at once if one old man of Syracuse were removed; as long as he was present they did not venture to attack."[15]

Abandoning the idea of taking Syracuse by storm, Marcellus resigned

* Lucian is our earliest, and not quite reliable, authority for the story that Archimedes set Roman ships on fire by concentrating the sun's rays upon them through the use of great concave mirrors.[13]

himself to a slow blockade. After a siege of eight months the starving city surrendered. In the slaughter and pillage that followed Marcellus gave orders that Archimedes should not be injured. During the sack a Roman soldier came upon an aged Syracusan absorbed in studying figures that he had traced in the sand. The Roman commanded him to present himself at once to Marcellus. Archimedes refused to go until he had worked out his problem; he "earnestly besought the soldier," says Plutarch, "to wait a little while, that he might not leave what he was at work upon inconclusive and imperfect, but the soldier, nothing moved by this entreaty, instantly killed him."[16] When Marcellus heard of it he mourned, and did everything in his power to console the relatives of the dead man.[17] The Roman general erected to his memory a handsome tomb, on which was engraved, in accordance with the mathematician's expressed wish, a sphere within a cylinder; to have found formulas for the area and volume of these figures was, in Archimedes' view, the supreme achievement of his life. He was not far wrong; for to add one significant proposition to geometry is of greater value to humanity than to besiege or defend a city. We must rank Archimedes with Newton, and credit him with "a sum of mathematical achievement unsurpassed by any one man in the world's history."[18]

But for the abundance and cheapness of slaves Archimedes might have been the head of a veritable Industrial Revolution. A treatise on *Mechanical Problems* wrongly attributed to Aristotle, and a *Treatise on Weights* wrongly ascribed to Euclid, had laid down certain elementary principles of statics and dynamics a century before Archimedes. Strato of Lampsacus, who succeeded Theophrastus as head of the Lyceum, turned his deterministic materialism to physics, and (about 280) formulated the doctrine that "nature abhors a vacuum."[19] When he added that "a vacuum can be created by artificial means," he opened the way to a thousand inventions. Ctesibius of Alexandria (ca. 200) studied the physics of siphons (which had been used in Egypt as far back as 1500 B.C.), and developed the force pump, the hydraulic organ, and the hydraulic clock. Archimedes probably improved—and unwittingly gave his name to—the ancient Egyptian water screw, which literally made water flow uphill.[20] Philon of Byzantium, about 150, invented pneumatic machines, and various engines of war.[21] The steam engine of Heron of Alexandria, which came after the Roman conquest of Greece, brought this period of mechanical development to a climax and close. The philosophical tradition was too strong; Greek thought went back to theory, and Greek industry contented itself with slaves. The

Greeks were acquainted with the magnet, and the electrical properties of amber, but they saw no industrial possibilities in these curious phenomena. Antiquity unconsciously decided that it was not worth while to be modern.

III. ARISTARCHUS, HIPPARCHUS, ERATOSTHENES

Greek mathematics owed its Hellenistic stimulus and blossoming to Egypt, Greek astronomy to Babylon. Alexander's opening of the East led to a resumption and extension of that trade in ideas which, three centuries earlier, had assisted at the birth of Greek science in Ionia. To this fresh contact with Egypt and the Near East we may ascribe the anomaly of Greek science reaching its height in the Hellenistic age, when Greek literature and art were in decline.

Aristarchus of Samos was a bright interregnum in the rule of the geocentric theory over Greek astronomy. He burned with such zeal that he studied almost all its branches, and achieved distinction in many of them.[22] In his only extant treatise, *On the Sizes and Distances of the Sun and the Moon,** there is no hint of heliocentricism; on the contrary it assumes that the sun and the moon move in circles about the earth. But Archimedes' *Sand-Reckoner* explicitly credits Aristarchus with the "hypothesis that the fixed stars and the sun remain unmoved; the earth revolves about the sun in the circumference of a circle, the sun lying in the middle of the orbit";[24] and Plutarch reports that Cleanthes the Stoic held that Aristarchus should be indicted for "putting the Hearth of the Universe" (i.e., the earth) "in motion."[25] Seleucus of Seleucia defended the heliocentric view, but the opinion of the Greek scientific world decided against it. Aristarchus himself seems to have abandoned his hypothesis when he failed to reconcile it with the supposedly circular movements of the heavenly bodies; for all Greek astronomers took it for granted that these orbits were circular. Perhaps a distaste for hemlock moved Aristarchus to be the Galileo as well as the Copernicus of the ancient world.

It was the misfortune of Hellenistic science that the greatest of Greek astronomers attacked the heliocentric theory with arguments that seemed

---

* Aristarchus estimated the volume of the sun as three hundred (it is over a million) times that of the earth—an estimate that seems low to us, but would have astonished Anaxagoras or Epicurus. He calculated the diameter of the moon as one third that of the earth—an error of eight per cent—and our distance from the sun as twenty (it is almost four hundred) times our distance from the moon. "When the sun is totally eclipsed," reads one proposition, "the sun and the moon are then comprehended by one and the same cone, which has its vertex at our eye."[23]

irrefutable before Copernicus. Hipparchus of Nicaea (in Bithynia), despite what seems to us an epoch-making blunder, was a scientist of the highest type—endlessly curious to know, devotedly patient in research, and so carefully accurate in observation and report that antiquity called him "the lover of truth."[26] He touched and adorned nearly every field of astronomy, and fixed its conclusions for seventeen centuries. Only one of his many works remains—a commentary on the *Phainomena* of Eudoxus and Aratus of Soli; but we know him from Claudius Ptolemy's *Almagest* (ca. A.D. 140), which is based upon his researches and calculations; "Ptolemaic astronomy" should be called Hipparchian. He improved, probably on Babylonian models, the astrolabes and quadrants that were the chief astronomical instruments of his time. He invented the method of determining terrestrial positions by lines of latitude and longitude, and tried to organize the astronomers of the Mediterranean world to make observations and measurements that would fix in these terms the location of all important cities; political disturbances frustrated the plan until Ptolemy's more orderly age. His mathematical studies of astronomic relations led Hipparchus to formulate a table of sines, and thereby to create the science of trigonometry. Helped, no doubt, by the cuneiform records which had been brought from Babylonia, he determined with approximate accuracy the length of the solar, lunar, and sidereal years. He reckoned the solar year as 365¼ days minus 4 minutes and 48 seconds—an error of 6 minutes according to current calculations. His time for a mean lunar month was 29 days, 12 hours, 44 minutes, and 2½ seconds—less than a second away from the accepted figure.[27] He computed, with impressive approximation to modern measurements, the synodic periods of the planets, the obliquity of the ecliptic and of the moon's orbit, the apogee of the sun, and the horizontal parallax of the moon.[28] He estimated the distance of the moon from the earth as 250,000 miles—an error of only five per cent.

Armed with all this knowledge, Hipparchus concluded that the geocentric view better explained the data than did the hypothesis of Aristarchus; the heliocentric theory could not stand mathematical analysis except by supposing an elliptical orbit for the earth, and this supposition was so uncongenial to Greek thought that even Aristarchus does not appear to have considered it. Hipparchus verged upon it by his theory of "eccentrics," which accounted for the apparent irregularities in the orbital velocities of the sun and the moon by suggesting that the centers of the solar and lunar orbits were slightly to one side of the earth. So near did Hipparchus come to being the greatest theorist, as well as the greatest observer, among ancient astronomers.

Watching the sky night after night, Hipparchus was surprised one evening by the appearance of a star where he was sure there had been none before. To certify later changes he made, about 129 B.C., a catalogue, a map, and a globe of the heavens, giving the positions of 1080 fixed stars in terms of celestial latitude and longitude—an immense boon to subsequent students of the sky. Comparing his chart with that which Timochares had made 166 years before, Hipparchus calculated that the stars had shifted their apparent position some two degrees in the interval. On this basis he made the subtlest of his discoveries*—the precession of the equinoxes—the slight advance, day by day, of the moment when the equinoctial points come to the meridian.† He calculated the precession as thirty-six seconds per year; the current estimate is fifty.

We have displaced from his chronological position between Aristarchus and Hipparchus a scholar whose ecumenical erudition won him the nicknames of *Pentathlos* and *Beta*—because he attained distinction in many fields, and ranked second only to the best in each. Tradition gave Eratosthenes of Cyrene exceptional teachers: Zeno the Stoic, Arcesilaus the skeptic, Callimachus the poet, Lysanias the grammarian. By the age of forty his reputation for varied knowledge was so great that Ptolemy III made him head of the Alexandrian Library. He wrote a volume of verse, and a history of comedy. His *Chronographia* sought to determine the dates of the major events in Mediterranean history. He wrote mathematical monographs, and devised a mechanical method for finding mean proportions in continued proportion between two straight lines. He measured the obliquity of the ecliptic at 23° 51′, an error of one half of one per cent. His greatest achievement was his calculation of the earth's circumference as 24,662 miles;[30] we compute it at 24,847. Observing that at noon on the summer solstice the sun at Syene shone directly upon the deep surface of a narrow well, and learning that at the same moment the shadow of an obelisk at Alexandria, some five hundred miles north, showed the sun to be approximately 7½° away from the zenith as measured on the meridian of longitude that con-

* If it was not taken from his Babylonian predecessor Kidinnu.[29]

† The equinoxes (lit., equal nights) are those two days of the year when the sun in its annual apparent motion crosses the equator northward (our vernal, Argentina's autumnal, equinox), or southward (our autumnal equinox), making day and night equal for a day. The equinoctial points are those points in the sky where the equator of the celestial sphere intersects the ecliptic.

nected the two cities, he concluded that an arc of 7½° on the earth's circumference equaled five hundred miles, and that the entire circumference would equal $360 \div 7.5 \times 500$, or 24,000 miles.

Having measured the earth, Eratosthenes proceeded to describe it. His *Geographica* brought together the reports of Alexander's surveyors, of travelers like Megasthenes, voyagers like Nearchus, and explorers like Pytheas of Massalia, who, about 320, had sailed around Scotland to Norway, and perhaps to the Arctic Circle.[31] Eratosthenes did not merely depict the physical features of each region, he sought to explain them through the action of water, fire, earthquake, or volcanic eruption.[32] He bade the Greeks abandon their provincial division of mankind into Hellenes and barbarians; men should be divided not nationally but individually; many Greeks, he thought, were scoundrels, many Persians and Hindus were refined, and the Romans had shown a greater aptitude than the Greeks for social order and competent government.[33] He knew little of northern Europe or northern Asia, less of India south of the Ganges, nothing of south Africa; but he was, so far as we know, the first geographer to mention the Chinese. "If," said another significant passage, "the extent of the Atlantic Ocean were not an obstacle, we might easily pass by sea from Iberia (Spain) to India, keeping in the same parallel."[34]

IV. THEOPHRASTUS, HEROPHILUS, ERASISTRATUS

Zoology never rose again in antiquity to the level that it had reached in Aristotle's *History of Animals.* Probably by an agreed division of labor his successor Theophrastus wrote a classic treatise, *The History of Plants,* and a more theoretical discussion called *The Causes of Plants.* Theophrastus loved gardening, and knew every aspect of his subject. In many ways he was more scientific than his master, more careful of his facts, and more orderly in his exposition; a book without classification, he said, was as untrustworthy as an unbridled horse.[35] He divided all plants into trees, bushes, shrubs, and herbs, and distinguished the chief parts of a plant as root, stem, branch, twig, leaf, flower, and fruit—a classification not improved on till A.D. 1561.[36] "A plant," he wrote, "has the power of germination in all its parts, for it has life in them all. . . . The methods of generation of plants are these: spontaneous, from a seed, a root, a piece torn off, a branch, a twig, pieces of wood cut up small, or from the trunk itself."[37] He had no clear idea of sexual reproduction in plants, except in a few species like the fig tree or the date palm; here he followed the Babylonians in describing fertilization and caprification. He discussed the geographical distribution of plants, their industrial uses, and the climatic conditions most conducive to their health. He studied the minutiae of half a thousand species with an accuracy of detail astonishing in an age that had no microscope. Twenty centuries before Goethe he recognized that the flower is a metamorphosed leaf.[38] He was a naturalist in more ways than one, stoutly rejecting the supernatural explanations current in his day for certain curiosities of botany.[39] He had all the inquisitiveness of a scientist, and did not think it beneath his dignity as a philosopher to write monographs on stones, minerals, weather, winds, weariness, geometry, astronomy, and the physical theories of the pre-Socratic Greeks.[40] "If there had been no Aristotle," says Sarton, "this period would have been called the time of Theophrastus."[41]

Theophrastus' ninth "book" summarized all that the Greeks knew about the medicinal properties of plants. One passage hinted at anesthesia in describing "dittany, a plant especially useful for labor in women; people say that either it makes labor easy, or it stops the pains."[42] Medicine progressed rapidly in this age, perhaps because it had to keep pace with the novel and multiplying diseases of a complex urban civilization. The Greek study of Egyptian medical lore stimulated a fresh advance. The Ptolemies were ruthlessly helpful; they not only permitted the dissection of animals and cadavers, but turned over some condemned criminals for vivisection.[43] Under these encouragements human anatomy became a science, and the absurdities into which Aristotle had fallen were substantially reduced.

Herophilus of Chalcedon, working at Alexandria about 285, dissected the eye and gave a good account of the retina and the optic nerves. He dissected the brain, described the cerebrum, the cerebellum, and the meninges, left his name in the *torcular Herophili,** and restored the brain to honor as the seat of thought. He understood the role of the nerves, originated their division into sensory and motor, and separated the cranial from the spinal nerves. He distinguished arteries from veins, discerned the function of the arteries as carrying blood from the heart to various parts of the body, and in effect discovered the circulation of the blood nineteen centuries before Harvey.[44] Following a suggestion of the Coan physician Praxagoras, he included the taking of the pulse in diagnosis, and used a water clock to measure its frequency. He dissected and described the ovaries, the uterus, the seminal vesicles, and the prostate gland; he studied the liver and the pancreas, and gave to the duodenum the name that it still bears.[45] "Science and art," wrote Herophilus, "have nothing to show, strength is incapable of effort, wealth is useless, and eloquence is powerless, where there is no health."[46]

Herophilus was, so far as we can now judge, the greatest anatomist of antiquity, and Erasistratus was the greatest physiologist. Born in Ceos, Erasistratus studied in Athens, and practiced medicine in Alexandria about 258 B.C. He dis-

* A confluence of blood sinuses in the dura mater, or outer membrane of the brain.

tinguished more carefully than Herophilus between cerebrum and cerebellum, and made experiments on living subjects to study the operation of the brain. He described and explained the working of the epiglottis, the lacteal vessels of the mesentery, and the aortic and pulmonary valves of the heart. He had some notion of basal metabolism, for he devised a crude respiration calorimeter.[47] Every organ, said Erasistratus, is connected with the rest of the organism in three ways—by artery, vein, and nerve. He sought to account for all physiological phenomena by natural causes, rejecting any reference to mystical entities. He discarded the humoral theory of Hippocrates, which Herophilus had retained. He conceived the art of medicine as prevention through hygiene rather than as cure through therapy; he opposed the frequent use of drugs and bloodletting, and relied upon diet, bathing, and exercise.[48]

Such men made Alexandria the Vienna of the ancient medical world. But there were great schools of medicine also at Tralles, Miletus, Ephesus, Pergamum, Taras, and Syracuse. Many cities had a municipal medical service; the physicians so employed received a modest salary, but were honored for making no distinction between rich and poor, free and slave, and for devoting themselves to their work at any time and risk. Apollonius of Miletus fought the plague in near-by islands without reward; when all the doctors of Cos were laid low by an epidemic which they had labored to control, others came to their rescue from neighboring towns. Many public decrees of gratitude were issued to Hellenistic physicians; and though ancient jests railed at mercenary incompetence, the great profession kept high that standard of ethics which had come down to it from Hippocrates as its most precious inheritance.

CHAPTER XXIX

The Surrender of Philosophy

THREE strains merged in Greek philosophy: the physical, the metaphysical, and the ethical. The physical culminated in Aristotle, the metaphysical in Plato, the ethical in Zeno of Citium. The physical development ended in the separation of science from philosophy in Archimedes and Hipparchus; the metaphysical ended in the skepticism of Pyrrho and the later Academy; the ethical remained until Epicureanism and Stoicism were conquered or absorbed by Christianity.

I. THE SKEPTICAL ATTACK

Amid this spreading Hellenistic culture Athens—mother of much of it, mistress of most of it—retained her leadership in two realms: the drama and philosophy. The world was not too busy with war and revolutions, new sciences and new religions, the love of beauty and the quest of gold, to spare some time for the unanswerable but inescapable problems of truth and error, matter and mind, freedom and necessity, nobility and baseness, life and death. From all the cities of the Mediterranean young men made their way, often through a thousand hardships, to study in the halls and gardens where Plato and Aristotle had left almost living memories.

At the Lyceum the industrious Theophrastus of Lesbos carried on the empirical tradition. The Peripatetics were scientists and scholars rather than philosophers; they devoted themselves to specialist research in zoology, botany, biography, and the history of science, philosophy, literature, and law. In his thirty-four years of leadership (322-288) Theophrastus explored many fields, and published four hundred volumes dealing with almost every subject from love to war. His pamphlet "On Marriage" severely handled the female sex, and was severely handled in turn by Epicurus' mistress Leontium, who wrote a learned and devastating reply.[1] Nevertheless it is to Theophrastus that Athenaeus attributes the tender sentiment that "it is through modesty that beauty becomes beautiful."[2] Diogenes Laertius describes him as "a most benevolent man, and very affable"; so eloquent that his original name was forgotten in that which Aristotle gave him, meaning that he spoke like a god; so popular that two thousand students flocked to his lectures, and Menander was among his most faithful followers.[3] Posterity preserved with especial care his book of *Characters*, not because it created a literary form, but because it sharply satirized the faults that all men ascribe to other men. Here is the Garrulous Man who "begins with a eulogy of his wife, relates the dream he had the night before, tells dish by dish what he had for supper," and concludes that "we are by no means the men we were" in former times. And here is the Stupid Man who "when he goes to the play, is left at the end fast asleep in an empty house . . . after a hearty supper he has to get up in the night, returns only half awake, misses the right door, and is bitten by his neighbor's dog."[4]

One of the few events in Theophrastus' life was the issuance of a state decree (307) requiring the Assembly's approval in the selection of leaders for the philosophical schools. About the same time Agnonides indicted Theophrastus on the old charge of impiety. Theophrastus quietly left Athens; but so many students followed him that the storekeepers complained of a ruinous fall in trade. Within a year the decree was annulled, the indictment was withdrawn, and Theophrastus returned in triumph to preside over the Lyceum almost till his death at eighty-five. "All Athens," we are told, attended his funeral. The Peripatetic school did not long survive him: science left impoverished Athens for affluent Alexandria, and the Lyceum, which had dedicated itself to research, subsided into a penurious obscurity.

Meanwhile Speusippus had succeeded Plato, and Xenocrates Speusippus, at the Academy. Xenocrates governed the school for a quarter of a century (339-314), and brought new credit to philosophy by the honorable simplicity of his life. Absorbed in study and teaching, he left the Academy but once a year, to see the Dionysian tragedies; when he appeared, says Laertius, "the turbulent and quarrelsome rabble of the city made way for him to pass."[5] He refused all fees, and became so poor that he was on the verge of being imprisoned for taxes when Demetrius of Phalerum paid his arrears and had him freed. Philip of Macedon said that among the many Athenian ambassadors sent to him Xenocrates was the only one who proved incorruptible. His reputation for virtue annoyed Phryne. Pretending that she was being pursued, she took refuge in his house; and seeing that he had but one bed she asked if she might share it with him. He consented, we are told, out of humane considerations; but he proved so cold to her entreaties and her charms that she fled from his bed and board, and complained to her friends that she had found a statue instead of a man.[6] Xenocrates would have no mistress but philosophy.

With his death the metaphysical strain in Greek thought neared exhaustion in the very grove that had been its shrine. The successors of Plato were mathematicians and moralists, and spent little time on the abstract questions that had once agitated the Academy. The skeptical challenges of Zeno the Eleatic, the subjectivism of Heracleitus, the methodical doubt of Gorgias and Protagoras, the metaphysical agnosticism of Socrates, Aristippus, and Eucleides of Megara resumed control of Greek philosophy; the Age of Reason was over. Every hypothesis had been conceived, aired, and forgotten; the universe had preserved its secret, and men had grown weary of a search in which even the most brilliant minds had failed. Aristotle had agreed with Plato on only one point—the possibility of acquiring ultimate truth.[7] Pyrrho voiced the suspicions of his time in suggesting that it was above all on this point that they had both been mistaken.

Pyrrho was born at Elis about 360. He followed Alexander's army to India, studied under the "Gymnosophists" there, and perhaps learned from them something of the skepticism for which his name became a synonym. Returning to Elis he lived in serene poverty as a teacher of philosophy. He was too modest to write books, but his pupil Timon of Phlius, in a series of *Silloi* or Satires, sent Pyrrho's opinions abroad into the world. These opinions were basically three: that certainty is unattainable, that the wise man will suspend judgment and will seek tranquillity rather than truth, and that, since all theories are probably false, one might as well accept the myths and conventions of his time and place. Neither the senses nor reason can give us sure knowledge: the senses distort the object in perceiving it, and reason is merely the sophist servant of desire. Every syllogism begs the question, for its major premise assumes its conclusion. "Every reason has a corresponding reason opposed to it";[8] the same experience may be delightful or unpleasant according to circumstance and mood; the same object may seem small or large, ugly or beautiful; the same practice may be moral or immoral according to where and when we live; the same gods are or are not, according to the different nations of mankind; everything is opinion, nothing is quite true. It is foolish, then, to take sides in disputes, or to seek some other place or mode of living, or to envy the future or the past; all desire is delusion. Even life is an uncertain good, death not a certain evil; one should have no prejudices against either of them. Best of all is a calm acceptance: not to reform the world, but to bear with it patiently; not to fever ourselves with progress, but to content ourselves with peace. Pyrrho tried sincerely to live this half-Hindu philosophy. He conformed humbly with the customs and worship of Elis, made no effort to avoid dangers or prolong his life,[9] and died at the age of ninety. His fellow citizens so approved of him that in his honor they exempted philosophers from taxation.

By the irony of time it was the followers of Plato who carried forward this attack upon metaphysics. Arcesilaus, who became head of the "Middle Academy" in 269, transformed Plato's rejection of sense knowledge into a skepticism as complete as Pyrrho's, and probably under Pyrrho's influence.[10] "Nothing is certain," said Arcesilaus, "not even that."[11] When he was told that such a doctrine made life impossible he answered that life had long since learned to manage with probabilities. A century later a still more vigorous skeptic took charge of the "New Academy," and pressed the doctrine of universal doubt to the point of intellectual and moral nihilism. Carneades of Cyrene, coming to Athens like a Greek Abelard about 193, made life bitter for Chrysippus and his other teachers by arguing with galling subtlety against every doctrine that they taught. As they had undertaken to make him a logician he used to say to them (turning the tables on Protagoras): "If my reasoning is right, well and good; if it is wrong, give me back my tuition fee."[12] When he set up shop for himself he lectured one morning for an opinion, the next morning against it, proving each so well as to destroy both; while his pupils, and even his biographer, sought in vain to discover his real views. He undertook to refute the materialistic realism of the Stoics by a Platonic-Kantian critique of sensation and reason. He attacked all conclusions as intellectually indefensible, and bade his students be satisfied with probability and the customs of their time. Sent to Rome by Athens as one of an embassy (155), he shocked the Senate by speaking one day in defense of justice, and on the morrow deriding it as an impracticable dream: if Rome wished to practice justice it would have to restore to the nations of the Mediterranean all that it had taken from them by superior force.[13] On the third day Cato had the embassy sent home as a danger to public morals. Perhaps Polybius, who was then a hostage with Scipio, heard these addresses or of them, for he speaks with the anger of a practical man against those philosophers

> who in the discussions of the Academy have trained themselves in extreme readiness of speech. For some of them, in their efforts to puzzle the minds of their hearers, resort to such paradoxes, and are so fertile in inventing plausibilities, that they wonder whether or not it is possible for those in Athens to smell eggs roasted in Ephesus, and are in doubt whether all the time they are discussing the matter in

the Academy they are not lying in their beds at home and composing this discourse in a dream. . . . From this excessive love of paradox they have brought all philosophy into disrepute. . . . They have implanted such a passion in the minds of our young men that they never give even a thought to the ethical and political questions that really benefit students of philosophy, but spend their lives in the vain attempt to invent useless absurdities.[14]

II. THE EPICUREAN ESCAPE

Though he described for many ages the theorist who loses his life in the cobwebs of speculation, Polybius was wrong in supposing that moral problems had lost their lure for the Greek mind. It was precisely the ethical strain that in this period replaced the physical and the metaphysical as the dominant note in philosophy. Political problems were indeed in abeyance, for freedom of speech was harassed by the presence or memory of royal garrisons, and national liberty was implicitly understood to depend upon quiescence. The glory of the Athenian state had departed, and philosophy had to face what to Greece was an unprecedented divorce between politics and ethics. It had to find a way of life at once forgivable to philosophy and compatible with political impotence. Therefore it conceived its problem no longer as one of building a just state, but as that of forming the self-contained and contented individual.

The ethical development now took two opposite directions. One followed the lead of Heracleitus, Socrates, Antisthenes, and Diogenes, and expanded the Cynic into the Stoic philosophy; the other stemmed from Democritus, leaned heavily on Aristippus, and drew out the Cyrenaic into the Epicurean creed. Both of these philosophical compensations for religious and political decay came from Asia: Stoicism from Semitic pantheism, fatalism, and resignation; Epicureanism from the pleasure-loving Greeks of the Asiatic coast.

Epicurus was born at Samos in 341. At twelve he fell in love with philosophy; at nineteen he went to Athens and spent a year at the Academy. Like Francis Bacon he preferred Democritus to Plato and Aristotle, and took from him many bricks for his own construction. From Aristippus he learned the wisdom of pleasure, and from Socrates the pleasure of wisdom; from Pyrrho he took the doctrine of tranquillity, and a ringing word for it—*ataraxia*. He must have watched with interest the career of his contemporary Theodorus of Cyrene, who preached an unmoralistic atheism so openly in Athens that the Assembly indicted him for impiety[15]—a lesson that Epicurus did not forget. Then he returned to Asia and lectured on philosophy at Colophon, Mytilene, and Lampsacus. The Lampsacenes were so impressed with his ideas and his character that they felt qualms of selfishness in keeping him in so remote a city; they raised a fund of eighty minas ($4000), bought a house and garden on the outskirts of Athens, and presented it to Epicurus as his school and his home. In 306, aged thirty-five, Epicurus took up his residence there, and taught to the Athenians a philosophy that was Epicurean in name only. It was a sign of the growing freedom of women that he welcomed them to his lectures, even into the little community that lived about him. He made no distinctions of station or race; he accepted courtesans as well as matrons, slaves as well as freemen; his favorite pupil was his own slave, Mysis. The courtesan Leontium became his mistress as well as his pupil, and found him as jealous a mate as if he had secured her by due process of law. Under his influence she had one child and wrote several books, whose purity of style did not interfere with her morals.[16]

For the rest Epicurus lived in Stoic simplicity and prudent privacy. His motto was *lathe biosas*—"live unobtrusively." He took part dutifully in the religious ritual of the city, but kept his hands clear of politics, and his spirit free from the affairs of the world. He was content with water and a little wine, bread and a little cheese. His rivals and enemies charged that he gorged himself when he could, and became abstemious only when overeating had ruined his digestion. "But those who speak thus are all wrong," Diogenes Laertius assures us; and he adds: "There are many witnesses of the unsurpassable kindness of the man to everybody—both his own country, which honored him with statues, and his friends, who were so numerous that they could not be contained in whole cities."[17] He was devoted to his parents, generous to his brothers, and gentle to his servants, who joined with him in philosophical studies.[18] His pupils looked upon him, says Seneca, as a god among men; and after his death their motto was: "Live as though the eye of Epicurus were upon thee."

Between his lessons and his loves he wrote three hundred books. The ashes of Herculaneum preserved for us some fragments of his central work, *On Nature;* Diogenes Laertius, the Plutarch of philosophy, handed down three of his letters, and late discoveries have added a few more. Above all, Lucretius enshrined the thought of Epicurus in the greatest of philosophical poems.

Perhaps already conscious that Alexander's conquest was letting loose upon Greece a hundred mystic cults from the East, Epicurus begins with the arresting proposition that the aim of philosophy is to free men from fear—more than anything else, from the fear of gods. He dislikes religion because, he thinks, it thrives on ignorance, promotes it, and darkens life with the terror of celestial spies, relentless furies, and endless punishments. The gods exist, says Epicurus, and enjoy, in some far-off space among the stars, a serene and deathless life; but they are too sensible to bother with the affairs of so infinitesimal a species as mankind. The world is not designed, nor is it guided, by them; how could such divine Epicureans have created so middling a universe, so confused a scene of order and disorder, of beauty and suffering?[19] If this disappoints you, Epicurus adds, console yourself with the thought that the gods are too remote to do you any more harm than good. They cannot watch you, they cannot judge you, they cannot plunge you into hell. As for evil gods, or demons, they are the unhappy fantasies of our dreams.

Having rejected religion, Epicurus goes on to reject metaphysics. We can know nothing of the suprasensual world; reason must confine itself to the experience of the senses, and must accept these as the final test of truth. All the problems that Locke and Leibnitz were to debate two thousand years later are here settled with one sentence: if knowledge does not come from the senses, where else can it come from? And if the senses are not the ultimate arbiter of fact, how can we find such a criterion in reason, whose data must be taken from the senses?

Nevertheless the senses give us no certain knowledge of the external world; they catch not the objective thing itself, but only the tiny atoms thrown off by every part of its surface, and leaving upon our senses little replicas of its nature and form. If, therefore, we must have a theory of the world (and really it is not altogether necessary), we had better accept Democritus' view that nothing exists, or can be known to us, or can even be imagined by us, except bodies and space; and that all bodies are composed of indivisible and unchangeable atoms. These atoms have no color, temperature, sound, taste, or smell; such qualities are created by the corpuscular radiations of objects upon our sense organs. But the atoms do differ in size, weight, and form; for only by this supposition can we account for the infinite variety of things. Epicurus would like to explain the operation of the atoms on purely mechanical principles; but as he is interested in ethics far more than in cosmology, and is anxious to preserve free will as the source of moral responsibility and the prop of personality, he abandons

Democritus in mid-air, and supposes a kind of spontaneity in the atoms: they swerve a bit from the perpendicular as they fall through space, and so enter into the combinations that make the four elements, and through them the diversity of the objective scene.[20] There are innumerable worlds, but it is unwise to interest ourselves in them. We may assume that the sun and the moon are about as large as they appear to be, and then we can give our time to the study of man.

Man is a completely natural product. Life probably began by spontaneous generation, and progressed without design through the natural selection of the fittest forms.[21] Mind is only another kind of matter. The soul is a delicate material substance diffused throughout the body.[22] It can feel or act only by means of the body, and dies with the body's death. Despite all this we must accept the testimony of our immediate consciousness that the will is free; else we should be meaningless puppets on the stage of life. It is better to be a slave to the gods of the people than to the Fate of the philosophers.[23]

The real function of philosophy, however, is not to explain the world, since the part can never explain the whole, but to guide us in our quest of happiness. "That which we have in view is not a set of systems and vain opinions, but much rather a life exempt from every kind of disquietude."[24] Over the entrance to the garden of Epicurus was the inviting legend: "Guest, thou shalt be happy here, for here happiness is esteemed the highest good." Virtue, in this philosophy, is not an end in itself, it is only an indispensable means to a happy life.[25] "It is not possible to live pleasantly without living prudently, honorably, and justly; nor to live prudently, honorably, and justly without living pleasantly."[26] The only certain propositions in philosophy are that pleasure is good, and that pain is bad. Sensual pleasures are in themselves legitimate, and wisdom will find some room for them; since, however, they may have evil effects, they need such discriminating pursuit as only intelligence can give.

> When, therefore, we say that pleasure is the chief good we are not speaking of the pleasures of the debauched man, or those that lie in sensual enjoyment . . . but we mean the freedom of the body from pain, and of the soul from disturbance. For it is not continued drinkings and revels, or the enjoyment of female society, or feasts of fish or other expensive foods, that make life pleasant, but such sober contemplation as examines the reasons for choice and avoidance, and puts to flight the vain opinions from which arises most of the confusion that troubles the soul.[27]

In the end, then, understanding is not only the highest virtue, it is also the highest happiness, for it avails more than any other faculty in us to avoid pain and grief. Wisdom is the only liberator: it frees us from bondage to the passions, from fear of the gods, and from dread of death; it teaches us how to bear misfortune, and how to derive a deep and lasting pleasure from the simple goods of life and the quiet pleasures of the mind. Death is not so frightful when we view it intelligently; the suffering it involves may be briefer and slighter than that which we have borne time and again during our lives; it is our foolish fancies of what death may bring that lend to it so much of its terror. And consider how little is needed to a wise content—fresh air, the cheapest foods, a modest shelter, a bed, a few books, and a friend. "Everything natural is easily procured, and only the useless is costly."[28] We should not fret our lives out in realizing every desire that comes into our heads: "Desires may be ignored when our failure to accomplish them will not really cause us pain."[29] Even love, marriage, and parentage are unnecessary; they bring us fitful pleasures, but perennial grief.[30] To accustom ourselves to plain living and simple ways is an almost certain road to health.[31] The wise man does not burn with ambition or lust for fame; he does not envy the good fortune of his enemies, nor even of his friends; he avoids the fevered competition of the city and the turmoil of political strife; he seeks the calm of the countryside, and finds the surest and deepest happiness in tranquillity of body and mind. Because he controls his appetites, lives without pretense, and puts aside all fears, the natural "sweetness of life" (*hedone*) rewards him with the greatest of all goods, which is peace.

This is a likably honest creed. It is encouraging to find a philosopher who is not afraid of pleasure, and a logician who has a good word to say for the senses. There is no subtlety here, and no warm passion for understanding; on the contrary Epicureanism, despite its transmission of the atomic theory, marks a reaction from the brave curiosity that had created Greek science and philosophy. The profoundest defect of the system is its negativity: it thinks of pleasure as freedom from pain, and of wisdom as an escape from the hazards and fullness of life; it provides an excellent design for bachelorhood, but hardly for a society. Epicurus respected the state as a necessary evil, under whose protection he might live unmolested in his garden, but he appears to have cared little about national independence; indeed, his school seems to have preferred monarchy to democracy, as less inclined to persecute heresy[32]—an arresting inversion of modern beliefs. Epicurus was ready to accept any government that offered no hindrance to the unobtrusive pursuit of wisdom and companionship. He dedicated to friendship the devotion that earlier generations had given to the state. "Of all the things that wisdom provides for the happiness of the whole life, by far the most important is friendship."[33] The friendships of the Epicureans were proverbial for their permanence; and the letters of the master abound in expressions of ardent affection.[34] His disciples returned this feeling with Greek intensity. Young Colotes, on first hearing Epicurus speak, fell on his knees, wept, and hailed him as a god.[35]

For thirty-six years Epicurus taught in his garden, preferring a school to a family. In the year 270 he was brought down with the stone. He bore the pains stoically, and on his deathbed found time to think of his friends. "I write to you on this happy day which is the last of my life. The obstruction of my bladder, and the internal pains, have reached the extreme point, but there is marshaled against them the delight of my mind in thinking over our talks together. Take care of Metrodorus' children in a way worthy of your lifelong devotion to me and to philosophy."[36] He willed his property to the school, hoping "that all those who study philosophy may never be in want . . . so far as our power to prevent it may extend."[37]

He left behind him a long succession of disciples, so loyal to his memory that for centuries they refused to change a word of his teaching. His most famous pupil, Metrodorus of Lampsacus, had already shocked or amused Greece by reducing Epicureanism to the proposition that "all good things have reference to the belly"[38]—meaning, perhaps, that all pleasure is physiological, and ultimately visceral. Chrysippus countered by calling the *Gastrology* of Archestratus "the metropolis of the Epicurean philosophy."[39] Popularly misunderstood, Epicureanism was publicly denounced and privately accepted in wide circles throughout Hellas. So many Hellenizing Jews adopted it that *Apiköros* was used by the rabbis as a synonym for apostate.[40] In 173 or 155 two Epicurean philosophers were expelled from Rome on the ground that they were corrupting youth.[41] A century later Cicero asked, "Why are there so many followers of Epicurus?"[42] and Lucretius composed the fullest and finest extant exposition of the Epicurean system. The school had professed adherents until the reign of Constantine, some of them, by their lives, degrading the name of the master to mean "epicure," others faithfully teaching the simple maxims into which he had once condensed his philosophy: "The gods are not to be feared; death cannot be felt; the good can be won; all that we dread can be conquered."[43]

III. THE STOIC COMPROMISE

Since an increasing number of Epicurus' followers interpreted him as counseling the pursuit of personal pleasure, the essential problem of ethics—what is the good life?—had reached not a solution but only a new formulation: how can the natural epicureanism of the individual be reconciled with the stoicism necessary to the group and the race?—how can the members of a society be inspired to, or frightened into, the self-control and self-sacrifice indispensable to collective survival? The old religion could no longer fulfill this function; the old city-state no longer lifted men up to self-forgetfulness. Educated Greeks turned from religion to philosophy for an answer; they called in philosophers to advise or console them in the crises of life; they asked from philosophy some world view that would give to human existence a permanent meaning and value in the scheme of things, and that would enable them to look without terror upon the certainty of death. Stoicism is the last effort of classical antiquity to find a natural ethic. Zeno tried once more to accomplish the task in which Plato had failed.

Zeno was a native of Citium in Cyprus. The city was partly Phoenician, chiefly Greek; Zeno is frequently called a Phoenician, sometimes an Egyptian; he was almost certainly of mixed Hellenic and Semitic parentage.[44] Apollonius of Tyre describes him as thin, tall, and dark; his head was bent to one side, and his legs were weak; Aphrodite, though Hephaestus was no better, would have surrendered him to Athena. Having no distractions, he rapidly amassed wealth as a merchant; when he first came to Athens, we are told, he had over a thousand talents. According to Diogenes Laertius he was shipwrecked on the Attic coast, lost his fortune, and arrived in Athens, about 314, almost destitute.[45] Sitting down by a bookseller's stall he began to read Xenophon's *Memorabilia*, and was soon fascinated by the character of Socrates. "Where are such men to be found today?" he asked. At that moment Crates, a Cynic philosopher, passed by. "Follow that man," the bookseller advised him. Zeno, aged thirty, enrolled in Crates' school, and rejoiced in having discovered philosophy: "I made a prosperous voyage," he said, "when I was wrecked."[46] Crates was a Theban who had turned over his fortune of three hundred talents to his fellow citizens and had taken up the ascetic life of a Cynic mendicant. He denounced the sexual looseness of his time, and counseled hunger as a cure for love. His pupil Hipparchia, having plenty to eat, fell in love with him, and threatened to kill herself unless her parents gave her to him. They begged Crates to dissuade her, which he tried to do by laying his beggar's wallet at her feet, saying: "This is all my fortune; think now what you are doing." Undiscouraged, she left her rich home, donned the beggar's garb, and went to live with Crates in free love. Their nuptials, we are informed, were consummated in public, but their lives were models of affection and fidelity.[47]

Zeno was impressed by the stern simplicity of the Cynic life. The followers of Antisthenes had now become the Franciscan monks of antiquity, vowed to poverty and abstinence, sleeping in any natural shelter that they came upon, and living upon the alms of people too industrious to be saints. Zeno took from the Cynics the outlines of his ethic, and did not conceal his debt. In his first book, *The Republic*, he was so far under their influence that he espoused an anarchist communism in which there should be no money, no property, no marriage, no religion, and no laws.[48] Recognizing that this utopia and the Cynic regimen offered no practicable program of life, he left Crates and studied for a time with Xenocrates at the Academy, and with Stilpo of Megara. He must have read Heracleitus receptively, for he incorporated into his own thought several Heracleitean ideas—the Divine Fire as the soul of man and of the cosmos, the eternity of law, and the repeated creation and conflagration of the world. But it was his custom to say that he owed most of all to Socrates, as the fountainhead and ideal of the Stoic philosophy.

After many years of humble tutelage Zeno at last, in 301, set up his own school by discoursing informally as he walked up and down under the colonnades of the Stoa Poecile, or Pointed Porch. He welcomed poor and rich alike, but discouraged the attendance of young men, feeling that only mature manhood could understand philosophy. When a youth talked too much Zeno informed him that "the reason why we have two ears and only one mouth is that we may hear more and talk less."[49] Antigonus II, when in Athens, attended Zeno's classes, became his admiring friend, sought his advice, seduced him into momentary luxury, and invited him to come and live as his guest in Pella. Zeno excused himself and sent his pupil Persaeus instead. For forty years* he taught in the Stoa, and lived a life so consistent with his teachings that "more temperate than Zeno" became a proverb in Greece. Despite his intimacy with Antigonus the Athenian Assembly gave him the "keys to the walls," and voted him a statue and a crown. The decree read:

> Whereas Zeno of Citium has passed many years in our city in the study of philosophy, being in all other respects a good man (*sic*),

* All dates for Zeno are disputed; the sources are contradictory. Zeller concludes to 350 for his birth and 260 for his death.[50]

> and also exhorting all the young men who have sought his company to the practice of temperance; making his own life a model of the greatest excellence . . . it has been resolved by the people to honor Zeno . . . to present him with a golden crown . . . and to build him a tomb in the Ceramicus at the public expense.[51]

"He died," says Laertius, "in the following manner," reputedly in his ninetieth year. "When he was going out of his school he tripped and broke a toe. Striking the ground with his hand, he repeated a line from the *Niobe:* 'I come; why call me so?' And immediately he strangled himself."[52]

His work at the Stoa was carried on by two Asiatic Greeks—by Cleanthes of Assus and then by Chrysippus of Soli. Cleanthes was a pugilist who came to Athens with four drachmas, worked as a common laborer, refused public relief, studied for nineteen years under Zeno, and lived a life of industry and ascetic poverty. Chrysippus was the most learned and prolific of the school; he gave the Stoic doctrine its historic form by expounding it in 750 books, which Dionysius of Halicarnassus held up as models of learned dullness. After him Stoicism spread throughout Hellas, and found its greatest exponents in Asia: in Panaetius of Rhodes, Zeno of Tarsus, Boethus of Sidon, and Diogenes of Seleucia. Out of the casual fragments that survive from a once voluminous literature we must piece together a composite picture of the most widespread and influential philosophy in the ancient world.

It was probably Chrysippus who divided the Stoic system into logic, natural science, and ethics. Zeno and his successors prided themselves on their contributions to logical theory, but the streams of ink that flowed from them on this subject have left no appreciable residue of enlightenment or use.* The Stoics agreed with the Epicureans that knowledge arises only out of the senses, and placed the final test of truth in such perceptions as compel the assent of the mind by their vividness or their persistence. Experience, however, need not lead to knowledge; for between sensation and reason lies emotion or passion, which may distort experience into error even as it distorts desire into vice. Reason is the supreme achievement of man, a seed from the *Logos Spermatikos*, or Seminal Reason, that made and rules the world.

The world itself, like man, is at once completely material and inherently divine. Everything that the senses report to us is material, and only ma-

* Except in certain additions to terminology, like the word *logic* itself. Zeno's pupil Aristo likened logicians to people eating lobsters, who take a great deal of trouble for a little morsel of meat concealed in much shell.[53]

terial things can cause or receive action. Qualities as well as quantities, virtues as well as passions, soul as well as body, God as well as the stars, are material forms or processes, differing in degrees of fineness, but essentially one.[54] On the other hand all matter is dynamic, full of tensions and powers, perpetually engaged in diffusion or concentration, and animated by an internal and eternal energy, heat, or fire. The universe lives through innumerable cycles of expansion and contraction, development and dissolution; periodically it is consumed in a grand conflagration, and slowly it takes form again; then it passes through all its previous history, even in minutest detail;* for the chain of causes and effects is an unbreakable circle, an endless repetition. All events and all acts of will are determined; it is as impossible for anything to happen otherwise than it does as it is for something to come out of nothing; any break in the chain would disrupt the world.

God, in this system, is the beginning, the middle, and the end. The Stoics recognized the necessity of religion as a basis for morality; they looked with a genial tolerance upon the popular faith, even upon its demons and its divination, and found allegorical interpretations to bridge the chasm between superstition and philosophy. They accepted Chaldean astrology as essentially correct, and thought of earthly affairs as in some mystic and continuous correspondence with the movements of the stars[55]—one phase of that universal *sympatheia* by which whatever happened to any part affected all the rest. As if preparing not only an ethic but a theology for Christianity, they conceived the world, law, life, the soul, and destiny in terms of God, and defined morality as a willing surrender to the divine will. God, like man, is living matter; the world is his body, the order and law of the world are his mind and will; the universe is a gigantic organism of which God is the soul, the animating breath, the fertilizing reason, the activating fire.[56] Sometimes the Stoics conceive God in impersonal terms; more often they picture him as a Providence designing and guiding the cosmos with supreme intelligence, adjusting all its parts to rational purposes, and making everything redound to the use of virtuous men. Cleanthes identifies him with Zeus in a monotheistic hymn worthy of Ikhnaton or Isaiah:

> Thou, O Zeus, art praised above all gods: many are thy names and thine is all power for ever.
>
> The beginning of the world was from thee: and with law thou rulest over all things.

---

* We are relieved to learn that some of the Stoics were not quite certain on this point.

Unto thee may all flesh speak: for we are thy offspring.

Therefore will I raise a hymn unto thee: and will ever sing of thy power.

The whole order of the heavens obeyeth thy word: as it moveth around the earth:

With little and great lights mixed together: how great art thou, King above all for ever!

Nor is anything done upon the earth apart from thee: nor in the firmament, nor in the seas:

Save that which the wicked do: by their own folly.

But thine is the skill to set even the crooked straight: what is without fashion is fashioned and the alien akin before thee.

Thus hast thou fitted together all things in one: the good with the evil:

That thy word should be one in all things: abiding for ever.

Let folly be dispersed from our souls: that we may repay thee the honor wherewith thou hast honored us:

Singing praise of thy works for ever: as becometh the sons of men."[87]

Man is to the universe as microcosm to macrocosm; he too is an organism with a material body and a material soul. For whatever moves or influences the body, or is moved or influenced by the body, must be corporeal. The soul is a fiery breath or *pneuma* diffused through the body, just as the world soul is diffused through the world. At death the soul survives the body, but only as an impersonal energy. At the final conflagration the soul will be reabsorbed, like Atman into Brahman, into that ocean of energy which is God.

Since man is a part of God or Nature, the problem of ethics can be easily solved: goodness is co-operation with God, or Nature, or the Law of the World. It is not the pursuit or enjoyment of pleasure, for such pursuit subordinates reason to passion, often injures the body or the mind, and seldom satisfies us in the end. Happiness can be found only through a rational adjustment of our aims and conduct to the purposes and laws of the universe. There is no contradiction between the good of the individual and the good of the cosmos, for the law of well-being in the individual is identical with the law of Nature. If evil comes to the good man it is only temporary, and is not really evil; if we could understand the whole we should see the good behind whatever evil appears in the parts.* The wise man will study science only sufficiently to find the law of Nature, and will then adapt his life to that Law. *Zen kata physin*, to live according to Nature—this is the purpose and sole excuse of science and philosophy. Almost in Newman's words Cleanthes surrenders his will to God's:

> Lead me, O God, and thou my Destiny,
> To that one place which you will have me fill.
> I follow gladly. Should I strive with thee,
> A recreant, I needs must follow still.[59]

The Stoic, therefore, will shun luxury and complexity, economic or political strife; he will content himself with little, and will accept without complaint the difficulties and disappointments of life. He will be indifferent to everything but virtue and vice—to sickness and pain, good or ill repute, freedom or slavery, life or death. He will suppress all feelings that may obstruct the course or question the wisdom of Nature: if his son dies he will not grieve, but will accept Fate's decree as in some hidden way the best. He will seek so complete an *apatheia*, or absence of feeling, that his peace of mind will be secure against all the attacks and vicissitudes of fortune, pity, or love.† He will be a hard teacher and a stern administrator. Determinism does not imply indulgence; we must hold ourselves, and others, morally responsible for every action. When Zeno beat his slave for stealing, and the slave, having a little learning, said, "But it was fated that I should steal," Zeno answered, "And that I should beat you."[61] The Stoic looks upon virtue as its own reward, and as an absolute duty or categorical imperative, derived from his participation in divinity; and he will console himself, in misfortune, by remembering that in following the divine law he becomes an incarnate god.[62] When he is tired of life, and can leave it without injuring others, he will have no scruples against suicide. Cleanthes, having reached his seventieth year, entered upon a long fast; and then, saying that he would not go back after coming halfway, continued it until he died.[63]

The Stoic, however, is not unsocial, neither so proud of poverty as the Cynic, nor so enamored of solitude as the Epicurean. He accepts marriage and the family as necessary, though he has no praise for romantic love; he

---

* Wars, said Chrysippus, are a useful corrective of overpopulation, and bedbugs do us the service of preventing us from oversleeping.[58]

† Chrysippus proposed to limit the care of dead relatives to the simplest and quietest burial; it would be still better, he thought, to use their flesh as food.[60]

dreams of a utopia in which all women will be in common.[64] He accepts the state, even monarchy; he has no fond memories of the city-state, and considers the average man a dangerous simpleton; he prefers the Antigonids to King Mob. In truth he cares little for any government; he wishes that all men might be philosophers, so that laws would be unnecessary; he thinks of perfection not, as Plato and Aristotle did, in terms of the good society, but in terms of the good man. He may take part in political affairs, and will support every move, however modest, toward human freedom and dignity; but he will not fetter his happiness to place or power. He may give his life for his country, but he will reject any patriotism that hinders his loyalty to all mankind; he is a citizen of the world. Zeno, in whose veins, as we have seen, there probably flowed both Greek and Semitic blood, longed like Alexander for a breaking down of racial and national barriers, and his internationalism reflects Alexander's passing unification of the eastern Mediterranean world. Ultimately, Zeno and Chrysippus hoped, all those warring states and classes would be replaced by one vast society in which there would be no nations, no classes, no rich or poor, no masters or slaves; in which philosophers would rule without oppression, and all men would be brothers as the children of one God.[65]

Stoicism was a noble philosophy, and proved more practicable than a modern cynic would expect. It brought together all the elements of Greek thought in a final effort of the pagan mind to create a system of morals acceptable to the classes that had abandoned the ancient creed; and though it naturally won only a small minority to its standard, those few were everywhere the best. Like its Christian counterparts, Calvinism and Puritanism, it produced the strongest characters of its time. Theoretically it was a monstrous doctrine of an isolated and pitiless perfection. Actually it created men of courage, saintliness, and good will like Cato the Younger, Epictetus, and Marcus Aurelius; it influenced Roman jurisprudence in building a law of nations for non-Romans; and it helped to hold ancient society together until a new faith came. The Stoics lent countenance to superstition, and had an injurious effect upon science; but they saw clearly the basic problem of their age—the collapse of the theological basis of morals—and they made an honest attempt to bridge the gap between religion and philosophy. Epicurus won the Greeks, Zeno won the aristocracy of Rome; and to the end of pagan history the Stoics ruled the Epicureans, as they always will. When a new religion took form out of the intellectual and moral chaos of the dying Hellenistic world, the way had been prepared for it by a philosophy that acknowledged the necessity of faith, preached an ascetic doctrine of simplicity and self-restraint, and saw all things in God.

IV. THE RETURN TO RELIGION

The conflict between religion and philosophy had now seen three stages: the attack on religion, as in the pre-Socratics; the endeavor to replace religion with a natural ethic, as in Aristotle and Epicurus; and the return to religion in the Skeptics and the Stoics—a movement that culminated in Neo-Platonism and Christianity. A like sequence has occurred more than once in history, and may be taking place today. Thales corresponds to Galileo, Democritus to Hobbes, the Sophists to the Encyclopedists, Protagoras to Voltaire; Aristotle to Spencer, Epicurus to Anatole France; Pyrrho to Pascal, Arcesilaus to Hume, Carneades to Kant, Zeno to Schopenhauer, Plotinus to Bergson. The chronology resists the analogy, but the basic line of development is the same.

The age of the great systems gave way to doubt in the ability of reason either to understand the world or to control the impulses of men into order and civilization. The skeptics were such not in the Humian but in the Kantian sense: they doubted philosophy as well as dogma, sapped the foundations of materialism, and advised a quiet acceptance of the ancient cult; in Pyrrho, as in Pascal, skepticism led not from but to religion, and Pyrrho himself ended as the venerated high priest of his city. The Epicurean abandonment of politics for ethics, the flight from the state to the soul, could only represent a moment in the return of the pendulum; and the concentration on individual salvation paved the way for a religion that would appeal to the individual rather than to the state. There were many who could not find in life the consolations that had satisfied Epicurus; poverty, misfortune, disease, bereavement, revolution, or war overtook them, and all the counsels of the sage left them empty-souled. Hegesias of Cyrene, though he started like Epicurus from the standpoint of the Cyrenaics, concluded that life has in it more pain than pleasure, more grief than joy, and that the only logical outcome of a naturalistic philosophy is suicide.* Philosophy, like a prodigal daughter, after bright adventures and dark disillusionments, gave up the pursuit of truth and the quest of happiness, returned repentant to her mother, religion, and sought again in faith the foundations of hope and the sanctions of charity.

* He argued the point so eloquently that a wave of suicides rose in Alexandria, and Ptolemy II had to banish him from Egypt.[86]

Stoicism, while seeking to construct a natural ethic for the intellectual classes, sought to preserve the old supernatural aids for the morality of the common man, and, as time went on, gave a more and more religious color to its own metaphysical and ethical thought. Zeno denied any real existence to the popular gods,[67] but a generation later Cleanthes proposed to prosecute Aristarchus for heresy. Zeno offered no personal immortality, but Seneca spoke of heavenly bliss in terms almost identical with those of the Eleusinian and Christian faiths.[68] After Zeno Stoicism became a theology rather than a philosophy, and nearly every proposition in it took a theological form. The greater part of the system was composed of arguments about the existence and nature of God, the emanation of the world from God, the reality of Providence, the correspondence of virtue with the divine will, the brotherhood of man under the fatherhood of God, and the final return of the world to God. In this philosophy we find the sense of sin that was to play so stern a role in primitive and in Protestant Christianity, the lofty inclusiveness that as in the new religions welcomed all races and ranks, and a celibate asceticism that derived from the Cynics and culminated in a long line of Christian monks. From Zeno of Tarsus to Paul of Tarsus was but a step, which would be taken on the road to Damascus.

Many components of the Stoic creed were Asiatic in origin, some were specifically Semitic. In essentials Stoicism was one elemental phase of the Oriental triumph over Hellenic civilization. Greece had ceased to be Greece before it was conquered by Rome.

CHAPTER XXX

The Coming of Rome

I. PYRRHUS

"WHO is so worthless or indolent," Polybius demands to know, "as not to wish to understand by what means and under what system of polity the Romans in less than fifty-three years have succeeded in subjecting the whole inhabited world to their sole government—a thing unique in history? Who is so passionately devoted to other studies as to regard anything of greater moment than the acquisition of this knowledge?"[1] It is a permissible inquiry, which may engage us later; but there have been so many conquests since Polybius wrote that we cannot spend much time on any of them. We have tried to show that the essential cause of the Roman conquest of Greece was the disintegration of Greek civilization from within. No great nation is ever conquered until it has destroyed itself. Deforestation and the abuse of the soil, the depletion of precious metals, the migration of trade routes, the disturbance of economic life by political disorder, the corruption of democracy and the degeneration of dynasties, the decay of morals and patriotism, the decline or deterioration of the population, the replacement of citizen armies by mercenary troops, the human and physical wastage of fratricidal war, the guillotining of ability by murderous revolutions and counterrevolutions—all these had exhausted the resources of Hellas at the very time when the little state on the Tiber, ruled by a ruthless and farseeing aristocracy, was training hardy legions of landowners, conquering its neighbors and competitors, capturing the food and minerals of the western Mediterranean, and advancing year by year upon the Greek settlements in Italy. These ancient communities, once proud of their wealth, their sages, and their arts, had been impoverished by war, by the depredations of Dionysius I, and by the growth of Rome as a rival center of trade. The native tribes that, centuries before, had been enslaved by the Greeks or pushed back into the hinterland, increased and multiplied while their masters cultivated comfort through infanticide and abortion. Soon the native stocks were contesting the control of southern Italy. The Greek cities turned to Rome for help; they were helped, and absorbed.

Taras, frightened by the growth of Rome, called to its aid the dashing young king of Epirus. In that picturesque and mountainous country, known to us as southern Albania, Greek culture had kept a precarious footing ever since the Dorians had raised a shrine to Zeus at Dodona.* In 295 Pyrrhus, who traced his ancestry to Achilles, became king of the Molossians, the dominant Epirote tribe. He was handsome and brave, a despotic but popular ruler. His subjects thought that he could cure the spleen by pressing his right foot upon their prostrate backs; nor was anyone so poor as to be refused his ministrations.[2] When the Tarentines appealed to him he saw an alluring opportunity: he would conquer Rome, the danger in the West, as Alexander had conquered Persia, the danger in the East; and he would prove his genealogy by his courage. In 281 he crossed the Ionian (Adriatic) Sea with 25,000 infantry, three thousand horse, and twenty elephants; the Greeks had taken elephants as well as mysticism from India. He met the Romans at Heracleia, and won a "Pyrrhic victory": his losses were so great, and his resources in men and materials were now so small, that when an aide complimented him on his success he created an historic phrase by replying that another such triumph would ruin him.[3] The Romans sent Caius Fabricius to treat with him for an exchange of prisoners. At supper, says Plutarch,

> amongst all sorts of things that were discoursed of, but more particularly Greece and its philosophers, Cineas [the Epirote diplomat] spoke of Epicurus, and explained the opinions his followers hold about the gods and the commonwealth, and the objects of life, placing the chief happiness of man in pleasure, and declining public affairs as an injury and disturbance of a happy life, removing the gods afar off both from kindness or anger, or any concern for us at all, to a life wholly without business and flowing in pleasures. Before he had done speaking, "O Hercules!" Fabricius cried out to Pyrrhus, "may Pyrrhus and the Samnites† entertain themselves with opinions as long as they are at war with us."[4]

Impressed by the Romans, and despairing of adequate aid from the Greeks of Italy, Pyrrhus dispatched Cineas to Rome to negotiate peace. The Senate was about to agree when Appius Claudius, blind and dying, had himself carried into the senate house and protested against making peace with a foreign army on Italian soil. Frustrated, Pyrrhus fought again, won another suicidal victory at Asculum, and then, hopeless of success against Rome, sailed to Sicily with the generous resolve to free it from the Carthaginians. There he drove the Carthaginians back with reckless heroism; but whether it was that the Sicilian Greeks

* Italian archeologists in 1929 unearthed at Butrinto (the ancient Buthrotum) numerous architectural and sculptural remains of Greek and Roman civilization, including a Greek theater of the third century B.C.

† The strongest of Rome's enemies in Italy.

were too timid to rally to him, or that he governed them as willfully as any tyrant, he received so little support that he had to abandon the island after a three years' campaign, making the prophetic remark, "What a battlefield I am leaving to Carthage and Rome!" Arriving with depleted forces in Italy, he was defeated at Beneventum (275), where for the first time the light-armed and mobile cohorts proved their superiority to the unwieldy phalanxes, and thereby wrote a chapter in military history.[5] Pyrrhus returned to Epirus, says the philosophical Plutarch,

> after he had consumed six years in these wars; and though unsuccessful in his affairs, yet preserved his courage unconquerable among all these misfortunes, and was held, for military experience and personal valor and enterprise, above all the other princes of his time; but what he got by brave actions he lost again by vain hopes, and by new desires of what he had not, kept nothing of what he had.[6]

Pyrrhus went out now to fresh wars, and was killed with a tile by an old woman in Argos. In that same year (272) Taras yielded to Rome.

Eight years later Rome began her century-long struggle against Carthage for the mastery of the western Mediterranean. After a generation of fighting Carthage ceded to Rome Sardinia, Corsica, and the Carthaginian portions of Sicily. In the Second Punic War Syracuse made the mistake of siding with Carthage, whereupon Marcellus starved it into surrender. The victors plundered the city so thoroughly that it never recovered. Marcellus "removed to Rome," says Livy, "the ornaments of Syracuse—the statues and pictures in which it abounded. . . . The spoils were almost greater than if Carthage itself had been taken."[7] By 210 all Sicily had fallen forfeit to Rome. The island was transformed into a granary for Italy, and relapsed into an agricultural economy in which nearly all the work was done by hopeless slaves. Industries were discouraged, trade was limited, wealth was sluiced off to Rome, and the free population withered away. Sicily disappeared from the history of civilization for a thousand years.

II. ROME THE LIBERATOR

At every step the expansion of Rome was aided by the mistakes of her enemies. In the year 230 two Romans were sent to Scodra, capital of Illyria (northern Albania) to remonstrate against the attacks of Illyrian pirates upon Roman shipping. Queen Teuta, who had been allowed to share the spoils, answered that "it was contrary to the custom of the Illyrian rulers to hinder their subjects from winning booty from the sea."[8] When one envoy threatened war Teuta had him killed. Pleased with so inexpensive an excuse for seizing the Dalmatian coast, Rome dispatched an expedition which reduced Illyria to a Roman protectorate almost as easily in 229 B.C. as in A.D. 1939. Corcyra (Corfu), Epidamnus (Durazzo), and other Greek settlements became Roman dependencies. Since Greek trade had also suffered from Illyrian piracy, Athens, Corinth, and the two leagues applauded Rome as a deliverer, accepted her ambassadors, and admitted the Romans to participation in the Eleusinian mysteries and the Isthmian games.

In 216 Hannibal annihilated the Roman army at Cannae, and marched up to the gates of Rome. While Rome faced the greatest crisis in the history of the republic, Philip V, King of Macedon, signed an alliance with Hannibal and prepared to invade Italy (214). In the conference at Naupactus (213) the Aetolian delegate Agelaus appealed for the unity of all Greeks, in this First Macedonian War, against the rising power in the west:

> It would be best of all if the Greeks never made war upon each other, but regarded it as the highest favor in the gift of the gods could they always speak with one heart and voice, and marching arm in arm like men fording a river, repel barbarian invaders and unite in preserving themselves and their cities. . . . For it is evident that whether the Carthaginians beat the Romans or the Romans the Carthaginians in this war, it is not in the least likely that the victors will be content with the sovereignty of Italy and Sicily, but they are sure to come here and extend their ambitions beyond the bounds of justice. Therefore I implore you all to secure yourselves against this danger, and I address myself especially to King Philip. For you, Sire, the best security is, instead of exhausting the Greeks and making them an easy prey to the invader, on the contrary to take thought for them as for your own body, and to attend to the safety of every province of Greece as if it were part and parcel of your own dominions.[9]

Philip heard him politely, and became for a moment the idol of Greece. But his treaty with Hannibal, if we may believe the too patriotic Livy, specified that in return for Philip's attack upon Italy, Carthage, if successful in the present war, would help Philip to subdue all mainland Greece to Macedonia.[10] Perhaps because the terms of such an agreement became known to the Greek states, most of them, including Agelaus' Aetolian League, entered into a pact with Rome against Macedon, and kept Philip so harassed at home that his invasion of Italy was indefinitely postponed. In 205 Rome signed a treaty with Philip so that she might give all her attention to Hannibal, and three years later the elder Scipio overwhelmed the Carthaginian at Zama. As the last great century of Greek civilization came to an end Egypt, Rhodes, and Pergamum appealed to Rome for help against Philip. Rome responded by inviting the Second Macedonian War. Opposed by nearly all of Greece as well as by Rome, Philip fought with the ferocity of a beast at bay. He used every treachery, stole whatever he found to his purpose, and treated captives with such cruelty that every man in Abydos, when Philip's siege was proving irresistible, killed his wife and children and then himself.[11] In 197 Titus Quinctius Flamininus, a patrician of the type that made Polybius a pro-Roman enthusiast, so overwhelmed Philip at Cynoscephalae that suddenly all Macedonia—indeed, all Greece—lay at the mercy of Rome. To the disgust of his Aetolian allies (who claimed that they had won the battle), Flamininus, after exacting severe indemnities and appropriating a shipload of spoils, allowed the safely weakened Philip to keep his throne, on the ground that Macedonia was needed as a bulwark against the barbarians in the north.

The Roman general had learned Greek at Tarentum (as Rome called Taras), and had known the fascination of Greek literature, philosophy, and art. It was apparently his sincere resolve to liberate the Greek city-states from Macedonian domination, and to give them every opportunity to live in freedom and peace. Having with some difficulty convinced the Roman commissioners that this was a wise policy, he went to the Isthmian games at Corinth (196), where all the important Greek world was gathered (each man telling the next, says Polybius, what the Romans would do now), and announced through a herald: "The Senate of Rome, and Titus Quinctius the proconsul, having overcome King Philip and the Macedonians, leave the following people free, without garrisons, subject to no tribute, and governed by their own laws: the Corinthians, Phocians, Locrians, Euboeans, Phthiotic Achaeans, Magnesians, Thessalians, and Perrhaebians"—i.e., all those mainland Greeks who were not already free. The greater part of the assemblage, unable to credit so unprecedented an act of liberality, cried out that the announcement should be repeated. When the herald read it again, "such a mighty burst of cheering arose," says Polybius, "that those who listen to the tale today cannot easily conceive what it was."[12] Many doubted the sincerity of the declaration, and looked for a trick behind it; but Flamininus that day began the removal of Roman troops from Corinth, and by 194 his entire army was back in Italy. Greece hailed him as "Savior and Liberator," and entered happily upon its last days of freedom.

III. ROME THE CONQUEROR

The Aetolians were not satisfied with these arrangements. Some of the cities that Rome had freed had once been under Aetolian domination, and were not now restored to the League. The Second Macedonian War was hardly over when the Aetolians invited Antiochus III to rescue Greece from Rome. Pergamum and Lampsacus, caught between the restless Gauls on the north and the expanding Seleucid power on the south, appealed to Rome for help against Antiochus. The Senate sent its ablest general, Publius Scipio Africanus, victor of Zama. With a few legions and the troops of Eumenes II, the Roman generals defeated Antiochus at Magnesia, and turning northward, drove back the Gauls. The Romans extended their protection over nearly all the Mediterranean coast of Asia, and then returned to Italy. Eumenes was grateful, but mainland Greece denounced him as a traitor to Hellas for calling in the barbarous Romans against his fellow Greeks.

For fickle Greece already regretted that she had ever accepted the favors of her rude rescuer from the west. It was observed that though Flamininus and his successors had given Greece freedom, they had taken in payment—from any city that had supported Philip or Antiochus or the Aetolians—so much booty that the Greeks dreaded another such liberation. For three days, in Flamininus' triumph, the spoils of his Grecian campaign passed in continuous train before the eyes of Rome: on the first day arms, armor, and innumerable statues of marble or bronze; on the second day 18,000 pounds of silver, 3,714 pounds of gold, and 100,000 silver coins; on the third day 114 coronets.[13] Moreover, the Romans had supported, and now through their representatives continued actively to support, the moneyed classes in Greece against the poorer citizens, and had forbidden all manifestations of class war. The Greeks did not want peace at such a price; they wished to be free to settle their own disputes, and to give play to national territorial ambitions; they could not bear changelessness. Soon the rival leagues were at odds, and faction ran rife everywhere. Each city or group laid conflicting claims before the Roman Senate; the Senate dispatched commissions to investigate and adjudicate; the Greeks denounced this interference as vassalage. The chains of foreign control were invisible but real; year after year the Greeks—all but the rich—felt them more sharply, and prayed for an end to this freedom. The Senate began to listen to those of its members who contended that there would never be order or quiet in Greece until Rome took full control.

In 179 Philip V died, and his eldest son Perseus, not without bloodshed, inherited his throne. Seventeen years of peace had restored the economy of Macedon, and had raised up a fresh generation of youths for the jaws of war. Perseus negotiated an alliance with Seleucus IV, and married Seleucus' daughter; Rhodes joined the alliance, and sent a great fleet to escort the bride. All Greece rejoiced, and saw in Perseus a living hope against the power of Rome. Eumenes II, fearful for the independence of Pergamum, journeyed to Rome and urged the Senate, for its own sake, to destroy Macedon. On his way home he was almost killed in a private quarrel. It suited Rome to interpret the brawl as a plot of Perseus to assassinate the king; and a patriotic exchange of diplomatic recriminations announced the Third Macedonian War. Only Epirus and Illyria had the courage to help Perseus; the Greek states sent him secret letters of sympathy, but did nothing. In 168 Aemilius Paulus annihilated the Macedonian army at Pydna, destroyed seventy Macedonian cities, banished their upper classes to Italy, and quartered the kingdom into four autonomous but tributary republics, among which all trade and intercourse were forbidden. Perseus was imprisoned in Italy, and died of maltreatment in two years. Epirus was devastated, and 100,000 Epirots were sold into slavery at a dollar a head.[14] Rhodes, which had played no active part in the war, was punished by the liberation of her possessions on the Asiatic coast, and by the establishment of a competitive and free port at Delos. The private papers of Perseus were captured, and all Greeks who had offered him aid or comfort were banished or jailed. A thousand of the Achaean League's most prominent representatives, including Polybius, were deported to Italy; they remained in exile there for sixteen years, during which seven hundred of them died. The admiration of Greece for Rome the liberator had never been so intense as was now the Greek hatred of Rome the conqueror.

The severity of the victors had unwilled results. The weakening of Rhodes ended her policing of the Aegean, and revived a trade-destroying piracy. The removal of so many aristocrats left the field open to radical leadership in the cities of the Achaean League, and the class war enjoyed one of its bitterest periods. The rich clung to the protection of Rome, the poor demanded the expulsion both of the rich and of the Roman power. In 150 the surviving Achaean exiles returned from Italy, and joined in the demand for the repudiation of Roman authority in Greece. To weaken the Achaean power Rome sent to Greece a commission that ordered Corinth, Orchomenos, and Argos to secede from the League. The ladies of Corinth replied by emptying pails of refuse upon the heads of the commissioners.[15] In 146 the League voted for a war of liberation, hoping that Rome's campaigns in Spain and Africa would divert her energies and incline her to a complaisant peace. A fever of patriotism swept the cities of the League. Slaves were freed and armed, a moratorium on debts was proclaimed, and land was promised to the poor, while the unhappy rich, trembling between socialism and Rome, reluctantly contributed their jewelry and their money to the cause of freedom. Athens and Sparta remained aloof, but Boeotia, Locria, and Euboea committed themselves bravely to the war. The republics of Macedonia joined in open revolt against Rome.

The angry Senate sent over an army under Mummius and a fleet under Metellus. Their combined forces overcame all resistance, and in 146 Mummius captured Corinth, the citadel of the League. Whether to destroy a commercial rival in the east as the younger Scipio was in that year destroying Carthage in the west, or to give rebellious Greece a lesson after the fashion of Alexander at Thebes, the rich city of merchants and courtesans was put to the flames, all the men were slaughtered, and all the women and children were sold into slavery. Mummius carried off to Italy whatever wealth could be moved, including the works of art with which the Corinthians had adorned their cities and their homes. Polybius tells how Roman soldiers used world-famous paintings as boards for their games of draughts or dice. The League was dissolved, and its leaders were put to death. Greece and Macedonia were united into one province under a Roman governor. Boeotia, Locris, Corinth, and Euboea were subjected to annual tribute; Athens and Sparta were spared, and were allowed to remain under their own laws. The party of property and order was upheld everywhere, and all attempts to wage war, or make revolutions, or change the constitution, were proscribed. The turbulent cities had at last found peace.

EPILOGUE

Our Greek Heritage

GREEK civilization was not dead; it had yet several centuries of life before it; and when it died* it bequeathed itself in an incomparable legacy to the nations of Europe and the Near East. Every Greek colony poured the elixir of Greek art and thought into the cultural blood of the hinterland—into Spain and Gaul, Etruria and Rome, Egypt and Palestine, Syria and Asia Minor, and along the shores of the Black Sea. Alexandria was the port of reshipment for ideas as well as goods: from the Museum and the Library the works and views of Greek poets, mystics, philosophers, and scientists were scattered through scholars and students into every city of the Mediterranean concourse. Rome took the Greek heritage in its Hellenistic form: her playwrights adopted Menander and Philemon, her poets imitated the modes, measures, and themes of Alexandrian literature, her arts used Greek craftsmen and Greek forms, her law absorbed the statutes of the Greek cities, and her later imperial organization was modeled upon the Greco-Oriental monarchies: Hellenism, after the Roman conquest of Greece, conquered Rome even as the Orient was conquering Greece. Every extension of Roman power spread the ferment of Hellenic civilization. The Byzantine Empire wedded Greek to Asiatic culture, and passed on some part of the Greek inheritance to the Near East and the Slavic north. The Syrian Christians took up the torch and handed it to the Arabs, who carried it through Africa to Spain. Byzantine, Moslem, and Jewish scholars conveyed or translated the Greek masterpieces to Italy, arousing first the philosophy of the Schoolmen and then the fever of the Renaissance. Since that second birth of the European mind the spirit of Greece has seeped so thoroughly into modern culture that "all civilized nations, in all that concerns the activity of the intellect, are colonies of Hellas" today.†[1]

If we include in our Hellenic heritage not only what the Greeks invented but what they adapted from older cultures and transmitted by these

* We may arbitrarily date this at A.D. 325, when Constantine founded Constantinople, and Christian Byzantine civilization began to replace the "pagan" Greek culture in the eastern Mediterranean.

† Increased knowledge of Egyptian and Asiatic civilization compels extensive modification of Sir Henry Maine's classic hyperbole: "Except the blind forces of nature, nothing moves in this world which is not Greek in its origin."[2]

diverse routes to our own, we shall find that patrimony in almost every phase of modern life. Our handicrafts, the technique of mining, the essentials of engineering, the processes of finance and trade, the organization of labor, the governmental regulation of commerce and industry—all these have come down to us on the stream of history from Rome, and through Rome from Greece. Our democracies and our dictatorships alike go back to Greek exemplars; and though the widened reach of states has evolved a representative system unknown to Hellas, the democratic idea of a government responsible to the governed, of trial by jury, and of civil liberties of thought, speech, writing, assemblage, and worship, have been profoundly stimulated by Greek history. These things above all distinguished the Greek from the Oriental, and gave him an independence of spirit and enterprise that made him smile at the obeisances and inertia of the East.

Our schools and universities, our gymnasiums and stadiums, our athletics and Olympic games, trace their lineage to Greece. The theory of eugenic mating, the conception of self-containment and of self-control, the cult of health and natural living, the pagan ideal of a shameless enjoyment of every sense, found their historic formulations in Greece. Christian theology and practice (the very words are Greek) stem in large part from the mystery religions of Greece and Egypt, from Eleusinian, Orphic, and Osirian rites; from Greek doctrines of the divine son dying for mankind and rising from the dead; from Greek rituals of religious procession, ceremonial purification, holy sacrifice, and the sacred common meal; from Greek ideas of hell demons, purgatory, indulgences, and heaven; and from Stoic and Neo-Platonic theories of the Logos, creation, and the final conflagration of the world. Even our superstition is indebted to Greek bogies, witches, curses, omens, and unlucky days. And who could understand English literature, or one ode of Keats, without some tincture of Greek mythology?

Our literature could hardly have existed without the Greek tradition. Our alphabet came from Greece through Cumae and Rome; our language is littered with Greek words; our science has forged an international language through Greek terms; our grammar and rhetoric, even the punctuation and paragraphing of this page, are Greek inventions. Our literary genres are Greek—the lyric, the ode, the idyl, the novel, the essay, the oration, the biography, the history, and above all the drama; again nearly all the words are Greek. The terms and forms of the modern drama—tragedy, comedy, and pantomime—are Greek; and though Elizabethan tragedy is unique, the comic drama has come down almost unchanged from Menander and Philemon through Plautus and Terence, Ben Jonson and Molière. The Greek dramas themselves are among the richest portions of our inheritance.

Nothing else in Greece seems so foreign to us as its music; and yet modern music (until its return to Africa and the Orient) was derived from medieval chants and dances, and these went back in part to Greece. The oratorio and the opera owe something to the Greek choral dance and drama; and the theory of music, so far as we know, was first explored and expounded by the Greeks from Pythagoras to Aristoxenus. Our debt is least in painting; but in the art of fresco a direct line can be traced from Polygnotus through Alexandria and Pompeii, Giotto and Michelangelo, to the arresting murals of our own day. The forms and much of the technique of modern sculpture are still Greek, for upon no other art has the Hellenic genius stamped itself so despotically. We are only now freeing ourselves from the fascination of Greek architecture; every city in Europe and America has some temple of commerce or finance whose form or columnar façade came from the shrines of Greek gods. We miss in Greek art the study of character and the portrayal of the soul, and its infatuation with physical beauty and health leaves it less mature than the masculine statuary of Egypt or the profound painting of the Chinese; but the lessons of moderation, purity, and harmony embodied in the sculpture and architecture of the classic age are a precious heirloom for our race.

If Greek civilization seems more akin and "modern" to us now than that of any century before Voltaire, it is because the Hellene loved reason as much as form, and boldly sought to explain all nature in nature's terms. The liberation of science from theology, and the independent development of scientific research, were parts of the heady adventure of the Greek mind. Greek mathematicians laid the foundations of trigonometry and calculus, they began and completed the study of conic sections, and they brought three-dimensional geometry to such relative perfection that it remained as they left it until Descartes and Pascal. Democritus illuminated the whole area of physics and chemistry with his atomic theory. In a mere aside and holiday from abstract studies Archimedes produced enough new mechanisms to place his name with the highest in the records of invention. Aristarchus anticipated and perhaps inspired Copernicus;* and Hipparchus, through Claudius Ptolemy, constructed a system of astronomy which is one of the landmarks in cultural history. Eratosthenes measured the earth and mapped it. Anaxagoras and Empedocles drew the outlines of a theory of evolution. Aristotle and Theophrastus classified the animal and plant kingdoms, and almost created the sciences of meteorology, zoology, embryology, and botany. Hippocrates freed medicine from mysticism and philo-

* Copernicus knew of Aristarchus' heliocentric hypothesis, for he mentioned it in a paragraph that disappeared from later editions of his book.[3]

sophical theory, and ennobled it with an ethical code; Herophilus and Erasistratus raised anatomy and physiology to a point which, except in Galen, Europe would not reach again till the Renaissance. In the work of these men we breathe the quiet air of reason, always uncertain and unsafe, but cleansed of passion and myth. Perhaps, if we had its masterpieces entire, we should rate Greek science as the most signal intellectual achievement of mankind.

But the lover of philosophy will only reluctantly yield to science and art the supreme places in our Grecian heritage. Greek science itself was a child of Greek philosophy—of that reckless challenge to legend, that youthful love of inquiry, which for centuries united science and philosophy in one adventurous quest. Never had men examined nature so critically and yet so affectionately: the Greeks did no dishonor to the world in thinking that it was a cosmos of order and therefore amenable to understanding. They invented logic for the same reason that they made perfect statuary: harmony, unity, proportion, form, in their view, provided both the art of logic and the logic of art. Curious of every fact and every theory, they not only established philosophy as a distinct enterprise of the European mind, but they conceived nearly every system and every hypothesis, and left little to be said on any major problem of our life. Realism and nominalism, idealism and materialism, monotheism, pantheism, and atheism, feminism and communism, the Kantian critique and the Schopenhaurian despair, the primitivism of Rousseau and the immoralism of Nietzsche, the synthesis of Spencer and the psychoanalysis of Freud—all the dreams and wisdom of philosophy are here, in the age and land of its birth. And in Greece men not only talked of philosophy, they lived it: the sage, rather than the warrior or the saint, was the pinnacle and ideal of Greek life. Through all the centuries from Thales that exhilarating philosophical bequest has come down to us, inspiring Roman emperors, Christian Fathers, Scholastic theologians, Renaissance heretics, Cambridge Platonists, the rebels of the Enlightenment, and the devotees of philosophy today. At this moment thousands of eager spirits are reading Plato, perhaps in every country on the earth.

Civilization does not die, it migrates; it changes its habitat and its dress, but it lives on. The decay of one civilization, as of one individual, makes room for the growth of another; life sheds the old skin, and surprises death with fresh youth. Greek civilization is alive; it moves in every breath of mind that we breathe; so much of it remains that none of us in one lifetime could absorb it all. We know its defects—its insane and pitiless wars, its stagnant slavery, its subjection of woman, its lack of moral restraint, its corrupt individualism, its tragic failure to unite liberty with order and peace. But those who cherish freedom, reason, and beauty will not linger over these blemishes. They will hear behind the turmoil of political history the voices of Solon and Socrates, of Plato and Euripides, of Pheidias and Praxiteles, of Epicurus and Archimedes; they will be grateful for the existence of such men, and will seek their company across alien centuries. They will think of Greece as the bright morning of that Western civilization which, with all its kindred faults, is our nourishment and our life.

TO THOSE WHO HAVE COME THUS FAR:
THANK YOU FOR YOUR UNSEEN BUT EVER FELT COMPANIONSHIP.

Glossary

Aperçus—instinctive insights.
Bizarreries—strange or extravagant expressions or actions.
Bourgeoisie—the middle classes.
Cujus regio ejus religio—the religion of the region must be that of the ruler.
De nobis fabula narrabitur—about us the story will be told.
Deus ex machina—the god from the machine.
Élan—spirited vitality.
In medias res—into the middle of things, or into the heart of the subject.
La Parisienne—The Parisian Woman.
Mater Dolorosa—The Sorrowful Mother.
Mise en scène—the surrounding situation.
Nouveaux riches—the newly rich.
Oikoumene (sc. *ge*)—the inhabited world.
Pace—despite, begging the pardon of.
Pinakotheka—picture gallery.
Plein air—open air.
Pornaia—brothels.
Soferim—scholars.

Bibliography

Of Books Referred to in Text or Notes

The starred volumes are recommended for further **study.**

ADAMS, B.: The New Empire. N. Y., 1903.
*AESCHYLUS: The Oresteia. Tr. G. Murray. London, 1928.
ANDERSON, W. J., and SPIERS, R. P.: The Architecture of Greece and Rome. London, 1902.
ARISTOPHANES: The Eleven Comedies. 2v. N. Y., 1928.
ARISTOPHANES: The Frogs, and Three Other Plays. Tr. Frere, etc., Everyman Library.
ARISTOTLE: Art of Rhetoric. Loeb Classical Library.
ARISTOTLE: Metaphysics. 2v. Loeb Library.
ARISTOTLE: Metaphysics. Tr. M'Mahon. London, 1857.
ARISTOTLE: Nicomachean Ethics. Tr. Chase. Everyman Library.
ARISTOTLE (?): Oeconomica and Magna Moralia. Loeb Library.
ARISTOTLE: On the Constitution of Athens. Tr. E. Poste. London, 1891.
ARISTOTLE: Physics. 2v. Loeb Library.
ARISTOTLE: Poetics. Loeb Library.
*ARISTOTLE: Politics. Tr. Lindsay. Everyman Library.
ARISTOTLE: Works. Tr. Smith and Ross. Oxford, 1931.
ARNOLD, M.: Essays in Criticism. A. L. Burt, N. Y., n.d.
ARRIAN: Anabasis of Alexander; Indica. London, 1893.
ATHENAEUS: The Deipnosophists, or Banquet of the Learned. 3v. London, 1854.

*BACON, F.: Philosophical Works. Ed. J. M. Robertson. London, 1905.
BAEDEKER, K.: Greece. Leipzig, 1909.
BAIKIE, J.: The Sea-Kings of Crete. London, 1926.
BAKEWELL, C.: Source Book in Ancient Philosophy. N. Y., 1909.
BALL, W. W. R.: Short Account of the History of Mathematics. London, 1888.
BARON, S. W.: Social and Religious History of the Jews. 3v. N. Y., 1937.
BEBEL, A.: Woman under Socialism. N. Y., 1923.
BECKER, W. A.: Charicles. Tr. Metcalfe. London, 1886.
BENSON, E. F.: Life of Alcibiades. N. Y., 1929.
BENTWICH, N.: Hellenism. Phila., 1919.
BERRY, A.: Short History of Astronomy. N. Y., 1909.
BEVAN, E. R.: House of Seleucus. 2v. London, 1902.
BEVAN, E. R., and SINGER, C., eds.: The Legency of Israel. Oxford, 1927.
BIBLE, THE
BLAKENEY, J. A.: Smaller Classical Dictionary. Everyman Library.
BOTSFORD, G. W.: The Athenian Constitution. N. Y., 1893.
BOTSFORD, G. W., and SIHLER, E. G.: Hellenic Civilization. N. Y., 1920.

BRECCIA, E.: Alexandrea ad Aegyptum. Bergamo, 1922.
BRIFFAULT, R.: The Mothers. 3v. N. Y., 1927.
BROWNE, H.: Handbook of Homeric Study. London, 1908.
BURY, J. B.: Ancient Greek Historians. N. Y., 1909.
*BURY, J. B.: History of Greece. London, 1931.

CALHOUN, G. M.: Business Life of Ancient Athens. Chicago, 1926.
CAMBRIDGE ANCIENT HISTORY (CAH): Vols. I-VIII. N. Y., 1924f.
CAPES, W.: University Life in Ancient Athens. N. Y., 1922.
CARPENTER, E.: Pagan and Christian Creeds. N. Y., 1920.
CARREL, A.: Man the Unknown. N. Y., 1935.
CARROLL, N.: Greek Women. Phila., 1908.
CHILDE, V. G.: Dawn of European Civilization. N. Y., 1925.
CICERO: De Finibus. Loeb Library.
CICERO: De Natura Deorum. Loeb Library.
CICERO: De Re Publica. Loeb Library.
CICERO: Tusculan Disputations. Loeb Library.
COOK, A. B.: Zeus. Cambridge Univ. Press, 1914.
COTTERILL, H. B.: History of Art. 2v. N. Y., 1922.
COULANGES, F. DE: The Ancient City. Boston, 1901.
CURTIUS, E.: Griechische Geschichte. 3v. Berlin, 1887f.

DAY, C.: History of Commerce. London, 1926.
DEMOSTHENES: On the Crown, etc. Loeb Library.
DEWEY, JOHN, etc.: Studies in the History of Ideas. N. Y., 1935.
DICKINSON, G. L.: The Greek View of Life. N. Y., 1928.
DIODORUS SICULUS: Library of History. 3v. Loeb Library.
DIODORUS SICULUS: Historical Library. 2v. London, 1814.
*DIOGENES LAERTIUS: Lives and Opinions of the Eminent Philosophers. London, 1853.
DRAPER, J. W.: History of the Intellectual Development of Europe. 2v. N. Y., 1876.
DUPRÉEL, E.: La Légende Socratique. Bruxelles, 1922.
DYER, T. H.: Ancient Athens. London, 1873.

ELLIS, H.: Studies in the Psychology of Sex. 6v. Phila., 1911.
ENCYCLOPAEDIA BRITANNICA, 14th ed. N. Y., 1929.
EURIPIDES: Electra. Tr. G. Murray. Oxford, 1907.
EURIPIDES: Iphigenia in Tauris. Tr. G. Murray. Oxford, 1930.
*EURIPIDES: Medea. Tr. G. Murray. Oxford, 1912.
EURIPIDES: Text and tr. by A. S. Way. 4v. Loeb Library.
*EURIPIDES: Trojan Women. Tr. G. Murray. Oxford, 1914.
EVANS, SIR A.: The Palace of Minos. 4v. in 6. London, 1921f.

FARNELL, L. R.: Greece and Babylon. Edinburgh, 1911.
FERGUSON, W. M.: Greek Imperialism. Boston, 1913.

FLICKINGER, R. C.: The Greek Theatre. Chicago, 1918.
FRAZER, SIR J. G.: Adonis, Attis, Osiris. 1935.
FRAZER, SIR J. G.: The Dying God. N. Y., 1935.
FRAZER, SIR J. G.: The Magic Art. 2v. N. Y., 1935.
FRAZER, SIR J. G.: The Scapegoat. N. Y., 1935.
FRAZER, SIR J. G.: Spirits of the Corn and of the Wild. 2v. N. Y., 1935.
FRAZER, SIR J. G.: Studies in Greek Scenery, Legend, and History. London, 1931.
FREEMAN, E. A.: The Story of Sicily. N. Y., 1892.

GARDINER, E. N.: Athletics of the Ancient World. Oxford, 1930.
GARDINER, PERCY: New Chapters in Greek History. N. Y., 1892.
GARDINER, PERCY: Principles of Greek Art. N. Y., 1914.
GARDNER, E. A.: Ancient Athens. N. Y., 1902.
GARDNER, E. A.: Handbook of Greek Sculpture. London, 1920.
GARDNER, E. A.: Six Greek Sculptors. London, 1910.
GARRISON, F. H.: History of Medicine. Phila., 1929.
GIBBON, E.: The Decline and Fall of the Roman Empire. 6v. Everyman Library.
GLOTZ, G.: Aegean Civilization. N. Y., 1925.
GLOTZ, G.: Ancient Greece at Work. N. Y., 1926.
GLOTZ, G.: The Greek City. London, 1929.
GLOVER, T. R.: Democracy in the Ancient World. Cambridge, Eng., 1927.
GOETHE, J. W. VON: Poetical Works. N. Y., 1902.
GOMME, A. W.: Population of Athens. Oxford, 1933.
GRAETZ, H.: History of the Jews. 6v. Phila., 1891f.
GREEK ANTHOLOGY: Tr. Shane Leslie. N. Y., 1929.
GREEK ANTHOLOGY: Tr. R. G. MacGregor. London, n.d.
GREEK DRAMAS: Tr. E. B. Browning, etc. N. Y., 1912.
GROTE, G.: Aristotle. 2v. London, 1872.
GROTE, G.: History of Greece. 12v. Everyman Library.
GROTE, G.: Plato and the Other Companions of Socrates. 3v. London, 1875.

HAGGARD, H. W.: Devils, Drugs, and Doctors. N. Y., 1929.
HAIGH, A. E.: The Attic Theatre. Oxford, 1907.
HALL, H. R.: Civilization of Greece in the Bronze Age. N. Y., 1927.
HALL, M. P.: Encyclopedic Outline of Masonic, Hermetic, Qabbalistic, and Rosicrucian Symbolical Philosophy. San Francisco, 1928.
HARRISON, J. E.: Prolegomena to the Study of Greek Religion. Cambridge, Eng., 1922.
HARRISON, J. E.: Themis. Cambridge, Eng., 1927.
HEATH, SIR T.: Aristarchus of Samos. Oxford, 1913.
HEATH, SIR T.: History of Greek Mathematics. 2v. Oxford, 1921.
HEITLAND, W. E.: Agricola: A Study of Agriculture and Rustic Life in the Greco-Roman World. Cambridge, Eng., 1921.
HERACLEITUS ON THE UNIVERSE. Tr. W. H. S. Jones. Loeb Library.

HERODES (HERODAS), CERCIDAS, AND THE GREEK CHOLIAMBIC POETS. Loeb Library.
*HERODOTUS: History. Tr. G. Rawlinson. 4v. London, 1862.
HESIOD, CALLIMACHUS, and THEOGNIS: Works. London, 1856.
HIMES, N. E.: Medical History of Contraception. Baltimore, 1936.
HIPPOCRATES: Works. 4v. Loeb Library.
HOBHOUSE, L. T.: Morals in Evolution. N. Y., 1916.
HOGARTH, D. G.: Ionia and the East. Oxford, 1909.
*HOMER: Iliad. Tr. W. C. Bryant. Boston, 1898.
HOMER: Iliad. Text and tr. by A. T. Murray. 2v. Loeb Library.
*HOMER: Odyssey. Text and tr. by A. T. Murray. 2v. Loeb Library.

ISOCRATES: Works. 2v. Loeb Library.

JEWISH ENCYCLOPEDIA. N. Y., 1901.
JONES, H. S.: Ancient Writers on Greek Sculpture. London, 1895.
JONES, W. H. S.: Malaria and Greek History. Manchester, Eng., 1909.
JOSEPHUS, F.: Works. 2v. Boston, 1811.
JOURNAL OF HELLENIC STUDIES. London, 1882f.

KELLER, A. G.: Homeric Society. N. Y., 1902.
KIRSTEIN, L.: Dance: A Short History. N. Y., 1935.
KÖHLER, C.: History of Costume. N. Y., 1928.

LACROIX, P.: History of Prostitution. 2v. N. Y., 1931.
LANGE, F. E.: History of Materialism. N. Y., 1925.
LESSING, G. E.: Laocoön. London, 1874.
LEWES, G. H.: Aristotle. A Chapter in the History of Science. London, 1864.
LINFORTH, I. M.: Solon the Athenian. Berkeley, Cal., 1919.
LIPPERT, J.: Evolution of Culture. N. Y., 1931.
LITCHFIELD, F.: Illustrated History of Furniture. Boston, 1922.
*LIVINGSTONE, R. W.: The Greek Genius. Oxford, 1915.
LIVINGSTONE, R. W., ed.: The Legacy of Greece. Oxford, 1924.
LIVY: History of Rome. 6v. Everyman Library.
LOCY, W. A.: Growth of Biology. N. Y., 1925.
LONGINUS: On the Sublime. Loeb Library.
LUCIAN: Works. 4v. Oxford, 1905.
*LUCRETIUS: De Rerum Natura. Loeb Library.
LUDWIG, E.: Schliemann. Boston, 1931.
LYRA GRAECA: 3v. Loeb Library.

MAHAFFY, J. P.: Empire of the Ptolemies. London, 1895.
MAHAFFY, J. P.: Greek Life and Thought. London, 1887.
MAHAFFY, J. P.: History of Classical Greek Literature. 4v. London, 1908.
MAHAFFY, J. P.: Old Greek Education. N. Y., n.d.
MAHAFFY, J. P.: Progress of Hellenism in Alexander's Empire. Chicago, 1905.

*MAHAFFY, J. P.: Social Life in Greece. London, 1925.
MAHAFFY, J. P.: What Have the Greeks Done for Modern Civilization? N. Y., 1909.
MASON, W. A.: History of the Art of Writing. N. Y., 1920.
MCCLEES, H.: Daily Life of the Greeks and Romans. N. Y., 1928.
MCCRINDLE, J. W.: Ancient India as Described by Megasthenes and Arrian. Calcutta, 1877.
MENANDER: Principal Fragments. Loeb Library.
MEYER, E.: Geschichte des Altertums. 4v. Stuttgart, 1884f.
MOMMSEN, T.: History of Rome. 5v. London, 1901.
MÜLLER, K. O.: The Dorians. 2v. Oxford, 1830.
MÜLLER-LYER, F.: Evolution of Modern Marriage. N. Y., 1930.
MÜLLER-LYER, F.: The Family. N. Y., 1931.
MURRAY, A. S.: History of Greek Sculpture. 2v. London, 1890.
MURRAY, G.: Aristophanes. N. Y., 1933.
*MURRAY, G.: Euripides and His Age. N. Y., 1913.
MURRAY, G.: Five Stages of Greek Religion. Oxford, 1930.
*MURRAY, G.: History of Ancient Greek Literature. N. Y., 1927.
MURRAY, G.: Rise of the Greek Epic. Oxford, 1924.

NAPLES MUSEUM, Guide to the Archeological Collections. Naples, 1935.
NIETZSCHE, F.: Early Greek Philosophy. N. Y., 1911.
NILSSON, M.: History of Greek Religion. Oxford, 1925.
NORWOOD, R.: The Greek Drama. N. Y., 1920.

OLMSTEAD, A.: History of Assyria. N. Y., 1923.
OVID: Heroides and Amores. Loeb Library.
OVID: Metamorphoses. Loeb Library.
OWEN, J.: Evenings with the Sceptics. 2v. London, 1881.
*OXFORD BOOK OF GREEK VERSE IN TRANSLATION. Oxford, 1938.
OXFORD HISTORY OF MUSIC: Introductory Volume. Oxford, 1929.
OXFORDER BUCH DEUTSCHEN DICHTUNG. Oxford, 1936.

PATER, W.: Plato and Platonism. London, 1910.
PAUSANIAS: Description of Greece. 2v. London, 1886.
PFUHL, E.: Masterpieces of Greek Drawing and Painting. London, 1926.
PHILOSTRATUS: Lives of the Sophists. Loeb Library.
*PIJOAN, J.: History of Art. 3v. N. Y., 1927.
PINDAR: Odes. Loeb Library.
PLATO: Dialogues. Tr. Jowett. 4v. N. Y., n.d.
PLATO: Epistles. Loeb Library.
PLINY: Natural History. 6v. London, 1855.
*PLUTARCH: Lives. 3v. Everyman Library.
PLUTARCH: Moralia. Vols. I-III. Loeb Library.
PÖHLMANN, R. VON: Geschichte der Sozialen Frage und des Sozialismus in der antiken Welt. 2v. München, 1925.

POLYBIUS: Histories. 6v. Loeb Library.
PRATT, W. S.: History of Music. N. Y., 1927.

QUINTILIAN: Institutio Oratoria. 4v. Loeb Library.

RAMSAY, SIR WM.: Asianic Elements in Greek Civilization. New Haven, 1928.
RANDALL-MACIVER, D.: Greek Cities in Italy and Sicily. Oxford, 1931.
REINACH, S.: Orpheus: A History of Religions. N. Y., 1930.
RENAN, E.: History of the People of Israel. 5v. N. Y., 1888.
RICHTER, G.: Handbook of the Classical Collection. Metropolitan Museum Of Art, N. Y., 1922.
RICKARD, T. A.: Man and Metals. 2v. N. Y., 1932.
RIDDER, A., and DEONNA, W.: Art in Greece. N. Y., 1927.
RIDGEWAY, SIR WM.: Early Age of Greece. Cambridge, Eng., 1901.
ROBINSON, D. M.: Sappho and Her Influence. Boston, 1924.
RODENWALDT, G.: Die Kunst der Antike. Berlin, 1927.
ROHDE, E.: Psyche. N. Y., 1925.
ROSTOVTZEFF, M.: History of the Ancient World. 2v. Oxford, 1930.
ROSTOVTZEFF, M.: Social and Economic History of the Roman Empire. Oxford, 1926.
RUSSELL, B.: Principles of Mathematics. 2v. London, 1903.

*SACHAR, A. L.: History of the Jews. N. Y., 1932.
SARTON, G.: Introduction to the History of Science. Baltimore, 1930.
SCHLEGEL, A. W.: Lectures on Dramatic Art and Literature. London, 1846.
SCHLIEMANN, H.: Ilios. N. Y., 1881.
SCHLIEMANN, H.: Mycenae. N. Y., 1878.
SEDGWICK, W. T., and TYLER, H. W.: Short History of Science. N. Y., 1927.
SEMPLE, E. C.: Geography of the Mediterranean Region. N. Y., 1931.
SEXTI EMPIRICI OPERA GRAECE ET LATINE. 2v. Leipzig, 1840.
SEYMOUR, T. D.: Life in the Homeric Age. N. Y., 1907.
SHOTWELL, J. T.: Introduction to the History of History. N. Y., 1936.
SINGER, C. E.: Studies in the History and Method of Science. Vol. II. Oxford, 1921.
SMITH, G. E.: Human History. N. Y., 1929.
SMITH, WM.: Dictionary of Greek and Roman Antiquities. Boston, 1859.
*SOPHOCLES: Tragedies. Tr. Plumptre. London, 1867.
SOPHOCLES: Plays. 2v. Loeb Library.
SPENCER, H.: First Principles. N. Y., 1910.
SPENGLER, O.: Decline of the West. 2v. N. Y., 1926f.
SPINOZA, B.: Ethics and De Emendatione Intellectus. Everyman Library.
STRABO: Geography. 8v. Loeb Library.
SUMNER, W. G.: Folkways. Boston, 1906.
SUMNER, W. G., and KELLER, A. G.: The Science of Society. 3v. New Haven, 1928.

SWINBURNE, A. C.: Poems. Phila., n.d.
*SYMONDS, J. A.: Studies of the Greek Poets. London, 1920.

TAINE, H.: Lectures on Art. N. Y., 1875.
TARN, W. W.: Hellenistic Civilization. London, 1927.
TAYLOR, A. E.: Plato. N. Y., 1936.
THEOCRITUS, BION, AND MOSCHUS: Poems. London, 1853.
THEOPHRASTUS: Characters. Loeb Library.
THOMPSON, SIR E. M.: Introduction to Greek and Latin Paleography. Oxford, 1912.
*THUCYDIDES: History of the Peloponnesian War. Everyman Library.
TOUTAIN, J.: Economic Life of the Ancient World. N. Y., 1930.
TUCKER, T. G.: Life in Ancient Athens. Chautauqua, N. Y., 1917.
TYLOR, E. B.: Anthropology. N. Y., 1906.

UEBERWEG, F.: History of Philosophy. 2v. N. Y., 1871.
USHER, A. P.: History of Mechanical Inventions. N. Y., 1929.

VERRALL, A. W.: Euripides the Rationalist. Cambridge, Eng., 1913.
VINOGRADOFF, SIR P.: Outlines of Historical Jurisprudence. 2v. Oxford, 1922.
VIRGIL: Works. 2v. Loeb Library.
VITRUVIUS: On Architecture. 2v. Loeb Library.
VOLTAIRE, F. M. A. DE: Works. 22v. N. Y., 1927.

WARD, C. O.: The Ancient Lowly. 2v. Chicago, 1907.
WARREN, H. L.: Foundations of Classic Architecture. N. Y., 1919.
WAXMAN, M.: History of Jewish Literature. 3v. N. Y., 1930.
*WEIGALL, A.: Alexander the Great. N. Y., 1933.
WEIGALL, A.: Sappho of Lesbos. N. Y., 1932.
WESTERMARCK, E.: History of Human Marriage. 3v. London, 1921.
WESTERMARCK, E.: Origin and Development of the Moral Ideas. 2v. London, 1917f.
WHEWELL, WM.: History of the Inductive Sciences. 2v. N. Y., 1859.
WHIBLEY, L.: Companion to Greek Studies. Cambridge, Eng., 1916.
*WILLIAMS, H. S.: History of Science. 5v. N. Y., 1909.
WINCKELMANN, J.: History of Ancient Art. 4v. in 2. Boston, 1880.
WRIGHT, F. A.: History of Later Greek Literature. N. Y., 1932.

XENOPHON: Works. Loeb Library.
XENOPHON: Memorabilia. Phila., 1899.
XENOPHON: Minor Works. London, 1914.

ZEITLIN, S.: History of the Second Jewish Commonwealth. Phila., 1933.
ZELLER, E.: Socrates and the Socratic Schools. London, 1877.
ZELLER, E.: Stoics, Epicureans, and Sceptics. London, 1870.
ZIMMERN, A.: The Greek Commonwealth. Oxford, 1924.

Notes

The full title of a book is given only at the first reference to it. Later references may be filled out by consulting the Bibliography. In references to modern works a Roman number (in capitals) indicates the volume, the Arabic number the page. In references to classical texts the Roman number (in small letters) indicates the "book" or main division; the Arabic number indicates the section, the marginal division, or the verse. Where sections are long a subdivision is indicated by an Arabic number after a period.

CHAPTER I

1. Plato, *Works*, Jowett tr.; *Phaedo*, 109.
2. Semple, Ellen, *Geography of the Mediterranean Region*, N. Y., 1931, 99, 507.
3. Evans, Sir Arthur, *Palace of Minos*, London, 1921f, I, 20.
4. Homer, *Odyssey*, tr. A. T. Murray, Loeb Classical Library, London, 1927, xix, 172-7.
5. Aristotle, *Politics*, 1271b.
6. Ludwig, Emil, *Schliemann*, Boston, 1931, 264-5; Glotz, G., *Aegean Civilization*, N. Y., 1925, 14; *Cambridge Ancient History* (hereafter referred to as CAH), N. Y., 1924f, I, 138.
7. Evans, I, 13; Hall, H. R., *Civilization of Greece in the Bronze Age*, N. Y., 1927, 24; Glotz, 30-1, 67, 348; CAH, I, 589-90.
8. Evans, I, 26.
9. Ibid., I, 27; Glotz, 38, 40; CAH, I, 597-8.
10. Glotz, 60-4; Baikie, Jas., *Sea-Kings of Crete*, London, 1926, 212-3.
11. Hall, 27; Glotz, 68-73.
12. Köhler, Carl, *History of Costume*, N. Y., 1928, frontispiece; Evans, III, 49.
13. CAH, I, 596; Glotz, 65-6, 75-8, 311, and fig. 6.
14. Cf. Evans, III, 227.

19. Glotz, 147-8; CAH, II, 437.
20. Thucydides, *History of the Peloponnesian War*, Everyman Library, I, 1.4; cf. Herodotus, *History*, tr. Rawlinson, London, 1862, vii, 170, and Diodorus Siculus, *Library of History*, v, 78.
21. Strabo, *Geography*, Loeb Library, x, 4.8; Glotz, 149; Evans, I, 2, IV, p. xxii; CAH, II, 442; Homer, *Odyssey*, xi, 568-70.
22. Ibid., iii, 296.
23. Glotz, 139-42, 173-4; Baikie, 120, 129-31.
24. Evans, I, facing 305, III, 13f; CAH, I, 591, 605, II, 432; Glotz, 106-9, 163-4; Baikie, 97.
25. Evans, I, facing 472; Glotz, 169-70, 293.
26. Evans, III, 213; Hall, 15; Glotz, 294-6, 312-3.
27. Evans, I, 15.
28. Ibid., 151; Glotz, 229, 237-41, 248-9, 255; Farnell, L. R., *Greece and Babylon*, Edinburgh, 1911, 228; Nilsson, M. P., *History of Greek Religion*, Oxford, 1925, 13, questions any worship of the bull in Crete.
29. Glotz, 146, 244-7; Evans, IV, 468-9.
30. Ibid.; Glotz, 252-4.
31. Ibid., 231-8, 265-70, 273-4; Farnell, 125; Reinach, S., *Orpheus*, N. Y., 1930, 83; Nilsson, 13, 16; CAH, II, 444-5.
32. Mason, W. A., *History of the Art of Writing*, N. Y., 1920, 315-23, 331; Evans, I, 15, 124f, IV, xx, 959; Glotz, 150, 196, 371-7, 381-7; *Encyclopaedia Britannica*, 14th ed., I, 213; CAH, II, 437; Whibley, L., *Companion to Greek Studies*, Cambridge U. P., 1916, 26.
33. Glotz, 165, 388; Baikie, 238.
34. Homer, *Iliad*, xviii, 590.
35. Glotz, 174, 321.
36. Evans, I, 342-4; Evans in Baikie, 71; Reinach, 82; Pliny, *Natural History*, London, 1855, xxxvi, 19; Glotz, 108.
37. Hall, 102.
38. Evans, I, 142, III, 252-3; Burrows, R. M., in Baikie, 99, and Semple, 570.
39. Evans, III, 116-22.
40. In Baikie, 129.

40a. Evans, Sir Arthur, "The Minoan and Mycenaean Element in Hellenic Life," *Journal of Hellenic Studies*, XXXII (1912), 277f; Hall, 27.

41. Evans, *Palace of Minos*, I, 17.
42. Ibid., 16-7; Smith, *Human History*, 378-90; Hall, 25; Glotz, 191-3, 209; Spengler, Oswald, *Decline of the West*, N. Y., 1926-8, II, 88.
43. Strabo, xiv, 2.27; Evans, "Minoan and Mycenaean Element," 283.

44. Herodotus, vii, 170; CAH, II, 475; Smith, G. E., 398.
45. Baedeker, K., *Greece*, Leipzig, 1909, 417.
46. CAH, I, 442-3.
47. Himes, Norman, *Medical History of Contraception*, Baltimore, 1936, 187.
48. Grote, G., *History of Greece*, Everyman Library, I, 190; Frazer, Sir Jas., *Dying God*, N. Y., 1935, 71.
49. Diodorus, iv, 76.
50. Ibid., 79; Ovid, *Metamorphoses*, Loeb Library, viii, 181f.
51. Pausanias, *Description of Greece*, London, 1886, ix, 40.
52. Plutarch, *Lives*, "Theseus"; Homer, *Odyssey*, xi, 321-5.
53. E.g., Polybius, *Histories*, Loeb Library, vi, 45.
54. Strabo, x, 4.16-22.

CHAPTER II

1. Schliemann, H., *Ilios*, N. Y., 1881, 3.
2. Ibid., 9.
3. Ibid., 17.
4. Ludwig, p. ix.
5. Schliemann, 14-15.
6. Ludwig, 137.
7. Ibid., 132-3, 153, 183, 234.
8. Schliemann, 26.
9. Ibid., 41; Ludwig, 139, 165.
10. Schliemann, H., *Mycenae*, N. Y., 1878, 101-2.
11. Homer, *Iliad.*, ii, 559.
12. Ludwig, 284.
13. Ibid., 256-7.
14. Pausanias, ii, 25.
15. Warren, H. L., *Foundations of Classic Architecture*, N. Y., 1919, 124-5; Pausanias, ii, 25.
16. Ibid., ii, 15.
17. *Iliad*, ii, 59, vii, 180; *Odyssey*, iii, 305.
18. Pausanias, ii, 16.
19. Schliemann, *Mycenae*, 293f; CAH, II, 452-3; Glotz, 46; *Enc. Brit.*, XVI, 38.
20. Hall, 1; Nilsson, 11; Glotz, 31-2; Whibley, 27.
20a. Murray, A. S., *History of Greek Sculpture*, London, 1890, I, 61.
21. Herodotus, ii, 53, 57.
22. Pausanias, vii, 2-3; Hall, 11.
23. Ibid.; Glotz, 47; Evans, I, 23; CAH, I, 608.
24. Lippert, J., *Evolution of Culture*, N. Y., 1931, 171.
25. Glotz, 47-8.
26. These frescoes are all in the National Museum at Athens. They are reproduced in Rodenwaldt, G., *Kunst der Antike*, Berlin, 1927, 143f.
27. Schliemann, *Ilios*, 281-3.
29. National Museum, Athens; Evans, III, 121; Rodenwaldt, 148-9.
30. Nat. Mus., Athens; Rodenwaldt, 152.
31. Evans, III, 183; Glotz, 338.
32. Gardiner, P., *New Chapters in Greek History*, N. Y., 1892, 178; Evans, "Minoan and Mycenaean Element," 283; Mason, 327-8; Farnell, 97-8.
33. Schliemann, *Ilios*, 587.
34. Ludwig, 280. He was later financed by Kaiser Wilhelm II.
35. CAH, II, 489-90.
36. Schliemann, *Ilios*, 453-505; *Enc. Brit.*, XXII, 502-3.
37. CAH, II, 488; Schliemann, *Ilios*, 123.
38. Bury, J. B., *History of Greece*, London, 1931, 46; CAH, II, 487.
39. *Iliad*, xx, 230f.
40. Herodotus, ii, 118; Strabo, xiii, 1.48.
41. Murray, G., *Rise of the Greek Epic*, Oxford, 1924, 49.
42. Ramsay, Sir W., *Asianic Elements in Greek Civilization*, Yale U. P., 1928, 109.
43. Bérard, M., in Semple, 699; Murray, *Epic*, 38.
44. Schliemann, *Ilios*, 240, 253; Bury, 48; Glotz, 197, 217.

CHAPTER III

1. CAH, II, 276-83; Glotz, 90.
2. *Iliad*, ii, 681.
3. Ridgeway, Sir Wm., *Early Age of Greece*, Cambridge U. P., 1901, 88-90, 337, 630, 682-4, etc.
4. CAH, II, 473; Hall, 248, 289.
5. Bury, 6; Glotz, 386-7.
6. Nilsson, 61.
7. *Odyssey*, xi, 582f; Diodorus, iv, 77.
8. Thucydides, i, 1.3, ii, 6.15.
9. Diodorus, iv, 9.
10. One form of the legend tells how Heracles triumphed over fifty virgins in a single night.—Athenaeus, *Deipnosophists, or Banquet of the Learned*, London, 1854, xiii, 4; Pausanias, ix, 27.
11. Diodorus, iv, 35, 53.
12. Ibid., iv, 57-8.
13. Ibid., iv, 41-8.
14. CAH, II, 475, III, 662.
15. *Iliad*, ii, 683, iii, 75.

16. Ibid., xxiii, 198.
17. xxiv, 228.
18. xxiv, 186.
19. xviii, 541, xxi, 257; Keller, A. G., *Homeric Society*, N. Y., 1902, 78.
20. *Iliad*, v, 87-9.
21. Glotz, G., *Ancient Greece at Work*, N. Y., 1926, 36.
22. *Odyssey*, xx, 72.
23. Seymour, T. D., *Life in the Homeric Age*, N. Y., 1907, 234, 209-10.
24. Glotz, *Ancient Greece*, 38; Ridgeway in Botsford, G. W., *Athenian Constitution*, N. Y., 1895, 82.
25. Ibid., 35; Pöhlmann, R. von, *Geschichte der sozialen Frage und des Sozialismus in der antiken Welt*, München, 1925, I, 29; Browne, H., *Handbook of Homeric Study*, London, 1908, 209; Seymour, 235, 273; Bury, 54.
26. *Iliad*, xxiii, 826.
27. Ibid., xiii, 341.
28. Glotz, *Ancient Greece*, 45.
29. Ibid., 42; Calhoun, G. M., *Business Life of Ancient Athens*, Chicago, 1926, 13.
30. *Odyssey*, xv, 82f.
31. Ibid., vi, 115.
32. xiv, 202.
33. Aeschylus, *Agamemnon*, 281f.
34. *Iliad*, xix, 247.
35. Ibid., ii, 210f.
36. *Odyssey*, xxi, 224-5.
37. Ibid., iv, 184.
38. *Iliad*, ix, 74.
39. *Odyssey*, vi, 207.
40. Ibid., iv, 20; ix, 267-8.
41. xv, 82f.
42. viii, 370f.
43. Gardiner, E. N., *Athletics of the Ancient World*, Oxford, 1930, 27; Mahaffy, J. P., *Social Life in Greece*, N. Y., 1925, 51.
44. Gardiner, E. N., 21-3; *Iliad*, xxiii, 166f.
45. Thucydides, i, 1.5.
46. *Odyssey*, viii, 158f.
47. Ibid., ix, 39f.
48. *Iliad*, x, 383.
49. *Odyssey*, xiii, 287-95.
50. Ibid., ii, 234, iv, 690, xiv, 138-141.
51. Ibid., i, 87, viii, 14; *Iliad*, ii, 169.
52. *Odyssey*, i, 57-9; *Iliad*, xx, 18.
53. *Odyssey*, xvii, 280.
54. Athenaeus, xiii, 2; Harrison, Jane, *Prolegomena to the Study of Greek Religion*, Cambridge U. P., 1922, 260-2.
55. Athenaeus, xiii, 4.
56. *Iliad*, xviii, 593.
57. Ibid., xviii, 490.
58. vi, 169.
59. *Odyssey*, i, 153, 325, viii, 43-64, xxi, 406-8.
60. Ibid., xxi, 46.
61. *Iliad*, vi, 313-7.
62. Ibid., i, 249.
63. iii, 222.
64. Murray, *Epic*, 129.
65. Sumner, W. G., and Keller, A. G., *Science of Society*, New Haven, 1928, I, 658.
66. CAH, II, 478; Murray, *Epic*, 174.
67. Whibley, 30.
68. Pliny, xxxvi, 64.
69. Grote, I, 77.
70. Plutarch, *De Stoicorum Repugnantiis*, 32, in Bakewell, C. M., *Source Book in Ancient Philosophy*, N. Y., 1909, 278.
71. *Iliad*, vi, 406.
72. Ibid., viii, 542.
73. CAH, III, 670.
74. *Odyssey*, iv, 521.
75. Butcher and Lang, *Odyssey*, N. Y., 1927, introd., xxiv.
77. Seymour, 73.
78. *Odyssey*, v, 151-8.
79. Ibid., vi, 239.
80. Nilsson, 4-5.
81. *Odyssey*, xix, 177.
82. Thucydides, i, 1.2.
83. Herodotus, i, 68.
84. Evans, IV, 477, 959.
85. Pausanias, iii, 2.
86. Ridder, A. de, and Deonna, W., *Art in Greece*, N. Y., 1927, 167.

CHAPTER IV

1. Plato, *Phaedrus*, 244; Frazer, *Magic Art*, N. Y., 1935, II, 358; Reinach, *Orpheus*, 98; CAH, II, 629.
2. Grote, IV, 196.
3. Mahaffy, J. P., *What Have the Greeks Done for Civilization?*, N. Y., 1909, 11.
4. Plato, *Timaeus*, 22-3.
5. Herodotus, ii, 143.
6. Ibid., ii, 53, 81, 123; Diodorus, i, 96; Harrison, *Prolegomena*, 574-5.
7. Herodotus, ii, 109; Strabo, xvii, 3; Diodorus, i, 69; Smith, G. E., 417-8; Ridder, 7, 341.
8. Ibid.; Smith, 418-22; Warren, *Foundations*, 193-4.

9. Glotz, *Ancient Greece*, 128; Day, C., *History of Commerce*, London, 1926, 14.
10. Olmstead, A. T., *History of Assyria*, N. Y., 1923, 537.
11. Herodotus, ii, 109.
12. Grote, IV, 124.
13. Heath, Sir Thos., *History of Greek Mathematics*, Oxford, 1921, I, 44, II, 21; CAH, IV, 539.
14. Ridder, 340; Anderson, W. J., and Spiers, R. P., *Architecture of Greece and Rome*, London, 1902, 49; Gardner, E. A., *Handbook of Greek Sculpture*, London, 1920, 51-2.
15. Cook, A. B., *Zeus*, Cambridge U. P., 1914, 777.
16. Strabo, viii, 6; CAH, III, 540-2; Grote, III, 96.
17. Herodotus, iii, 131.
18. Gardner, E. A., *Handbook*, 365.
19. Pausanias, iv, 6-14.
20. Strabo, viii, 5.4.
21. Müller, K. O., in Rawlinson's Herodotus, vii, 234n. The calculation is for 480 B.C., Meyer, Ed., *Geschichte des Alterthums*, Stuttgart, 1884f, III, §§263-4, gives the population of Laconia ca. 470 as 12,-000 Spartans (4000 adult males), 80,000 Perioeci, and 190,000 Helots.
22. CAH, V, 7.
23. Plutarch, *Spartan Institutions*, in *Lyra Graeca*, London, 1928, III, 287; Mahaffy, *Social Life*, 451; Cicero, in Cotterill, H. B., *History of Art*, N. Y., n.d., I, 61.
24. Grote, IV, 264.
25. *Greek Anthology*, ix, 488, in *Lyra Graeca*, I, 29.
26. Grote, III, 195; Murray, Sir G., *History of Ancient Greek Literature*, N. Y., 1927, 80.
27. In Ridder, 106.
28. Grote, III, 195.
29. Mahaffy, J. P., *History of Classical Greek Literature*, London, 1908, I, 189; Lacroix, Paul, *History of Prostitution*, N. Y., 1931, I, 149-50.
30. Alcman, Frag. 36 in *Lyra Graeca*, I, 77.
31. *Das Oxforder Buch Deutschen Dichtung*, Oxford, 1936, 117.
32. Goethe, J. W. von, *Poetical Works*, tr. Cobb, N. Y., 1902, 61.
33. Glover, T. R., *Democracy in the Ancient World*, Cambridge U. P., 1927, 84.
34. Herodotus, i, 65.
35. Aristotle, *Politics*, 1271b.
36. Plutarch, "Lycurgus."
37. Ibid.
38. Ibid.; Polybius, vi, 48.
39. Thucydides, i, 6.
40. E.g., Polybius, vi, 10.
41. Plutarch, "Lycurgus."
42. Glotz, *Ancient Greece*, 88.
43. Coulanges, Fustel de, *Ancient City*, Boston, 1901, 460.
44. Plutarch, l.c.
45. Ibid., Grote, III, 148.
46. Thucydides, iv, 14.
47. Coulanges, 294; Glotz, G., *Greek City*, London, 1929, 300; Carroll, M., *Greek Women*, Phila., 1908, 136.
48. Mahaffy, J. P., *Old Greek Education*, N. Y., n.d., 10.
49. Hesiod, Callimachus, and Theognis, *Works*, tr. Banks and Frere, London, 1856, 441n.
50. Plutarch, l.c.; Grote, III, 157; Müller-Lyer, F., *Family*, N. Y., 1931, 45.
51. Thucydides, i, 3.
52. Nilsson, 94.
53. Mahaffy, *Greek Education*, 46.
54. Plutarch, "Demetrius."
55. Xenophon, *Anabasis*, Loeb Library, iv, 6.15.
56. Symonds, J. A., *Greek Poets*, London, 1920, 159.
57. Becker, W., *Charicles*, London, 1886, 246, 297.
58. Carroll, 138-40; Weigall, A., *Sappho of Lesbos*, N. Y., 1932, 105.
59. Plutarch, "Lycurgus"; Lippert, 301.
60. Athenaeus, xiii, 2.
61. Whibley, 613.
62. Grote, III, 155-6; Sumner, W. G., *Folkways*, Boston, 1906, 351.
63. Athenaeus, xiii, 2.
64. Plutarch, "Numa and Lycurgus Compared."
65. Aristotle, *Politics*, 1270a; Grote, III, 153-7; Briffault, R., *Mothers*, N. Y., I, 399.
66. Plutarch, "Lycurgus"; Glotz, *Ancient Greece*, 89.
67. Athenaeus, xii, 74.
68. Plutarch, l.c.
69. Grote, III, 131, IX, 298; Rawlinson's Herodotus, iii, 148n, calls the roll of Spartan venality.
70. Herodotus, iii, 148.
71. Grote, III, 132, 158.
72. Plutarch, "Pelopidas."
73. E.g., Herodotus, i, 82.
74. Ibid., vii, 104.

75. Xenophon, "Constitution of the Lacedaemonians," in *Minor Works*, London, 1914, i, 1.
76. Pausanias, v, 1.
77. Ibid., vii, 21.
78. Frazer, Sir J., *Studies in Greek Scenery, Legend, and History*, London, 1931, 224-5.
79. Pausanias, ii, 1; Glotz, *Ancient Greece*, 116.
80. Strabo, viii, 6.21.
81. *Iliad*, ii, 570.
82. Aristotle (?), *Economics*, Loeb Library, ii, 2.
83. Aristotle, *Politics*, 1315b.
84. *Enc. Brit.*, XVI, 616. Others attribute the first Corinthian coinage to Cypselus; cf. CAH, III, 552.
85. Glotz, *Greek City*, 113, *Ancient Greece*, 86; Weigall, *Sappho*, 46.
86. Plutarch, *Moralia*, Loeb Library, 147D.
87. Herodotus, iii, 50-3; Diogenes Laertius, *Lives and Opinions of the Eminent Philosophers*, London, 1853, "Periander."
88. Aristophanes, *The Eleven Comedies*, N. Y., 1908, *Frogs*, 133; Lacroix, I, 110.
89. Pindar, *Odes*, Loeb Library, Frag. 122.
90. Strabo, viii, 6.20.
91. Athenaeus, xiii, 32.
92. Ibid., 33.
93. St. Paul, I Cor. vi, 15-18.
94. Semple, 669.
95. Pausanias, vi, 17-19; Litchfield, F., *History of Furniture*, Boston, 1922, 13.
96. CAH, III, 554.
97. Glotz, *Greek City*, 113.
98. Grote, III, 264-5.
99. Theognis, 237, in Dickinson, G. L., *Greek View of Life*, N. Y., 1928, 186.
100. Theognis in Hesiod, Callimachus, and Theognis, *Works*, 444-5.
101. Ibid., 448, ll. 373f.
102. Ibid., ll. 349f.
103. Symonds, 161.
104. Botsford, G. W., and Sihler, E. G., *Hellenic Civilization*, N. Y., 1920, 198-9; Coulanges, 369.
105. Symonds, 162.
106. Theognis in Hesiod, etc., 442.
107. Ibid., 470-1, 447-8, 489-90.
108. 479-81.
109. 477, 491-2.
110. 454-5.
111. Ridgeway, 33.
112. Calhoun, 30-1; Semple, 669.
113. Pausanias, ii, 26.
114. Pindar, Pythian iii, 47-58.
115. Gardner, E. A., *Ancient Athens*, N. Y., 1902, 431.

CHAPTER V

1. Strabo, viii, 6.21; ix, 2.25.
2. Pausanias, ix, 31.
3. Mahaffy, *Greek Literature*, I, 117.
4. *Enc. Brit.*, XI, 529.
5. Hesiod, *Works and Days*, 640.
6. Ibid., 655.
7. Gardiner, E. N., *Athletics*, 30.
8. Pausanias, ix, 31; cf. Mahaffy, *Greek Literature*, I, 125; CAH, IV, 474; Grote, I, 12.
9. Hesiod, *Theogony*, 1-6.
10. Ibid., 120f.
11. Nilsson, 185-6.
12. *Theogony*, 166f.
13. Ibid., 735f.
14. *Works and Days*, 285.
15. Ibid., 286f.
16. 504f.
17. 54f.
18. *Theogony*, 585f.
19. *Works and Days*, 695f.
20. Ibid., 109f.
21. Mahaffy, *Social Life*, 72.
22. Mahaffy, *Greek Literature*, 54.
23. Diodorus, xvi, 28; Frazer, *Studies*, 374-5.
24. Pope, A., *Essay on Man.*
25. Bury, 95; CAH, III, 619. Others (Murray, *Epic*, 43, and *Enc. Brit.*, XII, 575) derive the Graii from Epirus.
26. Cicero, *De Fato*, 7.
27. Baedeker, xxvii; Zimmern, A., *Greek Commonwealth*, Oxford, 1924, 38.
28. Hippocrates, *Works*, Loeb Library, Introductory Essay I to Vol. II, by W. H. S. Jones; cf. Jones, W. H. S., *Malaria and Greek History*, Manchester U. P., 1909.
29. Isocrates, *Works*, Loeb Library, *Panegyricus*, 24.
30. Ridder, 122.
31. Grote, III, 270-4; Vinogradoff, Paul, *Outlines of Historical Jurisprudence*, Oxford, 1922, II, 85-6.
32. Frazer, *Studies*, 58-9.
33. Aristophanes, I, 196, editor's note.
34. Baedeker, 104.
35. CAH, III, 579-80.
36. Aristotle, *Constitution of Athens*, London, 1891, sect. 57; Grote, III, 290; Coulanges, 331.

37. Meyer, Ed., in Zimmern, 396.
38. Aristotle, *Constitution*, 2, says that these "sixth-sharers" paid one-sixth of their product to the owner, and Plutarch ("Solon") follows him; but recent scholarship inclines to believe that the sixth part was the amount kept, not paid. Cf. Bury, 174; Glotz, *Greek City*, 102.
39. Botsford, *Athenian Constitution*, 141.
40. Aristotle, *Constitution*, 2.
41. Glotz, *Ancient Greece*, 61, 80, *Greek City*, 102.
42. Glotz, *Ancient Greece*, 71.
43. CAH, IV, 33.
44. Ibid.
45. Grote, III, 293-4; Coulanges, 418.
46. Plutarch, "Solon."
47. Botsford, *Constitution*, 143.
48. Pöhlmann, 158; Glotz, *Ancient Greece*, 71.
49. Glotz, *Greek City*, 119.
50. Plutarch, *Amatorius*, 751c, in Linforth, I. M., *Solon the Athenian*, Berkeley, Cal., 1919, 156-7.
51. Diog. L., "Solon," ii.
52. Plutarch, "Solon."
53. Diog. L., "Solon," ix.
54. Aristotle, *Constitution*, 5; Grote, III, 313; Botsford, 158.
55. Aristotle, 6, 12.
56. CAH, IV, 38.
57. Aristotle, 6.
58. Plutarch, "Solon."
59. Grote, III, 319.
60. Aristotle, 10.
61. Plutarch, l.c.
62. Grote, III, 316; Mahaffy, *What Have the Greeks Done for Civilization?*, 186.
63. CAH, IV, 134; Bury, 183.
64. Plutarch, l.c.
65. Aristotle, 12; Grote, III, 331-2.
66. Plutarch, l.c.
67. Ibid.; Aristotle, 9.
68. Coulanges, 420; CAH, IV, 43; Grote, II, 350.
69. Plutarch, l.c.
70. Diog. L., "Solon," vii.
71. Athenaeus, xiii, 25; Lacroix, I, 68-70; Bebel, A., *Woman under Socialism*, N. Y., 1923, 35.
72. Plutarch, l.c.; Grote, III, 351; Tucker, T. G., *Life in Ancient Athens*, Chautauqua, N. Y., 1917, 159.
73. Plutarch.
74. Ibid.
75. Diog. L., "Solon," xvi.
76. Grote, III, 344.
77. Diog. L., l.c.
78. *Enc. Brit.*, XX, 955.
79. Herodotus, i, 29.
80. Plato, *Amatores*, 133, in Linforth, 130.
81. Herodotus, i, 30.
82. Plutarch, l.c.
83. Diog. L., "Solon," iii.
84. Diodorus, ix, 20.
85. Herodotus, i, 60; Athenaeus, xiii, 89.
86. Aristotle, *Constitution*, 16.
87. Glotz, *Greek City*, 121.
88. Calhoun, 29.
89. Aristotle, *Politics*, 1310a.
90. Thucydides, vi, 19.
91. Athenaeus, xiii, 70; Lacroix, I, 153.
92. Aristotle, *Politics*, 1300b.

CHAPTER VI

1. Pater, W., *Plato and Platonism*, London, 1910, 246.
2. Thucydides, i, 1.
3. CAH, II, 558.
4. Strabo, x, 5.6; Plutarch, *Moralia*, Loeb Library, 249D.
5. *Lyra Graeca*, II, 639.
6. Aristophanes, *Peace*, 695.
7. Cicero, *De Oratione*, ii, 86, in *Lyra Graeca*, II, 306.
8. *Lyra Graeca*, II, 257.
9. Ibid., III, 297, 339; tr. J. A. Symonds, *Greek Poets*, 155, 167.
10. Cicero, *De Natura Deorum*, Loeb Library, i, 22.
11. Thucydides, iii, 103.
12. Glotz, *Ancient Greece*, 113.
13. Botsford and Sihler, 188.
14. Carroll, 99.
15. CAH, IV, 483.
16. Symonds, 169.
17. Herodotus, iii, 57.
18. Ovid, *Metamorphoses*, Loeb Library, x, 243.
19. Herodotus, i, 142.
20. Ibid., i, 146.
21. Ibid., i, 170; Diog. L., "Thales."
22. Aristotle, *Poetics*, Loeb Library, 1259a.
23. Diog. L., "Thales," iii-viii; Plutarch, "Solon."
24. Heath, *Greek Mathematics*, I, 130; Ueberweg, F., *History of Philosophy*, N. Y., 1871, I, 34-5.
25. Heath, I, 137; Herodotus, i, 74.
26. Aristotle, *Metaphysics*, tr. M'Mahon. London, 1857, i, 3.

27. Ibid.
28. Diog. L., "Thales," iii.
29. Ibid., "Thales," viii.
30. Ibid.
31. Ibid., "Thales," xii.
32. Strabo, xiv, 4.7.
33. Spencer, *First Principles of a New System of Philosophy*, N. Y., 1910, 367.
34. Bakewell, 5.
35. Heath, II, 38; Grote, V, 94.
36. Bakewell, 6.
37. Aristotle, *Metaphysics*, i, 3; Bakewell, 7; CAH, IV, 554.
38. Athenaeus, xii, 26, xiii, 29, xiv, 20.
39. Ibid., xii, 26.
40. Diog. L., "Bias," i-iv.
41. CAH, IV, 92-3.
42. Herodotus, ii, 134.
43. Plutarch, *Moralia*, 16C.
44. Leslie, Shane, *Greek Anthology*, N. Y., 1929, x, 123.
45. Pfuhl, Ernst, *Masterpieces of Greek Drawing and Painting*, London, 1926, Fig. 79.
46. Sarton, Geo., *Introduction to the History of Science*, Baltimore, 1930, I, 75.
47. Pausanias, viii, 14; Glotz, *Ancient Greece*, 132; Jones, H. Stuart, *Ancient Writings on Greek Sculpture*, London, 1895, 24-5.
48. Ridder, 174.
49. Pliny, xxxv, 46.
50. Ibid., xxxvi, 21.
51. Athenaeus, xii, 29.
52. Carroll, 102.
53. Frag. 78 in *Herodes, Cercidas, and the Greek Choliambic Poets*, Loeb Library, 55.
54. Diog. L. in Heracleitus, *On the Universe*, Loeb Library, 464.
55. Cf. Mahaffy, *What Have the Greeks?*, 219.
56. Bakewell, 33.
57. Nietzsche, F., *Early Greek Philosophy*, N. Y., 1911, 103-4.
58. Diog. L., "Heracleitus," v.
59. Strabo, xiv, 1.28; Weigall, *Sappho*, 155; Webster's *Dictionary*, s.v. *colophon*.
60. Weigall, 186; Symonds, 150.
61. Tr. in Harrison, *Prolegomena*, 173.
62. *Lyra Graeca*, III, 636, II, 126, 131.
63. Athenaeus, x, 33.
64. *Lyra Graeca*, II, 125, 139.
65. Ibid., 145, frag. 15.
66. *Greek (Palatine) Anthology*, vii, 24.
67. Diodorus, xx, 84.
68. Herodotus, viii, 105; Glotz, *Ancient Greece*, 85.
69. Athenaeus, vi, 88-90; Ward, C. O., *Ancient Lowly*, Chicago, 1907, I, 123f.
70. Eratosthenes in Grote, II, 159.
71. *Lyra Graeca*, I, 333; Athenaeus, xiv, 23.
72. Tr. by Symonds, 197.
73. Stobaeus, *Anthology*, xxix, 58, in *Lyra Graeca*, I, 141.
74. *Greek Anthology*, ix, 506.
75. Strabo, xiii, 2.3.
76. Ovid, *Heroides*, Loeb Library, xv, 31; scholiast on Lucian, *Imag.*, 18, in *Lyra Graeca*, I, 160.
77. Weigall, *Sappho*, 76.
78. Ibid., 175.
79. Symonds, 196.
80. Weigall, 86.
81. *Lyra Graeca*, I, 437.
82. Athenaeus, xii, 69.
83. Weigall, 119.
84. Longinus, *On the Sublime*, Loeb Library, ix, 15.
85. *Berliner Klassikertexte*, p. 9722, in *Lyra Graeca*, I, 239.
86. Murray, *Greek Literature*, 92; Weigall, 173, 90; Robinson, D. M., *Sappho and Her Influence*, Boston, 1924, 58.
87. Mahaffy, *Greek Literature*, I, 202.
88. Weigall, 321.
89. Suidas, *Lexicon*, s.v., *Phaon*, in *Lyra Graeca*, I, 153; Strabo, x, 2.8.
90. Ovid, *Heroides*, xv.
91. Oxyrhynchus Papyrus 1231, in Weigall, 291.
92. *Lyra Graeca*, I, 435.
93. Athenaeus, xiii, 89.
94. Strabo, xii, 3.11.
95. Ramsay, *Asianic Elements*, 118.
96. Diodorus, iv, 49.
97. Polybius, iv, 38.
98. Semple, 72-3, 214.
99. Murray, *Greek Literature*, 86.

CHAPTER VII

1. Pausanias, iii, 23.
2. Ludwig, 266; Cook, *Zeus*, 776.
3. Schliemann, *Ilios*, 41.
4. Strabo, x, 2.9.
5. *Journal of Hellenic Studies*, LVI, 170-89, London, 1882f.
6. Grote, IV, 150-1.
7. Mahaffy, *Greek Literature*, I, 97-8; *J. H. Studies*, LV, 138.

8. Randall-MacIver, D., *Greek Cities in Italy and Sicily*, Oxford, 1931, 75; CAH, III, 676.
9. Diodorus, iii, 9.
10. Athenaeus, xii, 20.
11. Ibid., xii, 15, 17.
12. Ibid., 58.
13. Herodotus, vi, 127.
15. Grote, IV, 168.
16. Athenaeus, xii, 19.
17. Diog. L., "Pythagoras," ix.
18. *Enc. Brit.*, XVIII, 802.
19. Diog. L., "Pythagoras," i-iii, xvii; Heath, *Greek Math.*, I, 4.
20. Cicero, *De Finibus*, Loeb Library, v, 29, 87; Diodorus, i, 98.
21. Cicero, *Tusculan Disputations*, Loeb Library, i, 16; *De Re Publica*, Loeb Library, ii, 15.
22. Carroll, 299, 307, 310.
23. Diog. L., "Pythagoras," viii.
24. Ibid., "Pythagoras," xix, vii, xviii; Grote, V, 103.
25. Diog. L., "Pythagoras," xix.
26. Ibid., "Pyth.," xviii.
27. Grote, V, 100-1.
28. Diog. L., "Pyth.," xxii; Cook, *Zeus*, 1.
29. Diog. L., "Pyth.," viii.
30. Heath, I, 10.
31. Proclus, in Heath, I, 141.
32. Diog. L., "Pyth.," xi.
33. Whibley, 229.
34. Heath, I, 70, 85, 145.
35. Whewell, W., *History of the Inductive Sciences*, N. Y., 1859, I, 106; *Oxford History of Music*, Oxford U. P., 1929, Introductory Volume, 3.
36. Aristotle, *Works*, ed. Smith and Ross, Oxford, 1931, *De Coelo*, ii, 9; *Metaphysics*, i, 5; *Oxford History of Music*, 27; Heath, I, 165, II, 107.
37. Heath, II, 65, 119; Berry, A., *Short History of Astronomy*, N. Y., 1909, 24.
38. Diog. L., "Pyth.," xxv.
39. Ibid., 9, Introd., xviii.
40. Livingstone, R. W., *Legacy of Greece*, Oxford, 1924, 59.
41. Diog. L., "Pyth.," xix.
42. Ibid.
43. Rohde, Erwin, *Psyche*, N. Y., 1925, 375; Pater, *Plato*, 54.
44. *Greek Anthology*, vii, 120.
45. Aristotle, *Nicomachean Ethics*, v, 8.
46. Diog. L., "Pyth.," xxi.
47. Grote, IV, 154-8; CAH, IV, 115-6.
48. Frag. 24 in Whibley, 89.
49. Heath, II, 52; Mahaffy, *Greek Lit.*, I, 138.
50. Frag. 7 in Bakewell, 9.
51. Frags. 14-5, 5-7, 1-3, in Bakewell, 8.
52. Diog. L., "Xenophanes," iii.
53. Frags. 9-10.
54. Bakewell, 10-11.
55. Warren, *Foundations*, 241; but Koldewey (ibid.) places it about 450.
56. Randall-MacIver, 9-10.
57. Childe, V. G., *Dawn of European Civilization*, N. Y., 1925, 93-100.
58. Thucydides, vi, 18; Diodorus, v, 2.
59. Grote, IV, 149.
60. Freeman, E. A., *Story of Sicily*, N. Y., 1892, 65.
61. Ibid.
62. Polybius, xii, 25.
63. Ibid., ix, 27.
64. Ibid., v, 2.
65. Herodotus, vii, 156.
66. Lucian, *Works*, tr. H. W. and F. G. Fowler, Oxford, 1905, "Hermotimus," 34.
67. Glotz, *Ancient Greece*, 116; Draper, J. W., *History of the Intellectual Development of Europe*, N. Y., 1876, I, 52.

CHAPTER VIII

1. In CAH, II, 610.
2. Cf. Sophocles, *Oedipus at Colonus*, 1470; Cook, *Zeus, passim*.
3. *Iliad*, iii, 277.
4. Frazer, *Magic Art*, I, 315.
5. Murray, G., *Five Stages of Greek Religion*, Oxford U. P., 1930, 50.
6. Nilsson, 91; Farnell, *Greece and Babylon*, 228.
7. Nilsson, 91-2; Heracleitus in Bakewell, 29.
8. Murray, G., *Aristophanes: A Study*, N. Y., 1933, 6.
9. Harrison, Jane, *Prolegomena*, 293; Glotz, *Aegean Civilization*, 391-2; Briffault, *Mothers*, III, 145.
10. Murray, *Five Stages*, 35-6; Reinach, S., *Orpheus*, 86; Frazer, Sir J., *Spirits of the Corn and of the Wild*, N. Y., 1935, I, 4.
11. Whibley, 387.
12. Murray, *Five Stages*, 31.
13. Ibid., 29, 33; Harrison, *Prolegomena*, pp. viii and 28.
15. Harrison, 18.
16. Rodenwaldt, 315.

17. Sophocles, *Philoctetes*, 1327-9; Harrison, 297f.
18. Ibid., 325.
19. Rohde, 159.
20. Nilsson, 123.
21. Rohde, 297.
22. Ibid., 172.
23. Seymour, 98; *Odyssey*, i, 65f; *Iliad*, iv, 14f.
24. Ibid., viii, 17-27.
25. Semple, 529.
26. *Iliad*, xvi, 651f.
27. Hesiod, *Theogony*, 887f.
28. *Iliad*, xv, 17.
29. Frazer, *Magic Art*, I, 14-15.
30. *Iliad*, viii, 330f.
31. Ibid., xx, 46, xxi, 406.
32. Smith, Wm., *Dictionary of Greek and Roman Antiquities*, Boston, 1859, 603.
33. CAH, II, 637; Glotz, *Ancient Greece*, 112; Blakeney, M. A., ed., *Smaller Classical Dictionary*, Everyman Library, 258.
34. CAH, l.c.
35. Diodorus, iv, 6.
36. Athenaeus, xii, 80.
37. Gardner, P., *New Chapters*, 157.
38. Frazer, Sir J., *Adonis, Attis, Osiris*, N. Y., 1935, 226; Gardner, *New Chapters*, 157.
39. Semple, 43-4.
40. In Symonds, 204.
41. Diodorus, iii, 62.
42. Herodotus, ii, 49-57.
43. Nilsson, 86; CAH, IV, 527.
44. Ibid., 535.
45. Rohde, 220; Gardner, *New Chapters*, 385.
46. Diodorus, iv, 25.
47. Harrison, *Prolegomena*, 465.
48. Reinach, 88; CAH, IV, 536-8; Harrison, 432; Murray, *Greek Literature*, 65; Carpenter, Edw., *Pagan and Christian Creeds*, N. Y., 1920, 64.
49. Harrison, p. xi.
50. Ibid., 588; Nilsson, 221; Rohde, 344.
51. Plato, *Republic*, ii, 364-5.
52. Harrison, 572.
53. Whibley, 402.
54. Nilsson, 247.
55. Symonds, 495.
56. Dickinson, G. L., *Greek View of Life*, N. Y., 1928, 1.
57. Grote, II, 101-2.
58. Coulanges, 223.
59. Xenophon, Anabasis, v, 3.4.
60. *Iliad*, xxi, 27; xxiii, 22, 175.
61. Pausanias, iv, 9, vii, 19; CAH, II, 621.
62. Pausanias, iii, 16; Plutarch, "Lycurgus"; Nilsson, 94.
63. CAH, II, 618; Grote, I, 111.
64. Frazer, Sir J., *Scapegoat*, N. Y., 1935, 253; Harrison, 107.
65. Aristophanes, *Frogs*, 734, and scholiast; Rohde, 296; Harrison, 103; Nilsson, 87; Frazer, *Scapegoat*, 253.
66. Harrison, 108.
67. Murray, G., *Epic*, 12-13, 317; Harrison, 103.
68. Plutarch, "Pelopidas."
69. Hesiod, *Theogony*, 557f.
70. *Odyssey*, iii, 338-41; CAH, II, 626.
71. Farnell, 237.
72. Harrison, 501.
73. Diodorus, iii, 66.
74. Grote, I, 145-6.
75. Harrison, 167.
76. Nilsson, 82-3; Rohde, 163.
77. Coulanges, 213; Rohde, 295-6.
78. Nilsson, 83.
79. Ibid., 85.
80. Theophrastus, *Characters*, Loeb Library, xvi.
81. Plutarch, "Solon."
82. Sophocles, *Trachinian Women*, 584; Lacroix, I, 117; Becker, 381.
83. Plato, *Laws*, 933; Harrison, 139.
84. Herodotus, ix, 95.
85. Coulanges, 291.
86. Carroll, 270; Rohde, 292.
87. Coulanges, 289.
88. Grote, III, 38-9; Benson, E. F., *Life of Alcibiades*, N. Y., 1929, 83.
89. Herodotus, v, 63, vi, 66; Grote, V, 431.
90. Ibid., III, 127.
91. CAH, III, 627-8.
92. Ibid., 604.
93. In Coulanges, 288.
94. Harrison, 121; Frazer, *Spirits of the Corn*, II, 17.
95. Harrison, 32.
96. Frazer, *Spirits of the Corn*, I, 30.
97. Rohde, 239.

CHAPTER IX

1. Herodotus, viii, 144.
2. Mahaffy, *Greek Literature*, IV, 24.
3. *Enc. Brit.*, I, 681.
4. Mason, W. A.. *History of the Art of Writing*, 344.

5. Mahaffy, *Old Greek Education*, 49; Thompson, Sir E. M., *Introduction to Greek and Latin Palaeography*, Oxford, 1912, 58.
6. Pliny, xiii, 11.
7. Shotwell, J. T., *Introduction to the History of History*, N. Y., 1936, 30; Becker, 162n.
8. Thompson, 39, 43; Mahaffy, l.c., 51.
9. Becker, 274.
10. Shotwell, 32.
11. Mahaffy, *Greek Literature*, I, 25-8.
12. Grote, II, 245; Murray, *Epic*, 238.
13. Diog. L., "Solon," ix.
14. Grote, II, 245; Murray, *Epic*, 147.
15. Ibid., 258.
16. *Iliad*, xxii, 106-13, tr. G. Murray.
17. Ramsay, *Asianic Elements*, 289.
18. *Iliad*, i, 477, etc.
19. Ibid., ii, 469-73.
20. Ibid., xx, 490, tr. Bryant.
21. Mahaffy, *Greek Literature*, I, 35, 81. Aristarchus of Samothrace wrote ca. 180 B.C.
22. Browne, 92.
23. Glotz, *Aegean Civilization*, 393; Ward, I, 41; Grote, II, 306-7.
24. Briffault, *Mothers*, I, 411.
25. *Odyssey*, iv, 120-36.
26. Herodotus, ii, 53.
27. Curtius, Ernst, *Griechische Geschichte*, Berlin, 1887f, I, 126, in Robertson, J. M., *Short History of Free Thought*, London, 1914, I, 127; Mahaffy, *Social Life*, 352; Murray, *Epic*, 267.
27a. Symonds, 187.
28. *Odyssey*, viii, 146.
29. Rodenwaldt, 233.
30. Gardiner, *Athletics*, 230.
31. Mahaffy, *Greek Education*, 18.
32. Gardiner, *Athletics*, 234.
33. Tucker, 222.
34. In Zimmern, 316.
35. Pausanias, v, 21.
36. Ibid., i, 44.
37. Gardner, *New Chapters*, 291.
38. Ibid., 294.
39. Ibid.
40. Gardiner, *Athletics*, 212f.
41. Pausanias, vi, 4.
42. Ibid., viii, 40.
43. Ibid., vi, 14.
44. Herodotus, iii, 106.
45. Pausanias, vi, 13.
46. Herodotus, viii, 26.
47. Grote, III, 352-3.
48. Athenaeus, x, 1; Gardiner, *Athletics*, 54-5.
49. Ferguson, W. M., *Greek Imperialism*, Boston, 1913, 58-9; Haigh, A. E., *Attic Theatre*, Oxford, 1907, 3.
50. Winckelmann, J., *History of Ancient Art*, Boston, 1880, II, 288.
51. Athenaeus, xiii, 90.
52. Ibid.
53. Symonds, 73.
53a. Richter G., *Handbook of the Classical Collection*, Metropolitan Museum of Art, N. Y., 1922, 76.
54. Rodenwaldt, 234.
55. Ridder, 171.
56. Pfuhl, 38.
57. Ridder, 181; Murray, A. S., *Greek Sculpture*, I, 11.
58. Rodenwaldt, 247.
59. Cf. Pijoan, J., *History of Art*, N. Y., 1927, I, figs. 351-2.
60. Ibid., p. 229.
61. Pliny, xxxv, 151.
62. Cotterill, H. B., *History of Art*, N. Y., 1922, 99-100.
63. Anderson and Spiers, 42; CAH, IV, 603-8.
64. Livingstone, *Legacy of Greece*, 412; Warren, 277-80; Smith, G. E., 422; CAH, IV, 99.
65. Polybius, iv, 20-1; Athenaeus, xiv, 22.
66. Lacroix, I, 122.
67. Pratt, W. S., *History of Music*, N. Y., 1927, 53.
68. Pausanias, x, 7.
69. Mahaffy, *Social Life*, 456.
70. Diodorus, iii, 67.
71. *Lyra Graeca*, III, 582.
72. Strabo, x, 3.17.
73. *Oxford History of Music*, 8.
74. Ibid.; Pratt, 55; Mahaffy, *What Have the Greeks?*, 143; id., *Social Life*, 463-5.
75. Aristotle, *Politics*, 1342b.
76. Athenaeus, xiv, 18.
77. Ibid., 10; *Lyra Graeca*, II, 498; Symonds, 180; Glotz, *Ancient Greece*, 279.
78. *Oxford History of Music*, 1, 30.
79. Haigh, 311.
80. Lucian, "Of Pantomime."
81. Ibid.
82. In Kirstein, L., *Dance*, N. Y., 1935, 26.
83. Athenaeus, i, 37.
84. Kirstein, 28-30.
85. Ibid., 30.
86. Athenaeus, xiv, 12, 32.
87. *Lyra Graeca*, III, 630.

88. Lucian, l.c.
89. Mahaffy, *Social Life,* 464-5.
90. Athenaeus, xiv, 17.
91. Aristotle, *Poetics,* iv; Murray, *Aristophanes,* 3.
92. *Enc. Brit.,* VII, 582.
93. Aristotle, *Politics,* 1336b.
94. Murray, l.c.; id., *Greek Literature,* 212; Haigh, 292; Sumner, W. G., *Folkways,* 447.
95. Aristophanes, *Eleven Comedies,* I, 327 and editor's note; Kirstein, 38.
96. *Enc. Brit.,* VII, 584.
97. Aristotle, *Poetics,* v, 3.
98. CAH, V, 117.
99. Aristotle, *Poetics,* iv, 17.
100. Ridgeway in Harrison, 76; Sumner and Keller, III, 2109.
101. *Enc. Brit.,* VII, 582.
102. Ibid., 583.
103. Athenaeus, i, 39.
104. Diog. L., 28, "Solon," xi.

CHAPTER X

1. Herodotus, vi, 98.
2. Grote, V, 16.
3. Ibid., 22.
4. Herod., vi, 102.
5. Rawlinson, app. to Herod., vi; Grote, V, 58; Pausanias, x, 20.
6. Plutarch, "Aristides."
8. Herod., vi, 132-6.
9. Plutarch, l.c.
10. Ibid.
11. Ibid.
12. Thucydides, i, 5.138.
13. Plutarch, "Themistocles."
14. Plutarch, "Aristides."
15. Herod., vii, 133-7.
16. Ibid., 184-6, 196.
17. Ibid., 146.
18. Ibid., 33-6.
19. Ibid., 56.
20. Athenaeus, iv, 27; Herod., vii, 118-9.
21. Ibid., viii, 4-6.
22. vii, 231-2.
23. viii, 24.
24. *Greek Anthology,* vii, 249; Strabo, ix, 4,12-16.
25. Plutarch, "Themistocles."
26. Mahaffy, *Social Life,* 223. Mahaffy considers the story a legend, but no lover of dogs will doubt it.
27. Herod., ix, 4-5.
28. Ibid., viii, 89.
29. Grote, V, 316f, and Freeman, 77, believe that the two actions were concerted; CAH, IV, 378, doubts it.
30. Grote, V, 319-20.
31. Herod., ix, 70.
32. Rawlinson, note to Herod., l.c.

CHAPTER XI

1. Shelley, P. B., "On the Manners of the Ancients," quoted by Livingstone, *Legacy,* 251.
2. Herod., viii, 111-12.
3. *Oxford Book of Greek Verse in Translation,* Oxford, 1938, 534; Plutarch, "Themistocles."
4. Plutarch, "Aristides."
5. Thucydides, i, 5.
6. Grote, VI, 6-7.
7. Aristotle, *Constitution,* 25.
8. Ibid., 41.
9. Plutarch, "Pericles"; Grote, VII, 16; CAH, V, 72.
10. Plutarch, l.c.
11. Ibid.
12. Ibid.
13. Glotz, *Greek City,* 241.
14. Plato, *Gorgias,* 515; Aristotle, *Constitution,* 27; Plutarch, l.c.
15. CAH, V, 100; Glotz, 210.
16. Glotz, 131.
17. Plutarch, l.c.
18. Ibid.
19. Plato, *Phaedrus,* 270.
20. Plutarch, l.c.
21. Carroll, 197.
22. Aristophanes, *Acharnians,* 514f; Athenaeus, xiii, 25-6.
23. Lacroix, I, 154; Carroll, 200.
24. Plato, *Menexenus,* 236; Carroll, 311; Benson, 58.
25. Lacroix, I, 156.
26. Plutarch, l.c.
27. Plato, l.c.; Benson, 57-8.
28. Plutarch, l.c.
29. Benson, 58.
30. Plutarch.
31. Plato, *Theaetetus,* 79, *Republic,* ii, 8, *Laws,* ix, 3; Thucydides, iii, 52; Mahaffy, *Social Life,* 178-9; Grote, VI, 305-6.
32. Botsford, 222.
33. Glotz, *Greek City,* 156; Carroll, 442.
34. Tucker, 251-2.
35. Isocrates, *Antidosis,* 320.
36. Coulanges, 248.

37. Tylor, E. B., *Anthropology*, N. Y., 1906, 217.
38. Vinogradoff, II, 61-2.
39. Aristotle, *Constitution*, 57.
40. Glotz, *Greek City*, 236.
41. Glotz, *Ancient Greece*, 153.
42. Botsford, 53-4.
43. Glotz, *Greek City*, 297.
44. Cf. Aristotle's will in Diog. L., 185, "Aristotle," ix.
45. Xenophon, *Memorabilia*, tr. Watson, Phila., 1899, x, 2.9.
46. Murray, *Greek Literature*, 328.
47. Glotz, *Ancient Greece*, 281.
48. Tucker, 263.
49. Isocrates, *Antidosis*, 79.
50. *Enc. Brit.*, X, 829.
51. Glotz, *Ancient Greece*, 316.
52. Glotz, *Greek City*, 263.
53. Herod., v, 77; Aristotle, *Ethics*, v, 7.
54. Glotz, *Greek City*, 220.
55. Zimmern, 290; Ferguson, 69.
56. CAH, V, 29; Grote, II, 55-7.
57. Thucydides, ii, 6.
58. *Lyra Graeca*, II, 337.

CHAPTER XII

1. Xenophon, *Economicus*, iv-vi, in *Minor Works*.
2. Ibid., xviii, 2.
3. Semple, 407, 414, 421.
4. Pausanias, ii, 38.
5. Zimmern, 52-4.
6. Aristophanes, II, 245; Athenaeus, vii, 43, 50f.
7. Ibid., xiv, 51.
8. Xenophon, *Memorabilia*, ii, 1.
9. Hippocrates, "Regimen in Acute Diseases," xxviiif.
10. Aeschylus, *Persian Women*, 238.
11. Aristotle, *Constitution*, 47; Baedeker, 123.
12. CAH, V, 16.
13. Rickard, T. A., *Man and Metals*, N. Y., 1932, I, 376; Calhoun, 142-3.
14. Ibid., 154-6.
15. Glotz, *Ancient Greece*, 225.
16. Semple, 678-9.
17. Ibid., 668.
18. Glotz, 205.
19. Vitruvius, *On Architecture*, Loeb Library, ii, 6.3.
20. Aeschylus, *Agamemnon*, 278f; Herod., ix, 3; Thucydides, viii, 26.
21. Aristophanes, *Frogs*, in *Eleven Comedies*, II, 194.
22. Plato, *Gorgias*, 511.
23. Glotz, 294.
24. Ibid., 233.
25. In Zimmern, 307.
26. Lucian, "Nigrinus," 1.
27. CAH, V, 22.
28. Zimmern, 218; CAH, V, 8.
29. Zimmern, 283.
30. Isocrates, *Panegyricus*, 42.
31. Thucydides, ii, 6.
32. Xenophon, *Economicus*, iv, 2.
33. Glotz, 218.
34. Gomme, A. W., *Population of Athens in the 5th and 4th Centuries B.C.*, Oxford, 1933, 21.
35. Athenaeus, vi, 103; Becker, 361.
36. Semple, 667; Glotz, 192-3.
37. Ibid., 208.
38. Aeschines, Epistle 12, in Becker, 361; CAH, V, 8.
39. In Botsford and Sihler, 225.
40. Glotz, 196.
41. Dickinson, 119; Ward, I, 93.
42. CAH, VI, 529-30.
43. Aristotle, *Ethics*, viii, 13.
44. Murray, *Epic*, 16; CAH, VI, 529.
45. CAH, V, 25.
46. Aristophanes, *Ecclesiazusae*, 307.
47. Ward, I, 98.
48. CAH, V, 12, 25.
49. Glotz, 237.
50. Ibid., 286.
51. Toutain, J., *Economic Life of the Ancient World*, N. Y., 1930; Introduction by Henri Berr, p. xxiii.
52. CAH, V, 32.
53. Semple, 425.
54. Glotz, 163.
55. Tucker, 251.
56. Coulanges, 451.
57. Ward, I, 424.
58. Glotz, 148.
59. Ward, I, 88, II, 48, 76, 263, 342.
60. Hall, M. P., *Encyclopedic Outline of Masonic, Hermetic, Qabbalistic, and Rosicrucian Symbolical Philosophy*, San Francisco, 1928, 64.
61. Aristophanes, II, 371f.
62. Ibid., 440f.
63. Thucydides, viii, 24.
64. Ibid., iii, 10, slightly transposed.
65. Aristotle (?), *Economics*, iii, 15.
66. Glotz, 296.
67. Ibid., 298.

68. Ibid., 298; Lysias, *Against the Grain-Dealers*, xxii, in Botsford and Sihler, 426; Semple, 365, 663; Zimmern, 362.
69. Glotz, 169.

CHAPTER XIII

1. Plato, *Republic*, 459f.
2. Aristotle, *Politics*, 1335.
3. Haggard, H. W., *Devils, Drugs, and Doctors*, N. Y., 1929, 19.
4. Himes, 82, 96. *Coitus interruptus* was apparently a popular method of family limitation throughout antiquity.
5. Athenaeus, xiv, 3.
6. Plutarch, "Themistocles," *Moralia*, 185D.
7. *Greek Anthology*, vii, 387.
8. McClees, H., *Daily Life of the Greeks and Romans*, N. Y., 1928, 41; Metropolitan Museum of Art.
9. Ibid., 41; Becker, 223; Mahaffy, *Greek Education*, 16, 19; Weigall, *Sappho*, 200.
10. Plato, *Laws*, vii, 84.
11. Plato, *Protagoras*, 326.
12. Mahaffy, op. cit., 39.
13. Becker, 224.
14. Winckelmann, II, 296.
15. Plato, *Protagoras*, 325.
16. Aristotle, *Constitution*, 42.
17. Gardner, *Ancient Athens*, 483; Mahaffy, op. cit., 76.
18. Lycurgus, *Against Leocrates*, 75-89, in Botsford and Sihler, 478. On its authenticity cf. Mahaffy, op. cit., 71.
19. Diog. L., "Aristippus," iv, "Aristotle," xi.
20. Tucker, 173; Weigall, 184.
21. Plutarch, *Moralia*, 249B.
22. CAH, II, 22-3.
23. Becker, 456.
24. Carroll, 172.
25. Tucker, 125-7.
26. Ibid.
27. Plutarch, *Moralia*, 228B; *Athenaeus*, xv, 34.
28. Weigall, 189, 206-7; Carroll, 173.
29. Eubulus, *Flower Girls*, in Tucker, 173-4, and Lacroix, I, 101-2.
30. Weigall, 187.
31. Athenaeus, xv, 45.
32. Glotz, 278.
33. Wright, F. A., *History of Later Greek Literature*, N. Y., 1932, 19.
34. Zimmern, 215.
35. Tucker, 120.
36. Coulanges, 294.
37. *Greek Anthology*, x, 125.
38. Voltaire, *Works*, N. Y., 1927, IV, 71.
39. Thucydides, ii, 6; Mahaffy, *Social Life*, 295; Hobhouse, L. Y., *Morals in Evolution*, N. Y., 1916, 347; Glotz, *Greek City*, 131.
40. Vinogradoff, II, 54-5.
40a. Aristotle, in Sedgwick and Tyler, *Short History of Science*, N. Y., 1927, 102.
41. Glotz, *Ancient Greece*, 290; Becker, 280; Tucker, 150.
42. Ibid., 123.
43. Grote, V, 53.
44. Thucydides, ii, 10.82.
45. Pausanias, vii, 9-10; Plutarch, "Artaxerxes II."
46. Xenophon, *Cyropaedia*, Loeb Library, i. 6.27.
47. Thucydides, i, 3.76.
48. Ibid., v, 17.
49. Ibid., iii, 9.34.
50. Ibid., v, 32.116; vi, 20.95; Polybius, iii, 86; Coulanges, 275.
51. Thucydides, ii, 7.67.
52. Plutarch, "Alcibiades."
53. Plato, *Laws*, viii, 831.
54. Herod., v, 78.
58. Aristophanes, *Eccl.*, 720; Becker, 241.
59. Ibid., 243.
61. Demosthenes, *Against Neaera;* Becker, 244.
62. Lacroix, I, 124, 129.
63. Ibid., 112.
64. Ibid., 85.
65. Briffault, II, 340.
66. Mahaffy, *Greek Life and Thought*, London, 1887, 72.
67. Lacroix, I, 88.
68. CAH, V, 175.
69. Lacroix, I, 166.
70. Ibid., 162.
71. Becker, 248.
72. Athenaeus, xiii, 59.
73. Ibid.
74. Ibid., 58.
75. Ibid., 52.
76. Lacroix, I, 180.
77. Ibid., 179.
78. Athenaeus, xiii, 54.
79. Lacroix, I, 182-3.
80. Ibid., 145-6.
81. Ellis, H., *Studies in the Psychology of Sex*, Phila., 1911, VI, 134.
82. Murray, *Aristophanes*, 45.
83. Plutarch, "Lycurgus"; Strabo, x, 4.21.

84. Plutarch, "Pelopidas."
85. Diog. L., "Xenophon," vi.
86. Cf. Plato, *Lysis*, 204.
87. Plato, *Symposium*, 180f, 192.
88. Lacroix, I, 118, 126.
89. Bebel, 37; Hime, 52.
90. Whibley, 612.
91. Carroll, 307.
92. Sophocles, *Trachinian Women*, 443.
92a. Tr. by J. S. Phillimore in *Oxford Book of Greek Verse in Translation*, 367.
93. Becker, 473.
94. Athenaeus, xiii, 16.
95. Sumner, *Folkways*, 362; Becker, 473.
96. Tucker, 83.
97. Carroll, 164.
98. Euripides, *Medea*, 233.
99. Coulanges, 63, 293; Becker, 475; Briffault, II, 336.
100. Zimmern, 334, 343.
101. Euripides, *Aeolus*, 22.
102. Demosthenes, *Against Neaera;* Smith, Wm., *Dictionary*, 349, s.v., *Concubium.*
103. Glotz, *Greek City*, 296; Zimmern, 340. Zeller, Ed., *Socrates and the Socratic Schools*, London, 1877, 62, questions the story and the law.
104. Westermarck, E., *History of Human Marriage*, London, 1921, III, 319; Becker, 497; *Lyra Graeca*, II, 135.
105. Lacroix, I, 114; *Enc. Brit.*, X, 828; Becker, 496.
106. Tucker, 84; Westermarck, op. cit., 319; Lacroix, I, 143.
107. Westermarck, l.c.; Coulanges, 119.
108. Thuc., ii, 6.
109. Lacroix, I, 143.
110. Becker, 464; Tucker, 83-4.
111. Sumner, *Folkways*, 497; Briffault, I, 405.
112. Tucker, 156.
113. Aristophanes, *Lysistrata*, 42f.
114. In Tucker, 84.
115. *Greek Anthology*, vii, 340.
116. Botsford and Sihler, 51.
117. Tucker, 90-6.
118. Semple, 490-1.
119. Athenaeus, i, 10.
120. *Greek Anthology*, xi, 413.
121. Athenaeus, v, 2.
122. Xenophon, *Banquet*, ii, 8.
123. Mahaffy, *Social Life*, 120-1.
124. Coulanges, 422.
125. Plato, *Republic*, iv, 425.
126. Tucker, 270.
127. Semple, l.c.
128. Rohde, 167.
129. Harrison, *Prolegomena*, 600; Westermarck, E., *Origin and Development of the Moral Ideas*, London, 1917-24, I, 715.

CHAPTER XIV

1. Xenophon, *Economicus*, viii, 19f.
2. Thuc., ii, 6.40.
3. Xenophon, *Banquet*, iv, 11.
4. In Ridder, 48.
5. Usher, A. P., *History of Mechanical Inventions*, N. Y., 1929, 106-7.
6. Cf. the gems in the Fourth Room of the Classical Collection, Metropolitan Museum of Art, New York.
7. Pfuhl, 5.
8. Ridder, 287.
9. Pliny, xxxv, 34.
10. Mahaffy, *Social Life*, 449-50; Ridder, 19.
11. Plutarch, "Cimon."
12. Pausanias, x, 25.
13. Pliny, xxxv, 35; Winckelmann, II, 296.
14. Pliny, xxxv, 36.
15. Ibid.
16. Plutarch, "Pericles."
17. Pliny, l.c.
18. Athenaeus, xii, 62.
19. Murray, A. S., I, 13.
20. Pliny, l.c.
21. Cicero, *De Invent.*, ii, 1, in Murray, A. S., I, 12. Pliny, l.c., places the story in Acragas.
22. National Museum, Naples; *Guide to the Archeological Collections*, Naples, 1935, 11.
23. National Museum, Athens.
24. Xenophon, *Memorabilia*, iii, 10.7.
25. Ridder, 177.
26. Gardner, *Greek Sculpture*, 20-1.
27. Pliny, xxxiv, 19.
28. Ibid.
29. Pijoan, I, 254.
30. Cf. Lucian, "A Portrait Study," in *Works*, III, 15-16.
31. Jones, H. S., *Ancient Writers on Greek Sculpture*, 78.
32. Glotz, *Ancient Greece*, 231.
33. Cf. Jones, op. cit., 76; Gardner, *Greek Sculpture*, 284; Frazer, *Studies in Greek Scenery*, 411; CAH, V, 479.
34. Pijoan, I, 269.
35. Pausanias, v, 11; Strabo, viii, 3.30.
36. *Iliad*, i, 528.
37. Pausanias, v, 11.
38. Polybius, xxx, 10.
39. Frazer, op. cit., 293.

40. Quintilian, *Institutes*, Loeb Library, xii, 10.7.
41. Plutarch, "Pericles."
42. Scholiast on Aristophanes, *Peace*, 605, in Jones, op. cit., 76.
43. Lucian, l.c.
44. Vitruvius, iv, 1.8.
45. Cotterill, I, 75.
46. Pausanias, v, 10.
47. Zimmern, 411. Grote (VI, 70) makes a smaller estimate ($18,000,000) for the architectural works in Athens proper.
48. Warren, 156.
49. Ibid., 331.
50. Vitruvius, iii, 5.
51. Ruskin, *Aratra Pentelici*, 174; in Gardner, *Ancient Athens*, 338; Gardner, *Greek Sculpture*, 324.
52. Warren, 327, 339-41; Mahaffy, *What Have the Greeks?*, 130.
53. Ludwig, 139f.
54. Warren, 310-11; Gardner, *Ancient Athens*, 258.

CHAPTER XV

1. Heath, *Greek Mathematics*, I, 46; Whibley, 228-9.
2. Heath, I, 150.
3. Sarton, 92.
4. Sedgwick and Tyler, 33.
5. Heath, I, 176, 178.
6. CAH, V, 383.
7. Heath, I, 93.
8. Diog. L., 384, "Parmenides," ii; Sarton, 85.
9. Aristotle, *De Coelo*, ii, 13; Heath, Sir Thos., *Aristarchus of Samos*, Oxford, 1913, 94.
10. Diog. L., 389, "Leucippus," iii.
11. Ibid., 390; Heath, *Aristarchus*, 125.
11a. Sarton, 92.
12. Heath, 78.
13. Anaxagoras, frags. 12 and 16, in Bakewell, 51; Ueberweg, I, 63-5; CAH, IV, 570.
14. Heath, 81.
15. Ibid., 82.
16. Ueberweg, I, 66.
17. Diog. L., 59-60, "Anaxagoras," iv.
18. Heath, 128.
19. Ibid., 70.
20. Anaxagoras, frag. 4, in Bakewell, 49.
21. Diog. L., l.c.
22. Frags. 5 and 17, in Bakewell, 50; Diog. L., l.c.
23. Frag. 9, in Bakewell, 51; Aristotle, *Metaphysics*, i, 3, *De Coelo*, iii, 3, *De Generatione et Corruptione*, i, 1; Lucretius, *De Rerum Natura*, Loeb Library, i, 830f.
24. Diog. L., l.c.
25. Aristotle, *De Partibus Animalium*, i, 10, iv, 10.
26. Aristotle, *Metaphysics*, i, 4.
27. Nilsson, 274.
28. Diog. L., 61, "Anaxagoras," viii; Robertson, J. M., I, 153.
29. Plutarch, "Pericles."
30. Murray, *Greek Literature*, 159.
31. CAH, IV, 569-70.
32. Heath, *Greek Math.*, I, 172.
33. Diog. L., 61, "Anaxagoras," ix.
34. Geminus in Heath, *Aristarchus*, 275.
35. Herod., ii, 4, and Rawlinson's note; Whibley, 71.
36. Grote, II, 29-30.
37. Herod., ii, 4.
38. Sarton, 83.
39. Semple, 35-7.
40. Ibid.
41. Cf. Sect. III of Chap. XVI, below; and cf. Aeschylus, *Prometheus Bound*, 442-506.
42. Gardner, *New Chapters*, 269.
43. Sarton, 83.
44. Herod., iii, 125-38.
45. Sarton, 77.
46. Ibid.; Livingstone, *Legacy*, 209.
47. Sarton, 102.
48. Garrison, F. H., *History of Medicine*, Phila., 1929, 95.
49. Hippocrates, *Works*, I, Introd., by W. H. S. Jones.
50. Ibid., IV, "Aphorisms," i.
51. "The Sacred Disease"; "Airs, Waters, Places," xxii.
52. Hippocrates, *Works*, II, Introd., viii; I, Introd., xxiv; Garrison, 94.
53. Ibid., IV, "The Nature of Man," iv, 10.
54. Ibid., "Regimen III," lxviii.
55. Livingstone, 234.
56. Garrison, 94; Hippocrates I, Introd., lvi.
57. IV, Introd., viii.
58. Harding, T. S., in *Medical Journal and Record*, Aug., 1, 1928.
59. Hippocrates, IV, Introd., vii. Hippocrates settles a very ancient problem when he writes: "It is best for flatulence to pass without noise and breaking, though it is better for it to pass even with noise than to be intercepted and accumulated internally." – *Works*, IV, "Prognostic," 11.

60. In Livingstone, 235.
61. Hippocrates, IV, "Regimen III," lxviii.
62. Sarton, 96.
63. Livingstone, 208.
64. Hippocrates, II, "The Sacred Disease," xvii.
65. Xenophon, "Constitution of the Lacedaemonians," xiii, 6; Mahaffy, *Social Life,* 293; Becker, 380; Garrison, 91; Hippocrates, *Works,* I, 299.
66. Garrison, 97; Livingstone, 225.
67. Ibid., 240.
68. I am indebted, for an explanation of the material at Epidaurus, to Dr. A. A. Smith, of Hastings, Neb.
69. Livingstone, 225.
70. Plato, *Laws,* iv, 720.
71. Carroll, 324-5; Mahaffy, *Social Life,* 297.
72. Xenophon, *Memorabilia,* iv, 2; Garrison, 91; Becker, 376.
73. Ibid., 291; Garrison, 90; Plato, *Statesman,* 259.
74. Hippocrates, II, "Law," i, and Introd. to Essay VI.
75. I, 291-5.
76. Ibid., 299.
77. Becker, 379.
78. Hippocrates, II, "Decorum," vii; "Precepts," vi.
79. "Decorum," v.

CHAPTER XVI

1. Athenaeus, xiii, 92.
2. Plato, *Protagoras,* 334, 339.
3. Symonds, 116; Owen, John, *Evenings with the Sceptics,* London, 1881, I, 177.
4. Bakewell, 11.
5. Ibid., 22; the conclusion is rephrased.
6. Plato, *Parmenides,* 127.
7. Russell, B., *Principles of Mathematics,* London, 1903, I, 347.
8. Plutarch, "Pericles."
9. Plato, l.c.
10. Diog. L., "Zeno," iv.
11. Ibid.
12. Tredennick, H., introd. to Aristotle, *Metaphysics,* Loeb Library, xvii; CAH, IV, 575-6.
13. Heath, *Aristarchus,* 105.
14. Tredennick, l.c.
15. Leucippus, frag. 2 in Bakewell, 7.
16. Diog. L., "Leucippus," i-iii.
17. Lange, F. E., *History of Materialism,* N. Y., 1925, 15.
18. Diog. L., "Democritus," ii-iii.
19. Ibid.
20. Lange, 17.
21. Ueberweg, I, 71.
22. *Enc. Brit.,* XVII, 39.
23. Grote, G., *Plato and the Other Companions of Socrates,* London, 1875, I, 68; Bakewell, 62.
24. Robertson, J. M., I, 158; Lange, 17.
25. Diog. L., "Democritus," xiii.
26. Heath, *Greek Math.,* I, 176.
27. Cicero, *De Oratore,* i, 11; Ueberweg, I, 68; Grote, *Plato,* I, 68, 96.
28. Bacon, F., *Philosophical Works,* ed. Robertson, London, 1905, 96, 471-2, 650.
29. Democritus, frag. O (Diels) in Bakewell, 60.
30. Frags. 117 and 9 in Bakewell, 59, slightly rephrased.
31. Ueberweg, I, 70.
32. Lange, 27.
33. Ueberweg, I, 69-70; Grote, *Plato,* I, 77.
34. Ibid., 76.
35. Diog. L., "Democritus," xii.
36. Heath, *Aristarchus,* 26, 127.
37. Ueberweg, l.c.
38. Grote, *Plato,* I, 78.
39. Lucretius, iii, 370.
42. In Plutarch, *Moralia,* 81.
43. Owen, I, 149.
44. Lange, 31; Diog. L., "Democritus," xii; Ueberweg, l.c.
45. Frag. 154a in Bakewell, 62.
46. Frag. 57.
47. In Owen, I, 149.
48. Ueberweg, I, 68.
49. Athenaeus, ii, 26.
50. Ibid.; Lucretius, iii, 1039.
51. Diog. L., "Democritus," xi.
52. Athenaeus, l.c.
53. Diog. L., "Democritus," viii.
54. Id., "Empedocles," ii.
55. In Symonds, 127.
56. Murray, *Greek Literature,* 76.
57. Symonds, 127.
58. Diog. L., "Empedocles," iii.
59. Ibid., "Empedocles," xi.
60. Ibid.; Symonds, 131.
61. Diog. L., "Empedocles," ix.
63. CAH, IV, 563.
64. Aristotle, *De Anima,* ii, 6; *De Sensu,* vi.
65. Symonds, 143.
68. Empedocles, frag. 82 in Bakewell, 45.
69. In Aristotle, *De Coelo,* iii, 2.
70. Ueberweg, I, 62.
71. Symonds, 143.
72. Frags. 17 and 35 in Bakewell, 44-5.

73. Cf. Frazer, *Spirits of the Corn*, II, 303.
74. Frags. 133-4 in Bakewell, 46.
75. Symonds, 137.
76. Livingstone, 46.
77. Symonds, 135.
78. Diog. L., "Empedocles," x.
79. Ibid., "Empedocles," xi.
80. Ibid.; Symonds, 131.
81. Plato, *Protagoras*, 316.
82. Grote, *History*, VI, 46.
83. CAH, V, 24, 377-8.
84. Plato, *Protagoras*, 309-10.
85. Ueberweg, I, 74.
86. Plato, *Protag.*, 311.
87. Ibid., 328.
88. Diog. L., "Protagoras," iv.
89. Plato, *Phaedrus*, 267.
90. Ueberweg, I, 75; Sarton, 88.
91. Euripides, frag. 189, quoted by Rohde, 438.
92. Plato, *Theaetetus*, 160; Bakewell, 67; Lange, 42.
93. Diog. L., l.c.; Bakewell, 67.
94. Diog. L., l.c.; Ueberweg, I, 74.
95. Bakewell, 67.
96. Isocrates, *Antidosis*, 155.
97. Philostratus, *Lives of the Sophists*, Loeb Library, §494.
98. Grote, VIII, 343.
99. Ueberweg, I, 77.
100. Philostratus, 483.
101. Plato, *Republic*, i, 336f; Oxyrhynchus Papyri xi, 1364, in Vinogradoff, II, 29; Murray, *Greek Literature*, 161.
102. Plato, *Sophist*, 265.
103. Murray, *Aristophanes*, 142.
104. Ibid.
105. Murray, *Greek Literature*, 160.
106. Zeller, 36.
107. Plato, *Gorgias*, 502.
108. Plato, *Cratylus*, 584.
109. Xenophon, *Memorabilia*, i, 6.13.
110. Plutarch, *Dec. Orat.*, iv, in Becker, 235.
111. Aristotle, *Soph. Elenchis*, i, 1.165.
112. Grote, VIII, 326.
113. Diog. L., "Plato," xxv.
114. Aristotle, *Ethics*, 1109, 1116, 1144, 1164.
115. Livingstone, 79.
116. CAH, VI, 303.
117. Plutarch, *De Malig. Herod.*, ix, 856, in Dupréel, E., *La Légende Socratique*, Bruxelles, 1922, 415.
118. Mahaffy, *Social Life*, 205-6.
119. Pausanias, i, 22.
120. Diog. L., "Socrates," iv.
121. CAH, V, 386.
122. Plato, *Apology*, 23; *Republic*, 337; Xenophon, *Memor.*, i, 2.1.
124. Plato, *Symposium*, 220-1.
125. *Republic*, 549.
128. Aristotle in Diog. L., "Socrates," x.
129. Cf. McClure, M., in Dewey, J., and Others: *Studies in the History of Ideas*, Columbia U. P., 1935, II, 31.
130. Plato, *Symposium*, 214.
131. Xenophon, *Banquet*, ii, 19.
132. Plato, *Phaedrus*, 229.
133. Diog. L., "Socrates," ix.
134. Xenophon, *Banquet*, ii, 24.
135. Diog. L., l.c.
136. Plato, *Charmides*, 154-5.
137. Id., *Protagoras*, 309.
138. Id., *Lysis*, 206; Xenophon, *Memor.*, iii, 11.
139. Ibid.
140. Ibid., iv, 8.
141. Plato, *Phaedo*, end.
142. CAH, V, 387-8.
143. Diog. L., "Socrates," iii; Robertson, J. M., I, 160.
144. Plato, *Apology*, 41.
145. Xenophon, *Banquet*, i, 5.
146. Diog. L., "Socrates," xviii.
147. Xenophon, *Memor.*, i, 2.16.
148. In Pater, 179.
149. Plato, *Protag.*, 338, 361.
150. Xenophon, iv, 4.9.
151. Plato, *Theaetetus*, 150.
152. Grote, VII, 92; Mahaffy, *Greek Education*, 84.
153. Cf., e.g., *Charmides*, 159, 161; *Protag.*, 331, 350; *Lysis*, *passim.*
154. Diog. L., "Crito," i.
155. Xenophon, ii, 6.28.
156. Ibid., i, 6.
157. Ibid.
158. Diog. L., "Socrates," xiv.
159. Xenophon, iv, 1.1.
160. Diog. L., "Crito," i.
161. Plato, *Symposium*, 215, 218.
162. Sextus Empiricus, *Opera*, Leipzig, 1840, *Adversus Mathematicos*, ix, 54; Botsford and Sihler, 369; Nilsson, 269; Symonds, 390.
163. Zeller, 205, 208.
164. Athenaeus, xii, 534.
165. Plato, *Meno*, 94.
166. Xenophon, *Memor.*, i, 1.2; i, 3.4; ii, 6.8; iv, 7.10; Plato, *Symposium*, 220; *Phaedo*, 118; *Apology*, 21.
167. Zeller, 82.
168. Plato, *Apology*, 29.

169. Id., *Cratylus*, 425.
170. Xenophon, *Memor.*, i, 1.11f.
171. Ibid., iv, 3.16.
173. iv, 7.
174. i, 1.16.
175. iv, 2.24.
176. iii, 8.3; iv, 5.9.
178. iii, 9.5.
179. i, 2.9.
180. iii, 5.15-17.
181. iv, 6.12.
182. CAH, VI, 309.
183. Xenophon, *Apology*, end.

CHAPTER XVII

1. Pausanias, ix, 22.
2. *Lyra Graeca*, III, 9; II, 264.
3. Pausanias, ix, 23.
4. Pindar, *Olympic Ode* xiv, 5.
5. *Olympic Odes* i-ii.
6. Frag. 76 in Pindar, *Odes*, p. 557.
7. CAH, IV, 511.
8. Symonds, 214.
9. *Lyra Graeca*, III, 7.
10. Pausanias, ix, 23.
11. *Olympic* i, 64.
12. Frag. 131.
13. *Olympic* ii, 56f, tr. C. J. Billson, in *Oxford Book of Greek Verse in Translation*, 294.
14. Pindar, *Pythian Ode* i, 81.
15. *Pythian* iv, 272
16. *Pythian* viii, 92, tr. G. Murray.
17. *Paean* iv, 32.
18. Symonds, 216.
19. S.v. Pratinas, *Lyra Graeca*, III, 49.
20. Aristophanes, II, 82, editor's note.
21. Haigh, 37.
22. Ibid., 64.
23. Mahaffy, *Social Life*, 469; Symonds, 380.
24. Haigh, 266.
25. *Lyra Graeca*, III, 283.
26. Aristotle, *Rhetoric*, Loeb Library, iii, 1.
27. Ward, II, 311.
28. Lucian, "Of Pantomime," 27.
29. Haigh, 325-7.
30. Ibid., 327, 335.
31. Flickinger, R. C., *Greek Theater and Its Drama*, University of Chicago Press, 1918, 132.
32. Haigh, 343.
33. Ibid., 345; Norwood, *Greek Drama*, 83.
34. Haigh, 344.
35. Ibid., 12, 24.
36. Ferguson, 59.
37. Haigh, 34.
38. Plato, *Laws*, 659, 700.
39. Herod., vi, 21.
40. CAH, IV, 172.
41. Haigh, 15.
42. Aeschylus, *Prometheus Bound*, 18f, tr. Elizabeth Barrett Browning, in *Greek Dramas*, N. Y., 1912, pp. 5-6.
43. Ibid., ll. 459f.
44. Tr. in Murray, *Greek Literature*, 219.
45. Schlegel, A. W., *Lectures on Dramatic Art and Literature*, London, 1846, 93. On the "paradox of *Prometheus Bound*," —an antitheistic play by the most pious of Greek dramatists, cf. *Journal of Hellenic Studies*, LIII, 40f, and LIV, 14f.
46. Mahaffy, *Social Life*, 150; Symonds, 260; Murray, *Greek Literature*, 221.
47. Aeschylus, *Agamemnon*, ll. 218f, tr. G. Murray, *Oresteia*, p. 44.
48. Tr. by Milman in Mahaffy, *Social Life*, 152.
49. *Agamemnon*, 1445f, *Oresteia*, p. 100.
50. *Choephoroe*, 1024f, *Oresteia*, 183.
51. Athenaeus, i, 39.
52. Schlegel, 95.
53. *Agamemnon*, ll. 55f.
54. Ibid., 160.
55. *Eumenides*, end.
56. Murray, *Greek Literature*, 215.
57. Botsford and Sihler, 34.
58. Athenaeus, i, 37; Schlegel, 97; Taine, H., *Lectures on Art*, N. Y., 1901, II, 483; Plumptre, E. H., Introd. to *Tragedies of Sophocles*, London, 1867, p. xxxvii.
59. Sophocles, *Works*, tr. F. Storr, Loeb Library, I, Introd., viii.
60. Symonds, 278.
61. Athenaeus, xiii, 81.
62. Mahaffy, *Greek Literature*, II, 57.
63. Murray, *Greek Literature*, 234.
64. Symonds, 290.
65. Sophocles, *Oedipus the King*, 980f.
66. *Oedipus at Colonus*, 668f, tr. Walter Headlam, *Oxford Book of Greek Verse in Translation*, 378.
67. *Oedipus at Colonus*, 607f, tr. Murray, *Greek Literature*, 249.
68. *Oed. Col.*, 1648f, tr. Murray.
69. *Antigone*, 332f, tr. Storr.
70. Ibid., 786f.
71. Ibid., 1220f.
72. Murray, *Greek Literature*, 238.
73. *Trachinian Women*, 1265f.
74. *Philoctetes*, 451-2.
75. *Electra*, 473f.

76. *Oedipus the King*, 863f.
77. *Oed. Col.*, 1211f, slightly transposed, tr. A. E. Housman, in *Oxford Book of Greek Verse in Translation*, 378. Cf. to like effect *Oedipus the King*, 1187-95 and 1529-30.
78. Athenaeus, xiii, 61.
79. Symonds, 278.
80. Mahaffy, *Greek Literature*, II, 97.
81. Murray, *Gk. Lit.*, 251.
82. Strabo, xiv, 1.36.
83. Diog. L., "Socrates," ii.
84. Euripides, *Hippolytus*, 191-7, in Murray, *Gk. Lit.*, 12.
85. Murray, op. cit., 34.
86. Euripides, *Medea*, 410f, tr. G. Murray, Oxford, 1912, p. 15.
87. Herod., ii, 120.
88. *Iphigenia in Aulis*, 636-54, tr. A. S. Way, Loeb Library.
89. *Iph. in Aulis*, tr. Webb in Mahaffy, *Social Life*, 202-4.
90. *Iph. in Aulis*, 1369-84, tr. A. S. Way.
91. *Hecuba*, 488f, tr. Way.
92. Murray, *Gk. Lit.*, 137.
93. *Trojan Women*, tr. G. Murray, Oxford, 1914.
94. Euripides, *Electra*, tr. Murray, Oxford, 1907, p. 77.
95. Euripides, *Iphigenia in Tauris*, tr. Murray, Oxford, 1930.
96. Aristotle, *Poetics*, xiii, 4.
97. Verrall, A. W., *Euripides the Rationalist*, Cambridge Univ. Press, 1913, 178 and *passim*.
98. Elizabeth Barrett Browning referred to "Euripides the human, with his droppings of warm tears."
99. *Iph. in Aulis*, 957.
100. *Helen*, 744f, tr. Way.
101. *Ion*, 374-8; *Iph. in T.*, 570-5; *Electra*, 400; *Bacchae*, 255-7; *Hippolytus*, 1059; Robertson, I, 162.
102. Euripides, *Electra*, tr. Murray, p. 37; *Heracles*, 1341; *Iph. in T.*, 386.
103. *Bellerophontes*, 293, tr. Symonds, 368; cf. *Helen*, 1137.
104. *Iph. in T.*, tr. Murray, p. 32.
105. *Helen*, 1688.
106. Verrall, 79.
107. *Trojan Women*, 884.
108. *Hecuba*, 282.
109. *Trojan Women*, prologue.
109a. *Cresphontes*, frag.
110. *Hippolytus* and the lost *Stheneboea* and *Chrysippus*.
111. *Andromeda*, 135, tr. Symonds, 363.
112. Norwood, 311.
113. Euripides, *Medea*, tr. Murray, p. 67.
114. Frag. 157 in Rohde, 438.
115. *Electra*, tr. Murray, p. 78.
116. Rohde, 437.
117. An uncertain frag. tr. Symonds, 367.
118. A frag. in Symonds, 366.
119. Aristophanes, *Frogs*, 552; Athenaeus, i, 41.
120. Symonds, 426.
121. Mahaffy, *Gk. Lit.*, II, 98.
122. Pater, 122.
123. Plutarch, "Nicias."
124. *Greek Anthology*, ix, 450.
125. Quoted by Murray, *Euripides and His Age*, N. Y., 1913, 10.
126. Murray, *Gk. Lit.*, 277.
127. Aristophanes, I, 117.
128. Haigh, 260.
129. Murray, *Aristophanes*, 102.
130. Zeller, 203.
131. Aristophanes, I, 91.
132. Ibid., 314, 319.
133. E.g., *Thesmophoriazusae* II, 286; *Knights*, I, 11; *Ecclesiazusae*, II, 378.
134. *Knights*, I, 31.
135. *Peace*, I, 194. In *The Birds* he calls Heracles a bastard (I, 173); and in *The Frogs* he makes Dionysus a coward, an onanist, a lecher, and a clown.
136. Philostratus, 483.
137. Lucian, "Herodotus and Aetion," 1; Bury, J. B., *Ancient Greek Historians*, N. Y., 1909, 65; Mahaffy, *Gk. Lit.*, II, 18; Murray, *Gk. Lit.*, 134.
138. Herod., i, 1.
139. Gibbon, Ed., *Decline and Fall of the Roman Empire*, Everyman Library, I, 77, ch. iii.
140. Strabo, xvii, 1.52.
141. Herod., iii, 101.
142. Ibid., i, 68.
143. iii, 38; ii, 3.
144. E.g., vii, 189, 191.
145. vii, 152.
146. Lucian, l.c.
147. Thuc., i, 1.21-23.
148. Mahaffy, *Social Life*, 208.
149. Thuc., ii, 45.
150. Ibid., viii, 24; ii, 17.
151. Murray, *Gk. Lit.*, 1.

CHAPTER XVIII

1. Diog. L., "Empedocles," vii.
2. Athenaeus, xii, 34.

3. Aristophanes, *Acharnians,* I, 111.
4. Glotz, *Ancient Greece,* 314.
5. Grote, V, 390.
6. Thuc., iii, 37.
7. Ibid., i, 3.75.
8. Plutarch, "Pericles."
9. Thuc., ii, 6.8.
10. Ibid., i, 2.58-65; i, 5.139-46.
11. Jones, W. H. S., *Malaria and Greek History,* 132.
12. Plutarch, "Tiberius Gracchus."
13. Aristotle, *Constitution,* 28.
14. Thuc., iii, 9.49-50.
15. Ibid., v, 15.22-3.
16. v, 17.84f.
17. Plutarch, "Alcibiades."
18. Ibid.
19. Xenophon, *Memor.*, i, 2.46.
20. Athenaeus, i, 5.
21. Benson, *Alcibiades,* 125.
22. Plutarch, l.c.
23. Thuc., vi, 18.18.
24. Ibid., 20.89.
25. viii, 24.18.
26. viii, 26.97; Aristotle, *Constitution,* 33.
27. Xenophon, *Hellenica,* Loeb Library, i, 4.13.
28. Aristotle, *Constitution,* 34.
29. Plutarch, "Lysander."
30. Isocrates, *Areopagiticus,* 66.
31. Aristotle, op. cit., 40.
32. Murray, *Gk. Lit.*, 176.
33. Xenophon, *Memor.*, i, 2.32.
34. Grote, IX, 63.
35. Ueberweg, I, 81.
36. In Reinach, 96.
37. Plato, *Apology,* 38.
38. Ibid., 27.
39. 18.
40. 29.
41. 30.
42. Diog. L., "Socrates," xxi.
45. Plato, *Crito.*
46. Xenophon, *Memor.*, iv, 8.1.
47. Plato, *Phaedo,* 59-60.
48. Ibid., 89.
49. Xenophon, *Apology,* 28.
50. Diodorus, xiv, 37.
51. In Zeller, 201.
52. Plutarch, *De Invid.*, 6, in Zeller, 201.
53. Diog. L., "Socrates," xxiii.
54. Grote, IX, 88.
55. Tertullian, *Apology,* 14, and Augustine, *City of God,* viii, 3, in Zeller, 201.

CHAPTER XIX

1. Aristotle, *Physics,* Loeb Library, 1269-70; Plutarch, "Lysander," "Lycurgus."
2. Glotz, *Greek City,* 300.
3. Aristotle, *Physics,* 1270.
4. Xenophon, *Anabasis,* iv, 7-22.
5. Plutarch, *Moralia,* 190F.
6. Plutarch, "Agesilaus."
7. Plutarch, *Moralia,* 39.
8. Ibid., 192C.
9. Aristotle, *Physics,* 1270.
10. Glotz, *Ancient Greece,* 199.
11. Xenophon, "On the Revenues," in *Minor Works.*
12. Calhoun, 46-8, 93-4, 101.
13. Glotz, *Anc. G.*, 304; CAH, VI, 72.
14. Calhoun, 109.
15. Ibid., 116; Glotz, 306.
16. Glotz, *Greek City,* 311; *Anc. G.*, 201.
17. Glotz, *Gk. City,* 312-3.
18. Plato, *Republic,* iv, 422.
19. Aristotle, *Politics,* 1310.
20. Isocrates, *Archidamus,* 67. Isocrates was writing of the Peloponnesian Greeks, but probably had his fellow Athenians in mind.
21. Pöhlmann, I, 147.
22. Plato, *Laws,* v, 736.
23. Vinogradoff, II, 113; Glotz, *Gk. City,* 318.
24. Vinogradoff, II, 205.
25. Isocrates, *Antidosis,* 159.
26. Glotz, *Gk. City,* 323; Rostovtzeff, M., *Social and Economic History of the Roman Empire,* Oxford, 1926, 2; id.. *History of the Ancient World,* Oxford, 1928, II, 362; Coulanges, 493.
27. Mahaffy, *Social Life,* 267, 273.
28. Glotz, *Gk. City,* 296.
29. Ibid.
30. Athenaeus, xiii, 38f; Lacroix, I, 168.
31. Athenaeus, xii, 43.
32. Aristotle, *Historia Animalium,* 583a.
33. Gomme, 18, 26, 47; Athenaeus, vi, 272; Müller-Lyer, *Family,* 203; Grote, IV, 338.
34. Xenophon, *Hellenica,* vi, 1.5.
35. Isocrates, *On the Peace,* 50.
36. Aristotle, *Problems,* 29, in Vinogradoff, II, 67.
37. Demosthenes in Glotz, *Gk. City,* 216.
38. Aristotle, *Constitution,* 41.
39. Aristophanes, *Clouds,* 991; Plato, *Theaetetus,* 173.
40. Isocrates, op. cit., 59.

41. Grote, XI, 198.
42. Diodorus, x, 4.
43. Aristotle (?), *Economics*, ii, 2.20.
44. *Lyra G.*, III, 366.
45. Diog. L., "Plato," xiv; Plutarch, "Dion"; Diodorus, xv, 7; Grote, XI, 34-5. Taylor, A. E., *Plato*, N. Y., 1936, 5, questions the story.
46. Plato, *Epistles*, Loeb Library, vii.
47. Athenaeus, x, 47.
48. Plutarch, l.c.
49. Plato, l.c.
50. Plutarch, l.c.
51. Athenaeus, xii, 58.
52. In Weigall, *Alexander the Great*, N. Y., 1933, 19.
53. Adams, Brooks, *New Empire*, N. Y., 1903, 36.
54. Athenaeus, xiii, 63.
55. Mahaffy, *Social Life*, 425-7.
56. Glotz, *Gk. City*, 339.
57. Philostratus, 507.
58. Plutarch, "Phocion."
59. Philostratus, 61.
60. Plutarch, "Alexander."

CHAPTER XX

1. Plutarch, "Demosthenes"; *Moralia*, 6.
2. Mahaffy, *Gk. Lit.*, IV, 137.
3. Demosthenes, *On the Crown*, Loeb Library, 126, 258-9, 265.
4. Murray, *Gk. Lit.*, 362.
5. Isocrates, *Antidosis*, 48.
6. Grote, G., *Aristotle*, London, 1872, I, 31; Murray, 344.
7. Isocrates, *Panegyricus*, 49.
8. Ibid., 167.
9. Ibid., 160.
10. Isocrates, *On the Peace*, 94.
11. Ibid., 13.
12. Isocrates, *Areopagiticus*, 15, 70.
13. *On the Peace*, 109.
14. *Areopag.*, 20.
15. Pausanias, i, 18; so Lucian and Philostratus; cf. Murray, 350.
16. Milton's phrase for Isocrates.
17. Diog. L., "Xenophon," i-ii.
18. Aristophanes, *Clouds*, 225.
19. Plutarch, *Moralia*, 212B.
20. Xenophon, *Economicus*, x, 1-10.
21. Ibid., xiv, 7.
22. Quoted by Shotwell, 180.
23. Pausanias, viii, 45.
24. Plutarch, "Alexander."
25. Cotterill, I, 108n.
26. Pliny, xxxv, 36, 40; Winckelmann, I, 219.
27. Pliny, xxxv, 32.
28. Ibid., xxxv, 36.
29. Ibid.
30. Aelian, *Varia Historia*, ii, 3, in Weigall, *Alexander*, 136.
31. Pliny, l.c.
32. Vitruvius, ii, 8.14.
35. Pausanias, i, 20.
36. Gardner, *Greek Sculpture*, 397.
37. Pausanias, v, 17.
38. Ibid., viii, 9.
39. They are listed in Murray, A. S., II, 253-4. Pliny alone mentions 28.
40. Pausanias, vi, 25.
41. Pliny, xxxvi, 41.
42. Ibid., xxxiv, 19.
43. Ibid.

CHAPTER XXI

1. Sarton, 127.
2. Plutarch, "Marcellus."
3. Aristotle, *Metaphysics*, i, 9.
4. Plato, *Hippias Major*, 303.
5. Sarton, 113.
6. Aristotle, *Politics*, 1340.
7. Sedgwick, 76.
8. Heath, *Greek Math.*, I, 209, 233, 252.
8a. Ibid., 354.
9. Diog. L., "Eudoxus," i-iii; Strabo, ii, 5.14; Heath, I, 320; id., *Aristarchus*, 192; Grote, *Plato*, I, 124n; Ball, W. R., *Short History of Mathematics*, London, 1888, 41.
10. Heath, I, 323.
11. Heath, *Aristarchus*, 208.
12. Sarton, 118.
13. Ibid., 141.
14. Heath, *Aristarchus*, 276.
15. Heath, I, 16.
16. Arrian, *Indica*, London, 1893, chaps. xx-xlii.
17. Sarton, 120-1.
18. Carroll, 325.
19. In Zeller, 266.
20. Zeller, 277.
21. Athenaeus, xiii, 55.
22. Vitruvius, ii, 6.1.
23. Athenaeus, xii, 63.
24. Zeller, 357, 361.
25. Ibid., 362b.
26. Diog. L., "Aristippus," iv.
27. Ibid.
28. Ibid.
29. Ibid.

30. Ibid.
31. Zeller, 367.
32. Carroll, 313.
33. Ibid.
34. Plato, *Phaedo*, 64.
35. Xenophon, *Banquet*, iii, 8.
36. Diog. L., "Antisthenes," iv.
37. Murray, *Five Stages*, 116.
38. Diog. L., "Diogenes," iii.
39. Ibid., iii, vi; Zeller, 326n.
40. Diog. L., "Diogenes," vi.
41. Ibid.
42. Ibid., x.
43. Ibid., vi.
44. Ibid.
45. Weigall, *Alexander*, 103.
46. Arrian, *Anabasis of Alexander*, vii, 2; Diog. L., "Diogenes," vi.
47. Ibid., xi.
48. Zeller, 308.
49. Diog. L., "Antisthenes," iv.
50. Ibid., "Diogenes," vi.
51. Plutarch, *Moralia*, 21F.
52. Diog. L., l.c.
53. Zeller, 319.
54. Ibid., 326.
55. Diog. L., "Diog.," xi.
56. Murray, *Five Stages*, 118.
57. Pöhlmann, 86-91.
58. Zeller, 317.
59. Plato, *Republic*, 372.
60. Diog. L., "Plato," i.
61. Ibid., v, x.
62. viii-ix; Cicero, *De Finibus*, v, 29.
62a. Plutarch, *De Exilio*, 10, in Capes, W. W., *University Life in Ancient Athens*, N. Y., 1922, 32.
63. Suidas, *Lexicon*, s.v. *Plato*, in Mahaffy, *Greek Education*, 122.
64. Diog. L., "Plato," xi.
65. Mahaffy, op. cit., 128; Grote, *Plato*, I, 125.
66. Heath, I, 11.
67. Plato, *Republic*, 539.
68. Heath, *Aristarchus*, 141.
69. Plutarch, *Moralia*, 79.
70. Plato, *Epistles*, vii, 531.
71. Taylor, 503.
72. Cf. *Epistles*, vii, 541.
73. Athenaeus, xi, 112.
74. Diog. L., "Cimon," i-iii, "Plato," xxxii.
75. Athenaeus, xi, 113.
76. Taylor, 20.
77. Plato, *Protag.*, 334.
78. *Symposium*, 175.
79. *Euthyphro*, 292.
80. *Charmides*, 169.
81. *Cratylus*.
82. *Phaedo*, 106.
83. *Theaetetus*, 161.
84. Ibid., 158; *Epistles*, vii, 344.
85. Aristotle, *Meta.*, i, 5-6; iii, 2; xiii, 4; *Cratylus*, 440.
86. Aristotle, *Meta.*, i, 9.16, etc.
87. Plato, *Phaedo*, 65.
88. Ibid., 74-5, *Theaetetus*, 185-7.
89. Carrel, Alexis, *Man the Unknown*, N. Y., 1935, 236.
90. Spinoza, *De Emendatione Intellectus*, Everyman Library, p. 259.
91. *Phaedrus*, 245.
92. *Philebus*, 22.
93. *Rep.*, 505.
94. *Laws*, 966; *Phaedo*, 96.
95. *Sophist*, 247.
96. *Phaedrus*, 245; *Philebus*, 30.
97. *Meno*, 81-2.
98. *Gorgias*, 523.
99. *Phaedo*, 69, 80-5, 110, 114; *Rep.*, 615f; *Timaeus*, 43-4.
100. *Phaedo*, 91, 114.
101. *Rep.*, 365.
102. *Symp.*, 209.
103. *Gorgias*, 482.
104. Ibid., 495; *Rep.*, 619; *Philebus*, 66.
105. *Rep.*, 441, 587.
106. *Philebus*, 64-6.
107. Ibid., 57-8.
108. *Crito*, 49.
109. Ibid.; *Laws*, 951; *Phaedo*, 82.
110. Aristotle, *Poetics*, i, 4.
111. *Rep.*, 424.
112. Quoted by Symonds, 411.
113. *Philebus*, 51; *Rep.*, 529.
114. *Symp.*, 206.
115. *Laws*, 636.
116. *Symp.*, 201; *Phaedrus*, 244f.
117. *Rep.*, 500.
118. *Epistles*, vii, 337.
119. *Rep.*, 555.
120. Ibid., 557.
121. 562.
122. 565.
123. 567.
124. 496.
125. *Phaedrus*, 239.
126. *Rep.*, 459.
127. 473.
128. *Statesman*, 297; *Epistles*, vii, 337.
129. *Laws*, 710.
130. Ibid., 704.
131. 968.

132. 761.
133. 742.
134. 744, 922-3.
135. 785.
136. 721, 774.
137. 672.
138. 885, 908-9.
139. *Phaedo*, 66.
140. Pater, 126.
141. *Laws*, 7.
142. Diog. L., "Plato," xxv.
143. Calhoun, 125-7.
144. Locy, W. A., *Growth of Biology*, N. Y., 1925, 27.
145. Athenaeus, xiii, 56.
146. Grote, *Aristotle*, I, 8.
147. Diog. L., "Aristotle," iv.
148. Grote, *Aristotle*, I, 43.
149. Murray, *Greek Epic*, 99; CAH, VI, 333.
150. Aristotle, *Meta.*, iii, 6.7-9.
151. Ibid., iv, 3.8.
152. Aristotle, *On Generation*, i, 2.
153. *Physics*, v, 3; vii, 1.
154. Aristotle, *Mechanics*, iii, 848-50.
155. *On the Heavens*, ii, 14.
156. *Meteorology*, i, 14.
157. *Meta.*, xii, 8.21.
158. Pliny, viii, 16.
159. Aristotle, *Parts of Animals*, i, 5.
160. *History of Animals*, v, 21-2; ix, 39-40.
161. Ibid., vi, 22.
162. Aristotle (?), *Economics*, i, 3; a typically Aristotelian sentence in a work long attributed to Aristotle, but probably from a later hand.
163. *History of Animals*, viii, 2.
164. *Reproduction of Animals*, i, 15.
165. Ibid., i, 21.
166. iv, 1.
167. *Hist. An.*, vii, 4.
168. *Reprod. An.*, ii, 1.
169. Ibid., ii, 3.
170. ii, 12.
171. *Hist. An.*, vi, 2-3.
172. Ibid.
173. i, 1.
174. viii, 1.
175. Ueberweg, I, 167.
176. Sedgwick, 14.
177. Lewes, G. H., *Aristotle: a Chapter in the History of Science*, London, 1864, 284, 361; Lange, 81.
178. Lewes, 159.
179. Aristotle, *Hist. An.*, ii, 3.
180. *Parts of Animals*, ii, 7.
181. Sarton, 128.
182. Aristotle, *Politics*, 1256b; Lewes, 322.
183. Aristotle, *On the Soul*, ii, 1.
184. Ibid., ii, 4.
185. iii, 8.
186. iii, 7.
187. *Reprod. An.*, ii, 3.
188. *Meta.*, viii, 4.4.
189. *Physics*, ii, 8.
190. *Meta.*, ix, 7.
191. *Poetics*, i, 3.
192. Ibid., vi, 2.
193. *Politics*, 1137b.
194. *Ethics*, 1097b, 1176b.
195. *Rhetoric*, i, 5.4, where, in a long list of things necessary for happiness, virtue comes in a poor last.
196. *Ethics*, 1099a.
197. Ibid., 1153b.
198. *Rhetoric*, ii, 16.2.
199. *Ethics*, 1178a.
200. Ibid., 1125b.
201. 1098a.
202. 1178b.
203. *Politics*, 1267a.
204. Ibid., 1275b.
205. 1253a.
206. 1296b.
207. *Ethics*, 1160ab.
208. *Rhetoric*, ii, 15.3.
209. *Politics*, 1258b.
210. Ibid., 1281a.
211. 1318b.
212. 1286a.
213. 1278a.
214. 1280a.
215. 1266b.
216. 1254b.
217. 1320a.
218. Ibid.
219. 1295a.
220. 1264a.
221. 1261b.
222. 1296b.
223. 1296a.
224. 1330a.
225. 1329b.
226. *Rhetoric*, i, 1.7.
227. *Politics*, 1287a.
228. Ibid., 1265b.
229. 1335b.
230. In Ueberweg, I, 177.
231. Pater, 141.

CHAPTER XXII

1. Plutarch, *Moralia*, 178F.
2. Mahaffy, *Greek Life and Thought*, 18.

3. Plutarch, "Alexander."
4. Weigall, *Alexander,* 235.
5. Ibid.
6. Plutarch, l.c.
7. Plutarch, *Moralia,* 127B.
8. Id., "Alexander."
8a. Id., *Moralia,* 180A.
9. Id., "Alexander."
10. Ibid.; Arrian, i, 17.
11. Weigall, 50.
12. Plutarch, *Moralia,* 179E.
13. Id., "Alexander."
14. Arrian, vii, 28.
15. Ibid., iii, 6.
16. Grote, *History,* XI, 85.
17. Weigall, 58.
18. Arrian, i, 3.
19. Weigall, 97.
20. Plutarch, "Alexander."
21. Ibid.
22. Arrian, vii, 9.
23. Plutarch, l.c.
24. Vitruvius, ii, 2.
25. Plutarch, *Moralia,* 180C.
26. CAH, VI, 384.
27. Arrian, iv, 7.
28. Ibid., vi, 26.
29. vii, 4.
30. Plutarch, "Alexander."
31. Grote, XII, 89.
32. Athenaeus, xii, 53.
33. Plutarch, *Moralia,* 180D.
34. Weigall, 146.
35. Plutarch, "Alexander"; Arrian, vii, 29.
36. Lucian, *Dialogues of the Dead,* xiv.
37. Cf. Arrian, iv, 9-11.
38. Ibid., vii, 11.
39. vii, 9-10.
40. ii, 12.
41. Plutarch, "Alexander"; Arrian, vii, 26.
42. Plutarch, l.c.
43. Grote, *Aristotle,* I, 23.
44. Diog. L., "Aristotle," vii.
45. Thrasybulus in Grote, *History,* VIII, 263.

CHAPTER XXIII

1. Mahaffy, *Greek Life and Thought,* pp. xxxv, 112.
2. Ibid., 56; Plutarch, "Demetrius."
3. Ibid.
4. Pausanias, x, 19.
5. Ibid., 22.
6. Livy, T. L., *History of Rome,* xxxviii, 16; CAH, VII, 103-7.
7. Polybius, iv, 77; Pausanias, ii, 9, vii, 7; Plutarch, "Aratus."
8. Athenaeus, vi, 103.
9. Heitland, W. E., *Agricola,* Cambridge University Press, 1921, 124-5.
10. Plato, *Critias,* 111.
11. Rostovtzeff, M., *History of the Ancient World,* Oxford, 1930, I, 320.
12. Cf. Tarn, W. W., *Hellenistic Civilization,* London, 1927, 90.
13. Vinogradoff, II, 108-9.
14. Glotz, *Ancient Greece,* 366.
15. Ibid., 364.
16. Ibid.
17. Ibid., 331-3; Tarn, 95.
18. Tarn, 102; Heitland, 63; Glotz, 359.
19. CAH, VII, 740.
20. Ibid.
20a. Ibid., 265, 741; Tarn, 104.
21. Ibid., 34.
22. Glotz, 333.
23. Polybius, vi, 9; vii, 10; xv, 21; Glotz, *Greek City,* 323.
23a. Diodorus Sic., V, 41-6.
24. Bentwich, Norman, *Hellenism,* Phila., 1919, 62.
25. Athenaeus, xiii, 18.
26. Tarn, 82.
27. Theocritus, Idyl ii.
28. Lacroix, I, 138-9.
29. Athenaeus, in Becker, 344.
30. Glotz, *Ancient Greece,* 298; Tarn, 86.
31. Ibid., 88.
32. Polybius, xxxvi, 17.
33. Plutarch, "Agis."
34. Glotz, *Ancient Greece,* 346.
35. Plutarch, l.c.
36. CAH, VII, 755.
37. Polybius, ii, 52; v, 38; Pausanias, ii, 9.
38. Coulanges, 467.
39. Pausanias, viii, 50.
40. Strabo, xiv, 2.5.
41. Ibid.
42. Polybius, v, 88.

CHAPTER XXIV

1. Meeting of the Oriental Institute, Chicago, Mar. 29, 1932.
2. Plutarch, *Moralia,* 183F.
3. Polybius, xx, 8.
4. Ibid., xxi, 3-7; xxx, 26.
5. Ibid., xxix, 27; xxxi, 9; Bevan, E. R., *House of Seleucus,* London, 1902, II, 131, 158.
6. Rostovtzeff, *Social and Economic History of the Roman Empire,* 3; Tarn, 79.

7. Toutain, 102-3.
8. Glotz, *Ancient Greece*, 353.
9. Rostovtzeff, *Roman Empire*, 3; id., *Ancient World*, I, 368-70; Glotz, 321.
10. Glotz, *Greek City*, 383.
11. Tarn, 254.
13. Josephus, *Against Apion*, I, 60; Bevan, 35; Tarn, 209.
14. CAH, VII, 193.
15. Sachar, A. L., *History of the Jews*, N. Y., 1932, 102. Cf. Zeitlin, S., *History of the Second Jewish Commonwealth*, Phila., 1933, 18f, or CAH, VIII, 501f, for an economic interpretation of these intrigues.
16. Graetz, H., *History of the Jews*, Phila., 1891f, I, 445-6; Zeitlin, 18.
17. Bevan, I, 171; Mahaffy, J. P., *Empire of the Ptolemies*, London, 1895, 341.
18. CAH, VIII, 507-8.
19. I Macc., i; Josephus, *Works*, Boston, 1811, I, 438; *Antiquities of the Jews*, xii, 5.
20. Bevan, II, 154.
21. I Macc., v-vi; Bevan, 174.
22. I Macc., ii.
23. Ibid., vi.
24. Ibid., ii.
25. Ibid., ii-v.
26. Sachar, 104.
27. Bevan II, 183, 223.

CHAPTER XXV

1. Breccia, E., *Alexandrea ad Aegyptum*, Bergamo, 1922, 96; Strabo, xvii, 1.8.
2. Mahaffy, *Empire*, 104; *Greek Life*, 204.
3. Athenaeus, xiii, 37.
4. Mahaffy, *Empire*, 162.
5. Draper, I, 190.
6. Tarn, 148; CAH, VII, 137.
7. Ibid., 27; Rostovtzeff, *Roman Empire*, 259.
8. Tarn, 149-51, 155; Glotz, *Ancient Greece*, 345.
9. Ibid., 343.
10. Usher, 80, 85.
11. Strabo, xvii, 1.25.
12. Glotz, *Ancient Greece*, 353.
13. Tarn, 152; Usher, 75.
14. Glotz, l.c.
15. Rostovtzeff, *Roman Empire*, 432.
16. Usher, 79, 119.
17. Pliny, xxxv, 42.
18. Rostovtzeff, *Ancient World*, I, 373; Tarn, 102; Glotz, 350.
19. Tarn, 155.
20. Botsford and Sihler, 597.
21. Athenaeus, v, 36.
22. Pliny, xxxvi, 18.
23. Breccia, 107.
24. Tarn, 198.
25. Calhoun, 130.
26. CAH, VIII, 662.
27. Mahaffy, *Greek Life*, 182.
28. Mahaffy, *What Have the Greeks?*, 195-7.
29. Tarn, 153; CAH, VII, 28.
30. Ibid., 139-40; Tarn, 153; Mahaffy, *Empire*, 182, 213; Breccia, 42.
31. Breccia, 69.
32. Strabo, xvii, 1.8-10; Tarn, 146.
33. Glotz, 336.
34. Athenaeus, iii, 47.
35. Herodas, *Mimiambi*, i.
36. Lacroix, I, 124.
37. Carroll, 326.
38. Graetz, I, 418; Mahaffy, *Empire*, 86.
39. Josephus, *Antiquities*, xii, 1-2.
40. Zeitlin, 6-8; Bevan, I, 165.
41. Bentwich, 36.
42. Renan, E., *History of the People of Israel*, N. Y., 1888, IV, 194; V, 189.

42a. Graetz, I, 504.

43. Bevan and Singer, *Legacy of Israel*, Oxford, 1927, 32.
44. Josephus, *Antiquities*, xii, 2; Sarton, 151.
45. Sachar, 109.
46. *Enc. Brit.*, XX, 335; Tarn, 177.
47. Glotz, *Ancient Greece*, 356; Tarn, 204.
48. Tarn, 158.
49. Mahaffy, *Greek Life*, 208.
50. Rostovtzeff, *Roman Empire*, 264.
51. Glotz, *Greek City*, 323.
52. Polybius, vii, 8.
53. Ibid.
54. Randall-MacIver, 138-9.
55. Athenaeus, v, 40.
56. Livy, xxiv, 4.

CHAPTER XXVI

1. Polybius, ix, 2.
2. Thompson, 71.
3. Strabo, xiii, 1.54.
4. Grote, *Aristotle*, 50.
5. Breccia, 47.
6. Ibid., 48.
7. Mahaffy, *Empire*, 208.
8. Oxyrhynchus Papyri X, 1241, p. 99; Breccia, 44.
9. Tarn, 238; Symonds, 21.
10. Tarn, 237; Mahaffy, 511.

11. Waxman, M., *History of Jewish Literature*, N. Y., 1930, I, 48.
12. Ibid., 49.
13. Ibid., 21.
14. Renan, IV, 258.
15. Lacroix, I, 166-7.
16. Wright, 22.
17. CAH, VII, 227.
18. Menander, *Arbitrants*, 679-85.
19. Bacchis in the *Phormio*.
20. St. Paul, I Cor., xv, 33.
21. Tarn, 219.
22. Frag. 40 in Murray, *Aristophanes*, 223.
23. Translation by Symonds, 454.
24. Ibid., 526.
25. Murray, *Greek Literature*, 381; Mahaffy, *Greek Literature*, I, 166; id., *Progress of Hellenism in Alexander's Empire*, Chicago, 1905, 112.
26. Theocritus, xv, tr. Lindsay, in *Oxford Book of Greek Verse*, 564.
27. Theocritus, i, 123-42; tr. Sir Wm. Marris, *Oxford Book*, 543.
28. Tarn, 52.
29. Frag. 54 in McCrindle, J. W., *Ancient India*, Calcutta, 1877, 120.
30. Bury, *Greek Historians*, 188.
31. Polybius, xii, 25, 27, etc.
32. Ibid., xxxiv, 6; xxxviii, 6.
33. xxx, 32.
34. iii, 2.
35. vi, 2.
36. vi, 3.
37. iii. 48, 59; xii, 25; Shotwell, 199.
38. xvi, 20.
39. xii, 28.
40. v, 75.
41. xxi, 32.
42. xvi, 12.
43. vi, 43.
44. iii, 31.
45. i, 1.
46. i, 35; i, 1.
47. i, 4.
48. ix, 1; ii, 56.
49. Dionysius of Halicarnassus in CAH, VIII, 10.

CHAPTER XXVII

1. Athenaeus, xiv, 33.
2. Mahaffy, *Social Life*, 467-8, 475-6.
3. Vitruvius, ix, 9; x, 13; Athenaeus, iv, 75; *Oxford History of Music*, Introd. Vol., 26.
4. Mahaffy, 455; id., *Greek Life*, 382.
5. Athenaeus, xiv, 31.
6. Strabo, xiv, 1.37.
7. In Gardner, *Ancient Athens*, 486.
8. Pliny, xxxv, 40.
9. Plutarch, "Aratus."
10. Strabo, xiv, 2.5.
11. Pliny, xxxv, 36.
12. Ibid., xxxv, 37; xxxvi, 60.
13. Lessing, G. E., *Laocoön*, London, 1874, 15.
14. Pliny, xxxiv, 18.
15. *Greek Anthology*, vi, 171.
16. Pliny, l.c.
17. Bostock's note, ibid.
18. Winckelmann, I, 229.
19. Virgil, *Aeneid*, ii, 49.
20. Pliny, xxxvi, 4.
21. Winckelmann, II, 325.
22. CAH, VIII, 675.
23. In Gardner, E. A., *Six Greek Sculptors*, London, 1910, 6.

CHAPTER XXVIII

1. Stobaeus, in Heath, *Greek Mathematics*, I, 357.
2. Plutarch, "Marcellus."
3. Ball, W. W. R., *Short History of Mathematics*, London, 1888, 64.
4. Ibid., 66-7.
5. Plutarch.
6. Cicero, *Tusc. Disp.*, i, 25.
7. Cicero, *Rep.*, i, 14.
8. Singer, C., *Studies in the History of Science*, Oxford, 1921, II, 502.
9. Heath, II, 18.
10. Plutarch.
11. Ibid.
12. Polybius, viii, 5; Livy, xxiv, 34.
13. Heath, l.c.
14. Plutarch.
15. Polybius, l.c.
16. Plutarch.
17. Livy, xxv, 31.
18. Heath, II, 20.
19. Sarton, 184; Usher, 44.
20. Ibid., 80.
21. Ibid., 41; Sarton, 184, 195.
22. Vitruvius, i, 1.16.
23. Heath, *Aristarchus of Samos*, 310, 383.
24. Ibid., 302.
25. Heath, *Greek Math.*, II, 2.
26. Williams, H. S., *History of Science*, N. Y., 1909, I, 233.
27. Heath, *Aristarchus*, 296-7; CAH, VII, 311.
28. *Enc. Brit.*, XI, 583.

29. Tarn, 230.
30. Heath, *Aristarchus*, 339-40.
31. Sarton, 144; Glotz, *Ancient Greece*, 375.
32. Strabo, i, 3.3.
33. Ibid., i, 4.7-9.
34. Ibid., i, 4.6.
35. Wright, 14.
36. Garrison, 102.
37. Theophrastus, *History of Plants*, ii, 1.1, in Livingstone, *Legacy*, 178.
38. Locy, 37.
39. Grote, II, 17.
40. Sarton, 143.
41. Ibid., 126.
42. In Wright, 14.
43. Celsus, *De Artibus*, i, 4, in Botsford and Sihler, 631.
44. Botsford and Sihler, 631.
45. Sarton, 159; Garrison, 153.
46. Sextus, Empiricus, *Adv. Math.*, xi, 50, in Livingstone, 201.
47. Garrison, 103.
48. Sarton, 159-60.

CHAPTER XXIX

1. Carroll, 316.
2. Athenaeus, xiii, 90.
3. Diog. L., "Theophrastus," iv-xi.
4. Theophrastus, *Characters*, Loeb Library, 1929, iii, xiv, etc.
5. Diog., "Xenophanes," iii.
6. Ibid., iii-v, x.
7. Aristotle, *Anal. Post.*, ii, 19.
8. Diog., "Pyrrho," viii.
9. Ibid., iii.
10. Zeller, E., *Stoics, Epicureans and Sceptics*, London, 1870, 99.
11. Ibid., 503.
12. Wright, 128.
13. Ueberweg, I, 136.
14. Polybius, xii, 26.
15. Diog., "Aristippus," xii-xiv.
16. Lacroix, I, 160-1.
17. Diog., "Epicurus," v.
18. Ibid., vi-viii.
19. Lucretius, v, 196; ii, 1090; Lucian, "Zeus Tragoedus," in *Works*, III, 97.
20. Lucretius, ii, 292; Plutarch, *Moralia*, 964C.
21. Cicero, *Nat. Deor.*, i, 20.
22. Diog., "Epicurus," xxiv.
23. Ibid., xxvii; Murray, *Greek Religion*, 168.
24. Diog., xxv.
25. Athenaeus, xii, 67.
26. Diog., xxxi.
27. Ibid., xxvii.
28. Ibid.
29. Ibid., xxxi, 31.
30. Ibid., xxvi.
31. Ibid., xxvii.
32. Zeller, 464.
33. Diog., xxxi, 28.
34. Cf. Frags. 165, 186, 194, and 213 in Murray, 130.
35. Murray, 138.
36. Frag. 138 in Murray, 141.
37. Diog., x.
38. Athenaeus, vii, 11.
39. Becker, 325.
40. *Jewish Enc.*, art. "Apiköros"; Bentwich, 77.
41. Zeller, 388.
42. Cicero, *De Fin.*, i, 7.25.
43. In Murray, *Greek Literature*, 372.
44. Diog., "Zeno," i-ii.
45. Ibid., xi, v.
46. Ibid., v.
47. Ibid., "Crates," i-iv; "Hipparchia," i-ii; Zeller, *Socrates*, 326n.
48. Diog., "Zeno," xxviii-xxix.
49. Ibid., xiv.
50. Zeller, *Stoics*, 37n.
51. Diog., "Zeno," ix.
52. Ibid., xxvii. Lucian, Lactantius, and Stobaeus tell the same story; cf. Zeller, 40.
53. Zeller, 59.
54. Ibid., 121.
55. Cicero, *Nat. Deor.*, ii, 7.
56. Diog., "Zeno," lxviii-lxxvii.
57. Tr. by Pater, 50.
58. Plutarch, *De Stoic. Repug.*, xxi, 4, in Zeller, 178; but Plutarch was intensely prejudiced against the Stoics.
59. *Oxford Book of Greek Verse*, 535.
60. Zeller, 288.
61. Diog., "Zeno," xix.
62. Ibid., lxiv.
63. Zeller, 316.
64. Diog., lxvi.
65. Zeller, 303.
66. Cicero, *Tusc. Disp.*, i, 34.83.
67. Zeller, 327.
68. Ibid., 207.

CHAPTER XXX

1. Polybius, i, 1.
2. Plutarch, "Pyrrhus."
3. Ibid.

4. Ibid.
5. Mommsen, T., *History of Rome*, London, 1901, II, 5.
6. Plutarch, l.c.
7. Livy, xxv, 40, 31.
8. Polybius, ii, 8.
9. Ibid., v, 103.
10. Livy, xxiii, 33.
11. Polybius, xvi, 30; Livy, xxxi, 18.
12. Polybius, xviii, 45.
13. Livy, xxxiv, 52.
14. Tarn, 29.
15. Strabo, viii, 6.23.
16. Polybius, xxxix, 2; Strabo, l.c.

EPILOGUE

1. Symonds, 579.
2. Rede Lecture for 1875, in Symonds, 578.
3. *Enc. Brit.*, II, 344.

Index

I am indebted for this index to the careful scholarship of Mr. Herbert Winer. The diacritical marks follow Webster's Dictionary.—W. D.

A

Aahmes (ä'-mēz) II, King of Egypt (reigned 570-526 B.C.), 173
Aaron (ā'-rŏn), 583
abacus, 338
Abdera (ăb-dē'-rȧ), 69, 149, 157, 352, 354, 358
Abélard, Pierre, French philosopher (1079-1142), 643
abortion, 287, 468, 567
Abydos (ȧ-bī'-dŏs), 135, 156, 544, 575, 663
Academus (ăk-ȧ-dē'-mŭs), 511
Academy, 226, 473, 474, 479, 486, 500, 501, 511-513, 524, 525, 553, 640, 641, 642, 644, 651
Acanthus (ȧ-kăn'-thŭs), 158
Acarnania (ăk'-ȧr-nā'-nĭ-ȧ), 105, 106, 542
Acco (ä'-kō), 580, 584
Achaea (ȧ-kē'-ȧ), 86, 88, 89, 198, 560, 569, 665
Achaean League, 560-561, 570, 585, 613, 665-666
Achaeans, 21*, 23, 37-38, 40, 42, 44-55, 62, 63, 64, 89, 106, 108, 128, 151, 160, 180, 203, 311, 613
Achaemenidae (ăk'-ē-mĕn'-ĭ-dē), 563
Achaeus (ȧ-kē'-ŭs), 39
Acharnae (ȧ-kär'-nē), 108
Acharnians (ȧ-kär'-nĭ-ănz), *The* (Aristophanes), 417, 422, 428
Achelous (ăk'-ē-lō'-ŭs), 106
Acheron (ăk'-ēr-ŏn), 67
Achilles (ȧ-kĭl'-ēz), 36, 43, 45, 46, 48, 52, 56, 58-59, 61, 150, 171, 183, 193, 208-209, 220, 302, 405, 406, 538, 541, 544, 546, 548, 551, 620, 660
Achilles and Briseis, 620*
Achilles and Penthesilea (pĕn'-thē-sĭ-lē'-ȧ), 315
Acontius (ȧkŏn'-tē-ŭs), 608
Acragas (ä'-krȧ-gŭs), 130, 170, 171, 172, 327, 339, 342, 355, 357, 438
Acre (ä'-kēr), 580, *see also* Acco
Acrocorinthus (ăk'-rō-kō-rĭn'-thŭs), 62, 89, 560
Acron (ȧ'-krŏn), physician (fl. 5th century B.C.), 342
Acropolis (ȧ-krŏp'-ō-lĭs) (Athens), 108, 120, 122, 178, 226, 251, 325, 330-331, 365, 377, 450, 543, 623
Acropolis (Pergamum), 623
Actium (ăk'-tĭ-ŭm), 89†
actors, 232, 379, 380-381, 383, 606
Adana (ä'-dä-nä), 576
Adasa (ä-däs'-ȧ), 584
Adeimantus (ȧ-dī-măn'-tŭs), 520
Aden (ä'-dĕn), 575, *see also* Adana
Admetus (ăd-mē'-tŭs), 402
Adonia (ȧ-dō'-nĭ-ȧ), 185*
Adonis (ȧ-dō'-nĭs), 13, 69, 178, 185, 467, 566
Adrastus (ȧ-drăs'-tŭs), 41, 232
Adriatic Sea, 67, 159, 660
adultery, in Homeric society, 51; in Sparta, 84; in Athens, 117, 305
Advokatenrepublik, 483
Aegaleus (ē'-gă-lē'-ŭs), Mt., 241
Aegean (ē-jē'-ăn) Islands, 3-4, 6, 8, 22, 27, 33, 59, 62, 70, 127, 128, 134, 158, 233, 234, 245, 441, 528, 570
Aegean Sea, 4, 5, 6, 10, 33, 70, 71, 106, 109, 128, 274, 275, 439, 445, 451, 463, 477, 571, 572, 578, 665
Aegeus (ē'-jūs), 23
Aegina (ē-jī'-nȧ), 29, 30, 72, 95, 240, 253, 279, 322, 342, 439
Aegira (ē-jī'-rȧ), 89
Aegisthus (ē-jĭs'-thŭs), 59, 386, 387, 388, 389, 409
Aegium (ē'-jĭ-ŭm), 89, 560
Aegospotami (ē'-gŏs-pŏt'-ȧ-mī), 295, 331, 450
Aegyptus (ē-jĭp'-tŭs), 49
Aenea (ē-nē'-ȧ), 60
Aeneas (ē-nē'-ăs), 58
Aeneas Tacticus (tȧk'-tĭ-cŭs), writer (4th century B.C.), 503
Aeneid (ē-nē'-ĭd), *The* (Virgil), 609*
Aeniania (ē'-nē-ăn'-ĭ-ȧ), 105, 106
Aenus (ē'-nŭs), 157
Aeolia (ē'-ō-lĭ-ȧ), 71, 128, 150, 151, 203, 238; dialect, 204
Aeolian League, 128
Aeolus (ē'-ō-lŭs), 177

B

D

N

Q

R

S

T

About the Authors

WILL DURANT was born in North Adams, Massachusetts, in 1885. He was educated in the Catholic parochial schools there and in Kearny, New Jersey, and thereafter in St. Peter's (Jesuit) College, Jersey City, New Jersey, and Columbia University, New York. For a summer he served as a cub reporter on the New York *Journal*, in 1907, but finding the work too strenuous for his temperament, he settled down at Seton Hall College, South Orange, New Jersey, to teach Latin, French, English, and geometry (1907–11). He entered the seminary at Seton Hall in 1909, but withdrew in 1911 for reasons which he has described in his book *Transition.* He passed from this quiet seminary to the most radical circles in New York, and became (1911–13) the teacher of the Ferrer Modern School, an experiment in libertarian education. In 1912 he toured Europe at the invitation and expense of Alden Freeman, who had befriended him and now undertook to broaden his borders.

Returning to the Ferrer School, he fell in love with one of his pupils, resigned his position, and married her (1913). For four years he took graduate work at Columbia University, specializing in biology under Morgan and Calkins and in philosophy under Woodbridge and Dewey. He received the doctorate in philosophy in 1917, and taught philosophy at Columbia University for one year. In 1914, in a Presbyterian church in New York, he began those lectures on history, literature, and philosophy which, continuing twice weekly for thirteen years, provided the initial material for his later works.

The unexpected success of *The Story of Philosophy* (1926) enabled him to retire from teaching in 1927. Thenceforth, except for some incidental essays, Mr. and Mrs. Durant gave nearly all their working hours (eight to fourteen daily) to *The Story of Civilization.* To better prepare themselves they toured Europe in 1927, went around the world in 1930 to study Egypt, the Near East, India, China, and Japan, and toured the globe again in 1932 to visit Japan, Manchuria, Siberia, Russia, and Poland. These travels provided the background for *Our Oriental Heritage* (1935) as the first volume in *The Story of Civilization.* Several further visits to Europe prepared for Volume II, *The Life of Greece* (1939) and Volume III, *Caesar and Christ* (1944). In 1948, six months in Turkey, Iraq, Iran, Egypt, and Europe provided perspective for Volume IV, *The Age of Faith* (1950). In 1951 Mr. and Mrs. Durant returned to Italy to add to a lifetime of gleanings for Volume V, *The Renaissance* (1953); and in 1954 further studies in Italy, Switzerland, Germany, France, and England opened new vistas for Volume VI, *The Reformation* (1957).

ABOUT THE AUTHORS

Mrs. Durant's share in the preparation of these volumes became more and more substantial with each year, until in the case of Volume VII, *The Age of Reason Begins* (1961), it was so pervasive that justice required the union of both names on the title page. The name Ariel was first applied to his wife by Mr. Durant in his novel *Transition* (1927) and in his *Mansions of Philosophy* (1929) —now reissued as *The Pleasures of Philosophy*.

The authors hope to present Volume IX in 1964 or 1965 as *The Age of Voltaire* (1715–56), and Volume X, the concluding work in the series, as *Rousseau and Revolution* (1756–89).

THE HELLENISTIC WORLD